Your UNIX

The Ultimate Guide

Your UNIX

The Ultimate Guide

Sumitabha Das
Internetworking Consultant

Boston   Burr Ridge, IL   Dubuque, IA   Madison, WI   New York   San Francisco   St. Louis
Bangkok   Bogotá   Caracas   Kuala Lumpur   Lisbon   London   Madrid   Mexico City
Milan   Montreal   New Delhi   Santiago   Seoul   Singapore   Sydney   Taipei   Toronto

McGraw-Hill Higher Education

*A Division of The **McGraw-Hill** Companies*

YOUR UNIX: THE ULTIMATE GUIDE

This book is printed on acid-free paper.

3 4 5 6 7 8 9 0 FGR/FGR 0 9 8 7 6 5 4 3 2

ISBN 0-07-240500-7

Publisher: *Thomas Casson*
Developmental editor: *Melinda Dougharty*
Marketing manager: *John Wannemacher*
Project manager: *Rebecca Nordbrock*
Production associate: *Gina Hangos*
Freelance design coordinator: *Pam Verros*
Senior media technology producer developer: *Phil Meek*
Cover design: *Pam Verros*
Interior design: *Z Graphics*
Cover image: *© Digital Vision*
Compositor: *Lachina Publishing Services*
Typeface: *10/12 Times Roman*
Printer: *Quebecor Fairfield Inc.*

Library of Congress Cataloging-in-Publication Data

Das, Sumitabha.
    Your UNIX : the ultimate guide / Sumitabha Das.
      p. cm.
    Includes bibliographical references and index.
    ISBN 0-07-240500-7 (alk. paper)
    1. UNIX (Computer file)   2. Operating systems (Computers)   I. Title.

QA76.76.O63 D3495 2001
005.4'32--dc21
                                            00-046052

www.mhhe.com

To the memory of my two uncles who both knew that it had to happen some day, but were no longer there when the day arrived.

Preface

The limits of my language mean the limits of my world.

—Ludwig Wittgenstein

In an article in *The Bell System Technical Journal* published in 1978, Ken Thompson and Dennis Ritchie introduced to the world a "general-purpose" operating system offering a "high degree of portability." That operating system was UNIX. It has come a long way since then, and it is firmly entrenched today in its famed position as the environment of choice for serious work. Whether it's used for computer-aided design or simulation in the laboratory, UNIX has been the platform that has aided their development. UNIX gave birth to the C language. Enterprise-scale database applications run on UNIX. UNIX systems have also been behind the creation of *Jurassic Park* and *Titanic*. Today, electronic commerce is fueled by UNIX.

However, the ride to fame hasn't always been smooth. UNIX has constantly drawn admirers and detractors alike. Beginners feel overwhelmed by its sheer weight and are often unable to comprehend why UNIX behaves in a radically different manner when compared with the Windows platform. Even experienced computer professionals feel lost in this mysterious universe, characterized by its arcane tools and cryptic syntax. Windows isn't like this at all; why was UNIX designed that way?

There's a reason behind all this. UNIX was never designed for the world. A group of programmers created it to run their own programs—programs that no one else required. But the fact that it still managed to gain wide acceptance without any serious marketing effort points to UNIX's inherent strengths. Because it is rooted in open standards, UNIX has shown up in every hardware and now powers the Internet.

Even though UNIX is based on a few simple ideas, it is extremely rich in features—features never seen or experienced before. UNIX has redefined what an operating system should be and why many people need to master it. The UNIX "command line," with its myriad options and complex syntaxes, drove many people away. But these features and the capability of these commands to act in combination are precisely what make UNIX seem irreplaceable. This is what this book attempts to explain and advise: *There is a method to this madness.*

A single textbook is never adequate to present all these features, but fortunately I could select from this ocean those essential concepts that require specific attention. This book makes no attempt to list all 24 options of the **ls** command or all of the shell's features. But it does discuss the ones that I consider important and shows you how to apply them to real-world situations. I have treated these concepts in some detail, which will benefit the beginner as well as the expert.

This book is well suited for use in a variety of UNIX courses related to introductory programming, operating systems and system administration—at both the introductory and more advanced levels. A knowledge of one operating system is preferable even though the book makes no such assumption. However, the programming features of the shell can be better understood by someone with a background of one programming language.

Why You Must Know UNIX Today

As I see it, UNIX had to grow through four important phases in its life cycle. Initially, it was considered a product for the engineering and scientific community. The initiated couldn't live without it; the others stayed away because it wasn't "friendly" enough. A lot of what we see in present-day UNIX is the result of the development work of these universities and research institutes.

Next, the corporates took to UNIX. UNIX made significant inroads into large corporations and government organizations. Its robustness established it as the operating system of choice for database work. Every RDBMS package, be it Oracle or Sybase or Informix, has long been available on the major UNIX platforms. If you wanted to be a good DBA (database administrator), you had to know UNIX.

The Internet is the third (and most significant) phase of the UNIX cycle. Many of the things you see on the Net and the Web owe their origin to the hard and inspiring work done by the UNIX community. TCP/IP was first ported to UNIX systems. Most servers on the Net are UNIX machines. Internet Service Providers use UNIX machines. **perl**, which operates behind all the forms that you see on the Web, is a UNIX product. In short, the Internet is UNIX, and to understand its workings and exploit this technology for local internets, one *must* know UNIX.

These years have also seen the silent but phenomenal growth of the Linux cult. Linux is the free UNIX that has captivated the new generation of college students and is now invading the commercial world. It is widely favored for its richness of Internet-related tools. I see a great future ahead for Linux and feel compelled to include its important features in this book. Even though Linux doesn't use any of the original AT&T code, it's just as UNIX as any other flavor—in spirit, in philosophy—in everything.

Why You Should Actually Like UNIX

I am distressed by one trend that seems to emerge from recent adoptions of UNIX. Many people are now entering UNIX through the "back door"—and this back door is the X Window system—the graphical windowing system offered on UNIX machines. These people use UNIX in the same way they handle DOS or Windows and expect the mouse to do all the work. They configure the system by filling up forms of menu-based GUI applications, and they don't even care to know the names of the files or which entries are affected. Let's make no mistake; you can't learn UNIX this way. It takes little time to get disillusioned and join the group of detractors.

Necessity apart, UNIX is actually fascinating. The system is based on its *commands*, programs that are meant to do specific jobs. Commands use *options*, and each option makes the command behave differently. Many of these commands can be combined with one another (as *filters*) to perform complex tasks. Some of them even use a powerful pattern matching feature (called *regular expressions*) that is used in locating and substituting text. Add to all this a scripting language, and you have a tool kit that sets no limits on the things that you can do with this system.

UNIX commands are generally noninteractive, and hence ideally suited for the development of automated systems. You can do things in UNIX at the drop of a hat—things which you simply can't do in the windowing environment. Ask a Windows user to convert a thousand files from BMP to GIF format; he'll run away. If you know your UNIX well, you can do that by writing just three or four lines of simple code. You don't need to click your mouse a thousand times (actually more).

The excitement that UNIX generates lies in the fact that many of its powers are hidden. It doesn't offer everything on a platter; it encourages you to create and innovate. Figuring out a command combination or designing a script that does a complex job is a real challenge to the UNIX enthusiast. This is what UNIX is, and it had better remain that way. If you appreciate this, then you are on the right track, and this book is for you.

How the Book Is Organized

UNIX versions can be broadly divided into two different schools—the *System V* school from AT&T Bell Laboratories and the *Berkeley* school from the University of California, Berkeley. More specifically, versions tend to be looked at as being either based on *SVR4* (System V Release 4—AT&T's last release before winding up its UNIX operations) or on *BSD UNIX* (the UNIX created by Berkeley). This books attempts to portray UNIX generically, keeping an eye on the adoption of its features by Solaris. Linux is primarily BSD-based and has been treated in separate sections.

The subject matter is organized differently from what you would find in other textbooks. Though a system component is often spread across multiple chapters, you'll find like material grouped together for ease of understanding and reference. Once you understand this organization, locating a feature or a command shouldn't be difficult:

Topic	Chapters
Editors	4 and 5
File system	6, 7 and 21
Shell	8, 17, 18 and 19
Process	10 and 22
TCP/IP and the Internet	11, 13, 14, 23 and 24
Regular expressions	4, 5, 15, 16 and 20
Filters	9, 15, 16 and 20
System and Network Administration	21, 22, 23 and 24

Allocation of a command or feature to a particular chapter is based on definite principles. You probably won't find a separate chapter on file attributes in other textbooks, but I have considered it necessary to maintain this arrangement. That's why the basic commands that act on file content (like **cp**, **rm**, **lp**, **compress** and **gzip**) have been separated from those that change or match the attributes only without disturbing the contents (like **ln**, **chown**, **chgrp** and **find**). The first group can be found in Chapter 6, while Chapter 7 exclusively handles file attributes.

In a similar manner, the shell makes its appearance in three distinct forms: as an interpreter (Chapter 8), as an environment customizer (Chapter 17) and as a programming language (Chapters 18 and 19). I haven't made the mistake of discussing shell programming and job control in a single chapter as some people have done. I feel that job control belongs to the realm of processes, even if it is a feature of the shell. That's why you'll find it in Chapter 10 along with its other companions that display, kill and schedule processes.

Now that you understand the basic overarching structure of the book, it's time you had a look at the organizational details of each chapter:

Chapter 1 takes you on a tour through two hands-on sessions to let you grasp some of the important features of the system. Try out some of the commonly used UNIX commands. Learn to use your keyboard when the system behaves unpredictably. This exposure, when set against the background, also gives you an indication of things to come. Learn the essential features of UNIX from this chapter.

Chapter 2 prepares you for understanding the syntax of UNIX commands—the various forms its options and arguments can take. Learn to use the on-line UNIX documentation, especially the **man** command. The various facilities available in the system not only let you find out what a command does but also locate the command that does a specific job.

Chapter 3 discusses some useful stand-alone utilities. Some of these commands report on the system's parameters like the date (**date**) or the machine name (**uname**). You'll learn to change your password (**passwd**) and set your terminal's characteristics (**stty**). Many of these commands have been used in command pipelines and shell scripts that are featured later in the book.

Chapter 4 presents comprehensive coverage of the **vi** editor, the most popular text editor used on UNIX systems. Get to know the three modes and the commands associated with each mode. Apart from performing the basic editing functions, learn how to use a number with a command to repeat it. Knowledge of searching and substitution techniques also leads you to the first discussion on *regular expressions*. The advanced features include configuration issues and are taken up in the "Going Further" section at the end of the chapter.

Chapter 5 presents yet another editor—GNU **emacs**, which is not universally available but is widely used. Learn the use of the *[Ctrl]* and the *[Meta]* keys in framing command sequences, and the fully-worded commands when no key bindings are available. Use *regions* and windows for productive editing and understand the superior pattern search and substitution techniques. Learn to use the *kill ring* for retrieving multiple sections of copied and deleted text. Customization of the editor and its advanced features are discussed in the end-of-chapter "Going Further" section.

Chapter 6 discusses files and directories. Understand the use of *pathnames* in describing the parent–child relationship between them. Create and remove directories (**mkdir** and **rmdir**) and navigate the file system (**pwd** and **cd**). Learn to create (**cat >**), copy (**cp**), remove (**rm**) and print (**lp**) files. Find out how free your disk is (**df**) and compress your files (**compress**, **gzip** and **zip**) to release space. No file attributes are discussed in this chapter.

All file and directory attributes are discussed in Chapter 7. Use the **ls** command with numerous options to display them. Change the permissions (**chmod**) and ownership (**chown** and **chgrp**) of a file. Understand how permissions acquire a different meaning when applied to directories. Use *links* (**ln**) to provide additional names to a file without changing the *inode number*. Finally, use the **find** command to locate any file or directory in the file system by specifying one or more file attributes. A file's contents are not disturbed in this chapter.

Chapter 8 is the first of four chapters reserved for the shell. Learn the use of *metacharacters* to match multiple filenames with a single pattern. Redirect the input and output *streams* of many commands to originate from or go to another file or another command. Use quotes and the \ to remove the special meaning of these metacharacters. The chapter also introduces the use of shell variables and shell scripts.

Chapter 9 develops on the stream-handling features of the shell to present a family of commands (*filters*) that use streams both for input and output. These are simple filters that manipulate content in a limited way, like extracting sections from different regions of a file (**head**, **tail**, **cut** and **paste**). Learn to sort a file (**sort**) and translate a character (**tr**) into something else. Finally, use these commands in combination to have a first taste of the much-hyped tool-building feature of UNIX.

The process management system comes next (Chapter 10). Find out how similar files and processes are, and discover three types of commands in the system when looked at from a process perspective. Understand how processes are created with **fork** and **exec**, display their attributes (**ps**) and kill a runaway process (**kill**). Learn to run jobs in the background (**nohup** and &) and move them between background and foreground (**bg** and **fg**). Also learn to change their priority (**nice**) and even schedule them (**at**, **batch** and **cron**) for later operation.

We venture into the TCP/IP networking world in Chapter 11. Get introduced to *hostnames*, *IP addresses* and *domain names*. Understand the role played by *ports* and *sockets* to move a packet from one host to another. You'll learn to log on to a remote machine with **telnet** and **rlogin**. Also copy files between machines with **ftp** and **rcp**. Use **rsh** to run a command remotely without logging in.

The GUI in UNIX comes next (Chapter 12) with a minimal discussion on the X Window system. Understand how X is ideally suited for working in a TCP/IP network. X clients need a separate program (the *window manager*) to control the look and feel of its windows. Use the **xterm** client as the launching pad to run all applications. Configure X to behave differently on startup (.xinitrc) and customize its *resources*.

Chapter 13 is all about electronic mail. Understand how the SMTP and POP protocols are used to handle mail. Here, apart from the standard **mail** command, use two menu-based programs, **elm** and **pine**. Forward your mail (.forward) or leave behind messages when you are away (**vacation**). Configure and use Netscape Messenger as a superior mail handling tool. Learn to compose a group of messages offline, use the address book and set up *spam* control. Mail can now handle multimedia attachments as a *multipart* message. Understand *MIME* theory in the "Going Further" section.

Chapter 14 extends Chapter 11 to focus on the Internet and the World Wide Web. Learn how the top-level *domains* are organized. Use a *mailing list*. Discover a domain-like structure in *newsgroups*, and access Net News using **tin** and Netscape. Communicate with multiple persons using the *Internet Relay Chat*. Use *URLs*, *HTTP* and

HTML to access the Web. Customize Netscape Navigator to make Web browsing very productive.

Filters make another appearance in Chapter 15 with two advanced text manipulators. Search for a pattern with commands of the **grep** family (also **egrep** and **fgrep**). Display lines containing and not containing the pattern, and their frequency of occurrence. Use **sed** as a multipurpose filtering tool and especially to substitute one pattern for another. Here, we have the most exhaustive presentation of regular expressions discussed in a phased manner in three sections.

awk as a filter and a programming language makes its appearance in Chapter 16. Break up a line into fields and manipulate each field individually. Use the comparison operators and decimal numbers for computation. Make decisions and iterate within a loop in true programming language style. Use the common **awk** variables and its built-in functions, especially those that relate to string handling. You'll need all this knowledge to understand **perl**, which uses many of **awk**'s features.

The UNIX shell provides excellent opportunities to customize your environment (Chapter 17). Use its variables to set the command search path, the terminal and the prompt. Use the *history* facility to edit and re-run previous commands with simple keystrokes. Devise *aliases* for frequently used commands, and let the shell *complete* filenames and command names for you. Learn to place all customized settings in a startup file. The discussions are presented separately for the Bourne shell, C shell, Korn shell and bash.

Shell programming is introduced in Chapter 18. Develop both interactive (**read**) and noninteractive scripts by passing arguments ($1, $2 etc.). Use the *exit status* of a command to control program flow ($?) and the || and && operators to act as simple conditionals. Learn to use **test** to check strings and the file attributes. Use the wild-card handling feature of **case** as a superior string checking tool. Exploit the $0 parameter to make a script do different things depending on the name by which it is called. Use the standard programing constructs **if**, **while**, **until** and **for** to develop three interesting scripts.

The shell's advanced features are presented in Chapter 19 and include the special features of the Korn and bash shells. Put values into positional parameters (**set** and **shift**). Have another look at stream redirection with the *here document* and learn to merge streams using special symbols. Use **export** to make variable values available in sub-shells. Learn to use arrays and shell functions. Evaluate a command line twice (**eval**) to develop scripts using numbered prompts and variables. Handle multiple streams using **exec**. Finally, use **trap** to determine script behavior when it receives a signal.

We encounter **perl** in Chapter 20 as the finest and most powerful filter in the UNIX world. Use the *default variable* $_ for condensing many statements. Split a line into a list of variables or an array. Use a nonnumeric subscript with the associative array. **perl** uses all the regular expressions discussed so far, but it uses some of its own too (the final discussion). Learn to handle external files and develop subroutines. **perl**'s dominant role in Internet CGI programming is discussed in the chapter's "Going Further" section using a simple form-based HTML application.

The file system comes up for the last time in Chapter 21—this time from the system administrative point of view. We discuss the device files and their unique attributes. Know all about *partitions*, *file systems* and *inodes*. Know the features of the various types of file systems and learn to *mount* and *unmount* them. Check the integrity of a file system with the **fsck** command.

General system administration is taken up in Chapter 22. Learn about the powers and privileges of the super user. Maintain user accounts and groups. Enforce security and learn two special permission modes of a file, the *sticky bit* and *set-user-id*. Understand the role of **init** in the startup and shutdown procedure, and grasp the significance of the fields in /etc/inittab. Make backups with **tar** and **cpio**. The end-of-chapter "Going Further" section discusses printer administration and the scripts used by **init**.

We turn to network administration in Chapter 23 and understand how IP addresses are allocated in a TCP/IP network. Learn to configure your network interface (**ifconfig**), routing (**route**) and display the network statistics (**netstat**). Understand how **inetd** controls the **ftp**, **telnet** and POP services. Connect your machine to the Internet with the *Point-to-Point Protocol* (PPP) using two tools, **dip** and **chat**. Make your directories and file systems shareable using the *Network File System* (NFS).

Finally, use your Linux machine to set up three important Internet services for a fictitious network—name service (DNS), email and Web (Chapter 24). Set up the master, slave and caching-only server using BIND 8. Understand how **sendmail** works, and configure the important parameters in /etc/sendmail.cf to set up standard mail server configurations. Understand the utility of *aliases* for forwarding mail and use **fetchmail** to download mail from a remote POP server. Also set up the **httpd** Web service using Apache. Learn to control CGI script execution, *virtual hosts* and directory access.

How This Book Is Different

At the outset, let me maintain that I made no conscious decision to make this book different from others. Facing a UNIX box was my first encounter with computers—even before I knew what an operating system was. I had no expectations, no sides to take and no one to offer me guidance. Having been out there "in the cold," I feel that the stumbling blocks to understanding UNIX are often different from what they are perceived to be. I couldn't wholeheartedly embrace the way people wrote on the subject, and instead conceived my own idea of the "true" UNIX book—a book that people would like to have with them all the time. The implementation of this idea, spurred by the instant delight that I developed in the subject, automatically sets this book apart from others. There are five important points to consider:

1. Clarity of Expression

UNIX concepts are sometimes abstract, and when they are not, their relevance to the real world is not often appreciated. I believe that every concept has to be dissected properly to expose its design considerations. Why was the feature conceived in the first place? Where can one apply it? Is the standard explanation clear? Do the examples leave behind gray areas of understanding? If we don't have positive answers to all these questions, then we are most certainly in a state of ambiguity and confusion.

This book makes sure every concept is explained the way it needs to be. Take, for instance, one of the basic tenets of the UNIX system, *standard output*. We are told what standard output is, but I have not been impressed with the way it has been explained in the books. On the other hand, I felt that the sequence **who > newfile** is better comprehended in this way *(p. 239)*:

The shell looks at the >, understands that standard output has to be redirected, opens the file **newfile**, writes the stream into it and then closes the file. And all this happens without **who** knowing absolutely anything about it!

How many people know for a fact that a command has no knowledge of the source of its input and output? Or that there are important implications involved when choosing to use **wc < foo** in preference to **wc foo** *(p. 240)*? When do you need to make a command ignorant of the source of its input *(p. 247)*? Does the \ in **echo "Enter your name \c"** really remove a special meaning as it is normally known to do *(p. 237)*? You must know the answers to these questions before you satisfy yourself that you have understood the shell.

To take another example, why do I often hear that the command line **find /home -name index.html -print** is difficult to remember? Only because many people don't care to split **find**'s arguments into three components *(p. 218)*:

---

find *path_list selection_criteria action*

- First, it recursively examines all files in the directories specified in *path_list*. Here, it begins the search from /home.

- It then matches each file for one or more *selection_criteria*. This always consists of an expression in the form *-operator argument* (-name index.html). Here, **find** selects the file if it has the name index.html.

- Finally, it takes some *action* on those selected files. The action -print simply displays the **find** output on the terminal.

Take a look at Table 7.5 *(p. 220)* and you'll find the selection criteria separated from the action, and presented in roughly the same sequence the **ls -l** command presents the file attributes. I haven't seen it organized this way in any other book, and yet I strongly feel that a power user of **find** needs to look at the command in this way.

There are so many other things that you need to know and yet aren't properly explained in the standard books. This book explains why file ownership is so important *(p. 208)* and how to use the sticky bit to implement group projects *(p. 680)*. You'll discover three important application areas where links can be used *(p. 215)*. How does the shell that greets you on login differ from the one that runs your scripts *(p. 523)*? Why mustn't the **cd** command run in a sub-shell *(p. 298)*? Will a message addressed to *joe winter <winterj@sasol.com>* reach him if we misspelled joe *(p. 368—Note)*? You'll find answers to all these questions (and many, many more) in this book.

2. Both Elementary and Comprehensive

One of my reviewers had earlier observed (before he reviewed this book) that the problem with writing a good semester-length UNIX book is that you need something ele-

GOING FURTHER

mentary enough for beginning students but comprehensive and "referency" enough for the same students to use as they advance. Making a book that fits into both slots was perhaps the most difficult task I faced, but it seems that this has now been achieved. The final judgment, however, is reserved for you.

This book has an enormous amount of information laid out in a structured manner—much more than can be expected from a book of this size. I have tried to present information that is easy to understand and yet devoid of verbiage. While I didn't deviate from the goal of grouping like material, I also made sure that advanced material was segregated from the essential by locating it at the end of a chapter. Each page there is highlighted with the "Going Further" tab. A beginner should simply ignore these portions during the initial pass.

I felt the need to provide as many examples as I could; in fact, some of the tables contain just examples. Just take a look at the ways **chmod** is used in Table 7.3 *(p. 205)* and discover an undocumented feature! Or the way the shell's wild cards are used with commands in Table 8.1 *(p. 231)*. Since **cron** is an indispensable scheduling tool, the significance of the fields of its configuration file is presented with a good number of examples in Table 10.3 *(p. 313)*. Sometimes, I have combined a concept and an example in the same table. You'll appreciate regular expressions better if you study the entries in Table 15.2 *(p. 441)*.

This book is also a comprehensive reference. Important commands have their options listed in their own tables, and the chapters on **vi** and **emacs** editors have lots of tables. Once you know how to use one editor, you'll find Appendix B *(p. 781)* useful (where **vi** and **emacs** are compared feature for feature) to learn the other. Does the C shell use functions? Or what's the role of the command that is itself named **command** in the Korn and bash shells? Just look up Appendix D *(p. 795)* where all the four shells are compared in detail. We all know that regular expressions are used differently by the major filters, but can you recall whether **grep** uses the \b escape sequence? There's no need to experiment any longer, the regular expression matrix says it all "in one place" *(Appendix C, p. 791)*.

This book is also characterized by the presence of section references everywhere. Each chapter opens with a statement of objectives with pointers to the section numbers. A list of the key terms introduced is also presented at the end with similar references. Both forward and reverse referencing have also been made in the main text:

> If you are afraid that you may accidentally overwrite a file, you can later use your knowledge of aliases (*17.4*) and shell functions (*19.10*) to make **cp** behave in this interactive manner by default.
>
> The same logic has already been implemented by using three commands in a pipeline--**cut**, **sort**, and **uniq** (*9.18.1*). That one used only a single line of code!

Sometimes, you'll want to know not what a command does, but the command that actually performs a specific function. How does one display lines in double space? Or select those that contain or don't contain a pattern? Does UNIX have any tool that presents lines in reverse order? What are the various copying facilities available? There's a specially prepared HOWTO document *(Appendix E, p. 807)* that you'll find enormously useful for these lookups, as these sample lines will reveal:

How to do or display	Command	Page no.
copy directory tree	cp -r	178
copy file between machines	ftp	329
copy file between machines without authentication	rcp	336
lines containing pattern	grep	434
lines in ASCII collating sequence	sort	275
lines in double space	pr -d -t	267
lines in reverse order	tail -r	272
lines not containing pattern	grep -v	438

If you fail to locate a key term, there's a comprehensive glossary that comes to your rescue *(Appendix G, p. 819)*. Special attention has also been given to the index. In addition to the general index, you have access to specially prepared indexes for the **vi** and **emacs** editors. A comprehensive set of over 200 commands discussed in this book has also been indexed separately. There's also a separate index for the shells that are featured in the book.

3. Realistic Illustrations

These days you'll find UNIX books filled with lots of illustrations, but how many of them truly explain a concept? Even though I probably have not used as many illustrations as some authors have, I have tried to make them more effective. For instance, the following illustration looks at standard output in a rather different way:

F I G U R E 8.2   *The Three Destinations of Standard Output*

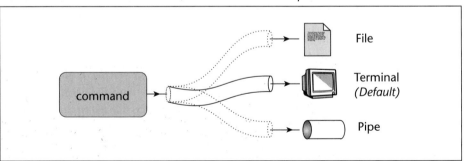

You probably won't have seen standard output portrayed in this manner, but this figure answers many queries. Did it ever occur to you that standard output has three possible destinations? This figure easily replaces a thousand words.

There are many more compelling illustrations. The complexity of the shell's behavioral pattern breaks down when you take a look at Fig 8.1 *(p. 229)*. The process killing mechanism becomes much easier to comprehend by drawing an analogy with a radar, a gun and an aircraft in Fig 10.2 *(p. 308)*. And you should find the presence of the postman in Fig. 13.7 *(p. 379)* quite meaningful when figuring out how SMTP and POP handle electronic mail.

4. Strong Learning Aids

The idea of reminding a reader about an important topic has always been uppermost in my mind, even though it may have already been mentioned in the text. In fact, these pedagogical aids are a strong feature of this book, and you'll find over 400 instances of such aids in this text. They take on various names, for example, Note, Caution, and Tip. Here's an instance of the first type:

Note

The caret has a triple role to play in regular expressions. When placed at the beginning of a character class (e.g., [^a-z]), it negates every character of the class. When placed outside it, and at the beginning of the expression (e.g., ^2...), the pattern is matched at the beginning of the line. At any other location (e.g., a^b), it matches itself literally.

UNIX is an unusual system; it seldom warns you when you are about to do something disastrous. Yet, the reader would like to be cautioned against taking this disastrous step. If you are going to schedule jobs using the **crontab** command, then this is something you must keep in mind:

Caution

If you use **crontab** - meaning to provide input through the standard input and then decide to abort it, you should terminate it with the interrupt key applicable for your terminal, rather than *[Ctrl-d]*. If you forget to do that, you'll remove all entries from your existing crontab file!

As mentioned before, many of UNIX's mysteries are hidden. A good tip can often save hours of effort, and I have chosen to provide lots of them in this book. Do you really have to quit the **vi** editor every time you want to execute the currently edited shell or **perl** script? No, you don't:

Tip

Can you execute a shell or **perl** script without leaving **vi**? Make this mapping of the function key *[F1]*:

```
:map #1 :!%^M
```
                                                                          File must have executable permission

This executes (!) the current file (%) at the : prompt. This is one important mapping which the author uses to run scripts without quitting **vi**. You should use it too, and then thank yourself (and the author) when you see how fast a script is debugged. Just remember that **vi** understands the current file as %—a poorly documented feature. If you want to compile the current file from the editor, you'll need to use the % as an argument to the compiling command (**cc** or **javac**, for example).

This book is not about Linux per se, but I consider Linux to be an important member of the UNIX family. In general, Linux commands have more options, and some of them are absolute beauties! I have highlighted features that are either unique to Linux or handled differently by it. Such instances are easily located; just look for the penguin:

GNU **grep** has a nifty option that locates not only the matching line, but also a certain number of lines *above* and *below* it. For instance, you may want to know what went before and after the **foreach** statement that you used in a **perl** script:

```
$ grep -1 "foreach" count.pl                    One line above and below
print ("Region List\n");
foreach $r_code sort (keys(%regionlist)) {
    print ("$r_code : $region{$r_code} : $regionlist{$r_code}\n") ;
```

The command locates the string `foreach` and displays one line on either side of it. Isn't this feature useful?

Even though I have used the Bourne shell as the "base" shell in this book, most discussions focus on the other shells—C shell, Korn shell and bash. Rather than have separate chapters for them, I have first discussed a concept in a general manner and then highlighted a shell-specific feature in a separate aside box:

The standard error is handled differently by the C shell, so the examples of this section won't work with it. In fact, the C shell merges the standard error with the standard output; it has no separate symbol for handling standard error only.

5. Numerous Questions and Exercises

This book features an enormous number of questions that test the reader's knowledge—over 900 of them. More than a third of them are Self-Test questions, and their answers are provided in Appendix H. These questions are all targeted toward beginners who will do well to answer them before moving on to the next chapter.

More rigorous and extensive questioning is reserved for the Exercises section. Some of them pose real challenges, and it may take you some time to solve them. These exercises reinforce and often add to your knowledge of UNIX, so don't ignore them. The answers to these questions are available to adopters of the book at the book's Web site *http://www.mhhe.com/das*. You'll find a lot of additional material on this site that you can use to supplement this book.

Final Words of "Wisdom"

All examples have been tested with a number of UNIX and Linux systems, but I simply can't guarantee that they will run error-free on every system. UNIX fragmentation makes sweeping generalizations virtually impossible. It is quite possible that some commands may either not be available or may throw out different messages on your system. You have to take this in your stride, and you need not automatically conclude that the system has bugs. Nevertheless, bugs in these examples are still possible, and I welcome ones (along with all your suggestions at *sumitabha@vsnl.com*) that you may hit upon.

Before I take leave, a note of caution would be in order. Many people missed the UNIX bus through confused and misguided thinking and are now regretting it. They fell for the mouse, and the mouse couldn't deliver much. Don't let this happen to you. It doesn't have to if you don't want it to—at least, not any longer. Learn to use the tools of the system and build on them without reinventing the wheel. You'll find a world of opportunity and excitement opening up. Approach the subject with zeal and confidence; I am with you.

Sumitabha Das

Conventions Used in This Book

The key terms used in the book (like **regular expression**) are shown in a bold font. Apart from this, the following conventions have been used in this book:

- Commands, internal commands and user input in examples are shown in bold constant width font:

  Many commands in **more** including **f** and **b** use a repeat factor.
  The shell features three types of loops—**while**, **until** and **for**.
  Enter your name: **henry**

- Apart from command output, filenames, strings, symbols, expressions, options and keywords are shown in constant width font. For example:

  Most commands are located in /bin and /usr/bin.
  Try doing that with the name gordon lightfoot.
  Use the expression wilco[cx]k*s* with the -l option.
  The shell looks for the characters >, < and << in the command line.
  The -mtime keyword looks for the modification time of a file.

- Machine and domain names, email addresses, newsgroups and URLs are displayed in italics:

  When henry logs on to the machine *uranus* ......
  The RFCs are available at *rs.internic.net.*
  User henry on this host can be addressed as *henry@calcs.planets.com.*
  Every beginner should subscribe to *news.announce.newusers.*
  Download the plugin software from *http://www.shockwave.com.*

- Place-holders for filenames, terms, header text, menu options and explanatory comments within examples are displayed in italics:

  Use the -f *filename* option if this doesn't work.
  ..... to develop a set of standard rules (*protocols*)
  We'll ignore the *C* header. *STIME* shows the time the process started.
  Use *Edit>Preferences* to configure Netscape.
  $ **cd ../..**   *Moves two levels up*

The following abbreviations, shortcuts and symbols have been used:

- SVR4—System V Release 4
- sh—Bourne shell
- csh—C shell
- ksh—Korn shell
- *ksh93*—The ksh93 version of the Korn shell
- $HOME/*flname*—The file *flname* in the home directory
- ~/*flname*—The file *flname* in the home directory
- foo, bar and foobar—Generic file and directory names as used on USENET
- .... for lines that are not shown
- This box □ indicates the space character.
- This pair of arrows ⇆ indicates the tab character.

Acknowledgments

A book of this type requires lots of input from people, and I have been fortunate enough to have all the support I needed. First and foremost, I must acknowledge the real debt of gratitude that I owe to Ananda Deb, without whom this book would not have seen the light of the day. Selflessly, he looked after all my hardware, software and system and network administration requirements, and if that is not enough, he is also responsible for rendering most of the illustrations of this book.

Thanks to all my reviewers for their positive and constructive suggestions related to the book organization and content:

Clare Nguyen	DeAnza College
Donald M. Needham	U.S. Naval Academy
John Berezinski	Northern Illinois University
Karen Atkinson	Rochester Institute of Technology
Ronald J. Thomson	Central Michigan University
Shashi Shekhar	University of Minnesota
Tony Marsland	University of Alberta

Vibha Mahajan deserves thanks for her initial groundwork. I can quite understand the pain she had to go through in allowing her own project to be put into abeyance while Thomas Casson engaged me in this one. Full marks to the publisher and his highly responsive team for the harmonious way they worked to ensure the smooth passage of this ambitious project. Thanks to the ubiquitous Melinda Dougharty for seeing to it that I stayed on course by constantly providing me with feedback and her own advice that helped me write the book. Her razor-sharp analysis of what this book should contain and how the material needed to be organized remains a classic piece of work by itself.

Rebecca Nordbrock deserves praise for the admirable way she conducted the editing and typesetting activities. She kept her cool throughout, even as last-minute changes were being carried out to make the book more reader-friendly. Heather Burbridge has been a real help to us through her activities as liaison and the special interest she has taken in this project. Thanks to Gina Hangos for taking care of the manufacturing process and making sure that deadlines were met.

If you find the book everywhere, it's simply because of John Wannemacher. The marketing manager, who also came up with the title of this book, has great faith in its potential and is responsible for creating the awareness that we all feel it deserves. If you have liked the cover and interior design, then think of Kiera Cunningham, who was instrumental in handling these elements. If the Web site for this book appeals to you, then we have Phil Meek to thank. Thanks are also due to designer, Pam Verros, and copy editor, Jill Barrie. The exhaustive set of indexes owes its origin to Richard Shrout. This book was a challenge for any compositor, but Lachina Publishing Services rose to the occasion admirably. Space constraints don't permit mentioning everyone by name; but thanks just the same.

Malay Mitra has been with me ever since I got into UNIX and has been providing me with valuable information and tips as and when I needed them. There have been helpful suggestions from J.P. Mathew on matters related to Linux. Kawaljit Gandhi was at my side when it came to the Internet and **perl**.

Aban Desai and Rajesh Choudhury were most generous in letting me treat their bookstores as my own private libraries. Dr. Gopal Saha, Trina Saha, Sunilabha Das and Mihir Das never faltered in providing whatever I had asked of them.

I also need to mention that my wife Julie and my daughter Sohini had to go through hell to provide a specially customized environment for me to work in. Thanks for emerging from this ultimate test of patience with the utmost calm. My parents too have been wonderfully restrained as they waited silently for the moment to come.

Finally, I can't help but acknowledge the constant support and blessings of my mentor—Dr. N. Subrahmanyam. The Managing Director of Tata McGraw-Hill believed several years ago that I could do it (when I myself didn't), and has not wavered in his support since.

List of Tables

Contents in Brief

Appendixes

Contents

Getting Started

In this opening chapter, we commence our journey into the world of UNIX. We'll discover why a computer needs an operating system and how UNIX more than fulfills that requirement. Through two hands-on sessions, we'll learn to play with the UNIX system. We'll gain firsthand knowledge of UNIX commands and how to handle files and directories.

As we absorb this knowledge, we'll place it against the rather turbulent background that UNIX had to grow through. We'll learn how contributions from different sources led to both the enrichment and the fragmentation of UNIX. Knowledge of the design considerations will also help us understand why UNIX sometimes behaves in a seemingly awkward manner.

In addition, we'll look at the features of UNIX and how two agencies between themselves handle all the work of the system. Some of the concepts you encounter may seem abstract, but you shouldn't be deterred if you don't understand them initially. Absorb as much as you can, and then move on to the other chapters.

Objectives

- Discover why a computer needs to have an operating system. *(1.1)*
- Learn how the block-building approach in UNIX lets you devise your own tools. *(1.2)*
- Understand the location and function of the special characters of the keyboard. *(1.4)*
- Log in and out of a UNIX system. *(1.6)*
- Learn the use of the commands **passwd**, **who**, **tty**, **set** and **echo** in the first session. *(1.7)*
- Evaluate the variables SHELL and TERM. *(1.7)*
- Know what can go wrong and how to use special keys to handle problems. *(1.9)*
- Handle directories using the **mkdir**, **ls**, **cd** and **pwd** commands in the second session. *(1.10)*
- Create, view and count the words of a file with the **echo**, **cat** and **wc** commands in the second session. *(1.10)*
- Understand how UNIX started from a single source and then steadily got fragmented by the emergence of other flavors. *(1.11)*
- Learn about the emergence of Linux as a strong, viable and free alternative. *(1.12)*
- Understand the concepts and features that characterize UNIX. *(1.13)*

1.1   The Operating System

You've heard of computer hardware and software, but have you ever wondered what an *operating system* is? Or why an entire book should be devoted to one? Isn't knowledge of your favorite word processing software enough? After all, we use cars but don't bother to understand exactly what happens when we change gears. As long as things work, why bother?

There's some merit in this argument—as long as you don't stray beyond your word processor application. But if you want to write some of these applications yourselves, you must know how a computer handles the instructions that you pass on to it. If you have aspirations to be a system administrator, you must understand how files are organized in the hard disk and how to ensure that one user can't intrude into another's territory. You must know your computer's operating system.

An **operating system** (the OS) is a life-giver to a computer—providing it with basic intelligence to work with. Technically speaking, it is a program that is loaded into the computer's memory when the system is booted, and it always remains there. It interacts with two agencies:

- **Applications** (like word-processing software) that run under its auspices.
- Users who pass commands to it using a **command language interpreter**. This too is a program; it translates commands to instructions that can be understood by the operating system.

Applications often require certain services that are controlled by the OS—like the opening and closing of files, accessing the printer, writing to tape, and so forth. When you compose a message, something has to move the disk head and write the data to the disk surface. The application, instead of doing it itself, relies on the OS to do the job. The OS also works behind the scenes on behalf of users who need to access these services. More specifically, an operating system offers these services:

- In systems where multiple programs are running concurrently, the OS decides which application to run at any one instant and how much time should be allocated for it before running the next application.
- It manages the memory shared by these multiple applications. When it's the next application's turn to run, the OS moves the data of the previous application to disk and keeps it ready to be reloaded.
- It directly controls access to all hardware devices like hard disks, terminals, printers and modems.
- When errors are encountered in operation, the OS reports these errors to the application and the user, depending on the agency from whom it received an instruction.
- It provides tools for the user to perform basic services like creating directories, copying and deleting files, sending mail or making backups.

Without an operating system, the most powerful computer in the world would be useless. No matter how powerful and elegant programs are, they simply can't function without its assistance, in the same way the most efficient chef can't display his talents without a properly furnished kitchen.

There have been many operating systems in the past, one at least from each hardware vendor. They all contributed to the chaotic situation that made programs developed on one machine incapable of running on another. Vendors required consumers to purchase expensive proprietary hardware and software if two dissimilar machines needed to talk to each other. We also had DOS and Windows (in all its manifestations) on our desktop computers providing us with a cheaper and thrilling way of computing.

Note An operating system runs programs and controls all resources that the program requires. It also provides services for the user to handle mail, files and processes.

1.2 The UNIX Operating System

Besides DOS and Windows, there's an operating system called UNIX. It arrived earlier than the other two, and has stayed long enough to give us the Internet. It has practically everything an operating system should have, and several features that other operating systems never had. Beginners with some experience in Windows think of UNIX in terms of it, quite oblivious to the fact that the similarities are only superficial. UNIX is a giant operating system and is way ahead of other systems in sheer power.

UNIX has introduced a number of profound and diverse concepts previously unknown to the computing community. It is a system developed by programmers for their own use, and thus many things that appear quite obvious to them don't appear obvious to us. However, that doesn't imply in any way that it is unconquerable; in fact, it's great fun. It only requires a different type of commitment to understand it. UNIX assumes a great deal; often, it doesn't tell you whether you are right or wrong, or warn you of the consequences of your actions.

UNIX also has a command language interpreter: you type in a word that is interpreted as a **command** by the system. A command may list files or count the number of words in a file. However, UNIX derives its power not from these simple commands, but their capability to combine with one another. Just as the English language lets you combine words to generate a meaningful idea, UNIX commands can be strung together to form complex tasks. In fact, the capabilities of UNIX are limited only by your imagination.

If you are willing to put in some *guided* effort, you'll gradually see the UNIX story unfold with clarity and simplicity. Focus your attention on the essentials and try to understand the designers' minds and objectives. Even though UNIX sometimes appears unfriendly, it in fact challenges you to unravel its mysteries. In this book, we take up this challenge.

Note The UNIX system doesn't offer a fixed set of services. In fact, you have to use your imagination in devising improvised tools from the existing ones. This is what makes UNIX so challenging and exciting.

1.3 Knowing Your Machine

Unlike Windows, UNIX can be used by several users concurrently. In other words, a single copy of the operating system installed on a single disk can serve the needs of hundreds of users. If you have access to such a *multiuser* system, then in all probability you'll be sitting with just a terminal (a monitor that looks more like a portable TV) and a keyboard. Like you, there will be others working on similar terminals. The rest of the equipment will probably be located in a separate room with restricted access. In this arrangement, you are expected to connect to your account, perform your work, disconnect and leave quietly.

Things are quite different, however, when you are using a **workstation**. This is a computer capable of producing high-quality graphics but meant to be used by a single user. Unlike a terminal, which is a pretty dumb device, a workstation has its own CPU (central processor unit), memory (the RAM—random access memory), hard disk, CD-ROM and printer. Since it has all the things that UNIX needs, a workstation can run its own UNIX. Desktop PCs are also often referred to as workstations.

Even though workstations run UNIX and can be used in a standalone mode, they are often connected to a larger, more powerful computer in the same way terminals are. There are a number of reasons you might want such an arrangement:

- The central computer is administered properly, and you might want to keep all your valuable files there so they are backed up regularly.
- You might like to use a powerful program that your workstation doesn't have but the central computer does.
- All your incoming and outgoing mail is handled by the central machine, which may be your only link with the outside world, i.e., the Internet.

To take advantage of these facilities, your workstation needs to be connected in a network to the central computer. To know whether you have a networked machine, just check whether any wire leads from the back of your workstation to the room housing the central computer.

Every workstation provides a **terminal emulation** facility that makes it abandon its normal mode and behave like a simple dumb terminal instead. The workstation then doesn't use its own hard disk, CPU or memory for doing any work except providing the minimal resources required by the terminal emulation software. However, there's one thing you ought to keep in mind at this stage: when you use a terminal or the terminal emulation facility to connect to a central computer, all files are created on the *remote* machine and not on your local machine. The programs you run also use the central computer's memory and CPU.

If you own a workstation or a PC, then you are directly responsible for its startup, shutdown and maintenance. If you lose a file, it's your job to get it from a backup. If things don't work properly, you have to try all possible means to set them right before you decide to call a maintenance person.

Note

Even if your workstation runs UNIX, you could still need to connect to a remote computer and run a program there. In that case, your workstation behaves like a simple dumb terminal. You'll surely want to have indicators that tell you whether you are working on the remote machine or the local one. You'll learn to do that in this book.

1.4 Knowing Your Keyboard

Before you start work, you need to know the functions of a number of keys on your keyboard. Many of these keys are either not used by Windows or have different functions there. We'll discuss the PC keyboard in this section but also note the possible deviations that you may find on other systems.

The portion of the keyboard at the left having the *QWERTY* layout (the letters Q, W, E, R, T and Y arranged in a line) resembles a typewriter (if you can find one today). The numeric keys are located above this line. The layout of the alphanumeric keys is standard for all systems. If you know typing, you are on familiar terrain and keyboard phobia shouldn't get in your way.

Apart from the alphanumeric keys, you'll observe a number of symbols as shown below:

`$ % * ( ) - = + [ ] { } ; : ' " , . ? & / ! @`

These symbols should be quite familiar to you as they are available on any typewriter or word processor. Some of them are invoked by pressing the *[Shift]* key with the corresponding key. But the keyboard also offers some characters which you may not have encountered before. They are shown in Table 1.1.

Every key on your keyboard has a function in UNIX, so you should be able to locate each one of these keys before you proceed further with this text. Many of these keys have multiple functions depending on the program that is using them. For instance, the | has a different meaning in the shell from the one it has in **vi**.

Each alphabet, number, or symbol is known as a **character** and represents the smallest piece of information that you can deal with. All these characters have unique values assigned to them, called the **ASCII value** (ASCII—American Standard Code for Information Interchange). For instance, the letter G has an ASCII value of 71, while the bang (!) has a value of 33. Many UNIX programs can also be used with ASCII values.

When you look at the screen, you'll see a blinking object called a *cursor*. When you key in a character, it shows at the location of the cursor, while moving the cursor itself right.

There's another important key that has no counterpart in the typewriter—the *[Enter]* key located at the right. On some machines, it may be labeled *[Return]*. This key is used to terminate a line, and its significance is taken up later in this chapter.

Directly above *[Enter]* is the *[Backspace]* key, which is often shown by the symbol ←. This key is used for correcting mistakes (hence the term **backspacing**). When

T A B L E 1.1 *Special Characters Used by UNIX*

Symbol	Name
`	Backquote or backtick
~	Tilde
#	Pound or number
^	Caret or hat
_	Underscore (different from -, the dash or hyphen)
\	Backslash
|	Pipe
<	Left chevron (the less than symbol)
>	Right chevron (the greater than symbol)

you need to erase a character that you have just entered, you have to press this key. The cursor then moves over that character to the left and removes it from sight.

Another important key is *[Ctrl]* (called *Control*) on the lower-left side. On PC keyboards, you'll find it in duplicate; there's one on the right as well. This key is never used singly but in combination with other keys. These combinations produce all the **control characters** that you'll encounter in this book. For instance, when you are advised to use *[Ctrl-s]* to stop a scrolling display, you should first press the *[Ctrl]* key and then the key labeled s—keeping *[Ctrl]* pressed all the time.

In the same line, you have the *[Alt]* key (in duplicate on PCs). This key too is used in combination. You'll need it when using **emacs** and the X Window system. Many systems don't have this key but have a *[Meta]* key instead. If a UNIX program requires you to use the *[Meta]* key and you don't have it on your keyboard, the *[Alt]* key can often take its place.

At the top-left corner, you can see the *[Esc]* key (called *Escape*). You'll require this key for performing file editing with the text editors **vi** and **emacs**. While you have alternatives to *[Esc]* in **emacs**, it's a vital component of **vi** functioning. This key often takes you to the previous menu in a menu-based program that doesn't use the mouse.

On the right is the *[Delete]* key. On some machines, you may see *[Del]* instead. This key is also used for backspacing on systems that either don't have the *[Backspace]* key or have one that doesn't function in that manner.

In the same line as the *[Esc]* key are the 12 function keys labeled *[F1]*, *[F2]*, and so on, up to *[F12]* (or *[F10]* on older systems). They are often located differently; you may find them on the left of your keyboard. You require them for invoking **virtual terminal** sessions (multiple sessions) on the same workstation or PC (but not on terminals). They are also needed for enhancing the capabilities of editors like **vi**.

Finally, let's turn to the keys that every Windows user is familiar with. The cursor control keys (the ones with four arrows) are required for navigation in **vi** and **emacs**. The same editors also use the *[Home]*, *[End]*, *[PageUp]* and *[PageDown]* keys in just the same way any word processor uses them. If your working environment permits it, you can use the keys with the up and down arrows to recall previous commands.

When you use *[Alt]* in combination with the function keys on your workstation or PC, you can have several **virtual terminal** sessions on a single machine. These virtual terminals let you log on several times to the *same* computer, with a separate "terminal" for each session. Since a single screen is shared by all sessions, the *[Alt]* key is used to step through these virtual terminals.

Note   Many of the keys representing the special characters, and even the *[Ctrl]* or *[Alt]* keys, are located differently on many systems and terminals. Some keyboards also have a *[Meta]* key, which is often functionally replaced by the *[Alt]* key on the PC keyboard.

1.5 The System Administrator

On a large system serving hundreds of users, someone has to be given charge of administration of the system. This person is known as the **system administrator**. The administrator is a very important person and is responsible for the proper management of the entire setup. She allocates user accounts, maintains file systems, takes backups, manages disk space and performs several other important functions. She is the person to be contacted in case of a genuine problem.

UNIX is security-conscious and can be used only by those persons who maintain an **account** with the computer system. This list of accounts is maintained separately in the computer. The administrator has a special user account for her own use; it's called **root**. root has near-absolute powers; some programs can only be run from this account—for instance, the program that creates the user account itself.

The administrator opens an account with a name for your use. This name is generally a meaningful string and is called the **user-id** or **username**. You'll also be provided with a secret code that you have to enter when the system prompts you for it. This string is called the **password**. Unlike the user-id, the password should be an unmeaningful string. You can't simply sit down at any terminal and start banging away unless you first *log in* to the system with a valid user-id and password. That's both an inadvisable and an impossible thing to do.

1.6 Logging In and Out

Seeing is believing as they say, so without further ado, let's get down to business and jump straight into a hands-on session on a UNIX system. See for yourself what a UNIX session is really like. A personal interaction with the system often drives home a point better than the preaching of textbooks (including this one).

1.6.1 Logging In

If you are working on a large system and have been provided with a terminal, ask the administrator for your user-id and password. If you are trying out UNIX on your own workstation, ask some experienced UNIX person to set up an account and provide you with these two parameters unless you decide to do that yourself.

If you have the name "romeo" as your user-id, you'll be expected to enter this name when you see a **prompt** similar to this on the terminal:

```
login:
```

There can be various prefixes to the word login: in the prompt string; sometimes you may see the machine name there too. (Yes, every machine has a name in UNIX.) On some systems, you may even see Username: instead. The login: prompt indicates that the terminal is available for someone to **log in** (i.e., connect to one's account on a machine). This message also indicates that the previous user has **logged out** (i.e., finished her work and disconnected).

Since you now have an account named romeo, enter this string at the prompt. Then press the *[Enter]* key after the string:

```
login: romeo[Enter]
password:
```

The system now requests you to enter the password—the secret code that was handed to you by your administrator. This code should be known to none except yourself. (The administrator doesn't even need to know!) It's something like the personal identification number that you have to key in before withdrawing cash from an automatic teller machine. Type the secret code, and then press the *[Enter]* key:

```
login: romeo
password:*********[Enter]                                          Entry not displayed
```

You may be surprised to see that the password you entered isn't displayed on the screen. This is another security feature built into the system, so someone standing beside you can't see what you have entered (unless, of course, she has been meticulously monitoring your finger movements!).

If you make mistakes while typing, you can try backspacing with the *[Backspace]* key if the system will permit it. You can also press the *[Enter]* key one or two times till the login prompt reappears on the screen. Be sure to terminate your responses with *[Enter]* to make the system "see" the input that you have entered. If you enter either the user-id or the password incorrectly, the system flashes the following message:

```
login incorrect
login:
```

Another level of security! You simply don't know what went wrong—your login name or password. The message `login incorrect` is quite deceptive in fact; in most cases, it's the password that's the culprit. When you get both these parameters correct, this is what you could be seeing:

```
Last login: Thu Sep 16 22:11:17 on tty2
$ _
```

The system here displays a message showing the last time you logged in. Your system may show other messages, but you'll finally see a prompt string (here, a simple one— a solitary $) with the cursor (the _ character) constantly blinking beside it.

Does it surprise you that while you are pondering what to do next, a program is *always* running at your terminal? This program produces the prompt and accepts all your input from the keyboard. It is known as the **shell**, and the UNIX system offers a variety of them for you to choose from. The shell is the command language interpreter— one of the two agencies that interacts with the operating system. When the administrator opens a user account, she also sets a specific shell for the user.

UNIX systems mostly feature $ as the default prompt. In the academic world, however, the % is more popular than the $. We don't show the cursor this time:

```
%                                                                  The C shell uses this
```

Depending on the shell you are using, prompts can be customized to show the user-id, the machine name, or the current date and time. Moreover, the system administrator will in all probability be using the # as her prompt. Here's another one:

```
[/home/romeo]                                        The Korn shell can show the directory
```

This one shows your *current directory*—a concept that should be familiar to most Windows users who use the statement **PROMPT [pg]** in their AUTOEXEC.BAT to customize their prompt string. For the time being, be content with whatever prompt you have to work with; it won't cause you any harm. We'll assume the $ as the prompt for most of this text.

Note

The shell is a program that keeps running all the time as long as you are logged in. Everything that you enter at the prompt is actually input to this program. The administrator sets your shell when opening your account, but you can sometimes change it yourself.

Linux

Linux systems hardly ever show the $ or % as the prompt. These systems come pre-configured with quite informative prompts like this one which shows the machine (*saturn*), username (romeo) and the current directory (/home/romeo):

```
romeo@saturn:/home/romeo >
```

1.6.2 Logging Out

Before you proceed to try out some of the UNIX commands available on your system, you must first know how to log out (take yourself out) of the system. The technique of doing that also depends on the shell you use, so you should try all of them in turn (mainly three). First try *[Ctrl-d]*:

```
$ [Ctrl-d]                                    Keep [Ctrl] pressed and then press d
login:
```

[Ctrl-d] is generated by pressing the *[Ctrl]* key and the character d. The `login:` message confirms that the session has been terminated, and the terminal is available for the next user. If you don't see the `login:` prompt but see this:

```
Use "logout" to log out.
```

it means that *[Ctrl-d]* won't work, and you should use the **logout** command instead. This usually happens on accounts that use % as the prompt:

```
% logout[Enter]                                              % is the prompt here
login:
```

If the **logout** command doesn't work, then the **exit** command should do the job. In most cases, this is the command that terminates a session. Don't forget to press the *[Enter]* key with both commands.

Tip

One of these three commands should log you out—*[Ctrl-d]*, **logout** or **exit**. The **logout** command is generally used by the C shell that produces the % prompt. *[Ctrl-d]* and **exit** are used by the other shells.

1.7 Trying Out Some Commands

Now log on to the system once again by providing the username (the user-id) and password at the two prompts. After you have successfully made your entry, you have free access to most of the wonderful things that UNIX offers. When you key in a word, the system interprets it as a **command**; you are in fact commanding the machine to do something. Not all commands are acknowledged, only those that are present in the system's predetermined list. We'll now acquaint ourselves with a few of these commands.

1.7.1   passwd: Changing Your Own Password

You can start your first meaningful dialogue with the system by changing your own password—the one you used to get in. The command needed to do that is called **passwd**:

```
$ passwd[Enter]
Old Password : ********[Enter]
New Password : ********[Enter]
Reenter Password : ********[Enter]
$ _                                      Prompt returns—command complete
```

When you enter the word passwd (note the spelling) and follow it with *[Enter]*, the system expects you to respond three times. First, it prompts you for the old password which you must key in at this prompt. Next, it checks whether you have entered a valid password, and if you have, it then prompts you for the new password. Enter the new password as required, using the password naming rules applicable for your system. Finally, the system asks you to reenter the new password.

As expected, the characters that you key in are not echoed to the terminal, so you must type carefully and slowly. Both entries for the new password must match; if they don't, the system will flash an error message and you'll be required to enter the **passwd** command again. Note that when the command has completed its run, the $ prompt is returned. Henceforth, we'll not indicate this return except in those situations where the return is significant.

The password framing rules depend on the brand of UNIX used and the security level that has been set for it. There is often a minimum length of the string. Many systems insist on using a mix of letters with numerals. Generally, a combination of upper-case and lowercase alphabets and numbers should make the password unmeaningful to others. This should prevent unauthorized users from intruding into your "territory" by pure guessing. You'll learn later of the terrible consequences that you may have to face if people with mischievous intent somehow come to know what your password is.

Next time you log in, remember that you'll need to enter the new password to gain entry into the system. Since you are expected to be the custodian of your password name, remember it as long as you don't change it again. If you still forget it, then rush to your system administrator.

passwd is one of the several hundred commands available in the UNIX system. We'll consider the **passwd** command in some detail in a later chapter.

Note

The return of the $ prompt indicates that all work relating to the previous command has been completed, and the system is ready to accept the next command.

Caution

Sometimes, the system may consider it is too soon to change your password. You'll then have to wait a specified period before you can change it. Ask the system administrator to relax the rules for this session.

1.7.2   who: Who Are the Users?

UNIX is a system used by multiple users, and you might be interested in knowing the people who are currently using the system. Use the **who** command:

```
$ who[Enter]
romeo        tty01        May 08 11:11
henry        tty02        May 08 14:18
steve        tty03        May 08 12:01
```

There are currently three users—romeo, henry and steve. These are actually the user-ids they used to log in. The terminal names and the date and time of login are also indicated.

You must also know who you are. Since you logged in with the name romeo, the system addresses you by this name, and associates romeo with whatever work you do. Sometimes, you may forget your own username, especially when you have a number of accounts on the system. To know who you are, use the same **who** command, but this time with two additional words am and i:

```
$ who am i[Enter]
romeo        tty01        May 08 11:11
```

Where else is the username required? Create a file and the system will make romeo the **owner** of the file. Send mail to another user and the system will inform the recipient that mail has arrived from romeo. The machine identifies you as romeo as if it's your real name. It may even be when the system administrator assigns you the user-id.

The additional words used with **who** are known as **arguments**, and most UNIX commands are used with a number of arguments. Arguments change the behavior of the command itself, and this text discusses the important arguments of the major UNIX commands.

Observe that the output of **who** doesn't include any headers to indicate what the various columns mean. This is an extremely important feature of the system, and is in great measure responsible for the unfriendly image that it has acquired. After you have completed Chapter 8, you'll discover that it is actually a blessing in disguise.

Note

The additional words used with **who** are referred to as *arguments*. And if am and i are two arguments there must be others, which you'll learn later.

1.7.3   tty: Know Your Terminal Name

Now that you know who you are, you should also know the name of your terminal. This seems to be tty01, but UNIX has a separate command to tell you that. It's the **tty** command:

```
$ tty[Enter]
/dev/tty01
```

It's tty01 alright, but observe that there's an extra component in this name. One of the notable features of UNIX is that it considers all devices as **files**, and tty01 is just a file in the system. For the time being, simply assume that it is placed inside a folder named dev.

Note

Just as all users have names, all terminals, disks and printers also have names. You'll see later that all these names are represented as *files* in the system. All commands are files too.

1.7.4   Know Your Shell and Terminal Type

It's possible that you are working with a prompt string that is different from the $. This is often determined by the shell you are using. The **echo** command when used with the $SHELL argument displays the name of your shell:

```
$ echo $SHELL[Enter]                                    Evaluation done with a $
/bin/ksh                                                        The Korn shell
```

This is the Korn shell represented by the file ksh located in the bin folder. Just as all commands are files, the shell is a file too. $SHELL (rather, SHELL) is a **variable** used by the UNIX environment. Like programming variables, shell variables also have values associated with them. The **echo** command is used in evaluating the value of any variable.

Like SHELL, there are many more variables. One of them, TERM, tells you the type of terminal you are using:

```
$ echo $TERM[Enter]
ansi
```

Note that your terminal has the name /dev/tty01 but its type is ansi. Different terminals have different characteristics, and some commands (like the **vi** editor) need to know the type of terminal you are using. If your terminal type is set incorrectly, you'll face other problems—especially when working on a remote machine.

1.7.5   set: Know Your Environment

Even though UNIX commands are generally in lowercase, uppercase is the rule with all system variables. SHELL and TERM are defined only in uppercase. If you use shell, you would be using a different variable altogether. (It could be undefined depending on the shell you are using.)

To display a list of all the system's variables, use the **set** command. The list is going to be long and would probably scroll off the screen. Here's a condensed list of the important variables:

```
$ set[Enter]
CDPATH=.:..:/home/romeo
HOME=/home/romeo
```

```
HOSTNAME=saturn
MAIL=/var/mail/romeo
MAILCHECK=60
PATH=/home/romeo/bin:/usr/local/bin:/usr/bin:/usr/X11R6/bin:/bin:.
PS1='$ '
SHELL=/bin/ksh
```

Each variable here controls an important aspect of system functioning. You can change the value of all these variables. For instance, you can determine what your prompt will look like by changing the value of PS1.

Note

The output of the **set** command varies with the shell you use. If **echo $SHELL** displays /bin/csh, then the output will be a little different (spaces in place of =). /bin/csh represents the C shell, which often behaves differently from its other counterparts. Throughout this book, we'll be noting the differences in shell behavior. If a command doesn't produce output as explained in this text, it could often be attributed to the shell.

We'll have one more session later in the chapter, but for the time being make room for the next user. You must know the technique of doing that by now. Generally, **exit** terminates most sessions:

```
$ exit[Enter]
login:
```

Tip

Make sure that you always log out of the computer after you have completed your work. If you don't, another user can easily remove all your files.

1.8 Two Important Observations

You've had your first interaction with the system after logging in. Before moving on to the next session, ponder the two important lessons that follow conclusively from the previous session. You could have made these observations yourself, but in case you didn't, the following paragraphs present them.

1.8.1 UNIX Commands Are in Lowercase

Case is significant in UNIX. UNIX commands are generally in lowercase, and if you use uppercase, the system will reject it. Try it out with the **passwd** command, but this time using **PASSWD** instead of **passwd**:

```
$ PASSWD[Enter]
/bin/ksh: PASSWD: command not found
```

There's no **PASSWD** command in the system. However, that doesn't prevent you from using uppercase for commands that you create. Lowercase is the custom rather than a rule.

Tip

Make sure that you never have the [CapsLock] key pressed when using a UNIX system. It will create problems everywhere except when inserting a block of text in uppercase in the editors like **vi** and **emacs**.

1.8.2 The *[Enter]* Key

You've been hitting the *[Enter]* key at the end of every line of input. The text that you type at the terminal remains hidden from the system until this key is pressed. As a rule, everything you enter at the $ or % prompt must be followed by *[Enter]*.

First-time users often fail to appreciate this point because there's no "[Enter] key" in the human information system. Humans register speech or text, as it is spoken or read, in a continuous manner. In this respect, *[Enter]* resembles the shutter of a camera: nothing gets into the film until the shutter is pressed. Since the requirement is obvious, henceforth, the explicit mention of this key will be avoided except in not-so-obvious circumstances.

1.9 When Things Go Wrong

Terminals and keyboards have no uniform behavioral pattern. Terminal settings directly impact keyboard operation; that's why you often need to check the value of the TERM variable. Though it's too early to discuss the significance of this variable, you should at least be able to wriggle out of some common traps. You must know which keys to press when things don't work quite as expected.

1.9.1 Backspacing Doesn't Work

You notice some mistakes in the command line and you press the *[Backspace]* key, but it doesn't erase text. For instance, if you wrongly entered password instead of passwd, you have to erase the last three characters (ord) and then enter d. It's quite possible then when you press the *[Backspace]* key three times, you may see this:

$ **password^H^H^H**

Backspacing is not working here; that's why you see the symbol ^H every time you press the key. This often happens when you log on to a remote machine whose terminal settings are different from your local one. In fact, Sun machines don't use the *[Backspace]* key at all. In that case, you should try these two key sequences:

[Ctrl-h]
[Delete] or *[Del]*

One of them should see you through. Pressing the appropriate key generates the **erase** character. You can change the key that produces this character, but these customization techniques are discussed in a later chapter.

1.9.2 A Command Has to Be Interrupted

Even though this is unlikely to happen with any of the commands featured in this chapter, it's a common problem. In the next session, you'll be using the **cat** command with a word representing the filename. Now, suppose you inadvertently pressed *[Enter]* just after entering cat:

$ **cat***[Enter]*

There's no action here; the command simply waits for you to enter something. Even if you do, you must know how to terminate your input. For commands which expect user input, enter a *[Ctrl-d]* to bring back the prompt:

```
$ cat[Enter]
[Ctrl-d]                                              Signifies end of file
$ _
```

This key represents the end-of-file mark and is termed the **eof** character. This character can also be changed.

Sometimes, a program goes on running for an hour but doesn't wait for user input. *[Ctrl-d]* here won't work, and you may have to interrupt the program using either of the two sequences:

[Ctrl-c]
[Delete]   *To interrupt programs*

Most UNIX systems use *[Ctrl-c]* to abnormally terminate a program, but some systems use the *[Delete]* key instead. The appropriate key generates the **interrupt** character.

1.9.3 Killing a Line

If the line contains many mistakes, you might prefer to kill the line altogether without executing it. In that case, use

[Ctrl-u]   *Kills the line*

This is known as the **line kill** character. Note that this is distinctly different from the interrupt character, which kills a program. The line kill character erases everything in the command line before the command is executed.

1.9.4 Other Problems

Besides the above, there are other problems that you could face. They are briefly described below:

- If a job is important enough not to be interrupted, you can suspend it with *[Ctrl-z]*. You can then run a more important job and resume the suspended job with the **fg** command.
- If the display from a command is scrolling too fast for you to see on the terminal, you can halt the output temporarily by pressing *[Ctrl-s]*. To resume scrolling, press *[Ctrl-q]*.
- The *[Enter]* key is used to complete the command line. If this key doesn't work, you can use either *[Ctrl-j]* or *[Ctrl-m]*.
- If you have a terminal that behaves in an erratic manner (especially when editing a file with a full-screen editor), use the command **stty sane** to restore sanity. Since the *[Enter]* key may not work either in these situations, use *[Ctrl-j]* or *[Ctrl-m]*.
- If you are unable to come out from one of those programs that features its own prompt, then try using **q**, **quit**, **exit** or *[Ctrl-d]* to close the program.

These key functions are summarized in Table 1.2. However, remember that these functions are system-dependent, and it's quite possible that some of the keys may not work in quite the same way as mentioned here. If you have problems, seek the assistance of the system administrator.

TABLE 1.2   *Keyboard Commands*

Keystroke or Command	Function
[Ctrl-j]	Alternative to *[Enter]*
[Ctrl-m]	As above
[Ctrl-h]	Erases text (if *[Backspace]* key doesn't work)
[Ctrl-c]	Interrupts a command (Use *[Delete]* or *[Del]* if this fails)
[Ctrl-u]	Kills command line without executing it
[Ctrl-\]	Kills running command but creates a core file containing the memory image of the program
[Ctrl-s]	Stops scrolling of screen output
[Ctrl-q]	Resumes scrolling of screen output
[Ctrl-d]	Terminates login session or a program that expects its input from the keyboard
exit	Terminates login session (always works)
logout	Terminates login session in the C shell
[Ctrl-z]	Suspends process and returns shell prompt (use **fg** to resume job)
stty sane	Restores terminal to normal status (a UNIX command)

Note

You can suspend a job with *[Ctrl-z]* only if your shell supports job control. The earlier shells didn't, but modern shells do.

1.10   Yet Another Session: Working with Files and Directories

Many of the commands you used in the previous session referred to files and **directories** (previously referred to as *folders*). The terminal name showed by **who am i** (tty01) is a file. The **tty** command showed /dev/tty01 as the complete *pathname* of the file tty01. Many of the variables seen in the **set** command output also pointed to files and directories.

Log in again using your username and password. Note that you have changed your password, and this time you need to supply the new one. Once you are at the $ prompt, you are ready to issue your next set of commands. You'll now learn to create files and directories and move from one directory to another.

1.10.1   mkdir: Creating a Directory

UNIX organizes all its files in separate folders called *directories*. You can create a directory with a command named **mkdir**:

```
$ mkdir docs
$ _                                                      Directory docs created
```

No output! Not all UNIX commands produce output; some just return the prompt after performing the job. Be assured that your directory is created.

1.10.2   ls: Listing Files and Directories

The **ls** command (a typically shortened command implying *list*) displays all files and directories. If you have so far run only the commands that were discussed in the previous session, **ls** won't display much since you didn't create a single file but a directory. Still it's worth trying out the command:

```
$ ls
docs
```

ls lists docs as the only file in the **current directory**. But is this a file or a directory? Or is it both? UNIX treats the term *file* quite liberally and also includes directories in the file definition. We'll have a lot to discuss about files and directories in Chapter 6.

1.10.3   pwd and cd: Navigating a Directory Structure

Apart from **mkdir**, UNIX has a special set of commands that handle directories. UNIX treats these directories in the dimension of space as if a user can be "placed" there. The **cd** command is used to change your current directory and place you in another directory. Before you do that, first find out what your current directory is. This is the job of the **pwd** command:

```
$ pwd
/home/romeo                                              The current directory
```

You have a directory named after your user-id. In fact, when a user account is opened, this directory is created. This is your **home directory**—the directory where you are placed after logging in. Now try to move to the directory docs that you just created using the **cd** command:

```
$ cd docs
$ _
```

Silence is often golden in UNIX. The absence of messages here implies that the command has been executed without encountering an error. You should be in the directory docs. To be sure, use the **pwd** command again:

```
$ pwd
/home/romeo/docs
```

This is a **pathname** that shows the directory docs as the last component. docs is placed under the romeo directory, which in turn is placed under the home directory. The topmost directory is the first / of the pathname (which is called the root directory).

1.10.4   echo and cat: Creating and Viewing Files

You are now in the docs directory. Why not create some files here? UNIX has two excellent editors (**vi** and **emacs**) which you'll later use to create and edit files, but in this section you'll use a simpler method. Use the **echo** command in this manner to place the words This is the first message inside the file note1:

```
$ echo This is the first message > note1                    Creates file with five words
$ _
```

The previous **echo** command (**echo $TERM**) displayed something on the terminal, but this one doesn't. But then the previous command didn't use the symbol > either—which has made all the difference. > saved the **echo** command output in the file note1.

Now create another file. Call this file note2:

```
$ echo This is the second message > note2
$ _
```

You have now created two files in the docs directory. Because you have not changed the current directory docs, **ls** should show the names of these two files. Run the **ls** command again:

```
$ ls                                                                        Lists two files
note1     note2
```

They are there of course, but that was to be expected. To see what's inside these files, use the **cat** command—the universal file viewer. You used this command before *(1.9.2)*, but pressed an *[Enter]* immediately after it. This time, enter the filename note1 after the command:

```
$ cat note1                                                          Shows contents of file
This is the first message
```

These were the same words that were used with the **echo** statement. It's pretty obvious what **cat note2** would display.

1.10.5   wc: Counting Lines, Words and Characters

Now, how many lines does this file note1 contain? The **wc** (word count) command more than answers this question:

```
$ wc note1                                                         wc shows five words
      1     5     26 note1
```

This is typical UNIX behavior—no headers to explain the meaning of the columns. You'll have to look up the manual or have this text in front of you to know that this file has 1 line, 5 words and 26 characters. But **wc** can also be used with a special argument -1 that counts only the number of lines:

```
$ wc -1 note1
      1 note1
```

-1 is also an argument to **wc**, but when an argument begins with a -, it acquires the name **option**. Like many commands, **wc** supports quite a few options. You'll see later how this command and option are used to count the number of users and files, apart from the standard function of counting lines in a file.

1.10.6   ls -l: Checking the File Attributes

Apart from its contents, every file has some **attributes** (or properties) associated with it. These attributes are not stored in the file itself but in a different area of the hard disk. Displaying a list of filenames is often not enough; you need to know more about these attributes. The same **ls** command does this job for us except that it has to be used with the -l option:

```
$ ls -l
total 2                                                          Ignore this
-rw-r--r--    1 romeo        dialout      26 Feb  8 11:17 note1
-rw-r--r--    1 romeo        dialout      27 Feb  8 11:18 note2
```

You see here a rather detailed listing of these files. One file has 26 characters and the other has 27, but they are both *owned* by romeo. (All files are owned by someone.) The files were last modified (here, created) on February 8 at 11:17 hours and 11:18 hours, and their names are shown in the last column.

The first column contains a rather interesting string which uses a combination of the characters r, w and -. The combination of these letters determines the users who can read and write a file. You, as owner, can read and write all files owned by you, but others will have some restrictions. These permissions can be manipulated with a special command (**chmod**), which you'll be using in Chapter 7.

That's enough for a day's work, so log out once again and make the terminal available for the next user. It's now time to know something about the background of UNIX.

1.11   How It All Clicked

Till UNIX came on the scene, operating systems were designed with a particular machine in mind. They were invariably written in a **low-level language** (like assembler, which uses humanly unreadable code). The systems were fast but were restricted to the hardware they were designed for. Programs designed for one system simply wouldn't run on another. That was the status of the computer industry when Ken Thompson and Dennis Ritchie, of AT&T fame, authored the UNIX system.

In 1969, AT&T withdrew its team from the MULTICS project, which was engaged in the development of a flexible operating system that would run continuously and be used remotely. Thompson and Ritchie then designed and built a small system having an elegant file system, a command interpreter (the shell) and a set of utilities. However, what they wanted was a general operating system running on more than one type of hardware. In 1973, they rewrote the entire system in C—a **high-level** (more readable than assembler) **language** that was invented by Ritchie himself. Portability became one of the strong features of UNIX.

1.11.1   Berkeley: The Second School

A U.S. government decree (subsequently revoked) prevented AT&T from selling computer software. The company had no option but to distribute the product to academic and research institutions at a nominal fee, but without any support. The University of California, Berkeley (UCB), created a UNIX of its own. They called it *BSD UNIX*

(Berkeley Software Distribution). These versions became quite popular worldwide, especially in universities and engineering circles. Later, UCB gave up all development work on UNIX.

Berkeley filled the gaps left behind by AT&T, and then later decided to rewrite the whole operating system in the way they wanted. They created the standard editor of the UNIX system (**vi**) and a popular shell (C shell). Berkeley also created a better file system, a more versatile mail feature and a better method of linking files (symbolic links). Later, they also offered with their standard distribution a networking protocol software (TCP/IP) that made the Internet possible. Like AT&T, they also offered it practically free to many companies.

1.11.2   The Others

When computer science graduates left academics for the commercial world, they took their UNIX aspirations with them. It was just a matter of time before business circles developed interest in the product, and they too joined in its development in a spree of unparalleled innovation. UNIX had turned commercial.

Sun used the BSD System as a foundation for developing their own brand of UNIX (then *SunOS*). Today, their version of UNIX is known as *Solaris*. Others had their own brands; IBM had *AIX*, HP offered *HP-UX*, while DEC produced *Digital UNIX*. The notable UNIX flavors are listed in Table 1.3.

As each vendor modified and enhanced UNIX to create its own version, the original UNIX lost its identity as a separate product. The BSD releases were much different from the System V releases, and the incompatibilities steadily mounted. While standards were being developed as to what a product had to satisfy to be called UNIX,

TABLE 1.3   *The UNIX Flavors*

Product	Company	Remarks
Xenix	Microsoft Corporation	Now discontinued
BSDi, BSD/OS and FreeBSD	Berkeley Software Design	Commercial venture started by some of the people who created BSD UNIX
SunOS	Sun Microsystems	No more independent existence. Bundled with Solaris
Solaris	Sun Microsystems	Has a version that runs on PC
HP-UX	Hewlett-Packard	
AIX	IBM	
Ultrix	DEC	Now discontinued; replaced by Digital UNIX
Digital UNIX	DEC	
IRIX	Silicon Graphics	
SCO Open Server	Santa Cruz Operation	Now discontinued; replaced by SCO UnixWare
SCO UnixWare	Santa Cruz Operation	Runs on PC (like Open Server)

AT&T took it upon themselves to rework mainly the BSD product, and ultimately unify their own System V 3.2, BSD, SunOS and XENIX flavors into its last release—*System V Release 4* (SVR4).

1.11.3   The Internet

Even before the advent of SVR4, big things were happening in the U.S. Defense Department. DARPA, a wing of this department, engaged several vendors to develop a reliable communication system using computer technology. Through some brilliant work done by Vinton Cerf and Robert Kahn, DARPA's ARPANET network was made to work using **packet-switching** technology. In this scenario, data is split into packets, which can take different routes and yet be reassembled in the right order. That was the birth of **TCP/IP**—a set of protocols used by the Internet for communication.

DARPA commissioned UCB to implement TCP/IP on BSD UNIX. ARPANET converted to TCP/IP in 1983, and in the same year, Berkeley released the first version of UNIX which had TCP/IP built-in. The computer science research community were all using BSD UNIX, and the network expanded like wild fire. The incorporation of TCP/IP into UNIX and its use as the basis of development were two key factors in the rapid growth of the Internet (and UNIX).

1.11.4   The Windows Threat

In the meantime, however, Microsoft was making it big with Windows—a **graphical user interface** (GUI) that uses the mouse rather than arcane and complex command options to execute a job. Options could be selected from drop-down menu boxes and radio buttons, which made handling some of the basic operating system functions easier. Windows first swept the desktop market (with Windows 3.1/95/98) and then made significant inroads into the server market (with Windows NT) which had for long been dominated by UNIX.

When UNIX badly needed a Windows-type interface for its survival, the Massachusetts Institute of Technology (MIT) introduced X Window—the first windowing system for UNIX. X Window has many of the important features of Microsoft Windows plus a lot more. Every flavor of UNIX now has X along with a host of other tools that can not only handle files and directories but also update the system's configuration files.

All said and done, the power of UNIX is derived from all the commands and their multiple options that one has to remember. No graphical tool can ever replace the `find` command that looks for files having all sorts of attributes using elaborate matching schemes.

1.11.5   Standards and POSIX

A number of significant developments have taken place in the last few years. In 1992, AT&T's UNIX business was sold to Novell, the people who produced a networking software called *Netware*. Later, Novell turned over the UNIX trademark to a standards body called X/OPEN. X/OPEN later merged with The Open Group which currently owns the UNIX standard. In 1997, The Open Group published the **Single UNIX Specification**, followed by **UNIX98** in the following year.

A set of standard operating interfaces now guides the development of UNIX. This set is called the **Portable Operating System Interface** (POSIX) and is based on

UNIX. People wanted to develop applications that could be moved freely across different UNIX systems without rewriting the code all over again. Though POSIX sets standards for operating systems in general, it was based on UNIX because UNIX was supposedly free from bias on account of its vendor-neutrality.

The POSIX interfaces were developed at the behest of the IEEE and comprise a set of standards. POSIX.1 specifies the C application program interface. POSIX.2 deals with the shell and utilities (the meat of this book). Today, both are included in the Single UNIX Specification. Most UNIX vendors now actively cooperate with The Open Group and also build products based on the UNIX standard. UNIX is now an open system.

1.12 Linux and GNU

Although UNIX finally turned commercial, Richard Stallman and Linus Torvalds had different ideas. Torvalds is the father of Linux, the free UNIX that has swept the computer world by storm. Stallman runs the Free Software Foundation (formerly known as GNU—a recursive acronym that stands for "GNU's Not Unix"!). Many of the important Linux tools were written and supplied free by GNU.

Linux is distributed under the GNU General Public License which makes it mandatory for developers and sellers to make the source code public. Linux is particularly strong in networking and Internet features, and is an extremely cost-effective solution in setting up an Internet server or a local internet. Today, development on Linux is carried out at several locations across the globe at the behest of the Free Software Foundation.

The most popular Linux flavors include Red Hat, SuSE and Caldera. These distributions, which are shipped on multiple CD-ROMs, include a plethora of software—from C and C++ compilers to Java, interpreters like **perl**, **python** and **tcl**, browsers like Netscape, Internet servers, and multimedia software. All this comes for just $50, and most of it can also be downloaded free from the Internet. All the major computer vendors (barring Microsoft) have committed to support Linux, and many of them have ported their software to this platform. This book also discusses Linux.

1.13 Inside UNIX

The entire UNIX system is supported by a handful of essentially simple, though somewhat abstract concepts. The success of UNIX, according to Thompson and Ritchie, "lies not so much in new inventions but rather in the full exploitation of a carefully selected set of fertile ideas, and especially in showing that they can be keys to the implementation of a small and yet powerful operating system."[1] UNIX is no longer a small system, but it certainly is a powerful one. Now, let's take a look at its foundation.

1.13.1 The Two Masters: Kernel and Shell

Foremost among these "fertile ideas" is the division of labor between two agencies—the **kernel** and the **shell**. The shell interacts with the user and the kernel with the

---

1. Ritchie, D. H., and K. Thompson. "The Unix Time-Sharing System." The Bell System Technical Journal *Vol. 57 No. 6, July–August, 1978.*

machine's hardware. The relationship between the two has been broadly explained (without naming them) in Section 1.1 and is depicted in Fig. 1.1.

The kernel is the center of the operating system—a collection of programs mostly written in C, which communicate with the hardware directly. It is that part of the UNIX system that is loaded into memory when the system is booted. It manages the system resources, allocates time between users and processes, decides process priorities and performs other tasks which you wouldn't like to bother about. Other programs (the applications) also access the services of the kernel through a set of functions called *system calls*. The kernel is in fact *the* operating system—a program's gateway to the computer's resources.

Computers don't have any inherent capability of translating commands into action. An interpreter is required, and that job in the UNIX system is handled by the "outer part" of the operating system—the shell. The shell takes a command from the user, deciphers the special characters that it hopes to find and rebuilds a simplified command line. It finally communicates with the kernel to see that the command is executed. It is actually the interface between the user and the kernel, which effectively insulates the user from knowledge of kernel functions.

FIGURE 1.1 *Kernel-Shell-User Relationship*

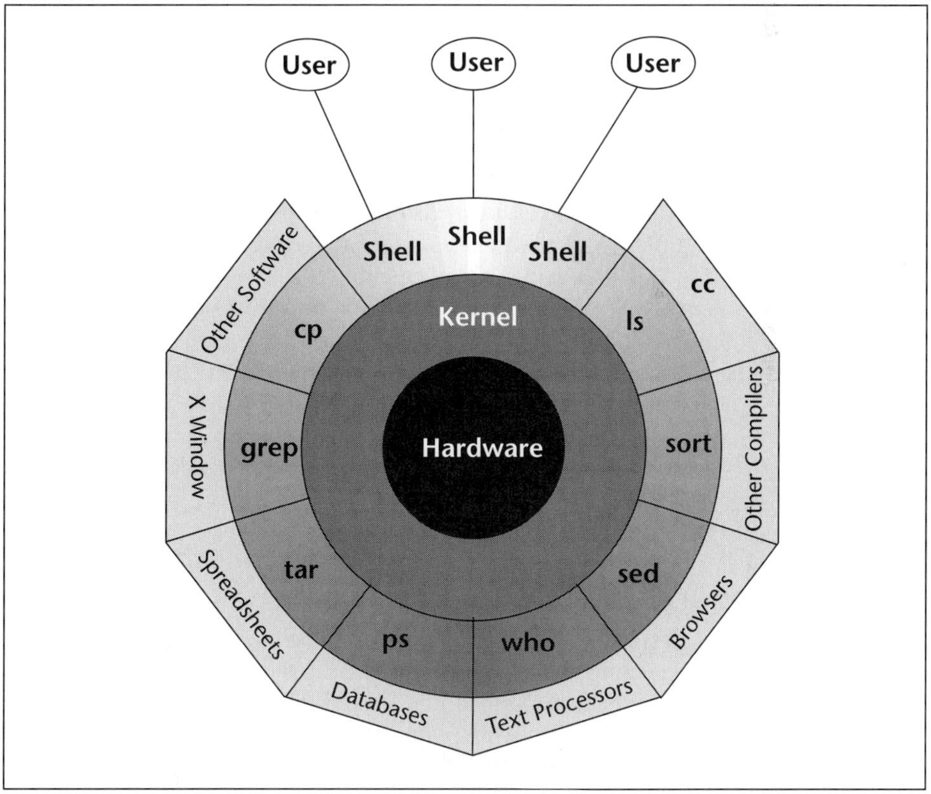

The kernel is represented by the file /stand/unix, /unix or /kernel/genunix (Solaris). The shell is represented by /bin/sh (Bourne shell), /bin/csh (C shell) or /bin/ksh (Korn shell). The system's bootstrap program loads the kernel into memory at startup. One of these shells will run to serve you when you log in. To know the one that is running for you, use the command **echo $SHELL**.

Linux

The kernel is represented by the file /boot/vmlinuz and the shell by /bin/bash (bash—the standard Linux shell).

1.13.2 UNIX Can Be Used by Multiple Users

The concept of multiple users working on a single system often baffles Windows users. Windows is essentially a single-user system where the memory, CPU and hard disk are all dedicated to a single user. In UNIX, the resources are actually shared between all users; UNIX is a **multiuser** system. Multiuser technology is the great socializer that has time for everyone.

For creating the illusory effect, the computer breaks up a unit of time into several segments, and each user is allotted a segment. So, at any point in time, the machine will be doing the job of a single user. The moment the allocated time expires, the previous job is kept in abeyance, and the next user's job is taken up. This process goes on till the clock has turned full-circle and the first user's job is taken up once again. This the kernel does several times in one second and keeps all ignorant and happy. All this is handled by the process management system, which is presented in Chapter 10.

1.13.3 One User Can Run Multiple Tasks

In UNIX, a single user can also run multiple tasks concurrently. It is usual for a user to edit a file, print another one on the printer, send email to a friend and browse the World Wide Web—all without leaving any of the applications. The kernel is designed to handle a user's multiple needs. In such a **multitasking** situation, only one job runs in the foreground while the rest run in the background. You can switch jobs between background and foreground, suspend, or even terminate them. Multitasking too is an important component of the process management system, which is discussed in Chapter 10.

Windows is also a multitasking system where you can work on several windows simultaneously. At any time, only one window is current (in the foreground)—the one whose title bar is highlighted.

1.13.4 Do One Thing Well

The designers never attempted to pack too many features into a few tools. Instead, their "do one thing well" approach resulted in the development of a few hundred commands each of which performed one simple job only. As stated before, UNIX tools singly aren't all that powerful (with few exceptions). However, using a supported **interprocess communication** feature, the shell can arrange for a command to pass on data to another command, and to another.

By interconnecting a number of tools, you can have an enormous number of combinations of their usage. That's why it's better to have a command handling a specialized function rather than one that tries to solve all problems itself. *Though UNIX started with this concept, it was somewhat forgotten when tools were added to the system later.* The device-independent features of UNIX are taken up in Chapter 8.

1.13.5   The Featureless File

Kaare Christian detects two powerful concepts in the UNIX system: "Files have places and processes have life."[2] The first assumes that files are situated in space which makes it easy to locate them with reference to a predetermined place. Moreover, you can be "placed" at a specific location in the file system, and you can also "move" from one place to another. This real-life model makes the UNIX file system easily comprehensible. The role of the process has already been explained in Sections 1.13.2 and 1.13.3.

UNIX doesn't really care to know the type of file you are using. It considers even directories and devices as members of the file system. A file to UNIX is just an array of bytes and can contain virtually anything—text, object code or a directory structure. The dominant file type is text, and the behavior of the system is mainly controlled by text files. UNIX provides a vast array of text manipulation tools that can edit these files without using an editor. The file system and file attributes are discussed in Chapters 6 and 7.

1.13.6   Pattern Matching

UNIX supports a pattern matching feature which helps in reducing your typing load. Characters like the * can be affixed to a string (like chap*) and then used to match multiple filenames. If you choose your filenames carefully, you can use a simple expression to access a whole lot of them. Apart from files, a special group of commands use a generalized pattern (called a **regular expression**), using characters like the *. This book emphasizes the importance of regular expressions and shows how you can perform complex pattern matching tasks using them. Matching filenames with these characters is taken up in Chapter 8. Chapter 15 covers regular expressions extensively.

1.13.7   Programming Facility

The UNIX shell is also a programming language; it was designed for a programmer, not a casual end user. It has all the necessary ingredients, like control structures, loops and variables, that establish it as a powerful programming language in its own right. These features are used to design **shell scripts**—programs that also include UNIX commands in their syntax. Shell scripts are extremely useful for text manipulation tasks.

Many of the system's functions can be controlled and automated by using these shell scripts. If you intend taking up system administration as a career, then you'll have to know the shell's programming features very well. Proficient UNIX programmers seldom take recourse to any other language (except **perl**) for text manipulation problems. Shell programming is taken up in Chapters 18 and 19.

2. *Kaare, Christian.* The UNIX Operating System. *New York: John Wiley, 1988.*

1.13.8   Portability and System Calls

UNIX is written in C. Though there are over a thousand commands handling special-ized functions, they all use a handful of functions called **system calls**. These calls are built into the kernel, and all library functions and utilities are written using them. All UNIX flavors have one thing in common: they all use the same system calls. If an oper-ating system used different system calls, then it wouldn't be UNIX.

Interaction through system calls represents an efficient means of communication with the system. A programmer writes a file with the **write()** system call without going into the programming innards that achieve the write operation. The same system calls are available to every C programmer who wants to develop tools of her own. This also means that once software has been developed on any UNIX system, it can be eas-ily ported to any other UNIX machine. It's only the implementation part of the system calls that then needs to be reprogrammed, not the system calls themselves.

1.13.9   Documentation

UNIX documentation is no longer the sore point it once was. Even though it's some-times uneven, at most times the treatment is quite lucid. The principal on line help facility available is the **man** command and remains the most important reference for commands and their configuration files. Thanks to O'Reilly & Associates, one can safely say that there's no feature of UNIX on which a separate textbook is not avail-able. UNIX documentation and the help facility are discussed in Chapter 2.

With this enormous base of text material and the availability of training courses, seminars and discussion groups on the Internet, UNIX is easier to tame today than it was even five years ago.

With the goal of building a comfortable relationship with the machine, Thomson and Ritchie designed a system for their own use rather than for others. They could afford to do this because UNIX wasn't initially developed as a commercial product, and the project didn't have any predefined objective. They acknowledge this fact too: "We have not been faced with the need to satisfy someone else's requirements, and for this freedom we are grateful."[3]

S U M M A R Y

An *operating system* interacts with the applications that require access to the machine's hardware. It also interacts with the user who passes commands to it using a *command language interpreter*. The OS handles program execution, memory allocation and pro-gram errors.

UNIX can be used by multiple users concurrently or on a standalone workstation. You enter a UNIX system by entering a username and a password, which are assigned by the system administrator. The password is not displayed on the screen for security reasons. You can log out of the session by pressing *[Ctrl-d]*, using the **logout** com-mand or entering **exit**.

3. Ritchie, D. H., and K. Thompson. "The Unix Time-Sharing System." The Bell System Techni-cal Journal *Vol. 57 No. 6, July–August, 1978.*

UNIX features a number of prompts like the $ and %. You can enter any legitimate command at this prompt. UNIX commands are in lowercase, and UNIX treats two uppercase and lowercase filenames as separate files.

You can change your own password with the **passwd** command. You can display the list of users with **who** and know the name of your terminal with **tty**.

SHELL and TERM are two important variables of the system, and you can evaluate their values by using **echo** with a $-prefixed variable name (e.g., **echo $SHELL**). **set** shows you a list of all system variables.

There are various key sequences that you can use when things go wrong. They are listed in Table 1.2.

Many commands can be used with additional words called *arguments*. A special argument beginning with a - is called an *option*.

You can create a directory with **mkdir**, change to it with **cd** and then check your current directory with **pwd**.

ls lists files of a directory, and when used with the -l option, shows their attributes. The **echo** command when used with the > symbol is used to place text in a file. **cat** displays a file's contents and **wc** counts the number of lines, words and characters.

UNIX was developed at AT&T Bell Laboratories by Ken Thompson and Dennis Ritchie with the intention of creating a portable operating system. It was finally written in C, and now runs on a wide range of machines.

A lot of development work was also done at the University of California, Berkeley, which gave rise to the BSD distributions. Berkeley is responsible for the C shell, the **vi** editor and the TCP/IP suite of networking utilities.

AT&T introduced SVR4 (System V Release 4) to merge their own version with some other versions. Both Bell Laboratories and Berkeley stopped further work on UNIX, and UNIX now is a trademark of The Open Group.

Also becoming popular is Linux, the free UNIX with contributions from GNU who also write and distribute free software. Linux is rich in Internet-related features.

The distribution of work is shared by the *kernel* which addresses the hardware directly, and the *shell* which interacts with the user. The shell processes the entered command, scans it for special characters and rebuilds it in a form that can be understood by the kernel. The kernel is resident in memory and is represented by the file unix or vmlinuz.

Several users can use the system together, and a single user can also run multiple jobs concurrently.

Each UNIX command does a simple job. UNIX lets you build complex command routines by connecting these basic building blocks.

UNIX files are conceptually simple. UNIX considers directories and devices as files. Text files control the system behavior, and UNIX has a wide range of tools that can modify them without using an editor.

UNIX features extensive facilities for matching patterns, has a library of system calls and a graphical user interface. UNIX documentation is quite extensive.

SELF-TEST

1.1   What are the two agencies that interact with the operating system?

1.2   Every character has a number associated with it. What is it called?

1.3   Which two keys are never used singly?

1.4   If you see a prompt like `mailserver login:`, what do you think `mailserver` represents?

1.5   Can you log in without using a password?

1.6   If the system echoes `Login incorrect`, does it mean that your login name is incorrect?

1.7   With which key will you interrupt a command?

1.8   You have forgotten the username that you used to log in. How can you find that out?

1.9   With which command do you see a detailed listing of files?

1.10   What is the **cat** command used for? Can it be used with two filenames?

1.11   Who are the principal architects of the UNIX operating system?

1.12   Why did AT&T virtually give away UNIX to the world?

1.13   Where did BSD UNIX originate?

1.14   What is Sun's version of UNIX known as?

1.15   Which flavors of UNIX run on the PC?

1.16   Who owns the UNIX trademark today?

1.17   Who are the two brains behind Linux?

1.18   What is the distinctive characteristic about the GNU General Public License?

1.19   Which part of the operating system gets loaded into memory as soon as the system is booted?

1.20   Why is UNIX more portable than other operating systems?

1.21   Can you divide UNIX into two major schools? To which school does Sun's UNIX belong?

1.22   What is the name of the kernel in (i) System V and (ii) Linux?

1.23   What does *multitasking* mean?

1.24   Why do UNIX tools perform simple jobs rather than complex ones?

1.25   What is the windowing system of UNIX known as?

1.26   Name some interpretive languages available on UNIX systems.

1.27   Name three notable Linux flavors.

E X E R C I S E S

1.1   Can you use the name of a friend as the password? Should you use one if permitted?

1.2   Which are the three commands that you would try in sequence to log yourself out of the system? Which one among them will always work?

1.3   Enter the two commands **finger** and **users** separately. What difference do you notice in their output?

1.4   If you don't have a *[Backspace]* key or it doesn't erase previous text, which key will you use?

1.5   If your *[Enter]* key is broken, how will you still enter commands?

1.6   How do you stop the screen output from scrolling? How will you resume scrolling?

1.7 Try out these two commands. How will you find out what happened and what would you conclude?

```
echo > README[Enter]
echo > readme[Enter]
```

1.8 What are TERM and SHELL? How do you evaluate their values?

1.9 How do the **tty** command and TERM differ?

1.10 You entered a command incorrectly and find that the prompt has not returned. What could be the reasons and what key sequences will you try to restore normalcy?

1.11 If your terminal produces strange output, which command will you try as a last resort? How will you execute that command in case your *[Enter]* key is also not working?

1.12 A job is running for an hour but is important enough not to be interrupted. Can you keep it in abeyance, run another job and then resume the first job?

1.13 Try to create this file with **echo > foo.bar.gz**. Can you do that?

1.14 Use the **wc** command with two filenames as arguments. What difference do you see?

1.15 Create a directory and change to that directory. Next, create another directory in the new directory and then change to that directory too. Now, run **cd** without any arguments followed by **pwd**. What do you conclude?

1.16 Why is the shell called a *command interpreter*?

1.17 What is the one thing that is common to directories, devices, terminals and printers?

1.18 When a UNIX system is moved to another machine, what needs to be changed?

K E Y   T E R M S

application *(1.1)*
ASCII value *(1.4)*
backspacing *(1.4)*
character *(1.4)*
command *(1.2 and 1.7)*
command argument *(1.7.2)*
command language interpreter *(1.1)*
command option *(1.10.5)*
control character *(1.4)*
current directory *(1.10.2)*
directory *(1.10)*
eof character *(1.9.2)*
erase character *(1.9.1)*
file *(1.7.3)*
file attribute *(1.10.6)*
file owner *(1.7.2)*

graphical user interface (GUI) *(1.11.4)*
high-level language *(1.11)*
home directory *(1.10.3)*
interprocess communication *(1.13.4)*
interrupt character *(1.9.2)*
kernel *(1.13.1)*
line kill character *(1.9.3)*
logging in *(1.6.1)*
logging out *(1.6.1)*
low-level language *(1.11)*
multitasking system *(1.13.3)*
multiuser system *(1.13.2)*
operating system *(1.1)*
packet switching *(1.11.3)*
password *(1.5)*
pathname *(1.10.3)*

Portable Operating System Interface (POSIX) *(1.11.5)*
prompt *(1.6.1)*
regular expression *(1.13.6)*
root account *(1.5)*
shell *(1.6.1 and 1.13.1)*
shell script *(1.13.7)*
shell variable *(1.7.4)*
Single UNIX Specification *(1.11.5)*
system administrator *(1.5)*

system call *(1.13.8)*
TCP/IP *(1.11.3)*
terminal emulation *(1.3)*
UNIX98 *(1.11.5)*
user account *(1.5)*
user-id *(1.5)*
username *(1.5)*
virtual terminal *(1.4)*
workstation *(1.3)*

## CHAPTER 2

Understanding the UNIX Command

The UNIX command family is quite large, built up steadily over a period of two decades. There are several hundred (sometimes, over a thousand) commands in the system. Even though most of these commands do simple jobs, many of them use terse syntax and throw out curt messages. If you enter a command incorrectly, the system may either flash a cryptic error message or none at all. Unlike Windows programs, UNIX commands are not interactive, which makes some of them initially difficult to use.

The UNIX designers appreciate that you can't remember the syntax and options of most of these commands. That's why they have provided some extensive documentation for your use. In this chapter, we examine closely the generalized UNIX command syntax, and understand the significance of its constituents—its options, arguments and other parameters. We'll also learn to use the on-line help facilities that are available in the system.

Objectives

- Understand the general features of a command like case-insensitivity and lack of extensions. *(2.1)*
- Learn how the PATH variable locates commands. *(2.2)*
- Distinguish between *internal* and *external* commands. *(2.3)*
- Break up a command into *arguments* and *options*, and note the possible variations that you may find. *(2.4)*
- Understand the flexibility of command usage. *(2.5)*
- Use the **man** command to browse the UNIX documentation. *(2.6)*
- Understand the organization of the documentation, especially the way the syntax is explained. *(2.7)*
- Use the **info** command for viewing Texinfo documentation. *(2.8)*
- Use the **apropos** and **whatis** commands for identifying the command that would do a job. *(2.9)*

2.1 General Features of a Command

A UNIX command consists of a single word generally using alphabetic characters. Since the designers created UNIX for their own use, they tried to ensure that a minimum number of keystrokes achieved the maximum amount of work. That's why the original UNIX commands are seldom more than four characters long. You've already used some of them—**ls**, **cat**, **who** etc. Some modern commands are long words and occasionally contain a numeral or an underscore.

The significance of a command can sometimes be guessed from the command name, but often it can't. For instance, intuition may lead us to believe that **ls** means list and **cp** implies copy. But can you guess that **grep** looks for a pattern and **sed** performs a substitution in a file?

As you know by now, commands are essentially *files* (we'll take up files in Chapter 6) representing programs—mainly written in C. These files are stored in certain folders which are better known as *directories*. For instance, the **ls** command is also a program represented by a file that's located in the directory /bin.

A UNIX command file doesn't need to have a special extension like .exe or .com, though you can provide one if you want to. There's hardly a practical restriction on length either; a command can be up to 255 characters long—a limit set for any file of the file system. Older UNIX systems, however, have a 14-character limit.

The introductory session of the previous chapter should have also taught you that UNIX is sensitive to case; the command **ls** is not the same as **LS**. If you enter **LS** instead of **ls**, this is how the system will respond:

```
$ LS
sh: LS: not found
```

There's obviously no command named **LS** in the UNIX system. If you have somehow acquired the habit of using uppercase for all commands, then it's time to shed the habit. The best way of doing that is to make sure that the *[CapsLock]* key of your keyboard is never set to produce uppercase letters.

Even though UNIX doesn't offer the **LS** command, that doesn't prevent you from creating a command with the name **LS**. Since all commands are represented as files in the system, you just have to create a file LS and place it at an "appropriate" location in the file system.

2.2   The PATH: Locating Commands

How does UNIX know whether a command is legitimate or not? When you enter a command, the system searches for its *file* in certain specified directories. If it finds the file in one of these directories, it executes it; otherwise it flashes the message as shown in the preceding example.

UNIX functioning is controlled by a number of variables. UNIX obtains the list of directories that has to be searched from one of its variables—the one named PATH. If you evaluate the value of this variable, you'll find a directory list separated by colons:

```
$ echo $PATH
/bin:/usr/bin:/usr/X116/bin:/oracle/bin:.
```
                                                                        Output in the C shell
                                                                        is a little different

Windows users also use a variable of this name in AUTOEXEC.BAT to specify the search path, except that here the delimiter is the : (; in Windows). There are five directories in this list, and when you issue a command, the system will search this list *in the sequence specified* to locate and execute it. This means that it will first search in /bin, then in /usr/bin, and so forth. We'll ignore the singular dot at the end for the time being.

But in which directory is the command located? The easiest way of knowing the location of a command file is to use the **type** command:

```
$ type ls
ls is /bin/ls
```

ls is located in the /bin directory, and because /bin is also a component of the value of the PATH variable, the system locates it easily and executes it.

Note

If a command can't be found in this list, that doesn't mean that it can't be executed. In this case, you have to use a **pathname** containing the exact location of the file *(6.6)*. Alternatively, you can modify the PATH variable *(17.3.1)* to add the directory containing the command file-name to its list. We'll learn to do both these things in later chapters.

2.3 Internal and External Commands

By a sweeping generalization, we have attributed all this hunting work to "system" as if there was such a thing as a system. The agency that actually does all this work is known as the **shell** (Chapter 8). This is a special command that starts running the moment you log in. The shell takes the command that you enter as its input and looks at its own PATH variable to find out where it is located.

Since **ls** is a file having an independent existence in the /bin directory (or /usr/bin), it is called an **external command**. Most commands are external in nature, but there are some that are not really found anywhere or not executed even if they are found. Take for instance the **echo** command:

```
$ type echo
echo is a shell builtin
```

When you type echo, the system (rather, the shell) won't look in its PATH to locate it (even if it can find it in /bin). Rather, it will execute it from its own set of built-in commands that are not stored as separate files. These built-in commands, of which **echo** is a member, are known as **internal commands**.

The **type** command itself is a shell built-in, and whether or not you are able to execute it depends on the shell you use. In some versions of the C shell, the command won't work. UNIX features a number of commands that reveal details of a command's attributes and location; some of them will surely be available on your system. If **type** doesn't work, then try **whence** or **which** in the same way you used **type**.

UNIX has a rather unusual history. Many a time, a command started off as an external command, but later was absorbed by the shell to become its own internal command. The shell has a number of such internal commands. Some systems today still maintain the external command in the file system even though it's not used by default (like **pwd**). The shell makes sure that even if there's a command of the same name in /bin or /usr/bin, top priority is accorded to its own internal command of the same name. This means that the external command is never executed.

This is exactly the case with **echo**, which is also found in /bin, but rarely ever executed because the shell built-in always makes sure that the internal **echo** takes precedence over the external. There's a way of executing this command too, but we'll do that after we have understood the workings of the shell and the file system.

Note

The essential UNIX commands for general use are located in the directories /bin and /usr/bin. The commands showing graphical output are usually found in /usr/X11R6/bin or /usr/dt/bin. The commands used by the system administrator are found in /sbin and /usr/sbin.

2.4 Command Structure

In Chapter 1, you entered commands that had multiple words (like **who am i**, **cat note1**). You also used a command which had an embedded minus sign (**ls -l**). It's time that we subjected a typical UNIX command to a dissective study. The structure of such a command is shown in Fig. 2.1.

The "entire" command here has five **words** separated by spaces. The first word (**ls**) is actually the command; the other words are called **arguments**. The **ls** command here has four arguments. Similarly, am and i are arguments of the **who** command. Because a command often accepts several types of arguments, it can be made to behave in numerous ways.

Commands and arguments are separated by any number of spaces or tabs to enable the system to interpret them as words. A contiguous string of spaces and tabs together form what is known as **whitespace**. Where the system permits the use of one whitespace character to separate words, it generally permits several, as in this command:

```
ls    -l    -t    note1 note2
```

You can enter the **ls** command like this. The UNIX system (rather, the shell) possesses a special mechanism of compressing these multiple consecutive spaces or tabs into a single space. The tab character is generated by hitting the *[Tab]* key on your keyboard, or using *[Ctrl-i]* in case there's none.

Beginners often forget to provide spaces between the command and the argument. If you have got away with **DIR/P** instead of **DIR /P** in Windows, don't expect UNIX to be equally accommodating:

FIGURE 2.1   *Structure of a UNIX Command*

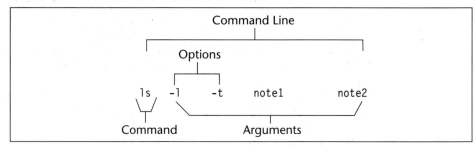

```
$ ls-l
ls-l: not found
```

The system fails to recognize -l as an option and treats **ls-l** as a single command. Obviously, this command doesn't exist.

Note

If you have found **whoami** working in addition to **who am i**, don't think that the theory breaks down here; it's just that **whoami** is also a command found on many UNIX systems. Further, if you feel that the system should also treat **ls-l** as a legitimate command, UNIX lets you create an *alias* with the name **ls-l** *(17.4)* which will actually execute **ls -l**.

2.4.1 Options and Filenames

There are two arguments in the example and Fig. 2.1 that begin with a - symbol. -l and -t are special arguments that are known as **options**. Options are given a special name because their list is predetermined; every command has a fixed set of options. An option changes a command's default behavior, so if **ls** shows only the filenames, the -l and -t options show their attributes as well.

Following the options are two more arguments (note1 and note2), which here represent filenames. Some commands use files and some don't. When you execute a command with a filename, the command opens the file and performs all its instructions on the contents of the file. If used at all, the filename will generally be its last argument, and certainly after the option. (This is not always true; some options use filenames as their own "arguments.")

The command with its arguments and options is entered in one line that is referred to as the **command line**. This line can be considered complete only after the user has hit the *[Enter]* key. The complete line is then fed to the shell as its input for interpretation and execution.

Some commands accept a single filename, some accept two and some accept an indefinite number (limited by the capacity of the system to accommodate them). Here are some examples of commands that use filenames as arguments:

```
ls -l -a -t chap01 chap02 chap03
cp chap01 chap02 progs
rm chap01 chap02
pine -f mail-feb                              mail-feb is an argument of -f
```

The last command here is a little different from the rest. Here, mail-feb (a filename) is also an argument of **pine**, but more specifically it's an argument of the -f option. This means that -f must be followed by a filename.

When you use a command with a wrong option, the shell locates the command alright, but the *command* this time finds the option to be wrong:

```
$ ls -z note
ls: ERROR: Illegal option -- z
usage: ls -1ACFLRabcdfgilmnopqrstux -W[sv] [files]
```

The above message has been generated by the command, and not by the shell. **ls** does have a large number of options (over 20), but it seems that -z is not one of them. Many commands also display the right syntax and options when you use them incorrectly.

Caution

An option is normally preceded by a minus sign (-) to distinguish it from other arguments which could consist of filenames. There must not be any whitespace between - and the option letter. Moreover, never have a filename which begins with a -; many commands just won't work!

2.4.2 Combining Options

UNIX has a few rules governing the use of options. Options that begin with a - sign can *normally* be combined with only one - sign. Take, for instance, this command line containing three options:

```
ls -l -a -t
```

Though **ls** is taken up in much detail in Chapter 7, it's good to know that the -l option provides most details of a file's attributes. If this had been the only option in the command line, the files would have been sorted in the alphabetic sequence (actually, the ASCII sequence). The -t option changes this behavior and sorts them according to the time of modification. Inclusion of the -a option changes the behavior further and includes the hidden files of the system. These are simple options and UNIX lets you combine them. You might just use

```
ls -lat
```

to obtain the same output. We might also use them in any combination:

```
ls -tal                          Sequence of combination not always
ls -atl                             important, but sometimes is
```

This facility reduces your typing load and makes some difference when you use commands with several options. The shell **parses** (breaks up) the option combination into separate options.

Some commands won't let you combine options in the way you did just now. Sometimes, options are followed by their own arguments like in this **tar** command:

```
tar -cv -f /dev/fd0 -b 18 *
```

There are four options here, but two of them (-f and -b) are special options; they both take further arguments. In a previous example, we saw **pine** using the -f option in a similar manner. We'll call them **option parameters**. The -f option is followed by the filename /dev/fd0. The -b option specifies the block size, which here is 18. This is how the **tar** command is used to back up all files in the current directory to a floppy diskette.

We combined the -c and -v options here, but can you combine the -f and -b options? Yes, you can, provided that you place their own parameters in the same sequence too. For instance, this combination is legal:

```
tar -cvfb /dev/fd0 18 *
```

The -f and -b options are followed by their parameters in the same order, and the command will work. But this one won't:

```
tar -cvfb 18 /dev/fd0 *
```

Here **tar** interprets 18 as the parameter to -f and /dev/fd0 as the parameter to -b. Obviously, this doesn't make sense.

Caution

Don't expect all commands to permit combining of options even if you line up their parameters correctly. In such cases, you have to specify the options separately.

2.4.3   Exceptions and Variations

All commands don't compulsorily use options and arguments. Commands like **clear** don't accept any arguments. The **who** and **date** commands are a little different; they may or may not be specified with arguments. The **ls** command permits more variations; it can be used in a number of ways:

- Without any arguments (**ls**).
- With only options (**ls -l**).
- With only filenames (**ls chap01 chap02**).
- Using a combination of both (**ls -la chap01 chap02**).

This text discusses a large number of commands that use options. The vast majority of them will conform to the option rules that have been discussed. Because UNIX was developed by people who had their own ideas as to what options should look like, there will invariably be exceptions to whatever rules we try to formulate.

Let's see some more examples. The word *option* turns out to be a misnomer in some instances; the **cut** command needs an option to work with:

```
cut -d: -f7 passwd
```

This command extracts the seventh field from the file passwd. While the -d option itself is optional (i.e., you may not use it), you have to specify either the -c or the -f option. In a sense, one of these options is compulsory.

The **pr** command here starts printing from page 5 of the file foo but uses the + as an option prefix instead of a -:

```
pr +5 foo
```

Here, the **dd** command copies the file boot.img to a floppy diskette. The command uses = with two keywords if and of:

```
dd if=boot.img of=/dev/rdsk/f0q18dt
```

Some of the advanced UNIX commands like **awk** and **perl** are programming languages by themselves. Further, there are some characters in the command line that are not really treated as arguments—the |, > and <, for instance. In Chapter 8, you'll see how some of them can even be placed *before* a command.

So what do we conclude from all this? It is simply not possible to specify a generalized syntax for a command; the syntax pertaining to a specific command is best taken from the UNIX manual. The syntax for some commands has been specified in this book. But don't let this deter you; you will have already built up a lot of muscle before you take on these commands.

2.5 Flexibility of Command Usage

The UNIX system provides a certain degree of flexibility in the usage of commands. A command can often be entered in more than one way, and if you use it judiciously, you can keep the number of keystrokes to a minimum. In this section, we'll see how permissive the shell is to command usage.

2.5.1 Combining Commands

So far you have been executing commands separately; each command was first processed and executed before the next could be entered. UNIX allows you to specify more than one command in the same command line. Each command has to be separated from the other by a **;** (semicolon):

who ; ls -l note   ls *executed after* who

When you learn to *redirect (8.6.1)* the output of these commands, you may even like to group them together within parentheses:

(who ; ls -l note) > newlist

The combined output of the two commands is now sent to the file newlist. Whitespace is provided here only for better readability; you might reduce a few keystrokes like this:

(who;ls -l note)>newlist   *Space around option always required*

The **;** is the first of the special characters that is understood by the shell. When a command line contains this character, the shell understands that the commands on either side of it need to be processed separately. These special characters, of which the **;** forms an element, are known as **metacharacters**. Like the **;**, there are several such metacharacters which have special meanings to the shell. Shell metacharacters are taken up in Chapter 8.

2.5.2 A Command Line Can Overflow

A command is normally entered in a line by typing from the keyboard. Though the terminal width is restricted to 80 characters, that doesn't prevent you from entering a command, or a sequence of them, in one line even though the total width may exceed 80 characters. The command simply overflows to the next line though it is still in a single "logical" line.

Some commands have lengthy syntaxes, and you may often find it desirable—and sometimes necessary—to spread the command line into multiple lines. The shell then issues a **secondary prompt**, usually > (or ?), to indicate to you that the command line isn't complete. This is how the **echo** command works on some systems:

```
$ echo "This is
> a three-line                        A second prompt (>) appears . . .
> text message"
This is                               Disappears after quote is closed
a three-line
text message
```

Here, you hit *[Enter]* twice before closing the double quote. The > appears every time *[Enter]* is pressed until the quote is closed. Apart from using a singular command, you'll also need to use a number of them in a *pipeline (8.8)*. Breaking up these command combinations into separate lines makes the command line more readable.

C Shell

The above **echo** command won't work when you use the C shell. You'll have to enter a \ (backslash) before you press *[Enter]*. Moreover, the C shell throws out a different secondary prompt (?). Its primary prompt is also different (%):

```
% echo "This is\
? a three-line\
? message"
```

Tip

Whenever you find the > or ? appearing after you have pressed *[Enter]*, it will generally be due to the absence of a matching quote or parenthesis. In case you find that the problem persists even after providing it, just kill the command line with *[Ctrl-c]*, *[Delete]* or *[Ctrl-u]*.

2.5.3   Wait till Previous Command Has Finished?

UNIX provides a full-duplex terminal which means that you can type your command at any time and feel satisfied that the system will interpret it. When you run a long program, the $ prompt won't appear till program execution is complete. Subsequent commands can be entered at the keyboard (as many commands as you wish) without waiting for the prompt; they may not be even displayed on your screen!

There is a type-ahead **buffer** (a temporary storage area) which stores all these commands and passes them on for execution after the previous program has completed its run. If you type correctly, simply don't bother to wait even if the output from the previous program garbles the display!

2.5.4   A Command May Not Work Properly

Since UNIX comes in many flavors, vendors have customized a number of commands to behave in the way they want, and not as AT&T decreed. Though DOS doesn't have such problems, by having only a single flavor (Microsoft), version differences exist. A DOS command often varies across versions in much the same way as a UNIX command, so much so that you are often forced to use the **VER** command to find out the version of DOS you are using. In UNIX, you do that with **uname**, but with the -r option:

```
$ uname -r                          This command can also show you the machine name!
4.0
```

This actually expands to UNIX System V Release 4.0. So if a command doesn't work properly, it could either belong to a different "system" (could be BSD) or a different "release" (may be 3.2). Higher releases usually don't take away features but add to them.

The **uname -r** command shows the version number of the kernel:

```
$ uname -r
2.2.7
```

2.6 man: **On-Line Help**

Once you understand how commands are broadly structured and the possible variations that you may see in them, you can take on the UNIX documentation. Today, it comes in a number of forms of varying complexity, and the earliest and most important is the one that is viewed with the **man** command—often called the **man documentation**. **man** remains the most complete (though not necessarily comprehensive) and authoritative guide to the UNIX system. You'll also use **apropos**, **whatis** and **info** later in the text, but we'll first discuss **man**.

The man facility is present in every system unless the system administrator has deliberately not installed it for the large footprint it occupies on disk. The documentation is also available in print. To view the manual page of the C shell, you have to use **man** with csh (the command representing the C shell) as argument:

```
man csh
```

The entire man page pertaining to the **csh** command is dumped on the screen. **man** presents the first page and pauses. This it does by sending its output to a **pager** program, which displays the contents of a file one page (screen) at a time. You have to press a key (generally, *[Spacebar]* or *[Enter]*) to see the next page. To quit the pager, and ultimately **man**, you have to press a **q**.

The pager is actually a UNIX command, and **man** is always preconfigured to be used with a specific pager. UNIX systems currently use these pager programs:

- **more**, Berkeley's pager now available universally and a superior alternative to the original AT&T **pg** command (now obsolete).
- **less**, the standard pager used by all Linux systems, but also available for all UNIX platforms. **less** is modeled on the **vi** editor and is more powerful than **more** because it replicates most of **vi**'s navigational and search functions.

When **man** displays a page, it doesn't tell you the pager it uses. You'll have to deduce that from the message it shows at the bottom line. If you see something like this:

```
--More--(29%)                                                      Pager is more
```

then you are using **more**, which shows the percentage of the file that has been displayed. However, if you see this:

:

then you could be using **pg**. (Some versions of **less** also show **:** as the prompt.) We'll not consider **pg** because it is obsolete.

A pager has keys defined for viewing the next page—and normally the previous page too. It has one for terminating the program which generally is the key labeled q. Some man pages run into several pages in which case you can search for strings as well.

The keys that you press when the pager is active could be termed its **internal commands**. These internal commands are conceptually different from the ones the shell uses (Chapter 8). Many UNIX commands like **pine**, **vi** and **emacs** also have their own internal commands that don't show up on the screen but perform some action. Though **more** and **less** are covered in Chapter 9, a minimum subset of their commands is shown in Table 2.1.

The man documentation is sometimes quite extensive, and the search facility lets you locate a page containing a keyword quite easily. For example, you can call up the page containing the word clobber by using the / (frontslash) with the term:

/clobber*[Enter]*

The / and search string show up on the screen this time, and when you press *[Enter]*, you are taken to the page. If that's not the page you are looking for, you can repeat the search by pressing **n**. Some pager versions even highlight the search term in reverse video.

TABLE 2.1 man*'s Pager Commands*

Action	more	less
Next page	*[Spacebar]* or f	*[Spacebar]* or f
Skip forward 10 pages	10f	—
Skip forward 1000 lines	1000s	1000z (sets window to 1000 lines)
Previous page	b	b
Skip back 15 pages	15b	—
Skip back 1000 lines	—	1000w (sets window to 1000 lines)
First page	—	p or 1G
Go to line 300	—	300G
Search for TCP	/TCP	/TCP
Repeat search	n	n
Repeat last command	. (dot)	—
Quit	q	q
View Help	h	h

You can see the man pages of multiple commands with a single invocation of **man**. Here's an example:

```
man cp mv rm
```

This command first shows you the page for the **cp** command (the command UNIX uses for copying files). To look up the next command, press **q**. A **q** at the page for **rm** will quit **man** altogether, but if you want to abort in the middle, just use the interrupt character of your system (*[Ctrl-c]* or *[Delete]*).

Since **man** also happens to be a UNIX command like **ls** or **cat**, you would probably first like to know how **man** itself is used. Use the same command to view its own documentation:

```
man man
```

And from this man page you'll learn that you can choose your pager too. The PAGER variable controls the pager **man** uses, and if you set it to less, then **man** will use **less** as its pager. Linux, however, uses the -P option to specify a different pager.

Tip

When viewing large man pages with the **more** pager, you may sometimes like to move in large blocks of lines or screens at a time. Even though **10f** skips 10 pages, you'll have to use the actual command only the first time. You can then repeat it with **more**'s dot (**.**) command. Navigation is much faster that way.

This facility is not available in **less**, but **less** has a similar acceleration feature. If you skip forward 200 lines with **200z**, you can repeat this command by pressing only **z**. **less** has a feature of resetting the window size when a number is used to prefix the **w** and **z** commands.

Note

On many UNIX systems, the pager used by **man** is available in the PAGER variable. To know it, use the command **echo $PAGER**. This may or may not show you any value at all, in which case **man** is using a default pager. Some systems set this variable in the file /etc/default/man instead. You'll learn later how to change the value of the PAGER variable for the current login session as well as for future sessions *(17.3.1)*.

2.7 The man Documentation

Vendors organize the man documentation differently, but in general you'll see eight sections of the UNIX manual. Later enhancements have added subsections (like 1C, 1M, 3N etc.), but we'll ignore them in this text. The basic manual sections for SVR4 and Linux are shown in Table 2.2.

Most of the commands you use are available in Section 1, and **man** searches the manuals starting from Section 1. If it locates a command in one section it won't continue the search even if the command also occurs in another section. Since **man** locates most user commands in Section 1, it means that you don't have to specify 1 as the argument:

```
man 1 cp
```
                                                              Same as man cp

Note that we are using an option (1) which doesn't begin with a -, the first deviation from the generalized command syntax. 1 is redundant here, but when a command is

TABLE 2.2 *Organization of the man Documentation*

Section	Subject (SVR4)	Subject (Linux)
1	User programs	User programs
2	Kernel's system calls	Kernel's system calls
3	Library functions	Library functions
4	Administrative file formats	Special files (in /dev)
5	Miscellaneous	Administrative file formats
6	Games	Games
7	Special files (in /dev)	Macro packages and conventions
8	Administration commands	Administration commands

found in multiple sections, you should use the section number additionally as an option:

```
man 4 passwd                              passwd also occurs in Section 4
man -s4 passwd                               Solaris uses the -s option
```

On Solaris machines, you'll have to use **man -s4 passwd** to specify a section. You can also specify multiple section numbers and multiple commands to look up. This is how you select the documentation of **mount** from Section 2 and **passwd** from Section 4:

```
man 2 mount 4 passwd                            Use q to exit in each case
```

This displays the pages of the **mount** command from Section 2 and a configuration file used by the **passwd** command from Section 4. This file also has the same name passwd but stores all users' details except the password!

Note The default order of search pursued by **man** starts from Section 1. So if a command (say **passwd**) occurs both in Sections 1 and 4, and you'd like to see the Section 4 man page only, then you must use the section number as argument with **man**—**man 4 passwd** (or **man -s4 passwd**).

2.7.1 Understanding a man Page

The structure of the man page has remained remarkably consistent over the years. It is divided into a number of compulsory and optional sections where each section is preceded by a header. The common headers are listed in Table 2.3.

Every command doesn't have all the headers but has most of them; the first three (*NAME, SYNOPSIS* and *DESCRIPTION*) are generally seen in all man pages. A compressed man page displaying some of these headers is shown in Fig. 2.2.

At the top of the manual page, you can see the title showing the command name with a number in parentheses. This command features in Section 1 of the manual. Now let's take a close look at the rest of the page:

TABLE 2.3   **man** *Page Headers*

Header	Significance
NAME	Shows the name of the command and its function
SYNOPSIS	Arguments and options used by the command
DESCRIPTION	Detailed account of how the command is used
EXAMPLES	Complex and unobvious examples of command usage
FILES	Other system files used by the command
SEE ALSO	Refers user to man pages of related commands for a fuller understanding
DIAGNOSTICS	When command generates error messages
BUGS	Bugs in the command that haven't been fixed yet
AUTHOR(S)	Author(s) of the command

- *NAME* This section shows the name of the command together with a brief description of its function. Some closely related commands can also feature together in this section. For instance, on some systems **grep**, **egrep** and **fgrep** share the same man page and the section for them looks like this:

```
grep, egrep, fgrep - print lines matching a pattern
```

- *SYNOPSIS* Here you'll find the syntax—the options and arguments used with the command. The synopsis follows certain conventions which every user must understand. However, these conventions differ a little between the hard-copy and on-line version of the manual. Expectedly, the hard copy takes advantage of bold, constant width font and italics, which most terminals are not able to handle. These are the rules that shape the *SYNOPSIS*:
    1. If you are viewing the printed manual, you'll find that the command name and its options are shown in constant width font. Anything shown in this font or in bold has to be entered as it is.
    2. If a command argument is enclosed in rectangular brackets, then it is optional; otherwise, the argument is required.
    3. Generally, files are shown in italics, which means that the actual filenames have to be inserted there. On terminals, you may see these filenames underlined or in reverse video.
    4. The ellipsis (a set of three dots) implies that there can be more instances of the preceding word.
    5. If you find a | character in any of these areas, it means that only one of the options shown on either side of the pipe can be used.

- *DESCRIPTION* This is the largest section in the manual page. It contains a detailed exposition of the command with specific explanation of every option. On some systems, the options themselves have their own separate header. Since UNIX was written by programmers for programmers, this section sometimes

F I G U R E 2.2   *A Censored man Page for the* **csh** *Command*

```
User Commands                                                    csh(1)

NAME
     csh - shell command interpreter with a C-like syntax

SYNOPSIS
     csh [ -bcefinstvVxX ] [ argument... ]

DESCRIPTION
     csh, the C shell, is a command interpreter with a syntax reminiscent
     of the C language.  It provides a number of  convenient features for
     interactive  use  that  are  not  available  with  the Bourne shell,
     including  filename  completion,  command aliasing,  history substi-
     tution, job control,  and a number of built-in commands. As with the
     Bourne shell,  the C shell  provides  variable,  command and filename
     substitution.

OPTIONS
     -b           Force a "break" from option processing. Subsequent command
                  line  arguments  are not  interpreted  as C shell options.
                  This  allows  the  passing  of options to a script without
                  confusion.  The  shell  does  not  run  set-user-ID or
                  set-group-ID scripts unless this option is present.

     -c           Execute  the  first  argument  (which  must  be  present).
                  Remaining arguments are placed in argv,  the argument-list
                  variable, and passed directly to csh.

FILES
     ~/.cshrc    Read at beginning of execution by each shell.
     ~/.login    Read by login shells after .cshrc at login.
     ~/.logout   Read by login shells at logout.

SEE ALSO
     bc(1),   echo(1),   login(1),   ls(1),   more(1),   ps(1),   sh(1),
     shell_builtins(1), tset(1B), which(1), df(1M), swap(1M), sysdef(1M),
     access(2),  exec(2),  fork(2),  pipe(2),  a.out(4),  environ(4)

DIAGNOSTICS
     You have stopped jobs.

          You attempted to exit the  C shell with stopped jobs under
          job control.  An immediate second attempt to exit will succeed,
          terminating the stopped jobs.

WARNINGS
     The use of setuid shell scripts is strongly discouraged.

BUGS
     As of this writing, the time built-in command does NOT compute the
     last  6 fields of output, rendering the output to erroneously report
     the value "0" for these fields.
```

assumes too much and presents information in a way that only an expert can comprehend. Here's an extract from the **find** man page:

```
find searches the directory tree rooted at each given file
name by evaluating the given expression from left to right,
according to the rules of precedence, until the outcome is
known (the left hand side is false for and operations, true
for or), at which point find moves on to the next file name.
```

Not many people can make sense out of this, but then such situations aren't all that common.

- *EXAMPLES* Sometimes, there will be an example or two to highlight the use of some of the complex options. You'll find that on some occasions they aren't all that obvious.
- *FILES* This shows all files used by the command. Sometimes, you'll need to see the contents of these files too.
- *SEE ALSO* It refers you to the other components of the system for a fuller comprehension. You may have to use **man** again with the commands and files listed there.
- *DIAGNOSTICS* It explains why and when the command generates error messages. Sometimes, it may list the error codes along with their meaning. These error codes can be used in shell scripts for controlling the flow of a program.
- *BUGS* As the name implies, this alerts you to the bugs in the program that could cause you some trouble.
- *AUTHOR(S)* Some systems, especially Linux, also show the authors of the command. Here, you may find their email addresses too.

There can be more sections, but we have covered the major ones. All said and done, it's still quite possible for a user to be misled into thinking that a particular feature isn't available with a command because it wasn't specifically mentioned in the section. Commands having one or two man pages are generally easy to use, but not the ones that have tens of pages. Often the manuals are good reading material only after you have sufficiently mastered the system.

2.8　`info`: **The Texinfo Documentation**

When you look for the man pages of the **tar** command in some implementations of Linux, this is what you could see:

```
$ man tar
No manual entry for tar
```

Many systems also support the Texinfo documentation (we'll call it the **info documentation**), and when you see a message like the one above, you should try the **info** command next. This command is a little difficult to use at first but is extremely suited for beginners. Like **man**, the info documentation is complete, but it also provides you with a lot of introductory material. It too is invoked with the command name:

```
info tar
```

You'll now see an **emacs**-type interface describing the table of contents of the **tar** command (Fig. 2.3). Info documentation is organized in **nodes** where one node represents a section of text at a certain level. There are multiple levels here, and the deeper you descend a level the more advanced the treatment becomes. Multilevel documents resemble the *hypertext* documents that are found in the World Wide Web.

In this system, you must first identify the nodes. These are marked with an asterisk at the beginning of the line. You can take the cursor to any of these lines and press *[Enter]*. This brings up another page showing further details. Often the screen will be split into two windows to facilitate viewing.

Within a page, you can use the *[PageUp]* and *[PageDown]* keys in the normal way for paging. To return to the previous level where you pressed *[Enter]*, press **u** (up). You can also move in a linear fashion using **p** (previous) and **n** (next). To quit **info**, use **q**. These are the only commands that you need to use for the time being. The essential commands are shown in Table 2.4.

FIGURE 2.3   *Info Pages of the **tar** Command*

```
        File: tar.info,  Node: Top,  Next: Introduction,  Prev: (dir),  Up: (dir)

        ┌─→* Menu:
        ├─→* Introduction::
Nodes ──┤
        ├─→* Tutorial::
        └─→* tar invocation::

          * operations::
          * Backups::
          * Choosing::
          * Date input formats::
          * Formats::
          * Media::
          * Index::

          -- The Detailed Node Listing --

          Introduction

          * Book Contents::          What this Book Contains
          * Definitions::            Some Definitions
          * What tar Does::          What `tar' Does
          * Naming tar Archives::    How `tar' Archives are Named
        --zz-Info: (tar.info.gz)Top, 248 lines --Top-- Subfile: tar.info-1.gz------
        Welcome to Info version 2.18. "C-h" for help, "m" for menu item.
```

TABLE 2.4 **info** *Commands*

Command	Function
[Enter]	Go to next level
u	Return to previous level
[Spacebar]	View next page
[Delete] or *[Backspace]*	View previous page
t	View top-most node
n	View next node at same level
p	View previous node at same level
q	Quit **info**
h	Help

You should be careful not to use any other keys because you may get stuck in the middle. In case that happens, and the **p** and **u** keys don't take you to the desired point, just quit **info** with **q**. When in doubt, press **h** to see the complete list of key sequences accepted by the **info** reader. The info documentation is detailed and very well organized, and it's no wonder that a lot of the Linux documentation is migrating to this form. You'll need **info** for a detailed study of the **emacs** documentation.

2.9   whatis **and** apropos: **Which Command Will Do the Job?**

man shows you the command syntax, but it doesn't show you how to apply the command in a particular situation. Sometimes, you would like to know just what the command does and not get into its syntax. The **whatis** and **apropos** commands are ideally suited for this purpose. If you don't have them, you can use **man** which has option equivalents for them.

What does the **cp** command do? The **whatis** command provides a one-line answer:

```
$ whatis cp
cp (1)            - copy files
```

You now know the command you have to use to copy a file. Once you have identified the command you need, you can use **man** with the command name to get further details. Note the number in the parentheses; the command is found in Section 1.

Wanting to know what a command does is one thing, but to find out the one that will actually do the job is quite another. If you have no idea about the command to use in a given situation, you should use the **apropos** command with one or more keywords. **apropos** then gives you the name and short description from all manual sections that contain the keyword:

```
$ apropos HTTP
Http (n)          - Client-side implementation of the HTTP/1.0 protocol.
b (8)             - Apache HTTP server benchmarking tool
```

```
apachectl (8)            - Apache HTTP server control interface
httpd (8)                - Apache hypertext transfer protocol server
```

There are four commands that deal with *HTTP* (the protocol used on the World Wide Web). The output also tells you the sections of the manual where they will be found.

Both **whatis** and **apropos** can be used with multiple arguments, but if your keyword itself contains more than one word, then you should surround them with quotes. This is how you can learn more about regular expressions:

```
$ apropos "regular expression"
re (3pm)                 - Perl pragma to alter regular expression behavior
regexp (n)               - Match a regular expression against a string
regsub (n)               - Perform substitutions based on regular expression pattern
 matching
zgrep (1)                - search possibly compressed files for a regular expression
```

Even if the first three lines may not interest you initially, you at least know that there's a command (**zgrep**) that can look for an expression in a compressed file.

Tip

If you don't have the **apropos** command on your system, you can use **man -k**. You can also use **man -f** in place of **whatis**.

Linux

While most UNIX options use a single letter with the - (e.g. -l), Linux also offers options using two hyphens and a multicharacter word. For instance, it offers the synonym **ls --all** in addition to **ls -a**. Though it means more typing load for the user, the words are quite meaningful and easy to remember; it's easier to remember --all than -a.

Some Linux commands don't have man pages, but almost all of them offer the --help option that displays a compact listing of all the options. You can spot the **find** option you are looking for by using this:

```
$ find --help
Usage: find [path...] [expression]
default path is the current directory; default expression is -print
expression may consist of:
operators (decreasing precedence; -and is implicit where no others are given):
      ( EXPR ) ! EXPR -not EXPR EXPR1 -a EXPR2 EXPR1 -and EXPR2
      EXPR1 -o EXPR2 EXPR1 -or EXPR2 EXPR1 , EXPR2
options (always true): -daystart -depth -follow --help
      -maxdepth LEVELS -mindepth LEVELS -mount -noleaf --version -xdev
tests (N can be +N or -N or N): -amin N -anewer FILE -atime N -cmin N
      -cnewer FILE -ctime N -empty -false -fstype TYPE -gid N -group NAME
      -ilname PATTERN -iname PATTERN -inum N -ipath PATTERN -iregex PATTERN
      -links N -lname PATTERN -mmin N -mtime N -name PATTERN -newer FILE
      -nouser -nogroup -path PATTERN -perm [+-]MODE -regex PATTERN
```

```
      -size N[bckw] -true -type [bcdpfls] -uid N -used N -user NAME
      -xtype [bcdpfls]
actions: -exec COMMAND ; -fprint FILE -fprint0 FILE -fprintf FILE FORMAT
      -ok COMMAND ; -print -print0 -printf FORMAT -prune -ls
```

A Linux command invariably offers far more options than its UNIX counterpart, and --help provides a single-page summary of all options. You'll find this lookup facility quite useful when you know the usage of the options, but can't recollect the one you require.

SUMMARY

UNIX is a command-based system. UNIX commands are generally short and are in lowercase. They need not have any specific extensions. Case is significant in UNIX.

The **type** command shows whether a command is *external* or *internal*. It also shows the location of an external command. Internal commands are built into the shell, and an internal command takes precedence over an external command of the same name.

The PATH shell variable specifies the search list of directories for locating external commands. The delimiter used in PATH is the colon (:). The system commands used by all users are located in the directories /bin and /usr/bin.

A command consists of *options* and *arguments*, and the vast majority of commands are used with files. An option changes the default behavior of a command, and most UNIX commands have a number of them. Options usually begin with a -, and commands and arguments must be separated by any number of spaces or tabs (*whitespace*). The command with all its options and arguments is called the *command line*.

Options can normally be combined with a single -, but some commands use options that have their own *parameters*. Generally, these options can also be combined if their parameters are lined up in the same sequence.

More than one command can be entered in one line, and a command sequence can overflow to the next line. You don't have to wait for the previous command to complete before you enter another one. If a command doesn't work properly, check the version of the operating system or kernel with **uname -r**.

The UNIX documentation is organized in eight sections and most of the user commands are found in Section 1. The **man** command used with a command name displays the synopsis (syntax), description and files used by the command. **man** uses the **more** or **less** pager to view the text one page at a time.

info organizes the documentation in multiple levels, and provides more details about command usage than **man**. Pressing *[Enter]* on a line that begins with an * provides more details on the topic.

whatis (or **man -f**) gives you a one-line introduction to the command. **apropos** (or **man -k**) provides a list of commands containing a keyword.

Linux options are complete words preceded by two hyphens (--). A Linux command generally supports the --help option that enables quick lookups of command usage.

SELF-TEST

2.1   Enter a : and then press *[Enter]*. What do you conclude?

2.2   Can you run UNIX commands in uppercase?

2.3   If a command has the `.txt` extension can it be executed?

2.4   Name two UNIX commands that are more than four characters long.

2.5   What is PATH?

2.6   What is the character used to separate the directories in the PATH list?

2.7   Is it possible to use `ls-l` instead of `ls -l`?

2.8   How many options are there in this command?

         `ls -lut chap01 note3`

2.9   If you find yourself using options preceded by two hyphens (like `--all`), which flavor of UNIX could you be using?

2.10   Do options necessarily need to begin with a -?

2.11   Is the option really optional?

2.12   What is the name given to the command, its options and arguments?

2.13   Which commands are actually programming languages?

2.14   How do you find out the version number of your operating system?

2.15   Why are the directories `/bin` and `/usr/bin` usually found first in the output of **echo $PATH**?

2.16   Do you really need to wait for a command to finish before entering the next one?

2.17   What is a command's man page?

2.18   What is the documentation viewer that organizes its pages in multiple levels or nodes?

2.19   You don't even know the name of the command that could do a job. What do you do?

EXERCISES

2.1   Enter a # before a command and press *[Enter]*. What do you see, and how do you think you can take advantage of the behavior?

2.2   Name three major differences between UNIX commands and Windows programs.

2.3   Where will you find the UNIX commands meant for general use?

2.4   Where are the commands used by the system administrator located?

2.5   You won't find the **cd** command either in `/bin` or `/usr/bin`. How is it executed then?

2.6   How do you find out whether these commands are internal or external—**echo**, **date**, **pwd** and `ls`?

2.7   If you find the **echo** command in the `/bin` directory, would you still call it an external command?

2.8   Is an option also an argument? How do an argument and an option differ?

2.9   Why shouldn't you have a filename beginning with a -?

2.10   Reduce the number of keystrokes to execute this command:

```
tar -t -v -f /dev/fd0
```

2.11   Consider the command **tar -x -v -f /dev/rct0 -b 20 ***. Can you combine the options in this way?

```
tar -xvfb 20 /dev/rct0 *
```

2.12   Name one command which uses a number as the option and a + as its prefix.

2.13   You need to save the output of the **who** and **date** commands in a single file. How will you do that?

2.14   What does the secondary prompt look like, and when does it appear?

2.15   What does the | in the *SYNOPSIS* section of this man page indicate as shown below?

```
/usr/xpg4/bin/tail [ -f | -r ]
```

2.16   What do the three dots in this *SYNOPSIS* section indicate as shown below?

```
ps [ -aAcdefjlLPy ] [ -g grplist ] [ -n namelist ] [[ -o format ] ... ]
```

2.17   What are the two pagers used by **man**? Which one is superior and why?

2.18   You have reached the end of the man page of **ksh** (the Korn shell) by pressing **f** repeatedly. How can you return to the beginning with the minimum keystrokes, assuming that the pager is **more**? What would you do if it were **less**?

2.19   You are unable to guess the pager used by **man** and find that the PAGER variable is also undefined. What will you try next?

2.20   You located the string crontab in a man page by searching with **/crontab**[*Enter*]. How do you find out the other occurrences of this string in the page?

2.21   When will you use the section number as an argument to **man**?

2.22   Your system doesn't have the **apropos** command. What will you do?

2.23   You used the command **apropos mount point** to list the commands that handle a file system's mount point, and you find that the output shows lines not connected with it. Why did that happen?

KEY TERMS

buffer *(2.5.3)*   **man documentation** *(2.6)*
command argument *(2.4)*   **metacharacter** *(2.5.1)*
command line *(2.4.1)*   **option parameter** *(2.4.2)*
command option *(2.4.1)*   **pager** *(2.6)*
command parsing *(2.4.2)*   **pathname** *(2.2)*
external command *(2.3)*   **secondary prompt** *(2.5.2)*
info documentation *(2.8)*   **shell** *(2.3)*
info node *(2.8)*   **whitespace** *(2.4)*
internal command *(2.3 and 2.6)*   **word** *(2.4)*

## CHAPTER 3

General-Purpose Utilities

The best way to start acquiring knowledge of the UNIX command set is to try your hand at some of the general-purpose utilities of the system. These commands have varied functions, but can be broadly divided into two categories. Some commands tell you the state of the system—the current users, the date, your machine and terminal names. Others can aid you directly in your work—like logging your session and providing a calculator service.

Every command featured in this chapter is useful, and has not been included here for cosmetic effect. Most also have been used in later chapters, especially in shell programming. A few are true dark horses. You'll need these commands in all sorts of situations in your daily life at the machine. The commands are simple to use, have very few options (except for **stty**), and hardly read from or write to files.

Objectives

- Change your own password with **passwd** and know the password framing rules for your system. *(3.1)*
- Find out the users of the system with **who** and **w**. *(3.2)*
- Know the device name of your terminal with **tty**. *(3.3)*
- Lock your terminal with **lock**. *(3.4)*
- Change your terminal's settings with **stty**. *(3.5)*
- Save all keystrokes and command output in a file with **script**. *(3.6)*
- Clear the screen and position the cursor with **clear** and **tput**. *(3.7)*
- Know your machine's name with **uname**. *(3.8)*
- Display the system date in various formats with **date**. *(3.9)*
- Display the calendar of any month or year with **cal**. *(3.10)*
- Generate a reminder service with **calendar**. *(3.11)*
- Use the calculator facility in **bc**. *(3.12)*

3.1 passwd: **Change Your Password**

Security wasn't much of a concern in the Windows environment (until NT), but that was because there wasn't really much this system could do to establish a secure environment. However, UNIX can, and if you really care about protecting your files, then make sure that no one else is able to use your account without your consent. If your account still doesn't have a password, or has one that is already known to others, you should change it immediately.

In Chapter 1, you used the **passwd** command to change passwords. The behavior of this command is heavily system-dependent. When used without arguments, it sets the user's own password:

```
$ passwd
(current) UNIX password: *******               Password not shown on screen
New UNIX password: *******
Retype new UNIX password: *******
```

When invoked by an ordinary user, **passwd** asks for the old password, after which it demands the new password twice. If everything goes smoothly, the new password is registered by the system, and the prompt is returned.

Depending on the way they are configured, many systems conduct certain checks on the string that you enter as password. They may either disallow you from framing easy-to-remember passwords or advise you against choosing a bad password. The following messages are quite common:

```
UX:passwd: ERROR: Passwords must differ by at least 3 positions
passwd(SYSTEM): The first 6 characters of the password must contain at least
two alphabetic characters and at least one numeric or special character.
passwd(SYSTEM): Password too short - must be at least 6 characters.
BAD PASSWORD: it does not contain enough DIFFERENT characters
BAD PASSWORD: it is based on a dictionary word
BAD PASSWORD: is too similar to the old one
```

These messages suggest that you are not able to choose any password you like. These are some of the rules that you are expected to follow when handling your own password:

- Don't choose a password similar to the old one.
- Don't use commonly used names like names of friends, relatives, pets and so forth. A system may check with its own dictionary and throw out those passwords which can be guessed.
- Use a mix of alphabetic or numeric characters. Enterprise UNIX systems won't allow passwords which are wholly alphabetic or numeric.
- Make sure the password is unmeaningful enough to prevent others from guessing it.
- Don't write down the password in an easily accessible document.
- Change the password regularly.

When you enter a password, the string is **encrypted** by the system. Encryption generates a string of seemingly random characters that UNIX uses subsequently to determine the authenticity of a password. This encryption is stored in a file named shadow in the /etc directory. Even if a user is able to see the encryption in the file, she can't work backwards and derive the original password string from the encryption.

There are elaborate rules governing the use of passwords and their expiry. And the command behaves differently when used by the system administrator. The command is revisited in Chapter 22.

Caution

It is possible that the system was set up for you without a password. This should be immediately corrected by running the **passwd** command. If others have acquired knowledge of your password, you should change it too.

3.2 who **and** w: **Know the Users**

UNIX maintains an account of all users who are logged on to the system. It's often a good idea to know their login names so that you can mail them messages or set up a chat session *(11.2)*. There are two commands which display an informative listing of users—**who** and **w**. **who** produces a simple three-columnar output:

```
$ who
root       console      Jan 30 10:32
romeo      tty01        Jan 30 14:09
andrew     tty02        Jan 30 14:15
juliet     pts/4        Jan 30 13:17
```

The first column shows the user-ids of the four users currently working on the system. The second column shows the device names of their respective terminals. romeo has the name tty01 associated with his terminal. The third column shows the date and time of logging in.

While it is a general feature of most UNIX commands to avoid cluttering the display with header information, this command does have a header option (-H). This option prints the column headers, and when combined with the -u option, provides a more detailed list:

```
$ who -Hu
NAME       LINE         TIME            IDLE      PID     COMMENTS
romeo      tty01        Jan 30 14:09    .         30
andrew     tty02        Jan 30 14:15   0:40       31
```

Two users have logged out, so it seems. The first three columns are the same as before, but it's the fourth column (*IDLE*) that is interesting. A **.** against romeo shows that activity has occurred in the last one minute before the command was invoked. andrew seems to be idling for the last 40 minutes. Ignore the PID attribute for the time being; you'll meet it in Chapter 10.

Tip

Know your own username with **who am i** or **whoami**. This has already been discussed in Chapter 1.

Note

The terminal names that you see in the **who** output are actually special files representing the devices. These files are available in /dev. For example, the file tty01 can be found in the /dev directory. pts/4 is the file named 4 under the pts directory, which in turn is under /dev.

The **w** command produces a more detailed output of users' activities, and additionally displays many details of the system:

```
$ w
  2:40pm  up  1:37,  3 users,  load average: 0.00, 0.00, 0.00
USER     TTY      FROM            LOGIN@   IDLE   JCPU   PCPU  WHAT
romeo    tty1                     1:24pm   6.00s 11.20s 11.01s vi ux3rd03
andrew   tty2                     2:20pm   6:35   0.68s  0.27s ispell ux3rd17
juliet   tty4                     2:42pm   1:10m  0.13s  0.13s -bash
```

Let's consider the first line of output first. This command was executed at 2:40 p.m. on a system having three users. The system itself has been up and running for 1 hour and 37 minutes. The system load averages for the past one, five and fifteen minutes are virtually negligible.

The remaining output is **who**-like except for the last three columns. The output shown under *JCPU* shows the total CPU time consumed by all processes at that terminal. The command the user is currently executing is shown in the last column. *PCPU* refers to the time consumed by that process. Because the multitasking nature of UNIX permits a user to run more than one job at the same time, the JCPU and PCPU times can often be different.

who and **w** are regularly used by the system administrator to monitor whether terminals are being properly utilized. Both offer a number of other options that are quite useful for administrative work. On large systems having hundreds of users, the output could be too long to be of any effective use. To obtain details for a single user only, use **w** with the username.

Tip

You can use the **users** command to get a single-line list of all users. **users** doesn't show details of either the users or the system. It's not available in all systems.

3.3 tty: **Know Your Terminal**

Since UNIX treats even terminals as files, it is reasonable to expect a command that tells you the filename of the terminal you are using. It is the **tty** (teletype) command, an obvious reference to the device that has now become obsolete. The command is simple and needs no arguments:

```
$ tty
/dev/term/2
```

The terminal filename is 2 (a file named 2) resident in the term directory. This term directory in turn is under the /dev directory. If the user logs in from another terminal next time, her terminal device name will be different.

You can use **tty** in a shell script to control the behavior of the script depending on the terminal it is invoked from. If a program must run from only one specified terminal, the script logic must use **tty** to take this decision.

3.4   lock: **Lock Your Terminal**

You sometimes have to be away from your terminal for a while, but don't want to log out because a job is running in the background. Many UNIX systems let you lock your terminal to prevent people with mischievous intent from gaining access to the system. This is done with the **lock** command (from Berkeley). It requires you to enter a password when you decide to lock it:

```
$ lock
Password: ********                              Password not shown on screen
Re-enter password: ********
terminal locked by romeo 0 minutes ago
```

The $ prompt disappears, and the system will remain locked in this condition for 30 minutes. If you are not back by that time, then it will log you out. Any time before that, you can unlock the terminal simply by re-entering the same password:

```
********
$ _
```

The password that **lock** prompts for need not be the same as that set with the **passwd** command. You may decide to set the duration of the lock (not exceeding 60 minutes) by using an option:

```
lock -45                                        Locks it for 45 minutes
```

These parameters are variable, and controlled by two settings in the file /etc/default/lock on some systems.

Note

Any file in the /etc directory can be changed only by the system administrator who uses root as the user-id.

3.5   stty: **Set Terminal Characteristics**

The terminal is the device with which a user communicates with the system. Depending on the user's choice, different terminals are configured differently. It's also possible that your terminal may not behave in the way it's meant to. The *[Enter]* key may not work, while aborting may not be possible with *[Ctrl-c]*. You may also need to set the parameters when you hook up a new terminal having different characteristics. The **stty** command helps straighten these things out.

     stty uses an enormous number of **keywords** (options that look different), but we'll consider only a handful of them. The -a (all) option displays the current settings. A trimmed output is presented below:

```
$ stty -a
speed 38400 baud; rows = 25; columns = 80; ypixels = 0; xpixels = 0;
intr = DEL; quit = ^\; erase = ^h; kill = ^u;
```

```
eof = ^d; eol = <undef>; eol2 = <undef>; swtch = <undef>;
start = ^q; stop = ^s; susp = ^z; dsusp = ^y;
isig icanon -xcase echo echoe echok -echonl -noflsh
```

The output shows, among other things, the **baud rate** (the speed) of the terminal, in this case 38,400. It also shows many of the parameters that were discussed in Chapter 1 *(1.9)*. In this system, the *[Delete]* key (rather than *[Ctrl-c]*) interrupts a program. The erase character is *[Ctrl-h]*, and the kill character is *[Ctrl-u]*.

Of special significance is the eof (end-of-file) character which here is set to *[Ctrl-d]*. You used this key sequence in Chapter 1 with the **cat** command *(1.9.2)*. For commands that accept input from the keyboard, this key signifies the end of input. In this chapter, we'll be using it with the **bc** command.

Following the fourth line, you see a series of keywords with a - prefixed to some of them. When an option doesn't have the -, it means that the option is turned on. You can use the **stty** command itself to set and unset these options.

Whether Backspacing Should Erase Character (echoe)   If you have worked on a number of terminals, you would have noticed that backspacing over a character sometimes removes it from sight and sometimes doesn't. This is decided by the keyword echoe. Since it is set here (no - prefix to it), backspacing removes the character from display.

You can use the same keyword to reverse this setting. Here, you need to prefix a - to the echoe keyword:

```
stty -echoe
```

Backspacing now doesn't remove a character from sight. This setting is inoperative in some systems.

Entering a Password through a Shell Script (echo)   The echo setting has to be manipulated to let shell programs accept a password-like string that you wouldn't like to be displayed on the screen. By default, the option is turned on, but you can turn it off in this way:

```
stty -echo                                                  Turns off keyboard input
```

With this setting, keyboard entry is not echoed. You should turn it off after the entry is complete by using **stty echo**, which again is not displayed, but makes sure that all subsequent input is.

Changing the Interrupt Key (intr)   **stty** also sets the functions for some of the keys. For instance, if you like to use *[Ctrl-c]* as the interrupt key instead of *[Delete]*, then you'll have to use

```
stty intr \^c                                                            ^ and c
```

Here, the keyword intr is followed by a space, the \ (backslash) character, a ^ (caret), and finally the character c. This is the way **stty** indicates to the system that the interrupt character is *[Ctrl-c]*.

When you insert control characters into a file, you'll see a ^ symbol apparently prefixed to the character. For example, *[Ctrl-l]* is seen as ^l (or ^L). However, it's actually a single character, occupying two slots on the terminal; no caret is actually present. Since you can't press *[Ctrl-c]* as an argument to **stty** (because that could abort the program), a literal caret is used, duly preceded by a backslash.

Changing the End-of-File Key (eof) When creating files with **cat**, you used *[Ctrl-d]* to terminate input. This eof character is also selectable. Instead of *[Ctrl-d]*, you can use *[Ctrl-a]* as the eof character:

```
stty eof \^a
```

Now, *[Ctrl-a]* will terminate input for those commands that expect input from the keyboard when invoked in a particular way. The **cat** and **bc** commands can be made to work in this way.

When Everything Else Fails (sane) **stty** also provides another argument to set the terminal characteristics to values that will work on most terminals. Use the word sane as a single argument to the command:

```
stty sane                                          Restores sanity to the terminal
```

There are other options, but you are advised against tampering with too many settings.

3.6 script: **Record Your Session**

This command, virtually unknown to many UNIX users, lets you "record" your login session in a file. All the commands, their output and the error messages are stored in the file for later viewing. If you are doing some important work, and wish to keep a log of all your activities, then you should invoke this command immediately after you log in:

```
$ script
Script started, file is typescript
$ _
```

The prompt returns, and *all* your keystrokes (including the one used to backspace) that you now enter here get recorded in the file typescript. After your recording is over, you can terminate the session by entering **exit**:

```
$ exit                                                    Or use [Ctrl-d]
Script done, file is typescript
$ _
```

You can now view this file with the **cat** command. **script** overwrites any previous typescript that may exist. If you want to append to it, or want to use a different log file, then you can consider these options:

```
script -a                             Appends activities to existing file typescript
script logfile                              Logs activities to file logfile
```

There are some activities that won't be recorded properly, for instance, the commands used in the full-screen mode (like **vi**, **emacs** and **pine**).

3.7   `clear` **and** `tput`: **Clear Your Screen**

There are two commands available in most UNIX systems to clear your screen—**clear** and **tput**. The first command is used without arguments:

```
clear
```
Prompt not shown

The screen clears and the cursor is positioned at the top-left corner of the screen. The second command is used with the `clear` argument:

```
tput clear
```
Also clears the screen

tput can also position the cursor at a specific location or be used to highlight text. Most of its arguments don't begin with a hyphen. You can use the `cup` argument to position the cursor at row number 10 and column 20:

```
tput cup 10 20
```

If you issue an **echo** command after this command in a shell script, you'll find the echoed text at that position. You'll be using this feature in one of the exercises when doing shell programming.

     You can boldface your text by using the `smso` and `rmso` arguments. The former starts the bold sequence, while the latter turns it off. These are generally used in conjunction with **echo**:

```
tput smso
```
Highlighting starts
```
echo Come to the Web
tput rmso
```
Highlighting ends

Later, you'll use a special feature of the shell that combines these sequences in a single command *(18.1)*.

3.8   `uname`: **Know Your Machine's Name**

If your machine is connected to a network, then it must have a name. If your network is connected to the Internet, then this name forms part of your machine's *domain name* (a series of words separated by dots, like *hillftp.planets.com*). The **uname** command with the -n option tells you the machine name in a network:

```
$ uname -n
hillftp
```
The first word of the domain name

Many UNIX networking utilities use the machine's name as an argument. To copy files from a remote machine, you have to specify it with the **ftp** command. Note that the same **uname** command when used with -r shows the operating system's version number *(2.5.4)*.

3.9   date: **Display the System Date**

The UNIX system maintains an internal clock meant to run perpetually. When the system is shut down, a battery backup keeps the clock ticking. This clock actually stores the number of seconds elapsed since January 1, 1970. A 32-bit counter stores these seconds, and the counter will overflow sometime in 2038.

You can display the current date with the **date** command, which shows the date and time to the nearest second:

```
$ date
Sat Feb 12 23:10:34 EST 2000
```

The command can also be used with suitable format specifiers as arguments. Each format is preceded by a + symbol, followed by the % operator and a single character describing the format. For instance, using the format +%m, you can print only the month:

```
$ date +%m
02
```

or the month name:

```
$ date +%h
Feb
```

You can also combine them in one command:

```
$ date +"%h (%m)"
Feb (02)
```

There are other format specifiers:

d—the day of the month (1 to 31)
y—the last two digits of the year
H, M, and S—the hour, minute and second, respectively

When you use multiple format specifiers (as in the previous example), you must enclose them within quotes (single or double), and use a single + symbol before the opening quote.

Note

You can't change the date as an ordinary user, but the system administrator uses the same command with a different syntax to set the system date! This is discussed in Chapter 22.

3.10   cal: **The Calendar**

cal is a handy tool that you can invoke anytime to see the calendar of any specific month or a complete year. To see the calendar for the month of December (of the current year), you have to provide the three-character month abbreviation as an argument:

```
$ cal dec
     December 2000
Su Mo Tu We Th Fr Sa
                 1  2
 3  4  5  6  7  8  9
10 11 12 13 14 15 16
17 18 19 20 21 22 23
24 25 26 27 28 29 30
31
```

cal can print the calendar for the entire year too. This time use the year as the argument:

```
cal 2000
```

You can't hold the entire calendar in one page of the screen; it scrolls off too rapidly before you can use *[Ctrl-s]* to make it pause. To make **cal** pause in the same way **man** pauses, just use **cal** with a pager (**more** or **less**) using the | symbol to connect them:

```
cal 2000 | more
```
                                                                                Or use less

The | symbol connects two commands (in a *pipeline*) where **more** takes input from the **cal** command. You can now scroll forward by pressing the *[Spacebar]*.

Unlike many similar utilities, the **cal** command is totally accurate, and also takes into account the leap year adjustments that took place in the year 1752.

3.11   calendar: A Useful Reminder Mechanism

The **calendar** command provides a useful reminder mechanism for a user. The command searches a file named calendar in the current directory for lines containing any date that either represents the current date or "tomorrow." It then displays the matched lines on the terminal. A typical calendar file could look something like this:

```
$ cat calendar
Mar 23, 2000 the target for this month is $3.2 million
The AGM is scheduled for March 24
Board meeting on 24th March, 2000 at 10 a.m.
On march 24 -- principals visiting us for discussion.
On Mar 27, demo -- to be arranged for a foreign delegation
On 03/27/00 -- meeting with all sales and marketing people
Half-yearly results should be published by Mar 25, 2000
Lunch with the Chairman on Mar 26
```

The file consists of a series of messages, each containing some date entered in a number of formats. To test how receptive **calendar** is to these formats, first execute the command after ascertaining today's date:

```
$ date
Thu Mar 23 16:09:35 EST 2000
$ calendar
Mar 23, 2000 the target for this month is $3.2 million
The AGM is scheduled for March 24
On march 24 -- principals visiting us for discussion.
```

calendar looks for those lines containing today's and tomorrow's dates. Note the differing formats that are accepted by this command; the current month has been spelled as "Mar," "March" and "march." **calendar** identifies all these formats as valid ones. However, the board meeting scheduled for the "24th March" has not been listed because that format isn't acceptable to **calendar**.

If the year is not specified, **calendar** assumes the current year by default. **calendar** also behaves differently when the command is run on a weekend. "Tomorrow" then includes not only the weekend holidays, but also the first working day beginning next week.

As you can see, the date format acceptable to **calendar** can take on a number of forms. However, if the date is specified as numerals, only the form *mm/dd/yy* is acceptable, but not *mm-dd-yy*.

Note

calendar is essentially a shell script, and it is worthwhile interpreting its structure after you have attained a fair amount of proficiency in shell programming. It's not offered in Linux.

3.12   bc: **The Calculator**

UNIX provides two types of calculators—a graphical object (the **xcalc** command) that looks like one, and the character-based **bc** command. The former is available in the X Window system, and is quite easy to use. The other one is less friendly, extremely powerful and remains one of the UNIX system's neglected tools.

When you invoke **bc** without arguments, the cursor keeps on blinking and nothing seems to happen. **bc** belongs to a family of commands (called *filters*) that expect input from the keyboard when used without any argument. Key in the following arithmetic expression:

```
$ bc
12 + 5
17                                          Value displayed after computation
```

bc added the two numbers and showed the output in the next line. To quit **bc**, you have to use *[Ctrl-d]* (the eof character) that marks the end of input. You can also ask **bc** to perform calculations together:

```
12*12 ; 2^32                                ^ indicates "to the power of"
144
4294967296                       Maximum memory possible in a 32-bit machine
[Ctrl-d]
$ _
```

Start **bc** again, and then divide two numbers. There's a surprise for you:

9/5
1   *Decimal portion truncated*

By default, **bc** performs *truncated* division, and you have to set `scale` to the number of digits of precision before you perform any division:

scale=2   *Truncate to 2 decimal places*
17/7
2.42   *Not rounded off, result is actually 2.42857.....*

bc is quite useful in converting numbers from one base to another. For instance, when setting IP addresses *(23.1)* in a network, you may need to convert binary numbers to decimal. Set `ibase` (input base) to 2 before you provide the number:

ibase=2
11001010
202   *Output in decimal—base 10*

The reverse is also possible, this time with `obase`:

obase=2
14
1110   *Binary of 14*

In this way, you can convert from one base to the other (not exceeding 16). **bc** also handles hexadecimal numbers perfectly well:

obase=16
14
E   *Hexadecimal value of 14*

bc can also be used with variables that retain their values until you exit the program. You can, however, use just 26 of them at a time as **bc** supports only single lowercase letters (a to z). While setting a variable is quite simple and straightforward, the evaluation is done by merely entering the variable name:

x=3 ; y=4 ; z=5
p = x+ y +z
p
12

bc is a pseudo-programming language featuring arrays, functions, conditionals (`if`) and loops (`for` and `while`). It also comes with a library for performing scientific calculations. It can handle very, very large numbers. If a computation results in a 900-digit number, **bc** will show each and every digit!

Apart from the commands that were discussed in this chapter, UNIX has many, many more general purpose commands that handle files. You may like to know what they do—and even try your hand at some of them:

- Copy, rename and delete files with **cp**, **mv** and **rm**. *(6.11 to 6.13)*
- View and print a file with **cat** *(6.14)*, **more** *(9.1)* and **lp**. *(6.16)*
- Compress a file with **compress** and **gzip**. *(6.19)*
- Find out disk space utilization with **df** and **du**. *(6.17 and 6.18)*
- Extract the two ends of a file with **head** and **tail**. *(9.8 and 9.9)*
- Cut a file vertically with **cut** and paste two cut segments with **paste**. *(9.10 and 9.11)*
- Find differences between two files with **comm**, **cmp** and **diff**. *(9.5 to 9.7)*
- Sort a file's contents with **sort**. *(9.12)*

Many of these commands have flexible usage and are placed in later chapters. To appreciate the power of these commands fully, you'll need to know the behavioral properties of the shell which manipulates the input and output of these commands.

SUMMARY

passwd is used to change a user's password which is not echoed to the screen for security reasons. Passwords must be unmeaningful, and some systems don't permit the use of easy-to-remember passwords. The system administrator doesn't need to know anyone's password to be able to change it.

who and **w** show you the users working on the system. They also show their time of logging in, and the time they have been idling. **w** provides details of CPU usage, and also shows the command each user is executing.

tty tells you the device name of your terminal. This will always be a file in the /dev directory.

Use **lock** to lock your terminal when you leave your place of work temporarily. The password used by **lock** need not be the same as the one used to log in.

stty is used to set various terminal attributes. You can define the key that interrupts a program (intr), erases text by backspacing (erase) and marks the end-of-file (eof). Setting the echo keyword disables display of keyboard input on the screen. If nothing works, you can use **stty sane** to set the terminal to some standard values.

script is the UNIX system's recorder which logs all activities of a user in a separate file. It stores both user input and command output in the file.

clear and **tput clear** are used to clear the screen. When used in combination with **echo**, **tput** can even highlight text or display it at a certain location on the screen.

uname -n displays the machine's name that is used by networking commands.

date can display the day, month or year, or any combination of them. The system administrator uses it to change the system date.

cal produces the calendar of a month or year.

calendar is used to remind you of your engagements. On a Friday, it considers "tomorrow" to mean the weekend holidays as well as the next Monday.

bc is the calculator. It can also handle binary, octal and hexadecimal numbers and convert from one to the other. You can store intermediate results of calculations in variables and use any degree of precision.

SELF-TEST

3.1   The **passwd** command didn't prompt for the old password. When do you think that can happen?

3.2   Where is the password stored?

3.3   Observe the calendar for the year 1752. Do you notice anything unusual?

3.4   Can you change the system date with the **date** command?

3.5   Where does **calendar** get its input from?

3.6   Which command clears the screen?

3.7   Enter the **uname** command without any arguments. What do you think the output represents?

3.8   Which command do you use to find out the length of time the system has been up?

3.9   How will you record your login session in the file **foo**?

3.10   How do you find out your terminal's device name?

3.11   How will you prevent others from using your terminal?

3.12   How will you ensure that **bc** displays the results of all divisions using three decimal places?

3.13   If a system is used by a hundred users, how will you list the activities of a single user, henry?

3.14   How do you list simply the names of the users logged in without displaying any further details?

EXERCISES

3.1   Display the current date in the form *dd/mm/yyyy*.

3.2   When does **calendar** treat "tomorrow" differently?

3.3   Is "17th October" treated by **calendar** as a valid date?

3.4   You suddenly found your keyboard is displaying uppercase letters even though your *[CapsLock]* key is set properly. What should you try?

3.5   Can you have the same login name more than once in the **who** output?

3.6   How do you find out the users who are idling?

3.7   With which command will you find out your machine's name and the version of the operating system?

3.8   Which command does the ordinary user use to change the system date and time?

3.9   How do you clear the screen and place the cursor at row 12, column 25?

3.10   If you find that your keystrokes are not being echoed, what remedies will you try?

3.11   How will you find out the decimal equivalent of 1101001?

KEY TERMS

baud rate *(3.5)*	**keywords** *(3.5)*
encryption *(3.1)*	

## CHAPTER 4

The vi/vim Editor

No matter what work you do with the UNIX system, you'll eventually write some C or Java programs or shell (or **perl**) scripts. You may also have to edit some of the system files at times. For all this, you must learn to use an editor, and UNIX provides two very versatile ones—**vi** and **emacs**. We look at **vi** in this chapter and **emacs** in the next.

vi is a full-screen editor now available with all UNIX systems, and is widely acknowledged as one of the most powerful editors available in any environment. It was created by a graduate student—Bill Joy—later to become the cofounder of Sun Microsystems. **vi** made its first appearance in BSD UNIX but is now standard on all UNIX systems.

vi offers cryptic, and sometimes mnemonic, internal commands for editing work. It makes near-complete use of the keyboard, where practically every key has a function. **vi** has innumerable features, and you really don't need to know all of them; a working knowledge initially should be fine. As a beginner, you should read on till you encounter the "Going Further" heading before Section 4.18 and move ahead only when you feel you must.

Linux

The most well-known "vi" editor in Linux is **vim** (vi improved). Bram Moolenaar has made three notable improvements to this program—multiple windows, highlighting text and command history. By virtue of a linking feature which lets one file have more than one name, **vi** in Linux calls up **vim**. We'll be discussing the features of **vim** in the Linux-specific sections.

Objectives

- Know the three modes of functioning. *(4.1.1)*
- Input and replace text and control characters. *(4.3)*
- Save your work, recover from a crash and quit **vi**. *(4.2 and 4.4)*
- Understand the significance of the *repeat factor*. *(4.6)*
- Navigate both across a file and along a line. *(4.8)*
- Understand the use of *operator-command* combinations to delete, move and copy text. *(4.9 and 4.10)*
- Change text including its case. *(4.11)*
- Repeat and undo the last command. *(4.12 and 4.13)*
- Search for a string in a file and a character in a line. *(4.14)*

- Extend the searching mechanism to include *regular expressions*. *(4.15)*
- Replace a pattern with another. *(4.16)*
- Edit multiple files and switch from one file to another. *(4.17)*

➤ *G O I N G   F U R T H E R*

- Mark text and access any mark. *(4.18)*
- Change screen text by running (*filtering*) a UNIX command on it. *(4.19)*
- Copy multiple text sections to separate buffers. *(4.20)*
- Recover up to nine complete line deletions. *(4.21)*
- Customize the editor's environment by defining abbreviations and key maps and setting variables. *(4.22, 4.23 and 4.24)*

4.1 vi **Preliminaries**

A **vi** session begins by invoking the command **vi** with (or without) a filename:

```
vi index.html
```

You are presented a full empty screen (Fig. 4.1), each line beginning with a ~ (tilde). This is **vi**'s way of indicating that they are nonexistent lines. For text editing, **vi** uses 24 of the 25 lines that are normally available in a terminal. The last line is reserved for some commands that you'll enter to act on the text. This line is also used by the system to display messages. The filename appears in this line with the message `"index.html" [New file]`.

4.1.1 The Three Modes

When you open a file with **vi**, the cursor is positioned at the top left-hand corner of the screen. You are said to be in the **Command Mode**. This is the mode where you pass commands to act on text. Pressing a key doesn't show it on screen, but may perform a function like moving the cursor to the next line, or deleting a line. You can't use the Command Mode to enter or replace text.

There are two Command Mode functions that you should know at this stage—the role of the *[Spacebar]* and the *[Backspace]* keys. The *[Spacebar]* takes you one character ahead, while *[Backspace]* (or *[Ctrl-h]*) takes you a character back. Backspacing in this mode doesn't delete text at all.

F I G U R E 4.1   *The* **vi** *Screen*

```
█
~
~
~
~
~
~
"index.html" [New file]
```

To enter text, you have to leave the Command Mode and enter the **Input Mode**. There are 10 keys which take you to this mode when pressed, and whatever you then enter shows up on screen. Backspacing in this mode, however, erases all characters that the cursor passes through. To leave this mode, you have to press the *[Esc]* key.

You have to save your work, leave **vi** or switch to editing another file. Sometimes, you'll need to make a global substitution in the file. Neither of the two modes will quite do the work for you. You have to use the **Last Line Mode** or **ex Mode**, where you enter the instruction in the last line of the screen. Some Command Mode functions also have Last Line Mode equivalents.

With this knowledge, we can summarize the three modes in which **vi** works:

- Command Mode—Where keys are used as commands to act on text.
- Input Mode—Where any key depressed is entered as text.
- Last Line Mode or ex Mode—Where commands can be entered in the last line of the screen to act on text.

The relationship between these three modes and the shell is depicted in Fig. 4.2.

4.1.2   The .exrc File

The behavior of **vi** is controlled by a configuration file—the one it reads on startup. Many UNIX commands have their own configuration files, and the one used by **vi**

FIGURE 4.2   *The Three Modes of* **vi**

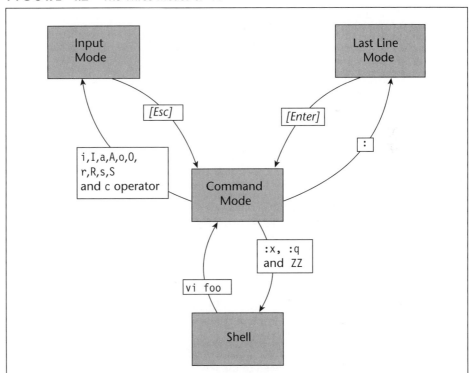

is .exrc. You may find this file in your home directory—the directory where you are placed upon logging in. Many of the commands used in the Last Line Mode can also be placed in this file.

The .exrc file is not displayed by the **ls** command unless it is used with a special option (-a). If it still doesn't show up, you can create one of your own, or ask the system administrator to give you a default file. We'll be customizing **vi** using this file in the "Going Further" section.

Caution

Before you move on, make sure that the *[CapsLock]* key on your keyboard is not activated. **vi** commands are case-sensitive; the command **a** is not the same as **A**. Even if you use *[CapsLock]* for entering a block of text in uppercase, make sure that you deactivate the key when you have finished entering text.

4.2 Quitting vi—The Last Line Mode

When you edit a file using **vi**, or for that matter any editor, the original file isn't disturbed as such. The editor works with a copy of the file which it places in a **buffer.** This is simply a temporary storage area that is associated with the file on disk. From time to time, you should save your work by writing the buffer contents to the disk file. It's the disk file that's permanent, not the buffer.

You should also know how to leave the editor. It would indeed be a tragedy if after entering a lot of text, you have to reboot the machine just because there is no one around to tell you how to

- Save the file (rather, the buffer) and quit.
- Abandon all changes and quit.

Even though we'll be saving a *file*, understand that to mean saving the *buffer*. Saving and quitting are handled by the Last Line Mode. Every command in this mode is preceded by a : (colon) and followed by the *[Enter]* key.

4.2.1 Saving and Quitting (:wq and :x)

The Last Line Mode offers two ways of saving and quitting—**:x** and **:wq**. The first requires one less keystroke, so we'll use it. The command returns you to the shell after saving your work (i.e., after writing the changed buffer to disk):

```
:x[Enter]                                          Must be in Command Mode first
"index.html", 8 lines, 303 characters
$ _
```

Enter a : (the Last Line Mode prompt), followed by x and the *[Enter]* key. This is a command in the Last Line Mode, and when you enter the :, you'll see it appearing in the last line of the screen. The message appears after pressing *[Enter]* only when the file is saved at the time of leaving **vi**.

Tip

The best way to save and quit the editor is to use the Command Mode command **ZZ** instead of **:x** or **:wq**. You need to use *[Esc]* first to be in this mode.

4.2.2 Aborting Editing (:q)

It's also possible to abort the editing process and quit the editing mode without saving the buffer. The **q** (quit) command takes you out of the editor *only if you don't have a changed buffer*:

:q*[Enter]*
$ _   *No message this time!*

vi also has a safety mechanism that prevents you from aborting accidentally if you have modified the file in any way. Now try the same command again on a modified but unsaved file:

:q*[Enter]*
No write since last change (use ! to override)

You haven't saved the changes and are trying to quit; that's what the message says. If you still want to abandon the changes, then use

:q!*[Enter]*   *! overrides many safety settings*

This will *always* return you to the prompt irrespective of the status of the buffer—no questions asked. Since all Last Line Mode commands need the *[Enter]* key to be seen by **vi**, we'll assume it henceforth and not show its use explicitly. The essential save and quit commands are shown in Table 4.1.

TABLE 4.1   *Save and Exit Commands in* **vi**

Command	Function
:w	Saves file and remains in editing mode
:x	Saves file and quits editing mode
:wq	As above
:q	Quits editing mode when no changes are made to file
:q!	Quits editing mode but after abandoning changes
:w n2w.pl	Saves to file n2w.pl (like *Save As* . . . in Microsoft Windows)
:w! n2w.pl	As above, but overwrites existing file
:w >> note1	Appends current file contents to file note1
:*n1*,*n2*w build.sql	Writes lines *n1* to *n2* to file build.sql
:.w build.sql	Writes current line to file build.sql
:$w build.sql	Writes last line to file build.sql
:sh	Escapes to UNIX shell (use **exit** to return to **vi**)
[Ctrl-z]	Suspends current session and escapes to UNIX shell (only for shells supporting job control; use **fg** to return to **vi**)

Note

In general, any Last Line Mode command used with a ! signifies some form of abortion. It can be used to switch to another file without saving the current one, or reload the last saved version of a file. You can even use it to overwrite a separate file.

4.3 Inserting and Replacing Text

Before you are able to enter text, you have to change from the default Command Mode to Input Mode. There are several methods of entering this mode, depending on the type of input you wish to key in, but in every case the mode is terminated by pressing the *[Esc]* key.

If you are a beginner to **vi**, it's better you issue the following Last Line Mode command after invoking it and before you start editing:

Tip

:set showmode*[Enter]*   *Press [Esc] first*

As with **:x**, enter this in the same way. This command sets one of the parameters of the **vi** environment, and displays a suitable message whenever the Input Mode is invoked. The message appears at the bottom line of the screen and is quite self-explanatory. Some versions of UNIX have **vi** configured in this mode, in which case this setting need not be made.

4.3.1 Inserting Text (**i** and **I**)

The simplest type of input is insertion of text. Whether the file contains any text or not, when **vi** is invoked, the cursor is always positioned at the first character of the first line. To insert text at this position, press

i   *Existing text will be shifted right*

The character doesn't show up on the screen, but pressing this key changes the mode from Command to Input. Since the showmode setting was made at the beginning (with **:set showmode**), you'll see the words INSERT or INSERT MODE in the last line. Further key depressions now will show text on the screen as it is being entered. Start inserting a few lines of text (Fig. 4.3) and follow each line with *[Enter]*.

The lines containing text along with the "empty lines" (actually nonexistent lines, shown with a ~ against each) approximate the screen shown here. The cursor is now positioned in the last character of the last line. This is known as the **current line**. The character where the cursor is stationed is known as the **current cursor position**. If you notice a mistake in this line, you can use *[Backspace]* to erase any inserted text—one character at a time. You can even erase the previous word using *[Ctrl-w]*.

After you have entered a few lines, you should press *[Esc]* to take you back to the Command Mode (from where you "came"). Note that your work is not saved yet. At this point, you can use the save and quit commands that were just discussed *(4.2)* and leave the editor if you want.

You started insertion with **i**, which put text at the left of the cursor position. If the **i** command is invoked with the cursor positioned on existing text, text on its right will be shifted further without being overwritten.

FIGURE 4.3   *Entering Text in* **vi**

```
This is the vi editor[Enter]
It is slow in getting started but is quite powerful[Enter]
It operates in three modes[Enter]
All the features of ex are also available[Enter]
You can even escape to the UNIX shell[Enter]
It maintains 26 buffers for storing chunks of text▌

~

~

~

~

~
```

While **i** can be used to insert text anywhere in a line, **I** inserts text only at the *beginning* of a line. Even if you are placed at the end of a line, you can move to line beginning with

I   *Cursor moves to line beginning first*

and then key in your text. This represents a quick way of navigating to the beginning of the current line too. The insertion of text with **i** and **I** is shown in Fig. 4.4. All figures in this chapter and the next use this shaded box ▌ to represent the cursor and the □ to signify a space (when its presence isn't all that obvious).

4.3.2   Appending Text (a and A)

There are other methods of inputting text. To append text to the right of the cursor position, use

a   *Existing text shifted right*

FIGURE 4.4   *Insertion of Text with the* **i** *and* **I** *Commands*

```
the vi ▌editor

      ifull-screen□[Esc]

the vi full-screen▌editor

      IThis is□[Esc]

This is▌the vi full-screen editor
```

followed by the text you wish to key in. This is slightly different from **i** as it places text on the right of the cursor. After you have finished editing, press *[Esc]*.

With **i** and **a**, you can append several lines of text in this way. But **a** too has an uppercase counterpart which acts in a completely opposite manner compared to **I**. To append text at the end of a line use

A   *Suitable for continuing a paragraph*

Like **I**, this also represents a fast way of navigating to the end of a line and adding text there. You'll frequently be using it to continue your text from the point you left off—adding a sentence to a paragraph, for instance. The use of the **a** and **A** commands is shown in Fig. 4.5.

4.3.3 Opening a New Line (o and 0)

You can also "open" (i.e., insert) a new line by positioning the cursor at any point in a line and pressing

o   *Opens new line below*

This inserts an empty line below the current line. To open a line above the current line, use

0   *Opens new line above*

In either case, the showmode setting tells you that you are in the Input Mode. You are free to enter as much text as you choose—spanning multiple lines if required. Press *[Esc]* after completing text input. The use of **o** and **0** is shown in Fig. 4.6.

4.3.4 Replacing Text (r, R, s and S)

Text is replaced with the **r**, **R**, **s** and **S** commands. To replace one single character with another, you should use

r   *No [Esc] required here*

FIGURE 4.5   *Insertion of Text with the **a** and **A** Commands*

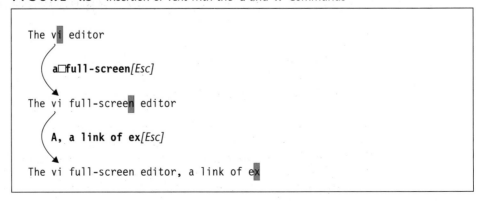

F I G U R E 4.6 *Opening a New Line with the* **o** *and* **0** *Commands*

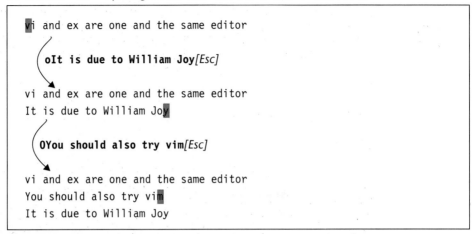

followed by the character that replaces the one under the cursor. You can replace only a single character in this way.

vi momentarily switches from the Command Mode to the Input Mode when **r** is pressed. It returns to the Command Mode as soon as the replacing character is entered. There's no need to press *[Esc]* after using **r** (and the character) since **vi** expects a single character anyway.

To replace more than a single character, use

R   *Replaces text as cursor moves right*

followed by the text. This is **emacs**' *overwrite* mode, where existing text is overwritten as the cursor moves forward. This replacement is, however, restricted to the current line only. The replacement commands **r** and **R** are depicted in Fig. 4.7.

Many a time, you'll need to replace a single character with multicharacter text. Take your cursor to the point and then press

s   *Replaces one with many*

F I G U R E 4.7 *Text Replacement with the* **r** *and* **R** *Commands*

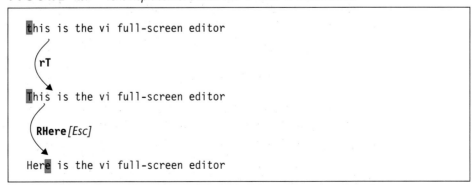

Now, enter as much text as you want and then press *[Esc]*. The **s** command is useful for changing the letter a to the. The text existing on the right is shifted further.

S replaces the entire line irrespective of the cursor position. You don't need to take your cursor to the beginning of the line to change the line's contents. Stay where you are, and press

S   *Current line vanishes*

The entire line vanishes from sight. Key in your text, and then (as you would have guessed by now), press *[Esc]*. Text replacement with **s** and **S** is shown in Fig. 4.8.

You have now been able to enter the Input Mode in 10 ways. You must switch to the Command Mode for doing many things that can't be done with these 10 commands. The functions of these 10 keys are summarized in Table 4.2. Strictly speaking, there's one more method of entering the Input Mode—with the **c** *operator*. To handle it, you'll have to understand operators first.

Caution

Remember to switch to the Command Mode from Input Mode by pressing the *[Esc]* key. If you forget to do that, all Command Mode commands will show up as text input. Repeated pressing of the *[Esc]* key won't make any difference to **vi** except that it has a built-in capability to indicate with a beep if a key has been pressed unnecessarily. Try this by pressing *[Esc]* several times. You are now in the Command Mode.

4.3.5 Entering Control Characters (*[Ctrl-v]*)

If you write shell scripts to send some escape sequences to your printer or terminal, then you would need to enter control characters. In **vi**, some of these characters are directly enterable, but generally a control character has to be preceded by another control character for it to be interpreted properly.

vi uses *[Ctrl-v]* to precede any control character. For instance, to enter *[Ctrl-h]*, you have to first press *[Ctrl-v]* and then *[Ctrl-h]*. You'll then see this on the screen:

^H   *Just one character here*

F I G U R E 4.8   *Text Replacement with the* **s** *and* **S** *Commands*

```
vi is a link of ex

    sone[Esc]

vi is one link of ex

    Sex and vi have the same inode number[Esc]

ex and vi have the same inode number
```

TABLE 4.2   *Input Mode Commands in* **vi**

Command	Function
i	Inserts text to left of cursor (existing text shifted right)
I	Inserts text at beginning of line (existing text shifted right)
a	Appends text to right of cursor (existing text shifted right)
A	Appends text at end of line
o	Opens line below
O	Opens line above
r*ch*	Replaces single character under cursor with *ch* (no *[Esc]* required)
R	Replaces text from cursor to right (existing text overwritten)
s	Replaces single character under cursor with any number of characters
S	Replaces entire line

Even though you feel you are seeing a ^ (caret) and an H, there's only a single character out there. You can position the cursor only on the ^ and not on the H; that's how you identify control characters anyway.

The same technique can be adopted for entering the *[Esc]* character. Press *[Ctrl-v][Esc]*, and you'll see the *[Esc]* character looking like this:

^[*Just one character here*

This too is a single character; you can place your cursor only on the ^. Insertion of a control character is shown in Fig. 4.9.

Note

If your version of **vi** doesn't let you enter the *[Esc]* character as advised above, then you can use this: *[Ctrl-v][Ctrl-[]* (Control with [). The *[Esc]* character may need special treatment in **vi** since it is the terminator of the Input Mode.

4.4 Saving Text (:w)

You have learned to leave the editor both after and without saving. You should be saving your work frequently (typically every five minutes), and **vi** offers commands for saving your work without leaving the editor. The essential save and exit commands of this mode are shown in Table 4.1.

FIGURE 4.9   *Inserting a Control Character*

To save a file and remain in the editing mode, use the **w** (write) command:

```
:w                                                         [Enter] assumed
"sometext", 8 lines, 275 characters
```

The message shows the name of the file, along with the number of lines and characters saved. With the **w** command, you can optionally specify a different filename as well:

```
:w anotherfile
"anotherfile" [New File] 8 lines, 275 characters written
```

In this case, the contents are separately written to anotherfile. *However, your current file continues to be* sometext *even though* **vi** *shows* anotherfile *in the last line.* Windows users should note that this alternate file saving facility is different from the *Save As . . .* option of the *File* menu, which also saves to a different file, but also makes the new file the current one.

Tip

Sometimes, a simple **:w** may not let you save a file. A file may be write-protected or owned by someone else. **vi** will still let you enter text, but to save it, you have to use **:w** with a different filename.

4.4.1 Writing Selected Lines

The **w** command can be used with one or two **line addresses** (one or two numbers representing one or more lines). If used with one address, **w** writes the specified line to the file. When used with two, it writes the group addressed by the line numbers. This is how you use them:

```
:5w n2words.pl                                    Writes 5th line to file n2words.pl
:10,50w n2words.pl                               Writes lines 10 through 50 to same file
```

vi has two symbols that denote the current line and last line of the file. The **.** represents the current line, while $ denotes the last line. For instance,

```
:.,$w n2words.pl                                            Current line till end
```

writes out the current line through the end. There are other methods of writing lines, but you can explore these opportunities later.

Note

In the Last Line Mode, the current line number is represented by **.** (dot), while the last line is denoted by $. Thus, **:1,$** addresses the entire file.

4.4.2 Recovering from a Crash

It's not always possible to save a file. Power glitches and blackouts or a kernel panic could leave some work unsaved. However, since **vi** works with a buffer on disk, you can often recover much of your work. You'll be informed by mail that a crash has occurred, or **vi** itself may inform you of the catastrophe. In that case, quit the editor and restart it with the **-r** (recover) option:

```
vi -r foo
```

Have a look at the contents now and satisfy yourself that you are seeing a version newer than the one seen without using the -r option. Save the file with :w and your salvage work is complete.

Some versions of **vi** (especially Linux) create a swap file (with the .swp extension) on **vi** invocation but remove it after completion. A crash doesn't remove the file, and **vi** complains of its existence on startup. Once the recovery operation is over, just manually remove the file (using the **rm** command—Section 6.12).

Caution

You can't be assured of complete recovery every time. Sometimes, **vi** may show you absolute junk when using the -r option. In that case, don't save the file and simply quit (with :q!). Start **vi** again normally; recovery is not possible here.

4.5 Exit to the UNIX Shell

Sometimes, you need to make a **shell escape** (temporary exit) which brings the shell prompt for you. You can do some work at the prompt and then come back to **vi**. The following Last Line Mode command provides this escape facility:

```
:sh
$ _                                                          Prompt returns
```

Pressing **exit** or *[Ctrl-d]* brings you back to **vi**. If you enter **vi** once again at this prompt, you'll simply have two instances of **vi**, which will cause a great deal of confusion. Just use a **ps** command to find out whether **vi** is still running *(10.6)*. If an **exit** doesn't return you the **vi** screen, it means that **vi** was not running or was killed. In that case, you would be logged out.

Note

The shell that shows its presence by the $ or % prompt is determined by the setting of your SHELL variable. This, by default, is the shell set for you by the system administrator. Even though sh actually represents the Bourne shell, :sh is a generic shell escape command. It could take you to the Korn shell, the C shell or bash depending on the value of $SHELL. Just try **echo $SHELL** to find out the shell you are using.

You can also run a single UNIX command without having a shell prompt in front of you. Use :! with the command name. This is how you find out the date from inside the editor:

```
:!date[Enter]
Sun Feb 13 10:26:53 EST 2000
Press RETURN or enter command to continue
```

An *[Enter]* here returns you to the editing screen you were in.

Tip

There's another method of escaping temporarily to the shell. If your shell supports *job control (10.11)*, you can press *[Ctrl-z]* to see the shell prompt. If it works, then the **fg** command should take you back to the editor. **fg** is an internal command of the shell that brings a background job to the foreground.

4.6   The Repeat Factor

One of the most notable features of **vi** (and **emacs**) is the facility of prefixing a number to a command. When this is done, most commands interpret the instruction to be repeated as many times. For instance, **3s** replaces the next three characters under the cursor. This number prefixing a command is called the **repeat factor** (term used by Sonnenschein in *A Guide to vi*, Prentice-Hall) or *preceding count*. The former term is mostly used in this book.

Suppose you wish to insert a series of 20 asterisks in one line. Instead of using **i** and then entering the * 20 times, you can use a shortcut:

20i*   *Only in Command Mode*

This must be followed by either *[Enter]* or *[Esc]*. You'll see a sequence of 20 *s in the line (Fig. 4.10).

The repeat factor not only applies to most commands of the Input Mode, but to the Command Mode commands also. In the following sections, you'll see how it helps in speedier navigation and editing.

4.7   The Command Mode

In the forthcoming sections, we'll mainly discuss the functions of the Command Mode. This is the mode you come to when you have finished entering or changing your text. This mode is meant for performing navigation and cut-and-paste operations. Keys here are used both singly and in combination.

Unlike in the Input Mode, when you press a key in the Command Mode, it doesn't show up on the screen, but simply performs its function. That's why you can see changes on the screen without knowing the command that has caused them. While beginners and **emacs** users may find this to be an irritant, things do get better with practice.

Note

Only the keys g, K, q, v, V and Z have no function in the standard UNIX implementation. Some of these keys do have functions in **vim**.

4.8   Navigation

If you have used a word processor like Microsoft Word, you must have extensively used the cursor motion keys (with arrows marked on them). Unless you are using terminals, these keys function in identical manner when using **vi** or **emacs**. In fact, if you

F I G U R E 4.10   *Using the Repeat Factor with the **i** Command*

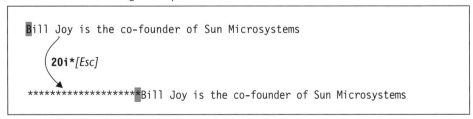

are using UNIX on a PC or a workstation, you could have been using the same keys till you reached this point in the text. However, like terminals, some older versions of UNIX don't recognize these keys.

vi has its own set of commands that move the cursor in the four directions—**h**, **l**, **j** and **k** (Table 4.3). They are located in a line in the middle row of your keyboard. The horizontal and vertical movements of the cursor are illustrated in Fig. 4.11.

All the navigation commands discussed here and in the next topic also use a repeat factor. **3h** moves the cursor three places to the left, while **7k** moves the cursor seven lines up.

4.8.1 Scrolling

You can use the control keys to change the view of displayed text on your window. **vi** lets you scroll in units of both half and full pages. The four essential scrolling commands are listed in Table 4.4, along with one that redraws the screen.

If for some reason the screen gets garbled, use *[Ctrl-l]* to redraw it. The repeat factor can also be used here. 5*[Ctrl-f]* scrolls five screens forward, while 10 *[Ctrl-u]* scrolls ten half-screens backward.

T A B L E 4.3   *Horizontal and Vertical Motion in* **vi**

Command	Function
h (or *[Backspace]*)	Moves cursor left
l (or *[Spacebar]*)	Moves cursor right
5l	Moves 5 characters right
k	Moves cursor up
10k	Moves 10 lines up
j	Moves cursor down

F I G U R E 4.11   *Horizontal and Vertical Motion with* **h, l, j** *and* **k**

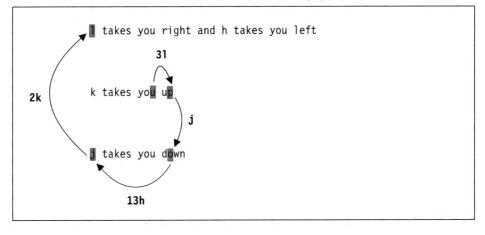

T A B L E 4.4 *Scrolling Commands in* **vi**

Command	Function
[Ctrl-f]	Scrolls full page forward
5 [Ctrl-f]	Scrolls 5 full pages forward
[Ctrl-b]	Scrolls full page backward
[Ctrl-d]	Scrolls half page forward
[Ctrl-u]	Scrolls half page backward
[Ctrl-l]	Redraws the screen (no repeat factor)

Note

emacs users should note that you can't move forward or back with these control keys unless you are in the Command Mode.

4.8.2   The Beginning or End of a Line (0, | and $)

Moving to the beginning or end of a line is a common requirement. This is handled by the commands **0** (zero), **|** and **$**. To move to the first character of a line, use

0 or | 30| *moves cursor to column 30*

and to move to the end of the line, use

$

The use of these two commands along with those that use units of words (**b**, **e** and **w**) is shown in Fig. 4.12.

F I G U R E 4.12 *Finer Navigation with* **b, e, w, 0** *and* **$**

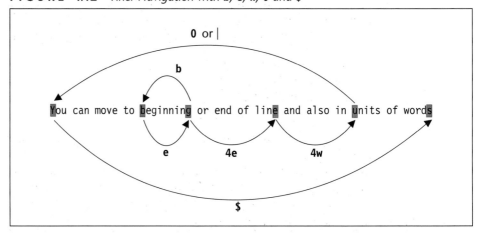

4.8.3   Moving by Words (b, e and w)

Movement by one character is not always enough, and you'll often need to move faster. **vi** understands a **word** as a navigation unit, and it provides commands which move the cursor in units of words. A word in **vi** has different meanings depending on the context it is used.

Word-oriented movement is achieved with the **b**, **e** and **w** commands. Their functions are shown below:

b—Moves back to beginning of word
e—Moves forward to end of word
w—Moves forward to beginning of word

A repeat factor speeds up cursor movement. For example, **5b** takes the cursor five words back, while **3w** takes the cursor three words forward.

A word here is simply a string of alphanumeric characters and the _ (underscore) character. bash is one word; so is sh_profile. tcp-ip is three words; the hyphen by definition becomes a word too.

The commands **B**, **E** and **W** perform similar functions to those of their lowercase counterparts except that they skip punctuation. The word definition also gets changed here, but we'll ignore these minor details.

4.8.4   Go to Line (G)

If you want to know the line number of your current cursor position, simply press *[Ctrl-g]*. You could see a line like this:

"salslip.pl" [Modified] line 403 of 541 —74%—

You instantly come to know the filename, the current line number, the total number of lines in the file and the relative location of the page expressed as a percentage. Some versions of **vi** (like **vim**) always show the current line and column number at the bottom right of the screen—*[Ctrl-g]* is not necessary there.

You can use the **G** command to move the cursor to a specific line number. This is prefixed by the line number. To move to the 40th line, use

40G   *Goes to line number 40*

and to move to the beginning of the file, use

1G   *Goes to line number 1*

The end of the file is reached by simply using

G   *Goes to end of file*

Note that no line number is prefixed for moving to the end of a file. **1G** and **G** are two commands that you should commit to memory immediately. The precise navigation commands that you learned in these three sections are grouped together in Table 4.5.

TABLE 4.5   *Precise Navigation Commands in* vi

Command	Function
b	Moves back to beginning of word
4b	Moves back 4 words to beginning of word
e	Moves forward to end of word
w	Moves forward to beginning of word
8w	Moves forward to beginning of 8th word
0 (zero) or |	Moves to beginning of line
30|	Moves to column 30
^	Moves to first *word* in line
$	Moves to end of line
1G	Moves to beginning of file
40G	Moves to line 40
G	Moves to end of file

Tip

The Last Line Mode offers equivalent commands for moving between lines. The previous three commands can be replaced by **:40**, **:1** and **:$**, respectively (along with *[Enter]*).

Tip

If you need to start up a file so that it shows the cursor at a certain line number, prefix the line number with a + and use it as an argument to **vi**. Using only a + will take you to the end of the file:

vi +40 chap01   *Cursor on 40th line*
vi + chap01   *Cursor on last line*

4.9   Operators

Before we move on to the basic editing functions like deleting and copying text, we must understand a very powerful feature that is supported by **vi**—**operators**. While **vi** has a number of single letter commands that work in the Command Mode, most of the actual *editing* work (actions that change the buffer) require the use of these operators.

There are only a few operators, and you must know at least the following ones:

d—Delete
y—Yank (copy)
c—Change
!—Filter to act on text

An operator alone can't perform any function unless it is combined with a command (or itself). The power of **vi** is mainly derived from the ease with which you can frame commands of your own using these operators. This opens up a new domain of commands for you to work with. Using *operator-command* combinations, you can frame a delete or yank command for practically any situation. We'll be using operators extensively in the next section.

Table 4.6 lists the various possible ways these operators are used in combination with other Command Mode editing commands.

Note

An operator, when doubled by itself (like **dd**, **cc**, **yy** and **!!**) acts only on the current line.

T A B L E 4.6 *The Editing Functions in* **vi**

Command	Function
x	Deletes character under cursor
6x	Deletes character under cursor and 5 characters on right
X	Deletes previous character
J	Joins current line with next line
d$ or D	Deletes from cursor to end of line
dd	Deletes current line
5dd	Deletes 5 lines
4dw or d4w	Deletes 4 words
d30G	Deletes from cursor to line number 30
df.	Deletes from cursor to first occurrence of a dot
d/endif	Deletes from cursor to first occurrence of string endif in forward direction
yy or Y	Yanks current line (Y is different from D and C in scope!)
y$	Yanks from cursor to end of line
6yy	Copies 6 lines
yw	Copies current word
3yw or y3w	Yanks 3 words
y?case	Yanks from cursor up to first occurrence of string case in reverse direction
p	Puts deleted or copied text below current line or on right of cursor
P	Puts deleted or copied text above current line or on left of cursor
c0	Changes from cursor to beginning of line
c$ or C	Changes from cursor to end of line
3cw or c3w	Changes 3 words
cc	Changes current line
cG	Changes from cursor to end of file
~	Reverses case of character under cursor
40~	Reverses case of 40 characters
.	Repeats last editing instruction
u	Undoes last editing instruction (previous instructions in Linux)
U	Undoes all changes made in current line
[Ctrl-r]	Redoes previous undo actions *(Linux only)*

4.10 Deleting, Moving and Yanking Text

Most of this section makes use of operators, but make sure that you are in the Command Mode when using them. While copying text is possible only with operators, there are two ways we can handle deletion:

- Using the Command Mode commands **x** and **X**.
- Using the **d** operator with a Command Mode command.

Moving text involves an additional step: *put* (place) the deleted text at the new location. We'll first learn to handle deletion in the simplest way.

4.10.1 Deleting Characters (x and X)

The simplest text deletion is achieved with the **x** command. This command deletes the character under the cursor. Move the cursor to the character that needs to be deleted and then press

x   *Deletes a single character*

The character is removed from sight, and the text on the right shifts left to fill up the space. A repeat factor also applies here, so **4x** deletes the current character as well as three characters from the right.

The unique feature of this command is that when you press **x** at the end of a line, you don't "pull up" the following line as most Windows editors (and even **emacs**) do. Instead, **vi** starts removing characters *on the left without joining the following line*.

To delete text on the left of the cursor use

X   *Deletes text on left*

Unlike **x**, **X** doesn't delete the character under the cursor. When you use **x** at the end of a line, it behaves like **X** except that it also deletes the character under the cursor. Use of **x** and **X** is shown in Fig. 4.13.

FIGURE 4.13   *Text Deletion with the* **x** *and* **X** *Commands*

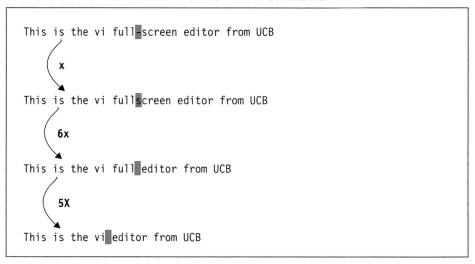

4.10.2 Joining Lines (J)

We just noted that when the deletion key is pressed at the end of the line, many editors join ("pull up") the current line with the following one. In **vi**, the same can be achieved with the **J** (join) command. To join the current line and the line following it, use

J   *4J joins following 3 lines with current one*

J removes the **newline** character between the two lines (Fig. 4.14). ASCII has the decimal value 10 for it and calls it **linefeed** (LF). Joining, however, is restricted to the maximum size that a line can have for editing. Early implementations of **vi** had the 1024-character limit, but modern systems have a higher limit (if at all).

4.10.3 Finer Deletion—Using the d Operator

Suppose you want to delete all text from the present cursor position to the end of line. Using the **d** operator, you can frame the command yourself if you recall the primary command that moves you to the end of a line. It is the **$**, so the command that should do the job is

d$ *Deletes till end ($) of line*

This command has a synonym though; it's a single **D**. Likewise, since **G** takes you to the end of the file, you should use the following combination to delete all text from the current cursor position to the end of the file:

dG   *Deletes till end of file (G)*

Using this simple logic, you can conclusively state that the command to delete a word is **dw**. You can also use a repeat factor and use **5dw** to delete five words. Note how specialized functions can be devised by following a simple set of rules. Such fine selection facilities are not available in **emacs**.

The *operator-command* theory takes a backseat when deleting lines. Entire lines are removed with the **dd** "command" (rather a doubled operator). Move the cursor to any line, and then press

dd   *Deletes a single line*

To delete a block of lines, use a repeat factor. Thus to delete the current line and five lines below it, use **6dd**. Fig. 4.15 illustrates the use of the **d** operator for line deletion and movement.

F I G U R E   4.14   *Joining Lines with the **J** Command*

```
if █ $x -gt 0 ] ;
then

        J

if [ $x -gt 0 ] ; then
```

FIGURE **4.15**   *Line Deletion and Movement with* **dd** *and* **p**

```
Press the Esc█key for entering command mode
Press the : to enter ex mode
dd is not really a command
It's a combination of an operator and a command

        ⟋
       (    dd
        ⟍
Press the : to enter ex mode
dd is not really a command
It's a combination of an operator and a command

        ⟋
       (    2dd
        ⟍
It's a combination of an operator and a command

        ⟋
       (    p
        ⟍
It's a combination of an operator and a command
Press the : to enter ex mode
dd is not really a command
```

4.10.4   Moving Text (d, p and P)

Text movement is an extension of the deletion operation; you just have to put the deleted text at the new location. **p** is used for putting back *entire lines* (those deleted with **dd**) below the current line; **P** places them above.

    The line that we "cut" above can now be "pasted" (put, in **vi** jargon) below the current line. Just move to the desired location and press

p   P *would paste the lines above*

p and **P** acquire different meanings when they are used to move words. Words are put at the left with **p** and right with **P**. These commands are also not restricted to moving text only. We'll use the same keys for copying operations.

Moving Text between Two Files   You can perform cut-and-paste operations between two files using a modified form of the above technique. To move a block of text from one file to another just follow these steps:

1. Delete the text into a buffer a. If you are deleting four lines, then use **"a4dd**, where the normal delete command is preceded by the string **"**a.
2. Save the current file with **:w**. To know how to skip this step, read Section 4.17.2.

3. Open a new file using the Last Line Mode command **:e foo.** This command has been discussed in Section 4.17.2.

4. To put back text, navigate to the desired location, press ", the buffer name (a) and p to place the copied text below the current line—**"ap** (the normal put command preceded by "a).

This technique is a special case of a general **vi** feature—the ability to copy or move up to 26 sections of text. This advanced feature is discussed in Section 4.20 (in the "Going Further" section).

Tip

For moving words and lines, delete them from their original location, move to the new location and press **p** or **P**.

4.10.5 Copying Text—Using the y Operator

Words and lines are copied (yanked—**vi** jargon) with the same commands used for deletion except that the operator to be used here is **y** instead of **d**. This means that **yy** (a doubled operator again) copies a line. To yank five lines of text, move the cursor to the first of these and press

5yy   *5 lines copied from source*

Next, move the cursor to the new location below which you want to insert these lines and press

p   *P would place lines above*

to put the copied text below the current line. Adopting the same logic, one can say that **y$** yanks text from current position to end of line, and **y1G** copies text from current cursor position to the beginning of the file. See for yourself where **p** places the copied text—right or below. Copying lines is illustrated in Fig. 4.16.

Copying Text between Two Files Using a technique similar to the one used in deleting text *(4.10.4)*, you can copy text between two files. To copy four words from one file to another, just use **4yw** instead of **4dd**; everything else remains the same, except that you don't need to save the original file this time.

Linux

To copy or move a block of text, **vim** doesn't need to use the "a symbols at all. Just delete or copy the text, save the file with **:w** if necessary, switch to the next file with **:e foo** and then paste the text with **p. vim** requires the buffer symbols only when multiple sections are copied or moved.

4.11   Changing Text (c and ~)

vi offers some techniques for changing text. Using the **c** operator, you can fine-tune your selection in the way we used **d** and **y**. You can also change the case of text. These techniques are discussed next.

F I G U R E   4.16   *Copying Lines with* **yy**

1. Copying is only possible with the y operator
2. You can use it with any navigation command
3. y$ copies text from the current position to line end

    First **yy** *then* **2j**

1. Copying is only possible with the y operator
2. You can use it with any navigation command
3. y$ copies text from the current position to line end

    p

1. Copying is only possible with the y operator
2. You can use it with any navigation command
3. y$ copies text from the current position to line end
1. Copying is only possible with the y operator

4.11.1   Changing with the c Operator

Text can be changed with the **c** (change) operator using the same techniques used by **d** and **y**. If **dw** deletes a word, **cw** changes it. This is the only operator which functions in the Input Mode. This means that you have to terminate the change operation with *[Esc]*.

When you use **c** with a valid Command Mode command, you are taken to the Input Mode. But this time the boundary limiting your area of operation could be indicated by a $. If you change three words with **3cw**, a $ should appear at the end of the third word (Linux excepted). The inserted text overwrites the characters delimited by the $ that temporarily appears on the screen. If the replaced text is larger, then once the cursor moves up to the $ marker, further insertion shifts existing text to the right.

To change text from the present cursor position up to the end of a line, use

c$ or C

To change entire lines, use

cc   *Behaves like* S *command*

Note

When you change text in a portion of a line with the **c** operator, you could find a $ appearing at the point up to which all existing text can be changed. Text on the right of the $ will not be overwritten but could be pushed further right. Many systems don't show the $, but simply remove the defined text the moment the change command is entered.

4.11.2 Changing Case (~)

vi uses the ~ (tilde) command to toggle the case of text—a facility available for a long time before it was finally documented. To reverse the case of a section of text, move the cursor to the first character of the section and then press

~

The case changes: upper becomes lower, and lower becomes upper. When you keep it pressed, the cursor moves forward and reverses the case of all subsequent text that it encounters. If you have to do this for a string of a hundred characters, use a repeat factor—**100~**. The changing of case is shown in Fig. 4.17.

The ~ is not suitable for changing an entire line to uppercase if some characters in the line are already in uppercase; those characters then turn to lowercase. To handle absolute case transformations, you should use the **!** operator with the UNIX **tr** command.

4.12 The Dot: Repeating the Last Command

Most editors (including **emacs**) don't have the facility to repeat the last editing instruction, but **vi** has. This repetition applies to commands of both the Input and Command Modes. For instance, if you want to insert the same text or delete the same number of lines at several places, you have to use the actual insertion or deletion command only once. To repeat the command at other places you have to use a simple **.** (dot) command. **more** also uses the same command.

Take a simple example. If you delete two lines of text at a time with **2dd**, then to repeat this operation elsewhere, all you have to do is to position the cursor at the desired location, and press

.   *A dot*

This will repeat the last editing instruction performed, i.e., it will also delete two lines of text.

Once you have acquired familiarity with the various commands of the Input and Command Modes, you'll find the **.** command extremely handy. For instance, if you insert the words DROP TABLE at the beginning of a line using the **I** command, you can move to another line and change it in the same way by pressing a dot.

FIGURE 4.17   *Changing Case with ~*

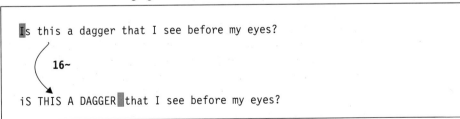

Note

The **.** command repeats only the most recent editing operation—one that modifies the buffer. Obviously, this doesn't include the navigation and search commands that don't modify the buffer contents in any way. Moreover, the search commands have their own set of characters for repeating a search. The **.** command cannot also repeat a Last Line Mode command.

4.13 Undoing Last Editing Instructions (u and U)

If you have inadvertently made an editing change that you shouldn't have, **vi** provides the **u** command for undoing the last change made. Before you do anything else, just press

u   *No repeat factor allowed*

If you were in the Input Mode, press *[Esc]* before using **u**. This facility is very useful, especially for beginners, who may accidentally delete a group of lines. They must use **u** immediately and *before fresh editing action has been performed*. Another **u** at this stage will undo this too, i.e., restore the original status.

When a number of editing changes have been made to a single line, **vi** allows you to discard all the changes *before you move away from the line*. The command

U   *No repeat factor allowed*

reverses all changes made to the current line, i.e., all modifications that have been made since the cursor was moved to this line.

Caution

Make sure the cursor has not been moved to another line before invoking **U**, in which case it won't work. This restriction doesn't apply in Linux.

Linux

Multiple Undoing and Redoing

vim lets you undo and redo multiple editing instructions. Here, **u** has a different role to play; it simply continues undoing whatever has been done before. To redo some of the actions, you have to use

[Ctrl-r]

Both **u** and *[Ctrl-r]* operate with a repeat factor; **5u** will undo the last five editing actions, while 3 *[Ctrl-r]* will redo the last three undone instructions.

The function of **U** is also different in **vim**. You can undo all changes made to the current line even if you have moved your cursor away from the line. But make sure that you have not performed any editing action after moving away.

The number of actions that can be undone in this way can be set externally (with the undolevels option), but the default setting (1000) is usually adequate.

4.14 String Search

vi's search capabilities are among its strongest features—not matched by any editor other than **emacs**. They are also quite elegant and simple to use. **vi** supports two forms of searches:

- Search for a string or a *regular expression* in the entire file.
- Search for a single character in the current line.

Both searches let you repeat the search in both directions (forward and backward). The search and repeat commands are listed in Table 4.7. In this section, we'll discuss searching with simple strings. In the next section, we'll take up regular expressions and see how generalized patterns enhance the search capability.

4.14.1 Search for a Pattern (/ and ?)

You can search for a pattern (string or regular expression) by prefixing the string or expression with a **/** (frontslash). To locate the first occurrence of the string UNIX, simply enter

/UNIX*[Enter]*   *Searches forward for string* UNIX

T A B L E 4 . 7   *Search and Replace Commands in* **vi**

Command	Function
/*pat*	Searches forward for pattern *pat*
?*pat*	Searches backward for pattern *pat*
n	Repeats search in same direction along which previous search was made (no repeat factor)
N	Repeats search in direction opposite to that along which previous search was made (no repeat factor)
f*ch*	Moves cursor forward to first occurrence of character *ch* in the current line
F*ch*	As above, but moves backward
t*ch*	Moves cursor forward onto but *before* first occurrence of character *ch* in the current line
T*ch*	As above, but moves backward
;	Repeats search in the same direction made with f, F, t or T
,	Repeats search in a direction opposite to that made with f, F, t or T
:*n1,n2*s/*s1*/*s2*/	Replaces first occurrence of string or regular expression *s1* with string *s2* in lines *n1* to *n2*
:1,10s/find/look/g	Replaces all occurrences of find with look in lines 1 to 10
:.,$s/find/look/gc	Interactively replaces find with look from current line through the end
:s	Repeats the last substitution on the current line *(Linux only)*

When you press the **/**, it is echoed in the last line of the screen. Enter the pattern and then press *[Enter]*. The cursor is then positioned on the first character of the first occurrence of this pattern, starting from the present location of the cursor. By default, the search **wraps around** the end of the text to resume from the beginning of the file if the pattern can't be located up to the end of the file.

To search in the reverse direction, you have to use the **?** instead of the **/**. The sequence

?UNIX*[Enter]*   *Searches backward*

searches backward for the most previous instance of UNIX. The wraparound feature also applies here, but in the reverse manner. In either case, if the pattern search fails, the message Pattern not found appears in the last line of the screen.

4.14.2   Repeating the Last Pattern Search (n and N)

For repeating searches **vi** uses the **n** and **N** commands. For repeating a search in the direction in which the previous search was made with **/** or **?**, use

n   *Need not necessarily mean forward*

For repeating the search in the reverse direction, use

N   *Need not necessarily mean backward*

The cursor will be positioned at the beginning of the character forming the pattern. In case the end or beginning of a file is reached while searching, the wraparound feature makes sure the entire file is scanned. The search and repeat commands discussed so far are shown in Fig. 4.18.

F I G U R E 4.18   *Pattern Searching and Repeating a Search*

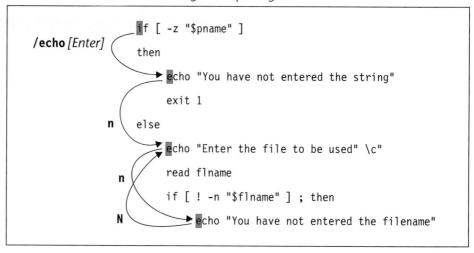

Note

The / searches in the forward direction while the **?** searches in the reverse direction. **n** repeats a search in the same direction the previous search was made—and not necessarily forward. If a search is made with **?**, **n** repeats this search and not **N**.

You can start up **vi** by specifying a pattern. Use the +/ symbols before the pattern:

vi +/scheduling chap01   *Cursor at* scheduling

Tip

The cursor will be located at the first instance of the pattern. You can then use **n** and **N** in the usual way for locating the next instance of the string. If the pattern contains multiple words, surround them with quotes.

4.14.3 Searching for a Character (f, F, t, T, ; and ,)

vi uses single-letter commands to move to a specific character in a line—**f** and **F** (for the reverse direction). Either of them is followed by the character that has to be located. For instance, to locate the next instance of the character (, use

f(*Use* F *for backward search*

Note that the search is restricted to the current line only. You can repeat the search using the commands **;** and **,** (comma). To search for the next occurrence of the previous character in the current line, use

;   *Use* , *for reverse search*

The **t** and **T** characters perform similar functions except that they stop just one character before the one that is targeted. All these single-character search and repeat commands also work with a repeat factor.

4.15 *Searching with Regular Expressions*

There's nothing very special about string search; every editor has this facility. **vi** also accepts a generalized pattern containing some special characters (**metacharacters**) as the search expression. This pattern is called a **regular expression** and is used to match a group of similar strings. There's a chapter reserved almost exclusively for regular expressions, but this discussion on searching can't be treated as complete unless we know some preliminaries of these expressions.

Let's say you want to search for michael, but don't how the word is spelled in the file; it could be michael or michel. Instead of searching twice—once with each string, you could search with a single expression that uses one or more of these metacharacters. The significance of these characters is shown in Table 4.8.

The * One of the metacharacters often used by a regular expression is the *. Let's understand its significance with reference to the two names michael and michel. If you want to locate both with a single expression, the * should be used with a to indicate *zero or more occurrences* of a. This should be pretty obvious as a may or may not occur in the pattern. This means that you can locate both names using

/micha*el*[Enter]*   a *may not occur at all*

TABLE 4.8   *The Regular Expression Characters Used by* **vi**

Symbols	Significance
*	Matches zero or more occurrences of the previous character
[*pqr*]	Matches a single character which is either a *p, q* or *r*
[^*pqr*]	Matches a single character which is not a *p, q* or *r*
.	Matches a single character
^*pat*	Matches pattern *pat* at beginning of line
pat$	Matches pattern *pat* at end of line
\<*pat*	Matches pattern *pat* at beginning of a word
pat\>	Matches pattern *pat* at end of a word

The pattern micha*el is termed a regular expression. Now, let's turn our attention to the other regular expression characters.

The Character Class ([])   Consider the names christie and christy. Here, the seventh character is either an i or a y; that is, it belongs to the **character class** [iy]. Since the last character e may also not occur at all, we can use the * as well to frame this expression:

/christ[iy]e*   *[iy] matches* i *or* y

This too locates both strings. The character class is also useful in matching strings which may be in both uppercase or lowercase. This pattern locates both strong and STRONG:

/[sS][tT][rR][oO][nN][gG]   *Case is insignificant here*

The ^ placed inside the character class negates the above, which means that it matches every character except those in the character class. So, **/[^a-zA-Z]** matches a nonalphabetic character. Note that ranges are allowed; the character on the left must be lower in ASCII value than the character on the right. Also note that ^ negates the class only when it is placed at the beginning of the class.

Anchoring the Pattern (^ and $)   The ^ has a different meaning when placed outside the class. Along with the $, it doesn't match anything but simply specifies the *position* of a match. ^ anchors the string at the beginning of a line and $ matches it at the end. If you are looking for comment lines in a C program, you must look for the # at the beginning of a line:

/^#   *^ matches at beginning of line*

A Single Character (.)   The . matches a single character. This is useful in locating a pattern at a specific column in a line. If you want to match the character w in the third column of a line, use the pattern

/^..w   *Matches w at third column*

Matching Words (\< and \>) The \< and \> are used to match a pattern at the beginning and end of a word, respectively. When scanning a program, you can locate all if statements without matching the endifs:

/\<if\>   *Doesn't match either* ifconfig *or* endif

You'll understand later why the \ was used, but for the time being just accept it as a necessity when used with < and >. Using only \>, you can select only the lines containing print but not printf:

/print\>   \> *matches at end of word*

All this makes the search facilities of **vi** and **emacs** superior to most other editors. Many UNIX commands like **grep**, **sed**, **awk** and **perl** also use regular expressions. The topic is considered in three sections in Chapter 15.

4.16 Search and Replace (:s)

vi uses the Last Line Mode's **:s** command to perform substitution—replacing one string or expression with another. Like in **w**, **s** can also be preceded by an address, in which case the substitution affects only the lines addressed. The syntax can be understood by the following example which replaces every occurrence of the string message with msg:

:1,$s/message/msg/g *[Enter]*

The address 1,$ represents all lines in the file. The patterns are separated by /s, and g makes the substitution **global**. If the g parameter is not used, only the first occurrence of the pattern in each line is replaced; the rest are left alone.

If the pattern can't be found, **vi** responds in this manner:

Substitute pattern match failed

You can also choose the range of lines that are to be affected by the substitution. The following examples should make addressing clear:

:3,10s/msg/message/g   *Lines 3 through 10*
:$s/msg/message/g   *Only the last line*
:1,$s/echo/print/   *Replaces first occurrence in every line*
:.,$s/christ[iy]e*/christie/g   *Replaces multiple patterns with one*
:.s/ *$//g   *Deletes trailing spaces in current line*
:1,$s/^#/dnl/   *Replaces # at beginning of line only*

The last three examples show that the pattern replaced can even be a regular expression. You can replace all christie's that match the expression with the singular string christie. The last but one example replaces zero or more occurrences of the space at the end of the line ($) with nothing (//). There are plenty of other possibilities, and the use of regular expressions makes the substitution feature of **vi** really powerful.

Sometimes the replaced pattern also has the original pattern embedded in it. You can use the & symbol in the replacement string to repeat the matched pattern:

```
:1,$s/Pentium/& II/g                    Replaces Pentium with Pentium II
:1,$s/[bB][oO][lL][dD]/<&>/g            Provides < and > around bold and BOLD
```

While you could have performed the first substitution without using the &, you couldn't have repeated a regular expression (the second example) in the replaced pattern without it. Here, bold is replaced with <bold>, BOLD with <BOLD> and so on.

Often, you'll want to replace a string interactively (*query replace* of **emacs**). In that case, add the c (confirmatory) parameter at the end. The substitution mechanism is shown in Fig. 4.19 and the commands are listed in Table 4.7.

Each line is selected in turn, followed by a sequence of carets (^) in the next line. The cursor is positioned at the end of this caret sequence and waits for your response. A y performs the substitution; any other response doesn't. This sequence is repeated for each of the matched lines in turn.

Substitution is also an important feature of the **sed** command, which uses a similar syntax. In fact many of the features discussed there also apply to **vi**. For a fuller exposition of this substitution feature look up Section 15.11.

Linux

Two Useful Features
Repeating Last Line Mode Commands

A generalized **history** feature in **vim** lets you recall and reexecute all Last Line Mode commands that have been used in the current session. This means that you can not only repeat the last substitution command but also repeat all previous substitutions made in the current session.

For instance, if you have made a substitution with **:s** and now want to repeat it, press **:** and then press the cursor Up key repeatedly to recall all previous Last Line Mode commands. Select the one you need and press *[Enter]*. This facility is also available for the search commands made with **/** and **?**. Press the **/** and then the Up key. This will recall the last search command.

Substitution

The substitution feature in Linux is not only more readable and friendly, but more powerful than its UNIX counterpart. The string to be replaced is shown in reverse video, and you have to enter your response against this prompt in the last line of the screen:

```
replace with msg (y/n/a/q/^E/^Y)?                                       5,1
```

Apart from y and n, you also have the option of aborting (q) the substitution process or making it noninteractive (a).

4.17 Handling Multiple Files

vi uses the Last Line Mode to handle multiple files and buffers. You can open as many buffers as you want and switch from one to the other. The basic file handling commands for both editors are already known to you; the advanced ones are presented in Table 4.9.

FIGURE 4.19   *Substitution (Command:* **:1,$s/message/msg/gc***)*

Before Substitution

```
message="has scheduled the $1 command"
~~~~~y
e_message="are not using the $1 command"
  ~~~~~n
if grep "$1" $crondir/henry ; then
    echo "henry $message"
              ~~~~~y
elif grep "$1" $crondir/julie ; then
    echo "julie $message"
              ~~~~~y
else
    echo "The three users $e_message"
                           ~~~~~n
fi
```

After Substitution

```
msg="has scheduled the $1 command"

e_message="are not using the $1 command"

if grep "$1" $crondir/henry ; then

    echo "henry $msg"

elif grep "$1" $crondir/julie ; then

    echo "julie $msg"

else

    echo "The three users $e_message"

fi
```

4.17.1   Inserting File and Command Output

With most Windows text editors, there's no easy way of inserting the contents of one file at a certain location in another file. You have to open the file, use something like *Select All* from the *Edit* menu, copy the entire text with *[Ctrl-c]*, switch to the original file, and then paste the contents with *[Ctrl-v]*. That involves a great deal of work by UNIX standards.

With **vi**, you don't have to visit the other file at all. Just insert its contents at the present cursor location:

:r note1   *Inserts file* note1

TABLE 4.9   *Advanced File Handling Commands in* **vi**

Command	Function
:r foo	Reads file foo below current line
:r !date	Reads output of date command below current line
:e foo	Stops editing current file, and edits file foo
:e! foo	As above, but after abandoning changes made to current file
:e!	Loads last saved edition of current file (like *Revert* in Microsoft Windows)
[Ctrl-^]	Returns to most recently edited file (requires *[Shift]* in Solaris)
:e#	As above
:n	Edits next file (when **vi** is invoked with multiple filenames)
:rew	Rewinds file list to start editing first file (when **vi** is invoked with multiple filenames)

You can also place the output of a command in your file. Use **:r** like before, but instead of specifying the filename, enter the command name preceded by the **!**:

:r !date   *Inserts output of* date *command*

This is a very useful feature for documentation authors, who need to feature command output in their text. There's no need to save this output in a file and then read in the file.

4.17.2   Switching Files

You may sometimes need to ignore all unsaved changes you made. You can reload the last saved version of the file:

:e!   *Like Revert in Microsoft Windows*

You can also edit multiple files without leaving the editor. While editing one file, you can easily switch to another:

:e note2   *Switches to* note2

You can return to the original file by using either of these:

[Ctrl-^]   *Returns to most recently edited file*
:e#

This has a toggling effect; the next time you use either of these sequences, you'll change the file again. The first sequence is easier to execute and you should use it whenever you use **vi** with multiple files.

Using vi with Multiple Filenames When **vi** is used with multiple filenames in the command line, it loads the first file into the buffer. You can move to the next file or rewind the file list to start from the beginning:

:n	*Next file in command line*
:rew	*Back to first file in command line*

vi's protection mechanism prevents a switch to another file if changes made to the current one remain unsaved. The **!** is the universal overriding switch. Use it freely (as you did with **:q!** and **:e!**) with any of the Last Line Mode commands whenever you want to ignore changes. You can also use **:n!** and **:rew!** in the same way.

Tip

You'll often need to copy or move text from one file to another. Saving the current file before switching to the other one is often an irritation. To have the files autosaved on switches, make the setting **:set autowrite** or **:set aw** in the file .exrc. This will enable you to use **:n** and toggle between two files with *[Ctrl-^]* without explicitly saving the file. But in many versions of UNIX it won't allow you to use **:e foo** without saving the file explicitly.

The features of **vi** that have been presented so far are good enough for a beginner, who shouldn't proceed any further before mastering most of them. If you already know **vi** quite well, read on.

Linux

Splitting the Window

You can split the screen into multiple windows in **vim**. The window can be empty or it can contain a file—even a copy of the same file. We'll restrict the discussion to two windows only as working with more than two is somewhat inconvenient.

To view the same file in two separate windows, use the **:sp** (split) command in the Last Line Mode:

:sp	*Splits existing window in two*

The split window is shown in Fig. 4.20. In this situation, changes made to the buffer in one window are also seen in the other window. You can also create a new window not associated with any file:

:new	*New blank window*

In either case, you'll see the screen split into two. You can move between the two windows by using this command:

[Ctrl-w][Ctrl-w]	*Cycles through windows*

In any window (empty or otherwise), you can open a new file by using **:e** *filename*. You can also increase or decrease the vertical size of a window:

[Ctrl-w] +   *Increases size of current window*
[Ctrl-w] –   *Reduces size of current window*

To make the current window the only window on the screen and close all other windows, use

    :on   *Removes all other windows*

You can kill the current window and move to the other window (if any):

    :q

Note that when you have multiple windows on, **:q** will quit editing from the *current* window and close it. To apply the save, quit and exit commands to *all* windows in **vim**, you have to append an a to the existing commands. To quit all windows without saving, use **:qa**. To save all buffers and quit, use **:xa**.

FIGURE 4.20   *A Split Window in* **vim** *(File:* backup.sh*)*

```
cd $HOME/project3
echo -e"\
1. Complete backup
2. Incremental backup
3. Complete restore
4. Incremental restore

backup.sh
cd $HOME/project3
echo -e"\
1. Complete backup
2. Incremental backup
3. Complete restore
4. Incremental restore

backup.sh
:sp
```

➤ *GOING FURTHER*

4.18 **Marking Text**

You can mark several positions in the file and later locate them. Unlike the *bookmarks* offered by browsers, these marks are invisible and disappear when you quit the editor. Both the mark and locate commands have to be used with a letter to mark a location or access a unique mark. To mark a location with the character q, move the cursor to the required location and press

mq   *Creates mark* q

After you have moved your cursor away from the portion of marked text, you can move back to this mark by using

'q   *Moves to mark* q

By using the different characters of the alphabet, you can mark up to 26 locations in the file in this way.

Tip

The **'** when doubled by itself toggles the motion of the cursor between its present and immediately previous locations. If you had first moved to a mark a with **'a** and then to mark b with **'b**, you can return to the mark a with **''** (two single quotes) and then again move back to mark b with the same command.

This also applies to those situations where the cursor is not explicitly moved away from a line. If you have moved to a line with **30G** and then to the end of the file with **G**, you can alternate between these two locations by using **''** (two single quotes).

4.19   Filtering Text—The ! Operator

Can you sort the contents of your editing window without leaving the editor? Yes, that's possible with the **!** operator. There's a family of UNIX commands that take input from one command and send output to yet another one. These commands are called **filters** and UNIX has lots of them. For instance, the **sort** command can sort a file and also the input it receives from the output of another command. Using this filtering property, we'll use **sort** to work on screen text.

Filtering text on the screen requires three steps:

1. Move to the beginning of the text to be acted upon and type **!**.
2. Move to the other end of the text using any navigation command like **G**.
3. Enter the UNIX command to act on the text. The text on the screen should change immediately.

For instance, to sort lines 21 to 40 of a file, move the cursor to the first character of line 21 (with **21G**), and then press the following sequence:

!40Gsort*[Enter]*

Nothing appears on the screen till the second address (40G) is entered. After you enter the word sort, the last line could look like this:

:21,40!sort   *You executed a Last Line Mode command!*

After you press *[Enter]*, the 20 specified lines are sorted and the output replaces the current contents. You have just executed the Last Line Mode command **:21,40!sort** without knowing it. You can enter this command directly as well. You can save the change if you want or undo it if it didn't do exactly what you wanted.

Note

Like the other operators, the **!** when doubled uses the command following it to operate on the current line.

Linux

Working with Regions

vim lets you mark a block of text as a **region** (using **emacs** lingo) and then use some command on this region. It uses the originally undefined v key for this purpose. This technique is often used when you are unable to define a section with simple keystrokes. The text is also highlighted, which makes it even easier to work with.

When you press **v**, **vim** enters the **visual mode**. The message --VISUAL-- appears in the last line. As you move your cursor with the navigation keys, text is progressively highlighted. The highlighted area is your region, and you can use any **vi** operator to act on this region. You can also undefine your region by pressing **v** again.

If you want to delete the region, just press the operator **d**. No additional command needs to be combined with **d** this time. In the same vein, use **y** to yank a selection. To filter screen text, use a **!**-prefixed command—like **!sort** to sort the region. Even though **~** is not an operator, you can use that too to change the case of text.

GOING FURTHER

4.20   Named Buffers: Copying and Moving Multiple Text Sections

You have copied and moved a single section of text—even between two files. Have you ever experienced the need to copy several sections of a program to another file in a single file switch? Both **vi** and **emacs** offer the facility to store up to 26 blocks of text (named after the letters of the alphabet) in a number of special **named buffers**.

You have already used the named buffer when working with two files *(4.10.4)*. At that time, you used "a to precede the copying or deleting operation. a is just one of the 26 buffers available in **vi**; you can actually choose any buffer name. This is how you yank four lines into the named buffer v:

"v4yy   *Copies 4 lines into buffer* v

To put back text, navigate to the desired location (possibly in another file) and use this:

"vp   *Use* P *to put text above*

In this way, you can yank up to 26 sections of text and restore the entire lot at different locations—even in different files. Windows and the mouse can never do all this! However, the X Window System and its **xclipboard** client *(12.11.1)* can do even better than this.

If you perform an operation on a named buffer which already contains some text, the contents of the buffer are overwritten. **vi** uses the uppercase letters to append to these buffers—**"Ayy** instead of **"ayy**.

Tip

If you want to copy text at different locations and later put the entire lot at a *single* location, then you should use the uppercase buffer name to append to the buffer. For instance, you can copy the current line at 10 locations by pressing **"Ayy** repeatedly at those 10 places. The buffer A now contains all the 10 lines which you can put with a *single* invocation of **"ap**.

4.21 Recovering Multiple Deletions

If you have deleted multiple text sections at different places, you can recover the last nine deletions of *complete* lines. Complete line deletions (not parts of lines) are stored in **numbered buffers** (1 to 9). The most recent deletion is stored in buffer 1, the next in buffer 2, and so forth. Like in named buffers, the same " prefix is used to access them. To restore the most recently deleted group of lines, use

`"1p`   *Restores most recent deletion*

If that is not the text you expected to restore, you can undo the last restoration with **u** and then use **"2p**. You can go on like this, using the rather tedious method of using ", a number and p every time.

There's a better way. **vi** uses the **.** command to also restore deleted lines apart from performing its usual function of repeating the last command. The command steps through the buffer set to restore the contents of the *next* buffer.

To make the dot work that way, you first have to restore at least one deletion using, say, **"1p**. If that's not the block you are looking for, you can undo with **u** and then press **.** to restore the next buffer (2). If the text resides in the buffer 4, you can start with buffer number 1, and then issue the following sequence of commands:

`"1pu.u.u.`

Note

The dot can recover up to the last nine deletions of entire lines only. Parts of lines can't be restored in this way. These restrictions don't apply to **vim**.

4.22 Abbreviating Text (:ab)

You can abbreviate long words to shorter uncommon strings. The moment you enter the abbreviation, followed by a space or a punctuation character, the string is expanded. Document authors and programmers use this feature to abbreviate frequently used long words and those that invariably are incorrectly spelled while typing.

To abbreviate text, you have to use the **:abbreviate** (itself abbreviated to **:ab**) command in the Last Line Mode. Here are two useful abbreviations that include the most often used command in Java:

`:ab varaible variable`   *Corrects the spelling*
`:ab sopl System.out.println`   sop *could be* System.out.print

The first one isn't really an abbreviation but makes use of the feature to correct frequently misspelled words. Next time you enter the word sopl, followed by a key which is nei-

GOING FURTHER

ther alphanumeric nor the _ (underscore) character, you'll see `System.out.println` in place of `sop1`.

Even though you can use these abbreviation commands at the Last Line Mode, you'll eventually like to make them permanent by placing the entries in the startup file `.exrc`. The entries should be placed there exactly in the same way they are entered at the Last Line Mode prompt (the colon is optional though). Abbreviations are listed with `:ab` and undone with `:unab`.

Note

The startup file `.exrc` should be placed in the *home directory*—the one where a user is placed immediately on login. You can know your home directory by issuing the **pwd** command immediately after logging in *(1.10.3)*.

4.23   Customizing the Keyboard (`:map`)

As you acquire proficiency in handling an editor, you'll find a number of keystroke sequences that are repeatedly executed to perform a job. It's time you mapped an oft-used sequence to a single key. You should be able to assign the undefined keys or reassign the defined ones so that, when such a key is pressed, it expands into a sequence of commands and does the work.

vi uses the **:map** command for mapping keys. The command is followed by the key which needs mapping and the key sequence that has to be mapped. For instance, if you want to save your buffer with a single keystroke, then you can map a certain key (let's say, q) to this sequence:

`:map q :w^M`   *^M signifies the [Enter] key*

This mapping also includes the *[Enter]* key, which **vi** understands as *[Ctrl-m]* (shown as ^M). This character is entered by first pressing *[Ctrl-v]* and then *[Ctrl-m]* *(4.3.5)*. Once q is mapped, you can just press it to save your file.

You can map keys in the Input Mode also. This requires the use of the ! after `map`. Let's map the second function key *[F2]* to the same function defined above:

`:map! #2 ^[:w^M`   *Function key [F2] is #2*

The first mapped character is the *[Esc]*, represented as ^[. You have to press this key to switch to Command Mode before you use `:w`. Note that this map will not work in the Command Mode.

Can you execute a shell or **perl** script without leaving **vi**? Make this mapping of the function key *[F1]*:

`:map #1 :!%^M`   *File must have executable permission*

Tip

This executes (!) the current file (%) at the : prompt. This is one important mapping which the author uses to run scripts without quitting **vi**. You should use it too, and then thank yourself (and the author) when you see how fast a script is debugged. Just remember that **vi** understands the current file as %—a poorly documented feature. If you want to compile the current file from the editor, you'll need to use the % as an argument to the compiling command (**cc** or **javac**, for example).

As with the abbreviation commands, you should save useful mappings in the .exrc. The **:map** command displays the mapped environment. **:unmap** cancels a Command Mode map and **:unmap!** cancels an Input Mode map.

Tip

You probably know by now that the keys g, q, v, K, V and Z are undefined in **vi**. You can use these keys for customizing your keyboard. Note that some of these keys are defined in **vim**.

4.24   Customizing the Environment (:set)

The behavior of **vi** is determined by its variable settings. Even though there are a large number of these variables, the default settings are generally adequate for normal editing work. But sometimes you might like to change them to suit your application. You can do that from the editor, but to make them permanent, you'd better place them in the file .exrc.

vi uses the **:set** command in the Last Line Mode to set its variables. (The : is optional when placed inside .exrc.) Here are two typical settings:

```
:set showmode
:set ignorecase                                    Can also use ic as a synonym
```

The second variable takes an abbreviation, which means that you can also use **:set ic**. Every variable can have the string no prefixed to its name, in which case the setting is negated or deactivated. For instance, noignorecase negates ignorecase. You can abbreviate this setting to **:set noic** also. Now, let's discuss the significance of some of the variables.

showmode   We used the command *(4.3)* to tell us the mode **vi** is currently in. Beginners tend to use the *[Esc]* key more often than they are required to, and it's good to see the words INSERT or REPLACE in the last line reminding you that you are not in the Command Mode.

showmatch   The showmatch setting enables the programmer to see momentarily the matching bracket to a) or }. The moment a) or } is entered, the cursor will jump to its matching counterpart, and stay there for a fraction of a second before returning to its current location. If a match is not found, it responds with a beep.

autowrite   When editing multiple files, **vi** refuses to make a switch to another file with **:n** or *[Ctrl-^]* if the current buffer is unsaved. This can be quite disconcerting at times, and the autowrite setting makes sure that the current buffer is automatically saved before moving to the next one.

You can make your searches case insensitive (ignorecase). This helps when you are not sure whether a word is available in lowercase or uppercase. You can also match strings literally by turning off the meaning of the regular expression characters (nomagic). You can set tab stops to 4 instead of the default 8 (tabstop 4). You can also number the lines in your program (number) to make it easier to debug it.

You can display all settings with the **:set all** command. The common **:set** options are summarized in Table 4.10.

TABLE 4.10   :set *Options in* **vi**

Option	Abbreviation	Significance
autoindent	ai	Next line starts at previous indented level
autowrite	aw	Writes current file automatically whenever switching files with :n or *[Ctrl-^]*
ignorecase	ic	Ignores case when searching for patterns
magic	–	Treats characters of regular expression set as special when searching for patterns
number	nu	Displays line numbers on screen
showmatch	sm	Shows momentarily match to a) and }
showmode	–	Displays a message when **vi** is in input mode
tabstop	ts	Sets tab for display (default: 8 spaces)
wrapscan	ws	Continues pattern search by moving to other end of a file so that entire file is scanned

SUMMARY

vi operates in three modes, and you can switch from one mode to the other quite easily.

The *Command Mode* is used to enter commands that operate on text or manipulate the cursor motion. Most of **vi**'s functions operate in this mode.

The *Input Mode* is used to insert (**i** and **I**), append (**a** and **A**), replace (**r** and **R**), change (**s** or **S**) text and open a line (**o** and **0**). The mode is terminated by pressing the *[Esc]* key. You can enter control characters using *[Ctrl-v]* first, and then the character.

The *Last Line Mode* is used for file handling and substitution. It is invoked by pressing a **:** in the Command Mode.

Most of the Input Mode and Command Mode commands also work with a *repeat factor* which generally performs the command multiple times.

You can use the Last Line Mode to save your work (**:w**), exit the editor after saving (**:x** and **:wq**) and quit without saving (**:q** and **:q!**). You can write selected lines to a separate file by using line addresses with **:w**. The current line in this mode is represented by a dot and the last line by $.

vi must be invoked with the **-r** option to salvage unsaved work that is lost in a system crash.

In the Command Mode, you can move along a line, using a *word* as a navigation unit. You can move back (**b**) and forward (**w**) to the beginning of a word, or to the beginning (**0**) or end (**$**) of a line. You can know your current line number (*[Ctrl-g]*) and go to a specific line number (**G**). You can use the control keys to page forward and back. You can move up (**k**), down (**j**), right (**l**) or left (**h**).

You can delete a character (**x** and **X**). With an *operator* and a Command Mode command, you can delete (**d**), move and yank (**y**) text in practically any manner. Text is put at the new location with **p** or **P**. When an operator is used by itself (like **dd**), the operation affects the current line only.

Text can be copied or moved from one file to another using the symbols "a before the copy or delete operation as well as the put operation.

You can reverse the case of text (**~**). Using the **c** operator, you can change text in more flexible ways.

vi can repeat (**.**) and undo (**u**) the last editing instruction. You can undo all changes made to the current line (**U**) before the cursor is moved away from the line. **vim** in Linux can perform multiple levels of undo and redo with **u** and *[Ctrl-r]*, respectively.

You can search for a pattern (**/** and **?**) and also repeat (**n** and **N**) the search in both directions. Using a *regular expression*, you can search for more than one pattern with a single expression. You can replace a pattern with another (**:s**), both globally and interactively. You can also search for a character in a line (**f**) and repeat the search (**;**).

You can insert the contents of another file (**:r**), move to an alternate file (**:e**), return to the last edited file (*[Ctrl-^]*) and revert to the last saved version (**:e!**).

You can also invoke **vi** with multiple filenames, edit each file in turn (**:n**) and rewind the file list (**:rew**) to start from the beginning. **vi** normally doesn't allow a change of file if changes in the current file are not saved, unless the ! suffix is used.

GOING FURTHER

You can mark up to 26 locations (a to z) with **m** and a letter, and then use the **'** and the letter to access the marked location.

Text can also be changed by filtering it (**!**) with a UNIX command.

You can use up to 26 buffers (a to z) to store text, using the " to precede the buffer name. The text can be put in another file with **p** or **P**.

You can undo up to 9 sets of deletions of *complete* lines using the numerals 1 to 9. The **.**, when used for restoring deleted lines, steps through the buffer and restores the previous line deletion.

You can abbreviate (**:ab**) long strings to short ones so that they are automatically expanded when they are input.

You can map a frequently used command sequence to a single key, both in the Command Mode (**:map**) and the Input Mode (**:map!**). Use *[Ctrl-m]* to signify *[Enter]*.

With the **:set** command, you can ensure that a file is saved before switching (autowrite). You can make searches case-insensitive (ignorecase) and turn off the significance of regular expressions (nomagic).

All **:ab**, **:map** and **:set** commands should be placed in the file .exrc so that they are always available on startup.

SELF-TEST

4.1   How will you partially overwrite the contents of a line?

4.2   How do you insert a line before the first line?

4.3   How do you change bad to bat?

4.4   How do you change the contents of the current line completely?

4.5   How do you abort an editing session?

4.6   How do you move to the 40th character of a line?

4.7   How do you move six lines up?

4.8   Your screen shows junk. How do you clear it?

4.9   How do you save the current line to a separate file?

4.10   How do you copy 10 words?

4.11   How are **d** and **y** different from the Command Mode commands?

4.12   How do you noninteractively and globally replace Internet with Web in all lines of a file?

4.13   How do you delete text from the current line to the beginning of the file?

4.14   How will you revert to the last-saved version of a file?

4.15   Name three major enhancements to **vi** that are found in **vim**.

4.16   How do you redo your undone instructions in **vim**?

EXERCISES

4.1   How do you add */ at the end of a line?

4.2   How will you replace has with have with the minimum keystrokes?

4.3   Name three ways of quitting **vi** after saving.

4.4   How will you quickly move to the fifth word of a line and replace its four characters with something else?

4.5   How do you move to the 100th line and then write the remaining lines (including that line) to a separate file?

4.6   In the midst of your work, how can you see the list of users logged in?

4.7   How many words are there in this string?
        02.29.2000 is_last_day_of_February

4.8   Explain which of the following commands can be repeated or undone: (i) **40k** (ii) *[Ctrl-f]* (iii) **5x** (iv) **J**

4.9   You have incorrectly entered the word Comptuer. How will you correct it to Computer?

4.10   How do you move two lines from the beginning of a file to the end?

4.11   How do you combine five lines into a single line?

4.12   You copied 20 lines with **20yy**, then switched to another file with **:e foo**, but when you tried to paste these lines back with **p**, it didn't work. Why?

4.13   Frame a command to change text from the current position to the first occurrence of the pattern Packet Switching.

4.14   How do you change an entire line consisting of only lowercase letters to upper-case?

4.15   How do you repeat a multicharacter string search? Will it search forward or back?

4.16   You need to shift the first five lines to the right by two spaces. How do you do that interactively?

4.17   How do you do the same thing noninteractively?

4.18   How will you search for the words Bill Joy, and then change Bill to William in some of them without entering the word William every time?

4.19   What is the difference between the commands **/*** and **f*** ?

4.20   Frame a command to delete the first two sentences of a line. How will you repeat it for subsequent lines?

4.21   How do you replace all leading spaces with one space in every line of a file?

4.22   What does the **U** command do? When will it fail to work?

4.23   How can you edit a second file without leaving **vi** and then toggle between the two files?

4.24   How will you ensure that **vi** automatically saves a file when moving from one file to another?

GOING FURTHER

4.25   Irrespective of the case of existing text, how do you change an entire line to uppercase? (HINT: first read Chapter 9.)

4.26   How do you repeatedly alternate between the beginning and end of a file?

4.27   How will you copy two groups of ten and five lines each from one file to another?

4.28   You have inadvertently deleted three groups of lines with **10dd**, **5dd** and **dd** (in that order). How will you restore the 10 deleted lines?

4.29   You defined an abbreviation re to expand to regular expression and when you try to input the word re-rating, you find the expansion getting in the way. What do you do?

4.30   Write a map which removes all leading spaces in a line.

4.31   How will you compile a C program currently being edited without leaving the editor?

4.32   Use one of the unused keys to create a map that locates the next blank line (which may or not contain spaces) and deletes it.

4.33   What are the two functions of the dot command?

KEY TERMS

character class *(4.15)*   **current cursor position** *(4.3.1)*
command history *(4.16—Linux)*   **current line** *(4.3.1)*
Command Mode *(4.1.1)*   **ex Mode** *(4.1.1)*

file buffer *(4.2)*

filter *(4.19)*

global substitution *(4.16)*

Input Mode *(4.1.1)*

Last Line Mode *(4.1.1)*

line address *(4.4.1)*

linefeed (LF) *(4.10.2)*

metacharacter *(4.15)*

named buffer *(4.20)*

newline *(4.10.2)*

numbered buffer *(4.21)*

operator *(4.9)*

region *(4.19—Linux)*

regular expression *(4.15)*

repeat factor *(4.6)*

shell escape *(4.5)*

visual mode *(4.19—Linux)*

word *(4.8.3)*

wraparound *(4.14.1)*

## CHAPTER 5

The GNU emacs Editor

UNIX features yet another powerful full-screen editor—**emacs**. It was created by Richard Stallman (the founder of GNU, now the Free Software Foundation). The program was originally written as a set of macros for the TECO editor, but was rewritten several times to make it an editor in its own right. Unlike **vi**, **emacs** is not available in all UNIX systems but is standard on Linux. It's the GNU version that we'll discuss in this chapter.

GNU **emacs** is more than an editor; it handles a number of nonediting functions as well. However, in this chapter we'll confine ourselves to its editing functions only. Users often have a near-fanatic attachment to their editors, but it's probably fair to say that both **vi** and **emacs** have their own strengths (and weaknesses). **vi** often does things with fewer keystrokes, but **emacs** easily surpasses **vi** when it comes to searching and replacing and using macros.

Is it worthwhile learning the commands of another editor? This question is not easily answered, but you would probably be better off knowing either one moderately well, and then taking up the other. This chapter is presented in the same manner as the previous one with a similar sequence of topics. If you have gleaned the essentials of **vi** from the previous chapter, then you'll know what to expect from **emacs** in this chapter.

Objectives

- Understand the use of the *[Ctrl]*, *[Alt]* and *[Esc]* keys. *(5.1.1)*
- Enter **emacs** commands with *[Alt-x]*. *(5.1.3)*
- Start a session and leave the editor. *(5.2)*
- Input text and control characters. *(5.3)*
- Save your work and recover from a crash. *(5.4)*
- Understand the significance of the *digit argument*. *(5.5)*
- Navigate the cursor both across a file and along a line. *(5.6)*
- Delete, move and copy text with or without using a *region*. *(5.8)*
- Understand the significance of the *kill ring*. *(5.8.2)*
- Change case of text with or without defining a region. *(5.9)*
- Complete a command without typing it entirely using the *command completion* feature. *(5.10)*

- Undo and redo previous commands. *(5.11)*
- Make an *incremental* and *nonincremental* search for a string. *(5.12)*
- Replace a string both noninteractively and interactively using the *query-replace* feature. *(5.14)*
- Extend the search and replace mechanisms to include *regular expressions. (5.13 and 5.14)*
- Work with two windows and edit multiple files. *(5.15)*
- Use the help facilities available. *(5.17)*

➤ *GOING FURTHER*

- Mark text and access any mark with and without using *bookmarks. (5.18)*
- Change screen text by running (*filtering*) a UNIX command on it. *(5.19)*
- Copy multiple text sections to separate buffers. *(5.20)*
- Recover copied and killed text from the kill ring. *(5.21)*
- Customize the editor's environment by defining abbreviations and macros and setting variables. *(5.22 to 5.25)*

5.1 emacs **Preliminaries**

Unlike **vi**, **emacs** may not be automatically installed in your system. Make sure that you have **emacs** installed and then invoke it with a filename:

```
emacs emfile
```

You have a full screen once again, but here just 22 of the 25 lines are available for editing. Two lines are shown in reverse video. The top one shows a menu and the lower one shows the **mode line**. Below this mode line is the last line—the **minibuffer** showing an **emacs**-generated message (Fig. 5.1).

There's a whole lot of useful information you can see in the mode line—like the filename (emfile) and the cursor position (L1) on line number 1. Note the three hyphens (---) on the left of F1; two of them will change the moment you enter text.

The last line (the minibuffer) is used by users to enter **emacs** commands. **emacs** also uses it to display system messages. There's one message here already showing one unique feature in the editor—autosaving a file.

FIGURE 5.1   *The* **emacs** *Screen*

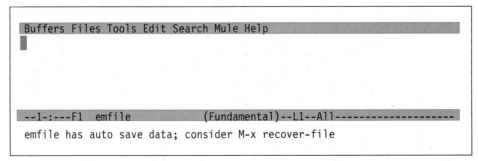

Note

If your version of **emacs** shows the menu at the top, then you can use it when running this editor from an **xterm** window *(12.9)* in the X Window system. Many **emacs** commands can be invoked from here.

5.1.1 The Control and Meta Keys

Like most word processors and unlike **vi**, **emacs** is a "mode-less" editor. You don't have to press a separate key (*[Esc]* in **vi**) to enter "Command Mode" (**vi** jargon) commands. Neither do you have to press a key (like **i** in **vi**) to begin insertion of text. In a sense, **emacs** is always in the "Input Mode" (**vi** jargon again), and you can start entering text any time.

Since you are always in the input mode in **emacs**, you have to use the control keys to execute commands to act on text. All functions in **emacs** are performed by using numerous combinations of the control keys. **emacs** also uses "meta" keys, and when you look up the **emacs** documentation, you'll find key sequences described like these:

C-e—This is *[Ctrl-e]*.
C-x C-b—This is *[Ctrl-x][Ctrl-b]*.
C-x b— *[Ctrl-x]*b is different from *[Ctrl-x][Ctrl-b]*.
M-e—This is *[Meta-e]*.

There are a lot of these sequences (much more than in **vi**), and most of them are neither mnemonic nor intuitive. There's also some confusion on the issue of whether a key is to be kept pressed or not. We'll settle this issue first.

5.1.2 How to Use the Keys

For entering editor commands, you'll require three special keys—*[Ctrl]*, *[Meta]* and *[Esc]*. These keys could by used with a printable character, and additionally, could be combined with one another. You won't see the *[Meta]* key on the PC keyboard, but we'll discuss its possible substitutes a little later.

Now, let's consider the sequence C-e. This is nothing but *[Ctrl-e]* and needs no elaboration. C-x C-b is actually *[Ctrl-x][Ctrl-b]*, where you need to do this:

1. Keep the *[Ctrl]* key pressed.
2. Press x and b in sequence.
3. Release both *[Ctrl]* and b.

Note that C-x C-b is distinctly different from *[Ctrl-x]*b; one command lists buffers, and the other is used to switch to one. To use *[Ctrl-x]*b, you'll have to press a different key sequence:

1. Enter *[Ctrl-x]* in the normal way.
2. Release both keys.
3. Singly press b.

Note

The generalized sequence *[Ctrl-x1][Ctrl-x2]* is different from *[Ctrl-x1]x2* where *x1* and *x2* are two printable characters. You need to keep the *[Ctrl]* key pressed in the first while hitting *x2*, but not in the second.

The M-e sequence is understood by **emacs** to represent *[Meta-e]* for those keyboards which have the *[Meta]* key. Many systems don't have this key on their keyboards but offer some alternative that can be used in its place. If the *[Alt]* key doesn't work on your Sun workstation, then you'll have to use the keys with the diamond symbol on them.

If you are using **emacs** on the PC, then you can try the *[Alt]* key. In most cases, *[Alt]* will work, so whenever you see M-e, just use *[Alt-e]* instead. In case this doesn't work, you have another choice—the *[Esc]* key. But here you have to be careful; press *[Esc]*, *release it*, and then press e. In this chapter, we'll use *[Alt]* to represent *[Meta]*, but you should use the key that actually works on your system.

There are other sequences that use both the *[Ctrl]* and *[Meta]* keys. To implement M-5 C-f, you'll have to do either of these two things:

- Press *[Alt-5]*, release both keys and then press *[Ctrl-f]*.
- Press *[Esc]*, release it, press 5, release it and then press *[Ctrl-f]*.

If the *[Alt]* key works on your system, you'll find it easier to use than *[Esc]*. In that case, you'll seldom need to use the *[Esc]* key. Even though you'll see *[Ctrl]*, *[Esc]* and *[Alt]* used in this chapter, you should also get used to the **emacs** form (C-, ESC and M-) because that's how they are represented in most texts and documentation featuring **emacs**.

Note

If you press *[Ctrl-x]* and take more than one second to press the next key, the string C-x- appears in the minibuffer. This is just to remind you that you have not yet completed your command.

5.1.3   Entering Commands Directly (*[Alt-x]*)

When you press a valid key sequence, **emacs** executes a command associated with the key. For instance, when you press *[Ctrl-n]*, **emacs** executes the **next-line** command that is *bound* to this key. You would, of course, prefer to use *[Ctrl-n]* rather than enter this long sequence because there is a **key binding** available between *[Ctrl-n]* and the **next-line** command.

emacs is a very powerful editor, and it has over a thousand of these commands. Some of them are very long words—like **nonincremental-repeat-search-forward**. Obviously, only a few of these commands have corresponding keys bound to them. If a command doesn't have a key binding, then you have no option but to enter the command yourself.

All **emacs** commands are entered first by pressing *[Alt-x]*, followed by the command text and then *[Enter]*. This is how you'll use the **next-line** command:

[Alt-x] next-line*[Enter]*   *Actually* M-x

When you enter *[Alt-x]*, you'll see the string M-x in the minibuffer. Enter the string next-line and then hit *[Enter]*. The cursor moves down one line. If your *[Alt]* key doesn't work, you would have to use *[Esc]* x next-line*[Enter]*. Make sure that you release *[Esc]* before you enter x.

Should you enter these rather long words every time you execute an **emacs** command? Wait, you don't need to enter the complete text ever. **emacs** has a *completion* feature *(5.10)* that will do part of the work for you.

There's a superb history facility available when you enter commands directly. **emacs** stores all commands that you issue *explicitly* with *[Alt-x]* or *[Esc]* x and retains them for the duration of the session. You can recall any command by first using *[Ctrl-x]* and then pressing *[Esc]* twice. You'll then see the last command that you issued in the minibuffer. Use the Up key to recall previous commands, edit and reexecute them. **vim** has a similar feature that works in the Last Line Mode *(4.16—Linux)*.

Tip

5.1.4 Canceling a Sequence (*[Ctrl-g]*)

emacs is an interactive editor. It often takes input from you at the minibuffer (the last line). It may ask you for a filename, an expression to be used for search or the text of an **emacs** command. As a beginner, you'll make mistakes and press the wrong keys. You must be able to cancel the current command when **emacs** is expecting something from you. This is done with *[Ctrl-g]*.

For instance, the **emacs** command for opening a file is *[Ctrl-x][Ctrl-f]*. It's possible that when meaning to edit another file, you pressed *[Alt-x]* instead of *[Ctrl-x]*. **emacs** then asks you for the command text rather than a filename:

M-x   *All* emacs *commands are entered here*

This is not what you wanted, so you have to get rid of this prompt and make **emacs** return to its normal mode. Whenever you are in a situation like this, just hit *[Ctrl-g]*. If it doesn't do what you expect, use it twice.

5.1.5 The .emacs File

Many UNIX commands read a configuration file at startup. Just as **vi** uses .exrc, **emacs** uses the file .emacs. The entries in .emacs are written in LISP—the language originally used to write **emacs**. These entries are not easily readable, so we'll be editing this file only in the "Going Further" section of this chapter.

It's possible that your login directory already contains .emacs. The file may also contain entries that change the defaults assumed in this chapter. This could make some of the commands either work differently or not at all. To eliminate the possibility of that happening, just rename the file to something else with the **mv** command *(6.13)*:

```
$ mv .emacs .emacs.bak                          Renames .emacs to .emacs.bak
$ _
```

Alternatively, you can invoke **emacs** with the -q option. This option ignores the .emacs file at startup.

Till you encounter the "Going Further" section, invoke **emacs** with the -q option. If you can rename the .emacs file, then the -q option is not required. Revert to the normal usage after you have learned to make use of .emacs.

Tip

5.2 Quitting `emacs`

You are now well aware that it's a **buffer** (a copy of the file) that you always edit and not the file directly. The buffer has a separate existence from the file it is associated with. Changes to the buffer are written to the disk file with a saving operation.

Before you start working in **emacs**, you must learn how to quit the editor. There are two choices that you have:

- Write the buffer changes to the file and quit.
- Abandon all changes to the buffer and quit.

emacs has a single command that handles these two issues. Keep the *[Ctrl]* key pressed and press x and c in sequence:

[Ctrl-x][Ctrl-c]   C-x C-c
$ _

If no changes have been made to the buffer after it was last saved by you, you are immediately returned the shell's prompt. But if you have made changes, then **emacs** produces this message:

```
Save file /home/romeo/project5/emfile? (y, n, !, ., q, C-r or C-h)
```

You now have to decide whether you would like to save your changes. There are six options here, but you need not know all of them. A y saves the file and quits the editor.

Sometimes, you won't want to answer these questions, but save and exit as quickly as possible. There is a special sequence for doing that:

[Ctrl-u][Ctrl-x][Ctrl-c]   *No questions asked!*

This uses three control keys. Keep the *[Ctrl]* key pressed and then hit u, x and c in sequence.

5.2.1 Aborting the Session

You'll sometimes enter some text and later decide that it isn't worth saving. In that case, you have to abort the session. If you use *[Ctrl-x][Ctrl-c]* on a modified buffer, you'll be asked the question as shown above. If you enter n here, the safety mechanism in **emacs** still makes sure:

```
Modified buffers exist; exit anyway? (yes or no)
```

Here, **emacs** is trying to tell you that you have modified the buffer since it was last saved. This time, you have to enter either yes or no (y or n won't do). A yes here aborts the editing process and returns you to the shell. no will continue with the editing process.

5.3 Inserting and Replacing Text

When you invoke **emacs**, the cursor is positioned on the first character of the first line. Insert a few lines of text as shown in Fig. 5.2. After you have entered the five lines, note

F I G U R E 5.2 *Entering Text*

```
Buffers Files Tools Edit Search Mule Help
This is the emacs editor.
When you start it without specifying a filename,
the system will show you a screenful of text.
Press the spacebar to clear the window and then start editing.
If you get stuck, then use C-x C-c to quit.█
 ... blank lines deleted ...
--1-:**-F1  emfile                 (Fundamental)--L5--Top--------------------
```

that the mode line shows the line number the cursor is currently on (L5). You are at the top of the file (Top) and the two asterisks at the left indicate that the buffer has been modified. We'll ignore the other symbols for the time being. In the figures, we'll continue to use this shaded box █ to represent the cursor.

You can use the *[Backspace]* key for erasing text to the left, but not *[Ctrl-h]*. This is the key **emacs** uses to call up its help facility. **emacs** does have a fairly extensive help feature; it is activated with *[Ctrl-h]*. You can also use *[Ctrl-d]* or *[Delete]* to delete the character under the cursor.

Caution

If the file is empty, you can still move vertically with the cursor keys. As you move down, **emacs** adds an extra line every time the Down key is pressed. If you are not careful, you'll unnecessarily add extra lines without pressing *[Enter]*.

5.3.1 Replacing Text (overwrite-mode)

By default, **emacs** works in the **insert mode**, which means that when you enter text, the existing text is shifted to the right. **emacs** can also work in the **overwrite mode** which replaces all characters the cursor moves over. You can switch to this mode in two ways:

- By pressing the *[Insert]* key which acts as a toggle switch. The first invocation takes you to overwrite mode; the next one returns you to insert mode.
- By issuing the **emacs overwrite-mode** command. When you enter *[Alt-x]*, **emacs** shows M-x at the minibuffer—waiting for input. Just enter overwrite-mode and press *[Enter]*:

M-x **overwrite-mode***[Enter]*

This also has a toggling effect, and you can go back to the insert mode by issuing the command once again. This implies a lot of typing, but the command completion feature *(5.10)* lets you enter part of the text and then complete it with the *[Tab]* key. You'll meet it soon.

Note

If you are in overwrite mode, you'll see the word Ovwrt in the mode line. To enter insert mode, press the *[Insert]* key or enter the **overwrite-mode** command with *[Alt-x]*.

5.3.2   Entering Control Characters (*[Ctrl-q]*)

emacs uses the control keys for everything. That's why it traps them as **emacs** commands when you try to enter them. To enter a control character literally, you have to precede it with *[Ctrl-q]*. To enter a *[Ctrl-m]*, you must use this sequence:

[Ctrl-q][Ctrl-m]   *Shows ^M*

This shows up on the screen as ^M (Fig. 5.3). As discussed in the chapter on **vi** *(4.3.5)*, this is actually a single character though it looks like two separate ones. The *[Esc]* key is also entered in a similar manner: *[Ctrl-q][Esc]*.

5.4   Saving Text

Even though **emacs** automatically saves a file (to a different filename), you should save your work regularly. The command to use is

[Ctrl-x][Ctrl-s]   *Saves in same file*

This saves the buffer in the same file that was used when invoking **emacs**. Often, you might like to provide a different name. In that case, you should use

[Ctrl-x][Ctrl-w]   *Saves in different file—prompts for filename*

The system shows the current directory and prompts for the filename. Enter a different filename (say emfile.txt) and press *[Enter]*:

```
Write file: ~/project5/emfile.txt
```

The new filename now appears on the mode line alright, *but the current buffer is also associated with it*. When writing to a different file, **emacs**' behavior stands in sharp contrast to **vi**'s; **vi** doesn't make the new file the current one *(4.4)*. The essential save and exit commands of this mode are shown in Table 5.1.

Tip

Sometimes, you may not be able to save the buffer in the current file. This happens when the file is write-protected. In that case, you should try saving the buffer with a different filename with *[Ctrl-x][Ctrl-w]*.

5.4.1   Recovering from a Crash

Unlike **vi**, **emacs** has an **autosave** feature which automatically saves a copy of the buffer every 300 keystrokes (or 30 seconds if the user is idle). You can at most lose 300

FIGURE 5.3   *Inserting a Control Character*

```
A DOS file has a Ctrl-m at the end of each line█

   ╱
  ⌠ [Ctrl-q][Ctrl-m]
  ⌡
   ↓
A DOS file has a Ctrl-m at the end of each line^M█
```

TABLE 5.1 *Save and Exit Commands in* **emacs**

Command	Function
[Ctrl-x][Ctrl-s]	Saves file and remains in editing mode
[Ctrl-x][Ctrl-w]	Saves to a different file (Like *Save As . . .* in Microsoft Windows)
[Ctrl-x][Ctrl-c]	Quits editing mode when (i) no changes are made to file or (ii) n and yes are entered at subsequent prompts if file is modified
[Ctrl-u][Ctrl-x][Ctrl-c]	Saves and exits without prompting
[Ctrl-x][Ctrl-z]	Suspends current session and escapes to UNIX shell (Use **fg** or **exit** to return to **emacs**)
[Ctrl-z]	As above
[Alt-x] shell	Escapes to UNIX shell in the current window (Use *[Ctrl-x]*b*[Enter]* to return to **emacs**.)

keystrokes of work in case of a system crash. However, **emacs** doesn't autosave in the same file, but to one which uses a # on either side of the original filename. For instance, the file emfile is autosaved as #emfile# in the current directory.

In case there's a power outage or a system crash, the latest status of the buffer may not have been saved by you. You can then replace your current buffer with the last autosaved file using the **recover-file** command:

[Alt-x] recover-file

After you have entered the filename (which must have a # on either side), **emacs** shows both files with their sizes and last modification times. It also prompts you for a fully worded answer. The screen featuring the prompt is shown in Fig. 5.4.

If you have made a lot of changes and then find that you shouldn't have made some of them, you'll find a useful companion in the autosave feature. Here, you have a version which is eight minutes newer than the last saved version; you may like to use it. **emacs** also makes sure of reminding you at startup whenever it finds the autosaved version to be of more recent origin.

FIGURE 5.4 *Recovering a File with* **recover-file**

```
-rw-r--r-- 1 romeo   dialout   2658 Sep 19 09:14 /home/romeo/p5/#note1#
-rw-r--r-- 1 romeo   dialout   2677 Sep 19 09:06 /home/romeo/p5/note1
....
--1-:%%-F1  *Directory*        (Help View)--L1--All-------------------------------
Recover auto save file /home/romeo/p5/#note1#? (yes or no) yes
```

5.5   The Digit Argument

Before you start using the editing functions, you should note that **emacs** also supports the facility of prefixing a number to a command. This number is called the **digit argument** and performs the command as many times. But here, the number is also prefixed by the *[Meta]* key.

Now, *[Ctrl-d]* deletes a single character. Thus, the generalized command to delete five characters is

[Meta-5][Ctrl-d]   5 *is the digit argument*

You should now be able to state with conviction that this can be implemented in either of two ways:

[Alt-5][Ctrl-d]   *Keep [Alt] pressed when entering* 5
[Esc]5 [Ctrl-d]   *Release [Esc] before entering* 5

The use of the character deletion command with and without the digit argument is shown in Fig. 5.5.

5.5.1   *[Ctrl-u]*: The Universal Argument

There's another way of entering the digit argument—with *[Ctrl-u]*, optionally followed by a number. The following command sequence also deletes five characters:

[Ctrl-u]5 [Ctrl-d]   *Same as [Alt-5][Ctrl-d]*

This looks like a bit of extra work, but *[Ctrl-u]* is a special key sequence; it's called the **universal argument**. It need not be used with a numeric argument and can be repeated as many times as required. When you use *[Ctrl-u][Ctrl-d]* (i.e., without using a numeric argument), the delete command is executed four times. Every additional *[Ctrl-u]* multiplies the number of repeats by a factor of 4. The following two sequences delete 16 characters and 64 characters, respectively:

[Ctrl-u][Ctrl-u][Ctrl-d]   *Deletes 16 characters*
[Ctrl-u][Ctrl-u][Ctrl-u][Ctrl-d]   *Deletes 64 characters*

FIGURE 5.5   *Deleting Characters with [Ctrl-d]*

```
Try X Window emacs if you have trouble learning emacs

    [Ctrl-d]

Try X Window emacs if you have trouble learning emacs

    [Alt-6][Ctrl-d]

Try X emacs if you have trouble learning emacs
```

This approach is sometimes preferable as it's easier to press the same key a number of times rather than move your hand away to enter a three- or four-digit number. You can use it to do part of your work too. To delete 66 characters, you can delete 64 of them by using *[Ctrl-u]* thrice with *[Ctrl-d]*, and then using *[Ctrl-d]* twice. The use of the universal argument is shown in Fig. 5.6.

5.6 Navigation

emacs uses the control keys to move in the four directions. These keys are quite intuitive—b (back), f (forward), p (previous line) and n (next line). Keeping these in mind, the keys to move left and right become:

[Ctrl-b]—Moves cursor left
[Ctrl-f]—Moves cursor right

and the keys to move up and down are:

[Ctrl-p]—Moves cursor up
[Ctrl-n]—Moves cursor down

The digit argument applies here too. Thus, *[Alt-4][Ctrl-b]* moves the cursor four places back, while *[Alt-200][Ctrl-n]* moves it down 200 lines. There is one notable distinction that must be made here between *[Ctrl-n]* and the other three control keys. When you encounter the end of the buffer, *[Ctrl-n]* adds extra blank lines in the same way the Down key does *(5.3—Caution)*. The basic navigation commands are shown in Fig. 5.7.

Caution

You must be careful to ensure that you don't press *[Ctrl-n]* unnecessarily when you have reached the end of the buffer. *[Ctrl-n]* then simply goes on adding lines to the buffer. You could find that you have generated a large number of blank lines in this way.

F I G U R E 5.6   *Using [Ctrl-u] as the Universal Argument*

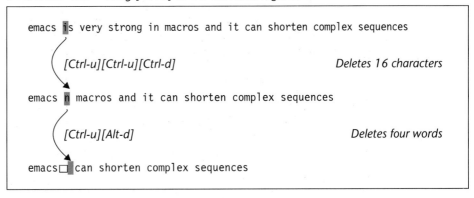

FIGURE 5.7   *Horizontal and Vertical Motion*

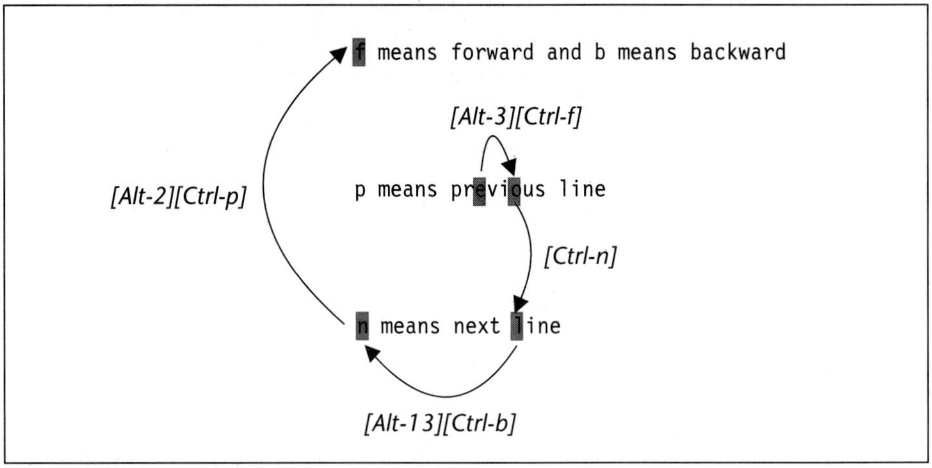

5.6.1   Paging and Scrolling (*[Ctrl-v]* and *[Alt-v]*)

For scrolling up and down, the key to remember is v. It's used with either the *[Ctrl]* or *[Alt]* key depending on whether you are scrolling forward or back. To scroll forward, use

[Ctrl-v]

and to scroll back, use

[Alt-v]   *[Alt] this time*

The digit argument applies here too, so you can scroll several screens at a time.

When the screen gets garbled, you'll have to use *[Ctrl-l]* to redraw it. You'll recall that **vi** also uses the same key combination. However, there is one difference; *[Ctrl-l]* in **emacs** also moves the current line to the center of the screen. This helps in bringing into view some text *without moving the cursor away from the current line*. The horizontal and vertical movements of the cursor and the paging commands are listed in Table 5.2.

T A B L E   5.2   *Horizontal and Vertical Motion in* **emacs**

Command	Function
[Ctrl-b]	Moves cursor left
[Ctrl-f]	Moves cursor right
[Ctrl-p]	Moves cursor up
[Ctrl-n]	Moves cursor down (adds blank lines when executed at end of buffer)
[Ctrl-v]	Scrolls full page forward
[Alt-v]	Scrolls full page backward
[Ctrl-l]	Clears screen and positions cursor at center of screen

5.6.2 The Beginning or End of a Line ([*Ctrl-a*] and [*Ctrl-e*])

You can move pretty swiftly to the beginning or end of a line. This is handled by the keys *[Ctrl-a]* and *[Ctrl-e]*. To move to the beginning of a line, use

[Ctrl-a]   *Like 0 in* vi

and to move to the end of the line, use

[Ctrl-e]   *Like $ in* vi

Do the digit arguments work here? Check that out for yourself. The use of these two commands along with those that use units of words (*[Alt-f]* and *[Alt-b]*) is shown in Fig. 5.8.

5.6.3 Navigating by Words ([*Alt-f*] and [*Alt-b*])

emacs also recognizes a *word* as a navigation unit. You can move with reference to one or more words. To move to the beginning of a word, use

[Alt-f]   *[Ctrl-f] would move one character forward*

and to move back by one word, use

[Alt-b]   *[Ctrl-b] would move one character backward*

A digit argument speeds up cursor movement along a line. For example, *[Alt-5][Alt-f]* takes the cursor five words forward, while *[Alt-3][Alt-b]* moves three words back.

5.6.4 Moving between Lines

By default, **emacs** shows you the current line number on the mode line, duly prefixed by L. If you don't see line numbers on your system, you can issue the

FIGURE 5.8 *Navigation Along a Line*

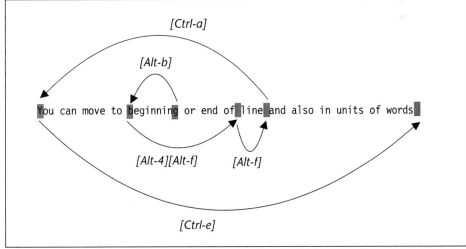

line-number-mode command. This is yet another **emacs** command that is not bound to a particular key sequence. This means that you have to use *[Alt-x]* before you enter the command:

[Alt-x] line-number-mode*[Enter]*

You'll now find an L appear on the mode line with the current line number. This again is a toggle switch; you can turn it off by issuing the command once again.

With the **goto-line** command, you can move to a specific line number. This is how you take your cursor to line number 40:

[Alt-x] goto-line*[Enter]*

emacs now asks you to enter the line number:

Goto line: **40***[Enter]*   *Like* 40G *in* vi

This looks like a lot of typing, but you'll soon see how the completion feature *(5.10)* can significantly shorten text entry. You can also go to a line without being prompted for by entering

[Ctrl-u] 40 *[Alt-x]* goto-line*[Enter]*

This implies a great deal of typing too, so you'll have to bind a key on your keyboard to simplify things. We'll be coming back to the **goto-line** command later in the chapter.

Tip

If you need to start up a file so that it shows the cursor at a certain line number (say, 40), prefix the line number with a + and use it as an argument to **emacs**:

emacs +40 chap01

5.6.5   Moving to Beginning or End of a File (*[Alt-<]* and *[Alt->]*)

emacs supports specific key sequences for moving to the beginning and end of file. To go to line number 1, you should use

[Alt-<]   *Like* 1G *in* vi

The end of a file is reached by using the > symbol:

[Alt->]   *Like* G *in* vi

On PC keyboards, the < and > symbols can be accessed by pressing the *[Shift]* key. To use the two commands shown above you actually have to use *[Shift]* with *[Alt]*:

[Alt] [Shift] <   *Beginning of file*
[Alt] [Shift] >   *End of file*

The precise navigation commands that you learned in these four sections are grouped together in Table 5.3.

TABLE 5.3 *Precise Navigation Commands in* emacs

Command	Function
[Ctrl-a]	Moves to beginning of line
[Ctrl-e]	Moves to end of line
[Alt-b]	Moves back to beginning of word
[Alt-f]	Moves forward by one word
[Alt->]	Moves to end of file
[Alt-<]	Moves to beginning of file
[Alt-x] goto-line*[Enter]* 40	Goes to line 40 (line number entered at prompt)
[Ctrl-u] 40 *[Alt-x]* goto-line	Goes to line 40 (no prompting)
[Alt-x] line-number-mode	Toggles line number display mode on mode line

Note

You have to use the *[Shift]* key for accessing some of the keys like >, <, | and ^. However, there are some key sequences that can be used both with or without using *[Shift]*—*[Ctrl-@]* and *[Ctrl-_]*, for instance. In this chapter, we won't normally be specifying *[Shift]* even if the command requires it. You shouldn't find it difficult to make that decision yourself; just add *[Shift]* to your sequence if the command fails to work without it.

5.7 Working with Regions

emacs lets you mark a block of text as a **region**. You don't need your mouse to do that; you can define a region using a few keystrokes. emacs supports deletion, case changing and copying functions that work on regions. By definition, a command that works on a region acts on the entire text defined by the region.

To define a region, you'll have to simply mark its two ends. Take your cursor to the point meant to mark the beginning of the region and press either of these key sequences:

[Ctrl][Spacebar]   *Mark set*
[Ctrl-@]   *May or may not use [Shift]*

This sets an invisible **mark** here. Now, move the cursor to the end of the section using the navigation keys. This process doesn't highlight the text, nor are the marks made visible, but it defines a region automatically. To toggle between the two ends, use

[Ctrl-x][Ctrl-x]   *Like '' in* vi

You'll see the cursor jumping back and forth—confirming that a region has been defined. You can now run some commands on this region.

The current position of the cursor (at the end of the region) is known to **emacs** as **point.** There's virtually no difference between cursor and point, except that the cursor always sits on top of a character, and the point is located just before it. We'll ignore this subtle difference in this text.

Tip

To mark the entire buffer as a region, **emacs** offers a shortcut—*[Ctrl-x]*h. You can issue this command anywhere in the text in which case there's no need to set mark and point separately.

5.8 Deleting, Moving and Copying Text

emacs has separate commands that can delete characters, words and lines. It can also delete text defined in a region. On the other hand, you can copy text *only* from a region. We'll first discuss the commands that don't require regions and then the ones that do. Table 5.4 lists the editing commands that are discussed in the forthcoming sections.

5.8.1 Deleting Words and Lines (*[Alt-d]* and *[Ctrl-k]*)

[Ctrl-d] deletes a character; you know that. **emacs** uses the *[Alt]* key instead for deleting words. The thumb-rule that you should immediately commit to memory is that *[Alt]* works on a larger group of characters—usually words. To delete a word, use

[Alt-d]   *Like* dw *in* vi

TABLE 5.4   *The Editing Functions in* **emacs**

Command	Function
[Ctrl-d] or *[Delete]*	Deletes single character
[Alt-6][Ctrl-d]	Deletes 6 characters
[Alt-d]	Deletes single word
[Ctrl-k][Ctrl-k]	Deletes current line
[Alt-6][Ctrl-k]	Deletes 6 lines
[Ctrl-x][Ctrl-o]	Deletes all following blank lines
[Ctrl-@]	Defines mark of region
[Ctrl][Spacebar]	As above
[Ctrl-w]	Deletes text in a region
[Alt-w]	Copies text in a region
[Ctrl-y]	Puts deleted or copied text on right of cursor
[Ctrl-t]	Interchanges character with previous one
[Ctrl-x][Ctrl-t]	Interchanges current line with previous one
[Alt-^]	Joins current line with previous line (requires *[Shift]*)
[Alt-u]	Converts word to uppercase
[Alt-4][Alt-u]	Converts 4 words to uppercase
[Alt-l]	Converts word to lowercase
[Alt-c]	Converts first character of word to uppercase
[Alt-5][Alt-c]	Converts first character of 5 words to uppercase
[Ctrl-x][Ctrl-u]	Converts entire text in region to upper
[Ctrl-x][Ctrl-l]	Converts entire text in region to lower
[Ctrl-x] u	Undoes last editing action
[Ctrl-_]	Undoes last editing action (control and underscore)
[Ctrl--]	Undoes last editing action (control and hyphen)

To delete a group of words, you should use the digit argument. To delete five words, use

[Alt-5][Alt-d]   *Like* 5dw *in* vi

This **kills** (a special form of deleting) five words. A **word** here has a different definition from what it has in **vi**; it's simply a string of alphanumeric characters (and doesn't include the _ character as the word in **vi** does).

      Apart from lines, you can also delete text up to the beginning or end of a line—and even the entire line itself. The key common to all these three operations is *[Ctrl-k]*. To delete text from the current cursor position to the end of the line, use

[Ctrl-k]   *Like* d$ *in* vi

To kill text till line beginning, you need to use *[Alt-0]* as well:

[Alt-0][Ctrl-k]   *Like* d0 *in* vi

Strange though as it may seem, there's no simple command to kill a line (unlike **dd** in **vi**). You have to use *[Ctrl-k]* twice, but at the *beginning* of the line. This means that you have to first use *[Ctrl-a]* to move to line beginning and then use

[Ctrl-k][Ctrl-k]   *Deletes the entire line*

The first *[Ctrl-k]* kills text till the last visible character in the line. The second *[Ctrl-k]* removes the newline character that remains after the first invocation.

      Using this reasoning, you may be tempted to suggest using *[Alt-6][Ctrl-k]* for deleting three lines (and not six). This reasoning, though apparently sound, is not correct. To kill six lines the extra *[Ctrl-k]* is not required:

[Alt-6][Ctrl-k]   *Kills 6 lines—like* 6dd *in* vi

emacs supports a special feature of removing a group of blank lines. The command to use is

[Ctrl-x][Ctrl-o]   *Deletes blank lines*

When executed from one of the blank lines, it kills all contiguous lines except one. When executed from the immediately preceding nonblank line, it kills all following blank lines. Line killing is shown in Fig. 5.9.

5.8.2   The Kill Ring

Have you noticed that we used the words "delete" and "kill" freely as if the two are interchangeable? Strictly speaking, they are not; **emacs** makes a clear distinction between the two. *[Ctrl-k]* is termed a kill operation because the removed text is sent to a storage area called the **kill ring**. By default, this ring stores the last 30 deletions (kills, actually), and any text sent to this ring can be recovered later.

      Commands that delete a single character and whitespace fall into the "delete" category. The text erased by these commands is not saved in the kill ring. On the other hand, when you kill one or more words or lines of text, the deleted text is saved in the kill ring. Except for *[Ctrl-d]*, practically all delete operations are actually kill operations. Henceforth, we'll be using the word "delete" in kill situations too, so take care not to interpret this word in its strictest sense.

FIGURE 5.9   *Killing Lines*

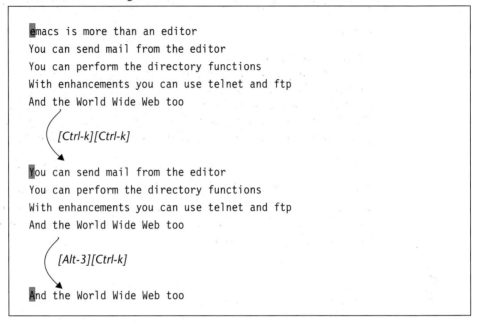

The kill ring doesn't just receive text from kill operations; *even copied text is sent to the kill ring.* We'll discover that when we learn to copy text.

Note

emacs stores a group of consecutive deletions as a *single* group in the kill ring (up to the next nonkill operation). You can delete four words with *[Alt-4][Alt-d]*, then eight lines with *[Alt-8][Alt-k]*, and then restore them together by using *[Ctrl-y]*—the key you'll be using for moving and copying text. In **vi**, **p** would have put back only the eight lines that you last deleted.

To be able to restore multiple deleted sections as a single block of text, make sure that all kill commands are executed in a sequence without a single nonkill sequence in between. If you have just moved the cursor a little between two kill operations, then you would have broken the chain. If that happens, then you'll only be restoring text deleted after the last nonkill operation. However, you can step through the kill ring and restore them too *(5.21).*

5.8.3   Deleting Text in a Region (*[Ctrl-w]*)

For deleting arbitrary sections of text, create a region as described previously. Just to make sure that mark and point are properly set, use *[Ctrl-x][Ctrl-x]* a couple of times, and then use

[Ctrl-w]   *Deletes text in a region*

The text in the region is deleted. You'll find that text after point has moved up to fill the vacuum caused by the disappearance of the region. The deletion of text in a region is shown in Fig. 5.10.

FIGURE 5.10   *Killing Text in a Region*

"A programmer is a person who passes as an exacting expert on the basis of being
 able to turn out, after innumerable punching, an infinite series of incomprehen
sive answers calculated with micrometric precisions from vague assumptions based
 on debatable figures taken from inconclusive documents and carried out on instr
uments of problematical accuracy by persons of dubious reliability and questiona
ble mentality for the avowed purpose of annoying and confounding a hopelessly de
fenseless department that was unfortunate enough to ask for the information in t
he first place." -- IEEE Grid news magazine

point

[Ctrl-w]

"A programmer is a person who passes as an exacting expert on the basis of being
 able to turn out, after innumerable punching, an infinite series of incomprehen
sive answers for the avowed purpose of annoying and confounding a hopelessly de
fenseless department that was unfortunate enough to ask for the information in t
he first place." -- IEEE Grid news magazine

Tip

To delete the contents of the entire buffer, define the region using *[Ctrl-x]*h and then use *[Ctrl-w]*.

5.8.4   Moving and Copying Text

Text can be moved by restoring it from the kill ring. *[Ctrl-y]* is universally used to restore text from the kill ring—even text killed in a region. For instance, if you kill a line with *[Ctrl-k][Ctrl-k]*, you can restore it at the new location by using

[Ctrl-y]   *Universal key for putting back text*

The deleted text is then put on the right of the cursor at the new location. You have just moved some text. You can delete three words with *[Alt-3][Alt-d]* and then use *[Ctrl-y]* to restore them too. If you have to put the text on a separate line by itself, then create the line before using *[Ctrl-y]*.

For copying text, you must work with a region. While *[Ctrl-w]* deletes text in a region, the command to copy text is

[Alt-w]   *Define a region first*

This copies the text to the kill ring. The copied text is also restored with *[Ctrl-y]* in the same way killed text is. It is also placed on the right of the cursor.

5.8.5 Transposing Text (*[Ctrl-t]*)

You can interchange two adjacent characters or lines quite easily. The key sequence to remember is *[Ctrl-t]*. If you have made a mistake of spelling `computer` as `compuetr`, then move the cursor to the `t` and press

[Ctrl-t]   *et becomes* `te`

You can transpose two sentences too. Just move the cursor to the lower line and use

[Ctrl-x][Ctrl-t]   *Like* `ddP` *in* `vi`

Transposing text is shown in Fig. 5.11.

Note

It's not true to state that text deleted with *[Ctrl-d]* is not saved. All editing actions are saved and can be undone. It's just that *[Ctrl-d]* doesn't send the deleted text to the kill ring. You'll appreciate this point better when you learn to restore text from the kill ring.

5.9 Changing Case of Text

`emacs` has comprehensive features for changing case of text. They can be used both on words and a region. To convert an entire word to uppercase, move to the beginning of the word and then press

[Alt-u]   *Entire word in uppercase*

In a similar manner, you have to use *[Alt-l]* for converting a word to lowercase. To capitalize a single character, position the cursor under it and then use

[Alt-c]   *First character to uppercase*

All three commands move the cursor to the next word, so if you keep the key pressed, you can convert 50 words in no time. Case changing of characters and words is shown in Fig. 5.12.

FIGURE 5.11 *Transposing Text*

```
They would be more convenient to use
The compue r is giving way to hand-held devices


      ( [Ctrl-t]


They would be more convenient to use
The computer  is giving way to hand-held devices


      ( [Ctrl-x][Ctrl-t]


The computer is giving way to hand-held devices
They would be more convenient to use
```

FIGURE 5.12 *Changing Case of Text*

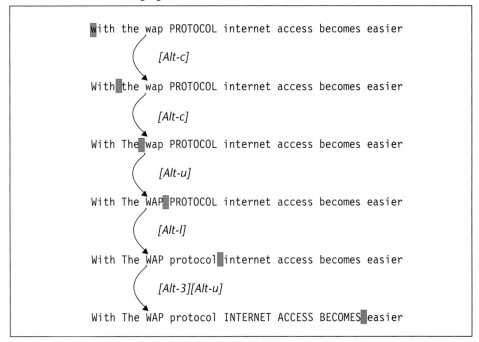

For transforming case in large blocks of text, use a region. The commands to convert text in a region are:

[Ctrl-x][Ctrl-u]   *Converts entire text in region to upper*
[Ctrl-x][Ctrl-l]   *Lower*

Note that these keys are entirely different from the ones used on words. This also makes them somewhat difficult to remember.

Tip

You may find the feature of case conversion of region disabled on your system. **emacs** then prompts you for enabling the feature permanently. This is controlled by the **upcase-region** and **downcase-region** commands. If you answer y at the final prompt when converting a region to uppercase, then **emacs** makes this setting in .emacs (a similar one for the **downcase-region** command):

```
(put 'upcase-region 'disabled nil)
```

5.10 Command Completion

This is the topic that you may have been eagerly waiting for. In a previous section you entered the complete text of two **emacs** commands—**line-number-mode** and **goto-line**. We'll now see how the **command completion** feature can reduce some of this typing work.

The guiding principle here is this: Enter as much of the command text as you want and then press the *[Tab]* key. **emacs** may either complete the command for you or present you with a list of all its commands that match the entered string. Enter a few more characters and press *[Tab]* again. This process should go on till **emacs** is able to fetch the complete command string from its list.

Let's consider one of the previous commands, **goto-line**. First press *[Alt-x]*, the key that is used as prefix to every **emacs** command. When the string M-x appears, enter the string go and press *[Tab]*:

M-x **go***[Tab]*

A new window opens up, and **emacs** shows six commands that the string go matches. Fig. 5.13 shows the completion list.

Observe the list carefully. If you now simply add a t to the existing substring (to make it got) and press *[Tab]* again, **emacs** will expand it to goto-:

M-x **got***[Tab]*   *This becomes* goto-

This matches five strings. You just need to enter an l to match goto-line:

M-x **got**o-l*[Tab]*   *This becomes* goto-line

You'll now see the complete command name in the minibuffer. The command has been completed, and you can now press *[Enter]* to enter the line number required by the **goto-line** command. To sum up, enter as much to make the string unique and use *[Tab]* to let **emacs** complete it to the extent it can.

We had to do quite a bit of typing for moving to a particular line; the completion feature didn't help much. But this feature works quite well with the **line-number-mode** command. Just the string lin will do the job:

M-x **lin***[Tab]*   *This becomes* line-number-mode

As you see more of the lists that **emacs** throws up on pressing *[Tab]*, you'll know the commands that begin with a particular string. You'll then know how much of a command to enter to make full use of the completion feature. Our previous experience has

F I G U R E 5.13   *The Command Completion Screen*

```
   In this buffer, type RET to select the completion near point.

   Possible completions are:
   gomoku                          goto-address
   goto-address-at-mouse           goto-address-at-point
   goto-char                       goto-line
   ... blank lines ...
  --1-:--F1  *Completions*      (Completion List)--L1--All---------------
   M-x go
```

now taught us this: we should have entered got*[Tab]*l*[Tab]* to complete the string goto-line with the minimum number of keystrokes. Table 5.5 shows the use of the command completion feature with some **emacs** commands.

5.11   Undoing and Redoing Editing

Like other editors, **emacs** also has an undo (and redo) feature which can reverse the editing actions performed. In contrast, **vi** (though not **vim**) can undo only the last editing action. According to the **emacs** documentation, the feature is useful and "worthy enough" to have two key sequences assigned to it. Actually, there are three:

[Ctrl-x] u
[Ctrl-_]   *With underscore–requires [Shift]*
[Ctrl--]   *With hyphen*

If you inadvertently make a change to your buffer, just press any of these key combinations. The first one is discussed in most textbooks, but the other two are easier to use. But before using them, check whether they work on your system. If you are using a PC, you'll find the - and _ keys grouped together, and the underscore is invoked by using *[Shift]*. *[Ctrl--]* is the easiest to use as it doesn't require *[Shift]*.

You can go on pressing any of these key sequences, say *[Ctrl--]*, repeatedly till you undo every single change you have made to the buffer. You'll finally see the two asterisks on the mode line disappear. This was the state of the buffer when you last saved the file. If you continue to press *[Ctrl--]*, you'll undo the changes made before the last save. Finally, the system may tell you this:

```
No further undo information
```

What happens if you press *[Ctrl--]* again? There's a surprise element here; **emacs** starts *redoing* everything that you had undone. In this way, you can go back to the point from where you came. The round-robin behavior continues as long as you persist. Unfortunately, this redoing feature is not well-documented.

TABLE 5.5   *Examples of Command Completion in* **emacs**

Entered String	Expanded String
got*[Tab]*	goto-
goto-l*[Tab]*	goto-line
lin*[Tab]*	line-number-mode
replace-s*[Tab]*	replace-string
repl*[Tab]*r*[Tab]*	replace-regexp
que*[Tab]*	query-replace
que*[Tab]*-*[Tab]*	query-replace-regexp
call*[Tab]*	call-last-kbd-macro

Note

You can't infinitely undo all your editing instructions. The limit is controlled by the **emacs** variable undo-limit. By default, it is set to 20,000 bytes of undo information which should be quite adequate for most purposes. When the undo information exceeds this limit, *garbage collection* takes place in FIFO style and the oldest commands are discarded.

5.12 String Search

emacs has a number of pattern matching schemes ranging from the simple to the elaborate, and is unmatched by **vi** in sophistication (though not in simplicity and ease of use). The search can be made both for a simple string as well as a *regular expression (4.15)*. In this section, we'll consider string searches and use two search techniques—the *incremental* and *nonincremental* search.

5.12.1 The Incremental Search (*[Ctrl-s]* and *[Ctrl-r]*)

In this method, **emacs** starts searching the moment the first character is entered, and positions the cursor at the first instance of the character. Subsequent characters are formed into substrings and searched again. This method of incrementing the search continues till the complete string is entered. **Incremental search** is invoked with *[Ctrl-s]* followed by the search string.

Consider that you are searching for the word mail. You'll first have to press *[Ctrl-s]* when **emacs** prompts for the search string in the minibuffer. Simply enter m, the first character of the string:

```
I-search: m
```

The search starts *immediately*. The cursor would relocate itself at the first instance of m—maybe on the word moon. Next, you enter a, and it could move to machine. The i could take it to maintain. Finally, if the string mail is there in the file, the cursor moves there. You should now press *[Enter]* to mark the termination of your search string.

There are a number of advantages of using incremental search:

- The search is faster than the conventional methods employed by other editors.
- **emacs** tells you instantly whether the string that you have entered so far exists in the file at all. If you are looking for quantum and you have just entered qa instead of qu, it's quite possible for **emacs** to protest immediately after qa is entered, because your file doesn't contain that string. (A word beginning with q is always followed by a u.)
- If there is a typo in the string, backspacing erases the error and moves the cursor back to the point from where it came. This goes on continuously as you backspace, and when you have erased the complete string, you'll find yourself at the point from where you launched the search.

If you are at the end of a file, you need to search backward as well. In that case, use *[Ctrl-r]* instead of *[Ctrl-s]*. Everything else remains the same, but don't forget to press *[Enter]* when you have located the string. Incremental search is shown in Fig. 5.14.

5.12.2 Repeating the Last Incremental Search (*[Ctrl-s]* and *[Ctrl-r]*)

To repeat a search, you'll have to use the same command—*[Ctrl-s]* or *[Ctrl-r]*—but without the string. Note that you'll have to press this key twice for the first repeat.

FIGURE 5.14   *Incremental Search for String* chop

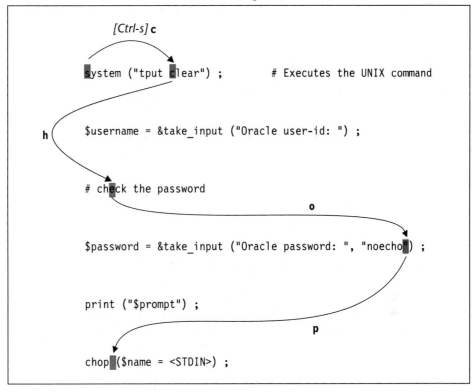

In case you are at the end or beginning of a file, **emacs** first issues this message:

`Failing I-search: quantum`

The wraparound feature *(4.14.1)* applies to **emacs** too. The next time you press *[Ctrl-s]*, the search wraps around the end to resume from the beginning of the file. The same applies for reverse search.

Caution

If you decide to cancel your search at any time, you must press the *[Esc]* or the *[Enter]* key. If you backspace to wipe out the entered string and then enter text, *the text will still be added to the search string and not to the buffer.* In most cases, **emacs** will beep and flash the error message shown above. *[Esc]* or *[Enter]* in the search mode cancels this action and takes you back to the normal mode.

5.12.3   Nonincremental Search

You can also opt for a simple "vanilla" (**nonincremental**) search in the way used in other editors. You require the same keys initially (*[Ctrl-s]* or *[Ctrl-r]*), but when the search pattern is asked for, just press *[Enter]*:

`I-search:[Enter]`

emacs now prompts you for the string:

Search: **quantum***[Enter]*

Effectively, this is how you would have performed a previous search in a non-incremental manner:

*[Ctrl-s][Enter]*quantum*[Enter]*

You can repeat a search in the same way you repeat an incremental search; there are no special considerations involved here. The search and repeat commands are summarized in Table 5.6. Nonincremental search is illustrated in Fig. 5.15.

Tip

If you happen to be near a word which is also the string you want to search for, then there's no need to enter the string. First move your cursor to the space before the word and press *[Ctrl-s]*. Instead of entering the string now, just press *[Ctrl-w]*. The word is then copied to the minibuffer and you can now use *[Ctrl-s]* to repeat the search. An extremely useful facility!

5.13   Searching with Regular Expressions

Like **vi**, **emacs** uses a pattern comprising some special characters to look for similar strings. This pattern is called a **regular expression** and is one of the important topics of this book. The topic was first introduced in Chapter 4, and even if you are not a **vi**

FIGURE 5.15   *Nonincremental Search for String* copies

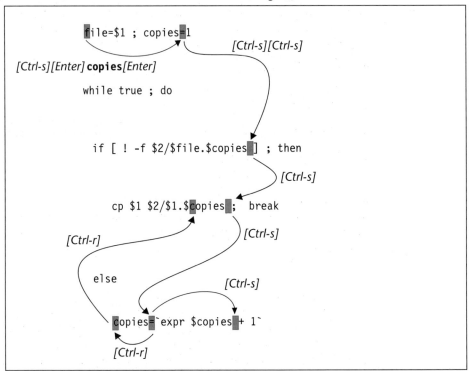

user, you must read that section *(4.15)* because all the concepts discussed there apply to **emacs** as well.

To recollect what has been discussed in Section 4.15, you can search for both michael and michel with this expression:

micha*el   a* *matches* a, aa, aaa—*or even no* a!

Here, the * indicates that the *previous* character a may occur any number of times or not at all. michae*l is a regular expression as it can match multiple strings.

You can also use a **character class** to specify a single character in that class. This means [iy] is a single-character regular expression which matches an i or y. The pattern that matches both christie or christy should be this:

christ[iy]e*   [iy] *means* i *or* y

You can use the anchoring characters ^ and $ to match an expression at the beginning and end of line, respectively. This expression looks for comment lines in a C program:

^#   ^ *matches at beginning*

The . signifies a single character, so a pattern of two dots matches two characters. But when the dot is combined with * (as in .*), it represents something quite significant—

T A B L E 5.6   *Search and Repeat Commands in* **emacs**

Command	Function
[Ctrl-s] pat	Incremental search forward for pattern *pat*
[Ctrl-r] pat	Incremental search backward for pattern *pat*
[Ctrl-s][Enter] pat	Nonincremental search forward for pattern *pat*
[Ctrl-r][Enter] pat	Nonincremental search backward for pattern *pat*
[Ctrl-s]	Repeats search in forward direction (incremental and nonincremental)
[Ctrl-r]	Repeats search in backward direction (incremental and nonincremental)
[Esc]	Cancels search
[Ctrl][Alt] s *pat*	Incremental search forward for regular expression *pat* (r for backward search)
[Ctrl][Alt] s *[Enter] pat*	Nonincremental search forward for regular expression *pat* (r for backward search)
[Ctrl][Alt] s *[Enter][Enter]*	Repeats search forward for regular expression (incremental and nonincremental)
[Ctrl][Alt] r *[Enter][Enter]*	Repeats search backward for regular expression (incremental and nonincremental)

TABLE 5.7   *The Regular Expression Characters Used by* **emacs**

Symbols	Significance
*	Matches zero or more occurrences of the previous character
[*pqr*]	Matches a single character which is either a *p, q* or *r*
[^*pqr*]	Matches a single character which is not a *p, q* or *r*
.	Matches a single character
^*pat*	Matches pattern *pat* at beginning of line
pat$	Matches pattern *pat* at end of line
\<*pat*	Matches pattern *pat* at beginning of word
pat\>	Matches pattern *pat* at end of word
\b*pat*	Matches pattern *pat* at beginning of word
pat\b	Matches pattern *pat* at end of word
\B*pat*	Matches pattern *pat* anywhere but at beginning of word
pat\B	Matches pattern *pat* anywhere but at end of word

any number of characters. Want to locate the **echo** command that also contains the string You or you? Just use the pattern echo.*[yY]ou.

emacs has some special characters of its own (Table 5.7). The \b matches a pattern at the beginning or end of the word depending on where it is placed:

\bfoot   *Doesn't match* lightfoot
wood\b   *Doesn't match* woodcock

The first matches michael foot but not lightfoot where foot is embedded. The second one selects wood but throws out woodcock. Similarly, \B negates \b; it matches at a nonword boundary, i.e., anywhere but not at the beginning or end of a word.

The regular expression characters are discussed in sufficient detail in Chapters 15, 16 and 20. These expressions are extremely important in UNIX as the power tools of the system like **grep**, **sed**, **awk** and **perl** also use them. You'll find them enormously useful when performing substitution also.

5.13.1   The Search Techniques

Let's now use our knowledge of regular expressions in searches. These searches can also be both incremental and nonincremental. To search forward in an incremental manner use this key sequence:

[Ctrl][Alt] s   *r for backward search*

emacs promptly responds at the minibuffer:

Regexp I-search: I *is incremental*

You can now enter any of the expressions that have just been discussed, followed by *[Enter]*. Note that this doesn't prevent you from specifying a simple string here also. The cursor progressively moves to the first occurrence of the string matching the regular expression as each character of the expression is entered. Don't forget to press *[Enter]* after you have completed input.

The forward nonincremental search is activated with *[Ctrl][Alt]* s *[Enter]*. Enter the regular expression and press another *[Enter]*. Thus, to locate all lines containing the string dn1 both at the beginning and end of the line, you'll need to conduct your search in this way: *[Ctrl][Alt]* s *[Enter]* ^dn1.*dn1$*[Enter]*. **emacs** can simplify this expression too, but that's another story *(15.12.2)*.

Repeating a regular expression search can be quite a bother; use the same keys till you enter the expression, but this time add another *[Enter]*—*[Ctrl][Alt]* s *[Enter][Enter]*. Further, the search doesn't wrap around when you encounter the terminal points of the file. All this can put off **vi** users who use **n** and **N** for repeating every type of search, and wraparound is never a problem.

5.14 Search and Replace

emacs offers powerful search-and-replace capabilities—both interactive and noninteractive. The reason why **vi** and **emacs** are way ahead of others is that they both use regular expressions to replace a group of similar strings with a compact expression. The replacement commands are shown in Table 5.8.

5.14.1 Noninteractive Replacement

To globally replace the word Internet with World Wide Web without interaction, first press *[Alt-x]*, the key sequence used to enter an **emacs** command. Now enter the **replace-string** command:

M-x **replace-string***[Enter]*

The command completion feature requires you to just use *[Alt-x]* repl *[Tab]* s *[Tab]*. You are prompted to enter the string to be replaced:

Replace string: **Internet***[Enter]*

TABLE 5.8 *Replacement Commands in* **emacs**

Command	Function
*[Alt-x]*replace-string	Replaces string noninteractively
*[Alt-x]*replace-regexp	Replaces regular expression noninteractively
[Alt-%]	Replaces string interactively (requires *[Shift]*)
*[Alt-x]*query-replace	Replaces string interactively
*[Alt-x]*query-replace-regexp	Replaces regular expression interactively

emacs now asks for the target string:

Replace string Internet with: **World Wide Web***[Enter]*

The substitution is now made throughout the buffer. If you feel that this hasn't done quite what you expected, then undo the operation with *[Ctrl-_]* or *[Ctrl--]*.

To replace a regular expression noninteractively, everything remains the same except that you have to use **replace-regexp** in place of the **replace-string** command.

5.14.2 Interactive Replacement

You can replace strings in an interactive manner with the **query-replace** facility that uses an **emacs** command of the same name. This time, we won't use *[Alt-x]* because the key binding *[Alt-%]* is available for the task. When you use this sequence, the system executes the **query-replace** command and asks you for the two strings:

Query replace: **Internet***[Enter]*
Query replace Internet with: **World Wide Web***[Enter]*

It then moves to the first instance of Internet and then poses this question:

Query replacing Internet with World Wide Web: (? for help)

There are 10 options that you have here, but in most cases, you'll need only these:

y or *[Spacebar]*—Replaces current occurrence and moves to next
n—Doesn't replace and skips to next
q or *[Enter]*—Exits without replacing
.—Replaces this instance only and quits
!—Replaces all remaining occurrences without asking

Similar options are offered by **emacs** when you try to quit without saving your buffer. They, however, have different meanings here. You can use q to abort the replace operation when you feel that you have performed all the replacements that you needed to make. On the other hand, you may have made a number of replacements already, and feel that no further confirmation is required for the rest. In that case, use ! to let **emacs** complete the remaining replacements. These features are not available in **vi**.

emacs uses the **query-replace-regexp** command to replace regular expressions interactively. It can also perform a very useful task in the middle of a replacement operation—**recursive editing**. This allows you to digress temporarily in the middle of the session to perform minor editing tasks.

5.15 Using Multiple Files, Windows and Buffers

When you open a file you associate a buffer with that file. This association lets you save the buffer to the disk file with a simple saving operation. You may view a buffer as the image of the file in one or more windows, but there's no relationship as such between the buffer and the window. The window merely acts as a viewer of the buffer.

When you close the window, the buffer is still open and can be called back any time. The difference between buffers and windows is subtle but distinct, and the following paragraphs should help in making this distinction.

5.15.1 Handling Windows

Unlike **vi** (but not **vim**), **emacs** lets you work with multiple windows. You can split your screen into as many windows as you like. The windows can contain anything; they may be either empty or contain the same or different files. We'll work with two windows since most of us feel comfortable with just two.

To view the same file in two separate windows, use

[Ctrl-x] 2   *Splits into 2 windows*

You'll see the screen split in two. The split window in Fig. 5.16 shows slightly different segments of the same file. In this way, you can view other parts of the program by scrolling text in the other window. Editing changes that you carry out in one window are also reflected in the other window since they show the same file (and buffer).

You'll often be editing two different files in two windows. To move to the other window, the command is:

[Ctrl-x] o   *To the other window*

FIGURE 5.16 *A Split Window*

```
Buffers Files Tools Edit Search Mule Insert Help
option=-e
while echo $option "Designation code: \c"
do
        read desig
            case "$desig" in
        [0-9][0-9]) if grep "^$desig" desig.lst >/dev/null # If code exists
                then echo "Code exists"
--1-:--F1  dentry1.sh          (Shell-script Abbrev)--L1--Top---------------------------
            case "$desig" in
        [0-9][0-9]) if grep "^$desig" desig.lst >/dev/null # If code exists
                then echo "Code exists"
                        continue                # Go to loop beginning
                    fi ;;
            *) echo "Invalid code" ; continue ;;
            esac
--1-:--F1  dentry1.sh          (Shell-script Abbrev)--L1--Top---------------------------
```

Every time you issue this command, the cursor alternates between the two windows. If you had three windows, you would be moving to each of these windows in turn. o is a mnemonic for *other*; it takes you to the other window.

If one window requires a larger screen, you can increase its vertical size:

*[Ctrl-x]^*   *Increases window's size*

Decreasing a window's size is a bit awkward. When working with two windows, it's easier to move to the other window with *[Ctrl-x]*o and then increase the size of that window.

You might now like to open a different file in one window. You probably know this command already:

[Ctrl-x][Ctrl-f]   *Like* :e foo *in* vi

After you have entered a different filename, you'll have two different files in two windows; you'll have two buffers as well. Now, suppose you opened the wrong file with this command. Will you use the same command again? No, if you don't need this file at all, then you should replace it with another file. The command to use is

[Ctrl-x][Ctrl-v]   *Replaces current buffer*

This kills the current buffer which you wrongly fetched with *[Ctrl-x][Ctrl-f]*. If you had used *[Ctrl-x][Ctrl-f]* yet again, you would have still held on to the buffer of the previous file that you wrongly called up. Unlike **vi**, **emacs** neither saves nor kills the current buffer before calling up another one, so it's easy to have a number of them in the buffer list if you don't use this command.

Note

The commands *[Ctrl-x][Ctrl-f]* and *[Ctrl-x][Ctrl-v]* are used to open a second file even when you are working in a single window (the normal **emacs** mode).

Sometimes, you would like to get rid of a window—at least temporarily. To make the current window the only window on the screen and close all other windows, use

*[Ctrl-x]*1   *Kills all other windows*

In a converse manner, you can also kill the current window and move to the other window:

*[Ctrl-x]*0 (zero)   *Kills this window*

The last two commands have important implications. Once again, killing a window doesn't kill the buffer which was being viewed in that window; it remains in the buffer list. The commands used to handle windows are shown in Table 5.9.

Tip

You can scroll forward in the other window without actually moving there by using *[Ctrl][Alt]*v, but unfortunately you can't scroll back. If you have to kill the other window now, use *[Ctrl-x]*1.

TABLE *5.9*   *Window Handling Commands in* **emacs**

Command	Function
[Ctrl-x] 2	Splits current window into 2 windows
[Ctrl-x] o	Moves between windows
[Ctrl-x] ^	Increases vertical size of current window (*[Shift]* required)
[Ctrl-x] 1	Kills all other windows and makes this window the only window
[Ctrl-x] 0	Kills this window only
[Ctrl][Alt] v	Scrolls text forward in other window (no scrolling back facility available)

5.15.2   Handling Buffers

You have been handling buffers all along. **emacs** offers a number of commands that show you the buffer list and let you select a buffer from this list. You can call back any buffer in its last unsaved condition by using this command:

[Ctrl-x] b   *Calls up another buffer*

When this command is used, it offers the last buffer name that was edited in that window as the default. In case you want to return to the last edited file, simply press *[Enter]*. When you are editing two files alternately, you can toggle between the current file and the immediately preceding file in this way.

When the buffer you want to edit is not the default one shown in the buffer list, you can enter the name yourself, or view the list and select one from there. Enter *[Ctrl-x]* b, and when the prompt appears, hit *[Tab]*. A typical buffer list is shown in Fig. 5.17.

The buffer list in the figure shows a *scratch* buffer that **emacs** always makes available to you for making notes. You can position yourself in the buffer list by using *[Ctrl-x]* o—twice, if required. You can then select any buffer by moving the cursor and

FIGURE *5.17*   *Displaying the Buffer List with [Ctrl-x] b*

```
In this buffer, type RET to select the completion near point.

Possible completions are:
*Messages*                          *scratch*
convert.sh                          dentry1.sh




--1-:--F1  *Completions*     (Completion List Abbrev)--L1--All-------------
Switch to buffer: (default *scratch*)
```

pressing *[Enter]*. You can close this window by using *[Ctrl-x]* 0 or cancel the entire action altogether with *[Ctrl-g]*.

There's a separate command for displaying the buffer list. It's a little different from the one that switches you to another buffer:

[Ctrl-x][Ctrl-b]   *Displays buffer list*

The output this time is quite informative (Fig. 5.18); it shows you the pathnames of all disk files whose buffers are held by **emacs**, their types and sizes.

Tip

If you have to work with a number of files, invoke **emacs** with multiple filenames. The buffers for all files are created by **emacs** and held in the buffer list. You can display the list with *[Ctrl-x][Ctrl-b]* and select any buffer for editing in a separate window. You can also use *[Ctrl-x]* b to replace the current window with a different buffer.

You may sometimes need to ignore all unsaved changes you made. You can reload the last saved version of the file:

[Alt-x] revert-buffer

This updates the buffer contents with the disk file. Note that this command is different from **recover-file** which loads the autosaved version of the file *(5.4.1)*.

Tip

The *[Ctrl-x]* b command in **emacs** is useful for another purpose; it can be used to create a "scratch" buffer—one that is not associated with any filename. If you receive a phone call from someone and are in the midst of an **emacs** session, just create this scratch buffer to make notes.

5.15.3 Inserting File and Command Output

You can insert the contents of a file at the current cursor location; you don't have to edit the other file and then copy its contents from there. Just use this command:

FIGURE 5.18   *The Buffer List Displayed by [Ctrl-x][Ctrl-b]*

```
 MR Buffer          Size  Mode            File
 -- ------          ----  ----            ----
 .   dentry1.sh       733  Shell-script  /home/romeo/project5/dentry1.sh
     convert.sh       520  Shell-script  /home/romeo/project5/convert.sh
     *Completions*    172  Completion List
     conv2pm6.sh      322  Shell-script  /home/romeo/project5/conv2pm6.sh
     *scratch*          0  Lisp Interaction
 *   *Messages*       240  Fundamental
 *% *Buffer List*    431  Buffer Menu


 --1-:%*-F1  *Buffer List*    (Buffer Menu Abbrev)--L3--All--------------------------
```

[Ctrl-x] i note1   *Filename entered at prompt*

You can also place the output of a command in your file:

[Ctrl-u][Alt-!] date   *Command output in file*

This is a very useful feature for documentation authors, who need to feature command output in their text. There's no need to save this output in a file and then read in the file. The file and buffer handling commands are listed in Table 5.10.

5.16   Escape to Shell

You can make a temporary exit to the shell without quitting the editor. Generally, with any of the shells that feature job control *(10.11)*, a *[Ctrl-z]* suspends the application and produces the shell prompt. This feature works both in **vi** and **emacs**, but **emacs** has a separate command of its own. Just press

```
[Ctrl-x][Ctrl-z]
[2]+ Stopped                    emacs emfile
$ _
```

There you see the suspension of editing and return of the shell prompt. You can do some work at the shell, and then enter **fg** to return to **emacs**. **fg** is an internal command of the shell that resumes the last foreground job.

If your shell doesn't support job control, you can still have the shell prompt in your editor window. Use the **shell** command:

[Alt-x] shell   *Like* :sh *in* vi

T A B L E 5.10   *File and Buffer Handling Commands in* **emacs**

Command	Function
[Ctrl-x][Ctrl-f]	Stops editing current file and edits another file
[Ctrl-x][Ctrl-v]	Replaces current buffer with another file
[Alt-x] revert-buffer	Loads last saved edition of current file (like *Revert* in Microsoft Windows)
[Alt-x] recover-file	Loads the autosaved file
[Ctrl-x] b[Enter]	Returns to most recently edited buffer
[Ctrl-x] b and select from list	Edits another buffer
[Ctrl-x][Ctrl-b]	Displays buffer list
[Alt-x] shell	Starts a UNIX shell session in a buffer named shell
[Ctrl-x] i foo	Reads file foo at current cursor position
[Ctrl-u][Alt-!] head -3 foo	Reads first three lines of foo at current cursor position
[Ctrl-x] k	Kills current buffer

This replaces the current window with a new buffer named she11. The session that you engage in at the prompt is held in this buffer. This means that all keystrokes and command output are stored in this buffer. You can return to the immediately previous buffer with *[Ctrl-x]* b *[Enter]*. Note that **exit** at the prompt will kill the shell but not the window.

If it's only a single command that you require to run, you don't need to escape to a shell prompt. Just use

[Alt-!]   *Prompts for UNIX command to be run*

After you key in the command to execute (using the *[Shift]* key if necessary for the !), **emacs** runs the command in a separate window (a buffer called *Shell Command Output*). Your cursor will, however, remain in the current window.

Tip

If the **script** command is not available in your system, you can record a UNIX session conducted at the shell prompt by saving the buffer named she11. This buffer is created with *[Alt-x]* she11.

5.17 Using the Help Facility (*[Ctrl-h]*)

emacs has quite an elaborate help facility which provides you with detailed information about its commands, keys, modes and variables. You can call up the tutorial or the multilevel info documentation as well. Together, they can assist you in knowing every aspect of the system. We can't discuss all these features in this chapter but only the ones that you'll require every day. The help facility is organized in a number of modules, and they are all invoked with *[Ctrl-h]* (Table 5.11).

5.17.1 Accessing Help by Key (*[Ctrl-h]*k)

There are two problems that beginners generally face; they are unable to remember the function of a key sequence or what a command does. The first problem is handled by *[Ctrl-h]* k (key). When you press this key, **emacs** asks you to enter a key sequence:

Describe key: *[Ctrl-y]*   *Seeking help for [Ctrl-y]*

TABLE 5.11   *The **emacs** Help Facility*

Command	Deals with
[Ctrl-h] k	Function performed by keystroke (detailed)
[Ctrl-h] c	Function performed by keystroke (one-line)
[Ctrl-h] f	Function performed by command
[Ctrl-h] w	Key binding available for command
[Ctrl-h] v	Function of variable and its current setting
[Ctrl-h] a	Commands that use a concept
[Ctrl-h] t	Runs tutorial
[Ctrl-h] i	Runs **info** reader

This is the command we use to paste copied or deleted text. **emacs** immediately responds with a detailed description of the key sequence in a separate window:

```
C-y runs the command yank
    which is an interactive compiled Lisp function.
(yank &optional ARG)

Reinsert the last stretch of killed text.
More precisely, reinsert the stretch of killed text most recently
killed OR yanked.  Put point at end, and set mark at beginning.
With just C-u as argument, same but put point at beginning (and mark at end).
With argument N, reinsert the Nth most recently killed stretch of killed
text.
See also the command M-y.
```

This explanation is quite detailed and should be quite useful. Since your cursor is still in the previous window, you can close the help window with *[Ctrl-x]* 1.

5.17.2   Accessing Help by Function Name (*[Ctrl-h]* f and *[Ctrl-h]* w)

emacs supports over a thousand commands, and it's practically impossible to remember the functions of all of them. Some of these commands have key bindings and some have not. *[Ctrl-h]* f and *[Ctrl-h]* w are two key sequences that you'll need to use to know more about these commands. To know what a command does, use *[Ctrl-h]* f (function) and then enter the command name at the prompt:

```
Describe function (default *): recover-file
```

Like before, **emacs** opens a separate window with a description of the function performed by the **recover-file** command:

```
recover-file is an interactive compiled Lisp function.
(recover-file FILE)

Visit file FILE, but get contents from its last auto-save file.
```

This description was short enough to fit in the window, but sometimes you'll need to scroll the other window (with *[Ctrl][Alt]* v) to see the rest of the text. Note that you can't scroll back; to do that, you'll have to visit that window first (with *[Ctrl-x]* o).

There's another problem you'll face sometimes; you'll remember the command name but not its key binding. For instance, you'll probably remember that interactive substitution is performed with the **query-replace** command, but can you recall the key binding that acts as a shortcut? Use the *[Ctrl-h]* w command (**where-is**):

```
Where is command (default *): query-replace
```

emacs shows you a single-line message at the minibuffer:

```
query-replace is on M-%, menu-bar search query-replace
```

This shows *[Alt-%]* as the shortcut, but it also guides you to the menu option *Search>query-replace* that is available at the top of the screen. You'll be able to take advantage of this menu facility when you use **emacs** in the X Window system.

5.17.3   Viewing the Tutorial and info Documentation (*[Ctrl-h]* t and *[Ctrl-h]* i)

Finally, let's have a look at two other help features that you'll find quite useful. You can invoke the **emacs** tutorial with *[Ctrl-h]* t (tutorial). This is an excellent introduction to the editor and serves as good reading material for beginners. Use *[Ctrl-x]* b to quit to the previous buffer.

More detailed than the tutorial is the info documentation that is invoked with *[Ctrl-h]* i (info). Depending on the system you are using, this could take you to the top of the "INFO tree." Linux systems offer a lot of info documentation for many commands, and you could see the opening screen showing all these commands. Now move your cursor across the window and locate the line showing emacs. Just press *[Enter]* to view the opening page of the **emacs** documentation.

You'll recall *(2.8)* that info documentation is organized in multiple nodes (levels). The nodes are indicated by asterisks at the beginning of the line. You can take your cursor to any of these nodes and press *[Enter]* to obtain detailed information on that topic. To return to the previous level, use **u**. To quit the info mode, use **q**. For refreshing your knowledge of the **info** commands, look up Table 2.4.

The features of **emacs** discussed so far should be quite adequate for your day-to-day editing tasks. After you feel comfortable using these techniques, you might like to use some of its powerful features which can improve your productivity even further. If you know **emacs** well by now, then just read on.

➤   *G O I N G   F U R T H E R*

5.18   Marking Text

You can mark several positions in the file and later locate them. Unlike *bookmarks* (which are also offered by **emacs**), these marks are invisible and disappear when you quit the editor. Both the mark and locate commands have to be used with a letter to make a unique mark. To mark a location with the character q, move the cursor to the required location and press

[Ctrl-x] /q   *Enter q at prompt*

After you have moved your cursor away from the marked location, you can move back to this mark by using

[Ctrl-x] jq   *Enter q at prompt*

In this way you can mark up to 26 locations in the file, using the different characters of the alphabet. Just remember to use / to mark and j to jump to that mark.

5.18.1   Using Bookmarks

Marks disappear as soon as you exit the editor. If you often edit multiple files existing in different directories, you must have felt the tedium of entering the pathname of a file every time you wanted to access it. **emacs** has a **bookmark** feature which not only marks a location in the current file, but in any file located anywhere. You can use this feature to call up other files with minimal keystrokes.

Let's say you want to bookmark the current location in the current file named news.1st. Just use

[Ctrl-x] rm

The prompt Set bookmark (news.1st): appears in the minibuffer. **emacs** asks you to enter a name for the mark, offering the current filename as default. The name of the bookmark need not be a single character; you can even have spaces in the name.

Once you have defined your bookmark, you can access the page *from any file* by using

[Ctrl-x] rb   *Enter the bookmark name here*

Tip

You can set bookmarks for the files that you edit regularly, especially the configuration files of your system—like .profile, .exrc, .emacs etc. **emacs** retains all bookmarks and stores them in the file .emacs.bmk in the home directory. No more *[Ctrl-x][Ctrl-f]* at least for these files!

5.19   Filtering Text

Like in **vi**, **emacs** also lets you run a UNIX command to change the text on the screen. This is possible with only those commands that take input from one command and send output to another one. These commands are called **filters**, and this book discusses all the important filters available in the system.

The UNIX **sort** command (a filter) can sort the contents of a file, but it can also sort the contents of an **emacs** screen. Generally, to filter text you have to do this:

1. First select a region, using *[Ctrl-x][Ctrl-x]* to confirm the location of point and mark if felt necessary.
2. Use *[Ctrl-u][Alt-|]*. When you use this sequence, **emacs** prompts you for the command:

   Shell command on region: **sort**

3. Enter the UNIX command to be run. After you enter sort and press *[Enter]*, the filtered output is shown in the same window.

To repeat the exercise that was done with **vi** *(4.19)*, you have to enter these key sequences:

1. *[Alt-x]* goto-line*[Enter]* 21—Goes to line 21
2. *[Ctrl][Spacebar]*—Marks beginning of text
3. *[Alt-x]* goto-line*[Enter]* 40—Goes to line 40
4. *[Ctrl-u][Alt-|]* sort—Runs **sort** command on region

Note

To have the output in a separate window, everything remains the same except that you don't use *[Ctrl-u]* with the *[Alt-|]* sequence.

Tip

emacs has a special command for sorting lines. Select a region and then use *[Alt-x]* sort-lines. The sorted output replaces the original lines.

5.20   Storing Multiple Text Sections

Like **vi**, **emacs** supports the retention of up to 26 blocks of text in a number of special buffers (named after the letters of the alphabet). To make use of these buffers, you have to first define a region for each one of them. Once a region is defined, use these commands with any buffer name, say v:

[Ctrl-x] xv	*Text copied to buffer* v
[Ctrl-u][Ctrl-x] xv	*Text deleted to buffer* v

The text in the region is copied or deleted to the buffer v. Move to the new location and use

[Ctrl-x] gv	*Text put from buffer* v

We carried out a similar exercise with **vi**, so let's consolidate our knowledge with a simple example. We'll copy 10 lines from one file to another file foo and put these lines below line 30. This is what we have to do:

1. Select region comprising the 10 lines.
2. *[Ctrl-x]* xa to copy those lines into buffer a.
3. *[Ctrl-x][Ctrl-f]* foo to switch to file foo.
4. *[Alt-x]* goto-line *[Enter]* 31 to move to line 31.
5. *[Enter]* to insert a blank line (cursor now on line 32).
6. *[Ctrl-p]* to move back to line 31.
7. *[Ctrl-x]* ga to put back the 10 lines after line 30.

Using this feature of named buffers, you can now copy and move text freely across a file, and even from one file to another. But do remember that you must not leave the editor at any time.

5.21   Recovering Multiple Deletions (*[Alt-y]*)

You can recover *many* of your deletions provided you follow certain rules. **emacs** allows the recovery of the last 30 entries in the kill ring. They need not all be deletions; copied text also goes to the kill ring. They need not be complete lines either; you can recover *any* text that is deleted with a kill operation. This basically means any deletion operation which is not *[Ctrl-d]*.

You have learned to delete text with *[Ctrl-k]* and *[Alt-d]*. You have also deleted or copied text in a region with *[Ctrl-w]* and *[Alt-w]*, respectively. When you have made multiple deletions or copies using these techniques, move to the new location and restore the most recent deletion or copy with *[Ctrl-y]*. If that is not the right one, this time use

[Alt-y]	*Works only after an initial [Ctrl-y]*

This undoes the last restoration or copy and restores the next entry—in a single keystroke. In this way, you can recover up to 30 entries from the kill ring, which should be quite adequate for most purposes.

5.22 Abbreviating Text (abbrev-mode)

emacs lets you abbreviate long words. Abbreviations can be **global** (available in all modes) or **local** (valid only for current mode). We need not go into the nuances of these modes but simply assume that we are working in the global mode. Unlike in **vi**, you have to switch on the abbreviation mode (off by default) before you can use the feature. To turn it on, use

[Alt-x] abbrev-mode*[Enter]*

The word Abbrev should now appear in the mode line. Once the mode is enabled, you can define an abbreviation by first typing it on the input screen where you type in your text. To take an example, we'll abbreviate the Java command System.out.println to sopl. We have to first enter sopl in any line, press *[Ctrl-x]*, and then input the string aig:

sopl*[Ctrl-x]*aig   *Use* ail *for local abbreviation*

emacs now prompts for the expansion. Type System.out.println in the minibuffer, and you'll see sopl expanded to this string. You have defined your abbreviation.

Once you have decided that you need all abbreviations on startup, you should save them from here. Use *[Alt-x]* write-abbrev-file and enter, say, .emacs_abbrevs as the name of the file that will hold your abbreviations. This saves all your abbreviations in that file. Now, you must tell **emacs** that it should enable abbreviation and load this file at startup. Place these lines in .emacs:

(setq-default abbrev-mode t)   t *indicates true value*
(read-abbrev-file "~/.emacs_abbrevs")

These are lines written in LISP, so don't worry too much about interpreting them. Your abbreviations are now available on startup. **setq-default** is the command used to set global variables, and we'll know about it shortly. If you want all future abbreviations to go to the file, then place an additional entry in .emacs:

(setq save-abbrevs t)

You can list (**list-abbrevs**), edit (**edit-abbrevs**) and disable your abbreviations (**kill-all-abbrevs**). Note that all these commands must be preceded by *[Alt-x]*.

Tip

emacs has a nifty abbreviation feature which doesn't require you to define the abbreviation at all. If you have already typed in a long word, next time enter enough of the word to make it unique, and then type *[Alt-/]*; emacs completes the abbreviation for you. If it's an abbreviation required only in the current document, you can use it like this instead of defining it.

5.23 Customizing the Keyboard

In **emacs**, every valid key sequence you press is bound to an **emacs** internal command. **emacs** has over a thousand such commands, only a few of which are actually bound to the keys. For mapping an often-used sequence, you'll have to use the **global-set-key** function.

vi users, who use **30G** to move to line 30, are generally horrified at having to use *[Alt-x]* goto-line for moving to a specific line number. We must have a key binding for this, and we propose to use *[Ctrl-x]* w for this purpose. But before that, let's check whether it already has one binding. Start help with *[Ctrl-h]*, and then press c to be prompted for the key sequence:

```
Describe key briefly: C-x w                            Enter [Ctrl-x] w
C-x w is undefined
```

Now that you know that this key combination is undefined, use the **global-set-key** command (with *[Alt-x]*) to map the **goto-line** command. **emacs** requires you to provide two inputs:

```
Set key globally: C-x-w                               The key sequence
Set key C-x w to command: goto-line                  The mapped command
```

The **goto-line** command is now bound to *[Ctrl-x]* w. You can press this key sequence and then enter the line number to navigate to a line. To make this binding permanent, just place this entry at the end of your .emacs file:

```
(global-set-key "\C-xw" 'goto-line)                   There's a ' here
```

Note the unusual LISP syntax which requires the key binding to be enclosed within double quotes. The command to run must be preceded by just one single quote. Note the conventions used: \C-x is *[Ctrl-x]*. The other escape sequences that you can use here are: \e for *[Esc]* and \r for *[Enter]*.

Tip

Use **emacs**' help facility to find out the **emacs** command that a key sequence executes internally. Invoke help with *[Ctrl-h]* c (or k) and enter any sequence. **emacs** will tell you the name of the internal command that is executed. If it is undefined, then you can safely use it for mapping purposes. Even if it is defined, decide for yourself whether you really need the existing function. If not, then you can redefine it.

5.24 Using Macros

The **global-set-key** function is useful for mapping a keyboard sequence to an **emacs** internal command. But we often need to map a set of keystrokes to a short sequence. In **vi**, the **:map** command handles this job moderately well; **emacs** needs to use a **macro**. This macro is a user-defined command that executes a group of key sequences.

Macro definitions start with the *[Ctrl-x]* (command. Once pressed, **emacs** goes into the "recording" mode and records all your keystrokes. The definition ends when you press *[Ctrl-x]*). (This sequence is not recorded, of course.)

emacs badly needs to have a short key sequence for copying the current line, so we'll use a macro:

[Ctrl-x] (	*Definition starts*
[Ctrl-a]	*Moves to beginning of line*
[Ctrl][Spacebar]	*Sets mark*
[Ctrl-e]	*Goes to end of line*
[Alt-w]	*Copies region*
[Ctrl-x])	*Definition ends*

This macro doesn't yet have a name, but you can execute it to copy the current line in this way:

[Ctrl-x] e   *Then place it anywhere with [Ctrl-y]*

This sequence executes the **call-last-kbd-macro** command. To save it to your .emacs file, you first need to give it a name (say, cpl). Just call up the command *[Alt-x]* name, press *[Enter]* and then input the name cpl to this macro:

Name for last kbd macro: **cpl***[Enter]*

This means that you can now go to any line and copy it by issuing the command *[Alt-x]* cpl. Open the file .emacs (with *[Ctrl-x][Ctrl-f]*), move to the end of the file, and then type this:

[Alt-x] insert-kbd-macro*[Enter]*   *Enter* cpl *at prompt*

The LISP code that **emacs** inserts into this file looks like this:

```
(fset 'cpl
   "\C-a\C-@\C-e\C-[w")                                                          C-[w is [Alt-w]
```

After you have saved .emacs, this macro named **cpl** is available for use. You can execute any named macro by using *[Alt-x]* and the macro name.

An **emacs** macro goes further and lets you define points where it will pause to take user input. We won't discuss this feature in this book.

5.25   Customizing the Editor Environment

emacs uses two types of commands to set its own variables. The **set-variable** command is used to assign values to variables from within the editor. But to make these values permanent, you have to use the **setq** and **setq-default** commands in .emacs. These variables may take on numeric, string or boolean values. Boolean values may be t or nil.

Let's consider the variable auto-save-timeout. This is set to a numeric value signifying the number of seconds of inactivity that results in an automatic saving operation. To know its default value, use the **describe-variable** command with *[Alt-x]*. This is a module of the help system that has the key binding *[Ctrl-h]* v. After you have entered this key sequence, **emacs** prompts for the variable name:

Describe variable: **auto-save-timeout**   *Use the completion feature*

emacs now shows you the current setting in a separate window along with a few lines of related documentation:

```
auto-save-timeout's value is
30

Documentation:
*Number of seconds idle time before auto-save.
Zero or nil means disable auto-saving due to idleness.
    .......
```

After you have finished viewing the documentation, kill this window with *[Ctrl-x]* 1. You can now change the value of this variable to 60 seconds with the **set-variable** command (with *[Alt-x]*):

```
Set variable: auto-save-timeout                                        Use completion
Set auto-save-timeout to value: 60
```

This sets the value for the rest of the session when using this buffer. To make it permanent, you have to use either **setq** or **setq-default** in .emacs:

```
(setq auto-save-timeout 60)                                 Note the enclosing parentheses
```

You can also set the number of keystrokes that result in an autosave operation. This is controlled by the variable auto-save-interval. By default, it is normally set to 300, but you can change it in .emacs:

```
(setq auto-save-interval 200)
```

emacs makes a distinction between **local** and **global variables**. A local variable applies only to the buffer in which it is defined and overrides any global values that may be defined for the variable. The **setq** command sets a local variable, and **setq-default** sets a variable to its default (global) value. We'll not go into further details except suggest that if the **setq** command doesn't work, use the **setq-default** command instead.

Now, let's discuss briefly the significance of some of the other important variable settings. This is how the settings are placed in .emacs:

```
(setq-default case-fold-search nil)
(setq tab-width 4)
(setq line-number-mode t)
(setq blink-matching-paren nil)
(setq kill-ring-max 50)
(setq abbrev-mode t)
```

When case-fold-search is set to nil searches become case-sensitive. You can set the number of spaces a tab is to expand to (tab-width). If the line number is not visible in the mode line, then check the value of line-number-mode. The cursor moves to the { or (and then comes back to their closing counterparts if blink-matching-paren is set to t. (Here, it is not.) If the default number of deletions that can be held in the kill ring proves to be inadequate, then you can increase the number (kill-ring-max). Sometimes, you might like to turn off the abbreviation feature (abbrev-mode nil).

Tip

After you have modified .emacs with **emacs** itself, you need not quit **emacs** and restart it for the changes to take effect. Just use the *[Alt-x]* load-file command to make **emacs** reread .emacs. This facility is not available in **vi**.

SUMMARY

emacs is a full-screen "mode-less" editor. The last line (*minibuffer*) shows system messages and accepts user input. The line above that (*mode line*) displays the editor modes and the filename. **emacs** reads the file .emacs on startup.

emacs uses the *[Ctrl]* and *[Meta]* keys for executing commands. The *[Esc]* or *[Alt]* keys can often be used in place of the *[Meta]* key. You can enter **emacs** commands using *[Alt-x]*, followed by the command text. A command sequence can be canceled with *[Ctrl-g]*.

To replace text, the **overwrite-mode** command has to be invoked with *[Alt-x]*. A control character is entered by preceding the command with *[Ctrl-q]*.

emacs autosaves a file every 300 keystrokes. You can save a file using the same name (*[Ctrl-x][Ctrl-s]*) or a different name (*[Ctrl-x][Ctrl-w]*). You can quit the editor with or without saving (*[Ctrl-x][Ctrl-c]*). You can recover an autosaved file (**recover-file**) in the event of a system crash.

You can use a *digit argument* (*[Alt-n]*, where *n* is an integer) to repeat a command. *[Ctrl-u]* executed a number of times in succession before the command multiplies the number of repeats by a factor of 4.

The keys b, f, p and n used with *[Ctrl]* move the cursor back, forward, to the previous and next lines. You can move to the beginning (*[Ctrl-a]*) or end (*[Ctrl-e]*) of a line. The *[Alt]* key, when used with b and f, moves the cursor by units of words. Scrolling is done with *[Ctrl-v]* (forward) and *[Alt-v]* (backward).

You require the **goto-line** command to move to a specific line number. You can also directly go to the beginning (*[Alt-<]*) or end (*[Alt->]*) of a file.

emacs lets you define a region by first marking its beginning (*[Ctrl][Spacebar]*) and then moving the cursor to the other end. You can view the extreme points (*[Ctrl-x] [Ctrl-x]*), and even define the entire buffer as a region (*[Ctrl-x]* h).

You can delete a character (*[Ctrl-d]*), kill a word (*[Alt-d]*) and a line (*[Ctrl-k][Ctrl-k]*). You can kill from the current cursor position to the beginning (*[Alt-0] [Ctrl-k]*) or end (*[Ctrl-k]*) of a line. You can also kill a group of blank lines (*[Ctrl-x][Ctrl-o]*). Killed text goes to the *kill ring* from where it can be recovered later.

You can kill (*[Ctrl-w]*) or copy text in a region (*[Alt-w]*). Killed or copied text is put in the new location with *[Ctrl-y]*.

Words are capitalized entirely (*[Alt-u]*) or only the first letter (*[Alt-c]*). *[Alt-l]* converts words to lowercase. A region is converted to uppercase with *[Ctrl-x][Ctrl-u]*.

emacs offers a *command completion* feature that lets you enter some text, and then use the *[Tab]* key to have the command completed without entering the rest of it.

Editing can be undone and redone with the same key—*[Ctrl-x]* u or *[Ctrl-_]*. **emacs** starts redoing when undoing is complete.

emacs offers an *incremental search* facility, by which the search starts the moment you enter part of the search string. It also offers the *nonincremental search*. *[Ctrl-s]* is used in both methods both to begin and repeat the search.

emacs supports *regular expressions* which let you use an expression containing some special characters to represent multiple strings. Using *[Ctrl][Alt]* s, these expressions can be used for both types of searches.

You can search and replace noninteractively (**replace-string**) or interactively using the *query-replace* feature (*[Alt-%]*). You can do both with regular expressions too (**replace-regexp** and **query-replace-regexp**).

You can split the screen into two (*[Ctrl-x]* 2) for viewing the same file. You can also open a new window (*[Ctrl-x]* b), switch between windows (*[Ctrl-x]* o) or increase the window size (*[Ctrl-x]* ^). You can display only the current window (*[Ctrl-x]* 1) and kill all other windows.

You can insert the contents of another file (*[Ctrl-x]* i), move to an alternate file (*[Ctrl-x][Ctrl-f]*), return to the last edited file (*[Ctrl-x]* b) and revert to the last saved version (**revert-buffer**).

You can run a UNIX command from inside the editor with *[Ctrl-u][Alt-!]*.

emacs supports an extensive help facility which uses *[Ctrl-h]* as the common keystroke. You can find out what a key does (*[Ctrl-h]* k), the function of a command (*[Ctrl-h]* f) or its key binding (*[Ctrl-h]* w). You can also view the tutorial (*[Ctrl-h]* t) or the info documentation (*[Ctrl-h]* i).

GOING FURTHER

You can mark up to 26 areas in a text with *[Ctrl-x]* / and a letter, and access the marked location with *[Ctrl-x]* j and the letter. You can even bookmark a location (*[Ctrl-x]* rm) and access it from any file (*[Ctrl-x]* rb). All bookmarks are automatically saved in .emacs.bmk.

You can run a UNIX command (*[Ctrl-u][Alt-|]*) on a region which *filters* the contents of the region.

emacs uses up to 26 buffers (named a to z) to store text, using *[Ctrl-x]* x to precede the buffer name. The text can be put in another file with *[Ctrl-x]* g and the name.

Killed text can be recovered with *[Alt-y]* which restores the next entry from the kill ring every time it is pressed.

Abbreviation has to be enabled (**abbrev-mode**) before a string can be abbreviated (*[Ctrl-x]* aig). Any **emacs** command can be bound to a key sequence (**global-set-key**). Abbreviations can be written to a separate file, but key bindings are stored in .emacs.

Macro definitions start with *[Ctrl-x]* (and end with *[Ctrl-x]*). You can execute the last defined macro (*[Ctrl-x]* e), name it (*[Alt-x]* name) and then store it in .emacs (**insert-kbd-macro**).

Variables are set with **setq** and **setq-default**. You can make your searches case-sensitive (case-fold-search), set the period of inactivity for autosaving (auto-save-timeout and auto-save-interval) and alter the size of the kill ring (kill-ring-max).

SELF-TEST

5.1   If you see three hyphens (---) on the mode line, what does that indicate?

5.2   You entered an incorrect command and find **emacs** asking you for more input. How do you get out of this mess?

5.3   Why doesn't *[Ctrl-h]* work in backspacing?

5.4   If the *[Insert]* key doesn't take you to overwrite mode, what command will you use?

5.5   Suppose you are editing a file foo1, and you now want to save the current buffer to foo2. How will you do it?

5.6   How do you delete all text from the current cursor position to the end of line?

5.7   How do you remove all text from a line without deleting the line?

5.8   What's the best way of deleting 16 words?

5.9   How will you locate the 40th character of a line?

5.10   With which commands do you scroll?

5.11   How do you reach the end of a file?

5.12   How do you append the string */ at the end of a line?

5.13   How will you search for the words Richard Stallman, and then change Richard to Dick in some of them?

5.14   How will you revert to the last-saved version of a file?

5.15   How do you globally replace CREATE with DROP using the minimum number of keystrokes?

5.16   In the midst of your session you want to find out the time. How do you do that without leaving **emacs**?

EXERCISES

5.1   What is the file **emacs** reads on startup? How can you make sure that it doesn't read the file?

5.2   If you see the string ^[, what could it represent? How do you enter it?

5.3   What's the difference between *[Ctrl-d]* and *[Alt-d]*?

5.4   What's the difference between the *digit argument* and the *universal argument*? Which keys do they use?

5.5   How will you delete 20 lines without using a digit argument?

5.6   You tried to delete three lines with *[Alt-3][Ctrl-k]*, and it didn't work. Why do you think it happened and what do you do?

5.7   If you delete four lines of text by using *[Ctrl-k]* four times, how can you recover all the four lines?

5.8   You have incorrectly entered the word Comptuer. How will you correct it to Computer?

5.9   Which editor will you use for joining all the 1000 lines in a file to form a single line, and how?

5.10   You executed a **goto-line** command in the current session and now want to use it again. Describe two ways of doing that using as few keystrokes as possible.

5.11   How will you toggle between the beginning and end of a file?

5.12   Use the command completion feature to complete the following commands with the minimum number of keystrokes:

(i) `replace-string`   (ii) `recover-file`   (iii) `query-replace`

5.13   How do you redo what you have just undone?

5.14   How will you convert the entire contents of a file to uppercase?

5.15   While undoing, how do you determine the point at which the buffer's status is the same as the last-saved version?

5.16   Explain which of the following commands can be undone:

(i) *[Ctrl-f]*   (ii) *[Ctrl-p]*   (iii) *[Ctrl-d]*   (iv) *[Ctrl-t]*

5.17   How do you move to the end of every sentence?

5.18   Is it possible to have the first few replacements done interactively and the rest automatically?

5.19   You made some substitution with *[Alt-x]* `query-replace`. How will you repeat this command without reentering it?

5.20   How do you increase the number of lines in the current window by four?

5.21   How do you delete text from the current line to the beginning of the file?

5.22   How can you edit a second file without leaving **emacs** and then toggle between the two files?

GOING FURTHER

5.23   You want to redefine one of your control keys. How do you find out whether it already has a key binding or not?

5.24   Devise two ways of sorting the entire buffer.

5.25   How do you delete line numbers 11 to 30 and then restore lines 11 to 20 and 21 to 30 at two different locations? What precaution do you need to take?

5.26   How do you copy several sections of text from one file to another?

5.27   You defined an abbreviation `re` to expand to `regular expression`, and when you try to input the word `re-rating`, you find the expansion getting in the way. What do you do?

5.28   Can you use an abbreviation without defining one?

5.29   Write a macro that removes all trailing spaces in a file.

5.30   How do you customize **emacs** so that it is always able to restore the last 50 kill operations?

5.31   What is the difference between **recover-file** and **revert-buffer**? Which file is generally more recent?

GOING FURTHER

KEY TERMS

autosave *(5.4.1)*
bookmarks *(5.18.1)*
character class *(5.13)*
command completion *(5.10)*
digit argument *(5.5)*
file buffer *(5.2)*
filter *(5.19)*
global abbreviation *(5.22)*
global variable *(5.25)*
incremental search *(5.12.1)*
insert mode *(5.3.1)*
key binding *(5.1.3)*
kill ring *(5.8.2)*
killing text *(5.8.1)*
local abbreviation *(5.22)*

local variables *(5.25)*
macro *(5.24)*
mark *(5.7)*
minibuffer *(5.1)*
mode line *(5.1)*
nonincremental search *(5.12.3)*
overwrite mode *(5.3.1)*
point *(5.7)*
query replace *(5.14.2)*
recursive editing *(5.14.2)*
region *(5.7)*
regular expression *(5.13)*
universal argument *(5.5.1)*
word *(5.8.1)*

## CHAPTER 6

The File System

U NIX looks at everything as a file. Any UNIX file system will have tens of thousands of files. If you write a program, you add one more file to the system. When you compile and run it, you add some more. Files grow rapidly, and if they are not organized properly, you'll find it virtually impossible to access them. Proper file organization requires an elaborate directory-based storage system so a user can "place" oneself in a directory (folder), or transfer files from one directory to another.

The file system in UNIX is one of its simple and conceptually clean features. The system has proved so useful that it has been widely adopted by other systems including Windows. In this chapter, you'll handle directories and navigate freely in the file system. You'll copy and remove files in these directories and learn to display and print files. You'll also use the commands that UNIX provides to use the disk space efficiently. This chapter handles files and directories, but not their attributes (properties). File attributes along with their commands are taken up in the next chapter.

Objectives

- Learn how UNIX divides files into three categories. *(6.1)*
- Understand the considerations involved in framing a filename. *(6.2)*
- Know the parent-child relationship between files. *(6.3)*
- Learn the important directories of the UNIX file system. *(6.4)*
- Understand the difference between *absolute* and *relative pathnames*. *(6.6 and 6.8)*
- Check and change your directory with **pwd** and **cd**. *(6.5 and 6.7)*
- Create and remove directories with **mkdir** and **rmdir**. *(6.9 and 6.10)*
- Copy, remove and rename files with **cp**, **rm** and **mv**. *(6.11, 6.12 and 6.13)*
- Display and create a file with **cat**. *(6.14)*
- Identify the type of file with **file**. *(6.15)*
- Print a file with **lp** (or **lpr**). *(6.16)*
- Find out disk space usage and free space with **df** and **du**. *(6.17 and 6.18)*
- Compress a file with **compress**, **gzip** and **zip**. *(6.19)*

6.1 The File

A UNIX file is a storehouse of information; for the most part, it's simply a sequence of characters. UNIX places no restriction on the structure of a file. A file contains exactly those bytes that you put into it—be it a source program, executable code or anything else. It neither contains its own size nor its attributes (properties), including the end-of-file mark. It doesn't even contain its own name!

The founders' vision of a file is all encompassing; it includes directories and devices in its definition. Whether it's a C program you execute, or a directory you use to house groups of such programs, they are all files in the UNIX sense. This concept also extends to each and every device you find in your machine—the hard disk, printer, tape, CD-ROM drive or terminal. The shell is also a file, and so is the kernel. And if you are wondering how UNIX treats the main memory in your system, it's a file too!

The most notable feature of the UNIX file system is that UNIX makes *little* distinction between these various types of files. Many commands (which are also files themselves) work with all types of files, and you don't need to indicate specifically the type of file you are using. Many of the commands used to access a disk file are also used to access the tape drive. With limited exceptions, UNIX doesn't offer separate commands to access CD-ROMs and tapes; the same command often accesses both.

Although everything is treated as a file by UNIX, it's still necessary to divide a file into three categories:

- Ordinary file—Also known as regular file. It contains only data as a stream of characters.
- Directory file—A folder containing the names of other files and directories.
- Device file—It represents all hardware devices.

The reason why we make this distinction is that the significance of a file's attributes depends on its type. Read permission for an ordinary file means something quite different from that for a directory or a device. Moreover, you can't directly put something into a directory file, and a device file isn't really a stream of characters. While the vast majority of commands work with all types of files, some don't. For a proper understanding of the file system, you must understand the significance of these files.

Note

A UNIX file doesn't contain any of its attributes nor does it contain the end-of-file mark. The name of the file is not stored in the file either.

6.1.1   Ordinary File

The traditional file is of the **ordinary** or **regular** type. It consists of a stream of data resident on some permanent magnetic media. You can put anything you want into this type of file. This includes all data, source programs, object and executable code, all UNIX commands, as well as any files created by the user. Commands like **cat**, **ls**, and so forth are treated as ordinary or regular files.

The most common type of ordinary file is the **text file**. This is just a regular file containing printable characters. The programs that you write are text files. The UNIX commands that you use, or the C programs that you execute, are not. The characteristic feature of text files is that the data inside them are divided into groups of lines, with each line terminated by the *linefeed* (LF) character (ASCII decimal value 10). On UNIX systems, the linefeed character is also known as the newline character *(4.10.2)*, and when we talk of newline, we actually mean LF. This character isn't visible and doesn't appear in hard copy output. It's generated by the system when you press the *[Enter]* key.

6.1.2 Directory File

A **directory file** contains no external data but maintains some details of the files and subdirectories that it contains. The UNIX file system is organized with a number of such directories and subdirectories, and you can also create them as and when you need. You often need to group a set of files pertaining to a specific application and have them under a directory. This allows two or more files in separate directories to have the same filename.

A directory file contains two fields for each file—its name and identification number. (Every file has a number called the **inode number**.) If a directory houses, say, 10 files, there will be 10 such entries in the directory file. You can't, however, write directly into a directory file; that power rests only with the kernel. When an ordinary file is created or removed, its corresponding directory file is automatically updated by the kernel with the relevant information about the file.

You don't need to concern yourself with further details at this stage. The directory file is further discussed in the next chapter.

Note

It is the directory file that contains the names of all files resident in the directory.

6.1.3 Device File

The definition of a file has been broadened by UNIX to consider even physical devices as files. This definition includes printers, tapes, floppy drives, CD-ROMs, hard disks and terminals. Although this may appear confusing initially, it's really an advantage; some of the commands used to access a disk file also work with **device files**.

The device file is special; it doesn't contain any data whatsoever. (This file is not a "sequence of characters" in contrast to what we had observed earlier.) Any output directed to it will be reflected onto the respective physical device associated with the filename. When you issue a command to print a file, you are really directing the file's output to the file associated with the printer. When you back up files onto tape, you are "symbolically" using the file associated with the tape drive. The kernel takes care of this by mapping these special files to their respective devices.

Now that you understand the three types of files, you shouldn't feel baffled by subsequent use of the word in the book. The term *file* will often be used in this book to refer to any of these types, though it will mostly be used to mean an ordinary file. The real meaning of the term should be evident from its context.

6.2 What's in a (File)name?

On most UNIX systems today, a filename can consist of up to 255 characters. Though this figure is normally never reached, if you enter more than 255 characters when specifying a filename, only the first 255 characters are effectively interpreted by the system. Some systems, however, report an error message.

Files may or may not have extensions and can consist of practically any ASCII character except the /. Just as you can have a filename beginning with a dot, you can have one which ends with a dot too. All these are valid filenames:

```
index       .last_time      LIST.
```

If you want, you can also use control characters or other unprintable characters in a filename. These filenames can be frightening, but they are still valid:

^V^B^D-++bcd   -{}[]   @#$%□*abcd   *Space before* *

The first filename contains three control characters (*[Ctrl-v]* being the first). The second begins with a hyphen (a filename that can cause a lot of trouble). The third one apparently shows an embedded space in the name. Later, you'll learn to find out whether it actually contains a space or an unprintable character.

Many of these characters have special significance when used in the command line. To be specific, the shell metes out different treatment for characters like $, `, ?, * and &, and commands behave unpredictably if filenames have these characters. You should also avoid using control characters. In fact, you should use only the following characters when framing filenames:

- Alphabets and numerals
- The period (.)
- The hyphen (-)
- The underscore (_)

UNIX imposes no restrictions on the extension, if any, that a file should have. A shell script doesn't need to have the .sh extension, even though it helps in identification. In all cases, it's the application that imposes this restriction. For instance, the C compiler expects C program files to have .c; Java expects its source files to have .java. Windows users must also keep these two points in mind:

- A file can have many dots embedded in its name; a.b.c.d.e is a perfectly valid filename. A filename can also begin with a dot or end with one.
- UNIX is sensitive to case; chap01, Chap01 and CHAP01 are three different filenames, and it's possible for them to coexist in the same directory.

Tip

Avoid using any characters other than alphabets, numerals, the dot, hyphen and underscore character in framing a filename. Use uppercase sparingly.

Caution

Never use a - at the beginning of a filename. You'll have a tough time getting rid of it! Moreover, many commands using this filename as an argument will instead treat it as an option and report errors. For instance, if you have a file named -z, **cat -z** won't display the file but interpret it as an invalid option.

6.3   The Parent–Child Relationship

All files in UNIX are "related" to one another. The file system in UNIX is a collection of all these related files (ordinary, directory and device files) organized in a hierarchical (an inverted tree) structure. This system has also been adopted by Windows, and is visually represented in Fig. 6.1.

The notable feature in every UNIX file system is that there is a supremo, which serves as the reference point for all files. This top is called **root**, and is represented by a / (frontslash). root is actually a directory file, and it has all the subdirectories of the system under it. These subdirectories, in turn, have more subdirectories and other files

FIGURE 6.1   *The UNIX File System*

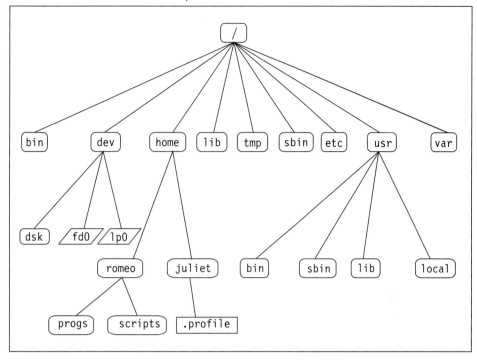

under them. For instance, bin and usr are two directories directly under root, while a second bin and lib are subdirectories under usr.

Every file, apart from root, must have a parent, and it should be possible to trace the ultimate parentage of a file to root. If the ancestry of a file can't be traced to root, the file is simply not part of the file system. This should be easy for you to understand as we all have our own families with similar *grandparent–parent–child* relationships. Thus, the home directory is the parent of romeo, while root is the parent of home and the grandparent of romeo. If you create a file login.sql under the romeo directory, then romeo will be the parent of this file.

It's also obvious that in these parent–child relationships the parent is always a directory. home and romeo are both directories as they are both parents of at least one file or directory. login.sql is an ordinary file and can't have a directory under it.

6.4   **The UNIX File System**

Now let's take a cursory look at the structure of the UNIX file system. This structure has been changing constantly over the years until AT&T proposed one in its SVR4 release. Though vendor implementations vary in detail, broadly the SVR4 structure has been adopted by most vendors.

Refer to Fig. 6.1 which shows a heavily trimmed structure of a standard UNIX file system. In real life, the root directory has many more subdirectories under it than shown, but for our initial comprehension, we'll stick to these:

- /bin and /usr/bin—These are the directories where all the commonly used UNIX commands (binaries, hence the name bin) are found. Note that the PATH variable *(2.2)* always shows these directories in its list.
- /sbin and /usr/sbin—If there's a command that you can't execute but the system administrator can, then it would probably be in one of these directories. On older systems, these directories may not exist, and /etc could then contain all administrative files. You won't be able to execute *most* (some, you can) commands in these directories. Only the system administrator's PATH has these directories in its list.
- /etc—This directory contains the configuration files of the system. You can change a very important aspect of system functioning by editing a text file in this directory. Systems not having /sbin and /usr/sbin have the administrative commands in /etc.
- /dev—This directory contains all device files. These files don't occupy space on the disk. There could be more subdirectories like dsk and rdsk in this directory.
- /home—All users are housed here. romeo would have his home directory in /home/romeo. Pre-SVR4 systems had home directories in /usr (and sometimes in other directories). The system administrator often uses a different directory for users—like /usr2, /u etc.
- /tmp—The directories where users are allowed to create temporary files. These files are wiped away regularly by the system.
- /var—The variable part of the file system. Contains all your print jobs, mail queues and incoming mail.
- /lib—Contains all library files.

There are a lot more directories, and unfortunately UNIX flavors differ in name and location of many of the system directories. Truly speaking, you really don't need to know more than this right now as file system internals are of interest mainly to the system administrator and a separate chapter has been earmarked for them.

6.5   pwd: **Knowing Your Current Directory**

It is a remarkable feature of UNIX that, like a file, a user is also placed in a specific directory of the file system on logging in. You can move around from one directory to another, but at any point of time, you are located in only one directory. This directory is known as your **current directory**.

You would often need to know what your current directory is. The **pwd** (present working directory) command tells you that:

```
$ pwd
/home/romeo                                                          This is a pathname
```

What you see above is a **pathname**—a sequence of directory names separated by slashes. This pathname shows your location with reference to the top—which is root. **pwd** here tells you that you are placed in the directory romeo, which has directory home as its parent, which in turn has root (the first /) as its parent. These slashes act as delimiters to file and directory names, except that the first slash is a synonym for root.

6.5.1   The Home Directory

When you log on to the system, UNIX automatically places you in a directory called the **home directory** (or **login directory**). It is created by the system when a user account is opened. If you log in using the login name romeo, you'll in all probability land up in a directory having the pathname /home/romeo or /usr/romeo. You can change your home directory when you like, but you can also effect a quick return to it, as you'll see soon.

The shell variable HOME knows your home directory. To evaluate it, issue this command from the shell prompt:

```
$ echo $HOME
/home/romeo
```

The home directory is decided by the system administrator at the time of opening a user account. This pathname is stored in the file /etc/passwd. On older systems, /usr/romeo would be romeo's default home directory, but modern systems use /home/romeo. It's also not uncommon to find home directories like /usr2/romeo or /u/romeo, especially in older systems.

Note

It's custom to refer to a file foo located in the home directory as $HOME/foo or as ~/foo. These naming conventions are followed throughout this text.

6.6   Absolute Pathnames

Many UNIX commands use file and directory names as arguments. These files and directories are presumed to exist in the current directory. For instance, the command

```
cat login.sql
```

will work only if the file login.sql exists in your current directory. However, if you are placed in /var and you want to access login.sql in /home/romeo, you can't obviously use the above command. There are two ways of accessing this file from your current directory /var:

- With an **absolute pathname** which uses the root directory as the ultimate reference for the file. All path references here originate from root.
- With a **relative pathname** which uses the current directory as point of reference and specifies the path relative to it.

We'll consider relative pathnames shortly. Using an absolute pathname for login.sql means that you have to use this command line from /var to display the file:

```
cat /home/romeo/login.sql                                    Can be used from any directory
```

cat here uses an absolute pathname, where the location of login.sql is specified with reference to root (the first /). When you have more than one / in a pathname, for each such /, you have to descend one level in the file system. Thus, romeo is one level below home, and two levels below root.

When you specify a file by using frontslashes to demarcate the various levels, you have a mechanism of identifying a file uniquely. No two files in a UNIX system can have identical absolute pathnames. If you have two files with the same name, they must be in different directories. This means that their pathnames will also be different. Thus, the file `/home/romeo/progs/count.pl` can coexist with the file `/home/romeo/safe/count.pl`.

Tip

If you are writing shell scripts that refer to files using an absolute pathname like /home/romeo/progs, you would do well to replace the component representing the home directory with the HOME variable—like $HOME/progs. If you now move your scripts to a different system where your home directory is, say /u2/romeo, the scripts will still work because $HOME always evaluates to the home directory in that system that's running the script.

6.6.1 Using the Absolute Pathname for a Command

A command runs in UNIX by executing its disk file. When you specify the **date** command, the system has to locate the file `date` from a list of directories specified in the PATH variable and then execute it. However, if you know the location of a particular command, you can also precede its name with the complete path. Since the file `date` resides in `/bin`, you can also use the absolute pathname:

```
$ /bin/date
Tue Feb 15 12:18:37 EST 2000
```

Nobody runs the **date** command like that. For any command that resides in the directories specified in the PATH variable, you don't need to use the absolute pathname. This PATH, you'll recall *(2.2)*, invariably has the directories `/bin` and `/usr/bin` in its list. Most UNIX commands meant for general use reside in these directories.

Note

If you execute programs residing in a directory that isn't in PATH, then the absolute pathname must be used. For example, to execute the program **less** residing in /usr/local/bin, you need to enter the absolute pathname:

```
/usr/local/bin/less
```

If you are frequently accessing programs in a certain directory, then it's better to include the directory itself in the PATH. The technique of doing that is shown in Chapter 17.

6.7   cd: **Changing Directories**

You can move around in the file system by using the **cd** (change directory) command. When used with an argument, it changes the current directory to the directory specified as the argument. To change to the directory `progs`, use **cd progs**. Check your current directory with **pwd** both before and after using **cd**:

```
$ pwd
/home/romeo
$ cd progs                                    progs must be in current directory
$ pwd
/home/romeo/progs
```

Though **pwd** displays the absolute pathname, **cd** doesn't need to use one when the directory that you are switching to is in the current directory itself. The command **cd progs** here means: "Change your subdirectory to progs that is under the current directory." Using an absolute pathname causes no harm either; use **cd /home/romeo/progs** for the same effect.

Now, if progs also contains a directory scripts under it, then you have to use this command from the home directory to change to that directory:

```
cd progs/scripts                                          progs is in current directory
```

You can also see the file convert.sh in that directory with this command:

```
cat progs/scripts/convert.sh
```

Here, we have pathnames that have slashes between the files, but they are not absolute pathnames—rather, **relative pathnames** in their simplest form. However, to change to the /bin directory you need the absolute pathname:

```
$ pwd
/home/romeo/progs
$ cd /bin                                          Absolute pathname required here because
$ pwd                                                       bin isn't in current directory
/bin
```

We can also navigate to /bin (or any directory) using a relative pathname; we are coming to that shortly. Navigation with the **cd** command using mostly absolute pathnames is illustrated in Fig. 6.2.

6.7.1   Using cd without Arguments

The **cd** command does something special when it is used without an argument:

```
$ pwd
/home/romeo/progs
$ cd
$ pwd
/home/romeo                              cd used without arguments reverts to home directory
```

Attention, Windows users! This command invoked without an argument doesn't indicate the current directory! It simply switches to the home directory—the directory where the user originally logged on to. Therefore, if you wander around in the file system, you can force an immediate return to your home directory by simply using **cd**:

```
$ cd /home/juliet
$ pwd
/home/juliet
$ cd                                                            Returns to home directory
$ pwd
/home/romeo
```

FIGURE 6.2 *Navigation with the* **cd** *Command*

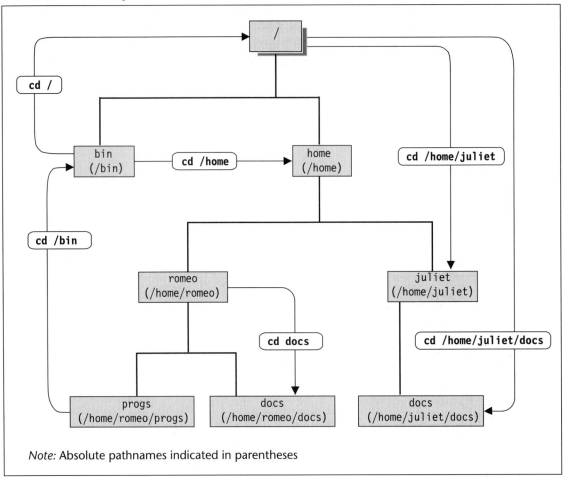

Note: Absolute pathnames indicated in parentheses

The **cd** command can sometimes fail if you don't have proper permissions to access the directory. This doesn't normally happen unless you deliberately tamper with the permissions of the directory. File and directory permissions are discussed in the next chapter.

Note

When **cd** is invoked without arguments, it simply reverts to its home directory. It doesn't show you the current directory!

6.8   Relative Pathnames (. and ..)

In the preceding example, you changed your directory from /home/romeo to /home/juliet by using **cd** with an absolute pathname:

```
cd /home/juliet
```

It's unusual that to move to a directory which has the same parent (/home) as the current directory, you have to use an absolute pathname! Further, how do you move from here to /home then? Will you use **cd /home**? This method can be tedious when the absolute pathname is long, i.e., when you are located a number of "generations" away from root. For this, UNIX offers a shortcut—the **relative pathname**. You have seen its rudimentary form before *(6.7)*, but it's best known for its use of two cryptic symbols:

- **.** (a single dot)—This represents the current directory.
- **..** (two dots)—This represents the parent directory.

We'll now use the **..** to frame relative pathnames. You would have already guessed that to move to the parent directory, you have to use **cd ..** (two dots). Now, try this out:

```
$ pwd
/home/romeo/progs
$ cd ..                                                          Moves one level up
$ pwd
/home/romeo
```

This method is compact and more useful when ascending the hierarchy. The command **cd ..** translates to this: Change your directory to the parent of the current directory.

The **..** can form a component of a pathname too. You can combine any number of such sets of **..** separated by /s. However, when a / is used with **..** it acquires a different meaning; instead of moving down a level, it moves one level *up*. For instance, to move to /home, you can always use **cd /home**. Alternatively, you can also use a relative pathname:

```
$ pwd
/home/romeo/progs
$ cd ../..                                                       Moves two levels up
$ pwd
/home
```

Now, how does one move from /home/romeo to /home/juliet? This requires a combination of the **..** and the destination directory name in the pathname:

```
$ pwd
/home/romeo
$ cd ../juliet                                           One level up and then down
$ pwd
/home/juliet
```

The use of relative pathnames using **..** is depicted in Fig. 6.3. Now let's turn to the solitary dot that refers to the current directory. Any command which uses the current directory as an argument can also work with a single dot. This means that the **cp** command *(6.11)* which also uses a directory as the last argument can be used with a dot:

```
cp ../juliet/pricelist.html .
```

FIGURE 6.3   *Navigation with Relative Pathnames*

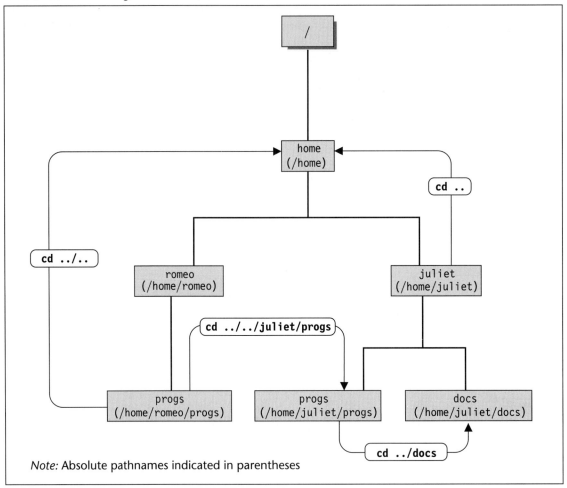

Note: Absolute pathnames indicated in parentheses

This copies the file `pricelist.html` to the current directory (`.`). Note that you didn't have to specify the filename of the copy; it's the same as the original one.

Note

When you use `../..`, the two dots on the right of the `/` represent the parent directory of the directory signified by the two dots on the left of the `/`.

You'll sometimes need to precede a *command* with `./` (a dot and a `/`). Let's assume that the current directory holds a **cat** program written by you, which is different from the UNIX **cat** in /bin. Now **cat note** will execute the **cat** command in /bin because /bin occurs earlier than . in PATH. (Use **echo $PATH** to check that out.) Using ./, you can run your own **cat** and ignore the one in /bin:

`./cat note`   cat *in current directory*

Observe that here both the command and its argument reside in the current directory.

Note

> Whether you should use an absolute or a relative pathname depends solely on the comparative number of keystrokes required to describe the pathname. In every case here, the relative pathname required fewer key depressions. Depending on where you are currently placed, an absolute pathname can sometimes require fewer keystrokes.

6.9 `mkdir`: **Making Directories**

Directories are created with the **mkdir** (make directory) command. The command is followed by the names of the directories to be created. A directory `patch` is created under the current directory like this:

```
mkdir patch
```

mkdir takes multiple arguments; you can create a number of subdirectories with one **mkdir** command:

```
mkdir patch dbs doc                                    Three directories created
```

So far, simple enough, but the UNIX system goes further and lets you create a directory tree with just one invocation of the command. For instance, the following command creates a directory tree:

```
mkdir pis pis/progs pis/data                          Creates the directory tree
```

This creates three subdirectories—`pis`, and two subdirectories under `pis`. The order of specifying the arguments is important; you obviously can't create a subdirectory before creation of its parent directory. For instance, you can't enter

```
$ mkdir pis/data pis/progs pis
mkdir: can't access pis/.
mkdir: can't access pis/.
```

Note that even though the system failed to create the two subdirectories `progs` and `data`, it has still created the `pis` directory.

Sometimes, the system refuses to create a directory:

```
$ mkdir test
mkdir: Failed to make directory "test"; Permission denied
```

This can happen for these reasons:

- The directory `test` may already exist.
- There may be an ordinary file by that name in the current directory.
- The permissions set for the current directory don't permit the creation of files and directories by the user.

We'll take up file permissions in the next chapter.

6.10   rmdir: **Removing Directories**

The **rmdir** (remove directory) command removes directories. You have to do this to remove the directory pis:

```
rmdir pis
```

Like **mkdir**, **rmdir** can also delete more than one directory in one shot. For instance, the three directories and subdirectories just created with **mkdir** can be removed by using **rmdir** with a reversed set of arguments:

```
rmdir pis/data pis/progs pis                              Arguments reversed this time
```

Note that when you delete a directory and its subdirectories, a reverse logic has to be applied. The following directory sequence used by **mkdir** is invalid in **rmdir**:

```
$ rmdir pis pis/progs pis/data
rmdir: pis: Directory not empty
```

Have you observed one thing from the error message? **rmdir** has silently deleted the lower level subdirectories, progs and data. There are two important rules that you should keep in mind when deleting directories:

- You can't use **rmdir** to delete a directory unless it is empty. In this case, the pis directory couldn't be removed because of the existence of the subdirectories progs and data under it.
- You can't remove a subdirectory unless you are placed in a directory which is hierarchically above the one you have chosen to remove. (This restriction doesn't apply in Linux.)

The first rule follows logically from the example above. But the UNIX **rm** command which works with ordinary files can be used with a special option (-r) to remove a complete directory structure. This is discussed in Section 6.12.1.

To illustrate the second cardinal rule, try removing the progs directory by executing the command from the same directory itself:

```
$ cd progs
$ pwd
/home/romeo/pis/progs
$ rmdir .                                      Trying to remove current directory works in Linux
rmdir: .: Can't remove current directory or ..
```

To remove this directory, you must position yourself in the directory above progs, i.e., pis, and then remove it from there:

```
$ cd ..                                                        Moves to parent directory
$ pwd
/home/romeo/pis
$ rmdir progs
$ _                                                               Command succeeded
```

The **mkdir** and **rmdir** commands work only with those directories *owned* by the user. Generally, a user is the owner of her home directory, and she can create and remove subdirectories (as well as regular files) in this directory or in any subdirectories created by her. However, she normally won't be able to create or remove files and directories in other users' directories. The concept of ownership will be discussed in the next chapter.

Note

Using **rmdir**, you can't remove a subdirectory unless it's empty, and you are positioned in its parent directory. However, with the **rm** command, you can remove any directory whether it is empty or not. Linux makes an exception; it allows you to delete the current directory with **rmdir .** but only if it is empty.

6.11   cp: **Copying Files**

We'll now take up the three basic commands that you'll need to use with files—**cp** (copy), **rm** (remove) and **mv** (move or rename). In this section, we take up **cp**; the other two are discussed in the next two sections.

The **cp** command copies a file or a group of files. It creates an exact image of the file on the disk with a different name. The syntax requires at least two filenames to be specified in the command line. When both are ordinary files, the first is copied to the second:

```
cp chap1 unit1
```

If the destination file (unit1) doesn't exist, it will first be created before copying takes place. If not, it will simply be overwritten without any warning from the system. So be careful when you choose your destination filename. Just check with an **ls** command whether or not the file exists.

What happens if unit1 exists and is a directory instead of an ordinary file? In that case, chap1 is copied to that directory with the same name. It's like using

```
cp chap1 unit1/chap1                                        Same as cp chap1 unit1
```

Using a directory name as the destination, you can copy multiple files into the directory using a single **cp** command.

cp is often used with the shorthand notation . (dot) to signify the current directory as the destination. For instance, to copy the file .profile from /home/juliet to your current directory, you can use either of the two commands:

```
cp /home/juliet/.profile .profile                              Destination is a file
cp /home/juliet/.profile .                              Destination is current directory
```

Obviously, the second one is preferable because it requires fewer keystrokes.

As discussed before, **cp** can also be used to copy more than one file with a single invocation of the command. In that case, the last filename *must* be a directory. For instance, to copy the files chap01, chap02 and chap03 to the progs directory, you'll have to use **cp** like this:

```
cp chap01 chap02 chap03 progs                                progs must be a directory
```

The files retain their original names in the progs directory. If these files are already resident in progs, **cp** will overwrite them. For the above command to work, the progs directory must exist because **cp** won't create it.

The UNIX system uses a set of special characters called **metacharacters** that you can use for matching more than one file. A detailed discussion on these characters is taken up in Chapter 8, but here we'll consider the *—one of the characters of the metacharacter set. If there were only three files in the current directory having the common string chap, you could compress the above sequence using the * as a suffix to chap:

cp chap* progs   *Copies all files beginning with* chap

We'll continue to use the * as a shorthand for multiple filenames sharing a common string. If you are keen on using the other special characters, then look up Section 8.2.

Caution

cp overwrites without warning the destination file if it exists. Before using it, run **ls** to check if the file exists, and then use **cat** to check the contents of the file.

6.11.1   cp Options

Interactive Copying (-i)   The -i (interactive) option warns the user before overwriting the destination file. If unit1 exists, **cp** prompts for a response:

$ **cp -i chap1 unit1**   unit1 *is an ordinary file here*
cp: overwrite unit1? **y**

A y at this prompt overwrites the file; any other response leaves it uncopied. If you are afraid that you may accidentally overwrite a file, you can later use your knowledge of *aliases (17.4)* and *shell functions (19.10)* to make **cp** behave in this interactive manner by default.

Copying Directory Structures (-r)   It's now possible to copy an entire directory structure with the -r (recursive) option. The following command copies all files and subdirectories in progs to newprogs:

cp -r progs newprogs

Since the process is recursive and copies all files resident in the subdirectories, **cp** here also has to create the subdirectories if it doesn't find them during the copying process. You can move entire directory structures this way.

Note

If the file to be copied is read-protected, it won't be possible to copy it. **cp** also won't work when the destination file exists and is write-protected. These issues are discussed and resolved in the next chapter.

6.12   rm: **Deleting Files**

The **rm** command deletes files and makes space available on disk. It normally operates silently and should be used with caution. It can delete more than one file with a single instruction:

rm chap01 chap02 chap03   *rm chap* should sometimes do*

Unless used with the -r option, **rm** won't remove a directory, but it can remove files from one. You can remove the two chapters from the progs directory without having to "cd" to it:

rm progs/chap01 progs/chap02   *Or* rm progs/chap0[12]

You may sometimes need to delete all files of a directory, as part of a cleaning-up operation. The *, when used by itself, represents all files, and you can then use **rm** like this:

$ **rm** *   *All files gone!*
$ _

Windows users, beware! When you delete files in this fashion, the system won't prompt you with the message Are you sure? or All files in directory will be deleted before removing the files! The $ prompt will return silently, suggesting that the work has been done.

Caution

Never issue a command like **rm** * before you check your current directory with **pwd** and use **ls** to list the files.

6.12.1   rm Options

Interactive Deletion (-i)   There will often be a number of files that you'd like to delete, and some you'd like to retain. If you have 20 files to delete, you really won't want to specify all their names in the command line. You can then use **rm**'s -i (interactive) option, which makes the command ask the user for confirmation before removing each file:

$ **rm -i chap01 chap02 chap03**
chap01: ?**y**
chap02: ?**n**
chap03: ?**y**

A y removes the file; any other response leaves the file undeleted.

Recursive (and Dangerous) Deletion (-r)   With the -r option, **rm** performs a tree walk—a thorough recursive search for all subdirectories and files within these subdirectories. It then deletes all of them. **rm** *won't normally remove directories, but when used with this option, it will.* Therefore, when you issue the command

rm -r *   *Current directory tree removed completely!*

you'll delete all files in the current directory, as well as all subdirectories and their files. You must be doubly sure of what you are doing before you execute an **rm** command like this: it can be even more disastrous than **rm** *. Check your current directory and look at the listing of all its files and directories to ensure that there is not a single file that is important to you. If you don't have a backup, then these files will be lost forever.

     rm won't delete any file if it's write-protected, but may prompt you for removal. The -f option overrides this protection also. It will force removal even if the files are write-protected:

rm -rf *   *This is even more dangerous!*

Note that you can't normally delete a file that you don't *own.* (Strictly speaking, this statement is not true.) **rm** doesn't send files to the Trash Bin (like Windows and X Window do); a file removed with **rm** is gone forever.

Caution

Unlike **rmdir**, **rm** **-r** can remove subdirectories even if they are not empty. If the root user (the super user) issues the command **rm** **-rf** * in the root directory, the entire UNIX system will be wiped out from the hard disk!

6.13 mv: **Renaming Files**

mv renames (moves) files and directories. It doesn't create a copy of the file but merely renames it. This means that no additional space is consumed in the disk by using **mv**. It has two functions:

- Renames a file (or directory).
- Moves a group of files to a different directory.

     We'll first use **mv** on an ordinary file. To rename the file chap01 to man01, you should use

mv chap01 man01   man01 *can also be a directory*

If the destination file doesn't exist, it will be created. By default, **mv** doesn't prompt for overwriting the destination file if it exists. So be careful, again.

     Like **cp**, a group of files can be moved, but only to a directory. The following command moves three files to the progs directory:

mv chap01 chap02 chap03 progs   progs *must be a directory*

mv can also be used to rename a directory and is used in exactly the same way as an ordinary file. There is a -i option available with **mv** also, which behaves exactly like in **cp**. So you can protect your files from being overwritten by using this option. The messages are the same, and require a similar response.

Even though the **cp**, **rm** and **mv** commands use simple syntaxes, you'll often be using them with pathnames—both absolute and relative. Table 6.1 shows how these commands can handle a wide variety of arguments.

6.14 cat: **Displaying and Creating Files**

Before you copy or remove files, you'll often want to see what's inside them. The **cat** command is the universal file viewer and is one of the most well-known commands of the UNIX system. It is mainly used to display the contents of a small file on the terminal:

```
$ cat note1
This is a file containing simply this sentence.
```

We used this command in Chapter 1 *(1.10.4)* to view a file created with **echo**. Like many UNIX commands, **cat** also accepts more than one filename as argument:

```
cat chap01 chap02
```

The contents of the second file are shown immediately after the first file without any header information. Here, **cat** concatenates the two files—hence its name. Displaying a single file is only a special case of concatenation.

    cat is normally used for displaying text files only. Executables, when seen with **cat**, simply display junk. If you have nonprinting ASCII characters in your input, you can use **cat** with the -v option to display these characters.

6.14.1 Using cat to Create a File

cat is also useful for creating a file. Though the significance of the following sequence can be appreciated only in Chapter 8, you should know how to create small files without

TABLE 6.1 *Usage of* **cp**, **rm** *and* **mv** *Commands*

Command line	Action
cp note ..	Copies file note to the parent directory
cp ../note .	Copies file note from the parent directory to the current directory
rm ../bar/index	Deletes file index in the bar directory placed at the same hierarchical location as the current directory
mv foo1 foo2 /foo1/foo2	Moves files foo1 and foo2 to the directory /foo1/foo2
rm -r bar	Deletes complete directory structure of bar. Will delete only bar if it is an ordinary file
cp -r . ../bar	Copies current directory tree to the directory bar under the parent directory (bar must exist)
mv ../* .	Moves all files from the parent directory to the current directory

using an editor like **vi**. Enter the command **cat**, follow it with > (the right chevron character) and the filename foo:

```
$ cat > foo                                             Creating a file this time
A > symbol following the command means that the
output goes to the filename following it. cat used
in this way represents a rudimentary editor.
[Ctrl-d]                                                           End of file
$ _                                                             Prompt returns
```

When the command line is terminated after hitting *[Enter]*, the prompt vanishes and **cat** waits to take input from the user. Enter the three lines, each followed by *[Enter]*. Finally, press *[Ctrl-d]* to signify the end of input to the system.

UNIX uses the *[Ctrl-d]* character to mark the end-of-file. You have used it in Chapters 1 and 3, and you also know how the **stty** command *(3.5)* can be used to change this character. When this character is entered, the system understands that no further text input will be made. The file is written and the prompt returned. To verify this, simply "cat" this file:

```
$ cat foo                                           No > required for viewing
A > symbol following the command means that the
output goes to the filename following it. cat used
in this way represents a rudimentary editor.
```

Note

The *[Ctrl-d]* character is used to terminate input not only with **cat**, but with all commands that accept input from the keyboard. We used it with **bc** too *(3.12)*.

cat can also append to files. The standard syntax won't permit this, but **cat** also works with a *stream*. You can provide input to **cat** not only by specifying a filename as argument, but also from the output of another command. Further, the output need not always go to the terminal but may go to a file instead. You'll learn about all this in Chapter 8.

6.15   **file: Know the File Types**

Even though there are basically three types of files (ordinary, directory and device), you may often need to know more about these files. For instance, a regular file may contain plain text, a C program or executable code. Instead of using the **cat** command on each file to find out the type of data it contains, you can use the **file** command which will do the work for you. **file** reports a file's "subtypes"—especially those of an ordinary file:

```
$ file emp.lst
emp.lst:    ascii text                                            A text file
```

When **file** is used on a wide variety of files, it displays quite an informative list. The output is system-dependent; some systems can identify a file better than others. We'll use the * to indicate all files:

```
$ file *
addressbook.gif:        GIF image data, version 87a, 482 x 345
backup.sh:              executable /bin/ksh script
basic1.html:            HTML document text
cmeri_dns.tar:          GNU tar archive
dialout.sh:             executable shell script
hosts.Z:                compress'd data 16 bits
ux3rd.gz:               gzip compressed data
wins.zip:               Zip archive data
wstovi.c:               C program text
```

This command has a built-in mechanism of identifying the type of file by context. It distinguishes between shell programs and C programs. It also identifies **tar** archives, images, HTML files and compressed files. While this method of identifying files isn't wholly accurate, it's quite a reliable indicator.

6.16   lp **and** cancel: **Printing a File**

No user is allowed direct access to the printer. Instead, one has to **spool** (or line up) a job along with others in a print queue. Spooling ensures the orderly printing of jobs and relieves the user from the necessity of administering the usage of print resources. The spooling facility in System V is provided by the **lp** (line printing) command.

The following **lp** command prints a single copy of the file chap01:

```
$ lp chap01
request id is pr1-320 (1 file)
$ _
```

Note that the prompt is returned *immediately* after the job is submitted. The file isn't actually printed at the time the command is invoked, but later, depending on the number of jobs already lined up in the queue. Several users can print their files in this way without conflict.

lp notifies the request-id—a combination of the printer name (*pr1*) and the job number (320)—which can later be accessed with other commands. The hard copy of the file is often preceded by a title page mentioning the username, request-id and date.

6.16.1   lp **Options**

lp uses a number of options, and they can vary across systems. We discuss below some of the common ones.

In the previous example, **lp** accepted the request because a default printer was defined by the administrator. If there is no default printer, or if there is more than one printer in the system, you have to use the -d option with the printer name (say, *laser*):

```
lp -dlaser chap01                                    Can also provide space after -d
```

The -t (title) option, followed by the title string, prints the title on the first page:

```
lp -t"First chapter" chap01                          Can also provide space after -t
```

You can notify the user with the -m (mail) option after the file has been printed. You can also print multiple copies (-n) :

lp -n3 -m chap01   *Prints 3 copies and mails message*

Even though we used **lp** with filenames, this will not always be the case. The UNIX system permits the output of another command to act as input to this commands, using the concept of a *pipeline* (Chapter 8).

6.16.2   cancel : Canceling a Job

Jobs queued by **lp** are canceled with the **cancel** command, which uses the request-ids of the jobs or the printer name as arguments:

cancel laser   *Cancels current job on printer laser*
cancel pr1-320   *Cancels job with request-id* pr1-320

Note

You can cancel (remove) only those jobs that you own (i.e., you have submitted yourself). However, the system administrator can cancel any job.

Linux

Printing with lpr, lpq and lprm

Linux uses Berkeley's printing system which supports the **lpr** command for printing and **lprm** for removing jobs. The command doesn't normally throw out the job number:

```
$ lpr typescript
$ _
```

To know the number of the job, use the **lpq** command:

```
$ lpq
lp is ready and printing
Rank    Owner     Job  Files                      Total Size
active  sumit     17   typescript                 3615 bytes
```

If you now have to remove this job from the queue before it gets printed, use

```
$ lprm 17                                          Removes job number 17
dfA017saturn dequeued
cfA017saturn dequeued
```

You can also remove all jobs owned by you by using a hyphen as a single argument:

lprm -   *Removes all jobs owned by the user*

Like System V **lp**, you can also print a specific number of copies, choose the title and direct output to a specific printer. You can also mail the completion of the job:

```
lpr -P dj500 foo                          Prints on the printer dj500
lpr -T "The List of RFCs" foo                          Uses this title
lpr -#3 foo                                            Prints 3 copies
lpr -m foo                              Mails message after completion
```

6.17   df: **Finding Out the Free Disk Space**

Even though we have considered the UNIX file system as one single tree structure with a single root directory, in real life things are quite different. You'll have multiple disks, and each disk will have at least one **file system** with its own root directory. Often, a single disk will have multiple file systems on it. The booting sequence merges all these tree-like structures into one and presents you the illusion of a single file system. However, they are distinct structures, and the free space of one can't be used by the other.

The concept of multiple file systems and their handling is discussed in Chapter 21. However, in this and the next chapter, we'll mostly understand them as one entity except when using the **df** (disk free) command. You should regularly use this command to display the amount of free space available on the disk. The output always reports for each file system separately:

```
$ df
/                 (/dev/dsk/c0t0d0s0 ): 4122488 blocks    446163 files
/proc             (/proc            ):       0 blocks     15861 files
/dev/fd           (fd               ):       0 blocks         0 files
/d01              (/dev/dsk/c0t8d0s0 ): 3197798 blocks    667713 files
/d02              (/dev/dsk/c0t8d0s1 ): 8587618 blocks    614579 files
/d03              (/dev/dsk/c0t8d0s3 ): 6435158 blocks    614547 files
/oracle           (/dev/dsk/c0t0d0s3 ): 6018636 blocks    495356 files
/tmp              (swap             ): 3649776 blocks    170946 files
```

There are eight file systems some of which are always created by the system during installation. The root file system (/ in the first column) has 4,122,488 **blocks** of disk space free. Many UNIX commands report space usage in units of blocks, where the size of a block is usually 512 bytes.

The root file system also has 446,163 **inodes** *(21.5.1)* free, which means that up to that many additional files can be created on this file system. (Some systems show the word "inodes" rather than "files" in the last column.) The system will continue to function until the free blocks or inodes are eaten away—whichever occurs earlier. The total free space in the system is the sum of the free blocks of these eight file systems, though the information is not of much use.

The -t (total) option includes the above output, as well as the total amount of disk space in each file system. This time, we'll find out the space usage of the oracle file system only:

```
$ df -t /oracle
/oracle              (/dev/dsk/c0t0d0s3 ):  6018636 blocks    495356 files
                              total:        6018654 blocks    495360 files
```

The interpretation is simple enough; the total space allocated to this file system is 6,018,654 blocks for files and 495,360 for inodes. The **df** command is regularly used by the system administrator for monitoring purposes.

Note

When the space in one file system is totally consumed, the file system can't borrow space from another file system.

Linux

Using df

The **df** command produces a different output; **df** here shows the percentage disk utilization also. The block size here is 1024 bytes:

```
$ df
Filesystem         1024-blocks  Used Available Capacity Mounted on
/dev/hdb3             485925   342168   118658    74%   /
```

Linux uses the -t option for a different purpose; the default output itself is informative enough.

6.18 du: **Finding Out Your Own Consumption**

You'll often need to find out the consumption of a specific directory tree rather than an entire file system. **du** (disk usage) is the command you need as it reports usage by a recursive examination of the directory tree. This is how **du** lists the usage of /home/sales/tml:

```
$ du /home/sales/tml
11554   /home/sales/tml/forms
12820   /home/sales/tml/data
638     /home/sales/tml/database
...
25170   /home/sales/tml                    Also reports a summary at end
```

By default, **du** lists the usage of each subdirectory of its argument, and finally produces a summary. The list can often be quite large, and more often than not, you may be interested only in a single figure that takes into account all these subdirectories. For this, the -s (summary) option is quite convenient:

```
# du -s /home/sales/tml
25170   /home/sales/tml
```

There is always a scramble for disk space. Users often don't delete the files they no longer require. This is the option the administrator needs to monitor the space used by each user's home directory tree *(22.10.1)*. Using shell scripts, she can use this command regularly to locate the notorious disk hoggers.

How do you find out the space utilization of your home directory tree? Use the -s option:

Tip

```
du -s /home/romeo
```

Using a metacharacter, you can also find out the space used by each user individually. This administrative function is taken up in Section 22.10.1.

6.19 `compress`, `gzip` **and** `zip`: **Compress Your Files**

To conserve disk space, you'll also be compressing large and infrequently used files so that they consume a fraction of their original size on disk. Every UNIX system comes with one or more compression utilities along with their decompression siblings. The most notable compression programs available are **compress**, **gzip** and **zip**. The last two are generally available on Linux systems as superior alternatives. **compress** and **gzip** work with multiple files and remove the original file after compression. **zip** retains the original file, but can also group multiple files into a single file (called an *archive*).

The degree of compression that you can achieve with these utilities depends on the compression utility you use and the type of file you compress. Postscript, PDF and text files compress more, but picture files with the `.gif` and `.jpeg` extensions won't compress at all as these files themselves hold graphic data in compressed form. The degree of compression typically achievable is shown in Table 6.2 for some of the popular file formats.

Using `compress` `compress` is one of the earliest compression utilities in UNIX. It's quite fast and compresses moderately well. It's simple to use too:

```
compress ux2nd22
```
                                                                     Original file transformed

This produces the file `ux2nd22.Z` and removes the original file. **compress** is also shipped with **uncompress** which is used to decompress this file:

```
uncompress ux2nd22.Z
```

T A B L E 6.2 *Compression of Files*

File Type	Percentage Compression with		
	`compress`	`gzip`	`zip`
JPG	0	1	1
GIF	0	0	0
BMP	5	15	15
HTML	81	89	89
PS (postscript)	57	64	63
Text Files	68	71	70
PDF (portable document format)	52	70	70

This returns the original file. **compress** also works with multiple files; you can use **compress** * to compact all files in the current directory. To view a file compressed with **compress**, you can use the **zcat** command, which uncompresses the file and displays the uncompressed contents on the terminal.

Note

You may be surprised to learn that on many UNIX systems **compress**, **uncompress** and **zcat** are one and the same program—having three *links*. Links are discussed in the next chapter.

Using gzip The most popular compression program for UNIX systems is available in Linux—GNU **gzip**. Free versions for use on UNIX systems are also available, and you could find it in your system. Compared to **compress**, it is a little slow but remarkably efficient. A compressed **gzip** file has the extension .gz. It is decompressed ("gunzipped") with the **gunzip** command:

```
gzip sales.dbf                                    Produces sales.dbf.gz
gunzip sales.dbf.gz                               Brings back sales.dbf
```

gunzip is a versatile command that can also decompress files compressed with **compress**. **gzip** today is a standard compression utility used on the Internet.

Using zip Many UNIX systems (like Linux) also offer Phil Katz's **PKZIP** program—**zip**. This program differs from the other compression utilities in that it compresses multiple files into an **archive** (a single file containing a group of files):

```
zip fin *.html                                          Produces fin.zip
```

This compresses all HTML files into a single file fin.zip. **unzip** is used for decompression. With the -r option, **zip** can also recursively compress an entire directory tree:

```
zip -r zipdir docs                            Compresses docs tree to zipdir.zip
```

This is something which **compress** and **gzip** can only do with the help of an external application like **tar** *(22.9.4)*. **zip** betters **compress** but very nearly equals **gzip**.

6.19.1   Compressed Files on the Internet

On the Internet, you'll often find these compressed files available for downloading on *anonymous ftp* sites *(11.7.1)*. Many of these files hold multiple files in a single archive. They may have any of the extensions discussed above, but they can also have multiple extensions. The extensions themselves are quite intuitive and you can make reasonable guesses about the way they were archived and compressed. In general, you'll see these extensions:

.zip—These are files compressed with **zip**.
.tar—Files archived into a single file with the UNIX **tar** command—there's no
           compression here.
.gz—These are compressed with **gzip**.

.tar.Z—Files archived into a single file with **tar** and then compressed with
    compress.

.tar.gz—As above, except that files are compressed with **gzip**.

Each tar.gz or tar.Z file is created in two stages: first, by grouping several files into
an archive with **tar**, and then by compressing the archive itself with **gzip** or **compress**.
The technique of doing this is discussed in Section 22.9.4.

Linux

The commands **gzip**, **gunzip** and **zcat** are actually one file having three *links*
(names). Besides, Linux has a vast array of "z" commands that can be used on files
compressed with **compress** and **gzip**—**zcmp**, **zgrep**, **zmore** and **zdiff**. The commands without their "z" prefixes are discussed in later chapters.

6.20 Conclusion

All the commands discussed in this chapter use file or directory names as their arguments. Some of these commands (**cat** and **lp**—also **lpr**, **compress** and **gzip**) also
support an alternate method of taking input. Further, **cat**'s output need not always
come to the terminal. For many commands, input can often come from the keyboard or
another program. Similarly, command output can also go to a file or serve as input to
another command.

This chapter didn't deal with these techniques, though this is how some of these
commands are generally used. After all, you wouldn't want to see the output of every
command on the screen. Often, you might want to perform some filtering action
on the output, or save it in a file. The discussion of these techniques is taken up in
Chapter 8.

SUMMARY

Everything is a file in UNIX, be it a C program, a UNIX command, the printer, tape
drive or the memory of your system. There are three types of files—*ordinary*, *directory*
and *device*.

An ordinary file contains data, and the most common type is text. A directory
holds files, and a directory file contains their names. The device file doesn't occupy
space on disk and deflects data directed to it to the actual physical device.

A file doesn't contain its attributes, nor does it contain the end-of-file mark. A
filename is restricted to 255 characters and can use practically any character (except
the /). Files are case-sensitive and accept any number of extensions and dots.

The file system is a hierarchical structure resembling an inverted tree, and the
top-most directory is called *root*. Directories and files have a parent–child relationship,
and the parent of any file must be a directory.

Commands used by users are located in /bin and /usr/bin. The administrative
commands are in /sbin and /usr/sbin, and their configuration files are in /etc.

/dev holds the device files. Users create temporary files in /tmp and spool all their mail and print jobs in /var.

pwd tells you the current directory, and **cd** is used to change it. When used by itself, **cd** switches to the *home directory*, the login directory of a user.

A *pathname* is a sequence of directory and filenames separated by slashes. An *absolute pathname* denotes the location of the file with respect to root. While two files may have the same name, they must have different absolute pathnames.

Files can also be represented by *relative pathnames*, which show the file's location relative to the current directory. The symbols . and .. are used universally to represent the current and parent directory, respectively.

mkdir and **rmdir** are used to create and remove directories. Multiple directories can also be created or removed with one invocation of **mkdir** and **rmdir**. You can't remove a directory with **rmdir** unless it's empty.

You can copy multiple files with **cp**, remove them with **rm**, and rename them with **mv**. **cp** and **mv** overwrite existing files, but all three commands can be used interactively (-i). **cp** and **rm** can work on a complete directory tree (-r) i.e., recursively. **mv** can also rename two directories. **rm -rf *** is the most potentially dangerous command that one can use.

cat can not only display one or more files but also create one. Input supplied from the keyboard to **cat** is terminated with *[Ctrl-d]*—the end-of-file character.

file tells you the type of file beyond the normal three categories. You can identify **tar** archives, images, HTML files and compressed files with this command.

lp prints a file, and can be used to print multiple copies (-n). It's also possible to mail (-m) a message to a user after printing is complete. You can cancel any submitted job with **cancel**. Linux uses **lpr** to print, but it uses **lprm** to cancel a job.

The **df** and **du** commands are used to manage the disk space. The former shows the free space available for each file system, while the latter lists the detailed usage of each file or directory. Both commands are used regularly by the system administrator.

The compression utilities **compress**, **gzip** and **zip** are used to compress files. **gzip** is quite popular and is widely used on the Internet. But **zip** can compress a group of files into an *archive*. Files are decompressed with **uncompress**, **gunzip** and **unzip**. The **zcat** command displays files compressed with **gzip** and **compress**.

SELF-TEST

6.1   There's a file /dev/mem in every UNIX system. What do think this file represents?
6.2   How long can a UNIX filename be?
6.3   Can you have the files note and Note in the same directory?
6.4   Which directory doesn't have a parent?
6.5   Try creating a file containing one and two dots. What do you conclude?
6.6   Which character does the *[Enter]* key generate?
6.7   Is this command legal—cat /bar/bar/bar/bar?
6.8   What does **cd** do when used without arguments?
6.9   Can you use **cd cd/mkdir/rmdir**?
6.10   Does **ls ..** work?

6.11   Can you execute any command in /sbin by using the absolute pathname?

6.12   Look in the UNIX documentation to find the easiest way of creating this directory structure—share/man/cat1.

6.13   Can you remove a directory even when you are located in the directory?

6.14   How will you copy a directory structure bar1 to bar2?

6.15   Will **mv bar1 bar2** work if bar1 and bar2 are directories?

6.16   Your file contains nonprintable characters. How do you view them?

6.17   Use the **file** command on all files in the /dev directory. Can you group these files into two categories?

6.18   If you see a file with extension .gz, what sort of file could it be?

E X E R C I S E S

6.1   Can you create a file of any number of dots, say five—.....?

6.2   Which are the characters that can't be used in a filename? Can a space be used in a filename?

6.3   Which are the characters that shouldn't be used in a filename?

6.4   State two reasons for not having a filename beginning with a hyphen.

6.5   What does the directory file contain?

6.6   Can you change the contents of a directory file?

6.7   charlie's home directory is /usr/charlie, and he has developed many scripts that refer to the pathname /usr/charlie/html. The system administrator now tells charlie that his home directory has changed to /home/charlie and advises him to change all his scripts. How could charlie have avoided this problem?

6.8   How will you move from /usr/spool/lp/admins to /usr/spool/mail?

6.9   You know that **echo** is a shell built-in. How do you then use the command of the same name that resides in /bin?

6.10   Discuss three ways of knowing your home directory.

6.11   If **mkdir foo** doesn't create the directory, what could be the possible reasons?

6.12   When will **rmdir bar** fail to work? How will you remove the directory bar?

6.13   When will you be compelled to run a command like this—./update.sh instead of update.sh?

6.14   Where are the system administrator's commands and configuration files stored?

6.15   What is the difference between **cd** and **cd $HOME**?

6.16   How do you copy all directories and files from the current directory bar1 to its parent bar2?

6.17   The command **cp hosts backup/hosts.bak** didn't work even though the file hosts exists in the current directory. What could be the reason?

6.18   What is a safer alternative to **rm ***?

6.19   What will **rm -fi *** do?

6.20   What happens if you issue the command **mv bar1 bar2** where bar2 may or may not already exist?

6.21   What will **cat foo foo foo** display?

6.22   Print three copies of /etc/passwd on the printer named *mainp* on System V.

6.23   How will you fire a printing job from a remote machine and make sure the job has been printed?

6.24   How do the **df** and **du** commands differ?

6.25   How will you find out the total disk usage of the current directory tree?

6.26   You have a complete directory structure to send to someone. Which command is most suitable for the task, and how do you do it?

6.27   You have a number of picture files having the .gif extension. Which command will you use to compress them?

KEY TERMS

absolute pathname *(6.6)*

archive *(6.19)*

current directory *(6.5)*

device file *(6.1.3)*

directory file *(6.1.2)*

disk block *(6.17)*

file system *(6.17)*

home directory *(6.5.1)*

inode *(6.17)*

inode number *(6.1.2)*

login directory *(6.5.1)*

metacharacter *(6.11)*

ordinary file *(6.1.1)*

pathname *(6.5)*

regular file *(6.1.1)*

relative pathname *(6.6, 6.7 and 6.8)*

root directory *(6.3)*

spooling *(6.16)*

text file *(6.1.1)*

## CHAPTER 7

File Attributes

In the previous chapter, you created directories, navigated the file system, and copied, moved and removed files without any problem. In real life, however, matters may not be so rosy. You may have problems when handling a file or directory. Your file may be modified or even deleted by others. A restoration from a backup may be unable to write to your directory. You must know why these problems happen and how to prevent and rectify them.

The UNIX file system lets users access other files not belonging to them—without infringing on security. A file also has a number of attributes which are changeable by certain well-defined rules. We'll be using the **ls** command in all possible ways to display these attributes. We'll also use other commands to change these attributes. Finally, we'll discuss **find**—one of the most versatile attribute handling tools of the UNIX system.

Objectives

- Use the **ls** command to list files in all possible ways. *(7.1)*
- Understand the significance of the seven fields of the **ls -l** *(listing)* output. *(7.2)*
- Learn the significance of file and directory permissions and how to change them with **chmod**. *(7.4 to 7.6)*
- Know how the **umask** setting determines the default permissions. *(7.7)*
- Learn the concept of file *ownership* and how to change it with **chown** and **chgrp**. *(7.8 and 7.9)*
- Use **ls** to display a file's last *modification* and *access times* and **touch** to change them. *(7.10 and 7.11)*
- Become familiar with *file systems* and the *inode* as a file identifier. *(7.12)*
- Create *hard links* to a file with **ln** and use **ls -i** to display the *inode number*. *(7.13)*
- Learn the practical applications of links. *(7.13.1)*
- Understand why *symbolic links* are superior to hard links. *(7.14)*
- Locate files by matching one or more file attributes with **find**. *(7.15)*

7.1   ls: **Listing Files**

In the introductory chapter, you used the **ls** command *(1.10.2)* to display some files in the current directory. The command displays practically every attribute of a file—at least the ones that concern us in this chapter. Let's execute it again in a directory which contains a good number of filenames:

```
$ ls
08_packets.html                                              Numerals first
TOC.sh                                                       Uppercase next
calendar                                                     Then lowercase
cptodos.sh
dept.1st
emp.1st
helpdir
progs
usdsk06x
usdsk07x
usdsk08x
```

What you see here is a list of filenames arranged in **ASCII collating sequence**, with one filename in each line. This sequence accords priority in the following order:

Whitespace (spaces and tabs)
Numerals
Uppercase letters
Lowercase letters

The list also includes directories which you'll be able to identify after using **ls** with suitable options. When the list is long, you won't be able to see all files. You may simply be interested in only knowing whether a particular file is available. In that case, just use **ls** with the filename:

```
$ ls calendar
calendar
```

And if **perl** isn't available in /usr/bin, **ls** clearly says so:

```
$ ls /usr/bin/perl
ls: /usr/bin/perl: No such file or directory
```

ls can also be used with multiple filenames. It has a host of options, not matched by many commands in number (over 20 in most versions). We'll discuss the important ones, especially those that reveal a file's or directory's attributes. Many of these options are discussed in the next section, but some are placed in the topical discussion of the attributes. The options are summarized in Table 7.1.

7.1.1   ls Options

Output in Multiple Columns (-x)   When you have several files, it is better to display the filenames in multiple columns. Use the -x option to produce a multicolumnar output:

TABLE 7.1 *Options to* ls

Option	Description
-x	Displays multicolumnar output
-F	Marks executables with *, directories with / and symbolic links with @
-a	Shows all files including ., .. and those beginning with a dot
-R	Recursive listing of all files in subdirectories
-L	Lists files pointed to by symbolic links
-d	Forces listing of a directory
-l	Long listing in ASCII collating sequence showing 7 attributes of a file
-n	Displays numeric user-id (UID) and group-id (GUID) instead of their names
-t	Sorts by last file modification time
-lt	Displays listing sorted by last modification time
-u	Sorts by last access time
-lu	Displays last access time in listing but sorts by ASCII collating sequence (by access time in Linux)
-lut	Displays and sorts by last access time (same as -lu in Linux)
-i	Shows inode number
-c	Sorts by last inode change time
-s	Shows file size in 512 K-byte blocks (1024 in Linux)
-r	Sorts files in reverse order (ASCII collating sequence by default)

```
$ ls -x
08_packets.html    TOC.sh       calendar      cptodos.sh
dept.lst           emp.lst      helpdir       progs
usdsk06x           usdsk07x     usdsk08x      ux2nd06
```

The display makes full use of the terminal width and is so convenient that many people have customized the command to display in this format by default (i.e., when used without options). You can do that too after you have learned to use *aliases (17.4)* and *shell functions (19.10)*.

Identifying Directories and Executables (-F) The output of ls that you have seen so far merely showed the filenames. You didn't know how many of them, if any, were directory files. To identify directories and executable files, the -F option should be used. Combining this option with the -x option produces a multicolumnar output:

```
$ ls -Fx
08_packets.html    TOC.sh*      calendar*     cptodos.sh*
dept.lst           emp.lst      helpdir/      progs/
usdsk06x           usdsk07x     usdsk08x      ux2nd06
```

Note the use of two symbols that tag some of the filenames. The * indicates that the file contains executable code; the / refers to a directory. You can now identify the two subdirectories in the current directory—helpdir and progs.

Showing Hidden Files (-a) By default, **ls** doesn't show all files in a directory. There are certain hidden files (those beginning with a dot) in every directory, especially in the home directory, that normally don't show up in the listing. The -a (all) option lists all the hidden files as well:

```
$ ls -axF
./              ../             .cshrc          .emacs
.exrc           .fetchmailrc    .netscape/      .profile
.rhosts         .sh_history     .xinitrc        08_packets.html*
TOC.sh*         calendar*
   .....
```

Generally, these "dot" files determine the behavior of their corresponding commands. **emacs** reads .emacs when invoked, and there are a lot of files in the .netscape directory which **netscape** reads on startup. The X Window system executes the instructions in .xinitrc.

The files .cshrc and .profile need special mention. They contain a set of instructions that are performed when a user logs in. They are conceptually similar to AUTOEXEC.BAT of Windows, and you'll know more about them later *(17.9)*. We'll discuss the significance of the various hidden files in some of the chapters of this text.

The first two files (. and ..) are special directories that should remind you of the symbols you used to represent the current and parent directories *(6.8)*. These symbols have the same meaning here, and whenever you create a subdirectory, these "invisible" directories are created automatically by the system. You can't remove them, nor can you write into them. They help in holding the file system together.

Note

All filenames beginning with a dot are displayed only when **ls** is used with the -a option. The directory . represents the current directory, while .. signifies the parent directory. You can also list a hidden file by specifying it as an argument to **ls**.

Listing Directory Contents We are not discussing an option here but just a way to list a directory's contents. In a previous example (**ls calendar**), you specified an ordinary filename to **ls** to check for its existence. However, the situation will be quite different if you specify a directory name progs instead:

```
$ ls -x progs
array.pl    cent2fah.pl    n2words.pl    name.pl
```

This time the *contents* of the directories are listed, consisting of a number of **perl** program files. Note that the output doesn't indicate the directory whose contents are displayed.

Note

If **ls** displays a list of files when used with a single filename as argument, you can conclude that the file is actually a directory. **ls** then shows the contents of the directory. The -d option suppresses this behavior. We'll discuss this option when we discuss directory attributes.

Recursive Listing (-R)   The -R (recursive) option lists all files and subdirectories in a directory tree. This traversal of the directory tree is done recursively till there are no subdirectories left:

```
$ ls -xR
08_packets.html    TOC.sh          calendar        cptodos.sh
dept.lst           emp.lst         helpdir         progs
usdsk06x           usdsk07x        usdsk08x        ux2nd06
./helpdir:
forms.hlp          graphics.hlp    reports.hlp
./progs:
array.pl           cent2fah.pl     n2words.pl      name.pl
```

The list shows files in three sections—the ones under the home directory and those under the subdirectories helpdir and progs. You should now find the subdirectory naming conventions familiar; ./helpdir is under the current directory. If this current directory is /home/romeo, the absolute pathname of helpdir expands to /home/romeo/helpdir.

Note

Any of these options can be used with the -r option to reverse the order of display. Here, this option would simply present files in reverse ASCII sequence.

7.2   ls -l: **Listing File Attributes**

The -l (long) option of **ls** reveals most attributes of a file—like its permissions, size and ownership details. The output in UNIX lingo is often referred to as the **listing**, and a typical listing is shown in Fig. 7.1.

The list is preceded by the words total 35; a total of 35 blocks are occupied by these files in the disk. (Each block contains 512 or 1024 bytes.) The -l option can be combined with other options to display more attributes—and in different ordering sequences. We'll now discuss the significance of each of the seven fields of the listing.

Type and Permissions   The first column shows the type and **permissions** associated with each file. The first character in this column shows a - for the first four files, which indicates that the file is an ordinary one. This is, however, not so for the directories helpdir and progs where there's a d at the same position.

You then see a series of characters that can take the values r, w, x and -. In the UNIX system, a file can have three types of permissions—read, write and execute. You'll see how to interpret these permissions and also how to change them in Section 7.5.

FIGURE 7.1 *Long Listing of Files with the* ls -l *Command*

```
$ ls -l
total 35
-rw-r--r--    1    romeo    metal    19514    May 10 13:45    chap01
-rw-r--r--    1    romeo    metal     4174    May 10 15:01    chap02
-rw-rw-rw-    1    romeo    metal       84    Feb 12 12:30    dept.lst
-rw-r--r--    3    juliet   metal     9156    Mar 12  1999    genie.sh
drwxr-xr-x    2    romeo    metal       64    May  9 10:31    helpdir
drwxr-xr-x    2    romeo    metal      320    May  9 09:57    progs
```

Permissions Links Owner   Group   Size   Last   Filename
                              Owner   Modification Time

Links The second column indicates the number of **links** associated with the file. This is actually the number of names maintained by the system of that file. UNIX lets a file have as many names as you want it to have, even though there is a single file on disk. Here, genie.sh has three links; the other links could be in different directories. This attribute will be discussed in Section 7.13.

Note

A link count greater than one indicates that the file has more than one name. That doesn't mean that there are multiple copies of the file.

Ownership and Group Ownership When you create a file, you automatically become its **owner.** The third column shows romeo as the owner of all files except genie.sh. The owner has full authority to tamper with a file's contents, permissions, and even ownership—a privilege not available with others except the root user. Here, romeo can alter the attributes of all files except genie.sh, which can be changed only by user juliet (and by root).

When opening a user account, the system administrator also assigns the user to some group. The fourth column stands for the **group owner** of the file. The concept of a group of users also owning a file has acquired importance today as group members often need to work on the same file. It's generally desirable that the group have a set of privileges distinct from others, as well as the owner. Ownership and group owner-ship are also elaborated in Section 7.8.

Size The fifth column shows the size of the file in bytes. This is actually a measure of the character count and not the disk space occupied by the file. The space used on disk is usually larger than this figure since files are written to disk in blocks of 1024 bytes (normally). In other words, even though the file dept.lst contains 84 bytes, it occu-pies 1024 bytes on the disk.

The two directories show smaller file sizes. A directory maintains a list of file-names along with an identification number (the *inode*) for each file. The size of the directory file depends on the size of this list—whatever the size of the files themselves.

Last Modification Time The next set of three columns indicates the last **modification time** of the file—a "time stamp" that is stored to the nearest second. A file is considered to be modified if its contents have changed in any way. The year is displayed if the file is more than a year old since its last modification date. This is true for the file `genie.sh`.

You'll often need to run automated tools that make decisions based on a file's modification time. This column shows two other time stamps when **ls** is used with certain options. The time stamps are discussed in Section 7.10.

Filename The last column displays the filenames arranged alphabetically. You already know *(6.2)* that UNIX filenames can be up to 255 characters long. We'll also stick to the alphanumeric characters, the hyphen (-), the underscore (_) and the dot (.) for framing all filenames. If you would like to see an important file at the top of the listing, then choose its name in uppercase—at least, its first letter.

Linux shows the year in the output of the listing if the file is just more than six months old. It also reports in 1024-byte blocks. For instance, the first line of the **ls -l** output (displaying the word `total`) uses a block size of 1024.

7.3 Listing Directory Attributes (`ls -d`)

ls lists files in the directory when used with a directory name. If you want to force **ls** to list the directory attributes rather than its contents, you require the `-d` (directory) option:

```
$ ls -ld helpdir progs
drwxr-xr-x    2 romeo    metal          48 Jan 30 14:21 helpdir
drwxr-xr-x    2 romeo    metal          96 Mar 12 14:50 progs
```

The `-l` option has been combined here to show that the listing for a directory is somewhat different from an ordinary file. Directories are easily identified in the listing by the first character of the first column; it's always a d. For ordinary files, this place always shows a - (hyphen), and for device files, either a b or a c. Directory attributes are discussed in Section 7.6.

Note

If you wish to see the attributes of a directory rather than the files contained in it, use **ls -d** with the directory name. Note that simply using **ls -d** will *not* list all subdirectories in the current directory. Strange though it may seem, **ls** has no option to list only directories!

7.4 File Permissions

UNIX has a simple, but well-defined system of assigning **permissions** to files. To understand them, you must understand the significance of ownership and group ownership as well. Issue the **ls -l** command once again to list some files in a directory:

```
$ ls -l chap02 dept.lst dateval.sh
-rwxr-xr--    1 romeo    metal       20500 May 10 19:21 chap02
-rwxr-xr-x    1 romeo    metal         890 Jan 29 23:17 dateval.sh
-rw-rw-rw-    1 romeo    metal          84 Feb 12 12:30 dept.lst
```

Observe the first column that represents the file permissions. These permissions are different for the three files. UNIX follows a three-tiered file protection system that determines the access rights that you have for a file. Each tier represents a **category**, and comprises a string of rs, ws and xs to represent three types of permissions.

r indicates read permission, which means **cat** will display the file. w indicates write permission; you can edit such a file with an editor. x indicates execute permission; the file can be executed as a program. To understand the significance of the entire string of rs, ws and xs, we must break it up into three groups as shown in Fig. 7.2.

In this figure representing the permissions of the file chap02, the first group (rwx) has all three permissions. The file is readable, writable and executable by the **owner** of the file. That's fine, but do we know who the owner is? Yes, we do; the third column of the listing shows romeo as the owner. You have to log in with the username romeo for these privileges to apply to you.

The second group (r-x) has a hyphen in the middle slot, and applies to the **group owner** of the file. This group owner is metal, and all users belonging to the metal group have read and executable permissions only.

The third group (r--) has the write and executable bits absent. This set of permissions is applicable for **others**—those who are neither the owner romeo nor belong to the metal group.

The **group** and **others** categories are often collectively referred to as the **world**. If you are told that a file is "world-writable," it means that there is a w in that part of the permissions string that applies to group and others (like r--rw-rw-).

Note

The group permissions don't apply to romeo (the owner) even if romeo is a member of the metal group. The owner has its own set of permissions that override the group owner's permissions. However, when romeo renounces the ownership of the file, the group permissions then apply to him.

You can change all these permissions, but you'll have to be careful. If you are generous enough (and careless, too) to have read, write and executable permissions for all categories of users, then the permissions field will look like this:

rwxrwxrwx   *All permissions for everyone!*

You shouldn't be able to read, write or execute every file; you can then never have a secure system. The UNIX system, by default, never creates files with these permissions. But don't get overly cautious and remove all permissions either:

---------   *No permissions for anyone!*

FIGURE 7.2   *Structure of a File's Permissions String*

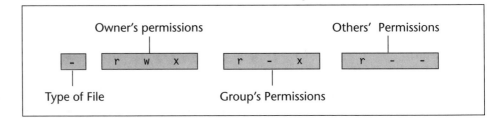

If chap01 had no permissions as shown above, we could test them quite easily:

```
$ cat chap01
cat: chap01: Permission denied                          File can't be read
$ echo "Come to the Web" > chap01
chap01: cannot create                                   File can't be written
$ chap01
chap01: cannot execute                                  File can't be executed
```

UNIX offers a well-defined protection mechanism by which you can set different permissions for the three categories of users—owner, group and others. This is applicable for all three types of files, and it's important that you understand them. A little learning here can be a dangerous thing; a faulty file permission is a sure recipe for disaster.

7.5   chmod: **Changing File Permissions**

The default security feature provided by UNIX write-protects a file from all except the owner of the file. Generally, all users have read access by default, but it could be different on your system. The default file permissions are easily revealed by creating a file small:

```
$ echo hello web > small
$ ls -l small
-rw-r--r--   1 romeo      metal        10    May 10 20:30 small
```

Observe that a file doesn't have executable permission by default—not even for the owner. So how does one execute such a file? Just change its permissions with the **chmod** (change mode) command. Only the owner of the file can use this command. **chmod** sets a file's permissions (read, write and execute) for all three categories of users (owner, group and others) and uses the following syntax:

chmod *category operation permission file(s)*

chmod is a rather unusual command, not quite fitting into the general command structure. The structure of a **chmod** command with its arguments is shown in Fig. 7.3. The expression used by the command contains three components:

- *Category* of user (owner, group owner or others)
- *Operation* to be performed (assign or remove a permission)
- *Permission* type (read, write or execute)

FIGURE *7.3   The Structure of a **chmod** Command*

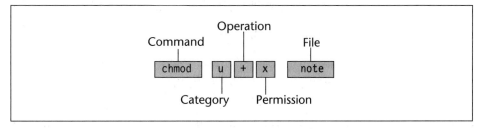

By using suitable abbreviations for each of these components, you can frame a compact string and then use the string as an argument to **chmod**. The abbreviations used for these three components are shown in Table 7.2.

Now, let's take an example. We'll assign executable permission to the owner (referred to as *user* in Table 7.2) of the file small without changing the other permissions. Look at the table closely; the expression required should be u+x:

```
$ chmod u+x small                                               Executable permission for owner
$ ls -l small
-rwxr--r--   1 romeo    metal      10    May 10 20:30 small
```

The command assigns (+) executable permission (x) to the user (u). (*User* in **chmod** is to be understood as *owner*.) romeo as owner can now execute the file, but the other categories (group and others) still can't. To enable execution by all, you should use more than one character for the category:

```
$ chmod ugo+x small ; ls -l small                                              x for all categories
-rwxr-xr-x   1 romeo    metal      10    May 10 20:30 small
```

ugo combines all three categories—user, group and others. **chmod** also offers a shorthand symbol a (all) as a synonym of ugo. As if that's not enough, there's an even shorter form—one that doesn't specify the category at all! So, the previous sequence can be replaced by either of the following:

```
chmod a+x small                                                              a implies ugo
chmod +x small                                                       By default, a is implied
```

Permissions are removed with the - operator. To remove the read permission from both group and others, use the expression go-r:

```
$ ls -l small
-rwxr--r--   1 romeo    metal      10    May 10 20:30 small
$ chmod go-r small ; ls -l small
-rwx------   1 romeo    metal      10    May 10 20:30 small
```

To remove all permissions from this file, you have to use

```
$ chmod u-rwx small ; ls -l small
----------   1 romeo    metal      10    May 10 20:30 small
```

T A B L E   7.2   *Abbreviations Used by* **chmod**

Category	Operation	Permission
u—User	+—Assigns permission	r—Read permission
g—Group	-—Removes permission	w—Write permission
o—Others	=—Assigns absolute permission	x—Execute permission
a—All		

What can you do with this file? You can't read, write or execute it, but can you remove it? Let's try that out:

```
$ rm small
rm: small: override protection 0 (yes/no)? yes
```

rm turns interactive when the owner attempts to delete a file that doesn't have write permission for her. On this Solaris system a yes at the prompt deletes the file; any other response leaves it alone. Some systems expect just a y. If you dislike **rm**'s prompting, then use **rm -f**.

Caution

An undocumented feature of **chmod** prevents +w from setting write permission for all categories. You must use a+w or ugo+w explicitly. Similarly, -w removes write permission only from owner; you have to use a-w or ugo-w to remove the permission from all users.

7.5.1   Using Multiple Expressions

Using multiple expressions and the comma as delimiter, **chmod** can set permissions in any manner you want. For instance, to restore the original permissions (rw-r--r--) to the file small (currently, ---------), you have to assign read permission to all and write permission to the owner:

```
$ chmod a+r,u+w small ; ls -l small
-rw-r--r--   1 romeo    metal        10   May 10 20:30 small
```

Removing write permission from the owner, assigning all permissions for the group and read and executable permissions for others require the use of three expressions:

```
$ chmod u-w,g+wx,o+x small ; ls -l small
-r--rwxr-x   1 romeo    metal        10   May 10 20:30 small
```

The permissions assigned so far were **relative**. When you use the expression u+r, you are assigning read permission to the owner without disturbing the other permissions—including those for group and others. **chmod** also uses an *absolute* assignment feature, which is taken up in the next topic.

7.5.2   Absolute Assignment

Absolute assignment by **chmod** is done with the = operator. Unlike the + or - operators, it assigns only those permissions that are specified along with it and *removes other permissions*. Thus, if you want to assign only read permission to all three categories and remove all other permissions from the file small, you can do it either by

```
chmod g-wx,o-x small
```

or simply by using the = operator in any of these ways:

```
chmod ugo=r small
chmod a=r small
chmod =r small
```

Sometimes, you don't need to know what a file's current permissions are but want to set all the nine permission bits *explicitly*. The absolute assignment method is then preferable and easier to use.

Note

A file's permissions can be changed only by its owner (understood by **chmod** as user). One user can't change the protection modes of files belonging to another user. However, the system administrator can tamper with all file attributes including permissions, irrespective of their ownership.

7.5.3 The Octal Notation

There's a shorthand notation available for representing file permissions. **chmod** also takes a numeric argument that describes both the category and the permission. The notation uses octal numbers (numbers using the base 8 contrasted with the standard decimal system which uses the base 10). Each type of permission is assigned a number as shown:

- Read permission—4
- Write permission—2
- Execute permission—1

When one category has multiple permissions, the respective numbers are added. For instance, if the owner has read and write permissions, the permissions for this category are represented by the number 6 (4 + 2). When this exercise is repeated for the other categories, you have a three-character octal number following this sequence: user, group and others. Like the = operator, the assignment is absolute.

You can use this method to assign read and write permission to all three categories. Without octal numbers, you will normally be using **chmod ugo+rw small** to achieve the task. Now you can use a different method:

```
$ chmod 666 small ; ls -l small
-rw-rw-rw-   1 romeo    metal          10    May 10 20:30 small
```

The 6 indicates read and write permissions (4 + 2). To restore the original permissions to the file, you need to remove the write permission (2) from group and others:

```
$ chmod 644 small ; ls -l small
-rw-r--r--   1 romeo    metal          10    May 10 20:30 small
```

To assign all permissions to the owner, read and write permissions to the group, and only executable permission to the others, you can use either of the two following forms:

```
chmod u=rwx,g=rw,o=x small
chmod 761 small                                          This is much simpler
```

The highest number possible for each category is 7 (4 + 2 + 1) and the lowest is 0. So, 777 signifies all permissions for all categories, while 000 indicates absence of all permissions for all categories. We know the consequences of using 000, but what happens if a file has all permissions?

You probably wouldn't have expected this answer, but a file writable by all can be edited, overwritten and appended to by all. But only the owner can delete the file. This really makes little difference since anyone can remove every byte from this file without actually deleting it. Table 7.3 shows the use of **chmod** both with and without using octal notation.

7.5.4   Recursive Operation (-R)

Even though we used **chmod** with only a single file, it works with multiple files also. You can assign the same set of permissions to a group of files using a single **chmod** command:

```
chmod u+x note note1 note3
```

It's now possible to apply the **chmod** command recursively to all files and subdirectories. This is done with the -R (recursive) option and needs only the directory name or the metacharacter * as argument:

```
chmod -R a+x progs          Acts recursively on all files in progs directory
chmod -R a+x *              Acts recursively on all files in current directory
```

You have used the * before *(6.12.1)* to match all files in the current directory. These two **chmod** commands make all files and subdirectories (in the progs directory or the current directory) executable by all users. If you want to use **chmod** for your home directory tree, then "cd" to it and use it like this:

```
chmod -R 755 .                              The dot is the current directory
```

There's an important observation to be made here. So far, we've been changing permissions of ordinary files. The commands used here with the -R option also change the permissions of all directories found in the tree walk. What do permissions mean when they are applied to a directory? Just read on.

T A B L E   7.3   **chmod** *Usage*

Initial Permissions	Symbolic Expression	Octal Expression	Final Permissions
rw-r-----	o+rw	646	rw-r--rw-
rw-r--r--	u-w,go-r	600	r--------
rwx------	go+rwx	777	rwxrwxrwx
rwxrw--wx	u-rwx,g-rw,o-wx	000	---------
---------	+r	666	r--r--r--
r--r--r--	+w	644	rw-r--r-- (Note this)
rw-rw-rw-	-w	466	r--rw-rw- (Note this)
rw-rw-rw-	a-w	444	r--r--r--
---------	u+w,g+rx,o+x	251	-w-r-x--x
rwxrwxrwx	a=r	444	r--r--r--

7.6 Directory Permissions

A directory stores the list of filenames along with an identification number for each file it houses. It's possible that a file can't be read even though it has read permission, and can be removed by others even when it's write-protected from them. This may come as a shock to you, but it's true; a file's access rights are also influenced by the permissions of its directory. Let's first check its default permissions:

```
$ ls -ld progs
drwxr-xr-x   2 romeo     metal          128 Jun 18 22:41 progs
```

Every directory shows a d in the first column of the permissions string. By default, all users are allowed read and execute access to a directory—something not allowed for ordinary files. The significance of a directory's permissions are also different.

Note

You can create a directory with **mkdir** and then view its permissions just to make sure that the default permissions are the same as shown here.

Read Permission Read permission for a directory means that **ls** can read the list of filenames stored in that directory. If you remove its read permission, **ls** won't work, and standard utilities won't be able to read the directory information:

```
$ chmod -r progs ; ls -ld progs
d-wx--x--x   2 romeo     metal          128 Jun 18 22:41 progs
$ ls -l progs                                               Trying to see the files inside it
ls: can not access directory progs: Permission denied (error 13)
```

However, if you remember the filenames, you can still read the files separately. It's just that **ls** won't display their names—a useful security feature.

Write Permission Write permission for a directory implies that you are permitted to create or remove filenames in it. Restore the read permission, remove the write permission and then try to copy a file to this directory:

```
$ chmod 555 progs ; ls -ld progs
dr-xr-xr-x   2 romeo     metal          128 Jun 18 22:41 progs
$ cp emp.lst progs
cp: unable to create file progs/emp.lst: Permission denied
```

The directory doesn't have write permission; you can't create or copy a file in it. Can you overwrite the existing files, or append to them? Does the directory file get changed in this way? You'll soon be able to answer these questions.

What happens if you allow all users to write to a directory?

```
$ chmod 777 progs ; ls -ld progs
drwxrwxrwx   2 romeo     metal          128 Jun 18 22:41 progs
```

This is the most dangerous thing you can ever do. Irrespective of the permissions that individual files may have, *every* user can remove *every* file in this directory!

Note

Write permission for the owner of a directory doesn't imply that the owner can directly edit the directory file; that power is reserved only for the kernel. If that were possible, then any user could destroy the integrity of the file system.

Execute Permission Execution privilege of a directory means that a user can "pass through" the directory in searching for subdirectories. When you issue the command

```
cat /home/romeo/progs/emp.sh
```

you need to have executable permission for each of the directories involved in the complete pathname. If a single directory doesn't have this permission, it can't be searched for the name of the next directory. It also means that you can't even switch to that directory with **cd**:

```
$ chmod 666 progs ; ls -ld progs
drw-rw-rw-   2 romeo    metal         128 Jun 18 22:41 progs
$ cd progs
progs: permission denied
```

Like for regular files, directory permissions are extremely important because system security is heavily dependent upon them. If you tamper with the permissions of your directories, then make sure you set them correctly. If you don't, be assured that an intelligent user could make life miserable for you!

Caution

If a directory is writable by group and others, then any user from these categories can delete every file in that directory. It doesn't matter who owns the file or whether the file itself has write permission for that user. As a rule, you should never make directories world-writable unless you have definite reasons to do so. Sometimes, you'll have a good reason *(22.4.2)*.

7.7   umask: **Default File Permissions**

When you create files and directories, the default permissions that are assigned to them depend on the system's default setting. These default permissions are inherited by files and directories created by *all* users:

- rw-rw-rw- (octal 666) for regular files
- rwxrwxrwx (octal 777) for directories

However, these are not the permissions you see when you create a file or a directory. Actually, this default is transformed by subtracting the **user mask** from it to remove one or more permissions. This mask is evaluated by using **umask** without arguments:

```
$ umask
022
```

This is an octal number, and subtracting this value from the file default yields 666 − 022 = 644. This represents the default permissions that you normally see when you create a regular file (rw-r--r--). Similarly, the default directory permissions are also rwxr-xr-x (777 − 022 = 755).

The **umask** setting can be changed only by the administrator who has to ensure that the setting is proper. Two extreme instances are shown below:

umask 666   *All permissions off*
umask 000   *All read-write permissions on*

The important thing to remember is that no one—not even the administrator—can turn on permissions not specified in the systemwide default settings. However, you can always use **chmod** as and when required. The effect of the **umask** settings on file and directory permissions is shown in Table 7.4.

7.8   File Ownership

The third and fourth fields of the listing show a file's owner and group owner. By default, the owner of a file is its creator. Consider this listing:

-rwxrw-r--   1 julie   dialout   717 Sep 14 20:37 wall.html

Only julie can change this file's attributes. But is julie a member of the dialout group? That depends on the user who created the file. If the creator is julie, her group automatically becomes the group owner. If she has not changed the default ownership pattern, dialout must be julie's group.

If you now copy this file to your directory, you become the owner of the copy and your group acquires group ownership (if your group is different). The file's permissions then change to the default—the form you see when you create a file. By virtue of being the owner, you can manipulate the attributes of the copy at will.

TABLE *7.4   Effect of* **umask** *Settings on Default Permissions*

umask Value	**Default File Permissions**	**Default Directory Permissions**
000	rw-rw-rw-	rwxrwxrwx
666	---------	--x--x--x
777	---------	---------
022	rw-r--r--	rwxr-xr-x
046	rw--w----	rwx-wx--x
066	rw-------	rwx--x--x
222	r--r--r--	r-xr-xr-x
002	rw-rw-r--	rwxrwxr-x
026	rw-r-----	rwxr-x--x
062	rw----r--	rwx--xr-x
600	---rw-rw-	--xrwxrwx

Here, any member of the dialout group can write to this file. This is an important requirement in group projects where you want group members to be able to read and write a group of files. Note, however, that none of the members of dialout (apart from julie) can change these permissions.

Tip

How do you know whether a file belongs to you? View the ownership column of its listing and then check with the **who am i** command. If they match, then you are the owner of the file.

7.8.1 /etc/passwd and /etc/group: How Ownership Details Are Stored

The usernames and the group names that you normally see in the listing and output of many UNIX commands are provided purely for your convenience. The system understands only numbers. Your user-id is actually a number (the **UID**) and this number is stored in the file /etc/passwd. Your group-id is a number too (the **GUID**) which is stored in both /etc/passwd and /etc/group. Here's a typical entry from /etc/passwd, often called the "password" file:

```
julie:x:508:100:julie andrews:/home/julie:/bin/csh
```

This is a line of seven fields showing the username in the first field. julie has 508 as the UID and 100 as the GUID. The name of this group-id can be found in /etc/group:

```
dialout:x:100:henry,image,enquiry
```

The first column shows the group name and the third column has the numeric group-id (the GUID). A user can belong to multiple groups, but the GUID shown in /etc/passwd is the **primary group**. /etc/group shows the usernames for **secondary groups**. Here, dialout is the secondary group for henry and two other users.

Using these two files, most commands translate these numbers to names before displaying ownership details. However, **ls** can be used with the **-n** option to display numbers instead of names.

7.8.2 An Intruder in the Listing

Sometimes, you'll see a set of numbers rather than the names of the owner and group owner in the ownership fields of the listing:

```
-rwxrw-r--    1    30    204       717 Sep 14 20:37 wall.html
```

Problems of this sort are often encountered when files are transferred from another system. This user probably has an identical account on the other system but with different values of the UID and GUID. The number-name translation wasn't done here because these numbers don't exist in /etc/passwd and /etc/group of this system. System administrators should draw a lesson from here.

Observe the listing of romeo's home directory in Fig. 7.1, and you'll see another intruder:

```
-rw-r--r--    3    juliet    metal    9156    Mar 12 1999    genie.sh
```

There's a file owned by juliet in romeo's directory. This can happen for a number of reasons:

- The directory was world-writable so juliet created a file in this directory.
- romeo copied a file from juliet's directory with **cp -p**—the command that preserves a file's attributes *(7.10—Tip)*.
- The file was transferred from a different system where romeo has the same UID that juliet has in this machine.

Now, what does a user like romeo do with these files if he finds them in his directory? Observe that neither file is writable by romeo since it is not owned by him. Even though wall.html is writable by members of the 204 group, romeo is not a member of this group. Even if romeo belongs to the metal group, genie.sh is not group-writable.

romeo can delete these files or copy them and then change their permissions. Alternatively, he can ask the system administrator to transfer the ownership to him. This has to be done with the **chown** and **chgrp** commands which are discussed next.

Tip

If you set up accounts of a user in two machines, then make sure that their numeric user-ids (the UIDs) match, as well as their group-ids (the GUIDs). Files can then be transferred freely between the two systems.

7.9 chown **and** chgrp: **Changing File Ownership**

There are two commands meant to manipulate the ownership of a file or directory—**chown** and **chgrp**. They can be used only by the owner of the file. Here's the syntax for both:

chown *options new_user file(s)*
chgrp *options new_group file(s)*

Before we proceed with **chown**, let's view the listing of the file note which will be used with these commands:

```
$ ls -l note
-rwxr----x   1 romeo    metal         347 May 10 20:30 note
```

Here, we assume that the user executing the **chown** and **chgrp** commands is also romeo—the owner of the file. Now, let's say that romeo wants to renounce the ownership of this file to juliet. To do that, he has to use **chown** (change ownership) which takes the new user's user-id as argument followed by one or more files:

```
$ chown juliet note ; ls -l note
-rwxr----x   1 juliet   metal         347 May 10 20:30 note
```

This does the job, but once the ownership of the file is transferred to juliet, the original ownership can't be reinstated:

```
$ chown romeo note
chown: cannot change owner ID of note: Operation not permitted
```

The file permissions pertaining to the owner are now applicable to juliet only. Thus, romeo can no longer edit the file note nor delete it since there is no write privilege for group and others. (He can copy it, of course.)

The **chgrp** (change group) command changes the group owner of a file. In the following example, romeo changes the group ownership of dept.1st to dba:

```
$ chgrp dba dept.1st ; ls -1 dept.1st
-rw-r--r--   1 romeo     dba            139 Jun  8 16:43 dept.1st
```

That's done, but what happens when he tries to get it back?

```
$ chgrp metal dept.1st ; ls -1 dept.1st
-rw-r--r--   1 romeo   metal            139 Jun  8 16:43 dept.1st
```

He does get back the group membership that he had surrendered. That's possible because he retains all rights related to the file as he's still the owner.

Like **chmod**, both **chown** and **chgrp** also work with the -R option to perform their operations in a recursive manner. All three commands place no restrictions whatsoever when used by the super user. In fact, the super user can change *every* file attribute that is discussed in this chapter.

Tip

If you want members of a project to be able to read and write a set of files, ask the system administrator to have a common group for them and then set the permissions of the group to rwx. There's a better way of doing this (with the *sticky bit*), and it is discussed in Section 22.4.2.

Linux

Restrictions on Use of chown **and** chgrp

In Linux, the **chown** command can only be used by the super user. When romeo attempts to use the command, the system refuses:

```
$ chown henry note
chown: note: Operation not permitted
```

A Linux user can use **chgrp**, but she can use it only for changing the group to one to which she also belongs. If juliet belongs to the dialout and uucp groups, she is confined to these two groups only for using **chgrp**. She can't give away ownership to root, which the System V user can do easily.

7.10   File Modification and Access Times

Apart from permissions and ownership, a UNIX file has three time stamps associated with it. In this section, we'll be discussing just two of them (the first two):

- Time of last file modification   *Shown by* ls -1
- Time of last access   *Shown by* ls -1u
- Time of last inode modification   *Shown by* ls -1c

When a file's contents are changed, its last **modification time** is updated by the kernel. Even though `ls -l` shows this time for a file, the `-t` option actually presents files in *order* of their modification time; the last modified file is placed first:

```
$ ls -lt
total 278
-rw-r--r--    1 romeo      metal          10411 May 10 15:56 chap02
-rw-r--r--    1 romeo      metal          19514 May 10 13:45 chap01
drwxr-xr-x    2 romeo      metal             64 May  9 10:31 helpdir
-rw-rw-rw-    1 romeo      metal             84 Feb 12 12:30 dept.lst
-rw-r--r--    1 romeo      metal           9156 Mar 12  1998 genie.sh
```

A file also has an **access time**—the last time someone read, wrote or executed the file. This time is also maintained by the system, and is distinctly different from the modification time that gets set only when the contents of the file are changed.

The `-u` option of `ls` displays a file's access time. When you use `ls -lu,` the access time is displayed against each file, but the sort order remains standard (the ASCII collating sequence). But when the `-t` option is coupled with `-u`, files are actually sequenced in order of their access time:

```
$ ls -lut unit02 unit03 unit04
-rw-r--r--    1 romeo      metal          48527 Mar 20 23:17 unit04
-rw-r--r--    1 romeo      metal          39480 Feb 28 16:35 unit02
-rw-r--r--    1 romeo      metal          27183 Feb 13 14:57 unit03
```

If you now view the contents of the file `unit03` with **cat**, you'll update its access time but not the modification time. This will be evident when you use the `ls -lu` command again:

```
$ ls -lu unit03                                              Check access time again
-rw-r--r--    1 romeo      metal          27183 Sep 30 23:30 unit03
$ date
Wed Sep 30 23:30:20 EST 1999
```

You can also use the `-r` option with both `-t` and `-ut`, in which case the files will be sorted in reverse order by the respective time (modification or access).

Knowledge of a file's modification and access times is extremely important for the system administrator. Many of the tools used by her have to look at these time stamps to decide whether a particular file will participate in a backup or not. A file is often incorrectly stamped when extracting it (using an option) from a backup with a file restoration utility (like **tar** or **cpio**). If that has happened to you, then you can use **touch** to reset the times to certain convenient values without actually modifying or accessing the file. **touch** is discussed next.

Note

It's possible to change the access time of a file without changing its modification time. In an inverse manner, when you modify a file, you generally change its access time as well. However, there is an exception; when you redirect command output (with the > and >> symbols) to a file, you do change the contents of the file, but this leaves the last access time unchanged. This feature is found on many UNIX and Linux systems.

Tip

What happens when you copy a file with **cp**? By default, the copy has both time stamps set to the time of copying. Sometimes, you may not like this to happen. In that case, use **cp -p** (preserve) to retain both time stamps. The option also preserves the existing ownership pattern.

7.11 touch: **Changing the Time Stamps**

As just discussed, you may sometimes need to set the modification and access times to predefined values. The **touch** command changes these times and is used in the following manner:

touch *options expression filename(s)*

When **touch** is used without *options* or an *expression*, both times are set to the current time. The file is created if it doesn't exist, but not overwritten if it does:

touch note   *Creates file if it doesn't exist*

When **touch** is used without options but with an expression, it changes both times. The expression consists of an eight-digit number—using the format *MMDDhhmm* (month, day, hour and minute). Optionally, you can suffix a two- or four-digit year string.

Now, let's use the command on emp.1st, but only after seeing its initial time stamps:

```
$ ls -l emp.1st                                        Modification time
-rw-r--r--   1 romeo    metal         870 May 11 12:49 emp.1st
$ ls -lu emp.1st                                           Access time
-rw-r--r--   1 romeo    metal         870 Jun  9 09:10 emp.1st
```

The first command shows the modification time, while the second one shows the access time of the file. **touch** here changes both times:

```
$ touch 03161430 emp.1st ; ls -l emp.1st
-rw-r--r--   1 romeo    metal         870 Mar 16 14:30 emp.1st
$ ls -lu emp.1st
-rw-r--r--   1 romeo    metal         870 Mar 16 14:30 emp.1st
```

It's also possible to change the two times individually. With the -m (modification) option, you can alter the modification time alone:

```
$ touch -m 02281030 emp.1st ; ls -l emp.1st
-rw-r--r--   1 romeo    metal         870 Feb 28 10:30 emp.1st
```

The -a (access) option changes the access time:

```
$ touch -a 01261650 emp.1st ; ls -lu emp.1st
-rw-r--r--   1 romeo    metal         870 Jan 26 16:50 emp.1st
```

The system administrator often uses **touch** to "touch up" these times so that a file may be included in or excluded from an *incremental backup* (that backs up only changed files). When the **find** command goes about locating files that have changed after a certain time, it may or may not locate these files depending on how the times have been set.

7.12 File Systems and Inodes

Before we take up links, we need some idea of the way files are organized in a UNIX system. A certain area of the disk is always set aside to store the attributes of files. All the attributes that we have discussed so far (along with links) are stored in a table called the **inode**. Every file has one inode and is accessed by a number called the **inode number**. The inode number for a file is unique in a single *file system.*

This brings us to the concept of the **file system**. We have casually used this term as if it referred to a single superstructure holding all files and directories together. That seldom is the case, and never so in large systems. The hard disk is split up into separate file systems, and each file system has its own root directory. If you have three file systems in one hard disk, then they will have three separate root directories.

Of these multiple file systems, one of them is considered the main one, and contains most of the essential files of the UNIX system. This is the **root file system**, which is more equal than others in at least one respect: its root directory is also the root directory of the UNIX system. At the time of booting, all the secondary file systems attach themselves to the main file system, creating the illusion of a single file system to the user.

Every file system has a separate area earmarked for holding inodes. **ls** fetches the attributes of files from their inodes. A file's inode number is unique only in that file system that holds the file. This means that if you see two files with the same inode number, then they must be on two different file systems.

This is all the knowledge we need to understand links. We won't go any further at this point as inodes and other file system concepts are covered in some detail in Chapter 21.

7.13 1n: Links

UNIX allows a file to have more than one name and yet maintain a single copy in the disk. The file is then said to have more than one **link**. A file can have as many names as you want to give it, but the only thing common to all of them is that they all have the same inode number.

You can easily know the number of links of a file from the second column of the listing. This number is normally 1, but this file has two links:

```
-rw-r--r--    2 sumit    dialout      504 Oct  4 16:29 alias.sam
```

A file is linked with the **1n** (link) command which takes two filenames as arguments. The first filename is the one that actually exists; the other filename is the alias we provide. The following command links the existing file display.sh with print.sh:

```
1n display.sh print.sh
```

The -i option of **1s** displays the inode number of a file. Here, the first column shows that both links have the same inode number, proving conclusively that they are actually one and the same file:

```
$ ls -li display.sh print.sh
29518 -rwxr-xr-x    2 romeo    metal      915 May  4 09:58 display.sh
29518 -rwxr-xr-x    2 romeo    metal      915 May  4 09:58 print.sh
```

The number of links is shown to be two. You can provide another link, say show.sh and increase the number to three:

```
$ ln print.sh show.sh ; ls -li display.sh print.sh show.sh
29518 -rwxr-xr-x   3 romeo    metal        915 May  4 09:58 display.sh
29518 -rwxr-xr-x   3 romeo    metal        915 May  4 09:58 print.sh
29518 -rwxr-xr-x   3 romeo    metal        915 May  4 09:58 show.sh
```

Note that even though **ls** shows three files, they are actually one. You can say that the file has two aliases. Links are equal in all respects; they have the same inode number, permissions and time stamps. Changes made to one link are automatically available in the others.

Links often occur in different directories, which makes it difficult to locate them—unless you are using the **find** command. For instance, the following command provides a link with the same name but in a different directory:

```
ln toc.txt ../project5_safe/toc.txt
```

We use **rm** to remove files. Technically speaking, **rm** actually removes a link from the file, so the following command removes the link show.sh and brings down the link count by one:

```
$ rm show.sh ; ls -l display.sh print.sh
-rwxr-xr-x   2 romeo    metal        915 May  4 09:58 display.sh
-rwxr-xr-x   2 romeo    metal        915 May  4 09:58 print.sh
```

Another **rm** will further bring the link count down to one. A file is considered to be completely removed from the system when its link count drops to zero. Links thus provide some protection against accidental deletion. If a file is linked and you have inadvertently used **rm** to delete the file, at least one link will still be available; your file is not gone yet.

7.13.1   Where to Use Links

When do you need to link a file? Well, one can think of three applications straightaway:

1. You can use a link to "notionally place" a file in a specific directory where many programs expect to find it. Say, you have a number of programs which invoke **perl** using the absolute pathname /usr/local/bin/perl. When you upgraded your system, you found **perl** has moved to /usr/bin. Would you change all your programs to point to this new path? Not necessary, just leave a link like this in /usr/local/bin:

    ```
    ln /usr/bin/perl /usr/local/bin/perl              root permission needed
    ```

2. C and the shell programming language support a feature which lets a program know the name by which it is called. Consider a program **display.sh** which formats its input and displays it on the terminal. Now, take another program, **print.sh**, which does a similar job but prints on the printer. Since both programs will have a substantial common portion, it makes sense to have all the logic in a single file.

A section of code in this file checks the name by which the file is called. It then executes the device-specific code to print the job either on the terminal or the printer. Once the program is developed, you can link the file to have two different names. Maintaining the program also becomes easy because there's only one file that does both jobs. There's a shell script using this feature in Section 18.12.

3. There's another useful application for links. Suppose you have a number of files that you use often but are placed in different subdirectories:

```
/home/henry/.profile
/home/henry/.elm/elmrc
/home/henry/Mail/received
```

All these are important files but have pathnames which are either long or difficult to remember. There's no need to use these pathnames at all; just place links of these files in a working directory, say $HOME/work:

```
cd $HOME/work
ln ../.profile prof.lnk
ln ../.elm/elmrc elmrc.lnk
ln ../Mail/received recd.lnk
```

Note how relative pathnames reduce your typing load. Once you have linked these files, you can consider them available in the work directory. To edit the file elmrc in the directory .elm, you no longer need to use **vi ../.elm/elmrc**; you can simply use **vi elmrc.lnk**. No more pathnames to access these files!

7.14 Symbolic Links

The preceding discussions throw up a couple of questions. Creating a link like the one we created for **perl** is fine as long as you are not linking too many files. But what if /usr/local/bin had originally contained a hundred programs, and all of them have now moved to /usr/bin? Use the **ln** command a hundred times? And what if the directory /usr/local/bin is on a different hard disk?

It's here that one encounters the limitations of links—at least the ones of the type described. These links have two serious drawbacks:

- You can't link a file across two file systems. In other words, if you have a file in the /usr file system, you can't provide a link for it in the /home file system.
- You can't link a directory even within the same file system.

A **symbolic link** overcomes both these problems. Unlike the other link, a symbolic link is a directory entry that points to the file or directory that actually has the contents. Being more flexible, it is also known as a **soft link**. The link that we discussed in the previous section has today come to be known as a **hard link**.

To return to the problem of linking the hundred programs in /usr/local/bin, you have to use a symbolic link to link these two directories. The command is the same, except that it uses the -s option. Let /usr/local/bin now point to /usr/bin:

```
cd /usr/local
ln -s /usr/bin bin                                    The second file must not exist
```

Because a symbolic link is just a directory entry containing a pathname, it doesn't occupy space on disk. For the **ln** command to work, make sure the destination filename doesn't exist. When you run **ls -l** now, two columns of the listing show up differently:

```
$ pwd
/usr/local
$ ls -l
lrwxrwxrwx     1 root     root        8 Mar 1 23:53 bin -> /usr/bin
```

You can identify symbolic links by the character l in the permissions field. The notation bin -> /usr/bin signifies that bin contains the pathname to the directory /usr/bin. You can now run all the hundred programs that once belonged to /usr/local/bin.

Many systems use symbolic rather than hard links to link regular files. The following **ln** command links two files in the same directory, and the -i (inode) option of **ls** has yet another story to tell:

```
$ ln -s note note.sym
$ ls -li note note.sym
 9948 -rw-r--r--     1 henry    group       80 Feb 16 14:52 note
 9952 lrwxrwxrwx     1 henry    group        4 Feb 16 15:07 note.sym -> note
```

The two files have different inode numbers (and hence a single link count) and file sizes; they are two separate files. However, it is note, and not note.sym, that actually contains the data. You can use relative pathnames here as well:

```
$ ln -s ../jscript/search.htm search.htm
$ ls -l search.htm
lrwxrwxrwx  1 sumit   dial  21   Mar 2 00:17 search.htm -> ../jscript/search.htm
```

Why should we use symbolic links for ordinary files? Unlike hard links, a symbolic link can link files across file systems. This means that two files in two hard disks can be connected with a symbolic link, where one of the files acts as one.

Even though a symbolic link can link directories, in a way it behaves like an ordinary file and is removed the same way. This means that the **rm** command removes a symbolic link—even if it points to a directory:

```
$ rm /usr/local/bin                                              An ordinary file
$ _
```

What happens when you delete the file pointed to rather than the symbolic link? The listing gives no indication, and it's only when you try to access the file that you'll find that it's no longer there:

```
$ rm ../jscript/search.htm
$ ls -l search.htm
```

```
lrwxrwxrwx  1 sumit   dial   21 Mar 2 00:17 search.htm -> ../jscript/search.htm
$ cat search.htm
cat: search.htm: No such file or directory
```

Symbolic links are used extensively in the UNIX system. System files constantly change locations with version enhancements. Yet, it must be ensured that all programs still find the files where they originally were.

Note

When you use **cd** with a symbolic link, the built-in **pwd** command shows you the path you used to *get* to the directory. This is not necessarily the same as the actual directory you are in. To know the "real" location, you should use the external command **/bin/pwd**.

7.15 find: **Locating Files**

find is one of the power tools of the system. It recursively examines a directory tree to look for files either by name or by matching one or more file attributes. It has a difficult command line, and if you have ever wondered why UNIX is hated by many, then you should look up the cryptic **find** documentation. However, **find** is easily tamed if you break up its arguments into three components:

find *path_list selection_criteria action*

Fig. 7.4 shows the structure of a typical **find** command. The command completely examines a directory tree in this way:

- First, it recursively examines all files in the directories specified in *path_list*. Here, it begins the search from /home.
- It then matches each file for one or more *selection_criteria*. This always consists of an expression in the form *-operator argument* (-name index.html). Here, **find** selects the file if it has the name index.html.
- Finally, it takes some *action* on those selected files. The action -print simply displays the **find** output on the terminal.

All **find** operators start with a - but the path list can never contain one. You can provide one or more subdirectories to act as the path list and multiple selection criteria to match one or more files. This makes the command difficult to use initially, but it is a program that every user must master since it lets her make file selection under practically any condition.

Let's run our first **find** command to locate all files named core (the process image that is dumped on disk):

```
$ find / -name core -print
/home/romeo/scripts/core
```

F I G U R E 7.4   *Structure of a* **find** *Command*

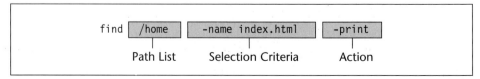

```
/home/andrew/scripts/reports/core
/home/juliet/core
```

Since the search starts from the root directory, **find** displays the absolute pathnames of the files. You can also use metacharacters in the name (like the *) to match a group of filenames, but then you need to enclose the pattern within quotes:

```
find . -name "*.lst" -print
```
Don't forget the quotes!

This matches all filenames having the .lst extension from the current directory tree (the . is current directory). Once you know how to use the special characters like the * *(8.2)*, you can use **find** as a real power tool. You can search for all filenames beginning with an uppercase letter in this way:

```
find . -name '[A-Z]*' -print
```
Single quotes will also do

Up to this point, **find** is already more powerful than its Windows counterpart. There are many features to follow.

Note

find accepts a set of metacharacters with the -name argument; the * is one of them. The shell also uses the same set *(8.2)*, and after you have learned to use them, you'll find pattern matching with find quite easy and useful. For instance, you can use find to locate all the .doc files irrespective of their case:

```
find -name "*.[Dd][Oo][Cc]" -print
```

find is probably the only UNIX command that supports this pattern matching feature in exactly the same way it's used in the shell.

7.15.1 find Options

-name is not the only operator used in framing the selection criteria; there are many others. Table 7.5 displays **find**'s selection criteria in nearly the same sequence **ls -lids** presents a file's attributes. Many of these options are intuitive enough, so let's see some of the ways you can put **find** to good use.

File Type and Permissions (-type and -perm) The -type operator followed by the letter f, d or l selects files of the ordinary, directory and symbolic link type. Here's how you locate all the directories of your home directory tree:

```
$ find /home/henry -type d -print
/home/henry
/home/henry/.elm
/home/henry/Mail
/home/henry/.netscape
```

You can also use the -perm operator to locate files having a specified set of permissions. For instance, -perm 666 selects files having read and write permission for all categories of users. Such files are security hazards. You'll often want to use two operators in combination to restrict the search to only directories:

TABLE 7.5   *Operators Used by* **find** *(+ can be replaced with - for reverse meaning)*

Selection Criteria	Significance
-inum *n*	Selects file having inode number *n*
-type *x*	Selects file if of type *x; x* can be f (ordinary file), d (directory) and l (symbolic link)
-perm *nnn*	Selects file if octal permissions match *nnn* completely
-perm -400	Selects file where owner has read permission irrespective of what the other bits may be
-links *n*	Selects file if having *n* links
-user *usname*	Selects file if owned by *usname*
-group *gname*	Selects file if owned by group *gname*
-size +*x[c]*	Selects file if size greater than *x* blocks (characters if c is also specified)
-mtime -*x*	Selects file if modified in less than *x* days
-mmin -*x*	Selects file if modified in less than *x* minutes *(Linux only)*
-newer *flname*	Selects file if modified after *flname*
-atime +*x*	Selects file if accessed in more than *x* days
-amin +*x*	Selects file if accessed in more than *x* minutes *(Linux only)*
-name *flname*	Selects file *flname*
-iname *flname*	As above, but match is case-insensitive *(Linux only)*
-follow	Selects file after following a symbolic link
-prune	Don't descend directory if matched
-mount	Don't look in other file systems *(Chapter 22)*

Action	Significance
-exec *cmd*	Executes UNIX command *cmd* followed by {} \;
-ok *cmd*	Like -exec, except that *cmd* is executed after user confirmation
-print	Prints selected file on terminal
-ls	Executes **ls -lids** command on selected files

```
find /home/henry -perm 777 -type d -print
```

Here, we are looking for directories that have all access rights for everyone—something even more hazardous than -perm 666 used with ordinary files. It's an AND condition that is implemented above; **find** selects the files only if both selection criteria (-perm and -type) are fulfilled.

Following Symbolic Links (-follow)   If a file is a symbolic link pointing to a directory, then **find** by default won't look in that directory if it is not in the path list. To illustrate this point, let's first symbolically link the directory ../jscript which contains a file night.gif:

```
ln -s ../jscript jscript
```

We now have a symbolic link jscript which points to a directory of the same name in the parent directory. When we run **find** to look for night.gif, it won't look in that directory:

```
$ find . -name night.gif -print
$ _
```

But when we combine this with the -follow operator, **find** locates the file:

```
$ find . -name night.gif -follow -print
./jscript/night.gif
```

Note the relative pathname **find** displays, but that is because the path list itself was relative (.).

Matching Modification Times (-mtime) You can use the -mtime operator to match a file's modification time. (-atime matches the access time.) This command shows the files that have been modified in less than two days—starting from the current directory:

```
$ find . -mtime -2 -print
.                                          Includes the current directory also
./unit13
./unit15
./unit14
```

As can be seen above, **find** doesn't necessarily display an ASCII sorted list. The sequence in which the files are displayed depends on the internal organization of the file system. Further, by using the same option twice, you can narrow down your search condition to represent a range:

```
$ find . -mtime +2 -mtime -5 -ls
 37353     2 -rwxr-xr-x   1 sumit     dialout        26 Apr 21 21:38 ./toc.sh
 37392   296 -rw-r--r--   1 sumit     dialout    150426 Apr 20 23:09 ./session4
 37393   146 -rw-r--r--   1 sumit     dialout     73728 Apr 20 23:10 ./session5
 37394    38 -rw-r--r--   1 sumit     dialout     17946 Apr 20 23:10 ./session6
```

find here uses the -ls action component to display a special listing of those files that were modified in more than two days *and* less than five days. -ls—an action component—runs the **ls -lids** command and shows the inode number (first column) and the file size in 512-Kbyte blocks (second column). Apart from -print and -ls, **find** uses two other action components that are discussed shortly.

Note

+365 means greater than 365 days, -365 means less than 365 days. For specifying exactly 365, use 365.

find also uses the operators -a and -o to signify the AND and OR conditions. Use of two selection criteria generally represents the AND condition; you know that already. But you need to use -o to locate both the **perl** and shell version of your script:

```
find /home -name binary.pl -o -name binary.sh -print
```

Note

When a series of selection criteria are specified without using the -a or -o operators, they translate into an AND condition. A previous example used -mtime twice without using -a; it is implied. Just to make sure, try both these commands and see if you notice any difference:

```
find . -mtime +2 -mtime -5 -ls
find . -mtime +2 -a -mtime -5 -ls
```

Taking Action on Selected Files (-exec and -ok) All these operators produce a list of files on the terminal (which you can save in a file using the operator >). In one instance, we displayed the listing of the files as well (with -ls). In real life, however, you'll want to take some action on them—like deleting them. This is done with the -exec operator, followed by the command to be executed and terminated with the sequence {} \;.

The following command removes all temporary files in /var/preserve that are more than a month old:

```
find /var/preserve -mtime +30 -exec rm -f {} \;                      {} represents filename
```

-exec permits execution of any UNIX command. The filename here is specified with the curly braces {} and **rm** forces removal. Note that the exec sequence is terminated with \;. The usage of this operator is quite cryptic, but it's one thing you can't afford to forget.

Removing a file without confirmation can be quite risky, so you can use the -ok operator instead of -exec for interactive deletion. This is how **find** selectively removes files that are larger than 2000 blocks and have not been accessed in 180 days:

```
$ find /home -size +2000 -atime +180 -ok rm {} \;
< rm ... /home/romeo/README >?    y
< rm ... /home/juliet/README >?   n
  .....
```

Each file is presented for your decision. A y executes the command; any other response leaves the file undeleted.

find is the system administrator's tool and in Chapter 22, you'll see it used for a host of tasks. It is especially suitable for backing up files and for use in tandem with the **xargs** command *(22.10).*

Note

When using -exec or -ok with **find**, represent the filename with {} but don't forget to terminate the UNIX command line with \;.

Linux

UNIX **find** displays the filenames only if the -print operator is used. However, GNU **find** doesn't need this option; it prints by default. It also doesn't need the path list; it uses the current directory by default. In other words, the command line **find -name "*.java"** matches and prints all .java files found in the current subdirectory tree. To "simplify" matters further, GNU **find** doesn't need any arguments at all; **find** used by itself displays recursively all files in the current directory tree!

The -iname operator makes the match case-insensitive. The options -mmin and -amin use the minute as the unit for matching rather than the hour used by -mtime and -atime.

SUMMARY

You can use the **ls** command to list files in any manner—in multiple columns (-x), to identify directories and executables (-F) and display hidden files beginning with a dot (-a). You can reverse the sort order (-r) and get a recursive list (-R).

By default, **ls** sorts files in *ASCII collating sequence*, which means numbers precede uppercase, which in turn precede lowercase.

The UNIX file has a number of attributes, and seven of them are listed with **ls -l**. They are the permissions, links, owner and group owner, size, date and time of last modification and the filename. **ls -ld** lists directory attributes.

The size of the file in bytes is not the actual space the file occupies on disk, but the number of bytes it contains. A file containing 1 byte will actually occupy 1024 bytes on disk.

A file can have read, write or executable permission, and there can be three sets of such permissions for the owner, the group owner of the file, as well as others.

chmod is used to alter these permissions, and can be used only by the owner of the file. The permissions can be *relative* when used with the + or - symbols, or *absolute* when used with octal numbers.

The significance of directory permissions differs from ordinary files. Read permission means that the filenames stored in the directory are readable. **ls** works by reading the directory file. Write permission allows you to create or remove files in the directory. Executable permission lets you "cd" to the directory.

The **umask** setting determines the default permissions that will be used when creating a file or a directory.

A file has an *owner*, usually the name of the user who creates the file. A file is also owned by a *group*, by default, the group to which the user belongs. Only the owner can change the file attributes. **chown** and **chgrp** are used to transfer ownership and group ownership, respectively.

A file has both a *modification* and an *access time*. **ls** can sort a file by its modification time (-t) or access time (-ut). **touch** changes these times to any arbitrary values.

Multiple *file systems*, each with its own root directory, merge at system startup to form a single file system. A file is identified by the *inode number*, and its attributes are stored in the *inode*. The inode number is displayed by **ls -i.**

A file can have more than one name (*hard link*). You can link files with **ln** and remove a link with **rm**. Links have the same inode number. A linked file can behave as two separate commands depending on the name by which it is invoked.

A *symbolic link* (soft link) is a directory entry that points to the location of another file even if it is in another file system. Unlike hard links, the soft link can also link directories. Symbolic links are created with **ln -s** but removed with **rm**.

find looks for files satisfying certain criteria which can be any file attribute. A file can be specified by type (-type), name (-name), size (-size), permissions (-perm) or by its time stamps (-mtime and -atime). Any UNIX command can be run on the selected files (-exec and -ok) with or without confirmation.

SELF-TEST

7.1   What is the sort order prescribed by the ASCII collating sequence?
7.2   Which **ls** option marks directories and executables separately?
7.3   What are hidden files?
7.4   What do you mean by the *listing* of a file?
7.5   How will you obtain a complete listing of all files and directories in the whole system?
7.6   How will you list the files of the parent directory?
7.7   How do you identify directories from the listing?
7.8   Who can change the attributes of a file or directory?
7.9   Does **ls -l** show all files?
7.10   When is the time (but not date) of modification not shown in the listing?
7.11   For a group member to be able to remove a file what does she require?
7.12   First create a file. How will you now assign all permissions to the owner and remove all permissions from others assuming that the default file permissions are rw-r--r--?
7.13   You removed the write permission of a file from group and others, and yet they could delete your file. How could that happen?
7.14   How do you display the inode number of a file?
7.15   Where are the ownership and group ownership details stored?
7.16   Transfer recursively the ownership of all files in the current directory to henry.
7.17   Change the modification time of a file to Sep 30, 10:30 a.m.
7.18   What will the command **touch foo** do?
7.19   What does the inode store?
7.20   What do you mean by saying that a file has three *links*?
7.21   How do you remove a linked file?
7.22   Frame a command to locate all the .html and .java files in the system.

EXERCISES

7.1   On executing **ls bar**, you see a list of 10 files of which bar is one of them. How can that happen?

7.2   How do you display all files recursively (including the hidden ones) in multiple columns with distinguishing marks on executables and directories?

7.3   Does the owner belong to the same group as the group owner of a file?

7.4   A file contains 1026 bytes. How many bytes of disk space does it occupy?

7.5   How do you list the attributes of the current directory?

7.6   Why is the size of a directory usually small?

7.7   If the file doesn't have write permission for the owner, can she remove it?

7.8   Show the octal representation of these permissions:
       (i) rwxr-xrw- (ii) rw-r-----

7.9   What will the permissions string look like for these octal values?—(i) 567 (ii) 623

7.10   You tried to copy a file foo from another user's directory, but you got the error message cannot create file foo. You have write permission in your own directory. What could be the reason and how do you copy the file?

7.11   What does **chmod -w foo** do?

7.12   If a directory has the permissions 777 and a file in it has the permissions 000, what are the important security implications?

7.13   What do you do to make sure that no one can see the names of the files you have?

7.14   If you are not able to change to a directory, what could be the likely cause?

7.15   Which file attributes change when you copy a file from another user account?

7.16   How can you copy a file while preserving the attributes?

7.17   If the owner doesn't have write permission on a file but her group has, can she edit it?

7.18   How is **chown** different from **chgrp** when it comes to renouncing ownership?

7.19   If you make one change to a file, undo it, and then exit the editor after saving, is the file considered to be modified?

7.20   How can you find out whether a program has been executed today?

7.21   What's the difference between **ls -l and ls -lt**?

7.22   What's the difference between **ls -lu and ls -lut**?

7.23   How can you make out whether two files are copies or links?

7.24   What are the two main disadvantages of the hard link?

7.25   You have a number of programs in $HOME/progs which are called by other programs. You have now decided to move these programs to $HOME/internet/progs. How can you ensure that users don't notice this change?

7.26   How does the administrator ensure that all files created by users will have the default permissions rw-rw----?

7.27   Find out from the /bin and /usr/bin directories all filenames that begin with z.

7.28   Use *only* **find** to locate the file login.sql in the /oracle directory tree, and then copy it to your own directory.

7.29   Use **find** to move all files modified within the last 24 hours to the posix directory under your parent directory.

KEY TERMS

absolute permission *(7.5.2)*

ASCII collating sequence *(7.1)*

file access time *(7.10)*

file group owner *(7.2 and 7.4)*

file link *(7.2 and 7.13)*

file modification time *(7.2 and 7.10)*

file owner *(7.2 and 7.4)*

file permission *(7.2 and 7.4)*

file system *(7.12)*

group owner *(7.4)*

GUID *(7.8.1)*

hard link *(7.14)*

inode *(7.12)*

inode number *(7.12)*

listing *(7.2)*

others category *(7.4)*

primary group *(7.8.1)*

relative permission *(7.5.1)*

root file system *(7.12)*

secondary group *(7.8.1)*

soft link *(7.14)*

symbolic link *(7.14)*

UID *(7.8.1)*

user mask *(7.7)*

world category *(7.4)*

## CHAPTER 8

The Shell

This chapter introduces the agency that sits between the user and the UNIX system. It is called the *shell*. All the wonderful things you can do with UNIX are possible because this agency understands so much by seeing so little code. It's like an efficient secretary who understands your directives from your gestures, and carries them out by specially devised means you don't need to know. The shell is a command processor; it processes the instructions you issue to the machine.

Conceptually, this is one of the most important chapters of the book, and it implements some of the brilliant ideas of the architects of UNIX. The concepts highlighted here must be understood clearly. They are based on the Bourne shell, named after its founder Steve Bourne. It's the earliest shell that came with the UNIX system. You probably won't be using this shell, but the Bourne shell is the lowest common denominator of them all, and most of its features are available in modern shells as well.

Objectives

- Understand what the shell does to a command. *(8.1)*
- Use *wild-card* characters in matching filenames. *(8.2)*
- Use the \ to *escape* (remove) the meaning of a special character. *(8.3)*
- Use single and double quotes to protect a group of characters and understand the difference between them. *(8.4)*
- Use the escape sequences used by the **echo** command. *(8.5)*
- Understand *streams* and how the shell treats them as files. *(8.6)*
- Redirect *standard output* to a file. *(8.6.1)*
- Redirect *standard input* to originate from a file. *(8.6.2)*
- Redirect *standard error* to a file. *(8.6.3)*
- Understand the significance of the files /dev/null and /dev/tty. *(8.7)*
- Learn the properties of a *filter* and how the | is used to set up a *pipeline* for connecting two or more commands. *(8.8)*
- Use *command substitution* to embed commands in command lines of other commands. *(8.10)*
- Learn the properties of *shell variables*. *(8.11)*
- Learn how commands can be grouped together in a *shell script*. *(8.12)*

You probably don't want to know this right now, but you could also be using any one of these widely used shells—the C shell, Korn shell and bash. Korn and bash are supersets of Bourne, so anything that applies to Bourne also applies to them. However, just a few of the shell's features discussed in this chapter don't apply to the C shell. These differences are noted as and when they are encountered.

Note

To know the shell you are using, invoke the command **echo $SHELL**. The output could show /bin/sh (Bourne shell), /bin/csh (C shell), /bin/ksh (Korn shell) or /bin/bash (bash shell). It does pay to know the shell you are using at this stage.

8.1   The Shell as Command Processor

When you log on to a UNIX machine, you see a prompt. The prompt could be a $, a % or anything; it really doesn't matter for most of this chapter. Even though it may appear that nothing is happening out there, a UNIX command is in fact running. This command is the **shell**. It starts functioning the moment you log in and withers away when you log out.

When you issue a command, the shell is the first agency to acquire the information. It accepts and interprets user requests; these are generally the UNIX commands we key in. The shell examines and rebuilds the command line and then leaves the execution work to the kernel. The kernel handles the hardware on behalf of these commands and all processes in the system. Users can thus afford to remain ignorant of the happenings behind the scenes. This is one of the beauties of UNIX design and philosophy.

The shell is generally *sleeping*. It *wakes* up when input is keyed in at the prompt. (**Sleeping**, **waiting** and **waking** are accepted terms in UNIX parlance.) This input is actually input to the program that represents the shell (sh for the Bourne shell). The following activities are typically performed by the shell (Fig. 8.1):

- It issues the prompt ($ or otherwise) and sleeps till you enter a command.
- After a command has been entered, the shell scans the command line for some special characters (*metacharacters*, the focus of attention in this chapter) that have a special meaning for it. Because it permits abbreviated command lines (like the use of * to indicate all files, as in **rm ***), the shell has to make sure the abbreviations are expanded *before* the command can act upon them.
- It then creates a simplified command line and passes it on to the kernel for execution. The shell can't do any work while the command is being executed, and has to wait for its completion.
- After the job is complete, the prompt reappears and the shell returns to its sleeping role to start the next "cycle." You are now free to enter some more commands.

Note that the shell has to interpret these metacharacters because they usually mean nothing to the command. In this chapter, you'll be mainly concerned with the activities that keep the shell preoccupied in its interpretative role.

8.2   Pattern Matching—The Wild Cards

In the last two chapters, you used commands with more than one filename (e.g., **cp chap01 chap02 chap03 progs**) as arguments. Often, you'll need to enter a number of similar filenames in the command line:

```
ls -l chap chap01 chap02 chap03 chap04 chapx chapy chapz
```

F I G U R E 8.1 *The Shell's Interpretive Cycle*

Since the filenames here have a common string chap, the lengthy command line using this string repeatedly looks rather wasteful. Why can't we have a single pattern comprising the string chap, along with one or two special characters? Fortunately, the shell does offer such a solution.

The shell recognizes some characters as special. You can use them to devise a generalized pattern or model that can often match a group of similar filenames. In that case, you can use this pattern as an argument to a command rather than supply a long list of filenames which the pattern represents. The shell itself performs this expansion on your behalf and supplies the expanded list to the command.

8.2.1 The * and ?

Now, let's get into the specifics. In Chapter 6, you used the command **rm** * *(6.12)* to delete all files in the current directory. The *, known as a **metacharacter**, is one of the characters of the shell's special set. This character matches any number of characters (including none).

When the * is appended to the string chap, the pattern chap* matches filenames beginning with the string chap—including the file chap. It thus matches all the filenames specified in the previous command line. You can now use this pattern as an argument to **ls**:

```
$ ls -x chap*
chap  chap01  chap02  chap03  chap04  chap15  chap16  chap17  chapx  chapy
chapz
```

When the shell encounters this command line, it immediately identifies the * as a meta-character. It then creates a list of files from the current directory that match this pattern. It reconstructs the command line as below, and passes it on to the kernel for execution:

```
ls -x chap chap01 chap02 chap03 chap04 chap15 chap16 chap17 chapx chapy chapz
```

What happens when you use **echo** with the * as argument?

```
$ echo *
array.pl back.sh calendar cent2fah.pl chap chap01 chap02 chap03 chap04 chap15 ch
ap16 chap17 chapx chapy chapz count.pl date_array.pl dept.lst desig.lst n2words.
pl name.pl name2.pl odfile operator.pl profile.sam rdbnew.lst rep1.pl
```

You simply see a list of files! The shell uses the * to match files in the current directory. All filenames match, so you see all of them in the output.

Note

Windows users may be surprised to know that the * may occur anywhere in a filename, and not merely at the end. Thus, *chap* matches all the following filenames—chap newchap chap03 chap03.txt.

The next metacharacter is the ?. This matches a single character. When used with the same string chap (as chap?), the shell matches all five-character filenames beginning with chap. Place another ? at the end of this string, and you have the pattern chap??. Use both these expressions separately, and the meaning of the ? becomes obvious:

```
$ ls -x chap?
chapx  chapy  chapz
$ ls -x chap??
chap01  chap02  chap03  chap04  chap15  chap16  chap17
```

These metacharacters relating to filenames are also known as **wild cards** (something like the joker that can match any card). The complete list of the shell's wild cards is shown with examples in Table 8.1. We'll now take up the significance of the other wild cards.

Note

The wild-card characters the shell uses to match patterns bear some resemblance to the ones used by **vi** and **emacs** in their regular expressions. But make no mistake, the similarities are only superficial. Regular expressions are understood and interpreted by the *command* (like **vi** and **emacs**) and have nothing to do with the shell.

8.2.2 The Character Class

Note that the patterns framed in the preceding examples are not very restrictive. It's not easy to list only the files chapy and chapz with a compact expression. Nor is it easy to pick out only the first four chapters from the numbered list. You need the **character class** for this matching work.

TABLE 8.1 *The Shell's Wild Cards and Application*

Wild Card	Significance
*	Matches any number of characters including none
?	Matches a single character
[*ijk*]	Matches a single character—either an *i, j* or *k*
[!*ijk*]	Matches a single character that is *not* an *i, j* or *k*
[*x-z*]	Matches a single character that is within the ASCII range of the characters *x* and *z*
[!*x-z*]	Matches a single character that is *not* within the ASCII range of the characters *x* and *z*

Examples

Command	Significance
ls *.lst	Lists all files with extension .lst
mv * ../bin	Moves all files to bin subdirectory of parent directory
compress .?*.?*	Compresses all files beginning with a dot, followed by one or more characters, then a second dot followed by one or more characters
cp foo foo*	Copies file foo to file foo* (* loses meaning here)
cp ?????? progs	Copies to progs directory all six-character filenames
cmp rep[12]	Compares files rep1 and rep2
rm note[0-1][0-9]	Removes files note00, note01 . . . through note19
lp *.[!o]	Prints all files having extensions except C object files
cp ?*.*[!1238] ..	Copies to the parent directory files having extensions with at least one character before the dot, but not having 1, 2, 3 or 8 as the last character

The character class uses two more metacharacters represented by a pair of brackets []. You can have multiple characters inside this enclosure, but matching takes place for a single character in the class. For example, a single character that can take one of the values 1, 2 or 4, can be represented by the expression

[124]   *Either 1, 2 or 4*

This can be combined with any string or another wild-card expression, so selecting the files chap01, chap02 and chap04 now becomes a simple matter:

```
$ ls -x chap0[124]
chap01   chap02   chap04
```

You can specify ranges inside the class with a - (hyphen). [a-h] is a character class using a range. This is normally done with numerals and alphabets because these are the characters mostly used in filenames. So, to select the first four numbered chapters, you have to use the range [1-4]:

```
$ ls -x chap0[1-4]
chap01   chap02   chap03   chap04
```

A valid range specification requires that the character on the left have a lower ASCII value than the one on the right. Using this property, the files chapx, chapy and chapz can also be listed in a similar manner:

```
$ ls -x chap[x-z]
chapx   chapy   chapz
```

Note

The expression [a-zA-Z]* matches all filenames beginning with an alphabet, irrespective of case. You can match a word character by including numerals and the underscore character as well—[a-zA-Z0-9_].

8.2.3   Negating the Character Class

The ! (bang) is the last character in the set of wild cards. Placing it at the *beginning* of this class reverses the matching criteria, i.e., it matches all other characters except the ones in the class. To reverse the earlier example made in the note, the pattern

[!a-zA-Z]*   *Won't work in the C shell*

matches all filenames where the first character is not alphabetic.

      The character class used with a ! represents the only means of negating a single character. To match all files having extensions except those having the .Z extension (those compressed with the **compress** command), you can use this pattern:

*.[!Z]   *All files with extensions but not ending with .Z*

When organizing information in groups of files, you should choose the filenames with care so that one, or at most two, metacharacter patterns can match all of them. If you don't do that, be prepared to specify them separately every time you use a command that accesses all of them!

8.2.4   When Wild Cards Lose Their Meaning

Now that you have seen all the wild cards, you should also know that some of these characters have different meanings depending on where they are placed in the pattern. It's important that you know them because you may sometimes find it difficult to match some filenames with a wild-card pattern.

      The metacharacters * and ? lose their meaning when used inside the class, and are matched literally. Similarly, - and ! also lose their significance when placed outside the class. Additionally, ! loses its meaning when placed anywhere but at the beginning of the class. The - also loses its meaning if it is not bounded properly on either side by a single character.

Note

[!!] matches a single character filename that is not a !. This doesn't work in the C shell and bash, which use the ! for a different purpose. bash needs to use [!\!] here, but the C shell can't negate a character class at all.

8.2.5   Matching the Dot

There are further restrictions. The * doesn't match all filenames *beginning* with a . (dot) or the / of a pathname. If you want to list all the hidden files in your directory having at least three characters after the dot, then the dot must be matched explicitly:

```
$ ls -x .???*
.exrc  .news_time  .profile
```

However, if the filename contains a dot anywhere but at the beginning, it need not be matched explicitly. For example, the expression emp*lst matches a dot embedded in the filename:

```
$ ls -x emp*lst
emp.lst  emp1.lst  emp221st  emp2.lst  empn.lst
```

Note

The * doesn't match all filenames beginning with a dot. Such filenames must be matched explicitly. One *, however, can match any number of embedded dots. For instance, the pattern fw*gz matches the filename fwtk2.1.tar.gz.

8.2.6   When Using **rm** with *

While these metacharacters help speed up your interaction with the system, there are great risks involved if you are not alert enough. A word of caution at this stage should be appropriate. When using shell wild cards, especially the *, you could be totally at sea if, instead of typing

```
rm chap*
```

which removes all the chapters, you inadvertently introduce a space between chap and *:

```
$ rm chap *                                              Very dangerous!
rm: chap: No such file or directory
```

The error message here masks a disaster that has just occurred; the **rm** command has removed all files in this directory! A singular * used with **rm** can be extremely dangerous as the shell treats it as a separate argument. In such situations, you should pause and check the command line before you finally press *[Enter]*.

What if the shell fails to match a single file with the expression chap*? There's a surprise element here; the shell also looks for a file named chap*. You should avoid using metacharacters when choosing filenames, but if you have to handle one, then you have to turn off the meaning of the * so that the shell treats it literally. This deactivation feature is taken up in the next section.

Wild cards represent a feature of the shell and not of the command using them. The shell has to do the wild-card expansion because chap* means nothing to **rm**—nor to any command that uses a filename as argument. The design of the UNIX system prevents the execution of a command till the shell has expanded all wild-card expressions.

It's not wholly true to suggest that wild cards mean nothing to a command, but only to the shell. The **find** command *(7.15)* accepts wild cards (probably the only UNIX command having this feature) as parameters to the -name keyword:

Note

```
find / -name "*.[hH][tT][mM][lL]" -print          All .html and .HTML files
find . -name "note??" -print                       Two characters after note
```

Here, we are using the same wild-card characters, but this time they are a feature of the **find** command, and not of the shell. By providing quotes around the pattern, we ensured that the shell can't even interpret this pattern. You'll learn about this insulating feature shortly.

Tip

To eliminate the danger of accidental deletion of your files, it makes sense to customize the **rm** command so that it always invokes the **rm -i** command. You can then make a decision on each file individually. This requires the use of an *alias (17.4)*, which is supported by the other shells. The alias definitions can be placed in a startup file *(17.9)*, which the shell reads every time a user logs in.

8.3 Escaping—The Backslash (\)

It's a generally accepted principle that filenames shouldn't contain the shell metacharacters. What happens if they do? The answer is tricky, and can cause a great deal of havoc before you realize it fully. Imagine a file named chap* created with the > symbol:

```
$ echo > chap*                                      Use chap\* if it doesn't work
$ _
```

The silent return of the prompt suggests that the file has been created. A suitable wild-card pattern used with **ls** confirms this:

```
$ ls -x chap*
chap    chap*  chap01  chap02  chap03  chap04  chap15  chap16  chap17  chapx
chapy   chapz
```

There's indeed a file with the name chap* in the current directory! The wild-card pattern matched this file along with the others. This file can be a great nuisance and should be removed immediately. But that won't be easy. You can't use **rm chap*** because that would remove all files in this list, and not this one only.

How do you remove this file then, without deleting the other files? For this to be possible, the shell has to treat the asterisk literally instead of interpreting it as a metacharacter. The answer lies in the \ (backslash)—yet another metacharacter, but one that removes the meaning of any metacharacter placed after it. Use the \ before the * and it solves the problem:

```
$ ls -x chap\*                                      Literally matches chap*
chap*
$ rm chap\*
$ ls -x chap\*
chap* not found
```

The expression chap* literally matches the string chap*. This is a necessary feature provided by the shell, and you'll see how this concept can be extended to other areas also. The use of the \ in removing the magic from any special character is called **escaping** or **despecializing**.

If you have the files chap01, chap02 and chap03 in your current directory, and then create a file chap0[1-3] by using

```
echo > chap0[1-3]
```

then you should escape the two rectangular brackets when accessing the file:

```
$ ls -x chap0\[1-3\]
chap0[1-3]
$ rm chap0\[1-3\]                                            Deletes chap0[1-3] — one file
$ ls -x chap0\[1-3\]
chap0[1-3] not found                                                        File removed
```

Sometimes, you would need to escape the \ character itself. Since the shell treats this as a special character, you need another \ to escape it:

```
$ echo \\
\
$ echo The newline character is \\n
The newline character is \n
```

Apart from the wild cards, there are other characters that the shell considers special. Many of them will often need escaping. Here are five of them:

```
$ echo \|\<\>\'\"
|<>'"
```

The shell uses these characters for its interpretive work. The |, < and > are required for handling command input and output. The ' and " also protect special characters, but a group of them. We'll take a detailed look at these characters in this chapter.

8.3.1 Escaping the *[Enter]* Key

Apart from these wild cards, there are other characters that are special to the shell—the newline character, for example. When you enter a long chain of commands or a command with numerous arguments, you can split the command line by hitting *[Enter]*, but only after the \ escapes this key:

```
$ find /usr/local/bin /usr/bin -name "*.pl" -mtime +7 -size -1024 \[Enter]
> -size +2048 -atime +25 -print                                            Note the >
```

This is the **find** command at work—a command often used with several arguments. Escaping is the best way of imparting readability to these lengthy command lines. The \ here escapes the meaning of the newline character generated by *[Enter]*. It also produces the second prompt (which could be a > or a ?), which indicates that the command line is incomplete.

Escaping is an unsatisfactory solution when you need to despecialize the meaning of a group of characters instead of a single one. Quoting is a better alternative.

Note

The second prompt could be a > or a ?, but in either case it implies that the command is not complete. The C shell uses the ?, but other shells use the >.

8.4 Quoting

There's another way to turn off the meaning of a special character. When a command argument is enclosed in quotes, the meanings of all enclosed special characters are turned off:

```
$ echo '*?[8-9]'                                    Can use double quotes also
*?[8-9]
```

The argument above is said to be **quoted**. Double quotes would also have served the purpose, but in some cases, use of double quotes does permit interpretation of some of the special characters (especially the $ and `—the backquote). This will become clear as more features of the shell are exposed. For a beginner, single quotes are the safest as they protect all special characters (except the quotes themselves!).

8.4.1 Quoting Preserves Spaces

The space is another character that has a special meaning to the shell. When the shell finds contiguous spaces and tabs in the command line, it compresses them to a single space. When you issue the following **echo** command, you'll find all spaces compressed:

```
$ echo The shell       compresses    multiple     spaces
The shell compresses multiple spaces
```

The above arguments to **echo** could have been preserved by escaping the space character wherever it occurs at least twice:

```
$ echo The shell \ \ \ compresses \ \ multiple \ \ spaces
The shell      compresses    multiple    spaces
```

When you have a large number of characters which you need to protect from the shell, quoting is preferable to escaping:

```
$ echo "The shell       compresses    multiple     spaces"
The shell      compresses    multiple    spaces
```

We used double quotes this time, and it worked just as well. Quotes also protect the \:

```
$ echo '\'
\
```

echo is an unusual command. So far, we used the \ to keep the shell out of the picture. The same character can be used to make **echo** behave differently—while the shell continues to stay out. This feature follows next.

8.5 Escaping and Quoting in echo

Apart from the shell, there are some commands that use the \ as part of their syntax. Rather than remove the special meaning, the \ is used to *emphasize* a character so that the command (and not the shell) treats it as special. Consider, for instance, the following **echo** command:

```
$ echo 'Enter Your Name : \c'
Enter Your Name : $ _
```

Observe that the prompt has been returned, not in the next line, but at the end of the echoed string. The shell can't interpret the \ this time because of the quotes. It's **echo** that interprets it and treats the character c as special. \c used here represents an **escape sequence**, which positions the cursor immediately after the argument instead of the next line.

     echo also accepts other escape sequences that manipulate the cursor motion in a number of ways:

\t—A tab
\f—A formfeed (page skip)
\n—A newline

This is how they are used:

```
$ echo '\tThis message is broken here\n\ninto three lines'
        This message is broken here                          Tab in effect
                                                      A blank line splits the message

into three lines
```

echo also accepts ASCII octal values as arguments. For instance, *[Ctrl-g]* results in the sounding of a beep. This key has the octal value 007. You can use this value as an argument to the command, but only after preceding it with a \:

```
$ echo '\007'                                        Double quotes will also do
. . . beep heard . . .
```

This is the first time we see ASCII octal values used by a UNIX command. (Very few commands use them.) Some people use **echo** to display the box-drawing characters on their terminal using the ASCII values of these characters.

BASH Shell

The escape sequences described with **echo** won't work in this form with the bash shell used in Linux. For using them, **echo** must be used with the -e option also:

```
echo -e "Enter your name:\c"
```

We'll be using these escape sequences extensively in this text, so if you are a Linux user, you must commit this option to memory. We'll also be designing a script *(19.13)* which checks the shell that is used and inserts this option automatically!

8.6 Redirection

Many of the commands that we used sent their output to the terminal. You've seen the **cat** *(6.14.1)* and **bc** *(3.12)* commands also taking input from the keyboard. Were these commands designed that way to accept only fixed sources and destinations? No, far from it. They are actually designed to use a **character stream** without knowing its source and destination. A stream is just a sequence of bytes that many commands see as input and output.

UNIX treats these streams as files, and a group of UNIX commands reads from and writes to these files. A command is usually not designed to send output to the terminal—but to this file. Likewise, it is not designed to accept input from the keyboard either—but only from a standard file which it sees as a stream. There's a third stream for all error messages thrown out by a program. This stream is the third file.

It's here that the shell comes in. The shell sets up these three standard files (for input, output and error) and attaches them to a user's terminal at the time of logging in. Any program that uses streams will find them open and available. The shell also closes these files when the user logs out.

The standard file for input is known as *standard input* and that for output is known as *standard output*. The error stream is known as *standard error*. By themselves, these standard files are not associated with any physical device, but the shell has set some physical devices as defaults for them:

- Standard input—The default source is the keyboard.
- Standard output—The default destination is the terminal.
- Standard error—The default destination is the terminal.

It's by design that both standard output and standard error share the same default device—the terminal. In the ensuing topics, you'll see how the shell reassigns (replaces) any of these files by a physical file in the disk the moment it sees some special characters in the command line. This means that instead of input coming from the keyboard and output and error going to the terminal, they can be **redirected** to come from or go to any disk file or some other device.

8.6.1 Standard Output

Commands like **cat** and **who** send their output as a character stream. This stream is called the **standard output** of the command; by default, it appears on the terminal. Using the symbols > and >>, you can redirect the output to a disk file. We'll now do that with the **who** command:

```
$ who > newfile
$ _                                          The prompt just returns
```

The shell looks at the >, understands that standard output has to be redirected, opens the file `newfile`, writes the stream into it and then closes the file. And all this happens without **who** knowing absolutely anything about it! `newfile` now contains a list of users (the output of **who**). This is the way we save command output in files.

If the output file doesn't exist, the shell creates it *before* executing the command. If it exists, the shell overwrites it; so use this operator with caution. Alternatively, you can append to a file using the >> (the right chevron used twice) symbols:

```
who >> newfile                                          Doesn't disturb existing contents
```

Redirection also becomes a useful feature when concatenating the standard output of a number of files. Using wild cards you can set up an abbreviated command line:

```
cat chap?? > textbook
```

You can also combine two or more commands and redirect their aggregate output to a file. A pair of parentheses groups the commands, and a single > symbol can be used to redirect both of them:

```
( ls -l ; who ) > lsfile
```

The previous chapters couldn't prove convincingly that UNIX makes very little distinction between various types of files. Redirection often doesn't care about file type. It can work with a device name to echo a message on someone's terminal. The following command redirects a message to the terminal /dev/tty02, and a user working on this terminal could see it (provided the terminal is enabled accordingly).

```
echo This message is for the terminal tty02 >/dev/tty02
```

The terminal is the first (and default) destination of standard output. The disk file is the second. There's a third destination—as input to another program, which we'll take up when discussing pipelines. The handling of the standard output stream using these three destinations is shown in Fig. 8.2.

F I G U R E 8.2   *The Three Destinations of Standard Output*

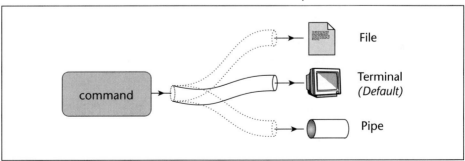

Note

When the output of a command is redirected to a file, the output file is created by the shell *before* the command is executed. Any idea what **cat foo > foo** does?

8.6.2 Standard Input

Some commands are designed to take their input also as a stream. This stream represents the **standard input** to a command. You used the **wc** command *(1.10.5)* for counting lines, words and characters in a file. But the same command expects input from the keyboard when the filename is omitted; you have to key it in:

```
$ wc                                              No filename!
      2 ^ 32                              Beginning of standard input
     25 * 50                             Spaces provided deliberately
30*25 + 15^2
[Ctrl-d]                                  End of standard input
      3        9        39                 No filename in output
```

You used **cat** *(6.14.1)* in a somewhat similar way too. Enter the three lines of text (a group of mathematical expressions), signify the end of input with *[Ctrl-d]*, and then press *[Enter]*. **wc** immediately counts 3 lines, 9 words and 39 characters in its standard input.

This input can be similarly redirected to originate from a file (the second source). First fill up the file `calc.lst` with the three expressions (using **cat > calc.lst**). Now, when the metacharacter < (left chevron) is used in this way, the shell redirects **wc**'s standard input to come from this file:

```
$ wc < calc.lst
      3        9        39
```

This too is standard input, but in its second form. Note once more that **wc** didn't open the file. It can do so, but only when it uses a filename as an argument:

```
$ wc calc.lst
      3        9        39 calc.lst
```

Note that **wc** this time shows the filename; it very well can because it opens the file itself.

You may have already framed your next question. Why bother to redirect the standard input from a file if the command can read the file itself as above? The answer is that there are times when you need to keep the command ignorant of the source of its input. This aspect, representing one of the most deep-seated features of the system, will gradually expose itself as you progress through these chapters.

To sum up, the standard input stream also has three sources:

* The keyboard, the default source.
* A file using redirection with <.
* Another program using a pipeline (to be taken up later).

The handling of the standard input stream from these three sources is shown in Fig. 8.3.

FIGURE 8.3   *The Three Sources of Standard Input*

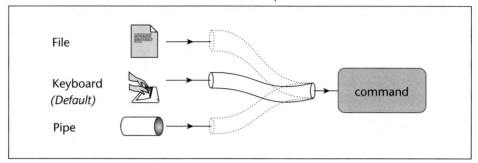

Note

When the standard input is redirected to come from a file (with <), it's the shell that opens the file. The command here is totally ignorant of the shell's activities. However, when the file-name is supplied as an argument to a command, it's the command which opens the file and not the shell.

Making Calculations in a Batch   You have used the **bc** command *(3.12)* as a calculator. This command still has a few surprises in store for us. Take, for instance, the file `calc.lst` that contains some arithmetic expressions. You can redirect **bc**'s standard input to come from this file:

```
$ bc < calc.lst > result.lst                    Using both standard input and output
$ cat result.lst
4294967296                                                      This is 2^32
1250                                                           This is 25*50
975                                                      This is 30*25 + 15^2
```

Look what's happened here. **bc** took each line from `calc.lst`, evaluated it and printed the result on the standard output. You don't need to perform your calculations "on-line" anymore. You can place them in a file and run the whole job as a batch. You can also save the output in a separate file (using >). It would be better still if we could have each expression in `calc.lst` beside the computed result. We'll do that too, but only after we learn how to use the **paste** command *(9.11)*.

Input Both from File and Standard Input   When a command takes input from multiple sources—say a file and standard input, the - symbol must be used to indicate the sequence of taking the input. The meaning of the following sequences should be quite obvious:

```
cat - foo                          First from standard input and then from foo
cat foo - bar                  First from foo, then standard input, and then bar
```

There's a fourth form of standard input which we have not considered here. It's the *here document* that has application in shell programming and hence discussed in Chapter 19.

8.6.3 Standard Error

When you enter an incorrect command or try to open a nonexistent file, certain diagnostic messages show up on the screen. This is the **standard error** stream. Like standard output, it too is destined for the terminal. Note that they are in fact two separate streams, and the shell possesses a mechanism for capturing them individually. Trying to "cat" a nonexistent file produces the third stream:

```
$ cat bar
cat: cannot open bar: No such file or directory
```

The standard error stream can also be reassigned to a file. Using the symbol for standard output obviously won't do:

```
$ cat bar > errorfile
cat: cannot open bar: No such file or directory
```

You tried to "cat" a file that doesn't exist, but the error message still shows up on the terminal. Before we proceed any further, you should know that each of these three standard files has a number, called a **file descriptor**, which is used for identification:

0—Standard input	*< is same as 0<*
1—Standard output	*> is same as 1>*
2—Standard error	*Must be 2> only*

These descriptors are implicitly prefixed to the redirection symbols. For instance, > and 1> mean the same thing to the shell, while < and 0< also are identical. You normally don't need to use the numbers 0 and 1 to prefix the redirect symbols because they are the default values. However, you need to use the descriptor 2> for the standard error:

```
$ cat bar 2>errorfile
$ cat errorfile
cat: cannot open bar: No such file or directory
```

This works. You can also append diagnostic output in a manner similar to the one in which you append standard output:

```
cat bar 2>> errorfile
```

You can now save error messages in a separate file. This enables you to run long programs and save error output to be viewed at the end of the day.

C Shell

The standard error is handled differently by the C shell, so the examples of this section won't work with it. In fact, the C shell merges the standard error with the standard output; it has no separate symbol for handling standard error only.

8.6.4 Combining Streams

When a command is used without a filename or with a -, it signifies that the input is from the standard input. You can redirect the output too. These two forms are equivalent:

```
cat > foo                                              - is not necessary here
cat - > foo                                    Both input and output redirected
```

You used the first command *(6.14.1)* to create a file by redirecting both input and output. You can also combine the < and > operators; there's no restriction imposed on their sequence either:

```
wc < infile > newfile                                   First input, then output
wc>newfile<infile                                       First output, then input
> newfile < infile wc                            As above, but command at end
```

The <, > and the >> operators are indifferent to the presence of spaces around them. In all these cases, the shell keeps the command ignorant of both source and destination. The last example illustrates a significant departure from a statement made previously *(2.4)* that the first word in the command line is the command. In the last example, **wc** is the last word in the command line.

The standard output and error symbols can also be used in the same command line:

```
cat newfile nofile 2> errorfile > outfile               But never to the same file!
```

Sometimes, you'll need to direct both the standard output and standard error streams to the same file. You'll have to use some more special symbols, and you'll learn about them in Chapter 19.

8.6.5   A New Categorization of Commands

Do all commands use the features of standard input and standard output? No, certainly not. From this viewpoint, the UNIX commands can be grouped into four categories:

Commands	Standard Input	Standard Output
mkdir, rmdir, cp, rm	No	No
ls, pwd, who	No	Yes
lp, lpr	Yes	No
cat, bc, wc	Yes	Yes

The indifference of a command to the source of its input and destination of its output is one of the most profound features of the UNIX system. It raises the possibility of commands "talking" to one another, so that the output of one command can be used as the input to another. We'll set up *pipelines* later that permit this communication. The handling of the three streams is shown in Fig. 8.4.

8.7   /dev/null **and** /dev/tty: **Two Special Files**

Quite often, you may want to test whether a program runs successfully without seeing the output or the error messages on the screen. You may not want to save this output in files either. You have a special file that simply accepts any stream without growing in size—the file /dev/null:

FIGURE 8.4   *The Three Standard Files*

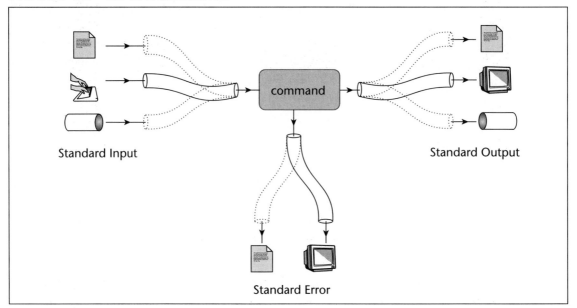

Standard Input

Standard Output

Standard Error

```
$ cal 1995 >/dev/null
$ cat /dev/null                                              Size is always zero
$ _
```

The device file /dev/null simply incinerates all output directed towards it. Its size always remains zero. This facility is useful in redirecting error messages away from the terminal so that they don't appear on the screen. The following sequence attempts to "cat" a nonexistent file without cluttering the display:

```
cat chap100 2>/dev/null                                Redirects the standard error
```

/dev/null is actually a pseudo-device because, unlike all other device files, it's not associated with any physical device.

The second special file in the UNIX system is the one indicating one's terminal—/dev/tty. Consider, for instance, that romeo is working on terminal /dev/tty01 and juliet on /dev/tty02. However, both romeo and juliet can refer to their own terminals with a single device file—/dev/tty. Thus, if romeo issues the command

```
who >/dev/tty
```

the list of current users is sent to the terminal he is currently using—/dev/tty01. Similarly, juliet can use an identical command to see the output on her terminal /dev/tty02. Like /dev/null, /dev/tty is another special file that can be accessed independently by several users without conflict.

You may ask why one should need to specifically redirect any output to one's own terminal since the default output goes to the terminal anyway. Sometimes, you do need to specify that explicitly. Apart from its use in redirection, this file can also be used as an argument to some UNIX commands. Section 8.9 makes use of this feature, while some situations are presented in Chapter 19 (featuring shell programming).

Tip

If you use **find** from an ordinary nonprivileged account to start its search from root, the command will generate a lot of error messages on being unable to "cd" to a directory. Since you might miss the selected file in an error-dominated list, the standard error of **find** should be directed to /dev/null—like **find / -name typescript -print 2>/dev/null**. Note that you can't do this in the C shell.

8.8 Pipes

To understand pipes, we'll set ourselves the task of counting the number of users currently logged in. We'll first attempt the task using the knowledge we possess already. **who** produces a list of users—one user per line, and we'll save this output in a file:

```
$ who > user.1st
$ cat user.1st
romeo       tty01        May 18 09:32
juliet      tty02        May 18 11:18
andrew      tty03        May 18 13:21
```

If we now redirect the standard input of the **wc -l** command *(1.10.5)* to come from user.1st, we would have effectively counted the number of users:

```
$ wc -l < user.1st
    3
```
The number of users

This method of using two commands in sequence has certain obvious disadvantages:

- The process is slow. The second command can't act unless the first has completed its job.
- You require an intermediate file that has to be removed after the **wc** command has completed its run.
- When handling large files, temporary files can build up easily and eat up disk space in no time.

Here, **who**'s standard output was redirected, and so was **wc**'s standard input. You may ask: Can't the shell connect these streams together so that one command takes input from the other? Yes, the shell can, using a special operator as the connector of two commands—the | (pipe). You can make **who** and **wc** work in tandem so that one takes input from the other:

```
$ who | wc -l
    3
```

Here, **who** is said to be *piped* to **wc**. No intermediate files are created when they are used. When a sequence of commands is combined together in this way, a **pipeline** is said to be formed. The name is appropriate as the connection it establishes between programs resembles a plumbing joint. It's the shell that sets up this interconnection, and the commands have no knowledge of it.

The pipe is the third source and destination of standard input and standard output, respectively. You can now use one to count the number of files in the current directory:

```
$ ls | wc -l
     15
```

Note that no separate command was designed to tell you that, though the designers could easily have provided another option to **ls** to perform this operation. And because **wc** uses standard output, you can redirect this output to a file:

```
ls | wc -l > fkount
```

There's no restriction on the number of commands you can use in a pipeline. But you must know the behavioral properties of these commands to place them there. Consider this generalized command line:

command1 | command2 | command3 | command4

It should be pretty obvious that *command2* and *command3* must support both standard input and standard output. *command1* requires to use standard output only, while *command4* must be able to read from standard input. If you can ensure that, then you can have a chain of these tools connected together as shown in Fig. 8.5. The commands *command2* and *command3* who support both streams are called **filters**. Filters are the central tools of the tool kit, and are discussed later in four entire chapters.

Printing the man Pages The online man pages of a command often show the keywords in boldface. These pages contain a number of control characters which have to be removed before you can print them. The **col -b** command can remove these characters from its input, which means that the **man** output has to be piped to **col -b**:

FIGURE 8.5 *A Pipeline of Three Commands*

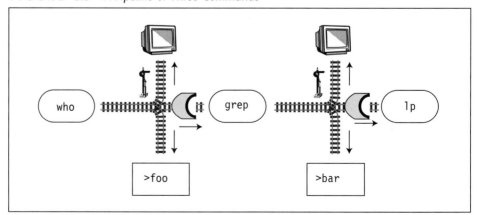

```
man grep | col -b > grep.txt
```

This sequence sends clear text to a text file, but we can pipe it again to print the page. The **lp** command *(6.16)* prints a file, but also accepts standard input:

```
man grep | col -b | lp
```

8.8.1   When a Command Needs to Be Ignorant of Its Source

Now where does all this discussion on redirection and piping lead us to? Let's consider the **grep** command which uses a filename as argument:

```
$ grep "print" foo1                                      grep opens the file foo1
print "Content-type: text/html\n\n";
print "</html>\n";
```

grep *(15.2)* locates lines containing a specified pattern in its input. Here it displays lines containing the string print. Since **grep** is also a filter, it should be able take input from the standard input as well:

```
grep "print" < foo1                                      Shell opens the file foo1
```

This also produces the same output, so what difference does it really make? This question was posed before *(8.6.2)*, but we'll have to answer it this time. To know why we sometimes need **grep** to handle a stream rather than a file, consider that **grep** also accepts multiple filenames:

```
$ grep "print" foo1 foo2 foo3
foo1:print "Content-type: text/html\n\n";
foo1:print "</html>\n";
foo2:find / -mtime +7 -print | perl -ne 'chop ; unlink ;'
foo3:$slno++ ; print ($slno . " " . $_ . "\n") ;
foo3:printf "File $file was last modified %0.3f days back \n", $m_age ;
```

grep prints the filenames this time; it can since it opens the files and knows their names. But sometimes you could be interested in only the content with the filenames removed. You can have that if you make **grep** ignorant of the source of its input. Concatenate the files with **cat** and pipe the combined output to **grep**:

```
$ cat foo[123] | grep "print"
print "Content-type: text/html\n\n";
print "</html>\n";
find / -mtime +7 -print | perl -ne 'chop ; unlink ;'
$slno++ ; print ($slno . " " . $_ . "\n") ;
printf "File $file was last modified %0.3f days back \n", $m_age ;
```

Since **grep** acts on a stream this time, the filenames vanish from the output. You'll come across similar situations as you work your way through.

Note

In a pipeline, the command on the left of the | must use standard output, and the one on the right must use standard input.

8.9   tee: **Splitting a Stream**

The UNIX **tee** command breaks up its input into two components; one component is saved in a file, and the other is connected to the standard output. **tee** doesn't perform any filtering action on its input; it gives out exactly what it takes. Even though it isn't a feature of the shell, it has been included in this chapter because it involves the handling of a character stream, which this chapter is mostly about.

Being also a filter (uses standard input and standard output), **tee** can be placed anywhere in a pipeline. You can use **tee** to save the output of the **who** command in a file and display it as well:

```
$ who | tee user.lst
romeo      tty01        May 18 09:32
juliet     tty02        May 18 11:18
andrew     tty03        May 18 13:21
```

You can crosscheck the display with the contents of the file user.lst:

```
$ cat user.lst
romeo      tty01        May 18 09:32
juliet     tty02        May 18 11:18
andrew     tty03        May 18 13:21
```

You can pipe **tee**'s output to another command, say **wc**:

```
$ who | tee user.lst | wc -l
      3
```

How do you use **tee** to display both the list of users and its count on the terminal? Since the terminal is also a file, you can use the device name /dev/tty as an argument to **tee**:

```
$ who | tee /dev/tty | wc -l          /dev/tty used as command argument
romeo      tty01        May 18 09:32
juliet     tty02        May 18 11:18
andrew     tty03        May 18 13:21
      3
```

The advantage of treating the terminal as a file is apparent from the above example. You couldn't have done so if **tee** (or for that matter, any UNIX command) had placed restrictions on the type of file it could handle. Here the terminal is treated in the same way as any disk file. **tee** also uses the -a (append) option which appends the output rather than overwrites it.

8.10 Command Substitution

The shell enables the connecting of two commands in yet another way. While a pipe connects the standard output of a command to the standard input of another, the shell enables the *argument* of a command to be obtained from the standard output of another. This feature is called **command substitution**.

To consider a simple example, suppose you wish to echo today's date with a statement like this:

```
The date today is Wed Oct 20 10:12:19 EST 1999
```

Now the last part of the statement (beginning from "Wed") represents the output of the **date** command. How does one incorporate this **date** command into the **echo** statement? With command substitution, it's a simple matter. Use the expression `date` as an argument to **echo**:

```
$ echo The date today is `date`
The date today is Wed Oct 20 10:12:19 EST 1999
```

When scanning the command line, the ` (backquote or backtick) is another metacharacter that the shell looks for. There is a special key on your keyboard (generally at the top-left) that generates this character, and should not be confused with the single quote ('). The shell then executes the enclosed command, and replaces the enclosed command line with the output of the command. For command substitution to work, the command so "backquoted" must use standard output. **date** does; that's why command substitution worked.

You can use this feature to generate useful messages. For example, you can use two commands in a pipeline, and then use the output as the argument to a third:

```
$ echo "There are `ls | wc -l` files in the current directory"
There are 58 files in the current directory
```

The command worked properly even though the arguments were double-quoted. It's a different story altogether when single quotes are used:

```
$ echo 'There are `ls | wc -l` files in the current directory'
There are `ls | wc -l` files in the current directory
```

We encounter the first difference between the use of single and double quotes. The ` is one of the few characters interpreted by the shell when placed within double quotes. If you want to echo a literal `, you have to use single quotes.

Command substitution has interesting application possibilities. It speeds up work by letting you combine a number of instructions in one. You'll see more of this feature in subsequent chapters.

Note

Command substitution is enabled when the backquotes and the enclosed command are placed within double quotes. If you use single quotes, then it's not.

KORN Shell

BASH Shell

The Korn shell and bash also offer a more readable synonym for the backquote. You can place the command inside parentheses and precede the string with a $:

```
$ echo $(date)
Mon Sep 20 20:09:23 EST 1999
```

If you are using either of these shells, then you should adopt this form rather than the unreadable and archaic form using backquotes. This is the form recommended by POSIX as well.

8.11 Shell Variables

You can define and use variables both in the command line and shell scripts. These variables are called **shell variables**. A shell variable is of the string type, which means that the value is stored in ASCII rather than in binary format. No type declaration is necessary before you can use a shell variable.

All shell variables take on the generalized form *variable=value* (except in the C shell). They are assigned with the = operator but evaluated by prefixing the variable name with a $. Here's an example:

```
$ x=37                                    No whitespace on either side of =
$ echo $x                                 $ required only at time of evaluation
37
```

A variable name comprises the letters of the alphabet, numerals and the underscore character; the first character must be a letter. Moreover, the shell is sensitive to case; the variable x is different from X. To remove a variable, use **unset**:

```
$ unset x
$ echo $x
                                          Variable removed
$ _
```

All shell variables are initialized to null strings by default. Sometimes, you'll need to explicitly set them to null values:

```
x=                    x=''                    x=""
```

Caution

For assigning values to shell variables, make sure that there are no spaces on either side of the =. If you provide them, the shell will treat the variable as a command and the = and value as its arguments! This restriction doesn't apply to the C shell.

To assign multiword strings to a variable, you can escape the space character, but quoting is the preferred solution:

```
$ msg='You have mail' ; echo $msg
You have mail
```

Now that you have another special character to deal with ($) that is gobbled up by the shell, you may still need to interpret it literally without it being evaluated. This can be done by either single-quoting the expression containing the $ or by escaping the $:

```
$ echo 'The average pay is $1000'
The average pay is $1000
$ echo The average pay is \$1000
The average pay is $1000
```

The output is predictable enough, but when you enclose the arguments within double quotes, you get a different result:

```
$ echo "The average pay is $1000"
The average pay is 000
```

Here is the second difference between the use of single and double quotes. Like the backquote, the $ is also evaluated by the shell when it is double-quoted. Here, the shell evaluated a "variable" $1; it's undefined, so a null string was output. $1 belongs to a set of parameters called *positional parameters (18.4)* that signify the arguments you pass to a script.

Note

Like command substitution, variable evaluation doesn't take place within single quotes but only within double quotes.

C Shell

The C shell uses the **set** statement to set variables. There either has to be whitespace on both sides of the = or none at all:

```
set x = 10
set mydir=`pwd`
```

The evaluation is done in the normal manner by prefixing a $ to the variable name. The C shell uses another statement, **setenv**, to set a different type of variable; you'll meet both **set** and **setenv** in Chapter 17.

8.11.1   Using Variables

Setting a Pathname to a Variable   In the command line, you can set a pathname to a variable and then use its shorthand representation with the **cd** command:

```
$ mfile='/usr/spool/mail'
$ cd $mfile
$ pwd
/usr/spool/mail
```

Now, suppose you have to use this absolute pathname (/usr/spool/mail) several times in a script. You can assign it to a variable at the beginning of the script and then use it everywhere—even in other scripts run by this script. Later, you may decide to change the location of the mail directory to /var/spool/mail. For everything to work as before, you need to just change the variable definition—nothing else.

Setting a UNIX Command to a Variable A shell variable can be used to replace even the command itself. If you are using a command with specific options many times, then set this command line to a variable. Just prefix the variable with a $ to execute it:

```
$ backup="tar -cvf /dev/fd0h1440 *"                          fd0 is a device name
$ $backup                                           Note how the variable is "executed"
....
```

The output you'll now see is from the execution of the **tar** command, a UNIX utility used for backing up files. Here again, you can appreciate the advantages of defining a variable and using it everywhere. If the backup device changes, just replace fd0h1440 with the new device name in the definition.

Using Command Substitution to Set Variables You can also use the feature of command substitution to set variables. For instance, if you were to set the complete pathname of the present directory to a variable mydir, you could use

```
$ mydir=`pwd`
$ echo $mydir
/home/romeo
```

Variable usage isn't restricted to the user alone. The UNIX system also uses a number of variables to control its behavior. There are variables that tell you the type of terminal you are using, the prompt string that you use, or the directory where incoming mail is kept. These variables are often called **environment variables** because they can alter the operation of the environment in many ways. A detailed discussion of the significance of these special shell variables will be taken up in Chapter 17.

8.12 Shell Scripts

The shell offers the facility of storing a group of commands in a file and then executing the file. All such files are called **shell scripts**. You'll also find people referring to them as *shell programs* and *shell procedures*. The instructions stored in these files are executed in the interpretive mode—much like the batch (.BAT) files of Windows.

The following shell script has a sequence of three commands stored in a file **script.sh**. You can create the file with **vi** or **emacs**, but since this takes only three lines, you can use **cat** instead:

```
$ cat > script.sh
directory=`pwd`                                  Beginning of standard input
echo The date today is `date`
echo The current directory is $directory
[Ctrl-d]                                              End of standard input
$ _
```

The extension .sh is used only for the purpose of identification; it can have any extension, or even none. Try executing the file containing these commands by simply invoking the filename:

```
$ script.sh
script.sh: execute permission denied
```

Executable permission is *usually* necessary for any shell procedure to run, and by default, a file doesn't have this permission on creation. Use **chmod** to first accord executable status to the file before executing it:

```
$ chmod u+x script.sh
$ script.sh
The date today is Thu Feb 17 11:30:53 EST 2000
The current directory is /home/sumit/project5
```

The script executes the three statements in sequence. Even though we used the shell as an interpreter, it is also a programming language. You can have all the standard constructs like **if**, **while** and **for** in a shell script. The behavior of the UNIX system is controlled by many prewritten shell scripts that are executed during system startup and those written by the system administrator. Two chapters in this text are reserved for shell programming (Chapters 18 and 19).

8.13 The Shell's Treatment of the Command Line

Now that you have seen the major features of the shell, it's time you understood the sequence of steps that it follows when processing a command. After the command line is terminated by hitting *[Enter]*, the shell goes ahead with processing the command line in one or more passes. The sequence is well-defined and assumes the following order:

- **PARSING** The shell first breaks up the command line into words, using spaces and tabs as delimiters, unless quoted. All consecutive occurrences of a space or a tab are replaced here with a single space.
- **VARIABLE EVALUATION** All words preceded by a $ are evaluated as variables unless quoted or escaped.
- **COMMAND SUBSTITUTION** Any command surrounded by backquotes is executed by the shell, and its output inserted in the place it was found.
- **REDIRECTION** The shell then looks for the characters >, < and >> to open the files that they point to.
- **WILD-CARD INTERPRETATION** The shell scans the command line for wild cards and replaces them with a list of filenames that match the pattern.
- **PATH EVALUATION** It finally looks for the PATH variable to determine the sequence of directories it has to search in order to hunt for the command.

The preceding sequence can be considered as a simplistic treatment of the Bourne shell's behavioral pattern; the C shell has a different pattern. Remember that there are several other things that the shell looks for that have been ignored here. For example, the character **;** (as well as || and &&) stops the shell from reading any further. There are other characters which are acted upon, and you'll come across them as the shell's features are gradually revealed. This revelation will be spread across several chapters.

8.14 The Other Shells

The original UNIX system came with the Bourne shell. Then came a plethora of shells offering new features. Two of them, the Korn shell (represented by the command file ksh) and the bash shell (bash) have been very well accepted by the UNIX fraternity. The Korn shell is offered as standard in SVR4, and bash is the standard shell in Linux. The C shell (csh) predates them both. It is still popular but will ultimately have to make way for Korn and bash.

Korn and bash maintain near-complete compatibility with the Bourne shell, which means that all shell programs developed under Bourne will also run under these two shells. Because commands like **kill** and integer and string handling features are built in, programs run under Korn and bash execute faster than under Bourne. In this book, the features of the C, Korn and bash shells are highlighted suitably. Further, the exclusive programming features of Korn and bash are discussed in Chapter 19. The C shell's programming constructs have been documented in Appendix A. All four shells are compared feature for feature in Appendix D.

➤ *GOING FURTHER*

8.15 More Wild Cards in the Korn Shell and bash

At times, you'll face situations when you can't frame a single expression to match a group of filenames. For instance, how do you match the following filenames?

```
chap01 chap02 chap03 chap16 chap17 chap18 chap19
```

The Bourne shell needs to use two expressions—chap0[1-3] chap1[6-9]—even though there's a common string (chap) in both of them. bash and Korn provide an important extension to the standard wild-card set (8.2) by letting you enclose differing expressions within curly braces. This expression matches them all:

```
chap{0[1-3],1[6-9]}
```
Note the comma

The comma here acts as the delimiter between the uncommon expressions placed within the braces. There must not be any whitespace on either side of it. And here's how you can copy the .txt and .gz versions of the files README and INSTALL:

```
cp {INSTALL,README}.{gz,txt} ../doc
```

This feature shortens the command line considerably; with Bourne, you would have had to specify all the four filenames separately. It also means that you can access multiple directories using a shortened syntax:

```
cp /home/romeo/{project,html,scripts}/* .
```

This copies all files from the three directories (project, html and scripts) to the current directory. Isn't this convenient? This feature is also available in the C shell, but not the one that is discussed next.

The Invert Selection Feature If you have used Windows Explorer, you would no doubt have used the *Invert Selection* feature. This option reverses the selection you make with your mouse and highlights the rest. bash and Korn also provide a similar feature of matching all filenames *except* those in the expression. For instance, this expression

```
!(*.exe)
```
All files without .exe *extension*

matches all except the .exe files. If you want to include multiple expressions in the exception list, then use the | as the delimiter:

```
cp !(*.jpg|*.jpeg|*.gif) ../text
```

This copies all except the graphic files in GIF or JPEG format to the text directory. Note that the parentheses and | can be used to group filenames only if the ! precedes the group.

Note

The exclusion feature won't work in bash unless you make the setting **shopt -s extglob**. Even if you don't understand what this means, simply place this statement in .bash_profile or .profile, whichever is your startup file *(17.9.6)*.

SUMMARY

The shell is a command that runs when a user logs in, and terminates when she logs out. It waits for a command to be entered and scans it for special characters (*metacharacters*). It rebuilds the command line before turning it over to the kernel for execution.

The shell matches filenames with *wild cards* that must be expanded before the command is executed. It can match any character (*) or a single one (?). It can also match a range ([]) and negate a match (!). These characters mean nothing to a command. However, **find** uses its own set of wild cards.

Any wild card or special character is *escaped* with a \ to be treated literally, and if there are a number of them, then they should be placed within quotes. The \ also escapes the *[Enter]* key, enabling you to split a lengthy command line into multiple lines.

Sometimes, escaping is used by a command to attach (rather than remove) a special meaning to a character. The **echo** command uses special escape sequences for echoing the formfeed character (\f), newline (\n) and tab (\t). **echo** also uses octal values. **echo** \007 produces a beep.

Many commands use data in the form of a *character stream*. They take input from the *standard input* stream and direct output to the *standard output* stream. By default, they are set to the keyboard and terminal, respectively. They can also be redirected to come from or go to a disk file or *pipeline*.

The symbol > overwrites an existing file and >> appends to it by redirecting standard output. < redirects standard input. Commands using standard input and standard output are called *filters*, a number of which are in the UNIX system.

The *standard error* represents error messages. Its default destination is the terminal, but it can also be redirected with 2>, but not in the C shell.

The file /dev/null is a special file that never grows in size even when a stream of data is directed to it. /dev/tty is a generic device name for every terminal which every user can use to direct output to.

Using a *pipeline*, the standard output of one command can be connected to the standard input of another. A combination of filters placed in pipelines can be used to perform complex tasks which the commands can't perform individually.

The **tee** command breaks the output into two streams. One stream goes to the standard output, and the other is saved in a file. **tee** is an external UNIX command and not a feature of the shell.

Command substitution enables a command's output to become the arguments of another command. It is specified within a pair of backquotes (` `` `).

Shell variables are used to store values that can be used in script logic. They are of the form *variable=value* but are evaluated by prefixing a $ to the variable name. The variables that control the workings of the UNIX system are known as *environment variables*.

Single quotes protect all special characters, while double quotes enable variable evaluation and command substitution.

The shell is also a programming language with its own set of constructs like **if**, **for** and **while**. These constructs can be used in combination with UNIX commands and variables in a *shell script*. A shell script generally requires executable permission.

The Bourne shell (sh) is the universal shell, though the C shell (csh) also has a significant user base. The Korn shell (ksh) and the bash shell (bash) are superior alternatives to the Bourne shell and C shell.

GOING FURTHER

The Korn shell and bash extend the wild-card matching features of the Bourne shell. They use the symbols {} to group multiple patterns using the , as the delimiter of patterns. The ! is used with the grouping operators () and the delimiter | for selecting all files except those matching an expression.

SELF-TEST

8.1   Why does the shell have to expand the wild cards?

8.2   What does the shell do when it encounters the * as a single argument to a command?

8.3   Match the filenames chapa, chapb, chapc, chapx, chapy and chapz with one expression.

8.4   Does **rm** * remove all files?

8.5   How do you list all filenames that have at least four characters?

8.6   Which UNIX command uses wild cards as part of its syntax?

GOING FURTHER

8.7   When using **cat > foo**, what happens if foo already contains something?

8.8   What happens when you use **who >> foo** and foo doesn't exist?

8.9   You have a long command sequence which you want to split into multiple lines. What precautions do you need to take?

8.10   What is this command meant to do? Is it legitimate in the first place?

```
>foo <bar bc
```

8.11   What is the best method of ensuring that error messages are not seen on the terminal?

8.12   Make this setting at the command prompt. Can you execute $x?

```
x='ls | more' or set x='ls | more' (C shell)
```

8.13   Enter the commands **echo "$SHELL"** and **echo '$SHELL'**. What difference do you notice?

8.14   How do you find out the number of users logged in?

8.15   Attempt the variable assignment x = 10 (space on both sides of the =). Does it work if you are not using the C shell?

8.16   What is the difference between directory='pwd' and directory=`pwd`?

8.17   What is the standard shell used in Linux?

8.18   The command **echo "Enter your name\c"** didn't put the cursor at the end of the prompt in Linux. Why?

EXERCISES

8.1   Using wild cards, frame a pattern where the first character is alphabetic and the last character is not numeric if you are not using the C shell.

8.2   What is the significance of the command **ls *.*** ? Does it match files that don't contain a dot?

8.3   Consider the pattern .*.*[!.]. How many dots could there be in filenames that match this pattern if you are not using the C shell?

8.4   How do you remove only the hidden files of your directory if you are not using the C shell?

8.5   How do you remove a file beginning with a hyphen in the foo directory if you are not using the C shell?

8.6   Is the expression [3-h]* valid?

8.7   Match all filenames not beginning with a dot.

8.8   Will **ls .*swp** show the filename .ux.2.swp if it exists?

8.9   How do you mark the completion of a command with a beep?

8.10   When does **cd *** work?

8.11   What happens when you use **cat foo > foo**?

8.12   Execute the command **ls > newlist**. What interesting observation can you make from the contents of newlist?

8.13   You want to concatenate two files, foo1 and foo2, but also insert some text in between from the terminal. How will you do this?

8.14   When will **wc < chap0[1-5]** work?

8.15   Is the output of the command **cat foo1 foo2 >/dev/tty** directed to the standard output?

8.16   What's the difference between the two lines produced by two invocations of **wc**? Why is the filename missing in the second line?

```
3       20      103 infile
3       20      103
```

8.17   What is a *filter*? Where does a filter get its input from?

8.18   What are the two consequences of using double quotes?

8.19   Using command substitution, write a command sequence which always prints the calendar of the current month.

8.20   For command substitution to work with a command, does the command have to be a filter?

8.21   A shell script **foo.sh** contains just this line—who >/dev/tty. Since the output of the command comes to the terminal, can you redirect the script by using foo.sh > bar?

GOING FURTHER

8.22   Without using a script, can you copy all files *not* having the .bak extension to a directory foobar? When will the command not work?

KEY TERMS

character class *(8.2.2)*
character stream *(8.6)*
command parsing *(8.13)*
command substitution *(8.10)*
despecializing *(8.3)*
environment variable *(8.11.1)*
escape sequence *(8.5)*
escaping *(8.3)*
file descriptor *(8.6.3)*
filter *(8.8)*
metacharacter *(8.2.1)*
pipeline *(8.8)*

quoting *(8.4)*
redirection *(8.6)*
shell *(8.1)*
shell script *(8.12)*
shell variable *(8.11)*
sleeping *(8.1)*
standard error *(8.6.3)*
standard input *(8.6.2)*
standard output *(8.6.1)*
waiting *(8.1)*
waking *(8.1)*
wild card *(8.2.1)*

## CHAPTER 9

Simple Filters

This chapter features the simple filters of the system—commands which accept data from standard input, manipulate it and produce standard output. Filters are the central tools of the UNIX tool kit, and each filter featured in this chapter performs a simple function. This chapter shows their use both in standalone mode and in combination with other tools using redirection and piping.

Many UNIX files have lines containing *fields*—strings of characters representing a meaningful entity. Some commands expect these fields to be separated by a suitable delimiter that's not used by the data. Typically this delimiter is a **:** (as in /etc/passwd and $PATH), but we have also used the | (pipe) as the delimiter for some of the sample files in this and other chapters. Many filters work well with delimited fields, and some simply won't work without them.

Most of the commands featured in this chapter are extremely important, and you'll see them used extensively in other chapters. After you have understood the use of these commands, you should read Section 9.18 where they are used in numerous combinations to perform content manipulations tasks—tasks which they can't do when acting alone.

Objectives

- View one screen of text at a time and search for a pattern with a pager like **more**. *(9.1)*
- Count the number of lines, words and characters with **wc**. *(9.2)*
- View the control and invisible characters by looking at their octal representations with **od**. *(9.3)*
- Format text to provide margins and headers, doublespacing and multiple column output with **pr**. *(9.4)*
- Find differences and commonalities between two files with **cmp**, **diff** and **comm**. *(9.5 to 9.7)*
- Pick up lines from the beginning with **head** and the end with **tail**. *(9.8 and 9.9)*
- Cut characters or fields vertically with **cut** and join two files laterally with **paste**. *(9.10 and 9.11)*
- Sort and remove duplicate lines with **sort**. *(9.12)*
- Change, delete or squeeze individual characters with **tr**. *(9.13)*

- Find out the unique and nonunique lines with **uniq**. *(9.14)*
- Number lines with **nl**. *(9.15)*
- Convert between DOS and UNIX files with **dos2unix** and **unix2dos**. *(9.16)*
- Check and list spelling errors with **spell**. *(9.17)*
- Combine these commands to perform content manipulating tasks in a special examples section. *(9.18)*

Linux

- Use the advanced paging facilities of **less**. *(9.1)*
- Use the **ispell** program to correct spelling both interactively as well as non-interactively. *(9.17)*

9.1   more: **Paging Output**

The **man** command displays its output a page at a time. This is possible because it sends its output to a pager program. UNIX offers two pagers, **more** and **less**, which have today replaced **pg**, the original pager of UNIX. **more** was developed at Berkeley but is available in every version of UNIX today. **less** is the standard pager in Linux. We'll discuss **more** in this section and note the exclusive features of **less** separately in the Linux-specific section. Many of their features have already been discussed in Section 2.7, so it could be worthwhile having a look at them before you continue.

To view the file chap01, enter **more** with the filename:

```
more chap01                                                        Press q to exit
```

You'll see the contents of chap01 on the screen, one page at a time. At the bottom of the screen, you'll see the string --More-- and probably the percentage of the file that has been viewed:

```
--More-- (17%)
```

To quit the pager at this point, enter a **q**. Like **vi** and **emacs**, **more** also has a number of internal commands of its own that don't show up on the screen when you invoke them. **q** is an internal command.

Navigation   The navigation features of **more** are quite system-dependent, and you have to try out the commands shown in Table 9.1 and Table 2.1 to know whether they apply to your system. If necessary, you may have to browse the man pages or use **more**'s online help facility (using **h**).

Irrespective of version, **more** uses the *[Spacebar]* to scroll forward a page at a time. You can also scroll by small and large increments of lines or screens. To move forward one page, use

```
f
```

and to move back one page, use

```
b
```

TABLE 9.1   *Internal Commands of* **more** *and* **less** *(See also Table 2.1)*

Action	more	less
One page forward	[Spacebar] or f	[Spacebar] or f
20 pages forward	20f	—
One line forward	[Enter]	j or [Enter]
1000 lines forward	1000s	1000j
One page back	b	b
15 pages back	15b	—
1000 lines back	—	1000k
Beginning of file	—	p or 1G
End of file	—	G
Go to line 300	—	300G
Search forward for *pat*	/*pat*	/*pat*
Repeat search forward	n	n
Search back for *pat*	—	?*pat*
Repeat search back	—	N
Skip to next file specified in command line	:n	:n
Skip to previous file specified in command line	:p	:p
Display current line number	=	=
Repeat last command	. (a dot)	—
Start up **vi** editor	v	v
Execute UNIX command *cmd*	!*cmd*	!*cmd*
Quit	q	q
View Help	h	h

Many commands in **more** including **f** and **b** use a repeat factor. This is a number prefixed to a **vi** command *(4.6)* to repeat the command that many times. This means you can also use **10f** for scrolling forward by 10 pages and **30b** for scrolling back 30 pages. Just remember that the commands themselves are not displayed on the screen—even for a moment.

     more has its own repeat command too. This is the dot (same command used by **vi**) that repeats the last command you used. If you scroll forward with **10f**, you can scroll another 10 pages by simply pressing a dot. This is a great convenience available in **more**!

Pattern Search   You don't need to learn new pattern searching techniques if you know **vi** well; **more** uses a subset of these techniques. To recapitulate the method of looking for a pattern, simply press a **/** and then the text you are looking for. Thus, to look for the word UNIX, you should use this:

```
/UNIX
```
Searches forward only

If that's not the pattern you are looking for, you can press **n** repeatedly till you have located the desired line. Some versions let you use **?** to search backward.

The patterns that you provide here need not be restricted to simple strings; they could be *regular expressions* as well. You have used these expressions with **vi** *(4.15)* and **emacs** *(5.13)*. These expressions use certain special characters to match more than one pattern—even at a certain location in the line. Consider these two searches; the first one matches two strings, and the second one matches all comment lines in a shell script:

```
/[sS]ystem
```
Searches for system *or* System
```
/^#
```
Searches for a # at the beginning (^)

Using Multiple Filenames **more** also works with multiple filenames:

```
more chap01 chap02 chap03
```
Same as more chap0[123]

You'll first see the contents of the first file. After you have finished viewing this file, you'll see a message similar to this:

```
chap01: END (next file: chap02)
```

more moves over to the next file chap02 when you press **f** or the *[Spacebar]* at this prompt.

In the middle of a session, you can switch to the next or previous file, using these sequences:

```
:n
```
Next file
```
:p
```
Previous file

more is often used in a pipeline with commands whose output won't fit in a single screen. We often use it with the **ls** command:

```
ls -l | more
```

more also has a fairly useful help facility. Hitting an **h** invokes this screen, where you'll see all its internal commands. The important ones are summarized in Table 9.1.

Tip

more can start up the **vi** editor from within **more** itself. Simply press **v**. After you have finished editing, use **ZZ**, **:x** or **:wq** to return to **more**.

Linux

less—The Standard Pager

Even though every Linux system also offers **more**, **less** is its standard pager. It's ironic that it bears such a name because it really is a superset of **more**. Feature for feature, it nearly matches **vi**, which means learning **less** should be a breeze for **vi** users.

Navigation is **vi**-compatible. You have to work with these keys:

f, *[Ctrl-f]* or *[Spacebar]*	Scroll forward one screen
b or *[Ctrl-b]*	Scroll backward one screen
j	One line up
k	One line down

In line with **vi** tradition, **less** uses the **G** command with a repeat factor to move to a specific line. For instance, **1G** takes you to the beginning of the file, **400G** goes to line number 400, while a simple **G** means the end of file.

Pattern searching techniques are similar. Unlike many versions of **more**, **less** can search for a pattern in the reverse direction also using the sequence ?*pattern*. But **less** does have one serious limitation. Unlike **more** (which uses the **.**), it can't repeat the last command. However, its acceleration feature enables you to skip forward 100 lines with **100z** and then repeat the command by using only **z** *(2.7—Tip)*.

9.2 **wc: Line, Word and Character Counting**

You have used the **wc** command a number of times already. The command counts lines, words and characters depending on the options used. We'll run it on a file, but first let's view its contents:

```
$ cat infile
I am the wc command
I count characters, words and lines
With options I can also make a selective count
```

wc displays a four-columnar output when you run the command on this file:

```
$ wc infile
      3      20     103 infile
```

The command counts 3 lines, 20 words and 103 characters. The filename has also been shown in the fourth column. The meanings of these terms should be clear to you as they are used throughout the book:

- A **line** is any group of characters not containing a newline character.
- A **word** is a group of characters not containing a space, tab or newline.
- A **character** is the smallest unit of information, and includes all spaces, tabs and newlines.

There are three options you can use with **wc** to make a specific count. The -l option counts only the number of lines, while the -w and -c options count words and characters, respectively:

```
$ wc -l infile
      3 infile                                          Number of lines
$ wc -w infile
     20 infile                                          Number of words
```

```
$ wc -c infile
    103 infile
```
Number of characters

When used with multiple filenames, **wc** produces a line for each file and displays a total count at the end:

```
$ wc chap01 chap02 chap03
    305    4058   23179 chap01
    550    4732   28132 chap02
    377    4500   25221 chap03
   1232   13290   76532 total
```
A total as a bonus

Applications   Since **wc** is a filter, it can count lines and words in the standard output of any UNIX command. For instance, it can count the number of files in a directory or the number of users:

```
ls | wc -l
```
Number of files

```
who | wc -l
```
Number of users

When handling multiple files, you may be interested in seeing a single figure that represents, say, the number of words. This can easily be done by using the same principle that we used earlier *(8.8.1)*; make **wc** ignorant of the source of its input. Concatenate the contents of multiple files with **cat** and send the output to **wc -w** as a stream:

```
$ cat ux3rd?? | wc -w
303254
```

If required, you can set this to a variable too:

```
$ count=`cat ux3rd?? | wc -w`
$ echo $count
303254
```
Use set *in the C shell*

and then use it as a control command in the shell's **if** statement:

```
if [ $count -gt 30000 ] ; then
    echo "Your files have exceeded 30K"
fi
```

These three lines belong to the domain of shell programming. We'll have enough opportunities to use UNIX commands and pipelines in these constructs.

9.3   od: **Displaying Data in Octal**

Many files (especially executables) contain nonprinting characters, and most UNIX commands don't display them properly. The file odfile contains some of these characters that don't show up normally:

```
$ more odfile
White space includes a
```

```
The ^G character rings a bell
The ^L character skips a page
```

The apparently incomplete first line actually contains the tab character that has been entered by hitting the *[Tab]* key. To make these characters visible, you have to use the **od** (octal dump) command that displays the ASCII octal value (numbering system of base 8) of a file's contents. The –b option displays this value for each character separately. Here's a trimmed output:

```
$ od -b odfile
0000000 127 150 151 164 145 040 163 160 141 143 145 040 151 156 143 154
0000020 165 144 145 163 040 141 040 011 012 124 150 145 040 007 040 143
. . . . .
```

Each line displays 16 bytes of data in octal, preceded by the position in the file of the first byte in the line. In the absence of proper mapping it is difficult to make sense out of this output, but when the –b option is combined with the –c (character) option, the output is friendlier:

```
$ od -bc odfile
0000000   127 150 151 164 145 040 163 160 141 143 145 040 151 156 143 154
          W   h   i   t   e       s   p   a   c   e       i   n   c   l
0000020   165 144 145 163 040 141 040 011 012 124 150 145 040 007 040 143
          u   d   e   s       a      \t  \n   T   h   e      \a       c
0000040   150 141 162 141 143 164 145 162 040 162 151 156 147 163 040 141
          h   a   r   a   c   t   e   r       r   i   n   g   s       a
0000060   040 142 145 154 154 012 124 150 145 040 014 040 143 150 141 162
          b   e   l   l  \n   T   h   e      \f       c   h   a   r
. . . . . . .
```

Each line is now replaced by two. The octal representations are shown in the first line, and the printable characters and escape sequences are shown as their equivalents in the second. The first character in the first line of the file contains the letter W, which also has the octal value 127. Now, pay attention to these characters:

- The tab character, *[Ctrl-i]*, is shown as \t and the octal value 011.
- The bell character, *[Ctrl-g]*, is shown as \a and 007.
- The formfeed character, *[Ctrl-l]*, is shown as \f and 014.
- The linefeed or newline character, *[Ctrl-j]*, is shown as \n and 012.

Note that **od** makes the newline character visible too. These escape sequences are also used with **echo** *(8.5)*. You should know them well as they are also used by the C language, **awk** and **perl**.

Detecting Nonprintable Characters in Filenames Now, where does one use this command? Sometimes, you can't access a file because it contains a nonprintable character in the filename:

```
$ ls P*
Program Files
```

There appears to be a space there, but how can you be sure? Use **od** to find out:

```
$ ls P* | od -bc
0000000 120 162 157 147 162 141 155 040 106 151 154 145 163 012
          P   r   o   g   r   a   m       F   i   l   e   s  \n
0000016
```

There's indeed a space (octal 040) between Program and Files. Removing this file should now be quite easy; just escape the space: **rm Program\ Files**.

9.4   pr: **Paginating Files**

The **pr** command prepares a file for printing by adding suitable headers, footers and formatted text. It has many options, and some of them are quite useful. Try it first without using any option and with a filename as argument:

```
$ pr group1
```

```
May 06 10:38 1999  group1               Page 1
```

```
root:x:0:root                           These seven lines are the original
bin:x:1:root,bin,daemon                            contents of group1
users:x:200:henry,image,enquiry
adm:x:25:adm,daemon,listen
dialout:x:18:root,henry
lp:x:19:lp
ftp:x:50:
. . . blank lines . . .
```

pr adds five lines of margin at the top (simplified here) and five at the bottom. The lower portion of the page has not been shown in the examples for reasons of economy. The header shows the date and time of last modification of the file, along with the filename and page number.

The **pr** output scrolls so fast that you won't be able to see it on your screen. You'd better use **more** or **less** with it too if you want to try out the examples in this section:

```
pr group1 | more
```

pr is generally used to impart cosmetic touches to text files before they are sent to the printer. If the **lp** command doesn't print headers, then it can be used in combination with **pr** as a "preprocessor":

```
$ pr group1 | lp
Request id is 334
```

9.4.1   pr Options

pr assumes a default page size of 66 lines which can be changed with the -l (length) option if your page size is different. It can also be instructed to start printing from a specific page number:

```
pr -l 72 chap01 | lp                              Page set to 72 lines
pr +10 chap01 | lp                          Starts printing from page 10
```

The +*k* option uses a +, so here's an option that doesn't begin with a - symbol.

How about printing the file group1 in two columns to save paper? And, how about removing all margins and headers from the file totally? The -t option removes these headers and -2 prints in two columns:

```
$ pr -t -2 group1
root:x:0:root                          dialout:x:18:root,henry
bin:x:1:root,bin,daemon                lp:x:19:lp
users:x:200:henry,image,enquiry        ftp:x:50:
adm:x:25:adm,daemon,listen
```

This is how the KEY TERMS section of the book was printed, but it was done by filtering the screen text *(4.19)*.

pr can also double-space text. People tend to use the **sed** command to do the job, but it is easier to use **pr** with the -d (double) option. We'll continue to suppress the margins and headers:

```
$ pr -t -d group1
root:x:0:root

bin:x:1:root,bin,daemon

users:x:200:henry,image,enquiry

adm:x:25:adm,daemon,listen
    . . . . . . .
```

pr has many other options. You can number lines (-n) and offset them (-o) so that every line is preceded by a specified number of spaces. The important options of **pr** are listed in Table 9.2.

Tip

If you find your print output wasting too much space, then you can reformat it to print in multiple columns using **pr**'s -*k* option, where *k* is an integer.

9.5 cmp: **Comparing Two Files**

You'll often need to know whether two files are identical. You could then delete one of them. Sometimes, you'll want to compare two configuration files of two UNIX systems to determine the additional work that needs to be done. There are three commands in the UNIX system that can tell you that—**cmp**, **diff** and **comm**. In this section, we'll have a look at the **cmp** (compare) command.

For illustrating the use of this command and some others, we'll be using two files, group1 and group2, which have slight differences between them. We have used group1 with **pr**, but here we need to see both files side-by-side. They are shown in Fig. 9.1.

TABLE 9.2   *Options to the* **pr** *Command*

Option	Significance
-l *n*	Sets length of page to *n* lines
-w *n*	Sets width of page to *n* characters
-h *stg*	Sets header for every page to string *stg*
-n	Numbers lines in output
-o*n*	Offsets output by *n* spaces
-d	Double-spaces output
-*k*	Produces output in *k* columns
+*k*	Starts printing from page *k*
-t	Eliminates headers, footers and margins totally

The second file has one extra line, but there are other differences which become evident when we use **cmp** with the two filenames as arguments:

```
$ cmp group1 group2
group1 group2 differ: char 47, line 3
```

The two files are compared byte by byte, and the location of the first mismatch (in the forty-seventh character of the third line) is echoed to the screen. **cmp**, when invoked without options, doesn't bother about possible subsequent mismatches.

Even though we could easily detect a discrepancy in the third line, there could be many others. The -l (list) option gives a detailed list of the byte number and the differing bytes in octal for each character that differs in both files:

```
$ cmp -l group[12]                                        Using a wild card
    47   62   61
   109   70   71
   128   71   70
cmp: EOF on group1                                        group1 finishes first
```

FIGURE 9.1   *Two Files* **group1** *and* **group2** *Having Some Differences*

```
$ cat group1                          $ cat group2
root:x:0:root                         root:x:0:root
bin:x:1:root,bin,daemon               bin:x:1:root,bin,daemon
users:x:200:henry,image,enquiry       users:x:100:henry,image,enquiry
adm:x:25:adm,daemon,listen            adm:x:25:adm,daemon,listen
dialout:x:18:root,henry               dialout:x:19:root,henry
lp:x:19:lp                            lp:x:18:lp
ftp:x:50:                             ftp:x:50:
                                      cron:x:16:cron
```

There are three differences up to the point the end-of-file is encountered in either of them. The forty-seventh character has the ASCII octal value of 62 in one file and 61 in another.

If the two files are identical, **cmp** displays no message, but simply returns the $ prompt. You can try it with two copies of the same file:

```
$ cmp group1 group1
$ _                                            No output—files identical
```

This follows the UNIX tradition of quiet behavior. This behavior is also very important because the comparison has returned a *true* value, which can be subsequently used in a shell script to control the flow of a program.

You can use **cmp** in a pipeline to count the number of differences between two files:

```
$ cmp -l group? | wc -l
3
```

cmp tells you the numerical positions where differences exist, but isn't much help except that it's the best way of knowing whether two files are identical or not. For identifying lines that contain the differences, we require the **diff** command.

9.6 diff: **Converting One File to Another**

diff takes a different approach to displaying file differences. Unlike **cmp**, it also tells you which lines in one file have to be changed to make two files identical. When used with the same files, it produces a detailed output:

```
$ diff group[12]
3c3                                            Change line 3 of first file
< users:x:200:henry,image,enquiry                   replacing this line
--                                                                  with
> users:x:100:henry,image,enquiry                                   this
5,6c5,6                                           Change lines 5 to 6
< dialout:x:18:root,henry                    replacing these two lines
< lp:x:19:lp
---
> dialout:x:19:root,henry                               with these two
> lp:x:18:lp
7a8                                       Append after line 7 of first file
> cron:x:16:cron                                                this line
```

diff uses certain special symbols with its **instructions** to indicate the changes needed to make two files identical. You should understand these instructions as they bear some resemblance to the ones used by one of the most powerful commands in the system—the **sed** command.

Each instruction is applied to the first file and comprises an **address** and an **action**. The instruction **3c3** changes line 3 with one line, which remains line 3 after the change. **7a8** means appending a line after line 7, yielding line number 8 in the second file. **5,6c** changes two lines. Look closely at both files to satisfy yourself that the recommended changes in these lines are sufficient to make the two files identical.

Tip

If you are simply interested in knowing whether two files are identical or not, use **cmp** without any options.

9.7 comm: **What Is Common?**

Suppose you have two lists of people, and you are asked to find out the names available in one and not the other, or even those common to both. **comm** is the command that you need for this work. It requires two *sorted* files, and lists the differing entries in different columns. Let's try it on these two files:

```
$ cat foo1            $ cat foo2
charlie               bob
henry                 charlie
julie                 harry
monty                 julie
sumit                 monty
                      sumit
```

Both files are sorted and have some differences. When you run **comm**, it displays a three-columnar output:

```
$ comm foo1 foo2
        bob                               Only in second file
                charlie                   Common to both files
        harry
henry                                     Only in first file
                julie
                monty
                sumit
```

The first column contains one line unique to the first file, and the second column shows two lines unique to the second file. The third column displays four lines common (hence its name) to both files.

This output would probably be of no use, but **comm** can also produce selective output using the options -1, -2 or -3. To drop a particular column, simply use its column number with the - sign. You can also combine options and display only those lines that are common:

```
comm -3 foo1 foo2            Selects lines not common to both files
comm -13 foo1 foo2           Selects lines present only in second file
```

The last example and one more with the other matching option (-23) has more practical value than you may think. We'll consider an example using this command at the end of this chapter.

9.8 head: **Displaying the Beginning of a File**

The **head** command, as the name implies, displays the top of the file. When used without an option, it displays the first 10 lines of the argument file:

```
head foo                                          Shows first 10 lines of foo
```

You can specify a linecount and display, say, the first three lines. Use the - symbol, followed by a numeric argument:

```
$ head -3 group1
root:x:0:root
bin:x:1:root,bin,daemon
users:x:200:henry,image,enquiry
```

head can be used in imaginative ways. For example, you resume an editing session the next day and find you are unable to recall the name of the file you last edited. Since **ls -t** displays files in order of their modification time, picking up the first file from the list and using it as an argument to the **vi** editor should do the job. This requires command substitution:

```
vi `ls -t | head -1`                            Opens last modified file for editing
```

You can define this as an *alias (17.4)* so that the aliased command is always available for you to use.

head is often used with the **grep** command *(15.2)* to restrict the display to a few lines. The following sequence picks up the first five lines containing the string GIF after the words IMG SRC:

```
grep "IMG SRC.*GIF" quote.html | head -5
```

Here, we have used a regular expression .* to signify the use of any number of characters. Here, it implies that there can be anything between SRC and GIF (even nothing at all).

Linux

Picking Up Bytes Rather than Lines

GNU **head** can pick up a specific number of characters, blocks, kilobytes and megabytes from the beginning of the file. So, if **cmp** didn't quite tell you where the forty-seventh character is located, the -c (character) option of **head** will show you exactly where the discrepancy is:

```
$ head -c47 group1
root:x:0:root
bin:x:1:root,bin,daemon
users:x:2
```

These are the 47 characters of group1. If you compare the last character here with group2, you'll find that there it is a 1 (the group-id there is 100). You can pick up in the other units too:

```
head -c 1b shortlist                                             First 512-byte block
head -c 2m README                                                    2 megabytes
```

Some programs (like **cmp**) point out errors and differences at a certain character location in a file, and it's here that the -c option can be very useful.

9.9 tail: Displaying the End of a File

Complementing its **head** counterpart, the **tail** command displays the end of the file. It provides an additional method of addressing lines, and like **head**, it displays the last 10 lines when used without arguments. The last three lines are displayed in this way:

```
$ tail -3 group1
dialout:x:18:root,henry
lp:x:19:lp
ftp:x:50:
```

Some versions of UNIX limit the size of the segment that can be extracted by **tail**. To get over this problem, you can address lines from the beginning of the file instead of the end. The +k option allows you to do that, where k represents the line number from where the selection should begin. If a file contains 1000 lines, selecting the last 200 implies using

```
tail +801 foo                                        801th line onwards, possible with + symbol
```

tail can also extract in units of blocks or characters. This command extracts the last 512 bytes:

```
tail -512c foo                                                        Use b for blocks
```

You probably wouldn't expect this from **tail**, but many versions of this command can also present lines in reverse order when used with the -r option.

Monitoring File Growth (-f) Many UNIX programs constantly write to the system's log files as long as they are running. System administrators need to monitor the growth of these files to view the latest messages. **tail** offers the -f (follow) option for this purpose. This is how you can monitor the installation of Oracle 8.1 by watching the growth of the log file install.log from another terminal:

```
tail -f /oracle/app/oracle/product/8.1/orainst/install.log
```

The prompt doesn't return even after the work is over. With this option, you have to abort the process to exit to the shell. Use the interrupt key applicable on your machine.

Tip

Use **tail -f** when you have a program running that constantly writes to a file, and you want to see how the file is growing. You have to terminate this command with the interrupt key.

Picking Up Bytes Rather than Lines

Linux

GNU **tail** also shares the options that were discussed in the Linux sidebar in the
section on **head**.

9.10 cut: **Slitting a File Vertically**

While **head** and **tail** are used to slice a file horizontally, you can slice a file vertically
with the **cut** command. **cut** identifies both columns and fields. We'll take up columns
first.

Cutting Columns (-c) Let's use **cut** to extract the first four columns of the group
file. This requires the -c option followed by the column specification:

```
$ cut -c1-4 group1                                    -c or -f option always required
root
bin:
user
adm:
dial
lp:x
ftp:
```

The specification -c1-4 cuts columns 1 to 4. You can also use **cut** with more than one
column specification. Ranges are permitted and commas can be used to separate the
column chunks:

```
cut -c -3,6-22,28-34,55- foo                              Must be an ascending list
```

There should be no whitespace in the column list. Observe that **cut** also uses a special
form for selecting a column from the beginning and up to the end of a line. The expression 55- indicates column number 55 to the end of the line. Similarly, -3 is the same
as 1-3.

Cutting Fields (-f) The -c option is useful for fixed-length lines. Most UNIX files
(like /etc/passwd and /etc/group) don't contain fixed length lines. Here, you'll need
to cut fields rather than columns.

   cut uses the tab as the default field delimiter, but can also work with a different
delimiter. You require two options here—-d for the delimiter and -f for specifying the
field list. This is how you cut out the first and third fields:

```
$ cut -d: -f1,3 group1
root:0
bin:1
users:200
adm:25
```

```
dialout:18
lp:19
ftp:50
```

When you use the -f option, you shouldn't forget to use the -d option too, unless the file has the default delimiter (the tab).

cut can be used to extract the first word of a line by specifying the space as the delimiter. The first example used in Section 3.2 now run in tandem with **cut** displays the list of users only:

```
$ who | cut -d " " -f1                                              Space is the delimiter
root
romeo
andrew
juliet
```

cut is a powerful text manipulator often used in combination with other commands or filters. You'll be using the command a number of times in this text.

Note

You must indicate to **cut** whether you are extracting fields or columns. One of the options -**f** and -**c** has to be specified. These options are really not optional; one of them is compulsory.

9.11 paste: **Pasting Files**

What you cut with **cut** can be pasted back with the **paste** command—but vertically, rather than horizontally. You can view two files side by side by pasting them. Like **cut**, **paste** also uses the -d option to specify the delimiter, which by default is also the tab.

Let's use **paste** to laterally join the two files calc.lst and result.lst that we generated in the last chapter *(8.6.2)*. We'll use = as the delimiter:

```
$ paste -d= calc.lst result.lst
     2 ^ 32=4294967296
    25 * 50=1250
30*25 + 15^2=975
```

You now have what you probably were looking for—both the expression and result in the same line. The -d option has played the trick in placing the = in between.

Even though **paste** uses at least two files for concatenating lines, we must not forget that it's also a filter. This means that the data for one file can be supplied through the standard input. Since **bc** displays its output on the standard output, we can use **bc** and **paste** in a pipeline:

```
$ bc < calc.lst | paste -d= calc.lst -
     2 ^ 32=4294967296
    25 * 50=1250
30*25 + 15^2=975
```

This is even better; we didn't create any intermediate file this time. Note the - symbol which indicates that **paste**'s second argument must come from the standard input. You can reverse the locations of calc.lst (the one used with **paste**) and -, and you'll find the result appears before the expression.

9.12   sort: **Ordering a File**

UNIX **sort** performs the usual sorting functions and works quite well with variable length lines. It has several options, but we'll consider only the important ones by sorting the file shortlist in all possible ways. This is a text file that contains five lines of a personnel database:

```
$ cat shortlist
2233|charles harris  |g.m.     |sales     |12/12/52|  90000
9876|bill johnson    |director |production|03/12/50|130000
5678|robert dylan    |d.g.m.   |marketing |04/19/43|  85000
2365|john woodcock   |director |personnel |05/11/47|120000
5423|barry wood      |chairman |admin     |08/30/56|160000
```

Each line has six fields delimited from one another by the |. The details of an employee are stored in each line. A person is identified by emp-id, name, designation, department, date of birth and salary (in the same order). The file has been deliberately designed in fixed format for easier readability. (You'll be using an enlarged version of this file in Chapter 15 to see the extent of manipulation possible with the UNIX tool kit.)

When **sort** is invoked without options, the entire line is sorted:

```
$ sort shortlist
2233|charles harris  |g.m.     |sales     |12/12/52|  90000
2365|john woodcock   |director |personnel |05/11/47|120000
5423|barry wood      |chairman |admin     |08/30/56|160000
5678|robert dylan    |d.g.m.   |marketing |04/19/43|  85000
9876|bill johnson    |director |production|03/12/50|130000
```

Sorting starts with the first character of each line, and proceeds to the next character only when the characters in two lines are identical. By default, **sort** reorders a line in ASCII collating sequence, starting from the beginning of the line. This default sorting sequence can be altered by using certain options.

9.12.1   sort Options

Sorting on Fields (-t) Like **cut** and **paste**, **sort** also works on fields, and the default field separator is the space (tab in **cut** and **paste**). Using the -t option, you can sort the file on any field, for instance, the second field (name):

```
$ sort -t \| +1 shortlist                                         Can use -t "|" also
5423|barry wood      |chairman |admin     |08/30/56|160000
9876|bill johnson    |director |production|03/12/50|130000
2233|charles harris  |g.m.     |sales     |12/12/52|  90000
```

```
2365|john woodcock  |director |personnel |05/11/47|120000
5678|robert dylan   |d.g.m.   |marketing |04/19/43| 85000
```

The | had to be escaped to prevent the shell from interpreting it as the pipeline character. The argument +1 indicates that sorting should start after skipping the first field. To sort on the third field, you should use

```
sort -t "|" +2 shortlist
```

The sort order can be reversed with the -r (reverse) option. The following sequence reverses a previous sorting order:

```
$ sort -t "|" -r +1 shortlist
5678|robert dylan   |d.g.m.   |marketing |04/19/43| 85000
2365|john woodcock  |director |personnel |05/11/47|120000
2233|charles harris |g.m.     |sales     |12/12/52| 90000
9876|bill johnson   |director |production|03/12/50|130000
5423|barry wood     |chairman |admin     |08/30/56|160000
```

sort combines options in a rather unusual way. The previous command sequence could also have been written as:

```
sort -t "|" +1r shortlist                      Reverse sorts second field
```

Note

By default, sorting takes place in this order—numerals, uppercase letters and then lowercase letters. You can change this order by using certain options with **sort**.

Sorting on a Secondary Key You can sort on more than one field, i.e., you can provide a secondary key to **sort**. If the primary key is the third field, and the secondary key the second field, you can use

```
$ sort -t \| +2 -3 +1 shortlist
5423|barry wood     |chairman |admin     |08/30/56|160000
5678|robert dylan   |d.g.m.   |marketing |04/19/43| 85000
9876|bill johnson   |director |production|03/12/50|130000
2365|john woodcock  |director |personnel |05/11/47|120000
2233|charles harris |g.m.     |sales     |12/12/52| 90000
```

This sorts the file by designation and name. -3 indicates stoppage of sorting after the third field, and +1 indicates its resumption after the first field. To resume sorting from the first field, use +0.

Note

+1 indicates that sorting should start from the second (not the first) field, and -4 signifies sort termination after the fourth field.

Sorting on Columns You can also specify a character position within a field to be the beginning of sort. If you have to sort the file according to the year of birth, then you need to sort on the seventh and eighth column positions within the fifth field:

```
$ sort -t"|" +4.6 -4.8 shortlist
5678|robert dylan    |d.g.m.    |marketing |04/19/43| 85000
2365|john woodcock   |director  |personnel |05/11/47|120000
9876|bill johnson    |director  |production|03/12/50|130000
2233|charles harris  |g.m.      |sales     |12/12/52| 90000
5423|barry wood      |chairman  |admin     |08/30/56|160000
```

The interpretation of the column specification here is quite unusual; +4.6 signifies the starting sort position—the seventh column of the fifth field. Similarly, -4.8 implies that sorting should stop after the eighth column of the same field.

Numeric Sort (-n) When **sort** acts on numerals, strange things can happen. When you sort the group file on the third field (containing the numeric group-id), you get a curious result:

```
$ sort -t: +2 -3 group1
root:x:0:root
bin:x:1:root,bin,daemon
dialout:x:18:root,henry
lp:x:19:lp
users:x:200:henry,image,enquiry                                  200 above 25!
adm:x:25:adm,daemon,listen
ftp:x:50:
```

This is probably not what you expected, but the ASCII collating sequence places 200 above 25 (0 has a lower ASCII value than 5). This can be overridden by the -n (numeric) option:

```
$ sort -t: +2 -3 -n group1                                      Can also use +2n -3
root:x:0:root
bin:x:1:root,bin,daemon
dialout:x:18:root,henry
lp:x:19:lp
adm:x:25:adm,daemon,listen
ftp:x:50:
users:x:200:henry,image,enquiry
```

Tip

Always use the -n option when you sort a file on a numeric field. If there are other sorting fields that require a plain ASCII sort, then affix the n to the column specification that requires numeric sort—like +2n.

Removing Duplicate Lines (-u) The -u (unique) option lets you purge duplicate lines from a file. If you cut out the designation field from shortlist, you can pipe it to **sort** to find out the unique designations that occur in the file:

```
$ cut -d"|" -f3 shortlist | sort -u | tee desigx.lst
chairman
```

```
d.g.m.
director
g.m.
```

We used three commands to solve a text manipulation problem. Here, **cut** serves to select the third field from the sorted output.

Other sort Options Since **sort** is also a filter, the sorted output can be redirected to a file with the > operator. **sort** and **uniq** are probably the only UNIX filters that also accept the output filename as an *argument*. **sort** uses the -o (output) option for this task, and curiously enough, the input and output filenames can be the same:

```
sort -o sortedlist +3 shortlist                         Output stored in sortedlist
sort -o shortlist shortlist                             Output stored in same file
```

And if you want to check whether the file has actually been sorted, you can do so with the -c (check) option:

```
$ sort -c shortlist
$ _                                                          File is sorted
```

Now, suppose you want to check whether the file has been sorted on the fourth field. **sort** points that out clearly:

```
$ sort -t \| +3 -c shortlist
sort: shortlist:2: disorder: 9876|bill johnson    |director |production|03/12/50
|130000
```

If there's more than one file in the command line, **sort** first concatenates the files and then sorts them collectively. When large files are sorted in this way, performance often suffers. It's sometimes preferable to sort files separately before merging them—a feature offered by **sort**'s -m (merge) option. The following command merges the three files provided they are sorted individually:

```
sort -m foo1 foo2 foo3
```

The important **sort** options are summarized in Table 9.3.

9.13   tr: **Translating Characters**

So far, the commands have been handling either entire lines or columns. The **tr** (translate) command manipulates individual characters in a character stream. It translates characters using one or two compact expressions and has an unusual syntax:

tr *options expression1 expression2 < standard input*

Note that this command takes its input only from the standard input; it doesn't take a filename as its argument. By default, it translates each character in *expression1* to

TABLE 9.3 sort *Options*

Option	Significance
-t*char*	Uses delimiter *char* to identify fields
-o *flname*	Places output in file *flname*
+*k*	Starts sort after skipping *k*th field
-*k*	Stops sort after *k*th field
+*m.n*	Starts sort after *n*th column of (*m+1*)th field
-*m.n*	Stops sort on *n*th column of (*m+1*)th field
-f	Folds lowercase to equivalent uppercase (case-insensitive sort)
-r	Reverses sort order
-c	Checks if file is sorted
-n	Sorts numerically
-m *list*	Merges sorted files in *list*
-u	Removes duplicate lines

its mapped counterpart in *expression2*. The first character in the first expression is replaced by the first character in the second expression, and similarly for the other characters.

You can use **tr** to replace the | with a ~ (tilde), and the / with a -. Simply specify two expressions containing them in the proper sequence:

```
$ tr '|/' '~-' < shortlist  | head -3
2233~charles harris   ~g.m.    ~sales     ~12-12-52~ 90000
9876~bill johnson     ~director ~production~03-12-50~130000
5678~robert dylan     ~d.g.m.   ~marketing ~04-19-43~ 85000
```

Note that the lengths of the two expressions should be equal. If they are not, the longer expression will have unmapped characters (not in Linux). Single quotes are used here because no variable evaluation or command substitution is involved. It's just as easy to define the two expressions as two separate variables, and then evaluate them in double quotes:

```
exp1='|/' ; exp2='~-'
tr "$exp1" "$exp2" < shortlist          Variable evaluation only in double quotes
```

Like wild cards, **tr** also accepts ranges in the expressions it uses. The same rules apply; the character on the right of the - (hyphen) must have an ASCII value higher than the one on the left. The escaping rules should also be obvious; the character [needs to be escaped if the special meaning is to be removed from it.

Since **tr** doesn't accept a filename as an argument, the input has to be redirected from a file. Alternatively, it can be supplied through a pipe. We'll use one to change the case of the first three lines from lower to upper:

```
$ head -3 shortlist | tr '[a-z]' '[A-Z]'
2233|CHARLES HARRIS  |G.M.     |SALES      |12/12/52| 90000
9876|BILL JOHNSON    |DIRECTOR |PRODUCTION|03/12/50|130000
5678|ROBERT DYLAN    |D.G.M.   |MARKETING |04/19/43| 85000
```

Reversing the two expressions will convert case from upper to lower. **tr** is often used to change the case of a file's contents.

Note

tr doesn't accept a filename as an argument, but takes its input through redirection or from a pipe (standard input only).

9.13.1   tr Options

Deleting Characters (-d) The file shortlist has fields separated by delimiters, and the date formatted in readable form with a /. In nondatabase setups, delimiters are never used, and the date is invariably used as a six-character field with the format *mmddyy*. If you need to convert this file into the traditional format, use the -d (delete) option to delete the characters | and / from the file. The following command does it for the first three lines:

```
$ tr -d '|/' < shortlist | head -3
2233charles harris  g.m.     sales      121252 90000
9876bill johnson    director production031250130000
5678robert dylan    d.g.m.   marketing 041943 85000
```

Compressing Multiple Consecutive Characters (-s) UNIX tools work best with fields, so you'll prefer to use files with delimited fields. You can, however, achieve a certain amount of compression by eliminating all redundant spaces. The -s (squeeze) option squeezes multiple consecutive occurrences of its argument to a single character:

```
$ tr -s ' ' <shortlist | head -3                             Squeezes spaces
2233|charles harris |g.m. |sales |12/12/52| 90000
9876|bill johnson |director |production|03/12/50|130000
5678|robert dylan |d.g.m. |marketing |04/19/43| 85000
```

Once you do the same thing with the **ls -l** output, you can select the individual fields from this output with **cut**. We'll do that in the last section of this chapter.

Complementing the Expression (-c) Finally, the -c (complement) option complements (negates) the set of characters in the expression. Thus, to delete all characters except the | and /, you can combine the -d and -c options:

```
$ tr -cd '|/' < shortlist
|||||//|||||//|||||//|||||//|||||//|||||//|||||//|||||//|||||//|||||//||||
|//||||||//|||||//|||||//|$ _
```

Unusual output indeed! **tr** has deleted all characters except the | and the / from the file. Even the newline character has not been spared. This is indicated by the prompt that appears at the immediate end of output, rather than on the next line. We'll use this -cd option combination to place each word in a separate line in our examples section *(9.18.1)*.

Using Octal Values Like **echo**, **tr** also uses the ASCII octal value of a character. So, if you want to have each field on a separate line, you can replace the | with the newline character (octal value 012):

```
$ tr '|' '\012' < shortlist | head -6
2233
charles harris
g.m.
sales
12/12/52
 90000
```

If you study these **tr** options closely, you'll discover many areas where you can apply them, especially in system administration work. We'll be using some of the **tr** options in the examples section of this chapter.

Linux

Using Escape Sequences with tr
The previous command could have been written with GNU **tr** in Linux like this:

```
tr '|' '\n' < shortlist | head -6
```

Linux also uses all the usual escape sequences used by the **echo** command *(8.5)*.

9.14 uniq: **Locate Repeated and Nonrepeated Lines**
When you concatenate or merge files, you'll face the problem of duplicate entries creeping in. You saw how **sort** removes them with the -u option. UNIX offers a special tool to handle these lines—the **uniq** command. The command is most useful when placed in pipelines and is also a useful tool for the system administrator.

Consider a sorted file dept.1st that includes duplicate lines:

```
$ cat dept.1st
01|accounts|6213
01|accounts|6213
02|admin|5423
03|marketing|6521
03|marketing|6521
03|marketing|6521
04|personnel|2365
05|production|9876
06|sales|1006
```

uniq simply fetches one copy of each line and writes it to the standard output:

```
$ uniq dept.lst
01|accounts|6213
02|admin|5423
03|marketing|6521
04|personnel|2365
05|production|9876
06|sales|1006
```

Since **uniq** requires a sorted file as input, the general procedure is to sort a file and pipe the process to **uniq**. The following pipeline also produces the same output:

```
sort dept.lst | uniq -
```

uniq is most useful when used in a pipeline. Before we use it with the other commands, we need to know its options first.

9.14.1   uniq Options

Selecting the Nonrepeated Lines (-u)   The -u option selects the unique lines in input—lines that are not repeated:

```
$ uniq -u dept.lst
02|admin|5423
04|personnel|2365
05|production|9876
06|sales|1006
```

Selecting the Duplicate Lines (-d)   The -d (duplicate) option selects only one copy of the repeated lines:

```
$ uniq -d dept.lst
01|accounts|6213
03|marketing|6521
```

Counting Frequency of Occurrence (-c)   The -c (count) option displays the frequency of occurrence of all lines, along with the lines:

```
$ uniq -c dept.lst
2 01|accounts|6213
1 02|admin|5423
3 03|marketing|6521
1 04|personnel|2365
1 05|production|9876
1 06|sales|1006
```

This is an extremely useful option, and we'll make best use of it in the examples section. It raises the possibility of printing a *word-count* list where the frequency of occurrence of each word is printed with it.

Caution

Like **sort**, **uniq** also accepts the output filename as an argument. If you use the command **uniq foo1 foo2**, **uniq** would simply process foo1 and overwrite foo2 with its output. Since this is done without using an option (unlike -o in **sort**), you should be sure of what you are doing when you use **uniq** with two filenames.

9.15   nl: **Line Numbering**

The **nl** command has elaborate schemes for numbering lines. Unlike **pr**, which numbers all lines irrespective of their contents, **nl** numbers only logical lines—those containing something apart from the newline character.

Consider the file desigx.1st, which was produced in a **sort** output *(9.12.1)*. With **nl**, you can number and print its lines in a space six characters wide:

```
$ nl desigx.1st
     1  chairman
     2  d.g.m.
     3  director
     4  g.m.
```

nl uses the tab as the default delimiter, but we'll change it to the : with the -s option. We'll specify the width (-w) of the number format too:

```
$ nl -w1 -s: desigx.1st
1:chairman
2:d.g.m.
3:director
4:g.m.
```

You now have a designation table created with the numbering and formatting capabilities of **nl**.

Note

nl won't number a line if it contains nothing. In that case, **pr** would be better.

9.16   dos2unix **and** unix2dos: **DOS and UNIX Files**

You may have to move files between UNIX and Windows systems. A UNIX file has a slightly different structure than the DOS type used in Windows. Every line in UNIX is terminated by the linefeed character (octal value 12). On the other hand, DOS uses two characters—carriage return (octal 15) and linefeed. Here are two lines from a DOS file viewed on a UNIX system:

```
Every line contains an extra character^M
DOS files are larger than UNIX files^M
```

When you edit a file containing these lines with a UNIX editor, you'll see a ^M (*[Ctrl-m]*) at the end of each line. What's the octal value of this character? Assume these two lines to be in the file foo, and then use a pipeline:

```
$ head -1 foo | od -bc
0000000 105 166 145 162 171 040 154 151 156 145 040 143 157 156 164 141
          E   v   e   r   y       l   i   n   e       c   o   n   t   a
0000020 151 156 163 040 141 156 040 145 170 164 162 141 040 143 150 141
          i   n   s       a   n       e   x   t   r   a       c   h   a
0000040 162 141 143 164 145 162 015 012
          r   a   c   t   e   r  \r  \n
```

The carriage return character is shown as the escape sequence \r and has the octal value 015. Every DOS file must have each line terminated by \r\n. Recall (*9.3*) that UNIX files just have a singular \n at the end of the line.

In many cases, this conversion takes place automatically, but sometimes you have to do it yourself. For this purpose, some UNIX systems feature two utilities—**dos2unix** and **unix2dos**—for converting files between DOS and UNIX. Sometimes, systems differ in their implementation.

To convert a file catalog.html from UNIX to DOS on a Solaris system, you can use either of the two commands:

```
unix2dos catalog.html catalogd.html                    catalogd.html is the new file
unix2dos catalog.html catalog.html                     Converted back to same file
```

Some systems require only one filename where the contents of the file are filtered and written back to the same file. Some again need to use redirection:

```
unix2dos catalog.html                                  Written back to same file
unix2dos catalog.html > catalogd.html
```

The same reasoning applies to **dos2unix** too. Now, if you find the entire contents of a file shown as a single line on a DOS system, you have to use **unix2dos**. If you find a ^M at the end of every line when a file is moved to UNIX, then you should use **dos2unix** first.

These two commands have been included in this chapter because they often behave like complete filters. This is how you can concatenate a group of UNIX files, and then save the output as a single file after conversion:

```
cat *.html | unix2dos > combined.html
```

Tip

You can use **dos2unix** to delete the ^M character that occurs at the end of every line of the file typescript. This is the file used by **script** to record a login session (*3.6*).

9.17   spell: **Check Your Spellings**

UNIX was originally used for the preparation of documents, and every version of it features a spell-checking facility. **spell** is normally found in most UNIX systems. The command reads a file and generates a list of all spellings that the program recognizes as mistakes:

```
$ spell note.txt
Admintrators
Commuicator
Comptuer
DAEMON
generalise
```
This is "generalize" in U.S. spelling

The first three are obvious mistakes, and even if the fourth one isn't (being a term used in UNIX), **spell** doesn't sense it as a valid word. By default, the spellings are checked with reference to the U.S. dictionary, but you can use the -b (British) option to use a different one:

```
spell -b
```
Uses the British dictionary

spell isn't interactive, and you can't correct the mistakes on-line as a Windows user would expect. This is sometimes an advantage because it can be used in a pipeline:

```
sort -u foo | spell
```

You can use the UNIX filters to produce a list of every word in a file with one word in a separate line. Can you then use some of these filters to generate a count of every word? You'll be doing that in the examples section.

Linux

Using ispell, an Interactive Editor

Linux has a better spell-checking program, **ispell**, which can operate in both an interactive mode as well as a filter. When used interactively (with a filename), it displays the text in the neighborhood of the word and highlights the line and the word. It also suggests some alternatives and offers you other options. Fig. 9.2 shows you the screen generated by ispell.

The word browing is suspect here. The system offers eight possible alternatives to correct it. You only have to type the number if the correct word is found in the list. Here, what the author intended to use was obviously browsing, judging by the context of the World Wide Web that's shown at the top. Pressing 4 corrects the word.

There are other options available. You can press **a** to accept the word for the rest of the session. In that case, **ispell** won't prompt you when it subsequently encounters the word in the same file. If it's a valid technical word, which you would like **ispell** to remember forever, then use **i** to insert the word into your own private dictionary. If you have a different replacement string to use, then use **r**. Quit **ispell** with **q** (without saving) and **x** (after saving).

When **ispell** is used with the -l option, it works noninteractively like **spell**. It imposes a certain restriction though; the input has to be supplied from a pipe:

```
cat foo | ispell -l
```
Redirection with < not allowed

FIGURE 9.2   *Editing with* `ispell`

```
browing                 File: ux3rd17


*** Messenger, which handles all email and newsgroups
*** Navigator for  browing  the World Wide Web, and additionally provides the ftp


0: blowing
1: bowing
2: brewing
3: browning
4: browsing
5: crowing
6: growing
7: rowing
.....
[SP] <number> R)epl A)ccept I)nsert L)ookup U)ncap Q)uit e(X)it or ? for help
```

This produces a list of misspelled words as they are encountered in the document. Run **sort -u** on this output to obtain a unique list—similar to what **spell** produces.

ispell stores all words inserted with **i** in the file $HOME/.ispell_english (in the home directory). You can edit this file directly with an editor to add all words which you don't consider to be errors in spelling. But the entries must be sorted.

9.18   Applying the Filters

You have now arrived at the examples section, well-armed with knowledge of the basic UNIX filters. There are another four that we have yet to cover (**grep**, **sed**, **awk** and **perl**), but the ones we know already can do a lot of work for us. In this section, we'll be using these commands in pipelines to solve content manipulating tasks.

9.18.1   Counting Frequency of Occurrences

Let's first consider the file `shortlist` *(9.12)* which contains six fields where the third field represents the designation. To determine the number of people having the same designation, we'll have to do this work in three stages:

1. First cut out the third field with **cut -d"|" -f3 shortlist**.
2. Sort it next with **sort**.
3. Finally, run **uniq -c** on the sorted output.

Using a pipeline, it's a simple matter to do everything together:

```
$ cut -d"|" -f3 shortlist | sort | uniq -c
      1 chairman
      1 d.g.m.
      2 director
      1 g.m.
```

To produce this output requires a great deal of effort in procedural languages. Later, you'll find how **perl** and **awk** also handle this situation using their own resources.

Document authors sometimes like to see the words they use along with the frequency of their occurrence. For this to be possible, each word has to be placed in a separate line. **tr** can do that by converting all spaces and tabs (octal 011) to newlines:

tr "☐\011" "\012\012" < fool   *Space is \040*

There's a space before \011; we won't be displaying the symbol subsequently. If we define a word as a contiguous group of alphabetic characters, we have to use **tr** again to delete all nonalphabetic characters (apart from the newline) from the output of the first **tr** command. This requires the use of the complementary (-c) and delete (-d) options:

tr " \011" "\012\012" < fool | tr -cd "[a-zA-Z\012]"

You now have a list of words, with each word on a separate line. Now, sort this output and pipe it to **uniq -c**:

```
$ tr " \011" "\012\012" < fool | tr -cd "[a-zA-Z\012]" | sort | uniq -c
     32 Apache
     18 DNS
     10 Directory
     16 FQDN
     25 addresses
     56 directory
```

You had to use four commands to display the word count. You'll need two more commands to sort the list in reverse numeric sequence and print it in three columns:

```
$ tr " \011" "\012\012" < fool | tr -cd "[a-zA-Z\012]" | sort | uniq -c \
> sort -nr | pr -t -3
     56 directory          25 addresses          16 FQDN
     32 Apache              18 DNS                10 Directory
```

This command line is pretty long, so for the sake of readability, we split it into two lines by using \ to escape the *[Enter]* key.

9.18.2 Finding Out the Difference between Two Password Files

When moving a set of users to another machine, the file the system administrator needs most is /etc/passwd of both machines. Some users may already have accounts on these machines, but some have to be created. These files often have hundreds of lines, but we'll work with smaller versions:

```
$ cat passwd1
joe:!:501:100:joe bloom:/home/henry:/bin/ksh
amadeus:x:506:100::/home/amadeus:/bin/ksh
image:!:502:100:The PPP server account:/home/image:/usr/bin/ksh
bill:!:503:100:Reader's Queries:/home/bill:/bin/sh
juliet:x:508:100:juliet:/home/julie:/bin/csh
charlie:x:520:100::/home/charlie:/usr/bin/ksh
romeo:x:601:100::/home/romeo:/usr/bin/ksh
ftp:x:602:50:anonymous ftp:/home/ftp:/bin/csh
$ cat passwd2
henry:!:501:100:henry blofeld:/home/henry:/bin/ksh
amadeus:x:506:100::/home/amadeus:/bin/ksh
image:!:502:100:The PPP server account:/home/image:/usr/bin/ksh
bill:!:503:100:Reader's Queries:/home/bill:/bin/sh
julie:x:508:100:julie andrews:/home/julie:/bin/csh
jennifer:x:510:100:jennifer jones:/home/jennifer:/bin/bash
charlie:x:520:100::/home/charlie:/usr/bin/ksh
romeo:x:601:100::/home/romeo:/usr/bin/ksh
harry:x:602:100:harry's music house:/home/harry:/bin/csh
```

Each file serves a group of users (the first field), but what concerns us is locating those users in the first file who *don't* have a presence in the second file. Let's first cut out the first field of passwd1 and save the sorted output:

```
cut -f1 -d: passwd1 | sort > temp
```

We could perform a similar exercise with the second file too:

```
cut -d: -f1 passwd2 | sort > temp2
```

We now have to compare these two files with the **comm -23** command. Since all these commands are filters, we should be able to do this part of the job in one invocation without creating the temporary file temp2:

```
$ cut -d: -f1 passwd2 | sort | comm -23 temp - ; rm temp
ftp
joe
juliet
```

comm -23 lists only those lines that are in the first file, and the - symbol ensured that the output from **sort** was supplied as standard input at the location of the second argument. The list shows three users for whom the administrator has to create accounts with the **useradd** command. Since the administrator is an expert shell programmer, she'll use a script to do this job automatically!

9.18.3   Displaying Both Modification and Access Times

Finally, let's use these tools to produce a list of files that shows both the modification and access times. We'll have to use **ls -l** twice for this job—once more, with the -u option *(7.10)* to extract the access time. Since the fields of the listing are separated by multiple spaces, we'll have to compress these spaces to enable **cut** to recognize them as fields.

We won't print all the seven fields of the listing, but just the filenames, permissions and the two time stamps. Let's first save the modification time details in a separate file:

```
ls -l | tr -s ' ' | cut -d" " -f1,6-9 > temp
```

Now, run the **ls -lu** command, but this time extract only the access time (with **cut -f6-8**). Finally, pipe this output to the **paste** command where the standard input is the first source of **paste**'s input:

```
$ ls -lu | tr -s ' ' | cut -d" " -f6-8  | paste - temp
         total
Mar 12 08:06    -rwxr-xr-x Feb 29 19:27 backup.sh
Mar 12 11:38    -rw-r--r-- Mar 12 11:37 foo2
Mar 12 08:06    -rwxr-xr-x Mar 8 07:51 leapyear.sh
Mar 12 12:17    -rw-r--r-- Mar 12 12:09 passwd1
Mar 12 12:20    -rw-r--r-- Mar 12 12:07 passwd2
Mar 12 12:34    -rw-r--r-- Mar 12 12:34 ux3rd09
```

The first set of three fields shows the access time, and the second set before the filename shows the modification time. The first line of **ls -l** shows a total line also. To get rid of this line, pipe this output further to the **tail** command:

```
ls -lu | tr -s ' ' | cut -d" " -f6-8  | paste - temp | tail +2
```

Caution

This example won't work in Linux because **ls -lu** behaves differently there (Table 7.1). This option displays the access time alright, but also sequences the listing in order of their access time. System V orders the listing by ASCII collating sequence both with -l and -lu, which is necessary for the output to be correct.

Pipelining represents one of the most important aspects of the UNIX system. It implements the UNIX philosophy that difficult jobs can be done by combining filters that do simple jobs in isolation. The UNIX manual doesn't tell you the combinations of filters required for each task, and this makes pipelines difficult to conceive initially. A lot is left to knowledge of these filters, perseverance and imagination.

S U M M A R Y

more is a pager that shows output of a file a page at a time. You can scroll both forward (**f**) and backward (**b**), and search for a pattern (*/pattern*). The pattern can be both a simple string as well as a regular expression. You can repeat the last command with a dot. You can also invoke the **vi** editor directly from the pager (**v**).

wc counts the number of lines, words and characters. When used with multiple filenames, it prints a total of everything.

od displays the octal value of a character, and is used to display invisible characters. When used with the -bc options, it shows you the escape sequences \f (form-feed), \n (newline), \r (carriage return) and \t (tab). **od** is useful in identifying unprintable characters.

pr formats its input to print headings and page numbers—mostly in conjunction with the **lp** command. The output can be double-spaced (-d), printed in multiple columns (-*k*), and set to start from a specific page number (+*k*). You can drop all headers and footers also (-t).

There are three file comparison utilities available. **cmp** tells you where the first difference was encountered, though you can have a detailed character-for-character listing (-1). **diff** actually shows the differing lines, using a set of instructions which, when applied to one file, converts it to the other. **comm** shows the lines that are common, and optionally shows you lines unique to either or both files.

head displays the beginning of a file, while **tail** displays the end. **tail** can also be used with a line number (with the +*k* option) to start extraction from a specific line. You can also use it to monitor the growth of a file (-f). The GNU versions of both these commands can extract characters, blocks and other units instead of lines (-c).

cut cuts columns (-c) from its input, as well as fields (-f). The field numbers have to be a comma-delimited sequence of ascending numbers with hyphens to denote ranges. What you cut with **cut** can also be pasted with **paste**. Both **cut** and **paste** use the tab as the default delimiter.

With **sort**, you can sort individual fields, and columns within these fields. You can sort numerically (-n), reverse the sort order (-r), check whether it is sorted (-c), merge two sorted files (-m) and purge duplicate lines (-u). The sort order can also be made case-insensitive (-f).

tr translates characters and can be used to change the case of letters. You can squeeze multiple consecutive occurrences (-s) and delete a specific character (-d). You can also use it with ASCII octal values. This is the only filter that works *only* with standard input.

uniq removes duplicate lines, but can also be used to list only nonduplicate lines (-u), as well as only the repeated ones (-d).

nl numbers only *logical* lines where you can set the width of the number (-w).

UNIX and DOS files differ in structure. Lines in DOS are terminated by the carriage return–linefeed characters, while a UNIX line uses only linefeed as the newline character. Two utilities—**unix2dos** and **dos2unix**—perform this conversion.

spell is used to spell-check a document. It displays a list of misspelled words.

Linux

SUMMING UP LINUX

less is a superior pager compared to **more**, and shares many of **vi**'s features. You can go to a specific line using the **G** command. You can scroll back (**b**) and also search in the reverse direction (**?***pattern*) for a pattern.

ispell can produce a list of misspelled words like **spell** (-1), but also lets you perform corrections on-line.

SELF-TEST

Some of the questions use the file shortlist whose contents are shown in Section 9.12.

9.1   Can you edit a file using **more**?

9.2   How do you search for the string Internet when viewing a file with **more**?

9.3   How do you repeat the search?

9.4   How is a *word* defined for most purposes?

9.5   Set the number of lines in a file to a variable.

9.6   How will you find out the ASCII octal values of the numerals and alphabets?

9.7   How will you double-space a file?

9.8   If **cmp foo1 foo2** produces no output, what does that indicate?

9.9   You have two sorted lists of persons. How will you find out the names common to both lists?

9.10   How do you display the length of a line in shortlist in a message used with the **echo** statement?

9.11   What happens when you use **head** with multiple filenames?

9.12   Can you present lines in reverse order?

9.13   A software installation process writes the progress of installation to the file install_log.lst. How do you continuously monitor the file?

9.14   Will this command work?

        cut -d: -c1 -f2 foo

9.15   Can you paste two files with **paste foo[21]**?

9.16   How do you remove duplicate lines from a file using **sort**?

9.17   Sort shortlist on the month of birth.

9.18   What is the difference between a DOS and a UNIX file?

9.19   How do you spell-check a document?

EXERCISES

9.1   Pressing **v** in **more** invokes **vi**. When will this command not work and why?

9.2   How will you count the number of ordinary files in your home directory tree?

9.3   There are two sorted lists of names. How will you find out the count of names that are common to both?

9.4   Create a filename containing just one space character. How will you later confirm from the **ls** output that it indeed contains a space?

9.5   How will you produce a list of all files in the current directory without headers, but in three columns?

9.6   Select lines 5 to 10 of a file in two ways.

9.7   Extract the names of the users from /etc/passwd after ignoring the first 10 entries.

9.8   Produce from `shortlist` a list of the years of birth, along with the number of people born in that year.

9.9   Invert the names in `shortlist` and place a comma after the last name.

9.10 If your system doesn't support **tail**'s `-r` option, how will you read a file backwards?

9.11 Generate a code list by selecting the departments from `shortlist`. Use the : as the delimiter.

9.12 Sort the file `/etc/passwd` on GUID (primary) and UID (secondary) so that the users with the same GUID are placed together. Users with a lower UID should be placed higher in the list.

9.13 How are these two commands similar and different?

```
sort -u foo
uniq foo
```

9.14 How will you find out the number of times the character ? occurs in a file?

9.15 Devise a sequence which lists the five largest files in the current directory.

9.16 List from `/etc/passwd` the UID and the user having the highest UID.

9.17 List the users logged in more than once.

9.18 A feature provided in a user's startup file appends the output of the **date** command to a file `foo` whenever a user logs in. How can the user print a report showing the day along with the number of times she logged in on that day?

9.19 While editing with **vi** a section of text that has one word in each line, how can you filter the screen text to print the words in two columns? Assume that the words are located between lines 30 and 130.

9.20 How can you convert a UNIX file to DOS format?

KEY TERMS

action *(9.6)*	**instruction** *(9.6)*
address *(9.6)*	**line** *(9.2)*
character *(9.2)*	**word** *(9.2)*

## CHAPTER 10

The Process

Everything, they say, in UNIX is a file. In this chapter, we change track and look at everything as a process. When working with files, you developed a feeling of being in space. You could locate both yourself and a file with reference to an absolute point (root). Now, consider processes in the dimension of time. Like living organisms, they have life, and are capable of dying, as well as giving birth to other processes. The striking similarity between mortals and processes makes it easy to understand them.

Since UNIX is a multitasking system, more than one process can run at a time. Typically, hundreds or even thousands of processes can run in a large system. In this chapter, we'll look at process attributes and the tools UNIX offers to view and control some of these attributes. Since most UNIX shells offer features to control processes, we'll use these facilities to kill runaway processes, as well as stop, suspend and move them between foreground and background. UNIX also offers tools to schedule processes.

Objectives

- Learn the general attributes of a process. *(10.1)*
- Understand the mechanism of process creation. *(10.2)*
- Discover how **init** creates the login shell. *(10.3 and 10.4)*
- Learn the three types of commands in the system from the process perspective. *(10.5)*
- View process attributes with **ps**. *(10.6)*
- Run jobs in the background with & and **nohup**. *(10.7)*
- Reduce job priority with **nice**. *(10.8)*
- Discover how *signals* communicate with a process. *(10.9)*
- Kill a process with **kill**. *(10.10)*
- Suspend jobs and move them between foreground and background. *(10.11)*
- Schedule one-time execution of jobs with **at** and **batch**. *(10.12)*
- Schedule jobs for periodic execution with **cron**. *(10.13)*
- Make comparative estimates of the efficiency of programs with **time**. *(10.14)*

10.1 Understanding the Process

A process is defined as an *instance* of a running program. Most programs give rise to a corresponding process, usually having the same name as the program itself. For example, when you execute the **grep** command, a process named **grep** is created. A program can also give rise to multiple processes. When you run a shell script or a group of commands in a pipeline, you are running one *job* alright—but multiple processes.

Because UNIX is both a multiuser and multitasking system, every user can run multiple processes at a time. The kernel (and not the shell) is ultimately responsible for the management of all these processes. It determines the time and priorities allocated to them so that multiple processes are able to share CPU resources. It provides a mechanism by which a process is able to execute for a finite period of time and then relinquish control to another process.

Processes use the memory of a system. When memory is full, the kernel moves the code and data of these processes to the **swap area**. This swap area is usually a separate file system on the disk. When the process is reallotted its time slice, its image is recalled from the swap area for running yet again. This happens more than once a second, making the user oblivious to the switching process. The busier the system, the greater the swap activity.

Each process is uniquely identified by a number called the **process identifier** (PID) that is allotted by the kernel when the process is born. Apart from the PID, a process also has the following attributes:

- The **real user-id** of the user who created the process. The user is then said to be the **owner** of the process.
- The real group-id of the owner of the process. Both user-id and group-id of the owner are stored in /etc/passwd.
- The priority with which it runs. The kernel's process scheduler uses this value to determine the process that has to run next.
- The current directory from where the process was run.

The use of the word *real* may amuse you, but a process can also behave as if it is owned by someone else while it is running. That's why every process also has an **effective user-id** (and group-id), which for most processes are synonymous with the real ones. We'll later consider a situation when they are not *(22.4.1)*.

Note

A process remembers the directory from where it was run. This attribute acquires importance when a process also changes a directory.

10.1.1   Birth and Death: Parents and Children

To borrow an idea from MULTICS, a process is said to be **born** when the program starts execution, and remains alive as long as the program is active. After execution is complete, the process is said to **die**. Just as a file has a parent, every process also has one. This **parent** itself is another process, and a process born from it is said to be its **child**. When you run the command

```
cat foo
```

from the keyboard, a process representing the **cat** command is started by the **sh** process (if your login shell is Bourne). This **cat** process remains active as long as the command is active. **sh** is said to be the parent of **cat**, while **cat** is the child of **sh**.

Since every process has a parent, you can't have an "orphaned" process (a process that has no parent) in the UNIX system. The ancestry of every process can be traced to one ultimate process—the first process (PID 0) set up when the system is booted. It's like the root directory of the file system.

The analogy with files and directories doesn't stop here. Like a file, a process can have only one parent. Moreover, just as a directory can have more than one file under it, the multitasking nature of UNIX permits a process to generate (or *spawn*) one or more children. This is most easily accomplished by setting up a pipeline. The command

```
cat emp.lst | grep 'director'
```

sets up two processes for the two commands. These processes have the names **cat** and **grep**, and both are spawned by the shell.

While the analogy between processes and mortals is striking, you might be amused by the attitude taken by the parent with respect to its child. Though the parent gives birth to a child, it also waits for its death. When a child process completes, it sends a signal to its parent informing it of its death. Control is thus reverted to the parent that can then give birth to other processes, and wait for them to die as well.

10.2 How a Process Is Created

As noted before, a process is just a program that is running. Like a file, a process is also a sequence of bytes interpreted as instructions to be run by the CPU. This is often an executable program, which contains the binary code to be executed, along with data that would be required for the program to run. These data comprise the variables and arrays that you find in program code.

The process image as viewed by the kernel runs in its own **user address space**— a protected space which can't be disturbed by other users. This address space has a number of segments:

- **TEXT SEGMENT** This contains the executable code of a program. Since several users may be using the same program, this area generally remains fixed.
- **DATA SEGMENT** All variables and arrays the program uses are held here. They include those variables and arrays that have values assigned to them during program execution.
- **USER SEGMENT** This contains all the process attributes that were discussed earlier—the UIDs and GUIDs and the current directory. The kernel uses the information stored in this segment to manage all processes.

There are three distinct phases in the creation of a process, using three important system calls—**fork()**, **exec()** and **wait()**. Knowledge of the role they play in process creation can often help you debug shell scripts and C programs. The three phases are discussed below:

- **FORK** A process in UNIX is created with the **fork** system call, which creates a copy of the process that invokes it. For example, when you enter a command at the prompt, the shell first creates a copy of itself. The image is practically identical to the calling process, except that the *forked* process gets a new PID. The forking mechanism is responsible for the multiplication of processes in the system.

- **EXEC** The parent then overwrites the image it has just created with the copy of the program that has to be executed. This is done with the **exec** system call, and the parent is said to *exec* this process. No additional process is created here; the existing program's text and data areas are simply replaced (or **overlaid**) with the ones of the new program. This process has the same PID as the child that was just forked.
- **WAIT** The parent then executes the **wait** system call to keep *waiting* for the child process to complete. When the child has completed execution, it sends a termination signal to the parent. The parent is then free to continue with its other functions.

When a process is forked, it inherits the environment of its parent, i.e., it responds to the same signals, has the same group- and user-ids, the same current directory, priority, and so forth. In other words, it inherits most of what is stored in the user segment of the user address space. In many cases, a process would like to modify these parameters, and is permitted to do so. But then there is a very serious consequence.

If a child process alters the operating environment it has inherited, *the modified environment is not available to the parent process, and disappears as soon as the child dies*. If you understand and remember this, then you'll understand why some variable values are not available everywhere, and why the **cd** command behaves in a special manner.

Note

The environmental parameters of a process are generally made available to all its children, but changes made by a child to its own environment are not communicated to the parent. This means that values of variables defined or redefined in the child are not visible in the parent.

10.3   The Login Shell: The First User Process

When you log on to a UNIX system, the shell process is immediately set up by the kernel. This program may be **sh** (Bourne shell), **csh** (C Shell), **ksh** (Korn shell), or **bash** (Bourne again shell); the process also has the same name. Any command you type in at the prompt is actually the standard input to the shell program. This process remains alive until you log out.

The shell maintains a set of variables that are available to the user. You have already encountered many of them like PATH and HOME. The PID of the login shell is stored in a special "variable" $$. To know the value for your current shell, simply type

```
$ echo $$                                          The PID of the current shell
659
```

The PID of your login shell doesn't change as long as you are logged in. When you log out and log in again, your login shell will be assigned a different PID. Knowledge of the PID is often necessary to control the activities at your terminal—especially when things go wrong.

You can start several processes from the login shell, each having a different PID. However, all of them will have the same parent—the login shell.

10.4 The `init` Process

Who's the parent of the login shell? Generally, it's a system process named **init**. This process has the PID 1—the second process of the system. **init** is a very important process and spawns a lot of children. In fact, many of the processes running on a UNIX system have **init** as their parent. We'll now examine its role in creating a user's shell.

According to classical theory, when the system starts up and moves to multiuser mode, **init** forks and execs a **getty** process at every port connected to a terminal. Each one of these **getty**s prints the login prompt on the respective terminal and then goes off to sleep.

When a user attempts to log in, **getty** wakes up and execs the **login** program to verify the login name and password entered. Generally, on successful login, **login** forks-execs the shell process—the login shell of the user. **getty** and **login** have now extinguished themselves by overlaying. The sequence of processes that leads to the shell process is shown in Fig. 10.1.

init, now the only living ancestor of the shell, goes off to sleep, waiting for the death of its children. When the user logs out, her shell is killed, and the death is intimated to **init**. **init** then wakes up and spawns another **getty** for that line to monitor the next login. You'll see in the chapter on system administration how all this is implemented in /etc/inittab—the configuration file used by **init**. It's quite fascinating, be assured!

Note

Some UNIX and Linux systems behave differently. In many of them, the **login** process is never overlaid with the **sh** program. For these systems, **login**, rather than **init**, is the parent of a user's login shell.

10.5 Internal and External Commands

We have looked at commands as being external or internal. The shell actually recognizes three types of commands:

- **EXTERNAL COMMANDS**—The most commonly used ones are the UNIX utilities and programs like **cat**, **ls** and so forth. The shell creates a process for each of these commands that it executes and remains its parent.
- **SHELL SCRIPTS**—The shell executes these scripts by spawning another shell (a sub-shell), which then executes the commands listed in the script. The sub-shell becomes the parent of the commands that feature in the script.
- **INTERNAL COMMANDS**—A programming language on its own, the shell has a number of built-in commands as well. Some of them like **cd** and **echo** don't generate a process and are executed directly by the shell. Similarly, variable assignment with the statement x=5 doesn't generate a process either.

F I G U R E 10.1   *The Sequence of Processes Leading to the Shell*

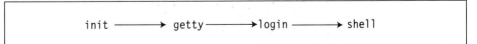

It's just as well that certain commands are built into the shell itself because it would be either difficult or impossible to implement them as separate external commands. You know that a child process inherits the current working directory from its parent as one of its environmental parameters. This inheritance has important consequences for the **cd** command.

It's necessary for the **cd** command *not* to spawn a child to achieve a change of directory. If it did so through a separate child process, then after **cd** had finished, control would revert to the parent and the original directory would be restored. It would then be impossible to change directories.

Note

All commands don't set up processes. Built-in commands of the shell like **pwd** and **cd** don't create processes.

10.6   ps: **Process Status**

Like a file, a process has many attributes, and for a proper understanding of its functioning, you need to know some of these attributes. The **ps** command is used to display the attributes of a process. It could be seen as the process counterpart of the file system's **ls** command. It's one of the few commands of the UNIX system that has knowledge of the kernel built into it. It reads through the kernel's data structures or process tables to fetch the characteristics of a process.

By default, **ps** displays the processes associated with a user at the terminal:

```
$ ps
   PID     TTY        TIME CMD
   659   tty03    00:00:01 sh            Shell of user who invoked ps
   684   tty03    00:00:00 ps
```

Like **who -H**, **ps** also generates header information. The first two columns show the PID and the terminal (*TTY*) with which the process is associated. Some processes are associated with a terminal but some are not. The login shell (**sh**) has the PID 659—the same number echoed by the special variable $$. *TIME* shows the total CPU time used by the process. This is generally a small figure; most programs usually complete their jobs quite fast. *CMD* shows the process name.

The user at this terminal is idling—only the login process is running. Because the **ps** command itself was used to obtain this output, some UNIX systems show **ps** in the output also (PID 684). These are the only commands associated with the terminal /dev/tty03.

10.6.1   ps Options

ps is a highly variant command; its actual output depends on the version of UNIX as well as the hardware used. The unusual aspect of this variation is that the options themselves mean different things to different systems. BSD and System V are at war here; none of their options seem to match. The options are listed in Table 10.1. We'll consider the System V options first.

T A B L E   10.1   *Options to* **ps**

Option	Significance
-f	Full listing showing the PPID of each process
-e	All processes including user and system processes
-u *usr*	Processes of user *usr* only
-a	Processes of all users excluding processes not associated with terminal
-l	A long listing showing memory-related information
-t *term*	Processes running on terminal *term* (say, tty03)

System Processes (-e)   Over and above the processes a user generates, there are a number of system processes that keep running all the time. Most of them are spawned during system startup, and some of them start when the system goes to the multiuser state. To list them you have to use the -e option:

```
$ ps -e
   PID    TTY        TIME CMD
     0      ?     00:00:00 sched
     1      ?     00:00:01 init          A very important process
     2      ?     00:00:00 vhand
     3      ?     00:00:01 bdflush
   260      ?     00:00:00 cron                        Chronograph
   282      ?     00:00:00 lpsched                  Printer daemon
   308      ?     00:00:00 rwalld
   336      ?     00:00:00 inetd                   Internet daemon
   339      ?     00:00:00 routed                   Routing daemon
   403      ?     00:00:00 mountd
   408      ?     00:00:00 nfsd                         NFS daemon
```

The characteristic feature of system processes is that most of them are not associated with any terminal at all (shown by the ?). Some of these processes, called **daemons**, do important work for the system. For instance, the **lpsched** daemon controls all printing activity. Your TCP/IP network will not run without the **inetd** daemon.

   These processes are known as *daemons* because they are called without a specific request from a user, and are not associated with any terminal. Many of these daemons are actually sleeping and wake up only when they receive input. One of them even looks at its control file once a minute to decide what it should do. You'll learn about some of these daemons and other system processes in subsequent chapters. We'll consider the **cron** daemon in this chapter.

Full Listing (-f)   To get a detailed listing which also shows the parent of a process, use the -f (full) option:

```
$ ps -f
     UID   PID  PPID  C    STIME     TTY        TIME CMD
   romeo   659    1   4 18:10:29   tty03   00:00:01 -sh
   romeo   685  659  15 18:26:44   tty03   00:00:00 ps -f
```

Here, you can see the parent (*PPID*) and owner (*UID*) of every process. The login shell (PID 659) has the PPID 1, which means that it was set up by a system process having this value as its PID. This is **init**, the creator of all login shells. Note that the PPID of **ps** also happens to be the PID of **sh** (659); **ps** is a child of **sh**. If you now issue a **vi** command from the shell, the PPID of **vi** will also be 659.

When the -f option is used, login shells are generally shown with a hyphen against the command name. This makes it easier to distinguish them from other shells (the sub-shells) which they may also run (through shell scripts, for example).

We'll ignore the *C* header for the time being. *STIME* shows the time the process started. *CMD* this time displays the full command line with its arguments. This is sometimes an advantage when you don't remember the exact options you have used. It can also be considered a serious detriment as others can easily know the name of the file you are working on; sometimes, you don't want that to happen.

Displaying Processes of a User (-u) The system administrator needs to use the -u (user) option to know the activities of any user, for instance, the user melinda:

```
$ ps -f -u melinda
     UID   PID  PPID  C    STIME     TTY        TIME CMD
 melinda   740   737  0 18:39:59   tty04   00:00:01 -ksh
 melinda   761   740  0 18:44:01   tty04   00:00:00 check_number.pl emp.lst
 melinda   840   837  0 18:41:09   tty05   00:00:01 -csh
```

melinda is logged in at two terminals, and this option shows all processes associated with both. We used the -f option also to display the complete command line of the programs. The user is using two types of shells at the two terminals.

Displaying All User Processes (-a) For displaying all processes run by all users including their login shells, use the -a (all) option:

```
$ ps -a
   PID    TTY        TIME CMD
   662  tty02   00:00:00 ksh
   705  tty04   00:00:00 sh
  1005  tty01   00:00:00 csh
  1017  tty01   00:00:04 vi
   680  tty03   00:00:00 ksh
  1056  tty02   00:00:00 sort
  1058  tty05   00:00:00 ksh
  1069  tty02   00:00:00 ps
```

Five users are at work here, as evident from the terminal names displayed. Two jobs are evident (**vi** and **sort**), and the users seem to differ in their preference for shells. Most seem to be users of the Korn shell (the most widely recommended shell today).

Linux

Linux uses the BSD version of the **ps** command, which has notable differences with its System V counterpart. **ps** in Linux uses two types of options—the BSD options that don't use a dash and the GNU-style options which use -- (2 hyphens). We'll consider the Red Hat Linux implementation in this discussion.

System Processes (ps ax) A typical Linux system shows a host of system processes, but Linux uses the ax option rather than the -e option to display them. Here's a vastly censored display:

```
$ ps ax
  PID TTY STAT TIME COMMAND
    1 ?   S    0:14 init                                                    Parent of login shell
    2 ?   SW   0:00 (kflushd)
    3 ?   SW   0:00 (kpiod)
    4 ?   SW   0:02 (kswapd)
    5 ?   SW   0:00 (mdrecoveryd)
  115 ?   S    0:00 inetd                                                        Internet daemon
  125 ?   S    0:00 named                                                          Name server
  133 ?   SW   0:00 lpd                                                          Printer daemon
  146 ?   SW   0:00 squid -D                                                        Proxy server
  148 ?   S    0:00 sendmail: accepting connections on port 25    Mail server
  160 6   SW   0:00 /sbin/mingetty tty6                              Process at the terminal
  161 ?   S    0:00 crond                                                  System's chronograph
  162 ?   S    0:03 httpd                                                            Web server
```

By default, Linux comes preconfigured with a number of network services, and the ax option should show them all. The system administrator needs to use this command when users have connectivity problems. If users are not able to do **ftp** or **telnet**, the administrator has to check whether **inetd** is running. If they can't print their files, the status of **lpd** has to be checked.

Full Listing (ps u) The **ps u** command approximates the **ps -f** (or, rather, **ps -l**) command of SVR4. The output, however, is more detailed:

```
$ ps u
USER    PID %CPU %MEM  SIZE   RSS TTY STAT START   TIME COMMAND
sumit   192  0.0  3.5  1892  1088   1 S    20:55   0:00 -bash
sumit   216  0.0  1.9  1576   600   5 S    20:59   0:00 sh /usr/X11R6/bin/sta
sumit   237  0.0  2.9  1908   904   5 S    20:59   0:01 fvwm95
sumit   321  0.0  4.1  1904  1260   1 S    21:02   0:03 vi +12 /home/sumit/pr
sumit  3708  0.1 28.4 20732  8728   4 S    09:17   0:04 /opt/netscape/netscap
```

There are a number of new columns here. The percentage CPU and memory usage of each command are shown under *%CPU* and *%MEM* respectively. Here, the Web browser **netscape** has taken up more than a fourth of the memory space. If you find degradation in your system's performance, this is the option that will help you locate the possible culprits. The amount of space the program occupies in memory (in Kilobytes) is shown under *SIZE* and *RSS*.

Displaying Process Ancestry (ps f) Locating ancestry by matching PIDs and PPIDs can be a grueling affair; a visual representation of the process tree is what you may be looking for. This is what Linux **ps** offers with the f option:

```
$ ps f
 PID TTY STAT TIME COMMAND
 3653   4 SW   0:00 (bash)
 3687   4 SW   0:00 \_ (startx)
 3696   4 SW   0:00  |  \_ (xinit)
 3700   4 SW   0:00  |     \_ (sh)
 3701   4 S    0:02  |        \_ kfm
 3708   4 R   24:25  |        |  \_ /opt/netscape/netscape
 3702   4 S    0:01  |        \_ fvwm95
 3969   4 S    0:00  |           \_ xterm -ls
```

It's easy to see from here that the **startx** process (PID 3687) is the parent of **xinit** (PID 3696) and the ultimate parent of many more processes that owe their origin to **xinit**. You don't need to know their PPIDs; you just have to terminate **startx** if you want to terminate all its children. This option doesn't have a close parallel in SVR4; but in its ability to display the parentage of a process, it somewhat resembles **ps -f** of SVR4.

Displaying User Processes (ps x) To display the processes run by all users, you have to use the x option (-a in SVR4):

```
$ ps x
 PID TTY    STAT  TIME COMMAND
 507 tty1   S     0:00 -bash
 593 tty4   S     0:00 -bash
 607 tty3   S     0:00 -bash
 686 tty1   S     0:00 sh /usr/X11R6/bin/startx
 693 tty1   S     0:00 xinit /etc/X11/xinit/xinitrc -- -auth /home/sumit/.Xa
 697 tty1   S     0:00 /usr/bin/gnome-session
 706 tty1   S     0:00 gnome-smproxy --sm-client-id default0
 712 tty1   S     0:02 enlightenment -clientId default2
 725 tty1   S     0:00 xscreensaver -no-splash -timeout 20 -nice 10 -lock-mo
 748 tty3   R     0:00 ps x
```

As also seen with **ps f**, you can see here the state of each process. Only one process is running; the rest are sleeping. An X Window session using GNOME as the windowing environment seems to be on.

Apart from **ps**, the **top** command also shows CPU usage in a more humanly readable form. This command available in Linux and some UNIX systems also shows **ps**-like output, but its first five lines make most interesting reading:

Note

```
11:14am  up  3:31,  6 users,  load average: 0.00, 0.00, 0.00
57 processes: 55 sleeping, 1 running, 1 zombie, 0 stopped
CPU states:  0.3% user,  0.9% system,  0.0% nice, 98.8% idle
Mem:   30628K av,  29092K used,   1536K free,  17144K shrd,   1376K buff
Swap:  40088K av,   9868K used,  30220K free               10636K cached
```

There's a whole lot of information here. From a process perspective, it shows the free and used memory of the system and the state of the CPU. Most of the memory is used up (1536K out of 30,628K available), but the CPU is idling 98.8 percent of the time. This is a very useful command for the system administrator.

10.7 Running Jobs in Background

A multitasking system lets a user do more than one job at a time. Since there can be only one job in the **foreground**, the rest of the jobs have to run in the **background**. There are two ways of doing this—with the shell's & operator and the **nohup** command. The latter permits you to log out while your jobs are running, but the former doesn't allow that (except in the C shell and bash).

10.7.1 &: No Logging Out

The & is the shell's operator used to run a process in the background (i.e., not wait for its death). Just terminate the command line with an &; the command will run in the background:

```
$ sort -o emp.1st emp.1st &
550
```
                                                                                The job's PID

The shell immediately returns a number—the PID of the invoked command (550). The prompt is returned, and the shell is ready to accept another command even though the previous command has not been terminated yet. When you execute the **ps -f** command now, you'll see something quite different:

```
$ ps -f
    UID   PID  PPID  C   STIME     TTY       TIME CMD
  romeo   541     1  4 08:22:05  tty02   00:00:00 -sh
  romeo   550   541 80 08:22:40  tty02   00:00:03 sort -o emp.1st emp.1st
  romeo   575   541  0 08:26:23  tty03   00:00:00 ps -f
```

Both **sort** and **ps** now have the same PPID—the PID of the shell. The shell has spawned two processes—one in the foreground and the other in the background. Using an & you can run as many jobs in the background as the system load permits; the shell will always be their parent.

Depending on the shell you are using, the standard output and standard error of a job running in the background may or may not come to the terminal. If they do, then make sure both streams are redirected suitably, using /dev/null if necessary. This precaution has to be taken when you are using the C shell. This shell, along with bash, allows you to log out without aborting the job.

You should use the & facility to run all your *noninteractive* jobs in the background while you keep working in the foreground. It's important that you don't idle after doing that; otherwise it makes no sense to have run those jobs in the background in the first place.

It's obvious that you can't run an interactive job in the background—like the **vi** editor for instance. If you do so, the job will remain suspended; you'll have to bring it to the foreground with **fg** *(10.11)* to work with it. This restriction doesn't apply to graphical editors like **emacs** and **xemacs**, which run in their own windows under the X Window system.

Caution

When running background jobs, take care that you don't run too many of them as significant deterioration of CPU performance may occur. It can also be a disservice to other users who might find the machine practically at a standstill owing to the multiplicity of these processes. UNIX can't prevent users from running multiple jobs.

10.7.2   nohup: Log Out Safely

Background jobs cease to run, however, when a user logs out (the C shell and bash excepted). That happens because her shell dies. And when the parent dies, its children also die. The UNIX system permits a variation in this default behavior. The **nohup** (no hangup) command, when prefixed to a command, permits execution of the process even after the user has logged out. You can use the & with it as well:

```
$ nohup sort emp.lst &
586
Sending output to nohup.out
```

The shell returns the PID this time too, and some shells display this message as well. When the **nohup** command is run in these shells, **nohup** sends the standard output of the command to a file nohup.out. If you don't get this message, then make sure that you have taken care of redirection or provided an output filename, wherever possible. You can now safely log out of the system without aborting the command.

When you use the **ps** command after using **nohup** from another terminal (and if it has not been completed already), you'll notice something quite significant:

```
$ ps -f -u romeo
    UID   PID  PPID  C    STIME TTY  TIME COMMAND
  romeo   586     1 45 14:52:09  01  0:13 sort emp.lst
```

Now, look what's happened this time. The shell died on logging out, but its child (**sort**) didn't. The kernel has simply reassigned the PPID of **sort** to the system's **init** process (PID 1)—the parent of all shells. When the user logs out, **init** takes over the parentage of any process run with **nohup**. In this way, you can kill a parent (**sh**) without killing its child (**sort**).

If you run more than one command in a pipeline, then you should use the **nohup** command at the beginning of each command in the pipeline:

```
nohup grep 'director' emp.lst & | nohup sort &
```

C Shell

BASH Shell

Jobs run in the background continue to send their standard output and standard error to the terminal, and have to be redirected to avoid screen clutter. The jobs are not aborted even after the user has logged out. This is not the case with the Bourne and Korn shells. Moreover, the **nohup** command in the C shell doesn't send the standard output of the command to nohup.out. It has to be separately redirected to a file.

Note

You should use the & symbol even if you are using **nohup**. Otherwise, the job won't run in the background. In some versions of the C shell, however, **nohup** itself runs a job in the background.

10.8   nice: **Job Execution with Low Priority**

Processes are usually executed with equal priority. This is not always desirable since high-priority jobs must be completed earliest. UNIX offers the **nice** command, which is used with the & operator to *reduce* the priority of jobs. More important jobs can then have greater access to the system resources (being "nice" to your neighbors).

To run a job with a low priority, the command name should be prefixed with **nice**:

```
nice wc -l uxmanual
```

or better still with

```
nice wc -l uxmanual &
```

nice is a built-in command in the C shell, where it has a default value of 4. **nice values** are system-dependent and typically range from 1 to 19. Commands execute with a nice value that is generally in the middle of the range—usually 10. A higher nice value implies a lower priority. **nice** reduces the priority of any process, thereby raising its nice value. You can also specify the nice value explicitly:

```
nice -5 wc -l uxmanual &                                   Nice value increased by 5 units
```

A nonprivileged user can't increase the priority of a process; that power is reserved for the super user. The nice and priority values are displayed with the -l option of **ps**.

Linux

Nice values range from -20 to 19, and commands run with a nice value of 0. **nice** raises the nice value of any process to 10. **nice** is also used with the -n option to specify the nice value.

10.9   Signals

If you have a program running longer than anticipated, or if you have changed your mind and want to run something else, you have to terminate the process. This is generally done by pressing the interrupt key of your machine. This simply sends a **signal** to the active process with a specific request of termination. The process is terminated if it has not been designed to handle the signal.

A signal is an interrupt generated by the shell or even another process in response to some error condition. This error condition can be a floating point exception, illegal instruction, memory violation or even the press of the interrupt key. After the event is communicated to the process, it has to do one of three things:

- **Do nothing**. The process won't take any action on its own and lets the signal take its own action. The default action is to terminate the process.
- **Ignore the signal**. The process code must be able to intercept the signal and then continue its normal processing as if nothing has happened.
- **Trap the signal**. The process "catches" the signal and decides to take some predetermined action on the signal. The process may still terminate but could remove some temporary files before it does so.

A signal is represented by an integer that represents a particular event, and the common ones that you'll find on any system are shown in Table 10.2. Since some of the signal numbers are system-dependent (not the common ones though), signals are better accessed by their names. The complete list of signals applicable to your machine can be found in the file /usr/include/sys/signal.h.

When you press the interrupt key, the SIGINT signal (number 2) is sent to the current foreground process. This kills the process if it is not designed to catch or ignore that signal. SIGQUIT (number 3) directs a process to produce a **core dump** (a file named core in the current directory).

However, even if a process decides to ignore all these signals, there's one signal that it can't ignore or catch—the SIGKILL signal (signal 9). No matter what signal handling routine a process may have, this signal will surely terminate the process with the

T A B L E   10.2   *List of Commonly Used Signals*

Signal Number	Signal Name	Function
1	SIGHUP	Hangup—modem connection is broken
2	SIGINT	Terminal interrupt—user hits the interrupt key
3	SIGQUIT	Quit from terminal—process produces a core dump file
9	SIGKILL	Surest kill—can't be trapped
15	SIGTERM	Default termination signal used by **kill** command.
24	SIGTSTP	Suspends process—user hits *[Ctrl-z]*

utmost "prejudice." The process makes an unclean exit and won't be able to remove any temporary files before terminating.

Programs like **vi** are designed to preserve their work even if a termination signal is received. These programs have to handle signals carefully.

10.10   kill: **Premature Termination of a Process**

You can terminate a process with the **kill** command—an internal command in most shells. The external command **/bin/kill** is executed only when the shell lacks the kill capability. The command uses one or more PIDs as its arguments, and by default uses the SIGTERM signal (15). Thus,

```
kill 105
```
Uses SIGTERM (15)

terminates the job with the PID 105. To facilitate premature termination, the & operator displays the PID of the process that's run in the background. If you don't remember the PID, then use the **ps** command to find out and then use **kill**.

If you run more than one job in the background, then you can kill them all with a single **kill** statement. Just specify all their PIDs with **kill**:

```
kill 121 122 125 132 138 144
```

If all these processes have the same parent, you may simply kill the parent in order to kill all its children. However, when you use **nohup** with a set of commands and log out, you can't kill the parent as **init** acquires their parentage. You have to individually kill the processes because you can't kill **init**.

10.10.1   Specifying Signals

By default, **kill** uses the SIGTERM signal (number 15) to terminate the process. You would have noticed that some programs simply ignore this interruption and continue execution normally. In that case, the process can be killed with the SIGKILL signal (number 9). This signal can't be generated at the press of a key, so **kill** lets you use the signal number or name as an option:

```
kill -9 121
kill -KILL 121
kill -s 9 121
```
Kills with signal number 9

Solaris use -s option

A simple **kill** command (used with signal 15) won't kill the login shell. You can kill your login shell by using any of these commands:

```
kill -9 $$
kill -9 0
kill -KILL 0
```
$$ stores PID of current shell

Kills all processes including the login shell

Same

The built-in **kill** also accepts a job number, but that is useful only when you use the shell's job control features *(10.11)*. Process killing is graphically depicted in Fig. 10.2.

FIGURE 10.2   *Killing a Process after Finding Out PID*

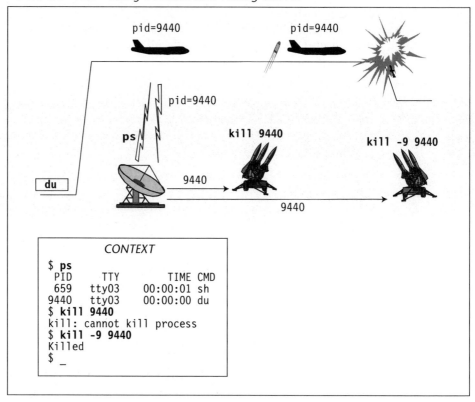

```
                        CONTEXT
$ ps
  PID      TTY          TIME CMD
  659     tty03      00:00:01 sh
 9440     tty03      00:00:00 du
$ kill 9440
kill: cannot kill process
$ kill -9 9440
Killed
$ _
```

Note

You can use signal names also with **kill**. For instance, signal 9 has the name SIGKILL, so you can also use **kill -KILL 121** instead of **kill -9 121**. You can run the **kill -l** (list) command to view the complete list of signals that are applicable for your machine or view the file /usr/include/sys/signal.h. On Solaris and Linux systems, you'll have to use **kill -s 9 121** or **kill -s KILL 121**.

10.10.2   Killing the Last Background Job

For most shells, the system variable $! stores the PID of the last background job—the same number seen when the & is affixed to a command. So you can kill the last background process without using the **ps** command to find out its PID:

```
$ sort -o emp.lst emp.lst &
345
$ kill $!                                          Kills the sort command
```

If your shell supports job control (as most shells do), you can use **kill** with one or more job identifiers. Thus, **kill -9 %1** kills the first background job with the signal number 9, while **kill %s** terminates the program with a name beginning with s.

The $! variable is not available in the C shell. To kill the first (or only) background job, you have to use **kill %** or **kill %1**.

C Shell

Note

Like files, you also own those processes spawned by commands you execute. It's natural that you can kill only those processes that you own, and you can't kill processes of other users. Moreover, certain system processes having the PIDs 0, 1, 2, 3 and 4 simply can't be killed in this manner.

10.11 Job Control

You expect a job to complete in 10 minutes, and it goes on for half an hour. If you kill the job now, then you'll lose a lot of work. If you are using the C shell, Korn shell or bash, you can use their job control facilities to manipulate jobs. Some systems also feature **jsh**—a job control version of the Bourne shell. Job control in these shells means that you can

- Relegate a job to the background (**bg**).
- Bring it back to the foreground (**fg**).
- List the active jobs (**jobs**).
- Suspend a foreground job (*[Ctrl-z]*).
- Kill a job (**kill**).

The commands needed to perform these activities are shown in parentheses. To begin our discussion, if you have invoked a command and the prompt hasn't yet returned, you can suspend the job by pressing *[Ctrl-z]*. You'll then see the following message:

```
[1] + Stopped                     spell uxtip02 > uxtip02.spell
```

Observe that the job has not been terminated yet; it's only suspended ("stopped"). You can now use the **bg** command to push the current foreground job to the background:

```
$ bg
[1]        spell uxtip02 > uxtip02.spell &
```

The & at the end of the line indicates that the job is now running in the background. So, a foreground job goes to the background, first with *[Ctrl-z]*, and then with the **bg** command. You can start more jobs in the background any time:

```
$ sort permuted.index > sorted.index &
[2]    530                                          [2] indicates second job
$ wc -1 uxtip?? > word_count &
[3]    540
```

Now that you have three jobs running, you can have a listing of their status with the **jobs** command:

```
$ jobs
[3]  +  Running                        wc -l uxtip?? > word_count &
[1]  -  Running                        spell uxtip02 > uxtip02.spell &
[2]     Running                        sort permuted.index > sorted.index &
```

You can now bring any of the background jobs to the foreground with the **fg** command. To bring the current (most recent) job to the foreground, use

```
fg
```

This will run the **wc** command in the foreground. The **fg** and **bg** commands can also be used with the job number, job name or a string as arguments, prefixed by the % symbol:

`fg %1`	*First job brought to foreground*
`fg %sort`	*Brings* `sort` *job to foreground*
`bg %2`	*Sends second job to background*
`bg %?perm`	*Sends to background job containing string* `perm`

At any time, however, you can kill any background job with the built-in **kill** command using the same identifiers.

Tip

You can have a temporary escape to the shell from a **vi** or **emacs** editing session by pressing *[Ctrl-z]*. Entering **fg** returns you to the editing mode. That also determines whether your shell supports job control.

At this point, it must be mentioned that the reason why we used *[Ctrl-z]* for suspending a job is that, by default, this is the character set by the **stty** command *(3.5)* for this purpose. When you use this command in those shells supporting job control, you'll probably see a line of output similar to this:

```
start = ^q; stop = ^s; susp = ^z; dsusp = ^y;
```

The third assignment shows the suspend character as ^z, which is **stty**'s way of representing *[Ctrl-z]*. You can change it if you want but that normally won't be necessary.

10.12   at **and** batch: **Execute Later**

UNIX provides sophisticated facilities to schedule a job to run at a specified time of day. If the system load varies greatly throughout the day, it makes sense to schedule less urgent jobs at a time when the system overheads are low. The **at** and **batch** commands make such scheduling possible.

at takes as its argument the time the job is to be executed. Input has to be supplied from the standard input:

```
$ at 14:08
empawk2.sh
[Ctrl-d]
warning: commands will be executed using /bin/sh
job 951035880.a-574:0 at Sun Feb 20 14:08:00 2000
```

The job goes to the **at** queue, and at 2:08 p.m. today, the script file `empawk2.sh` will be executed. **at** shows the job number, the date and time of scheduled execution. This job number is derived from the number of seconds that have elapsed since 1970. It's the most meaningful method of making such numbers unique across several years.

      at doesn't indicate the name of the script to be executed; that is something the user has to remember. The standard output and standard error of this shell script will be mailed to the user, who can use any mail reading program to view it. Alternatively, a user may prefer to redirect the output of the command itself:

```
at 15:08
empawk2.sh > rep.lst
```

You can also use the **-f** option to take commands from a file. However, any error messages that may be generated when executing a program will, in the absence of redirection, continue to be mailed to the user. To mail job completion to the user, use the **-m** option.

      at accepts a large number of time formats using keywords like now, noon, midnight, today and tomorrow:

```
at 15                                24-hour format assumed
at 5pm
at 3:08pm
at noon                                       At 12:00 hours today
at now + 1 year               At the current time after one year
at 3:08pm + 1 day                           At 3:08 p.m. tomorrow
at 15:08 December 18, 2001
at 9am tomorrow
```

Jobs can be listed with the **at -l** command and removed with **at -r**. *Unfortunately, there's no way you can find out the name of the program scheduled to be executed.* This can create problems, especially when you are unable to recall whether a specific job has actually been scheduled for later execution.

      Solaris uses the -c and -k options to have the command executed by the C shell and Korn shell, respectively. It also uses the -t option to accept the time in the format allowed by **touch**.

Note

The month name and day of the week, when used at all, must be either fully spelled out, or abbreviated to three letters.

10.12.1 The batch Command

The **batch** command also schedules jobs for later execution, but unlike **at**, jobs are executed as soon as the system load permits. The command doesn't take any arguments but uses an internal algorithm to determine the execution time. This prevents too many CPU-hungry jobs from running at the same time. The response of **batch** is similar to **at** otherwise:

```
$ batch < empawk2.sh
warning: commands will be executed using /bin/sh
job 951018281.b-581:0 at Sun Feb 20 09:14:41 2000
```

Any job scheduled with **batch** also goes to the **at** queue, and can also be removed with the command **at -r**.

10.12.2   Restricting Use of at and batch

All users may not be able to use the **at** and **batch** commands. The access to these commands is restricted and controlled by the files at.allow and at.deny in /etc/cron.d. Some systems maintain these files in /usr/lib/cron, and Linux uses /etc. However, it's not necessary that all systems will have any of these files.

The primary level of security is controlled by at.allow. If it is present, only the users listed in the file are permitted to use **at** and **batch**. If it is not present, the system checks at.deny for a list of users who are barred from using these commands. If neither file is present, only the system administrator is permitted to invoke **at** and **batch**. Both files are normally readable by all, but writable only by the system administrator.

10.13   cron: **Running Jobs Periodically**

The **ps -e** command always shows the **cron** daemon (one whose name doesn't end with a "d") running. This is the UNIX system's chronograph, ticking away every minute. Unlike **at** and **batch** that are meant for one-time execution, **cron** executes programs at regular intervals.

cron is mostly dormant, but every minute it wakes up and looks in a control file (the **crontab** file) in /var/spool/cron/crontabs for instructions to be performed at that instant. After executing them, it goes back to sleep, only to wake up the next minute. A user may also be permitted to place a crontab file named after her login name in this directory. romeo has to place his crontab commands in the file /var/spool/cron/crontabs/romeo. This location is, however, system-variant.

Each crontab file contains a list of commands along with the schedule of execution. A specimen crontab entry is shown in Fig. 10.3.

Each line contains a set of six fields separated by whitespace. The complete command line is shown in the last field. Together they determine when and how often the command will be executed.

FIGURE 10.3   *The Components of a crontab Entry*

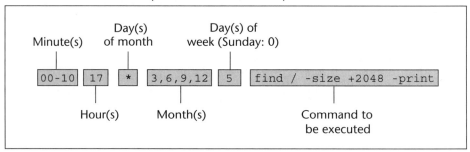

cron uses an unusual number matching system. A set of numbers is delimited by a comma. A * used in any of the first five fields implies that the command is to be executed every period depending on the field where it is placed.

The first field (legal values 00 to 59) specifies the number of minutes after the hour when the command is to be executed. The range 00-10 schedules execution every minute in the first 10 minutes of the hour. The second field (17, i.e., 5 p.m.) indicates the hour in 24-hour format for scheduling (legal values 1 to 24).

The third field (legal values 1 to 31) controls the day of the month. This field (here, an asterisk), read with the other two, implies that the command is to be executed every minute, for the first 10 minutes, starting at 5 p.m. every day. The fourth field (3,6,9,12) specifies the month (legal values 1 to 12). The fifth field (legal values 0 to 6) indicates the days of the week, Sunday having the value 0.

So what's the frequency of execution of this command? Even though the third field uses a * to indicate execution every day, the fifth field overrides the entry and limits execution to every Friday. The **find** command will thus be executed every minute in the first 10 minutes after 5 p.m., every Friday of the months March, June, September and December (of every year). Some specimen crontab entries are shown in Table 10.3.

10.13.1 The crontab Command

You can also create your own crontab files with **vi** or **emacs** in the format shown previously. But, since **cron** reads the file only during system startup, you'll have to use the **crontab** command for **cron** to read the file again:

```
crontab cron.txt                                    cron.txt contains cron commands
```

If romeo runs this command, a file romeo will be created in /var/spool/cron/crontabs containing the contents of cron.txt. In this way, different users can have crontab files named after their user-ids.

TABLE 10.3 *Sample crontab Entries*

Crontab Entry	Significance
0,30 * * * * int_connect.sh	Runs script **int_connect.sh** every 30 minutes on the half-hour.
0 0 * * * backup.sh	Runs script **backup.sh** at midnight every day.
55 17 * * 4 find / -name core -print	Runs **find** command every Thursday at 17:55 hours.
30 0 10,20 * * du.sh	Runs script **du.sh** at 00:30 hours on the tenth and twentieth of every month.
00,30 09-17 * * 1-5 mail.sh	Runs script **mail.sh** on weekdays every half hour between 9 and 17 hours.

It's also possible to enter **cron** commands by using **crontab** with the -e option. **crontab** calls up the editor defined in the EDITOR variable (often, **vi**). After you have edited your commands and quit **vi**, the commands are automatically scheduled for execution.

When the system clock is reset, **cron** is aborted and restarted. **cron** should never be killed, not even by the system administrator. It is mainly used by her to perform housekeeping chores, like removing outdated files or collecting data on system performance. It's also extremely useful to periodically dial up to an Internet mail server to send and retrieve mail.

You can see the contents of your crontab file with **crontab -l** and remove them with **crontab -r**.

10.13.2   Controlling Access to cron

All users may not be able to use the **cron** facilities. Like **at** and **batch**, the authorization to use it is controlled in identical manner by two files, cron.allow and cron.deny in /etc/cron.d or /usr/lib/cron.

If cron.allow is present, only users included in this file are allowed to use this facility. If this file is not present, then the file cron.deny is checked to determine the users who are prohibited. In case neither of them is present, only the system administrator is authorized to use **cron**.

Caution

If you use **crontab -** meaning to provide input through the standard input and then decide to abort it, you should terminate it with the interrupt key applicable for your terminal, rather than *[Ctrl-d]*. If you forget to do that, you'll remove all entries from your existing crontab file!

Linux

cron looks in a control file in /var/spool/cron in Red Hat. It additionally looks up the file /etc/crontab which has the instructions in a different format. For details, look up the **cron** or **crond** documentation.

10.14   **time: Timing Processes**

When you have multiple versions of a program, you'll want to find out how efficiently they use the system resources. The **time** command accepts a command to be timed as its argument and does this work. It executes the program and also displays the time usage on the terminal. This enables programmers to tune their programs to keep CPU usage at an optimum level.

You can find out the time taken to perform a sorting operation by preceding the **sort** command with **time**:

```
$ time sort -o newlist invoice.lst
real    0m1.18s
user    0m0.73s
sys     0m0.38s
```

The *real* time shown is the clock elapsed time from the invocation of the command till its termination. This time can differ on multiuser systems where several programs may be running concurrently. The *user* time shows the time spent by the program in executing itself, while *sys* indicates the time used by the UNIX system in doing work on behalf of the user.

The sum of the user time and the system time actually represents the CPU time. It's not necessary that this sum be equal to the real time or clock elapsed time since some time is consumed in doing other work in the system. The more heavily loaded a system is, the greater is the difference.

SUMMARY

A process is simply an instance of a running program. It lives as long as the program is running. The kernel makes sure that processes get their due time slice and are swapped out to disk as and when needed.

A process is identified by the process-id (*PID*), and every process has a parent whose PID is also available (*PPID*). Its other attributes include the user-id, group-id, priority and the current directory from where it runs. A process can also *spawn* (generate) multiple children.

Every process comprises code and data. It is created by the parent with the **fork** system call, which creates a copy of itself. The parent then overwrites the copy (*execs*) with the **exec** system call to create the child. It also waits for the death of the child, i.e., for the process to finish.

Built-in shell commands like **pwd** and **cd** don't fork a separate process. The shell also spawns a separate sub-shell to execute a shell script. The child's environment inherits some of the parameters from the parent, but changes in the child are *not* made available in the parent.

The login shell is a user process that keeps running as long as the user is logged in. Its PID is stored in the parameter $$. It is the parent of all commands and scripts run from the shell.

The **init** process with PID 1 is the parent of most system processes and all login shells. **init** fork-execs a **getty**, which fork-execs a **login**. On most systems, **login** fork-execs a shell.

The **ps** command lists the attributes of processes. You can view a full listing (-f), the processes of a user (-u), all users (-a) and all system processes (-e).

A job can be run in the background by affixing an & at the end of the command line. **nohup** ensures that a background job remains alive even after the user has logged out. **init** takes over the parentage of all such jobs when the user logs out. You can also lower the priority of a job with **nice**.

You can kill a process by sending a *signal* to it. The process may terminate, ignore the signal or do something else. The **kill** command is used with a signal number to terminate a process. If the default signal number 15 doesn't work, then signal 9 will (**kill -9**). The last background job can be killed with **kill $!** on most shells.

The C shell, bash and the Korn shell enable job control. You can move jobs between foreground and background (**fg** and **bg**) and suspend (*[Ctrl-z]*) them. **fg %2** brings the second job to the foreground and **kill %grep** kills the **grep** command running in the background.

You can schedule a job for one-time execution with **at**, or run it when the system load permits with **batch**. To control access, the system checks at.allow to allow users listed there, failing which it tries at.deny to deny access to users in that file. If that fails, only the system administrator is allowed to use these services.

cron lets you schedule jobs so that they run repeatedly. It takes input from a user's *crontab* file. The file contains multiple fields that specify the time of execution of the command, its frequency and the command to be executed. The **crontab** command is used to make entries in the crontab file. Access to **cron** services are also controlled by cron.allow and cron.deny in identical manner as at.allow and at.deny.

Jobs are timed with **time**, a useful tool for the programmer to make comparisons between different versions of a program.

Linux

SUMMING UP LINUX

Linux uses the BSD **ps** command without using a dash before an option, and the GNU type which uses --. With **ps**, you can view a full listing (u), all users' processes (x) and all system processes (ax). **ps** also shows a hierarchical process diagram when **ps f** is used.

SELF-TEST

10.1   What are the two system calls used to create a process?

10.2   What's the easiest way of finding out the PID of your login shell?

10.3   When does the login shell spawn another shell?

10.4   Which is the process that listens on every terminal for a login request?

10.5   Name some processes that aren't associated with a terminal.

10.6   How can you remove the header line from the **ps** output?

10.7   Why is **ps -f** considered to be an intrusion into a user's privacy?

10.8   Can you increase the priority of a process?

10.9   Which option will you use with **kill** to make sure that a process is killed?

10.10 Can you kill processes of other users?

10.11 How do you display the signal list?

10.12 The **jobs** command issued the message jobs: not found. When does that normally happen?

10.13 You are editing a file with **vi** and you want to make a temporary exit to the shell. How will you do it and then come back to **vi** again? (Assume that you are using one of these shells: the C shell, Korn shell and bash.)

10.14 How do you find out the name of the job scheduled to be executed with **at** and **batch**?

10.15 Frame an **at** command to run the script **dial.sh** tomorrow at 8 p.m.

10.16 You invoked the **crontab** command to make a crontab entry and then changed your mind. How do you terminate the standard input that **crontab** is now expecting?

10.17 How do you compare the efficiency of two programs?—fool and foo2?

EXERCISES

10.1 What is the role of the *swap area* in the control of processes?

10.2 If two users execute the same program, are the memory requirements doubled?

10.3 First create a directory foo and then fill up a shell script with two commands shown below. What happens when you execute this script and why?

```
cd foo; pwd
```

10.4 Which process do you think may have the maximum number of children? What is its PID? Can you divide its children into two categories?

10.5 What does **init** do when a user logs out?

10.6 What's the role of the **login** program?

10.7 If this pipeline is run from a shell script, who will be the parent and grandparent of all these processes?

```
nl foo | sort -nr | cut -f2-
```

10.8 How do you find out the complete command line of a process run by user romeo?

10.9 What is the difference between **ps -e** and **ps -a**?

10.10 What are the major attributes of a *daemon*?

10.11 If you want to edit a file but don't want the filename to be shown by any **ps** command, how do you go about it with (i) **vi** (ii) **emacs**?

10.12 If you are not able to print, which process will you look for in the **ps** output?

10.13 Which process does **kill -9 0** terminate?

10.14 How will you kill the last background job without knowing its PID? Will it run in all shells?

10.15 What is the difference between a process run with & and one run with **nohup**?

10.16 Should you run a command like this?

```
nohup compute.sh
```

10.17 If you run a program with **nohup** and then log out, what happens to the parentage of the process?

10.18 Name some commands that don't require a separate process.

10.19 What does the **exit** command do?

10.20 How are the signal numbers 2 and 9 generated? What are their names and how do they differ in function?

10.21 The **ps** command shows the **emacs** command running on the same terminal. Yet, you don't see the **emacs** screen but only the shell prompt. When can that happen, and what do you do?

10.22 Interpret these crontab entries:

```
(i) * * * * * dial.sh
(ii) 30 21 * * * find /tmp /usr/tmp -atime +30  -exec rm -f {} \;
```

10.23   There are some errors in this crontab entry; what are they?

```
00-60 22-24 30 2 * find.sh
```

10.24   Frame a crontab entry to execute the **int_connect.sh** script every 15 minutes on every Monday, Wednesday and Friday between the times 9 a.m. and 9 p.m.

10.25   The administrator has decided that most users would be allowed to use **at** and **cron**. What should she change that requires the minimum effort?

10.26   How does the system administrator become the exclusive user of **at** and **cron**?

KEY TERMS

background job *(10.7)*

child process *(10.1.1)*

core dump *(10.9)*

crontab *(10.13)*

daemon *(10.6.1)*

data segment *(10.2)*

effective user-id *(10.1)*

exec *(10.2)*

foreground job *(10.7)*

fork *(10.2)*

nice value *(10.8)*

overlay *(10.2)*

parent process *(10.1.1)*

process birth *(10.1.1)*

process death *(10.1.1)*

process identifier (PID) *(10.1)*

process owner *(10.1)*

real user-id *(10.1)*

signal *(10.9)*

swap area *(10.1)*

text segment *(10.2)*

user address space *(10.2)*

user segment *(10.2)*

wait *(10.2)*

## CHAPTER 11

TCP/IP Networking Tools

In the beginning, there were only stand-alone computers. Later, people realized that stand-alone computers made no sense: they needed to talk to one another. The origins of TCP/IP were firmly rooted in the belief that stand-alone networks made little sense either. Networks also needed to communicate with other networks irrespective of the hardware, software and operating system used. What was needed was a set of protocols that took all these heterogeneities into account. This set of protocols is known as *TCP/IP*.

The characteristic thing about TCP/IP is that the development of the technology went hand-in-hand with the invention of the tools that exploited the technology. This practice continues till this day. Many stand-alone UNIX applications were also modified to work in the network. Today, TCP/IP networking tools are found in every major implementation of the UNIX system as a built-in feature of its kernel. TCP/IP is also the protocol of the Internet. All the TCP/IP tools that we discuss in this chapter will also work on the Internet.

Objectives

- Understand how a *packet-switching* network works. *(11.1)*
- Learn how hostnames are converted to *IP addresses* using the file /etc/hosts. *(11.1.2)*
- Learn how hostnames are replaced with *fully qualified domain names* (FQDN) on the Internet. *(11.1.3)*
- Use **talk** to conduct a real-time, text-based conversation with another user. *(11.2)*
- Display details of users on a remote system with **finger**. *(11.4)*
- Use **telnet** and **rlogin** to log on to a remote machine. *(11.5 and 11.6)*
- Use **ftp** and **rcp** to transfer files between two machines. *(11.7 and 11.8)*
- Execute a command remotely with **rsh**. *(11.9)*
- Learn the configuration settings needed to enable the use of **rlogin**, **rcp** and **rsh**. *(11.10)*

11.1 TCP/IP Basics

TCP/IP is a set of networking **protocols**. These protocols define a set of rules that each machine must comply with to communicate with another machine in the network. The term expands to Transmission Control Protocol/Internet Protocol, but the name is somewhat of a misnomer because TCP/IP is a collection of several protocols (of which TCP and IP are the most important ones). The features of TCP/IP include:

- Independence of vendor, type of machine and operating system.
- The delivery of data in multiple packets.
- Ability to divert data immediately through other routes if one or more parts of the network went down.
- One-hundred percent reliability of transmission with facilities for full error control.

Unlike our telephone system, TCP/IP is a **packet-switching** system. In a packet-switched network, there is no dedicated connection between sender and receiver. Rather, the data is broken into packets, and each packet is provided with a header (**envelope**). This header contains the sequence number and a checksum, which is a simple number determining the exact information in the packet. These packets are put inside envelopes, the sender's and recipient's addresses are written on them, and the packets are sent on their way.

As the packets travel along a vast network like the Internet, they encounter **routers** everywhere. These are special computers or intelligent devices that look at the envelope addresses and then determine the most efficient route each packet has to take to move closer to its destination. Because the load on the network varies constantly, packets may move along different routes and arrive out of order. The packets are reassembled in the correct order from the information provided in them.

Before assembly, the checksum of each packet is calculated and checked with the number that has been sent in the packet. If the checksums don't match, the packet is corrupted and has to be resent. When all clean packets are received, they are assembled, their headers discarded and data fed to the application in their original form.

These functions are not built into the applications that work in the network—like `ftp` and `telnet`. They are totally independent of the underlying hardware details or the operating system used by the machines.

11.1.1 Hostnames and IP Addresses

In a network, a computer is known as a **host**, and every such host has a **hostname**. This name is unique throughout the network. The easiest way of knowing your own machine's hostname is to use the **hostname** command:

```
$ hostname
saturn.planets.com
```

This is a rather longish name of the type used by hosts on the Internet, where the first word actually signifies the name of the host. *planets.com* is the name of the *domain* to which the host belongs. Some systems omit the domain name from the output of the **hostname** command, but if your system doesn't, then you can use the -s option with **hostname** (if that is supported too):

```
$ hostname -s
saturn
```

Apart from the hostname, every host in the network has an address called the **IP address** which is used by other machines to communicate with it. This address is a series of four dot-delimited numbers which could typically look like this:

```
192.168.0.1
```

The IP address too is independent of the networking hardware and is set at the time of booting by the system's startup scripts. TCP/IP applications can address a host by its hostname as well as its IP address:

```
ftp 192.168.0.1
telnet saturn
```

Because numbers are difficult to remember, users prefer to access machines by their hostnames rather than their IP addresses. But ultimately, machines understand only IP addresses, and the conversion from the hostname to the IP address has to be made before two machines can set up a connection between them.

Note

Like the **date** command, the **hostname** command can be used with an argument by the system administrator to actually set the hostname.

11.1.2   /etc/hosts: Mapping Hostnames to IP Addresses

On a small network, the name-address mappings are placed in the file /etc/hosts in every host of the network. This is often called the **hosts file**. This database allows the applications to look up a name and find out its corresponding IP address. A look at a sample file reveals its flexible structure:

```
$ cat /etc/hosts
127.0.0.1      localhost
192.168.0.1    saturn
192.168.0.2    uranus
192.168.0.3    jupiter j2                                      Aliases permitted
```

For each host in the network, this table contains a line mapping the IP address to its respective hostname. It contains at least two fields in each line. The last line shows that TCP/IP also permits the use of aliases. This makes addressing even simpler as you can now use **telnet jupiter** instead of **telnet 192.168.0.3**. And, if that seems a lot of work, you can use **telnet j2** too.

Tip

You don't need to be connected to a network to use the TCP/IP services running there. You can access your own machine using the name **localhost** or the IP address 127.0.0.1. You'll always find a line mapping this name to this IP address in every /etc/hosts file. This applies even if your machine is not on the network.

Note

You also have a *hosts* file in Windows which offers the **telnet** and **ftp** facilities. The location of this file is typically \WINDOWS (Win95/98) or \WINDOWS\SYSTEM32\DRIVERS\ETC (Win 2000/NT). If you access a UNIX machine with the hostname from a Windows host, then you'll need to edit this file.

11.1.3   DNS: The Domain Name System

Maintaining a hosts file in every machine of a large network is a painful task for the network administrator. It is an impossible task on the Internet which uses a different system—the **Domain Name System (DNS)**. DNS theory treats a host not as a simple name, but as a constituent of one or more **domains**. Domains follow a hierarchical pattern and are administered locally. Yet the data of each domain is made available globally to all other domains.

In this scenario, the Internet **namespace** (the domain tree) is equated with the UNIX file system. Likewise, it too has an unnamed root domain called . (dot). This root domain has a number of root-level or top-level domains under it. *edu* and *com* are examples of top-level domains. These domains, in turn, have second-level domains or sub-domains under them in the same way a directory has subdirectories under it. Second-level domains also have sub-domains, and this nesting can descend several levels.

For instance, if *binghamton* is a second-level domain under *edu*, and *cs* a sub-domain under *binghamton*, then the host *ralph* could be uniquely described as

ralph.cs.binghamton.edu.   *Note the dot at the end*

This represents a **fully qualified domain name (FQDN)** of the host *ralph*—something like the absolute pathname of a file. Another **site** (a collection of hosts of a single organization) can also have the *ralph* hostname, or the *cs* sub-domain name, but the FQDN will always be different. This name will be unique throughout the Internet.

Domain names are case-insensitive; you can use *CS.BINGHAMTON.EDU* in the same way you can use *Cs.BiNghAmtOn.eDU*. An organization must have a short FQDN; it should be easy to remember, and should identify the organization easily.

However, eventually every FQDN has to be mapped to its corresponding IP address using BIND—the software used universally to implement DNS on the Internet. This name service follows certain well-defined rules to refer domain names to different machines for resolution. The theory governing the resolution process and DNS implementation is discussed in Chapter 24.

Note

The email address, domain name and IRC (Internet Relay Chat) are probably the only entities in UNIX where case is irrelevant.

11.1.4   Daemons, Ports and Sockets

TCP/IP and the Internet operate on the **client-server** principle—the division of labor between two computers connected in a network. An **ftp** application is split up into a server and a client component—two separate programs by themselves. The Web server's job is to send an HTML document, which the client software (the browser) formats on the user's screen.

The server programs are called **daemons** in UNIX, and you have seen many of them in the output of the **ps** command *(10.6.1)*. They are not associated with any terminal and always run in the background, listening for input from the clients. The **httpd** daemon listens for a Web page request. **sendmail** is the daemon which handles your mail.

How does an **ftp** packet know that it has to connect to another **ftp** application at the other end and not to a Web browser? Specifying the IP address in an **ftp** packet is not enough; a separate **port number** has to be included as well. This number is always associated with the **ftp** service, so the packet reaches the **ftp** server. Port numbers are like telephone extension numbers in an office. Specifying the office telephone number is not enough; one must know the extension number also to reach the right person.

Daemons listen for requests at certain specific port numbers assigned to them. **sendmail** listens on port 25, **ftp** on 21 and **telnet** on 23. However, their client counterparts use *random* port numbers at their ends. For instance, **ftp** will open a connection using some random number at the client end, but will specify port number 21 for the server end.

These port numbers used by the server programs are listed in /etc/services. The important services have these entries in the file:

```
ftp         21/tcp
telnet      23/tcp
smtp        25/tcp          mail
www         80/tcp          http      # WorldWideWeb HTTP
pop3        110/tcp         # POP version 3
```

Every packet includes a set of four numbers—the IP addresses and TCP port numbers at each end. This set is called a **socket**—sometimes a **connection**. No two sockets can have the same set of numbers. If two users with the same IP address request a Web page from the same server, their sockets will be different because the port numbers they will be using at the client end will be random—and different.

With this knowledge of the functional aspects of TCP, we now proceed to discuss the well-known networking tools which are covered in the rest of this chapter. Two of them (**ftp** and **telnet**) are widely used on the Internet as well. The addresses and hostnames listed in our sample /etc/hosts will often be assumed.

11.2 talk: **Real-Time Conversation**

talk is a popular network communications program available in all versions of UNIX. It enables you to have a two-way communication with any person who is currently logged in. This is a text-based conversation where text entered by one user appears on the terminal of the other. **talk** makes obsolete the **write** command (not discussed in this text) and is the ancestor of the Internet Relay Chat.

You can use **talk** to exchange messages with another user on the same or a remote host. This is how henry invokes **talk** to communicate with user charlie:

```
talk charlie                                            User on the same host
talk charlie@saturn                                     User on a remote host
```

Note the second form of addressing. This is also the form used to address an email message to someone. The address here consists of two components—username and hostname—separated by the @.

If charlie is logged in, he will be informed that henry wants to talk to him. This is what he could see on his display:

```
Message from Talk_Daemon@uranus at 10:20 ...
talk: connection requested by henry@uranus
talk: respond with: talk henry@uranus
```

Now, charlie has to respond by invoking **talk**, and then entering his message. He should use either of these commands depending on whether henry is on the same or on a different host:

```
talk henry                                              henry on same host
talk henry@uranus                                       henry on different host
```

Once this command is entered by charlie and received by henry, a connection is set up between the two users. **talk** then splits the screen horizontally into two windows on both machines (Fig. 11.1).

There's no chance of incoming and outgoing messages being grouped together. This makes it easier to distinguish between messages sent and received. The conversation is in real-time: the message appears on each recipient's screen simultaneously as it is being typed. In this way, it's possible to continue a conversation until such time as one or both the users decide to terminate it. **talk** is terminated by either user pressing the interrupt key.

Tip

If you have the **ytalk** command on your system, you can use it to set an Internet-style chat session with several users. **talk** is restricted to just two.

11.3 mesg: **Your Willingness to Talk**

Communication—single or two-way—can be disconcerting to someone who might be watching the output of an important program on their terminal at that instant. Whether you can "write" or "talk" to another user also depends on what the **mesg** setting is. The command

FIGURE 11.1 *A Split Window Created by* **talk**

```
[Connection established]
What is that you wanted to say?


------------------------------------------------------------------------

Was just wondering whether you received the message from jim.



```

```
mesg n                                                    Can't receive messages
```

prevents other people from writing to a terminal. y enables receipt of such messages. To know the status of your terminal, simply use **mesg** without arguments:

```
$ mesg
is y                                                        Can receive messages
```

mesg is one command typically kept in the startup file executed by the shell every time the user logs in. An entry in this file ensures that the terminal is always set to a desired state *for that user*. We'll be discussing this file and its variants later in the text. If neither **write** nor **talk** works, check the **mesg** setting.

11.4 finger: **Details of Users**

finger (from Berkeley) is a useful command that reveals details of users. Like **talk**, the command can be used both for the local and a remote system. By default, **finger** simply produces a list of all logged users on the local machine. But you can use it with an @-prefixed hostname to obtain similar details for the remote users:

```
$ finger @jupiter
Login      Name              Tty   Idle  Login Time    Where
henry      henry blofeld     *p1         Sep  4 12:15
sumit      sumitabha das     2           Sep  4 08:27
root       root              4     45    Sep  4 10:19
charlie    charlie greene    p0          Sep  4 12:14
```

The second field shows the user's full name obtained from /etc/passwd. The third field shows the terminal of the user. An asterisk here implies that the terminal doesn't have write permission. The fourth field shows the idle time—the time that has elapsed since the last keystroke was entered on that terminal. Here root has been idling for the last 45 minutes. The last field is often blank, but could show either the office location (taken from the fifth field of /etc/passwd) or the hostname.

Unlike **who**, **finger** can also provide details about a single user on the remote machine:

```
$ finger romeo@jupiter
[jupiter]
Welcome to Linux version 2.2.5 at jupiter!
12:22pm  up  3:51,  2 users,  load average: 0.00, 0.03, 0.00


Login: romeo                          Name: romeo cox
Directory: /home/romeo                Shell: /bin/bash
On since Sat Sep  4 12:14 (EST) on tty2, idle 0:01 (messages off)
Mail forwarded to romeo@yahoo.com
New mail received Sat Sep 4 16:45 1999 (EST)
Mail last read Sat Sep 4 11:28 1999 (EST)
No Plan.
```

You get to see something more here. The operating system is Linux, romeo is using the bash shell, has disabled his terminal (`messages off`) and has "no plan." If romeo is not logged in, the output will show the last login time. He has also forwarded his mail to *romeo@yahoo.com* by placing an entry in his `.forward` file *(13.5)*. This version of **finger** features two lines showing the date and time the user last received and read mail.

If you don't know a user's login name, but you do know the full name or even part of the name, you can try using either the first name or the last name as the argument to **finger**. If henry was set up with the following entry in /etc/passwd:

```
henry:x:200:50:henry james:/home/henry:/bin/ksh
```

you can use **finger** with his last name as well:

```
finger james
```

If you want to find out a person's telephone number or address, try using **finger** with her email address. If you don't know her email address, try her first or last name. You never know, you might just be lucky and get the information.

The .plan and .project Files It's often necessary to leave behind your schedule and other important information for others to see, especially if you are going on vacation. Since it's not possible to send mail to all users, you can use **finger** to display the contents of two files $HOME/.plan and $HOME/.project. If romeo has these two files in his home directory, this is what **finger** could show at the end of its normal output:

```
Project:
The tulec2 project should be completed by Feb 28, 2001
Plan:
The DTP people have to be contacted on Feb 25, 2000
A number of diagrams need to be drawn with illustrator.
```

Many people resent the loss of privacy that **finger** causes. They feel that an individual's personal details must not be divulged to outsiders without his or her consent. Consequently, the **finger** service is disabled on many systems, especially on the Internet.

In the forthcoming sections, we'll discuss the tools developed when TCP/IP was in its infancy. Every UNIX system offers these tools, and many of them are still used on the Internet.

11.5 `telnet`: **Remote Login**

Initially, the development of TCP/IP applications was confined to mainly two sources—DARPA (the organization ultimately responsible for the birth of the Internet) and Berkeley. Today we call them the **DARPA set** and the **r-utilities** because all the tools in this suite begin with r.

Every UNIX vendor offers DARPA's **telnet** and Berkeley's **rlogin** commands in their TCP/IP package to log on to a remote multiuser system. **rlogin** also requires a UNIX machine at the other end, but **telnet** does not. For **telnet**, the server side could be any time-sharing system offered by IBM, Digital, Sun and so forth. If you have an account on a host in a local network (or on the Internet), you can use this tool with the hostname or the IP address as argument:

```
$ telnet saturn
Trying 192.168.0.1...                    Name resolved by /etc/hosts
Connected to saturn
Escape character is '^]'.
login: henry                             Enter username and password
Password: ********
Last login: Thu Sep 23 12:19:42 on ttyp0 from ppp112-202.pppc.
You have mail.
$ _
```

You can quit **telnet** by using the **exit** command at the prompt. Once you are in and can see a shell prompt, anything you type is sent to the remote machine, and your machine behaves like any other dumb terminal. You can issue commands that are understood by the remote machine, have them executed there, and yet have their output displayed on your terminal. Let's find out the release of the remote machine's operating system:

```
$ uname -r
5.7                                      Solaris 7 with SunOS 5.7
```

It's sometimes difficult to find out which machine you are logged on to, especially when both machines use identical versions of UNIX. That's why the facility available in bash to use the hostname in the prompt *(17.3.4)* becomes quite useful when using **telnet**.

Tip

You'll sometimes find you are not able to delete characters with the same key that you use locally. This would mean that the remote machine has assigned a different key for this purpose. Try these key sequences—*[Delete]*, *[Ctrl-h]* or *[Backspace]*. If that doesn't help, look up Sections 1.9.1 and 3.5.

11.5.1 The telnet> Prompt

When **telnet** is used without the address, the system displays the telnet> prompt from where you can use its internal commands. You can now invoke a login session from here with **open**, one of **telnet**'s internal commands:

```
telnet> open 202.54.54.35                Using IP address this time
Trying 202.54.54.35...
Connected to 202.54.54.35.
Escape character is '^]'.
        .....
```

In the midst of a **telnet** session, you might need to check the name of a file that resides on your local machine. The "Escape character" lets you make a temporary escape to the `telnet>` prompt so that you can execute a command on your local machine. To invoke it, press *[Ctrl-]]* (*[Ctrl]* and the *]*). You can then use the ! with a UNIX command, say **ls**, to list files on the local machine:

```
$ [Ctrl-]]
telnet> !ls -l *.sam                                    Executed on local machine
```

You can terminate either your current session or **telnet** itself from this prompt. Use either of these commands:

- Log out with **logout**. This terminates **telnet** as well.
- Close the current connection with **close**. If you invoked **telnet** with the hostname as argument, then this command also behaves like **logout**. Otherwise, it merely closes the current connection, and you can then open a new one from here with **open**. Some systems, however, behave differently.

Note

Even though Windows doesn't offer the **telnet** service, you can use the **telnet** client available there to connect to a UNIX machine. Invoke the MS-DOS command prompt, and then enter the **telnet** command with a hostname or IP address.

11.5.2   telnet from the Browser

If you are surfing the Web and need to make a quick **telnet** connection, you can do that from your Netscape browser. You just have to enter this string in the small window at the top of your browser:

telnet://sasolution.com[Enter]   *This is a URL*

First, enter the protocol (`telnet`), followed by a `:` and then two slashes. Next, enter the FQDN of the site before you press the *[Enter]* key. The browser here calls up an **xterm** window *(12.9)* which behaves like a VT100 terminal. Log in as usual, do your work and then close the connection (with **exit**) before closing the window. You are back to the browser.

     telnet is the ideal tool for administering a remote machine. Most UNIX programs still use the command line interface, and administration frequently requires editing of simple text files. This is easily done with **telnet**. You can even shut down a remote machine with **telnet**.

Note

What you entered just now from your browser window is the **Uniform Resource Locator (URL)** of the telnet site. This is Web terminology which is adequately explained in Chapter 14.

Tip

To know whether a particular service is running on a host, you can use the port number as the second argument to **telnet**. For instance, to check whether the POP3 service is running on the host *cal.vsnl.net.in,* use 110 (the port number used by POP-3 in /etc/services) as an additional argument to **telnet**:

```
$ telnet cal.vsnl.net.in 110
Trying 202.54.9.25...
```

```
Connected to cal.vsnl.net.in.
Escape character is '^]'.
+OK QUALCOMM Pop server derived from UCB (version 2.1.4-R3) at cal.vsnl.net.in s
tarting.
```
quit   *Quits* telnet *when in this mode*
```
+OK Pop server at cal.vsnl.net.in signing off.
```

The POP3 service is running, and you are seeing POP-related messages emanating from the server. Here, you'll have to use POP3's **quit** command to quit **telnet**.

11.6 rlogin: **Remote Login without Password**

rlogin is Berkeley's implementation of the remote login facility, but works only on UNIX systems. It lets you log on to your own identical remote account without using either the username or password:

```
$ rlogin jupiter
Last login: Mon Oct 25 09:26:46 from saturn
$ _                              Logged in without entering username or password
```

Here, a user accesses her own account on a remote system without authenticating herself. Both machines must have entries for this user in their /etc/passwd files. That's not sufficient of course; the remote machine must also be configured properly for this to be possible. We'll be discussing the configuration issues in Section 11.10.

You can also use the -l option to log on to a different user account without having a similar account on the local machine:

```
rlogin -l franklin saturn                         User logs in with username franklin
```

This time, the user *may* have to enter a password but need not have the franklin user account on the local machine. However, "proper" configuration allows a user entry without using the password.

rlogin is terminated in the same way a login session is terminated—*[Ctrl-d]*, **exit** or **logout**.

Tip

If you are using **rlogin** from a like-to-like account on a Linux machine to access a UNIX machine, you may not be able to gain password-free access unless you turn off Kerberos authentication with the -K option (on the Linux machine).

11.7 ftp: **File Transfer Protocol**

TCP/IP offers two commands for transferring files—DARPA's **ftp** (file transfer protocol) and Berkeley's **rcp**. In this chapter, we take a look at **ftp** which is more widely used than **rcp**. We'll use it on the same host that we used with **telnet**:

```
$ ftp saturn
Connected to saturn.
220 saturn FTP server (Version wu-2.4.2-academ[BETA-17](1) Tue Jun 9 10:
43:14 EDT 1998) ready.
```

```
Name (saturn:sumit): henry
331 Password required for henry.
Password: *********
230 User henry logged in.
Remote system type is UNIX.
Using binary mode to transfer files.
ftp> _
```

It's fairly common for one host to offer several services if it can handle the traffic. The same login techniques are applied here, and you find yourself in the home directory. To quit **ftp**, you can optionally use **close** and then use **bye** or **quit**:

```
ftp> close                                              You can skip this if you want
221 Goodbye.
ftp> bye                                                You can use use quit also
```

ftp has a host of internal commands that you can use at the ftp> prompt (Table 11.1), and some of them have identical names in UNIX. For instance, you can create and remove directories (**mkdir** and **rmdir**) and also change file permissions (**chmod**).

You can also use **ftp**'s trinity of the **pwd**, **cd** and **ls** commands to navigate the file system and list files in the same way you use them on your UNIX system:

```
ftp> pwd
257 "/home/henry" is current directory.
ftp> cd download
250 CWD command successful.
ftp> ls                                                 Which ls does it use?
200 PORT command successful.
150 Opening ASCII mode data connection for /bin/ls.     The UNIX command!
total 142720
drwxr-xr-x    2 root      users        1024 Sep  7 15:34 .
drwxr-xr-x    8 adeb      users        1024 Jun  2 11:26 ..
-rw-r--r--    1 root      root        30520 Feb 17  1999 1req.htm
-rw-r--r--    1 root      root        48761 Feb 17  1999 2pre.htm
-rw-r--r--    1 root      root        37899 Feb 17  1999 3inst.htm
...
```

Even though these are internal commands of **ftp**, one of them (the **ls** command) uses the operating system's **ls** command in /bin. That's why the **ls** output differs across machines depending on the way it's implemented in the operating system.

Local machine commands need the ! prefix. Since the ! doesn't work with the **cd** command, **ftp** offers the **lcd** (local cd) command to do the job. You can use **cd ..** (remote) and **lcd ..** (local) whenever you wish to move to the parent directory.

11.7.1 Transferring Files

For the purpose of transfer, files can be seen as belonging to two types—*ascii* (text) and *binary*. All executables, graphic, word processing and multimedia files belong to the binary type. These files need special attention, so you should set the transfer mode to **binary** before initiating file transfer.

TABLE 11.1 **ftp** *Commands*

Command	Significance
open *hname*	Connects to host *hname*
user *uname*	Logs in with username *uname*
bye or quit	Quits **ftp**
mkdir, rmdir, cd and pwd	Same as in UNIX except that commands are executed on remote machine
cdup	Changes directory to parent directory on remote machine
ls	Lists files on remote machine
!ls	Lists files on local machine
lcd ..	Changes to parent directory on local machine
get *f1 f2*	Copies remote file *f1* to local file *f2* (the same filename if *f2* not specified)
restart *n*	Resumes an aborted file transfer from remote machine after skipping *n* bytes
reget *flname*	Resumes an aborted transfer of file *flname* from remote machine *(Linux only)*
put *f1 f2*	Copies local file *f1* to remote file *f2* (the same filename if *f2* not specified)
mget *filenames*	Copies multiple remote files to local machine (wild cards interpreted remotely)
mput *filenames*	Copies multiple files to remote machine (wild cards interpreted locally)
binary or ascii	Sets transfer type to binary or ascii
delete and mdelete	Deletes single or multiple files on remote machine
verbose	Toggle switch—turns on/off messages
prompt	Turns on/off interactive behavior when using mput and mget

Uploading (put and mput) If you are a Web site developer, you'll frequently need to upload your Web pages and graphic files to your Web site. The **put** command sends (uploads) a single file penguin.gif to the remote machine:

```
ftp> binary
200 Type set to I.
ftp> put penguin.gif                              Copied under same name
local: penguin.gif remote: penguin.gif
200 PORT command successful.
150 Opening BINARY mode data connection for penguin.gif.
226 Transfer complete.
6152 bytes sent in 0.04 seconds (150.20 Kbytes/s)
```

You can change your destination filename, and you can also copy multiple files with
mput:

```
put penguin.gif pelican.gif
mput t*.sql                                       * interpreted on local machine
```

Downloading (get and mget) To download files from the remote machine, you'll
require the **get** and **mget** commands which are used in a similar manner as their "put"
counterparts. This time, we'll turn off all messages with **verbose**:

```
ftp> verbose                                                      Turns off noise
ftp> ls
drwxr-xr-x   14 888        999           4096 Jun 15 16:46 communicator
drwxr-xr-x    2 888        999             26 May 14 00:47 communicator_for_france
-rw-r--r--    1 888        999         323393 Sep  7 17:22 ls-lR
-rw-r--r--    1 888        999          28360 Sep  7 17:22 ls-lR.gz
.....
ftp> binary                                               Default on most systems
ftp> get ls-lR.gz
ftp> _                                           No statistics this time—file copied
```

Like in **put**, you can change your destination filename, and you can also copy multiple files with **mget**:

```
get ls-lR.gz netscape_filelist
mget t*.sql                                      * interpreted on remote machine
```

On the Internet, there are several sites which offer trial and public domain software for
downloading. There, you don't have a separate account and password for every user.
These sites offer a special user account, "anonymous," that has to be used for logging
in. Though not always mandatory, you are also expected to provide your email address
as the password. These sites are known as **anonymous ftp** sites. You can only download files from an anonymous ftp site.

Tip To know the default file transfer type, use the **type** command at the ftp> prompt. Generally, it shows binary. Working in the binary mode is an advantage because even ASCII files
can be faithfully transferred in the binary mode.

Tip **mput** and **mget** generally prompt for transfer of every file, which could be a bother when you
need noninteractive behavior for speedier transfer. Just use the command **prompt** to turn off
prompting. The command acts like a toggle switch; use the command again to reactivate
prompting.

11.7.2 Connecting from the ftp> Prompt

ftp displays the ftp> prompt when used without an argument. You can then establish
a connection with its **open** command:

```
$ ftp
ftp> open saturn
Connected to saturn.
220 saturn FTP server (Version 2.1WU(1)) ready.
```

You can log in as usual, but if you have incorrectly entered the user details, then **ftp** refuses you entry. *You, however, remain connected to the site.* To log in at this stage, you have to use the **user** command and then go through the usual login sequence:

```
ftp> user charlie
331 Password required for charlie.
Password: ********
```

11.7.3 .netrc: Using ftp Noninteractively

You always use the same username and password for anonymous ftp sites. So, why enter them every time and not take them from a file instead? **ftp** allows you to do that. It also lets you specify the authentication parameters for each host individually. The file **ftp** uses for this purpose is $HOME/.netrc.

Here are three entries in .netrc. Two of them are for hosts *jupiter* and *neptune*. The other is for all anonymous ftp sites where you use the same username and password to log in. Each line in this file specifies the parameters for connecting to an ftp site:

```
machine jupiter login sasol password 11u2dw3ig
machine neptune login romeo password b1e6e37nn
default login anonymous password romeo@vsnl.com
```

The first two lines apply to "private" ftp sites where the user has individual accounts. machine, login and password are keywords, and each keyword is followed by its corresponding parameter. The last line contains the keyword default and generally applies to all other sites. Here, it is used for anonymous ftp sites. This line has one word less than the previous ones.

Since the file contains the clear-text password, it *must* be made unreadable to group and others (with **chmod 600 .netrc**). Your **ftp** client will now use this file for logging on to *jupiter*, *neptune* and anonymous ftp sites without prompting.

Automatic File Transfer How about also transferring a file without interaction? Since **ftp** accepts commands from the standard input, we can keep all these commands in a file:

```
$ cat ftpparam.lst
cd download
prompt                                          For noninteractive transfer
mget *.gif
bye
```

These represent four **ftp** commands which we'll use noninteractively to fetch all the GIF files from the download directory of the *jupiter* site. We'll use the same parameters for logging in as shown in the previous .netrc file. We'll just have to redirect

ftp's standard input like this:

```
$ ftp jupiter < ftpparam.lst
$ _
```

The command acts silently and returns you to the prompt after copying the files from the sasol account in *jupiter*. Amazing, isn't it?

11.7.4   Other ftp Features

Resuming an Aborted File Transfer   This is a problem on the Internet where file transfers sometimes get aborted. Some versions of **ftp** allow you to resume the transfer from the point you left off. You need to use the **restart** command before you use **get**:

```
restart 846913                              The number of bytes to be skipped and then
get exceptions                                get the file after skipping 846913 bytes
```

Restarting an aborted file transfer in Linux is quite easy. Just use **ftp**'s **reget** command:

```
reget exceptions                                  Makes all calculations automatically
```

Viewing Documents without Downloading   You may often want to view text documents before you decide to download them. Sometimes, you can use a pager too:

```
get root-servers.txt /dev/tty                          /dev/tty is your terminal
get root-servers.txt - \| more                                  Works sometimes
```

If the second command works on your machine, then you can step forward and back in the document without actually downloading it! This feature is, however, not available on most systems, so don't be disappointed if it doesn't work on yours.

Note

Even though Windows doesn't offer the **ftp** service, you can use the **ftp** client there to connect to an ftp site. Invoke the MS-DOS command prompt, and then enter the **ftp** command in the way used here.

11.7.5   ftp from the Web Browser

If it's just a matter of getting a single file, and you know where it is, connecting from the browser is the best solution. All browsers support the FTP protocol, and you can specify it in the window of your Netscape browser:

ftp://ftp.javasoft.com[Enter]

No further typing is needed; Netscape supplies the word "anonymous" and the password automatically. The area where you normally see a Web page now shows the root directory structure of the site (Fig. 11.2). Once you are in this mode, navigating and

FIGURE 11.2   **ftp** *from the Browser*

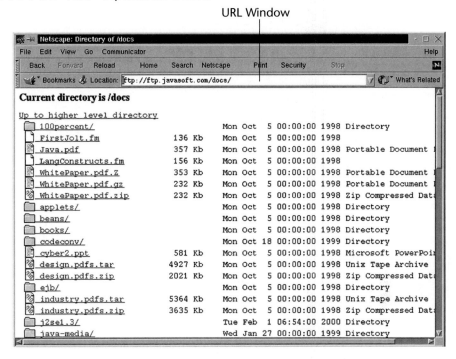

downloading become exceedingly simple. Click on an underlined directory link, and you'll see its file listing. Click on a file, and one of these things will happen:

- If it's a binary file, you are asked to choose the destination filename before it is saved on your disk.
- If it's a text file, you actually see the contents of the file on your screen. To save it, you have to use the Netscape menu in this sequence—*File>Save As*.

Usually, a few mouse clicks do the entire job. However, you must be aware of the limitations of this method:

- You can download only one file at a time.
- You can't upload files to the server.
- Transfers can't be resumed if the transfer was interrupted by an external phenomenon and not directly by the user.

Before you use the anonymous ftp feature, make sure that it's enabled. The browser configuration window (*Edit>Preferences>Advanced*) lets you click on a checkbox which sets the email address as the anonymous ftp password.

Tip

If you already know the complete pathname of the file containing the Java documentation, then you can directly retrieve the file by following the URL string with the pathname:

ftp://ftp.javasoft.com/docs/tutorial.zip   *[Enter] presumed*

11.8   rcp: **Remote File Copying**

rcp is Berkeley's counterpart of the **ftp** command. It behaves like **cp** except that it's used for copying files and directory structures from and to a remote system. A file on the remote machine is known to **rcp** as a combination of the hostname and filename, separated by a **:**. We'll copy a file from the host *uranus* in two ways:

```
rcp uranus:/home/henry/cent2fah.pl c2f.pl
rcp uranus:/home/henry/cent2fah.pl .                    Copied to same filename
```

If the file is copied from henry's home directory, then you can shorten the command line further:

```
rcp henry@uranus:cent2fah.pl c2f.pl
rcp henry@uranus:cent2fah.pl .
```

Multiple files may be copied, but then the last argument of **rcp** must be a directory. You can use shell wild cards too, but whether they will be interpreted remotely or locally depends on whether they are quoted or not:

```
rcp uranus:/home/henry/"*" .                         * interpreted remotely
rcp * uranus:/home/henry                              * interpreted locally
```

Though **rcp** has been virtually replaced by **ftp**, it retains one important advantage over **ftp**: it can copy subdirectory structures (recursive copy). This it achieves with the -r option:

```
rcp -r uranus:/home/henry/cgi-bin .              Copies cgi-bin directory tree
```

rcp has been created in the UNIX tradition, and requires both source and destination filenames to be provided. Unlike **ftp**, it's also totally quiet, and doesn't show what's going on during the transfer process. Access to this facility is also determined in a similar manner that also affects **rlogin**, and is dealt with shortly.

Tip

It makes sense to use the *username@hostname* format when using **rcp**. If you use the command **rcp foo juliet@uranus:docs**, it doesn't matter what the absolute pathname of juliet's home directory is. The file would be copied to the docs directory just the same.

Note

Although **ftp** doesn't permit recursive copying, you can use it to copy an **archive**. This is a group of files combined in a single file. The **tar** command *(22.9)* can archive an entire directory tree into a single file. You can compress this archive with **compress** or **gzip** *(6.19)* and then give it away to someone either by **ftp** or as an email attachment *(13.7.6)*.

11.9   rsh: **Remote Command Execution**

Sometimes, you require the resources of a larger system to run a CPU-intensive program without going through the formalities of logging in. **rsh** allows you to request a remote computer to run a particular program on that machine. It needs the machine name and the command:

```
rsh uranus ls -l
```
Executed in the user's home directory

Though **ls** is run remotely, the output is seen on *your* terminal. You have to escape the redirection character if you want to save the output in a file on the remote machine:

```
rsh uranus ls -l \> dir.lst
```
> interpreted remotely

The absence of the \ would have saved the output in a local file. If you use wild cards that have to be interpreted remotely, you need to quote or escape them too. **rsh** also has a **-l** option which lets henry run the same command in franklin's account remotely.

11.10 Enforcing Security for the Berkeley r-Utilities

Berkeley created the r-utilities to make it easier (and less secure) to access a remote machine. If you have failed to run **rlogin**, **rcp** and **rsh** in the way they are meant to, then this section is compulsory reading—even for the nonprivileged user.

UNIX systems don't come with any entries in the configuration files, so you have to insert them before you can use the r-utilities. UNIX provides two levels of authorization at

- The system level which applies to all users of a host. Authorization here is controlled by the file /etc/hosts.equiv on the remote machine.
- The user level where any user can set access restrictions to her account in the file $HOME/.rhosts.

The entries in these files determine two things:

- Whether you can use **rlogin** without using a password.
- Whether you can use **rcp** and **rsh** at all since these commands don't prompt for a password.

We'll take up system-level authorization first. We assume three possible situations where a user on *saturn* attempts to connect to the host *uranus*. A line in /etc/hosts.equiv of *uranus* can contain

- Simply the word saturn. This means that any user from *saturn* can log on to her account in *uranus* without using a password. The host is said to be **trusted**, and users are said to have **user equivalence** with their respective accounts in the remote host. No password is required for like-to-like accounts if the entry contains just the hostname.
- The two words saturn henry. The remote system then behaves in a more permissive manner. henry from *saturn* can log on to *any* account in *uranus* without using a password (root excepted, of course). This confers absolute powers on henry to use any account (**-l** option required for **rlogin**).
- No entry. henry can still log in but only after supplying a password.

Unhindered access is something no administrator would generally allow as it presents a potential security hazard. A better idea would be to enforce access at the user level with the file .rhosts. This file is edited by the concerned user.

Now, let's consider the same example, but this time we assume that there's no entry related to *saturn* in /etc/hosts.equiv of *uranus*. If henry (from *saturn*) is to be allowed access to charlie's account (on *uranus*) without using a password, then charlie's `.rhosts` should contain this:

```
saturn henry
```

However, if the line contains just the word `saturn`, then only the same user (i.e., charlie) can log in without a password. The guiding principle is this: When there are two fields in a line of `.rhosts`, the corresponding user is trusted; otherwise, the same user is trusted.

rcp and **rsh** also use `/etc/hosts.equiv` and `.rhosts` except that they either run or don't. They don't prompt for a password.

Tip

It's always preferable to enforce security at the user level. The safest and most restrictive entry would be to have just the hostname in `.rhosts` of the concerned user.

11.11 Prelude to the Internet

You have now learned to use the essential TCP/IP tools that you'll find in any UNIX system. Commands like **ftp** and **telnet** are still widely used on the Internet. Besides, the rapid growth of the Internet and the World Wide Web have also led to the development of a new generation of tools. These tools let you fetch news, subscribe to mailing lists and browse the Web. Netscape's browser software also provides graphic and easy-to-use alternatives to many of these tools. You'll meet TCP/IP again, but in an enlarged and modern form in the chapter on the Internet.

SUMMARY

TCP/IP is a suite of *protocols* used to connect heterogeneous machines running diverse operating systems. It is a *packet-switching* system where data is broken down into packets and these packets are reassembled at the destination. It is vendor-independent and ensures reliable transmission with full error control.

TCP/IP works in the *client-server* model. The client application (like **ftp**) communicates with its server counterpart at the other end to achieve its task. The server programs are known as *daemons*, which run in the background and listen for requests.

Every host in a network has a name which is found in the output of the **hostname** command. A host also has an *IP address* consisting of a set of four dot-delimited numbers. TCP/IP lets you access a host both by name as well as by IP address. Since users find names easier to remember, the name-address mappings are kept in the file `/etc/hosts` in all machines of a small network.

Large networks use the *Domain Name System* (DNS) where a host is described by its *fully qualified domain name* (FQDN). This is a series of dot-delimited names arranged in a hierarchical manner.

To have a two-way dialogue with another user, you have to set **mesg** to y. **talk** lets you have an on-line and interactive chat. It splits the screen into two and makes it easy to view both incoming and outgoing messages. **ytalk** can communicate with more than two users.

finger displays **who**-like details of all logged users in a remote machine. It can also reveal a number of details of a user even if the user is not logged in. A **finger** enquiry of a user displays the contents of two files, .plan and .project, in the user's home directory.

telnet lets you log on to a remote machine by supplying a username and password. After logging in, the files you create will be on the remote machine, but the display of commands will be on your local host. To run a command on the local machine, you need to escape to the telnet> prompt with *[Ctrl-]]*, and then prefix the command with a !.

rlogin is also used for remote login, but doesn't require a password for like-to-like accounts. It can also be used with the -l option to access other accounts.

ftp is used to upload (**put** and **mput**) and download (**get** and **mget**) files between two hosts. The name "anonymous" and the email address are used to access an *anonymous ftp* site. You can restart an aborted transfer and log in noninteractively by reading the authentication information from .netrc.

rcp can also transfer files but without having to log in. Unlike **ftp**, it can also copy an entire directory tree.

rsh is used in executing a command on a remote machine. It's possible to save command output both on the remote and local machine.

The r-utilities **rlogin**, **rcp** and **rsh** can only be used if proper authorization is provided at the server end. System level authorization is controlled by /etc/hosts.equiv. Authorization can also be enforced at the user level with .rhosts.

SELF-TEST

11.1   In how many ways does the system administrator use the **hostname** command?

11.2   What is a *socket*?

11.3   What is the problem with /etc/hosts?

11.4   What is an *FQDN*?

11.5   Is the domain name *FTP.download.Com* valid?

11.6   Name some common networking daemons and their functions.

11.7   How do you use **talk** to communicate with user brenda on host *uranus*?

11.8   How will someone using **finger** know whether you are on vacation or not?

11.9   How will you find out the details of all logged-in users on a remote machine *saturn*?

11.10 How do you invoke the telnet> prompt in the midst of a **telnet** session?

11.11 How can you be sure whether you are working on the local machine or used **telnet** to log on to a remote machine?

11.12 How will you connect to the telnet site *saturn.planets.com* from your Web browser?

11.13 To be able to use **rlogin** without using a password, what is the basic criterion that you have to fulfill?

11.14 If you rename /bin/ls to something else, will you be able to use **ftp**'s internal **ls** command?

11.15 When using **ftp**, how do you change your directory on the local machine?

11.16   With which command do you upload files to an anonymous ftp site?

11.17   What does this command do?

```
rsh jupiter date \> .date
```

EXERCISES

11.1   How is a TCP/IP network different from a telephone network?

11.2   Why is TCP termed a *reliable* protocol?

11.3   Can you use **telnet** on a standalone machine?

11.4   What is a *hosts* file and what does it contain?

11.5   Why are hostnames not used on the Internet, but only FQDNs?

11.6   How will you find out the port number **finger** uses?

11.7   If two users on the same host request the same Web page from a common host, how can you still maintain that they are using different sockets?

11.8   If **talk** throws up a message Your party is refusing messages, what could be the cause?

11.9   A remote machine offers only the **telnet** service but not **ftp**. You want to transfer the remote machine's /etc/passwd to your machine. What do you do?

11.10   You are in the middle of a **telnet** session, and you have to run a number of programs on the local machine. How can you invoke the local machine's shell prompt?

11.11   You have to log on to several remote machines with **telnet**. How will you do that without invoking **telnet** every time?

11.12   Why is **telnet** generally used on the Internet in preference to **rlogin**?

11.13   The **cp -i** command behaves interactively only when the destination file exists. How can you use TCP/IP to copy files interactively in your own host even if the destination files don't exist? When will this facility not work?

11.14   When you change your local directory from inside **ftp**, will the changed directory still be in place after you quit **ftp**, and why?

11.15   You copied a graphics file with **ftp**, and the file appears to be corrupted. What could be the possible reason?

11.16   356789 bytes of the file ie4.exe had been transferred from an ftp site when the transfer was interrupted. How will you restart the transfer from the point you left off?

11.17   You have to "ftp" to your own account on another host, but when you use the **ftp** command with the hostname, you find that you have logged in to a different account. When does that happen, and how will you rectify the situation?

11.18   How will you view a text file on an anonymous ftp site without downloading it?

11.19   How will you connect to an anonymous ftp site noninteractively?

11.20   What are the disadvantages of using **ftp** from the browser?

11.21   When will you be compelled to use **rcp** in preference to **ftp**?

11.22   If /etc/hosts.equiv on a host *neptune* contains just the word mars, how do you interpret the entry?

11.23   If you now remove this entry, what do you think will happen?

11.24 How should the remote machine on *neptune* be configured if user henry on *mars* is to be allowed to access (i) any account (ii) only his own account without using a password?

KEY TERMS

anonymous ftp *(11.7.1)*
archive *(11.8)*
client-server *(11.1.4)*
connection *(11.1.4)*
daemon *(11.1.4)*
DARPA command set *(11.5)*
domain *(11.1.3)*
Domain Name System (DNS) *(11.1.3)*
envelope *(11.1)*
**fully qualified domain name
  (FQDN)** *(11.1.3)*
host *(11.1.1)*
hostname *(11.1.1)*
hosts file *(11.1.2)*

IP address *(11.1.1)*
localhost *(11.1.2)*
namespace *(11.1.3)*
packet-switching *(11.1)*
port number *(11.1.4)*
protocol *(11.1)*
r-utilities *(11.5)*
router *(11.1)*
site *(11.1.3)*
socket *(11.1.4)*
trusted host *(11.10)*
uniform resource locator (URL) *(11.5.2)*
user equivalence *(11.10)*

## CHAPTER 12

The X Window System

The command line and the dumb terminal have always dominated the user interface of UNIX systems. But terminals can't produce the high-quality graphics required by advanced scientific and engineering applications. Apple and Microsoft made the graphical user interface (GUI) popular, and users were also getting tired of complex command line syntaxes. This was the scene in the UNIX arena when a group of graduates at the Massachusetts Institute of Technology (MIT) came up with the X Window system.

The X Window system was developed as part of Project Athena at MIT. Snubbed by one as "the Vietnam of UNIX," X (i.e., X Window) wasn't originally designed with any particular operating system in mind. However, it has now been adopted as the standard windowing system by practically all UNIX vendors. There are versions available for Windows as well. In 1987, MIT released X version 11—referred to as X11. It also has its own share of releases, the latest one being Release 6.4 (X11R6.4). X is controlled and maintained by the Open Group.

In this chapter, we'll take a look at the X Window system (not X Windows, as most mistakenly refer to it)—the X server and clients (the tools) usually shipped with it. We'll examine two sides of X. First, we'll learn to handle X the way we handle any GUI, using the mouse as the navigation tool. We'll also see how X is designed and ideally suited for running in a network.

Objectives

- Find out why one would need to use X. *(12.1)*
- Learn to start X and quit an X session. *(12.3)*
- Understand the role of the server and client. *(12.4)*
- Allow a command to be run by a remote user with **xhost**. *(12.5.1)*
- Display the output on a remote machine with the DISPLAY variable and the -display option. *(12.5.2)*
- Understand how X is split into two components. *(12.6)*
- Discover the role of the window manager. *(12.7)*
- Learn about the emerging standard in the Common Desktop Environment (CDE). *(12.8)*
- Use the **xterm** client. *(12.9)*

- Learn the general command line options used with X programs. *(12.10)*
- Copy data between different windows using the mouse and **xclipboard**. *(12.11)*
- Use some common clients like **xclock**, **xcalc**, **xkill** and **xload**. *(12.12)*
- Configure the file `.xinitrc`, the startup file used by **xinit**. *(12.13)*
- Specify X *resources* and override them with **xrdb** and the `-xrm` option. *(12.14)*

Note

This chapter presupposes knowledge of some windowing system—Apple, Windows or Presentation Manager. You also need to use the knowledge of TCP/IP that you acquired in the previous chapter. We won't go through the nitty-gritty of the various options of the window menus except briefly. It's presumed that you know how to select an object, highlight text with your mouse, or move and resize windows.

12.1   Why Use X?

Why do we need to use a graphical user interface? There can be a handful of reasons, and you have to assess the suitability of each reason to your environment. There's no sense in using X just because it's fashionable. There have to be strong reasons to do so.

First, let's consider that you want to remove a file. You can always use **rm foo** to do so. But if you have the file's icon (a small image) in front of you, and another one representing the Trash Can (the counterpart of Windows' Recycle Bin), then you can easily pick up your mouse, click on the file icon and drag it to the Trash Can. It's somewhat faster that way.

But what happens if it's a group of files that match the wild-card expression `*.txt`? The UNIX command line clearly comes on top in this case. **rm *.txt** can be entered faster than you can ever select a group of files and then drag the whole bunch to the Trash Can.

Whether you use X or the command line to do your job is a decision you have to make after making suitable comparisons of the time and effort needed. You'll come across situations when it's easier to do a thing in X. File and directory management with the command line sometimes fare poorly.

However, when it comes to viewing graphics, the command line has no answer. Traditionally, UNIX terminals have been character displays where a group of pixels constitutes one character. Terminals can handle a fixed set of these characters representing all the keys on your keyboard and some box drawing characters. A terminal typically displays 80 characters horizontally and 25 characters vertically.

Pictures, however, require individual manipulation of each pixel. X uses a **bit-mapped** display, where there can be several of these pixels on your screen. It's common for a screen to have a resolution of 800 × 600 pixels, which means that you can have 800 pixels in one horizontal line. The availability of multiple pixels along with the capability to handle each one of them individually gives X the power to handle graphics. That's why you need as much memory as possible—both on the machine and on your video graphics (VGA) card—to run X.

There's a third reason for using X. Applications are quickly moving to this platform. You'll be surprised at the spate of applications being developed for X. If you don't know X, you can't use Netscape—the tool with which we access the Internet and the Web.

12.2 The Graphical User Interface in X

If you have used any windowing system (the GUI) like Microsoft Windows, then you would have worked with multiple windows; they represent the applications (the programs). You would have used one window for Wordpad, one for Excel, and yet another one for Windows Explorer. Having multiple windows is like having multiple terminals in front of you, where you can move data from one application to the other. The number of windows you work with is limited by the size of your screen or your capacity to handle them.

X is also a windowing system, and it too has its own GUI. But, unlike the windowing systems of Microsoft or Apple, the look and feel of its GUI is not standard. You can have several types of these looks in X because the design of X separates the application from its appearance.

It's possible to change the appearance of a window instantly by running a separate program after starting X. This program is called the **window manager**, and there are several such window managers available in X. We'll postpone discussion on the reason behind this separation to a later topic, but be prepared to see X windows of different types wherever you go.

12.3 Starting and Stopping X

There are basically two ways of starting X. One method is to have it started automatically with the **xdm** command. This command is run during boot time from /etc/inittab by **init**—the process with PID 1. You'll see a graphical screen which requires you to authenticate yourself by entering your username and password to enter the system. **xdm** can otherwise be run only by the root user account.

If you are the sole user of your system (as is the case with most desktop owners using Linux or UNIX), then you should use the **startx** command to invoke X:

```
startx
```

The command starts the X *server* and loads a number of icons onto the desktop. Unless you are clicking on these icons, further work from here can commence by invoking an **xterm** *client* which simulates a terminal—the most often used client of the X Window system. We'll take up the X server and client very soon.

If you are not using **startx** to initiate an X session, you can use the **xinit** command:

```
xinit
```

This also starts up the X server, and if you have not customized X yet, the command simply places a single **xterm** window at the top-left corner of the screen. In fact, **startx** is only a frontend to **xinit**. The behavior of **xinit** is determined by its configuration file .xinitrc, which we'll discuss later.

There's no standard way of quitting X. One of these two should work on most systems:

- Point the cursor anywhere on the desktop or an edge of the screen and press one of the mouse buttons. If this brings up a menu, see if you can find options like *Exit Session* or *Log out*.

- For sessions started with **xinit**, it may be possible to use the **exit** command in that **xterm** window seen on starting X.

Before we proceed further, we must first understand the rather different client-server mechanism that characterizes X, and how it makes X especially suited for running in a TCP/IP network. This discussion follows next.

12.4   The X Architecture

X is a truly revolutionary product—not just a mere windowing system. When MIT started work on the project, they were aware that people were working with several types of graphic displays. Every display had its own methods for drawing lines and shapes on the screen. If an application were to write to all these displays, then there had to be several versions of the application—one for each type of display.

It's absurd to imagine designing a hundred versions of a program for a hundred types of displays, so the folks at MIT decided that the display should be handled by a separate program. The application would instead send its output to this display-handling program. This led to a very important splitting of the application into *client* and *server* components.

In a typical Windows application, the job of handling the PC's display is handled by the client application (on the PC) itself. X reverses this paradigm, and its architecture places the responsibility of handling the display on the **server**. The application itself runs as a **client**. The X server and clients may be on the same machine, but X shines when they are separated, and was primarily designed to run over a TCP/IP network. The transmission is totally reliable; X uses the TCP protocol *(23.1)*.

Now, what does the X server have? To derive the answer, let's consider that you want to run a program on a remote machine either because of its superior computing power or simply because you don't have it on your machine. *X technology lets you run an X client on a remote machine, and yet have the display on your own local machine.* It sounds amazing, but it's true! If the server has to handle the display, then it must take care of all input to the display as well (for instance, the input to a calculator program). This means that the server also comprises the mouse and keyboard.

This has important implications in X. Freed from the rather complex tasks of window drawing, X programs become quite portable. To run an X client on a different terminal, all one has to do is to write the server component of X for that terminal. Once written, future X programs can then write to this new server program.

Note

An X display includes the mouse and keyboard. It can also comprise multiple screens on multiple monitors. In fact, many UNIX systems offer support for multiple screens.

12.5   Running X Programs Remotely

On single-user systems, the server and client run on the same machine, and you don't have to bother about controlling the display. The situation is quite different when running X over a network. Consider that you want to use the **xcalc** calculator program which is not available on your machine (*saturn*) but in a remote one (*uranus*). You would like to run the program there, but have the display here so you can input data from your keyboard. There are two things you must ensure before you can make that happen:

- The server on your machine, *saturn*, must enable others to write to its display.
- The client programs on the remote machine, *uranus*, must be directed to write their output to *saturn*'s display.

The first requirement is met by using the **xhost** command, and the other is enforced by setting either the DISPLAY variable, or by using the -display option with the client. We'll take up these two features in the upcoming paragraphs. Though a discussion on **xterm** follows much later, it's good to know now that all X clients can be run from the UNIX command line offered by **xterm**. In fact, that's what we'll be doing in this chapter.

Tip

If you don't find an **xterm** window on your desktop on starting X, then place the entry **xterm &** in the file $HOME/.xinitrc and restart X. The file is discussed in Section 12.13.

12.5.1   xhost: Let Others Write to Your Display

To run remote programs locally, you have to first ensure that the X server is running on your machine. The **startx** and **xinit** commands ensure that, so make sure X is started. You now have to use the **xhost** command from an **xterm** window on your local machine:

```
$ xhost +uranus
uranus being added to access control list
```

Any user on *uranus* can now write to your display. You can turn off the **xhost** setting with the - symbol or enable your display for all machines with +:

```
$ xhost -                                           Disables display for others
access control enabled, only authorized clients can connect
$ xhost +                                            Enables display for others
access control disabled, clients can connect from any host
```

Make sure your display is enabled (with **xhost +uranus** or **xhost +**). We'll describe two techniques of running a command remotely. The first is with **telnet** and the second with **rsh**.

Tip

If you have a fixed list of machines that are permitted to write to your display, rather than set DISPLAY every time, it's better to store the hostnames (one per line) in the file /etc/X*n*.hosts where *n* is the number of the display.

12.5.2   The DISPLAY Variable: Where to Send Output

We all know that **telnet** lets you run a remote program, so let's "telnet" to *uranus* from here:

```
$ telnet uranus
Trying 192.168.0.4...
Connected to uranus.
Escape character is '^]'.
```

```
login: henry
Password: ********
```

Once you are at the prompt, just define and export the DISPLAY variable in the new shell:

```
DISPLAY=saturn:0.0                                    saturn must be in /etc/hosts
export DISPLAY                                   See Section 17.2.2 for C shell syntax
```

The output of the DISPLAY variable is of the form *hostname:server.screen. saturn* is the hostname, :0 is the instance of the X server program and .0 is the screen number of the display. Both server and screen are usually 0 for single-user systems, and the screen number (.0) may be omitted. If *saturn* is not defined in /etc/hosts, then you have to use the IP address in its place.

The above setting signifies that any X client on *uranus* will use the display of *saturn*'s machine, rather than its own. Now you can run the program **xcalc** on *uranus* and have the display on your own machine:

```
xcalc &
```

The calculator pops up on your machine, and you can now use it to perform all your calculations. X allows the use of the local keyboard with a remote client simply because the keyboard is a component of the server definition, and this server runs locally.

12.5.3 Using rsh with the -display Option

Instead of using **telnet** which requires you to log in and then use the command from there, you can also use **rsh** to execute the command on the remote machine and have the output locally.

Here, you need to use the -display option offered by every X client. This option is also followed by the complete display name (in the form *hostname:server.screen*). Here's how you run the same **xcalc** client on *uranus* using your own local display:

```
rsh uranus xcalc -display saturn:0                        Screen number dropped
```

This is the most efficient way of running a command remotely; use the absolute pathname of **xcalc** if necessary. However, there's a very important consequence when you the run the **xterm** client in this way:

```
rsh uranus xterm -display saturn:0
```

The **xterm** window appears on *saturn*'s display as usual, *but now any further programs run from this* **xterm** *window will continue to write to the same display without using the* -display *option*. This isn't an obvious consequence, but it's true. However, for this to be possible, you must have adequate authorization to use **rsh** *(11.10)*.

Note

Any remote program run with **telnet** or **rsh** will always save files in the remote machine, even though the display appears on the local machine. When **rsh** is used with a character-based client using standard output, make sure you escape the > character with the \ to save output remotely. This has already been discussed *(11.9)*.

12.6 X Techniques and Components

The complete screen (the **desktop**) in X is usually filled with multiple windows (Fig. 12.1). The navigation tool in any GUI is the mouse. Every mouse has generally two or three buttons, and the left button is used most. The mouse pointer is used to click on something or drag it. When you click the pointer on some text in an editor, the pointer changes to an I-beam cursor. When you drag it (by keeping the left mouse button pressed) over text, the text gets highlighted.

A menu comes up when you click one of the mouse buttons on the desktop (also known as the **root window**)—sometimes at one of the edges. Called the **Root Menu**, it offers important X applications like calendar and mail, the Web browser, terminals or the option to exit the X session.

Every window on the desktop shows a **title bar** unless it is **iconified** (minimized). Iconifying a window is converting it to an icon which sits on the desktop. You can see one at the top-left corner of the desktop shown in Fig. 12.1. You can rejuvenate an iconified window by clicking on it.

Before you can work with a visible window, you have to make sure the **input focus** is on it. In other words, the window has to be selected for keyboard input to reach the application in the window. A selected window will have a different color title bar, and at any time only one window will have this color.

FIGURE 12.1 *The Desktop in X*

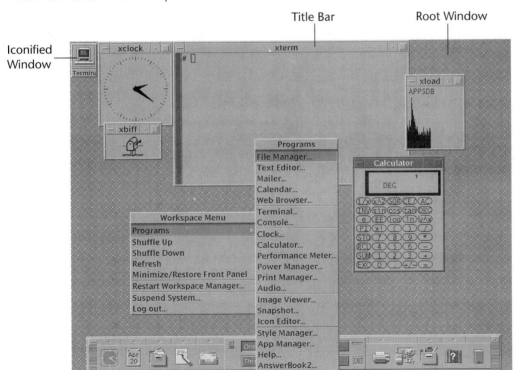

In Windows, you select a window by clicking anywhere on it with your mouse. Window selection techniques in X depend on the window manager you use. The CDE and Motif follow the Windows system; others require you to click on the title bar. On some systems you may even have to move the cursor over a window to select it (no clicking required).

If a window is not visible (being at the bottom of the window stack), then try using the Windows-type *[Alt][Tab]* combination to bring it to the top. You should position your windows in such a way that some part of each window is always visible. To move a window, click on its title bar and drag it. You can resize a window by dragging any of the four corners. Once you are able to do all this, you are ready to start work in X.

Tip

Windows users should note that X has an additional way of moving windows. You can move a window without selecting it. Just press the *[Alt]* key, click on the title bar of any window and move it. The window doesn't get selected, and yet it gets moved!

12.6.1 The X Widgets

X works with a number of components—called **widgets**. X widgets comprise the buttons, scrollbars, checkboxes and all the other objects that respond to your mouse clicks. Fig. 12.2 shows these components in the two overlapping configuration windows of Netscape.

You can see a scrollbar on the left. You can either drag this scrollbar with your mouse or click at its two ends to display text not currently visible. You can also see a set of three radio buttons displaying a set of mutually exclusive options. On the other

FIGURE 12.2 *X Widgets*

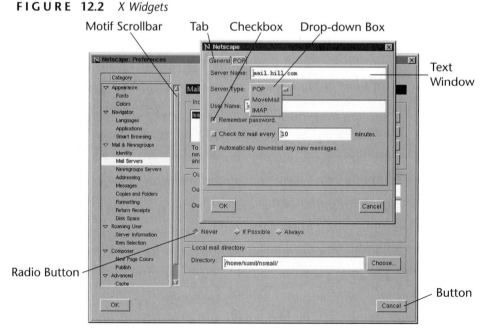

hand, checkboxes let you select one or more items. Enabling an option could mean adding a tick mark or depressing a small box or a diamond. You'll also encounter tabs and drop-down boxes.

12.7 The Window Manager—A Special Client

X clients display their output on separate windows on the display, but the X server doesn't provide any frames or menus for them. The clients don't provide them either. In addition, there's no way you can move or resize a "frameless" window. Who provides these then? The specific look and feel of X clients is determined by a special X client—the **window manager**.

The window manager imparts more than a cosmetic touch to all X applications. It is built on the client programs and ensures that all clients have the same appearance irrespective of the vendor they come from. The irony is that the window management functions of all clients are performed by another client—albeit a very important one. The server has no role to play here. The window manager provides the frames and buttons and lets you resize and move windows. It also provides the Window Menu.

There have been a number of window managers in the past—like **twm**, Open Look (**olwm**) and Afterstep. We very nearly had a standard one—**mwm** (the Motif window manager) and yet another one in **dtwm** (the window manager used by the Common Desktop Environment). **dtwm** is based on Motif which in turn was deliberately designed to resemble the look and feel of IBM's Presentation Manager. Linux also has its own standards—**fvwm**, **fvwm95** (Windows-based) and **kwm** (CDE-based).

The **dtwm** window manager is shown in Fig. 12.3 embracing an **xterm** client (a client that gives you the shell prompt). The title bar shows a button at the top left and two on the right. It's here that we encounter the first characteristic feature of X. Both the number and shape of these buttons depend on the window manager you have chosen. You could very well see an X system with different buttons.

FIGURE 12.3 *The* **xterm** *Window and the* **dtwm** *Window Menu*

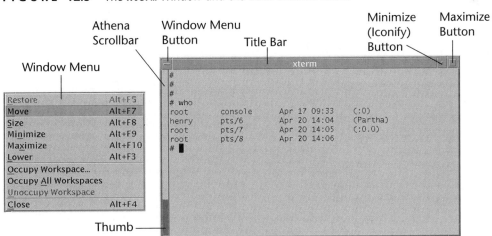

One of the two buttons on the right of the title bar is represented by a tiny square and is used to minimize a window, i.e., convert it into an icon. The other button beside it is shown by a "raised" rectangle (initially) and is used to maximize a window. Once it is blown up full-screen, the rectangle appears depressed.

The left button has a totally different function. When you click on it, the **Window Menu** pops up. Many of the window management functions mentioned above can also be handled by this Window Menu. If the buttons on the right are not visible, but the left one is, you can use its menu options to minimize, maximize, close, move—and even resize—a window.

No matter how you start X, you have to make sure the window manager is run from one of the configuration files used by X. If that's not done, you can run it from an **xterm** window immediately after starting X. If you are using the Motif window manager, run the client in the background:

mwm &   *Use the appropriate window manager program*

Enter this command at an **xterm** window only if you find the window frames missing upon starting X. All existing and future windows will then have a characteristic look similar to the one shown in the **xterm** window in Fig. 12.3.

12.8   CDE: The Common Desktop Environment

A number of developments have taken place that hopefully will make a user comfortable in any X environment. In the past, even if Motif was adopted by most vendors as the standard window manager, implementations of X still differed across vendors. The desktop appearance was not uniform, nor was the method of using the applications. This made it difficult for a user to feel at home when she encountered a different X version even though both implementations used Motif. Motif remained a standard of sorts for some time before the "desktop environment" wave changed the look and feel of the entire desktop (the entire screen)—and not merely the window manager.

Based on Motif, industry leaders IBM, HP, Sunsoft and Novell started the COSE (Common Open Software Environment) movement in 1993. They introduced the **Common Desktop Environment** (CDE)—a standard desktop that made sure once and for all that all vendors' implementations of X not only had the same look and feel for all windows, but for the complete desktop as well.

The window manager used on CDE is **dtwm** (desktop window manager). It is quite similar to Motif, so if you are comfortable with Motif, you'll find little difficulty in handling CDE. The window manager has an enhanced role to play in this environment. In addition to handling windows, **dtwm** features a Front Panel, a virtual Workspace Switch, a File Manager and a Trash Can. It's the CDE that is shown in Fig. 12.1.

From the Front Panel (Fig. 12.4), you can launch subpanels by clicking on the triangular symbols on the top. The most exhaustive option list is provided by the subpanel *Programs* (Fig. 12.1), and you can start many X clients from here. The most commonly used clients are also provided as icons in the Front Panel itself. You can start the clock, a calendar scheduling service or the File Manager directly by clicking on their icons.

File Manager resembles Windows Explorer and lets you perform basic file functions. You can delete files by dragging them to the Trash Can. Files deleted in this way can be recovered later.

FIGURE 12.4 *The CDE Front Panel*

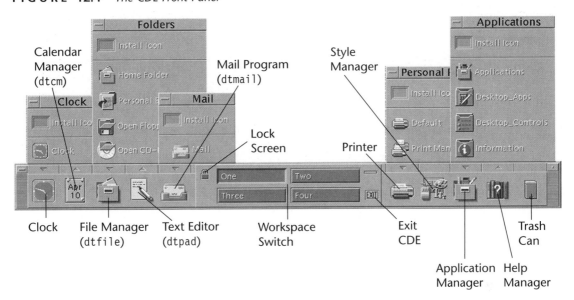

At the center of the Front Panel is the Workspace Switch. This is a set of four buttons that let you create multiple "desktops" on your machine. You can have one set of windows on one desktop, another set on another, and you can select your desktop by clicking on the respective workspace button. With four buttons, you can have up to four such desktops. It's like having a screen four times as large.

Further discussion on CDE is beyond the purview of this text. What follows is a generic presentation of the features of X—sometimes assuming Motif as the window manager. Remember that the appearance of windows and the desktop on your systems can be different if you use a different window manager or desktop environment.

Linux

Not to be left behind, Linux also has started its own "desktop" movement, and now has two products—KDE and GNOME (from GNU). KDE has **kwm** as its window manager. Like CDE, KDE also features a panel (CDE's Front Panel), virtual desktops, the K File Manager and the Trash Bin. However, GNOME is rapidly acquiring popularity and may eventually become the standard.

12.9 xterm: **The Main Client**

As mentioned before, **xterm** is probably the most important X client. By default, it comes up when X is started with **xinit** (Fig. 12.3). If you find the frames around the window missing, then the first thing you should do before anything else is to invoke the window manager in the background *(12.7)*.

xterm behaves just like any character-based terminal, and is simply an instance of the shell. You'll see the shell prompt in this window from where you can launch all UNIX commands and other X programs. You can run several jobs by affixing an & against each to run them in the background:

```
xclock &
xfm &                                                    The file manager
netscape &
```

This is the same technique you use in the command line except that this time you see a number of overlapping windows in front of you—each a separate application by itself. With X, you really get the feeling of working on several machines at a time.

You need multiple **xterm** windows if you want to run foreground jobs—like **vi** or **emacs**, for example. You can even edit a program on one, and run it on another. However, input to an **xterm** window is only possible when you click on it—or select it by other means (like *[Alt][Tab]*).

Note

The desktop environment offers a superior terminal emulation client—**cdterm** (CDE) and **kvt** (KDE). Unlike **xterm**, they always display a scrollbar and have a separate menu bar. From this menu, you can set the font size and color, and also copy and paste text.

Caution

If you don't affix the & to an X client command, the issued command becomes the child of the **xterm** window that created it. If you kill this parent window, the child window then gets terminated as well. This is not what you would want normally, so all X clients should be run asynchronously, i.e., in the background.

12.9.1   Using the Scrollbar

You can activate the scrollbar facility available in **xterm**. To be able to recall previous commands and their output, use **xterm** with the -sb and -sl options:

```
xterm -sb -sl 10000 &                                 Saves the last 10,000 lines
```

The number of lines saved is determined by the -sl option. An Athena scrollbar (the original scrollbar from MIT) now appears at the left of the **xterm** window. This scrollbar contains a grayed-out **thumb** which initially occupies the entire column, but reduces in size as commands are entered. To recall the history, you have to drag the thumb with the middle button.

12.10   Command Line Options

Most X client programs are built to handle a large number of options, and their sheer number can put commands like **find** to shame. Many of these options (Table 12.1) are common to practically all commands. They often take on abbreviations, which are shown in parentheses in the table. We'll discuss their significance briefly.

12.10.1   Window Position and Size (-geometry)

When you invoke an X client without specifying any options, it will be set up at a default location and with a default size. When you need to place several such clients on your desktop, you'll have to size and place them properly so they can easily be selected. Most X clients offer the -geometry option to determine the location and size of the client. The option is followed by a two-part component—the size of the window and the location of one of its corners from the respective edge of the screen.

TABLE 12.1   *Common Command Line Options Used by X Clients*

Option	Significance
-display	The display specification of host on which client should display its output
-geometry	Size and location of window (-g)
-foreground	Window foreground color (-fg)
-background	Window background color (-bg)
-reverse	Reverses foreground and background colors (-rv)
-iconic	Starts client in minimized form
-title	Name of window to be displayed in title bar
-name	The name of the application
-xrm	Resource specification overriding settings of resource files

For **xterm**, the size of the window is specified in characters and the location (or offset) in pixels. The following command line sets up an **xterm** with a window size of 40 by 12 characters, with its top-left corner offset by 10 pixels from the left side of the display and 20 pixels from the top:

```
xterm -g 40x12+10+20 &
```

For other clients, 40x12 would mean 40 pixels by 12 pixels—a very small window to be of any use. By default, **xterm** windows have the size 80 by 24 characters. You can have multiple **xterm**s at different areas of the screen; the size can also be omitted:

```
xterm -g -10-20 &                          Offset from lower-right corner of display
xterm -g +10-20 &                               Offset from lower-left corner
xterm -g -10+20 &                               Offset from upper-right corner
```

It should be quite obvious that when both numbers are zeros, the window is placed at the corner of the display. (-g -0-0 should place it at the bottom right.)

12.10.2   Setting Colors (-fg, -bg and -rv)

The -foreground (-fg) and -background (-bg) options determine the respective colors of the client. You can set these colors for your **xterm** windows in this manner:

```
xterm -fg darkslategrey -bg lightblue &
```

X maintains this database of colors in the text file /usr/lib/X11/rgb.txt. (This location can vary.) This file contains over 700 color descriptions, with each line containing three numbers representing the amount of red, green and blue (the **RGB values**). The file also contains variations in these spellings—often with spaces between the words. Here are some typical entries in this file:

```
255 255 240              ivory
 47  79  79              dark slate gray
 47  79  79              DarkSlateGray
  0   0 128              navy blue
135 206 235              sky blue
  0 255 255              cyan
224 255 255              light cyan
```

The foreground and background colors can be reversed with the -reverse (-rv) option. This option comes in handy when you need to have a distinctly different appearance for a window, say the parent **xterm**. A different color setting for an **xterm** window will prevent you from accidentally killing it.

12.10.3   Other Options

Starting as an Icon (-icon)   You can start any **xterm** client, but in an iconic form, with the -iconic option. This option is required especially when there isn't sufficient space on your root window to accommodate all of them. You can activate the window either by clicking (single or double depending on the window manager). You can keep your parent **xterm** window permanently iconified so that you don't kill it by mistake.

Providing a Title (-title)   You can provide a title (-title) to be displayed in the title bar at the top. When running multiple instances of **xterm**, it's better that you have separate names for them. You could name them after the machines on which they are running or the applications running on them:

```
xterm -fg red -bg lightblue -title "sqlplus on uranus"
```

Providing a Name (-name)   The -name option lets you provide a name which can be identified by the server; you'll see the name in the icon label. X resources understand the string provided with -name. For this reason, it's often preferable to use this option rather than the -title option.

Two other options, -bd and -bw, set the border color and border width, respectively.

12.11   Copy and Paste

Neither **xterm** nor the window manager (like **mwm** or **dtwm**) offers any specific menu options for copying or moving text. (**cdterm** displays the Windows-like *Edit* menu in the menu bar having the usual copy, cut and paste functions.) X offers a general facility to copy and paste text using only the mouse buttons. With them, you can move text from one window to another—perhaps between **vi** and **emacs** sessions.

To copy text, highlight it by dragging it in the usual manner with the left mouse button; *the text automatically gets copied into the buffer.* Then, click on the other window with the left button, move the cursor to the point where you want to paste it, and click the middle button. The copied text is inserted into the window. If you are using **vi**, make sure you are in the input mode before pasting back text. You can also copy and paste a command line in another **xterm** window to reexecute the command.

Instead of dragging, text can also be selected by clicking multiple times on the text. Double-clicking selects a word; the triple click selects the entire line. X offers no facility for cutting text. This has to be done by using the editor's own facilities.

Tip

If you are using **xterm** for selecting a block of text in one screen, click with the left button at the starting point of text, and right-click at the end of the text; the entire text gets selected. To extend the selection on either side, right-click at the respective text boundary.

12.11.1   xclipboard: Advanced Copy and Paste

The standard copy and paste feature has its limitations. You can only act on single sections of text at a time; you can't copy multiple sections in one shot for later pasting. This is also a problem with software running Microsoft Windows, where a user has to repeatedly switch between two files for performing this dual operation. **vi** and **emacs** handle this problem with the named buffers, but X solves the problem with a Macintosh-like tool—the **xclipboard** program.

xclipboard (Fig. 12.5) is a typical MIT X application using the Athena widgets. There are six buttons at the top of the window; the last two are grayed out initially. To use this tool, copy text from one **xterm** window in the usual manner and then paste it in a blank window on **xclipboard**. The counter at the right, which initially showed 1, continues to do so.

If the text is too large to fit in the window, the Athena scrollbar appears, and you can then drag the thumb of the scrollbar with the middle button. Unlike **xterm**,

F I G U R E   12.5   *The* **xclipboard** *Client*

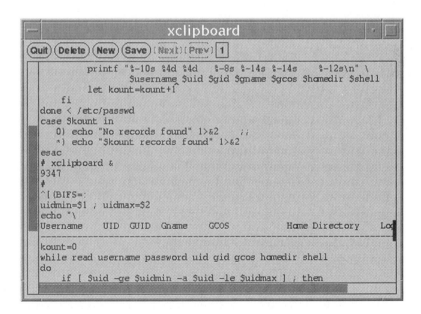

xclipboard also displays a horizontal scrollbar if the window width is insufficient to display the text.

To repeat the copying operation with another text segment, you have to click on *New* first. This clears the **xclipboard** display and advances the counter to 2. You can now paste the text that you have copied into this region. In this way, you can have multiple text sections stored in the clipboard. You can step through the various clipboard buffers by using the buttons *Next* and *Prev*.

The important thing to remember is that *once you have a text section on display on the clipboard window, that section is deemed to be copied.* You can then paste it at any place you want by using the middle mouse button. If it doesn't work, then select the text. You can delete a clipboard section (*Delete*) and even store it (*Save*) in a file. Nothing in Microsoft Windows can match this method of copying and pasting text.

12.12 Standard X Clients

MIT ships X with over 50 clients, ranging from desktop accessories, font and graphic utilities to special tools related to window and resource management. Linux has many more clients. In the following sections, we'll discuss a handful of X accessories available in standard X distributions. You should look up the directory /usr/X11R6/bin for the list of X clients or /usr/dt/bin if you are using CDE. The ones we are going to discuss now can all be seen in Fig. 12.1 featuring the entire desktop.

12.12.1 xclock: The Analog Clock

All X distributions come with the analog clock **xclock**. It has a number of useful options, as the following command lines show:

```
xclock -chime &                                          Chime sounds every half-hour
xclock -digital &                                           Prints in character format
xclock -update 5 &                                          Shows a seconds dial
```

Besides these options, there are other options to set the color of the hands of the analog clocks. It always helps keeping the clock at some corner of the screen.

12.12.2 xcalc: The Calculator

X also features a calculator, the **xcalc** client. You can run it in two modes—the Texas Instruments TI-30 mode or the Hewlett-Packard 10C mode. The first mode is emulated by using **xcalc** without arguments.

There is nothing special about this calculator except that its -rpn option lets you use **reverse polish notation** (i.e., the HP-10C mode). This notation often uses a reduced set of keystrokes compared to the number used in standard notation. The calculation 3 + 5 + 9 = becomes 3 *[Enter]* 4 *[Enter]* 9 + in reverse polish notation.

12.12.3 xload: Displaying the System Load

xload displays a histogram of the system load average. This is a useful program which you can run on multiple remote machines and have the histograms of the load data on your local machine. You can then run your next program on the machine with the lowest load, other things being equal (the processing power, for instance). The command should be used with two useful options—-update and -jumpscroll:

```
xload -update 15 -jumpscroll 1 &
```

By default, **xload** pools the machine every 5 seconds (10 in Linux). The -update option sets this time to 15 seconds. The -jumpscroll option ensures that the graph shifts to the left by 1 pixel when the histogram reaches the end on the right. This ensures smooth scrolling of the display. Because the command is most often used to run on multiple machines, the window shows the name of the host at the top.

12.12.4   xkill: Killing a Window

Any window can be closed either by clicking on the respective button on the title bar, or using an option from the menu button. Sometimes, windows don't respond, in which case, you have to use **xkill** to kill a single window or all windows together. When used without arguments, X displays this message:

```
Select the window whose client you wish to kill with button 1....
```

You now have to move the cursor to the window and do exactly as told. If this happens to be the parent window of a number of child windows, this action will kill the child windows as well. The -all option lets you kill all root level windows in one go, except that X makes sure you select the root window three times—once with each button. This gives you a number of chances to change your mind.

12.13   .xinitrc: **The Startup File**

Like most applications, X can be customized to present a specific look and feel upon startup. If you use **startx** to invoke X, it will invoke **xinit**, and **xinit** will always look up the file .xinitrc in the home directory. Generally, all X sessions place an **xterm** window on the desktop. From that window, you'll have to invoke other X clients to continue your session.

If you want your desktop to be loaded with a number of X clients upon startup, you have to place the command sequences in .xinitrc. This is a shell script (not the C shell) where every command, *except the last*, is placed in the background. A sample .xinitrc is shown below:

```
$ cat $HOME/.xinitrc
xrdb -load $HOME/.Xdefaults
mwm &
xclock -g 100x100-0+0 -bg tomato3 -fg white -update 1 -chime &
xterm -g -80-55 -sb -sl 300 -bg darkslategrey -fg ivory -rv -iconic &
xterm -g -0-0 -sb -sl 3000 -bg darkslategrey -fg ivory &
xbiff -g +0+0 &
netscape
```

Make sure you start the **mwm** client; otherwise you won't be able to move or resize any of the windows. **xbiff** is a mail notification tool (Fig. 12.1) which beeps and puts up a flag when mail lands in your mailbox. **netscape** is a very important client that you'll use in the next two chapters.

12.14 X Resources

Every X client is composed of a number of objects (widgets) like scrollbars, buttons and so forth. There are attributes (*resources*) that are associated with both a class of objects as well as individual instances of these objects. For instance, every application button has a foreground color, termed as the **resource** for the button. Every possible resource of every object of an application can be customized so that you need not invoke the client with complex options.

The sample .xinitrc file above shows **xterm** invoked with the same set of background and foreground colors (darkslategrey and ivory) and with a scrollbar. Now, if that is how you want **xterm** to always appear, you can set these attributes in a special file, $HOME/.Xdefaults. This file is read by X when it is started, but you can make X reread this file after you have made changes to it in the middle of a session. To customize **xterm** as above, you have to place the following entries in this file:

```
XTerm*ScrollBar: True
XTerm*saveLines: 10000
XTerm*background: darkslategrey
XTerm*foreground: ivory
```

The definitions on your system could look different, but the same principles apply. A resource definition begins with the name of the client (the class), which may be followed by either the widget hierarchy (a series of objects separated by dots) or an asterisk which matches all objects at that location. In either case, the resource attribute follows, terminated by a :, and then the value of the attribute. These values can be boolean (True or False), a string (ivory), or a number (10000).

Once you set resources this way, henceforth, you need not use the -sb, -sl, -fg and -bg options with **xterm** if you want it to always appear with these attributes. However, you would certainly want to leave the -geometry option out of this, being the only variable part of the **xterm** command line.

12.14.1 xrdb: Loading the Resources

You need not quit and restart X if you have made changes to .Xdefaults during your session. You can simply use the **xrdb** command to signal to X that it should reread the configuration file:

```
xrdb $HOME/.Xdefaults
```

X starts with a number of defaults for these resources, some of which are specified in the application itself. There are yet others which are set in a systemwide configuration file in /usr/lib/X11/app-defaults (location can vary). You'll find a file named after each configurable client in this directory.

CDE uses the directory /usr/dt/app-defaults. Depending on the language used by the system, you have to use one of the subdirectories of this directory. For U.S. English, it is en_US.UTF-8.

If a user has no .Xdefaults in her home directory, the specifications of the systemwide file are applicable when X is started. If you have created a customized .Xdefaults file, then you should also put the **xrdb** statement in the .xinitrc so that clients are invoked with the right resource values.

12.14.2   The -xrm Option: Overriding the Resources

There are situations when you need not only ignore the systemwide default settings but also the ones you have put in your .Xdefaults. A specific instance of an application may also require a different setting. You can sometimes override these settings by invoking the command with suitable options. However, not all resources have corresponding option equivalents, but a special option, -xrm, can let you specify any resource value.

For example, you can change the background color of **xclock** with the -bg option. But you can also use the resource specification for the class:

```
xclock -xrm 'xclock*background: lightblue' &
```

Besides these simple resources, there are other settings related to the translation of events. A typical event could be the interpretation of mouse clicks or movements. They are not quite intuitive, and a discussion on them is beyond the scope of this text.

This is all you need to know about X to ready yourself for the Internet and the World Wide Web. In the next two chapters, we'll be using Netscape extensively as a universal Internet and mail-handling tool.

S U M M A R Y

X Window uses a *bit-mapped* display where each pixel can be manipulated individually. The entire display is known as the *root window*, and individual applications are displayed as windows on this root window.

X is started with the **startx** or **xinit** commands. X can also be invoked during system startup with the **xdm** command. **xdm** can otherwise be invoked by the root user only.

X splits an application into two components—*client* and *server*. The server program controls the monitor, keyboard and mouse, while the application itself is the client. X programs are thus portable since they don't have to bother about window drawing.

X also runs in a TCP/IP network, and it is possible for a client to run on one machine and have its display on another. The **xhost** client controls access to the server, while the environment variable DISPLAY determines where the client should display its output. The -display option can also be used with any X client to direct program output.

All windows have a *title bar* comprising a number of buttons. The left button brings up the *Window Menu*. A window can be moved, resized, minimized, maximized and closed using these buttons. A window is brought to *focus* generally by clicking on the window or its title bar.

X windows comprise a number of *widgets* (components). They can be buttons, scrollbars, checkboxes, radio buttons, tabs and drop-down boxes.

By default, X clients don't have any window management functions. A special client, the *window manager*, must be invoked once, at the start of an X session, to make these functions available to all windows. A window manager makes it possible to move and resize windows. The standard window manager for UNIX has been Motif (**mwm**), but it is now being replaced by **dtwm** of CDE. **fvwm** and **kwm** are two of the many window managers available in Linux.

The Common Desktop Environment (CDE) provides a standard look for both the desktop and the window manager. It features a Front Panel from which you can launch many applications. The File Manager handles the file and directory functions, and the Trash Can stores deleted files. The Front Panel also offers a Workspace Switch that lets you create virtual desktops to accommodate clients that won't fit in one screen.

You can invoke all UNIX commands and X programs from the UNIX command line available in an **xterm** window. **xterm** can also be used with a scrollbar (-sb), and the number of lines saved can be specified (-sl).

X programs run with a number of common options. You can position and specify the size and position of a window (-geometry) and its foreground and background colors (-fg and -bg). You can start a program as an icon (-icon) and provide a name (-name) or title (-title).

You can copy text from any window by merely selecting it with the mouse button. The copied text is pasted back by clicking the middle button. Multiple sections of copied text can be stored in the **xclipboard** client from which it can be pasted anywhere.

There are several clients available in X. X offers a clock (**xclock**) and a calculator (**xcalc**). **xload** displays the system load, and is often used with remote machines. **xkill** kills a window. It can kill all root-level windows in one invocation (-all).

X can be easily customized. You can start X clients from the file .xinitrc, the startup file used by **xinit**. X *resources* enable you to change practically any X feature. These features can be stored in .Xdefaults, and **xrdb** can be used any time to read this file. These settings can also be overridden with the -xrm option available in every X client.

SELF-TEST

12.1   Why does X require a lot of video memory?

12.2   Name two commands that can be used to start X. Can you use **xdm** to start X?

12.3   How do you invoke the Root Menu?

12.4   Which component of X is responsible for displaying a window on the screen?

12.5   Can an X client like **xterm** running on a Solaris machine display its output on a HP-UX machine?

12.6   What is the function of the **xhost** command? What does **xhost** + signify?

12.7   How do you identify the selected window?

12.8   Can you move a window without selecting it?

12.9   What is the difference between a checkbox and a radio button?

12.10   How do you invoke the Window Menu?

12.11   What is **mwm**?

12.12   How will you invoke an **xterm** with a scrollbar and a saving facility of 1000 lines?

12.13   If the **xinit** command doesn't place an **xterm** window on the desktop, how will you configure it to do so?

12.14   What entries do you place in the file $HOME/.Xdefaults?

E X E R C I S E S

12.1   Why can't you display graphics on a character-based terminal?

12.2   What is the difference between removing a file with **rm** and dragging it to the Trash Can?

12.3   How does X solve the problem of running the same program on different displays with different characteristics?

12.4   What are the elements that comprise an X display?

12.5   How can romeo running **netscape** on his machine *saturn* display its output on juliet's display in a remote machine *uranus*? Do both users need to run X?

12.6   What is wrong with this command when run from host *venus*?

        rsh saturn xload &

12.7   How is the DISPLAY variable more convenient to use than the -display option?

12.8   A remote machine *saturn* doesn't have telnet facilties. Can you still run its programs remotely from *venus* without using the -display option with every client?

12.9   Who places the frames, borders and buttons on the windows? Is it a server or a client?

12.10   Which program represents the window manager in CDE?

12.11   What happens if there is no window manager running on your system? Can you still work?

12.12   If you have five X clients on your desktop, how many times do you need to run the window manager?

12.13   What's the function of the four rectangles that you see on the Front Panel at the center of Fig. 12.4?

12.14   Which shell does **xterm** use?

12.15   How can you make one **xterm** window show a different name in its title bar?

12.16   What is the essential difference between these two commands?

        xterm -g 40x14+0+0
        xclock -g 40x14+0+0

12.17   Why do you need to run X clients in the background?

12.18   How do you copy text from one window to another?

12.19   If you are copying text to the **vi** editor running on an **xterm** window, what additional step do you have to take?

12.20   How do you copy multiple sections of text from a window?

12.21   How can you use **xkill** to terminate an X session?

12.22   What happens if all commands in .xinitrc are placed in the background?

12.23   How do you override a resource setting when invoking a client?

KEY TERMS

bit-mapped display *(12.1)*

Common Desktop Environment
 (CDE) *(12.8)*

desktop *(12.6)*

iconified window *(12.6)*

input focus *(12.6)*

reverse polish notation *(12.12.1)*

RGB value *(12.10.2)*

Root Menu *(12.6)*

root window *(12.6)*

thumb *(12.9.1)*

title bar *(12.6)*

widget *(12.6.1)*

window manager *(12.2 and 12.7)*

Window Menu *(12.7)*

X client *(12.4)*

X resource *(12.14)*

X server *(12.4)*

## CHAPTER 13

Electronic Mail

Email is fast replacing the fax as a data communication medium, while taking a load off the post office. UNIX systems provide an impressive collection of email communication tools. The users of these tools can be on the same host, different hosts in a TCP/IP network or on any host on the Internet. Their features are so useful that, for some people, UNIX means electronic mail.

The medium of email is informal, fast and quite cheap. Today, it can handle graphics, sound and video files as well. To send an email message, one has to simply type it in, write the address (or probably select it from an address book) and then issue a send command or click on a button. No affixing stamps, sealing the envelope and rushing to the post office. The message is usually received in a few seconds, sometimes in minutes, but rarely in hours. That's why email users dub post office mail "snail mail."

In this chapter, we'll take up three character-based mailing programs—**mail**, **elm** and **pine**. We'll also discuss Netscape Messenger, a very popular and powerful client that runs under the X Window system.

Objectives

- Understand the organization of mail folders and the format of a mail message. *(13.1)*
- Acquire a working knowledge of the **mail** command. *(13.2)*
- Use a menu-based program like **elm** to handle mail. *(13.3)*
- Use the superior features of **pine**, another menu-based program. *(13.4)*
- Learn the significance of the .signature and .forward files. *(13.5)*
- Understand the role of the *SMTP* and *POP* protocols in transporting mail. *(13.6)*
- Configure and use Netscape Messenger as a superior mail client. *(13.7)*
- Use the **vacation** command as an automated mail generation system when you are away. *(13.8)*

➤ *GOING FURTHER*
- Learn the role of *MIME* in the transmission of binary files as mail attachments. *(13.9)*

13.1 Email Basics

Mail addressed to you with a special addressing scheme lands in your mailbox even when you are not logged in. This is a distinct advantage over the **talk** command, where two users need to be logged in to communicate. A mailed message never appears directly on your terminal. If you are running a program, the system waits for program execution to finish before flashing the following message:

```
You have new mail in /var/mail/romeo
```
                                                                                  romeo is the user

When you log in and have unviewed mail, the system will greet you with a similar message. You need not handle it immediately; the mail will remain in your mailbox till you view it. However, it's good practice to see incoming mail immediately upon arrival rather than defer it for future viewing. After you have viewed it on your terminal, there are several things you can do with it:

- Reply to the sender and all recipients.
- Forward it to others.
- Save it in a mailbox folder.
- Save it in a separate file.
- Delete it.
- Print it.
- Add the address of the sender and all recipients to the address book.
- Call up a helper application to view it if it is not in plain text format.

Mail is marked with the name of the sender and the date and time it was sent. All incoming mail is saved in a **mailbox**. This is a text file normally placed in the directory /var/mail (/var/spool/mail in Linux), and it has the same name as the login name. All mail gets appended to the mailbox file. charlie's mail is saved in /var/mail/charlie.

Note

Older UNIX systems use /usr/spool/mail as the spool directory. You can find out the location of your mailbox by evaluating the value of the shell's MAIL variable:

```
$ echo $MAIL
/var/mail/sumit
```

However, changing the value of this variable won't change the location of your mailbox. It's just that mailers like **mail** and **elm** read the file defined in this variable for knowing the location of the mailbox.

When the content (not the header) of a mail message has been viewed by any of the character-based mailers like **mail**, **elm** or **pine**, the message may get deleted from there and end up in $HOME/mbox. These mailers use different *folders* (their lingo—actually ordinary files) for saved, sent and even unsent messages, and they are located in $HOME/Mail. Netscape, on the other hand, maintains all its folders in $HOME/nsmail.

To sum up, these are the possible areas where you may find a received mail message:

- /var/mail (/var/spool/mail in Linux)—Mail is stored in a file named after the user-id. It's from here that a message moves to other locations. If you are retrieving mail through a dialup line, you'll have to access this directory.
- $HOME/mbox—**mail** and **pine** move viewed mail to this file, but the other mailers don't on their own.

- $HOME/Mail/received—**elm** and **pine** often prompt to save viewed mail in this file.
- $HOME/nsmail/Inbox—Used exclusively by Netscape.

The directory locations, and sometimes the filenames, can be changed by configuring the mailers, but we'll leave them undisturbed. All these mail programs, however, look at the mailbox file in /var/mail for all incoming mail.

13.1.1 The Addressing Scheme

UNIX is a time-sharing system where several users miles apart can log on to a central machine and use it to send messages. The email addressing scheme in the early days simply used the recipient's username (as registered in /etc/passwd). The primitive **mail** command was used in this way:

```
mail henry
```
                                                                henry is on same host

Later, when machines got connected in a network, a combination of the username and the hostname was required to make the address unique in the entire network. This addressing scheme uses the @ as the delimiter. This is how you would address mail to henry having an account on a different host *calcs*:

```
mail henry@calcs
```
                                                               henry is on host calcs

That's how we used **talk** earlier *(11.2)*. The Internet's Domain Name System *(11.1.3)* extended the addressing scheme even further. Since the address had to be unique throughout the world, hosts are associated with domains. For instance, the host *calcs* in the domain *planets.com* would be known to any email application as *calcs.planets.com*, and a user henry on this host can be addressed as *henry@calcs.planets.com*. This combination will be unique in the Internet. The *From:* and *To:* lines in a message received by henry could typically look like this:

```
From: charlie@mumcs.net
To: henry@calcs.planets.com
```
                                                      Mail from a different domain

This naming scheme brought all hosts in the world under one roof, and email became the most popular application on the Internet (until overtaken by the Web).

13.1.2 Anatomy of a Mail Message

Every mail message consists of several lines of header information. You may or may not be able to see all the headers depending on the application used to compose the message and the one used to handle it. However, a typical message will show at least the first four fields as shown below:

```
Subject: creating animations in macromedia director from GIF89a images
   Date: Mon, 08 Nov 1999 15:42:38 +0530
   From: joe winter <winterj@sasol.com>
     To: heinz@xs4all.nl
     Cc: psaha@earthlink.net
```

When you compose a mail message, the subject is optional, but it's good discipline to fill up the subject field, especially when you are trying to draw the attention of the recipient. The *Date:* and *From:* fields are automatically filled in by the system. When sending a message, you have to enter the recipient's email address carefully as the mail will bounce back if there's a single mistake in it.

You may also want to send copies of your message to other people; the term *carbon copy* (Cc) seems to have stuck in this regard. When you send multiple copies of your message to other people on the same host, unlike in the postal system only a single copy is sent out by your mailer. The copies are made at the destination and then delivered to the users' mailboxes.

Note

The *From:* line in the example above shows the full name of the sender. If your mail systems are Internet-compliant, you should be using this form since it provides more information about the sender than the minimal form does (shown inside the < and >). However, the string on the left (joe winter) is not used for routing the message, and a mistake here won't bounce the mail. If you reply to the sender, and winterj or sasol.com is incorrectly spelled, the mail is most certainly going to bounce. This point will be taken up in Section 13.7.4.

13.2   `mail`: **The Good Old Mailer**

The earliest mail handling tool still offered by all UNIX systems is the primitive **mail** program. Its simplicity and convenience can be aptly compared to **cat**'s creating a file (**cat > foo**) with no editing facilities whatsoever. However, **mail** is a very convenient tool if you have to send a line or two to someone. In fact, it's simpler sending a message with **mail** than handling a received one.

There are two ways of invoking **mail**. When you use it with the recipient's email address, you are using it in the sending mode. **mail** expects standard input, which you terminate with a *[Ctrl-d]* on some systems and a **.** on others:

```
$ mail henry                                                henry on same host
Subject: RealAudio — TCP or UDP?
Dear henry:
which protocol does RealAudio use — TCP or UDP?
I think it's UDP
[Ctrl-d]                                                     Solaris uses .
$ _
```

Sending a message is as simple as this. The mail lands in henry's mailbox, which is usually /var/mail/henry. As observed before, all email programs read this file for incoming mail.

The contents of a mail message can also be supplied by redirecting the standard input. The *Subject:* line remains blank when the input is redirected in this way:

```
mail henry < note.1st
```

This is an advantage with this "brain-dead" program—the only reason we have retained this command in this text. Since **mail** operates here noninteractively, you can use it in shell scripts to automatically mail messages. **elm** also allows this, but not **pine**—and certainly not Netscape.

To view mail, henry can also invoke the **mail** program, but this time without any arguments:

```
$ mail
Mail version 8.1 6/6/93.  Type ? for help.
"/var/mail/henry": 1 message 1 new
>N  1 sumit@saturn  Sat Sep 25 17:34  15/455    "RealAudio — TCP or UDP?"
?  _                                                        The mail prompt
```

mail first shows the header of the message, which reveals the sequence number, the sender's email address (*sumit@saturn*), the date and time, number of lines and byte count (15/455), and finally the header of the message. It then waits for user input at the ? prompt. **mail** has a number of single-letter internal commands that can be used at this prompt. We'll discuss only a few of them here.

To view the message marked 1, henry has to enter the message number, followed by *[Enter]*. He can save it to a separate file with **w 1**, or delete it with **d 1**. Finally, he has to use **q** to quit **mail**. Once a message is viewed, it is deleted from /var/mail/henry and appended to $HOME/mbox. This migration always takes place for **mail** and **pine**, but not for **elm**. We won't go into any further details of the workings of the **mail** program.

Though the limitations of **mail** restricted its use, it formed the basis of development of better mail tools. UNIX systems offer two outstanding programs—**elm** and **pine**, which are even easier to use. Both are completely menu-driven, extremely simple to use and yet quite powerful.

13.3 elm: **A Screen-Oriented Mail Handler**

elm fills up the entire screen when invoked by the command name. At the bottom of the screen, you'll find its internal commands. In this universal mode, you can use **elm** both for sending and receiving messages. On invocation, it shows the headers of received messages, suitably numbered, in **mail**-style. A typical **elm** screen is trimmed and shown in Fig. 13.1.

The menu is fairly straightforward and shouldn't pose a problem—even for beginners. New and unread messages are indicated with an N at their left. The size of the message in bytes is shown within parentheses. To view any message, just move the highlight up and down to select that message, and then press *[Enter]*:

```
Message 1/3 Julie Brown                    Apr 30, 98 10:02:12 am +0530

Return-Path: <local>
Date: Thu, 30 Apr 1998 10:02:12 +0530
To: henry@saturn
Subject: Going Out?

Dear Henry:
Let's eat out since Sonu doesn't need to go to school
for the next three days
```

Selecting **q** from the main menu quits **elm**, but not before it makes sure that you have answered these questions:

F I G U R E 13.1   *The* **elm** *Screen*

```
Mailbox is '/var/mail/henry' with 3 messages [ELM 2.4ME+ PL37 (25)]


     1    Sep 24 Julie Brown          (55)    Going Out?
     2    Sep 25 system PRIVILEGED     (30)    Accounting time less than 50 hours
  N  3    Sep 24 Kothari Pioneer       (269)   KPMF InstaNAV 24.09.99


... blank lines removed ...


  You can use any of the following commands by pressing the first character;
d)elete or u)ndelete mail,  m)ail a message,  r)eply or f)orward mail,  q)uit
   To read a message, press <return>.  j = move down, k = move up, ? = help


Command: _                                                        Cursor waiting here
```

```
Command: Quit              Move read message to "received" folder? (y/n) y
Command: Quit              Keep unread messages in incoming mailbox? (y/n) y
```

You should now understand what **elm** means by all this. Entering a y at the first prompt means that read messages will be appended to the file $HOME/Mail/received. A y at the second prompt means that **elm** will keep unread messages in /var/mail/henry; otherwise it will move these messages to the same received folder. Note that **elm** doesn't use mbox.

Note

If you are addressing someone on the same machine as yours, you can drop the machine name and simply use the username in the *To:* field.

13.3.1   Sending a Message

Sending a mail message is quite simple. You have to first select **m** from the main menu, and then respond to the following prompts:

```
Send the message to: jackie@caltiger.com
Subject of message: Yet another proposal
Copies to: hillary@caltiger.com
```

elm then opens up the **vi** (or **emacs**) editor where you can key in your message. Whether you send or forward a new message, or reply to one, you can always mark copies to other people. After you have quit the editor, you still have a few options to choose from:

```
Please choose one of the following options by parenthesized letter: s
             e)dit message, edit h)eaders, s)end it, or f)orget it.
```

You can do all the usual things now like editing and canceling a message, but note that a very important option is missing here—the facility to defer sending a message. Sometimes, we don't want to send a message in its present condition; we don't like to "forget" it either. This is where **pine** and Netscape Messenger score over **elm**.

13.3.2   Handling a Received Message

You can reply to, forward or delete a message. To reply, select the message and then press **r**. You have the option to send copies to others:

```
Command: Reply to message                          Copy message? (y/n) n
Subject of message: Re: The forthcoming holidays
Copies to:
```

The editor will come up once again. Compose your message, and then save your work before you exit. **elm** finally offers you the same options that you have seen when sending a new message.

With **f**, you can forward a message to someone else. You can delete a message with **d**, but **elm** makes sure you are doing the right thing when you exit the program with **q**:

```
Command: Quit                                      Delete message? (y/n) y
```

13.3.3   Controlling Spam

As you become an active email user, you'll subscribe to mailing lists and surrender your email address to Web sites. Eventually, a lot of people will acquire your address, and your mailbox will pile up with hundreds of messages every day—something you never expected to happen. You have unwittingly become the victim of **spam** (junk) mail. Most email programs including **elm** support a filtering scheme that identifies a search string in the mail and deletes from your mailbox all messages that contain the string.

You can specify a pattern to search for (in **vi**-style) with the **/** command (or **//** to search in message body). Once you find that the search correctly identifies messages that you don't want to see, you can use *[Ctrl-d]* to delete them without prompting.

13.3.4   **elm** Options

elm can be used to read any mail folder located anywhere. This requires the use of the -f option. Using it, you can read the Inbox folder of Netscape. You'll recall that Netscape keeps all its mail files in $HOME/nsmail:

```
elm -f $HOME/nsmail/Inbox
```

If you just want to check whether there is any mail in your mailbox, then use **elm** with the -z option:

```
$ elm -z
You have no mail.                                  The program also quits
```

elm can also be used with the username as argument. The text can also be taken from the standard input:

```
elm -s "The forthcoming holidays" henry          -s specifies Subject: line
elm henry < holiday.txt                          Message from standard input
```

elm's behavior can be tailored by editing the file $HOME/.elm/elmrc. You can choose your editor (editor = vi), set the directory to save mail (maildir = $HOME/Mail), or save messages by user-id of sender or recipient (savename = on). You can also set some of these features by using **elm**'s **o** command. The important commands for **elm** are shown in Table 13.1.

Tip

You need to know the **vi** editor to use **elm** in its default configuration. If you want to use **emacs** or a simple editor like **pico**, use the **o** command to change **elm**'s configuration, change the relevant line with **E**, press *[Enter],* and then use **>** to save the new configuration.

Note

The characteristic feature of the **mail** and **elm** commands (**pine** excluded) is that they are often used with a special redirection (<<), known as the *here document (19.2),* where the input is placed in the same script file. This is an important feature provided by the shell that you'll find quite useful.

13.4   pine: **Yet Another Mail Program**

pine, the program for Internet news and e-mail, is arguably the most popular character-based mailer, and is widely used on the Internet. Developed at the University of Washington, it combines simplicity and power using a core set of minimal functions. Like **elm**, it too can be used without reading the manuals.

The mailer can be called up simply by invoking **pine**. The interface looks so simple, you'll hardly realize its true power. The opening screen of **pine** is shown in Fig. 13.2.

TABLE 13.1   *Internal Commands Used by* **elm**

Command	Significance
m	Mails a message
r	Replies to current message
d	Deletes current message
f	Forwards current message
q or Q	Quits with (q) or without prompting (Q) for deleting or moving messages
s	Saves current message or tagged messages to a folder ($HOME/Mail, by default)
/	Searches the *From:* and *Subject:* lines for pattern
//	Searches entire message for pattern
[Ctrl-d]	Deletes messages containing pattern
o	Opens **elm**'s options screen

FIGURE 13.2   *The Opening* **pine** *Screen*

```
 PINE 4.05    MAIN MENU                        Folder: INBOX   5 Messages


          ?     HELP                -  Get help using Pine


          C     COMPOSE MESSAGE     -  Compose and send a message


          I     MESSAGE INDEX       -  View messages in current folder


          L     FOLDER LIST         -  Select a folder to view


          A     ADDRESS BOOK        -  Update address book


          S     SETUP               -  Configure Pine options


          Q     QUIT                -  Leave the Pine program


      Copyright 1989-1998.  PINE is a trademark of the University of Washington.
                  [Folder "INBOX" opened with 5 messages]
 ? Help                     P PrevCmd                   R RelNotes
 O OTHER CMDS L [ListFldrs] N NextCmd                   K KBLock
```

The menu items are neatly laid out. It seems that you can maintain an address book—a feature missing in **elm**. Though the main menu offers a general help feature, **pine** also has a context-sensitive help that is invoked by using ? in most cases, and ^G in others. (^G is *[Ctrl-g]*.)

13.4.1   Viewing Mail

pine breaks up incoming and outgoing mail into a number of folders. **elm** also does that, but **pine** can display the list of folders. Pressing **l** or **L** shows the list, and a sample one is shown in Fig. 13.3.

You can highlight any of these five (sometimes, more) folders, and then press *[Enter]* for further details. Note that this option (**l** or **L**) lets you see the messages that you have already sent or postponed. The INBOX folder (same term used by Netscape) refers to the user's spool file in /var/mail or $HOME/mbox. When you highlight this folder and press *[Enter]* (or **i**), a screenful of viewed headers (the message index) is displayed (Fig. 13.4).

pine displays context-sensitive help in the last two lines of the screen. As you move from one screen to another, you'll find the options changing in these two lines. The options shown in the figure are helpful enough and should need no elaboration.

Like in **elm**, just select a message with the cursor keys, and then press *[Enter]* or **>** to show the message contents. Let's have a look at the only unread message (the one marked + N) in this folder (Fig. 13.5).

FIGURE 13.3   *The Folder List in* **pine**

```
                        Local folders in Mail/
        ----------------------------------------------------------
        INBOX          sent-mail      saved-messages    postponed-msgs
        received
```

FIGURE 13.4   *The Message Header Window in* **pine**

```
     PINE 4.05    MESSAGE INDEX              Folder: INBOX  Message 1 of 26   NEW


            1 Aug 23 isingh@elnet-31.com    (304) Mail server working fine
            2 Aug 22 sujit lala           (3,993) Fw: GOT IT
        + N 3 Aug 23 henry blofeld        (8,174) RE: RealAudio -- TCP or UDP?
            4 Aug 23 Kothari Pioneer     (15,561) KPMF InstaNAV 23.08.1999
            5 Aug 26 The Economist        (9,639) Politics This Week August 21st
        ... lines deleted ...


        ? Help        < FldrList   P PrevMsg      - PrevPage D Delete      R Reply
        O OTHER CMDS > [ViewMsg]  N NextMsg    Spc NextPage U Undelete    F Forward
```

FIGURE 13.5   *The Message Content Window in* **pine**

```
        Date: Mon, 23 Aug 1999 13:12 +0500 (GMT)
        From: henry blofeld <henry@vsnl.com>
        To: joe winter <winterj@sasol.com>
        Subject: RE: RealAudio -- TCP or UDP?


        dear joe:


        RealAudio has to come streaming in. If it has to wait for
        retransmission of segments, will you ever hear the sound properly?
        It has to use UDP.
        ... lines deleted ...


        ? Help        < MsgIndex   P PrevMsg      - PrevPage D Delete      R Reply
        O OTHER CMDS > ViewAttch  N NextMsg    Spc NextPage U Undelete    F Forward
```

The help menu changes yet again, even though in only two options. If you have more messages to view, you can use **n** to see them in turn, and **p** to view a previous one. Pressing **i** returns you to the message index.

Tip

The keys **>** and **<** are extremely useful and can make your work in **pine** very productive. Using **>** repeatedly, you can move from the folder list to the header list, and then to the screen featuring the message contents. If the message has any attachments, another **>** will take you to the attachment index and finally to the attached contents. If you are using **pine** from X, a series of >s executed in sequence (with the cursor keys thrown in between) can quickly call up an external graphic viewing program and show you an image. Use **<** to trace your path back—right up to **pine**'s opening screen.

13.4.2   Composing a Message

Pressing **c** (from the main menu) makes **pine** bring up its built-in **pico** editor for composing your message. We'll send a copy of our message to a local user this time. Fig. 13.6 shows the composition window.

This editor is fairly easy to use—even for doing things that you can't easily do in **elm**. You can cut (^K) and paste (^U) text and search for a string (^W). After you have finished composing your text, you can use ^X to send it. **pine** is built on the principle that the user must confirm every action that she can't undo later:

```
Send message?
```

pine differs from **elm** in another way; it allows you to postpone (^O) transmission of a message. This is a useful feature (also available in Netscape) that lets you edit a message later before you are sure of sending it. You can also run a spell-checking program (^T); this would normally use the program shipped with the system—**spell** or **ispell**. This is also controlled by the setting of the speller variable in $HOME/.pinerc. Linux users must make sure that they explicitly set this variable to /usr/bin/ispell.

Note

The control keys you see in Fig. 13.6 are visible only when the cursor is positioned in the content section of the screen. You'll see a different set of keys when the cursor is in the header section.

Tip

With the cursor positioned in the content section, you can use ^R to insert a file's contents into your message, for instance, a program listing or its output. To send a file as an attachment, move the cursor to the appropriate header *(Attchmnt:),* and use ^J.

13.4.3   Forwarding and Replying

The forwarding and replying functions are similar to **elm**, and need no elaboration here. Use **f** and **r** for these purposes from either the message index window or when viewing the message contents. **pine** does ask you these questions when you decide to reply:

```
Include original message in Reply?
Use "Reply-To:" address instead of "From:" address?
Reply to all recipients?
```

F I G U R E   13.6   *The Composition Window in* **pine**

```
   To      : bruno@elnet-31.com                Someone on the Internet
   Cc      : henry                             User on the same host
   Attchmnt:
   Subject : how does one start Star Office?
   ---- Message Text -----
   dear bruno:


   i am unable to invoke Star Office from an ordinary user account. well,
   henry is using some word processor on linux (I don't know which one), and
   he may be able to help too. do either of u know?


   sumit
   ... lines deleted ...


   ^G Get Help  ^X Send      ^R Read File ^Y Prev Pg  ^K Cut Text   ^O Postpone
   ^C Cancel    ^J Justify   ^W Where is  ^V Next Pg  ^U UnCut Text^T To Spell
```

The *Reply-To:* prompt appears when the sender's message contains this field. It's possible that the sender's machine may be down, and she may be using her friend's machine to mail the message. Understandably, she doesn't want the reply to be directed to this address but to her actual email address. This feature is not available to you when you compose a message with **elm** and **pine**. So, if you see a message with the *Reply-To:* field, it must have been composed in another mailer (probably Netscape).

You can include as much of the original message in your reply. This often helps the recipient in correlating the messages; people do tend to forget what they had written. You also don't have to reply to all recipients separately—a feature that looks forward to *mailing lists (14.3)*, which are widely used on the Internet.

13.4.4   The Address Book

An interesting feature of **pine** is its **address book** (also available in Netscape), where you enter a person's details just once so they can be picked up from the "book" subsequently. You can select the address book from the main menu and then press **@** to add a new entry:

```
Nickname : chris
Fullname : christopher flynn
Fcc      :
Comment  :
Addresses : chris@lakeerie.edu
```

Fill in the fields just like you would in the composer.
To form a list, just enter multiple comma-separated addresses.

It is ok to leave fields blank. Press "^X" to save the entry, "^C" to cancel.
If you want to use quotation marks inside the Fullname field, it is best
to use single quotation marks; for example: George 'Husky' Washington.

A helpful message appears from **pine**. After you have saved the entry with ^X, you can
later pick up the address when composing a message. At the first prompt (*To:*), press
^T to invoke the address book, then highlight the entry you want and select it with **s**.
The field gets automatically filled in.

13.4.5 pine Options and Configuration

pine also has a number of options. The -I option lets you supply a sequence of keystrokes that **pine** will execute on startup. Since you press **c** at the main menu to open
the composition window, you can have this window in front of you when you start **pine**:

    pine -I c   *Executes c command on startup*

You can also use **pine** with the address directly:

    pine henry@saturn   *The composition window appears*

You can view the messages that **elm** has saved by default in the received folder of
$HOME/Mail:

    pine -f received

pine can be configured from the main menu itself. It uses the startup files
/usr/lib/pine.conf for systemwide settings, and /usr/lib/pine.conf.fixed for
options that can't be overridden. **pine** also supports a user-specific file $HOME/.pinerc.
The files are very well documented, and you'll have no problem editing them.

      elm and **pine** are used on the Internet for at least one reason: they can both be
used to send multimedia attachments *(13.9)*. With the advent of the World Wide Web,
their charm has somewhat declined because Netscape's Communicator software also
handles mail. Netscape is the last mail handling program that we'll be considering in
this chapter.

Note

You can send a text or binary file as an attachment with **pine** using its -attach option. **elm**
does the same with the -A option. However, the type of file that is sent must feature in an
important configuration file used by these mailers. To handle multimedia attachments, you
need to understand MIME first, which is taken up in the "Going Further" section.

13.5 .signature and .forward: Two Important Files

Most mailers make use of a facility to affix a section of text to every message you send.
You probably have seen details of a person's address and telephone number at the end
of every message. In all likelihood, the sender has not entered these details every time
she sent the message. Rather, she used a mailer which attaches the contents of a file,
.signature, automatically.

If you feel you should also do the same, then place all these details in .signature in your home directory. Both **elm** and **pine** use these files by default. Netscape, while maintaining its own set of configuration files for everything, also uses this file. All these mailers can, however, be configured to use a different file.

The next file, $HOME/.forward, provides an automatic mail forwarding facility. When you travel, you may want your mail redirected to another host (say, at one of the free email sites offered on the Web). You can then place an entry like this in the .forward file:

romeo@yahoo.com

That's all that is required. When a message addressed to romeo is received by the mail server, it forwards the message to Yahoo's site without delivering it to romeo's local mailbox. No mailer needs to be configured to use this facility because forwarding through .forward is a feature of **sendmail**—the program that uses SMTP and delivers most of our mail on the Internet.

A problem arises when you forward mail with .forward to another host and then set up a reverse forwarding facility there to redirect it back. This situation can occur for mobile users who depend on .forward to ensure they don't miss a single mail message. Forwarding at both ends creates a loop, and your message never gets the opportunity to "land"; it shuttles to and fro before **sendmail** intervenes and breaks the loop.

Tip

*If **elm** is not using .signature, then edit the file $HOME/.elm/elmrc, and set either localsignature or remotesignature to $HOME/.signature, depending on whether you want to use it for local or remote mail. If **pine** is ignoring .signature, then set signature-file in $HOME/.pinerc. Netscape makes the setting in Edit>Preferences> Mail & Newsgroups>Identity.*

13.6   How Mail Works

Before we take on Netscape, we need to know how mail works. You can skip this section if you intend to stick to character-based clients like **elm** and **pine**. But if you'd rather be a power user of Netscape and would also like to configure it, then this section is compulsory reading.

Unlike **telnet** and **ftp**, which work within a simple client-server framework, mail handling requires the work of three agencies:

- Mail user agent (MUA)—For reading and sending mail.
- Mail transport agent (MTA)—For forwarding mail between machines.
- Mail delivery agent (MDA)—For delivering mail to the recipients' mailboxes.

In this three-tiered arrangement, the **mail user agent** (MUA) like **pine** or **elm** acts as the user's front-end. By itself, it is not designed to transport mail across the network. Some MUAs like **pine** and Netscape have capabilities to transport mail too, but UNIX systems have a separate agency earmarked for the job.

The **mail transport agent** (MTA) has two functions: it both sends and receives mail. At the sending end, the MTA identifies the recipient's address and delivers the message *directly* to the MTA at the other end. Both sending and receiving mail are handled universally by the **Simple Mail Transfer Protocol** (SMTP).

The MTA is not responsible for ultimate delivery of the message. It's the **mail delivery agent** (MDA) that accepts mail from the receiving MTA and delivers it to the actual user's mailbox. This is handled by separate programs like **/bin/mail** (This is an MDA too.) and **deliver**. (**procmail** is the standard MDA for Linux systems.)

A fourth tier comes in when the MTA is unable to deliver mail to the MDA. This is true for dialup lines where the receiving host connects to the network intermittently. In this arrangement, users typically use their Internet Service Provider's (ISP's) facilities to handle both incoming and outgoing mail. The ISP stores the user's mail on their server, and the user fetches the mail using a separate program. There are two protocols in use today for fetching mail—**Post Office Protocol** (POP3) and **Internet Message Access Protocol** (IMAP).

Fig 13.7 shows how SMTP and POP move mail in a network. Netscape has many built-in mail functions and is often configured to ignore some of the mail handling services provided by the operating system. We'll now study Netscape.

13.7 Netscape Messenger: The Most Powerful Mailer

Netscape Messenger is an excellent mail user agent that runs as an X client. It is actually a component of the Netscape Communicator suite which also features Navigator as the other major component. To invoke Messenger, run the **netscape** command in either of these ways from an **xterm** window:

```
netscape &
netscape -messenger &                                  Only Messenger will be invoked
```

While the first command would generally invoke Navigator with or without Messenger (depending on the way Communicator is configured), the second one makes sure you have only the Messenger window in front of you. In any case, the Menu Bar at the top will always show *Communicator* as one of the items. In case you see the Navigator window, just use *Communicator>Messenger* to activate Messenger. (Click on *Communicator* in the menu bar at the top and then *Messenger* from the menu that follows.)

FIGURE 13.7   *Mail Movement Using SMTP and POP*

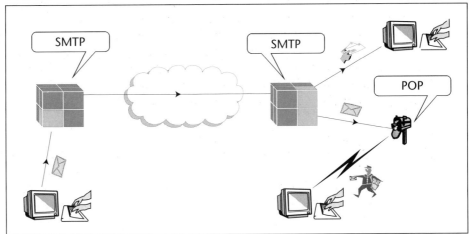

Messenger is a multipurpose mail client. Apart from performing the usual mail handling functions, it uses its internally built SMTP facilities to transport mail to an outgoing mail server. It also acts as a POP client to fetch mail from the incoming server and deliver it to the mailbox. In short, it handles some of the functions that were explained in the previous section—but only for a single user. That's why it's possible to send and receive mail on a machine running Messenger, but not any of the mail services offered by the operating system. This section should be interesting reading both for beginners and power users.

13.7.1   Configuring Netscape Messenger

Before you start using Messenger, you have to set it up. All Netscape settings are initiated with *Edit>Preferences*. A new window shows up on the screen. Now, expand the *Mail & Newsgroups* category by clicking on the triangle on its left. You'll find a host of items in this menu, but in this section we'll stick to the first two—*Identity* and *Mail Servers*.

First, move to the *Identity* group. You'll have to enter your full name and email address. Note that Netscape shows the location of a `.signature` file, which was discussed in Section 13.5. This is a file whose contents are attached to every mail message sent from Netscape. We'll ignore the other fields.

Next, click on the *Mail Servers* group (Fig. 13.8). Here, you'll have to enter the hostnames or the fully qualified domain names (FQDNs) of the mail servers—both incoming and outgoing. If your outgoing and incoming mail is handled by another host—probably a central host in your campus—then enter its hostname or FQDN depending on the addressing scheme followed in your environment. If your mail is handled by your ISP, then enter the names of the ISP's mail servers; these will be FQDNs since your ISP's mail server would probably be on the Internet.

In the mail configuration screen shown in Fig. 13.8, the domain names of both incoming and outgoing mail servers are shown to be the same—*cal.vsnl.net.in*. They need not be so; often incoming and outgoing mail are handled by different hosts. The username for both mail servers is also shown. For individual accounts, this is generally the same as the name component of your email address. For the incoming mail server, you also have to decide whether

- The password can be stored so it need not be entered every time.
- Mail is to be checked regularly and new messages automatically downloaded.
- Messages are to be left on the server. As a beginner, you should make sure that they are, so you should check this box (default: unchecked).

Observe from this screen that the mail directory `$HOME/nsmail` is set here. You can change it to `$HOME/Mail` if you want all mailers to use the same directory. You are now ready to use Messenger.

13.7.2   Messenger: A Frontal View

Messenger's features are quite intuitive, so you can get up to speed in no time. From version 4.5 onwards, it shows a three-pane window (Fig. 13.9). All message folders are shown on the left (the Message Center) along with the number of read and unread messages. A boldfaced folder name means that there are unread messages inside. The messages here are divided into two categories—email and newsgroups.

FIGURE 13.8 *Netscape Mail Server Configuration Screen*

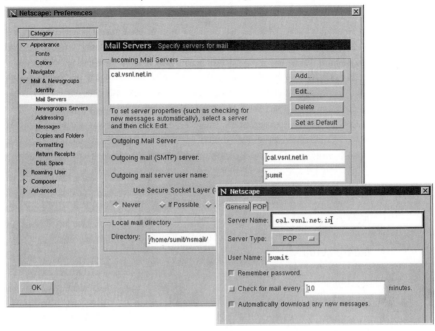

FIGURE 13.9 *Netscape Messenger: A Frontal View*

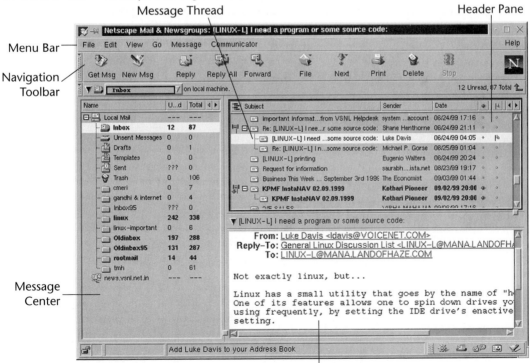

The message list on the right is split into two panes. Message headers are shown in the top pane (Header Pane), and the contents of the currently selected message in the bottom pane (Content Pane). Double-clicking on a message header brings up a new window with a larger viewing area. You can stretch and compress these panes with your mouse to suit your convenience.

At the top is the Menu Bar, where you can see the traditional *File*, *Edit* and *View* menus, apart from three more. In the next row is Messenger's Navigation Toolbar containing clickable icons. The basic functions are all handled here—ones that any mail handler is supposed to perform. Table 13.2 shows the mail handling functions of Messenger.

You have seen how most of these functions are implemented in the character-based mailers. Doing all this in Netscape is a breeze, requiring only simple mouse clicks. In fact, you'll find Messenger effortlessly doing things that aren't possible at all in `elm` and `pine`.

You can create folders for different subjects under `Local Mail` (*File> New Folder*). The windowing drag-and-drop features have been well implemented. To move a message to a folder, simply drag the message header to the folder with your left mouse button.

In the Header Pane, you can sort messages, in both ascending and descending sequence on any header field—by subject, sender and date. If you want messages sorted by date, just click once on the *Date* title. Click it again, and the sort order is reversed.

When a group of messages is exchanged in response to one another, a message **thread** is said to be formed. Messenger supports such threads as can be seen by the hierarchical structure of the messages in the header pane. To view threads, click on the icon on the left of the *Sender* title; a second click reverses the order.

Tip

There are several ways of doing the same thing in Messenger. You can use the Menu Bar, the Navigation Toolbar, or you may right-click in the context area. When in doubt, just right-click to bring up a context-sensitive menu.

TABLE 13.2   *Mail Handling Functions of Netscape Messenger*

Icon or Label	Function
Get Msg	Retrieve messages from the mail server
New Msg	Compose a mail message
Reply	Reply to sender of message
Reply All	Reply to sender and other recipients
Forward	Forward a received message to one or more people
File	Save a message in a folder like `Sent`, `Inbox`, `Unsent` etc.
Next	View next *unread* message in current folder
Print	Print message on printer
Delete	Delete current message and move it to the `Trash` folder (unless used on the `Trash` folder itself)

13.7.3 Composing and Receiving Messages

To compose a message, use *New Msg* to open a composition window (Fig. 13.10). You can pick up the address from an address book (*Address* from the Toolbar) or enter just as much to enable Messenger to complete it for you. This is a superb completion feature which should enthuse **emacs** users. You can check the spelling or send a file as an attachment with the message.

The *Bcc:* (Blind carbon copy) feature allows you to mark a copy of your message to yourself without the recipients knowing about it. A message can also be addressed to a *newsgroup (14.4)*. Messenger lets you generate the *Reply-To:* and *Followup-To:* headers, something which you couldn't do in the other mailers.

You can send (*Send*) a message immediately or defer it (*File>Send Later*). Sent and unsent messages are stored in separate folders. You can compose a group of messages offline and later send them in a bunch (*File>Send Unsent Messages*).

To receive a message, click on *Get Msg* (Fig. 13.9). If you have opted for saving your password, then you'll be prompted for the password only the first time. All messages end up in the Inbox folder. You can then reply to or forward a message by clicking on the respective icon in the Toolbar.

13.7.4 The Address Book and Mailing List

The address book (*Communicator>Address Book*) is well implemented in Messenger (Fig. 13.11). Like in the Header Pane, you can click on any title to have the contents sorted by that title. Addresses can be sorted by name, nickname or by email address—either ascending or descending.

FIGURE 13.10 *Netscape Messenger: The Composition Window*

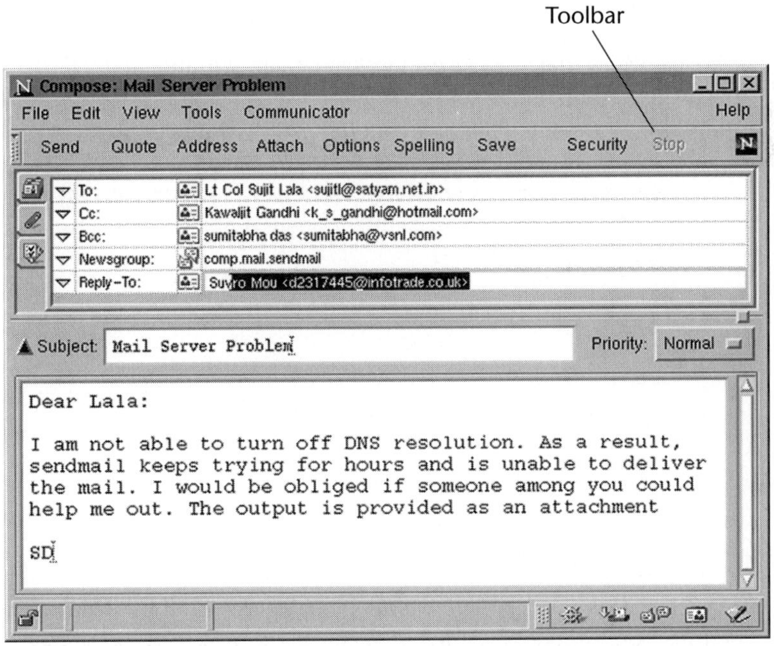

FIGURE 13.11   *Netscape Messenger: The Address Book*

If you are looking for someone, enter only a few characters that will make the address unique. Here, we entered only a p to locate an entry. Messenger highlights that entry, and even lets you initiate a mail communication from here. Just click on *New Msg*, and you'll see the composition window popping up.

When you make an entry in the address book, make sure you include the first and last names as well. Many people leave them out and simply enter the email address. Contrary to popular belief, these names also feature in the message header. The first and last names help in identifying the actual recipient when a single email account is shared by many.

The nickname lets you adopt short names which you can enter in the *To:* or *Cc:*, and have the system automatically expand it. Let's say you have an entry in the address book filled up this way:

```
First Name: christopher
Last Name: jenkins
Nickname: kris
Email Address: momsgrace@elnet-31.com
```

This is how the *To:* line will finally look like when you enter the string kris in its window:

```
christopher jenkins <momsgrace@elnet-31.com>
```

This is the form of an email address as specified by RFC 822. You need not always fill up the address book manually. Whenever you receive a message, you can send the sender's (and all recipients') address directly to the address book by right-clicking on the message and using *Send to Address Book*.

Tip

When you have a number of entries in your address book, you should save them in a text file (*File>Export*). You can carry this file with you wherever you go and import this list on another machine (*File>Import*).

Extending the idea of the address book is the **mailing list**. This list acts as an alias for multiple email accounts. A message addressed to this list name automatically reaches all its members. The list is invoked by clicking on *New List* in the address book. Give the list a name (say, friends) or a nickname, and then drag the entries from the address book to the mailing list window. Your mailing list is created.

When you address a message to the list name or the nickname, Messenger performs the expansion automatically. Even though Netscape calls this a *mailing list*, it's really an *alias*, and we must be able to distinguish between a true mailing list *(14.3)*, a centralized facility that reflects mail automatically, and a mere alias.

13.7.5 Filtering Out Spam

As you become an active email user, you'll find a lot of junk mail (**spam**) in your mailbox. Presumably, you divulged your address at every Web site when asked for it or subscribed to a number of mailing lists. You can set up a filtering mechanism in Messenger which searches for a string and then acts on the message in the way you specify.

The search may be conducted in the sender's email address, message body, *Subject:* line, or even in the *Cc:* line. You can delete those messages, move them to other folders or mark them as read. There can be a vast number of selection criteria and a great deal of action you can specify to control spam.

Messenger handles spam rather well. Choose *Edit>Message Filters*, and you'll see a window with the names of the existing filters (in case there are some). We'll create a new one with *New* (Fig. 13.12) which searches the subject or the body for the word Netphonic. We'll move this message to the Trash folder. The available search criteria are quite adequate for most tasks, and you can specify up to five of them to narrow your search. Don't forget to put a tick mark on the third column of the filter list to activate the filter (in case it's not there).

13.7.6 Mailing Attachments

The SMTP protocol handles only 7-bit text files where each line is restricted to 1000 characters. So mail messages and attachments have traditionally been restricted to text; binary files couldn't be included. This situation has changed today. Messenger handles both text and binary attachments rather well—an area where **elm** and **pine** do have certain deficiencies.

pine and **elm** can also view text attachments, but Messenger views them **inline** (along with the main message). Messenger also goes one step further and displays inline graphics that are in GIF and JPEG format. These two formats are standards on the Web, and every browser can also display them without seeking help. **pine** would need to call up an external program to view a picture.

FIGURE 13.12   *Netscape Messenger: Creating a Message Filter*

To send a file as an attachment, select *Attach* from the composition window. Choose the file and click on *Open*. (Perhaps this should have been called *Attach*.) When the message is sent, it goes as a **multipart** message—a single message containing the main message and the attachment as multiple parts. The "Going Further" section of this chapter takes up some important aspects of the specification that determines the structure of this message.

When you download this mail at the receiving end, you'll see an icon near the headers. If it's an attachment that Messenger can handle, the contents of the file are shown just below the main mail message with a line separator in between. Note that even though the attachment was sent as a separate file, it actually goes as a *single* message containing both the message text and the contents of the attached file. This attached file may be a picture, an audio or a video file.

If Messenger can't view an attachment on its own, it will call up a **helper application**. This is simply an external application having no relationship with Messenger—or for that matter, any mailer. You can also invoke this application independently from the shell prompt. The technique of identifying and calling up a helper application is explained in Section 13.9 in the "Going Further" section.

13.8   vacation: **Going on Leave**

You may need to let other people know that you are going on a long vacation so that mail doesn't pile up in your mailbox. The Berkeley **vacation** command uses the mail forwarding facility of the .forward file. The command is used only when the recipient is away on vacation (or for some other purpose).

The SVR4 **vacation** command uses a totally different syntax from the Berkeley version and has now fallen out of favor. Solaris and Linux use the BSD version which is invoked without arguments:

```
vacation
```

This brings up an editor containing the following message or one similar:

```
Subject: away from my mail
I will not be reading my mail for a while. Your
mail regarding "$SUBJECT" will be
read when I return.
```

You can edit this message, but it's not necessary to add the *From:* and *To:* lines since these are generated by **vacation** automatically. When you quit the editor, the four lines are saved in a file $HOME/.vacation.msg. **vacation** also puts this entry in the .forward file:

```
\sumit, "|/usr/bin/vacation sumit"
```

This is a different format we are using with .forward. Messages addressed to sumit are forwarded to the **vacation** program which then issues the message stored in .vacation.msg to all senders. However, all incoming messages will be saved; \sumit here indicates that one copy of the message is saved in /var/mail/sumit.

When you have both .vacation.msg and .forward in place, you'll just have to execute **vacation** with the -I option. To turn off **vacation**, remove the .forward file or rename it.

On Solaris systems, **vacation** creates two additional files—.vacation.pag and .vacation.dir. These files contain the list of senders who sent messages when **vacation** was enabled. **vacation -I** clears these files.

➤   *GOING FURTHER*

13.9   **MIME: Handling Binary Files**

What happens if the mail reading application can't handle a particular file? And how does the SMTP protocol handle multimedia attachments when it can't use the eighth character of the ASCII code? Today, there's a separate protocol that handles these attachments—**Multipurpose Internet Mail Extensions** (MIME), which is now the de facto standard on the Internet.

MIME extends the definition of mail to include binary files and multiple data formats in a *single* message. While the earlier protocol, RFC 822, was concerned with message headers, MIME is concerned with the format of the *content*. It imposes no restriction on line length. (RFC 822 restricted it to 1000 characters.) MIME encodes a message before sending, and sends with this data sufficient information on how to handle it.

The data is subsequently decoded at the other side by a MIME-compliant mail reader. If the user agents on both sides understand MIME, then MIME messages can be easily exchanged between them. The mail reading program at the receiving end may have a capability of displaying it, or it may refer it to a helper application (an external program) which can do that job on its behalf.

13.9.1 Two Important MIME Headers

When you send an attachment, the multipart message shows distinct divisions. The first part shows two headers followed by the message text. The second part (representing here an attached JPEG file—an image) has its own set of headers too. This is followed by the encoded data. A section of a mail message containing an attachment is shown in Fig. 13.13.

There are two MIME fields here which are generally found in every mail message— *Content-Type:* and *Content-Transfer-Encoding:*. Note that they are both different for the different parts.

FIGURE 13.13   *A Mail Message Containing an Attachment in MIME Format*

```
This is a multi-part message in MIME format.
--------------4369A7A6B4A758020BD17F87
Content-Type: text/plain; charset=us-ascii
Content-Transfer-Encoding: 7bit


Here you can see the picture of marc andreesen. Did you know that he
designed the browser at Illinois University for $6.85 an hour?
--------------4369A7A6B4A758020BD17F87
Content-Type: image/jpeg;
name="andreesen.jpg"
Content-Transfer-Encoding: base64
Content-Disposition: inline;
filename="andreesen.jpg"


/9j/4AAQSkZJRgABAgEASABIAAD/7RfQUGhvdG9zaG9wIDMuMAA4QklNBAQAAAAAwOcAgAA
AgACHAJ4AkBNYXJjJjIEFuZHJlZXNlbjbiwgTmVOc2NhcGGUgQ29tbXVuaWNhdGlvbnMgY28tZm91
bmRlciBhbmQgc2VuW9yIHZpY2UgcHJlc2lkZW5OIG9mIHR1Y2hub2xvvZ3ksIHBhdXN1cyBk
dCBicm93c2VyLCBhbm5vdW5jZWQgYSBtYWpvciBleHBhbnNpb24gb2YgaXRzIGxpbmUgb2Yg
     .... base64-encoded data ....
```

The **Content-Type** header defines the type of data found in the message body of the respective part. This type comprises two parts—a main type and a subtype. The main type can be `text`, `image`, `audio` and `video`. It is followed by a / and then a subtype. `plain` is a subtype of `text`. One type generally has multiple subtypes. For instance, the image type can have `jpeg` as its subtype (as here) or `gif`. Video data could be represented by `video/mpeg` while `audio/aiff` is used for audio files.

MIME also specifies the **Content-Transfer-Encoding**—another header that defines the encoding techniques used for the data. There are three well-known techniques that are used universally. `7bit` and `quoted-printable` are used for ASCII data, while `base64` is recommended for images, audio and video. `base64` encodes three octets of data as four six-bit characters. This consequently increases the file size by 33 percent. The content of the second part of the message shows you what `base64` does to the data containing Andreesen's image.

What does all this mean for us? Messenger views JPEG binary files inline—no helper application is needed. But the user agents **pine** and **elm**—even though MIME-compliant—can't view these files without assistance. This assistance is partly provided by a multimedia mail handler called **metamail**. This program reads the file `/etc/mailcap` to determine the helper application that has to be used to handle a particular Content-Type.

pine has **metamail** support built-in. But it does read `/etc/mailcap`. The relevant line that determines which application to call up for handling data having `image/jpeg` as the Content-Type looks like this on one system:

```
image/jpeg; xv %s;  test=test -n "$DISPLAY"
```

This means that **pine** will use the **xv** image program to view this Content-Type. `%s` acts as a placeholder for the filename. When you are viewing the message, you have to press **v** once to see the part list as shown in Fig. 13.14.

Move the highlight to select the image part, and press *[Enter]* or **v** again. This launches the **xv** helper application—an external program that displays the picture file `andreesen.jpg` in a separate window (not inline). But **pine** first has to decode the content using the same technology that was used in encoding it (`base64`). (Note that for seeing the image, you must use **pine** from an **xterm** window under X.)

Netscape has MIME built-in; it also has its own set of MIME files in the `$HOME/.netscape` directory. MIME plays an important part in the Web also, and this is taken up in the next chapter.

FIGURE 13.14 *The Attachment Index Displayed by* **pine**

```
    PINE 4.10   ATTACHMENT INDEX      Folder: INBOX  Message 67 of 68


     1     1 lines   Text/PLAIN
     2    17 KB      Image/JPEG
```

SUMMARY

Email is a cheap, informal and fast method of off-line communication. An email address may consist of only the username if the user is on the same host or may have the form *username@hostname* or *username@domainname*. The latter is followed on the Internet.

Incoming mail is appended to a text file (the *mailbox*) named after the user-id in /var/mail (SVR4) or /var/spool/mail (Linux). The earliest mail handling program is **mail**, but **elm** and **pine** are more powerful and user-friendly. Viewed mail is often stored in $HOME/mbox, but **elm** and **pine** also use separate folders in $HOME/Mail.

You can reply to mail, forward, delete or save a mail message with simple keystrokes. You can search for a pattern, and also take suitable action on junk mail (*spam*). Using **pine**, you can also defer dispatch of mail, maintain an address book and spellcheck your messages. **pine** can be configured to automatically execute a series of keystrokes on startup.

elm can be configured by editing the file $HOME/.elm/elmrc. **pine** uses $HOME/.pinerc.

You can redirect your mail by placing the desired email address in $HOME/.forward. You can ensure that every message is accompanied by your personal details by placing them in the .signature file, which all mailers use by default.

Mail is transported using the *Simple Mail Transfer Protocol* (SMTP). SMTP hands over the message to the delivery agent. Mail is fetched from a remote site with the *Post Office Protocol* (POP)—often using a dialup line.

Netscape Messenger uses its own SMTP and POP client features to send mail and fetch it from a POP server. Mail messages can be sorted in any sequence or moved to any folder by using the mouse. Messenger can group messages that emanate from another as a *thread*. It can view GIF and JPEG graphics *inline* (along with the message).

The **vacation** command sends a predetermined message to everyone who sends a message to a user on vacation. It is invoked from a user's .forward file.

GOING FURTHER

Internet mail uses *Multipurpose Internet Mail Extensions* (MIME) to enable transmission of multimedia attachments. It uses the *Content-Type* header to determine the *helper application* needed to handle the content. The *Content-Transfer-Encoding* defines the encoding techniques used. base64 is the encoding technique used for images, audio and video files.

SELF-TEST

13.1   What are *folders* as the term is used in email?
13.2   If you find a message in $HOME/mbox what does that indicate?
13.3   From where is all mail picked up by the mail readers?
13.4   What is the difference between invoking **mail** with a username and without it?

13.5 Using **mail**, send the **ps** output showing all system processes to user charlie.

13.6 Where is **elm**'s configuration file stored?

13.7 How do you send an attachment with **pine**?

13.8 Why are **elm** and **pine** so useful on the Internet?

13.9 How do you turn off the **vacation** feature?

13.10 Whom does the Mail Transport Agent (MTA) hand over mail to?

13.11 How do you invoke Netscape to bring up Messenger only?

EXERCISES

13.1 How do mailers like **elm** and **pine** know the location of your mailbox?

13.2 If a mail message addressed to user john shows *bill johnston <john@planets.com>* in the *To:* line, will the message reach john?

13.3 If you send copies of a message to a hundred people on the same host, which is different from yours, where are the copies made?

13.4 How in **elm** do you delete all messages in your mailbox containing the string prize in the header?

13.5 If a mailer can't understand the format of a message, what should it ideally do?

13.6 How can you use **elm** to read those messages that were sent out with Netscape?

13.7 If you want to use the **vi** editor for composing a message in **elm**, what setting will you make?

13.8 How do you simply check with **elm** whether you have any mail?

13.9 Name three features of **pine** not available in **elm**.

13.10 How will you call up **pine** so that it first shows the address book and not the main menu?

13.11 If you want to ensure that your address and phone number accompany every message you send, what would you do?

13.12 You sent a mail to your account in a remote host, and it didn't reach you. Instead, it ended up in another host where you also have an account. What could be the reason?

13.13 How is SMTP different from POP3?

13.14 How long should a message take to reach its destination under normal circumstances and why?

13.15 Which are the two protocols used for downloading mail from a remote host connected by a dialup line?

13.16 What is a *thread* when applied to the context of email and newsgroups?

13.17 You want to send a copy of a message to someone else without the other recipients knowing about it. How can you do that?

13.18 What is a *mailing list* as the term is used in email?

13.19 When you send one picture file and one audio file as attachments to your message, how do they leave your machine?

13.20 Which two files does **vacation** modify on invocation?

13.21 What is a *helper application*? What is its role in handling mail?

GOING FURTHER

13.22 What is the protocol used in mailing multimedia attachments? Why is a separate protocol required at all?

13.23 Why does MIME send the Content-Type of the data to the other end?

13.24 What technique is used for encoding binary files, and what is its effect on the file size?

13.25 While trying to view a GIF attachment with **pine**, you got this message:

```
Don't know how to display Application/OCTET-STREAM attachments. Try Save.
```

What is **pine** trying to say, and what should you do?

13.26 Which file does a mailer look up to determine the helper application needed to view a file that it can't handle?

KEY TERMS

address book *(13.4.4)*

Content-Transfer-Encoding *(13.9.1)*

Content-Type header *(13.9.1)*

helper application *(13.7.6)*

inline graphic or text *(13.7.6)*

Internet Message Access Protocol (IMAP) *(13.6)*

mail delivery agent (MDA) *(13.6)*

mail transport agent (MTA) *(13.6)*

mail user agent (MUA) *(13.6)*

mailbox *(13.1)*

mailing list *(13.7.4)*

message thread *(13.7.2)*

multipart message *(13.7.6)*

Multipurpose Internet Mail Extensions (MIME) *(13.9)*

Post Office Protocol (POP) *(13.6)*

Simple Mail Transfer Protocol (SMTP) *(13.6)*

spam *(13.3.3 and 13.7.5)*

## CHAPTER 14

The Internet

The Internet is the unintended outcome of research by ARPA (Advanced Research Projects Agency) of the United States Defense Department to develop a reliable computer-based communications system. The Net is a collection of TCP/IP networks, and is often referred to as the "network of networks." It is also the biggest client-server experiment in computer history that embodies open architecture networking using TCP/IP's packet-switching technology.

One of the main reasons for UNIX's rise to fame was the predominant role it played over a period of 20 years to evolve a communications technology that helped bring the Internet to the world. UNIX was adopted as the platform of choice for the development of the TCP/IP tools and services that are used on the Net. Today, most Internet servers offer these services on UNIX and Linux machines. UNIX is the language of the Internet.

Some of the TCP/IP applications used on the Net have already been discussed in Chapter 11. In this chapter, we take on the late entrants to the Internet, including the World Wide Web. We'll consider a mix of character-based and graphic tools, but we'll use Netscape exclusively for handling the Web.

Objectives

- Learn the naming and organization of the Internet domains. *(14.1)*
- Discover how to use a mailing list. *(14.3)*
- Understand how *Network News* works and how newsgroups are organized. *(14.4)*
- Use **tin** and Netscape Messenger to handle newsgroups. *(14.5 and 14.6)*
- Conduct an online *Internet Relay Chat* with multiple people using the **irc** command. *(14.7)*
- Learn how the *World Wide Web* links documents across machines. *(14.8)*
- Analyze the different components of the Netscape Navigator browser. *(14.9)*
- Discover how the Web works using the *Hypertext Transfer Protocol* (HTTP). *(14.10)*
- Understand how the Web uses the *Hypertext Markup Language* (HTML) to hold text and graphics together. *(14.11)*
- Save Web pages and their associated graphics. *(14.12)*
- Enhance browser performance. *(14.13)*

➤ *G O I N G   F U R T H E R*
  • Learn how MIME technology is used on the Web. *(14.15)*

Tip

A detailed history of the Internet authored by its architects can be found at the Web site of the Internet Society, *http://www.isoc.org/internet/history/brief.html.* There are also other interesting documents in the `history` directory.

14.1 The Internet Top-Level Domains

The Internet doesn't use single-word hostnames like the ones used in a TCP/IP network. Hosts belong to domains, and these domains and sub-domains constitute the backbone of the Internet. The Net originally had eight top-level (more proposed now) three-character domains—mostly represented by U.S. organizations. Every country today has a single domain at this level (Table 14.1). The top-level domains are organized like an inverted tree (Fig. 14.1), with each domain having its own sub-domains.

The three-character domains are called **generic** or **organizational domains**. MIT belongs to the *edu* domain, Sun Microsystems to the *com* domain, and InterNIC to *net*. The Internet originated in the United States, so it's natural that most U.S. organizations find their place in these generic domains. However, apart from *mil* and *arpa*, the other generic domains are not reserved for U.S. organizations—contrary to what many people believe. Many non-U.S. organizations also belong to these domains.

Every country, including the United States, is represented by a two-character domain name. Apart from Great Britain (which uses *uk* instead of *gb*), all names are drawn from the ISO-3166 specification. Germany has *de*, France has *fr*, India has *in* and Japan has *jp*. These country domains have the same hierarchical status as the generic domains.

Sub-domain naming conventions vary across countries. Some countries organize them by geography, some by function, using a similar structure as the generic domains. You can see *co* and *com* domains under the top-level domains of many countries (like *mirc.co.uk*, *sun.com.sg*). The *us* domain uses geography as basis for its 50 sub-domains— one for each state.

T A B L E 14.1   *The Internet Top-Level Domains*

Domain Name	Represents
int	International organizations
edu	Educational institutions
gov	U.S. government organizations
mil	U.S. military organizations
org	Nonprofit organizations
com	Commercial organizations
net	Networking organizations
arpa	Domain for Reverse Resolution
uk, ch, us, de, etc.	United Kingdom, Switzerland, USA, Germany, etc.

FIGURE **14.1** *The Internet Domain Tree*

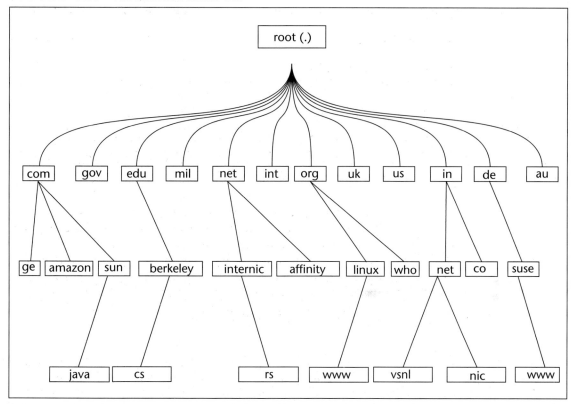

Typically, a company gets one domain name and uses sub-domains for its branches or divisions. For instance, the second-level domain *binghamton* was allotted by Inter-NIC, an organization that was once solely responsible for registering domain names. They ensure that *binghamton* is unique within *edu*, and won't be allotted to anyone else in the future. The authority to create sub-domains under *binghamton* now rests with the local authorities. The administration of the sub-domain also gets delegated accordingly.

14.2 The Services on the Internet

Internet services have evolved with time. Some were developed by Bolt, Beranek and Newman (BBN) under the auspices of DARPA before being later incorporated into BSD UNIX. Other applications followed suit, but some were to drop out to make way for the Web. Today, these are the applications used on the Net:

- Electronic mail—By far the most widely used application for personal communication.
- Telnet—For logging on to a remote machine and treating that machine as a local one.
- FTP—For transferring files between two machines.
- Mailing Lists—For mailing messages automatically to a group of persons.

- Newsgroups—Let users post and share information on topics of interest.
- Internet Relay Chat (IRC)—Enables an on-line chat session similar to **talk**.
- The World Wide Web—A vast storehouse of linked documents and images where one document can be accessed from within another.

Email and the specifications for **ftp** and **telnet** were in place by 1972—just a year before Thompson and Ritchie presented their first paper on UNIX. We have already discussed these features in previous chapters because they also are useful in standalone networks. Newsgroups, IRC and the Web are late entrants into the Internet arena. Table 14.2 shows the Internet services used today along with the clients needed to access them. It does not include the tools **archie** and **gopher**, which have faded into oblivion.

As you might expect, all these applications originally used character-based tools, with each tool having its own set of internal commands. These tools generally provide more functionality, but the graphic software that emerged later is much easier to use. In this chapter, we'll consider some of these tools, but also discuss Netscape Communicator—the most widely used graphic Internet tool on UNIX systems.

14.3 Mailing Lists

Mail aliases help in sending a message to several people. Modifications caused by additions and dropouts have to be maintained at every place the alias is used. A **mailing list**, on the other hand, is centralized, and messages are sent out automatically. There are over 100,000 such lists on the Internet covering practically every subject that can interest a human being.

TABLE 14.2   *The Internet Applications*

Application/Protocol	Character-Based Client	GUI Client
File Transfer Protocol (FTP)	**ftp** command	(i) *ftp://* URL prefix in Netscape Navigator (ii) **xftp**
Telnet protocol	**telnet** command	*telnet://* URL prefix in Netscape Navigator
Email (SMTP)	**mail**, **pine** and **elm** commands	(i) Netscape Messenger (ii) *mailto:* URL prefix for sending messages in Netscape Navigator
Mailing lists	Any email client	Any email client
Newsgroups (NNTP)	**tin** and **trn** commands	(i) Netscape Messenger (ii) *news:* URL prefix for subscribing to a newsgroup in Netscape Navigator
Internet Relay Chat (IRC)	**irc** command	**xirc**
World Wide Web (HTTP)	**lynx** command	Netscape Navigator (**netscape** command)

You **subscribe** to a mailing list (no payment involved) on a topic that interests you. Any query sent by a member of the list (including you) reaches all list members, and your mailbox piles up with messages regularly. If you feel you've had too much, you can **unsubscribe** (take yourself off) to the list. A list can be **moderated** (managed by a human being) or automated (handled by a program).

14.3.1 Subscribing and Unsubscribing

When viewing the man pages of a once-popular text browser named **lynx**, the author encountered these three paragraphs which can be considered reasonably representative of the mailing list mechanism:

```
If you wish to contribute to the further development of Lynx, subscribe to our m
ailing list. Send email to <majordomo@sig.net> with "subscribe lynx-dev" as the
only line in the body of your message.

Send bug reports, comments, suggestions to <lynx-dev@sig.net> after subscribing.

Unsubscribe by sending email to <majordomo@sig.net> with "unsubscribe lynx-dev"
as the only line in the body of your message. Do not send the unsubscribe messag
e to the lynx-dev list, itself.
```

Observe from the above that every mailing list has a name related to the topic it discusses. Here, *lynx-dev* is a list that discusses the Lynx software—the text browser that helped launch the World Wide Web revolution. It is handled by a program named **majordomo**. Before you can send queries to the list, you should first subscribe to the list by addressing this simple message to *majordomo@sig.net*—the **administrative address** of the list:

```
subscribe lynx-dev                                    To be sent to administrator
```

Leave the *Subject:* line blank; most mailing list programs don't care what you put there. The **majordomo** program (written in **perl**) interprets every line of message you put in the body as a *command* to be executed. It adds your email address to the list and automatically sends out a confirmatory message. You are now subscribed to the list.

As a subscriber, you can send your queries, but they have to be addressed, this time, not to the administrative address, but to the **list address**. This address is *lynx-dev@sig.net*—named after the name of the list. The list server makes multiple copies of your message and sends them out to list members. The server simply acts as a reflector of these messages.

You need to address the administrator once again to take yourself off the list, this time by sending this message:

```
unsubscribe lynx-dev                                    Again to administrator
```

Note

You use the list address to send your messages concerning the subject, and the administrative address for subscribing or unsubscribing to the list. The list address generally features the topic in the user component of the email address (here, *lynx-dev*).

Tip

Many of your queries are already answered in some newsgroup or another, so it's better to check the relevant FAQ *(14.4.2)* before you decide to fire your missive.

14.3.2   Listserv Programs

The three most popular mailing list programs in use today are **listserv**, **listproc** and **majordomo**. The **listserv** program is the earliest, and the reason why all these programs are known generically as **listserv programs**. Each program carries out both administrative as well as mail reflecting tasks.

Listserv programs support a number of internal commands (shown subsequently in parentheses); **subscribe** and **unsubscribe** are just two of them. The commands these server programs use are often identical, but sometimes have distinct differences. For instance, **unsubscribe** is used only by **listproc** and **majordomo**; **listserv** uses **signoff** instead.

If you are new to mailing lists and have the address of a server program like *listserv@lists.colorado.edu*, then you should send a message to this address containing these two lines:

```
help                                              For a list of commands this server recognizes
lists                                                      All lists hosted by the server
```

When you place these two commands in your message, you'll receive by email two files—containing all instructions accepted by the server and the lists available. You can also seek more information about a specific list (**info** *listname*).

Tip

Two Web sites can help you locate a list. The first is *http://www.liszt.com*, which contains details of over 90,000 mailing lists, newsgroups and IRC chat directories. The other site is *http://paml.net*. Both sites provide search windows to track down a list easily. Mailing list information is also archived at the anonymous ftp site *ftp://rtfm.mit.edu/pub/usenet/ news.answers/mail/mailing-lists*.

14.4   Newsgroups

Since before the Internet, UNIX users have participated in a discussion forum known as **USENET** (Users' Network). It's a collection of discussion groups (or **newsgroups**) where users pose problems on any topic. Someone somewhere usually cares to provide a suitable reply. USENET initially worked on a now-obsolete protocol named UUCP, but has since migrated to TCP/IP. There are over 100,000 newsgroups on the Internet with no central authority whatsoever.

The term *USENET* is often used to refer to newsgroups, but it would probably be more accurate to use the term **Network News** or simply **news**. (The UNIX **news** command is obsolete.) Network News uses the **Network News Transfer Protocol** (NNTP) at port 119.

News is maintained in a number of news servers by ISPs. Every news server gets **newsfeeds** from other news servers on the Internet at regular intervals by virtue of agreements which the administrators of these servers conclude among themselves. Because of the increasing volume of traffic that news encounters and the amount of disk space required, your ISP or the network administrator at your campus will not host all newsgroups. If your server doesn't host a particular newsgroup, you can contact another server.

Before you can use Network News, you must have a **newsreader** client on your machine. This is a program that fetches news from a news server and displays headers or contents. UNIX systems have a number of character-based news reading tools—**nn**, **trn** and **tin**. They have their own advantages and drawbacks, but **tin** is the easiest to use. We'll look at **tin** and Netscape Messenger, our mail handler that also serves as a useful GUI news client.

To receive news, you have to **subscribe** to one or more newsgroups (news is free). This means that you have to tell your newsreader (not the server) the names of the newsgroups you would like to see on a regular basis. Unlike in email, news is fetched in two stages:

- First, the article headers are downloaded so you may look at them and then decide whether you would like to see their contents.
- A second fetch operation downloads the articles (the contents).

The articles are stored in separate files so they don't get mixed up with normal email messages. The newsreader keeps track of all subscribed newsgroups and article headers that have been downloaded. Because of the sheer volume of data generated by network news, the news server has to **retire** (throw out) old articles to make place for new ones. It's quite possible that when you attempt to fetch the contents of a message, you'll find that it's no longer there.

You can participate in a newsgroup by **posting** (sending) an article or a message. In response, someone will post an article of her own. When a series of postings emanate from one posting, a particular message constitutes a **thread**. You can view messages as threads or in chronological order. If you have used Netscape Messenger for handling mail, then you have already done this.

However, if you download news from your ISP's server over a dialup line using NNTP, then you must be very selective about the groups you would like to subscribe to. There are simply too many groups and too many messages. Downloading the list of newsgroups itself takes considerable time. **tin** works best with a local server, but Netscape is good enough for both.

Note

In a large organization, it's common to find news hosted on the server in which you have an account. This server has to download the articles from an ISP's server every day through a high-speed line. Since news resides on your local machine, it's relatively easy and fast to view it.

14.4.1 Newsgroup Naming Conventions

Like domain names, newsgroups are organized with dot-delimited names—but in a reversed hierarchical manner. A typical newsgroup where you may pose all the problems you encounter in **perl** takes this form:

comp.lang.perl

The name on the left of the dot represents a higher level than the one on the right. *comp* is the main group (computers), and *lang* (languages) is a sub-group under it. There are several newsgroups with the prefix *comp.lang* and even more under *comp*.

Most newsgroups you see on the Net, especially the serious ones, can be traced back to USENET. These are the major ones that you'll see everywhere:

- *biz*—Business activities. Advertising permitted.
- *comp*—Computers. There are two major subgroups—*comp.lang* (for languages) and *comp.os* (for operating systems).
- *news*—All about USENET.
- *rec*—Recreation.
- *sci*—Group for the sciences, both hard and soft (like psychology and economics).
- *soc*—Social and cultural issues.
- *misc*—Miscellaneous group. Deals with matters not found anywhere else.
- *talk*—A free discussion on many contemporary topics.

There have been in recent years several additions outside USENET. Moreover, there's often a great deal of overlap in the subjects addressed by these groups. Thus it's not uncommon for a message to be posted to multiple newsgroups.

14.4.2   Newsgroup Conventions

The immense popularity of newsgroups can be partly attributed to the **FAQ** (**Frequently Asked Questions**), a compilation carried out from USENET postings by certain volunteers. A broad range of topics each have their own FAQs. For routine queries, you should look up the relevant FAQ before posting an article to a newsgroup. The FAQ is periodically posted, generally at the beginning of the month, in the relevant newsgroup itself and in *news.answers*. FAQs are archived permanently at the anonymous ftp site *rtfm.mit.edu*.

Flames (tempers) are widespread on newsgroups, and smileys have their origin in USENET. These are ASCII characters which convey certain feelings, and when used judiciously can be remarkably effective. You most likely have seen the expression :-) in email and news messages.

USENET is also responsible for the birth of the terms *foo*, *bar* and *foobar*. You'll often find these words used as generic file and directory names. It's now customary to say, To create a directory, use the command `mkdir foo`. Or, Copy a file with `cp foo bar`. This book also uses these generic names.

Tip

You can access most of the newsgroups on the Web itself. The site of choice is Deja News (*http://www.dejanews.com*), a vast resource handling over 30,000 newsgroups—both inside and outside USENET. In fact, if you don't find a newsgroup on your campus's or ISP's news server, chances are that you'll find it here.

14.4.3   The `.newsrc` File

Whether news is read from the local server or from the Net using NNTP, a character-based newsreader like **tin** works by first looking up the file $HOME/`.newsrc`. Each line in this file contains the name of a newsgroup, followed by a `:` or a `!`, and optionally followed by a set of numbers. A look at a few lines of this file reveals some interesting details:

```
alt.animal.dolphins!                                            Unsubscribed
alt.rec.movies: 1-561                                   Articles 1 to 561 are read
comp.os.linux.networking: 1-721
comp.mail.sendmail: 1-250, 255-270, 275
rec.humor! 1-352                                          Was subscribed once
```

Each line in this file specifies a newsgroup, optionally followed by one or more numbers. They are delimited either by a **:** or a **!**. When the name of a newsgroup is followed by a **:**, it means the user is subscribed to that group and has read the articles whose numbers are shown alongside. Numbers are delimited by commas, and ranges are allowed.

Some entries show a **!** in place of the **:**. A **!** in that position means the user is unsubscribed. The final entry shows a mix of both. *rec.humor* was subscribed once, and the first 352 articles were read at that time.

Since this is a text file, you can edit it with an editor. You can subscribe to a newsgroup by inserting an entry in this file. You can unsubscribe to a group by deleting its line altogether. Articles can also be marked as read by manipulating the numbers. Note that the modifications you carry out will apply to all character-based newsreaders (like **tin**, **trn**, **nn** etc.); it's only Netscape that doesn't read this file.

14.5 Using `tin` to Read Newsgroups

We'll now consider the most popular and versatile character-based network news-reader—**tin**. When **tin** is invoked without arguments, it fetches news from the local news server. It then compares the user's list as noted in `.newsrc` with the active list of newsgroups maintained by the server. If there are any new newsgroups, **tin** shows you the list, and you then have the option to subscribe.

The list can be very large, often exceeding several thousand groups. If news is fetched for the first time, this process can take a long time before the list shows up on your display. You can use *[PageUp]* and *[PageDown]*, or the **k** and **j** commands (in **vi**-fashion) to navigate the list. If there's a newsgroup that you'd like to subscribe to, simply press **s**. To unsubscribe, use **u**. The list of subscribed groups is then stored in `.newsrc`.

After you have chosen a group, press *[Enter]* to see the article threads (the message headers really). **tin** consolidates a group of related articles as a single thread and displays a list of these threads. This is shown in Fig. 14.2 for the *comp.os.sendmail* newsgroup.

Each thread in the list is shown with a serial number at left and the name of its originator at right. All threads here show a **+**, implying that there are unread articles in the thread. The tenth thread has 11 followup articles, while the one numbered 12 has none. The description is usually truncated, but can be expanded by pressing **d**, in which case the author's name vanishes from sight. (Press it again to restore normalcy.)

Tip

Every beginner should subscribe to *news.announce.newusers*. It contains a lot of information regarding the functioning of USENET, the code of conduct that one ought to follow and discussions on some of the other groups under the *news* newsgroup itself. It's also a good idea to subscribe to the groups containing the word "answers."

FIGURE 14.2 *Viewing News Thread Lists with* **tin**

```
            comp.mail.sendmail (114T(B) 157A OK OH R )           h=help

10   +  11  25 how to delete spam from mailq?          jose
11   +   2  46 pop accounts                            G. Roderick Singleto
12   +      53 Sendmail warning about "World Writable   G. Roderick Singleto
13   +   2  27 8.10.0.Beta6 SMTP Authentication         Claus Assmann
14   +      89 Secondary mail                           Rob McMillin
15   +      69 HELP!  sendmail 8.9.3 on RH-6.1 thinks   Fisch
16   +   2  34 mailertable:how to send mail to relati   jlshan@wiscom.com.cn
17   +       6 forwarding e-mail                        amahcush@wt.net


<n>=set current to n, TAB=next unread, /=search pattern, ^K)ill/select,
a)uthor search, c)atchup, j=line down, k=line up, K=mark read, l)ist thread,
|=pipe, m)ail, o=print, q)uit, r=toggle all/unread, s)ave, t)ag, w=post
```

14.5.1 Handling a News Article

As noted before, news headers are downloaded first. Even if you have not seen any articles yet, there are a number of things you can do with a thread. Here are some of **tin**'s commands which you might like to use:

o — Print the thread.
s — Save it to a file.
w — Post a new message not connected to the current thread.
m — Mail the thread to a friend.
K — Mark thread as read.

Marking a thread as read allows you to use *[Tab]* to view unread threads only. Read articles are noted in .newsrc so they are not displayed by **tin** the next time you fetch articles of this newsgroup.

When you make a posting, make sure the header of your article contains sufficient material to attract the attention of the audience. Most people decide to download the message content by seeing the header, and if your message has a drab and routine header like pppd problem, most people will ignore the message completely. Instead, something like pppd hangs in kernel 2.2 won't be ignored easily.

tin operates at a number of levels—group level, thread level and article level. The display shown in Fig. 14.2 was obtained at the thread level. From any level, you can use **q** to return to the previous level. When you do that at the group level, you quit **tin**. You can also unconditionally quit **tin** with **Q**.

To enter the article level, select any thread from the list and press *[Enter]*. Doing so on thread number 10 displays the articles, and one of them is shown in Fig. 14.3. Here, you see someone answering a query posed by one Roger Marquis concerning the disposal of junk mail. Similar options are also displayed at this level, but these two are additional:

FIGURE 14.3   *An Article Viewed with* **tin**

```
Sun, 24 Oct 1999 20:41:25      comp.mail.sendmail      Thread   10 of  114
Lines 25            Re: how to delete spam from mailq?   10 Responses
jose <jose@biocserver.cwru.edu> at Case Western Reserve University, Cleveland O


Newsgroups: alt.spam,comp.os.linux.misc,comp.mail.sendmail,comp.security.unix


Roger Marquis wrote:


> Don't delete all your mail, just the spam.  The best way to do that
> is to find a unique character string used by the spam source, say
> the original IP address, then delete all messages containing that
> string.

then why not just set up a sendmail.cf config to do this? block relaying,
accepting mail from known spammers (not relays but spammers), all of this
can be done very VERY easily in a sendmail.cf file. a simple m4 config
   .........


    <n>=set current to n, TAB=next unread, /=search pattern, ^K)ill/select,
     a)uthor search, B)ody search, c)atchup, f)ollowup, K=mark read,
     |=pipe, m)ail, o=print, q)uit, r)eply mail, s)ave, t)ag, w=post
```

     r — Reply to the author of the article (an email message).
     f — Follow up (as a newsgroup message).

14.5.2   **tin** Options

tin can also be used with one or more newsgroup names as arguments:

```
tin comp.os.linux.networking
```

This retrieves the articles of a single newsgroup and is comparatively faster in operation. You can also bypass the complete loading of newsgroups in these ways:

`tin -q`	*Doesn't check for new newsgroups*
`tin -z`	*Only if there are new articles*
`tin -z  rec.animals.wildlife`	*Same, but only if there are new articles in this newsgroup*

Finally, you can also use **tin** to read news from an Internet news server—for instance, the one maintained by your ISP. For this, simply set the variable NNTPSERVER to the FQDN of the news server, export the variable (with the **export** command) and then start **tin** with the -r option:

```
NNTPSERVER=news.vsnl.net.in                              See Sec. 8.11 for C shell assignment
export NNTPSERVER
tin -r                                                                       Reads news remotely
```

Everything works mostly like before, except that when you use an ordinary dialup line to connect to a news server, things work much slower. However, Netscape Messenger is adept at these tasks as it stores the article headers permanently in the disk. The news handling features of Netscape are taken up in the next section.

Tip

Post your first message (like This is a test) to *misc.test* to make sure you can send and receive messages. You can then see how long it takes the message to reach the main host and then return to your news server.

14.6   Using Netscape Messenger for Net News

Henceforth, we will mostly be using Netscape Communicator for handling news and browsing the Web. This workhorse software suite consists mainly of three components:

- Messenger—Handles all email and newsgroups. This component has been used in Chapter 13 for email. From version 4.5, Netscape has integrated the news function (once in Collabra) into Messenger.
- Navigator—Browses the World Wide Web and additionally provides **ftp** and **telnet** services.
- Composer—Offers an editing facility to create Web pages. In this chapter, we'll be using it only for downloading complete Web pages.

The Communicator suite has grown in size and complexity in a very short time and now runs as a fat X Window client. The executable is over 12 MB in size. Unless you are running it on state-of-the-art hardware, its startup time can be frustratingly long.

Invoke Communicator with the **netscape &** command from an **xterm** window. As mentioned before *(13.7)*, this could show you either Navigator or Messenger. In either case, the frontal view (Fig. 14.4) presents six or seven menu items in the Menu Bar at the top (including *Help*). Apart from the usual *File*, *Edit*, and *View* options, observe that there is also a *Communicator* menu. You can select any Communicator component from this menu:

- *Navigator*—the browser.
- *Messenger*—handles all your mail.
- *Newsgroups*—lets you read and compose network news.
- *Address Book*—stores email addresses.
- *Composer*—the Web page editor that lets you create Web pages.

At the bottom right is the Component Bar containing a set of five icons. All the five Communicator functions are replicated here. It's easier to invoke the components from here rather than from the menu.

There's a great deal of overlap between email and newsgroup functions. Netscape uses the same user interface for both, so make sure you know how to use Messenger for handling mail *(13.7)* as we are going to use it to fetch news from a remote news server. Configuration requires just one simple setting. Start with *Edit>Preferences*, select *Newsgroup Servers* and add the FQDN of your news server. Make sure the port number is set to 119.

FIGURE 14.4 *Netscape Messenger: Frontal View of Newsgroups*

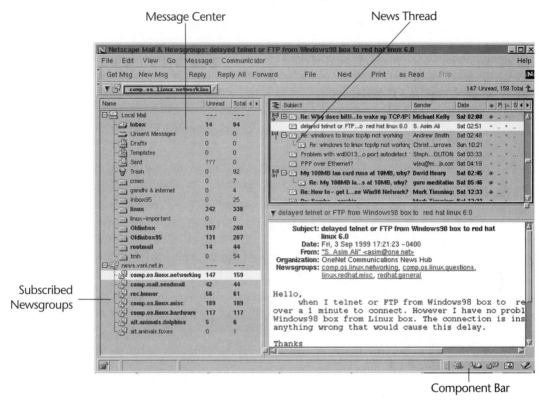

14.6.1   **Subscribing**

To subscribe to newsgroups, choose *File>Subscribe* and Messenger instantly contacts the news server and starts downloading the list. If you are downloading these groups from your ISP's server over a dialup line, the whole process could take up to half an hour (or more). The newsgroup hierarchy finally appears in the window (Fig. 14.5) showing the number of messages available on the server for each newsgroup.

Select a group and then click on *Subscribe*—or alternatively, double-click on it. To locate a group in a huge list, use the search facility to enter the group name. You'll need this facility if you are not sure of the complete name of the newsgroup.

When you subscribe to a newsgroup, a folder is created for it in the Message Center labeled with your server's name (here, `news.vsnl.net.in`) (Fig. 14.4). Subscribed newsgroups now feature as sub-folders in this folder. You can now select each newsgroup with your mouse, and post or receive messages.

Tip

If you have the name of a newsgroup ready, your Web browser offers a better way of subscribing to it. For this, you have to use the *news* protocol prefix in the URL string, say, *news:alt.animals.dolphins*. No // are used here unlike in *http://*. After pressing *[Enter]*, you'll see a folder named `alt.animals.dolphins` created in the Message Center window. You are now ready to retrieve messages for this group.

FIGURE 14.5   *Newsgroup Subscribing in Netscape Messenger*

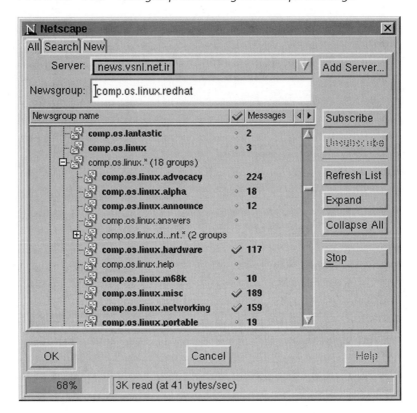

14.6.2   Fetching Messages

The technique of fetching messages is the same as in email, but you have to select the newsgroup first. Select the group from the Message Center, and then use *Get Msg*. The headers (threads) are downloaded and appear in the right upper pane. Note that you have not downloaded the articles yet.

When you select a header with the mouse, its content is *temporarily* downloaded (the second fetch) and appears on the lower pane. As in **tin**, you can save a message in a file or mark it as read. Messenger also lets you move a message to a folder by dragging the header with your mouse.

What about retrieving the contents of a group of headers? Downloading the contents permanently is a tricky operation, and it's here that **tin** and the Windows version of Netscape score over UNIX Netscape. However, a workaround makes things a lot easier if you follow these steps:

- First, create a folder for the newsgroup under the Local Mail folder (*File>New Folder*). The Local Mail folder should be clicked with your mouse before you do this.

- Select the messages in the header pane with the mouse. If you are selecting a contiguous group of headers, click on the first header, and then, keeping the *[Shift]* key pressed, click on the last header. The entire group then gets highlighted. For noncontiguous selections, use the *[Ctrl]* key instead when selecting individual headers.
- While you are connected, drag the selected messages from the header pane to the folder just created, or use the *File* icon to save them to this folder.

This time the contents are downloaded permanently. You can now go offline and view the messages.

Tip

When you have clicked on the header and seen its contents appear in the lower pane, you can also save the article using the conventional route—*File>Save As>File*. Each message then gets saved in a separate file.

14.7   irc: **Internet Relay Chat**

Today, we have graduated from the essentially offline methods of email and newsgroups to a truly online service—the **Internet Relay Chat** (IRC). It bears resemblance to the UNIX **talk** command, but with IRC you can have a chat session (written text, not voice) in real-time with several users. IRC normally uses port number 6667, but some servers use 6666.

A group of IRC servers are connected to form an IRC network, and when you connect to any of these servers, you have instant access to all *channels* currently hosted by all servers in that network. *For two users to converse with IRC, they need to be on the same network and need not be on the same server.* There are several such networks on the Internet—like EFnet (Eris Free Net), Undernet and Dalnet.

In IRC, all discussions are organized in **channels**. To join, you'll need to use a unique *nickname* in the network. After you join a channel, anything you type (unless it is an IRC command) is displayed on the terminals of all users of that channel. You can switch channels and send files too.

The most important IRC client for UNIX systems is the character-based **irc** command. It is heavily command-based (Table 14.3), characterized by the absence of man and info documentation. It, however, offers an extensive help facility.

14.7.1   Connecting and Listing Channels

To connect to an IRC network, you'll have to provide a **nickname** by which you'll be known to your friends for the session. This name must be unique in the particular network. The **irc** command requires both the nickname and the server name to connect:

```
$ irc wolfgang irc.cs.cmu.edu                          Nickname is wolfgang
     ......
There are 5186 users and 44782 invisible on 42 servers
*** There are 170 operators online
*** 20683 channels have been formed
*** This server has 2990 clients and 1 servers connected
*** Current local  users:  2990  Max: 4678
```

TABLE 14.3   *Commands Used by* **irc**

Command	Function
/list	Lists channels
/list -min 5 -max 10	Lists channels with minimum 5 and maximum 10 users
/list *98	Lists channels matching wild card
/server *sname*	Connects to server having FQDN *sname*
/join *#ch*	Joins channel *#ch*
/part *#ch*	Leaves channel *#ch* (the current channel if *#ch* is not specified)
/msg *usname mesg*	Sends personal message *mesg* to *usname*
/query *usname mesg*	Sends personal message *mesg* to *usname* (No need to use /query again)
/notify *usname*	To be notified if *usname* connects to the network
/whois *usname*	Lists details of *usname* like idle time
/away	Leaves temporarily without leaving channel
/invite *usname #ch*	Invites *usname* to channel *#ch* (the current channel if *#ch* is not specified)
/dcc chat *usname*	Starts direct client connection with *usname*
/dcc send *usname flname*	Sends file *flname* to *usname* through DCC
/dcc get *flname*	Receives file *flname* sent with /dcc send
/quit	Quits **irc**

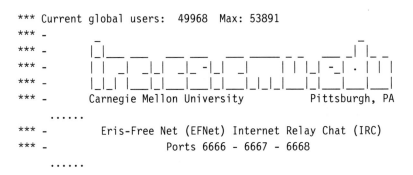

```
*** Current global users:  49968  Max: 53891
*** _      _                                              _
*** _     |_|___  __  ___  __  ____  __ __   __  _| |__ _
*** _     | |  _| _|_| _|_ -|_|  _|  | | |_| -_| . | | |
*** _     |_|_| |__|_|__|__|_|__|_|_|_|_|_|__|_|__|__|__|
*** _     Carnegie Mellon University          Pittsburgh, PA
   ......
*** _           Eris-Free Net (EFNet) Internet Relay Chat (IRC)
*** _                    Ports 6666 - 6667 - 6668
   ......
```

This vastly trimmed output shows you connected to a server of the EFnet network, which hosts over 20,000 channels at a time. Some of these channels are always alive with contributors dropping in and out, while others last only for a limited time. The cursor will now settle in the last line of the screen. From here, you'll enter all IRC commands—in this case, the internal commands of **irc**.

To distinguish between text messages and **irc** commands, **irc** requires all its commands to be preceded with a /. For instance, to list all channels currently available in the entire network (and not merely on this server), you need to use **/list**:

```
/list
*** #utah        5       Nothing but good people in here.
*** #beatles     2       damn the man, save the Empire!
*** #polska      1
*** #linux       2       Support A Channel NOT Run By The Frankie BOT!!
*** #gemini      2       Let Kids Berkeley Kids...They Grow Up Too Fast!! :o/
*** #macintosh 3       PowerBook G3's Delayed, Fair-Poor Reviews Of Windoze 98,
*** #giggles     4       Have a Wonderfull Day!!! :)
        .....
```

Most of the channels show a # beside them; they are public channels. The second column shows the number of users of the channel, and the third displays some text—often quite bizarre and obscure. You might feel lost in a channel having too many users, so you could choose to impose some selection criteria—using wild cards, if necessary:

`/list -min 5`	*Minimum 5 users*
`/list -min 10 -max 15`	*Between 10 and 15 users*
`/list #Win98`	*Single-line output—doesn't list* `#win98`
`/list *98`	*All channels containing* 98

Connections often get disrupted in IRC, and if that happens you don't need to quit **irc**. Just use the **/server** command to reconnect.

Tip

If **irc** doesn't connect to a server, try a different port number with the -p option. To use the DALnet server in Hollywood, you can also use **irc –p 6662 wolfgang sodre.dal.net**.

14.7.2 Joining, Inviting and Leaving Channels

You can join a channel with the **/join** command. Most channels are public channels, so don't forget to use the prefix # before the channel name:

`/join #Win98`   *A public channel*

If the channel doesn't exist, it's created by your joining instruction. You then become the **operator** of the channel and acquire some special rights. If the channel exists, your nickname is announced instantly to all users of the channel:

```
*** wolfgang (henry@203.197.102.56) has joined channel #Win98
```

Anything you enter now through your keyboard gets relayed in real-time to all users. Every message is preceded by the nickname. Here's a sample session:

```
<wolfgang> Does Windows 98 accept encrypted passwords?
<DeNIaL> Sure it does
<wolfgang> That's why it doesn't connect to my Samba server
<DeNIaL> You have to make one important change
<DeNIaL> in the Windows registry.
<wolfgang> What's that?
```

Make sure that lines are not too long, and press *[Enter]* as soon as you have entered about five or six words. A line is only transmitted when *[Enter]* is pressed, so you might want to let the other side see text in rapid succession rather than see it all together.

You can also invite a user (say julie) to your current channel or any other:

```
/invite julie                                          Invites julie to current channel
/invite julie #y2k_help                               Invites julie to channel #y2k_help
```

julie will then see the following message on her screen:

```
*** wolfgang invites you to join #y2k_help
```

If interested, she can then join that channel with the **/join** command.

You can quit **irc** itself with **/quit** or **/bye**, but you should first formally take leave from the channel. The **/part** command, when used by itself, leaves the current channel, but you can also leave a specific channel:

```
/part                                              Leaves IRC—can also use /leave
/part #Win98                                           Leaves the channel only
```

Tip

You can use the **/msg** *nickname message* command to converse with someone personally without quitting a channel and joining a new one. Your message will then be displayed only on the intended recipient's computer and not on others'. To avoid using **/msg** every time, you can also use the **/query** command. Once it is used, all successive messages will be seen only on the individual's screen.

14.7.3   DCC: Direct Connections and Exchanging Files

On a congested network, and especially on an active IRC server, response often suffers. **irc**'s **Direct Client Connection** (DCC) facility permits you to directly communicate with another person in private. You don't need to join any channels or have the IRC server in between. The feature is useful for exchanging files as well.

DCC is invoked with the **/dcc** command. The command has a few reserved arguments. To start a DCC chat with monty, you have to use the chat argument:

```
/dcc chat monty                                        chat is a /dcc argument
```

You can use DCC to send both text and binary files. Sending files is a two-step process using two **/dcc** arguments—send and get. The sender initiates the transfer:

```
/dcc send monty penguin.gif
```

The news is conveyed to monty, who in turn has to invoke **/dcc get** to start the transfer (unless the auto-get file option is used):

```
/dcc get penguin.gif                              Can drop filename if it's the only file
```

The transfer is direct, uses fewer overheads compared to email attachments, and, more importantly, is instantaneous. The above DCC session is closed with **/dcc close chat monty**.

The DCC facility is IRC's strongest feature. It's the most convenient way of sending a file to someone without either machine needing to have a permanent IP address. It's also the best way to conduct closed-door discussions. It avoids the hassles of anonymous ftp and the obvious limitations of email attachments. It's quite easy to send a 5-MB file through IRC. If you tried to do that with email, your ISP may not provide you with a mailbox that large.

14.8 The World Wide Web

As the content on the Internet increased (and grew more disorganized), users found they had to work harder than ever to retrieve information on a topic; they had to try a host of telnet and ftp sites, mailing lists and newsgroups. What was needed was an organization of information that made retrieval faster. People also needed a single tool—a "one-stop shop"—from where they could navigate to the right places with simple keystrokes.

The next-generation tools Archie and Gopher did make a serious attempt in that direction—and achieved a moderate amount of success. But it wasn't until 1991 that Tim Berners-Lee at CERN, Switzerland devised a means of interconnecting documents. In this system, a document contains sufficient information to direct the reader not only to another remote machine, but also to the right document there. He called this interlinked network of documents a *web* where people could "wander and roam" without knowing where they were. A document viewer (*browser*) followed suit, and the web soon changed to the **World Wide Web**.

Like the Internet, the Web also works on the client-server model. The Web's access (client) tool is called the **browser**. A Web browser fetches a document and pictures (the *resources*) residing in Web servers and formats it using the formatting instructions provided in the document itself. It also displays pictures if they are in GIF and JPEG formats. If there's a format it can't understand, it will call up a helper application—an external program that can do the job.

A resource is described by a **Uniform Resource Locator** (URL)—a form of addressing that combines the FQDN of the site and the pathname of the file. We access a Web site through its URL, which in its most common form looks like this:

http://www.who.org   *World Health Organization*

The basic resource unit on the Web is a **Web page**, generally consisting of two or three screens of text and pictures. The common denominator in this blended mix is the **Hypertext Markup Language** (HTML)—a text-based language the documents are written in. An HTML document can be viewed by *any* browser on *any* hardware using *any* operating system; Web documents are fully portable.

Text in a document contains **hypertext links** (or **hyperlinks**) to other Web pages. Activating a link can take you to another place in the same document, another document in the same server, or any page anywhere on the Internet. Text can also link to pictures, and what's more, even pictures themselves can contain links to other pictures. A connection can be initiated with a simple keystroke or a mouse click.

The Web uses the **Hypertext Transfer Protocol** (HTTP) at port number 80 for fetching all linked resources. Because of this, Web servers are also known as HTTP servers, and browsers are also referred to as HTTP clients.

You can see much of the old Internet with your browser because it supports most of its basic services. You must know this already; you have used both **ftp** *(11.7)* and **telnet** *(11.5)* from the browser (using *ftp://* and *telnet://* as the URL prefixes). You often don't need a separate **ftp** or **telnet** client; the browser is the true "one-stop shop" to the Internet.

We've encountered quite a bit of jargon already—URL, HTML and HTTP. We'll now be discussing these concepts in the following sections.

14.9 Using The Web Browser: Netscape Navigator

The Web **browser** is the HTTP client. It fetches a document from an HTTP server and displays it on screen. Initially, the Web had only text, so the first browsers were text browsers. **lynx** is the most well-known text browser, and document retrieval with it is probably the fastest. However, not many people use it any more because it can't handle graphics.

The next wave of browsers brought graphics to the Web, and today we have graphic browsers running under the X Window system. Netscape is the standard browser for UNIX systems. Irrespective of type, however, every browser is expected to offer these features:

- Step back and forth through documents viewed in a session.
- Save HTML files (and graphics) to the local machine.
- *Bookmark* important URLs so they can be fetched later without actually entering the URL.
- Support other application protocols like FTP and Telnet.
- Automatically invoke helper applications and special software (*plugins*) when encountering a file format it can't handle.

Make sure you have the Navigator window in front of you (Fig. 14.6). In case you see Messenger, just select *Communicator>Navigator* from the Menu Bar. Below the top menu are three toolbars of labeled icons. The Navigation Toolbar contains the following buttons:

- *Back* and *Forward* The browser remembers the sequence of the URLs visited, so these buttons are required to step back and forth through the session. This means you can redisplay all documents viewed in a single session without having to reenter the URL.
- *Reload* You need this button to fetch the latest page from the server. Many pages are dynamically created (like stock quotes and baseball scores), and you have to click on this button repeatedly to get the latest information.

The Location Toolbar contains the URL window and the *Bookmarks* icon. We'll take up bookmarks later in this chapter. We'll ignore the last toolbar (Personal Toolbar) which contains links to various resources of the Netscape site.

Tip

You can increase the content area by removing the Personal Toolbar. Select *View* from the menu bar and unselect *Personal Toolbar*. You can further increase the area by removing the graphic icons from the toolbars. Using *Edit>Preferences>Appearance*, check the last radio button which sets the toolbar as Text Only. The same area also lets you decide whether Navigator or Messenger will be launched on startup.

FIGURE 14.6 *A Web Page Viewed with Netscape Navigator*

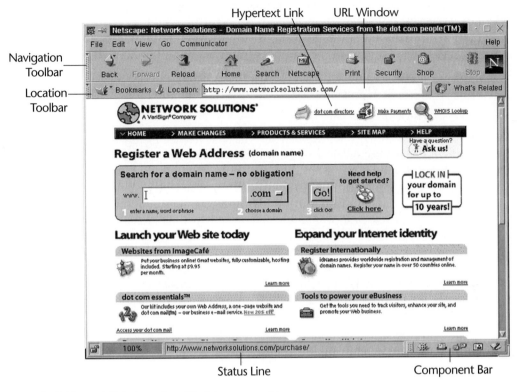

When connecting to Web sites, always keep an eye on the status line at the bottom. When you click on a hyperlink or an icon, you'll see messages on this line showing what your Web browser is doing at that instant. There are various things you may see here:

- When a site is contacted and before the Web page is fetched, the first message appears here.
- When the mouse is moved over a hyperlink, you can instantly know the URL the link is pointing to.
- You'll know the speed at which a resource is being transferred and the percentage progress of transfer.
- Sometimes, it shows you the IP address of the site.
- You'll know that a page has completed downloading when you see the message Document Done.

When Navigator is started, what you see on the browser window depends on the way it is configured. By default, it tries to connect to the **home page** of Netscape's site *home.netscape.com*. The home page is the one first presented to you when you enter the site's FQDN in the URL window—the page that introduces the organization to the viewer. You can configure Navigator to change the default to display an empty page or the last site visited (*Edit>Preferences>Navigator*).

Note

All Communicator functions can be configured from the *Edit* menu (*Edit>Preferences*). The items are neatly laid out by function, and you should have no difficulty in configuring any parameter.

14.9.1   Connecting to New Sites

To connect to a new Web site, you'll have to enter its URL in the URL window and then press the *[Enter]* key. The URL could look something like this:

http://www.nasdaq.com   *Web site of NASDAQ*

The *http://* prefix is not required but widely advertised merely to indicate that this is a Web site and should be accessed with a browser. The browser connects to the site and fetches the home page from the server. Keep an eye on the status line to see the usual connecting messages. A message like Waiting for reply confirms connectivity, so do keep a watch on the happenings in this line.

The home page will have a number of hyperlinks which you can easily identify by locating underlined text. A picture can also act as a hyperlink if the cursor changes to a hand when moving over it. As you branch out from the home page by clicking on hyperlinks, you'll find the URL window updating its contents automatically. You can copy a URL simply by highlighting it with your mouse and then pasting it elsewhere with the middle button. Just to make sure, you can also use *[Alt-c]* for copying and *[Alt-v]* for pasting.

Sometimes, the URL string will be very long—too long to show in the fixed-length box. The entire string is there alright, and to view it, you have to insert an I-beam cursor at some point in the box. Then you have to use the cursor keys to move to the right. You'll often find characters like ?, + and = in this string. Like commands, URLs also have arguments (or parameters).

If you have visited a number of Web sites by entering their URLs in the URL window, then you have automatically built up a history of URLs. This means you can trace back the path you followed, and call back all documents you have seen in that session. You have to remain connected to the Net, of course (unless the documents are fetched from the browser's cache). This is where the *Back* and *Forward* buttons come into play. Click on *Back* continuously and you'll arrive at the first document viewed in that session.

14.9.2   URL History and Bookmarks

When you've had a long session, this tracing back could be a wasteful exercise. After all, you may be looking for only one document, and there's no reason why you should sequentially step through pages you aren't really interested in seeing. There are two facilities that let you select a site from a list:

- Keep the left mouse button pressed on the *Back* (or *Forward*, if required) button and select the site from the pop-up list. This list remains in memory as long as you don't quit the browser.
- The list of visited sites is also available in the drop-down box of the URL window. There, you'll find sites of previous sessions too. This history expires in nine days, but you can set it to a convenient value (*Preferences>Navigator>History*).

There is one problem with the history feature of the URL window. What the browser shows you is the URL of the site you have *entered*, and not the URLs of those pages viewed by following links. It's here that **bookmarks** play a more meaningful role. Like its namesake, a bookmark marks a page by storing the URL of any Web page, and not just the URL you enter at the URL window.

The bookmark icon is located on the Location Toolbar. When you click on it, you see a list of bookmarked sites. Rather than show the URLs (which may not be very suggestive), the bookmark shows the title of the Web page. When you select a bookmark, you are connected to that site and resource immediately. There's no limit on the number of bookmarks you can have; you can follow 10 links from a home page, and you can bookmark all of them.

The top section of the bookmarks drop-down list lets you add, edit or file a bookmark. When you are on a page that you want bookmarked, select *Add Bookmark* from this list. The page gets bookmarked, and the bookmark is added to the list at the end.

Netscape provides extensive facilities for organizing your bookmarks. Once you have a number of them, it makes good sense to organize them into proper folders. Select *Edit Bookmark*, and you'll see a window of bookmarks organized in a hierarchical manner (Fig. 14.7). The bookmarks window also shows the time of last visit of that URL. As in Messenger, you can sort the list in any order by simply clicking on the title line. Here, we have it ordered by the date of last visit—obtained by clicking on the Last Visited title. You can right-click on any bookmark to obtain context-sensitive options.

To create a folder Books and Magazines at the level shown, use *File>New Folder* (or right-click and select *New Folder*). Enter the name Books and Magazines, and you'll see a folder created. You can now move the relevant bookmarks of these sites into this folder in two ways. One way is to simply drag each one and drop it into this new folder. Alternatively, you can select them as a group with the *[Ctrl]* key (for non-contiguous selections) or *[Shift]* (for contiguous selections), cut (*[Alt-x]*) and then paste (*[Alt-v]*) them.

FIGURE 14.7 *The Bookmarks Window*

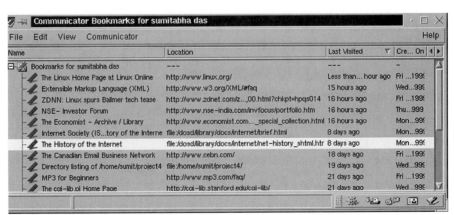

Tip

Apart from bookmarks, there's another facility available to access previously visited sites. On its own, Netscape stores the details of *all* URLs visited and retires them after nine days by default. If you have seen 10 different pages on one site, Netscape stores the URLs of all 10 of them. You can view these URLs on a separate window by using *Communicator>Tools>History*. This window shows for each URL the times of first and last visit, the expiry date and the number of times visited. You can invoke any URL from here by double-clicking an entry. This is a very useful feature, and you can even use it to locate pages whose URLs you can't remember.

14.10 Hypertext, HTTP and the URL

To understand how Web documents are organized, a simple analogy with a textbook would be appropriate. You read a book from the first page to the last in a linear fashion. But that's not always the most effective way of comprehending its contents. You might get stuck in the middle and have to refer back to something that has been defined or explained in a previous chapter—or even in a different book.

The Web is a lot like that. It uses *hypertext*: the word found in the expansion of the two keywords of the Web—HTTP and HTML—the protocol and language used in the Web, respectively. It is a system of organizing text so it can be read in a nonlinear manner. Web pages contain references to other Web pages, and such references are known as **hypertext links**—or simply **hyperlinks**. These links are embedded in the main text of an HTML document in this way:

```
<A HREF="http://www.sonu.com/docs/email.html">The email debate</A>
```

We'll take up HTML later, but for now, note two important keywords of this language—A and HREF. When a browser encounters this line, it underlines the words The email debate and displays them in a different color. This underlined text is what is known as a *hypertext link*. A mouse click on this link fetches the document (the file email.html) from the Web server specified in the link (*www.sonu.com*) and displays it in the browser window.

The text on the right of the = shows the site's Uniform Resource Locator (URL)—a form of addressing which uniquely identifies a resource (in this case, the file email.html) on the Internet. The fetched document in turn can contain further A HREF references to other documents and pictures, leading to a vast and intricately woven web. What's more, even pictures can point to other resources. For this reason, the term *hyperlink* is increasingly used these days to refer to a link, and sensibly so.

Note

Most Web sites have the prefix *www* in their FQDNs. However, it's not mandatory for all Web sites to have this prefix. A single company may have several prefixes (or none at all) depending on the content it offers.

14.10.1 HTTP: The Protocol of the Web

The Web runs on the **Hypertext Transfer Protocol** (HTTP) on port number 80. Unlike SMTP, HTTP transports 8-bit data across the network. This means it can handle binary files without encoding the data. Because of the predominance of graphics in HTTP traffic, the protocol had to be specially designed. As in **ftp**, a connection is made in stages:

- The client contacts the server at the FQDN specified in the URL and opens a connection at port number 80.
- The client then requests the Web server for some service. This service may be to *get* some data from or *post* some data to the server. The request consists of a **request header** followed by the data sent by the client.
- The server now sends a response which consists of a **response header**, followed by the data.
- The server waits for more requests and finally closes the connection.

The above is the behavioral pattern of a Web server that runs HTTP 1.1. In HTTP 1.0, every resource is fetched from a Web server through separate connections. (Some servers allow fetching of multiple resources using a single connection.) This implies that if a Web page contains five graphic files, six connections are required to transfer them (one for the HTML document itself). HTTP 1.1 supports **persistent connections** by default, which means that a single connection can do the job. In either case, the protocol is **stateless** in that each connection is unaware of the other, even though they all took place sequentially.

The request header that a client sends to the server contains, among other things, the *method* used to send data. HTTP uses the **get** method for requesting a document from the server. When form data is sent from the browser to the server, the **post** method is often specified. The server understands from the <FORM> tag that the data following the header has to be forwarded to a **gateway program** (like **perl**) for further processing. The get and post methods are discussed in Section 20.20.3; a CGI programmer needs to know how data is formatted when it is sent using these methods.

The server's response header describes the type of data sent from the server. MIME's "Content-Type" *(13.9.1)* comes into play here. For sending an HTML document, the response header will use Content-Type: text/html as one of its header fields. However, if the server passes form-data to a gatewaying program, then the header has to be generated by the gatewaying program, and not the server. If you are going to write CGI programs in **perl**, then you must know the exact format of these header fields because you will have to generate them through your program.

14.10.2 The Anatomy of a URL

To access a Web site, you have to input the **Uniform Resource Locator** (URL) of the site in the URL window located at the top of every browser:

http://java.sun.com[Enter]   *Can enter IP address instead of FQDN*

The syntax is a bit awkward; the word http (the protocol to be used) is followed by a colon, two frontslashes and the FQDN of the Web site (*java.sun.com*). The starting point of a connection is the home page—generally, the file index.html. You can specify the default filename explicitly in the URL just to make sure:

http://java.sun.com/index.html   *index.html is the default*

The file /index.html is located at the server's root directory (different from the system's root directory). On the home page, you'll see plenty of links, and you can follow these links to other documents by clicking on them. Alternatively, you can also specify the complete path of the document to go there directly:

http://java.sun.com/docs/books/tutorial/index.html

The Web has a strong UNIX tradition, so frontslashes are the rule. You can specify a directory name too, but in that case, follow it with a /:

http://java.sun.com/docs/books/tutorial/   `tutorial` *is a directory*

The URL syntax ranges from the simple to the complex, but in general, a URL is a combination of three things:

- The protocol (here, *http://*) used in transferring the resource.
- The FQDN of the host (here, *java.sun.com*).
- The pathname of the file (here, `/docs/books/tutorial/index.html`).

There are two words of significance in the expansion of the URL acronym—*uniform* and *resource*. The data fetched from a Web server is termed a resource because it doesn't have to be a file every time. A Web server can create **dynamic HTML** content on-the-fly without actually sending a file. As for the use of the term *uniform*, because HTTP allows the use of other protocol prefixes like *ftp://* and *telnet://*, the method of addressing has been kept uniform—hence the word. In fact, the uniformity of URL schemes is evident from these examples that show the usage of different protocols supported by the browser:

- *ftp://ftp.tucows.com* When you use anonymous ftp from the browser using this URL, you'll see a directory listing of the files.
- *telnet://sasolution.com* The X Window system uses a simple **xterm** client which invokes **telnet**.
- *gopher://manuel.brad.ac.uk/11/.faq/.unix* Connects to a Gopher site.
- *mailto:thathc@netscape.com* A mouse click on this link calls up the composition window of Netscape Messenger which you can use to send email.
- *file:///home/henry/download/penguin.gif* Used to view files on the local machine. The Explorer-type interface also helps in navigation. (Note the three /s.)

Strictly speaking, every URL also features the port number in its syntax. A previous URL could also have been written as

http://java.sun.com:80/docs/books/tutorial/   *Port number shown*

We don't use port numbers in the URL string since they normally default to 80 on the Web. However, if you are setting up an internet or a special service, then you would probably want to set up separate port numbers for the various services. If you do see a port number in any URL that is not 80, then don't forget to put it there.

Do you need to type in *http://* every time? No, just the FQDN of the site will do if you want to see the home page. If you are using Netscape as your browser, then you can condense the URL string further. If the FQDN has the *www* prefix and *com* suffix, you can drop them. This means that you can enter a URL simply as `redhat` and see it expanded to *http://www.redhat.com*. Some abbreviation facility indeed!

Note

If you see a ~ in a pathname (like in ~docs/index.html), then don't forget to insert the tilde character (~) before docs. UNIX systems use the ~ to mean the home directory *(17.8.3)*, so ~docs could mean /home/docs on modern UNIX systems. If you see a tilde, the server's operating system is probably UNIX.

Caution

The URL string is not fully case-insensitive. As discussed before *(11.1.3)*, the FQDN is case-insensitive; *JAVA.SUN.COM* is the same as *java.sun.com*. But whether the pathname is case-insensitive or not depends on the operating system used by the server. Most Web servers use UNIX, and UNIX is case-sensitive. If you have seen the pathname /Docs/index.html, then enter it just that way.

14.11 HTML: The Language of the Web

Even though the HTML acronym expands to **Hypertext Markup Language**, it's not really a programming language like C or Java, which produces binary executables from text sources. You can copy the source of any HTML document on the Web to your local machine and see it there. This makes it even easier to learn the language. In addition, HTML has a number of other features that make it suitable for creating Web pages:

* It is cross-platform—It doesn't matter whether you are viewing a page on a Windows, UNIX or a Macintosh system.
* It is browser-independent—A document would look *similar* whether it's viewed by Netscape or Internet Explorer (for Windows).
* It allows easy editing—Since an HTML document is a text file, you can create and modify it with even the most rudimentary editor. Pictures and other multimedia elements are stored as separate files, and the document files merely provide links to their location.
* It uses small-sized files—An HTML document is often a fraction of the size of its word-processing counterparts like .doc (Microsoft Word), .ps (Postscript) or .wp (Corel WordPerfect). This makes it specially suitable for transmission over the Net. The Web works simply because the .html (and the .gif and .jpeg) files are quite small in size.

HTML documents use the extension .html. Most browsers are configured to also accept .htm as valid extensions. The language uses embedded commands within text. The commands themselves don't show up but control the layout and format of the contents. A document looks similar (but not identical) on two different systems. To understand why, read on.

14.11.1 Markup and Tags

HTML's origin can be traced back to the **nroff/troff** suite that was the standard typesetter of UNIX systems in the 70s and 80s. HTML uses tags for formatting text. The tags always begin with a < and end with >, and most tags have some formatting capability. For instance, <I> and its closing counterpart, </I>, serve to italicize text. If the word protocol has to be shown in italics, you need to put these two tags on its two sides—<I>protocol</I>.

Every HTML document consists of a number of these tags used to *mark* the text (hence the term **markup**). Instead of specifying an exact formatting attribute, each tag is meant to *advise* the browser as to how it should go about interpreting the text.

For example, an author marks a second-level heading with the <H2> and </H2> tags. She doesn't direct the browser to use the Arial font of size 14 in boldface. It's left to the browser to determine how the heading should be displayed. Unfortunately, all browsers don't agree on interpretation, which is why a page in Internet Explorer looks different from one rendered with Netscape.

Note

Netscape and Microsoft each have their own tags, and one browser often doesn't recognize the other's. HTML 4.0 has adopted some of these vendor-specific tags as standard, but has rejected some of the others. It remains to be seen when these nonstandard tags will be dropped from future browser releases.

14.11.2   Anatomy of an HTML Document

Armed with some basic knowledge of the capabilities of HTML, let's now see what an HTML document looks like. Every HTML document should begin with the <HTML> tag and end with a matching one (</HTML>). The document is then divided into two sections—head and body, named after their respective tags. Fig. 14.8 shows the source of the document that is displayed in Fig. 14.9.

<HEAD> contains information applicable to the document as a whole. There are a few tags that can go inside the <HEAD> tag—<TITLE> is one of them. The text that you insert between <TITLE> and </TITLE> appears in the title bar of your browser. Next comes the body, delimited by <BODY> and </BODY>, which has all the HTML content and all other tags.

The browser ignores extra spaces and blank lines and combines multiple adjacent spaces into a single space. The <IMG> tag is responsible for placing the picture of a pearl in the page. The entire text appears as a single paragraph and flows around the image, keeping a respectable distance from it (because of VSPACE and HSPACE). The

F I G U R E 14.8   *The Text of an HTML Document*

```
<HTML>
  <HEAD>
     <TITLE>
          Perl: Larry Wall's Brainchild
     </TITLE>
  </HEAD>
  <BODY>
    <H1> Perl: Larry Wall's Brainchild </H1>
     <B>perl</B> is an interpretive language and is probably the
     best     language yet          available for text manipulation.
     <IMG SRC="pearl.gif" ALIGN=LEFT VSPACE=10 HSPACE=10>
     It was created by Larry Wall, and made freely available to the world.
     <EM><STRONG> You don't have to pay for using perl</STRONG></EM>,
     It's     distributed      under the GNU General Public License,
     which means that no one can impose any restrictions on its distribution.

     You can know more about <STRONG>perl</STRONG> by visiting
     <A HREF="http://www.perl.org"> the Perl site</A>.
  </BODY>
</HTML>
```

FIGURE 14.9 *An HTML Document Viewed with Netscape*

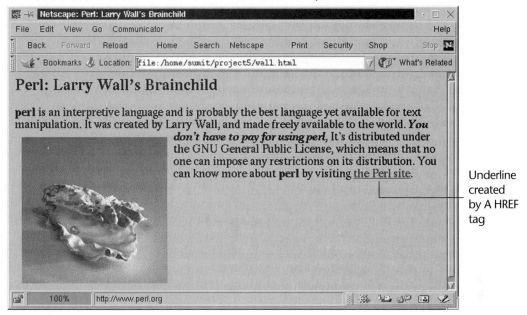

power of HTML is quite obvious here; you would have to struggle with a word processor to keep text and pictures together. And the file would have been much larger.

A portion of the text (the words `the Perl site`) appears underlined and in a different color. This is a hypertext link pointing to the URL *http://www.perl.org*. When you move the cursor over the linked text, it changes into a hand, and you see the URL appearing in the status bar at the bottom. If you click here, the home page of *www.perl.org* would replace this page.

Some tags have attributes, and most attributes take the form *attribute=value*. `SRC` and `ALIGN` are two attributes of the `<IMG>` tag, and here have the values `pearl.gif` and `LEFT`, respectively. Tags and attributes are case-insensitive; `<TITLE>`, `<Title>` and `<tiTLe>` are interpreted by the browser in identical manner. However, some attribute values are case-sensitive. Filenames are entirely dependent on the operating system used for hosting these pages. UNIX is case-sensitive and treats `pearl.gif` and `Pearl.gif` as two separate files.

14.11.3   HTML: Its Capabilities

HTML is a markup language where tags indicate the true meaning of the enclosed content rather than the way it should look to the user. HTML does have some basic word processing capabilities, however. You can break text into paragraphs, and impart to it the normal visual attributes like bold and italics. You can change font size, type, line and paragraph spacing and their indentation. You can provide headings of six different sizes.

You can also place pictures anywhere in a document provided they are in GIF or JPEG format. Both GIF and JPEG use compression technology to keep file sizes small. GIF can handle 256 colors and is suitable for line drawing, small pictures and icons using few colors. JPEG handles up to 16.7 million colors and is used for displaying landscapes. However, JPEG compression is lossy, and may cause perceptible degradation in quality. Images having other formats have to be viewed with helper applications.

At the heart of HTML is the hyperlink. Text can be marked up to point to other documents anywhere on the Web. You can link to a specific location in the same document too. Like documents, images can be loaded from anywhere on the Internet. Images can also be links: an entire image can point to another resource. In addition, images serve as good clickable image-maps where different parts of the image have different clickable properties.

Apart from the above, you can create the following with HTML:

- **Lists** You can create both ordered and unordered lists, and even nest them.
- **Tables** You can design tables with varying number of rows and columns to suit every requirement.
- **Frames** You can split your display screen into multiple frames and have each frame display a different document. You can use this feature to have a table of contents in one frame and details in another.
- **Multimedia** The browser uses freely available software which is installed in the browser to handle special file formats, or it calls up helper applications to handle them. You can also view Java applets on your Web browser.
- **Cascading stylesheets for fine-tuning your output** Font types, alignment, size and color can be set as styles that can be applied to most tags.
- **Embedded Javascript programs** You can now embed a Javascript program into an HTML document. Javascript has all the usual programming constructs, and is particularly useful in validating form data, which otherwise has to go to the server for validation.

HTML is highly extensible. The HTML 4.0 specification proposes the adoption of many more tags which are yet unimplemented. There will be many more features to come, which ultimately would lead to the replacement of the language itself by XML (Extended Markup Language).

14.11.4   Forms and the Common Gateway Interface

The <FORM> tag adds a new dimension to HTML and to the Web. Forms provide inter-activity to your documents and are the means by which electronic commerce is transacted on the Web. This tag lets you use all the usual windows input "devices" like checkboxes, radio buttons and drop-down menus. The inputs you provide are passed on to the server in the form of variables. You can ask for a document or direct the server to process some data supplied through these input devices.

By itself, a Web server has no special processing capability. If the server receives a request to process the data, then it has to rely on some *gatewaying* (external) program to do the job. This server-side program processes the form input, inserts the HTML tags and HTTP headers and sends back **dynamically created HTML** content for presentation at the client end. These programs are known as **CGI programs** (Common Gateway Interface)—named as such because of the gatewaying nature of their functions. The instruction to run a CGI program is embedded in the <FORM> tag itself:

```
<FORM METHOD="POST" ACTION="/cgi-bin/getname.pl">
```

The server here has to run the **getname.pl** script. This is a program written in **perl**—the language of choice for CGI programming. **perl** programs can easily parse form data into *name-value* pairs and store these names and values in separate variables. After processing the data, the **perl** script generates the response header and the HTML content dynamically. It finally passes this on to the server for onward transmission to the client. We'll develop some **perl** CGI scripts in Chapter 20.

14.12 Saving Web Pages and Graphics

Many Web resources can be downloaded onto your local hard disk. This includes all HTML files and both static and animated graphics, but leaves out executable content like Java applets. This is a great convenience because it lets you view your documents and the associated graphics offline, i.e., without being connected to the Internet. Netscape has a limited cache facility which stores the immediately visited sites, but you may not find a recently visited page in the cache.

To download Web pages, you first need to create a directory for storing them. When you use *File>Save As*, the current page on the browser is saved to disk. You can change the default filename as it is stored on the server if it doesn't appear to be meaningful enough.

Sometimes you need to download a graphic. The technique used here is different. Take your cursor to any point in the graphic and right-click. Select *Save Image As*, choose or change the default filename, and you have saved the graphic file. If the page contains 20 pictures, you have to move your cursor to those 20 locations, and repeat the process.

The problem with this approach is that graphics are not always easy to identify. A perfectly simple table could be a graphic while a block of text under a blue background could be plain and simple HTML. A small graphic icon can easily escape your attention. Netscape has a solution to this problem, and we'll take it up shortly.

If you see a moving graphic, it could be an animated GIF—a special GIF format that permits limited animation. It could also be a Java applet which is executed by the Java virtual machine that is installed in your browser. Animation can also be rendered with Shockwave—which can be viewed by special software (a *plugin*) that needs to be installed in your browser. You can save animated GIFs using the technique described here, but not Java applets and Shockwave files.

Tip

The best way of identifying a plain graphic is to right-click on a suspected image. If you see the option *Save Image As*, then it's a graphic but only in GIF or JPEG format. This includes animated GIF files, but obviously leaves out Java applets and Shockwave files.

14.12.1 Viewing Downloaded Files

After you have disconnected from the Net, you can view the downloaded files with *File>Open*. If it's an HTML file, you'll see the text exactly as you had seen it online. Sometimes, you want only text, in which case this method should suit you fine. If you have also downloaded an associated graphic file, whether or not you are able to see it depends on the way the <IMG> tag has been used in the document.

The above point needs some elaboration. If the <IMG> tag uses an absolute pathname like *http://www.sasol.com/pics/wall.gif* for the hypertext link, the browser will attempt to fetch the graphic from the Web even if has been downloaded onto your disk. This is generally not the practice, and more often than not, relative pathnames are used.

An <IMG> reference like IMG SRC="wall.gif" (a relative pathname) means the graphic is stored in the *same* directory and on the *same* server as the HTML page itself. The browser should then be able to display the graphic automatically after you have saved it to disk in the same directory.

Local files are viewed using the *file://* protocol prefix. With *File>Open*, you are, in fact, using this protocol. Alternatively, you can enter a URL like *file://localhost/home/henry/download/wall.html* in the URL window to show the HTML file on your browser. If the file is a GIF or JPEG image, it shows up on the browser. In fact, this is the easiest way of viewing a graphic file. You don't really need external viewing programs if you have the browser open at all times.

What happens if the last component of the URL using the *file://* prefix is a directory? You'll then see a directory listing similar to the way the *ftp://* prefix shows files in the browser window (Fig. 11.2). You have a Windows Explorer–like interface here. Click on a directory, and you see that directory's listing. Click on an HTML, JPEG or GIF file; it's displayed straightaway. The author prefers to view files this way rather than use *File>Open*.

Tip

The URL with the *file://* prefix that was just discussed uses the name *localhost* as the FQDN. This is the name you use to address your own machine *(11.1.2—Tip)*. There's a synonym, however, that you can use—the // string. The above URL thus reduces to *file:///home/henry/download/wall.html* (3 slashes). Try using one / instead of three. Does it work?

14.12.2   When Downloaded Graphics Don't Show Up

Sometimes, you may see a relative pathname in the value of the <IMG> tag—like pics/banner1.gif or ../../images/banner1.gif. If both references are found in the same document, then they exist on the same server. The first one exists in the pics directory under the directory that hosts the HTML page. The second one takes you two levels up from the document's directory and then descends one level to the images directory.

If you have downloaded both the GIF files and the associated HTML document to the *same* directory, the graphics won't show up when you view the document. To view them, you also need to maintain a similar directory structure in your local hard disk. This is often a troublesome procedure, especially when there are a lot of these directories. You'll find it easier to edit the HTML file to remove all /s and directory names from these values. You can then maintain all files in one directory. **sed** and **perl** are quite adept at these tasks, and we'll be considering one such task as an example *(15.12.2)*.

14.12.3   Saving a Web Page with All Graphics

How does one download a complete Web page with all its associated graphics in one shot? This is one of Netscape's strong features, but the job is done not by Navigator but by Netscape Composer—another component of the Communicator suite.

When you are on a graphic-rich page, invoke the Composer's editing mode *(File>Edit Page)*. You'll see a different type of window this time, and find pictures gradually appearing on this window. You don't have to wait for all of them to appear. Just call *File>Save As*; use the default HTML filename if it doesn't conflict with any existing ones in the directory you use for downloading files. You are not prompted to supply the names of the pictures at all. Composer now saves not only the HTML file but all its associated graphics too. Look at your directory to check that out for yourself.

14.13   Enhancing Browser Performance

Browsing requirements vary widely; some people don't want to view pictures, and some would rather do without Java applets. Some might be browsing in a network using a *proxy server*. In this section, we'll see how the browser can be customized to render optimum performance.

14.13.1   Disabling Pictures and Applets

Pictures and Java applets take time to load, and on a congested network, you need to disable the downloading of these media in the browser configuration. Use *Edit>Preferences >Advanced* and uncheck the first two boxes (*Automatically load images* and *Enable Java*). You can sometimes effect further time savings by disabling JavaScript.

Henceforth, your browser will show only text and leave marks on the image locations. When you need to see all images of a page, you can press the *Images* button (which appears after image loading is disabled) on the Navigation Toolbar. You can also retrieve a single image by clicking on its location where it would have normally appeared. The first click fetches the image, and a second click fetches the resource if the image points to it.

14.13.2   Using Your Machine's Cache

Every browser has a cache—both in memory and disk—to store recently visited Web resources. When you enter a URL, the browser first attempts to load it from this cache. The disk cache can be carried over to the next session, but the memory cache obviously can't. A large cache value means you can store a lot of pages, but that also means it would take some time to retrieve them. If you are using a computer with 32 MB RAM, then you shouldn't use more than 4 MB of memory cache and 20 MB of disk cache. You can tune the cache in Netscape using *Edit>Preferences>Advanced>Cache*.

Most Web pages have static content. But if you are viewing stock prices online, then you have to make sure that pages are not retrieved from the cache but from the network every time you use the *Reload* button. In that case, you need to check the radio button which lets you check the document in cache with the one in the network every time you ask for it.

Tip

You'll sometimes want your browser to fetch data from the network rather than from the proxy or Netscape's internal cache. Press *[Shift]* while clicking on the *Reload* button in case the page is still fetched from the cache.

14.13.3   Access through Proxy

If you are in a network, you may be able to access the Net only through a gateway host which has direct access to the Net. This machine will probably be running **proxy** software, and you may have to access the Net through this proxy. The proxy server gets a page from the Net on your behalf (by proxy) and maintains a large cache for this purpose. So, if someone from one machine has already requested a page once, you can retrieve it faster from the proxy cache next time. These pages reside in the cache for several days if not weeks.

Consider that the gateway machine has the IP address 192.168.0.100 and is using the Squid proxy server. You must communicate with this proxy using the port number 3128—the default port used by Squid. Move to *Edit>Preferences>Advanced> Proxies*, opt for *Manual proxy configuration* and select *View*. Enter 192.168.0.100 or the FQDN in the *HTTP Proxy:* line, and enter 3128 as the port number. You are now ready to use the proxy service.

14.14   The Bubble that Didn't Burst

Scott McNealy once said: "The network is the computer." At that time, very few people understood what he meant. A lot has happened since to foster the spirit of cooperation that has brought the world a great deal closer. This cooperation has already created a superb product that goes by the name Linux. It has also produced over a billion static Web pages. Information on every conceivable topic is being added daily. A host of high-quality freeware and shareware programs are being made available. There is so much more to come.

Christopher Anderson (of *The Economist*) observed that the Net ". . . has challenged the corporate-titan model of the information superhighway."[1] As corporations invade the Web, one wonders whether the core group of designers who worked with open standards will be able to face the onslaught of the stakeholders. If we hold our heads high, and uphold openness and nonproprietary standards, the Net could well turn out to be the bubble that didn't burst.

➤ *G O I N G   F U R T H E R*

14.15   MIME Technology on the Web

When the Web adopted graphics as constituents of Web pages, the choice was quite limited. Every browser then was expected to view GIF and JPEG files inline, i.e., without using any external programs. As expectations from the Web increased, so have the types of media. Today, we have Java, RealAudio, RealVideo and Shockwave technology, which together are responsible for the bells and whistles that we see on Web pages—animation, audio and video.

Even though the browser is progressively getting loaded with more and more features, it can't handle these files. It either has to call up a built-in *plugin* or a **helper application**. Helper applications are external applications which often have large footprints and take a long time to load. Moreover, invoking an entire application that also has editing and composing features makes no sense when all we want is to view a file (or play a sound file). The Web has the answer to this in plugin technology.

_____

1. *Anderson, Christopher.* The Economist. *July 1, 1995.*

14.15.1 Plugins

A **plugin** is a piece of software installed ("plugged") in the browser. It is normally small in size and has the minimal features required for simple viewing (or, in case of audio and video, playing). You can't invoke a plugin separately as you can call up a helper application like WordPerfect. When a file is viewed with a plugin, it appears inline with the HTML text, and not in a separate window.

To install the Shockwave plugin on a Linux machine, download the plugin software from the Web (*http://www.shockwave.com*). Use the **tar** command *(22.9)* to extract the contents, and then simply copy these two files to the directory .netscape/plugins:

```
cp ShockwaveFlash.class $HOME/.netscape/plugins
cp libflashplayer.so $HOME/.netscape/plugins
```

Plugins once installed in $HOME/.netscape/plugins are registered with Netscape. To view the ones installed, simply enter this in the URL window:

```
about:plugins[Enter]
```

Netscape also comes with the built-in Java plugin that lets you see Java applets on your browser. Apart from Java and Shockwave Flash, more plugins are increasingly being made available.

14.15.2 Helper Applications

When a browser encounters an unfamiliar data format, it first sees whether there is a plugin in its arsenal. If there is none, then depending on the way it is configured, Netscape may give you these two choices:

- Open the file after you specify the **helper application**.
- Save the file to disk so you can deal with it later.

The MIME technology that we used in email *(13.9)* also applies to multimedia files on the Web. However, these files are sent by Web servers not as multipart messages but as independent files. The server sends the Content-Type to the client before it sends the file by looking up a database that associates the Content-Type with the file's extension. The client (browser) looks up yet another database to associate this Content-Type with the right helper application. These databases are actually two simply-structured text files:

- /etc/mime.types or $HOME/.mime.types (used by Netscape).
- /etc/mailcap or $HOME/.mailcap (used by Netscape).

The first file which maps file extensions to the Content-Type is used by a Web server—and sometimes by a client as well. The mapping is shown below for RealPlayer data:

```
audio/x-pn-realaudio ra rm ram
audio/vnd.rn-realaudio ra rm ram
application/smil smi
```

GOING FURTHER

There are three possible Content-Types here, mapped to different file extensions. If the server sees an extension which is, say, `.ra`, it looks up `mime.types` and associates the sound file with the Content-Type shown in the first line above. It then sends this Content-Type header to the client before sending the file.

Note

When a browser fetches a file through **ftp** (using *ftp://*) or locally (using *file://*), there's no Content-Type explicitly preceding the file content. The browser must be able to guess the file's type by looking at the extension, for which it needs a `mime.types` at its end as well. That's why you can often click on a file icon in your browser window and view its contents when using these protocols.

At the other end, the browser looks up `audio/x-pn-realaudio` in `mailcap` to locate the helper application. The corresponding entries for RealPlayer data in `mailcap` could look like this:

```
audio/x-pn-realaudio; /usr/local/RealPlay7/realplay %u
audio/vnd.rn-realaudio; /usr/local/RealPlay7/realplay %u
application/smil; /usr/local/RealPlay7/realplay %u
```

The second field specifies **realplay** as the helper application that handles the content types. The browser now calls up this application to play the file. This executable today handles a host of multimedia data types including MP3 and Shockwave Flash files.

Netscape follows roughly the same procedure except that it uses the files `.mailcap` and `.mime.types` in the home directory. But the files are edited directly by Netscape when you configure the browser using *Edit>Preferences>Navigator>Applications*.

To install the Realplayer helper application, download the executable (currently named `rp7_redhat6.bin` for Red Hat Linux) and execute it as a root user. By default, it is installed in `/usr/local/RealPlayer7` as the executable **realplay**. It comes with a README file which contains its configuration details.

Note

The file `mime.types` contains a list of all filename extensions. `mailcap` contains the name of the helper application programs that must be used to view files having specified extensions. Both files contain the Content-Type.

SUMMARY

The Internet is a collection of networks running on TCP/IP. Apart from **ftp** and **telnet**, the Internet also offers mailing lists, newsgroups, the Internet Relay Chat and the World Wide Web as additional services.

The Internet namespace is divided into domains and sub-domains. The top-level domains include the three-character generic domain names like *com*, *net*, *edu* and *org*. All countries including the United States have two-character top-level domain names. The authority to create sub-domains is delegated to the local authorities.

A *mailing list* is handled by a program to reflect a message automatically to members of a list. The request for *subscription* and other information is addressed to the administrator, while the message itself is addressed to the list address.

Newsgroups serve news using the *Network News Transfer Protocol* (NNTP) at port 119. You have to *subscribe* to a newsgroup, which uses a hierarchical naming scheme similar to that used by domains. A *newsreader* fetches the headers first, and only the selected contents are downloaded. `tin` is a versatile character-based newsreader, but you can also use Netscape for handling news.

Internet Relay Chat (IRC) enables several users to join *channels* using unique *nicknames* to carry on an online chat session. A message sent to the channel reaches all users of that channel unless the `/msg` or `/query` commands are used. You can also bypass the server and initiate a direct connection (`/dcc`) and exchange files.

The Web uses *hypertext* to link one document with another or any *resource* anywhere in the Internet. A document can refer to pictures, and pictures can also link to other documents or pictures. A *browser* views all documents and the pictures they point to.

A document is accessed by using a *Uniform Resource Locator* (URL) which combines the FQDN of the site with a pathname. URLs may be *bookmarked* for quick access later. Netscape saves the URLs of all pages visited. URLs can also point to ftp and telnet sites.

The Web works on the *Hypertext Transfer Protocol* (HTTP) at port 80 and can transport 8-bit data. HTTP is a *stateless* protocol where separate connections fetch resources with one connection having no knowledge of the previous one. The server sends a *response header* specifying the Content-Type of the document.

A Web document is written in the *Hypertext Markup Language* (HTML). An HTML document is cross-platform and can be viewed in any environment. The language can specify the placement of text and pictures together in the same document. GIF and JPEG pictures are viewed *inline* with the browser.

HTTP behaves differently when used with forms. Form data is generally passed on to the *Common Gateway Interface* (CGI)—a separate program which processes the data, creates the HTML code and returns it to the server. `perl` is the language of choice for CGI programming.

All documents and graphics can be saved on the local machine so they can be viewed offline. A downloaded file can be viewed using a URL of type *file://*. A document's graphics will show up as well if the <IMG> tag doesn't specify relative pathnames. Using Netscape Composer, you can save a document with its associated graphics and not worry about relative pathnames.

To enhance browser performance, you may disable pictures or Java. You can tune the size of the cache or access the Web through a *proxy server.* You may need to use the *[Shift]* key with the *Reload* button to refetch a document from the network instead of the cache.

GOING FURTHER

If the browser can't handle a data format, it will either invoke a *plugin* or a *helper application*. Unlike helper applications, plugins are small pieces of software which can be invoked only from the browser. The server looks up mime.types to determine the Content-Type from the file's extension, and the browser uses mailcap to associate the Content-Type with the right helper application.

GOING FURTHER

SELF-TEST

14.1 Name three generic domains that can be used by non–U.S. organizations.

14.2 Can you send a query on a topic of your interest to this address? *listserv@lists.colorado.edu*

14.3 Why does a news message need to be retired?

14.4 To test whether you are able to send a message to a newsgroup, where should you first try sending it?

14.5 What is an *FAQ*?

14.6 Can two users connect to two different servers and still manage to communicate using IRC?

14.7 Why is the performance of **lynx** better than that of Netscape?

14.8 What is the protocol and port number used on the Web to access HTML documents?

14.9 Using Netscape Navigator, how do you *directly* go back to a previous page of the current session without going through the intermediate pages?

14.10 If you are going to visit a Web site regularly, what should you do for quick access?

14.11 Is hypertext confined to text only?

14.12 What is the default filename of the page shown by a browser when you use only the FQDN as the URL?

14.13 How do you access the home page of the Web server running on your own machine?

14.14 Why is HTTP called a *stateless* protocol?

14.15 What's the Content-Type for Web pages?

14.16 Why does an HTML document look different on different browsers?

14.17 What is a clickable image map?

14.18 How do you identify a graphic in a Web page viewed with Netscape?

EXERCISES

14.1 How do you use **telnet** to connect to the site *patvolkcal.com* from the browser?

14.2 What is a true *mailing list*? How does it differ from an *alias*?

14.3 How will you quickly check whether the news service is available on the host *news.planets.com*?

14.4 How is a newsgroup message different from an email message?

14.5 While communicating with the user anna on IRC, you want to send her a private message before inviting her to a different channel. How do you do that?

14.6 How will you send the file **wozniak.gif** directly to the user anna using IRC?

14.7 Can the Netscape browser display a picture in any format without using external help? Do the pictures appear in a separate window?

14.8 What is *hypertext*?

14.9 What is the significance of the word "uniform" in the Uniform Resource Locator (URL)?

14.10 Can you use *WWW.PLANETS.COM/CATALOG.HTML* instead of *www.planets.com/catalog.html* as the URL?

14.11 If you place a file `foo.html` in `/etc` in the host with the FQDN *www.planets.com*, can you access it as *http://www.planets.com/etc/foo.html* from the browser?

14.12 To connect to the site *http://www.ge.com*, what's the minimal string you need to enter as the URL in the Netscape browser?

14.13 To download a Web page with 10 graphics, how many connections does HTTP require?

14.14 Why is HTML specially suited for the Web?

14.15 If a browser passes data from an HTML form to the server, how does the server handle the data?

14.16 When do you need to use the *Reload* button in the browser? What do you do if it still doesn't do what it's meant to do?

14.17 How do you save a Web page with all its graphics in one shot?

14.18 You first downloaded a Web page and then all graphics separately. When you view the file offline, you find that the graphics don't appear. What could be the most likely reason?

14.19 What statement will you place in an HTML document to make the mail composition window pop up on clicking it?

GOING FURTHER

14.20 If HTTP can handle 8-bit files, why does it still need MIME?

14.21 What is a *plugin*? How does it differ from a *helper application*?

KEY TERMS

administrative address of mailing list *(14.3.1)*

article thread *(14.4)*

bookmark *(14.9.2)*

browser *(14.8 and 14.9)*

channel operator *(14.7.2)*

chat channel *(14.7)*

chat nickname *(14.7.1)*

Common Gateway Interface (CGI) *(14.11.4)*

Direct Client Connection (DCC) *(14.7.3)*

dynamic HTML *(14.10.2 and 14.11.4)*

Frequently Asked Question (FAQ) *(14.4.2)*

gateway program *(14.10.1)*

generic domain *(14.1)*

get method *(14.10.1)*

helper application *(14.15 and 14.15.2)*

home page *(14.9)*

hyperlink *(14.8 and 14.10)*

hypertext link *(14.8 and 14.10)*

HyperText Markup Language (HTML) *(14.8 and 14.11)*

HyperText Transfer Protocol (HTTP) *(14.8 and 14.10.1)*

Internet Relay Chat (IRC) *(14.7)*

list address of mailing list *(14.3.1)*

listserv program *(14.3.2)*

mailing list *(14.3)*

markup *(14.11.1)*

moderated mailing list *(14.3)*

network news *(14.4)*

Network News Transfer Protocol (NNTP) *(14.4)*

news *(14.4)*

newsfeed *(14.4)*

newsgroup *(14.4)*

newsreader *(14.4)*

organizational domain *(14.1)*

persistent connection *(14.10.1)*

plugin *(14.15.1)*

post method *(14.10.1)*

posting article *(14.4)*

proxy server *(14.13.3)*

request header *(14.10.1)*

response header *(14.10.1)*

retiring article *(14.4)*

stateless protocol *(14.10.1)*

subscribing *(14.3 and 14.4)*

Uniform Resource Locator (URL)
    (14.8 and 14.10.2)

unsubscribing *(14.3 and 14.4)*

USENET *(14.4)*

Web page *(14.8)*

World Wide Web *(14.8)*

CHAPTER 15

Filters Using Regular Expressions—grep and sed

You often need to search a file for a pattern—either to see the lines containing (or not containing) it or to have it replaced by something else. This chapter discusses two important filters that are specially suited for these tasks—**grep** and **sed**. **grep** takes care of all search requirements you may have—and does the job well. **sed** goes further and can even manipulate the individual characters in a line. In fact **sed** can do several things, some of them quite well.

This chapter also takes up *regular expressions*—one of the fascinating features of UNIX. You've already had a taste of these expressions when using the search capabilities of **vi** and **emacs**. But it's in this chapter that you'll see them in all their manifestations. The rules for framing the patterns are well defined, and in no time you'll be able to devise compact expressions that perform amazing matches. In fact, it's common to find just a single line of **grep** or **sed** code replacing several lines of C code.

The system administrator must be adept in understanding and framing regular expressions. Learning to use them along with **grep** and **sed** serves as a suitable prelude to learning **perl** which uses many of their features. These features are discussed here but assumed in the chapter on **perl**.

Objectives

- Output lines containing a simple string with **grep**. *(15.2)*
- Use **grep**'s options to display their count, line numbers and lines not containing a pattern. *(15.3)*
- Use a *regular expression* to search for multiple similar strings. *(15.4)*
- Use **egrep** and **fgrep** with multiple patterns. *(15.5)*
- Learn how **egrep** uses a special regular expression that can group and delimit multiple patterns. *(15.6)*
- Use **sed** to select and edit lines. *(15.7 to 15.10)*
- Replace one pattern with another in **sed**, using regular expressions where necessary. *(15.11)*
- Use the *interval* and *tagged* regular expressions to enhance the power of **grep** and **sed**. *(15.12)*

15.1 The Sample Database

In this chapter and the ones dealing with filters and shell programming, you'll often be referring to the file emp.1st. Sometimes, you'll also be using another file or two derived from it. It's a good idea to have a close look at the file now and understand the organization:

```
$ cat emp.1st
2233|charles harris  |g.m.     |sales     |12/12/52| 90000
9876|bill johnson    |director |production|03/12/50|130000
5678|robert dylan    |d.g.m.   |marketing |04/19/43| 85000
2365|john woodcock   |director |personnel |05/11/47|120000
5423|barry wood      |chairman |admin     |08/30/56|160000
1006|gordon lightfoot|director |sales     |09/03/38|140000
6213|michael lennon  |g.m.     |accounts  |06/05/62|105000
1265|p.j. woodhouse  |manager  |sales     |09/12/63| 90000
4290|neil o'bryan    |executive|production|09/07/50| 65000
2476|jackie wodehouse|manager  |sales     |05/01/59|110000
6521|derryk o'brien  |director |marketing |09/26/45|125000
3212|bill wilcocks   |d.g.m.   |accounts  |12/12/55| 85000
3564|ronie trueman   |executive|personnel |07/06/47| 75000
2345|james wilcox    |g.m.     |marketing |03/12/45|110000
0110|julie truman    |g.m.     |marketing |12/31/40| 95000
```

The first five lines of this file were used as the file shortlist in the section on **sort** *(9.12)*. The significance of the fields have also been explained there, but we'll recount them just the same. This is a text file containing 15 lines of a personnel database. There are six fields—empid, name, designation, department, date of birth and salary using the | as the field delimiter. This character has a special meaning to the shell, so we must remember to escape it whenever we specify the delimiter.

15.2 grep: Searching for a Pattern

UNIX has a special family of commands for handling search requirements, and the principal member of this family is the **grep** command. It scans a file for the occurrence of a pattern and, depending on the options used, displays

- Lines containing the selected pattern.
- Lines not containing the selected pattern. (-v)
- Line numbers where the pattern occurs. (-n)
- Number of lines containing the pattern. (-c)
- Filenames where the pattern occurs. (-1)

grep is exceedingly simple to use too. Its syntax treats the first argument as the pattern and the rest as filenames:

grep *options pattern filename(s)*

We'll first use simple strings as search patterns and later use regular expressions. This is how **grep** displays lines containing the pattern sales from the file emp.1st:

```
$ grep sales emp.lst
2233|charles harris  |g.m.      |sales     |12/12/52| 90000
1006|gordon lightfoot|director |sales     |09/03/38|140000
1265|p.j. woodhouse  |manager  |sales     |09/12/63| 90000
2476|jackie wodehouse|manager  |sales     |05/01/59|110000
```

We didn't quote the pattern here; quoting is essential if the search string comprises multiple words or uses any of the shell's characters like *, ? and so forth. However, quoting doesn't cause any harm either; **grep "sales" emp.lst** works in just the same way.

Because **grep** is also a filter, it can search its standard input for the pattern and store the output in a file:

```
who | grep henry > foo
```

When **grep** is used with a series of strings, it interprets the first argument as the pattern and the rest as filenames. Every line displayed is prefixed by its filename:

```
$ grep director emp1.lst emp2.lst
emp1.lst:1006|gordon lightfoot|director |sales     |09/03/38|140000
emp1.lst:6521|derryk o'brien  |director |marketing |09/26/45|125000
emp2.lst:9876|bill johnson    |director |production|03/12/50|130000
emp2.lst:2365|john woodcock   |director |personnel |05/11/47|120000
```

15.2.1 Quoting in grep

When you use multiword strings as the pattern, you must quote the pattern. If you don't, **grep** treats its first argument as the pattern and the rest as filenames. Try using **grep** with the name gordon lightfoot:

```
$ grep gordon lightfoot emp.lst
grep: lightfoot: No such file or directory
emp.lst:1006|gordon lightfoot|director |sales     |09/03/38|140000
```

grep interprets lightfoot as a filename, and obviously fails to open such a file. However, its search continues by using the next argument, i.e., emp.lst. Now, quote the pattern:

```
$ grep 'gordon lightfoot' emp.lst
1006|gordon lightfoot|director |sales     |09/03/38|140000
```

Now, let's try to locate neil o'bryan from the file:

```
$ grep 'neil o'bryan' emp.lst
>
```

What happened here? The Bourne, Korn and bash shells interpret this as an incomplete command by issuing a secondary prompt string (>). The same command run in the C shell even causes an error:

```
% grep 'neil o'bryan' emp.lst
Unmatched '.
```

The pattern itself contains a single quote. The shell looks for even numbers of these quotes to determine the boundaries of noninterference. We should have remembered that single quotes don't protect single quotes, only double quotes do:

```
$ grep "neil o'bryan" emp.lst
4290|neil o'bryan     |executive|production|09/07/50| 65000
```

Though quotes are redundant in single-word fixed strings, it's better to enforce their use. It sets up a good habit with no adverse consequences. You can then use regular expressions inside them.

Note

> You need to quote the pattern in **grep** if the pattern contains more than one word or special characters that can be interpreted otherwise by the shell. You can generally use either single or double quotes, but if you need command substitution or variable evaluation, you must use double quotes.

15.2.2 When grep Fails

grep is a representative UNIX command that silently returns the prompt when the pattern can't be located:

```
$ grep president emp.lst
$ _                                                            No president found
```

There's more to it here than meets the eye. The command **failed** because the string `president` couldn't be located. Though the feature of scanning a file for a pattern is available in both **sed** and **awk**, these commands are not considered to fail if they can't locate a pattern in their input.

Don't, however, draw the wrong conclusion from the above behavioral pattern of **grep**. The silent return of the shell prompt is no evidence of failure. In fact, the silent behavior of **cmp** denotes success. Success or failure is determined by the value of a special variable ($?) that gets set when a command has finished execution. You'll see in the chapter on shell programming *(18.5.1)* how this variable is applied in the command line of the shell's programming constructs.

15.3 grep **Options**

grep is one of the most frequently used UNIX commands. It uses a few options (Table 15.1), and is one command most of whose options you must know. Fortunately, there aren't too many of them.

Solaris maintains a POSIX-compliant version of **grep** in /usr/xpg4/bin. This version uses the -E and -F options that are also used by Linux. If you want to use this executable, then either use the absolute pathname or change the PATH setting *(17.3)*.

Counting Occurrences (-c) How many directors are there in the file? The -c (count) option counts the occurrences; the following example reveals that there are four of them:

TABLE 15.1   *Options Used by the* **grep** *Family*

Option	Significance
-c	Displays count of number of occurrences
-l	Displays list of filenames only
-n	Displays line numbers along with lines
-v	Doesn't display lines matching expression
-i	Ignores case when matching
-h	Omits filenames when handling multiple files
-w	Matches complete word (**grep** only)
-e *pat*	Also matches pattern *pat* beginning with a - (hyphen)
-e *pat*	As above, but can be used multiple times (*Linux and some UNIX versions*)
-E	Treats pattern as an **egrep** regular expression (*Linux and Solaris-xpg4*)
-F	Matches pattern in **fgrep**-style (*Linux and Solaris-xpg4*)
-*n*	Displays line and *n* lines above and below (*Linux only*)
-A *n*	Displays line and *n* lines after matching lines (*Linux only*)
-B *n*	Displays line and *n* lines before matching lines (*Linux only*)
-f *file*	Take patterns from *file*, one per line (*Linux only*)

```
$ grep -c 'director' emp.lst
4
```

This is one of the few **grep** options that doesn't display the lines at all. If you use this command with multiple files, the filename is prefixed to the line count:

```
$ grep -c director emp*.lst
emp.lst:4
emp1.lst:2
emp2.lst:2
empold.lst:4
```

Sometimes, you need to get a single count from all these files so that you can use it in script logic. You have already handled a similar situation before *(8.8.1)*, and you should be able to use **grep** in a manner that drops the filenames from the output. Try the -h option.

Displaying Line Numbers (-n)   The -n (number) option can be used to display the line numbers containing the pattern, along with the lines:

```
$ grep -n 'marketing' emp.lst
3:5678|robert dylan    |d.g.m.    |marketing |04/19/43| 85000
11:6521|derryk o'brien  |director |marketing |09/26/45|125000
14:2345|james wilcox    |g.m.      |marketing |03/12/45|110000
15:0110|julie truman    |g.m.      |marketing |12/31/40| 95000
```

The line numbers are shown at the beginning of each line, separated from the actual line by a `:`. If you use this option with multiple filenames, then you would have two additional fields—the filename and the count:

```
$ grep -n 'marketing' emp?.lst | head -2
emp1.lst:2:5678|robert dylan     |d.g.m.    |marketing |04/19/43| 85000
emp1.lst:6:6521|derryk o'brien   |director  |marketing |09/26/45|125000
```

Deleting Lines (-v)   The `-v` (inverse) option selects all but the lines containing the pattern. Thus, you can create a file `otherlist` containing all but directors:

```
$ grep -v 'director' emp.lst > otherlist
$ wc -l otherlist
     11 otherlist                              There were 4 directors initially
```

This is a useful option for "deleting" lines, but you can use it effectively only by applying redirection. Obviously, the lines haven't been deleted from the original file as such. We had to create a separate file `otherlist` containing all but the directors' lines.

Note

The `-v` option removes lines from **grep**'s output, but doesn't actually change the argument file.

Displaying Filenames (-l)   The `-l` (list) option displays only the names of files where a pattern has been found:

```
$ grep -l 'manager' *.lst
desig.lst
emp.lst
emp1.lst
empn.lst
```

So, if you have forgotten the filename where you last saw something, just use this option to find out which one has it. This is the second option that doesn't display the lines.

Ignoring Case (-i)   When you look for a name, but are not sure of the case, **grep** offers the `-i` (ignore) option. This makes the match case-insensitive:

```
$ grep -i 'WILCOX' emp.lst
2345|james wilcox     |g.m.      |marketing |03/12/45|110000
```

This locates the name `wilcox`. However, a simple string like this can't match the name `wilcocks` that also exists in the file but is spelled with minor differences. **grep** supports very sophisticated techniques of pattern matching, and this is the ideal forum for regular expressions to make their entry.

Patterns Beginning with a - (-e)   What happens when you look for a pattern that begins with a hyphen? Most systems will show you something similar to this:

```
$ grep "-mtime" /var/spool/cron/crontabs/*
grep: -mtime illegal option
grep [-E|-F] [-c|-l|-q] [-bhinsvx] [-e pattern_list] [-f pattern_file] [pattern_
list] [file...]
```

grep treats -mtime as an option of its own, and finds it "illegal." To locate such patterns, you must use the -e option:

```
$ grep —e "-mtime" /var/spool/cron/crontabs/*
romeo:55 17 * * 4 find / -name core —mtime +30 —print
```

Solaris offers this option only in its POSIX-compliant version in /usr/xpg4/bin. On some systems (especially Linux), the -e option can also be used multiple times to let you match multiple patterns.

Linux

Some More Options

Matching Multiple Patterns (-e and -f) As just mentioned, the -e option has an additional use in Linux. With this option, you can match multiple patterns using a single invocation of the command:

```
$ grep -e woodhouse -e wood -e woodcock emp.1st
2365|john woodcock   |director |personnel |05/11/47|120000
5423|barry wood      |chairman |admin     |08/30/56|160000
1265|p.j. woodhouse  |manager  |sales     |09/12/63| 90000
```

Quotes aren't really necessary for single-word arguments, so for a change we dropped them here. However, the tedium of entering such a lengthy command line is compelling enough to use regular expressions, which we'll discuss shortly.

You can put all the three patterns in a separate file, one pattern per line. GNU **grep** takes input from there with the -f option:

```
grep -f pattern.1st emp.1st
```

The -f option is also offered by **egrep** and **fgrep**, though it is used in different ways.

Printing the Neighborhood GNU **grep** has a nifty option that locates not only the matching line, but also a certain number of lines *above* and *below* it. For instance, you may want to know what went before and after the **foreach** statement that you used in a **perl** script:

```
$ grep -1 "foreach" count.pl                    One line above and below
/print ("Region List\n") ;
foreach $r_code sort (keys(%regionlist)) {
   print ("$r_code : $region{$r_code} : $regionlist{$r_code}\n") ;
```

The command locates the string foreach and displays one line on either side of it. Isn't this feature useful? Using this numeric option, you can locate a section of code by supplying a unique string that exists in the middle of the code segment.

You can be selective and prefer to display, along with the matched line, a certain number of lines either above or below. This requires the -A and -B options:

```
grep -A 5 "do loop" update.sql                  5 lines after matching lines
grep -B 3 "do loop" update.sql                  3 lines before matching lines
```

It's easier to identify the context of a matched line when the immediate neighborhood is also presented. These options are also useful when searching sorted files. The previous user-id or the next date of birth are often important things to look for.

15.4   Regular Expressions—Round One

View the file emp.lst *(15.1)* once again, and you'll find some names spelled in a similar manner—like trueman and truman, wilcocks and wilcox. You'll often want to locate both truman and trueman without using **grep** twice. The command

$ grep truman emp.lst
```
0110|julie truman     |g.m.     |marketing |12/31/40| 95000
```

doesn't help here as it lists only one line—the one exactly matching the pattern. Like the shell's wild cards *(8.2)* which match similar filenames with a single expression, **grep** also uses an expression of a different sort to match a group of similar patterns. Unlike wild cards, however, this expression is a feature of the *command* that uses it and has nothing to do with the shell. It has an elaborate metacharacter set (Table 15.2) overshadowing the shell's wild cards and can perform amazing matches. If an expression uses any of these characters, it is termed a **regular expression**.

Regular expressions take care of some common query and substitution requirements. You may want the system to present a list of similar names, so you can select exactly the one you require. Or you may want to replace multiple spaces with a single space or display lines that begin with a #. You may even be looking for a string at a specific column position in a line. All this is possible (and much more) with regular expressions as you'll discover in the three rounds of discussions that feature the subject in this chapter.

Some of the characters used by regular expressions are also meaningful to the shell—enough reason why these expressions should be quoted. We'll first start with a minimal treatment of regular expressions and then expand the coverage when we discuss **sed**.

Note

Regular expressions are interpreted by the command and not by the shell. Quoting ensures that the shell isn't able to interfere and interpret the metacharacters in its own way.

15.4.1   The Character Class

Like the shell's wild cards, a regular expression also uses a character class that encloses a group of characters within a pair of rectangular brackets [ ]. The match is then performed for a single character in the group. Thus, the expression

TABLE 15.2   *The Regular Expression Characters Used by* **grep**, **sed** *and* **perl**

Pattern	Matches
*	Zero or more occurrences of previous character
g*	Nothing or g, gg, ggg, etc.
gg*	g, gg, ggg, etc.
.	A single character
.*	Nothing or any number of characters
[*pqr*]	A single character *p*, *q* or *r*
[abc]	a, b or c
[*c1-c2*]	A single character within the ASCII range represented by *c1* and *c2*
[1-3]	A digit between 1 and 3
[^*pqr*]	A single character which is not a *p*, *q* or *r*
[^a-zA-Z]	A nonalphabetic character
^*pat*	Pattern *pat* at beginning of line
pat$	Pattern *pat* at end of line
bash$	bash at end of line
^bash$	bash as the only word in line
^$	Lines containing nothing
\{*m*\}	*m* occurrences of the previous character (no \ in **perl**) *(15.12.1)*
^.\{9\}nobody	nobody after skipping nine characters from line beginning (no \ in **perl**) *(15.12.1)*
\{*m*,\}	At least *m* occurrences of the previous character (no \ in **perl**) *(15.12.1)*
\{*m*,*n*\}	Between *m* and *n* occurrences of the previous character (no \ in **perl**) *(15.12.1)*
\(*exp*\)	Expression *exp* for later referencing with \1, \2, etc. (no \ before (and) in **perl**) *(15.12.2)*
\(BOLD\).*\1	At least two occurrences of the string BOLD in a line (no \ before (and) in **perl**) *(15.12.2)*

[od]   *Either* o *or* d

matches either an o or a d. You can also use ranges, both for alphabets and numerals. Thus, the pattern

[a-zA-Z0-9]

matches a single alphanumeric character. This property can now be used to match woodhouse and wodehouse. These two patterns differ in their third and fourth character positions—od in one and de in the other. To match these two strings, we'll have to use the model [od][de] which in fact matches all these four patterns:

od   oe   dd   de

The first and fourth are relevant to the present problem. Using the character class, the regular expression required to match woodhouse and wodehouse should be this:

wo[od][de]house

Let's use this regular expression with **grep**:

```
$ grep "wo[od][de]house" emp.lst
1265|p.j. woodhouse  |manager  |sales     |09/12/63| 90000
2476|jackie wodehouse|manager  |sales     |05/01/59|110000
```

A single pattern has located two similar strings; that's what regular expressions are all about.

When ranges are used, the character on the left side of the - must be lower (in the ASCII collating sequence) than the one on the right. The character class [X-c] is, therefore, quite legitimate, as X has a lower ASCII value than c. However, that doesn't mean you can match an alphabetic character in either case with the expression [A-z] because, between Z and a, there are a number of other nonalphabetic characters as well (the caret, for example).

Negating a Class Regular expressions use the ^ (caret) to negate the character class, while the shell uses the ! (bang). When the character class *begins* with this character, all characters other than the ones grouped in the class are matched. So a single nonalphabetic character string is represented by this expression:

[^a-zA-Z]

Note

The feature of the character class is similar to the wild cards except that negation of the class is done by a ^ (caret), while in the shell it's done by the ! (bang).

15.4.2   The *

The * (asterisk) refers to the immediately preceding character. However, its interpretation is the trickiest of the lot. Keep in mind that it bears absolutely no resemblance to the * used by wild cards or DOS. Rather, it matches *zero or more* occurrences of the *previous* character. In other words, the previous character can occur many times, or not at all. The pattern

e*

matches the single character e and any number of es. Because the previous character may not occur at all, *it also matches a null string.* Thus, apart from this null string, it also matches the following strings:

e   ee   eee   eeee   .....

Mark the words "zero or more occurrences of the previous character" that are used to describe the significance of the *. Don't make the mistake of using this expression to match a string beginning with e; use ee* instead. Recall that the * used by wild cards doesn't relate to the previous character at all.

Note

The expression e* indicates that e might not occur at all!

How do you now match `trueman` and `truman`? The first pattern contains an e, while the other pattern doesn't. This means that e may or may not occur at all in the expression, and the regular expression that signifies that is e*. This means that

```
true*man
```

matches the two patterns. Now use this expression with **grep** and you would have done the job:

```
$ grep "true*man" emp.1st
3564|ronie trueman    |executive|personnel |07/06/47| 75000
0110|julie truman     |g.m.     |marketing |12/31/40| 95000
```

A simple regular expression using the unusual significance of the * matches both names! But note that these are not the only strings it can match; the expression is general enough to include other patterns. It would have also matched `trueeman` had there been such a pattern in the file.

Using both the character class and the *, we can now match `wilcocks` and `wilcox`:

```
$ grep "wilco[cx]k*s*" emp.1st
3212|bill wilcocks    |d.g.m.   |accounts  |12/12/55| 85000
2345|james wilcox     |g.m.     |marketing |03/12/45|110000
```

The expression k*s* means that k and s may not occur at all (or as many times as possible); that's why the expression used with **grep** also matches `wilcox` which doesn't contain these two characters at its end. You can feel the power of regular expressions here—and how they easily exceed the capabilities of wild cards.

Note

The * in its special sense always refers to the character preceding it, and has significance in a regular expression only if it is preceded by a character. If it's the first character in a regular expression, then it's treated literally (i.e., matches itself).

15.4.3   The Dot

A . matches a single character. The shell uses the ? character to indicate that. The pattern

```
2...
```

matches a four-character pattern beginning with a 2. The shell's equivalent pattern is 2???.

The Regular Expression .*   The dot along with the * (.*) constitutes a very useful regular expression. It signifies any number of characters, or none. Say, for instance, you are looking for the name p. woodhouse, but are not sure whether it actually exists in the file as p.j. woodhouse. No problem, just embed the .* in the search string:

```
$ grep "p.*woodhouse" emp.1st
1265|p.j. woodhouse  |manager  |sales     |09/12/63| 90000
```

Note that if you literally look for the name p.j. woodhouse, then the expression should be p\.j\. woodhouse. The dots need to be escaped here with the \—the same character you used in the shell for despecializing the next character.

Note

What ? means to the shell, the . (dot) means to a regular expression.

15.4.4 The ^ and $: Specifying Pattern Locations

A regular expression possesses one more property in that it can match a pattern at the beginning or end of a line. These are the two characters that are used:

^ (caret) — for matching at the beginning.
$ — for matching at the end.

Anchoring a pattern in this way is often necessary when it can occur in more than one place in a line, and you are interested in its occurrence only at a particular location.

Consider a simple example. Try to extract those lines where the empid begins with a 2. What happens if you simply use

```
2...
```

as the expression? This won't do because the character 2, followed by three characters, can occur anywhere in the line. You must indicate to **grep** that the pattern occurs at the beginning of the line, and the ^ does it easily:

```
$ grep "^2" emp.1st
2233|charles harris  |g.m.     |sales     |12/12/52| 90000
2365|john woodcock    |director |personnel |05/11/47|120000
2476|jackie wodehouse|manager  |sales     |05/01/59|110000
2345|james wilcox     |g.m.     |marketing |03/12/45|110000
```

Similarly, to select those lines where the salary lies between 70,000 and 89,999 dollars, you have to use the $ (nothing to do with the currency) at the end of the pattern:

```
$ grep "[78]....$" emp.1st
5678|robert dylan     |d.g.m.   |marketing |04/19/43| 85000
3212|bill wilcocks     |d.g.m.   |accounts  |12/12/55| 85000
3564|ronie trueman     |executive|personnel |07/06/47| 75000
```

How can you reverse the search and select only those lines where the empids *don't* begin with a 2? You need the expression ^[^2], and the following command should do the job:

```
grep "^[^2]" emp.1st
```

UNIX has no command that lists only directories. However, we can use a pipeline to "grep" those lines from the listing that begin with a d:

```
ls -l | grep "^d"
```
Shows only the directories

It's indeed strange that in an operating system known for its commitment to brevity and options, you have to type such a long sequence simply to list the directories! You should convert this into an alias *(17.4)* or a shell function *(19.10)* so that it is always available for you to use.

Here's how **grep** can add power to the **ls -l** command. This pipeline locates all files which have write permission for the group:

```
$ ls -l | grep '^.....w'                          Locates w in sixth position
drwxrw-r-x   3 sumit     dialout        1024 Oct 31 15:16 text
-rwxrw----   1 henry     dialout       22954 Nov  7 08:21 wall.gif
-rw-rw-r--   1 henry     dialout         717 Oct 25 09:36 wall.html
```

This sequence matches a w at the sixth column location of the **ls -l** output—the one which indicates the presence or absence of write permission for the group.

Note

The caret has a triple role to play in regular expressions. When placed at the beginning of a character class (e.g., [^a-z]), it negates every character of the class. When placed outside it, and at the beginning of the expression (e.g., ^2...), the pattern is matched at the beginning of the line. At any other location (e.g., a^b), it matches itself literally.

15.4.5 When Metacharacters Lose Their Meaning

It's possible that some of these special characters actually exist as part of the text. If a literal match has to be made for any of them, the "magic" of the characters should be turned off. Sometimes, that is automatically done if the characters violate the regular expression rules. Like the caret, the meaning of these characters can change depending on the place they occupy in the expression.

The - loses its meaning inside the character class if it's not enclosed on either side by a suitable character, or when placed outside the class. The . and * lose their meanings when placed inside the character class. The * is also matched literally if it's the first character of the expression. For instance, when you use **grep "*"**, you are in fact looking for an asterisk.

Sometimes, you may need to escape these characters, say, when looking for a pattern g*. In that case, **grep "g*"** won't do, and you have to use the \ for escaping. Similarly, to look for a [, you should use \[, and to look for the literal pattern .*, you should use \.*.

Regular expressions are found everywhere in the UNIX system. You have already used them with **vi** and **emacs**—and now with **grep**. Apart from them, some of the most powerful UNIX commands like **egrep**, **sed**, **awk**, **perl** and **expr** also use regular expressions. You must understand them because they hold the key to the mastery of the UNIX system.

We'll introduce some more metacharacters used by regular expressions later in this chapter and when we take up **perl**. To understand some of them, you need to know the **egrep** command first.

Note

You should always keep in mind that a regular expression tries to match a string nearest to the beginning of the line. The match is also made for the longest possible string. Thus, when you use the expression 03.*05, it will match 03 and 05 as close to the left and right of the line, respectively. This point acquires significance when these expressions are used for substitution.

15.5 egrep **and** fgrep: **The Other Members**

The **egrep** and **fgrep** commands extend **grep**'s pattern-matching capabilities. They both use most of **grep**'s options, but have some special features of their own. They can search for multiple patterns and also take them from a file.

How do you now locate both woodhouse and woodcock from the file, a thing that GNU **grep** achieves by using multiple -e options? This is easily done with **egrep**. Delimit the two expressions with the | and the job is done:

```
$ egrep 'woodhouse|woodcock' emp.1st
2365|john woodcock    |director |personnel |05/11/47|120000
1265|p.j. woodhouse   |manager  |sales     |09/12/63| 90000
```

The | is a regular expression character used by **egrep**; we'll discuss the characters that are special to **egrep** in the next section. With **fgrep**, you would have to place each pattern on a separate line by itself:

```
fgrep 'woodhouse
woodcock' emp.1st
```

C shell users should escape the newline character by using a \ at the end of the first line. **fgrep** doesn't use any regular expression character—including the | used by **egrep**. If the pattern to search for is a simple string or a group of them, **fgrep** is recommended. It is arguably faster too, the reason why it's known as fast **grep**.

15.5.1 Storing Patterns in a File: (-f)

So far, you have been scanning the file for two or three patterns at the most. What do you do if there are quite a number of them? Both commands support the -f (file) option to take such patterns from the file. The patterns should be stored in exactly the same way you use them in the command line. Here's how you'll fill up a file for use by **egrep**:

```
$ cat pat.1st
admin|accounts|sales
```

And, here's how the file should look like if **fgrep** were to use it:

```
$ cat pat.1st
admin
accounts
sales
```

To look for these three patterns the **egrep** and **fgrep** commands should now be used in these ways:

```
egrep -f pat.lst emp.lst
fgrep -f pat.lst emp.lst
```

The principal disadvantage with the commands of the **grep** family is that none of them has separate facilities to identify fields, and it's not easy to search for an expression in a field. This is where **awk** and **perl** score over them.

    egrep accepts all the regular expression characters discussed previously (though not necessarily all the ones **grep** actually supports), but uses some special characters too. This calls for the second round of discussions on regular expressions.

15.6   Regular Expressions—Round Two

The regular expressions we have used so far in **grep** can also be used as patterns in **egrep** (and also in **awk**). While **grep** and **sed** use some more characters not recognized by **egrep**, **egrep**'s set includes some additional characters (Table 15.3) not used either by **grep** or **sed**.

15.6.1   The + and ?

egrep's extended set includes two special characters—+ and ?. They are often used in place of the * to restrict the matching scope. They signify the following:

+ — Matches one or more occurrences of the previous character.
? — Matches zero or one occurrence of the previous character.

Now, what all this means is that b+ matches b, bb, bbb, etc; it doesn't match nothing—unlike b*. The expression b? matches either a single instance of b or nothing. These characters restrict the scope of match as compared to the *.

    In the two *trueman*s that exist in emp.lst *(15.1)*, note that the character e either occurs once or not at all. So, e? is the expression to use here:

```
$ egrep "true?man" emp.lst
3564|ronie trueman   |executive|personnel |07/06/47| 75000
0110|julie truman    |g.m.     |marketing |12/31/40| 95000
```

TABLE 15.3   *The Extended Regular Expression Set Used by* **egrep** *and* **awk**

Expression	Matches
ch+	One or more occurrences of character *ch*
g+	At least one g
ch?	Zero or one occurrence of character *ch*
g?	Nothing or one g
exp1 | *exp2*	Expression *exp1* or *exp2*
GIF|JPEG	GIF or JPEG
(*x1*|*x2*)*x3*	Expression *x1x3* or *x2x3*
(lock|ver)wood	lockwood or verwood

The + is a pretty useful character too. When you are looking for two consecutive words but don't know how many spaces separate the two, you can follow the space with a + to represent at least one space. Thus the expression a□+b matches these patterns:

a□b   a□□b   a□□□b   a□□□□b   ......

15.6.2   The |, (and): Searching For Multiple Patterns

In the previous section, we used the | to match multiple patterns in this way:

```
egrep 'woodhouse|woodcock' emp.lst
```

The | is yet another character used by **egrep**'s regular expression set. There are more; using the parentheses, **egrep** offers an even better alternative. You can use parentheses to group patterns and the pipe to act as delimiter:

```
$ egrep 'wood(house|cock)' emp.lst
2365|john woodcock    |director |personnel |05/11/47|120000
1265|p.j. woodhouse   |manager  |sales     |09/12/63| 90000
```

You can now combine the other regular expression characters that were used in **grep** to form a rather complex sequence:

```
$ egrep 'wilco[cx]k*s*|wood(house|cock)' emp.lst
2365|john woodcock    |director |personnel |05/11/47|120000
1265|p.j. woodhouse   |manager  |sales     |09/12/63| 90000
3212|bill wilcocks    |d.g.m.   |accounts  |12/12/55| 85000
2345|james wilcox     |g.m.     |marketing |03/12/45|110000
```

Even though it appears that **egrep** supports the regular expressions used by **grep**, that's not true. There are some characters and examples listed in Table 15.2 which are not supported by **egrep**. We'll discuss them when we take up **sed**. Our coverage of regular expressions is not over yet.

Linux

You can use **grep -E** also to use **egrep**'s extended regular expressions. The **-F** option makes **grep** behave like **fgrep**.

15.7   sed: **The Stream Editor**

sed is a multipurpose tool which combines the work of several filters. Designed by Lee McMahon, it is derived from the **ed** line editor, the original editor of UNIX (not discussed in this text). **sed** is used for performing noninteractive operations. It acts on a data stream, hence its name.

     sed has very few options, and its power is derived from the ease with which you can both select lines and frame instructions to act on them. It has numerous features—almost bordering on a programming language. Due to obvious constraints, we'll have to stop short of its limits because its functions have been taken over by **perl**. In fact, **perl** often handles them better—and faster.

Everything in **sed** is an **instruction**. An instruction combines an **address** for selecting lines with an **action** to be taken on them:

sed *options* '*address action*' *file(s)*

The address and action are enclosed within single quotes. The action component is drawn from **sed**'s family of internal commands (Table 15.4). It can either be a simple display (print) or an editing function like insertion, deletion or substitution of text. The components of a **sed** instruction are shown in Fig. 15.1.

You can have multiple instructions in a single **sed** command, each with its own address and action components. This is what makes the command so powerful.

FIGURE 15.1   *Components of a **sed** Instruction*

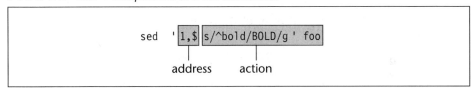

TABLE 15.4   *Internal Commands Used by **sed***

Command	Significance
i, a, c	Inserts, appends and changes text
d	Deletes line(s)
1,4d	Deletes lines 1 to 4
r foo	Places contents of file foo after line
w bar	Writes addressed lines to file bar
p	Prints line(s) on standard output
3,$p	Prints lines 3 to end (-n option required)
$!p	Prints all lines except last line (-n option required)
/begin/,/end/p	Prints lines enclosed between begin and end (-n option required)
q	Quits after reading up to addressed line
10q	Quits after reading the first 10 lines
=	Prints line number addressed
s/*s1*/*s2*/	Replaces first occurrence of string or regular expression *s1* in all lines with string *s2*
10,20s/-/:/	Replaces first occurrence of - in lines 10 to 20 with a :
s/*s1*/*s2*/g	Replaces all occurrences of string or regular expression *s1* in all lines with string *s2*
s/-/:/g	Replaces all occurrences of - in all lines with a :

Before proceeding further, C shell users must note that when a **sed** command is continued in the next line by pressing the *[Enter]* key, the shell generates an error and complains of an "unmatched" quote. As a general rule, escape all lines except the last with a \ to generate the ? prompt. (Some systems like Solaris don't display this prompt.) The situations where such escaping is required are pointed out sometimes, but not always. Sometimes, escaping doesn't work, which means the command in that form simply won't work in this shell.

Note

Chapter 17 emphasizes that the Korn and bash shells are far superior to Bourne and the C shell. You'll find **sed** easier to use if you choose either Korn or bash as your login shell—or at least the Bourne shell. If you still don't want to change your working C shell, at least use a different shell for running the **sed** commands and **awk** programs discussed in the next chapter. Simply execute **sh**, **ksh** or **bash**—whichever is available on your system—and continue working normally. At the end of your session, run **exit** to return to your login shell.

15.8   Line Addressing

Addressing in **sed** is done in two ways:

- By line number (like **3,7p**).
- By specifying a pattern which occurs in a line (like **/From:/p**).

In the first form, the address specifies either one line number to select a single line or a set of two (**3,7**) to select a group of contiguous lines. Likewise, the second form uses one or two patterns. In either case, the action (**p**, the print command) is appended to this address. We'll consider line addressing first.

Let's first consider the instruction **3q**—using a **line address**. This can be broken down to the address 3 and the action q (quit). When this instruction is enclosed within quotes and followed by one or more filenames, you can simulate **head -3** in this way:

```
$ sed '3q' emp.lst                                      Quits after line number 3
2233|charles harris  |g.m.      |sales      |12/12/52| 90000
9876|bill johnson    |director  |production|03/12/50|130000
5678|robert dylan    |d.g.m.    |marketing |04/19/43| 85000
```

sed also uses the **p** (print) command to print the output. But notice what happens when you use two line addresses with the **p** command:

```
$ sed '1,2p' emp.lst
2233|charles harris  |g.m.      |sales      |12/12/52| 90000
2233|charles harris  |g.m.      |sales      |12/12/52| 90000
9876|bill johnson    |director  |production|03/12/50|130000
9876|bill johnson    |director  |production|03/12/50|130000
5678|robert dylan    |d.g.m.    |marketing |04/19/43| 85000
2365|john woodcock   |director  |personnel |05/11/47|120000
...more lines with each line displayed only once...
```

By default, **sed** prints all lines on the standard output *in addition* to the lines affected by the action. So the addressed lines (the first two) are printed twice. But this is not what you wanted, and you need to use an option with **sed** to suppress this printing. The solution is discussed next.

Suppressing Duplicate Line Printing (-n) To overcome the problem of printing duplicate lines, you should use the -n option whenever you use the **p** command. Thus, the previous command should have been written as follows:

```
$ sed -n '1,2p' emp.lst
2233|charles harris  |g.m.     |sales    |12/12/52| 90000
9876|bill johnson    |director |production|03/12/50|130000
```

And, to select the last line of the file, use the $:

```
$ sed -n '$p' emp.lst
0110|julie truman    |g.m.     |marketing |12/31/40| 95000
```

The address and action are normally enclosed within a pair of single quotes. As you have already learned by now, you should use double quotes only when parameter evaluation or command substitution is embedded in a **sed** instruction.

Reversing Line Selection Criteria (!) You can use **sed**'s negation operator (!) with any action. So selecting the first two lines is the same as *not* selecting lines 3 through the end. The command sequence prior to the previous one can be written in this way too:

```
sed -n '3,$!p' emp.lst                        Don't print lines 3 to the end
```

Selecting Lines from the Middle **sed** can also select lines from the middle of a file—something that's not possible with either **head** or **tail** (acting alone):

```
sed -n '9,11p' emp.lst                                      Lines 9 to 11
```

Selecting Multiple Sections **sed** is not restricted to selecting contiguous groups of lines. By placing each instruction on a separate line, you can select as many sections from just about anywhere:

```
sed -n '1,2p                           3 addresses in one command,
7,9p                              using only a single pair of quotes
$p' emp.lst                                    Selects the last line
```

You can place all these instructions in a single line too, but each instruction has to be preceded by the -e option:

```
sed -n -e '1,2p' -e '7,9p' -e '$p' emp.lst                  Same as above
```

Tip

Use the -n option whenever you use the **p** command, unless you deliberately want to select lines twice. Very rarely will you need to print every line twice.

15.9   Context Addressing

The second form of addressing lets you specify a pattern (or two) rather than line numbers. This is known as **context addressing** where the pattern has a / on either side. You can locate the senders from your mailbox ($HOME/mbox) in this way:

```
$ sed -n '/From: /p' $HOME/mbox                                  A simple grep!
From: janis joplin <joplinj@altavista.net>
From: charles king <charlesk@rocketmail.com>
From: Monica Johnson <Monicaj@Web6000.com>
From: The Economist <business@lists.economist.com>
```

Both **awk** and **perl** also support this form of addressing. Ideally, you should only be looking for From: at the beginning of a line. **sed** also accepts regular expressions of the type we used with **grep**. The following command lines should refresh your memory:

```
sed -n '/^From: /p' $HOME/mbox                         ^ matches at beginning of line
sed -n '/wilco[cx]k*s*/p' emp.lst                       Both wilcox and wilcocks
sed -n "/o'br[iy][ae]n/p                                Either the o'briens or
/lennon/p" emp.lst                                                   lennon
```

Note that we had to use double quotes in the third example because the pattern itself contains a single quote. Double quotes protect single quotes in just the same way single quotes protect double.

C Shell   C shell users should note that you must add a \ at the end of the first line in the third example above. Otherwise, the shell will generate the error message Unmatched ". as it always does whenever it sees a line containing an unclosed double or single quote.

You can also specify a comma-separated pair of context addresses to select a group of contiguous lines. What is more, line and context addresses can also be mixed:

```
sed -n '/johnson/,/lightfoot/p' emp.lst
sed -n '1, /woodcock/p' emp.lst                          Space after comma—OK
```

In a previous example *(15.4.4)*, we used **ls** and **grep** in a pipeline to list files which have write permission for the group. We can do that with **sed** as well:

```
ls -l | sed -n '/^.....w/p'
```

Regular expressions in **grep** and **sed** are actually more powerful than the ones we have used so far. They use some more special characters, and we'll meet them in the third round of discussions at the end of the chapter.

Note   All context addresses, whether single or double, must be enclosed within a pair of /s. Inside them, you can use regular expressions of the type understood by **grep** (but not the **egrep**-variety).

15.10 Editing Text

Apart from selecting lines, **sed** can also edit text itself. Like **vi**, **sed** uses the **i** (insert), **a** (append), **c** (change) and **r** (read) commands in similar manner. These commands are discussed next.

15.10.1 Inserting and Changing Text (i, a and c)

For appending text, you have to use the **a** command and then enter as many lines as you want. Each line except the last must have a \ at the end. You can append these two lines to the end of this **perl** library file in this way:

```
$ sed '$a\                                           Appending to end of file
> # You must place the following line at the end\
> 1 ;
> ' www_lib.pl > $$
```

You can actually key in as many lines as you wish, but you have to precede the *[Enter]* key in each line except the last with a \. This technique has to be followed when using the **i** and **c** commands also. $$, which signifies the shell's PID, is used here to frame a numeric filename. You can use any filename here you want; it's just that you are unlikely to overwrite any existing file if you use $$.

Double-Spacing Text What is the consequence of not using an address with these commands? The inserted or changed text is then placed after or before *every* line of the file. The following command:

```
sed 'i\                                              Inserts before every line
                                                               this blank line
' foo
```

inserts a blank line before each line of the file is printed. This is another way of double-spacing text *(9.4.1)*. The difference between **i** and **a** is that **i** inserts text before the addressed line, while **a** does the same after the line.

C Shell

These commands won't work in the C shell in the way described here. You have to use two /s for lines that already have one /, and one / when there is none. The previous command will work in this way in the C shell:

```
sed 'i\\                                                      Two \s here
\                                                             and one here
' foo
```

This is an awkward form of usage and is not intuitive at all. The **sed**, **awk** and **perl** commands should be run in the other shells.

Reading in a File (r) The **r** command lets you read in a file at a certain location of the file. This is how you can insert a form's details from an external file `template.html` after the `<FORM>` tag:

```
sed '/<FORM>/r template.html' form_entry.html
```

15.10.2   Deleting Lines (d)

Using the **d** (delete) command, **sed** can emulate **grep**'s -v option to select lines not containing the pattern. Either of these commands removes comment lines of a shell or **perl** script:

```
sed '/^#/d' foo > bar
sed -n '/^#/!p' foo > bar                                    -n option to be used here
```

Deleting Blank Lines   A blank line consists of any number of spaces, tabs or nothing. How do you delete these lines from a file? Frame a pattern which matches zero or more occurrences of a space or tab:

```
sed '/^[□ ⇥]*$/d' foo                                        A space and a tab
```

You need to press the *[Tab]* key or *[Ctrl-i]* inside the character class—immediately after the space. Providing a ^ at the beginning and a $ at the end matches only lines that contain nothing but whitespace. Obviously, this expression also matches those lines that contain nothing.

15.10.3   Writing to Files (w)

The **w** (write) command writes the selected lines to a separate file. You can save the lines contained within the <FORM> and </FORM> tags in a separate file:

```
sed '/<FORM>/,/<\/FORM>/w forms.html' pricelist.html
```

Every <FORM> tag in an HTML file has a corresponding </FORM> tag. The / here needs escaping as / is **sed**'s pattern delimiter. Here, the form contents are extracted and saved in forms.html. To go further, you can save all form segments from all HTML files in a *single* file:

```
sed '/<FORM>/,/<\/FORM>/w forms.html' *.html
```

sed's power doesn't stop here. Since it accepts more than one address, you can perform a full context splitting of its input. You can search for three patterns and store the matched lines in three separate files—all in one shot:

```
sed '/<FORM>/,/<\/FORM>/w forms.html
     /<FRAME>/,/<\/FRAME>/w frames.html
     /<TABLE>/,/<\/TABLE>/w tables.html' pricelist.html
```

Note

The **w** command outputs *all* lines on the terminal irrespective of the lines actually written to separate files. If you prefer silent behavior, then use the -n option.

Tip

When there are numerous editing instructions to perform, use the -f option to accept instructions from a file. For the example above, you can use **sed -f instr.fil emp.lst** where instr.fil contains the instructions in this format:

```
/<FORM>/,/<\/FORM>/w forms.html
/<FRAME>/,/<\/FRAME>/w frames.html
/<TABLE>/,/<\/TABLE>/w tables.html
```

You can specify some more instructions with the -e option in the command line and let **sed** take the rest from the file.

15.11 Substitution

sed's strongest feature is undoubtedly substitution, achieved with its **s** (substitute) command. It lets you replace a pattern in its input with something else. You have encountered the syntax in **vi** before *(4.16)*:

*[address]*s*/expression1/string2/flag*

Here, *expression1* (which can also be a regular expression) is replaced by *string2* in all lines specified by the *[address]*. Unlike in **vi**, however, if the address is not specified, the substitution will be performed for all lines containing *expression1*. This is how you replace the | with a colon:

```
$ sed 's/|/:/' emp.lst | head -2
2233:charles harris  |g.m.      |sales     |12/12/52| 90000
9876:bill johnson    |director |production|03/12/50|130000
```

But notice what happened. Just the first (left-most) instance of the | in a line has been replaced. You need to use the g (global) flag to replace all the pipes:

```
$ sed 's/|/:/g' emp.lst | head -2
2233:charles harris  :g.m.      :sales     :12/12/52: 90000
9876:bill johnson    :director :production:03/12/50:130000
```

We used **global substitution** to replace all pipes with colons. Though we are seeing two lines here, the substitution has been carried out for the entire file.

You can limit the vertical boundaries too by specifying an address:

```
sed '1,3s/|/:/g' emp.lst
```
                                                                        First three lines only

Substitution is not restricted to a single character; it can be any string. The string to be replaced can even be a regular expression:

```
sed 's/<I>/<EM>/g' foo.html
sed -n 's/gilmo[ur][re]/gilmour/p' emp.lst
```
                                                                        1,$s implied here

Note the use of the -n option in the second example which not only converts gilmour and gilmore into a single gilmour, but selects just those lines as well.

Checking Whether Substitution Is Performed sed shows you the contents of the entire file on the screen (unless redirected); it doesn't tell you whether it has been able to perform any substitution at all. Unlike **grep** which *fails* when it can't find a pattern, **sed** is not considered to fail when it is unable to substitute.

In that case, how does one know whether a substitution has been performed at all? Using our knowledge of the other UNIX filters, we can find out the number of pipes that will be replaced by this **sed** command:

```
$ sed 's/|/:/g' emp.lst | cmp -l - emp.lst | wc -l
   75
```

sed's output here is compared with the original file. (**cmp**'s -l option produces a line for each unmatched character.) When **wc** counts these lines, it effectively tells us that 75 pipes have been replaced. A count of 0 would mean that no substitution has been performed.

Performing Multiple Substitutions You can perform multiple substitutions with one invocation of **sed**. Simply press *[Enter]* at the end of each instruction, and then close the quote at the end:

```
$ sed 's/<I>/<EM>/g                                    For csh add a \ at end
> s/<B>/<STRONG>/g                                        for every line
> s/<U>/<EM>/g' form.html                                   except last
```

sed is a stream editor; it works on a data stream. This means that an instruction processes the output of the *previous* one. This is something users often forget; they don't get the sequence right. Note that the following sequence finally converts all <I> tags to <STRONG>:

```
$ sed 's/<I>/<EM>/g
> s/<EM>/<STRONG>/g' form.html
```

When there are a group of instructions to execute, you should place these **s** instructions in a file instead, and then use **sed** with the -f option.

Note

When a g is used at the end of a substitution instruction, the change is performed globally along the line. Without it, only the left-most occurrence is substituted.

Compressing Multiple Spaces How do you delete the trailing spaces from the second, third and fourth fields of the employee database? The regular expression required in the source string needs to signify zero or more occurrences of a space, followed by a |:

```
$ sed 's^ *|^|^g' emp.lst | head -2                            Space before *
2233|charles harris|g.m.|sales|12/12/52| 90000
9876|bill johnson|director|production|03/12/50|130000
```

We've used the ^ instead of the / this time. **sed** (and **vi**) allows any character to be used as the pattern delimiter as long as it doesn't occur in any of the strings. Most UNIX system files (like /etc/passwd) follow this variable-length format because UNIX tools can easily identify a field by seeing the delimiter. This is the file format you'll be using with the **awk** command later.

Note

The -n option and print (**p**) command are generally not used when performing substitution. This means that all lines will be displayed, whether a substitution has been performed or not. This is what we normally want **sed** to do.

15.11.1 The Remembered Pattern

So far, we've looked for a pattern and then replaced it with something else. Truly speaking, the three commands below do the same job:

```
sed 's/director/member/' emp.lst
sed '/director/s//member/' emp.lst
sed '/director/s/director/member/' emp.lst
```

The second form suggests that **sed** "remembers" the scanned pattern, and stores it in // (2 frontslashes). The // representing an empty (or null) regular expression is interpreted to mean that the search and substituted patterns are the same. We'll call it the **remembered pattern**.

However, when you use // in the target string, it means you are removing the pattern totally:

```
sed 's/|//g' emp.lst
```
                                                                          Remove every | from file

The address /di rector/ in the third form appears to be redundant. However, you must understand this form also because it widens the scope of substitution. It's possible that you may like to replace a string in all lines containing a *different* string:

```
$ sed -n '/marketing/s/director/member/p' emp.lst
6521|derryk o'brien  |member    |marketing |09/26/45|125000
```

Note

The significance of // depends on its position in the instruction. If it is in the source string, it implies that the scanned pattern is stored there. If the target string is //, it means that the source pattern is to be removed.

15.11.2 The Repeated Pattern

There are further surprises in store. When a pattern in the source string also occurs in the replaced string, you can use the special character & to represent it. All these commands do the same thing:

```
sed 's/director/executive director/' emp.lst
sed 's/director/executive &/' emp.lst
sed '/director/s//executive &/' emp.lst
```

The &, known as the **repeated pattern**, expands to the entire source string. Apart from the numbered tag *(15.12.2)*, the & is the only other special character you can use in the replacement string. All other characters are treated literally.

15.12   Regular Expressions—Round Three

We haven't exhausted the regular expression set yet; there are more characters used by **grep** and **sed**. This is the third time we encounter regular expressions, and this time be prepared to see and use a \ before every metacharacter discussed in this section. We'll learn to use two types of expressions:

- The *interval regular expression*—This expression uses the characters { and } with a single or a pair of numbers between them.
- The *tagged regular expression*—This expression groups patterns with (and).

In both these expressions, the metacharacters need escaping so the command understands them as special. The shell has nothing to do with this escaping because the expressions themselves are quoted and insulated from its interpretation.

15.12.1   Interval Regular Expression (IRE)

We have matched a pattern at the beginning and end of a line. But what about matching it at any specified location—or within a zone? **sed** and **grep** also accept a special form of a regular expression that uses an integer to specify the number of characters preceding a pattern.

Let's consider the listing where the write permission bit is located at the third, sixth and ninth character positions. We can use this sequence to display files which have write permission set for group:

```
$ ls -l | grep "^.\{5\}w"
-r-xrw-r-x   1 sumit      dialout        527 Apr 23 07:42 valcode.sh
-r-xrw-r-x   2 sumit      dialout        289 Apr 23 07:42 vvi.sh
```

Now, let's dissect the regular expression ^.\{5\}w. This matches five characters (.\{5\}) at the beginning (^) of the line, followed by the pattern (w). The expression \{5\} signifies that the previous character (.) has to occur five times. This expression using the escaped pair of curly braces will be referred to as the **interval regular expression** (IRE). It takes three forms:

- $ch\backslash\{m\backslash\}$—Here, the metacharacter *ch* can occur *m* times.
- $ch\backslash\{m,n\backslash\}$—Here, *ch* can occur between *m* and *n* times.
- $ch\backslash\{m,\backslash\}$—Here *ch* can occur at least *m* times.

All these forms have the single character regular expression *ch* as the first element. This can either be a literal character, a . (dot), or a character class. It is followed by a pair of escaped curly braces containing either a single number *m*, or a range of numbers lying between *m* and *n* to determine the number of times the character preceding it can occur. The values of *m* and *n* cannot exceed 255.

Now, let's consider the second form of the IRE. Since this matches a pattern within a "zone," we can display the listing for those files that have the write bit set either for group or others:

```
$ ls -l | grep "^.\{5,8\}w"
-r-xr-xrwx   3 sumit      dialout        426 Feb 26 19:58 comj
-r-xr-xrwx   3 sumit      dialout        426 Feb 26 19:58 runj
```

```
-r-xrw-r-x   1 sumit    dialout        527 Apr 23 07:42 valcode.sh
-r-xrw-r-x   2 sumit    dialout        289 Apr 23 07:42 vvi.sh
```

We used five dots in a previous example *(15.4.4)* to anchor a pattern at a certain location in a line. But would you like to use 100 dots to locate a string preceded by 100 characters? Surely not; in the sample database, the year begins from column 50, so we can easily locate the people born in 1945. We'll use **sed** this time:

```
$ sed -n '/^.\{49\}45/p' emp.lst
6521|derryk o'brien  |director |marketing |09/26/45|125000
2345|james wilcox    |g.m.     |marketing |03/12/45|110000
```

Extracting Lines Based on Length With the IRE, you can use these commands to select lines longer than 100 characters. The second one additionally imposes a limit of 150 on the maximum length:

```
sed -n '/.\{101,\}/p' foo                              Line length at least 101
grep '^.\{101,150\}$' foo                       Line length between 101 and 150
```

The ^ and $ are required in the second example; otherwise lines longer than 150 characters would also be selected. A regular expression always tries to match the longest pattern possible *(15.4.5—Note)*.

15.12.2   The Tagged Regular Expression (TRE)

We'll first discuss this feature with reference to **sed**, though our observations apply to **grep** as well. In real life, you'll probably be using it more with **sed** than with **grep**.

   sed uses the & for reproducing the entire source string. But it can reproduce a *part* of the string as well. If you group a pattern in the source string with an escaped pair of parentheses, **sed** attaches a *numbered tag* to it. The tag can then be used anywhere where it will be expanded automatically.

   For instance, if **sed** sees \(higgins\) as the first group in a line, it understands it as higgins alright, but it remembers and abbreviates it to \1. This means that anywhere in the line—in the source or the target string—higgins can be represented as \1. Subsequent tags are numbered \2, \3, and so on.

   Consider a simple example. Suppose you want to replace the words henry higgins by higgins, henry. The **sed** substitution instruction will then look like this:

```
$ echo "henry higgins" | sed 's/\(henry\) \(higgins\)/\2, \1/'
higgins, henry
```

Here, we have two tagged patterns \(henry\) and \(higgins\) in the source string. They are automatically reproduced in the target string with the numbered tags \1 and \2, respectively. Each grouped pattern is called a **tagged regular expression** (TRE). The (,), 1 and 2 have to be escaped as they all need to be treated specially by **sed**. The , in the replacement string is treated literally, so you have it (and a space) between the words higgins and henry.

Searching for Repeated Words   Now, let's consider another example that benefits document authors. The TRE raises the possibility of detecting words that are inadvertently repeated—like the the. Since the TRE remembers a grouped pattern, you can look for these repeated words like this:

```
$ grep "\([a-z][a-z][a-z]*\)□□*\1" note                          Two spaces before *
You search search for a pattern with grep.
sed    sed can perform substitution too.
But the grand-daddy of them all is perl perl.
```

Each line here contains consecutive instances of a word (search, sed and perl). What does the group match? A word containing at least two alphabetic characters in lowercase. This group is followed by one or more spaces (note the two spaces before the second *) and the repeated pattern.

Generating Email Addresses   Suppose all the people in emp.1st *(15.1)* have user accounts named after their last name in the domain *planets.com*. Can you generate a list of email addresses for them so that they can be used in a shell script? For the TRE, it's a simple matter. Extract the second field with **cut** and then form two groups where each group contains a word. You'll have to consider a word as a group of nonblank characters:

```
$ cut -d\| -f2 emp.1st | sed 's/\([^ ]*\) \([^ ]*\)/\2@planets.com/'
harris@planets.com
johnson@planets.com
dylan@planets.com
woodcock@planets.com
    . . . . . . . .
```

The first or last name is quite adequately expressed by the TRE \([^]*\). This expression expands to zero or more occurrences of a nonspace character. In the target string, use only the last name (\2) and append @planets.com to it. It's as simple as that!

Converting Pathnames in URLs   Finally, let's take up a very important application of the TRE. You may have faced the problem of displaying links of an HTML document even though the linked documents are all available in the current directory *(14.12.2)*. This happens because the link tags often have relative pathnames in the URLs they point to. For instance, consider this section showing a list of four items:

```
$ cat httplinks.html
<LI><A HREF="smail.html">Sendmail</A> The Universal Mail Transport Agent
<LI><A HREF="http://www.sonu.com/docs/ftpdoc.html"File Transfer Protocol</A>
<LI><A HREF="../../public_html/news.html">Newsgroups</A> Usenet News
<LI><A HREF="../irc.html">Internet Relay Chat</A> On-line text conversation
```

Note that the last three items have pathnames using directories, and one of them points to a different host altogether. If you have downloaded all these HTML files to your current directory, you won't be able to access them by clicking on these links unless you remove all protocol, FQDN and directory references from each document. For instance, the anchor tag (<A>) in the second line should specify A HREF="ftpdoc.html" instead of the complete URL shown. Let's use the TRE to extract only the filenames from these URLs.

The task isn't as daunting as you might think. If you observe these A HREFs closely, you'll find the source string for substitution to have three components:

- \(A HREF="\)—This is the first group and should be printed with \1.
- .*\/—This takes care of all characters following the opening " up to the last /. Note that this matches the pathname of the directory, but we won't be printing this. The frontslash also needs to be escaped.
- \([^/]*"\)—This matches all nonfrontslash characters followed by a ". The matched expression is the base filename and should be printed with \2.

Now run **sed** using these three components in a regular expression:

```
$ sed 's/\(A HREF="\).*\/\([^/]*"\)/\1\2/' httplinks.html
<LI><A HREF="smail.html">Sendmail</A> The Universal Mail Transport Agent
<LI><A HREF="ftpdoc.html">File Transfer Protocol</A>
<LI><A HREF="news.html">Newsgroups</A> Usenet News
<LI><A HREF="irc.html">Internet Relay Chat</A> On-line text conversation
```

There you see only the base filenames after conversion! This is a useful sequence that you'll need often, and you may also need to modify it. The IMG SRC tag also refers to URLs, so you have to add another **s** command for it. You can try this out as an exercise for yourself.

The TRE is probably the most useful feature of **sed**. You'll find numerous uses for it. Though it's quite cryptic and difficult to comprehend initially, you must understand it if you want **sed** to serve as a gateway to learning **perl**. **perl** also uses these numbered tags, but with a more readable form.

sed also features *pattern* and *hold spaces*, and *branches* and *labels*. They are difficult to use and hence left out of our discussions. This power tool is best mastered by sheer practice, by repeated attempts to figure out the exact command sequence that will perform a specific job. You don't always get it right the first time, but don't worry; hardly anybody does, not with this command at least.

Note

Apart from the commands **grep** and **sed**, regular expressions are used by the power filters **awk** and **perl** and the editors **vi** and **emacs** also. The GNU versions of these commands support some more metacharacters and POSIX too specifies some special patterns. For a detailed and complete picture of their usage, look up Appendix C.

SUMMARY

The grep Family

grep is a filter used to search a file for a pattern. You can count only the occurrences (-c) without displaying the selected lines, the names of the files (-l) and the line numbers (-n) where the pattern occurs. You can also ignore case when performing a match (-i) and select only lines not containing the pattern (-v).

Unlike **awk** and **sed**, **grep** returns a false exit status if it fails to find a match. This exit status is stored in a special shell variable ($?).

egrep extends **grep**'s capabilities. It uses the | to delimit multiple patterns. **fgrep** accepts only fixed strings and is faster than the other two.

GNU **grep** in Linux uses the -A and -B options to show both lines above or below the matched line. **grep -2** shows two lines on either side of the matched line. It can also match multiple patterns (-e) and take patterns from a file (-f).

sed

A **sed** *instruction* consists of an *address* and an *action* (command). Lines can be addressed by line numbers or by specifying one or more context patterns enclosed by /s. The instruction must be enclosed within quotes.

sed accepts multiple instructions which can be used to print lines from various sections of a file. The action **p** prints a file, and the -n option makes sure that lines are not printed twice. The ! reverses the selection criteria.

Lines can be inserted (**i**), appended (**a**), changed (**c**) and deleted (**d**). **sed** can also read in a file at any location (**r**). Different segments of a file can be written to separate files too (**w**).

sed is mostly used for replacing one pattern with another (**s**), both on selected lines as well as globally. The search and substitution patterns can also be regular expressions of the type understood by **grep**.

A set of two slashes (//) matches the expression used for scanning a pattern (the *remembered* pattern). The & reproduces the entire source string in the target string (the *repeated* pattern).

Regular Expressions

Both **grep** and **sed** support the use of a *regular expression* as a pattern for search or substitution. **egrep** and **awk** also support regular expressions but of a different form. There are some metacharacters that are common to the two groups. The enlarged metacharacter set for **grep** and **sed** is shown in Table 15.2 and that for **egrep** and **awk** in Table 15.3.

The **.** matches a single character, while * matches zero or more occurrences of the *previous* character. The character class uses a set of characters within rectangular brackets to match a single character in the class. Ranges are similar to that used by the wild cards, except that negation is done with a ^.

A pattern can be matched at the beginning of a line with a ^, and at the end with a $. Because it is the command that interprets these characters, a regular expression should be quoted to prevent the shell from interfering.

The + and ? (used by **egrep** and **awk**) are used in a more restrictive way than *. + matches one or more occurrences, while ? matches zero or one occurrence of the previous character. Multiple patterns can be grouped within parentheses using the | as the delimiter.

The *interval regular expression* (IRE) uses a single or a pair of numbers surrounded by escaped curly braces—like \{m,n\}. The expression is preceded by a single character and signifies the number of times the previous character can occur. The IRE is useful in locating a pattern at a specific column location or in a range.

The *tagged regular expression* (TRE) uses \(and \) to enclose a pattern. The command remembers the pattern and attaches a tag to it. The tags can be referenced anywhere with \1, \2 etc. The feature is useful in reproducing a portion of the source string in the target expression in **sed**, and has very wide application in the real world.

SELF-TEST

When filenames are not specified, emp.lst *(15.1)* is to be often assumed.

15.1   What happens when you use **grep a b c**?
15.2   Store a single figure in a variable representing the number of lines containing the word HTML in the files foo1, foo2 and foo3.
15.3   Display the files in the current directory that contain the string A HREF in either upper- or lowercase.
15.4   Do you need to quote the pattern <TABLE> if you are trying to locate it in a file?
15.5   Can you use **grep** to display lines containing the pattern <TABLE> and five lines below?
15.6   What does the expression gg* signify?
15.7   How do you locate lines containing harris and harrison using **grep**?
15.8   What will the regular expression a.*b match?
15.9   Show two ways by which **grep** can locate lines longer than 15 characters.
15.10   Using **egrep**, locate lines containing lockwood and harwood.
15.11   When do you use **fgrep**?
15.12   How do you use **egrep** and **fgrep** to take patterns from a file?
15.13   Print every line of a file twice.
15.14   Select all but the last line of a file.
15.15   How do you insert a blank line after each line that is read?
15.16   How will you replace the string Linux by Red Hat Linux?
15.17   Use a command sequence to locate the line containing the last occurrence of a pattern.

EXERCISES

15.1   What's the difference between a *wild card* and a *regular expression*?
15.2   What does this command do? What are the two $s doing here?

```
grep "$SHELL$" /etc/passwd | cut -d: -f1
```

15.3   If you did not have the **wc** command on your system, how would you use **grep** to count the number of users currently using the system?
15.4   Use a command sequence to start the **vi** editor with the cursor on the last line of occurrence of the string APPENDIX.
15.5   How will you remove blank lines from a file using **grep**?
15.6   What does **grep "^*"** do? Is the \ really necessary?

15.7   How will you list the ordinary files in your current directory that are not writable by the owner?

15.8   Locate lines beginning and ending with a dot and containing anything between them.

15.9   Locate lines containing the string `plugin` or `plugins` as the only characters in the line.

15.10   Frame regular expressions to match lines containing (i) `jefferies jeffery jeffreys` (ii) `hitchen hitchin hitching` (iii) `Heard herd Hird` (iv) `dix dick dicks dickson dixon` (v) `Mcgee mcghee magee`.

15.11   Use command substitution with **grep** to list the names of the persons from `emp.lst` who were born today.

15.12   Find out the name and designation of the youngest person who is not a director.

15.13   What does **grep "**" foo** match?

15.14   What does **grep *** do? When will it not work?

15.15   Interpret this command:

```
grep "^[^^]" foo
```

15.16   You are looking for one `bill christie` in a file, but are not sure whether `bill` exists as `william` or `bill`, and whether `christie` exists as `christy`. How do you frame a compact expression?

15.17   Match the names `wood`, `woodcock` and `woodhouse` using **egrep**.

15.18   Frame an **egrep** regular expression to extract lines containing the section and subsection numbers of this book.

15.19   Frame a command sequence that looks at romeo's mailbox to tell him that either he has received a message from henry or the `Subject:` line contains the word `urgent` or `immediate`.

15.20   Add the tags <HTML> at the beginning and </HTML> at the end of a file.

15.21   How do you delete all lines beginning with a # except the line `#!/bin/ksh`?

15.22   Find out the occurrences of three consecutive and identical word characters (like `aaa` or `bbb`) using (i) **grep** and (ii) **sed**.

15.23   Locate lines that are less than 100 characters in length using (i) **grep** and (ii) **sed**.

15.24   How do you delete all spaces at the end of every line?

15.25   What is wrong with this command? How do you correct it?

```
sed 's/compute/calculate/g
s/computer/host/g' foo
```

15.26   Will this command leave the input unchanged?

```
sed 's/print/printf/g
s/printf/print/g' foo
```

15.27   Write a command sequence to find out the number of occurrences of the word `encryption` in a file. (Note: A word may occur more than once in a line.)

15.28   How do you add the century (the string 20) to the date field of `emp.lst`?

15.29 Every <B> tag in an HTML file has a closing </B> tag as well. Convert them to <STRONG> and </STRONG>, respectively, using **sed** with a single **s** command.

KEY TERMS

command failure *(15.2.2)*

context address *(15.9)*

global substitution *(15.11)*

interval regular expression
   (IRE) *(15.12.1)*

line address *(15.8)*

regular expression *(15.4)*

remembered pattern *(15.11.1)*

repeated pattern *(15.11.2)*

sed action *(15.7)*

sed address *(15.7)*

sed instruction *(15.7)*

tagged regular expression
   (TRE) *(15.12.2)*

## CHAPTER 16

Programming with awk

The **awk** command made a late entry into the UNIX system in 1977 to augment the tool kit with suitable report formatting capabilities. Named after its authors Aho, Weinberger and Kernighan, **awk** remains the most powerful native text manipulation utility of the UNIX system. (The almighty **perl** is not available in all systems.) Like **sed**, it combines features of several filters, though its report writing capability is the most useful. **awk** appears as **gawk** (GNU **awk**) in Linux.

awk doesn't belong to the do-one-thing-well family of UNIX commands. In fact, it can do several things—and some of them quite well. Unlike other filters, it operates at the *field* level and can easily access, transform and format individual fields in a line. It also accepts regular expressions for pattern matching, has C-type programming constructs, variables and several built-in functions.

We'll discuss the important **awk** features in some detail because that will also help you in understanding **perl**. **perl** uses most of the **awk** constructs—sometimes in an identical manner.

Objectives

- Understand **awk**'s unusual syntax with its *selection criteria* and *action* components. *(16.1)*
- Split a line into *fields* and format the output with **printf**. *(16.2 and 16.3)*
- Use the comparison operators to select lines on practically any condition. *(16.4)*
- Use the ~ and !~ operators with **egrep**-type regular expressions for pattern matching. *(16.4.1)*
- Handle decimal numbers and use them for computation. *(16.4.2 and 16.5)*
- Use variables without declaring or initializing them. *(16.6)*
- Do some pre- and post-processing with the BEGIN and END sections. *(16.8)*
- Run a program from a shell script and make **awk** read the arguments supplied to the script. *(16.9)*
- Use the **getline** function to take input from the terminal. *(16.10)*
- Use arrays and access an array element with a nonnumeric subscript. *(16.12)*
- Use the built-in functions for performing string handling tasks. *(16.13)*
- Make decisions with the **if** statement and its compact one-line conditional. *(16.14)*
- Use the **for** and **while** loops to perform advanced text manipulation. *(16.15)*

16.1   awk **Preliminaries**

awk is not just a command, but a programming language too. It uses an unusual syntax that uses two components and requires single quotes and curly braces:

awk *options* '*selection criteria {action}*' *file(s)*

The constituents resemble those of **find**. The *selection criteria* (a form of addressing) filters input and selects lines for the *action* component to act on. This component is enclosed within curly braces. The address (rather, the selection criteria) and action constitute an **awk** *program* that is surrounded by a set of single quotes. These programs are often one line long though they can span several lines as well. A sample **awk** program is shown in Fig. 16.1.

The selection criteria in **awk** have wider scope than in **sed**. Like there, they can be patterns like /negroponte/ or line addresses using **awk**'s variable NR. Further, they can also be conditional expressions using the && and || operators as used in the shell *(18.6)*. You can select lines practically on any condition.

A typical and complete **awk** command specifies an address and an action. The following command selects the Subject: lines from mbox, the mailbox file:

```
$ awk '/^Subject:/ { print }' $HOME/mbox
Subject: RE: History is not bunk
Subject: Mail server problem
Subject: Take our Survey, Win US$500!
```

The selection criteria section (/^Subject:/) selects lines that are processed in the action section ({ print }). If the selection criteria are missing, the action applies to all lines. If the action is missing, the entire line is printed. One of them has to be specified.

When used without any field specifiers, the **print** statement prints the entire line. Moreover, since printing is the default action of **awk**, all the following three forms could be considered equivalent:

```
awk '/^Subject:/' mbox                        Printing is the default action
awk '/^Subject:/{ print }' mbox                     Whitespace permitted
awk '/^Subject:/ { print $0}' mbox               $0 is the complete line
```

So far, the programs have produced readable output, but that's because the file emp.lst contains fixed-length lines. Henceforth, the input for many **awk** programs used in this chapter will come from the file empn.lst. The lines here are of variable length:

FIGURE 16.1   *Components of an* **awk** *Program*

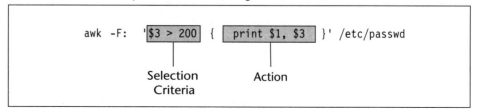

```
$ head -4 empn.1st
2233|charles harris|g.m.|sales|12/12/52| 90000
9876|bill johnson|director|production|03/12/50|130000
5678|robert dylan|d.g.m.|marketing|04/19/43| 85000
2365|john woodcock|director|personnel|05/11/47|120000
```

Pattern matching is done in **sed**-style, but **awk** uses the **egrep**-type of regular expressions *(15.6).* This type allows you to use the | as the pattern delimiter and the + and ? to restrict the occurrences of the previous character:

```
$ awk '/wilco[cx]k?s?|wood(cock|house)/' empn.1st
2365|john woodcock|director|personnel|05/11/47|120000
1265|p.j. woodhouse|manager|sales|09/12/63| 90000
3212|bill wilcocks|d.g.m.|accounts|12/12/55| 85000
2345|james wilcox|g.m.|marketing|03/12/45|110000
```

Note

So far, we have used single-line **awk** programs. It won't be long before we see these programs spanning multiple lines. C shell users have to note yet again that they must escape the *[Enter]* key for the programs to run. Refer to the Section 15.7 "Note" for the author's suggestions in this matter.

Caution

An **awk** program must be enclosed within single quotes. Double quotes will create problems unless used judiciously.

16.2 Splitting a Line into Fields

Unlike the other UNIX filters which operate on fields, **awk** uses a contiguous sequence of spaces and tabs (whitespace) as a *single* delimiter. No other UNIX command is so liberal in its interpretation of the field delimiter. We have used **cut**, **paste** and **sort**, and they all use a single character as the separator.

   awk breaks up a line into fields on whitespace or on the delimiter specified with the -F option. These fields are represented by the variables $1, $2, $3 and so forth in the order specified. There's another one, $0, that represents the entire line. Since these parameters are evaluated by the shell in double quotes, **awk** programs must be single-quoted. This is how we use these variables:

```
$ awk -F"|" '/sales/ { print $2,$3,$4,$6 }' empn.1st
charles harris g.m. sales  90000
gordon lightfoot director sales 140000
p.j. woodhouse manager sales  90000
jackie wodehouse manager sales 110000
```

awk extracts the fields from its input, something we could do only with **cut**. We'll now use a line address to select lines using the built-in variable NR to specify the line numbers:

```
$ awk -F"|" 'NR == 3, NR == 6 { print NR, $2,$3,$6 }' empn.1st
3 robert dylan d.g.m.   85000
4 john woodcock director 120000
```

```
5 barry wood chairman 160000
6 gordon lightfoot director 140000
```

Here, we see **awk** combining the functions of three filters (**cut**, **sed** and **nl**). The line address NR == 3, NR == 6 is really **awk**'s way of expressing **sed**'s **3,6p**. Further, NR == 3 is a condition that is tested rather than an assignment, and should appear familiar to C programmers. == is one of the many operators employed in comparison tests.

Note

A , (comma) is generally used to delimit the field specifications to ensure that each field is separated from the other by a space. If you don't put in the comma, the fields will be glued together.

16.3   `printf`: **Formatting Output**

awk's C-like **printf** statement produces formatted output. **awk** accepts most of the formats used by C's **printf** function. There are a host of them, but in this chapter, we'll stick to these formats:

%s — String
%d — Integer
%f — Floating point number

Since **awk** also accepts regular expressions, we can use them and these print formats to display readable output:

```
$ awk -F"|" '/true*man/ {
> printf "%3d %-20s %-12s %6d\n",NR,$2,$3,$6 }' empn.lst
13 ronie trueman         executive    75000
15 julie truman          g.m.         95000
```

C shell users should note that **awk** gets multiline here. The name and designation have been printed in placeholders 20 and 12 characters wide, respectively; the - symbol left-justifies the output. Note that **printf** requires a \n to print a newline after each line. Using the various formats in an **awk** program, you can now have complete control over the way the output is presented.

Note

As shown in the preceding example, the built-in variable NR is not suitable for printing a display line number if all lines are not selected. You then need to define and use a separate variable to start numbering from 1.

16.3.1   **Redirecting Standard Output**

Every **print** and **printf** statement can be separately redirected with the > and | symbols. However, make sure the filename or the command that follows these symbols is enclosed within *double* quotes. For example, the following statement sorts the output of the **printf** statement:

```
printf "%s %-10s %-12s %-8s\n", $1, $3, $4, $6 | "sort"
```

If you use redirection instead, the filename should be enclosed in quotes in a similar manner:

```
printf "%s %-10s %-12s %-8s\n", $1, $3, $4, $6 > "mslist"
```

awk thus provides the flexibility of separately manipulating the output of the different output streams. But don't forget the quotes!

16.4   The Comparison Operators

How do you print the three fields for the directors and the chairman? You can do that by matching a pattern against a specific *field*—here $3:

```
$ awk -F"|" '$3 == "director" || $3 == "chairman" {
> printf "%-20s %-12s %d\n", $2,$3,$6 }' empn.lst
bill johnson          director     130000
john woodcock         director     120000
barry wood            chairman     160000
gordon lightfoot      director     140000
derryk o'brien        director     125000
```

This is the first time we matched a pattern with a field. In fact, field matching is implemented in only **awk** and **perl**. For negating the above condition, you should use the != and && operators instead:

```
$3 != "director" && $3 != "chairman"
```

The address here translates into this: Select those lines where the third field doesn't (!=) completely match the string director and (&&) also doesn't (!=) completely match the string chairman. Note that the match is made for the *entire* field, rather than a string embedded in the field space. We couldn't verify that because the file empn.lst has all trailing spaces trimmed. But will this program work with emp.lst which has trailing spaces attached to the strings?

```
$ awk -F"|" '$3 == "director" || $3 == "chairman"' emp.lst
$ _
```

No, it won't; the third field contains trailing whitespace, so a perfect match wasn't found. Field matching is better done with regular expressions as you'll see in the next topic.

16.4.1   ~ and !~: The Regular Expression Operators

How does one match regular expressions? Previously we had used **awk** with regular expressions in this manner:

```
awk '/wilco[cx]k*s*|wood(cock|house)/' empn.lst
```

This matches a number of patterns anywhere in the line and not in a specific field. For matching anywhere in a field, **awk** offers the ~ operator; !~ negates the match. With these operators, matching becomes more specific as seen in the following examples:

```
$2 ~ /wilco[cx]k*s*|wood(cock|house)/
$2 ~ /wilco[cx]k*s*/ && $2 ~ /wood(cock|house)/
$3 !~ /director|chairman/
```
Matches second field
Same as above
Neither directors nor chairman

Remember that the operators ~ and !~ work only with field specifiers (like $1 and $2). The delimiting of patterns with the | is an **egrep** feature which **awk** also uses. In fact, **awk** uses all the regular expression characters used by **egrep**, but doesn't accept the IRE (interval regular expression) and TRE (tagged regular expression) used by **grep** and **sed** *(15.12)*.

Tip

To match a string embedded in a field, you must use ~ instead of ==. Similarly, to negate a match, use !~ instead of !=.

To locate those people whose designation is g.m., you would probably try this:

```
awk -F"|" '$3 ~ /g\.m\./ { printf " .....
```

This selects those with designation d.g.m. also because g.m. is embedded in d.g.m.. Locating just g.m. requires use of the anchoring characters ^ and $. These characters have slightly different meanings when used by **awk**. Here, they are used to indicate the beginning and end of a *field*, unless you use them with $0. Anchor the pattern in this way:

```
awk -F"|" '$3 ~ /^g\.m\./ { printf " .....
```

The ^ here matches g.m. at the beginning of the third field; this discards d.g.m..

Tip

To match a string at the beginning of a field, precede the search pattern with a ^. Similarly, use a $ for matching a pattern at the end of a field.

16.4.2   Number Comparison

awk can also handle numbers—both integer and floating type—and make relational tests on them. Using operators from the set shown in Table 16.1, you can now print the pay slips for those people whose salary exceeds 120,000 dollars:

```
$ awk -F"|" '$6 > 120000 {
> printf "%-20s %-12s %d\n", $2,$3,$6 }' empn.lst
bill johnson        director     130000
barry wood          chairman     160000
gordon lightfoot    director     140000
derryk o'brien      director     125000
```

You can also combine regular expression matching with numeric comparisons to locate those, either born in 1945 or drawing a salary greater than 100,000 dollars:

```
awk -F"|" '$6 > 100000 || $5 ~/45$/' empn.lst
```

Recall that the context address /45$/ matches the string 45 at the end ($) of the field. With all these operators, you can now select lines by locating a pattern as a simple string or a regular expression, or by making a numerical comparison.

TABLE 16.1   *The Comparison and Regular Expression Matching Operators in* **awk**

Operator	Significance
<	Less than
<=	Less than or equal to
==	Equal to
!=	Not equal to
>=	Greater than or equal to
>	Greater than
~	Matches a regular expression
!~	Does not match a regular expression

16.5   Number Processing

awk can perform computations on numbers using the arithmetic operators +, -, *, / and % (modulus). It also overcomes one of the most major limitations of the shell—the inability to handle decimal numbers.

Salespeople often earn a bonus apart from their salary. We'll assume here that the bonus amount is equal to one month's salary. The pay slip of these people should look like this:

```
$ awk -F"|" '$4 == "sales" {
> printf "%-20s %-12s %6d %8.2f\n",$2, $3, $6, $6/12 }' empn.lst
charles harris       g.m.          90000  7500.00
gordon lightfoot     director     140000 11666.67
p.j. woodhouse       manager       90000  7500.00
jackie wodehouse     manager      110000  9166.67
```

The last column shows the bonus component, obtained by dividing the salary field by 12 ($6/12). To print the decimal part, we had to use the %f format—the one universally used for printing floating point numbers.

16.6   Variables

While **awk** has certain built-in variables, like NR (for line number) and $0 (the entire line), it also lets you use variables of your choice. A user-defined variable used by **awk** has two special features:

- No type declarations are needed.
- By default and depending on its type, variables are initialized to zero or a null string. **awk** has a mechanism of identifying the type of variable used from its context.

You can now use these properties to print a serial number for those directors drawing a salary exceeding 120,000 dollars:

```
$ awk -F"|" '$3 == "director" && $6 > 120000{
> kount = kount + 1
> printf "%3d %-20s %-12s %d\n", kount,$2,$3,$6 }' empn.lst
1 bill johnson          director     130000
2 gordon lightfoot      director     140000
3 derryk o'brien        director     125000
```

The initial value of kount is 0 (by default). That's why the first line is correctly assigned the number 1. **awk** also accepts the C-style incrementing forms:

```
kount++                                     Same as kount = kount + 1
kount += 2                                   Same as kount = kount + 2
printf "%3d\n", ++kount                      Increments kount before printing
```

Note

No type declarations or initial values are required for user-defined variables used in an **awk** program. **awk** identifies their type and initializes them to zero or null strings.

16.7   Reading the Program from a File (-f)

You should hold large **awk** programs in separate files and provide them with the .awk extension for easier identification. Let's first store the previous program in the file empawk.awk:

```
$ cat empawk.awk
$3 == "director" && $6 > 120000 {
printf "%3d %-20s %-12s %d\n", ++kount,$2,$3,$6 }
```

Observe that this time we haven't used any quotes to enclose the **awk** program. You can now use **awk** with the -f *filename* option to obtain the same output:

```
awk -F"|" -f empawk.awk empn.lst
```

Caution

If you use **awk** with the -f option, make sure the program stored in the file is not enclosed within quotes. **awk** uses single quotes only when the program is specified in the command line.

16.8   The BEGIN and END Sections

If you have to print something before you process input, the BEGIN section can be used quite gainfully. Similarly, the END section is equally useful for printing some totals after the processing is over. Both sections are optional and take this form:

```
BEGIN { action }                            Both require curly braces
END { action }
```

When present, these sections are delimited by the body of the **awk** program. You can use them to print a suitable heading at the beginning and the average salary at the end. Store this **awk** program in a separate file empawk2.awk:

```
$ cat empawk2.awk
BEGIN { printf "\n\t\tEmployee abstract\n\n"
}
$6 > 120000 {   # Increment variables for serial number and pay
                kount++ ; tot+= $6
                printf "%3d %-20s %-12s %d\n", kount,$2,$3,$6
}
END { printf "\n\tThe average salary is %6d\n", tot/kount
}
```

awk also uses the # for providing comments. The BEGIN section here is meant to print a suitable heading, offset by two tabs (\t\t), while the END section should print the average salary (tot/kount) for those lines selected. To execute this program, use the -f option:

```
$ awk -F"|" -f empawk2.awk empn.lst
```

```
            Employee abstract

    1 bill johnson         director     130000
    2 barry wood           chairman     160000
    3 gordon lightfoot      director     140000
    4 derryk o'brien        director     125000

        The average salary is 138750
```

Caution

Always start the opening brace in the same line the section (BEGIN or END) begins. If you don't, **awk** will generate some strange messages!

16.9 Positional Parameters

The previous program could take a more generalized form if the number 120000 is replaced by a variable. **awk** uses some special variables called **positional parameters**. These parameters are also represented by $1, $2 and so forth, but have a different meaning from field identifiers that use the same notation. When you provide arguments to a shell script containing an **awk** program, these arguments are stored in these positional parameters.

Because the shell also uses identical parameters (*18.4*) to represent the arguments of a shell script, the positional parameters in **awk** have to be placed in *single* quotes. This would enable **awk** to distinguish between a positional parameter and a field identifier.

To use positional parameters, the entire **awk** command (not just the program) should be stored in a shell script (say, **empabs.sh**) after making this nominal change:

$6 > '$1'   *Instead of* $6 > 120000

Every shell script will need executable permission to be able to execute. (Follow the instructions given in Section 8.12.) Now, invoke the shell script with an argument, and the argument will be visible inside the **awk** program:

```
empabs.sh 100000
```

You are now able to build a facility of querying a database to select those lines that satisfy a selection criterion, i.e., the salary exceeding a certain figure. With a nominal amount of **awk** programming, you could also calculate the average salary of the persons selected. You couldn't have done all this with **grep** or **sed**; they simply can't perform computations.

16.10 getline: **Making** awk **Interactive**

Every programming language uses a statement to withhold program execution and take some input from the terminal. **awk** uses the **getline** statement. This statement has a diverse syntax, but you'll want to use it like this:

```
getline cop < "</dev/tty"                          Standard input assigned to cop
```

Using the device name /dev/tty to represent the terminal, you can replace the previous sequence by placing the **getline** statement in the BEGIN section. We won't print the average this time. Use the script file empawk3.awk to reflect these changes:

```
$ cat empawk3.awk
BEGIN { printf "Enter the cut-off salary : "
        getline cop < "/dev/tty"
        printf "\n\t\tEmployee abstract\n\n"
}
$6 > cop { printf "%3d %-20s %-12s %d\n", ++kount,$2,$3,$6
}
```

Remember to double-quote any filename used inside an **awk** program (like "/dev/tty"); single quotes won't do. When you execute this script, it asks you for the value that has to be used as the cut-off point:

```
$ awk -F"|" -f empawk3.awk empn.lst
Enter the cut-off salary : 130000                            Interactive behavior!

              Employee abstract

  1 barry wood          chairman     160000
  2 gordon lightfoot    director     140000
```

This script pauses at the beginning of the program to take input from the user. The **getline** feature lets you use **awk** like a shell script. We haven't seen any filter behave like this as interactivity runs counter to the principle of filtering.

16.11 **Built-In Variables**

awk has several built-in variables (Table 16.2). They are all assigned automatically though it's sometimes possible for a user to reassign them. You have already used NR to print the current line number. We'll now have a brief look at some of the other variables.

TABLE 16.2 *Built-In Variables Used by* **awk**

Variable	Function
NR	Cumulative number of lines read
FS	Input field separator
OFS	Output field separator
NF	Number of fields in current line
FILENAME	Current input file
ARGC	Number of arguments in command line
ARGV	List of arguments

As stated elsewhere, **awk** uses a contiguous string of spaces as the default field delimiter. FS redefines this field separator, which in the sample database happens to be the |. When used at all, it must occur in the BEGIN section so that the body of the program knows its value before it starts processing:

```
BEGIN { FS="|" }
```

This is an alternative to the -F option of the command which does the same thing.

Note

awk is the only filter that uses whitespace as the default delimiter instead of a single space or tab.

NF comes in quite handy when cleaning a database of lines which don't contain the right number of fields. You can easily locate lines not having six fields which have crept in due to faulty data entry:

```
$ awk  'BEGIN { FS = "|" }
> NF != 6 {
> print "Record No ", NR, "has ", NF, " fields"}' foo
Record No 6 has 4 fields
Record No 17 has 5 fields
```

FILENAME stores the name of the current file being processed. Like **grep** and **sed**, **awk** can also handle multiple filenames in the command line. By default, **awk** doesn't print the filename, but you can instruct it to do so:

```
'$6 < 4000 { print FILENAME, $0 }'
```

With FILENAME, you can devise logic that does different things depending on the file being processed.

16.12 Arrays

awk handles one-dimensional arrays. The index for an array can be virtually anything; *it can even be a string.* No array declarations are necessary; an array is considered declared the moment it is used. It is also automatically initialized to zero unless initialized explicitly.

You can use arrays to store the totals of the salary and commission (@20% of salary) for the sales and marketing people. We'll use the tot[] array here:

```
$ cat empawk4.awk
BEGIN { FS = "|" ; printf "%44s\n", "Salary     Commission" }
/sales|marketing/ {
    commission = $6*0.20
    tot[1] += $6 ; tot[2] += commission
    kount++
}
END { printf "\t     Average    %5d    %5d\n", tot[1]/kount, tot[2]/kount }
```

Note that this time we didn't match the patterns sales and marketing specifically in a field. We could afford to do that because the patterns occur only in the fourth field, and there's no scope here for ambiguity. When you run the program, it outputs the averages of the two elements of pay:

```
$ awk -f empawk4.awk empn.lst
                        Salary    Commission
        Average    105625    21125
```

C programmers should find the program quite comfortable to work with except that **awk** simplifies a number of things that require explicit specification in C. There are no type declarations, no initializations and no statement terminators.

16.13 Functions

awk has several built-in functions performing both arithmetic and string operations (Table 16.3). The arguments are passed to a function in C-style—delimited by commas and enclosed by a matched pair of parentheses. In contrast to C, however, when a function is used without any argument, the symbols () need not be used.

Some of these functions take a variable number of arguments, and one (**length**) uses no argument as a variant form. The functions are adequately explained here so you can confidently use them in **perl** which often uses identical syntaxes.

length() **length()** determines the length of its argument, and if no argument is present, then it assumes the entire line as its argument. You can use **length** (without any argument) to locate lines whose length exceeds 1024 characters:

```
awk -F"|" 'length > 1024' empn.lst
```

TABLE 16.3 *Built-In Functions in* **awk**

Function	Significance
int(x)	Returns integer value of x
sqrt(x)	Returns square root of x
length	Returns length of complete line
length(x)	Returns length of x
substr(stg,m,n)	Returns portion of string of length n, starting from position m in string stg
index(s1,s2)	Returns position of string s2 in string s1
split(stg,arr, ch)	Splits string stg into array arr using ch as delimiter; optionally returns number of fields
system("cmd")	Runs UNIX command cmd, and returns its exit status

You can use **length()** with a field as well. The following program selects those people who have short names:

```
awk -F"|" 'length($2) < 11' empn.lst
```

index() **index**(*s1,s2*) determines the position of a string *s2* within a larger string *s1*. This function is especially useful in validating single character fields. If you have a field which can take the values a, b, c, d or e, you can use this function to find out whether this single character field can be located within the string abcde:

```
x = index("abcde","b")
```

This returns the value 2.

substr() The **substr**(*stg,m,n*) function extracts a substring from a string *stg*. *m* represents the starting point of extraction, and *n* indicates the number of characters to be extracted. Because string values can also be used for computation, the returned string from this function can be used to select those born between 1946 and 1951:

```
$ awk -F"|" 'substr($5,7,2) > 45 && substr($5,7,2) < 52' empn.lst
9876|bill johnson|director|production|03/12/50|130000
2365|john woodcock|director|personnel|05/11/47|120000
4290|neil o'bryan|executive|production|09/07/50| 65000
3564|ronie trueman|executive|personnel|07/06/47| 75000
```

Note that **awk** does indeed possess a mechanism of identifying the type of expression from its context. It identified the date field as a string for using **substr()** and then converted it to a number for making a numeric comparison.

Note

awk makes no distinction between numeric and string variables. You can use a string for numeric computations as well.

split() **split**(*stg,arr,ch*) breaks up a string *stg* on the delimiter *ch* and stores the fields in an array *arr*[]. Here's how you can convert the date field to the format *YYYYMMDD*:

```
$ awk -F\| '{split($5,ar,"/") ; print "19"ar[3]ar[1]ar[2]}' empn.1st
19521212
19500312
19430419
   .....
```

You can also do this with **sed**, but this method is superior because it explicitly picks up the fifth field, whereas **sed** would transform the only date field that it finds. **split()** also returns a value, and we'll learn to use this value in a later example.

system() You may want to print the system date at the beginning of the report. For running any UNIX command within **awk**, you'll have to use the **system()** function. Here are two examples:

```
BEGIN { system("tput clear")                                    Clears the screen
        system("date") }                             Executes UNIX date command
```

You should be familiar with all the functions discussed in this section as they are used in a wide variety of situations. We'll use them again in **perl**.

16.14 Control Flow—The if Statement

awk has practically all the features of a modern programming language. It has conditional structures (the **if** statement) and loops (**while** and **for**). They all execute a body of statements depending on the success or failure of the **control command**. This is simply a condition that is specified in the first line of the construct.

The **if** statement has been elaborated in Chapter 18, but **awk** uses a different form:

```
if ( condition is true ) {                               Must use parentheses
    statements
} else {                                                      else is optional
    statements
}
```

As in C, the control flow constructs require the terminators { and } only when multiple actions are specified. Moreover, the control command itself must be enclosed in parentheses.

Most of the addresses used so far reflect the logic normally used in the **if** statement. In a previous example, you selected lines where the salary exceeded 120,000 dollars by using the condition as the address:

```
$6 > 120000 {
```

An alternative form of this logic places the condition inside the action component rather than the address. But this form requires the **if** statement:

```
awk -F"|" '{ if ($6 > 120000) printf  .....
```

if can be used with the comparison operators and the special symbols ~ and !~ to match a regular expression. When used in combination with the logical operators || and &&, **awk** programming becomes quite easy and powerful. Some of the earlier pattern matching expressions are rephrased in Table 16.4—this time in the form used by **if**.

To illustrate the use of the optional **else** statement, let's assume that the commission is 15 percent of salary when the latter is less than 100,000 dollars, and 10 percent otherwise. The *if-else* structure that implements this logic looks like this:

```
if ( $6 < 100000 )
   commission = 0.15*$6
else
   commission = 0.10*$6
```

You can even replace the above **if** construct with a compact conditional structure:

```
$6 < 100000 ? commission = 0.15*$6 : commission = 0.10*$6
```

This is the form that C and **perl** use to implement the logic of a simple *if-else* construct. The ? and : act as separators of the two actions.

Note

There is no **endif** or **fi** terminator for the **if** statement used in **awk**.

T A B L E 16.4   *Usage of* **awk***'s* **if** *Construct*

Command	Significance
if (x)	x is non-null
if (NR >= 3 && NR <= 6)	Lines 3 to 6
if ($3 == "director" || $3 == "chairman")	Third field matches director or chairman
if ($3 ~ /^g.m/)	Third field contains g.m at beginning of field
if ($2 !~ /[hH]o?uston/)	Second field doesn't match the regular expression

16.15 Looking: `for` and `while`

`awk` supports two loops—`for` and `while`. They both execute the loop body as long as the control command returns a true value. `for` has two forms. The easier one resembles its C counterpart. A simple example illustrates the first form:

```
for ( k=1 ; k<=9 ; k+= 2 )                    Like FOR K = 1 TO 9 STEP 2 in BASIC
```

This form also consists of three components; the first component initializes the value of k, the second checks the condition with every iteration, while the third sets the increment used for every iteration.

16.15.1 Creating Email Addresses from `/etc/passwd`

We have here an interesting application which uses the `for` loop, the `split()` function and the one-line conditional. We'll use them to generate email addresses using the GCOS field (the fifth) of `/etc/passwd`. Let's first view a few lines of the password file:

```
henry:!:501:100:henry higgins:/home/henry:/bin/ksh
julie:x:508:100:julie andrews:/home/julie:/bin/ksh
steve:x:510:100:steve wozniak:/home/steve:/bin/ksh
```

The addresses have to be of the form *henry_higgins@planets.com*. The following **awk** program should do it:

```
$ cat email_create.awk
BEGIN { FS = ":" }
{ array_length = split($5, name_arr," ") ;
  fullname = "" ;
  for (x = 1 ; x <= array_length ; x++)  {
    name_arr[x] =  x < array_length ? name_arr[x] "_" : name_arr[x] ;
    fullname = fullname name_arr[x] ;
  }
  printf "%s@planets.com\n", fullname
}
```

This program extracts the GCOS field ($5) and splits it on the space to the array name_arr. **split** also returns the number of elements found, and the variable array_length stores this value. The **for** loop picks up each name from the array and concatenates it with the previous one with the _ character. This has to be done for all elements except the last one. When you run the program with the password file, you'll see properly formatted email addresses created:

```
$ awk -f email_create.awk /etc/passwd
henry_higgins@planets.com
julie_andrews@planets.com
steve_wozniak@planets.com
....
```

Note

Variable concatenation in **awk** is done by placing them side by side with one space in between; no operators are needed. To concatenate the values of x and y, use **print x y**.

16.15.2 Using **for** to Count Number of Occurrences

The second form of the **for** loop doesn't have a parallel in any known programming language except **perl**. It has an unusual syntax:

```
for ( k in array )
    commands
```

This form uses an array where k is the subscript. The subscript here is not restricted to integers, and can even be a string! This makes it very simple to display a count of the employees, grouped according to designation (the third field). You can use the string value of $3 as the subscript of the array kount[]:

```
$ awk -F"|" '{ kount[$3]++ }          Add a \ at the end of first
> END { for ( desig in kount)              2 lines when using csh
> print desig, kount[desig] }' empn.1st
g.m.      4
chairman  1
executive 2
director  4
manager   2
d.g.m.    2
```

The program here analyzes the database to group employees according to their designation and count their occurrences. The array kount[] takes as its subscript nonnumeric values like g.m., chairman, executive, and so forth. **for** is invoked in the END section to print the subscript (desig) and the number of occurrences of the subscript (kount[desig]). Note that you don't need to sort the input file to print this report!

Note

The same logic has already been implemented by using three commands in a pipeline—**cut**, **sort** and **uniq** *(9.18.1)*. That one used only a single line of code!

16.15.3 Looping with **while**

The **while** loop has a similar role to play; it repeatedly iterates the loop till the control command succeeds. For example, the previous **for** loop used for generating email addresses can be easily replaced with a **while** construct:

```
fullname = "" ; x=0 ;
while ( x++ <= array_length )  {
    name_arr[x] =  x < array_length ? name_arr[x] "_" : name_arr[x] ;
    fullname = fullname name_arr[x] ;
}
```

There are just two differences in this construct. x is set to 0 before the loop commences and its incrementing is done in the control command itself.

16.16 Conclusion

awk, like **sed**, violates the "do one thing well" philosophy that generally characterizes all UNIX tools. Although presented in this chapter as a utility filter, it's more of a programming language. There are far more features than one would ever require, reflecting not "poverty of imagination" (Kernighan makes this aspersion on the authors, of whom he himself is one), but rather a surfeit of it.

awk has a number of advantages which make it an important member of the tool kit. At the time of its entry, you didn't have regular expressions in other languages. You couldn't intermingle strings with numbers. Partly because of the absence of type declarations and initializations, an **awk** program is often a fraction of the size of its C counterpart. However, **awk** resembles C, and for large programs, it can be used as an intermediate platform to code in C. Eric Raymond has in fact written such a converter—**awk2c**.

awk has been completely overwhelmed in sheer power by **perl**—the latest and most notable addition to the UNIX tool kit for several years. There is nothing that any UNIX filter can do and which **perl** can't. In fact, **perl** is even more compact, is faster, and in every sense better than them. This chapter was prepared for you to understand **perl** better because so many of the constructs are also used there. **perl** is taken up in Chapter 20.

SUMMARY

The **awk** filter combines features of several filters. **awk** can manipulate individual fields ($1, $2, etc.) in a line ($0). It uses **sed**-type addresses and the built-in variable NR to determine line numbers.

Printing can be formatted with **printf**. The format specifiers can be used to format strings (%s), integers (%d) and floating point numbers (%f). Each print statement can be used with the shell's operators for redirection and piping.

awk uses all the comparison operators (like >, ==, <= etc.). The special operators ~ and !~ are used to match (or negate) regular expressions at specific fields. The ^ and $ are used to anchor a pattern at the beginning or end of a field rather than the line.

awk can perform numeric computation using the standard operators +, -, *, / and %. It overcomes the shell's limitation by handling decimal numbers.

Variables are used without initializing them or declaring their type. **awk** accepts x++ as a way of incrementing variables.

awk can take instructions from an external file (-f). In this case, the program must not be enclosed within quotes.

The BEGIN and END sections are used to do some pre- and post-processing work. A report header is generated by the BEGIN section, and a numeric total is computed in the END section.

You can run an **awk** command from a shell script and pass arguments to the script. These arguments are understood by **awk** as '$1', '$2' and so forth. The parameters have to be single-quoted.

The **getline** statement stops processing to take input from the keyboard. Using **getline**, **awk** can be used like a shell script in an interactive manner.

awk's built-in variables can be used to specify the field delimiter (FS), the number of fields (NF) and the filename (FILENAME). **awk** uses one-dimensional arrays where the array subscript can be a string as well.

awk has a number of built-in functions, and many of them are used for string handling. You can find the length (**length**), extract a substring (**substr**) and find the location (**index**) of a string within a larger string. The **system()** function executes a UNIX command.

The **if** statement uses the return value of its control command to determine program flow. The **else** statement is optional. **if** uses all the operators available for comparison, but additionally uses the operators || and && to handle complex conditions.

The first form of the **for** loop uses an array and can be used to count instances of occurrence using a nonnumeric subscript. The other form resembles its C counterpart. The **while** loop repeats a set of instructions as long as its control command returns a true value.

perl is better than **awk**.

SELF-TEST

16.1 What is the difference between **print** and **print $0**?

16.2 What is wrong with this statement?

```
printf "%s %-20s\n", $1, $6 | sort
```

16.3 Select every alternate line of a file starting with the first line.

16.4 Select those people from emp.lst *(15.1)* who were born either in September or December.

16.5 Locate lines longer than 100 and smaller than 150 characters.

16.6 Find out the total space usage of files in the current directory.

16.7 Calculate from emp.lst the average pay, and store it in a variable.

16.8 Use a **for** loop to center the output of the command **echo "DOCUMENT LIST"**, where the page width is 55 characters.

EXERCISES

16.1 Display from /etc/passwd a list of users and their shells for those using the Korn shell or bash. (The shell is specified in the seventh field).

16.2 List the users from /etc/passwd who don't have a password. Assume that the password field is null for these users.

16.3 Find out the next available UID in /etc/passwd after ignoring all system users placed at the beginning and up to the occurrence of the user nobody.

16.4 How do you delete all blank lines (including those that contain spaces) from a file?

16.5 Display a recursive listing of the files in your home directory that have been last modified on January 6 of the current year at the 11th hour.

16.6 Generalize the sequence in question 16.5 so that the date and time can be supplied externally to a script.

16.7 The **tar** command on your system can't back up files that have more than 100 characters in the pathname. How can you use **find** and **awk** to generate a list of such files?

16.8 Print the next available UID in /etc/passwd.

16.9 Split empn.1st so that lines are saved in two separate files depending on whether the salary exceeds 100,000 dollars.

16.10 Invert the name of the individual in empn.1st so that the last name occurs first.

16.11 Frame an **awk** sequence that prints the total of a specific column from the data that's supplied to it as standard input. The column number should be passed as an argument to **awk**. For instance, **ls -l |** *program_name* **5** should print the fifth column of the listing (the total).

16.12 Use a script to kill a process by specifying its name rather than the PID.

16.13 How can you print the last field of a line even if all lines don't contain the same number of fields? Assume the field delimiter is the **:**.

16.14 Repeat the exercise set in 16.8 (Self-Test) with a **while** loop.

16.15 List the users currently using the system along with a count of the number of times they have logged in.

KEY TERMS

control command *(16.14)*   positional parameter *(16.9)*

## CHAPTER 17

Customizing the Environment

Interaction with the operating system takes a significant chunk of the user's time. One has to constantly change directories, list files, edit and compile programs and repeat previous commands. Users might like to use shortcuts if they were available or could be devised. Incorrect or inconvenient environmental settings can also make life difficult for the UNIX programmer or administrator. As a user, you'll surely want to establish a pleasant environment for yourself. Though not realized by many people, UNIX is second to none in environment control.

This chapter focuses on the environment-related features of the shell—in fact, four shells. UNIX can be highly customized by manipulating the settings of the shell alone. Commands can be made to change their default behavior. You can recall, edit and reexecute previous commands. You can devise shortcuts to commands or make the shell complete commands and filenames for you. You can also make these settings permanent so they are always available when you log in, and in your shell scripts. The degree of customization possible depends mainly on the shell you use. After reading this chapter, you may want to select your shell.

Objectives

- Understand the general environment-related features of the Bourne, Korn, bash and C shells. *(17.1)*
- Learn the significance of the *environment variables. (17.2 and 17.3)*
- Use *aliases* to shorten command line sequences. *(17.4)*
- Use the *history* feature to recall, edit and reexecute previous commands. *(17.5)*
- Use the **vi**- and **emacs**-like *in-line editing* facilities available in the Korn shell and bash. *(17.6)*
- Use the filename and command name *completion* features of the Korn shell and bash. *(17.7)*
- Protect your files from accidental overwriting with noclobber and accidental logging out with ignoreeof. *(17.8.1 and 17.8.2)*
- Use the ~ (tilde) to represent the home directory. *(17.8.3)*
- Execute a shell script without spawning a sub-shell using the . and **source** commands. *(17.9.1)*
- Configure the startup files to execute instructions on login or starting a sub-shell. *(17.9.3 to 17.9.6)*

17.1 Which Shell?

In the previous chapters, we've often faced situations when a command would work in one shell but not in another. We sometimes had to use the \ with some of these commands (like **echo** and **sed**) to make things work. This represents a different form of fragmentation where a command behaves in different ways—even within the same system. This can happen primarily due to these reasons:

- You are actually using a shell's internal command without knowing it. Every shell has its own set of internal commands, and a command in one shell often doesn't behave in an identical manner in another.
- The settings of the common environmental parameters are different in the different shells.
- The shell interferes with your work and doesn't let you run the command. You have already encountered situations which required you to enter a \ before pressing *[Enter]*.

The shell is the primary agency that determines your environment—and consequently the comfort level that you can hope to achieve. The modern shells like the Korn shell and bash are feature-rich and highly customizable. You'll have a headstart over others if you select one of them as your login shell. However, people do have their own favorite shells and often stick to the C shell because it was the first shell to offer certain features which were later incorporated into the modern shells. It's the history substitution feature that keeps the C shell alive today.

You can ask the system administrator to set your login shell, or if your system supports the **chsh** command, you can do that yourself. Let's select Korn as our login shell:

```
$ chsh
Password: ********
Changing the login shell for henry
Enter the new value, or press return for the default
Login Shell [/bin/csh]: /bin/ksh                              Use this shell!
$ _
```

The command changes the last field of /etc/passwd to /bin/ksh which the system administrator would otherwise have done either manually or with **usermod**:

```
henry:x:501:100:henry blofeld:/home/henry:/bin/ksh
```

Before you embark on customizing your environment, just make sure you know the shell you are using by issuing this command:

```
$ echo $SHELL
/bin/ksh
```

In this chapter, we'll present the environment-related features of the following shells:

- The Bourne shell (sh), the first shell of the UNIX system.
- The C shell (csh) introduced by Berkeley as a superior interpreter but an inferior programming language.
- The *ksh93* version of the Korn shell (ksh)—a vastly superior shell compared to the other two. If you don't have this version on your system, then download a free

version for noncommercial use from *http://www.kornshell.com* and place it in /bin (after renaming the existing one). However, most of the Korn shell's features discussed in this chapter are also available in the earlier version—*ksh88*—which could be in your system. The "Tip" in Section 17.7.1 shows the technique of finding out the version number of your Korn shell.

- bash, the Bourne Again shell (bash)—the standard shell used by Linux systems and comparable to Korn in power. bash is also available free for use on other flavors of UNIX.

Table 17.1 presents the comparative features of the shells that we'll consider in this chapter. Each shell is presented in its own section, and a section often presents the common features of two or more shells.

TABLE 17.1 *Comparative Features of the Shells*

Feature	sh	csh	ksh	bash
Pathname	/bin/sh	/bin/csh	/bin/ksh	/bin/bash
Defining local variable *var*	*var=value*	set *var=value*	*var=value*	*var=value*
Defining environment variable *var*	As above, then export *var*	setenv *var value*	export *var=value*	export *var=value*
Displaying environment variables	export	setenv	export	export
Aliases	—	Offered	Offered	Offered
Defining alias *name*	—	alias *name value*	alias *name=value*	alias *name=value*
Command history and substitution	—	Offered	Offered	Offered
Extracting arguments of previous commands	—	Offered	—	Offered
Truncating pathnames	—	Offered	—	Offered
In-line command editing	—	—	Offered	Offered
Filename completion	—	Offered	Offered	Offered
Toggling between directories with cd -	—	—	Offered	Offered
Shortcut to home directory with cd ~*user*	—	Offered	Offered	Offered
Command to run script without creating a sub-shell	.	source	.	. or source
Login file	.profile	.login	.profile	.bash_profile, .profile or .bash_login
Environment file	—	.cshrc	Determined by ENV (often .kshrc)	.bashrc or determined by BASH_ENV
Logout file	—	.logout	—	.bash_logout

Note

Though each shell is taken up in its own section, a lot of conceptual detail is found in the introductory material of each topic as well as the Bourne shell-specific sections. This has been done to avoid redundancy of the information presented. You must read these sections even if you are using a different shell and would like to read only its specific section.

17.2 Environment Variables

The UNIX system is controlled by a number of special shell variables *(8.11.1)*. Some are set during the boot sequence and some after logging in. When you start a new sub-shell, some of these variables are inherited by the sub-shell from its parent. In this section, we'll discuss the significance of these **environment variables** or *system variables* and also learn to alter them to suit our convenience.

Environment variables are different in scope from simple (local) shell variables; they are available globally (are *exported*). This means that they are visible in the user's total environment—the sub-shells that run shell scripts, mail commands and editors. The major environment and special variables for the shells considered in this text are classified in Table 17.2.

TABLE 17.2   *Predefined System Variables*

sh	csh	ksh	bash	Significance
HOME	home	HOME	HOME	Home directory—the directory a user is placed on logging in
PATH	path	PATH	PATH	List of directories searched by shell to locate a command
LOGNAME	user	LOGNAME	USER or LOGNAME	Login name of user
MAIL	mail	MAIL	MAIL	Absolute pathname of user's mailbox file
MAILCHECK	mail	MAILCHECK	MAILCHECK	Mail checking interval for incoming mail
—	history	—	HISTSIZE	Number of commands saved in memory
—	savehist	HISTSIZE	HISTFILESIZE	Number of commands saved in history file
—	Always .history	HISTFILE	HISTFILE	History file
TERM	term	TERM	TERM	Type of terminal
—	cwd	PWD	PWD	Absolute pathname of current directory
CDPATH	cdpath	CDPATH	CDPATH	List of directories searched by **cd** when used with a nonabsolute pathname
PS1	prompt	PS1	PS1	Primary prompt string
PS2	Always ?	PS2	PS2	Secondary prompt string
SHELL	shell	SHELL	SHELL	User's login shell and one invoked by programs having shell escapes
—	Always .cshrc	ENV	BASH_ENV	Environment file used when running a sub-shell

17.2.1 Using Variables in the Bourne, Korn and bash Shells

The **set** statement displays a complete list of all variables—both simple and environment *(1.7.5)*. It's the **env** command (or **export** statement) that shows only the environment variables. A concise list is displayed here for the Bourne shell:

```
$ env
CDPATH=.:...:$HOME
HOME=/home/romeo
LOGNAME=romeo
MAIL=/var/mail/romeo
MAILCHECK=60
PAGER=/usr/bin/more
PATH=/bin:/usr/bin:/usr/dt/bin:/home/romeo/bin:.
PWD=/home/romeo/project5
PS1='$ '
SHELL=/bin/sh
TERM=ansi
....
```

By convention, environment variables are defined in uppercase so you can define your own variables in lowercase. The output also shows the way variables are defined or reassigned. For instance, this is how you can change your terminal type:

```
$ TERM=vt220
$ _
```

Can a variable be defined at the prompt like this and still be made available in a shell script? Yes, that's true for some variables like TERM, but what about this assignment?

```
x=5                                                              x is a local variable
```

The value of x here is not available globally but only in the current shell. However, when you **export** it, it is converted into an environment variable:

```
export x                                          x becomes an environment variable
```

The Korn shell and bash can combine the two operations in a single statement (**export x=5**). The reason why we don't use **export** with the variables displayed by **env** (and many of the ones shown by **set**) is that the job has already been done before. When you log in, the system variables are exported by one or more startup scripts run by the login shell. In Section 19.6.1, we'll use the **export** command to see the difference made in exporting and not exporting variables.

Tip

To avoid confusion with system variables, you should define your own variables in lowercase.

17.2.2 Using Variables in the C Shell

The C shell uses different methods for assigning nonglobal and global variables. Nonglobal variables are assigned with the **set** statement:

```
% set x = 20                                    No whitespace required around =
% echo $x
20
```

The C shell doesn't require whitespace around the =; but we'll provide spaces for the sake of readability. This value of x is not available globally. To make it visible in all your shell scripts, you should use the **setenv** statement for assignment:

```
setenv x 30                                                              No =
```

setenv doesn't use the = (a mistake often committed by beginners); the variable and its value are placed side by side. We used the same variable name here with both **set** and **setenv**. So, what is the value of x?

```
% echo $x
20                                                              The local value
```

echo displays the local value. But when you use the same statement from a sub-shell, you'll get the global value:

```
% csh                                                    Creates a C sub-shell
% echo $x
30                                                            The global value
```

The local variable overrides the value of the global variable in the shell where they are both defined. However, if you define just the global one (with **setenv**), then its value is also available in the current shell. To avoid this confusion, it's better that you have separate names for local and environment variables.

The **set** statement displays all shell variables available in the current shell but not the ones available globally. There's no = symbol here; the variable and value are separated by whitespace:

```
% set
cwd       /home/julie/docs
history   100
home      /home/julie
mail      /var/mail/julie
path      (/bin /usr/bin /usr/ucb .)
prompt    %
savehist  100
shell     /bin/csh
term      AT386
user      julie
x         20                                              Shows local value
```

Note that **set** shows 20 as the value of x. We also see a number of "environment-like" variables, but they are *not* environment variables. Only the variables set with **setenv**

can truly be called environment variables. These variables are displayed by using
setenv without arguments:

```
% setenv
HOME=/home/julie
PATH=/bin:/usr/bin:/usr/ucb:.                              A different format
LOGNAME=julie
TERM=AT386
SHELL=/bin/csh
MAIL=/var/mail/julie
PWD=/home/julie/docs
USER=julie
OPENWINHOME=/usr/openwin
x=30                                                      Shows environment value
```

The output appears in the same format used by the **set** command of the other
shells. **setenv** shows the global value of x (30). (**set** shows 20—the local value.) Have
you noticed that it also shows many of the lowercase system variables—like home,
term and path—in uppercase? This is where all the confusion begins, so we must
address this issue first.

While programs like **vi** read the uppercase environment variables, the C shell
itself uses lowercase local variables for its own use. For instance, it uses path rather
than PATH to find out where a command is located. Many of these local variables have
corresponding environment variables; **echo $TERM** and **echo $term** output the same
value. On some systems, changing term and user automatically updates TERM and
USER, but the reverse is often not true. While it appears that the environment variable
is copied from its corresponding shell variable, the relationship between the two is
somewhat complex, and we'll not attempt to explain in this book.

There's one variable here whose "set" format differs from its "setenv" format; it's
path which shows a space-delimited list of directories surrounded by parentheses. The
reason behind this will be apparent after we learn to assign values to a C shell array
(Appendix A).

Note

External programs read environment variables rather than the simple shell variables. Some
of them like TERM, PATH and USER are copied from their corresponding shell variables.
Strangely enough, the C shell itself uses the lowercase variables, some of which are not available globally!

17.3   Significance of the Environment (System) Variables

The variables you see in the output of the **set**, **env**, **export** or **setenv** statements control the behavior of the system. You have encountered them on many occasions, and in
the course of your UNIX experience, you'll modify many of them. We'll first discuss
the Bourne shell, whose variables are also used by Korn and bash. Some of them are
used in the C shell as well. Irrespective of the shell you use, you must read the following section to know the significance of these variables.

17.3.1   Environment Variables of the Bourne, Korn and bash Shells

The Command Search Path (PATH)   PATH is one of the important system variables that determine whether or not you need to use an absolute pathname when executing a command. Let's see its current value:

```
$ echo $PATH
/bin:/usr/bin:/usr/dt/bin:/home/romeo/bin:.
```

This variable instructs the shell about the route it should follow to locate any executable command. We have here a list of five directories separated by a colon (:). Note that there's a singular dot at the end. This is the current directory *(6.8)*, and placing it last means that the shell will look for a command in the current directory only after the search in the previous directories fails. This has already been discussed *(2.2)*.

If you wish to include the directory /usr/xpg4/bin in your search list, you'll have to redefine this variable:

```
PATH=$PATH:/usr/xpg4/bin                          Adding old value to new value—OK
```

Note that now the new directory will be searched last—even after the current directory. This new directory is the place where Solaris places its POSIX-compliant tools. The **grep** command here behaves a little differently from the one in /bin (or /usr/bin).

Note

If there are two commands having the same name in two different directories, that command will be executed whose directory name appears first in the PATH list. That's why if you have a **cat** command in your home directory and you invoke **cat foo**, it's only **/bin/cat** that is executed and not the one in your home directory. It's assumed that the current directory occurs later than /bin in the PATH setting.

Your Home Directory (HOME) When you log in, UNIX normally places you in a directory named after your login name. This directory is called the *home* or *login* directory *(6.5.1)* and is available in the variable HOME:

```
$ echo $HOME
/home/romeo
```

A user's home directory is specified in the line pertaining to that user in /etc/passwd. This file contains a line for every user with seven fields per line. The line for this user could look like this:

```
romeo:x:208:50::/home/romeo:/bin/sh
```

The home directory is specified in the second-to-last field. When a user logs in, the **login** program reads the file *(10.4)* and sets HOME and SHELL accordingly. /etc/passwd can be edited only by the system administrator—either manually or with the **useradd** or **usermod** commands. You have to request the administrator if you desire a change of HOME.

You can change the value of HOME, but it will not change the home directory as such but only the directory that **cd** switches to when used without arguments. This happens because a simple **cd** implies **cd $HOME**.

If you want to use someone else's .xinitrc *(12.13)* because of her choice and placement of X clients, you can start X after manipulating the value of HOME:

Tip

HOME=/home/julie xinit   *In the same line*

You don't need to copy julie's .xinitrc to your directory; X automatically reads this file rather than the user's own. When the command line is preceded by a variable assignment (as above and without a ; to act as command delimiter), the value of the variable is changed only temporarily. It returns to its original value after the program completes execution.

Your Username (LOGNAME)   This variable shows your username. When you wander around in the file system, you may sometimes forget your login name. (It's strange, but it happens when you have multiple accounts!) From time to time, just make sure you know which account you logged in to:

$ **echo $LOGNAME**   *Or try* whoami
romeo

Where else will you use this variable? You can use it in a shell script which does different things depending on the user actually invoking the script.

The Pager Used by man (PAGER)   On many systems, the **man** command uses the value of the PAGER variable to determine the program that will be used to produce paged output. On modern UNIX systems, you are likely to see more as its value, but older systems show pg. If your system shows pg, and it supports **more**, you should immediately change the value of PAGER:

$ **PAGER=/usr/bin/more ; echo $PAGER**
/usr/bin/more

If your system supports **less** (as Linux systems do and use it as default for **man**), then you should use **less** instead. **less** in every way is superior to **more** (not to speak of **pg**)—and easier to use too.

Note

Some UNIX systems don't use this variable, but rather define the pager in the file /etc/default/man. If you have this file on your system, then you are likely to see an entry there like this: PAGER=/usr/bin/more. Solaris uses **more -s** if PAGER is undefined.

Mailbox Location and How Often Checked (MAIL and MAILCHECK)   The UNIX mail handling system doesn't inform the user that mail has arrived; that job has to be done by the shell. It knows the location of a user's mailbox from MAIL. This mailbox is generally /var/mail, /var/spool/mail or /usr/spool/mail (on older systems). romeo's mail is saved in /var/mail/romeo on an SVR4 system.

MAILCHECK determines how often the shell checks the file for the arrival of new mail—typically 600 seconds on a large system. If the shell finds the file modified since the last check, it informs the user with this familiar message:

```
You have mail in /var/mail/romeo
```

If romeo is running a command, he will get this message on his terminal only after the command has completed its run.

The Prompt Strings (PS1 and PS2) The shell has two prompts stored in PS1 and PS2. The primary prompt string PS1 is the one you normally see. You also know that if you continue a command to the next line, the shell responds with a >:

```
$ sed 's/STRONG/BOLD/g
> s/html/HTML/g'
```

The > is the secondary prompt string stored in PS2. Normally, PS1 and PS2 in the Bourne shell are set to the characters $ and >, respectively.

You can change the primary prompt string to C> if you find the Windows environment more reassuring:

```
$ PS1="C> "
C> _
```

While the $ is the most commonly used primary prompt string, the system administrator uses the # as the prompt. We have a little more to discuss about PS1 when we take up the Korn and bash shells *(17.3.3 and 17.3.4)*.

The Directory Search Path (CDPATH) You may be regularly visiting other directories located elsewhere in the file system. Say, for instance, you have two directories bar1 and bar2 under your home directory, and you are currently in bar1. If you have to move to bar2, you would normally use **cd ../bar2**. You can cut a few keystrokes here by first setting CDPATH:

```
CDPATH:.:..:/home/romeo/project5
```

This again is a string of three directories which the shell searches (in that sequence)—this time to look for a directory. When you use **cd bar2** from bar1, the shell will first search the current directory (.) for bar2, failing which it will search the parent directory (..). Since both bar1 and bar2 are at the same hierarchical level, it will locate it:

```
$ pwd
/home/romeo/bar1
$ cd bar2 ; pwd
/home/romeo/bar2
```

In case the shell didn't find bar2 in /home/romeo, then it would have looked in /home/romeo/project5.

Shell Used by Commands with Shell Escapes (SHELL) SHELL tells you the shell you are using. You have seen how programs like **vi**, **emacs** and **telnet** take the escape route to the shell. SHELL determines the shell these programs use. Even though **vi** uses the **:sh** command to escape to the shell, the shell that is actually invoked is determined by SHELL, and need not necessarily be the Bourne shell, which sh represents.

Like HOME, the administrator sets up your login shell in /etc/passwd when creating a user account. Just have a look at the sample line in the discussion on the HOME variable; the last field sets the value of SHELL. The **chsh** command also changes this field.

The Terminal Type (TERM) TERM indicates the terminal type that is used. Every terminal has certain characteristics that are defined in a separate control file in the directory /usr/lib/terminfo (/usr/share/lib/terminfo in Solaris). This directory contains a number of subdirectories named after the letters of the alphabet. A terminal's control file is available in a directory having a one-letter name that is the same as the first letter of the terminal name. For instance, ansi terminals use the file /usr/lib/terminfo/a/ansi.

Some utilities like the **vi** editor are terminal-dependent, and they need to know the type of terminal you are using. If TERM isn't set correctly, **vi** won't work and the display will be faulty. TERM is also important when you log on to a remote machine. Often many UNIX tools don't work or produce garbage on the screen because of the incorrect setting of TERM.

17.3.2   Special Variables of the C Shell

Though the C shell uses uppercase variables names for environment variables, you'll mostly be manipulating the values of the lowercase C shell variables. In fact, some of these variables don't have uppercase counterparts, but are required for interactive use. These variables are assigned with the **set** statement.

The Primary Prompt (prompt) The C shell stores the prompt string in the prompt variable. You normally see the % as the prompt string, but you can use **set** to customize it:

```
% set prompt = "[C>] "
[C>] _
```

The secondary prompt string is the ?, but that value is not stored in any environment variable. Moreover, prompt doesn't have an uppercase counterpart (but is nonetheless available in sub-shells!).

Using the Event Number in Prompt (!) The C shell was the first to introduce a *history* feature that allowed users to reexecute previous commands without reentering them. We'll discuss this history feature later; just let it be known that every command in the history list has an **event number** assigned to it, and you can access and execute a command from this list with this number.

Many people use this property to assign the event number to all commands. The character required is the ! but has to be escaped:

```
% set prompt = '[\!] '
[12] _
```
set prompt *is 11th command in list*

Note that the ! is hidden by a \ because it has a special significance in this shell. (We escaped it here, but later we'll get away without escaping!) Next time you enter a command, it is added to the history list, and the event number is incremented. We'll take up command history separately.

Note

We used the \ to escape the ! in the prompt definition because it was followed by a non-whitespace character (]). The C shell interprets anything following the ! as a command and tries to repeat the last command beginning with the string.

The Command Search Path (path) This is the C shell's way of representing Bourne's PATH. The path list is also displayed differently:

```
% echo $path
/bin /usr/bin /usr/lib/java/bin /usr/dt/bin
```

Unlike in Bourne, you see a space-delimited list of directories. What is even more significant is that the output of **set** shows them enclosed within parentheses as well:

```
path        (/bin /usr/bin /usr/lib/java/bin /usr/dt/bin)
```

This is actually an array of four elements. We won't go into the details of array handling, which is taken up in Appendix A. What we need to know is the way this variable is reassigned. To add /usr/xpg4/bin to the path list, we have to do this:

```
% set path = ($path /usr/xpg4/bin)
% echo $path
/bin /usr/bin /usr/lib/java/bin /usr/dt/bin /usr/xpg4/bin
```

The **setenv** command shows PATH with the same list of directories, but in Bourne-shell format *(17.2.2)*. Changing path updates PATH and vice versa.

The Mailboxes and Checking Interval (mail) The C shell combines the functions of the MAIL and MAILCHECK variables of Bourne in the mail variable. Even though the **set** option in Section 17.2.2 shows a single filename (/var/mail/julie) as the value of mail, the variable can be set to multiple file names, optionally prefixed by a number:

```
set mail = (600 /var/mail/julie /opt/Mail/julie)
```

Every 600 seconds, the shell checks the last modification times of these two files for arrival of new mail. The environment variable MAIL simply stores a single filename that is read by some external programs.

Other Variables Now let's take a brief look at some of the other variables:

cwd — This stores the current directory.
user — The name of the user logged in (Bourne's LOGNAME).

home, `cdpath`, `shell` and `term` — They have the same meaning as their uppercase counterparts of the Bourne shell. The C shell also uses `SHELL` and `TERM` as environment variables.

`history` and `savehist` — They are required by the history facility and are discussed in Section 17.5.1.

Besides these variables, there are a group of special variables that have no value but are either set or unset. They take on the form **set** *variable*. Here are four of them:

`notify` — Notifies users when a background job is completed.

`filec` — It enables filename completion and is discussed in a C shell side box in Section 17.7.2.

`noclobber` and `ignoreeof` — They are discussed in Section 17.8.1.

We have now encountered three types of C shell variables. Variables like `prompt` are set to a single value. The second type is the array which can take multiple values (like `path`). The third type doesn't take a value at all (like `noclobber`).

17.3.3   Other Environment Variables of the Korn Shell

The Korn Shell is a superset of Bourne, so all the Bourne variables that we discussed earlier apply to Korn as well. But Korn has some variables of its own too.

Current Directory in Prompt (PWD and PS1)   The Korn shell uses the PWD variable to store the pathname of the current directory. It's more useful than the `cwd` of the C shell; `$PWD` can be used in a PS1 assignment:

```
$ PS1='[$PWD] '                                          Only single quotes
[/home/romeo] _
```

Just see how the prompt changes from $ to [/home/romeo]. Now change your directory to `cgi`;

```
[/home/romeo] cd cgi
[/home/romeo/cgi] _                             Prompt reflects changed directory
```

PWD is a rather unusual variable; it is reevaluated every time the working directory changes. The prompt accordingly changes to reflect the new value of PWD. Try the same thing with `cwd` in the C Shell; it won't work. (Using aliases, it can be made to behave that way, though.)

Using Event Number in PS1 (!)   The Korn shell also supports a *history* facility that lets you recall and execute previous commands. You can set the PS1 prompt to show the current event number. This feature is borrowed from the C shell and uses the ! to signify the event number in the assignment:

```
$ PS1="[!] "                                        The \ is not required in Korn
[42] _
```

or better still, include the PWD variable to also reflect the current directory. This time, we must switch to single quotes because $PWD doesn't work in double quotes when set as a variable value:

```
$ PS1='[! $PWD] '                                    Variable evaluation within single quotes!
[43 /home/romeo/project3]
```

Every time you execute a command, the event number is incremented (here, from 42 to 43). Knowledge of the event number is quite useful because you can reexecute a previous command by referring to this number.

Other Variables There are other variables used by the Korn shell, and they may or may not appear in the **set** output:

HISTFILE and HISTSIZE are used by the command history mechanism and are
    discussed in Section 17.5.
ENV specifies the script that is executed whenever a shell is invoked. This is treated in
    Section 17.9.5.
EDITOR and VISUAL determine the mode (vi or emacs) used by the *in-line editing*
    facility. This is discussed in Section 17.6.

17.3.4   Other Environment Variables of bash

Like the Korn shell, bash is also a superset of Bourne, so many of the features described in the section on Bourne also apply to bash. bash too has some variables specific to itself.

Current Directory in Prompt (PWD and PS1) Like Korn, bash also uses the PWD variable as a substitute for the **pwd** command. We can use it in identical manner:

```
$ PS1='$PWD> '                                          Single quotes must be used!
/home/juliet> _
```

PWD is reevaluated every time your current directory changes. This means that if you change your directory, the prompt also changes:

```
/home/juliet> cd cgi                                   Prompt shows changed directory
/home/juliet/cgi> _
```

PWD is a rather unusual variable; it is reevaluated every time the working directory changes. Try using cwd in an assignment of the C shell's prompt variable; it's never reevaluated.

Using Event Number in PS1 (!) bash also supports a *history* facility, but in this respect it resembles the C shell. You can recall previous commands where each command is assigned an event number. The ! is used to signify this number, but has to be escaped so that the shell doesn't treat the string following it as a command:

```
$ PS1='<\!> '                                          The \ is required in bash
<508> _
```

You can include the PWD variable with it as well:

```
$ PS1='<\! $PWD> '
<509 /home/juliet/cgi> _
```

We used single quotes here without any problem. This is the 508th command in the history list which just got incremented in the last invocation of the PS1 assignment. Event numbers are extremely useful in calling up previous commands.

Customizing PS1 Further   bash uses a number of escape sequences to make your prompt string as informative as possible. For instance, the \h string shows the host-name of your computer:

```
$ PS1="\h> "
saturn> _                                     saturn is the machine's name
```

When you use **telnet** to get into other machines in the network, you often get confused as to where you actually are. This prompt keeps you informed at all times. If you set PS1 to include your hostname and see some other name in the prompt string, then you must be logged on to a remote machine.

There are other escape sequences you can use:

\s — Name of the shell.
\t — Current time in *HH:MM:SS* format (\T for 12-hour format).
\@ — Current time in am/pm format.
\w — Current directory relative to the home directory.
\u — The username of the current user.

Combine some of these escape sequences and you have a reasonably informative (though longish) prompt string:

```
$ PS1="\h \@ \w>"
saturn 09:55am ~/project5/cgi> _
```

The ~ (tilde) is a shorthand representation of the home directory in all shells except Bourne. The user here is in the project5/cgi directory (under the home directory). The ~ is discussed later *(17.8.3)*.

Other Variables   There are other variables used by bash:

HISTFILE, HISTSIZE and HISTFILESIZE are used by the command history
      mechanism and are discussed in Section 17.5.1.
BASH_ENV specifies the script executed whenever a shell is invoked. This is treated in
      Section 17.9.6.
USER stores the login name of the user. It's an alternative to using LOGNAME.

17.4   Aliases

All the sample shells apart from Bourne support the use of **aliases** that let you assign shorthand names for frequently used commands. This means that if **l** is an alias of

ls -lids, you might just use **l** instead of **ls -lids**. You may also want to redefine an existing command so that it is always invoked with certain options. For instance, many people customize the **ls** command to always execute **ls -xF**. Aliasing is done with the **alias** statement but is defined differently in the C shell compared to Korn and bash. The following features are common to all shells though:

- When used without arguments, **alias** displays all defined aliases.
- The **alias** statement when used with an alias name displays the definition.
- An alias is **unaliased** (definition removed) by using the **unalias** statement with the alias name.
- An alias is recursive, which means that if **a** is aliased to **b** and **b** is aliased to **c**, **a** should run **c**.

We'll now take up the aliasing features offered by the three shells. This discussion is more extensive for the C shell than for Korn and bash, but that is because Korn and bash also support *shell functions (19.10)* which are superior to aliases in every possible way. The C shell doesn't support functions, so aliases are the only way you can condense command sequences without incurring the overhead of using shell scripts.

17.4.1 Using Aliases in the C Shell

The C shell offers extensive features in its aliases, including command line arguments. The **alias** statement uses two arguments—the alias name and the alias definition. The following statement abbreviates the **ls -l** command:

```
alias l ls -l                                                    No = symbol in C shell
```

Once defined in this way, you just have to invoke **l** to execute **ls -l**. This is true even if you have an external command or built-in by that name. Now look what happens when you use the alias with some filenames:

```
$ l relaydenied.html blankdel.sh
-rwx------   1 sumit     dialout        75 May 23 16:22 blankdel.sh
-rw-r--r--   1 sumit     dialout      7899 Jun 14 20:04 relaydenied.html
```

It's tempting to think that the alias **l** has worked with two command line arguments, but it has not. It's just that the shell replaced the alias with the command it represents, and then executed the entire command line with the additional arguments. But the C shell **alias** does accept arguments, which are read into special **positional parameters** inside the alias. You must know at least these two parameters:

\!* — Represents all arguments in the command line.
\!$ — Represents the last argument in the command line.

The expressions are derived from the history mechanism which uses them with similar meanings except that it relates them to the previous command. We can use the last expression to devise an alias for finding a file:

```
alias where 'find / -name \!$ -print'                                    ! is special
```

Now, we can run this alias to locate a file, starting the search from the root directory:

```
where pearl.jpg                                    pearl.jpg accepted into !$
```

We had to escape the parameter !$ to prevent the shell from replacing it with the last argument of the previous command. Instead, \!$ provides a placeholder for the last argument of the *current* command. If you had gone along with the old maxim that single quotes protect all special characters, then here's the first deviation. They don't protect the !, only the \ does. In fact, the quotes are not required here at all.

But the quotes are surely required if you have to use the other special characters, like the |. Here's one alias that shows the listing of files, one page at a time:

```
alias lsl 'ls -l \!* | more'
```

We had to use \!* this time because the alias has to work with multiple filenames:

```
lsl 123.html thanks.ppt r*.html                              Wild cards allowed
```

If we had used \!$ here, we would have seen the listing of only the *last* filename. This alias can also be run without arguments, in which case it executes **ls -l | more**. But what happens when we run the alias **where** without arguments? You probably wouldn't have expected this, but the alias **where** looks for the *file* where. It interprets \!$ as the last word in the command line—the command or alias itself!

The C shell goes further than this and lets you access every argument individually. This feature is also derived from the history mechanism, and uses the expression \!:*n* where *n* can represent a number or a range, or even some special characters. Let's modify the **where** alias to accept a second argument that will hold the saved output:

```
alias where 'find / -name \!:1 -print > \!:2'
```

This time, the \! is followed by a : and then a number representing the position of the argument in the command line. You can use a range too; \!:3-6 represents arguments three through six. This numbering system is used by the history facility, and the complete list of these characters is provided in Section 17.5.1.

There are simple uses of aliases too. If you are visiting a directory that has a long pathname, then you can alias the complete command line itself:

```
alias cddoc cd /usr/documentation/packages
```

Or you may like to redefine the **ls** command itself to always display in multiple columns and mark executables and directories:

```
alias ls ls -xF
```

You can remove an alias by using the **unalias** command:

```
unalias where
```

The **alias** command without arguments lists all alias definitions. But, you can also use it with an argument to display a particular alias:

```
% alias where
find / -name !:1 -print > !:2                                    Doesn't show \
```

If you have no option but to use the C shell, then you must be proficient in handling aliases. Other users can simply use them as a stepping stone to learning shell functions which use the *positional parameters* $1 and $2 instead of \!:1 and \!:2. Believe it or not, C shell aliases also use conditional statements of the form *if-then-else-endif*, except that they have to be used with plenty of \s!

Note

If you are converting an external command or a built-in to an alias, you can still execute the original command by simply preceding the command with a \. That is, you can still run the **where** command, if such a command exists on your system, with **\where**.

17.4.2   Using Aliases in the Korn Shell and bash

The Korn and bash shells also use the **alias** command to precede an assignment. Any user will probably use the **ls -l** command more often than others, and if you don't have the **l** command in your system, then you can create an alias for the command:

```
alias l='ls -l'                                               = symbol required here
```

alias here requires the =, but there must not be any whitespace on either side of the =. If the value contains whitespace (as here), then it should be quoted. You can now execute **ls -l** by simply using

```
l                                                         This executes ls -l
```

We often use the **cd** command with long pathnames. If there's a sequence that you use often, then it would be sensible to convert it into an alias. Consider this alias:

```
alias intcd="cd /usr/spool/lp/interface"
```

Do these aliases accept command line arguments in the same way shell scripts do? Can we run the **l** alias with some filenames? Let's try it out:

```
$ l addbook.ldif apacheFAQ.html
-rw-r--r--   1 sumit    dialout      1555 Feb  8 14:03 addbook.ldif
-rw-r--r--   1 sumit    dialout    103485 Dec 13  1999 apacheFAQ.html
```

This works, but that is because the shell expands the alias **l** to **ls -l** and then runs **ls -l** with the two arguments. Though it appeared that we used an alias with arguments, it is not true; Korn and bash aliases don't use arguments. But if a command uses filenames as its *last* arguments, we can use this property to redefine existing commands. This is what we are going to do next.

The **cp -i** command behaves interactively when the destination file exists. Using aliases, you can make **cp** always behave interactively. Similarly, as a precautionary measure, you can also do that with **rm**:

```
alias cp="cp -i"
alias rm="rm -i"
```

Now, every time you invoke these commands, their aliased versions are executed. How can you now use the original external commands? Just precede the command with a \. This means that you have to use **\cp foo1 foo2** to override the alias.

You can display an alias definition by using **alias** with the name:

```
$ alias cp
cp='cp -i'                                                          bash output differs a little
```

You can list all aliases by using **alias** without arguments and unset an alias with the **unalias** statement. To unset the alias **cp**, use **unalias cp**.

Aliases can make a great difference to your productivity. Here are some important aliases used by the author:

```
alias ..='cd ..'
alias ...='cd ../..'
alias dial='/usr/sbin/dip -v $HOME/internet/int3.dip'
alias dialk='/usr/sbin/dip -k'
alias mailg='fetchmail && elm'
alias mails='/usr/sbin/sendmail -q'
```

Many of them are predefined, and some were defined by the author to speed up Internet activities. You'll find the **..** and **...** aliases quite useful if you use **cd ..** and **cd ../..** very often. **dial** uses the **int3.dip** script to dial the modem and log on to the ISP's computer; **dialk** kills the connection. **mailg** gets mail from the mail server and calls up the **elm** mailer if there is new mail. **mails** sends spooled mail to the outgoing server. All these features are discussed in this book, but just note how the basic Internet activities are handled using only a handful of aliases!

Tip

Do exercise some restraint when defining aliases; too much aliasing can be confusing and difficult to remember. Moreover, aliases have been entirely superseded by *shell functions (19.10)*, which offer a superior form of aliasing. Aliases are good to begin with, but eventually you'll be using shell functions.

17.5 Command History

A serious drawback of the Bourne shell is that a command has to be retyped to be reexecuted. The other three shells support a versatile **history** feature that lets you recall previous commands (even those executed in previous sessions), edit them if required and reexecute them. The shell assigns each command an **event number** and may (depending on the shell used) save all commands in a history file.

The **history** command displays the history list showing the event number of every command. A command is recalled by using this event number with a symbol like **!** or **r**. The maximum size and name of this file are determined by two shell-specific variables. The C shell and bash have similar facilities but Korn uses different symbols for the job. The history functions are summarized in Table 17.3.

17.5.1   The History Feature in C Shell and bash

Like **alias**, **history** is also a built-in command. By default, the command displays all events in its list:

TABLE 17.3   *The History Functions*

csh, bash	ksh	Significance
history 12	history -12	Lists last 12 commands
!!	r	Repeats previous command
!7	r 7	Repeats event number 7
!24:p	—	Prints without executing event number 24
!-2	r -2	Repeats command before last
!ja	r ja	Repeats last command beginning with ja
!?size?	—	Repeats last command with embedded string size
!find:s/pl/java	r find pl=java	Repeats last **find** command after substituting java for pl
^mtime^atime	r mtime=atime	Repeats previous command after substituting atime for mtime
!cp:gs/doc/html	—	Repeats last **cp** command after globally substituting html for doc
!! | sort	r | sort	Repeats previous command but after piping it to **sort**
!find | sort	r find | sort	Repeats last **find** command but after piping it to **sort**
cd !$	cd $_	Changes directory to last argument of previous command ($_ used by bash also)
rm !*	—	Removes files expanded from all arguments of previous command
vi !:2	—	Runs **vi** with second argument of previous command
grep http !30:4	—	Runs **grep http** with fourth argument of event number 30
more !:$	—	Runs **more** on last argument of previous command (: not necessary)
!:0 foo	—	Runs previous command with argument foo
echo !$:h	—	Displays head of previous command's pathname
echo !$:t	—	Displays tail (filename) of previous command's pathname
echo !$:r	—	Removes extension from previous command's filename

```
12 % history
..... lines not shown .......
 8    grep "William Joy" uxadv??
 9    cd
10    pwd
11    doscp *.awk /dev/fd1135ds18
12    history
```

Each command is shown prefixed with the event number. Every command you run gets added to the list. The last command shows the **history** command itself. The list can be pretty big, so you can use **history** with a numeric argument to restrict the size. For instance, **history 7** shows only the last seven commands.

These shells can save commands both in memory and a file. They use one variable to determine the size of the history list in memory and yet another to determine the maximum size of the saved file. This distinction is shown below:

csh	bash	Significance
$HOME/.history	$HOME/.bash_history	File containing history list
savehist	HISTFILESIZE	Size of saved history list
history	HISTSIZE	Size of history list in memory

Otherwise, the C shell and bash have virtually identical commands and statements to handle the history facility. You won't normally change the history file, but you can override its default size:

```
set savehist = 1000                          Saves in .history — C shell
HISTFILESIZE=1000                       Saves in .bash_history — bash
```

Likewise, you can also set the number of commands to be saved in memory:

```
set history = 500                          Saves in memory — C shell
HISTSIZE=500                               Saves in memory — bash
```

Tip

Make this alias definition for displaying only the last 15 commands:

```
alias h 'history 15'                                          C shell
alias h='history 15'                                            bash
```

C Shell

The history facility is not activated unless the history variable is set. If it is not set, then only the last command is saved, that too only in memory.

BASH Shell

Unlike in the C shell, the history file is determined by the setting of the HISTFILE variable. If it is not set, then $HOME/.bash_history is used.

Repeating Previous Commands (!) The ! command is used to repeat previous commands. It's the key symbol of the history mechanism. It can be used with a positive or a negative integer, a string or with another !. A world of opportunities opens up when you start using this symbol, as you'll see in the following pages.

To repeat the last command, you have to use ! twice:

    !!   *Repeats previous command*

You can also repeat any command in the history list by using ! with the event number. There must not be any whitespace between the ! and the event number:

    % !11   *Repeats event number 11*
    11 doscp *.awk /dev/fd1135ds18

The command line is displayed and executed. Working like this, you might execute a wrong command (like **rm**), so by using a **modifier** (or operator) p (print), you can display the command without executing it:

    % !11:p
    11 doscp *.awk /dev/fd1135ds18

The **doscp** command copies files from disk to diskette and vice versa. You should make sure of what you are doing by using the :p modifier first. If this is the command line you want to execute, you can now use !! to run it.

You can use relative addressing for commands you executed very recently. Recall the command used before the last one by using a negative number with !:

    !-2   *No space between ! and -*

You probably won't remember the event numbers of the commands except for the immediately preceding two or three, but you could at least remember that the command started with a specific letter or a string. For instance, if you remember that the last command name beginning with v was the **vi** command, you can use ! with either v or vi:

    !v   *Repeats last command beginning with v*

If matching a string at the beginning won't serve your purpose, you can match an embedded string. Just provide a ? on both sides of the pattern. This command matches xvf *anywhere* in any previous command:

    !?xvf?   *Runs last command having xvf embedded*

tar uses the xvf options to extract files from a floppy and cvf to write to one. Calling up the last **tar** command with **!tar** is quite risky as it might overwrite your floppy when you actually wanted to restore from it. **!?xvf** is certainly a safer bet. Yes, it might execute the wrong command with these options, but then no other command uses the xvf options anyway. Note that the second ? is not required if you follow the string with an *[Enter]*.

Searching for an embedded pattern is not possible in the Korn shell. There are many more commands that perform substitution and extract the components of a pathname. They are taken up next.

Tip   Follow the ! with a string to recall the last command beginning with the string. Enclose the string with ? on either side to execute any command that has the string embedded in the command line (including at the beginning). The second form is more useful when you have used a command repeatedly with various options; a search for the command argument is what is needed here. If you feel that using history in these ways might ruin your system, then use **:p** to produce a simple display before you decide to repeat the command with **!!**.

Substitution in a Previous Command (:s)   There are a number of modifiers that enable you to make simple and noninteractive editing operations. Using the :s modifier, you can rerun the previous **grep** command, but after replacing William with Bill:

```
!grep:s/William/Bill
```
: acts as the delimiter

To use **sed** jargon, this substitution is not global; only the first occurrence of the string is replaced. Global substitution is achieved with the g parameter (also used by **sed**). The following command repeats the last **cp** command after globally replacing all instances of doc with bak:

```
!cp:gs/doc/bak
```
Not possible in Korn

To make a substitution in the immediately previous command, you have a shortcut available. There's no need to use !, just use the ^ (caret) as the delimiter of strings (no regular expressions here!). Restore the original command line partially by replacing bak with doc in this way:

```
^bak^doc
```
Substitutes first instance only

Using Arguments of the Previous Command (!$ and !*)   We create a directory with **mkdir foo** and then change to it with **cd foo**. The C shell and bash use a special pattern which can abbreviate our command lines; it's the !$. This expression signifies the last argument of the previous command. We have already used it in our aliases, but here we'll use the !$ as a shorthand feature to represent the directory used by the previous command:

```
mkdir programs
cd !$
```
Changes directory to programs

To consider another example, if you have edited a shell script **cronfind.sh** with **vi** or **emacs**, you can execute this file by simply entering this:

```
!$
```
Executes cronfind.sh

What better way can you imagine of executing a shell or **perl** script that you just edited with **vi** or **emacs**!

You can also use the !* to signify *all* arguments of the previous command. We have used it in our aliases as well. So if you made a check to find out whether these files exist:

```
ls runj count.pl script.sh
```

you can remove them by using !* as the argument to **rm**:

```
rm !*                                          This is rm runj count.pl script.sh
```

This facility is not available in the Korn shell. There's a limitation here, of course. If you used **ls -l** instead and then used the **rm** command, **rm** would have run with the -l argument as well and reported an error.

Using History Modifiers (:*n*) Now, suppose you have just listed some files with this command:

```
ls runj count.pl script.sh add.sh binary.pl
```

You can use the :*n* word modifier to fetch individual arguments of the previous command. The value of *n* can begin from 0 (the command) and optionally accept both a range and an * to retrieve up to the last argument. You can also use the ^ and $ to represent the first and last argument, respectively. Table 17.4 shows how you can edit one or more of these files with **vi**.

The :*n* word specifier is not restricted to the last command alone. You can run a command of a certain event with selected arguments of another event. We have accessed command arguments, but to access a previous command (without the argument), we need to use the modifier :0 (zero). For instance, this one

```
!com:0 !47:1-3
```

TABLE 17.4   *Using History Modifiers*
                 (Last Command: `ls runj count.pl script.sh add.sh binary.pl`*)*

Command with History Modifier	Actually runs
`vi !:1`	`vi runj`
`vi !^`	Same as above (: not needed)
`vi !:2-3`	`vi count.pl script.sh`
`vi !:3-$`	`vi script.sh add.sh binary.pl`
`vi !:3*`	Same as above
`vi !*`	`vi` with all arguments
`vi !:3-`	`vi script.sh add.sh` (excludes last argument)
`vi !$`	`vi binary.pl` (: not needed)

runs the command beginning with com (possibly intending to use **compress**) with the first three arguments of event 47. You can also run the previous command but with arguments from another command:

!:0 !-2:*   *!:0 is previous command without arguments*

This extracts only the command from the previous command line and runs it with all arguments of the command prior to the previous one. It takes time to get used to these cryptic symbols, but this is probably the only reason people still use the C shell today.

BASH Shell

Apart from !$, bash also uses the $_ to represent the last argument of the last command—the same variable used by the Korn shell.

Tip

If you have performed some action on a group of files, you can run another command on the same set of files by using the special symbol !*. If you want to use only the last filename, then use !$. You can also extract only the command using the modifier :0.

Pathname Modifiers (:h, :t and :r) There are three important operators you can use to extract sections from a pathname. If you have used one in a previous command, then you can run the same (or a different) command with a derivative of this pathname.

Let's consider the :h (head) modifier first. This extracts the head of a pathname, which means that if you have just displayed a listing of a directory like this:

ls /var/spool/lp/admins

you can repeat the process for its parent directory, or even switch to this directory:

ls !$:h   *# Runs* ls /var/spool/lp
cd !$:h   *# Runs* cd /var/spool/lp

The :t (tail) operator extracts just the base filename. This lets you provide an extension to a file when copying it from another directory:

% **cat /etc/skel/profile**
    ... Displays file contents ...
% **cp !$!$:t.txt**   *Copies to* profile.txt
cp /etc/skel/profile profile.txt   *Message from system*

The :r (root) operator drops a file's extension and fetches the rest. This feature is useful in running Java programs:

% **javac hello.java**   *Compiles* hello.java
hello.java compiled successfully
% **java !$:r**   *Runs* java hello
java hello

There's one more modifier, `:e`, which extracts just the extension from a filename. While both the C shell and bash use these modifiers with arguments of previous commands, the C shell also makes them work with variables:

```
% set domain=planets.com
% echo $domain:e                                          C shell only
com
```

There are four important history features of the C shell and bash that are yet unmatched by the Korn shell:

- You can search for an embedded string (as in `!?xvf?`) in the history file. Korn can only search for a command beginning with the string.
- You can make a global substitution in a previous command (as in **`!cp:gs/doc/bak`**). Korn can only repeat a previous command *beginning* with a string and substitute only the *first* occurrence in a line.
- You can use a special notation `!*` to signify all arguments of the previous command and the modifier `:n` to access arguments selectively. Korn can only access the last argument.
- Korn doesn't also offer pathname modifiers but has better pattern matching schemes *(19.8.1)*.

Note

17.5.2 The History Feature in the Korn Shell

The **history** command run without arguments lists the last 16 commands maintained in the history file. You can list the last five commands by using –5 as an argument:

```
$ history -5                                      Note the - symbol this time
36 exit
37 alias l='ls -l'
38 doscp *.pl a:
39 fc -l
40 history -5                            Also includes command invoked to obtain list
```

The commands are saved in the file defined in the HISTFILE variable. If it is not set, then $HOME/.sh_history is used. The number of commands stored in the event list is determined by HISTSIZE. By default, it saves the last 128 commands, but you can set it to a large number to store commands of multiple login sessions:

```
HISTSIZE=1200                                     Will store last 1200 commands
```

Every time you execute a command, the event number is incremented. Knowledge of the event number is quite useful because you can reexecute a previous command by referring to this number.

Repeating Previous Commands (r) Korn uses the **r** command to repeat previous commands. When used without arguments, **r** repeats the last command:

```
r                                   Repeats previous command — same as r -1
```

You can repeat other commands using **r** with the event number as argument:

$ **r 38**   *Space between r and 38*
38 doscp *.pl a:

There are times when you run two commands alternately but repeatedly (a **cc** and a **vi** command for compiling and editing a C program, for instance). You can call up each command alternately by using relative addressing to execute the command used prior to the last one:

r -2   *Alternates function*

Sometimes, accessing a command with an event number is an impossible task—especially in calling up old events. You can access a command with a string, and the command must *begin* with that string (embedding not permitted). For instance, if you remember that the last command name beginning with v was the **vi** command, you can use **r** with either v or vi:

r v   *Repeats last command beginning with* v

Substitution in Previous Command (=) You'll sometimes reexecute a previous command but only after making a replacement. Use the **r** command with the command name, and follow the command line with the old string, an = sign and the new string. So, if you want to repeat the previous **cp** command, but this time only on the **awk** programs, replace the string pl by awk:

r cp pl=awk

However, this substitution is made only for the *first* occurrence in a line; two or more substitutions are not permitted. (The C shell and bash allow this too.) If you face situations that require global substitution or extensive editing, then you should use in-line command editing instead. This is discussed in the next section.

Tip

If you are a programmer, you'll find the feature of accessing previous commands with a substring extremely useful—especially when you are repeatedly editing and compiling programs. For instance, if you alternately use the command **vi appl.java** and **javac appl.java**, you need to explicitly invoke the commands only once. Subsequently, you can go on using **r v** and **r j** alternately if you are using Korn, and **!v** and **!j** for the other shells. There's no need to remember their line numbers!

Using Last Argument of Previous Command ($_) We often run several commands on the same file, and this file is often the last argument. Instead of specifying the filename every time, we can now use $_ to represent the last argument of the last command. For example, if you have just used **vi applet.java**, you can call up **javac** with $_ to compile the program:

vi applet.java $_ *becomes* applet.java

```
javac $_                                                    Executes javac applet.java
```

How does one run a shell script that's just been edited with **vi foo**? Simple, use $_ to execute foo:

```
$_                                                    Runs last argument of last command
```

Unlike the C shell, the Korn shell doesn't have too many history features, but the ones discussed so far are adequate for most tasks. It more than compensates for this deficiency by offering in-line editing instead. **vi** or **emacs** users might also like to use commands like */pattern* or *[Ctrl-r] pattern* to call back previous commands. bash and Korn support this feature and it is discussed next.

17.6 In-Line Command Editing in Korn Shell and bash

Korn and bash provide **vi**- and **emacs**-like capabilities of editing the command line—both of the current command and its predecessors. This feature is known as **in-line editing**. The basic features of both editors are built into these shells. Before you can use these capabilities, you have to make one of the following settings:

```
set -o vi                                                    Only one, but not both
set -o emacs
```

You can switch off either mode by using the +o option instead. Now, let's see how the shell's **vi**-like editing capabilities help enhance command line editing. If you know **emacs**, then you'll know how to adapt yourself to this environment. A working subset of their editing commands drawn from Chapters 4 and 5 is listed in Table 17.5.

Now, let's say you notice a mistake in the command line. Since you have **vi**-editing enabled, you need no longer erase all previous text to take the cursor to that point. First press *[Esc]* to take you to **vi**'s "Command Mode." You can now use all **vi** navigation commands to move across a line (with ^, **$**, **b** and **e**)—using a repeat factor too, if necessary and relevant.

You can also invoke the commands used to enter the "Input Mode"—like **i**, **a**, **A**, and so forth. You can delete a character with **x** and a word with **dw**. You can even put this word elsewhere in the line (or even in a different line!) with **p** or **P**. The command can now be executed by hitting *[Enter]*.

The **k** command, which in **vi** takes the cursor up, calls up previous commands here (but only after first hitting *[Esc]*). And, since the repeat factor applies here too, you can also use **5k** to present the fifth-most recent command (barring the present). If that's not the command you are looking for, then use **j** to show the next command.

You can use **vi**'s search techniques to call previous commands. Even though the search is in the reverse direction, you'll have to use the */pattern* sequence—with regular expressions too if required:

```
/find[Enter]                                          Locates last occurrence of string find
/^find                                                       Locates last find command
```

You can use *?pattern* only when you have already conducted a search backward and now want to conduct a forward search. You can repeat the search by pressing **n** repeat-

TABLE 17.5 *Useful In-Line Editing Commands*

vi *Command*	**emacs** *Command*	*Action*
i	—	Inserts text
A	—	Appends text at end of line
j	[Ctrl-n]	Next command
k	[Ctrl-p]	Previous command
l	[Ctrl-f]	One character right
h	[Ctrl-b]	One character left
w	[Alt-f]	One word forward
b	[Alt-b]	One word back
0 (zero)	[Ctrl-a]	Beginning of line
$	[Ctrl-e]	End of line
x	[Delete] or [Ctrl-d]	Deletes character
dw	[Alt-d]	Deletes word
D	[Ctrl-k]	Deletes till end of line
/pat	[Ctrl-r] pat	Gets last command containing pattern *pat*
?pat	—	Searches forward for command containing pattern *pat*
n	[Ctrl-r]	Repeats search in same direction of initial search
N	—	Repeats search in opposite direction of initial search
u	[Ctrl-_]	Undoes last editing instruction

edly. If you overshoot, come back with **N**. Edit the line and run it again. Now, isn't this something!

We have claimed that the in-line editing feature more than compensates for the lack of the history modifiers that make the C shell so popular. A proficient **vi** (or **emacs**) user will easily exploit these editing facilities to run a command with selected arguments of previous commands. If you remember having executed the command **vi foo1 foo2 foo3 foo4**, then you can easily run the **compress** command with some or all of these arguments. Press *[Esc]*, search for the command with **/vi**, change vi to compress with **cw**, and hit *[Enter]*. If you need to delete the last argument, move to the fourth argument with **4w**, and then press **dw**. It's as simple as that!

KORN Shell

Apart from using **set -o**, the Korn shell can also enable command line editing by setting either of these two variables:

```
EDITOR=/usr/bin/vi
VISUAL=/usr/bin/emacs
```

Strangely enough, the pathname doesn't have to be correct; it doesn't matter whether VISUAL is set to /usr/bin/vi or abcd/vi. The shell first looks at VISUAL and then the EDITOR variable for a string that *ends* with vi or emacs and enables the mode accordingly.

BASH Shell

bash lets you use the cursor motion keys to recall the previous commands in "DOSKEY"-style. Neither **set -o** command can be used for this mode to function. If you have used **set -o vi**, then turn off the setting with **set +o vi**.

17.7 Filename Completion

Korn and bash support a feature called **filename completion**, which has been enhanced in the modern versions of these shells to support

- Completion of a filename used as an argument to a command.
- Completion of the command name itself.

This means that you may not have to enter the complete command or filename—even for the first time. Enter just a part of it and let the shell complete it to the extent it can. If you have used a similar facility in **emacs** *(5.10)*, then you are on familiar terrain. Most versions of the C shell support only completion of a filename but not of a command. The key sequences required for completion work are listed in Table 17.6 for the three shells.

17.7.1 Filename and Command Completion in the Korn Shell

The discussions on the Korn shell are drawn up with reference to the *ksh93* version which supports both features. If you are using an older version, you won't be able to use the command completion feature. Before using this facility, activate the completion mechanism by entering any of the commands that enable **vi**-like command editing:

```
set -o vi
EDITOR=vi                                          Only vi-like editing permitted
VISUAL=vi
```

To use the completion feature, we need just two commands; both require the *[Esc]* key. Let's say that you have the following files beginning with p:

```
$ ls -x p*
passwd              patlist              pattern.lst
planets.local.sam   planets.master.sam   planets.reverse.sam
problems.sam        profile.sam          pstree.sam
```

T A B L E 17.6 *Filename and Command Name Completion Characters*

	csh	ksh	bash
Completing filename	*[Esc]*	*[Esc]* \	*[Alt-/]* or *[Tab]*
Displaying file list	*[Ctrl-d]*	*[Esc]* =	*[Ctrl-x]/* or *[Tab][Tab]*
Completing command name	—	*[Esc]* \	*[Alt-!]* or *[Tab]*
Displaying command list	—	*[Esc]* =	*[Tab][Tab]*

You now want to edit the file planets.master.sam with **vi**. Enter vi, and then enter just a part of the string—only up to pl initially. After that, hit the sequence *[Esc]*\:

$ **vi pl***[Esc]*\   *Becomes* planets.

This command line immediately expands to vi planets. (including the dot). The shell found that there were three files in the current directory which begin with pl, but they also have planets. as their common string. Now, you can enter an m and use *[Esc]*\ again:

$ vi planets.**m***[Esc]*\   *Becomes* vi planets.master.sam

Only one of the three files has an m after the common string planets. (the second one). You'll find the shell has completed the command line for you. You entered just three characters and pressed *[Esc]*\ twice—that's all! Filename completion is depicted in Fig. 17.1.

There's another way of using the completion feature. Instead of asking the shell to complete the command line for you, you can ask for the file list that matches the entered string. In this case, you have to use *[Esc]*=. When you repeat the previous exercise using this feature, this is what you'll see:

$ **vi pl***[Esc]*=
1) planets.local.sam
2) planets.master.sam
3) planets.reverse.sam
113 $ vi pl

F I G U R E 17.1   *Filename Completion in the Korn Shell*

```
$ vi pl▌

    [Esc]\

$ vi planets.▌

    m[Esc]\

$ vi planets.master.sam▌


    CONTEXT

    $ ls -x p*
    passwd              patlist             pattern.lst
    planets.local.sam   planets.master.sam  planets.reverse.sam
    problems.sam        profile.sam         pstree.sam
```

The shell this time shows three files with the cursor sitting on the last character of the incomplete command line. Now that you have three filenames in front of you, you know what to do; repeat what you did previously. Press *[Esc]* to expand the string to planets., then enter an m and press *[Esc]* once again. The job's done.

Filename completion has now been extended in *ksh93* to work on command names too. Say you want to uncompress a file with the **uncompress** command. Enter the first three letters and then use both sequences (*[Esc]* and *[Esc]=*) in turn. When you use it like this:

unc*[Esc]*

the shell expands unc to uncompress. The command is completed by using a total of five keystrokes. If you had pressed *[Esc]=* instead, you would have seen a single file-name matching the pattern. Try the exercise using a shorter string to obtain a list.

Tip   To know the version of your Korn shell, enable command line editing mode using the techniques stated at the beginning of this section and then press *[Ctrl-v]*. You should see something like this—Version 12/28/93f. This is *ksh93*.

17.7.2   Filename and Command Completion in bash

The technique used in Korn also works in bash. But bash has a superior completion feature that can complete hostnames and email addresses also. Here, we'll confine ourselves to filename and command completion using different key sequences that require in-line editing (with **set -o vi**) to be *disabled* rather than enabled. Let's use the same files that we used with Korn—but those beginning with pl:

```
$ ls -x pl*
planets.local.sam     planets.master.sam     planets.reverse.sam
```

To edit the file planets.master.sam, enter just the unique part of the string—only up to pl. After that, use *[Alt-/]*:

$ **vi pl***[Alt-/]*   *Becomes* planets.

bash performs filename completion by expanding pl to planets. (including the dot). Since all three files that begin with pl also have planets. as their common string, you can enter an m and use *[Alt-/]* to complete the string:

$ vi planets.**m***[Alt-/]*   *Becomes* vi planets.master.sam

Note that only one file has an m after the string planets. (the second one). We had to use three letters and press *[Alt-/]* twice to complete this filename comprising 18 characters! Filename completion is depicted in Fig. 17.2.

Instead of using **ls** to display the list, you can also let bash do the job for you. This time, you have to use a different key sequence—*[Ctrl-x]/*. Let's repeat the previous exercise but use this key sequence instead:

FIGURE 17.2   *Filename Completion in bash*

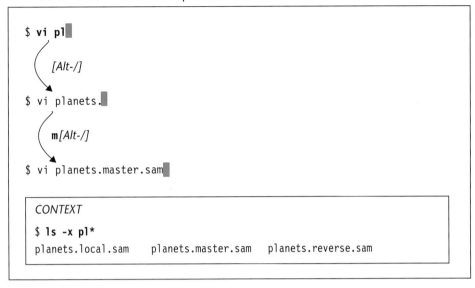

```
$ vi pl▌
        [Alt-/]

$ vi planets.▌
        m[Alt-/]

$ vi planets.master.sam▌

  ┌──────────────────────────────────────────────────────────────────┐
  │ CONTEXT                                                            │
  │ $ ls -x pl*                                                        │
  │ planets.local.sam    planets.master.sam    planets.reverse.sam    │
  └──────────────────────────────────────────────────────────────────┘
```

```
$ vi pl[Ctrl-x]/                               Release [Ctrl-x] before hitting /
planets.local.sam    planets.master.sam    planets.reverse.sam
$ vi pl
```

By looking at the list, you can figure out your next move. Press *[Alt-/]* to expand the string to planets., then enter an m and press *[Alt-/]* again. That's all that you need to do.

bash supports command name completion too. Say you want to uncompress a file with the **gunzip** command. Enter the first two letters and then use *[Alt-!]*:

```
gu[Alt-!]                                                     Requires [Shift]
```

The shell expands gu to gunzip. If you want to see all commands in the directories held in PATH that match an entered string, hit the *[Tab]* key twice after the string.

Tip

A half-documented feature of bash lets you enter the *[Tab]* key both to complete a filename or a command. Enter part of the string and press *[Tab]* once; the filename or command is completed to the extent possible. To display the list, press *[Tab]* twice. This is unquestionably the most preferred method as it doesn't matter whether in-line editing is enabled or not with **set -o vi**.

C Shell

Most versions of the C shell also support filename completion but not command name completion. The command has to exist in the current directory so that it can be treated as a file. If your version supports filename completion, then enable it with **set filec**. For completion, use *[Esc]*, and for displaying the list, use *[Ctrl-d]*.

17.8   Miscellaneous Features

Before moving on to the shell's initialization scripts, let's consider a few features which you may sometimes need to use:

- Protecting files from accidental overwriting. This feature is known as **noclobber**. Once set, you can protect your files from being overwritten with the shell's > and >> symbols.
- Preventing *[Ctrl-d]* from logging out. Users often inadvertently press *[Ctrl-d]* with intent to terminate the standard input, but end up logging out of the system. The **ignoreeof** feature provides a safety lock to prevent this.
- Using the tilde (~) as a shorthand representation of the home directory.

These features are not available in the Bourne shell. They are also implemented somewhat differently in the other shells.

17.8.1   noclobber and ignoreeof in the C Shell

The C shell uses the **set** statement with the noclobber argument to prevent accidental overwriting of files:

```
set noclobber                                   No more overwriting files with >
```

If you now redirect command output to an existing file foo, the shell will retort with a message:

```
foo: File exists.
```

To override this protection feature, you have to use the ! after the >:

```
head -5 emp.lst >! foo
```

Accidental logging out with *[Ctrl-d]* is prevented with the ignoreeof argument:

```
set ignoreeof                                   [Ctrl-d] won't log you out
```

Now, when you use *[Ctrl-d]* to terminate your session, you'll see this typical response from the shell:

```
Use "logout" to logout.
```

You now have to use the C shell's **logout** command to take you out of the session. You can also use the **exit** command.

17.8.2   noclobber and ignoreeof in Korn and bash

The **set** statement supports a -o option that must be used to take advantage of these features. To prevent you from accidentally overwriting the contents of a file, you have to use the noclobber argument in this way:

```
set -o noclobber
```
                                                              No more overwriting files with >

This means that if you redirect output to an existing file foo, the shell will retort with
a message:

```
bash: foo: cannot overwrite existing file                                        bash
ksh: foo: file already exists                                                     Korn
```

To override this protection feature, use the | after the >:

```
head -5 emp.lst >| foo
```

Accidental logging out with *[Ctrl-d]* is prevented by using the ignoreeof argument
with **set -o**:

```
set -o ignoreeof
```
                                                              [Ctrl-d] won't log you out

Now, when you use *[Ctrl-d]* to terminate your session, here's a typical response from
the shell:

```
Use 'exit' to terminate this shell
```

You now have to use the **exit** command to take you out of the session; *[Ctrl-d]* won't
do any more (unless executed repeatedly).

    A **set** option is turned off with **set +o**. To restore the noclobber feature, use
set +o noclobber. The complete list of **set**'s special options is obtained by using
set -o or **set +o** without any additional arguments.

BASH Shell

bash supports a C shell-styled **logout** command which also terminates a login
session.

17.8.3   Tilde Substitution

The ~ acts as a shorthand representation of the home directory and is used by all the
non-Bourne shells. When the ~ is followed by a login name, as below:

```
cd ~juliet
```
                                                      Effectively becomes cd $HOME/juliet

it switches to juliet's home directory. If the value of $HOME is /home/juliet/html,
then this is the directory where **cd ~juliet** switches to.

    Interestingly, the ~ when used by itself refers to the home directory. If you have
logged in as juliet, you can access the html directory under your home directory by
using **cd ~/html**. That's why we often find a configuration file like .profile referred
to both as $HOME/.profile and ~/.profile.

KORN Shell

BASH Shell

You can also toggle between your current directory and the last visited directory by using a hyphen with **cd** (**cd -**). This is like the button many TV remote units have that lets you alternate between the current and last visited channels. Here is how you use it:

```
[/home/image] cd /bin                                    Switch to /bin from /home/image
[/bin] cd -                                                      Revert to /home/image
/home/image                                                     Shell displays this
[/home/image]                                                 PS1 of current directory
```

You should now be using this command several times every day.

17.9   The Initialization Scripts

We have assigned values to many of the environment variables, defined aliases and used **set** options. These settings are applicable only for the session; they revert to their default values when the user logs out. To make these settings permanent, you'll have to place them in the system's startup scripts.

Every shell uses at least one startup script that is placed in the user's home directory—much like the AUTOEXEC.BAT file of Windows. This script is executed when the user logs in. Some shells also make use of a separate file that is run before logging out. Look in your home directory with **ls -a**, and you'll find one or more of these files:

- .profile (Bourne shell)
- .login, .cshrc and .logout (C Shell)
- .profile and .kshrc (Korn Shell)
- .bash_profile (or .profile or .bash_login), .bashrc and .bash logout (bash)

A script here can belong to one of three categories. (See also last three entries in Table 17.1):

- Login script—This is a startup script that is executed when a user logs in. The C shell uses .login, Bourne and Korn use .profile and bash uses .bash_profile as the login script.
- Environment script—This file is executed when a sub-shell is run from the login shell. It is often referred to as the **rc script**, and every shell except the Bourne shell has one (.cshrc, .kshrc and .bashrc). Strictly speaking, the Korn shell's *rc* script doesn't have to be .kshrc, but often is.
- Logout script—Only the C shell and bash use a logout script (.logout and .bash_logout) which is run before the user logs out.

In the following sections, we'll have a look at the working of these files and decide on the useful entries that one could place in them. Before that, we must be able to make a distinction between the shell that receives us at login and the one that runs our scripts. We must also learn to execute these scripts without creating sub-shells.

17.9.1   The . and source Commands

When you execute a shell script, the current shell spawns a sub-shell that executes commands in the script. Variable assignments and change of directories made in the script are not seen in the shell that ran the script. This is to be expected because changes made in a child shell are not seen in the parent *(10.2)*.

It's a different story altogether when the login shell executes the initialization files. Variables defined in these files are indeed seen in the login shell. A change of directory remains permanent even after script execution is complete. We can safely conclude that these scripts are executed by the login shell *without creating a sub-shell*.

There are two commands which run any shell script without creating a sub-shell—the **.** (dot) and **source** commands. The C shell uses **source**, Bourne and Korn use the dot, and bash uses both. Contrary to what some people believe, you don't have to log out and log in again if you have made a change to a startup script. Just execute the script in these ways:

`. .profile`	*Bourne and Korn shell*
`source .login`	*C shell*
`. .bash_profile`	*bash*
`source .bash_profile`	*bash—uses both* `.` *and* `source`

Once executed in this way, the changes are made available in the current shell. You'll also need this facility in a later chapter to execute files containing shell functions.

Note

The dot and **source** commands execute a script without using a sub-shell. They also don't require the script to have executable permission. Most of these commands exhibit an unusual behavioral pattern if the current directory doesn't feature in PATH. They fail to locate a file in the current directory unless a relative or absolute pathname is used for the file. If `.` doesn't appear in PATH, the command `. .profile` won't execute; you then have to use `. ./.profile`. The C shell behaves normally though.

17.9.2   Interactive and Noninteractive Shells

From another perspective, every shell can be further divided into two types—interactive or noninteractive. When you log in, you see an **interactive shell** that presents a prompt and waits for your requests. An interactive shell permits job control, command-line editing and history. It also responds to signals in a different manner than noninteractive shells. Some UNIX commands like **vi** and **emacs** have shell escapes that let you work at the prompt of an interactive sub-shell.

When you execute a shell script from this shell, you call up a **noninteractive shell**. Because many of the interactive shell's parameters are not passed to a noninteractive shell, we have to make separate arrangements to make them available there. The interactive shell runs a startup (login) script and a separate *rc* (environment) script. When a noninteractive shell is run from the interactive shell, it runs only the *rc* script. This *rc* script contains all settings the sub-shell needs to know.

We'll now discuss the `.profile` used by the Bourne shell. Even if your shell is different, you should still read this section because it also discusses certain concepts applicable to the other shells.

Note

A distinction must be made between environment variables and aliases (as well as **set** options). These variables are available in all sub-shells. However, aliases and **set** options are not automatically made available to sub-shells. Hence they are always placed in the *rc* files and propagated to *interactive* shells. The C shell goes further than this; aliases are also available in C shell scripts.

17.9.3 The Bourne Shell: The Initialization Scripts (.profile)

Issue the `ls -a` command and see whether you can locate the `.profile` in your home directory. This login script should be added to your home directory at the time of user creation, but you can create one even if it's not there. When a user logs in, the shell executes these two files:

- A global initialization file, `/etc/profile`, that sets the variables and issues commands meant to be common to all users.
- The user's own `.profile` containing settings made by the user.

A `.profile` can be quite large depending on the user's requirements, but an abridged one should do for initial comprehension:

```
$ cat .profile
# User $HOME/.profile - commands executed at login time
MAIL=/var/mail/$LOGNAME                              # mailbox location
IFS=
PATH=$PATH:$HOME/bin:/usr/ucb:.
CDPATH=.:..:$HOME
PS1='$ '
PS2=>
TERM=ansi
MOZILLA_HOME=/opt/netscape ; export MOZILLA_HOME
calendar
mesg y
stty stop ^S intr ^C erase ^?
```

Some of the system variables have been assigned in this script. The later statements show that the file has been edited to taste. The PATH has been modified to contain three more directories. CDPATH now lets you directly access directories under your home and parent directory. It's a good thing to be reminded of your engagements (by **calendar**). **mesg y** expresses your willingness to receive messages from people using the **talk** command *(11.2)*. Some **stty** settings have also been made here.

Many of the variables defined in the script have been inherited from `/etc/profile` which the shell executes before running `.profile`. We had to export MOZILLA_HOME because the variable was defined here and has to be exported if Netscape has to run properly. The other variables (like PATH) have already come "exported," so you don't have to export them again just because you have changed their values.

The Bourne shell doesn't support aliases or any of the advanced features discussed in this chapter, so it doesn't need an *rc* script. All variables defined in the .profile must be exported in the script itself so that they are available in sub-shells. Bourne doesn't run a logout script either, though with knowledge of shell programming it can be made to emulate that behavior.

Note

The .profile is executed after /etc/profile—the universal profile for all users. Universal environment settings are kept by the administrator in /etc/profile so that they are available to all users. If your system has the directory /etc/skel (for skeleton), then it would also have a file .profile (or local.profile) in that directory. This is the file that is added to the user's home directory by the **useradd** command.

17.9.4   The C Shell: The Initialization Scripts (.cshrc, .login and .logout)

The C shell doesn't use a .profile for startup instructions; it uses two other files instead. The ~/.logout file is executed (if present) before logging out of the system. When a user logs in, the shell runs three scripts in the order shown:

- A global initialization file, which could be /etc/login or /etc/.login (Solaris). Any instructions meant to be executed by all users are placed there. This file may not be present in all systems.
- The ~/.cshrc—containing instructions that are executed whenever a C shell is started.
- The ~/.login which is executed only when the user logs in.

Note the adoption of ~/ as a synonym for the home directory. There's something to note in this sequence because it's not exactly what one would expect. It also differs from the behavioral pattern of Korn and bash. First, the shell runs the login file in /etc. It then runs ~/.cshrc, and after determining whether it is a login shell, it runs ~/.login. While ~/.cshrc is run for every sub-shell called up, /etc/login and ~/.login are run only once.

The C shell's environment files follow a simple behavioral pattern. Whether you run an interactive or a noninteractive shell, the file .cshrc is always executed. (Korn behaves differently.) The .login should contain only environment variable settings like TERM and those instructions you need to execute only once:

```
calendar
mesg n
stty stop ^S intr ^C erase ^?
setenv MOZILLA_HOME /opt/netscape                    Required by Netscape
setenv TERM vt220
```

MOZILLA_HOME and TERM have to be explicitly specified as environment variables by the **setenv** statement. The special C shell variables not automatically inherited by sub-shells should be defined in the ~/.cshrc:

```
set prompt = '[\!] '
set path = ($path /usr/local/bin)
set history = 500
set savehist = 50
set noclobber
set ignoreeof
```

`prompt`, `path` and `history` are C shell (local) variables whose values are made available to child shells when placed in this file. Moreover, the `noclobber` and `ignoreeof` settings are not exported to sub-shells, and must be used every time a child shell is created. Since alias definitions can't be inherited by child shells, they must also be placed in `~/.cshrc`:

```
alias l ls -l
alias ls-l ls -l
alias h "history | more"
alias ls ls -aFx
alias h history
alias rm rm -i
```

You'll find that over a period of time, your `~/.cshrc` builds up faster than `~/.login`. Note that most of these settings are either useful or relevant only in interactive shells. But they will still be available in shell scripts!

17.9.5   The Korn Shell: The Initialization Files (`.profile` and ENV)

Since the Korn shell is a superset of Bourne, everything discussed in Section 17.9.3 applies to the Korn shell as well. However, Korn is rich in features and needs its own environment (*rc*) script. This script name can be anything but is determined by the setting of the ENV variable. This often is the file `~/.kshrc` as most users migrate to this shell from the C shell.

When a user logs in to the system, these are the scripts that are executed in this order:

- A global initialization file, `/etc/profile`, containing settings common to all users.
- The user's own `~/.profile`.
- The file defined in the ENV variable, which is usually `~/.kshrc`.

As Korn's behavioral pattern is somewhat different from Bourne's, it's no wonder that its `.profile` also contains different and fewer entries:

```
export ENV=$HOME/.kshrc                    Exporting and assigning together
calendar
mesg n
stty stop ^S int ^C erase ^?
```

We see a special variable ENV which must be present in every .profile used by Korn. The ENV variable serves two purposes:

- It defines the file that is also run on login and when invoking a sub-shell.
- It also executes the environment file.

Since the .profile is executed only on login, place in this file those statements that need to be executed only once. The remaining statements should go to the environment file. Here are some sample entries in the .kshrc:

```
MAIL=/var/mail/$LOGNAME          # mailbox location
PATH=$PATH:$HOME/bin:/usr/dt/bin:.
CDPATH=.:..:$HOME
PS1='[$PWD] '
PS2=>
HISTSIZE=2000

set -o noclobber
set -o vi

alias h="history -10"
alias cp="cp -i"
alias rm="rm -i"
```

Strictly speaking, the environment variable settings in .kshrc can be placed in the .profile instead of here. In that case, many of them would need to be exported explicitly since the profile is not executed by child shells. But the **set -o** and **alias** commands must remain here. Unlike in the C shell, Korn shell aliases are available only in interactive shells and not in shell scripts. (The -x option of **alias** allows this too, but the feature has been obsoleted by *ksh93*.)

Tip

Cleaner still would be to place the aliases in a separate file, say ~/.aliases. If you need to use these aliases in your shell scripts, then place the statement . ~/.aliases at the beginning of the script. It doesn't then matter which version of the Korn shell you are using.

17.9.6   bash: The Initialization Files (.bash_profile, .bash_logout and .bashrc)

Like Korn, bash is also a superset of Bourne, so the discussions in Section 17.9.3 apply to this shell as well. bash draws features from the C shell too; as a result it supports a rather elaborate set of initialization files. When a user logs in to the system, these are the scripts that are executed—and in this order:

- A global initialization file, /etc/profile, containing settings common to all users.
- The user's own "profile." bash looks for these three files in the sequence specified—~/.bash_profile, ~/.bash_login and ~/.profile. The moment it finds one file, it ignores the others.
- An environment file set by the variable BASH_ENV, but only if explicitly specified in the profile. This file is generally ~/.bashrc.

bash also executes the file ~/.bash_logout before a user quits the system. For the purpose of these discussions, we'll assume .bash_profile as the profile of bash. Like in the C shell and Korn, place only those statements in .bash_profile that have to be executed only on login:

```
stty stop ^S int ^C erase ^?
mesg n
export BASH_ENV=$HOME/.bashrc
. ~/.bashrc
```

BASH_ENV here specifies the environment file. If this entry is missing, place it there because sub-shells also execute this file. But the login shell won't do it automatically unless specifically instructed in .bash_profile to do so. That's why you should find the last entry (. ~/.bashrc) in every .bash_profile.

The environment file should contain all environmental settings, **set -o** statements and aliases:

```
MAIL=/var/spool/mail/$LOGNAME            # mailbox location
PATH=$PATH:$HOME/bin:/usr/X11R6/bin:/usr/lib/java/bin:/opt/kde/bin:.
CDPATH=.:.:.:$HOME
PS1="\u@\h:\w > "
PS2='> '
HISTSIZE=1000
HISTFILESIZE=1000
TERM=linux
set -o emacs
set -o ignoreeof

alias dial='/usr/sbin/dip -v $HOME/internet/int3.dip'
alias dialk='/usr/sbin/dip -k'
alias mailg='fetchmail && elm'
alias mails='/usr/sbin/sendmail -q'
```

By seeing the value of the MAIL variable, you can guess that this is a Linux system. Note that PS1 here shows the username, hostname and the current directory. The alias definitions have already been explained *(17.4.2)*.

Strictly speaking, the environment variables could have been assigned in the .profile (or .bash_profile) instead of here. But then the ones that are already not exported have to be exported explicitly since the profile is not executed by sub-shells. TERM and PATH are reassigned here and would need no exporting, but HISTSIZE and HISTFILESIZE would probably need to be exported.

Aliases and **set** options must be placed in .bashrc because they are not exported. Unlike in the C shell, bash aliases are available only in interactive shells and not propagated to shell scripts. You cannot even use the technique of placing them in a separate .aliases file as described in the "Tip" of Section 17.9.5.

Tip

You can use the file .bash_logout to store any commands that you want to be executed before logging out, like displaying the time, for example. Korn doesn't have a similar file.

bash and the Korn shell are supersets of the Bourne shell, while bash also has features borrowed from the C shell. It's always advisable to use the Korn shell or bash (if you are using Linux) as your default login shell. If this chapter has convinced you, ask your system administrator to set it that way. In either case, you are assured of a fruitful and rewarding experience.

SUMMARY

General

A command in one shell may either not be available in another or behave in a different manner. The Bourne shell has the fewest features followed by the C shell. The Korn and bash shells are feature-rich and recommended for use.

An *environment variable* is a shell variable that is *exported* to make it available in all sub-shells. The behavior of the UNIX system is largely determined by the settings of these variables.

The login shell and the shell run from shell escapes in **vi**, **emacs** and **telnet** are *interactive* shells. Shell scripts are run with *noninteractive* shells. There is a difference in behavioral pattern between these two shells.

Every initialization script is executed without spawning a sub-shell and thus makes variables defined in the script also available in the login shell and sub-shells. The dot (`.`) command does this job in Bourne, Korn and bash, but the **source** command is used by the C shell (and also by bash).

In the non-Bourne shells, *aliases* help to shorten long command sequences with the **alias** statement. These shells also support a *history* feature that lets you recall previous commands (*events*), performing a substitution if necessary. You can protect your files from accidental overwriting (noclobber) and prevent *[Ctrl-d]* from logging you out (ignoreeof). The tilde (~) acts as a shorthand representation of the home directory.

The Korn and bash shells are recommended both for interactive and noninteractive use.

The Bourne Shell (Also Applicable for Korn and bash)

Using environment variables, you can set the command search path (PATH) and the directory search path (CDPATH). Your home directory and login shell are determined from /etc/passwd and are available in HOME and SHELL. For a terminal to work properly, TERM must be correctly set. The shell knows the location of your mailbox (MAIL) and how often to look there to detect new mail (MAILCHECK).

export turns ordinary variables into *environment variables*. Changes to these variables are stored in $HOME/.profile which is executed by the shell when a user logs in.

The C Shell

The **set** statement assigns values to local variables and also displays them. **setenv** sets environment variables, and displays their settings when used without arguments. The uppercase variables like TERM are read by programs, but the C shell uses the lowercase ones for its own use.

You can set the command search path (path) and prompt string (prompt). Your home directory is available in home, the current directory in cwd, the shell in shell and the mail directory in mail. Many of these special variables are also available in upper-case as environment variables.

An alias is defined without an = symbol. The symbol \!$ represents the last or only parameter to an alias, while \!* signifies all parameters.

Previous commands can be saved in memory (history) or in the file .history (savehist). The ! when used with a string runs a previous command, while !! repeats the last command. !$ and !* represent the last argument and all arguments, respectively, of the last command.

Using :s, you can make a substitution in a previous command. Substitution can be performed on the last command using the sequence ^*s1*^*s2*.

The :*n* operator (where *n* begins from 0) extracts one or more arguments of a previous command. You can also run a previous command with a different set of arguments (:0). From a pathname, you can extract the head (:h), tail (:t) and the root file-name without its extension (:r).

Accidental file overwriting and logging out are prevented with **set noclobber** and **set ignoreeof**.

The files ~/.cshrc and ~/.login are executed when a user logs in. .cshrc is also used when running a sub-shell. .logout is run when the user logs out. Aliases and settings of the special lowercase variables should be kept in .cshrc.

The Korn Shell

The Korn Shell uses all variables found in the Bourne shell. You can include the current directory (PWD) and event number (!) in the prompt string to make it reasonably informative.

Aliases are defined with the = symbol and accept no command line arguments.

Previous commands are saved in ~/.sh_history (or in a file defined by HISTFILE). **r** used with a string repeats a previous command. When used by itself, **r** repeats the last command. $_ represents the last argument to the last command.

The **vi**- or **emacs**-like *in-line* editing features are enabled with **set -o** (with vi or emacs as argument). You can use the command and filename *completion* feature to let the shell expand an entered string into a command line.

The **set -o** command is used to protect files from overwriting (noclobber) and accidental logging out (ignoreeof). You can use the shortcut **cd -** to revert to the previous directory.

In addition to the .profile, both the login shell and interactive sub-shells also execute an environment file defined by the ENV variable—often the file .kshrc. Environmental variables, **set -o** statements and aliases should be stored in the environment file.

bash

bash is a superset of the Bourne shell and uses all its variables. The prompt string (PS1) can include the current directory (PWD) and the event number (!). You can also include the username, hostname and the current time in the prompt.

An alias is defined with the = symbol and accepts no command line arguments.

Previous commands are saved in .bash_history (or the file defined by HISTFILE). A ! followed by a string runs the most recent command beginning with the substring. You can repeat the last command (!!). Both $_ and !$ represent the last argument to the last command while !* signifies all arguments to the previous command.

You can make a substitution in a previous command (:s and :gs). bash also offers a shortcut to perform substitution on the last command (^s1^s2).

You can extract one or more arguments of a previous command (:*n*) or run a previous command with a different set of arguments (:0). From a pathname, you can extract the head (:h), tail (:t) and the root filename without its extension (:r).

You can perform **vi**- and **emacs**-like *in-line* editing of the command line by using **set -o** with either vi or emacs as argument. You can also use the command and filename *completion* feature to let the shell expand a partially entered command line.

set -o noclobber is a safety mechanism that prevents files from being accidentally overwritten. *[Ctrl-d]* won't log you out if ignoreeof is set. The command **cd -** reverts to the previous directory.

When a user logs in, bash executes .bash_profile, .profile or .bash_login, whichever is found first. The variable BASH_ENV determines the file that is executed when a sub-shell is run—often the file .bashrc. All environment variables, **set -o** statements and aliases are kept in this file.

SELF-TEST

Some questions assume that the user has Korn or bash as her login shell. You'll have to deduce that from context.

17.1   If TERM has the value vt220, where will you expect to find its control file?

17.2   How often is your mailbox checked by the shell for incoming mail?

17.3   If **man** uses a variable to set its pager, how can you change the pager to **less**?

17.4   Which variable contains the output of the **who am i** command?

17.5   You are afraid that you may accidentally overwrite files with the > symbol. What precaution will you take?

17.6   If you run a shell script, does the sub-shell also read the login file (.login or .profile)?

17.7   When does a shell variable become an *environment variable*?

17.8   If you have the files .bash_profile and .profile in your home directory, will bash read them both on login?

17.9   How will you make the history facility store the last 200 commands in *memory* in the (i) C shell (ii) Korn (iii) bash?

17.10   How will you repeat the last command in the (i) C shell (ii) Korn (iii) bash?

17.11   To enable **vi**-like editing of the command line, what setting will you have to make first in the (i) Korn shell (ii) bash?

17.12   You don't know the absolute pathname of henry's home directory. How will you "cd" to it in the non-Bourne shells?

17.13   What is the significance of the symbols :h and :t?

EXERCISES

17.1   Do you have to contact the system administrator to change your login shell?

17.2   Which two environment variables are set by reading /etc/passwd?

17.3   How will you add the parent directory to your existing PATH?

17.4   If you want your mailbox to be checked every minute, what setting will you make?

17.5   How can you create a prompt like this in bash (user is romeo, machine name is *niccomail* and project5 is the current directory)?

        [niccomail-romeo ~/project5]

17.6   Assume you are in /home/romeo/cgi and you want **cd perl** to always take you to /home/romeo/perl. What setting do you need to make?

17.7   If you have PS1='\!$', what sort of prompt will you have in Korn and bash?

17.8   Write a Korn or bash alias to show only the hidden files of the current directory. If the hidden file is a directory, how will the output be different?

17.9   Write a Korn or bash alias that (i) lists only the executables in the current directory (ii) brings up the last modified file for editing with **vi**.

17.10   How will you set your prompt in the C shell to reflect the current directory? (HINT: Devise an alias for the **cd** command.)

17.11   If you have set noclobber to prevent overwriting, how will you overwrite files when you really need to in the (i) C shell (ii) Korn and bash?

17.12   There is a file profile (no dot) in /etc. Is this file executed at all?

17.13   If you have kept all your aliases in the file .alias, how can you ensure that they are available in all sub-shells of the (i) C shell (ii) Korn (iii) bash?

17.14   How can you quickly reexecute the last **fdformat** command with a few keystrokes in the (i) C shell (ii) Korn (iii) bash?

17.15   What is the significance of this command?

        ^htm^pdf

17.16   You have just used the command **tar -cvf /dev/fd0 *.sh**. How will you repeat the command to use the .pl files this time in the (i) C shell (ii) Korn (iii) bash?

17.17   You issued the command **$_** and got the message foo.sh: Permission denied. What does all this indicate?

17.18   Assuming you have enabled in-line command editing, how can you pull up the last command containing the name perl for editing in (i) **vi**-mode (ii) **emacs**-mode?

17.19   What's the easiest way of listing all command names beginning with z in the directories specified by PATH in the (i) Korn shell (ii) bash?

17.20   Can you condense this sequence in the (i) C shell (ii) Korn (iii) bash?

        vi script.c ; cc script.c

17.21   How do you switch to the directory where you last were in the (i) C shell (ii) Korn (iii) bash?

17.22   What is the difference between an *interactive* and *noninteractive* shell? Which features of the shell have significance only in an interactive shell?

17.23   When the command **. .profile** was used, the system generated an error message `ksh: .profile: not found`. Why did that happen even though the file `.profile` exists in the current directory?

17.24   If your `.profile` contains a statement like `PATH=$PATH:$HOME/bin`, and you make repeated changes to the file, how should you activate the changes?

17.25   What is the significance of this statement? `vi !un:1:r`

KEY TERMS

alias *(17.4)*

environment variable *(17.2)*

event number *(17.3.2 and 17.5)*

export *(17.2.1)*

filename completion *(17.7)*

history *(17.5)*

history modifier *(17.5.1)*

ignoreeof *(17.8)*

in-line editing *(17.6)*

interactive shell *(17.9.2)*

noclobber *(17.8)*

noninteractive shell *(17.9.2)*

positional parameter *(17.4.1)*

rc script *(17.9)*

unalias *(17.4)*

## CHAPTER 18

Shell Programming

The activities of the shell are not restricted to command interpretation alone; they involve much more than that. The shell has a whole set of internal commands that can be strung together as a language—with its own variables, conditionals and loops. Most of its constructs are borrowed from C, but they are compact and simpler to use than those in C. What makes shell programs powerful is that the external UNIX commands blend easily with the shell's internal constructs.

We need two chapters to discuss the programming features of the shell in some detail and to put them into productive use in real-world situations. In this chapter, we'll focus on the Bourne shell—the lowest common denominator of all shells. We have reserved the discussion of the advanced features of the Korn and bash shells for the next chapter. However, everything discussed here applies to both these shells too. The C shell uses totally different programming constructs and has been separately treated in Appendix A.

Shell programs run in *interpretive mode*—one statement at a time. They consequently run slower than those written in high-level languages. Speed is not a factor in many jobs we do, and in many cases, using the shell is an advantage—especially in system administrative tasks. *The UNIX system administrator must be an accomplished shell programmer.*

Objectives

- Learn the various ways of executing a shell script. *(18.2)*
- Take input from the keyboard and a file with **read**. *(18.3)*
- Understand how command line arguments are passed to and interpreted as *positional parameters* inside a script. *(18.4)*
- Learn the significance of the *exit status* of a command and the parameter $?. *(18.5)*
- Use simple one-line conditionals with the && and || operators. *(18.6)*
- Use the **if** statement for multiway branching using a UNIX command as its *control command*. *(18.8)*
- Compare strings and integers and test file attributes with **test**. *(18.9)*
- Use the pattern matching features of **case** for matching strings with wild cards. *(18.10)*
- Perform integer computation and manipulate strings with **expr**. *(18.11)*

- Learn how to design a script that behaves differently depending on the name by which it is invoked. *(18.12)*
- Run a set of commands repeatedly using the **while** and **until** loops. *(18.14)*
- Execute a set of statements for each member of a list using a **for** loop. *(18.16)*
- Change filename extensions with **basename**. *(18.16.4)*

Note

The discussions and examples in this chapter are drawn from the Bourne shell, though practically everything here applies equally well to the Korn and bash shells. Hardly anything here applies to the C shell. There are two things you have to take care of when using bash. First, you have to use **echo -e** whenever you use the escape sequences \c and \n. Second, a special variable $0 shows up differently from its Bourne and Korn counterparts. You'll note this difference later in the chapter.

18.1 Shell Variables

Shell variables were introduced in Chapter 8 as a convenient way of storing values. In this chapter, we'll be using them in shell scripts. To briefly recapitulate, a variable name must start with a letter but can contain numerals and the underscore character. A variable is assigned with the = symbol without using the $, but is evaluated by prefixing it with a $:

```
$ fname=profile
$ echo $fname
profile
```

The **unset** statement removes a variable from the shell. Variables are concatenated by placing them side by side; no operators are needed, unlike in other programming languages:

```
$ x=foo ; y=.doc              Can make multiple assignments in one line
$ z=$x$y                        Variable assigned by other variables
$ echo $z
foo.doc
```

The shell uses an alternative notation when evaluating variables—a pair of curly braces that enclose a variable name. Here's another way of evaluating the variable fname:

```
$ echo ${fname}
profile
```

The shell often requires a variable to be evaluated in this form to enable its manipulation in various ways. However, a variable and a string can't be concatenated in the same way as two variables can. To affix an x to a variable's value, you have to use either of these two forms:

```
$ echo ${fname}x
profilex
$ echo $fname"x"              Single quotes will also do
profilex
```

These forms have at least one advantage; you can generate a second set of filenames by modifying the original name. You'll find these concatenation features useful when changing a file's extension.

Command substitution and shell variables acting in concert often help produce clean and compact scripts. Using curly braces, the multiple command sequence in Section 3.7 can be rewritten like this:

```
boldon=`tput smso` ; boldoff=`tput rmso`
echo ${boldon}Come to the Web$boldoff
```

This displays the words Come to the Web in boldface on the terminal. Note that the curly braces are required in the first variable but not in the second. Once the **tput** sequences have been set to variables in this way, you can later use the variables directly in your shell scripts.

18.2 Shell Scripts

Theoretically, all shell statements and UNIX commands can be entered in the command line itself. However, when a group of commands have to be executed regularly, they are better stored in a file. All such files are called **shell scripts** or *shell programs*. There's absolutely no restriction on the extension such filenames should have, though it is helpful to use .sh as the extension. This makes it easy to match scripts with wild cards.

The following shell script **script.sh** has a sequence of five UNIX commands; four of them are **echo**:

```
$ cat script.sh
# Sample shell script
echo "The date today is `date`"                # Using command substitution
echo Your shell is $SHELL
echo Your home directory is $HOME
echo The processes running on your system are shown below:
ps
```

You can use **vi** or **emacs** to create this script. Note the comment character (#) that can be placed anywhere in a line; the shell ignores all characters placed on its right.

You can execute this file in two ways. The common way of running a shell script is to first make it executable with **chmod** before running it:

```
$ chmod +x script.sh ; ls -l script.sh
-rwxr-xr-x    1 romeo      dialout       154 Feb 25 22:33 script.sh
```

Now that there's executable permission for the script, you can run it by simply invoking its filename:

```
$ script.sh
The date today is Fri Feb 25 22:35:49 IST 2000
Your shell is /bin/sh
Your home directory is /home/romeo
The processes running on your system are shown below:
```

```
PID TTY STAT TIME COMMAND
192  1 S    0:00 sh
588  1 R    0:00 ps
```

All the statements have been executed in sequence. The script is too simple to require any explanation—no inputs, no command line arguments and no control structures. We will be progressively adding these features to our future scripts.

Shell scripts are always run in a separate shell—a sub-shell. When a script is running, the **ps** command always shows at least two **sh** (**ksh** and **bash** for the other shells) processes running. The login shell is the parent of the sub-shell that actually runs the script. When running loops like **while** inside a script, more sub-shells are created, but keep in mind that there are at least two shell processes running when a script is in execution.

Now, which shell will you use to execute a shell script? You'll naturally want to use your login shell, but what happens if you have a script written in the Bourne shell, and your login shell is Korn? You might just try running it by calling it like this:

script.sh   *Or use* ./script.sh

But then this will call a Korn sub-shell to execute it—and possibly produce errors. Since the Bourne shell is generally available in every system, you can call it as your sub-shell:

sh script.sh   *Invokes a sub-shell explicitly*

Here, you are executing the **sh** command which uses the script name as its argument. **sh** opens the file and executes all statements in the script file in sequence. No executable permission for the script file is then required. Since you called up the sub-shell explicitly, you are sure of your shell too.

Note

You can execute a script foo by invoking the filename only when the current directory features in PATH. In case it doesn't, then you can still execute the script without using the absolute pathname. Use **./foo**.

If you are using the **vi** editor to edit your shell and **perl** scripts, then you need not leave the editor to execute the script. Just make this mapping of the *[F1]* function key in $HOME/.exrc:

:map #1 ^[:w^M:!%^M

Tip

This saves the buffer before executing the file (:!%). ^[and ^M represent the *[Esc]* and *[Enter]* key, respectively *(4.3.5)*. You can now press *[F1]* to run your current script. (But first use **chmod** to make the script executable.) If your script accepts arguments, then make a similar mapping of *[F2]* with the last ^M removed. Provide them in the last line after you have pressed *[F2]*.

Specifying the Interpreter It's also possible to specify the shell inside the script itself. So instead of executing a script with **sh** *filename*, it's better to place the following statement at the beginning of the script:

```
#!/bin/sh
```
                                                          Assuming sh *is in* /bin

The # is treated as the comment character by the shell, but when you follow it with a !, the shell interprets the remainder of the string as the interpreter specification. You can now execute the script without calling **sh** explicitly. If your script will run properly only under a specific shell, put the interpreter at the top of the script (and before you enter anything else).

Note

On some UNIX systems, the C shell behaves differently in choosing the shell for running a script. On these systems, you still need to have this statement at the beginning even if your login shell is **csh**:

```
#!/bin/csh
```

As a safety measure, you'll do well to have the interpreter line at the top of every shell script.

18.3   read: **Making Scripts Interactive**

The **read** statement is the shell's internal tool for taking input from the user, i.e., making scripts interactive. It is used with one or more variables. Input supplied through the standard input is read into these variables. When you use a statement like

```
read name
```

the script pauses at that point to take input from the keyboard. Whatever you enter is stored in the variable name. Since this is a form of assignment, no $ was used before name. Our first script **emp1.sh** uses **read** to take a search string and filename from the terminal:

```
$ cat emp1.sh
#!/bin/sh
# Script: emp1.sh - Interactive version
# The pattern and filename to be supplied by the user
echo "Enter the pattern to be searched: \c"              # \n for a newline
read pname
echo "Enter the file to be used: \c"
read flname
echo "Searching for $pname from file $flname"
grep "$pname" $flname
echo "Selected lines shown above"
```

Shell scripts accept comments prefixed by # anywhere in a line. You know what the sequence \c does *(8.5)*. Run the script and specify the inputs when the script pauses twice:

```
$ emp1.sh
Enter the pattern to be searched: director
Enter the file to be used: emp2.lst
Searching for director from file emp2.lst
```

```
9876|bill johnson      |director |production|03/12/50|130000
2365|john woodcock     |director |personnel |05/11/47|120000
Selected lines shown above
```

First, the script asks for a pattern to be entered. Input the string di rector, which the shell assigns to the variable pname. Next, it asks for the filename; enter the string emp2.1st, which goes to the variable flname. After accepting these inputs from the keyboard, the **grep** and **echo** statements are executed.

You can enter both arguments in one line before hitting *[Enter]*, but then you would have to use the **read** statement with two variables:

```
echo "Enter the pattern and filename: \c"
read pname flname
```

Note

If the number of arguments supplied is less than the number of variables accepting them, any leftover variables will simply remain unassigned. However, when the number of arguments exceeds the number of variables, the remaining words are assigned to the *last* variable.

18.3.1 Redirecting read Input

That was an interactive script; its arguments were read from the standard input by **read**. The obvious question that would arise is this: Can't the script be redirected to take input from a file instead? To answer that, let's insert the two responses into a file list:

```
$ cat list
director
emp2.1st
```

Now, run the script **emp1.sh** but redirect it this time to take input from this file:

```
$ emp1.sh < list
Enter the pattern to be searched: Enter the file to be used:
Searching for director from file emp2.1st
9876|bill johnson      |director |production|03/12/50|130000
2365|john woodcock     |director |personnel |05/11/47|120000
Selected lines shown above
```

The script shows the two prompts alright but doesn't pause this time. You have been able to run an interactive script noninteractively. You'll find this technique useful in running a menu-driven program that is normally used with a fixed set of responses. You can make the program read these responses from a file rather than from the keyboard.

Well, if that be so, can't **vi** take all its commands from a file? After all, we pass instructions to **vi** through the standard input!

18.4 Positional Parameters

Shell scripts accept arguments in another manner—from the command line itself. The C and **perl** languages also use arguments in this way. In fact, this is how you use UNIX tools (which are written in C) all the time. This noninteractive method of specifying command line arguments forms the basis of developing tools that can be used with redirection and pipelines.

When arguments are specified with a shell script, they are assigned to certain special "variables"—rather **positional parameters**. The first argument is read by the shell into the parameter $1, the second argument into $2, and so on. You can't technically call them shell variables because all variables are evaluated with a $ before the variable name. In case of $1, you really don't have a variable 1 that is evaluated with $.

We'll now rewrite the previous script to accept command line arguments. We'll use these special parameters inside the script:

$1 — The first argument.
$2 — The second argument.
$0 — The name of the script.
$# — The number of arguments.
$* — The complete set of positional parameters as a single string.

In addition to the parameters signifying the arguments, the shell also uses three special parameters—$0, $# and $*. We'll use them several times in this chapter, but first let's use them in a "passive" way in the script **emp2.sh**:

```
$ cat emp2.sh
#!/bin/sh
echo "Program: $0"                              # $0 contains the program name
echo "The number of arguments specified is $#"
echo "The arguments are $*"                     # All the arguments stored in $*
grep "$1" $2
echo "\nJob Over"
```

Recall the discussion on links *(7.13.1)*, where we discussed calling a program with different names. $0 tells you the name of the script by which you invoked it. If the shell can also count the number of arguments with $#, you can design scripts that check whether the right number of arguments have been entered. Invoke this script with the pattern director and the filename emp1.lst as the two arguments:

```
$ emp2.sh director emp1.lst
Program: emp2.sh
The number of arguments specified is 2
The arguments are director emp1.lst
1006|gordon lightfoot|director |sales     |09/03/38|140000
6521|derryk o'brien  |director |marketing |09/26/45|125000

Job Over
```

When arguments are specified in this way, the first word (the command itself) is assigned to $0, the second word (the first argument) to $1, and the third word (the second argument) to $2. You can use more positional parameters in this way up to $9 (and, using the **shift** statement, can go beyond).

Since the script accepts two arguments, how do you search for a multiword pattern, say, robert dylan? When the string is quoted, the shell understands it as a single argument:

```
$ emp2.sh "robert dylan" emp1.lst
Program: emp2.sh
The number of arguments specified is 2
The arguments are robert dylan emp1.lst
5678|robert dylan    |d.g.m.    |marketing |04/19/43| 85000

Job Over
```

$# is still set to 2, as you can see above. If you had not used quotes, the number of arguments would have been three, **grep** would have interpreted dylan as a filename, and the script would have aborted.

Note

Using $0, a shell script knows its own name. If a script filename has links, you can make it behave differently depending on the name by which it is invoked. We'll take advantage of this feature but only after we have learned to use the **case** statement.

BASH Shell

$0 in bash is set a little differently. In the example above, it would have shown ./emp2.sh instead of emp2.sh. Later scripts will match the value of $0 with a filename, in which case the symbols ./ have to be removed before performing the match. We'll learn to do that as well.

18.5 Exit Status of a Command

Once **grep** couldn't locate a pattern *(15.2.2)*; we said then that the command **failed**. Any command can fail, and you should know the consequences of this failure. You used UNIX commands in every chapter; some commands executed in the way you wanted, and some didn't. For example, the command

```
$ cat foo
cat: can't open foo
```

fails and generates an error message to the standard error, probably because the file is not present or is unreadable. You already know that **grep** simply returns the prompt when it fails to find the pattern.

Every command *returns* a value after execution. This value is called the **exit status** or **return value** of the command. This value is said to be true if the command executes successfully and false if it fails. The **cat** command shown above didn't succeed and is said to return a false exit status.

The return value is extremely important for programmers. They use it to devise program logic that branches into different paths depending on the success or failure of a command. For example, there's no point in continuing with script execution if an important file doesn't exist or can't be read. The shell offers a statement (**test**) that tests a return value.

18.5.1 The Parameter $?

There's another special parameter used by the shell; it's the $?. It stores the exit status of the last command. It has the value 0 if the command succeeds, and a non-zero value if it fails. For example, if **grep** fails to find a pattern, the return value is 1, and if the file scanned is unreadable in the first place, the return value is 2. In any case, return values exceeding 0 are to be interpreted as failure of the command. Try using **grep** in different ways:

```
$ grep director emp.1st >/dev/null; echo $?
0                                                    director found
$ grep manager emp.1st >/dev/null; echo $?
1                                                manager doesn't exist
$ grep manager emp3.1st >/dev/null; echo $?
grep: can't open emp3.1st
2
```

You should note that all assignments to the positional and special parameters are automatically made by the shell. You can't really tamper with their values except in an indirect fashion. But you can use them to great advantage in several ways. They will be used over and over again in shell scripts, so make sure that you have understood them. They are reproduced in Table 18.1. Two of them have already been discussed in previous chapters; one will be taken up later.

Tip

To find out whether a command executed successfully or not, simply use **echo $?** after the command. 0 indicates success; other values point to failure.

18.6 The Logical Operators && and ||—Conditional Execution

The script **emp1.sh** has no logic to prevent display of the Selected lines shown above message even when the pattern search fails. That is because we didn't use **grep**'s exit status to control the flow of the program. The shell provides two operators that allow conditional execution—the && and ||, which typically have this syntax:

TABLE 18.1 *Special Parameters Used by the Shell*

Shell Parameter	Significance
$1, $2, etc.	Positional parameters
$*	Complete set of positional parameters as a single string
$#	Number of arguments specified in command line
$0	Name of executed command
$@	Same as $* except when enclosed in double quotes
$?	Exit status of last command
$$	PID of the current shell *(10.3)*
$!	PID of last background job *(10.10.2)*

cmd1 **&&** *cmd2*
cmd1 **||** *cmd2*

The **&&** delimits two commands; the command *cmd2* is executed only when *cmd1* succeeds. You can use it with **grep** in this way:

```
$ grep 'director' emp1.lst && echo "pattern found in file"
1006|gordon lightfoot|director |sales    |09/03/38|140000
6521|derryk o'brien   |director |marketing |09/26/45|125000
pattern found in file
```

The **||** operator plays an inverse role; the second command is executed only when the first fails. If you "grep" a pattern from a file without success, you can notify the failure:

```
$ grep 'manager' emp2.lst || echo "Pattern not found"
Pattern not found
```

You'll be using these compact operators a number of times in developing shell scripts later in this chapter. **awk** *(16.4)* and **perl** *(20.7)* also use them.

18.7   exit: **Script Termination**

Sometimes, you test for a condition and find that it fails. You'd then like the program to terminate since there's no point in continuing further if an essential resource is missing—say, the file that you want to search. The **exit** statement is used to prematurely terminate a program. When this statement is encountered in a script, execution is halted and control is returned to the calling program—in most cases the shell. You used the same statement *(1.6.2)* to terminate the introductory session in the first chapter.

You don't need to place **exit** at the end of every shell script because the shell knows when script execution is complete. Rather, it's quite often used with a command when there are chances that it may fail. Now, let's modify the previous program (**emp2.sh**) to show the results of a search if a pattern is found, but terminate if the search fails for any reason:

```
$ cat emp2a.sh
#!/bin/sh
echo "Program: $0"                                    # $0 contains the program name
echo "The number of arguments specified is $#"
echo "The arguments are $*"                           # All the arguments stored in $*
grep "$1" $2 >patlist 2>/dev/null  || exit 2          # exit with an argument
echo "Pattern found -- Contents shown below"
cat patlist
```

The program is aborted when the **grep** command fails, but the contents are shown if it succeeds. Errors are directed to /dev/null, so even if the file represented by $2 doesn't exist, **grep**'s error message won't show up on the screen. We'll come to **exit**'s argument in a moment, but let's first run the script with a file that doesn't exist at all:

```
$ emp2a.sh manager emp3.lst
Program: emp2a.sh
The number of arguments specified is 2
The arguments are manager emp3.lst
```

The last **echo** statement has not been executed nor are the contents of patlist displayed. This confirms that the script had a premature termination. But what was its return value? Check the value of $?:

```
$ echo $?
2                                                                    Because of exit 2
```

This was the value specified as **exit**'s argument in the script. The argument is optional, but when you specify one, the script returns that value but only if it terminates *at that point*. If no return value is specified, $? would show zero—a true value. So you can still return a true value even if there was an error! Control your return values; UNIX is that flexible!

By using the logical operators && and || in these ways, we have approached the territory that belongs to the shell's conditionals. These operators have their limitations and are recommended for making simple decisions. When complex decision making is involved, they have to make way for the **if** statement.

18.8 The if Conditional

The **if** statement takes two-way decisions depending on the fulfillment of a certain condition. In the shell, the statement uses the following forms, much like the one used in other languages:

if *command is successful*	if *command is successful*	if *command is successful*
then	then	then
execute commands	*execute commands*	*execute commands*
else	fi	elif *command is successful*
execute commands		then...
fi		else...
		fi
Form 1	Form 2	Form 3

As in BASIC, **if** also requires a **then**. It evaluates the success or failure of the *command* that is specified in its "command line." If the *command* succeeds, the sequence of commands following it is executed. If the command fails, then the **else** statement (if present) is executed. This statement is not always required, as shown in Form 2. Every **if** is closed with a corresponding **fi**, and you'll encounter an error if one is not present.

What makes shell programming so powerful is that the success of the command is determined by the return value of any UNIX program. All commands return a value as we saw with **cat** and **grep**, so you can imagine where shell programming can lead us.

In the next example, **grep** is first executed and **if** uses its return value to control the program flow:

```
$ cat emp3.sh
if grep "^$1" /etc/passwd 2>/dev/null    # Search username at beginning of line
    then
        echo "Pattern found - Job Over"
    else
        echo "Pattern not found"
fi
```

This is a simple *if-else* construct where **if** tests the return value of **grep**. The rest of the script should be pretty self-explanatory, but this time we'll search /etc/passwd for the existence of the user firewall:

```
$ emp3.sh firewall
firewall:x:41:31:firewall account:/tmp:/bin/false
Pattern found - Job Over
```

This seems to be an unusual user account with /tmp as the home directory and /bin/false as the "shell," but we'd rather not bother with such things now. You can test the working of the **else** statement by entering a pattern which doesn't exist in the file:

```
$ emp3.sh mail
Pattern not found
```

Why did we use **grep** to locate the pattern? Couldn't we have used **awk**, in which case we could have matched the pattern in a specific field? Let's modify the script by replacing the **grep** command with **awk**:

```
$ cat emp3a.sh
#!/bin/sh
if awk -F: '$1 ~ '/$1/' { print }' /etc/passwd 2>/dev/null ; then
        echo "Pattern found - Job Over"
    else
        echo "Pattern not found"
fi
```

Note that there are two $1's here. The first one is **awk**'s field identifier, and the second signifies the first argument to the script. Recall *(16.9)* that script arguments need to be surrounded by single quotes to be properly interpreted by **awk**. We also changed the location of the **then** line; you can have it in the same line as the **if** but only after you delimit them by a **;**. Now let's run the script with a user-id which exists:

```
$ emp3a.sh firewall
firewall:x:41:31:firewall account:/tmp:/bin/false
Pattern found - Job Over
```

This was no problem and was to be expected, but you could be in for a surprise when you use this:

```
$ emp3a.sh mail
Pattern found - Job Over
```

The string `mail` doesn't exist, **awk** was unable to locate it, but it didn't return a false exit status. **if** detected no error condition but misguided us just the same. How does one generate an error condition here? Can we count the number of characters in **awk**'s output and then check with **wc** whether **awk** really produced any output at all?

```
if awk -F: '$1 ~ '/$1/' { print }' /etc/passwd | wc ; then
```

The bad news is that **wc** also returns a true value even if it counts nothing. However, the good news is that we can check **wc**'s character count to see whether it's really zero or not. We'll take up this problem after we have learned to handle numbers.

18.8.1 if-elif: Multiway Branching

We saw two forms of the **if** conditional—*if-then-fi* and *if-then-else-fi*. There's a third form also—*if-then-elif-then-else-fi*. In this form, you can have as many **elif**s as you want, while the **else** remains optional. Let's use this form to search the crontab files of henry, romeo and juliet for a command which a user may have scheduled:

```
$ cat cronfind.sh
#!/bin/sh
crondir=/var/spool/cron/crontabs
message="has scheduled the $1 command"
if grep "$1" $crondir/henry ; then
    echo "henry $message"
elif grep "$1" $crondir/romeo ; then
    echo "romeo $message"
elif grep "$1" $crondir/juliet ; then
    echo "juliet $message"
else
    echo "None of the users is using the $1 command"
fi
```

Here, we have made proper and effective use of shell variables. Abbreviating the crontab directory shortens the code; you can refer to it as `$crondir`. Since the same basic message is echoed for every search, it makes sense to convert the common part of the message to a variable too.

If you find unusual and prolonged disk activity, you can use this script to find out whether any of the three users has scheduled a **find /** command (a search from the root directory) in their crontab files:

```
$ cronfind.sh "find */"
59 16 * * * find      / -name "*.html" -print |mail romeo
romeo has scheduled the find */ command
```

romeo tried to outsmart the administrator by providing a lot of whitespace between `find` and `/` to avoid detection. But the administrator was smarter and used the regular expression □* (space before the *) between `find` and `/` to match whitespace too. Need to be reminded that a * after a space expands to zero or more occurrences of the space?

All these scripts have a serious shortcoming. They don't indicate why a pattern wasn't found. The `not found` or `None of the users` messages appear even if the files looked at don't exist, and the redirection of the diagnostic stream with 2> ensures that **grep**'s and **awk**'s complaints are not seen on the terminal. A script ideally should check the existence of a file before starting a search. We'll take up this matter shortly.

The condition placed in the command line of the **if** statement will henceforth be referred to as the **control command**. Any UNIX command can be a control command to an **if**, **while** or **until** construct. Amazing power indeed!

Note

Every **if** must have an accompanying **then** and **fi**, and optionally an **else**. The **else** clause may include another nested **if** statement (**else if**), and each one of these **if**s must be closed with its matching **fi**. The **elif** clause doesn't require this termination and produces more compact code.

18.9 test and []: Companions of if

When you utilize **if** to evaluate expressions, the **test** statement is often used as its control command. **test** uses certain operators to evaluate the condition on its right and returns either a true or false exit status, which is then used by **if** for making decisions. **test** works in three ways:

- Compares two numbers.
- Compares two strings or a single one for a null value.
- Checks a file's attributes.

These tests can be made by **test** in association with the shell's other statements also, but for the present we'll stick with **if**. **test** doesn't display any output but simply returns a value that sets the parameter $?. In the following sections, we'll actually check this value.

18.9.1 Numeric Comparison

The numerical comparison operators (Table 18.2) used by **test** have a form different from what you would have seen anywhere. They always begin with a - (hyphen), followed by a two-character word and enclosed on either side by whitespace. Here's a typical operator:

-ne   *Not equal*

TABLE 18.2   *Numerical Comparison Operators Used by* **test**

Operator	Meaning
-eq	Equal to
-ne	Not equal to
-gt	Greater than
-ge	Greater than or equal to
-lt	Less than
-le	Less than or equal to

The operators are quite mnemonic; -eq implies equal to, -gt implies greater than, and so on. You should also know that numeric comparison in the shell is confined to *integer* values only; decimal values are simply truncated.

We'll assign some values to three variables and check whether they are equal or not. The last test proves conclusively that numeric comparison is restricted to integers only:

```
$ x=5; y=7; z=7.2
$ test $x -eq $y ; echo $?
1                                                                Not equal
$ test $x -lt $y ; echo $?
0                                                                    True
$ test $z -gt $y ; echo $?
1                                                       7.2 is not greater than 7!
$ test $z -eq $y ; echo $?
0                                                         7.2 is equal to 7!
```

Having used **test** as a stand-alone feature, you can now use it as **if**'s control command. The next script uses **test** and the special shell variable $#—this time for testing a condition. The script simply checks whether the right number of arguments have been entered:

```
$ cat arg_number_check.sh
if test $# -ne 3 ; then
    echo "You didn't enter three arguments"
else
    echo "You entered the right number"
fi
```

Now, run it twice, first with a single argument and then with three:

```
$ arg_number_check.sh 1024
You didn't enter three arguments
$ arg_number_check.sh /home list.tar 1024
You entered the right number
```

Now that we can use **test** to make a numeric comparison, we'll take up the problem of looking for a pattern with **awk**. Will **test** work like this?

```
if test awk -F: '$1 ~ '/$1/' { print }' /etc/passwd | wc -c -ne 0
```

test here works with too many arguments and reports an error. **wc** also generates an error because it interprets -ne as an illegal option. What we need to check is the output of this pipeline (a number) and not its return value. We'll have to use command substitution to output **wc**'s character count and then check that value with **test**. The following line should do the job:

```
if test `awk -F: '$1 ~ '/$1/' { print }' /etc/passwd | wc -c` -ne 0
```

This time we just enclosed the pipeline within backquotes. But this doesn't display the selected line on the screen. Obviously, we would like to have both. We'll resolve these issues in our next script:

```
$ cat emp3b.sh
#!/bin/sh
if test $# -ne 1; then                              # 1 argument not entered
    echo "Usage: $0 pattern"; exit 3
else
    if test `awk -F: '$1 ~ '/$1/'' /etc/passwd \
    | tee /dev/tty | wc -c` -ne 0                    # Display on screen also
    then
        echo "Pattern found - Job Over"
    else
        echo "Pattern not found"; exit 2
    fi
fi
```

Here, you have two nested **if** constructs—one enclosed by the other and each terminated with its own **fi**. We have used **awk** differently here; the **{ print }** statement is missing since **awk** prints by default if the selection criterion is specified. We used the **tee** command to produce output on the screen as well. Note that the \ breaks up this pipeline of three commands to appear in two lines. **wc -c** now checks **awk**'s output (filtered through **tee**); a count of zero means that the pattern couldn't be found. The script should now work:

```
$ emp3b.sh
Usage: emp3b.sh pattern
$ emp3b.sh image
image:x:502:100:The PPP server account:/home/image:/bin/ksh
Pattern found - Job Over
$ emp3b.sh mail
Pattern not found
$ echo $?
2
```

So, finally we could use **if** both with a command and with command substitution (which required the use of **test**) to make searching with **grep** and **awk** possible.

Shorthand for test **test** is so widely used that fortunately there exists a shorthand method of executing it. A pair of rectangular brackets enclosing the expression can replace it. Thus, the following two forms are equivalent:

```
test $x -eq $y
[ $x -eq $y ]
```

The [and] must have spaces on their inner sides. The second form is easier to handle and will be used henceforth. But don't forget to be liberal in the use of whitespace here!

Note

It is a feature of most programming languages that you can use a condition like **if x**, where x is a variable. If x is greater than 0, the statement is said to be true. We can also apply the same logic here and use **if [$x]** as a shorthand form of **if [$x -gt 0]**.

Tip

Although we didn't use quotes with $-prefixed variable names when conducting numeric tests on them, you'll have to be more careful when using strings. If the variable expands to a single word, no quotes will also do, but when it expands into multiple words, a script will fail if quotes are not used. Moreover, when a variable expands to a null string, you'll often encounter errors with unquoted variables.

Set up a good habit of using quotes wherever there are chances of these events taking place. In like manner, also quote the strings these variables match—like in "$file" = "j".

18.9.2   String Comparison

test can be used to compare strings with yet another set of operators. Equality is performed with = and inequality with the C-type operator !=. Like the other **test** operators, these too should have whitespace on either side. Table 18.3 lists the string handling tests.

Our next script should be useful for C and Java programmers. Depending on the option used, it stores the last modified C or Java program in the variable file. It then compiles the program. You have to provide one argument to the script—the file type which could be c (for C files) or j (for Java files):

```
$ cat compile.sh
#!/bin/sh
if [ $# -eq 1 ] ; then
    if [ $1 = "j" ] ; then
        file=`ls -t *.java | head -1`
        javac $file
    elif [ $1 = "c" ] ; then
        file=`ls -t *.c | head -1`
        cc $file && a.out
    else
        echo "Invalid file type"
    fi
else
    echo "Usage: $0 file_type\nValid file types are c and j"
fi
```

javac and **cc** are the compilers for Java and C programs, respectively. The script proceeds with the checking of $1 only when it finds one argument. Otherwise, it just displays the usage and quits. We have even used **cc**'s exit status to run the file a.out—the default file produced by the C compiler. Let's run the script now:

TABLE 18.3 *String Tests Used by* **test**

Test	True if
s1 = s2	String *s1* = *s2*
s1 != s2	String *s1* is not equal to *s2*
stg	String *stg* is assigned and not null
-n *stg*	String *stg* is not a null string
-z *stg*	String *stg* is a null string
s1 == s2	String *s1* = *s2* (Korn and bash only)

```
$ compile.sh
Usage: compile.sh file_type
Valid file types are c and j
$ compile.sh c
hello world
```

The last modified C program actually contained a **printf** statement echoing the most famous words of the language. Wouldn't it be much better if the script itself identified the last modified program file and then chose the appropriate compiler without the user having to supply anything at all? We'll do that only after we have learned to use the **case** statement.

Now, let's see how we can check for null values of input. You can use the string comparison features in the next script to check whether the user actually enters a string or simply presses the *[Enter]* key:

```
$ cat emp4.sh
#!/bin/sh
echo "Enter the string to be searched: \c"
read pname
if [ -z "$pname" ] ; then                           # -z checks for a null string
    echo "You have not entered the string" ; exit 1
else
    echo "Enter the file to be used: \c"
    read flname
    if [ ! -n "$flname" ] ; then                    # ! -n is the same as -z
        echo "You have not entered the filename" ; exit 2
    else
        grep "$pname" "$flname" || echo "Pattern not found"
    fi
fi
```

A **test** is negated by the ! (bang) operator. The script pauses at two points—first in accepting the pattern, and next in accepting the filename. Note that the check for a null string can be made in both ways:

```
[ -z "$x" ]
[ ! -n "$x" ]
```

They are really two different ways of saying the same thing. The script aborts if one of the inputs is a null string:

```
$ emp4.sh
Enter the string to be searched: director
Enter the file to be used: [Enter]
You have not entered the filename
$ emp4.sh                                                        Invoke it again
Enter the string to be searched: director
Enter the file to be used: emp1.1st
1006|gordon lightfoot|director |sales    |09/03/38|140000
6521|derryk o'brien  |director |marketing |09/26/45|125000
```

test also permits checking of more than one condition in the same line, using the **-a** (AND) and **-o** (OR) operators. You can now simplify the earlier script to illustrate this feature. Remove the first **if** construct and use this sequence after both strings have been accepted:

```
if [ -n "$pname" -a -n "$flname" ] ; then
     grep "$pname" "$flname" || echo "Pattern not found"
else
     echo "At least one input was a null string" ; exit 1
fi
```

The **test** output is true only if both variables are non-null strings, i.e., the user enters some non-whitespace characters when the script pauses twice.

18.9.3 test: File Tests

test can be used to test various file attributes. For example, you can test whether a file has the necessary read, write or executable permissions. Except for **perl**, you won't find these elaborate testing arrangements (Table 18.4) in other languages where these file attributes are either not available to a program or tested by using a good deal of programming.

The file testing syntax used by **test** is quite compact, so let's use it to test some attributes of the file emp.1st at the prompt:

```
$ ls -l emp.1st
-rw-rw-rw-  1 romeo    group        870 Jun  8 15:52 emp.1st
$ [ -f emp.1st ] ; echo $?
0                                                              An ordinary file
$ [ -x emp.1st ] ; echo $?
1                                                           Not an executable
$ [ ! -w emp.1st ] || echo "False that file is not writable"
False that file is not writable
```

TABLE 18.4   *File-Related Tests with* **test**

Test	True If File
-f *fname*	*fname* exists and is a regular file
-r *fname*	*fname* exists and is readable
-w *fname*	*fname* exists and is writable
-x *fname*	*fname* exists and is executable
-d *fname*	*fname* exists and is a directory
-s *fname*	*fname* exists and has a size greater than zero
-e *fname*	*fname* exists *(Korn and bash only)*
-u *fname*	*fname* exists and has SUID bit set
-k *fname*	*fname* exists and has sticky bit set
-L *fname*	*fname* exists and is a symbolic link *(Korn and bash only)*
f1 -nt *f2*	*f1* is newer than *f2* *(Korn and bash only)*
f1 -ot *f2*	*f1* is older than *f2* *(Korn and bash only)*
f1 -ef *f2*	*f1* is linked to *f2* *(Korn and bash only)*

The ! negates a test, so [! -w file] negates [-w file]. Using these features, you can design a script that accepts a filename as argument and then performs a number of tests on it:

```
$ cat filetest.sh
#!/bin/sh
if [ ! -f $1 ] ; then
    echo "File does not exist"
elif [ ! -r $1 ] ; then
    echo "File is not readable"
elif [ ! -w $1 ] ; then
    echo "File is not writable"
else
    echo "File is both readable and writable"
fi
```

Test the script with two filenames—one that doesn't exist and one that does:

```
$ filetest.sh emp3.lst
File does not exist
$ filetest.sh emp.lst
File is both readable and writable
```

Caution

Some people make the mistake of using the shell's wild cards with **test**. For instance, you can't use [-w inde*.html] to test whether the file that matches the pattern is writable.

18.10 The case **Conditional**

The **case** statement is the second conditional offered by the shell. It doesn't have a parallel in most languages including **perl**. The statement exactly matches an expression for more than one alternative and uses a compact construct to permit multiway branching. It matches strings with wild cards, which makes the command an indispensable string matching tool. Here is its syntax:

```
case expression in
    pattern1) commands1 ;;
    pattern2) commands2 ;;
    pattern3) commands3 ;;
        . . . . .
esac
```

case first matches *expression* with *pattern1*. If the match succeeds, then it executes *commands1*, which may be one or more commands. If the match fails, then *pattern2* is matched, and so forth. Each command list is terminated with a pair of semicolons, and the entire construct is closed with **esac** (reverse of **case**).

We'll now use a simple script to display some important data of our file system. It has four options, which are displayed by a multiline **echo** statement:

```
$ cat filesys.sh
#!/bin/sh
tput clear
echo "\n  1. Find files modified in last 24 hours\n  2. The free disk space
  3. Space consumed by this user\n  4. Exit\n\n SELECTION: \c"

read choice
case $choice in
    1) find $HOME -mtime -1 -print ;;
    2) df ;;
    3) du -s $HOME ;;
    4) exit ;;
    *) echo "Invalid option"
esac
```

case matches the value of $choice with the strings 1, 2, 3 and 4. The first three options execute the **find**, **df** and **du** commands, respectively, and you know well by now what they do. Option 4 quits the program. The last option (a *) matches any option not matched by the previous options. We'll make fruitful use of this feature later.

To find out how much space your files are occupying on your disk, invoke the script and choose option 3:

```
$ filesys.sh
```

```
    1. Find files modified in last 24 hours
    2. The free disk space
```

```
   3. Space consumed by this user
   4. Exit

SELECTION: 3
269440  /home/sumit
```

sumit is using this many blocks of disk space (of 512 bytes each) in his home directory. The same logic can also be implemented using the **if** statement, but **case** obviously is more compact. Now, let's have a look at its other features.

18.10.1   Matching Multiple Patterns

case can also match more than one pattern in **egrep**-style. If you have a file backup schedule that specifies a complete backup on, say, Wednesdays and Fridays, and an incremental backup for the other days, then **case** can provide an extremely compact construct to implement this logic. Since the day can be "cut" from the **date** command output, we'll use command substitution to provide the string to **case** in our next script:

```
$ cat back.sh
case `date | cut -d" " -f1` in          # Outputs three-character day string
   Wed|Fri) tar -cvf /dev/fd0 * ;;
        *) find . -newer .last_full_backup_time -print > tarilist
           tar -I tarilist -cvf /dev/fd0 ;;         # -I option in Solaris
esac
```

The first field of the **date** output displays the day, which we extracted with **cut** to provide input to **case**. The first option shows two patterns; like **egrep** and **awk**, **case** also uses the | as the pattern delimiter when matching multiple patterns. This option matches the day with a Wed or a Fri and executes the **tar** command. We haven't bothered to explicitly match the other days, since the * takes care of this; it matches all options not matched by any of the previous options.

The script can be run on any day, and the right command will be automatically invoked. How the **tar** command accomplishes the complete and incremental backups is discussed in Section 22.10.2.

Now consider another example. Programmers frequently encounter a logic that tests a user response for both y and Y (or n and N). To implement this logic with **if**, you need to use the compound condition feature:

```
if [ "$choice" = "y" -o "$choice" = "Y" ]
```

case takes care of this with the compact expression y|Y, which matches both upper- and lowercase:

```
echo "Do you wish to continue? (y/n): \c"
read answer
case"$answer" in
   y|Y) ;;                              Null statement, no action to be performed
   n|N) exit ;;
     *) echo "Invalid option" ;;
esac
```

18.10.2 Wild Cards: case Uses Them

case has a superb string matching feature that uses the wild cards. It uses the filename matching metacharacters *, ? and the character class *(8.2)—but only to match strings and not the files in the current directory.* The revised **case** construct for a previous example lets the user answer the question in several ways:

```
case "$answer" in
        [yY][eE]*) ;;                        Matches YES, yes, Yes, etc.
        [nN][oO]) exit ;;                     Matches NO, no, nO and No
                *) echo "Invalid response"        When everything else fails
esac
```

Wild-card usage in the first two options appears simple enough. Note that the * appears in two options but has slightly different meanings. In the first option, it behaves like a normal wild card. In the last option, it provides a refuge for all other nonmatched options. Note that the last **case** option doesn't need ;; but you can provide them if you want.

Using the ?, you can match a four-character string with the model ????, and if it must contain numerals only, [0-9][0-9][0-9][0-9] will be just right. This is how you can validate a six-character numeric field from the terminal:

```
n="[0-9][0-9][0-9][0-9][0-9][0-9]"
echo "Enter a date string\c "
read dstring
case $dstring in
  ???????*) echo "String exceeds six characters" ;;
        $n) echo "A six character numeric field" ;;
        *) echo "The string is either non-numeric"
            echo "or less than six characters long" ;;
esac
```

Now that we have a powerful string matching feature with us, can we make the **compile.sh** script *(18.9.2)* more powerful still? Our revised program should compile the last modified C or Java program that a user was working on and choose the compiler automatically:

```
$ cat compile2.sh
file=`ls -t *.java *.c 2>/dev/null | head -1`
case $file in
        *.c) cc $file && a.out ;;
    *.java) javac $file ;;
        *) echo "There's no Java or C program in the current directory "
esac
```

The first statement has done most of the work for us. It selects the last modified .c or .java file and stores the value in the variable file. After that, it's a simple matter for **case**. It matches the extensions and calls up the right compiler. All this with just six lines of code; no wonder some people can't get away from UNIX!

Note

The * is used in two ways in **case** though it behaves like a wild card each time. A * embedded in a pattern matches any number of characters, but a singular * is placed as the last **case** option for matching anything *not* matched by the previous options.

18.11   expr: **Computation and String Handling**

The Bourne shell can check whether an integer is greater than another, but it doesn't have any computing features at all. It has to rely on the external **expr** command for that purpose. This command combines two functions in one:

- Performs arithmetic operations on integers.
- Manipulates strings.

We'll use **expr** to perform both these functions, but with not-very-readable code when it comes to string handling. If you are using the Korn shell or bash, you have better ways of handling these things *(19.8)*, but you must also understand the helplessness of Bourne. It's quite possible that you have to debug someone else's script which contains **expr**.

18.11.1   The Arithmetic Functions

expr can perform the basic four arithmetic operations, as well as the modulus (remainder) function:

```
$ x=3 ; y=5                                        Multiple assignments
$ expr 3 + 5
8
$ expr $x - $y
-2
$ expr 3 \* 5                                      Asterisk has to be escaped
15
$ expr $y / $x
1                                                  Decimal portion truncated
$ expr 13 % 5
3
```

The operand, be it +, -, * etc., must be enclosed on either side by whitespace. Observe that the multiplication operand (*) has to be escaped to prevent the shell from interpreting it as the filename metacharacter. Since **expr** can handle only integers, division yields only the integral part.

     expr is often used with command substitution to assign a variable. For example, you can set a variable z to the sum of two numbers:

```
$ x=6 ; y=2 ; z=`expr $x + $y`
$ echo $z
8
```

Perhaps the most common use of **expr** is in incrementing the value of a variable. All programming languages have a shorthand method of doing that, and it is natural that UNIX should also have its own:

```
$ x=5
$ x=`expr $x + 1`                                    Same as C's x++
$ echo $x
6
```

If you are using the Bourne shell, you'll have to adopt this usage of **expr** in many of your shell scripts.

18.11.2   String Handling

Though **expr**'s string handling facilities aren't exactly elegant, Bourne shell users hardly have any choice. For manipulating strings, **expr** uses two expressions separated by a colon. The string to be worked upon is placed on the left of the **:**, and a regular expression is placed on its right. Depending on the nature of the regular expression, **expr** can perform three important string functions:

- Determine the length of the string.
- Extract a substring.
- Locate the position of a character in a string.

The Length of a String   The length of a string is a relatively simple matter; the regular expression **.*** signifies to **expr** that it has to print the number of characters matching the pattern—which effectively simplifies to the length of the entire string:

```
$ expr "robert_kahn" : '.*'                    Note whitespace around :
11
```

Here, **expr** has counted the number of occurrences of any character (**.***)—something quite different from the output when used with **grep** or **sed**. This feature is useful in validating data entry. Consider that you want to validate the name of a person accepted through the keyboard so that it doesn't exceed, say, 20 characters in length. The following **expr** sequence can be quite useful for this task:

```
echo "Enter your name: \c"
read name
if [ `expr "$name" : '.*'` -gt 20 ] ; then
    echo "Name too long"
fi
```

Extracting a Substring   **expr** can extract a string enclosed by the escaped characters \(and \). If you wish to extract the 2-digit year from a 4-digit string, you must create a pattern group and extract it this way:

```
$ stg=2001
$ expr "$stg" : '..\(..\)'                     Extracts last two characters
01
```

Note the pattern group \(..\). This is the tagged regular expression (TRE) that we used with **sed** (15.12.2), but here it has a somewhat different meaning. It signifies that the first two characters in the value of $stg have to be ignored and two characters have to be *extracted* (not remembered) from the third character position. (There's no \1 or \2 used here.)

Locating Position of a Character **expr** can also return the location of the first occurrence of a character inside a string. To locate the position of the character b in the string value of $stg, you have to count the number of characters which are not b ([^b]*), followed by a b:

```
$ stg="paul_baran"
$ expr "$stg" : '[^b]*b'
6
```

expr also duplicates some of the features of the **test** statement and uses the numerical comparison operators in the same way. They are not pursued here because **test** is a built-in feature of the shell and is consequently faster. The Korn shell and bash have built-in computational and string handling facilities; they don't need **expr**. They are taken up in the next chapter.

18.12 $0: Calling a Script with Different Names

In our discussion on links *(7.13.1)*, we raised the possibility of calling a file by different names and doing different things depending on the name by which it is called. In fact, there are a number of UNIX commands which do exactly that. Now that we know how to use **case** and extract a string with **expr**, it's time we designed a single script that compiles, edits or runs the last Java program. The script file will have three names, but before developing it, let's understand some essential aspects of Java programming.

A Java program must have the .java extension. When compiled with **javac** *filename*, it produces a .class file. However, you must not use the extension when executing the program with the **java** command. This means you'll compile a program hello.java to produce hello.class and then run **java hello** to execute the program. We must be able to extract the "base" filename after dropping the extension, and with **expr** it should be a simple matter.

We remarked at the beginning of the chapter about bash showing a ./ before the command name when $0 is evaluated. We'll make this script shell-independent too by removing the ./ when it senses bash as the shell. The script **comj** which performs all these functions is shown below:

```
$ cat comj
# Script that is called by different names
lastfile=`ls -t *.java |head -1`

case $SHELL in
*/ksh|*/sh) command=$0 ;;
    *bash) command=`expr $0 : '.*/\([^/]*\)'`  ;;        # Removes ./
esac
```

```
case $command in
        runj) lastfile=`expr $lastfile : '\(.*\).java'`      # Removes .java
              java $lastfile ;;
         vij) vi $lastfile ;;
        comj) javac $lastfile && echo "$lastfile compiled successfully" ;;
esac
```

There are two **case** constructs here. The first one extracts the name of the script from $0. For the Bourne and Korn shells, there is really nothing to do except assign $0 to the variable command. For bash, the .⁄ is removed by the **expr** command. **expr** ignores the group .*⁄ which signifies any number of characters followed by a ⁄. It then extracts a group of non-frontslash characters. This effectively extracts the command name which it stores in the variable command.

The second **case** conditional now checks the name by which the program is invoked. Observe that the first option (runj) extracts the base filename of the file by dropping the .java extension. Since the last modified filename is held in the lastfile variable, the rest of the job becomes a simple matter. The only thing left to do is to create the links for **comj** with the **ln** command:

```
ln comj runj
ln comj vij
```

Now you can run **vij** to edit the program, **comj** to compile it and **runj** to execute the compiled code. We'll only compile it here:

```
$ comj
hello.java compiled successfully
```

Isn't all this exceedingly simple? Make it simpler still by mapping the two function keys to these tasks when using **vi**. Place these two entries in your .exrc:

```
:map #1 :w^M:!comj^M                                          Saves file first with :w^M
:map #2 :!runj^M
```

While editing a program, you can press *[F1]* to compile the program and *[F2]* to run it. Is there anything else you want UNIX to do?

18.13   sleep **and** wait

You may occasionally need to introduce some delay in a shell script to let the user see some message on the screen before the script starts doing something else. You may also want to make a check regularly (say, once a minute) for an event to occur (say, for a file to spring into existence). **sleep** is a UNIX command that introduces this delay. It is used with an argument that specifies the number of seconds for which the shell will pause or *sleep* before it resumes execution:

```
$ sleep 100 ; echo "100 seconds have elapsed"
100 seconds have elapsed
```

The message appears 100 seconds after the commands have been invoked. This command's special feature is that it doesn't incur significant overheads while it is sleeping.

wait is a shell built-in that checks whether all background processes have been completed. This can be quite useful when you have run a job in the background and now want to make sure the command is completed so you can run yet another program. You can use the **wait** command to wait for the completion of the last background job with or without the process PIDs:

```
wait                                    Waits for completion of all background processes
wait 138                                           Waits for completion of PID 138
```

18.14 `while` **and** `until`: **Looping**

None of the pattern scanning scripts developed so far offers the user another chance to rectify a faulty response. Loops let you perform a set of instructions repeatedly. The shell features three types of loops—**while**, **until** and **for**. All of them repeat the instruction set enclosed by certain keywords as often as their control command permits.

The **while** statement should be quite familiar to most programmers. It repeatedly performs a set of instructions till the control command returns a true exit status. The general syntax of this command is as follows:

```
while condition is true
do                                                      Note the do keyword
        commands                                             Loop body
done                                                    Note the done keyword
```

The *commands* enclosed by **do** and **done** are executed repeatedly as long as the *condition* remains true. You can use any UNIX command or **test** as the control command (condition here), as before.

We'll start with an orthodox **while** loop application. The **emp5.sh** script accepts a code and description in the same line and writes out the line to newfile. It then prompts you for more entries:

```
$ cat emp5.sh
#!/bin/sh
# Program: emp5.sh -- Shows use of the while loop
answer=y                                # Must set it to y first to enter the loop
while [ "$answer" = "y" ]                             # The control command
do
      echo "Enter the code and description: \c"
      read code description                                 # Read both together
      echo "$code|$description" >> newlist         # Append the line to file
      echo "Enter any more (y/n)? \c"
      read anymore
      case $anymore in
            y*|Y*) answer=y ;;                      # Anything starting with y or Y
            n*|N*) answer=n ;;                      # Anything starting with n or N
                *) answer=y ;;                      # Any other reply means y
      esac
done
```

Like the one above, a program well commented doesn't need much explanation. Let's run this first:

```
$ emp5.sh
Enter the code and description: 03 analgesics
Enter any more (y/n)? y
Enter the code and description: 04 antibiotics
Enter any more (y/n)? [Enter]                        No response, assumed to be y
Enter the code and description: 05 OTC drugs                  Three words here
Enter any more (y/n)? n
```

That was a fairly simple script that didn't feature any validation whatsoever. Whatever you enter goes to the file newlist:

```
$ cat newlist
03|analgesics
04|antibiotics
05|OTC drugs
```

18.14.1   Using while to Wait for a File

Let's now consider an interesting **while** loop application. There are situations when a program *b* needs to read a file created by another program *a*. *b* can run only after the file is created by *a*. We'll implement this logic in the next example.

The **monitfile.sh** script periodically monitors the disk for the existence of the file (here, invoice.lst) and then executes the **alloc.pl** script once the file is located:

```
$ cat monitfile.sh
while [ ! -r invoice.lst ]        # While the file invoice.lst can't be read
do
   sleep 60                               # Look for the file every 60 seconds
done
alloc.pl                   # Execute this program after exiting the while loop
```

The loop executes as long as the file invoice.lst can't be read (! -r means not readable). If the file becomes readable, the loop is terminated and the program **alloc.pl** is executed. This script is an ideal candidate to be run in the background like this:

```
monitfile.sh &
```

We used the **sleep** command to check every 60 seconds for the existence of the file.

18.14.2   Finding Out Users' Space Consumption

Refer to Section 22.10.1 to view the output of the **du -s /home/*** command. The command when run with /home/* as argument displays the disk usage summary of every user. Here are a few sample entries:

```
166      /home/enquiry
4054     /home/henry
```

```
647     /home/image
64308   /home/sumit
```

We assume here that home directories are maintained in /home. We can use a **while** loop to read every line of this output and then mail a message to root for every user who has either exceeded a specified figure or a default of 4000 blocks. This means the script **du.sh** either accepts no arguments or just one:

```
$ cat du.sh
# du.sh -- Program to monitor free space on disk
case $# in
    0) size=4000 ;;                         # Default size without user input
    1) size=$1 ;;                           # Specified on invocation
    *) echo "Usage: $0 [blocks]" ; exit ;;
esac
du -s /home/* | while read blocks user
do
  [ $blocks -gt $size ] && echo "$user has consumed $blocks blocks" \
                          | mail root                # List goes to root
done
```

Here, the **while** loop takes input from the standard output of the **du** command and reads each line into two variables blocks and user. It then compares the **du** summary figure either with 4000 (if no arguments are specified) or with the number specified as argument. For every line, a separate message is mailed to root. We can run this command in two ways:

```
du.sh
du.sh 8000                                 Selects only those users who exceed 8000 blocks
```

Now, when the root user opens her mailbox, she'll see a message for every user who has exceeded the limit. The message looks like this:

```
/home/sumit has consumed 64308 blocks
```

This script is useful for the system administrator who has to constantly monitor the disk space and identify the users who consume more space than they are supposed to. And what better way of running it than as a crontab job that's executed on working days every 3 hours between 10 a.m. and 7 p.m.:

```
0 10,13,16,19 * * 1-5 /home/admin/scripts/du.sh                    crontab entry
```

There's a drawback in this script which could prove serious for large installations. Even though it does the job, it sends a separate message for each user. Ideally, there should be a *single* mail message containing the entire list. Even though this isn't exactly intuitive, we should have piped the **echo** output at the **done** keyword:

```
done | mail root
```

We'll have a second look at redirection in the next chapter. For the time being, this script should serve our purpose.

18.14.3 Setting Up an Infinite Loop

Suppose, as the system administrator, you want to monitor the free space available in your disks every five minutes. You could use an infinite loop, and the easiest way to do that is to use a dummy command as **while**'s control command. This command does nothing except return a true value. There is, in fact, such a command named **true** in /bin, and you can set up the loop in the background as well:

```
while true ; do
    df -t
    sleep 300
done &
```

Once you have started this program in the background, you can continue your other work except that every five minutes you may find your screen filled with **df** output *(6.17)*. To kill this process, you have to use **kill $!**—the command that kills the last background job *(10.10.2)*.

Like **true**, there's also a command **false** that always returns a false value. They are the simplest commands available in the UNIX system:

```
$ cat /bin/true
$ _                                      File contains nothing—returns true
$ cat /bin/false
exit 255
```

The Linux versions of these two commands have some more features, but we'll ignore them. Remember that unless you run these infinite loops in the background, you have to terminate them by pressing the interrupt key. However, inside the loop you can use the **break** keyword for termination. **break** and **continue**—two keywords used in loops—are taken up in the next section.

18.14.4 until: while's Complement

The **until** statement complements the **while** construct in that the loop body here is executed repeatedly as long as the condition remains false. It's simply another way of viewing the whole thing. Either form can be used interchangeably, except for the fact that the expression has to be negated when switching from one form to another.

Some people would have preferred to have written a previous **while** control command in this way:

```
until [ -r invoice.lst ]                 Until invoice.lst can be read
```

and they probably would be right. The line translates into this: "Until the file invoice.lst is made readable, . . ." This form is certainly more intelligible.

18.15   Two Sample Scripts

We'll now consolidate the knowledge that we have acquired so far by developing two interesting scripts. One is an enhanced **cp** command that provides a file with a numeric extension if it exists at the destination. The other is a data entry script featuring validation.

Before we take up these scripts, you must know two keywords that are used by the shell's loops—**break** and **continue**. They have their namesakes in the C and Java languages. The **continue** statement suspends execution of all statements following it and switches control to the top of the loop for the next iteration. The **break** statement causes control to break out of the loop. They both work with arguments too.

18.15.1   cpback.sh: Backing Up a File with a Numeric Extension

Have you ever lost an important file by overwriting it with something else? The script **cpback.sh** shown in Fig. 18.1 protects your files from accidental overwriting by the **cp** command. The first version of this program accepts the filename to be copied and a directory name as the two arguments. It checks whether a file foo exists at the destination, and if it does, it affixes a numeric extension—beginning with foo.1. This could exist too, so it increments the number repeatedly to finally copy the file without overwriting.

FIGURE 18.1   cpback.sh: *Script to Copy a File without Overwriting*

```
# Program cpback.sh -- Copies a file to a directory
# Makes a backup instead of overwriting the destination file
# Copies foo to foo.1 if foo exists or foo.2 if foo.1 exists .......

if [ $# -ne 2 ] ; then                          # Script requires two arguments
    echo "Usage: $0 source destination" ; exit
elif [ ! -d $2 ] ; then
    echo "Directory $2 doesn't exist"
else
    file=$1
    if [ ! -f $2/$file ] ; then                 # File doesn't exist at destination
       cp $1 $2
    else
       copies=1                                 # Start checking if file with
       while true ; do                          # numeric extensions exist
          if [ ! -f $2/$file.$copies ] ; then
             cp $1 $2/$1.$copies                 # Provide a numeric extension and copy
             echo "File $1 copied to $1.$copies"
             break                              # Job done -- exit the loop
          else                                  # If file with numeric extension
             copies=`expr $copies + 1`          # also exists, go for the next one
          fi
       done
    fi
fi
```

The **break** statement terminates the loop iteration once the file has been copied. Now let's create a directory safe and copy the file vvi.sh to this directory. We'll play with the script for a little while though:

```
$ cpback.sh
Usage: cpback.sh source destination
$ cpback.sh vvi.sh safe1
Directory safe1 doesn't exist
$ cpback.sh vvi.sh safe
$ _                                                     File copied as vvi.sh
```

This hopefully should have copied the file, but to be sure let's repeat the copy operation a couple of times:

```
$ cpback.sh vvi.sh safe
File vvi.sh copied to vvi.sh.1
$ cpback.sh vvi.sh safe
File vvi.sh copied to vvi.sh.2
```

The script is working correctly. You can now save all versions of a program in a separate directory by copying the file with this script. We'll modify the script later to handle multiple files.

18.15.2   dentry1.sh: A Data Entry Script

The next script **dentry1.sh** shown in Fig. 18.2 accepts a code and its corresponding description from the terminal, performs some rudimentary validation checks, and then adds an entry to a file desig.lst. It validates the code entered with the ones that already exist in the file. The script repeatedly prompts the user till the right response is evoked.

The script prompts for two fields—the designation code and the description. It also uses two loops—one enclosed by the other. The code has to be reentered if it exists in the file or doesn't have a two-digit structure. Similarly, the description has to be reentered if it contains a nonalphabetic character other than a space (*[!\□a-zA-Z]*). The **continue** statements let you reenter the data or start a fresh cycle. The **break** statement in the inner loop quits the loop after adding the line.

The logic becomes convincing after you undertake a dialogue with the script:

```
$ dentry1.sh
Designation code: 01
Code exists
Designation code: 07
Description     : security officer

Wish to continue? (y/n): Y
Designation code: 8
Invalid code                                            Must have two digits
Designation code: 08
Description     : vice president 1
```

Can contain only alphabets and spaces
Description   : **vice president**

Wish to continue? (y/n): **n**

When you "cat" the file newlist, you'll see the two appended entries:

$ **cat newlist**
07|security officer
08|vice president

We have used the **while** loop in a number of ways already—to wait for a file to spring
into existence, increment a number repeatedly and continue prompting the user for a
valid entry. This is a very important shell construct that every proficient shell programmer needs to master.

18.16 for: **Looping with a List**

The **for** loop is different in structure from the ones used in other programming languages. BASIC users are in for a new treat—no **next** statement, no **step** specification.

FIGURE 18.2   *The* **dentry1.sh** *Script*

```
#!/bin/sh
while echo "Designation code: \c" ; do                        # Use -e in Linux
    read desig
    case "$desig" in
    [0-9][0-9]) if grep "^$desig" desig.lst >/dev/null ; then  # If code exists
                  echo "Code exists" ; continue                # Go to loop beginning
            fi ;;
        *) echo "Invalid code"  ; continue ;;                  # Not a 2-digit code
    esac

    while echo "Description     : \c"   ; do
        read desc
        case "$desc" in
    *[!\ a-zA-Z]*) echo "Can contain only alphabets and spaces" ; continue ;;
              "") echo "Description not entered" ; continue ;;
              *) echo "$desig|$desc" >> newlist ; break   # Terminate loop
        esac
    done

    echo "\nWish to continue? (y/n): \c"
    read answer
    case "$answer" in
        [yY]*) continue ;;                                 # Go to loop beginning
          *) break ;;                                      # Terminate loop
    esac
done
```

Unlike **while** and **until**, **for** doesn't test a condition but uses a *list* instead. The syntax of this construct is quite simple:

```
for variable in list ; do
    commands                                                          Loop body
done
```

The loop body is the same (with the same keywords **do** and **done**), but the additional parameters here are *variable* and *list*. The loop body is executed as many times as there are items in the list. A simple example can help you understand things better:

```
$ for file in chap20 chap21 chap22 chap23 ; do
>     cp $file ${file}.bak
>     echo $file copied to $file.bak
> done
chap20 copied to chap20.bak
chap21 copied to chap21.bak
chap22 copied to chap22.bak
chap23 copied to chap23.bak
```

The *list* here comprises a series of character strings (chap20 and onwards) separated by whitespace. Each item in the list is assigned to *variable* file. file is first assigned the value chap20, then chap21, and so on. Each file is copied with a .bak extension and the completion message is displayed after every file is copied.

You can also use a series of variables in the command line. They are evaluated by the shell before executing the loop:

```
$ for var in $PATH $HOME $MAIL ; do echo "$var" ; done
/bin:/usr/bin:/home/local/bin:/usr/bin/X11:.:/oracle/bin
/home/romeo
/var/mail/romeo
```

You have to provide the semicolons at the right places if you want to enter the entire loop in a single line. The three lines represent the values of the three environment variables.

You can also use command substitution to produce the list. The following **for** command line picks up its list from the file clist:

```
for file in `cat clist`
```

When the list is large and you don't consider it practicable to specify its contents individually, this method is most suitable. It's also a clean arrangement because you can change the list without having to change the program.

What else can this list be made up of? It can consist of practically any of the expressions that the shell understands and processes. We have already seen it generated by variables and command substitution. In the following paragraphs, we'll generate the list from wild cards and positional parameters. **for** is probably the most often used loop in the UNIX system, and it's important that you understand it thoroughly.

18.16.1　List from Filenames and Wild Cards

Like **case**, **for** also uses wild cards, *but it actually matches them against files in the current directory*. In the first example, where we used **for** to copy a group of files, we could have easily used a wild-card pattern:

```
for file in chap2[0-3] ; do
```

The shell produces an alphabetically sorted list of filenames and then instructions in the body act on each file in turn. We'll consider two more examples using **for** to work on a group of files.

Compiling a Group of C Programs　Since the * matches any number of characters, you can use it to compile all C programs:

```
$ for file in *.c ; do
>     cc -o $file{x} $file                     x appended to each object filename
> done
```

The -o option of **cc** lets you choose the output executable filename. Here, we are using the original filename with an x appended. The loop picks up each C program, say stringfind.c, and then creates the file stringfind.cx as the executable.

Making Substitution in a Group of Files　The **for** loop is indispensable for making substitutions in a set of files with **sed**. Since the standard output is redirected to a separate file, you can do the entire job inside a **for** loop to write back the output to the same file. Take for instance this script which works on every HTML file in the current directory:

```
$ cat lower2upper.sh
for file in *.htm *.html ; do
    sed 's/strong/STRONG/g
    s/img src/IMG SRC/g' $file > $$
    mv $$ $file
    compress $file
done
```

for here picks up each HTML file, performs some substitution with **sed**, moves the output to a temporary variable $$ (the PID of the current shell) and writes the changes back to the original file. It finally compresses each file.

18.16.2　List from Positional Parameters

One of the most important uses of **for** lies in its ability to process positional parameters that are supplied externally. The next script **emp6.sh** scans the file repeatedly for each argument:

```
$ cat emp6.sh
for pattern in $* ; do
```

```
        grep "$pattern" emp.lst || echo "Pattern $pattern not found"
done
```

Recall that $* holds the complete list of arguments as a space-delimited list of strings *(18.4)*. These strings are understood by the shell as $1, $2, and so on. We don't have to work with these individual positional parameters here. The loop iterates with each parameter and assigns it to the variable `pattern`. Now execute the script by passing four arguments:

```
$ emp6.sh 2345 1265 4379 367
2345|james wilcox       |g.m.      |marketing |03/12/45|110000
1265|p.j. woodhouse  |manager  |sales      |09/12/63| 90000
Pattern 4379 not found
Pattern 367 not found
```

Since **for** is mostly used with $* (or "$@") to access command line arguments, a blank list defaults to this parameter. These two statements mean the same thing:

for pattern in $*   *Actually, "$@"—see Section 18.16.3*
for pattern   *"$@" is implied*

Tip

For better readability, use **for** *variable* **in $*** rather than **for** *variable* in your scripts. Brevity can sometimes be confusing. See next section for use of "$@" in place of $*.

18.16.3 $@: Another Special Parameter

The script **emp6.sh** scanned emp.lst with four-character empids. The **for** loop creates problems when you use names instead. Just run the same script with two names:

```
$ emp6.sh "robert dylan" "ringo lennon"
5678|robert dylan    |d.g.m.   |marketing |04/19/43| 85000
5678|robert dylan    |d.g.m.   |marketing |04/19/43| 85000
Pattern ringo not found
6213|michael lennon  |g.m.      |accounts  |06/05/62|105000
```

This produces some interesting but deceptive output. **for** treats robert as one argument, dylan as another, ringo as one argument and lennon as another. Though ringo couldn't be found, lennon was found as michael's surname. Note that one line is shown twice.

Enclosing $* in quotes (like **for pattern in "$*"**) makes matters worse:

```
$ emp6.sh "robert dylan" "ringo lennon"
Pattern robert dylan ringo lennon not found
```

Both arguments here are viewed as a single argument by "$*". It's the shell's most neglected special parameter—the $@—that comes to your rescue in these critical situations. It behaves exactly like $* when used without quotes. When used with them, however, *it treats each quoted argument as a separate one*—exactly what is required here. Modify the **for** statement to look like this:

```
for file in "$@"
```

and then invoke the script as you have done before:

```
$ emp6.sh "robert dylan" "ringo lennon"
5678|robert dylan    |d.g.m.   |marketing |04/19/43| 85000
Pattern ringo lennon not found
```

This output has important implications. When you employ multiword strings as arguments of a shell script, you must use "$@" with the relevant programming construct to iterate for each argument of the script. The use of "$@"—rather than $*—is highly recommended because "$@" can handle single-word arguments in just the same way $* has been handling all along.

Tip

Use "$@" (within quotes) instead of $* if you have to use multiword strings as arguments to your scripts. Even otherwise, "$@" behaves exactly like $* when you use it for single-word strings. In fact, the statement **for pattern** actually means **for pattern in "$@"**.

18.16.4 basename: Changing Filename Extensions

We'll discuss yet another external command, **basename**, only because it's most effective when used inside a **for** loop. Working in tandem, they are quite useful in changing the extensions of a group of files. Windows users would be disappointed to learn that UNIX doesn't accept the following sequence:

```
mv *.txt *.doc                          Trying to convert all .txt extensions to .doc
```

You need to use a script in UNIX to achieve what Windows does with a single-line **RENAME** command. We did extract the base filename once with **expr** *(18.12)*, but the **basename** command can do the same job—and it doesn't use regular expressions:

```
$ basename /home/henry/project3/dec2bin.pl
dec2bin.pl
```

When **basename** is used with a second argument, it strips off the string represented by this argument from the first argument:

```
$ basename hello.java .java
hello                                                       .java stripped off
```

You can now use this feature inside the loop to change filename extensions from txt to doc:

```
for file in *.txt ; do
  leftname=`basename $file .txt`                Stores left part of filename
  mv $file ${leftname}.doc
done
```

If **for** picks up seconds.txt as the first file, leftname stores seconds (without a dot). **mv** simply adds a .doc to the extracted string (seconds). You don't need **expr** for this job at all!

18.17 cpback2.sh: **The Final Script**

Now that we understand the use of **while** and **for**, let's develop our last script for this chapter by enhancing the previous script **cpback.sh** (*18.15.1*) to accept multiple file-names. Since this script now uses at least two arguments, the last argument must be a directory. The text of the script is shown in Fig. 18.3.

From the argument list, we must be able to construct a second list that excludes the directory name. In other words, we must be able to use a **for** loop to iterate for all script arguments except the last one. The UNIX shell doesn't have any symbol that identifies the last argument or parameter, so we'll have to use our knowledge of filters to do this job.

F I G U R E 18.3 cpback2.sh: *Script to Copy Multiple Files without Overwriting*

```
#!/bin/sh
# Program cpback2.sh -- Copies multiple files to a directory
# Makes backups instead of overwriting the destination files
# Copies foo to foo.1 if foo exists or foo.2 if foo.1 exists .......

if [ $# -lt 2 ] ; then
    echo "Usage: $0 source(s) destination" ; exit
fi

echo $* | tr ' ' '\012' > $$              # Place each argument in a separate line
destination=`tail -1 $$`                  # The last line is the directory
if [ ! -d $destination ] ; then
    echo "Directory $destination doesn't exist"
else
    count=`expr $# - 1`                    # To iterate for 1 less than argument count
    for file in `head -$count $$` ; do
        if [ ! -f $destination/$file ] ; then
            cp $file $destination                           # No overwriting here
        else
            copies=1
            while true ; do
                if [ ! -f $destination/$file.$copies ] ; then
                    cp $file $destination/$file.$copies
                    echo "File $file copied to $file.$copies"
                    break                           # No further iteration needed
                else
                    copies=`expr $copies + 1`                # Go for the next number
                fi
            done
        fi
    done
fi
rm $$                                      # Remove this temporary file
```

To create the new list, we used **tr** to convert the space in the argument list to the newline character. This ensures that each script argument is placed in a separate line in the file represented by $$. The last line of this file is the directory name (`tail -1 $$`), so we store it in the variable destination. We now subtract the number of arguments by 1 (count=`expr $# - 1`) and then use **head** to pick up all lines except the last one (**head -$count $$**) and provide this list to **for**.

Don't forget to remove the temporary file (**rm $$**) after your work is over. Everything else remains much the same, so let's continue the copying exercise to the same safe directory—this time using some more filenames. We'll assume that the file toc.pl (but not index) also exists in the directory safe. We'll run the same command line a number of times:

```
$ cpback2.sh vvi.sh toc.pl index safe
File vvi.sh copied to vvi.sh.3
File toc.pl copied to toc.pl.1
$ cpback2.sh vvi.sh toc.pl index safe                          Run again
File vvi.sh copied to vvi.sh.4
File toc.pl copied to toc.pl.2
File index copied to index.1
$ cpback2.sh vvi.sh toc.pl index safe                          ... and again
File vvi.sh copied to vvi.sh.5
File toc.pl copied to toc.pl.3
File index copied to index.2
```

The script works fine with multiple filenames too. Do you realize that you now have a tool that will copy one or more files but never overwrite the destination? Whenever you modify a program, you can use the **cpback2.sh** script to copy it to a directory, and the numeric extension will be provided automatically! If you are still not sure how all this happened, then turn to Section 19.15.

Note

You can imagine a host of applications for the **while** loop. For instance, it can be run in the background to issue reminders. If you can't bring yourself to use the **:w** command regularly to save a file, then you can use **while** to throw up an alert on your screen when you are using **vi**. This is set as an important exercise at the end of this chapter.

This completes the first of the two chapters that we have reserved for shell programming. You have seen for yourself the remarkable power of the shell programming language. Be sure that you have gleaned everything discussed here before we take up the shell's advanced features—including the exclusive features of the Korn and bash shells. We'll learn new techniques, develop even better and more compact code and do things we have never done before.

SUMMARY

The shell is also a programming language that executes shell scripts in the interpretive mode—one line at a time. Shell scripts run slower than compiled languages like C, but for many jobs speed is no hurdle.

Shell variables can be evaluated by using curly braces around the variable name. These braces also enable concatenation of a variable and a string.

A shell script is executed after assigning executable permission to the script file. It can also be run with the **sh** command. You can specify the shell a script must use by placing the statement #!/bin/sh in the first line of the script. sh should be replaced by ksh and bash when working with the Korn and bash shells.

The **read** statement accepts input to a script from the keyboard. The input is read into one or more variables. A script containing a **read** statement can be redirected to take input from a file.

You can also run a script noninteractively by specifying arguments in the command line. These arguments are accepted into the positional parameters $1, $2, and so on. The shell parameter $# stores the number of arguments and $* contains all the arguments. $0 contains the name of the script that is executed.

Every command or script returns an *exit status* (or *return value*) on termination. This value is stored in the parameter $?. 0 signifies a true value; any non-zero value points to failure.

The && and || operators act as simple one-way conditionals. When && delimits two commands, the second command is executed only when the first command succeeds. The reverse is true for the || operator.

The **exit** statement terminates a script. It can be used with a number signifying the success or failure. This number is stored in $?.

The **if** statement takes three forms and is closed with **fi**. It evaluates the return value of the *control command* to perform a set of instructions. The optional **else** and **elif** components are used to specify another set of instructions if the previous control command fails. The control command can be a UNIX command.

The **test** statement has a synonym []. It can be used with numerous operators to compare numbers and strings, as well as test the file attributes. **test** doesn't produce any output but simply stores the result of its tests in $?.

case is a compact string-matching construct and is closed with **esac**. It uses the shell's wild cards to match multiple patterns in **egrep**-style. The * when used as the last option matches everything not matched by the previous options. The wild cards match strings and not files.

case is specially suitable for matching the filename $0. It lets you design a script that does different things depending on the name by which it is invoked.

expr is used for integer computation and string manipulation. It is used with the Bourne shell for incrementing the value of a variable. It uses regular expressions to extract a substring, locate the position of a character and evaluate the length of a string. Korn and bash don't need **expr**.

The **while** loop executes its body as long as the control command returns a true value. It is used in scripts that repeatedly increment the value of a variable or provide multiple chances to a user. You can set up an infinite loop using **true** as the control command. The **until** loop complements **while**.

for works with each element of a list at a time. The list can be generated by variables, wild cards, positional parameters and command substitution. You can compile a group of C programs or perform mass substitution with **sed** on a group of files by placing their code inside the loop.

All loops use the keywords **do** and **done**. The **break** statement terminates a loop, while **continue** starts the next iteration.

You should use "$@" with a **for** loop when using multiword arguments. You can use **basename** inside a **for** loop to change the extensions of files.

SELF-TEST

18.1   If x has the value 10, what are the values of xx and xx?

18.2   A shell script run as **foo.sh** did something quite different from what you had put inside the script. Why do you think that happened, and what do you do?

18.3   If you have developed a script using the Korn shell, how will you make sure the script will use that shell even if the login shell is different?

18.4   If a script calls itself, what do you think will happen?

18.5   If a script is run as **foo -l -t bar[1-3]**, what are the values of $# and $* ? Does it make any difference if the options are combined?

18.6   What is the *exit status* of a command? What is its normal value, and where is the value stored?

18.7   If a file containing nothing is executed, what will be the return value?

18.8   Search for a pattern with **grep**, **sed** and **awk**. Test the return value of each command when it fails in its search. What conclusions would you draw?

18.9   What are the external UNIX commands that were introduced in this chapter? Why were they located here?

18.10 Can you use **sh < foo.sh** instead of **sh foo.sh** to execute the script?

18.11 How can you run the **emp4.sh** script *(18.9.2)* noninteractively so that it displays the final output without prompting?

18.12 Write a script which accepts a file containing a list of arithmetic expressions as argument, and then uses **bc** to print both the expression and the value in the form *expression=value*.

18.13 What will this construct do and why?

```
while [ 5 ]
```

18.14 How can you repeat a command 10 times using only a **for** loop?

18.15 What is the unusual feature of this program?

EXERCISES

18.1   How can you prevent a user from executing a shell script? Should you remove the executable permission from the script file?

18.2   If x has the value 5, and you reassign it with x="expr $x + 10", what is the new value of x? What would have been the value if single quotes were used? What's wrong with all this anyway?

18.3   A script named **test** containing the **df** and **du** commands displays nothing when executed. Why does that happen? State two ways of making the script behave properly.

18.4 Devise a script that locates all the hard links of the argument file from the home directory. The filename provided as argument must exist in the current directory.

18.5 Write a shell script that lists files by modification time when called with **lm** and by access time when called with **la**. What else do you have to do before you execute it?

18.6 Write a script that accepts a pattern and filename as arguments and then counts the number of occurrences of the pattern in the file. (A pattern may occur more than once in a line and comprise only alphanumeric characters and the underscore.)

18.7 Use a script to display a special listing of files showing their date of modification and access time (side by side) along with their permissions, sizes and filenames. The script should accept any number of arguments to display a selective listing and should abort if no filenames are specified as arguments. Provide headers for the columns.

18.8 Accept a string from the terminal and use **case** to echo a suitable message if the string doesn't have at least 10 characters.

18.9 How will you do the same thing using **expr**?

18.10 Use **expr** to extract the parent directory from a file's absolute pathname.

18.11 There are at least six syntactical mistakes in this program. Locate them. (Line numbers are shown on left.)

```
1    ppprunning = yes
2    while $ppprunning = yes ; do
3       echo "   INTERNET MENU\n
4       1. Dial out
5       2. Exit
6       Choice:
7       read choice
8       case choice in
9          1) if [ -z "$ppprunning" ]
10               echo "Enter your username and password"
11             else
12                chat.sh
13             endif ;
14          *) ppprunning=no
15       endcase
16   done
```

18.12 Display the processes in the system five times every 30 seconds using a (i) **while** loop (ii) **for** loop.

18.13 Send the contents of the file msg.lst as a message to all users who are logged in. Users logged in more than once should get a *single* message.

18.14 Write a script that displays, in **head**-style, the last three lines of each file in the current directory, duly preceded by the filename.

18.15 Write a script that accepts one or more filenames as arguments and converts the filenames to uppercase.

18.16 Devise a script that accepts two directory names bar1 and bar2, and deletes those files in bar2 whose contents are identical to their namesakes in bar1.

18.17 Develop script logic that allows only romeo and henry to execute it, and only from the terminals tty05 and tty06.

18.18 Call up **vi** from a script so that every three minutes you hear a beep and see a message in the last line. This message appears in reverse video and reminds you to save the buffer. (Hint: Use **tput** to position the cursor. Set up a loop in the background and kill it when **vi** terminates.)

KEY TERMS

command failure *(18.5)*

control command *(18.8.1)*

exit status *(18.5)*

positional parameter *(18.4)*

return value *(18.5)*

shell script *(18.2)*

## CHAPTER 19

Advanced Shell Programming Including Korn and bash

In this chapter, we'll discover the shell's advanced features. We'll analyze the environment created by a shell and devise means of handling the shell's streams. Some shell statements run in sub-shells which often don't let us do the things we want. We'll learn to pass environmental parameters to a sub-shell and run commands without spawning one. We'll also discuss those features that previously belonged to the domain of external commands but now are built into the modern shells.

This chapter also features some of the important features of the Korn shell and bash. Both borrow features from the modern procedural languages and can handle computation, strings and arrays. Korn's *ksh93* version elevates the shell's status even further and gives us a portent of things to come—incorporating many of **awk**'s and **perl**'s features in the shell itself.

The other features discussed in this chapter are also available in the Bourne shell, but to smoothly work your way through all the examples discussed in this chapter, you are strongly advised to switch to either the Korn shell or bash. We'll discuss those features common to both Korn and bash, and every such feature is indicated in the section heading itself.

Objectives

- Use **set** and **shift** to extract fields from single-line command output. *(19.1)*
- Place data for a program in the same script with the *here document*. *(19.2)*
- Use **let** for computation in the Korn shell and bash. *(19.3)*
- Provide redirection at the keywords of a loop or conditional. *(19.4.1)*
- Merge the standard output and standard error streams with the symbols 1>&2 and 2>&1. *(19.4.2 and 19.4.3)*
- Make variables visible in sub-shells with **export**. *(19.6.1)*
- Understand the significance of the () and {} operators in relation to the process. *(19.6.2)*
- Use arrays supported by the Korn shell and bash. *(19.7)*
- Handle strings with the built-in facilities of the Korn shell and bash. *(19.8)*
- Evaluate variables in different ways depending on whether they are set or not. *(19.9)*
- Understand how *shell functions* are superior to aliases. *(19.10 and 19.11)*

- Use **eval** to evaluate a command line twice and produce generalized prompts and variables *(19.12 and 19.13)*
- Overlay the current program with another and handle multiple streams with **exec**. *(19.14)*
- Debug shell scripts with **set** **-x**. *(19.15)*
- Use **trap** to determine the action a script is to take on receiving a signal. *(19.16)*

19.1 set: Assigning Values to Positional Parameters

Some UNIX commands like **date** produce single-line output. Output of other commands is often filtered through line extractors like **grep** and **head** to produce a single line. Sometimes you need to access one or more fields in this line. We faced a similar situation in the previous chapter *(18.10.1)* when we had to use **cut** to extract a field from the **date** output:

```
case `date | cut -d" " -f1` in
```

Calling up an external command merely to extract a single field is sure overkill. The shell has an internal command to do this job—the **set** statement. It performs a very simple function: it assigns the positional parameters $1, $2 and so on to its arguments. This feature is especially useful for picking up individual fields from the output of a program. Using **date** with command substitution, you can now assign values to the positional parameters:

```
$ set `date`
$ echo $*
Thu Sep 30 08:27:50 EST 1999
$ echo "The date today is $2 $3, $6"
The date today is Sep 30, 1999
$ echo $#
6
```

When using **set**, $* and $# are also set in the usual way. You no longer need to use **cut** to extract any field; **set** does it easily. By default, **set** parses the string of values on whitespace and inserts values into the positional parameters. The Bourne shell allows *direct* access of up to nine parameters, but Korn and bash can access any parameter. If you set the contents of this entire chapter to **set**, you can access each and every word provided you use curly braces from the tenth parameter onwards:

```
$ set `cat ux3rd19`
$ echo $#
20202                                          This many words in this chapter
$ echo $4 $5
SHELL PROGRAMMING
$ echo ${12}                                   Works only with bash and ksh
BASH
```

The possibilities are immense. The output of any command or pipeline can be parsed into words with **set** without using any external command. The fact that **set** uses whitespace as the delimiter is no restriction as this delimiter also can be changed with the shell variable IFS.

Caution

If a script accepts command line arguments and also uses the **set** statement, don't forget to save the command line arguments in separate variables before using **set**. Because **set** uses the same notation for its own parameters, it will overwrite those used by the arguments.

KORN Shell

BASH Shell

Unlike in the Bourne shell, there are no restrictions on the number of parameters that you can directly access. For instance, you have to use curly braces to access the fortieth parameter:

```
echo ${40}
```

19.1.1   The IFS Variable: set's Default Delimiter

IFS contains a string of characters that are used as word separators in the command line. The string normally consists of the space, tab and the newline characters. None of these characters is visible, so **echo $IFS** outputs a blank line:

```
$ echo $IFS
```
blank line

Even though nothing shows up, there is something there. You can confirm the contents of this variable by taking its octal dump:

```
$ echo "$IFS" | od -bc
0000000 040 011 012 012                    Space, tab and newline constitute IFS
          \t  \n  \n
0000004
```

The space is represented by the ASCII octal value 040; you have used \t and \n with **echo**. **set** uses the value of IFS to determine its delimiter. You normally don't bother about this variable, but if a line has to be parsed on some other delimiter, then you need to make a temporary change to IFS. For instance, consider this line of /etc/passwd:

```
$ grep henry /etc/passwd
henry:x:501:100:henry blofeld:/home/henry:/bin/ksh
```

If you encounter a line like this when reading a file with the **read** statement, you can easily extract the sixth field by changing the value of IFS before using **set**:

```
$ IFS=:
$ set `grep "^henry" /etc/passwd`
$ echo $6
/home/henry
```

We'll need to change the IFS variable in some examples in this chapter. **set** and IFS are useful accessories that one would like to have, but they become more useful still when used in tandem with **shift**.

19.1.2   shift: Shifting Arguments Left

Many scripts use the first argument to indicate a separate entity—say a filename. The other arguments could then represent a series of strings—probably different patterns to be selected from a file. We know how to exclude the last argument from a list *(18.17)*; this time we'll have to exclude the first argument. This is the job of the **shift** statement.

    shift renames a positional parameter to its immediate lower numbered one. When called once, $2 becomes $1, $3 becomes $2, and so on. Try this on the positional parameters that were filled up with the **date** command:

```
$ echo $*
Thu Sep 30 08:27:50 EST 1999
$ echo $1 $2 $3
Thu Sep 30
$ shift                                                    $1 gets lost
$ echo $1 $2 $3
Sep 30 08:27:50
$ shift 2                                                  Shifts 2 places
$ echo $1 $2 $3
08:27:50 EST 1999
```

Note that the leftmost parameter, $1, is lost every time **shift** is invoked. So if a script uses 12 arguments, you can shift three times and then use $9. This makes it possible to design a script that accepts both a filename and a set of patterns as arguments:

```
$ cat emp7.sh
# Script using the shift feature

case $# in
    0|1) echo "Usage: $0 file pattern(s)" ; exit 2 ;;
      *) flname=$1                    # Store $1 as variable before it gets lost
         shift
         for pattern in "$@" ; do              # We'll use "$@" instead of $*
             grep "$pattern" $flname || echo "Pattern $pattern not found"
         done ;;
esac
```

You can now use the script with a variable number of arguments (not less than two):

```
$ emp7.sh emp.lst
Usage: emp7.sh file pattern(s)
$ emp7.sh emp.lst wilcocks 1006 9877
3212|bill wilcocks   |d.g.m.    |accounts  |12/12/55| 85000
1006|gordon lightfoot|director  |sales     |09/03/38|140000
Pattern 9877 not found
```

Note that here `flname` stores the string emp.lst, and the **for** loop iterates with the three strings `wilcocks`, 1006 and 9877.

Tip

Every time you use **shift**, the leftmost variable gets lost; so it should be saved in a variable before using **shift**. If you have to start iteration from the fourth parameter, save the first three parameters and then use **shift 3**.

19.1.3   set --: Helps Command Substitution

You'll often need to use **set** with command substitution. There is a small problem though, especially when the output of the command begins with a -:

```
$ set `ls -l unit01`
-rw-r--r--: bad option(s)
```

Since the permissions string begins with a - (for regular files), **set** interprets it as an option and finds it to be a "bad" one. **set** creates another problem when its arguments evaluate to a null string. Consider this command:

```
set `grep PPP /etc/passwd`
```

If the string PPP can't be located in the file, **set** will operate with no arguments and puzzle the user by displaying all variables on the terminal (its default output)! The solution to both these problems lies in the use of -- (two hyphens) immediately after **set**:

```
set -- `ls -l unit01`                          The first - now taken care of
set -- `grep PPP /etc/passwd`                     Null output is no problem
```

set now understands that the arguments following -- are not to be treated as options. The two hyphens also direct **set** to suppress its default behavior if the arguments evaluate to a null string.

19.1.4   Using set to Find Out Free Disk Space

Observe the output of the **df** command in Section 6.17, which displays the used and free disk space for every file system. A typical line of the output reads like this:

```
/home           (/dev/dsk/c0t0d0s3 ): 107128 blocks    495356 files
```

We can devise a script that accepts the file system *mounting directory* (the first field) as argument and extracts the free space (the first of the two numbers) from the line matching it. It can even mail a message if the free space falls below a critical figure. The **df.sh** script does this job:

```
$ cat df.sh
# df.sh -- Program to monitor free space on disk
# Uses the name of the file system as argument
set -- `df | grep "^$1"`
if [ $4 -lt 200000 ] ; then
    echo "Free space in $1 has dropped to $4 blocks" | mail root
fi
```

In this UNIX system, the file system is shown in the first column, the reason why **grep** is used with the ^ to anchor the pattern. The numeric comparison is made for the fourth field. A message is mailed to root when the free space in that file system falls below 200,000 blocks. The script is invoked like this with the name of the mounting directory:

```
df.sh /home                                        Finds free space of /home file system
```

This is a script a system administrator would like to run repeatedly, so it's best placed in the administrator's crontab file for execution by **cron**. This entry should run the job every hour on every working day between 9 a.m. and 5 p.m.:

```
0 09-17 * * 1-5  /home/admin/scripts/df.sh
```

19.2   The Here Document (<<)

There are occasions when the data your program reads is fixed and fairly limited. The shell uses the << symbols to read data from the same file containing the script. This is referred to as a **here document**, signifying that the data is here rather than in a separate file. Any command using standard input can also take input from a here document.

This feature is useful when used with commands that don't accept a filename as argument (like the **mail** command, for instance). If the message is short (which any mail message is normally expected to be), you can have both the command and message in the same script:

```
mail juliet << MARK
Your program for printing the invoices has been executed
on `date`. Check the print queue              Command substitution permitted
The updated file is known as $flname                Variable evaluation too
MARK
```

The here document symbol (<<) is followed by three lines of data and a delimiter (the string MARK). The shell treats every line following the command and delimited by MARK as input to the command. juliet at the other end will only see the three lines of message text; the word MARK itself doesn't show up. When this sequence is placed inside a script, execution is faster because **mail** doesn't have to read an external file—it's *here*.

Note

The contents of a here document are interpreted and processed by the shell before it goes as input to a command. This means you can use command substitution and variables in its input. You can't do that with normal standard input.

19.2.1   Using the Here Document with Interactive Programs

Many commands require input from the user. Often, it's the same input that is keyed in response to a series of questions posed by the command. For instance, you may have to enter a y two or three times when the command pauses, but the questions may not come in quick succession. Rather than wait for the prompt, we can instruct the script to take input from a here document.

Consider the Linux **fdisk** command *(21.9.1)* which uses the internal commands **p** for displaying the file partitions and **q** for quitting **fdisk**. As a system administrator, you'll have to make sure you are using the right device names of your hard disk partitions when doing your job. You can perform a quick check by using this script:

```
# cat showpart.sh                                    Using the root prompt—#
fdisk << END
p
q
END
```

Now, when you run **showpart.sh** from the root prompt (#), you instantly have the partition information in front of you. We have done it once before *(18.3.1)*, and we have done it again; we have made an interactive program behave noninteractively. A typical **fdisk** output is shown in Section 21.9.1.

Tip

If you write a script that uses one or more **read** statements and which you are always running with a predefined set of replies, you can run the script with a here document for noninteractive operation. It aids in automation too.

19.3   **let: Computation—A Second Look** (ksh **and** bash)

Korn and bash come with a built-in integer handling facility that totally dispenses with the need to use **expr**. You can compute with the **let** statement:

```
$ let sum=256+128                                    No whitespace after variable
$ echo $sum
384
```

If you use whitespace for imparting better readability, just quote the expression:

```
$ let sum="3 * 6 + 4 / 2" ; echo $sum
20
```

Let's see how **let** handles variables. First define three variables; a single **let** does it:

```
$ let x=12 y=18 z=5
$ let z=x+y+$z                                        $ not required by let
$ echo $z
35
```

let permits you to get rid of the $ altogether when making an assignment. Since this computational feature is built-in, scripts run much faster than when used with **expr**. Later, we'll be using **let** in place of **expr** in one of our scripts.

Computation with **let** is still restricted to integer handling. However, the *ksh93* version of the Korn shell handles floating point numbers too. Since **printf** is also now built into both these shells, there's a lot we can do without using even **awk**!

A Second Form of Computing with ((and)) The Korn shell and bash use the
(( )) operators that replace the **let** statement itself:

```
$ x=22 y=28 z=5
$ z=$((x+y + z))                              Whitespace is unimportant
$ echo $z
55
$ z=$((z+1))                                  Can also use z=$((z+=1))
$ echo $z
56
```

The POSIX specification recommends the use of ((and)) rather than **let**, and this
form is likely to become a standard feature of the shells. It's easier to use too because
a variable doesn't have to be preceded by the $. The entire arithmetic operation, how-
ever, needs to be preceded by a single $.

19.4 Redirection—A Second Look

We are not done with redirection yet. So far, we have been using redirection in a sim-
plistic manner—providing the redirection symbols with commands that needed them.
We have also been treating each stream separately rather than combining these streams.
In the following paragraphs, we'll learn to apply redirection at other places where it can
be more effective. We'll also use some new symbols for merging two different streams.

19.4.1 Redirection at Keywords

Refer to the script **emp5.sh** *(18.14)* where we added a line to newlist with the >>
symbol:

```
echo "$code|$description" >> newlist
```

Redirecting the **echo** statement causes newlist to be opened every time **echo** is called
up—not an efficient way of working at all. The shell avoids such multiple file openings
and closures by providing a redirection facility at the **done** keyword itself:

```
done > newlist
```

Here, the file is opened and closed only once, but it also leads to a very serious consequence: all commands inside the loop using standard output also get redirected to
newlist. Some command output still needs to come to the terminal, so you should
explicitly redirect them to /dev/tty. Here's the revised version of the program
emp5.sh:

```
$ cat emp5a.sh
answer=y                               # Must set it to y first to enter the loop
while [ "$answer" = "y" ]              # The control command
do
    echo "Enter the code and description: \c"  >/dev/tty
    read code description              # Read both together
```

```
        echo "$code|$description"        # No redirection here
        echo "Enter any more (y/n)? \c"  >/dev/tty
        read anymore
        case $anymore in
            y*|Y*) answer=y ;;                # Anything starting with y or Y
            n*|N*) answer=n ;;                # Anything starting with n or N
                *) answer=y ;;                # Any other reply means y
        esac
done > newlist                           # Only one echo statement goes to file
```

There are two statements here that are directed to /dev/tty. Even if redirection at the **done** keyword collectively redirects the standard output of all statements inside the loop, these two statements will be exempted as they have been explicitly redirected to the terminal.

Redirection is also available at the **fi** and **esac** keywords, and includes input redirection and piping:

```
fi > foo                                 All statements between if and fi
esac > foo                               All statements between case and esac
done < param.lst                         Entire loop takes input from param.lst
done | while true                        Pipes output to a while loop
```

We have surreptitiously used the last form in the previous chapter *(18.14.2)*. Now, we have sanction to use it.

19.4.2   Merging Streams (1>&2)

Redirection with /dev/tty also has its share of problems. A stream redirected once can't be redirected again. It also means typing out the nine characters in >/dev/tty every time you want to send output to the terminal. The shell supports a feature of stream merging which can often make things a lot easier.

The idea is simple. Since the standard error stream goes to the terminal, terminal-destined statements can be directed to merge their standard output with this stream. You then need to handle only the standard error stream for controlling these statements. This merger uses the & operator with the redirection symbol. When you use an **echo** statement in a script in this way:

```
echo "None of the patterns found" 1>&2                          >&2 will also do
```

you are in fact saying: "Merge the two streams and send the merged stream to the destination of the standard error—by default, the terminal." This means that if you redirect the loop—or even the entire script to a separate file—the output of this statement will *always* be seen on the terminal. Since 1 is the default file descriptor for standard output, you can also use >&2.

Note

You can redirect the merged stream in the normal manner. When you use **find_number.sh > foo 2> bar**, all script statements having the symbols 1>&2 affixed will actually write to bar. The rest of the script output will be saved in foo.

19.4.3   Saving Error Messages and Output in the Same File (2>&1)

You can reverse the roles of the standard output and standard error streams. The following command merges the two streams as usual, but this time the standard error stream goes where standard output also goes:

```
cat foo1 foo2 foo3 > bar 2>&1
```

Does it make any difference whether we use 1>&2 or 2>&1? Yes, it does. In this example, if foo3 can't be opened, **cat**'s error message will be saved with the contents of foo1 and foo2 in bar. We now have a facility of saving error messages in the same file as the normal output. If you have understood this, then you would agree that the above statement can also be expressed in this way:

```
cat foo1 foo2 foo3 2> bar 1>&2
```

This feature has great implications for you—both as script developer and system administrator. If you have to run a program when you are away, you can redirect the script so that both output and error messages are saved in the same file:

```
content.sh 2>&1 | sort > bar                           Sorting merged output
content.sh 2> bar 1>&2
```

bar now contains the output of both streams. The first form even lets you pipe the stream to another command. If you are using **cron** to run the script, then this is the only way you'll know what went wrong with your program. You must understand and remember this.

Note

When you affix the symbols 1>&2 or 2>&1 to a command using standard output, you are only merging the standard output and standard error streams and not redirecting them. You have to provide the redirection symbol additionally if you want to redirect the merged stream.

19.5   user_details.sh: A Script to List User Details

Now, let's consider an interesting application of loop redirection and stream merging by printing the user details from /etc/passwd and /etc/group. This Korn shell script accepts a range of UIDs as two arguments and reads in the fields related to each UID from /etc/passwd. It also looks up /etc/group for the numeric GUID and extracts the group name as well.

The script also uses the **printf** command available in most UNIX systems. It is now a built-in in bash and *ksh93*. There's nothing new about **printf**; you have used it in **awk** already for formatting the output. The script **user_details.sh** is shown in Fig 19.1.

printf here uses no commas; that's all you need to remember. The two arguments are held in the variables uidmin and uidmax, and the **while** loop reads each line of /etc/passwd in turn. Each line is split into seven fields as shown in the **read** statement. The fourth field (gid) is searched in /etc/group with the **set** statement. The variable kount counts the number of lines read from /etc/passwd.

FIGURE 19.1 *The* `user_details.sh` *Script*

```
#!/bin/ksh
case $# in
  2) ;;                                      # Needs two arguments
  *) echo "Usage: $0 min_guid max_guid" 1>&2 ; exit
esac

IFS=:
uidmin=$1 ; uidmax=$2              # Save $1 and $2 before set replaces them
echo "\
Username     UID  GUID  Gname     GCOS          Home Directory    Login Shell
---------------------------------------------------------------------------"
kount=0
while read username password uid gid gcos homedir shell
do
    if [ $uid -ge $uidmin -a $uid -le $uidmax ] ; then
        set -- `grep ":$gid:" /etc/group`    # Replaces previous $1 and $2
        gname=$1
        printf "%-10s %4d %4d   %-8s %-14s %-14s    %-12s\n" \
                $username $uid $gid $gname $gcos $homedir $shell
        kount=`expr $kount + 1`
    fi
done < /etc/passwd
case $kount in
  0) echo "No lines found" 1>&2     ;;
  *) echo "$kount lines found" 1>&2
esac
```

This loop takes its input at the **done** keyword. Note the three statements that merge the standard output stream with the standard error (with 1>&2). This means that you can now safely redirect the entire script to a file and yet have any of those messages on the terminal. We'll run the script in three ways:

```
$ user_details.sh  > newlist                      Without arguments
Usage: user_details.sh min_guid max_guid
$ userdetails.sh 701 703 > newlist                With invalid arguments
No lines found
$ userdetails.sh 601 603 > newlist                Valid arguments
3 lines found
```

Stream merging is working fine, so it seems. Let's now see what `newlist` contains:

```
$ cat newlist
Username    UID  GUID  Gname   GCOS           Home Directory    Login Shell
-------------------------------------------------------------------------
romeo       601  100   users   Romeo N.       /home/romeo       /bin/ksh
juliet      602  100   users                  /home/juliet      /bin/bash
henry       603  100   users   henry blofeld  /home/kaust       /bin/bash
```

Look how the standard output of two other statements (**echo** and **printf**) made their way to this file. You looked up two files, and produced formatted output from them with **printf**—using a script that used only one external command (**grep**)!

Note

If you had run the script from the Bourne shell, you would have used two external commands (**grep** and **printf**). But you would have also obtained the message No lines found even if you find them in `newlist`. The **while** loop in Bourne runs in a sub-shell, so the value of `kount` inside the loop is not available outside it. The **exec** statement *(19.14)* can solve this problem.

19.6   Problems with Sub-Shells

When a process is created by the shell, it makes available certain features of its own environment to the child. The created process (representing the command) can also make use of these inherited parameters for it to operate. These parameters include:

- The PID of the parent process.
- The UID (owner) and GUID (group owner) of the process.
- The current working directory.
- The three standard files.
- Other open files used by the parent process.
- Some environment variables available in the parent process.

We have used variables like HOME and SHELL inside shell scripts (which run in a sub-shell) without ever defining them. But what happens to those variables that we define in the `.profile` or other scripts? Are they also passed on to a sub-shell? There are a number of other issues related to the shell's environment that should concern us and they are taken up in the following paragraphs.

19.6.1   export: Exporting Shell Variables

By default, the values stored in shell variables are not passed on to a child shell. But the shell can also **export** (with the **export** statement) these variables recursively to all child processes so that they are available globally. You have used this statement before, but now you should understand why you have done so.

Consider a simple script which echoes the value of a variable x that is defined in the shell before the script is executed:

```
$ cat var.sh
echo The value of x is $x
x=20                                      # Now change the value of x
echo The new value of x is $x
```

First assign the value 10 to x at the prompt and then execute the script:

```
$ x=10 ; var.sh
The value of x is                              Value of x not visible in sub-shell
The new value of x is 20
$ echo $x                                      Value set inside script doesn't
10                                             affect value outside script
```

Because x is a local variable in the login shell, its value can't be accessed by **echo** in the script, which is run in a sub-shell. To make x available globally, you need to use the **export** statement before the script is executed:

```
$ x=10 ; export x
$ var.sh
The value of x is 10                           Value set outside script now visible here
The new value of x is 20
$ echo $x
10                                             Reset value in script still not available outside
```

When x is exported, its assigned value (10) is also available in the script. But when you export a variable, it has another important consequence; a reassignment (x=20) made in the script (the sub-shell) is not seen in the parent shell that executed the script.

You must export the variables you define unless you have strong reasons not to let sub-shells inherit their values. To know whether you have already done so, use **export** without arguments. It lists all environment variables (which are already exported) and user-defined variables (like x) that you have exported. The **env** command also lists the exported variables.

Note

A variable is only local to the process in which it's defined. But when exported, it is available recursively to all child processes. However, when the child alters the value of the variable, the change is not seen in the parent. Many people make the mistake of using the **export** command every time they change the value of a variable. It's simply not necessary.

19.6.2   Command Grouping

Apart from the parentheses *(2.5.1)*, the shell also uses the { } to group commands. The difference between the two is that the former executes the command group in a sub-shell, while the other uses the current shell only. This becomes quite evident when we use both operators with the built-in **cd** and **pwd** commands:

```
$ pwd
/home/romeo
$ ( cd progs ; pwd )
/home/romeo/progs
$ pwd
/home/romeo                                    Back to original directory
```

Working from a sub-shell, **cd** changed the working directory (one of the environmental parameters) to /home/romeo/progs. The parent (login shell) can't adopt this change, so the original directory is back in place. The same command group—this time using the {} operators—tells a different story:

```
$ pwd
/home/romeo
$ { cd progs ; pwd
> }
/home/romeo/progs
$ pwd
/home/romeo/progs                                 Directory change is now permanent
```

The two commands have now been executed without spawning a shell; the change of directory is now permanent.

Tip

The closing curly brace is placed on a separate line by itself. If, however, you want both braces in the same line, simply terminate the last command with a semicolon:

```
{ cd progs ; pwd ; }
```

But where does one use these command grouping features? Review the scripts developed in Chapter 18, and you'll notice that in many of them you can replace certain sections with a suitable command grouping sequence. For example, this one:

```
[ $# -ne 1 ] && { echo "Usage: $0 pattern" ; exit 3 ; }
```

can easily replace the opening section of the script **emp3b.sh** *(18.9.1)*. The program here is aborted if the user doesn't specify one argument.

Note

The () operators execute the enclosed commands in a sub-shell, while the {} operators do the same in the current shell. This means that if there is an **exit** statement in the command group, you must use {}, otherwise you won't be able to exit at all!

19.7 Arrays (ksh and bash)

Korn and bash support one-dimensional arrays where the first element has the index 0. While *ksh93* works within a limit of 4096 elements, bash suffers from no such restrictions. Here's how you set and evaluate the value of the third element of the array prompt:

```
$ prompt[2]="Enter your name"
$ echo ${prompt[2]}
Enter your name
```

Note that evaluation is done with the curly braces, and prompt[2] is treated just like a variable. It, however, doesn't conflict with a variable prompt that you may also define in the same shell. When a group of elements needs to be assigned, you can use a space-delimited list enclosed within parentheses:

```
month_arr=(0 31 29 31 30 31 30 31 31 30 31 30 31)
```

This defines the array `month_arr`. This syntax is used by bash and *ksh93*. If you are using an older version of Korn, then you can use the **set -A** statement:

```
set -A month_arr 0 31 29 31 30 31 30 31 31 30 31 30 31
```

In either case, the array stores the number of days available in each of the 12 months. **perl**'s arrays also use the first form for assignment. The first element had to be deliberately assigned to zero for obvious reasons. Finding out the number of days in June is simple:

```
$ echo ${month_arr[6]}
30
```

Using the @ or * as subscript, you can display all the elements of the array as well as the number of elements. The forms are similar except for the presence of the # in one:

```
$ echo ${month_arr[@]}
0 31 29 31 30 31 30 31 31 30 31 30 31
$ echo ${#month_arr[@]}                                          Length of the array
13
```

Can we use arrays to validate an entered date? The next script **dateval.sh** shown in Fig. 19.2 does just that and takes into account the change made to February in leap years (except the one that takes place at the turn of every fourth century).

The first option of the outer **case** construct checks for a null response. The second option uses the expression $n/$n/$n to check for an eight-character string in the form *mm/dd/yy*. Using a changed value of IFS, the components of the date are set to three positional parameters and checked for valid months. The second **case** construct makes the leap year check and then uses an array to validate the day. The **continue** statements take you to loop beginning whenever the test fails the validity check.

Now, let's test the script:

```
$ dateval.sh
Enter a date: [Enter]
No value entered
Enter a date: 13/28/00
Illegal month
Enter a date: 04/31/00
Illegal day
Enter a date: 02/29/01
2001 is not a leap year
Enter a date: 02/29/00
02/29/00 is a valid date
[Ctrl-c]
```

FIGURE 19.2   `dateval.sh`: *A Date Validation Script Using Arrays*

```
#!/bin/ksh
IFS="/"
n="[0-9][0-9]"
set -A month_arr 0 31 29 31 30 31 30 31 31 30 31 30 31

while echo "Enter a date: \c" ; do
  read value
  case "$value" in
        "") echo "No value entered" ; continue ;;
  $n/$n/$n) set $value
            let rem="$3 % 4"                          # Checks for leap year
            if [ $1 -gt 12 -o $1 -eq 0 ] ; then
                echo "Illegal month" ; continue
            else
                case "$value" in
                02/29/??) [ $rem -gt 0 ] &&           # 29 or 28 for Feb?
                            { echo "20$3 is not a leap year" ; continue ; } ;;
                      *) [ $2 -gt ${month_arr[$1]} -o $2 -eq 0 ] &&
                            { echo "Illegal day" ; continue ; } ;;
                esac
            fi;;
        *) echo "Invalid date" ; continue ;;
  esac
  echo "$1/$2/$3" is a valid date
done
```

Since the script has no clean exit path, we had to use the interrupt key to terminate execution. We'll discuss ways of handling that too.

19.8   String Handling (ksh **and** bash)

Korn and bash don't need **expr** as they have adequate string handling features themselves. Unlike **expr**, they use wild cards but not regular expressions. All forms of usage require curly braces to enclose the variable name along with some special symbols. The subtle variations in their forms make them difficult to remember and sometimes uncomfortable to work with.

Length of String   The length of a string is easily found by preceding the variable name with a #. Consider this example:

```
$ name="vinton cerf"
$ echo ${#name}
11
```

We used **expr** to compute the length of a string *(18.11.2)*, but the built-in feature is far easier to use:

```
if [ `expr "$name" : '.*'` -gt 20 ] ; then                        Using expr
if [ ${#name} -gt 20 ] ; then                                     Korn and bash
```

The second form looks more readable and is also faster since no external command is called up. It should eventually be easier to remember because **perl** uses a similar form to evaluate the length of an array *(20.8)*.

Extracting a Substring *ksh93* and bash offer simple techniques to extract a substring in ways any high-level language handles them. Using the same value of the variable name, here's how you can implement the **substr()** function used in **awk** and **perl**:

```
$ echo ${name:3:3}                                                First position is zero
ton
$ echo ${name:7}                                                  Extracts rest of string
cerf
```

This feature is much easier to use than the regular expression-oriented technique adopted by **expr**.

19.8.1 Extracting a String by Pattern Matching

You can extract a substring using a special pattern matching feature. These functions make use of two characters—# and %. Their selection seems to have been based on mnemonic considerations. # is used to match at the beginning and % at the end, and both are used inside curly braces when evaluating a variable.

To remove the extension from a filename, previously you had to use an external command—**basename** *(18.16.4)*. This time, you can use a variable's ${*variable%pattern*} format to perform the extraction. This is how you should go about it:

```
$ filename=quotation.txt
$ echo ${filename%txt}
quotation.                                                        txt stripped off
```

The % symbol after the variable name deletes the *shortest* string that matches the variable's contents at the *end*. If there were two %s instead of one, it would have matched the *longest* one. The %s have to be used with wild cards when extracting the hostname from an FQDN:

```
$ fqdn=java.sun.com
$ echo ${fqdn%%.*}
java
```

You'll recall that **basename** can also extract the base filename from a pathname. This requires you to delete the longest pattern which matches the pattern */, but at the beginning of the variable's value:

```
$ filename="/var/spool/mail/henry"
$ echo ${filename##*/}
henry
```

This deletes the segment /var/spool/mail—the longest pattern that matches the pattern */ at the beginning. Since you know the matching rules now, you can try matching with one #. The pattern matching forms of Korn and bash are listed in Table 19.1.

19.9 Conditional Parameter Substitution

To continue on the subject of variable evaluation, you can evaluate a variable depending on whether it has a null or defined value. You need the curly braces here too, but this time you'll have to use a : after the variable name, followed by any of the symbols +, -, = or ?. The symbol is followed by a string. This feature is known as **parameter substitution**, and is available in the Bourne shell also.

The + Option This uses the ${*variable*:+*string*} format. Here, *variable* is evaluated to *string* if it has a non-null value. It's the best way of echoing something if a directory is not empty:

```
found=`ls`
echo ${found:+"This directory is not empty"}
```

ls displays nothing if it finds no files, in which case the variable found is set to a null string. However, the message is echoed if ls finds at least one file.

The - Option This is the inverse of the + function. This can be used in a script which prompts for a filename, and then uses a default value when the user simply presses *[Enter]*:

```
echo "Enter the filename : \c"
read flname
fname=${flname:-emp.lst}                        Instead of using if [ -z $flname ]
```

If nothing is entered at the prompt, flname is evaluated to emp.lst. But fname actually contains this value. This compact assignment dispenses with the need for an **if** conditional.

TABLE 19.1   *Pattern Matching Operators of* **bash** *and* **ksh**

Form	Evaluates to segment remaining after deleting
${*var#pat*}	shortest segment that matches *pat* at beginning of *$var*
${*var##pat*}	longest segment that matches *pat* at beginning of *$var*
${*var%pat*}	shortest segment that matches *pat* at end of *$var*
${*var%%pat*}	longest segment that matches *pat* at end of *$var*

The = Option This also works similarly except that it goes a step further and *makes the assignment* to the variable that is evaluated. Instead of using separate statements for initializing and testing a loop variable, like this:

```
x=1 ; while [ $x -le 10 ]
```

you can combine them in a single statement:

```
while [ ${x:=1} -le 10 ]
```

The ? Option It works like the - option, except that it aborts and kills the shell if the value is null. You can terminate a script if the user fails to respond:

```
echo "Enter the filename : \c"
read flname
grep $pattern ${flname:?"No filename entered .... quitting"}
```

Except for the =, all these operators can also be used with positional parameters. Later in the chapter, you'll use this knowledge to compress some of the earlier script sequences. The shell's parameter substitution functions are listed in Table 19.2.

Note

The string handling techniques discussed in these two sections are merely ways of evaluating a variable. Except when used with the = option, they don't alter the value of the variable in any way. But you can set them to other variables, for instance: bname=${filename##*/} or fname=${flname:-emp.lst}.

19.10 Shell Functions

A **shell function** consists of a group of statements that are executed together as a bunch—a feature available in the Bourne shell too. A function goes further than a shell alias *(17.4)* in devising shortcuts to command sequences. Optionally, it also returns a value (which an alias can't):

```
function_name(){
        statements
        return value                                          Optional
}
```

TABLE 19.2 *Parameter Substitution Operators*

Form	Evaluates to
${*var*:+*pat*}	*pat* if *var* is set; otherwise null
${*var*:-*pat*}	$*var* if *var* is set; otherwise *pat*
${*var*:=*pat*}	As above, but set *var* to *pat*
${*var*:?*pat*}	$*var* if *var* is set; otherwise print *pat* and abort

The function definition is followed by (), and the body is enclosed within curly braces. When the function is called, it executes all statements in the body. The **return** statement, when present, returns a value representing the success or failure of the function (and not a string value). Since shell statements are executed in the interpretive mode, a shell function must precede the statements that call it.

Let's first consider a simple application. When viewing the listing of a large number of files in a directory, you are often compelled to use **ls -l | more**. Sometimes, you may like to use **ls** with select filenames as well. This command sequence is an ideal candidate for a shell function, which we can call **ll**:

```
$ ll () {
> ls -l $* | more
> }
```

Even though you need the () in the definition, you must not use them when invoking the function. You can now invoke the function with or without arguments:

ll	*Executes* ls -l | more
ll ux3rd??	*Executes* ls -l ux3rd?? | more

A C shell alias here would also have worked fine, but an alias has its limitations. Like shell scripts, shell functions also use command line arguments (like $1, $2, etc.). $* and $# also retain their usual significance in functions. Aliases don't recognize them, however.

Where does one define a shell function? A function can be defined at a number of places:

- At the beginning of every script using them.
- In the .profile (or the startup file specific to the shell), so it is available in the current session.
- In a separate "library" file so other applications can also use them.

We have used the **ll** function more like a procedure, but a shell function can also return a value with the **return** statement. This value signifying the success or failure of the function is stored in $?.

Note

The positional parameters set by shell scripts from command line arguments are not available *directly* to a shell function. They either have to be stored in separate variables or passed on to the function as its own arguments:

```
ll $2
```

Here the second argument ($2) of the shell script is accepted inside the function **ll** as its first parameter ($1). This means that $1 inside and outside a function represent different entities.

19.11   Devising Shell Functions

If you have developed a number of shell programs by now, you would most certainly have used repetitive sequences. A sequence could ask whether a user wants to continue or it could validate user input. In the forthcoming paragraphs, we'll craft some useful shell functions which you'll want to use in your scripts. We'll develop a "library" for them too so they are easily accessible.

19.11.1   Generating a Filename from the System Date

As a system administrator, you'll often need to maintain separate files for each day of a specific activity. If these filenames are derived from the system date, you can easily identify a file related to a certain day. It's a good idea to have this filename evaluated by a shell function **dated_fname()**, which in turn derives it from the **date** output. Let's define this function at the prompt:

```
$ dated_fname () {
> set -- `date`
> year=`expr $6 : '..\(..\)'`          Picks up last two characters from year
> flname="$2$3_$year"
> }
```

We stored the required value in `flname` because shell functions can return only true or false values, and not literals. Moreover, the positional parameters set inside a function are *not* available in the current shell. After you have executed the function, the value of `flname` should now be available in the current shell:

```
$ echo $flname
Sep22_00
```

This string can be used to frame unique filenames—one for each day. Instead of using **expr**, Korn and bash users should prefer to use the statement `year=${6##??}`. Oracle users can easily use this function to have a system-generated dump filename for the **exp** (export) command:

```
exp scott/tiger file=$flname
```

This will generate the export dump file Sep22_00.dmp. Create a library file **mainfunc.sh** and place this function definition there. We'll use this file later—after we have added two more functions to it.

19.11.2   To Continue or Not to Continue

We'll now consider a shell function that returns a value. Recall the sequence used at the end of the script **dentry1.sh** *(18.15.2)* which prompts the user for a y to continue, or an n to terminate the outermost loop. This routine is very often used inside shell scripts, and it's a good idea to convert this into a function **anymore()**:

```
anymore () {
   echo "\n$1 ?(y/n) : \c" 1>&2          Prompt supplied as argument
   read response
   case "$response" in
     y|Y) echo 1>&2 ; return 0 ;;
       *) return 1 ;;
   esac
}
```

The function uses its argument $1 to determine what the entire prompt will look like. When this function is invoked with the string `Wish to continue`, you are prompted for a response:

```
$ anymore "Wish to continue"

Wish to continue ?(y/n) : n
$ echo $?
1                                               Value specified in return statement
```

We'll make use of the return value of this function later in the chapter. Place this function definition too in **mainfunc.sh**.

19.11.3   Validating Data Entry

Review the script **dentry1.sh** once again *(18.15.2)*. Note the **while** loop that repeatedly prompts the user for a valid entry. This sequence also deserves to be converted to a shell function. We expect our function **valid_string()** to check two things—first that something is entered at all, and next whether it exceeds a certain length:

```
valid_string () {
    while echo "$1 \c"  1>&2 ; do
        read name
        case $name in
            "") echo "Nothing entered"  1>&2 ; continue ;;
             *) if [ `expr "$name" : '.*'` -gt $2 ] ; then
                    echo "Maximum $2 characters permitted" 1>&2
                else
                    break
                fi ;;
        esac
    done
    echo $name
}
```

The function takes two arguments—the prompt string and the maximum length of the response string. Korn and bash users would like to replace the section using the **expr** command with `[ ${#name} -gt $2 ]`. We'll also place this function in our library file **mainfunc.sh**. Now that this file holds three shell functions, you can make them available in any shell script by executing the library file with the dot command from inside the script. We'll do that in the script **user_passwd.sh**:

```
$ cat user_passwd.sh
# Script to validate user input -- uses a shell function twice

. mainfunc.sh                        # Makes function valid_string available

user=`valid_string "Enter your user-id :" 16`
stty -echo                           # Password not to be echoed
```

```
password=`valid_string "Enter your password:" 9`
stty echo                                       # Turns on echoing facility
echo "\nYour user-id is $user and your password is $password"
```

This small script accepts the user's name and password and validates them to ensure that they don't exceed 16 and 9 characters in length, respectively. A sample session shows how shell functions can reduce script size:

```
$ user_passwd.sh
Enter your user-id : robert louis stevenson
Maximum 16 characters permitted
Enter your user-id : scott
Enter your password:
Nothing entered
Enter your password: *****                        Doesn't show on screen
Your user-id is scott and your password is tiger
```

Because they accept all shell constructs including positional parameters, shell functions can often replace shell scripts. Invocation of a shell function reduces disk I/O since the function is resident in memory. Moreover, because a shell function is executed in the current shell, variables defined in the shell are also visible inside the function and vice versa (but not positional parameters). However, make sure you invoke just as many functions as you require for your current login session.

Tip

If a number of shell functions are used by multiple programs, you should place all of them in a single "library" file, and store the file at a convenient location. At the beginning of every script which requires these functions, insert a statement that executes the library file with the dot command.

19.12 eval: **Evaluating Twice**

Have you ever tried setting a variable to a pipeline and then executing it? Try running this:

```
cmd="ls | more"
$cmd                                             | and more are arguments to ls!
```

This doesn't produce paged output as you might expect. Now, define a "numbered prompt" and try to evaluate it:

```
$ prompt1="User Name:" ; x=1
$ echo $prompt$x                                 $prompt is undefined
1
```

In the first case, the shell identifies the | and more as arguments to **ls** and evaluates the variable later. As a result, **ls** treats them as two arguments and produces unpredictable output. In the second example, the shell first evaluates $prompt; it is undefined. It then evaluates $x, which has the value 1.

To make these command sequences run properly, we must be able to *postpone* evaluation of portions of the command line. We'll do that by using the **eval** statement (also available in Bourne) to evaluate a command line twice. In the first pass, it suppresses some evaluation and performs it only in the second pass.

We can make the first sequence work by using **eval** like this:

```
eval $cmd
```

In its first pass, **eval** locates three arguments—ls, | and more. It then reevaluates the command line and splits them on the | into two commands. The command should now run properly.

The second sequence can be made to work by hiding the first $ with a \, and then using **eval**:

```
$ x=1 ; eval echo \$prompt$x
User Name:
```

The first pass ignores the $ escaped with a \; this evaluation results in \$prompt1. The second pass ignores the \ and evaluates $prompt1 as a variable—exactly what we want. We'll now consider a useful application using multiple numbered variables.

If a script has to take input from the terminal 10 times, you need to define and use 10 variables to hold them. Sometimes, you won't even know the number of variables that are required at run time. We would prefer to have a more general script where the *variable name itself can be generated by the script on-the-fly*. We would store the prompts as variables and read the input into "numbered variables."

We have used a numbered prompt; we now need to use numbered variables like value1, value2, value3, and so on to hold the input:

```
$ { x=1
> eval echo \$prompt$x '\\c'
> read value$x                                    OK—no problems
> eval echo \$value$x ; }
User Name: kleinrock
kleinrock
```

The statement **read value$x** reads the response into the variable value1; **eval** makes two passes to echo this value. What you have achieved just now has far-reaching consequences which we'll exploit in our next script.

We can access a positional parameter with $1 or whatever, but can we access the last parameter directly? Since we have the value of $# available, we can use the services of **eval**:

```
$ tail -1 /etc/passwd
martha:x:605:100:martha mitchell:/home/martha:/bin/ksh
$ IFS=:
$ set `tail -1 /etc/passwd`                      set -- not required here
$ eval echo \$$#
/bin/ksh
```

Look, we don't even have to know the number of fields in a line of /etc/passwd. Since we can easily isolate the last script argument in this way, do we need to use **head** and **tail** in the script **cpback2.sh** *(18.17)* to exclude the directory from the list? There's an exercise on this topic for you in this chapter.

19.13   createuser.sh: **Using** eval **to Create a User**

We'll now develop a script to create a user with the **useradd** command *(22.3.2)*. This is the only script (**fdisk** discussed in Section 19.2.1 is also run from root) in the chapter which requires root permission. All arguments required by **useradd** are to be supplied interactively. The script should have the following features:

- Accept inputs into six fields using a numbered prompt and variable.
- Use the **anymore()** function placed in the file **mainfunc.sh**.
- Decide whether **echo** is to be used with the -**e** option, depending on whether the shell is bash or otherwise.

Since we'll have to prompt the user six times, it's quite tempting to use **eval** in producing a compact script. The **createuser.sh** script is shown in Fig. 19.3. This time the **mainfunc.sh** script is executed somewhat differently. The current directory is generally absent in the super user's PATH, and the dot command (in all shells except bash)

FIGURE 19.3   createuser.sh: *Script That Uses* **eval** *to Create a User*

```
# Program to create user -- uses eval to create prompts and variables
# Will run in the Korn and bash shells without modification

option=
[ $SHELL = "/bin/bash" ] && option=-e
. ./mainfunc.sh                                # Makes anymore() function available

prompt1="User Name:"      ; prompt2="User-id:"     ; prompt3="Group-id:"
prompt4="Home Directory:"; prompt5="Login Shell:"; prompt6="GCOS Details:"

while true ; do
    x=1
    while [ $x -le 6 ] ; do
        eval echo $option \$prompt$x '\\c' 1>&2       # Produces six prompts
        read value$x
        x=`expr $x + 1`
    done
    useradd -u $value2 -g $value3 -d $value4 -s $value5 -c "$value6" -m $value1
    anymore "More users to create" 1>&2 || break
done
```

doesn't look for the script in the current directory. That's why the relative pathname had to be used *(17.9.1—Note).*

The six prompts are defined at the beginning of the script as numbered variables. The inner **while** loop issues all of them in turn. The values are read into the variables value1, value2, and so on. We'll now create a user ppp:

```
# ./createuser.sh                          Required as . is not in root's PATH
User Name: ppp
User-id: 520
Group-id: 100
Home Directory: /home/ppp
Login Shell: /etc/ppp/ppplogin
GCOS Details: PPP Server Account
More users to create ?(y/n) : n
```

Hopefully, this should have created a new user account, but let's be sure by observing the last line of /etc/passwd:

```
# tail -1 /etc/passwd
ppp:x:520:100:PPP Server Account:/home/ppp:/etc/ppp/login
```

Now, this is amazing; thanks to **eval**, we have managed to read six user responses into six variables with a miniscule script! As **echo** automatically uses the -e option if bash is the user's login shell, the script will run without modifications in all shells. We had to execute the script with **./createuser.sh** because the current directory doesn't feature in the super user's PATH.

Note

The login shell that we specified when creating the ppp user is not a shell at all. Truly speaking, this can be any executable command (even a shell script), and need not be restricted to a shell. In fact, if you are creating a PPP server, you must not allow users access to the shell. The login process will run the **ppplogin** script and then log the user out. It's generally done that way.

19.14   The exec **Statement**

Your study of the mechanism of process creation *(10.2)* led you to the **exec** system call—one that overlays a forked process. This property has some importance to shell scripters who sometimes need to overwrite the current shell itself with another program's code. This is something we haven't done yet, but if you precede any UNIX command with **exec**, the command overwrites the current shell. This has the effect of logging you out after the completion of the command:

```
$ exec date
Sun Apr  9 14:12:03 EST 2000
login:
```

Sometimes, you might want to let a user run a single program automatically on logging in and deny her an escape to the shell. You can place the command in the .profile, duly preceded by **exec**. The command starts when the user logs in, but when command execution is complete, she is logged out. There was no shell there in the first place.

exec is useful in replacing the current shell with another one. When you use **exec ksh**, the current shell's environment is completely replaced by the new shell. This feature also lets you log in to a different user account by using **exec login** *userid*. This technique is useful when working on remote machines with **telnet**.

19.14.1 Effecting Redirection in the Current Shell

exec has another important property; it can redirect the standard streams for an entire script. If a script has several commands whose standard output go to a single file, then instead of using separate redirection symbols for each, you can use **exec** to reassign their default destination like this:

```
exec > found.lst
```
Can use >> also

What's the big deal you might say; one could redirect the script itself. But **exec** can create several streams apart from the standard three (0, 1 and 2)—each with its own file descriptor. For instance, you can create a file descriptor 3 for directing all output and associate it with a physical file foundfile:

```
exec 3>foundfile
```

You can now write the file by merging the standard output stream with the file descriptor 3:

```
echo "This goes to foundfile" 1>&3
```

In programming language this means that you can use **exec** to provide a logical name to a file (a *filehandle* in **perl**). With this powerful I/O handler, you should now be able to handle files in a simpler and more elegant way. Let's design a script which reads empids from a file. It then searches emp.1st and saves in three separate files the following:

- The lines found.
- The empids not found.
- Badly formed empids.

First, here's the file that contains the empids. It contains two three-digit empids which should be trapped by the script:

```
$ cat empid.lst
2233
9765
2476
789
1265
9877
5678
245
2954
```

FIGURE 19.4   `countpat.sh`: *Script Using* **exec** *to Create Multiple Streams*

```
exec  > $2                     # Open file 1 for storing selected lines
exec 3> $3                     # Open file 3 for storing patterns not found
exec 4> $4                     # Open file 4 for storing invalid patterns


[ $# -ne 4 ] && { echo "4 arguments required" ; exit 2 ; }


exec < $1                                   # Redirecting input
while read pattern ; do                     # read now reads from $1
    case "$pattern" in
        ????) grep $pattern emp.lst ||
            echo $pattern not found in file 1>&3 ;;
         *) echo $pattern not a four-character string 1>&4 ;;
    esac
done
exec 0<&- ; exec >&- ; exec 3>&- ; exec 4>&-          # Close the files
exec >/dev/tty              # Redirects standard output back to terminal
echo Job Over
```

The **countpat.sh** script shown in Fig. 19.4 divides the standard output into three streams and redirects them to three separate files. It requires four arguments—the file containing the patterns and the files for the three streams.

The standard output streams are merged with the file descriptors 1, 3 and 4. Note that we have also set $1 as the source of all standard input. This means that the **read** statement in the loop will take input from $1—the file containing the patterns. Once all file writing is over, the standard output stream has to be reassigned to the terminal (**exec >/dev/tty**), otherwise the message Job Over will also be saved in the filename passed to $2.

This script is quite clean and has two statements using the merging symbols. The **grep** statement uses the standard output's file descriptor so no merging is required. The script takes four arguments and diverts the output into three of them:

```
$ countpat.sh empid.lst foundfile notfoundfile invalidfile
Job Over
```

The message appears on the terminal instead of going to any of these files. Now, just have a look at the three files and see for yourself what has actually happened:

```
$ cat foundfile
2233|charles harris  |g.m.     |sales     |12/12/52| 90000
2476|jackie wodehouse|manager  |sales     |05/01/59|110000
1265|p.j. woodhouse  |manager  |sales     |09/12/63| 90000
5678|robert dylan    |d.g.m.   |marketing |04/19/43| 85000
```

```
$ cat notfoundfile
9765 not found in file
9877 not found in file
2954 not found in file
$ cat invalidfile
789 not a four-character string
245 not a four-character string
```

This then is the power of **exec**. It opened several files together and accessed each one separately in the same way **perl** uses its own filehandles. It's always preferable to use file descriptors instead of filenames because it makes shell scripts independent of them.

19.15   set -x: **Debugging Shell Scripts**

The shell also supports a feature often used to debug scripts—its -x option. When used inside a script (or even at the $ prompt), it echoes each statement on the terminal, preceded by a + as it is executed. Modify the **cpback2.sh** script *(18.17)* to turn on the **set** option by placing the following statement at the beginning of the script:

```
set -x
```

set +x turns off **set -x**, and you can place this at the end of the script. Continuing from the position we left off, let's run the script but this time with only one filename—index (copy index.2 already available in safe). The annotated output is shown below:

```
$ cpback2.sh index safe
+ [ 2 -lt 2 ]                                      Checks number of arguments
+ tr ' ' '\012'
+ echo index safe                                  This is echo $*
+ 1> 707
+ tail -1 707                                      Identifies the directory name
+ destination=safe                                 and sets it to variable
+ [ ! -d safe ]
+ expr 2 - 1
+ count=1
+ head -1 707                                      To copy only one file
+ [ ! -f safe/index ]
+ copies=1
+ true
+ [ ! -f safe/index.1 ]
+ expr 1 + 1
+ copies=2                                         index.1 exists
+ true
+ [ ! -f safe/index.2 ]
+ expr 2 + 1
+ copies=3                                         index.2 also exists
+ true
```

```
+ [ ! -f safe/index.3 ]
+ cp index safe/index.3                                              File copied to index.3
+ echo 'File index copied to index.3'
File index copied to index.3
+ break
+ rm 707                                                            Temporary file removed
```

This is an ideal tool to use if you have trouble finding out why scripts don't work in the manner expected. Note how the shell prints each statement as it is being executed, affixing a + to each. It shows you the command line of the **head**, **tail** and **cp** commands. It even shows you how **expr** increments the value of the variable copies at every iteration!

19.16   trap: **Interrupting a Program**

By default, shell scripts terminate whenever the interrupt key is pressed. It's not a good idea to terminate shell scripts in this way because that can leave a lot of temporary files in the disk. The **trap** statement lets you do the things you want in case the script receives a signal. The statement is normally placed at the beginning of a shell script and uses two lists:

trap '*command_list*' *signal_list*

When a script is sent any of the signals in *signal_list*, **trap** executes the commands in *command_list*. The signal list can contain the integer values or names of one or more signals—the ones you use with the **kill** command. So instead of using 2 15 to represent the signal list, you can also use INT TERM.

     If you habitually create temporary files named after the PID number of the shell, you should use the services of **trap** to remove them whenever an interrupt occurs:

trap 'rm $$* ; echo "Program interrupted" ; exit' 1 2 15

Now, when you send the signals 1, 2 or 15, **trap** intercepts ("catches") the signal, removes all files expanded from $$*, echoes the message and terminates the script. When the interrupt key is pressed, it sends the signal number 2. It's a good idea to include this number in all advanced scripts.

     You may also like to ignore the signal and continue processing. In that case, you should make the program immune to such signals by using a null command list:

trap '' 1 2 15   *The script can't be killed*

It's not mandatory to have a **trap** statement in your shell scripts. However, if you have one, don't forget to include the **exit** statement at the end of the command list unless you want the script to ignore the specific signals. The Korn and Bourne shells don't execute a file on logging out, but using **trap**, you can make them do that. You'll have to use the 0 to represent the signal number. These shells also use the statement **trap -** to reset the signals to their default values. You can also use multiple **trap** commands in a script; each one overrides the previous one.

We have finally come to the end of our journey with the shell. Along with **awk** and **perl**, the shell too has to be taken seriously if the power of the UNIX system is to be exploited to the hilt. Though shell programs run slower than C programs, for most administrative tasks the shell's speed and solution are quite acceptable.

SUMMARY

set puts values into positional parameters, and **shift** shifts them to the left. The leftmost variable is lost and should be stored in a variable before using **shift**. The field delimiter used by **set** is determined by the IFS variable. **set --** must be used if output could be null or begin with a hyphen.

The *here document* (<<) provides input to a script from the script itself. It can be used with both command substitution and variables. It is often used with commands that don't use a filename as argument or for running interactive programs noninteractively.

let performs computing as a built-in feature of the Korn shell and bash. It doesn't require the $ prefix when assigning a value. The Korn shell and bash use the ((and)) operators as an additional POSIX-compliant computing tool.

A conditional or loop can be redirected or piped at the **fi** or **done** keyword. All terminal-destined standard output inside redirected constructs must be separately directed with >/dev/tty. The shell can also merge the standard output and standard error streams using the symbols 1>&2 and 2>&1.

A variable defined in the parent is visible in the child only when it is exported (**export**). However, when the child alters the value of the variable, the changed value is not seen by the parent. The matching operators () run a group of commands in a subshell, but the {} don't spawn one.

Korn and bash support one-dimensional arrays. An array serves to validate a date.

String handling features are well-developed in Korn and bash. Variable contents can be matched with wild cards. Using the characters # and %, you can match a pattern at the beginning or end of a string and extract the nonmatched portion.

Shell variables can be evaluated in a conditional manner depending on whether they are assigned a non-empty value. The = operator additionally assigns a value to the variable, while ? prints an error message and exits the shell.

Shell functions let you condense important and repetitive sequences, and are more powerful than aliases. They accept positional parameters, but not the arguments passed on to the script, unless passed to them as arguments as well. A function can return only a true or false value.

eval processes a command line twice and is used to simulate arrays and execute variables. With **eval**, you can create generalized numbered prompts and variables that significantly compact code.

exec overlays the current shell when prefixed to a command. It can create multiple streams and associate each stream with its own file descriptor. For instance, it writes to a nonstandard file descriptor 7 by using 1>&7.

To debug shell scripts, use **set -x** at the beginning of the script so that every command line is echoed to the screen. The command shows the entire iterative process of a loop.

Use **trap** if you want your script to respond to an interrupt in a specific way. It is useful in removing temporary files when a script receives a signal. You can make your scripts immune to interrupts also.

SELF-TEST

19.1   Observe this command—Does it make any sense?

```
set `set`
```

19.2   If a script uses 12 parameters, how will you access the last one?

19.3   What could be the problem with this command?

```
set `grep -c "A HREF" catalog.html`
```

19.4   If a directory change is made inside a shell script, why is the original directory restored after the completion of the script? How do you overcome this problem?

19.5   If you define a variable at the command prompt, how can you make its value available in a shell script?

19.6   Invoke the **script** command and define a variable at the prompt. Now quit **script** with **exit**, and then echo the value of this variable. What do you see and why?

19.7   The command **echo ${#x}** produces the output x: Undefined variable. When does that happen and what was the expression designed for?

19.8   What will this statement do?

```
flname=${1:-emp.lst}
```

19.9   When do you need to use a *here document* with a command?

19.10 Write a shell function that removes the current directory by invoking the function from there.

19.11 In the script **var.sh** *(19.6.1)*, how can you make x have the same value that is set outside without using **export**?

19.12 How will you make sure that a specific program is executed immediately on logging in and the user is logged out when the program finishes?

EXERCISES

19.1   If the command **set `cat foo`** generates the error unknown option, what could be the reason assuming that foo is a small readable file?

19.2   Write a script which accepts a filename as argument and displays the last modification time if the file exists, and a suitable message if it doesn't.

19.3   Write a script which accepts a single- or multi-word pattern as argument, searches it from a group of files (foo*) and starts up the **vi** editor with only those files containing the pattern. How do you then locate the pattern in each file?

19.4   Write a script which accepts an anonymous ftp site (like ftp.planets.com) and any number of **ftp** commands (like "cd pub", "get cp32.tar.gz") as arguments. It should then connect to this Internet site, log in automatically, and execute the **ftp** commands.

19.5 Repeat Exercise 19.3 by searching for the pattern recursively in the current directory.

19.6 Why won't the **exit** command, when placed in a shell script like this, terminate the script? How do you get over this?

(*statements*; exit)

19.7 Invoke the **su** command (if you know the root password), and then run **ps -t** with the terminal name. What conclusion would you make?

19.8 You have a small script **cman** containing these two lines:

```
#!/bin/ksh
x=`find $HOME -name $1 -print`
cd $x
```

When you run **cman man1**, you find that the current directory hasn't changed even though the directory man1 exists somewhere in your home directory tree. Why did that happen, and how do you change to the directory anyway? How can you make the sequence run in the Bourne shell?

19.9 What's wrong with this statement? How do you modify it to execute correctly?

```
[ $# -ne 2 ] && echo "Usage: $0 min_guid max_guid" ; exit
```

19.10 You have to run a job at night and need to have both the output and error messages in the same file. How will you run the script?

19.11 How do you use **exec** to save the output of a script in one file and the error messages in yet another?

19.12 Using arrays, how can you extract the last command line argument to a script?

19.13 A script containing the statement **while [${count:=1} -lt 50]** is not executing the loop at all. What could be the possible reason?

19.14 Write a shell function for **rm** which goes to the interactive mode whenever you use it with more than three filenames.

19.15 Write a shell function **lstot()** which lists the total size of the files of the arguments (all files without arguments).

19.16 Modify the example in Section 19.13 to use arrays instead of **eval**.

19.17 Why can't you use the **exit** statement inside a function to return control to the calling program?

19.18 Modify the script **cpback2.sh** *(18.17)* to copy files to a directory only when they don't exist there. You are allowed to use only one external command (**cp**) and exploit the features of the Korn and bash shells. The last argument to the script is the directory. (Hint: Use the **eval** statement to identify the directory name.)

19.19 Modify the program developed in Exercise 19.18 so that only older files are overwritten.

19.20 You have used a loop in a script and want to see the values of the variables at each iteration of the loop. How do you do that without using any **echo** statements?

19.21 How will you make sure that a script prompts you before exiting on interruption?

19.22 How will you ensure that all filenames beginning with a numeral are removed on logging out of the Bourne or Korn shell?

KEY TERMS

export *(19.6.1)*

here document *(19.2)*

parameter substitution *(19.9)*

shell function *(19.10)*

perl—The Master Manipulator

Perl is UNIX's latest major acquisition, and one of its finest. Developed by Larry Wall, it is often hailed as the "Swiss Army Officer's Knife" of the UNIX system, in that it does several things well. It was meant to expand to a Practical Extraction and Report Language, but has gone far beyond its original purpose. In **perl**, Wall has invented a general-purpose tool which is at once a programming language and the mother of all filters. **perl** is not available in all systems but is standard on Linux and Solaris 8. However, it is free, and executables are available for all UNIX flavors (*http://www.perl.com*).

perl combines the power of some of the most powerful UNIX tools—the shell, **grep**, **tr**, **sed** and **awk**. In fact, there's nothing these tools can do, which **perl** can't. It has all the control structures that you could possibly have seen anywhere. It also has hundreds of other features related to handling of files, directories, processes, and so on, most of whom have counterparts in UNIX and C. **perl** also knows all the regular expressions that we have discussed so far. In spite of being a large executable, **perl** is faster than the shell and **awk**.

Objectives

- Gain an overview of a sample **perl** program. *(20.1)*
- Use **chop** to remove the last character of a line or variable. *(20.2)*
- Use the escape sequences and the concatenation operators. *(20.3)*
- Use the superior string handling features. *(20.4)*
- Specify loops both in command line and inside script for reading files. *(20.5)*
- Understand the significance of the *default variable* $_. *(20.6)*
- Use lists and arrays and their operators. *(20.8)*
- Use the **foreach** loop for working with a list. *(20.10)*
- Split and join a line with **split** and **join**. *(20.11 and 20.12)*
- Handle associative arrays with a nonnumeric subscript. *(20.14)*
- Handle substitution with regular expressions, the **s** and **tr** commands. *(20.15)*
- Use *filehandles* to access a file or stream. *(20.16)*
- Test the file attributes. *(20.17)*
- Develop *subroutines* for repeated use. *(20.18)*

➤ *GOING FURTHER*
   • Use **perl**'s features to develop a CGI program which is activated from the browser. *(20.20 and 20.21)*

Note

You should have a working knowledge of C—or at least **awk**—to be able to understand **perl** from this text because many features of **perl** are assumed here but explained in the chapter on **awk**. They are also found in textbooks featuring C. You also need to be familiar with regular expressions before you can comprehend some of the examples in this chapter. If necessary, turn back to Chapters 15 and 16 before you take the plunge.

Tip

You can run your **perl** scripts from within the **vi** editor. The technique of doing that is detailed in the "Tip" of Section 18.2.

20.1   perl **Preliminaries**

A **perl** program runs in a special interpretive mode; the entire script is compiled internally in memory before being executed. Unlike other interpreted languages like the shell and **awk**, script errors are generated before execution itself.

   perl in Linux is located in /usr/bin, but other UNIX systems may have it elsewhere—possibly in /usr/local/bin. If you have the directory in your PATH, this is how you can test whether it's working:

```
$ perl -e 'print ("GNUs Not Unix\n") ;'
GNUs Not Unix
```

perl doesn't behave like a filter here in printing the GNU acronym, but more like **echo**. Unlike **awk**, printing isn't **perl**'s default action, so you have to specify it explicitly. Like in C, all **perl** statements end with a semicolon.

   perl can do a lot of useful things from the command line when used with the -e option. However, most **perl** programs are big—often very big—and are better placed in .pl files. Here's a simple one which shows the use of variables and computation:

```
$ cat sample.pl
#!/usr/bin/perl
print ("Enter your name: ") ;
$name = <STDIN> ;                              # Input from the keyboard
print (  "Enter a temperature in Centigrade: "  ) ;
$centigrade=<STDIN> ;                          # Whitespace unimportant
$fahrenheit=$centigrade*9/5 + 32 ;             # Here too
print "The temperature $name in Fahrenheit is $fahrenheit\n" ;
```

The first line (the interpreter line) specifies the program that would be used to execute the script; the shell here uses **perl** rather than itself. You have used a similar feature in your shell scripts also, so this should need no elaboration. Make sure you have this statement as the first line of every **perl** program.

   perl variables need to be prefixed with $ both in the definition ($name = <STDIN>), as well as in evaluation (The temperature, $name .....). <STDIN> is a *filehandle* (a logical name for a file) representing the standard input.

Notice that the last **print** function doesn't use parentheses. *In general, functions in* **perl** *require the parentheses only when their omission leads to ambiguity.* It may take you some time to realize this, but you'll eventually welcome this simplification.

Let's execute this program in the same way we execute a shell script. This time, we'll enter a lot of spaces before keying in the actual input:

```
$ sample.pl
Enter your name:                        stallman
Enter a temperature in Centigrade:                      40.5
The temperature                         stallman
in Fahrenheit is 104.9
```

Note that **perl** reads the spaces provided before stallman but not those entered before the number 40.5. **perl** is also quite indifferent to the presence of whitespace around its symbols and operators as the variable nature of the statements seems to suggest.

Note

You can also execute a **perl** script using **perl** *scriptname*. In that case, you don't need to provide the interpreter line in the first line of the script.

20.2   chop(): **Removing the Last Character**

Why did **perl** show the output in two lines? That's because it included the newline generated by *[Enter]* as part of $name. (The shell's **read** statement doesn't do that.) So $name is now actually stallman\n (ignoring the spaces at the front). In many instances, we need to remove the last character—especially when it's newline. This is done by the **chop()** function. Let's consider this program:

```
$ cat name.pl
#!/usr/bin/perl
print ("Enter your name: ") ;
$name = <STDIN> ;
chop ($name) ;                          # Removes newline character from $name
if ( $name ne "" ) {
    print ("$name, have a nice day\n" ) ;
} else {
    print ("You have not entered your name\n" ) ;
}
```

The **if** conditional here differs from its namesake in C and **awk** in that the curly braces are *always* required—whether it's one or multiple statements to be executed. **chop** (we won't be showing the () with functions henceforth) has removed the last character alright, but here it has also assigned the "chopped" value to the same variable. This time, you'll find the output in a single line:

```
$ name.pl
Enter your name: larry wall
larry wall, have a nice day
```

There are other ways of using **chop**:

```
chop ($name = <STDIN>) ;                              Reading and assigning together
$lname = chop($name) ;                               lname stores last character chopped
```

The first statement combines, in C-style, both reading and chopping in a single statement. The second one is a special case of the **substr** function for extracting the last character of a string.

Tip

You should remember to use **chop** whenever you read a line from the keyboard or a file unless you deliberately want to retain the newline character. You'll find some programmers using **chop** to remove this newline and then adding it back in the **printf** statement. This is a senseless thing to do.

20.3 Variables and Operators

As you would have already seen, **perl** variables have no type and need no initialization. Strings and numbers can be as large as the machine permits. These are some of the variable attributes that one should remember:

- When a string is used for numeric computation or comparison, **perl** immediately converts it into a number.
- If a variable is undefined, it's assumed to be a null string and a null string is numerically zero.
- If the first character of a string is not numeric, the entire string becomes numerically equivalent to zero.

perl uses the same set of operators as **awk** for numeric comparison *(16.4)* with ==, !=, >, <, >= and <=. For string comparison, you'll have to use similar operators the shell uses—eq, ne, gt, lt, ge and le. Note that these operators don't need to be prefixed with a hyphen (which the shell uses). The comparison here is made according to the ASCII collating sequence.

You can use practically any character as a variable's value—including all the escape sequences we know. In addition, **perl** has some special ones that convert the case of a string. The following assignments show the versatility of **perl**'s variables:

```
$x = $y = $z = 5 ;                                         Multiple assignments
$name = "larry\t\twall\n" ;                               Two tabs and newline
$y = "A" ;    $y++ ;                                          This becomes B
$z = "P01" ; $z++ ;                                        This becomes P02!
$todays_date = `date` ;                            Uses command substitution
$name = "steve jobs" ;
$result = "\U$name\E" ;                                $result is STEVE JOBS
$result = "\u$name\E" ;                                $result is Steve jobs
```

There's some unusual stuff here. You can expect **perl** to offer the feature of incrementing P01 and returning P02. The escape sequences \U and \u convert to uppercase the entire string and the first character, respectively. The end of the affected area is marked by \E. Expectedly, \L and \l convert strings to lowercase.

perl also offers the C and **awk** feature of conditional assignment, using the ? and :. The following assignment determines whether February has 28 or 29 days:

```
$feb_days = $year % 4 == 0 ? 29 : 28 ;
```

perl can also set the return value of a comparison to a variable. The following statement sets the value of $x, depending on the result of the comparison:

```
$x = $y == $z ;
```

The return value of a comparison (here, $y == $z) is *non-zero* if the result of the comparison is true. Here, $x has the value 1 if $y and $z are equal; otherwise it has no value. *Note that here **perl** deviates from the general UNIX feature of using zero to signify a true return value.*

20.3.1 The Concatenation Operators . and x

Unlike in the shell, the expression xy (or ${x}${y}) isn't interpreted as variable concatenation. Rather, **perl** uses the . (dot) operator for concatenating variables:

```
$ perl -e '$x=ford ; $y=".com" ; print ($x . $y . "\n") ;'
ford.com
```

Note that $y itself contains a dot, so it had to be placed within quotes. For the sake of readability, it's preferable to have whitespace on either side of the dot operator.

    perl uses the x operator to repeat a string. The following statement prints 40 asterisks on the screen:

```
$ perl -e 'print "*" x 40 ;'
****************************************
```

The string to print isn't restricted to a single character; it can even be an expression. This operator is most useful in printing rulers for reports.

20.4 The String Handling Functions

perl has all the string functions that you could have possibly seen anywhere. **length** and **index** play their usual role *(16.13)*, but the **substr** function is quite versatile. The following examples tell the story:

```
$x = "abcdijklm" ;                           This is 9
print length($x) ;                           This is 5
print index($x,j) ;                    Stuffs $x with efgh
substr($x,4,0) = "efgh" ;         $x is now abcdefghijklm
print "$x" ;                         Extracts from right
$y = substr($x,-3,2) ;                         $y is kl
print "$y" ;
```

Note that **index** and **substr** consider the first character to be at position 0 (expectedly). **substr** in **perl** can extract a string as usual, but it can also *insert* a string. For instance, **substr($x,4,0)** stuffs the string $x with efgh without replacing any characters; 0 denotes nonreplacement. **substr($x,-3,2)** extracts two characters from the third position on the *right*. Note that you can specify the position at both left and right.

There are four functions for changing the case of text. **uc** converts to uppercase its entire argument, while **ucfirst** converts only the first character to uppercase:

```
$name = "larry wall" ;
$result = uc($name)                                    $result is LARRY WALL
$result = ucfirst($name)                               $result is Larry Wall
```

The functions **lc** and **lcfirst** perform opposite functions of their "uc" counterparts. Apart from converting case, **perl** can filter the contents of variables in the same way UNIX filters manipulate text. We'll be discussing the **tr** and **s** functions later—two important functions that **perl** uses for substitution.

20.5 Specifying Filenames in Command Line

perl provides a number of methods for accessing data from a file. Here are two ways of reading dept.1st:

```
perl -e 'print while (<>)' dept.1st
perl -e 'print <>' dept.1st                                          Loop implied
```

<> generally represents a null *filehandle*—the filenames supplied as arguments to the command. The contents of dept.1st are printed till **while** is able to read input (<>). But **perl** also has a -n option which implies this loop:

```
perl -ne 'print' dept.1st                                       -en won't work here!
```

Both **perl** forms can be used with multiple files for concatenation. The advantage of this form is that you can use simple one-line conditionals in the command line itself. Here is a bare-bones **grep** command at work:

```
$ perl -ne 'print if /wood\b/' emp.1st
5423|barry wood      |chairman |admin     |08/30/56|160000
```

This one-line conditional uses the regular expression /wood\b. **perl** uses an enlarged regular expression set (Table 20.1), where \b is used to match on a word boundary. This eliminated woodcock and woodhouse from the output. We'll see more of **perl**'s regular expressions later.

The above **perl** statement could have been placed in a script. This time, a loop is implied, so we have to specify the interpreter with the -n option:

```
#!/usr/bin/perl -n
print if /wood\b/ ;
```

We often need to do some processing outside the loop—like printing a heading or a total. The -n option doesn't allow that, so we have to set up the **while** loop inside the script:

```
#!/usr/bin/perl
printf ("%30s", "LIST OF EMPLOYEES\n") ;
while (<>) {
```

```
        print if /wood\b|light.*/ ;                        egrep-type of expression
    }
    print "\nREPORT COMPLETE\n" ;
```

What you see above is something that we do many a time: print a heading before the detail and then something after the detail.

Tip

For pure filtering, use **perl -n** as the interpreter name at the beginning of the script. No separate **while** loop is then required. If you have headers and footers to print, then drop the -n option and set up a **while** loop inside the script.

20.6 $_ : The Default Variable

The previous programs used **print** without specifying what to print; **perl** automatically understood it to be the entire line. **perl** assigns the line read from input to a special variable $_—often called the **default variable**. This is an extremely important variable, and you must understand its magical properties if you want to write abbreviated code.

Suppose you have to prefix a line number to every line. This is where you need $_ to explicitly specify the line. The comments in the following script show what **perl** does internally with $_:

```
$ cat grep1a.pl
#!/usr/bin/perl
while (<>) {                                  # Actually ($_ = <>)
    chop() ;                                  # chop($_)
    if (/From:.*\@velvet.com/) {              # if ($_ =~ /From:.*\@velvet ...)
        $slno++ ;
        print ($slno . "  " . $_ . "\n") ;
    }
}
```

$_ acted as the default variable in three situations here. Though its function is difficult to define exactly, it often represents the last line read or the last pattern matched. Many functions act on $_ when the variable name is omitted, so you shouldn't be surprised if you see functions used with fewer arguments. Whether or not you'll be able to use $_ isn't always intuitive; experience here is the best guide.

The $_ appears—implicitly or otherwise—at four places though it is compulsorily required at only one—in the print line. <>, **chop** and pattern matching operate on $_ by default. We used it with the **print** statement only because it had to be concatenated with $slno; otherwise **print** also operates on $_ by default. The program locates the email addresses of all senders from the *velvet.com* domain:

```
$ grep1a.pl $HOME/mbox
1  From: "Caesar, Julius" <Julius_Caesar@velvet.com>
2  From: "Goddard, John" <John_Goddard@velvet.com>
3  From: "Barnack, Oscar" <Oscar_Barnack@velvet.com>
```

Tip

You can reassign the value of $_. Since many of **perl**'s functions operate on $_ by default, you may often want to set $_ to the expression you are working with. This allows you to apply all the major functions available in **perl** on the expression without specifying either $_ or any variable name. All this ultimately leads to trimming of code.

20.7 Current Line Number ($.) and the Range Operator (..)

perl stores the current line number in another special system variable $. ($ followed by a dot). You can use it to represent a line address and select lines from anywhere in a file:

```
perl -ne 'print if ($. < 4)' foo                                    Like head –3
perl -ne 'print if ($. > 7 && $. < 11)' foo                    Like sed -n '8,10p'
```

But **perl** has shortcuts to these commands too. Use its range operator **..** (2 dots):

```
perl -ne 'print if (1..3)' foo
perl -ne 'print if (8..10)' foo
```

For selecting multiple segments from a file, you can use multiple **print** statements, or you can use compound conditions:

```
if ((1..2) || (13..15)) { print ; }
```

Unlike $_ which can be reassigned, $. always retains the current line number. If all input lines are passed through, you can use $. to number lines; a separate variable like $slno is not required.

20.8 Lists and Arrays

Lists and arrays lie at the very heart and soul of **perl**. **perl** has a large number of functions which can manipulate them. The following is an example of a list:

```
( "Jan", 123, "How are you", -34.56, Dec )
```

A list may either be assigned to an array or formed into a set of variables. These arrays are of two types—*scalar lists* and *associative arrays*. We'll be looking at **scalar lists** in this section. Let's assign the following list to an array @month:

```
@month = ("Jan", "Feb", "Mar") ;                               $month[0] is Jan
```

This sets up a three-element array @month from a list. The first value, $month[0], yields the string Jan. Note that even though the array itself is defined with the @ symbol, each individual element is accessed with $mon[*n*]. Array assignment is also quite flexible in **perl**. You can use the range operator or even assign values selectively:

```
@x = (1..12) ;
@month[1,3..5,12] = ("Jan", "Mar", "Apr", "May", "Dec") ;
```

The first example assigns the first 12 integers (1..12) to the first 12 elements of the array @x. In the second example, note that $month[4] is now Apr and $month[2] is null if it wasn't defined previously. The following script illustrates some features of **perl** arrays:

```
$ cat ar_in_ar.pl
#!/usr/bin/perl
@days_between = ("Wed", "Thu") ;
@days = (Mon, Tue, @days_between, Fri) ;                 # No quotes, OK
@days[5,6] = ("Sat", "Sun") ;
$length = @days ;                           # @days becomes array length here
@r_days = reverse @days ;                   # Reverses the array

print ("The third day of the week is $days[2]\n") ;
print ("The days of the week are @days\n") ;
print ("The days of the week in reverse are @r_days\n") ;
print ("The number of elements in the array is $length\n") ;
print ("The last subscript of the array is $#days\n") ;
```

Observe that **perl** permits a second array (@days_between) to become a part of another array @days. **perl** also offers a smart way of choosing your own subscripts (@days[5,6] = ...). With **reverse**, you can reverse the array too.

The length of the array can be determined from two functions—$#days and @days. $#days actually stores the last subscript of the array, which should remind you of a similar construct used by the Korn shell and bash to determine the length of a string *(19.8)*. The actual length of the array is stored in @days *when it is placed on the right side of an assignment*. Because the index of an array starts from 0, $length is one greater than $#days:

```
$ ar_in_ar.pl
The third day of the week is Wed
The days of the week are Mon Tue Wed Thu Fri Sat Sun
The days of the week in reverse are Sun Sat Fri Thu Wed Tue Mon
The number of elements in the array is 7
The last subscript of the array is 6
```

Note that @days evaluates differently depending on the way it is used. **print @days** displays all the elements, but when @days is assigned to a variable ($length = @days), it becomes the *length* of the array!

Reading a File into an Array   The easiest way to fill up an array is to read a file into it. Each line becomes an element of the array:

```
@line = <> ;                                Reads entire file from command line
print @line ;                                              Prints entire file
```

The entire file is read with a single statement (@line = <>), and each element of the array @line contains a line of the file (including the newline).

Note

When you read a file into an array, every element will have newline as the last character. The **chop** function, when applied to arrays, removes the newline from each and every element of the array, and not just the last element.

Caution

You can make the array index start from 1 and not 0 by making the following setting at the beginning of your **perl** program: $[= 1 ;. However, this represents a nonstandard way of working and can easily confuse people who are used to seeing 0 as the first index.

20.9   ARGV[ ]: **Command Line Arguments**

perl also uses command line arguments which are stored in the system array @ARGV[ ]; the first argument is $ARGV[0]. Note that the command name itself isn't stored in this element; it's held in another system variable $0. The following program expects a year string as argument and determines whether it's a leap year or not:

```
$ cat leap_year.pl
#!/usr/bin/perl
die ("You have not entered the year\n") if (@ARGV == 0 ) ;
$year = $ARGV[0] ;                                    # The first argument
$last2digits = substr($year, -2, 2) ;                 # Extract from the right
if ($last2digits eq "00") {
    $yesorno = ($year % 400 == 0 ? "certainly" : "not" ) ;
}
else {
    $yesorno = ($year % 4 == 0 ? "certainly" : "not" ) ;
}
print ("$year is " . $yesorno . " a leap year\n") ;
```

Note that the value of @ARGV (without the subscripts) equates to the length of the array. You also see here the rather unusual use of the **substr** function. Let's run the program:

```
$ leap_year.pl
You have not entered the year
$ leap_year.pl 2000
2000 is certainly a leap year
$ leap_year.pl 1997
1997 is not a leap year
```

There is one drawback with the above script; you have to invoke the program five times if you want to subject five numbers to leap year checks. This can be taken care of by the **foreach** loop which is taken up next.

Note

die() simply prints its argument and exits a script. It's most often used to handle errors in opening a file or in discarding erroneous user input.

20.10 foreach: **Looping through a List**

perl provides an extremely useful **foreach** construct to loop through a list. The construct borrowed from the C shell has a very simple syntax:

```
foreach $var (@arr) {
    statements
}
```

In spirit, this works like the **for** loop of the shell as well. Each element of the array *@arr* is picked up and assigned to the variable *$var*. The iteration is continued as many times as there are items in the list. The following program uses **foreach** to calculate the square root of some numbers:

```
$ cat square_root.pl
#!/usr/bin/perl
print ("The program you are running is $0\n") ;
foreach $number (@ARGV) {              # Each element of @ARGV goes to $number
    print ("The square root of $number is " . sqrt($number) . "\n") ;
}
```

Every element in the array @ARGV is assigned to the variable $number. You can now supply as many arguments to the script as you like:

```
$ square_root.pl 123 456 25
The program you are running is ./square_root.pl
The square root of 123 is 11.0905365064094
The square root of 456 is 21.3541565040626
The square root of 25 is 5
```

We have previously noted $_ making its presence felt everywhere, and this is no exception. In the above example, you need not use $number at all. **foreach** stores each item in $_, and **sqrt** works on it as well:

```
foreach (@ARGV) {                                          $_ is the default variable
    print ("The square root of $_ is " . sqrt() . "\n") ;
```

It's not that **foreach** is used with named arrays only. It can be used with lists generated by UNIX commands as well. You can use command substitution to generate the list:

```
foreach $file (`ls`) {
```

This loop construct picks up each file in the current directory, and assigns it to the variable $file. We'll use this feature later in the chapter.

Note

perl has a **for** loop as well. This construct performs its enclosing code block three times:
```
for ($i=0 ; $i<3 ; $i++) {
```

20.11 split(): **Splitting into a List**

CGI programmers using **perl** need to understand two important array handling functions—**split** and **join**. **split** breaks up a line or an expression into fields. These fields are assigned either to variables or an array. Here are the two syntaxes:

($*var1*, $*var2*, $*var3*.....) = split(/*sep*/, *stg*) ;
@*arr* = split(/*sep*/, *stg*) ;

split takes up to three arguments but is usually used with two:

- The expression *sep* on which splitting takes place. This can be a literal character or a regular expression which could expand to multiple characters.
- The string *stg* to be split. It is optional, and in its absence, $_ is used as default.

The fields resulting from the split are assigned either to the variables $*var1*, $*var2* and so on, or to the array @*arr*. We'll now use the first syntactical form to parse /etc/passwd to create a list of email addresses for nonprivileged users:

```
$ cat email_create.pl
#!/usr/bin/perl -n
chop() ;
($uname, $password, $uid, $gid, $gcos, $home, $shell) = split (/:/, $_) ;
print "\"$gcos\" <$uname\@planets.com>\n" if ( $home =~ /\/home\// ) ;
```

Since $_ is the default string used by **split**, we'll drop it in the future. Nonprivileged users are identified by matching $home for /home/. Note that we used the regular expression operator =~ for matching the sixth field. Since the addresses will be in RFC 822 format *(13.7.4)*, double quotes have to be provided around the GCOS field. Both " and / are special and need to be hidden. Let's now execute the script:

```
$ email_create.pl /etc/passwd
"george kennedy" <george@planets.com>
"henry blofeld" <henry@planets.com>
"enquiry for products" <enquiry@planets.com>
```

What do you do when a split results in a large number of fields? In that case, it's better to split on an array (the second form). The previous **split** statement could have been used to fill up the array @profile instead:

```
@profile = split (/:/) ;                                    $_ is the default string
```

The first field then goes into $profile[0]. You can now use the individual elements of the array like this:

```
$uname = $profile[0] ;
$gcos = $profile[4] ;                                       GCOS is the fifth field
```

Note that it's quite possible to use an assignment like this: $profile = $profile[3];
identical variable and array names don't conflict with each other. The **split** statement
can also be used without an explicit assignment:

split (/:/) ;   *Fills up the array @_*

split gets shortened further. This fills up **perl**'s built-in array @_ having elements
$_[0], $_[1] and so forth. You should get used to this form also as you'll see it used
in many programs.

   perl's penchant for brevity allows you to use **split** without any arguments
whatsoever:

split() ;   *Splits $_ on whitespace*

The line ($_) here is broken up on whitespace into the array @_. If that's not enough,
you can drop the parentheses too!

Note

When **split** is used as a statement without an array name (rather than as an assignment on
the right of the =), the built-in array @_ is used. The elements of this array are $_[0], $_[1],
$_[2] and so on. Moreover, when **split** is used with the null string (//) as delimiter, it stores
each character of the string as a separate element.

20.12   join(): **Joining a List**

The **join** function acts in an opposite manner to **split**. It combines all array elements
into a single string. It uses the delimiter as the first argument. The remaining arguments
could be either an array name or a list of variables or strings to be joined. This is how
you provide a space after each day:

```
$weekstring = join (" ", @week_array) ;
$weekstring = join (" ", "Mon", "Tue", "Wed", "Thu", "Fri", "Sat", "Sun") ;
print $weekstring ;
```

Either statement should produce this output:

```
Mon Tue Wed Thu Fri Sat Sun
```

Joining has a very important application. If you split a line into fields and then edit a
field or two, then you must use **join** to paste them back. Let's consider these lines of
/etc/passwd:

```
mdom:x:28:28:mailing list agent:/usr/lib/majordomo:/bin/ksh
yard:x:29:29:yARD database admin:/usr/lib/YARD:/bin/ksh
wwwrun:x:30:65534:daemon user for apache:/tmp:/bin/ksh
fax:x:33:14:facsimile Agent:/var/spool/fax:/bin/ksh
```

To convert the fifth field (GCOS) to uppercase, the following program splits each line
into fields, applies the **uc** function on the fifth field and then joins all fields back:

```
#!/usr/bin/perl -n
split (/:/) ;                           # Splits $_ on @_ array
$_[4] = uc($_[4]) ;                     # Fifth field converted to uppercase
$_ = join(":", @_) ;                    # Line recreated
print if (1..3) ;                       # This prints $_
```

When this program is executed with /etc/passwd as argument, the first three lines are displayed:

```
mdom:x:28:28:MAILING LIST AGENT:/usr/lib/majordomo:/bin/ksh
yard:x:29:29:YARD DATABASE ADMIN:/usr/lib/YARD:/bin/ksh
wwwrun:x:30:65534:DAEMON USER FOR APACHE:/tmp:/bin/ksh
```

Joining on a delimiter has common applications in everyday programming. First and last names often require a space between them. The month, day and year may need to be separated by a -. You'll see some of these applications later.

20.13   Modifying Array Contents

perl has a number of functions for manipulating the contents of an array. For deleting elements at the beginning or end of an array, **perl** uses the **shift** and **pop** functions:

```
@list = (3..5, 9) ;                                        This is 3 4 5 9
shift(@list) ;                                     The 3 goes away, becomes 4 5 9
pop (@list) ;                             Removes last element, becomes 4 5
```

The **unshift** and **push** functions add elements to an array. Let's apply them to the residual value of @list at the end of the previous example:

```
unshift(@list, 1..3) ;                              Adds 1, 2 and 3—1 2 3 4 5
push (@list, 9) ;                                   Pushes 9 at end—1 2 3 4 5 9
```

The **splice** function can do everything these four functions can do. Additionally, it uses up to four arguments to add or remove elements at *any* location of the array. The second argument is the offset from where the insertion or removal should begin. The third argument represents the number of elements to be removed. If it is 0, elements have to be added. The new replaced list is specified by the fourth argument (if present):

```
splice (@list, 5, 0, 6..8) ;                    Adds at 6th location—1 2 3 4 5 6 7 8 9
splice (@list, 0, 2) ;                          Removes from beginning—3 4 5 6 7 8 9
```

We'll now consolidate our knowledge of array handling functions by developing a script. The script accepts an IP address (like 202.54.9.1) as an argument and converts it to binary:

```
$ cat ipadd2binary.pl
#!/usr/bin/perl
split(/\./, $ARGV[0]) ;
```

```
        print "The IP address in binary is " ;
        foreach $number (@_) {
            $original_number = $number ;
            until ($number == 0 ) {
                $bit = $number % 2  ;                    # Find the remainder bit
                unshift (@bit_arr, $bit) ;               # Insert bit at beginning
                $number = int($number / 2 ) ;
            }
            $binary_number = join ("", @bit_arr) ;       # Join on nothing!
            substr($binary_number,0,0) = "0" x (8 - length($binary_number)) ;
            print ("$binary_number ") ;
            splice(@bit_arr, 0, $#bit_arr+1) ;           # Delete all array elements
        }
        print chr(10) ;                                  # Prints newline -- same as print "\n"
```

split here breaks up the dotted IP address into four fields and stores them in the array @_. You'll recollect that for converting a decimal number into binary, you have to repeatedly divide the quotient by 2 and then reverse all the collected remainders. **unshift** does this job of reversal.

substr pads extra 0s at the beginning so that each octet of the IP address is displayed as 8 bits. The body of **foreach** prints the binary equivalent for each octet. **splice** flushes the array before the next iteration is started. Let's run the script:

```
$ ipadd2binary.pl 224.67.34.06
The IP address in binary is 11100000 01000011 00100010 00000110
```

You can use this program to convert the subnet mask also *(23.1)* and then check whether two hosts are on the same subnet.

20.14 Associative Arrays

perl uses yet another type of array—the **associative array**. It alternates the array subscripts and values in a series of comma-delimited values. For instance, the associative array %region could be defined like this:

```
%region = ("N", "North", "S", "South", "E", "East", "W", "West") ;
```

This array uses the % symbol to prefix the array name. This assignment creates an array of four elements where the subscript precedes the value in the array definition. The array subscript, which can also be a string, is enclosed within a pair of curly braces rather than []. For instance, $region{"N"} produces North. CGI programmers must feel totally at home with associative arrays.

The following program uses the %region array to expand region codes. It also shows how to use two associative array functions **keys** and **values**:

```
$ cat region.pl
#!/usr/bin/perl
%region = ("N", "North", "S", "South", "E", "East", "W", "West") ;
```

```
foreach $letter (@ARGV) {
    print ("The letter $letter stands for $region{$letter}" . "\n" );
}
@key_list = keys(%region) ;                              # List of subscripts
print ("The subscripts are @key_list\n") ;
@value_list = values %region  ;                          # List of values
print ("The values are @value_list\n") ;
```

keys stores the list of subscripts in a separate array (here, @key_list), while **values** holds the value of each element in yet another array (here, @value_list). (We didn't use the parentheses here.) Let's test the script by supplying a couple of single-character strings:

```
$ region.pl S W
The letter S stands for South
The letter W stands for West
The subscripts are S E N W
The values are South East North West
```

There are important implications here. You can separately extract both the keys and their values from an associative array. You can also present these values in the same way the **set** statement shows all environment variables:

```
foreach $key (keys %region) {
    print "$key" . "=" . "$region{$key}\n" ;
}
```

We found out the value of each key and stored it in turn in the variable $key. It's then a simple matter to use it as the subscript of %region. The element $region{$key} stores the value of each key as shown by this output:

```
S=South
E=East
N=North
W=West
```

Normally, **keys** returns the key strings in a random sequence. To order the list alphabetically, you'll often find the **sort** function used with **keys**. You can have both a normal and a reverse sort:

```
foreach $key (sort(keys %region)) {
@key_list = reverse sort keys %region  ;                            No ()—OK
```

Note

perl's built-in array %ENV stores all the shell's environment variables. For instance, $ENV{'PATH'} contains the value of the shell's $PATH. You can easily access these variables using the techniques discussed here.

20.14.1   Counting Number of Occurrences

Associative arrays are extremely useful in counting the number of occurrences of an item. From the sample database, you can create a report showing the number of people in each department. We tried a similar exercise before with **awk** *(16.15.2)* and the basic UNIX filters *(9.18.1)*, and we'll complete this exercise with **perl**. For a programming language, this is quite some work, but a small **perl** program does the job:

```
$ cat count.pl
#!/usr/bin/perl
while (<>) {
    split (/\|/) ;                          # | has to be escaped
    $dept = $_[3] ;                         # Department is fourth field
    $deptlist{$dept} += 1 ;                 # Same as ++
}
foreach $dept (sort (keys %deptlist)) {
    print ("$dept: $deptlist{$dept}\n") ;
}
```

The program is divided into two parts. The **while** construct first filters out the values of $dept for each line read, and increments the counter of the respective element of the array %deptlist. After all input has been read, the **foreach** construct assigns each value of the key from %deptlist to the variable $dept. $deptlist{$dept} now contains the accumulated total for each key. This sorted output shows the power of **perl**:

```
$ count.pl emp.lst
accounts  : 2
admin     : 1
marketing : 4
personnel : 2
production: 2
sales     : 4
```

With only a few lines of **perl** code you have been able to list out the department-wise distribution of people.

20.15   Regular Expressions and Substitution

perl offers a grand superset of all possible regular expressions that are found in the UNIX system (except the ones specified by POSIX). You have already used some of them for pattern matching. **perl** understands the types used by **egrep** and **awk**, as well as those known only to **grep** and **sed**. It has some of its own too (Table 20.1). We'll now use them for substitution.

20.15.1   The s and tr Functions

The **s** and **tr** functions handle all substitution in **perl**. The **s** function is used in the same way as the **s** command in **sed**. **tr** translates characters in just the same way the

TABLE 20.1　*Additional Regular Expression Sequences Used by* **perl**
　　　　　　　　(See also TABLE 15.2)

Symbols	Significance
\w	Matches a word character (same as [a-zA-Z0-9_])
\W	Doesn't match a word character (same as [^a-zA-Z0-9_])
\d	Matches a digit (Same as [0-9])
\D	Doesn't match a digit (Same as [^0-9])
\s	Matches a whitespace character (Same as [□⇥])
\S	Doesn't match a whitespace character (Same as [^□⇥])
\b	Matches on word boundary
\B	Doesn't match on word boundary

UNIX **tr** command does, but with a slightly different syntax. This is how we use them on $_:

```
$ cat substitute.pl
#!/usr/bin/perl -n
s/\|/:/g ;                    # | to be escaped
tr/a-z/A-Z/ ;
s#/#-#g ;                     # Delimiter changed to # here
s/ +:/:/g ;                   # Compresses multiple spaces before delimiter
print if (1..3) ;
```

All the five actions here are performed on $_. The first **s** function replaces the | with a :, and **tr** changes everything to uppercase. The second **s** function changes every / to a -. We changed the separator here from the default / to a #, the reason why the / to be replaced was not escaped.

　　　　As in **sed**, each **perl** statement acts on the line resulting from the immediately previous action. Since the | was replaced with : by the first **s** function, the last **s** function can now access the :. **s** here uses the **egrep**-type + metacharacter to delete spaces on the left of the :. Here's the output:

```
$ substitute.pl emp.lst
2233:CHARLES HARRIS:G.M.:SALES:12-12-52: 90000
9876:BILL JOHNSON:DIRECTOR:PRODUCTION:03-12-50:130000
5678:ROBERT DYLAN:D.G.M.:MARKETING:04-19-43: 85000
```

Both functions work on variables too. In that case, you'll have to use the operator =~ for performing a match and !~ for negating it:

```
$line =~ s/:/-/g ;                                    $line is reassigned
$line =~ tr/a-z/A-Z/ ;                                      Here too
```

Both **s** and **tr** also accept flags. **s** accepts the g flag (shown above) for global substitution, and yet another (e) for indicating that the replaced pattern is to be evaluated as an expression. **tr** uses all the UNIX **tr** options as flags—s squeezes multiple occurrences, c complements and d deletes the character *(9.13.1)*.

The last **s** function in `substitute.pl` could be modified by using \s instead of a space:

```
s/\s+:/:/g ;
```

perl offers some escaped characters to represent whitespace, digits and word boundaries (Table 20.1). You can often compact your regular expressions by using these characters:

\s — A whitespace character
\d — A digit
\w — A word character

All these escaped characters also have uppercase counterparts that negate their lowercase ones. Thus, \D is a nondigit character. We have already used the anchoring sequence \b for matching a pattern on a word boundary *(20.5)*. For a complete list of the regular expressions used by **perl** and others, look up Appendix C.

20.15.2   The IRE and TRE Features

perl also accepts the IRE and TRE used by **grep** and **sed** *(15.12)*, except that the curly braces and parentheses are not escaped. For instance, this is how you locate lines longer than 512 characters:

```
perl -ne 'print if /.{513,}/' foo                        No \ before { and }
```

Let's consider an important application of \d using the TRE feature. IP addresses use four decimal digits, and if you want to change your network address from 192.168.*x*.*x* to 172.16.*x*.*x* in some of your configuration files, the tag feature becomes very useful:

```
s/192.168.(\d+).(\d+)/172.16.\1.\2/g ;                    No \ before ( and )
print ;
```

(\d+) stands for a group of digits—a more compact form compared to **sed**'s \([0-9][0-9]*\). We now have two groups of digits separated by any character (.). These groups appear as \1 and \2 in the replaced string.

As an added bonus, **perl** also uses the variables $1, $2 and so on to remember the grouped patterns till the next grouping is done. You can recall them later in the program:

```
if (/(\d+)\.(\d+)\.(\d+)\.(\d+)/) {
   if ($1 < 127) {
      print "Host Address is $2.$3.$4\n" ;
   }
   elsif ($1 < 192) {
      print "Host Address is $3.$4\n" ;
   }
   else {
      print "Host Address is $4\n" ;
   }
}
```

This section of code locates a line containing an IP address and extracts the four components. It then applies the rules discussed in Section 23.1 to determine the host component of the address. Note that the scope of the grouped patterns extends beyond the current pattern and can be easily used in subsequent statements. Test this program by assigning an IP address to the variable $_ at the beginning.

Note

\d represents a digit, \s identifies a whitespace character, \w is the word character and \b matches a pattern at the word boundary. Their uppercase counterparts negate the lowercase ones.

20.15.3   Editing Files In-Place

Instead of writing to the standard output or to a separate file, **perl** can edit and *rewrite* the input file itself. With **sed**, you would have redirected the output to a temporary file and then renamed it back to the original file. For a group of files, you would have used a **for** loop as well. Not so for **perl**; the -i option can edit multiple files **in-place**:

```
perl -p -i -e "s/<B>/<STRONG>/g" *.html *.htm
```

This changes <B> in all lines where they occur in all HTML files to <STRONG>. The files themselves are rewritten with the new output. If in-place editing seems a risky thing to do, you can back the files up before undertaking the operation:

```
perl -p -i.bak -e "tr/a-z/A-Z/" foo1 foo2 foo3 foo4
```

This first backs up foo1 to foo1.bak, foo2 to foo2.bak, and so forth, before converting all lowercase letters in each file to uppercase.

20.16   File Handling

So far, we have been specifying the input filenames from the UNIX command line. **perl** also provides the low-level file handling functions that let you hard-code the source and destination of the data stream in the script itself. A file is opened for reading like this:

```
open (INFILE, "/home/henry/mbox") ;
```
                                                                    Don't forget the quotes!

INFILE here is a **filehandle** (a shorthand representation) of the file mbox (file presumed to be in current directory if a pathname is not used). Future **perl** statements will use the filehandle rather than the filename to access the file. The advantage here is that if you change the filename, you have to modify the filehandle definition just once.

A file is opened for writing with the shell-like operators > and >> having their usual meanings:

```
open (OUTFILE, ">rep_out.1st") ;
open (OUTFILE, ">>rep_out.1st") ;
```

perl's filehandles can be associated with pipelines also. To shell programmers, the meanings of these statements should be quite obvious:

```
open (INFILE, "sort emp.lst |" ) ;                    Input from sort output
open (OUTFILE, "| lp" ) ;                             Output to print spooler
```

The next script has the input and output filenames hard-coded. It also closes the files at the end:

```
$ cat rw.pl
#!/usr/bin/perl
open (FILEIN, "desig.lst") || die ("Cannot open file") ;
open (FILEOUT, ">desig_out.lst") ;
while (<FILEIN>) {                        # Till there are lines in the file
    print FILEOUT if ($. < 4 ) ;         # Can also use if (1..3)
}
close (FILEIN) ;
close (FILEOUT) ;
```

The statement **while (<FILEIN>)** reads a line at a time from the file represented by the FILEIN filehandle and stores it in $_. Every time the <FILEIN> statement is executed, the next line is read. You can read and print a single line in this way:

```
$_ = <FILEIN> ;                                            Assign to $_
print ;                                             print uses $_ by default
```

Note that **print** uses the filehandle as an optional argument. When you specify it, the output is written to that file. In the script **rw.pl**, **print** writes $_ directly to desig_out.lst—the file assigned to the filehandle FILEOUT.

Even if you don't close the files before terminating the script, **perl** closes them on its own. The **close** statement also brings back the pointer to the beginning of the file in case you decide to reopen the file later in the program. When we run the script without arguments, the output doesn't come to the terminal this time, but goes to the file desig_out.lst.

Tip

If a number of **print** statements have to write to the same filehandle (say, FILEOUT), then you can assign this filehandle as the default using **select (FILEOUT) ;**. Subsequent **print** statements don't need to use the FILEOUT argument in that case.

20.17   File Tests

perl has an elaborate system of file tests. It overshadows the capabilities of the Bourne shell—and even the **find** command in some ways. The following statements test some of the most common attributes of a file:

```
$x = "rdbnew.lst" ;
print "File $x is readable\n" if -r $x ;
print "File $x is executable\n" if -x $x ;
print "File $x has non-zero size\n" if -s $x ;
print "File $x exists\n" if -e $x ;
```

```
print "File $x is a text file\n" if -T $x ;
print "File $x is a binary file\n" if -B $y ;
```

perl's file tests go further; it can tell you a file's modification and access times very accurately. The following script uses the C- and **awk**-like **printf** statement with its standard formats. It detects files which were modified less than 2.4 hours ago:

```
$ cat when_last.pl
#!/usr/bin/perl
# Finds out files less than 2.4 hours old
foreach $file (`ls`) {
  chop ($file) ;
  if (($m_age = -M $file) < 0.1) {          # tenth of a day i.e., 2.4 hours
    printf "File %s was last modified %0.3f days back \n", $file, $m_age ;
  }
}
```

-M $file returns the time elapsed in hours since $file was last modified. It's a general **perl** feature (an idea borrowed from C) that you can make a test (< 0.1) and assignment ($m_age = ...) at the same time. Let's observe the output:

```
$ when_last.pl
File bf2o.sh was last modified 0.063 days back
File profile.sam was last modified 0.082 days back
File when_last.pl was last modified 0.000 days back
```

It seems that the last file has just been modified; three decimal places are not enough. You have to increase the length of the **printf** format if you need to know the exact time.

Apart from testing file attributes, **perl** can manipulate files and directories very easily. It uses **chmod**, **chown**, **chgrp**, **chdir** (like **cd**), **mkdir**, **rmdir**, **rename** (like **mv**), **link**, **unlink** (like **rm**) and **umask** in the same way. Like filehandles, it can also open directories with directory filehandles.

20.18   Subroutines

perl handles subroutines—both as procedures and functions that return values. Subroutines are called by the & symbol followed by the subroutine name. A subroutine's arguments are stored in the array @_. Variables inside the subroutine can be declared as local if their values are not meant to be visible in the calling program.

Many applications require the user to supply a username and password. Since this involves executing the same amount of code twice, it becomes an ideal candidate for a subroutine. The following program uses the subroutine **take_input()**, which accepts the prompt string as an argument, validates the input for word characters and returns the value that was input:

```
$ cat input.pl
#!/usr/bin/perl
system ("tput clear") ;                    # Executes the UNIX command
$username = &take_input ("Oracle user-id: ") ;
```

```
$password = &take_input ("Oracle password: ", "noecho") ;
print "\nThe username and password are $username and $password\n" ;
system ("sqlplus $username/$password @query.sql >/dev/null" ) ;

sub take_input {
    local ($prompt, $flag) = @_ ;          # @_ stores arguments of subroutine
    while (1)  {                            # (1) is always true
        print ("$prompt") ;
        system("stty -echo") if (@_ == 2 ) ;            # Echo mode off
        chop ($name = <STDIN>) ;
        system("stty echo") if (@_ == 2 ) ;             # Echo mode on
        last if $name =~ /\w/ ;            # Quit the loop if $name has at
    }                                      # least one word character
    return $name ;                         # Just $name will also do
}
```

The subroutine arguments are accepted into the system array @_ and then reassigned to the two local variables $prompt and $flag. What is checked in the subroutine is just the number of arguments passed (@_ == 2). When you pass two arguments to it, the UNIX **stty** command blanks out the display during password entry.

last is **perl**'s equivalent of the shell's **break** statement that exits a loop. (**perl** also uses **next** instead of **continue**.) Here, control breaks out of the loop when there is at least one word character in the input. This is how you can ensure that the password is not displayed:

```
$ input.pl
Oracle user-id: !@#$%^&*                              Nonword characters
Oracle user-id: scott
Oracle password: *****                                Password not echoed
The username and password are scott and tiger
     ...... Executes SQL*Plus script query.sql .........
```

You should store frequently used subroutines in separate files. Instruct the calling program to read a file containing a subroutine by placing the **require** statement at the beginning. If you save the **take_input** subroutine in the file oracle_lib.pl, you should do these two things:

- Insert the statement **require "oracle_lib.pl" ;** in the calling program immediately after the line specifying the **perl** interpreter.
- Place the statement 1; at the end of the *file* containing one or more subroutines. The **perl** documentation requires every "required" file to end with a true value. Any non-zero value is a true value in **perl**, so 1; returns true. We'll illustrate these features in the sections featuring CGI programming.

Note

In the above example, you can use $_[0] instead of $prompt and $_[1] in place of $flag. You can also drop the word local when assigning the subroutine arguments in case you want the variables to be visible outside the subroutine.

20.19 Conclusion

This is a fairly large and dense chapter for just one application, and yet there still remains much to be discussed. **perl** has specific functions for networking and inter-process communication which have not found a place here. Its object-oriented tools and techniques have been ignored. **perl** is also shipped with two useful utilities—**s2p** for converting **sed** programs to **perl**, and **a2p** for converting **awk** programs.

perl is Larry Wall's implementation of the three virtues he expects a programmer to have—laziness, impatience and hubris. It's a real gold mine of techniques where someone discovers a new feature every day. The UNIX spirit lives in **perl**. Think of the essential and fascinating UNIX features; they are all there in **perl**. **perl** is the pride of UNIX.

➤ *GOING FURTHER*

20.20 CGI Programming with perl—An Overview

When you fill up a form on your Web browser and press the *Submit* button, the browser transmits the form data to the Web server at the other end. A Web server by itself doesn't have any inherent capability of processing this data, so it passes it on to an external application. This application extracts the meat from the sent data and performs some job. It may access a database to add, modify or delete the data, or query it and send back the results of its search. The Web server here acts as a link to the application—the **Common Gateway Interface** (CGI) to pass information to and from the (gatewaying) application.

A CGI program needs to do some filtering of form data—like separating the variables from their values and converting encoded characters to ASCII. The program often has to generate HTML on-the-fly with all its tags, and send the document to the browser. This program can be written in any language—C, Java, the shell or **perl**. When it comes to text parsing, **perl**'s filtering capabilities are second to none, which is why **perl** is the language of choice for CGI programming.

In the remaining sections, we'll use **perl** to do two things—filter form data and generate the HTML. We'll present some more **perl** features needed to develop a small application that exploits its well-known filtering capabilities.

20.20.1 Understanding the HTML Form

We'll use a similar employee database *(15.1)* in our CGI application, but this time we'll access it from our Web browser. Before you embark on this venture, you need to know some HTML *(14.11)* to understand the significance of its tags. You should then be able to make the CGI **perl** program generate the right tags when it sends back data to the browser.

The HTML code presented in Fig. 20.2 specifies a form with the <form> tag. The action attribute of this tag specifies a URL pointing to a **perl** program (**emp_add.pl**) on the server. This program adds a line to the database. The form that accepts user input is shown in Fig 20.1; the code for it is shown in Fig. 20.2.

Every HTML document consists of some header code (the first five lines) and some footer code (the last two lines). Since **perl** has to generate these lines in most CGI applications, we'll create two subroutines to be used by our CGI programs.

FIGURE 20.1   `emp_form.html`: *An HTML Form Viewed by Netscape*

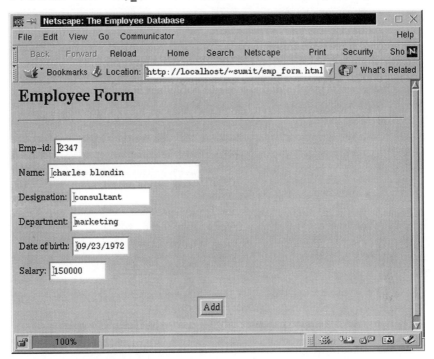

The body of the HTML document consists of a simple form enclosed between the `<form>` and `</form>` tags. There are six text boxes here—for accepting the six fields of the employee database. The values entered into these fields are paired with their corresponding variable names—`empid`, `ename`, `desig`, and so on. The `<br>` tag is required to place each text box in a separate line.

The `action` attribute of the `<form>` tag specifies a URL on the localhost itself. This URL points to a **perl** program **emp_add.pl** in `/cgi-bin` (the directory where CGI programs are generally kept). This program is executed the moment the button labeled *Add* and of type `submit` is clicked with the mouse.

20.20.2   The Query String

As you know by now *(14.10.1)*, the browser sends data to the server through its request header. To understand how form data is structured, consider a form that has only three fields with names `empid`, `ename` and `desig` (the `name` attribute of the `<input>` tag). Let's put the values `1234`, `henry higgins` and `actor` into these three fields. On submission, the browser strings together the entire data as *name=value* pairs into a **query string** in this manner:

`empid=1234&ename=henry+higgins&desig=actor`

This single string is sent to the server specified in the URL. The & here acts as the delimiter of each *name=value* pair. Note that the browser has encoded the space character to

F I G U R E   20.2   emp_form.html: *The HTML Code of a Form Document*

```
<html> <head>
    <title>The Employee Database</title>              Appears on title bar
</head>
<body>
<h1> Employee Form </h1>                           Appears in a large bold font
<hr>                                                 Adds a horizontal rule
<form action="http://localhost/cgi-bin/emp_add.pl" method=get>
        Emp-id: <input type="text" name="empid" size=4> <br>
          Name: <input type="text" name="ename" size=30> <br>
   Designation: <input type="text" name="desig" size=15> <br>
    Department: <input type="text" name="dept" size=15> <br>
 Date of birth: <input type="text" name="dtbirth" size=10> <br>
        Salary: <input type="text" name="salary" size=10> <br> <br>
<center>
<input type=submit value="Add">                      The "Add" button is centered
</center>
</form>
</body>
</html>
```

a +. To be able to use this data, **perl** has to split this string twice—once to extract all *name=value* pairs and then to separate the names from their values. This can be done in two ways depending on the *method* specified, and is taken up next.

20.20.3   GET and POST: The Request Method

The <form> tag shows another attribute—method. This signifies the way data is transmitted to the server. Generally, the query string shown above is sent in two ways:

- **GET**—This method appends the query string to the URL using the ? as the delimiter. With this string, the URL will now look like this:

  http://localhost/cgi-bin/emp_add.pl?empid=1234&ename=
  henry+higgins&desig=actor

  The server parses the get statement in the request header and stores the data following the ? in its environment variable QUERY_STRING. This variable can be used by any CGI program.

- **POST**—With this method, the browser precedes this string with a number signifying the number of characters the string holds. The server stores this number in the CONTENT_LENGTH variable. It supplies the string as standard input to the CGI program. **perl** reads this data with its **read** function, and reads just as much as specified by CONTENT_LENGTH.

GOING FURTHER

The method itself is available as REQUEST_METHOD in the server's environment. Our sample HTML form uses GET as the method. GET has the limitation that the string size is restricted to 1024 characters. If you have a lot of data to transmit, then use POST. However, the structure of the query string is the same in both cases, so the **emp_add.pl** program should be able to handle the data using both methods. There was no compelling reason to choose GET rather than POST for this example.

20.21 Handling Form Data

The **emp_add.pl** CGI program (shown later) has to parse the data in QUERY_STRING (for GET) or STDIN (for POST). It then has to combine the extracted data into a single line and add it to a text file that acts as the database. To better understand what's going on, we'll print the contents of the important CGI environment variables on the browser window. The CGI program must be able to generate the HTML required to display these messages.

20.21.1 Creating the Subroutines for Header and Footer

Since all HTML documents have a common header and footer segment, let's first frame two subroutines for them. **Htmlheader** prints the header:

```
sub Htmlheader {
  local ($title, $h1) = @_;
    print << "MARKER";                          A here document
    <html>
    <head>
    <title>$title</title>                       Variable substitution enabled
    </head>
    <body>
    <h1>$h1</h1>
MARKER                                          Don't indent this!
}
```

Htmlheader accepts two arguments which are accepted into the placeholders $title and $h1. This means you have the option of specifying the title and first level header when calling the subroutine. Here, we have used a single **print** statement like a here document. The double quotes surrounding the marker tag ensure that variable substitution is enabled (required for $title and $h1).

The subroutine for the footer is simpler still:

```
sub Htmlfooter {
print "</body>\n</html>\n";
}
```

Place these two subroutines (and another one that we'll be discussing shortly) in a separate file **web_lib.pl**. They will be required at runtime by our CGI program. Make sure you add the statement 1; at the end of the file *(20.18)* so that it always returns a true value.

20.21.2   emp_add.pl: The Main CGI Program

Before we take up the third subroutine, let's have a look at the CGI program **emp_add.pl** specified in the URL. It requires the two subroutines just discussed to add a line to the text database:

```
$ cat emp_add.pl
#!/usr/bin/perl
require "web_lib.pl" ;

open (OUTFILE, ">>/home/sumit/public_html/emp_out.1st") ;
&Parse(*field) ;
print "Content-type: text/html\n\n";
&Htmlheader("Testing Query String", "The QUERY_STRING Variable") ;

print "The query string is $ENV{'QUERY_STRING'}<br>\n" ;
print "The method of sending data to server is $ENV{'REQUEST_METHOD'}<br>\n" ;
print "THE content length is $ENV{'CONTENT_LENGTH'}<br>\n" ;
print OUTFILE "$field{'empid'}|$field{'ename'}|$field{'desig'}|$field{'dept'}|
$field{'dtbirth'}|$field{'salary'}<br>\n" ;
print "A record has been added <a href=\"http://localhost/cgi-bin/emp_query.pl\"
>Click here to see the records</a><br>\n" ;
&Htmlfooter ;
close (OUTFILE);
```

Since this program has to generate the HTML, it has to explicitly spell out its Content-Type and then leave a blank line (\n\n) before sending back data. The HTML header is then printed with the **Htmlheader** subroutine. The footer is printed at the end with **Htmlfooter**.

Note from the **open** statement that the script writes to the file emp_out.1st. The child HTTP process that communicates form data to the server runs as an ordinary user *(24.14.1)*. For the process to be able to create this file, the directory public_html must be world-writable (with **chmod 777**). This is necessary for entering the first detail. Once the file is created, the directory can have its old permissions.

20.21.3   The Parse Subroutine

Parse is the third subroutine that we need to use here. **Parse** makes each *name=value* pair available as separate entries in the associative array %field. Note that the array %field is passed *by reference* with the * prefix to **Parse** in the **emp_add.pl** script.

The next three **print** statements following &Htmlheader display the contents of the server's environment variables on the browser window. The fourth one uses the filehandle OUTFILE to add a line to the database, using the | as the field delimiter. The final **print** statement prints a completion message and offers a hyperlink (with A HREF) to the **emp_query.pl** program. You should be able to see all the lines of the file emp_out.1st (including the one that you just added) when you click on this link.

To understand how **perl** makes the form values available in the associative array %field, we need to study closely the **Parse** subroutine:

```perl
sub Parse {
  local (*in) = @_ ;
  local ($i, $key, $val) ;                              # Local variables

  if ($ENV{'REQUEST_METHOD'} eq "GET") {                # Takes care of both GET
    $in = $ENV{'QUERY_STRING'} ;
  } elsif ($ENV{'REQUEST_METHOD'} eq "POST") {          # ... and POST
    read(STDIN, $in, $ENV{'CONTENT_LENGTH'}) ;
  }                                                     # Query string in $in

  @in = split(/&/, $in) ;                               # Break up into name=value pairs
  foreach $i (0 .. $#in) {
    $in[$i] =~ s/\+/ /g ;                               # Decode a + to a space
    ($key, $val) = split(/=/, $in[$i], 2) ;             # Splits on the first =
    $key =~ s/%(..)/pack("c",hex($1))/ge;
    $val =~ s/%(..)/pack("c",hex($1))/ge;
    $in{$key} = $val ;                                  # Name and value in associative array
  }
  return %in ;
}
```

Parse here accepts an array by reference. This array is copied to %in inside the subroutine. We used the associative array %ENV to evaluate the server's three environment variables we have just discussed. The query string is assigned to the variable $in irrespective of the method used. POSTed data is also read into $in, but from standard input (STDIN is the filehandle) with the **read** function. The number of characters read is determined by **read**'s third argument (the content length).

Because the query string uses the & as the delimiter of the *name=value* pairs, the first **split** stores every such pair in the scalar array @in. The **s** function decodes every + to a space as encoding (space to a +) takes place whenever there are spaces in the data. Many characters are encoded into hexadecimal strings because they have special significance in the URL string. For instance, the / that separates the elements of the date field is used to delimit directories in the URL string. As you can see in Fig. 20.3,

FIGURE 20.3   *Output of CGI Program* **emp_add.pl**

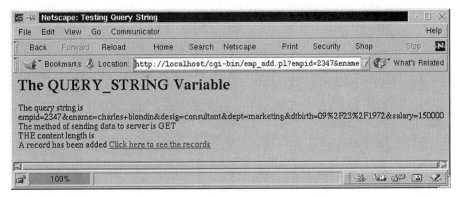

it is encoded to %2F before the query string is sent to the server. The **pack** function converts these hex values back to their original ASCII characters. Note how the **s** function identifies these characters with the pattern %(..) that uses a TRE. The ge flags ensure that **pack** is interpreted as an expression and not treated literally.

The **foreach** loop picks up each *name=value* pair from the array @in. After decoding, each element of the array is split again, this time on the =, and stored in the variables $key and $val. The first is set as the subscript and the other as the value in the associative array %in. This array is returned to the calling program. Note that in this program we used in as a variable ($in), as a scalar list (@in) and an associative array (%in) without conflict.

20.21.4   emp_query.pl: The Query Program

Fig 20.3 shows the output of **emp_add.pl** on the browser window after you have pressed the *Add* button of the form shown in Fig 20.1. Note the hyperlink which offers to show all the lines of the database including the one you just added. A click here runs the **emp_query.pl** program and displays the list of people as elements of a table (Fig. 20.4). Here's the listing of the program:

```
$ cat emp_query.pl
#!/usr/bin/perl
require "web_lib.pl" ;

open (OUTFILE, "/home/sumit/public_html/emp_out.lst") ;
print "Content-type: text/html\n\n";
&Htmlheader("Retrieving from Database", "Result of Query:") ;
print "<table border=1 bordercolor=magenta bgcolor=cyan>" ;
print "<tr><th>Emp-id</th><th>Full Name</th><th>Designation</th>" ;
print "<th>Department</th><th>Date of Birth</th><th>Salary (\$)</th></tr>" ;
while (<OUTFILE>) {
    ($empid, $ename, $desig, $dept, $dtbirth, $salary) = split (/\|/) ;
    print "<tr><td>$empid</td><td>$ename</td><td>$desig</td>" ;
    print "<td>$dept</td><td>$dtbirth</td><td>$salary</td></tr>" ;
}
print "</table>" ;
&Htmlfooter ;
```

This time the file emp_out.lst is opened for reading. The table headers are printed with the <tr> and <th> tags. The program picks up each line of OUTFILE, splits it and then prints it as a table row with the <tr> and <td> tags.

With **perl**, all this looks so ridiculously simple that you wouldn't dream of using any other language for text manipulation—not for CGI, at least. It's no wonder that **perl** is the most widely used language for CGI programming on the Internet.

Note

CGI is a security threat on the Internet as a result of which the server administrator often disables CGI operation by individual users. In case you find this restriction on your system, contact the administrator.

FIGURE 20.4 *Output of CGI Program* `emp_query.pl`

> **Netscape: Retrieving from Database**
>
> File   Edit   View   Go   Communicator   Help
>
> Back   Forward   Reload   Home   Search   Netscape   Print   Security   Sho
>
> Bookmarks   Location: http://localhost/cgi-bin/emp_query.pl   What's Related
>
> ## Result of Query:
>
> | Emp–id | Full Name | Designation | Department | Date of Birth | Salary ($) |
> |--------|-----------|-------------|------------|---------------|------------|
> | 2347 | charles blondin | consultant | marketing | 09/23/1972 | 150000 |

SUMMARY

perl is a superset of **grep**, **tr**, **sed**, **awk** and the shell. It can be used from the command line with the -e option, but a **perl** program is better placed in a file with the interpreter specified in the first line. All **perl** statements are terminated with semicolons.

Input is read from the keyboard by assigning the *filehandle* <STDIN> to a variable. **perl** reads everything that is entered including spaces and the newline character. The last character of a line is removed by **chop**.

Variables need the $ both for assignment and evaluation. They need no type declarations and can store a number with a very high degree of precision. Variable values can include the escape sequences like tab (\t) and newline (\n). You can capitalize the first character of a string (\u) or the entire string (\U).

The . is used for string concatenation. x is used for repetition. **substr** extracts a string both from right and left, and also inserts a string. **uc** and **ucfirst** convert into uppercase the entire argument and the first character, respectively.

perl uses the -n option to set up an implicit loop for reading files. An explicit loop can also be set up with the symbols <>—representing the filenames specified in the command line. **while (<>)** is quite often used inside a script to read a file.

$. stores the current line number, and the range operator (..) specifies a group of lines.

$_ is the *default variable* used by many **perl** functions. It stores the last line read or the last pattern matched. **print**, **chop**, **split**, pattern matching and substitution operate on $_ by default.

perl uses lists and arrays extensively. @*arr* when assigned to a variable represents the length of the array. $#*arr* stores the last subscript of the array @*arr*. @ARGV[ ] stores all command line arguments, but the command name is available as $0.

The **foreach** construct loops through an array and assigns each element in turn to a variable. The list can also be provided by command substitution.

split breaks up a list into variables or an array. @_ is the default array and whitespace the default delimiter. Elements of a split line can be glued together with **join**.

Elements can be deleted from an array (**shift** and **pop**) or inserted (**unshift** and **push**). **splice** can do everything at any array location.

The *associative array* uses the % symbol and alternates the array subscript and value in a series of comma-delimited values. The subscript of this array can also be a character string. The **keys** function extracts these subscripts, and **values** filters out the values. **sort** may be used to order the extraction.

perl accepts all regular expressions used by all UNIX commands, and has some of its own. Now, you can match a digit (\d), a word character (\w), the beginning of a word (\b) and a whitespace character (\s). The uppercase counterparts negate the lowercase ones.

The **s** and **tr** functions are used for substitution and character translation in the same way done in **sed** and **tr**. The operators =~ and !~ are used to match regular expressions with variables. Files can be edited "in-place" with the -i option, and can be optionally backed up with a separate extension.

The IRE and TRE work in the same way as before except that the \ is not required before the () and {} characters. A grouped pattern can also be reproduced elsewhere with $1, $2 and so on, till the next grouping is done.

perl uses a *filehandle* to access a file. A filehandle can represent a pipeline as well. **print** also uses a filehandle to write to a file. The **select** *filehandle* statement makes **print** use that filehandle as the default.

perl's file tests can store the age of a file (modification and access) to several places of decimals.

Subroutines are invoked with an &, and its arguments are stored in the array @_. Subroutines can be held in an external file but must have the statement 1; at the end of the file. The calling program "includes" subroutines placed in an external file with the **require** statement.

GOING FURTHER

perl is the language of choice for CGI programming. A **perl** program can be specified in the action attribute of the <form> tag. The GET method passes data to the program through the QUERY_STRING environment variable. POST data is passed as standard input. The program extracts the *name=value* pairs, separates the name from the value, and also generates the HTML code required to be sent back to the browser.

SELF-TEST

20.1   What's wrong with this program? What is it supposed to print anyway?

```
#!/usr/bin/perl
x = 2;
print x ** 32 ;
```

20.2   Number all lines of a file, separating the line from the line number by a tab.

20.3   List the lines in /etc/passwd having 100 as the GUID.

20.4 Print the string UNIX 20 times without using a loop.

20.5 How will you convert all characters in a file to uppercase without using shell redirection?

20.6 Write a program which accepts a positive integer from the keyboard and then displays all integers from 1 up to that number, each on a separate line.

20.7 Accept a string from the keyboard and then print each character of the string on a separate line.

20.8 Ask the user repeatedly to enter a number, and when the user enters 0, print the total of all numbers entered so far.

20.9 Accept a four-digit year from the keyboard and then check whether it's a leap year or not. (Note: Years ending with 00 must be divisible by 400.)

20.10 Find at least four errors in the following program (line numbers shown on the left):

```
1    #/usr/bin/perl
2    print "what is your age ?;
3    $a = <STDIN>
4    chop ($a) ;
5    if ( $a < 18 )
6        print "Not old enough to vote yet  /n ";
7    } else {
8        print "You are old enough to vote ";
9    }
```

20.11 Write a program that prompts a user to input a string and a number, and prints the string that many times, with each string on a separate line.

EXERCISES

20.1 How do you double-space a file with **perl**?

20.2 Instead of numbering lines, add the letters A., B., C. and so on at the beginning of every line.

20.3 How do you print lines in reverse order?

20.4 How will you print just the first occurrence of a string in a file? (The string and filename are the first and second arguments.)

20.5 Capitalize the first character of every word in a file.

20.6 How will you convert a binary number (supplied as argument) to decimal?

20.7 Find out the occurrences of three consecutive and identical alphabetic characters (like aaa or bbb).

20.8 Devise a script which lists all words used in one or more files and displays their count (in the form *word:count*).

20.9 How do you print a sorted list of all environment variables in the form *variable=value*?

20.10 How will you use **find** and **perl** to delete all files modified more than a year back? What's the advantage of using this method compared to using **find** with -exec rm?

20.11   Change the interpreter line to `#!/usr/local/bin/perl` in all **perl** scripts in the current directory.

20.12   A closing HTML tag starts with /. For instance <b> is closed with </b>. Convert all these tags comprising single words (without attributes) to uppercase. (`<img src=`.... will not get converted.)

20.13   Display the listing in the current directory of only those files that have multiple links.

20.14   Refer to the example of converting URLs in HTML documents in Sec. 15.12.2, and implement it in **perl**. This time take care of the <IMG SRC> tag which also refers to URLs.

GOING FURTHER

20.15   Write a CGI script which displays the **df** command output on your browser.

KEY TERMS

associative array *(20.14)*

Common Gateway Interface (CGI) *(20.20)*

default variable *(20.6)*

filehandle *(20.16)*

GET method *(20.20.3)*

in-place editing *(20.15.3)*

POST method *(20.20.3)*

query string *(20.20.2)*

scalar list *(20.8)*

## CHAPTER 21

System Administration I—
The File System Revisited

So far, we have been looking at the UNIX file system as one large tree-like structure. In real life, it is seldom so. In fact, it is often a combination of a number of such structures—the *file systems*. These file systems are probably the most sensitive components of the UNIX system. In this chapter, we'll delve deeply into the file system and understand some of its internals. We'll learn to create partitions and file systems, mount and check them.

A file system maintains all information related to files, directories and devices. The system administrator must understand its internals well because it's her job to maintain it in a healthy and correct state. She must be able to fix inconsistencies that tend to crop up from time to time and ensure that loss of data is minimal. When the system refuses to boot, she must not panic and reinstall the entire system. It is considered a serious demerit if she is not able to rectify *most* of the damage. The task need not be daunting though as UNIX provides the utilities needed for maintaining file systems.

Objectives

- Learn the significance of the two types of device files and their names. *(21.1 and 21.2)*
- Understand how files are held in separate *partitions* and *file systems*. *(21.4)*
- Know the functioning of the four components of a file system. *(21.5)*
- Learn how the inode keeps track of all disk block addresses used by a file. *(21.5.3)*
- Know the role of the directory in the kernel's handling of files. *(21.6)*
- Learn the different types of file systems that you'll find on UNIX systems. *(21.8)*
- Create a partition and a file system on a Linux machine with **fdisk** and **mkfs**. *(21.9)*
- *Mount* and *unmount* file systems with the **mount** and **umount** commands. *(21.10)*
- Learn how **mount** uses /etc/fstab to obtain mounting information. *(21.10.3)*
- Conduct checks on and repair file systems with **fsck**. *(21.11)*

Note

System administration commands are quite system-dependent, and their functions and output vary widely from one system to another. Sometimes a command may not be available on a system at all. In case you are unable to execute a command discussed in this chapter, look up the system's documentation; the command could either have a different name or use a different option there.

You have to log in as root to use most of the commands featured in this chapter. If required, have a look at Section 22.2 of the next chapter to make yourself fully aware of the consequences of acquiring super user powers. For most of the chapter, you'll have to work at the # prompt—the one used by root.

21.1 The Device

All devices are also files. You open a device, read and write into it and then close it like you do to any file. The functions for doing all this are built into the kernel for each and every device of the system. All device files are stored in /dev or in its subdirectories. Here's a concise listing of these devices for a system running System V:

```
$ ls -l /dev
total 52
brw-rw-rw-  1 root     sys       51,   0 Aug 31 07:28 cd0              CDROM
brw-rw-rw-  2 bin      bin        2,  64 Feb 23  1997 fd0    Default floppy drive
brw------   1 sysinfo  sysinfo    1,   0 May  7  1996 hd00       First hard disk
crw------   2 bin      bin        6,   0 Dec  5 14:12 lp0              Printer
cr--r--r--  1 root     root      50,   0 Aug 31 07:28 rcdt0          Tape drive
crw------   1 henry    terminal   0,   0 Oct 15 10:23 tty01           Terminal
crw-rw-rw-  2 bin      bin        5,   0 May  7  1996 tty1a        Serial port 1
crw-rw-rw-  1 bin      bin        5,128 Feb 23  1997 tty1A        Modem port 1
```

SVR4 also has two additional directories—/dev/dsk and /dev/rdsk containing some more files. The files in those directories sometimes have equivalents (or even links) in /dev. The lists in real life are much larger than this and includes every possible device in your system—including even the main memory of your computer. This listing reveals two vital points:

- Device files can be grouped into mainly two categories depending on the first character of the permissions field (b or c).
- The fifth field—normally representing the size for other files—consists of a pair of numbers. A device file contains no data.

The significance of these attributes is taken up next.

21.1.1 Block and Character Devices

First, a word about disk reading and writing. When you issue an instruction to save a file, the request is combined with other users' requests and the write operation takes place in chunks or blocks. Each block here represents an integral number of disk sectors. When you read from disk, a **buffer cache** is first accessed which contains the most recently used data. If the data is found there, the disk access is avoided. This saves a great deal of time. You may also decide to ignore this facility and access the device directly. Many devices allow you to do that, and the access method is determined by the *name* of the device that is called up.

Note that generally the first character in the permissions field is c or b. The floppy drive, CD-ROM and the hard disk have b prefixed to their permissions. All data is read from and written into these devices in blocks and use the buffer cache. That's why they are referred to as **block special devices**. On the other hand, the terminal, tape drive and printer are **character special** or **raw devices**, indicated by the letter c. The read/write operations ignore the buffer cache and access the device directly.

Note

Many devices have both a raw and a block counterpart in System V. Hard disks, floppy drives and CD-ROMs have both block and character devices. Generally, an r prefixed to a block device name makes it a character device. Block devices are also found separately in /dev/dsk and character devices in /dev/rdsk.

21.1.2 Major and Minor Numbers

The set of routines needed to operate a specific device is known as the **device driver**. When a particular device is accessed, the kernel calls the right device driver and passes some parameters for it to act properly. The kernel must know not only the type of device but also certain details about the device—like the density of a floppy or the partition number of the disk.

The fifth column of the previous listing doesn't show the file size in bytes, but rather a pair of two numbers separated by a comma. These numbers are called the **major** and **minor device numbers**, respectively. The major number represents the device driver; this is actually the type of device. All hard disks will have the same major number if they are attached to the same controller.

The minor number is indicative of the parameters that the kernel passes to the device driver. Often, it indicates the special characteristics of the device. For example, fd0h1440 and fd1h1440 represent two floppy devices attached to a particular controller. So both of them will have the same major number but different minor numbers.

Device files also have permissions with the same significance. To send output to a terminal, you need to have write permission for the device, and to read a floppy, you must have read permission for the device file. However, most device permissions and other attributes can only be set by the system administrator.

21.2 Significance of Device Names

The characteristic feature of UNIX device files is that the same device can often be accessed with several different filenames. This has sometimes been done for backward compatibility and sometimes for associating a separate device with a specific function.

The devices that you'll normally encounter on UNIX and Linux systems are shown in Table 21.1. Though the device names in Linux have been known to be remarkably invariant, the same can't be said of the System V devices. Different SVR4 systems often have different names. If you are using Solaris or HP-UX, the names *will* be different.

You'll see a lot of 0s, 1s and other digits in the device names. Often, you'll be able to identify a device from its filename. System V device files are resident in /dev/dsk (and /dev/rdsk for raw devices). The name /dev/dsk/f0q18dt represents a 3.5″ floppy (block) device. It is bootable (0), of quad density and has 18 sectors/track—a 1.44 MB diskette. There is also a default name for many devices; the floppy drive can be accessed by /dev/fd0.

TABLE 21.1   *Typical Device Names (Directory: /dev)*

SVR4 Device	Linux Device	Significance
cd0 or dsk/c0t6d0s2	cdrom	CD-ROM
fd0 or diskette	fd0	Default floppy drive
dsk/f0q18dt	fd0H1440	1.44 MB floppy
rdsk/f0q18dt	fd0H1440	1.44 MB raw floppy
hd00 or dsk/c0t0d0s2	hda	First hard disk
hd10 or dsk/c1t3d0s2	hdb	Second hard disk
lp0	lp0	Printer
rcdt0 or rmt/0	st0	Tape drive
term/1	tty1	Terminal
tty1a	cua0	Serial port 1
tty2A	ttyS1	Modem port 2

On older systems, you may see the file fd0135ds18 representing the 3.5″ floppy drive. It is bootable (0), double-sided, has 135 tracks and 18 sectors/track. It can also be accessed as a raw device—/dev/rfd0135ds18. These files were used by the XENIX system, and are still provided by many vendors for backward compatibility.

Note

Unlike ordinary and directory files, device files don't contain any data. They merely point to the actual physical device.

Linux

Device Names and Significance

Linux files are mostly in /dev. Their names are also quite different:

```
lrwxrwxrwx  1 root  root       3 Mar 11 20:54 cdrom -> hdc
crw-rw----  1 root  uucp   5,  64 Nov 30 18:55 cua0              Serial port 1
brw-rw-rw-  1 root  root   2,  40 Nov 30 18:55 fd0H1440          First floppy
brw-rw-rw-  1 root  root   2,  41 May  1 04:19 fd1H1440          Second floppy
brw------   1 root  root   3,   0 Nov 30 18:55 hda               First hard disk
crw-rw----  1 root  lp     6,   0 Nov 30 18:55 lp0               Printer
lrwxrwxrwx  1 root  uucp      10 Apr 24 15:04 modem -> /dev/ttyS0
lrwxrwxrwx  1 root  root       9 Apr 24 15:04 mouse -> /dev/cua1
crw------   1 henry tty    4,   1 Apr  3 17:31 tty1              Terminal
crw-rw----  1 root  uucp   4,  64 Nov 30 18:55 ttyS0             Serial port 1
```

Linux uses only the block device for the 3.5″ bootable floppy drive—/dev/fd0H1440. It also supports an extensively linked system of device files. You can see that /dev/modem is linked to /dev/ttyS0 (the first outgoing serial port). The mouse is linked to /dev/cua1 (the second incoming serial port). The CD-ROM is linked to one of the devices representing the hard disk (/dev/hdc).

21.3 **The Hard Disk**

As system administrator, you'll need to know hard-disk lingo when you create partitions and file systems. Every disk contains one or more **platters**, each having two surfaces. A magnetic head reads and writes each surface. If there are eight usable surfaces, they'll require eight heads. The heads move in tandem, but their movements can't be controlled individually.

Each surface is composed of a number of concentric serially numbered **tracks**. There are as many tracks bearing the same track number as there are surfaces. You can then visualize a **cylinder** comprising all tracks bearing the same number on each disk surface. There will be as many cylinders in the disk as there are tracks on each usable surface. Each track is further broken up into **sectors** or **blocks**. So if each track has 32 sectors, and a disk has eight surfaces, then there are 256 sectors per cylinder. All this is visually represented in Fig. 21.1.

The disk is spinning constantly (typically 3600 r.p.m.). The disk heads move radially from track to track, and when the head is positioned above a particular track, all its sectors pass through the head in a very short time.

F I G U R E 21.1   *The Hard Disk*

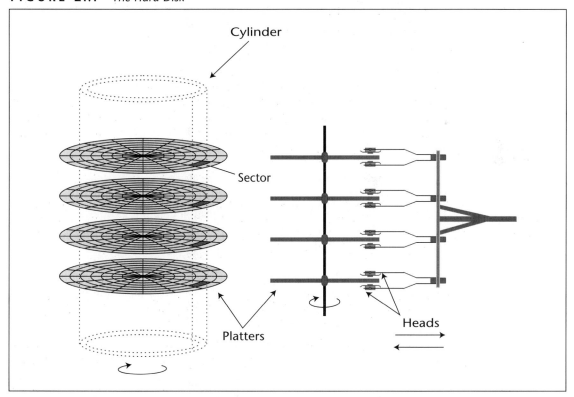

21.4   Partitions and File Systems

Like other operating systems, UNIX requires a formatted hard disk. The formatting operation lies outside the operating system's domain. It marks the defective tracks so read-write operations avoid them. This operation was once carried out by special utilities supplied by the vendor. Today, disks (both IDE and SCSI) come preformatted, so this is one thing you don't have to bother about.

To use your disk, you have to divide it into **partitions**. Each partition can be considered a logically independent disk and accessed by its own device file. By itself, a partition is not ready for use unless you create one or more **file systems** on it. Unlike a partition, a file system has a directory structure containing the various components of the UNIX system. Finally, you'll have to make sure that all file systems unite to form a *single* file system to make it easy for you to work with.

21.4.1   Partitions

We begin with partitions. The term is used interchangeably with **slices** by BSD UNIX and Solaris. Dividing a disk into a number of distinct partitions has advantages from the administrative point of view:

- Separate partitions prevent potential encroachment conflicts that may arise between the various data areas. As user data grows constantly and unpredictably, it should not be allowed to spill over to the system's main partition.
- If there is corruption in one area, other areas are effectively shielded from this evil influence. The system administrator can attend to one partition without shutting down the system.
- Large number of small partitions means that fragmentation *(21.5.2)* will be limited. Fragmentation adversely affects disk performance.
- If the system has an adequate number of partitions, each partition can be backed up separately onto a single volume of tape. The administrator can also have different backup schedules for the different partitions.
- Dual boot systems (like Linux and SCO UNIX) require separate partitions for different operating systems.

When you create partitions, you'll have to make sure that a partition always begins and ends on a cylinder boundary. If a partition begins in the middle of a cylinder, then disk performance will be impeded. Partition creating utilities usually round this off to the nearest complete cylinder, but you'll have to take care if they don't. If you are asked to specify tracks instead of cylinders, it's easy to miss the boundaries if you don't do your arithmetic properly.

Note

Dual boot systems (like Linux and SCO UNIX) allow multiple operating systems to be loaded on the same machine. In that case, every operating system requires a separate partition for itself. The system prompts the user for the operating system to be booted at startup.

21.4.2   File Systems

After the disk has been partitioned, you'll have to create a **file system** in each partition. A UNIX system is usually configured into multiple file systems, where each file system has its own directory tree headed by root. If you don't see multiple "roots" on your machine it's because all these file systems become a single one at the time of use. How all this happens will be discussed later, but let's first see how a file system is organized.

Every file system is organized in a sequence of blocks of 1024 bytes and generally has these four components:

- The boot block—This block contains a small boot program and the partition table.
- The superblock—It contains global information about the file system. Additionally, it also maintains a free list of inodes *(21.5.1)* and data blocks that can be immediately allocated by the kernel when creating a file.
- The inode blocks—This region contains a table for every file of the file system. All attributes of a file and directory are stored in this area except the name of the file or directory itself.
- The data blocks—The operating system's files, all data and programs created by users reside in this area.

The file system layout is shown in Fig. 21.2. In the upcoming sections, we'll have a detailed look at the way the kernel and these components work in tandem to organize allocation of space for files. Before we do that, we'll familiarize ourselves with the device naming schemes of these file systems.

Note

The words *partition* and *file system* are often used synonymously, especially when a partition contains a single file system. However, this is not always the case. Some systems like SCO UNIX break up a partition into *divisions*, with a file system in each division. Linux allows the creation of an **extended partition**, with multiple **logical partitions** in each extended partition. Each logical partition then contains a file system. In this way, it's possible to have multiple file systems in a single partition.

21.4.3 Devices for File Systems

SCSI disks normally support up to eight partitions while IDE disks hold four. Every file system (and partition) has a device name associated with it, and these names vary across UNIX flavors. In fact, nowhere is UNIX so disgustingly fragmented as in these naming conventions.

SVR4 uses the directories /dev/dsk and /dev/rdsk to hold block and character devices, respectively. It also employs a naming scheme which includes the controller number, the drive number on the controller and the partition number. Here are two device names on a Solaris system which uses this scheme:

- /dev/rdsk/c0t3d0s4 — This is the fifth partition (s4) for the first drive (d0) in the first controller (c0).

FIGURE 21.2 *The File System Layout*

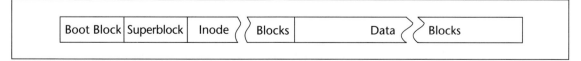

- /dev/rdsk/c0t3d0s2 — This is the third partition 3 (s2) representing the entire disk.

Note that apart from having specific devices for partitions (or file systems), UNIX systems also have a special device denoting the *entire* disk. This device name denotes the partition 2 (the third partition) in Solaris. For other systems, the naming scheme is different.

Note

If a partition contains multiple file systems, every file system and partition will have its own device file. There will also be a separate device for the entire hard disk.

Linux

Devices for File Systems

Linux has a simpler naming mechanism. SCSI disks have the sd prefix and IDE disks have hd in the base filename. This is followed by the drive letter and partition number:

/dev/hda1 — Partition 1 on first (a) IDE hard disk.
/dev/sdb3 — Partition 3 on second (b) SCSI hard disk.
/dev/hdb — Entire second IDE hard disk.
/dev/sda — Entire first SCSI hard disk.

As can be seen above, Linux too has a special device denoting the *entire* disk. This device name has no partition number in the file naming scheme.

What happens if /dev/hda1 is an extended partition and contains two logical partitions? In that case, these two logical partitions will have the device names /dev/hda5 and /dev/hda6. The **fdisk** output will drive home this point in a later topic.

21.5   File System Components

We'll now discuss the functionalities of the four components of a file system in reverse order. We'll take up the inode and data blocks first, followed by the superblock and boot block. This unconventional approach actually helps us understand the working of the file system better.

21.5.1   Inode Blocks

Every file has an **inode**—a 128-byte table that contains virtually everything you could possibly need to know about a file (except its name). All inodes are stored in contiguous (in continuity) **inode blocks** in a user-inaccessible area of the file system. Each inode contains the following attributes of a file:

- File type (regular, directory, device, etc.).
- Number of links (the number of aliases the file has).
- The numeric UID of the owner.
- The numeric GUID of the owner.
- File mode (the triad of the three permissions).
- Number of bytes in the file.
- Date and time of last modification of file data.

- Date and time of last access of file data.
- Date and time of last change of the inode.
- An array of 15 pointers to the file.

The inode is accessed by a number called the **inode number**. This number is unique for every file in a *single* file system. It is actually the position of the inode in these inode blocks, and hence can be located using simple arithmetic. As discussed before *(7.13)*, the inode number is displayed with the -i option of ls.

Observe that neither the name of the file nor its inode number is stored in the inode. Both parameters are actually stored in the directory that houses the file. Except for the array of 15 pointers, all these file attributes can be revealed by different options of the ls command. The command has to look up the directory file as well to display the filename.

When a file is opened, its inode is copied from the hard disk to the system's own inode table maintained in memory. The kernel always works with the memory copy (the **inode buffers**), but it periodically updates the disk copy with the contents of the memory copy. Because the two copies are not in *sync* (one more recent than the other), the integrity of the file system is compromised when the power to the machine is cut off abnormally. You'll have to conduct file system checks when UNIX refuses to come up.

Note

The inode contains all attributes of a file except the filename. The filename is stored in the directory housing the file. The UNIX inode structure is in sharp contrast to the system followed in the Windows FAT file system, which stores the file attributes, including the modification time, the number of bytes and the address of the starting disk cluster in the directory part of the system area itself.

21.5.2   Data Blocks

On most systems, the smallest block that can be read and written by the disk controller is 512 bytes. It's often called a **physical block**. The kernel reads and writes data using a different block size, and this block is often referred to as a **logical block**. Many UNIX tools report their output in physical blocks, but the performance of your system is determined by the logical block size that you set when creating your file systems.

Unlike terminals and printers (character devices), which read and write one character at a time, hard disks (block devices) handle data in chunks or blocks. The standard (logical) block size varies from 1024 to 8192 bytes (Solaris). Using an entire block for read/write operations means that even if you have to write three bytes of data into a 1024-byte disk block, 1021 bytes will simply be wasted. A pity, but that is the price one has to pay for having a well-organized and consistent file system.

The **data blocks** commence from the point the inode blocks terminate. Every block is identified by an address—a number that refers to the position of the block in the data block area. The blocks containing data are known as **direct blocks**.

Even though the blocks are numbered consecutively, you'll hardly ever find the data of a frequently modified file arranged in contiguous blocks. When a file expands, the kernel may not find the adjacent block free. It has to locate a free one from the blocks scattered randomly throughout the disk. This slows down read/write operations and leads to **disk fragmentation**. However, this fragmentation also allows files to be enlarged or reduced at will.

All this means that the inode has to keep track of all direct block addresses. However, the inode can store only some (12) of them. You may find this incredible, but the file system also contains some **indirect blocks**. These themselves don't contain data but only the addresses of those direct blocks which couldn't be accommodated in the inode (13th block onwards). But the inode maintains a list of these indirect block addresses as well, and we'll soon see how this arrangement helps to keep track of all blocks used by a file.

Note

Even though a logical block on your system may be 1024 or 8192 bytes in size, many UNIX commands use the physical block for reporting their output. This block has a size of 512 bytes. On most systems, the `ls -s`, `df`, `du` and `find` commands understand and report in physical blocks only.

21.5.3 The Block Addressing Scheme

The discussions in this section are drawn up with reference to the standard file system (*ufs*) used by Solaris, but the concepts are applicable universally. We'll now see how the array of 15 disk block addresses in the inode suffice to keep track of a file's data blocks.

The first 12 entries contain the addresses of the first 12 blocks of the file. However, if a file is only three blocks large, the first three entries are utilized and the remaining entries are flushed out with zeroes. The three entries from the 13th onward don't point to direct blocks but only to indirect ones. The situation gets a bit complex here, but the rules are well laid down.

The 13th entry has the address of a **single indirect block** which contains many more direct block addresses. When the file size increases further, the 14th entry points to a **double indirect block**, which contains the addresses of single indirect blocks. The 15th and final entry points to a **triple indirect block**, which points to double indirect blocks. Ultimately, all these indirect blocks form a **linked list** to store all the blocks used by a file. The organization of data blocks is depicted in Fig. 21.3.

Note

The maximum size of a file in the *ufs* file system discussed above is 2 GB on a 32-bit machine. Now that UNIX has gone 64-bit thanks to Digital, Sun and IBM, it's now possible to have file sizes exceeding several terabytes (1 TB = 1000 GB).

21.5.4 The Superblock

The inode blocks are preceded by the **superblock**—the "balance sheet" of every UNIX file system. It contains global file information about disk usage and availability of data blocks and inodes. Its information should, therefore, be correct for healthy operation of the system. This is mainly what it contains:

- The size of the file system.
- The length the file system's logical block.
- Last time of updating.
- The number of free data blocks available and a partial list of immediately allocable free data blocks.
- Number of free inodes available and a partial list of immediately usable inodes.
- The state of the file system (whether "clean" or "dirty").

FIGURE 21.3   *The Disk Block Addressing Scheme (Triple Indirect Block Not Shown)*

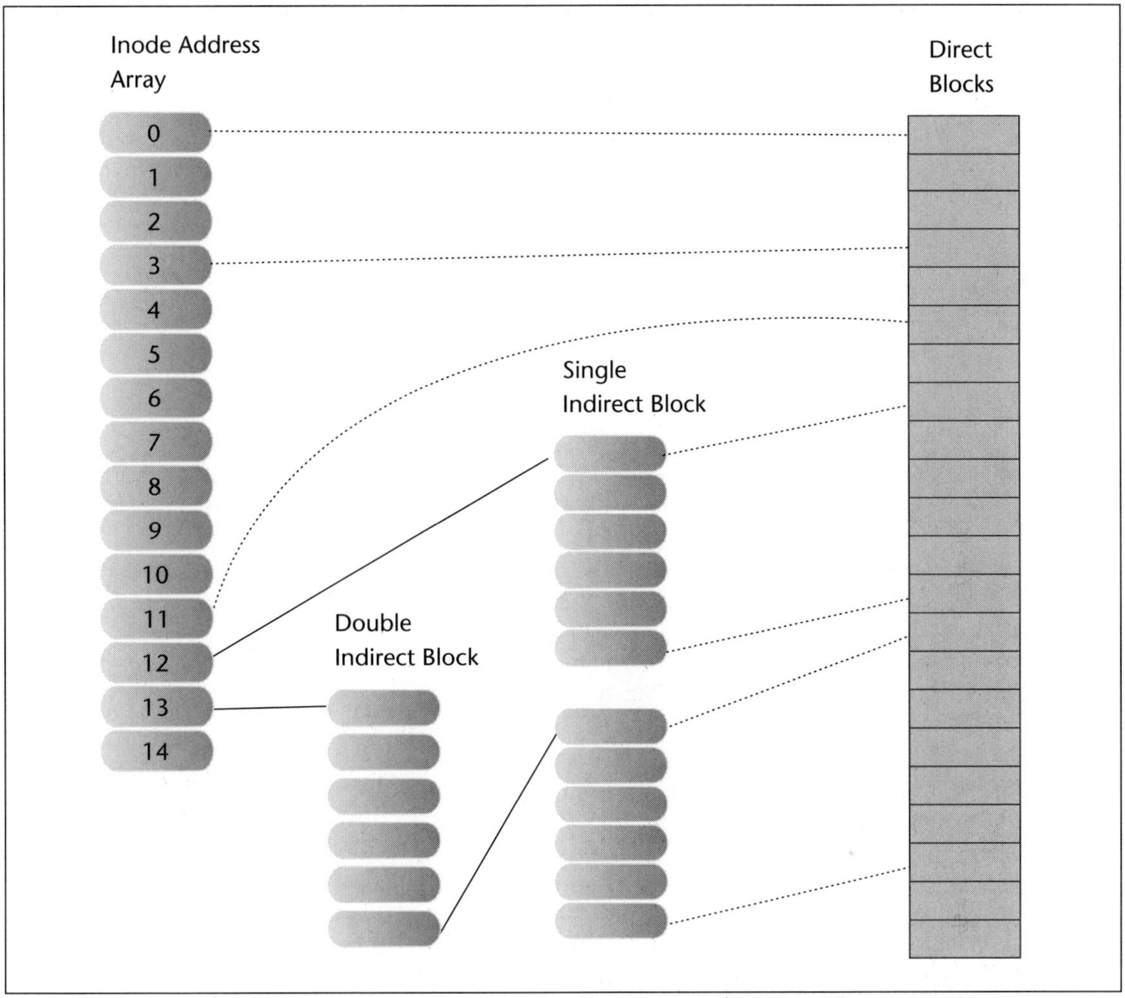

Inode Address
Array

Direct
Blocks

0
1
2
3
4
5
6
7
8
9
10
11
12
13
14

Single
Indirect Block

Double
Indirect Block

As with inodes, the kernel also maintains a copy of the superblock in memory. It reads and writes this copy when controlling allocation of inodes and data blocks. From time to time, the kernel uses the **sync** operation to update the disk copy with the memory copy. This means that the disk copy can *never* be newer than the memory copy, but nearly as recent. This flushing also takes place just before the machine is shut down.

Note

UNIX refuses to boot if the superblock is corrupt. To overcome this problem, many systems (like Solaris and Linux) have multiple superblocks written in different areas of the disk. If one superblock is corrupt, the system can be directed to use another.

21.5.5   The Boot Block

Continuing our reverse viewing of the file system, we have finally come to its beginning. Preceding the superblock is the **boot block**. This is the **Master Boot Record**

(MBR) that Linux users would recall seeing as a LILO option when installing the system. The boot block contains the partition table and a small "bootstrapping" program.

When the system is booted, the system BIOS checks for the existence of the first hard disk and loads the entire segment of the boot block into memory. It then hands over control to the bootstrapping program. This in turn loads the kernel (the file unix, genunix or vmlinuz) into memory. However, the bootstrapping program is read in from the boot block of the root (main) file system. For other file systems, this block is simply kept blank.

21.6 The Directory

The directory contains just two file attributes—the filename and inode number. Because the inode itself can be accessed by this number, the directory and the inode can be said to form a relational database, with the two *tables* related to each other through the inode number. To use RDBMS jargon, you can fetch a file's attributes by *joining* the respective *rows* of these two tables.

When you create a link to a file, its link count in the inode is incremented. A directory entry is also created with the new filename, and the inode number copied from the original file entry. When you remove a linked file with **rm**, the link count in the inode is decremented, and the directory entry is also removed for that link. A file is considered to be removed when the link count drops to zero. The associated disk blocks are then freed and made available for fresh allocation.

21.6.1 How the Kernel Accesses a File

Now that you know the addressing mechanism used by the kernel for accessing files and directories, what happens when you issue the command **cat foo**? The file must be located and displayed on the standard output, but the kernel also has to determine when the end of file has been reached. A great deal of work is involved here:

1. The kernel always maintains in memory the inode number for the current directory. Using this number it searches the inode blocks and locates the inode for this directory.
2. It fetches from this inode the address of the data block that contains the directory file.
3. From the directory file the kernel looks for the file foo and its inode number.
4. It then goes back to the inode blocks and locates the inode for foo.
5. The kernel now reads the file size and disk address entries, goes to the indirect blocks (if any) and reads all associated direct block entries.
6. Finally, it instructs the disk driver to move the disk heads to the respective blocks, counts the number of bytes read, matches it with the file size and reads till the two numbers match. There's no other way to know that the end of file has been reached.

Tip

You should not add to the kernel's misery by creating large directories occupying more than one (perhaps noncontiguous) block. This will only slow down file access. Create multiple directories instead.

21.7   The Standard File Systems

The preceding discussions related to a single file system. In real life, most UNIX systems split a disk into as many as eight partitions. Moreover, if you have multiple disks, every such disk must have at least one file system on it. In general, most UNIX systems will always have these two file systems:

- *root* This file system must be present in every UNIX system. It contains the bare-bones UNIX—the root directory, /bin, /usr/bin, /etc, /sbin, /usr/sbin, /dev and /lib directories—all the tools and utilities that are just adequate to keep the system going. When the system is booted in single-user mode, this is the only file system available to the system administrator.
- *swap* Every system should have a swap file system which is used by the kernel to control the movement of processes. When the system memory is heavily loaded, the kernel has to move processes out of memory to this file system. When these swapped processes are ready to run, they are loaded back to memory. Users can't access data in this file system directly.

A UNIX system—especially a large one—contains many more file systems. System files should be kept separate from data files created by users, and hence a separate file system is usually made for them. Linux and SVR4 create users' home directories in /home, but older systems use /usr. /home is often maintained as a separate file system. If there's no space left on /home, the administrator uses other file systems like /usr2 or /u.

You can have additional file systems for /tmp and /var/tmp so that temporary and log files can't grow indefinitely. If the system is handling a lot of mail, it makes sense to have /var/mail as a separate file system. There may also be other file systems where the administrator may want to install the database software—for instance, /oracle for the Oracle RDBMS.

21.8   File System Types

Initially, there were only two types of file systems—the ones from AT&T and Berkeley. Over time, many more file system types have made their entry into the UNIX system. You need to know the following file systems which you'll encounter often:

- *s5* Before SVR4, this was the only file system used by System V, but today it is offered by SVR4 by this name for backward compatibility only. This file system uses a logical block size of 512 or 1024 bytes and a single superblock. It also can't handle filenames longer than 14 characters.
- *ufs* This is how the Berkeley Fast File System is known to SVR4 and adopted by most UNIX systems. Because the block size here can go up to 64 KB, performance of this file system is considerably better than *s5*. It uses multiple superblocks with each cylinder group storing a superblock. Unlike *s5*, *ufs* supports 255-character filenames, symbolic links and disk quotas.
- *ext2* This is the standard file system of Linux. It uses a block size of 1024 bytes and, like *ufs*, uses multiple superblocks and symbolic links.

- *iso9660* or *hsfs* This is the standard file system used by CD-ROMs and uses DOS-style 8+3 filenames. Since UNIX uses longer filenames, *hsfs* also provides Rock Ridge extensions to accommodate them.
- *msdos* or *pcfs* Most UNIX systems also support DOS filesystems. You can create this file system on a floppy diskette and transfer files to it for use on a Windows system. Linux and Solaris can also directly access a DOS file system in the hard disk.
- *swap* This file system has already been discussed.
- *bfs* The boot file system. This is used by SVR4 to host the boot programs and the UNIX kernel. Users are not meant to use this file system.
- *proc* or *procfs* This can be considered a pseudo-file system maintained in memory. It stores data of each running process and appears to contain files, but actually contains none. Users can obtain most process information including their PIDs directly from here.

Some of these file systems have certain unique characteristics, but we'll ignore them. Besides the above, UNIX vendors also have their own proprietary file systems, but they also support most of the types discussed above. Commands handling file systems (like **mkfs** and **mount**) use an option to describe the file system, the reason why you should know the file system you are using.

21.9 Creating Partitions and File Systems

UNIX fragmentation is also quite evident when it comes to creating partitions. Different versions of UNIX use different tools for partitioning a disk. Though the principles are broadly similar, the differences in details sometimes make the similarities insignificant. The system administrator probably won't allow you to create or delete partitions on her system, so we'll create them on a Linux system.

21.9.1 fdisk: Creating Partitions

Both Linux and SCO UNIX allow a user to have multiple operating systems on Intel machines. It's no wonder then that both offer the Windows-type **fdisk** command to create, delete and activate partitions. **fdisk** in Linux, however, operates differently from Windows.

We'll now create a partition on the first IDE hard disk to hold the Oracle RDBMS software. Let's run **fdisk** and then use the **p** command to view the partition table:

```
Disk /dev/hda: 255 heads, 63 sectors, 784 cylinders
Units = cylinders of 16065 * 512 bytes

    Device Boot    Start      End   Blocks   Id  System
/dev/hda1    *        1      217  1743021    5  Extended
/dev/hda2            218      478  2096482+   6  DOS 16-bit >=32M
/dev/hda4            620      784  1325362+  83  Linux native
/dev/hda5              1        5    40099+  82  Linux swap
/dev/hda6              6      217  1702858   83  Linux native
```

This disk contains 784 cylinders of 16065×512 bytes each. This is a 6.5 GB disk ($784 \times 16065 \times 512$) containing a number of partitions. Partitions in Linux behave more like their DOS counterparts. As stated before, you can create a primary partition with one file system in it, or an extended partition containing multiple logical partitions.

Observe that partition 1 (hda1) uses the same cylinders as partitions 5 (hda5) and 6 (hda5). This partition (hda1) is really an extended partition containing these two logical partitions. One of them contains the system's swap partition (hda5) and the other contains a Linux system (hda6). The size of each partition can be seen under *Blocks*, where one block is 1024 bytes. The active partition is indicated by an * in the second column.

You can see the presence of other operating systems on this disk. There is another Linux system on partition 4 (hda4) and a DOS file system (running Windows) on partition 2 (hda2). Since hda5 and hda6 can be considered to be "subsets" of hda1, we have here three "top-level" partitions. We also have cylinders between 479 and 619 unused, so we can use that space to create a partition. This will be partition 3.

The **fdisk m** command shows you all its internal commands of which the following subset should serve our purpose:

```
Command (m for help): m
Command action                                          Condensed list
   a   toggle a bootable flag
   d   delete a partition
   l   list known partition types
   m   print this menu
   n   add a new partition
   p   print the partition table
   q   quit without saving changes
   w   write table to disk and exit
```

To create a partition, we have to use the **n** command, supply the partition number and the starting and ending cylinder numbers:

```
Command (m for help): n
Command action
   l   logical (5 or over)                              Note this
   p   primary partition (1-4)
p
Partition number (1-4): 3
First cylinder (479-784, default 479): 479
Last cylinder or +size or +sizeM or +sizeK (479-619, default 619): 619
```

Linux is smart enough to suggest default cylinder values, but we preferred to enter the values explicitly. Now, use **p** again to view the new partition:

```
   Device Boot  Start    End    Blocks  Id  System
/dev/hda1    *      1    217  1743021    5  Extended
/dev/hda2         218    478  2096482+   6  DOS 16-bit >=32M
/dev/hda3         479    619  1132582+  83  Linux native        New partition
```

```
/dev/hda4        620      784    1325362+  83   Linux native
/dev/hda5          1        5      40099+  82   Linux swap
/dev/hda6          6      217    1702858   83   Linux native
```

We now have a new partition, hda3, occupying over 1 GB of space. Now that the partition table has been modified, we have to write it to the boot block with the **w** command. You'll be prompted to reboot the system which will make the new file system available for use.

Note

To have multiple file systems in one Linux partition, you must first have an extended partition and then create multiple logical partitions in this extended partition. If all this seems difficult to achieve with **fdisk**, then use the menu-based program **cfdisk**.

21.9.2   **mkfs**: Creating File Systems

Now that you have created a partition, you need to create a file system on this partition to make it usable. Though front-end tools are available today, they generally operate through **mkfs**—the universal file system creation tool. Sticking to Linux and the partition that we created recently, we'll use **mkfs** with the -t option to specify the type of file system:

```
# mkfs -t ext2 /dev/hda3
mke2fs 1.14, 9-Jan-1999 for EXT2 FS 0.5b, 95/08/09
Linux ext2 filesystem format
Filesystem label=
283560 inodes, 1132582 blocks
56629 blocks (5.00%) reserved for the super user
First data block=1
Block size=1024 (log=0)
Fragment size=1024 (log=0)
139 block groups
8192 blocks per group, 8192 fragments per group
2040 inodes per group
Superblock backups stored on blocks:
        8193, 16385, 24577, 32769, 40961, 49153, 57345, 65537, 73729, 81921,
        90113, 98305, 106497, 114689, 122881, 131073, 139265, 147457, 155649,
    .......                                                      Condensed list
Writing inode tables: done
Writing superblocks and filesystem accounting information: done
```

This creates an *ext2* file system—the standard Linux file system that uses a block size of 1024 bytes. Note the multiple superblocks that are uniformly (8192 blocks) spaced apart. The *ufs* and *ext2* file systems also use *fragments* to minimize wastage; discussion on this is beyond the scope of this text. For details, look up *System Performance Tuning* (O'Reilly & Associates) by Mike Loukides.

    mkfs in Linux acts as a front-end to **mke2fs** which actually creates the file system. Since we didn't specify the number of blocks, **mkfs** used default values for the number of inodes and data blocks. The increase of one can only be achieved at the expense of the other. The file system fills up whenever either figure is reached. Generally, you won't need to disturb the default values unless you are handling a huge number of very small files.

Tip

From the output of the **mkfs** command you should keep a record of the block addresses that contain copies of the superblock. If the main superblock gets corrupt, then you would need to use **fsck** with an alternate superblock number.

Note

Solaris uses the menu-based **format** command to create partitions. You have to invoke **partition** at the format> prompt to bring up the partition menu. The menu lets you change up to eight partitions, where partitions numbered 1 and 2 (the second and third) are reserved for the swap and entire partition, respectively. To write the partition table to disk, you finally have to use the **label** command. Solaris (and HP-UX) also uses the **newfs** command as a frontend to **mkfs**:

newfs /dev/rdsk/c0t3d0s0

21.10 **File System Mounting and Unmounting**

The file system now has all its standard four components including an empty root directory and an inode area. However, the root (main) file system (created at the time of installation) doesn't even know of its existence. This new file system can store data only after you have attached it to the main file system (which could be hda4 or hda6).

This attachment happens by **mounting**—a process by which a file system mounts (attaches) itself to the main file system at different points. The point at which this linkage takes place is called the **mount point**. After mounting, the root file system becomes the "main" file system, and its root directory also becomes the root directory of the unified file system.

21.10.1 **mount: Mounting File Systems**

The **mount** command is used to mount file systems. When mounting a *new* file system, it takes two arguments—the device name of the file system and the directory under which it is to be mounted. Before mounting a file system, an empty directory (say, /oracle) must first be made available in the main file system. The root directory of the new file system has to be mounted on this directory.

mount uses an option to specify the type of file system. This option varies across UNIX flavors. This is how we use **mount** to mount a file system on the /oracle directory on Solaris and Linux systems:

```
mount -F ufs /dev/dsk/c0t3d0s5 /oracle                        Solaris
mount -t ext2 /dev/hda3 /oracle                               Linux
```

After the device is mounted, the root directory of the file system created by **mkfs** loses its separate identity. It now becomes the directory /oracle and is made to appear as if it is part of the main file system. The end result of mounting is that the user sees a single file system in front of her, quite oblivious of the possibility that a file moved from /oracle to /home may have actually moved between two hard disks!

The file systems that were mounted above were the default ones, so the -F (or -t) option was redundant. However, if you mount other file systems, the option has to be used:

```
mount -F hsfs -r /dev/dsk/c0t6d0s0 /cdrom                          CDROM — Solaris
mount -F pcfs /dev/diskette /floppy                           DOS diskette — Solaris
mount -t iso9660 /dev/cdrom /mnt/cdrom                               CDROM — Linux
mount -t vfat /dev/hda1 /msdos                           Windows hard disk — Linux
mount -t msdos /dev/fd0 /floppy                               DOS diskette — Linux
```

mount -a mounts all file systems that are listed in a configuration file. **mount**, when used by itself, lists all mounted file systems:

```
# mount
/ on /dev/dsk/c0t0d0s0 read/write/setuid/largefiles on Thu Apr 20 10:00:10 2000
/proc on /proc read/write/setuid on Thu Apr 20 10:00:10 2000
/dev/fd on fd read/write/setuid on Thu Apr 20 10:00:10 2000
/oracle on /dev/dsk/c0t0d0s3 setuid/read/write/largefiles on Thu Apr 20 10:00:15 2000
/u01 on /dev/dsk/c1t3d0s1 setuid/read/write/largefiles on Thu Apr 20 10:00:15 2000
/u02 on /dev/dsk/c1t3d0s3 setuid/read/write/largefiles on Thu Apr 20 10:00:15 2000
/u03 on /dev/dsk/c1t3d0s4 setuid/read/write/largefiles on Thu Apr 20 10:00:15 2000
```

mount fetches this information from /etc/mnttab (Solaris) or /etc/mtab (Linux). We'll be discussing the contents of **mount**'s configuration file shortly.

Linux makes a distinction between a plain DOS file system with 8+3-style file-names (*msdos*) and Windows 95/98/2000-type file systems (*vfat*) which accommodate long filenames. So if you find a ~ (tilde) in a filename in your mounted DOS disk, then you must have incorrectly mounted it as *msdos* instead of *vfat*.

Note

The mount point is normally an empty directory, but if it contains some files, these files won't be seen after mounting. The files are back when the file system is unmounted.

21.10.2   umount: Unmounting File Systems

Unmounting is achieved with the **umount** command (note the spelling!), which requires either the file system name or the mount point as argument. For the file system that we just created and mounted, we can use either of the first two commands to unmount the file system:

```
umount /oracle                                       Specify either mount point
umount /dev/hda3                                     or device name—Linux
umount /dev/dsk/c0t3d0s5                                              Solaris
```

Unmounting a file system is not possible if you have a file open in it. Further, just as you can't remove a directory unless you are placed in a directory above it, you can't unmount a file system unless you are placed above it. If you try to do that, this is what you'll see:

```
# umount /dev/hda3
umount: /oracle: device is busy
```

You can also unmount all file systems or some of them depending on their type:

```
umount -t ext2                                          Only ext2 file systems—Linux
umount -a                                               Unmounts all file systems
```

The `-a` option unmounts all currently mounted file systems except the ones required for running of the system. The list of mounted file systems is available in `/etc/mtab` (Linux) or `/etc/mnttab` (Solaris).

21.10.3   mount Options (-o) and /etc/fstab

mount can be run with a number of special options which themselves are preceded by the `-o` option. Many of these options are file system–specific. These options are grouped together with the comma as delimiter. Although they are used here with Linux device names, most of the options are universally applicable:

```
mount -o ro /dev/sdb3 /usr/local                                      Read only
mount -o exec /dev/cdrom /mnt/cdrom                          Allow binary execution
mount -o rw,remount /dev/hda3 /home                     Remount in read-write mode
```

The first one mounts a file system in read-only mode; **mount** has a synonym for it though—the `-r` option. The second one lets you run executable files directly from the CD-ROM itself (`exec`). If you have mounted a file system as read-only, then to remount it as read-write, you don't need to unmount it first. Just use the `rw` and `remount` options together.

    mount uses a configuration file, and when you use **mount -a**, all file systems listed in that file are mounted sequentially. At system startup, the same command is executed, so you always find mounted file systems available on your machine. This file is generally `/etc/fstab`, but Solaris uses the SVR4-styled `/etc/vfstab` having a different format. There are some minor differences in options too. We'll consider a few lines of `/etc/fstab` on a Linux system:

```
# Mount device   Mount Point   File System Type   mount Options
/dev/hda5        swap          swap               defaults          0     0
/dev/hda6        /             ext2               defaults          1     1
/dev/hda2        /dosc         vfat               defaults          0     0
/dev/hda3        /oracle       ext2               defaults          1     2
/dev/hdc         /mnt/cdrom    iso9660            ro,noauto,user    0     0
/dev/fd0         /floppy       auto               noauto,user       0     0
none             /proc         proc               defaults          0     0
```

Each line provides the mounting specifications of a single file system. The list includes the floppy drive and CD-ROM too. The first four columns should make plain reading. The `noauto` option ensures that the file system is not mounted even when **mount -a** is used. This file system has to be mounted "by hand."

    Having the mounting specifications for the CD-ROM (or any device) in `/etc/fstab` means that now you can use **mount** *with either the device name or the mount point as argument*:

```
mount /dev/hdc                                          mount takes the other argument
mount /mnt/cdrom                                             from the configuration file
```

The `user` option implies that you can issue the command as an ordinary user. The `auto` file system type for the floppy device means that **mount** will look in `/proc/filesystems` and try each and every type listed there.

A 1 in the fifth field indicates that the file system has to be backed up (dumped) with the **dump** command. The sixth field shows the order in which the file systems are to be checked by the **fsck** command during a system boot.

Note

mount -a mounts all file systems in `/etc/fstab` or `/etc/vfstab` (Solaris) that are also mounted at boot time. Similarly, **umount -a** unmounts all these file systems whose information is held in `/etc/mnntab` (Solaris) or `/etc/mtab` (Linux). Some systems like Solaris also use the **mountall** and **umountall** commands (actually shell scripts) to mount and unmount all file systems.

21.11   fsck: **File System Checking**

The built-in UNIX feature of delaying the updating of the disk superblock and the inode blocks by their memory copies *(21.5.1)* leaves a lot of scope for file system inconsistency. If the power goes off before the superblock is written to disk, the file system loses its integrity. There are many discrepancies that could lead to file system corruption, and the most common ones are listed below:

- Two or more inodes claiming the same disk block.
- A block marked as free but not listed in the superblock.
- A used block marked as free.
- An inode neither marked free nor in use, or having a bad block number that is out of range.
- Mismatch between the file size specified in inode and the number of data blocks specified in the address array.
- A corrupt superblock containing erroneous summary data.
- A file not having at least one directory entry or having an invalid file type specified in the inode.

The **fsck** (file system consistency check) command is used to check and repair a damaged file system. The command generally acts as a front-end to the file system-specific program (like **fsck_ufs** or **fsck.ext2**) that actually does the job. It is generally run when a file system fails to mount.

On many systems including Solaris, file systems are marked as "dirty" or "clean." **fsck** then checks only the dirty file systems during the next startup. **fsck** can also be directed to check all file systems listed in `/etc/fstab` (`/etc/vfstab` in Solaris) in the sequence specified in the sixth field—starting with the root file system first. The command can also be used with the name of the file system as argument:

```
# fsck /dev/rdsk/c0t3d0s5
** /dev/rdsk/c0t3d0s5
** Phase 1 - Check Blocks and Sizes
```

```
** Phase 2 - Check Pathnames
** Phase 3 - Check Connectivity
** Phase 4 - Check Reference Counts
** Phase 5 - Check Free List
```

fsck conducts a check in five phases, and the output above is obtained when the file system is consistent. However, when it is corrupt, messages and questions are seen on the system console, which you have to answer correctly. This is what **fsck** does in each phase:

- *Phase 1* Validates the inodes for correctness of format and the block numbers for bad and duplicate blocks. **fsck** declares a block BAD if the block number is out of range and DUP if it is claimed by another inode.
- *Phase 2* Checks all directory entries, starting from root, for OUT OF RANGE inode numbers detected in Phase 1. **fsck** corrects the errors either by removing the entire directory or the file.
- *Phase 3* Looks for unreferenced directories and stores their files in /lost+found for later examination. The files here are named after their inode numbers. You must make sure this directory is always available for every file system because **fsck** won't create it on its own.
- *Phase 4* Checks the link count as stored in the inode with the directory entries, and prompts for the file's removal or reconnection (to the /lost+found directory), depending on the extent of damage caused. **fsck** then compares the free inode count it computes with the figure stored in the superblock.
- *Phase 5* Finally, **fsck**'s free-block count is compared with the figure maintained in the superblock. A salvage operation may be carried out with the user's approval, which will replace the erroneous free block list with a newly computed one.

When used without options, **fsck** prompts you before repairing any damage that it has detected. It's generally safe to answer every question with a y. **fsck -y** (-p used by **e2fsck** in Linux) assumes that all answers are in the affirmative and proceeds without waiting for any response. On Solaris systems, **fsck -m** performs no rectification but merely detects flaws.

fsck works with both block and character devices, but the check on the character device is faster. The administrator should always perform this check with the file systems in unmounted condition. Since the root file system can't be unmounted, the check on this file system should be made in single-user mode.

If the superblock is corrupt beyond repair, then **fsck** must be used with the -b option (-o b=*n* in Solaris, where *n* is the block number) to specify an alternate superblock number. This list is displayed by **mkfs** when initializing the file system. (**newfs —Nv** in Solaris displays them too.) Occasionally, the file system is so corrupt that rectification simply becomes impossible, and reinstallation of the system remains the only alternative.

Tip

fsck often outputs the inode numbers of files which it considers suspect in integrity. You should note down these numbers for further investigation. You should also have a look at the /lost+found directory if you find a file missing after a system crash.

21.11.1   The Problem with `sync`

The **update** daemon calls **sync** every 30 seconds to flush the superblock, inodes and data blocks cached in memory. When the command is entered manually, the prompt is returned, signifying that writing has been scheduled, but a second **sync** won't start until the first one is finished.

When **fsck** rebuilds the file system, the in-memory copies of the superblock and other tables may sometimes contain old and inaccurate information. In this unusual case, the information on the disk becomes more *recent* than the memory copy. **fsck** may then flash the following message:

```
***** BOOT UNIX (NO SYNC!) *****
```

This happens when the root file system contains a serious problem. The message signifies that if you use **sync** or **/sbin/shutdown** to write the incorrect superblock to disk, all the good work done by **fsck** would then be lost. Instead, you should immediately press the reset button without using **sync** and reboot the system. This must be done before the next **sync** operation automatically writes this incorrect information to disk.

SUMMARY

All device files are stored in /dev. A device file's inode contains a pair of numbers (*major* and *minor*). The major number represents the device driver—the type of device. The minor number is a serial number representing the parameters the kernel passes to the device driver.

Devices can be *block-special* or *character-special* devices, depending on the way the data is read from or written into them.

SVR4 uses the /dev/dsk directory for block devices and /dev/rdsk for *raw* (character) devices. The same device can often be accessed with different filenames either for backward compatability or for a specific function.

A hard disk consists of a number of surfaces representing *cylinders* of concentric *tracks*. Data is written to *sectors* in these tracks.

The UNIX file system is generally composed of multiple file systems, each having its own root directory and device file. A file system is held in a separate *partition*. Partitioning limits fragmentation of data and ensures that data from one partition doesn't affect another. There is a separate device file representing the entire hard disk.

Every file system consists of the boot block, superblock, inode and data blocks. The *boot block* contains boot information and the partition table. The *superblock* contains global information on the file system, including details of free inodes and free data blocks. The superblock in memory is periodically written to disk with **sync**. Many systems maintain multiple superblocks in different areas of the disk.

An *inode* contains all file attributes except the filename. It contains an array of 15 addresses where the first 12 store the addresses of the first 12 data blocks. The other three are formed into a *linked list* to eventually hold the remaining disk block numbers used by a file. Like the superblock, the inode in memory is also written to disk to keep the two in sync.

A directory contains only the inode number and the filename, and is related to the inode of the file with the inode number. When a file is linked, its inode count is increased by one. A file is considered deleted when its inode count drops to zero.

Every UNIX system will have the *swap* and *root* file systems. Most systems today use the *ufs* file system which permit multiple superblocks, symbolic links and disk quotas. Linux uses the *ext2* file system. There are different file system types for CD-ROMs (*hsfs* or *iso9660*), DOS disks (*pcfs*, *vfat* or *msdos*) and a pseudo-file system for processes (*proc* or *procfs*).

On some systems, the **fdisk** command is used to create, delete and activate partitions. Linux systems allow the creation of one *extended* partition to hold multiple *logical* partitions. **mkfs** is used to create file systems and is often used with front-end tools.

Each file system is unknown to the root file system until it is *mounted* (**mount**). **mount** takes mounting instructions from /etc/fstab (/etc/vfstab in Solaris). A file system can't be unmounted unless the user is placed above the mount point or a file in it is being used by someone. File systems can also be unmounted (**umount**).

File system corruption occurs if the memory copies of the superblock and inodes are not written to disk before shutdown. **fsck** checks the integrity of file systems—generally in unmounted condition. It corrects inconsistencies by either deleting files or moving the unconnected ones to /lost+found. The root file system must be checked in single-user mode.

shutdown uses **sync** to write the memory contents of the superblock to the file system. Sometimes, when the disk status is newer, "syncing" should not be done.

SELF-TEST

21.1   What is the common device name for the floppy used both by System V and Linux?
21.2   What are the device names of your bootable 3.5″ 1.44 MB floppy drive?
21.3   Explain the concept of an *extended* partition in a Linux system.
21.4   Which is the only file attribute not stored in the inode? Where is it stored then?
21.5   When a file is deleted, what change occurs in the inode?
21.6   Where are the number of free inodes and data blocks stored?
21.7   In which directory is the kernel stored on SVR4 and Linux systems?
21.8   How will you find out the inode number of a file?
21.9   How many partitions can you have in IDE and SCSI hard disks?
21.10 Which command do front-end software programs invoke to create a file system?
21.11 When is unmounting a file system not possible?
21.12 What does **fsck** normally do with an unconnected file?
21.13 How do you normally run **fsck** in the root file system?

EXERCISES

21.1   What are the *major* and *minor* numbers of a device?
21.2   If a directory tends to fill up and use all the disk space, how should you modify the file system organization?
21.3   Which partition does the device /dev/rdsk/c0t3d0s2 represent in Solaris, and what is special about it?
21.4   What is the device name of the entire IDE hard disk on the first drive in Linux? If you have one extended partition and two logical partitions here, what would be the device names of the logical partitions?

21.5   Can two files in a host have the same inode number?

21.6   What does the directory store?

21.7   What is the common component in the inode and directory?

21.8   Since a UNIX file has no end-of-file mark, how does the kernel know that the end of file has been reached when displaying a file?

21.9   What is the role of **sync** in relation to the superblock and inodes? Why are two **sync**s generally required when shutting down a system?

21.10   Where is the partition table stored? What is it known as in Linux?

21.11   Why do you need to have a swap file system?

21.12   Name three important features of the *proc* or *procfs* file system.

21.13   What is the standard file system used by SVR4? What are its special features?

21.14   Which file system do CD-ROMs use? What is the role of Rock Ridge here?

21.15   What facilities do UNIX systems have to counter superblock corruption?

21.16   If the mount directory is not empty, can you still mount a file system on it?

21.17   Which file does **mount** read at startup to mount the file systems?

21.18   If your Linux machine shows a ~ (tilde) in most filenames on your DOS or Windows partition, what is the mistake you have made? How do you get back the long filenames?

21.19   If a file system is mounted read-only, do you have to unmount it first before mounting it in read-write mode?

21.20   Is the memory copy of the superblock always more recent than the disk copy?

KEY TERMS

block *(21.3)*

block special device *(21.1.1)*

boot block *(21.5.5)*

buffer cache *(21.1.1)*

character special device *(21.1.1)*

cylinder *(21.3)*

data block *(21.5.2)*

device driver *(21.1.2)*

direct block *(21.5.2)*

disk fragmentation *(21.5.2)*

double indirect block *(21.5.3)*

extended partition *(21.4.2)*

file system *(21.4 and 21.4.2)*

indirect block *(21.5.2)*

inode *(21.5.1)*

inode block *(21.5.1)*

inode buffer *(21.5.1)*

inode number *(21.5.1)*

linked list *(21.5.3)*

logical block *(21.5.2)*

logical partition *(21.4.2)*

major number *(21.1.2)*

Master Boot Record (MBR) *(21.5.5)*

minor number *(21.1.2)*

mount point *(21.10)*

mounting *(21.10)*

partition *(21.4)*

physical block *(21.5.2)*

platter *(21.3)*

raw device *(21.1.1)*

sector *(21.3)*

single indirect block *(21.5.3)*

slice *(21.4.1)*

superblock *(21.5.4)*

track *(21.3)*

triple indirect block *(21.5.3)*

unmounting *(21.10.2)*

## CHAPTER 22

System Administration II— The General Duties

After the file system, it's time to make a visit to the world of general system administration. This task is usually entrusted to a single person—the **system administrator**, also known as the **super user** or **root user**. She has vast powers, having access to practically everything. The success and stability of any UNIX installation depends, in great measure, on the effectiveness of the system administrator.

The job of system administration involves the management of the entire system—ranging from maintaining security, performing backups and managing the disk space to maintaining user accounts. Scripts have to be devised for automating operations that are carried out regularly. Services have to be started or stopped by running and editing the system's configuration files. All this requires from the administrator an in-depth knowledge of the different components of the system. The burden is not overwhelming though because UNIX is more easily maintained and well documented than most other systems.

Today, every user must know some of the important functions that she may be called upon to perform at any time. For this, she must have sound knowledge of some of the advanced filters and also be quite proficient in shell programming. Even if you are a nonprivileged user, you should read most of this chapter.

Objectives

- Log in to root and become a super user with **su**. *(22.1)*
- Change any user's password with **passwd**. *(22.2.1)*
- Change the system date with **date** or communicate with all users with **wall** and **calendar**. *(22.2.2 and 22.2.3)*
- Create, modify and delete user accounts with **useradd**, **usermod** and **userdel**. *(22.3)*
- Make programs run with root's powers by setting the *set-user-id* bit. *(22.4.1)*
- Make directories sharable with the *sticky bit*. *(22.4.2)*
- Restrict a user's activities with the *restricted shell*. *(22.4.3)*
- Learn the role of **init** and /etc/inittab in startup and shutdown, and control the system's *run levels*. *(22.5 and 22.6)*
- Format and copy diskettes with **format**, **fdformat** and **dd**. *(22.7.1 and 22.7.2)*
- Handle DOS files on diskettes with a set of "DOS" commands. *(22.7.3)*
- Use **cpio** to back up and restore files. *(22.8)*

- Use **tar** to back up a directory tree and append files to an archive. *(22.9)*
- Use **du**, **find** and **xargs** to manage disk space. *(22.10)*

➤ *G O I N G   F U R T H E R*

- Enforce *password aging* with **passwd** so that passwords are changed regularly. *(22.11)*
- Understand how **init** uses *rc* scripts to start and stop the system's daemons. *(22.12)*
- Learn how **getty** is executed and sets the parameters for a terminal. *(22.13)*
- Learn the printing preliminaries, administer the printer and control the print spooler with the lp subsystem of System V. *(22.14 and 22.15)*
- Do the same with the **lpd** system used by Linux. *(22.15)*

22.1 root: The System Administrator's Login

The UNIX system provides a special login name for the exclusive use of the administrator; it is called **root**. This account doesn't need to be separately created, but comes with every system. Its password is generally set at the time of installation of the system and has to be used on logging in:

```
login: root
password: *******[Enter]
# _
```

The prompt of root is #, unlike the $ or % used by the nonprivileged users. Once you log in as root, you are placed in root's home directory. Depending on the system, this directory could be / or /root.

On modern systems, most administrative commands are resident in /sbin and /usr/sbin, but if you are using an older system, you could find them in /etc. root's PATH list is also different from other users:

```
/sbin:/bin:/usr/sbin:/usr/bin:/usr/dt/bin
```

Since the super user is always moving around in the file system, it is possible that she might inadvertently execute programs and scripts written by other users. *That's why the PATH for a super user doesn't include the current directory.*

Note

Many of the standard scripts supplied with UNIX systems for system administration work (especially the scripts related to booting) rely on the Bourne shell for execution. As an administrator, you have to carefully weigh the consequences of using the Korn shell since scripts developed under this shell may not run on another host, which may not have this shell. But you must not under any circumstances use C shell scripts. Linux uses bash—both for normal and system administrative activities; there's no problem there.

22.1.1 su: Acquiring Super User Status

Any user can acquire super user status with the **su** command if she knows the root password. For example, the user local (with the home directory /home/local) can also become a super user:

```
$ su
Password: ********[Enter]                              Has to be root's password
```

```
# pwd
/home/local
```
Prompt changes, but directory doesn't

su here expects root's password. The # prompt indicates that the user is a super user. The user-id ($LOGNAME) is still local, and the current directory doesn't change. User local now has powers of a super user.

Creating a User's Environment Users often rush to the administrator with the complaint that a program has stopped running. The administrator first tries running it in a simulated environment. **su**, when used with a -, recreates the user's environment without taking the *login-password* route:

```
su - henry
```
No password required

This sequence executes henry's startup file (`.profile` or any other) and creates henry's environment for the administrator. Since **su** runs in a sub-shell, this mode is terminated by hitting *[Ctrl-d]* or using the **exit** command.

Rather than log on to another user's account, the super user can run a program in another user's environment using the -c option. For instance, you can start up the Oracle database with its **dbstart** command from root even though the command is normally run by the oracle user account:

```
su oracle -c dbstart
```

You should place commands like these in the system's startup scripts so the database is automatically started when the system boots.

22.2 The Administrator's Privileges

The super user has enormous powers, and there are several commands reserved for her exclusive use. Some commands also behave differently when executed by the administrator. The super user authority is mainly derived from the power to

- Change the attributes of any file—its contents, permissions and even ownership. She can delete any file with **rm** even if it is write-protected!
- Initiate or kill any process. The administrator can directly kill all processes except the ones essential for running the system. Only the super user can run the **shutdown** command to power down the system.
- Change any user's password without knowing the existing one.
- Set the system clock.
- Address all users concurrently.
- Limit the maximum size of files that users are permitted to create.
- Control users' access to the scheduling services like **at** and **cron**.
- Control users' access to the TCP/IP services **rlogin**, **rcp** and **rsh**.

You can well appreciate that the administrator has to use these powers with utmost caution. An apparently innocent and unplugged loophole can cause disaster if that knowledge is acquired by a mischievous person. We have already discussed users' access to the scheduling and TCP/IP services. In the forthcoming sections, we take up the rest.

22.2.1   passwd: Changing Any Password

passwd prompts for the existing password when the command is used by a nonprivileged user *(3.1)*. However, when the super user uses the command, the system behaves in a more lenient manner:

```
# passwd
Changing password for root
Enter the new password (minimum of 5, maximum of 8 characters)
Please use a combination of upper and lower case letters and numbers.
New password: *********
Re-enter password: *********                                To be entered twice
Password changed.
```

Note that the system doesn't prompt for the old password this time. The administrator must not only closely guard the super user password but remember it too. Otherwise, the entire UNIX system may have to be reloaded! UNIX also allows the administrator the privilege of changing anybody's password without knowing it:

```
passwd henry
```

Once again, the old password is not prompted for; the new one has only to be entered twice.

Modern times have seen several instances of hackers who manage to get into a system. Users often give out their passwords to others, thus jeopardizing the security of the system. As a result, passwords tend to be known to others over time. What makes matters worse is that users themselves are quite averse to changing their own passwords. The **passwd** command offers features that force users to change their passwords after a specific time. These features are discussed in the "Going Further" section *(22.11)*.

Note

passwd doesn't prompt for the old password when the command is used by the super user—even for changing the root password.

22.2.2   date: Setting the System Date

We have used **date** as a "passive" command before *(3.9)*—to display the system date. The same command, in the hands of the administrator, can be used with a numeric argument to actually set the system date. This argument is usually an eight-character string of the form *MMDDhhmm*, and optionally followed by a two- or four-digit year string:

```
# date 06010735
Fri Jun  1 07:35:00 EST 2000
```

UNIX systems will continue to understand the century for some time (till the year 2038, at least). Ensure that the date is reasonably accurate as the **cron** scheduler *(10.13)* uses the clock time to run jobs.

Note

The system date can be set only by the administrator.

22.2.3 `wall` and `calendar`: Communicating with Users

wall The **wall** command addresses all users simultaneously. Most UNIX systems don't permit users to use this command (Linux excepted), and reserve it for the sole use of the administrator:

```
# wall
The machine will be shut down today
at 14:30 hrs. The backup will be at 13:30 hrs
[Ctrl-d]
```

All users currently logged in will receive this message on their terminal. The **mesg** setting is ignored by **wall**. This command is routinely executed by the administrator—especially before shutdown of the system.

calendar You have seen **calendar** used *(3.11)* as a useful reminder service. As an administrator, you can use it with an argument (-) to remind all users about their appointments:

```
calendar -                                    Reads all users' calendar files
```

calendar now reads every user's `calendar` file, and mails the output to the user. The command is best placed in the administrator's profile (`/.profile`), or in a startup script that is executed at the time of booting. Better still is to let **cron** execute it at a specific time every day.

22.2.4 `ulimit`: Setting Limits on File Size

Faulty programs or processes can eat up disk space in no time. The **ulimit** command imposes a restriction on the maximum size a user is permitted to create. When used by itself, **ulimit** displays the current setting:

```
# ulimit
2097151                                Linux and Solaris show "unlimited"
```

The default limit expressed in units of 512 (or 1024 for some systems) bytes is set inside the kernel. Though an ordinary user can only *reduce* this default value, the super user can increase it:

```
ulimit 20971510                         Maximum file size increased 10 times
```

You'll often place this statement in `/etc/profile` so that every user has to work within these restrictions. This command is now a built-in of all shells. The built-in offers many options which we'll not discuss in this text.

22.3 Maintaining User Accounts

The term *user* in UNIX is not meant to be only a person; it can represent a project or an application as well. A group of users having similar functions can use the same username to use the system. It's thus quite common to have usernames like marketing, accounts, mis, and so forth. For the creation and maintenance of user accounts, UNIX provides three commands—**useradd**, **usermod** and **userdel**.

When opening a user account, you have to associate the user with a *group*. A group usually has more than one member with a different set of privileges. People working on a common project should be able to read one another's files, which is possible only if they belong to the same group. The **chmod** and **chgrp** commands can change those file attributes that apply to the group.

Creating a user involves setting of the following parameters:

- A user identification number (UID) and username.
- A group identification number (GUID) and group name.
- The home directory.
- The login shell.
- The mailbox in /var/mail.
- The password.

Most of these parameters are found in a single line identifying the user in /etc/passwd. In early days, the system administrator had to manually create the home directory and the mailbox, but today there is a command which does all the work. We'll now create a group for a user and then add a user to the system.

22.3.1   groupadd: Adding a Group

If the user is to be placed in a new group, an entry for the group has to be created first in /etc/group. A user always has one primary group and may also have one or more secondary groups. This file contains all the named groups of the system and a few lines of this file reveal the structure:

```
root:x:0:root
bin:x:1:root,bin,daemon
lp:x:7:
uucp:x:14:uucp,fax,root,fnet,sumit
users:x:100:henry,oracle,image,enquiry
pppusers:x:230:                                                    GUID is 230
```

Each line contains four fields. Let's consider the entry for the group users:

- The first field (users) shows the group name. This is the same name you see in the group ownership column of the listing.
- The second field is either blank or contains an x. This originally contained the group password but is not generally used today.
- The third field shows the numeric group-id (GUID) of the user (here, 100). Two users belonging to the same group have the same GUID.
- The last field contains a list of comma-delimited usernames (henry,oracle, image,enquiry). These are the *additional* users for whom this is the secondary group. A blank at this position doesn't mean that no one is a member of this group.

To create a new group dba with a GUID of 241, you have to use the **groupadd** command:

```
groupadd -g 241 dba                                              241 is the GUID
```

The command places this entry in /etc/group which you can also insert manually:

dba:x:241:

Once an entry for the group has been made, you are now ready to add a user with this group to the system.

Note

Apart from **groupadd**, you can also use the **groupmod** and **groupdel** commands to modify and delete groups.

22.3.2   useradd: Adding a User

The **useradd** command adds new users to the system. All the parameters related to the user have to be provided in the command line itself:

```
# useradd -u 210 -g dba -c "THE RDBMS" -d /home/oracle -s /bin/ksh -m oracle
# _
```

This quietly creates the user oracle with a UID of 210 and group name dba. The home directory is /home/oracle, and the user will use the Korn shell. The -m option ensures that the home directory is created if it doesn't already exist and copies a sample .profile and .kshrc to the user's home directory. The line **useradd** creates in /etc/passwd is shown in Fig. 22.1.

You now have to set the new user's password with the command **passwd oracle**. Once all this has been done, the oracle user account is ready for use.

22.3.3   /etc/passwd and /etc/shadow: User Profiles

All user information except the password encryption is now stored in /etc/passwd. It contained the password once, the reason why it continues to be known by that name. The encryption itself is stored in /etc/shadow. This is now the control file used by **passwd** to ascertain the legitimacy of a user's password.

Let's take the line pertaining to oracle in /etc/passwd. There are seven fields here, and their significance is noted below (in the order they appear in /etc/passwd):

- Username—The name you use to log on to a UNIX system (oracle).
- Password—No longer stores the password encryption but contains an x.

FIGURE 22.1   *A Line from /etc/passwd*

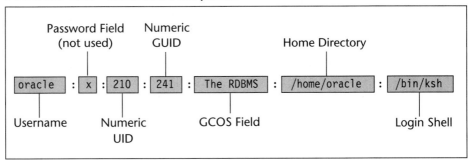

- UID—The user's numerical identification (210). No two users should have the same UID.
- GUID—The user's numerical group identification (241). This number is also the third field in /etc/group. Commands like **ls** have to read this file to print the group name.
- Comment or GCOS—User details, e.g., her name, address and so forth (The RDBMS). This name is used at the front of the email address. Any mail sent from this user account will show the sender as *"The RDBMS" <oracle@planets.com>*—assuming the user belongs to the domain shown.
- Home directory—The directory where the user ends up on logging in (/home/oracle).
- Login shell—The first program executed after logging in. This is usually the shell (/bin/ksh).

While this file can normally be changed by only the administrator, users can use the **chsh** command to change their shells without having to contact the administrator *(17.1)*.

Note

The last field in /etc/passwd is actually the command that has to be executed when a user logs in. This is usually the shell, but the administrator may choose a different program to restrict the user's actions (like **pppd**).

For every line in /etc/passwd, there's a corresponding entry in /etc/shadow. The relevant line in this file could look something like this:

```
oracle:$1$07VbeHwq$OqHKOW73boShhrO93.txp.:10846:-1:99999:-1:-1:-1:135365660
```

The password encryption is shown in the second field. It's impossible to generate the password from this encryption. However, an intelligent hacker can use an encryption algorithm to generate a sequence of encrypted patterns. Such algorithms are also widely available on the Internet. It's quite possible that she might just find a match, so this file *must* be made unreadable to all but the super user.

22.3.4   usermod and userdel: Modifying and Removing Users

usermod is used for modifying some of the parameters set with **useradd**. Users sometimes need to change their login shell, and the following command line sets bash as the login shell for the user oracle:

```
usermod -s /bin/bash oracle
```
                                                                                   Use if chsh *is not available*

Users are removed from the system with **userdel**. The following command removes the user oracle from the system:

```
userdel oracle
```
                                                                                   Doesn't delete user's files

This removes all entries pertaining to oracle from /etc/passwd, /etc/group and /etc/shadow. The user's home directory doesn't get deleted in the process and has to be removed separately if required.

22.4 Maintaining Security

Because security in a computer system eventually involves files, a faulty file permission can easily be exploited by a malicious user in a destructive manner. As administrator, you have to ensure that the system directories (/bin, /usr/bin, /etc, /sbin etc.) and the files in them are not writable by others. We'll now discuss some of the other security-related features found in a UNIX system.

22.4.1 Set-User-Id—Power for a Moment

Many UNIX programs let users update sensitive system files like /etc/shadow—something they can't do directly with an editor. This is possible because these programs have a special permissions mode which lets a user get the privileges of the owner of the file *during the instance of the program*. This is true of the **passwd** program:

```
-rwsr-xr-x   1 root      shadow      34808 Nov 30 17:55 /usr/bin/passwd
```

The character s in the permissions field is a special mode known as the **set-user-id** (SUID). When a nonprivileged user executes **passwd**, the *effective* UID of its process is not the user's, but of root's—the owner of the program. This SUID privilege is then used by **passwd** to edit /etc/shadow. This privilege vanishes with the termination of the program.

The SUID for any file can be set only by the super user with a special syntax of the **chmod** command:

```
# chmod u+s filex ; ls -l filex                          Same as chmod 4711
-rws--x--x   1 root      bin        113 Mar 24 11:18 filex
```

The SUID is a potential security hazard. Once a user has access to such a file owned by root, she acquires hidden powers (even though she may not be aware of it). As administrator, you must keep track of all SUID programs owned by root that a user may try to create or copy. The **find** command easily locates them:

```
find /home -perm -4000 -print | mail root
```

The extra octal bit (4) signifies the SUID mode, but **find** treats 000 as representing *any* other permissions. You can use **cron** to run this program at regular intervals and mail the file list to root.

The SUID mechanism, invented by Dennis Ritchie, is the only patented part of UNIX. The **set-group-id** (SGID) is similar to set-user-id except that a program with SGID set allows the user to have the same power as the group which owns the program. The SGID bit is 2.

Note

The fourth bit is used only when the special modes of a file are set. It has the value 4 for the SUID, 2 for SGID and 1 for the sticky bit. The other 3 bits have their usual significance.

22.4.2 The Sticky Bit

Programs on heavily loaded systems are swapped out to disk and reloaded when required. The **sticky bit** ensures that swapping takes place only once and permanently stores the text image of the program *(10.2)* in the swap area. It is indicated by the letter t in the permissions field (fourth octal bit 1):

```
-rwxr-xr-t  2 root     root       2878448 Sep 25  1999 /usr/bin/emacs
```

This means that if you have used **emacs** once, it remains in the swap area till the machine is shut down. That's why on old hardware the editor takes quite some time to start the first time, but not after subsequent invocations. However, this bit has lost most of its charm because it once made sense on machines with slow disk drives and scarce RAM. Modern machines with ultra-fast disk drives and lots of cheap memory don't need this bit for ordinary files.

Using the Sticky Bit with a Directory However, the sticky bit becomes a useful security feature when used with a directory. The UNIX system allows users to create files in /tmp and /var/tmp, but no one can delete files not owned by her. Strange, isn't it? This is possible because both directories have their sticky bits set:

```
# ls -ld /tmp /var/tmp
drwxrwxrwt  15 root     root       6144 Nov 28 22:26 /tmp
drwxrwxrwt  37 root     root       1024 Nov 27 23:46 /var/tmp
```

The directories are writable by all, but that extra t bit ensures that henry can't remove romeo's files in these directories. Using **chmod**, you can set the bit on a directory by using 1 as the additional bit:

```
# chmod 1775 bar
# ls -l bar
drwxrwxr-t  2 sumit    dialout    1024 Apr 13 08:25 bar
```

The sticky bit is extremely useful for implementing group projects. To let a group of users work on a set of files without infringing on security, you'll have to do this:

- Create a common group for these users in /etc/group.
- Create separate user accounts for them but specify the same home directory.
- Make sure the home directory and all subdirectories are not owned by any of the users. Use **chown** to surrender ownership to root.
- Make the directories group- or world-writable but also set their sticky bits with **chmod 1775**.

In this scenario, every user of the group has write permission on the directories and can create files and directories, but can only delete those she owns. A very useful feature indeed!

Tip

Set the sticky bit for a directory that is shared by users belonging to a group. The files owned by each user are then protected from tampering by other users of that group. The directory must not be owned by any of the users.

22.4.3 Restricted Shell

To restrict the activities of a user, you should set up the user account with a special restricted shell. This shell once had the name **rsh**, but today **rsh** represents the command with which you remotely run a program. The better shells today have restricted versions—**rbash** and **rksh**. Either of them has to be specified in the last field of /etc/passwd. A user with a restricted shell can't do any of the following things:

- Use the **cd** command, which means that she can't change directories.
- Redefine the PATH, which makes it impossible to access commands placed in other directories.
- Redefine the SHELL so the user can't change to a nonrestricted shell.
- Use a pathname containing a /, which means a command can't be executed with either a relative or an absolute pathname.
- Use the > and >> operators to create or append to files.

In this environment, a user can only execute programs in the directories specified in a new unchangeable PATH. This generally is set to *only* the current directory. If the user needs to run some of the system commands in /bin and /usr/bin, place links of those commands in the user's restricted directory.

Some commands have shell escapes (like **vi** and **mail**), and some versions of UNIX let you use these escapes to execute any UNIX command by using the absolute pathname. Make sure these commands don't behave in that manner in your system. If they do, disallow their use.

Tip

If you don't have a separate restricted shell on your system, use the standard shells with the -r option to enforce that behavior (**sh -r**, **bash -r** or **ksh -r**). Since you can't put these entries in /etc/passwd, run a normal shell there and use **exec** to execute them from the startup file. Make sure to set the PATH to just one directory.

22.5   Booting

The startup and shutdown procedures are controlled by automated shell scripts which are changed quite infrequently. Yet the administrator needs to know the exact sequence of steps the system follows during the two events. Things do go wrong, especially during startup, and she must be able to fix them.

22.5.1   init: The Prime Mover

There are several processes initiated at system startup. The kernel (**/stand/unix**, **/kernel/genunix** or **/vmlinuz**) is loaded into memory, and it then starts spawning further processes. The most important of these is **/sbin/init** with PID 1, which is responsible for the birth of all subsequent processes. You must know the behavioral pattern of **init** for two vital reasons:

- It controls the *run levels* (the system states) and decides which processes to run (and kill) for each run level.
- It spawns a **getty** process at every terminal or modem port so that users can log in.

init also makes sure all system daemons are running. **lpsched** monitors the line printer spooler for jobs that have been queued for printing. **cron** is the system's chronograph. **httpd** is the Web server daemon and **sendmail** looks for all incoming and outgoing mail. However, **init** remains the parent (and sometimes grandparent) of them all.

22.5.2   **init Run Levels**

init is responsible for keeping the system in different *states*—which we call **run levels**. Each run level here is normally a single digit (0 to 6), or an **s** or S. A distinct set of processes is scheduled to run at each of these states. Normally, the system would be in any one of these run levels:

0—System shutdown.
1—System administration mode (local file systems mounted).
2—Multiuser mode (NFS not available).
3—Full multiuser mode.
6—Shutdown and reboot mode.
s or S—Single-user mode (file systems mounted).

We'll not consider run levels 4 and 5 as they are either unused or used in situations which won't interest us. When the system is booted, **init** first enters the run level 1— the system administration mode. You can't use either the printer or the terminals because the system daemons are not running.

The single-user mode is used by the administrator to perform her administrative tasks—like taking an offline backup. The role of run level 1 is system-variant; on some systems, 1 and S have identical roles.

Depending on your system, the normal multiuser mode is implemented in either of the two run levels—2 or 3. You can change your run level by using the **init** command with the run level as argument:

```
init 2                                          Switches to multiuser mode
init 3
```

If you look at the boot messages carefully (or /etc/inittab), you can find out the normal multiuser run level of your system.

Tip

To know the run level you are in, use the **who -r** command. Linux users can use the **runlevel** command.

22.5.3   **/etc/inittab: init's Startup File**

The behavior of **init** is controlled by /etc/inittab. **init** reads all entries of this file just once—when it is invoked. Its fields determine the processes that should be spawned for each of the **init** run levels, and the programs to run at the communication ports. Let's have a look at a few sample lines which are shown in Fig. 22.2.

All the things you see happening on startup owe their ultimate origin to entries like these. The *label* is simply used to identify the entry and has no real significance. The second field shows the *run levels* for which this line is applicable. The *action* and the *command* to execute comprise the last two fields (if we consider *command arguments* to be part of *command*).

FIGURE 22.2   *An* /etc/inittab *File*

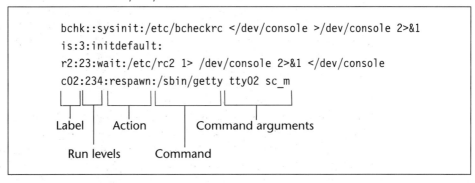

Let's now dissect one of the lines of inittab. The line with the label r2 provides this directive: "For run levels 2 or 3, run the **/etc/rc2** program and wait for it to complete before moving on to the other lines of this file." All input, output and error messages must be directed from or to the console. We'll consider the significance of the other lines later.

When **init** is executed with a specific run level as argument, it reads all lines that match that run level, and executes the commands specified there in sequence. A blank run level (here, in the first line) means the command has to be run for all run levels. **init** also obtains the default run level by reading the line that shows initdefault as the action. Here, the system boots to run level 3.

initdefault and wait are two of the actions that **init** understands. There are others:

- sysinit—Used for initializing the system. The system may check the "dirtiness" of file systems, activate swap partitions and set the hostname. It may also ask for input from the administrator.
- respawn—Makes sure a process restarts on termination. This is always required for the **getty** process.
- once—Runs process only once, and doesn't wait for its completion.
- boot—Executes only when inittab is read the first time. **init** ignores any run level fields placed here.
- bootwait—Same as above, but waits for its completion.
- off—Kills process if it is running.
- ctrlaltdel—Executes **shutdown** command (Linux only).

Using telinit q   As administrator, you can also insert or modify statements in /etc/inittab. You can change the default run level, or add and modify entries when adding a new terminal or modem to the system. But then you have to use the **telinit** command to let **init** reread its configuration file:

telinit q   *Or* init q

init and **telinit** are links, so **telinit** can always be created (if it doesn't exist) with the **ln** command. You can also use **init q**.

Note

You can obtain the default run level by looking for the entry containing `initdefault` in /etc/inittab.

22.6 Shutdown

The administrator also has the duty of shutting down the machine at the end of the day (if it's ever shut down). The **shutdown** command controls this sequence. **shutdown** usually performs the following activities:

- Notifies users with **wall** about the system going down with a directive to log out. Users are then expected to close all their files and log out of the system within a minute or so. **shutdown** itself sleeps for a minute after mailing the first message and may issue a reminder or two.
- Sends signals to all running processes so they can terminate normally.
- Logs users off and kills remaining processes.
- Unmounts all secondary file systems.
- Writes information about file system status to disk *(21.5.4)* to preserve the integrity of the file system.
- Notifies users to reboot or switch off or moves the system to single-user mode.

When messages of this type

```
Reboot the system now or turn power off
System halted
```

appear on the console, the machine can be considered to have completed the shutdown sequence successfully. You can now turn the power off, or reboot the system.

The -g option overrides the default waiting time of one minute. The command can be used in these ways:

```
shutdown -g2                          Powers down machine after 2 minutes
shutdown -y -g0                                   Immediate shutdown
shutdown -y -g0 -i6                       Shut down and reboot (run level 6)
```

Since **init** uses the run levels 0 and 6 for shutting down the system, you can also use **init** for this purpose, but in a less disciplined way compared to **shutdown**:

```
init 0                                        Shuts down the system
init 6                               Shuts down and reboots the system
```

Note

Some systems like Solaris have the **reboot** and **halt** commands that also shut the system down without warning the users. Yet another, **haltsys**, brings down the system instantly. Unless you know what you are doing, you should stick to **shutdown** if you are administering a multiuser system.

Linux

The *[Ctrl][Alt][Del]* sequence also shuts down the system. Every Linux system will invariably contain a line like this in its `inittab`:

```
ca::ctrlaltdel:/sbin/shutdown -t3 -r now
```

Linux also uses the **-t** option to override the default waiting time of one minute. **shutdown** can also be used in these ways:

```
shutdown 17:30                                    Shut down at 17:30 hours
shutdown -r now                          Shut down immediately and reboot
```

22.6.1   Allowing a User to Only Shut Down

The **shutdown** command can only be executed by the super user. However, she sometimes needs to grant root access to a backup user to perform this function in her absence. This user shouldn't be allowed entry into the shell at all. This means that she has to create another "root"-like account. There's a way of solving this problem that still bothers many system administrators.

The super user's powers originate from one simple entry in /etc/passwd. This is the only user which has a UID 0. The trick is to first create an ordinary user account (say, shut) with **useradd**:

```
useradd -u 210 -g users -s /bin/sh -d /home/shut -m shut
```

You now have to confer root status on this user by changing the UID in /etc/passwd from 210 to 0. **useradd** may not permit reuse of the root user-id, so you may have to do that manually by editing /etc/passwd. Now, place the **shutdown** command in shut's .profile (preferably with **exec**) so that shut can't do anything else. This feature isn't explicitly documented, but it works quite well with our sample UNIX systems. You may additionally need to set the GUID to zero as well.

The trouble with this approach is that someone who manages to sneak in to the root account will take a few seconds to do this job. There's no way the administrator can control the powers of this account except by changing the UID (or the password).

22.7   Handling Floppy Diskettes

Although the tape is the most common backup device, floppy diskettes are used extensively on desktop systems. The diskette is the most convenient means of exchanging files between machines at work and home. For our examples, we'll be using the 3.5″ 1.44 MB diskette.

22.7.1   **format** and **fdformat**: Formatting Diskettes

Before you use a floppy for backup purposes, you need to format it. This is done with the **format** or **fdformat** commands (whichever is available on your system) with the device name as argument:

```
format /dev/rdsk/f0q18dt                                              System V
```

This command formats a 1.44 MB floppy. System V uses a raw device for formatting. The formatting process is followed by verification where most of the errors are encountered.

The **format** command in Solaris is used to create partitions. Solaris uses the **fdformat** command for formatting a diskette:

fdformat
Press return to start formatting floppy.

The -d option uses the DOS format.

Linux too uses the **fdformat** command for formatting a floppy. The device name has to be specified:

fdformat /dev/fd0H1440

22.7.2   dd: Copying Diskettes

dd (disk dump) is a versatile command that can be used to perform a variety of tasks. It is somewhat dated as some of its filtering functions have been taken over by other UNIX tools. It can be invoked by any user, but is really the administrator's tool. It has a strange command line having a series of options in the form *option=value*.

dd was extensively used in copying file systems, but today its role is mainly restricted to copying media—like floppies and tapes. It is not interactive, and a pair of **dd** commands is needed to complete the operation.

We'll now use **dd** to make a copy of a 1.44 MB floppy diskette. The first step is to create the image of the floppy on disk:

dd if=/dev/rdsk/f0q18dt of=$$ bs=147456
10+0 records in
10+0 records out

The keywords are if= (input filename), of= (output filename) and bs= (block size). The above command copies the "raw" contents of a 1.44 MB floppy to a temporary file $$ using a block size of 147456—exactly one-tenth the capacity of a 1.44 MB diskette.

Next, take out the source floppy from the drive and insert a formatted target floppy. A second reversed **dd** command copies this temporary file onto the diskette:

dd if=$$ of=/dev/rdsk/f0q18dt bs=147456
10+0 records in
10+0 records out

You should copy your boot floppies in this way. In the same manner, you can copy a tape, but if there are two tape drives, a single **dd** command can do the job:

dd if=/dev/rct0 of=/dev/rct1 bs=9k

Note

dd only uses raw devices—those in /dev/rdsk or those files in /dev beginning with an r— like /dev/rdiskette, or /dev/rct0. Linux doesn't have separate devices for the two modes but selects the right mode automatically.

22.7.3   Handling DOS Diskettes

It has now become quite common to see both Windows and UNIX systems on the desktop. UNIX today provides a family of commands (Table 22.1) with which one can read from and write onto DOS floppy diskettes. These commands begin with the string dos in SVR4. They are modeled after UNIX commands performing similar functions.

The command required most is **doscp**, which copies files between disk and diskette:

```
doscp emp.lst /dev/dsk/f0q18dt:/per.lst
```

There are two components in the target specification—the device name (1.44 MB floppy drive) and the filename (/per.lst), with the : used as a delimiter. As in **cp**, multiple file copying is also possible:

```
doscp emp[123].lst /dev/dsk/f0q18dt
```

doscat performs a simple "cat" of its arguments in the command line. When more than one filename is specified, the standard output for each is concatenated:

```
doscat /dev/dsk/f0q18dt:/CHAP01 /dev/dsk/f0q18dt:/CHAP02 > newchap
```

Like UNIX, DOS also features a hierarchical file system with its own root directory. Its files are also similar to UNIX files except that the line terminator in UNIX is the LF (line feed—octal value 012) character, which we have been referring to as newline. In DOS, the line terminator is a combination of CR (carriage return—octal value 015) and LF *(9.16)*. When files are copied and displayed with these commands, the relevant conversion takes place. Both **doscp** and **doscat** also work with the -r option, in which case the files are copied or concatenated without newline conversions.

On some machines, these "DOS" commands also work with a DOS hard disk partition if the machine has a separate partition for DOS. The device name for the fixed disk is system-dependent; some systems use c: and d:. To see the files in the root directory of the DOS partition, any of these commands can be used on a SCO UNIX system:

```
dosdir c:
dosdir /dev/hd0d              Xenix device name of the DOS partition
dosdir /dev/dsk/0sC
```

Table 22.1 shows the use of these commands with varying device names. One of them should work on your system. If a: and b: don't work, then use the appropriate file in /dev or /dev/dsk.

Linux

The Linux "DOS" commands begin with the string m and use the corresponding DOS command as the rest of the string. Here are some examples:

```
mcopy emp.lst a:
mcopy emp[1-3].lst a:

mdir a:
mdel a:*.txt
```

Note that Linux uses the DOS drive name. All these commands belong to the "mtools" collection. For details, use **man mtools**.

TABLE 22.1   *The Family of DOS Commands (Linux command name in parentheses)*

Command	Action
`doscp /dev/fd0135ds18:/tags .`	Copies `tags` from DOS diskette (`mcopy`)
`doscat a:readme a:setup.txt`	Concatenates files `readme` and `setup.txt` in DOS diskette (`mtype`)
`dosdir /dev/dsk/f0q18dt`	Lists files in DOS diskette in DOS-style (`mdir`)
`dosls /dev/dsk/f0q18dt`	Lists files in UNIX `ls`-style
`dosmkdir a:bin`	Creates directory `bin` on DOS diskette (`mmd`)
`dosrmdir a:bin`	Removes directory `bin` on DOS diskette (`mrd`)
`dosrm /dev/dsk/f0q18dt:setup.inf`	Deletes file `setup.inf` on DOS diskette (`mdel`)
`dosformat b:`	Formats diskette in nonbootable drive for use on DOS systems (`mformat`)

22.8   `cpio`: **Copy Input-Output**

The importance of performing regular backups isn't usually appreciated till a crash has occurred and a lot of data has been lost. As an administrator, you are partly responsible for the safety of the data that resides in the system. It is part of your duties to decide which files should be backed up—and to determine the periodicity of such backups. The effectiveness of the backup is determined by your ability to easily restore lost or corrupted data files.

Today, the two most popular programs for backups are **cpio** and **tar**. Both combine a group of files into an archive, with suitable headers preceding the contents of each file. Each command has definite advantages over the other, and the formats they use to record data are not *fully* compatible with each other. **tar** archives can sometimes be read by **cpio**, but not vice versa.

The backup device can be a magnetic or a cartridge tape, a floppy diskette—or even a disk file. Small systems may not be having the tape facility, so the floppy drive will be used here to illustrate the features of both commands.

Note

Before you try out the **cpio** and **tar** commands on a Solaris machine, make sure you have inactivated its volume management daemon with **/etc/init.d/volmgt stop**. This daemon (**vold**) which mounts CD-ROMs automatically can be reactivated by using the command with the `start` argument. The diskette must not be in the drive when you `stop` the daemon.

The **cpio** command (copy input-output) copies files to and from a backup device. It uses standard input to take the list of filenames. It then copies them with their contents and headers into a stream which can be redirected to a file or a device. This means that **cpio** can be (and is) used with redirection and piping.

cpio uses two "key" options— -o (output) and -i (input), either of which (but not both) must be there in the command line. All other options have to be used with either of these key options. The examples in this section and the next use System V device names. Linux users should use /dev/fd0H1440 and Solaris users should use /dev/rdiskette as the device names.

22.8.1 Backing Up Files (-o)

Since **cpio** uses only standard input, you can use **ls** to generate a list of filenames to serve as input to **cpio**. The -o key option creates the archive on the standard output, which you need to redirect to a device file. This is how you copy files in the current directory to a 1.44 MB floppy:

```
# ls | cpio -ov > /dev/rdsk/f0q18dt                    Use /dev/rdiskette in Solaris
array.pl
calendar
cent2fah.pl
convert.sh
xinitrc.sam
276 blocks                                             Total size of the archive
```

The -v option makes **cpio** operate in the verbose mode so each filename is seen on the terminal when it's being copied. What **cpio** needs as input is a list of files to be backed up, with one file in each line. If this list is available in a file, redirection can be used too:

```
cpio -o >/dev/rdsk/f0q18dt < flist
```

Incremental Backups **find** can also produce a file list, so any files that satisfy its selection criteria can also be backed up. You'll frequently need to use **find** and **cpio** in combination to back up selected files—for instance, those that have been modified in the last two days:

```
find . -type f -mtime -2 -print | cpio -ovB >/dev/rdsk/f0q18dt
```

Since the path list of **find** is a dot, the files are backed up with their relative pathnames. However, if it is a /, absolute pathnames are used.

The -B option sets the block size to 5120 bytes for input and output, which is 10 times the default size. For higher (or lower) sizes, the -C option has to be used:

```
ls *.pl | cpio -ovC51200 >/dev/rdsk/f0q18dt                        100 times the default
```

Multivolume Backups When the created archive in the backup device is larger than the capacity of the device, **cpio** prompts for inserting a new diskette into the drive:

```
# find . -type f -print | cpio -ocB >/dev/rdsk/f0q18dt
Reached end of medium on output.
If you want to go on, type device/filename when ready
```

/dev/fd0   *Device name entered*
3672 blocks

Enter the device name when **cpio** pauses to take input. If there are two floppy drives on a machine, you can alternate between two device names. This lets **cpio** do the copying while the diskettes are being changed. In this way, an archive can be split into several *extents* (volumes).

22.8.2 Restoring Files (-i)

A complete archive or selected files can be restored with the -i key option. To restore files, use redirection to take input from the device:

```
# cpio -iv < /dev/rdsk/f0q18dt
array.pl
calendar
cent2fah.pl
convert.sh
xinitrc.sam
276 blocks
```

When restoring subdirectories, **cpio** assumes that the subdirectory structures are also maintained in the hard disk; it can't create them in case they aren't. However, the -d (directory) option overrides that.

    cpio also accepts a quoted wild-card pattern, so multiple files fitting the pattern can be restored. Restoring only the shell scripts becomes quite easy:

```
cpio -i "*.sh" < /dev/rdsk/f0q18dt
```

Tip

A file is restored in that directory that matches its pathname. That is, if the absolute pathname has been used to back up a file (e.g., /home/romeo/unit13), then it will be restored only in the same directory (/home/romeo). However, when relative pathnames are used, they can be restored anywhere. The "relative filename" method is normally recommended because the administrator often likes to back up files from one directory and restore them in another. Make sure you use **find** with a dot, rather than a /, to specify the path list.

Handling Modification Times (-m) By default, when a file is extracted, its modification time is set to the time of extraction. This could lead to problems as this file will participate in future incremental backups even though it has not *actually* been modified after restoration. In such an eventuality, you should use **touch** *(7.11)* to change the modification time. Alternatively, you can use the -m option to tell **cpio** that the modification time is to be retained.

    cpio compares the modification time of a file in the media with the one in disk (if any). If the disk file is newer than the copy, or of the same age, then it won't be restored, and **cpio** echoes this message:

```
"current <unit14> newer"
```

This is a useful built-in protection feature that safeguards the latest version of a file. (**tar** doesn't have this feature.) However, this can be overridden with the -u (unconditional) option.

Tip

If you are often moving files from one machine to another, use **cpio** instead of **tar**. You are then assured that a newer file on one machine is not overwritten by an older one from another.

22.8.3   Displaying the Archive (-it)

The -t option displays the contents of the device without restoring the files. This option *must* be combined with the -i key option:

```
# cpio -itv </dev/rdsk/f0q18dt
100755 henry       605  Oct 18 23:34:07 1997  cent2fah.pl
100755 henry       273  Oct 18 23:34:07 1997  check_number.pl
100755 henry       531  Oct 18 23:34:08 1997  dec2bin.pl
100755 henry       214  Oct 18 23:34:08 1997  get_home.pl
```

The files are displayed in a format resembling the listing. (Linux and Solaris output is identical to the listing.) This format shows the octal representation of the permissions as well as the modification time of the file (to the nearest second!).

22.8.4   Other Options

There are three important options that can be used with both the -o and -i modes:

- The -r (rename) option lets you rename each file before starting the copying process. The system presents each filename, and prompts you for a response. If you enter a filename, copying is done to that file; a null response leaves the file uncopied.
- The -f option, followed by an expression, causes **cpio** to select all files *except* those in the expression:

  ```
  cpio -ivf "*.c" </dev/rdsk/f0q18dt          Restores all except C programs.
  ```

- The -c option tells **cpio** to use ASCII characters, rather than the binary format, for creating headers. When using media on different machines, you should select this option to produce portable backups.

The **cpio** options are shown in Table 22.2. **cpio** relies on another command (usually **find**) or a file to provide its file list. It can't accept filename arguments in the command line. A **cpio** archive is also overwritten with every invocation of the command. There's no way a file can be appended to the archive (Solaris and Linux excepted). This is where **tar** comes in.

22.9   tar: The "Tape" Archive Program

The **tar** (tape archive) command has been in existence since before the emergence of **cpio**. Today, it not only creates archives on tapes, but supports floppies as well. Unlike **cpio**, **tar** doesn't normally write to the standard output (though it can be made to), but

TABLE 22.2 **cpio** *Nonkey Options (used with* -i *or* -o *as relevant)*

Option	Significance
-d	Creates directories as and when needed
-c	Writes header information in ASCII character form for portability
-r	Renames files in interactive manner
-t	Lists files in archive (only with -i option)
-u	Overwrites newer file with older version
-v	Verbose option—prints list of files that are being copied
-m	Retains original file modification time
-f *exp*	Copies all files except those in *exp*
-C*size*	Sets input-output block size to *size* bytes
-A -0 *device*	Appends files to *device (Solaris and Linux only)*
-H tar	Creates or reads a **tar** header format *(Solaris and Linux only)*
-E *file*	Extracts only those files listed in *file (Solaris and Linux only)*

creates an archive in the media. It is a versatile command with certain exclusive features not found in **cpio**:

- It doesn't use standard input to obtain its file list. **tar** accepts file and directory names as arguments.
- It copies one or more entire directory trees; i.e., it operates recursively by default.
- It can create several versions of the same file in a single archive (**cpio** in Solaris and Linux also).
- It can append to an archive without overwriting the entire archive (**cpio** in Solaris and Linux also).

tar is used with one of a number of key options—the common ones are -c (copy), -x (extract) and -t (list). The -f option additionally has to be used for specifying the device name. The **tar** options are listed in Table 22.3.

22.9.1   Backing Up Files (-c)

tar accepts directory and filenames directly on the command line. The -c key option is used to copy files to the backup device:

```
# tar -cvf /dev/rdsk/f0q18dt /home/sales/SQL/*.sql
a /home/sales/SQL/invoice_do_all.sql 1 tape blocks
a /home/sales/SQL/load2invoice_do_all.sql 1 tape blocks
a /home/sales/SQL/remove_duplicate.sql 1 tape blocks
a /home/sales/SQL/t_mr_alloc.sql 10 tape blocks
```

This backs up all SQL scripts with their absolute pathnames to the floppy diskette. The single character a before each pathname indicates that the file is appended. The verbose option (-v) shows the number of blocks used by each file.

TABLE 22.3 **tar** *Options*

Key Options (only one to be used)	
Option	**Significance**
-c	Creates a new archive
-x	Extracts files from archive
-t	Lists contents of archive
-r	Appends files at end of archive
-u	Like r, but only if files are newer than those in archive
Nonkey Options	
Option	**Significance**
-f *device*	Uses pathname *device* as name of device instead of the default
-v	Verbose option—lists files in long format
-w	Confirms from user about action to be taken
-b *n*	Uses blocking factor *n*, where *n* is restricted to 20
-m	Changes modification time of file to time of extraction
-I *file*	Takes filenames from *file (Solaris only)*
-T *file*	Takes filenames from *file (Linux only)*
-k *num*	Multivolume backup—sets size of volume to *num* kilobytes *(Solaris only)*
-M	Multivolume backup *(Linux only)*
-z	Compresses/uncompresses with **gzip** *(Linux only)*
-Z	Compresses/uncompresses with **compress** *(Linux only)*
-X *file*	Excludes filenames in *file (Solaris and Linux only)*

Note

tar is quite liberal in its handling of options. **tar cvf** is the same as **tar -cvf**. The - symbol is not required at all! However, future versions of **tar** will not support this.

When files are copied in this way with absolute pathnames, the same restrictions apply; they can only be restored in the same directory. However, if you choose to keep the option open of installing the files in a different directory, you should first "cd" to /home/sales/SQL and then use a relative pathname:

```
cd /home/sales/SQL
tar -cvf /dev/rdsk/f0q18dt ./*.sql                          Using the ./
```

The command will also execute faster if used with a block size of 18 (i.e., 18 × 512 bytes):

```
tar -cvfb /dev/rdsk/f0q18dt 18 *.sql                  ./ is really not required
```

Since both -f and -b have to be followed by an argument, the first word (/dev/rdsk/f0q18dt) after the option string -cvfb denotes the argument for -f, and the second word (18) will line up with -b.

Tip

Never use **tar** and **cpio** with their default block sizes. Choose as high a value as the system permits. Higher block sizes speed up I/O operations.

The advantage of **tar** lies in that it can copy an entire directory tree with all its subdirectories. The current directory can be backed up with or without the hidden files:

```
tar -cvfb /dev/rdsk/f0q18dt 18 *                            Doesn't back up hidden files
tar -cvfb /dev/fd0 18 .                                     Backs up hidden files also
```

The files here are backed up with their relative pathnames, assuming they all fit in one diskette. If they don't, **tar** in System V may accommodate them as much as possible, and then quit the program without warning.

Caution

There is one problem with copying deeply recursive directory structures. **tar** was developed at a time when the UNIX filename was restricted to 14 characters. Even today, **tar** can't handle a pathname exceeding 100 characters. On modern UNIX systems which have great depth in their directory structures, this proves to be a serious limitation. Solaris, however, has a higher limit, which is enhanced even further with the -E option.

Multivolume Backup (-k) For multivolume diskette backups, **tar** in Solaris (and SCO UNIX) uses a special option (-k), followed by the volume size in kilobytes. This is how the file index is backed up in SCO UNIX:

```
# tar -cvfkb /dev/rdsk/f0q18dt 1440 18 index
Volume ends at 1439K, blocking factor = 18
tar: large file index needs 2 extents.
tar: current device seek position = 0K
+++ a index 1439K [extent #1 of 2]
```

tar estimates that two 1440 KB (the argument of -k) diskettes will be required. After the first volume is full, **tar** prompts for a new volume:

```
tar: please insert new volume, then press RETURN.
```

At the time of restoration, the same option has to be used.

22.9.2 Restoring Files (-x)

Files are restored with the -x (extract) key option. When no file or directory name is specified, it restores all files from the backup device. The following command restores the files just backed up:

```
# tar -xvfb /dev/rdsk/f0q18dt 18
x /home/sales/SQL/invoice_do_all.sql, 169 bytes, 1 tape blocks
x /home/sales/SQL/load2invoice_do_all.sql, 456 bytes, 1 tape blocks
x /home/sales/SQL/remove_duplicate.sql, 237 bytes, 1 tape blocks
x /home/sales/SQL/t_mr_alloc.sql, 4855 bytes, 10 tape blocks
```

Selective extraction is also possible by providing one or more directory or filenames:

```
tar -xvf /dev/rdsk/f0q18dt tulec1 project2
```

Unlike **cpio**, when files are extracted, the modification times of the files also remain unchanged. This can be overridden by the -m option to reflect the system time at the time of extraction.

Note

Unlike **cpio**, some versions of **tar** (like in Solaris) don't read wild-card patterns. If you use **tar -xvf /dev/fd0 *.pl**, it's the *shell* that tries to expand the pattern, which means that the files have to reside in the current directory. In many cases, they won't, so extraction may be incomplete. You'll then have to specify the filenames explicitly in the command line.

Some versions of **tar** (like in Linux) do permit the use of the wild cards; it doesn't matter whether the files exist at all in the disk. **tar** uses the wild-card pattern to match files in the *media*—a significant departure from the theory that unquoted wild cards are meaningful only to the shell. This is one of the first things you should check when using **tar**.

Caution

When restoring from a multivolume backup, you have to make sure you start with the right volume. **tar** won't point out that you have not started with the right one, nor will it tell you that the disk you inserted is not the right one in the sequence. It will simply go on extracting files as much as it can. A file can easily get truncated if you are not careful.

22.9.3 Displaying the Archive (-t)

Like in **cpio**, the -t key option simply displays the contents of the device without restoring the files. When combined with the -v option, they are displayed in a long format similar to the listing:

```
# tar -tvf /dev/rdsk/f0q18dt
rwxr-xr-x203/50      472 Jun  4 09:35 1991 ./dentry1.sh
rwxr-xr-x203/50      554 Jun  4 09:52 1991 ./dentry2.sh
rwxr-xr-x203/50     2299 Jun  4 13:59 1991 ./func.sh
```

There's something here that you ought to pay attention to. The files here have been backed up with relative pathnames. Each filename here is preceded by ./. If you don't remember this but want to extract the file func.sh from the diskette, you'll obviously first try this:

```
# tar -xvf /dev/fd0 func.sh                          Using generic floppy device
tar: func.sh: Not found in archive
```

tar failed to find the file because it existed there as ./func.sh and not func.sh. Put the ./ before the filename, and get it this time. Remember this whenever you encounter extraction errors as above.

22.9.4 Using tar with Compression Utilities

tar need not always be used with a device name; the -f option can also be used with an ordinary filename. This means you can archive a group of files into a single disk file. Since **tar** operates recursively, you can use it to archive an entire directory tree:

```
tar -cvf quotes.tar quotes.dir                       quotes.dir is a directory
tar -cvf quotes.tar *
```

The first command uses a directory name as an argument, and the second one uses all files in the current directory. In either case, the file `quotes.tar` is created containing multiple files (and directories). You can now mail this file to someone and let her work with your files and directories without letting her "telnet" or "ftp" to your account. Normally, the file is compressed with **compress** or **gzip** before it is mailed. The output of these commands is written back to the same file with a `.Z` or `.gz` extension:

```
compress quotes.tar                                          Creates quotes.tar.Z
gzip quotes.tar                                              Creates quotes.tar.gz
```

It may seem strange, but **cpio**, **tar** and the compression tools **compress** and **gzip** can also operate as filters. You can combine the archiving and compressing activities in a pipeline:

```
tar -cvf - quotes.dir | compress > quotes.tar.Z
tar -cvf - quotes.dir | gzip > quotes.tar.gz
```

Note that this time we deliberately provided the `.tar`, `.Z` and `.gz` extensions. Both **compress** and **gzip** look for these extensions because they can handle multiple compression formats. This file can then be mailed as an attachment with any of the mailers that we have discussed—**elm**, **pine** and Netscape.

At the receiving end, the attachment has to be saved to a file—preferably with the same extensions. The extraction procedure is similar but works in a reverse manner. Here's how it works with **uncompress**:

```
uncompress quotes.tar.Z                                      Creates quotes.tar
tar -xvf quotes.tar                                 Gets back directory quotes.dir
```

A "tar-gzipped" file can also decompressed in a similar manner:

```
gunzip quotes.tar.gz                                         Creates quotes.tar
tar -xvf quotes.tar                                 Gets back directory quotes.dir
```

When creating the archive, we used a pipeline to avoid creating the intermediate file. In a similar vein, we can use one for extraction:

```
uncompress -c quotes.tar.Z | tar -xvf -
gunzip -c quotes.tar.gz | tar -xvf -
```

Large files containing text compress more. GIF and JPEG files are hardly affected by compression because they already hold data in compressed form *(6.19)*. Note that **tar** uses the `-` to signify both standard input and standard output, and additionally uses the key option (`-c` or `-x`) to specify the stream.

22.9.5 Other Options

There are a number of other options of **tar** that are worth considering:

- The `-r` key option is used to *append* a file to an archive. The unusual outcome of this is that an archive can contain several versions of the same file.

- The -u key option also adds a file to an archive but only if the file is not already there or is being replaced with a newer version. You can't use the -c option when using either -r or -u.
- The -w option permits interactive copying and restoration. It prints the name of the file and prompts for the action to be taken (y or n).
- Some versions of **tar** use a special option to pick up filenames from a file. You might want to use this facility when you have a list of over a hundred files, which is impractical (and sometimes, impossible) to enter in the command line. Unfortunately, this option is not standard; Solaris uses -I and Linux uses -T.

Tip

Use the -r key option to append files to an archive. Use the -u option to store only newer files. **tar** can also store multiple copies of a file in a single archive.

Caution

When using **cpio** or **tar**, make sure that raw devices are used, i.e., those in /dev/rdsk (and not /dev/dsk), or those files in /dev beginning with r. If block devices are used, there could be problems with multivolume backups. Linux users need not bother.

Linux

The GNU **tar** command is more powerful than its System V counterpart and supports a host of exclusive options. Unfortunately, there is sometimes a mismatch with the options used by System V. Portability problems are sometimes encountered.

Compression (-z and -Z)   GNU **tar** supports a compression facility while backing up files. The -z option is used for compressing with **gzip** and -Z for **compress**:

```
tar -cvzf /dev/rft0 .                          Compresses with gzip
tar -cvZf /dev/rft0 .                          Compresses with compress
```

At the time of extraction or for displaying with -t, the -z or -Z options have to be used in just the same way.

Multivolume Backup (-M)   If the files don't fit on a floppy, **tar** issues a warning. However, it behaves more intelligently when used with the -M option:

```
# tar -cvf /dev/fd0H1440 -M *
.....
Prepare volume #2 for /dev/fd0H1440 and hit return:
```

tar identifies the volume size from the device name itself. System V versions of **tar** are not able to do this.

22.10 Managing the Disk Space

Managing disk space is one of the important functions of the administrator. There are a number of files, especially in the directories /tmp and /var/tmp that tend to accumulate during the day. If this build-up is not checked, the entire disk space will eventually be eaten up, resulting in a slowdown of system functioning. The administrator uses the **df** *(6.17)*, **du** *(6.18)* and **find** *(7.15)* commands to monitor the disk space. We'll take up two of these commands again—this time from the administrative point of view.

22.10.1   Assessing Space Consumed by Users (du -s)

Most of the dynamic space in a system is consumed by users' home directories and data files. You should use **du -s** with the /home/* argument to report on each user's home directory. The output is brief and yet quite informative:

```
# du -s /home/*
1204      /home/ftp                                            root of anonymous ftp
144208    /home/henry
1536      /home/httpd                                          root of Web server
98290     /home/image
28346     /home/sales
```

du can also report on each file in a directory (-a option), but the list would be too big to be of any use. You may instead look for some of the notorious disk eaters, and exceptional reporting is what you probably need. **find** does this job better.

22.10.2   find Revisited: The Administrator's Tool

The **find** command *(7.15)* can match a file with practically every attribute. We'll consider some more options here that make it a powerful disk management tool.

Locating Large Files (-size) **find** uses the -size operator to locate large files. Multiple selection criteria can also be specified:

```
find /home -size +2048 -print                                   Files above 1 MB
find /home -size +2048 -size -8192 -print              Above 1 MB and below 4 MB
```

find here uses a block size of 512 bytes. It also lets you track down a file if you know its exact size. If you recall having placed a file with 38,765 bytes somewhere, but can't remember where, this is how **find** can help you:

```
find / -size 38765c -print
```

Finding Unused Files (-mtime and -atime) Many files remain unaccessed or unmodified for months—even years. **find**'s -mtime and -atime operators can easily match a file's modification and access times to select them. This is how the administrator regularly scans the /home directory for files that have either not been accessed for a year or not modified in six months:

```
find /home -atime +365 -o -mtime +180 -print | mail root
```

Incremental Backups (-newer) You can also use **find** for performing incremental backups. First, you have to stamp a zero-byte file with the present system date and time whenever you go in for a backup. Subsequent backups will only select those files newer than this file. The following script lines show a simple implementation:

```
find /home -newer .last_time -print | cpio -o > /dev/rct0
touch .last_time
```

These two lines can be used together any time, and **touch** ensures that the last backup time is stored in the file's modification time stamp. You can use **tar** too:

```
tar -cvf /dev/rct0 `find /home -type f -newer .last_time -print`
touch .last_time
```

The type has to be specified as f because if it is not, **find** shows the directory as part of its output, which is interpreted by **tar** to include *all* files of the directory. This means files would be backed up twice.

Avoiding Mounted File Systems (-mount) Backing up the root file system generally requires other file systems to be dismounted. You need not do that any longer as **find** today offers the -mount keyword to restrict this tree walking. Backing up files of the root file system modified in less than a day is quite easy:

```
find / -depth -mount -mtime -1 -print | cpio -ocvB -O /dev/rct0
```

This time **find** doesn't traverse the other file systems. The -depth keyword makes sure the files in the directories are acted upon before the directory itself. If the -mtime keyword is omitted, then the pipeline sequence makes a complete backup of the root file system. The **find** options are listed in Table 7.5.

Tip

You must back up the root file system on tape immediately after installation of the system. Subsequently, you must take further backups (normally, incremental) whenever the root system files are modified.

22.10.3   xargs: Building a Dynamic Command Line

There's one problem with using **find**'s -exec operator *(7.15.1)* with a UNIX command. If **find** produces a list of 200 files for removal, **rm** has to be executed 200 times. **xargs** comes to our rescue here as it lets **rm** (or, for that matter, any UNIX command) be used just *once* with 200 filenames as arguments.

     xargs is one of UNIX's dark horses—a command not well appreciated or understood. It breaks up data supplied as standard input into a list, and provides this list to the command used as its argument. The following command lines do the same thing except that the second one does it much faster:

```
find /usr/preserve -mtime +30 -exec rm -f {} \;
find /usr/preserve -mtime +30 -print | xargs rm -f
```

xargs here obtains the file list from **find** and supplies a *single* set of arguments to **rm**. So, even if **find** selects 30 files, **rm** will be executed only once.

     Commands usually have limits on the number of arguments they can handle. **xargs** uses the -n option to provide the specified number of arguments for a single invocation of the command:

```
find / -name core -size +1024 -print | xargs -n20 rm -f
```

If **find** locates 100 files, **rm** will be invoked five times—each time with 20 filenames as arguments. Isn't this a useful tool?

➤ *GOING FURTHER*

22.11 Password Administration with `passwd`

The **passwd** command offers a number of options which help in administering passwords. When a user forgets her password or when assigning a password to a new user, the system administrator has to make arrangements for them to login unhindered and then set a new password themselves. This is easily done by deleting the password altogether so a user can go straight in:

```
passwd -d henry
```
                                              No password required now

This could be risky and could create additional problems; the user may be unable to set any password at all for some time. So the administrator might want to set one herself and force the user to change it on first login. This is done with the `-f` option (not in Linux):

```
passwd -f henry
```
                                        Password has to be changed on login

UNIX systems originally stored passwords in encrypted form in `/etc/passwd`. Because the file is readable and vulnerable to attack by intelligent and mischievous hackers, modern systems have moved the location to `/etc/shadow`. `shadow` contains nine fields, including the encryption, and is not world-readable. Most of the fields in `/etc/shadow` can be updated by using **passwd** with suitable options.

For administering the change of password, `shadow` also provides an elaborate scheme called **password aging**. You can force a user to change her password after a predetermined number of days have elapsed. You can also prevent her from doing so too frequently:

```
passwd -n 14 julie
passwd -x 30 julie
```
                                                      Minimum 14 days
                                                      Maximum 30 days

`-n 14` prevents julie from changing her password before two weeks, while `-x 30` forces her to change it after thirty days.

In the interests of security, it may be sometimes necessary for you to lock a user account. You can do that with **passwd**'s `-l` (lock) option.

22.12 The *rc* Scripts Used by `init`

init and `/etc/inittab` completely control the way the system is booted and powered down. Moreover, when the system changes a run level, **init** looks up `inittab` to find out the processes that should and shouldn't be running for the new run level. It first kills the processes that shouldn't be running and then spawns those that should be.

Every `inittab` specifies the execution of some **rc** (run command) **scripts** placed in `/etc` or `/sbin`. These scripts have the names **rc0**, **rc1**, **rc2**—one for each run level. This is evident from the following lines in `/etc/inittab`:

```
s0:0:wait:/sbin/rc0            >/dev/console 2<>/dev/console </dev/console
s1:1:wait:/sbin/shutdown -y -iS -g0 >/dev/console 2<>/dev/console </dev/console
s2:23:wait:/sbin/rc2           >/dev/console 2<>/dev/console </dev/console
s3:3:wait:/sbin/rc3            >/dev/console 2<>/dev/console </dev/console
s6:6:wait:/sbin/rc6            >/dev/console 2<>/dev/console </dev/console
```

init executes the script specific to that run level. However, **rc2** runs in both states 2 and 3. Each *rc* script further specifies the execution of a series of scripts in the directory /etc/rc*n*.d. This means that for run level 2, **init** executes **/etc/rc2**, which in turn executes the scripts in /etc/rc2.d.

Linux

The *rc* Files

The initialization files in Linux were originally based on BSD, but now have a strong System V flavor. However, the *rc* files and directories here are all under one roof—/etc/rc.d. Moreover, instead of using **rc*n***, Linux uses a single **rc** with different arguments as shown below:

```
l0:0:wait:/etc/rc.d/rc 0
l1:1:wait:/etc/rc.d/rc 1
l2:2:wait:/etc/rc.d/rc 2
```

All scripts in the rc*n*.d directories are executed from **/etc/rc.d/rc**. The sequence for Linux goes like this: For switching to run level *n*, **init** executes **/etc/rc.d/rc** *n*, which executes the scripts in /etc/rc.d/rc*n*.d.

22.12.1 The Start and Kill Scripts

Now, let's turn our attention to the scripts in the /etc/rc*n*.d directories. These directories host two types of files as shown by this listing of /etc/rc3.d:

K60nfs.server	S69inet	S75cron	S91agaconfig
K76snmpdx	S70uucp	S76nscd	S91leoconfig
K77dmi	S71rpc	S80lp	S92rtvc-config
S20sysetup	S73cachefs.daemon	S85power	S99audit
S21perf	S73nfs.client	S88sendmail	S99dtlogin
S30sysid.net	S74autofs	S88utmpd	

The scripts in these rc*n*.d directories fully initialize the system by mounting file systems, setting up the network and activating the daemons. They are executed in two batches. When the system enters run level 3, **rc** executes (in ASCII sequence) all scripts beginning with K (the "kill" scripts) with the stop argument. This kills all processes that shouldn't be running at this level. It then executes the scripts beginning with S (the "start" scripts) with the start argument. If you look up the **rc3** script, you'll find two **for** loops doing that.

Because a script may be executed in more than one run level, the scripts also have links pointing to the files placed in /etc/init.d. The files in this directory have similar names with the three-character prefix chopped off. This is a clean and sensible arrangement as you need to modify a file at only one place.

GOING FURTHER

As system administrator, you must understand how these scripts work. You should also be able to identify the script that starts a specific service. The filenames often provide the clue, but sometimes you need **grep** for locating a script. This is how we identify the script that starts up the Internet daemon:

```
# grep -l inet *
S69inet
S72inetsvc
```

It's probably the first one that does the job. To be sure, we have to look inside the script.

Note

A script in r*cn*.d beginning with S is meant to start a service, while one beginning with K is meant to kill one. The kill scripts are executed before the start ones. They are all run from the corresponding /etc/r*cn* (or /etc/rc with the argument *n* in Linux) script where *n* signifies the run level.

22.13   Terminal Management

Before the advent of workstations and PCs, terminals once ruled the UNIX world. They are still used today in situations not requiring graphic output. (Only one chapter—Chapter 12—of this book exclusively discusses graphics.) A terminal can be connected to a UNIX machine either through one of the serial ports provided or through a separate serial port card offering multiple ports. PCs come with two serial ports (COM1 and COM2), and they can also be used to connect terminals, modems and mice.

UNIX is unmatched in versatility and ease with which these devices can be configured. Very rarely does one need to write a device driver for a terminal. Even X Window **xterm** windows use the same drivers and configuration files as dumb terminals. You'll find it's easy to change a terminal's characteristics.

22.13.1   getty and /etc/gettydefs

Apart from starting system daemons via startup scripts, **init** directly handles the terminal. It spawns a **getty** at every serial port connected to a terminal. On System V, each terminal requires a separate entry in /etc/inittab with a corresponding matching entry in /etc/gettydefs. Here are two typical entries:

```
c02:234:respawn:/sbin/getty tty02 m          Terminal connected
c03:234:off:/sbin/getty tty03 m              Terminal not connected
```

The first line translates to this: "For run levels 2, 3 or 4, run the **getty** program with the two arguments tty02 and m." The respawn setting makes sure the terminal is always enabled; i.e., **getty** is respawned every time it is killed when a user logs out. You won't see the login prompt on the terminal tty03 because the action here is set to off.

getty, you'll recall *(10.4)*, is fork-execd by **init** to produce the login: prompt on the screen. It also matches its second argument (m) with the first field of /etc/gettydefs. This file contains the terminal definitions:

```
l # B4800 HUPCL # B4800 CS8 SANE HUPCL TAB3 ECHOE IXANY #\r\nlogin: # m
m # B9600 HUPCL # B9600 CS8 SANE HUPCL TAB3 ECHOE IXANY #\r\nlogin: # n
n # B19200  HUPCL # B19200  CS8 SANE HUPCL TAB3 IXANY #\r\nlogin: # l
```

Here, **getty** initially uses the second line which starts with m. It *attempts* to set the terminal speed to 9600 bauds and produce the login prompt. The last field in the same line is another label (n), which **getty** tries next to match if a break is received in the line. A cyclic search has been set up here—first 9600, then 19200, and then 4800, and back again to 9600. If the first label of a line is the same as the last label in the matching line, no such cycling will be possible.

Once the terminal has been set up and entries made in the two files, **init** has to be told to reread /etc/inittab. Similarly, changes made in /etc/gettydefs should be checked with **getty**'s -c option:

telinit q	*Read* inittab *again*
getty -c /etc/gettydefs	*Check* gettydefs *for correctness*

Solaris doesn't use gettydefs. **getty** here is a symbolic link to the **ttymon** port monitor program which is invoked with options in inittab.

Linux

Linux has a number of "getty" daemons—**agetty**, **mingetty** and **uugetty**. It also uses a separate daemon for handling modems connected to serial ports—**mgetty**. None of them use **gettydefs**. They either use different configuration files or are invoked with a number of "gettydefs"-like options.

22.13.2 Setting the Terminal Type

Apart from terminal definitions, many systems use a separate file for storing terminal types. This is often the file /etc/ttytype. It contains a line for each terminal device name and contains two fields—the terminal type and the terminal name:

```
vt220     tty01
ansi      tty1a
dialup    tty2A
```

The terminal type is simply the entry in /usr/lib/terminfo—a database controlling terminal characteristics. For example, the vt220 attributes will be found in the binary file /usr/lib/terminfo/v/vt220. By default, the TERM variable is set by reading **/etc/ttytype**. Other terminal characteristics can be set with **stty** *(3.5)*.

Note

If a terminal is connected through a multiport card, there will be as many entries in inittab as the number of ports. Make sure the action field is enabled for each terminal; otherwise it won't work.

22.13.3 Using Virtual Terminals

If you are using UNIX or Linux on your PC, you can log in more than once from multiple "terminals" on the same machine. If that sounds incredible, then just use *[Alt][F2]* or *[Alt][F3]*. You'll see the login: prompt on that screen. UNIX supports a number of **virtual terminals** (or screens), each accessible by using the *[Alt]* key with a function key. You can log on to any of these virtual terminals and start a separate login session—with same or different usernames.

You can edit a program on one terminal and compile or run it on another. The technique is pretty simple. Invoke your editor (**vi** or **emacs**) with the program in one screen. Save your editing changes without quitting the editor, before you switch to the other screen to run the compilation or run command. This command line is entered only once (assuming you are not using the Bourne shell). Subsequently, you need to use only **!!** or **r** (to repeat the last command).

When you start using your virtual terminals like this, you'll find (and this is not an exaggeration) that you can do things faster than you'll ever be able to do in a windowing environment. That's why some people use UNIX!

22.14   Printing Preliminaries

Printer administration is an important part of the administrator's job, and in large installations, can often take a lot of time. UNIX provides a spooling subsystem featuring a number of commands which ensure that spooling takes place in an orderly manner. This involves managing the print queues, adding and removing printers, starting and stopping the subsystem, and administering specific printers. The administration commands are different for SVR4 and Linux.

When a user uses **lp** to print a file, the file is spooled and submitted to a queue. Spooling in SVR4 is performed by the **lpsched** daemon. The daemon is invoked by one of the start scripts in the rc*n*.d directories when the system moves to multiuser mode. The moment printing activity ceases, you should use this sequence to first check whether **lpsched** is running:

```
ps -e | grep lpsched
```

If it is not running, look for "S" scripts matching the patterns S*lp (for **lpsched**) in rc2.d or rc3.d:

```
ls /etc/rc2.d/S*lp
```

The "lp" suffix refers to the once-popular line printers, which have been made obsolete today by laser and inkjet printers. However, just as the suffix has remained unchanged so has the basic technology. The printers of today are mostly **bitmap** devices where the output is composed of innumerable dots. A printer having a resolution of 600×600 d.p.i. will print 600 dots per inch both vertically and across. UNIX systems were not designed to handle such printers.

These modern printers accept input that is formatted in a **page description language** (PDL). Today, these PDL options have narrowed down to just two—Adobe's Postscript and Hewlett Packard's PCL. Postscript is a programming language characterized by the presence of a host of parentheses, curly braces and slashes. UNIX commands don't produce output in this format, which means the traditional UNIX character output is totally unacceptable to a Postscript printer.

To harmoniously blend the two technologies, the character data is passed through an **interface program**. This interface is simply a shell script which controls some options like printing the banner page, setting the page dimensions and specifying the control codes used by the printer. The interface often calls up an external program like Ghostscript (**gs**) or **netpr** to finally print the file.

Note

The interface program can be considered equivalent to Microsoft Windows print driver, which you need to specify when installing a printer. If you don't specify the interface program correctly, the printer will not print correctly (if at all).

Linux

The lpd System

Spooling is performed by the **lpd** daemon in Linux, which uses the BSD system. To check whether it is running, use this:

```
ps ax | grep lpd
```

If it is not running, look for "S" scripts matching the pattern S*lpd (for **lpd**) in rc2.d or rc3.d:

```
ls /etc/rc.d/rc2.d/S*lpd
```

Linux has a number of utilities that can generate Postscript output. **gs**, **a2ps** and **enscript** are some of them. Use the **a2ps** command to generate Postscript from ASCII input. For inverse conversion, use **ps2ascii**.

22.15 Administering an SVR4 Printer

Apart from **lp**, the spooling system consists of these major components:

- User commands like **cancel** (for canceling jobs) and **lpstat** (for monitoring the print queue). A user can cancel only jobs submitted by her.
- The administrator's commands like **lpadmin**, **lpsched**, **lpshut**, **accept** and **reject**, **enable** and **disable**.

Unfortunately, there's no standard location for these commands. You may find some of them in /usr/lib and some in /usr/sbin. The chief command in the set is the **lpadmin** program. This command is used to add or remove a printer, or modify its configuration. It has a number of options that are used to

- Assign the printer name (-p).
- Define a class (-c).
- Specify the interface script (-e and -i).
- Specify the printer's device file (-v).
- Define the printer model (-m).
- Set the default printer (-d).
- Remove a printer (-x).

lpadmin considers the final recipient of the print output to be the *destination* rather than a printer. This destination may be a single printer or a *class* of similar printers. The ability to define a class is most useful when there are a group of identical printers. If three jobs are fired to the same class, **lpsched** would direct them to separate printers of that class. If all printers are busy, the job would be automatically diverted to the one that is freed first.

lp spools all requests in the directory /var/spool/lp/request. Every printer defined by **lpadmin** has a directory here. Unlike the BSD system, this directory doesn't hold a copy of the file unless **lp** is used with the -c option. If you make changes to a file after it has been spooled, the method of invocation of **lp** determines whether the changes are seen in the final output.

lp also creates a lock file /usr/spool/lp/SCHEDLOCK to make sure a second instance of **lpsched** is not started. If printing terminates abnormally—say on account of a power outage—this file is not removed. In that case, remove this file before you reinvoke **lpsched**.

22.15.1 Adding a Printer

The significance of these options and commands is best understood by adding a printer to the system. If **lpsched** is running, you have to stop it first with **lpshut** (Solaris excepted) and then use **lpadmin** to install the printer:

```
# lpshut
Print services stopped
# lpadmin -p pr1 -m epson -v /dev/lp0
```

This assigns the name *pr1* to the printer having the model type epson and attached to the device /dev/lp0. This also copies the interface program for the printer from /usr/spool/lp/model to /usr/spool/lp/interface (/etc/lp/interfaces in Solaris). Standard interface programs are kept in the model directory, and the installation process copies the right one to the interface(s) directory. **lp** uses the copied program rather than the original one.

The interface program is actually a shell script invoked by **lpsched** with a number of arguments. These include the username, number of copies, filenames and the job-id. The script takes input from the specified filenames, formats it to suit the printer for which it is designed and dispatches it to the standard output. This output is redirected to the device file that was set when configuring the printer with the -v option.

The above invocation defined a simple printer. You can also define it to belong to a class with the -c option. The class is created if it doesn't exist:

```
lpadmin -p pr1 -m epson -v /dev/lp0 -c c1                    pr1 belongs to class c1
```

The -p option is used both to add a printer and to modify its configuration. Further, many commands of the lp subsystem use this option to specify the printer. Now, start **lpsched**, direct **lp** to start accepting requests, and then enable the printer:

```
# lpsched
Print services started.
# accept pr1
destination "pr1" now accepting requests
# enable pr1
printer "pr1" now enabled                                   Printer now installed and ready
```

We haven't yet defined a default printer (or class) for the system, and it's time we defined one. The -d option sets the default printer:

```
lpadmin -d pr1                                          Sets default printer to pr1
lpadmin -d cla1                                          Sets default to class cla1
```

You have to use the -m option to change the interface program if the existing one doesn't work properly. If you are satisfied with your interface, then when you add a similar printer, you can instruct **lpadmin** (with -e) to copy the interface program of an existing printer:

```
lpadmin -ppr1 -m HPLaserJet                       Uses interface program of HPLaserJet
lpadmin -ppr3 -e pr1                                   Uses interface program used by pr1
```

The -x option removes a printer from the system provided there are no jobs queued on that printer:

```
lpadmin -x pr1                                             Removes printer pr1
```

Note

The default printer is first set by the LPDEST variable. If it is undefined, then the default value set by **lpadmin -d** is used. If there is no default printer defined, the print request is rejected by **lp**.

22.15.2   lpstat: Obtaining Printer and Job Status

lpstat has a number of options that provide the status information of printers and jobs. The -r option shows whether lpsched is running:

```
# lpstat -r
scheduler is running
```

Without options, **lpstat** shows the status of all requests submitted by the user who executed the command. The administrator can also obtain the list of jobs lined up for a specific printer:

```
# lpstat -ppr1                                            Can also use -p pr1
pr1-323      romeo      345670     Jan 10 13:26    on laser
pr1-324      romeo        3659     Jan 10 13:30
pr1-325      juliet      23678     Jan 10 13:40
```

Jobs can also be listed by user (-u), and an informative listing can be obtained with the -t option:

```
# lpstat -t
scheduler is running
system default destination: pr1
device for pr1: /dev/lp0
pr1 accepting requests since Fri Dec 12 10:06:04 1997
printer pr1 waiting for auto-retry. available.
     stopped with printer fault
pr1-1                        henry                1897    Dec 12 10:37
```

Note

The scheduler is stopped with **lpshut** and started with **lpsched**. When **lpsched** is restarted, all suspended jobs will start printing from the beginning.

22.15.3 `accept and reject`: Controlling Spooling

A number of commands control the spooling activity. You often have to resort to their use when the traffic is high or a printer is down. You must be able to control input coming to the spooler and divert jobs from one printer to another.

The **cancel** *(6.16.2)* command is used to cancel any job. However, when the spooler traffic is high, you should use the **accept** and **reject** commands to control input to the spooler itself. **reject** inhibits spooling, and if the `-r` option is used to specify the reason, a user attempting to print a job on a "rejected" printer will see the reason as the message:

```
# reject -r"Spooler very busy" laser epson
destination "laser" will no longer accept requests
destination "epson" will no longer accept requests
```

The **accept** command is used to permit spooling. This command has to be run every time a new printer is added to the system. However, both **accept** and **reject** can't affect the status of pending jobs.

22.15.4 `enable and disable`

accept allows spooling, but that doesn't automatically imply that jobs will be printed. For that to happen, the target printer has to be *enabled*, which is also done once—when a printer is added. But there are situations when a particular printer has to be shut down, for instance, when there is a jamming of paper. The **disable** command halts printing activity on the printer:

```
disable -r"Jamming of paper; just a minute" lwriter
```

Unlike **reject**, **disable** doesn't prevent jobs from being submitted to the spooler nor does it abort printing of a current job. All jobs meant for a disabled printer can only be printed when the printer is enabled with **enable**.

22.15.5 `lpmove`: Moving Jobs to a Different Printer

When a printer is disabled in this way, you can use **lpmove** to move jobs to another printer. The command can be used in two ways:

```
lpmove prl-321 prl-322 laser              Moves the two jobs to laser
lpmove prl laser                          Moves all jobs of prl to laser
```

In the second case, **lpmove** invokes an implicit **reject** on the source printer. Here, it means that printer *prl* can no longer accept requests after all jobs on it have been moved.

Linux

Administering a Linux Printer

Linux uses the older Berkeley print system. It is somewhat crude and is not as comprehensive as the AT&T system. Jobs here are printed with the **lpr** command

(6.16—Linux) and uses the **lpd** daemon. Compared to its SVR4 counterpart, the printing system has fewer commands in its arsenal:

- User commands like **lprm** (for canceling jobs) and **lpq** (for monitoring the print queue).
- The administrator's command **lpc** which takes care of all printer and spooling functions that are performed by separate commands in SVR4.

Unlike AT&T's **lpadmin**, Linux doesn't have a command line tool to install a printer. Linux systems offer menu-based software for configuring a printer. Most of the input you provide through front-ends ultimately end up in a text file—/etc/printcap. This database stores all printer attributes like its name, the interface script, spool directory, device file and so on. You can edit the file directly, but that is something you should only attempt when you are familiar with the variables and codes used in the file.

When a user submits a job to the print spooler, **lpr** looks up /etc/printcap for the directory where the file is to be placed. A copy of the file is then placed there. This queue is monitored by the printer daemon **lpd**. When **lpd** finds a job waiting to be printed, it spawns another copy of itself. The new **lpd** process then invokes the interface program specified in /etc/printcap to print the job.

Most of the commands in this system understand the -P option (-p in System V), which is used to specify the printer. If this option is not used, the command uses the default printer defined for the system.

lpq and lprm: Obtaining Printer and Job Status

lpq prints the print queue. If it is used with the -P printer option, the queue of that printer is displayed. By default, **lpq** prints the status of jobs on the default printer:

```
# lpq
lp is ready and printing
Rank    Owner    Job  Files                        Total Size
active  sumit     48  (standard input)             1972 bytes
1st     sumit     49  searchlist.html              61061 bytes
2nd     henry     50  (standard input)             17746 bytes
```

The fact that **lpq** shows the first job as "active" confirms that the **lpd** daemon is running. Otherwise, it would have been shown as the "1st" job. The job number is shown in the third column. Unlike **lpstat**, **lpq** also shows the filename unless the input is fed from a pipeline, in which case, it is shown as standard input.

You can obtain a comprehensive output of the status of your print queue by using **lpq** with the -l option:

```
# lpq -l
lp is ready and printing

sumit: active                              [job 048uranus]
        (standard input)                   1972 bytes
```

```
sumit: 1st                                    [job 049uranus]
        searchlist.html                       61061 bytes
```

The **lprm** command removes jobs from the print queue. A nonprivileged user can also use this command, but the command works only on jobs owned by her. However, when the command is used by the super user with a - as argument, all jobs are dequeued. **lprm** can also remove all jobs associated with a printer or those owned by a user:

```
lprm -                                          Removes all jobs in queue
lprm −Phpl                                      Removes all jobs in printer hpl
lprm henry                                      Removes all jobs owned by henry
```

Note

The default printer is first set by the PRINTER variable. If it is undefined, then the default value set in /etc/printcap is used. If there is no default printer defined there, the print request is rejected by **lpr**.

/etc/printcap: The Master Database

The BSD lpd system uses /etc/printcap as its database for storing all printer specifications. The file has a cryptic structure similar to /etc/termcap—one that stores terminal definitions. Some of the variables with all the :s and #s can sometimes be difficult to interpret. Unless you are sure of what you are doing, it's better you let your front-end software (like **printtool** in Red Hat) modify this file—at least initially.

printcap is divided into sections, and each section stores a printer definition. The definition starts with the name of the printer, delimited from its aliases by a |. Let's have a look at a sample printcap entry for an HP Deskjet 500 printer:

```
lp|lwriter|cdj500-a4-auto-mono-300|cdj500 a4 auto mono 300:\
        :lp=/dev/lp0:\
        :sd=/var/spool/lpd/cdj500-a4-auto-mono-300:\
        :lf=/var/spool/lpd/cdj500-a4-auto-mono-300/log:\
        :af=/var/spool/lpd/cdj500-a4-auto-mono-300/acct:\
        :if=/var/lib/apsfilter/bin/cdj500-a4-auto-mono-300:\
        :la@:mx#0:\
        :tr=:cl:sh:sf:
```

The printer here has the name lp, lwriter or cdj500-a4-auto-mono-300. You can use any of these names with the -P option. The other lines contain a printing attribute each, and they are delimited by colons. All newlines in printcap have to be escaped by the \ except in the last line of a definition.

Every printing attribute is of the form *variable=value*. printcap accepts a number of these variables which control things like the printer device name, the spool directory, page dimensions, filtering programs and access to printers. In this section, we'll confine ourselves to just a few essential ones.

lp here is both a printer name and a variable, and you should make no mistake about its significance from the context in which it is used. The lp variable here sets the printer to /dev/lp0—a parallel port. There are three parallel ports Linux systems use (lp1 and lp2 are the others), so make sure you have selected the device name correctly.

The spool directory (sd) is the directory in /var/spool/lpd where **lpr** dumps files for printing. Notice that it has the printer name as the directory name. For each file, **lpr** creates two files with cf and df prefixes in the spool directory. The "df" file contains the file's unfiltered data, while the "cf" file contains control information.

if sets the input filter. Here, it refers to an interface shell script stored in /var/lib/apsfilter/bin. Input filters usually call up an X Window–based graphic program (like **gs**, the Ghostscript program) to print graphic output. We'll ignore the other printing attributes.

The spool directory also contains a lock file which prevents two jobs from accessing the printer at the same time. The lock file contains the "cf" number of the currently active job and the PID of the **lpd** daemon. This file is removed after the printing is complete and a new one created for the next job. If there is a power outage in the midst of printing, you have to remove this file manually.

After you make changes to the printcap file, you must restart the **lpd** daemon. The **lpd** script in init.d supports the reload and restart arguments in addition to start and stop. You can either use this script or the *rc* script that is linked to it:

```
/etc/rc.d/init.d/lpd restart                                    Or reload
/etc/rc.d/rc3.d/S60lpd restart                                  The rc script
```

lpc: Printer Control

The **lpc** command handles all printer control functions. The command when used by itself produces the lpc> prompt. You can enter all internal commands from this prompt. They are used to

- Enable and disable spooling (**enable** and **disable**).
- Enable and disable the printer (**start** and **stop**).
- Enable and disable everything (**up** and **down**).
- Control the printer daemon (**abort** and **restart**).
- Display spooling and printing status (**status**).
- Move a job to the top of the queue (**topq**).

Enter **help** at the lpc> prompt to display a list of the complete functions. **lpc** can also be run in the noninteractive mode by using any of these commands as its own argument. Some of these functions are common to the AT&T system, so we'll briefly describe them here.

All these commands except **topq** use the printer name as an optional argument. If it is not supplied, the default printer is used. System V users need to note that **lpc** uses the functions **enable** and **disable** to control *spooling* and not printing. We'll use one of them from the shell's command line, and the other at the lpc> prompt:

```
# lpc enable lwriter                                            Shell prompt shown
lpc> disable lwriter                                            lpc's prompt shown
```

GOING FURTHER

The **start** and **stop** commands control the printing activity (like **enable** and **disable** in AT&T), but they additionally control the starting and stopping of **lpd**. To control everything including spooling and printing, you have to use the **up** and **down** commands. Like the **reject** command of the AT&T system, **down** also accepts a message as an argument:

```
up lwriter
down lwriter "Printer is down"                          This is stop and disable
```

You can change a job's priority in a "limited" way; you can only move it to the top of the queue and not anywhere else:

```
topq lwriter 52                                 Moves job number 52 to top
topq lwriter henry                             Moves all of henry's jobs to top
```

The **status** command shows the current state your printing system is in. The command can be used by any user:

```
lpc> status lwriter
lwriter:
        queuing is enabled
        printing is enabled
        no entries
        printer idle
```

Tip

To terminate printing of the current job immediately, use **lpc**'s **abort** command.

SUMMARY

The root user account is used for system administration. The **su** command can also be invoked from any user account to acquire root's powers. Most of the administrative commands are resident in /sbin and /usr/sbin. The PATH doesn't include the current directory.

The administrator can change the attributes of any file, kill any process and change any user's password. She sets the system date, addresses all users simultaneously (**wall**), reminds them about their engagements (**calendar**) and sets a limit on the file size (**ulimit**).

A user can be added (**useradd**), modified (**usermod**) and removed from the system (**userdel**). User details are maintained in the files /etc/passwd, /etc/shadow and /etc/group. The password is kept in an encrypted manner in shadow. Users on some systems can change their login shell themselves (**chsh**).

The *set-user-id* bit (SUID) of a file allows a user to run a program that temporarily acquires the powers of its owner during the instance of the program. This lets a user modify system files or write into system directories by using these commands rather than directly.

The *sticky bit* on an ordinary file keeps the file permanently in the swap area. When used on a directory, it lets users belonging to a group create and remove their own files but not those of other group members. Many UNIX system directories like /tmp and /var/tmp have this bit set, the reason why users can write to these directories without infringing on security.

A restricted shell doesn't allow a user to change her directory, execute commands placed in other directories, or even create files. To be accessible, system commands must be linked to files placed in a user's nonchangeable directory.

The **init** process maintains the system at specific *run levels* and spawns a **getty** at every terminal to enable users to log in. **init** reads its instructions from /etc/inittab and is responsible for running the system *daemons* (processes) associated with a specific run level. Run level 2 or 3 represents the normal multiuser operation, and 1 or s represents single-user operation.

The **shutdown** program kills processes and unmounts file systems before powering down a machine. **init** can also be used with the run level as argument (0 or 6) to power down the machine. In Linux, the *[Ctrl][Alt][Del]* sequence also shuts down a machine.

Floppies are formatted with **format** or **fdformat**. **dd** uses a raw device and is used to copy diskettes and tapes. UNIX provides an entire group of commands to handle DOS diskettes. They start with the string dos for System V and m for Linux.

cpio takes a list of files from the standard input to group them into an archive. It is quite suitable for use with **find** in a pipeline. It uses key options for copying to a media (-o), restoring from it (-i) and displaying the archive (-it). It won't, by default, overwrite an older file unless the -u option is specified. Wild cards can be used to restore groups of files.

tar is more suitable for backing up a directory tree. It too uses key options for copying to a media (-c), restoring from it (-x) and displaying the archive (-t). It can append to an archive (-r and -u) and also keep several versions of the same file. GNU **tar** adds compression (-z and -Z) to the archiving activity.

The **du** command reports the usage of every user's home directory tree. The administrator uses **find** to locate files that have not been used for prolonged periods. The power of **find** is enhanced when used with **xargs**, which runs a command just once or a specified number of times, rather than every time a file is found.

GOING FURTHER

For enforcing security, the administrator uses the **passwd** command to implement *password aging* so users are forced to change their passwords after a certain time has elapsed (-x). A user's account can be locked (-l), or the user can be forced to change her password on first login (-f).

The system processes are started from the *rc* scripts in /etc and other scripts in its subdirectories. The scripts to be executed for a specific run level are maintained in separate directories. The "K" scripts are used to kill processes, and the "S" scripts are meant to start them. All these scripts are linked to the ones held in /etc/init.d.

The terminal definitions are accessed by **getty** from /etc/gettydefs. The file can be configured to let **getty** attempt to match sets of parameters in turn. The default terminal types are stored in /etc/ttytype on many systems. You can set up multiple login sessions on your PC, using a virtual terminal for each. You can run different jobs on them and have separate displays for each.

On System V, the **lpsched** daemon monitors and activates the print queue. **lpadmin** is used to add, modify and set the default printer. **lpstat** displays the status of print requests. **accept** makes the print queue ready for accepting jobs, and **reject** inhibits spooling altogether. The printer must be enabled (**enable**) for printing, but sometimes has to be disabled (**disable**). Jobs in the queue can be moved (**lpmove**) to another printer.

Linux uses the BSD printing system. **lpd** is the printer daemon that monitors the print queue. **lpq** prints the status of the queue, and **lprm** removes jobs from the queue. The printer specifications are stored in /etc/printcap. Printing and spooling control is achieved with **lpc**. You can enable and disable printers (**start** and **stop**), and turn spooling on and off (**enable** and **disable**). A job can also be moved to the top of the queue (**topq**).

UNIX printing programs pass print data to an *interface* program—a filter which formats it in accordance with the printer's specifications. The filter often calls up an external program to do the actual printing.

SELF-TEST

22.1   Where are the administrator's commands located?
22.2   How does the behavior of the **calendar** command change when invoked by the super user?
22.3   Where is the password stored?
22.4   How does the administrator address all users simultaneously?
22.5   Create a user john with user-id 212 and belonging to the dialout group. john will use bash as his shell and be placed in the /home directory.
22.6   How can you change your shell without using the root account?
22.7   What is the name of the UNIX kernel?
22.8   How do you determine the default run level of the system?
22.9   What is the fastest method of initiating the shutdown procedure in Linux?
22.10 How will you use **shutdown** to bring down the system immediately?
22.11 What are the two important roles of **init**?
22.12 What is the difference between run levels 0 and 6?
22.13 Can you print a file when the system is in single-user mode?
22.14 What should you do immediately after you have made changes to /etc/inittab?

EXERCISES

22.1   How does the behavior of the **passwd** command change when invoked by the super user?
22.2   Which variable is set by reading the first field of /etc/passwd?
22.3   **telnet** sometimes doesn't permit root logins. How will you then change a file writable only by root on a remote host?
22.4   Why was the password encryption moved from /etc/passwd to /etc/shadow?

22.5   How can you prevent user kathy from logging on to her account without using the **passwd** command?

22.6   A user after logging in is unable to change directories or create files in her home directory. How can that happen?

22.7   How is a user able to update /etc/shadow with **passwd** even though the file doesn't have write permission?

22.8   The letter t was seen in the permissions field of a listing. What does this t indicate?

22.9   How will you arrange for a group of users to write to the same directory and yet not be able to remove one another's files?

22.10 How can you create another user with the same powers as root?

22.11 What does this command do?

```
find / -perm -4000 -mount -print
```

22.12 What is run level 1? Name four activities that you can't perform in this state.

22.13 How can the system administrator arrange to monitor the free disk space every hour on a working day between 9 a.m. and 10 p.m.?

22.14 Write a shell script to implement the **DISKCOPY** command of DOS.

22.15 How do you copy all HTML files to a DOS floppy in (i) SVR4 (ii) Linux?

22.16 You plan to back up all files you have worked with today. What should you do first after logging in, and how do you back them up with **cpio**?

22.17 Archive a directory structure /home/local/bin with **tar** and compress it to a disk file with **gzip**.

22.18 Archive the directory tree htmldoc on a remote machine *jupiter* with **tar** but create the archive on your local hard disk. When will the command not work?

GOING FURTHER

22.19 Where is the password aging information kept? How will you ensure that a user changes her password every four weeks?

22.20 Use the **passwd** command to prevent kathy from using her account.

22.21 What is the significance of the *start* and *kill* scripts?

22.22 If a terminal is not showing the login prompt, what's the first thing you should check?

22.23 Where are the speed and terminal settings kept on an SVR4 system? How will you ensure that a terminal is connected at one and only one speed?

22.24 Devise a sequence which shows whether the printer daemon is running irrespective of whether the system is using SVR4 or Linux.

22.25 What is an interface script?

22.26 Is the data to be printed held in a spool directory? If so, where?

22.27 Even though **lpsched** is running, you are not able to print on your printer *laser1*. What commands would you first try?

22.28 What is the difference between **accept** and **enable** as the terms are applied to printing in SVR4?

KEY TERMS

bitmap device *(22.14)*

page description language
  (PDL) *(22.14)*

password aging *(22.11)*

printer interface program *(22.14)*

rc **script** *(22.12)*

root user *(22.1)*

run level *(22.5.2)*

set-group-id (SGID) *(22.4.1)*

set-user-id (SUID) *(22.4.1)*

sticky bit *(22.4.2)*

super user

system administrator

virtual terminal *(22.13.3)*

## CHAPTER 23

TCP/IP Network Administration

In the two concluding chapters of the book we visit TCP/IP again—this time from the network administrator's point of view. The age of standalone machines is over; today users even run applications across the network. Network administration has thus become an essential and specialized component of administrative activity. In large installations, the network administrator is often different from the system administrator.

A certain amount of TCP/IP theory has been provided at the beginning of the chapter. We'll learn to set up a simple TCP/IP network and configure it to access hosts in other networks. We'll set up the basic Internet services with the Internet daemon and also connect to the Internet using a dialup line. This chapter also introduces two late entrants to the TCP/IP family—PPP and NFS. The power services used by a network, like DNS, SMTP email and HTTP are taken up in the last chapter.

Objectives

- Understand the functioning of a TCP/IP network and the IP addressing system. *(23.1)*
- Install the network interface card and configure it with **ifconfig**. *(23.2 and 23.3)*
- Troubleshoot a network with **ping**. *(23.4)*
- Learn how TCP/IP handles *routing* and create routes using **route**. *(23.5)*
- Display the network statistics with **netstat**. *(23.6)*
- Learn the role of **inetd** in handling the basic TCP/IP services like **ftp** and **telnet**. *(23.7)*
- Understand the characteristics of the *Point-to-Point Protocol. (23.8)*
- Connect your Linux machine to the Internet with **dip** and **chat**. *(23.9)*
- Understand the two important protocols used for authentication over PPP—*PAP* and *CHAP*. *(23.10)*
- Learn the functioning and configuring of the *Network File System. (23.11)*

23.1 TCP/IP and the Addressing System

TCP/IP is a layered product, and various logical layers handle its various functions. Two protocols handle a lot of the important work:

- **Transmission Control Protocol** (TCP) — TCP is responsible for ensuring the reliability of transmission and has robust error-detection and recovery facilities. It divides the data it receives from the application into segments (or packets) and encapsulates each with a checksum and a sequence number to facilitate reassembly in the right order at the other end. This packet also contains the source and destination port numbers *(11.1.4)*. It resends a segment if it is not received in uncorrupted form on the other side.

TCP is also *connection-oriented*; it makes sure the remote system is ready to exchange data by first undertaking a handshaking exercise with its peer. A **connection** is established when this handshaking is successful, and TCP then proceeds with data transfer. Most applications use TCP, but some applications (like RealVideo) can't afford these overheads, and use an alternate protocol like UDP instead. UDP doesn't guarantee reliability, nor is it connection-oriented.

- **Internet Protocol** (IP) — A packet passing through the TCP layer moves next to the IP layer. IP determines where a packet has to go and where it comes from. It provides the source and destination IP addresses to a TCP segment and also has a vital role to play in *routing* (i.e., directing) the packet to its proper destination. If a packet is meant for a host on the same network, IP sends it directly to the network. If it is meant for a host on a different network, IP directs the packet to the nearest router, "hoping" that this router is indeed the closest one to the destination.

Note the two distinct roles played by TCP and IP. TCP specifies the port numbers—the *applications* that have to be connected. IP knows which *machine* a packet goes to and where it comes from.

Before taking on a TCP/IP network, you ought to know something about the way machines are addressed in a network. Each machine is fitted with a network interface card which is connected by wire to the corresponding cards in other machines. All communication between hosts normally takes place through these network interfaces only.

Every Ethernet network card has a 48-bit physical address hard-coded into the board by the hardware manufacturer. This address is known as the **MAC address** (Media Access Control) or **Ethernet address**. It comprises a set of six colon-delimited hexadecimal numbers and typically looks like this:

```
00:00:E8:2E:47:0C
```

Apart from this address, TCP/IP also understands an **IP address**—a logical software address (the Internet address) that you have used with some of the TCP/IP tools. Even though every hostname is converted to its corresponding IP address, TCP/IP has to finally convert the IP address to the corresponding MAC address of the host.

There are also a number of rules governing the allotment of these IP addresses. Consider the following 32-bit address, which is broken up for convenience into four octets:

```
11000000 10101000 00000001 10100000
```

This binary form converts to 192.168.1.160 in decimal. This address consists of two portions—a **network address** and a **host address**. The maximum number each octet can have is 255. The network address is common to all hosts in the same network and may use one to three octets from the left; the remaining octets are used by the host. Here, 192.168.1 is the network address. By convention, we fill up the host portion with zeroes, so this should actually read 192.168.1.0.

The number of octets that go into the network component is determined by the **subnet mask**. This again is a series of four octets, where the individual bits of the network portion of the address are set to 1. The above network would have 255.255.255.0 as the subnet mask. The number of octets set to 255 by this mask is determined by certain rules. TCP/IP uses this mask to determine whether a packet belongs to the current network or not. We have something more to discuss about this mask a little later.

On the Internet, addresses are considered to belong to one of three **classes**. The number of octets reserved for the network address and the *value of the first octet* determine the class to which the network belongs. The three classes are as shown in Table 23.1.

You can easily tell the type of network by looking at this first octet. For instance, 148.27.3.12 is a Class B address, and 192.142.3.67 is a Class C address. 148.27.0.0 is the network address in one, and 192.142.3.0 in the other.

When you have a Class B network, you can have 65,534 hosts in it—a number which you may never need. If you "subnet" the network by using up the third octet, you can have 126 hosts, which could be lower than your requirements. TCP/IP also allows "borrowing" bits from an octet that normally forms the component of the host address. So if the first two bits are borrowed from the third octet by the above Class B network (148.27), then the subnet mask changes to 255.255.192.0 (128 + 64 = 192).

When allotting IP addresses, you'll have to keep these points in mind:

- TCP/IP needs a separate address for each machine for *broadcasting* a message to all hosts. The **broadcast address** is obtained by setting the host portion of the IP address to 255. This means that our network 192.168.1.0 has 192.168.0.255 as the broadcast address and 255.255.255.0 as the subnet mask.
- TCP/IP treats a machine without an interface card as a **localhost** which needs a separate address—a **loopback address**. This is the address 127.0.0.1, and you can use it to run networking services on a stand-alone host.
- The addresses used on the Internet should not be used in the local network even if the network is not connected to the Internet. A block of addresses from each class has been reserved for use by local internets and is shown in the last column of Table 23.1.

With this background, you should be able to set the addresses for a network. For instance, you could choose the Class C address 192.168.5.0 as your network address. In that case, you can have host addresses between 192.168.5.1 and 192.168.5.254. The network and broadcast addresses then become 192.168.5.0 and 192.168.5.255, respectively, and are unavailable for allocation.

TABLE 23.1 *The Network Classes and Reserved Addresses*

Network Class	Value of First Octet	Subnet Mask	Network Addresses for Intranets
A	1–126	255.0.0.0	10.0.0.0 – 10.255.255.255
B	128–191	255.255.0.0	172.16.0.0 – 172.31.255.255
C	192–223	255.255.255.0	192.168.0.0 – 192.168.255.255

Tip

The respective octets of the subnet mask and the broadcast address always add up to 255. You can easily calculate one if you know the other.

23.2   Setting Up the Network Interface Card

You need an Ethernet card on every machine that has to be connected in a network. The UNIX system identifies the network interface at the time of booting just as it identifies hard disks and CD-ROM drives. Most systems install the interface along with the necessary drivers at the time of system installation, but vendors also provide specific tools to add a card later.

When you set up your network interface card, the system *may* try to set two hardware parameters automatically, but you'll have to provide them if it can't. In general, these are the parameters that have to be set if your UNIX machine has to function properly in the network:

- The I/O address (a hardware parameter).
- The interrupt vector (a hardware parameter).
- The IP address.
- The subnet mask.
- The broadcast address.
- The gateway address.
- The hostname.
- The domain name.

The I/O address is a hexadecimal number (typically 0x300). IRQ is an integer (typically 2 or 9). If your machine sets values for these parameters automatically, then you need not bother. Otherwise, you have to set them yourself on the card before you proceed. For PCs, you may have to run a small DOS program provided by the manufacturer after the card is inserted into the machine. You have to make sure the I/O address and IRQ don't conflict with the ones used by the other devices of your system (like the keyboard, hard disks and serial ports).

After these two parameters are supplied, the machine must identify the card correctly at the time of booting. Many systems support the **dmesg** command which simply prints the boot messages. If the interface is installed properly, you should see something like this in the **dmesg** output:

```
ne2k-pci.c:vpre-1.00e 5/27/99 D. Becker/P. Gortmaker
ne2k-pci.c: PCI NE2000 clone 'RealTek RTL-8029' at I/O 0x6200, IRQ 10.
eth0: RealTek RTL-8029 found at 0x6200, IRQ 10, 00:80:C8:02:24:78.
```

The system here recognizes an NE2000 PCI network card, and shows the I/O address set to 0x6200 and IRQ to 10. The MAC address of the card is also shown at the end. This interface has a name, and it's known as eth0 to the system. Many of the networking tools specifically display this name in their output. If this machine has another interface, it would have been named eth1. eth is the prefix Linux uses to name its interface cards, so this must be a Linux system. Other UNIX systems follow a naming pattern derived from the manufacturer of the card or the chip set. You may have seen names like ie0, en0, le0 and so forth.

This brings us to the second part of the configuration—the software part. You must now define sets of four octets—for IP address, subnet mask, broadcast address and gateway address. This information is used by the **ifconfig** and **route** commands at the time of startup. The machine also uses the **hostname** command to set your machine's FQDN from the input you provide. The subnet mask and broadcast address are often determined automatically by the system from the IP address you provide when your network is not subnetted.

You have to provide the gateway address only if your machine is connected to a gateway or router. TCP/IP banishes the distinction between the two that has traditionally been made by networking technology. A gateway may sometimes be the only way for your host to connect to the Internet or to another network. It is generally a dedicated device, but a machine with two interface cards can also act as a gateway—one for each network. In fact, if a machine is connected to four networks, it must have four such cards.

23.3   ifconfig: **Configuring the Network Interface**

Since TCP/IP is independent of the network hardware, the IP addresses are not built into the kernel, but rather reside in the networking software. You have to use the **ifconfig** command to set the IP address of your interface. The command is used like this:

```
ifconfig eth0 192.168.0.3
```

The syntax requires the command to be followed by the interface name (here, eth0) and the IP address. This not only sets an IP address to the interface, but also brings it up. On non-Linux machines, this command is adequate to prepare your machine for use on the network. **ifconfig** doesn't set the interface permanently as it doesn't change any of the system's files. The command has to be run from the *rc* scripts every time the system is booted.

ifconfig optionally uses the subnet mask and the broadcast address as arguments. We didn't provide them here as they are not required if the network is not subnetted. If your network conforms to the class rules (A, B or C), then **ifconfig** computes the subnet mask and broadcast address automatically. For subnetted networks, the netmask and broadcast parameters have to be provided separately. This is how we have to use **ifconfig** for one of the hosts in a subnet:

```
ifconfig le0 147.35.3.45 netmask 255.255.192.0 broadcast 147.35.63.255
```

It's a different interface (le0) we are using this time. The broadcast address also has been specified even though it could have been derived from the subnet mask. (The corresponding bits of the host part of both always add up to 255.) It's always safe to keep it this way as many old BSD 4.2 systems used 0 instead of 1 to set the broadcast bits.

To know more about all the interfaces on your system, depending on the system you use, you may simply have to use **ifconfig** (as in Linux) or provide the -a option. This output was obtained on a machine running System V:

```
# ifconfig -a
le0: flags=4043<UP,BROADCAST,RUNNING,MULTICAST> mtu 1500
        inet 147.35.3.45 netmask ffffff00 broadcast 192.168.0.255
```

```
       perf. params: recv size: 4096; send size: 8192; full-size frames: 1
       ether 00:20:18:62:47:e0
lo0: flags=4049<UP,LOOPBACK,RUNNING,MULTICAST> mtu 8232
       inet 127.0.0.1 netmask ff000000
       perf. params: recv size: 57344; send size: 57344; full-size frames: 1
```

The output is system-variant, but you can know all the static parameters of the interface from this output. **ifconfig** here not only tells you the IP address of your machine but also its status. The system is UP, supports BROADCASTs and is currently RUNNING. Note that it also shows you the MAC address of the interface card.

There seems to be yet another interface, lo0; this is the loopback interface which every host must have. Even though **ifconfig** was not explicitly used to set its IP address to 127.0.0.1, it was actually done at the time of system installation.

ifconfig can be invoked with a specific interface name. Linux provides even the hardware parameters (the IRQ and the base address) of the interface:

```
# ifconfig eth0
eth0      Link encap:Ethernet   HWaddr 00:20:18:62:47:E0
          inet addr:192.168.0.1  Bcast:192.168.0.255  Mask:255.255.255.0
          UP BROADCAST RUNNING MULTICAST  MTU:1500  Metric:1
          RX packets:0 errors:0 dropped:0 overruns:0
          TX packets:9 errors:0 dropped:0 overruns:0
          Interrupt:9 Base address:0x300
```

ifconfig doesn't merely set or display the interface attributes. It can also be used to activate and deactivate the interface. Sometimes, that is necessary if the IP address has to be changed. The command is used in these ways:

ifconfig eth0 down	*Interface disabled*
ifconfig eth0 up	*Interface enabled*
ifconfig eth0 192.168.0.5 up	*Interface set and up*

ifconfig ensures that you'll be able to connect to all hosts in the same network (provided they too are properly set up), but you still won't be able to connect to hosts in another network. For that to happen, your system must be provided with a *route* to the network. Routing is considered shortly.

Linux

If you look at the *rc* script (or any other script executed at boot time) that contains the **ifconfig** statement, you'll often find that it is used with variables as arguments, rather than with explicit values. These scripts are meant to be general, and all variables are defined in another file. The variables are brought into the script by first executing the script containing them with the **.** or **source** commands *(17.9.1)*. This is a sensible approach followed by most Linux flavors.

23.4   ping: **Checking the Network**

Once the network interface has been configured, you have to send packets to a machine known to be working in the network. The command people use most in troubleshooting a network is **ping**. The command sends 56-byte packets to a remote destination which answers back on receipt:

```
# ping 192.168.0.4
PING 192.168.0.4 (192.168.0.4): 56 data bytes
64 bytes from 192.168.0.4: icmp_seq=0 ttl=255 time=1.442 ms
64 bytes from 192.168.0.4: icmp_seq=1 ttl=255 time=0.735 ms
64 bytes from 192.168.0.4: icmp_seq=2 ttl=255 time=0.708 ms
64 bytes from 192.168.0.4: icmp_seq=3 ttl=255 time=0.711 ms
64 bytes from 192.168.0.4: icmp_seq=4 ttl=255 time=0.744 ms
[Ctrl-c]                                                    Display interrupted
-- 192.168.0.4 ping statistics ---
5 packets transmitted, 5 packets received, 0% packet loss
round-trip min/avg/max = 0.708/0.868/1.442 ms
```

The time shown in each line is the "round-trip" time taken by a special (ICMP) packet to reach its destination and come back. Here, we see a well-connected local area network with a good response time and no "packet loss." For wide area networks, the round-trip time would be in the order of several milliseconds—which could still be within the acceptable range. If the packets arrive randomly, there could be some packet loss as well. However, TCP/IP is designed to retransmit data whenever it is lost in the network, and you need not consider packet loss as data loss.

When the host is "down or unreachable," you'll see this after the interrupt key is pressed:

```
-- 192.168.0.3 ping statistics ---
50 packets transmitted, 0 packets received, 100% packet loss
```

Note

"Pinging" a host doesn't require any server process to run at the other end. However, a successful **ping** output doesn't necessarily imply the services themselves are running. For instance, if **inetd** is not started up on the remote machine, neither **ftp** nor **telnet** will work even if **ping** reports success.

Tip

Failure to ping one host doesn't imply a connectivity problem. The remote host could be down or taken off temporarily from the network. Just try pinging another host.

23.5 Routing

A packet needs to be handled by a *router* if it is destined for a host on another network. Each host on the network maintains a **routing table** in the kernel that contains at least three fields—the name of the interface, the destination address and the IP address of the router. When IP receives a packet, it uses the subnet mask to extract from it the network portion of the destination address. It then compares this address with every entry in the table. (Note that an IP packet doesn't contain this mask.)

If IP finds the address in the routing table, it routes the packet through the gateway specified there. If not, then IP has to send the packet through a **default route**, which is also specified in the table. *IP, thus, only specifies the route to the network rather than the route to the host itself.* This is one of the most important features of IP.

Every network has a minimal routing table even if there is actually no router present. For small sized networks, the network administrator can create a **static routing** table when there are limited routes to a host.

However, the Internet uses **dynamic routing** since there are often several routes to a host on it. Here, routing daemons (like **routed**) communicate with other routing daemons on other machines to build dynamic routing tables. Routes are adjusted dynamically if the network topology changes or parts of the network go down. Routing protocols can also decide the most cost-effective route to a host. They make IP look "intelligent."

23.5.1 route: Building a Static Routing Table

The **ifconfig** command builds a minimal routing table which is good enough for hosts on the same network (Linux excepted). To forward packets to a host on another network, the routing information for the gateway has to be added to the routing table. If dynamic routing is not involved, the administrator has to manually build a static routing table. This is done with the **route** command.

To demonstrate how to set up a static routing table, let's consider the Class C network 192.168.0.0 which has the address 192.168.0.10 for the host *sunny*. The network has two gateways—*michael* (192.168.0.1) which accesses the Internet, and *fredo* (192.168.0.20) which is connected to another network 172.16.1.0. We'll have to configure the routing table on *sunny* to install the routes through the two gateways. We assume that the network interfaces on *michael* and *fredo* have already been configured with **ifconfig**.

We'll use the **route** command on *sunny* to first install the route to the non-Internet gateway (on *fredo*):

```
route add 172.16.1.0 192.168.0.20
```

We added a route (add) 172.16.1.0 to the routing table and specified that the gateway to be contacted for forwarding packets is 192.168.0.20 (the address of *fredo*).

Since *michael* acts as the gateway to the Internet, it obviously handles more *routes* (not necessarily traffic), and should, therefore, be set as the default gateway. This is done using the keyword default instead of a specific route:

```
route add default 192.168.0.1
```

Once you set up the default route this way, all packets not meant for the local network and for 172.16.1.0 are forwarded to this gateway (192.168.0.1). You can then have unhindered access to the Net. This assumes, of course, that the gateway machine is configured as a *firewall* to support *IP forwarding* or as a proxy server (not considered in this book) and has allowed this host to forward packets to this machine.

To remove a route, the delete keyword is used. The routes created above can be deleted by simply replacing the add keyword with delete:

```
route delete 172.16.1.0 192.168.0.20
route delete default 192.168.0.1
```

Linux uses a slightly different syntax for the **route** command; it uses the keyword gw to indicate a gateway. The **route add** and **route delete** commands in Linux would have to be entered as:

```
route delete 172.16.1.0 gw 192.168.0.20                          Linux uses gw
route add default gw 192.168.0.1
```

Expectedly, **route** doesn't need to know the subnet mask as long as the network is not subnetted. But when it is, the subnet mask has to be specified with the netmask keyword. Sometimes, you have to use the keyword net with the destination address to make **route** understand that we are referring to a network route. Occasionally, you may require to specify a host route, in which case the host keyword has to be used. Linux and Solaris use -net and -host instead.

As with **ifconfig**, these **route** statements will be valid as long as the machine is up. They will have to be executed every time the system is booted, so they are invariably kept in the system's startup scripts.

23.6 netstat: **Displaying the Network Parameters**

The **netstat -rn** command displays the routing table. The -r option lists the table, and -n prints the numeric form of the IP addresses. After executing the two **route add** statements in the previous section, this is what the table looks like on a Linux system:

```
# netstat -rn
Kernel IP routing table
Destination     Gateway         Genmask          Flags   MSS Window  irtt Iface
172.16.1.0      192.168.0.20    255.255.255.255 UGH      0 0         0 eth0
192.168.0.10    0.0.0.0         255.255.255.255 UH       0 0         0 eth0
192.168.0.0     0.0.0.0         255.255.255.0   U        0 0         0 eth0
127.0.0.0       0.0.0.0         255.0.0.0       U        0 0         0 lo
0.0.0.0         192.168.0.1     0.0.0.0         UG       0 0         0 eth0
```

The first line shows that any packet destined for the network 172.16.1.0 is forwarded to the machine with the IP address 192.168.0.20. The G under *Flags* indicates a gateway; if it is absent, then the hosts are directly connected. Providing a network address here makes sense as it reduces the size of the routing table.

The third line shows that packets meant for the network 192.168.0.0 are forwarded to the machine 0.0.0.0—the machine whose routing table is displayed. This machine is using its own interface to communicate with other machines of the same network. If a packet's destination address doesn't match any of the entries in the first column, then the last line is decisive. Since the destination here is 0.0.0.0, the default gateway 192.168.0.1 will be used. Here, 0.0.0.0 represents addresses not matched by any previous addresses (like the * used by **case**). Sometimes, you may see the word default in this position.

You can see that every host in a network has two interfaces—the Ethernet address (here, eth0) and the loopback address (lo). All the interfaces are up and running (*Flag* shows U). H indicates that you can reach only a single host through the route. A packet meant for the localhost (127.0.0.0) uses the same machine (0.0.0.0) as its gateway. If you have understood all this, you should be able to conclude that the machine on which this command was run has the IP address 192.168.0.10.

Note

If a machine is not connected to any host, the routing table displays only a single entry for the loopback interface. The presence of this route in the routing table means that you can use TCP/IP tools on that host.

23.7   inetd: **The Internet Daemon**

UNIX has a large number of daemons, each listening at a specific port number for a request from its respective client. Can we afford to run all these daemons constantly even though some of them may not be used most of the time? Certainly not, it makes sense to invoke them as and when required. The **inetd** daemon solves this problem.

Many TCP/IP daemons like those for the **telnet** and **ftp** services are started neither by the client nor by the system's startup scripts in rc*n*.d, but by the master Internet daemon **inetd**. **inetd** listens on *multiple* ports for any connection requests. When it detects one, it launches the program that's defined for that port in its configuration file /etc/inetd.conf. This file contains one line for each service:

```
ftp        stream   tcp    nowait    root    /usr/sbin/tcpd   in.ftpd -l -a
telnet     stream   tcp    nowait    root    /usr/sbin/tcpd   in.telnetd
talk       dgram    udp    wait      nobody  /usr/sbin/tcpd   in.talkd
pop-3      stream   tcp    nowait    root    /usr/sbin/tcpd   ipop3d
#imap      stream   tcp    nowait    root    /usr/sbin/tcpd   imapd
#tftp      dgram    udp    wait      root    /usr/sbin/tcpd   in.tftpd
```

The first column shows the service. The protocol it uses is shown in the third column. If the fourth column shows nowait, it means that multiple connections can be made for the same service. The last two columns show the absolute pathname of the server program and the complete command line of the program the server *ultimately* invokes.

All these lines have one thing in common. They are invoked, not directly by **inetd**, but through a wrapper program called **tcpd**. **tcpd** first checks in its configuration files whether the client is authorized to use this service. If it is, **tcpd** then invokes the corresponding server program. For **ftp**, this daemon is the server program **in.ftpd**, which is run with the arguments -l -a. **tcpd** also logs the request in a separate file. Network access through **tcpd** is controlled by the file hosts.deny and hosts.allow.

UNIX systems start up with a number of services, many of which may not be required at all. In that case, it's better to disable the service itself by commenting out the line. You can now understand why the trivial file transfer protocol (**tftp**) doesn't run by default on most UNIX systems.

Now, which port number does **ftp** use? This number is determined by a lookup of /etc/services. This file is related to inetd.conf through their first fields—the service name. The file contains two fields:

```
ftp             21/tcp
telnet          23/tcp
smtp            25/tcp              mail
pop3            110/tcp             # POP version 3
pop3            110/udp
```

The port number has the protocol tag affixed to it. A lookup of this table not only determines the port number used by a service but also the protocol. Many services in this file have two entries—one for tcp and the other for udp.

Note

The **tcpd** program isn't available on all systems. On some systems (like Solaris), the server program is directly started by **inetd**. For the **ftp** service, this means that **inetd** starts **in.ftpd** (or **ftpd** on older systems) directly rather than through the wrapper program **tcpd**. The last two columns of /etc/inetd.conf in that case show the same command name.

23.8 pppd: **The Point-to-Point Protocol (PPP)**

Your computer may not have a network card, or you may be living where the only means of communication with the outside world is the telephone. Today, you can link up two machines through the serial ports (COM1 and COM2 in DOS), and run TCP/IP on this link. A special protocol makes this possible—**Point-to-Point Protocol** (PPP). In the sphere of serial port communication, PPP has replaced SLIP and UUCP, which have already seen their best days. Today, it's the standard way users access the Net using a modem on their computer's serial port (though it too is making way for newer technologies).

PPP is an unusual protocol. It sets up a connection between two hosts, using its own set of IP addresses so the other protocols like **ftp** and **telnet** can run thereafter. PPP then takes no further part in the communication process except to ensure the continuity of the link. It also doesn't have separate client and server components. The same **pppd** command has to be invoked with the right options to act either like a client or a server. In this section, we'll discuss the BSD PPP package, which is used by Linux and many UNIX systems (but not Solaris).

The **pppd** command resides in /usr/sbin in Linux systems. We assume you are logged in as a root user since running **pppd** from an ordinary user account requires some configuration. If you are connecting to your ISP, you have to start the **pppd** process on your local machine like this:

```
/usr/sbin/pppd /dev/ttyS0 115200 crtscts modem defaultroute noipdefault -detach
```

/dev/ttyS0 is the modem device attached to the first serial port (COM1), and the port speed (here 115,200 bauds, i.e., bits per second) is set to at least three times the maximum speed the modem can handle. There's a reason behind this *(23.9.2)*. The command sets up another interface (ppp0) whose attributes can be displayed by the **ifconfig** and **netstat -rn** commands.

You need to run PPP between your computer (client) and your ISP's (server) to access the Internet. This implies that a similar PPP process has to run at the other end too. If the client PPP interface is set up without a separate IP address (as above), then the server has to provide this before establishing the link.

Tip

If you always have to use **pppd** with a fixed set of options, then you may keep most of these options in **pppd**'s configuration file, /etc/ppp/options. This file holds one option per line.

pppd has a complex command line, and you'd better know the complete syntax in case you have to start the process manually using a tool like **chat**. You must also understand why the command above is invoked with these options:

- Since PPP uses all 8 bits, **hardware flow control** must be used (crtscts) so the system can adjust the flow of the stream.
- **Software flow control** must be switched off. We don't want the characters *[Ctrl-s]* and *[Ctrl-q]* to be interpreted by the modem as the start and stop characters. This is assured as **pppd** here is not using the xonoff option.
- The default route (defaultroute) for any IP packet not meant for the local network has to be routed through the PPP interface.
- Most ISPs feature **dynamic addressing**, which means the server has to provide the client's IP address (noipdefault). PPP also allows you to set the IP address yourself.
- **pppd** must *not* be allowed to be detached from the terminal (-detach) or else the connection will not persist.

We'll not consider the server's options as we can safely assume your ISP knows what it is doing. However, if you set up a PPP connection between your machines at home and work, then you must know the server options too.

Note

PPP is probably the only TCP/IP tool that doesn't have separate client and server components. It is neither started by the system's startup scripts nor handled by **inetd**.

Tip

If you are using **pppd** from an ordinary user account, then you may have to set its SUID bit *(22.4.1)*. This is easily done by using **chmod a+s /usr/sbin/pppd**. Some versions of Linux merely expect the user to belong to the same group as the one that owns **pppd**.

23.9 Using PPP to Connect to the Internet

You'll now use a Linux machine to connect to an ISP—and through their gateway—to the Internet. You'll have to connect a modem to a serial port (say, COM1) and use it to dial out to the ISP. Modem installation in Linux is a straightforward affair; just set up a symbolic link between /dev/modem and /dev/ttyS0 (assuming you are using the first serial port). The listing of /dev/modem should look like this:

```
lrwxrwxrwx   1 root      root            10 Dec  5 08:44 /dev/modem -> /dev/ttyS0
```

ISPs normally use UNIX machines, and you have to log in to their computer using a username and password that have been registered with them. Once logged in, the PPP process has to be started at the server end. If the ISP's machine doesn't do it automatically (normally it does), then you have to start it. After that, you have to quit the ISP's machine *without resetting the modem* and then start PPP on your machine.

The ISP's PPP process generally allots your IP address—often dynamically from its pool of addresses. After you have started **pppd** on your machine, the link is established between your computer and the ISP's host. This link also provides you with a default route (the `defaultroute` option in **pppd**) to the Net. Your computer then becomes part of the Internet. The ISP's machine has no further role to play except to provide the PPP link which remains till we hang up.

Your ISP will also probably maintain one or more **name servers** *(24.2)* for you. These are machines that perform hostname to IP address resolution. Access to the name service is necessary because all domain names must be resolved and their IP addresses inserted inside the PPP packets before they move out of your machine. The ISP will also normally offer email services and maintain a news server so you can access newsgroups.

23.9.1 Specifying the Name Server and Resolver

Your ISP should provide you with the IP addresses of their name servers. You now need to modify two files on your Linux system. Simply insert these two lines in `/etc/host.conf`:

```
order hosts bind                                          Name service enabled with BIND
multi on
```

A **resolver** is a client *(24.2.1)* which acts on behalf of the application to request a name server to convert an FQDN to the IP address. The resolver on UNIX systems uses the configuration file `/etc/resolv.conf`. Place your ISP's name server addresses in this file (the ones shown here are used by the author's ISP):

```
nameserver 202.54.1.30                                    The IP addresses of the primary
nameserver 202.54.9.1                                     and the secondary name servers
```

This completes the resolver configuration. Your machine now knows it has to use BIND (after `/etc/hosts` fails) to resolve FQDNs, and it also knows which machines to contact for this purpose.

23.9.2 Obtaining Script Parameters

To connect to the Net, you'll use two character-based tools. Eventually, you'll learn to pass all input to the remote end through a script, but you must know what strings to expect from that side. So just dial out, observe the prompts and input the appropriate strings. **minicom** is an ideal tool for this purpose as it can be used with the Hayes' "AT" commands. These are strings starting with AT, which can dial a modem and perform some initializations too.

Before you dial out, make sure you have set the modem speed to the highest throughput that it can handle. Most modems and ISPs support data compression, which has the effect of increasing the modem's rated speed—often by a factor of 4. This means that you can safely use 115,200 bps (bits per second) as the speed for a 33.6 kbps (kilo bits per second) modem. If you are using **minicom** and a 33.6 or 56 kbps modem, invoke **minicom -s** and then set the serial port speed to the inflated figure. Quit **minicom** and then reenter normally.

You'll now have to use a couple of "AT" commands. First, reset the modem with **atz**, and then dial out with **atdt**, followed by the telephone number of the ISP. Input

FIGURE 23.1   *Logging on to an ISP's PPP Server*

```
Press ALT-Z for help on special keys

AT S7=45 S0=0 L1 V1 X4 &c1 E1 Q0
OK
atz                                                   Resetting the modem
OK
atdt5599001                                        Phone number is 5599001
CONNECT 28800/ARQ/V34/LAPM/V42BIS
User Access Verification


Username:  sumit                                  The first input string
Password:  *********                              The second input string
gicaro31> ppp                               The third input string. Note that
Entering PPP mode.                          server PPP is started manually with ppp
Async interface address is unnumbered (Ethernet0)
Your IP address is 202.54.52.240. MTU is 1500 bytes
~~y}#.!}!q} }4}"}&} }*} } }%}&Tb..}'}"}(}"!.~~y}#.!}!r} }4}"}&} }*} } }%}&Tb..}~
~~y}#.!}!q} }4}"}&} }*} } }%}&Tb..}'}"}(}"!.~~y}#.!}!r} }4}"}&} }*} } }%}&Tb..}~
 .....
```

the usual things at the two prompts requiring user verification. We assume the ISP doesn't start the **pppd** process automatically, so we'll do it ourselves. This is shown in Fig. 23.1.

The figure shows dynamic IP addressing at work; your ISP has assigned you the IP address 202.54.52.240. The "junk" you see is simply PPP packets generated at the server end. On examining this output you'll note that the three strings you should be expecting are Username:, Password: and gicaro31>. The strings you should send in return are shown beside them. We'll now develop the scripts using this information.

23.9.3   Using dip

Among the character-based dialing tools, **dip** is available in a wide variety of UNIX systems like SunOS, AIX, Ultrix and Linux. It has rudimentary programming constructs and provides logic for error-handling. It can be programmed to perform redialing too. Here's the script that you should use with the *expect-send* strings derived above:

```
# cat dipdial.dip                                  Customary to use .dip extension
get $local 0.0.0.0                                 Local IP address is dynamic
port modem                                         The symbolic link should be set up
```

```
speed 115200                                    Recommended for a 33.6 kbps modem
dialstart:
reset
flush
send atdt5599001\r                              Can also use dial 5599001
sleep 2
wait CONNECT
wait name: 20                                    Wait up to 20 seconds for name: prompt
if $errlvl != 0 goto redial                      If everything not OK
send sumit\r
wait word:
send a9h4uil\r                                    Password is visible!!
wait >                                           This takes care of gicaro31>
send ppp\r                                        Starts pppd at server
mode PPP                                          Starts pppd at client
exit
redial:
sleep 1
goto dialstart
```

This script needs little explanation as most of it has been provided already. Note that the *[Enter]* key is represented here by \r—an escape sequence understood by the **echo** command also. We used substrings to allow for minor variations in the prompt strings. For instance, name: takes care of both username: and Username:. The $errlvl variable is set to 0 when the connection is successful. The **if** statement ensures that the modem will redial if errors are encountered. Note that **dip** starts the **pppd** process at the client end with a simple statement (**mode PPP**). This has the effect of starting the **pppd** command line shown earlier.

After you have saved this in a file dipdial.dip, you have to run the **dip** command:

```
/usr/sbin/dip -v dipdial.dip
```

That's all there is to it. This should dial the modem, log you in, start PPP processes at both ends and return you the prompt. You are now on the Internet and should be able to use any of the Internet tools and the ones featured in this chapter. Use **dip -k** to terminate **pppd**. If this method works, then drop the -v (verbose) option because that displays your password on the screen.

Note

If the server starts PPP on its own, the two statements **wait >** and **send ppp\r** have to be dropped from the script.

Tip

If you have a pulse-dialing telephone system, use **atdp** instead of **atdt**. If you use a slower modem, say, 14.4 kbps, set the speed to 38,400. If your modem won't dial, try using **atx3dt** instead of **atdt**. If all this fails, try the **wvdial** and **wvdialconf** commands if they are available on your Linux system. **wvdialconf** can often configure these settings for you.

23.9.4 Using chat

If your system doesn't have **dip**, you can try the **chat** command. **chat** also uses a script, and each line in a **chat** script (barring a few lines containing ABORT) contains an *expect-send* string pair. **chat** uses a much simpler and less sophisticated script:

```
# cat chatdial.chat
'' atz                              Expect nothing before executing atz
OK atdt5599001                            Expect OK and then dial
ABORT BUSY                        Check whether your modem shows BUSY
ABORT 'RING - NO ANSWER'                    or RING - NO ANSWER
CONNECT ''                          Expect CONNECT and send nothing
name: sumit                       Now the three expect-send string pairs
word: a9h4uil
> ppp                            Not needed if server starts pppd on its own
```

A null string or response is indicated by `''`. This script takes care of BUSY and RING - NO ANSWER messages that your modem may throw up, and uses the keyword ABORT to terminate. Note that the script doesn't start PPP at the client end. We adopt a different approach here: run the **pppd** command and use its `connect` option to execute the **chat** script. The entire operation can take place in the background:

```
/usr/sbin/pppd /dev/ttyS0 115200 connect "/usr/sbin/chat -f chatdial.chat" \
crtscts modem defaultroute noipdefault -detach  &
```

Unlike **dip**, **chat** has no option to kill the **pppd** process. You can run **ps** and then kill **pppd** in the usual way. But since the PID of the **pppd** process is stored in a text file `/var/run/ppp0.pid`, you can also kill it like this:

```
kill -9 `cat /var/run/ppp0.pid`                 Define an alias for this
```

There is no facility for redialing here, so if you always manage to connect to your ISP in a single attempt, then you can use **chat**. Put this sequence in a shell script or frame an alias for easier handling.

23.9.5 After Establishing the Link

It's possible that **dip** and **chat** went through without a hitch, but you are still unable to connect to a remote site. In that case, you should first test whether your PPP interface is up by using **netstat -rn** or **route -n**:

```
# netstat -rn                              Can also use route -n
Kernel IP routing table
Destination     Gateway         Genmask           Flags Metric Ref    Use Iface
192.168.0.3     0.0.0.0         255.255.255.255 UH    0      0        0 dummy0
202.54.1.30     0.0.0.0         255.255.255.255 UH    0      0        0 ppp0
192.168.0.0     0.0.0.0         255.255.255.0   U     0      0        0 eth0
127.0.0.0       0.0.0.0         255.0.0.0       U     0      0        1 lo
0.0.0.0         202.54.1.30     0.0.0.0         UG    0      0        0 ppp0
```

You should now see two lines pertaining to ppp0. The second one shows the effect of using the `defaultroute` option with the **pppd** command. "Ping" the server, and if this works, then try pinging a known host with, say, **ping rs.internic.net**. If **ping** doesn't produce the usual output, then check the speed set for the modem in the dialing script.

pppd invokes the script **/etc/ppp/ip-up** after the link setup and **/etc/ppp/ip-down** before the link is brought down. Users whose activities are restricted to using the Web generally may not need to use these files. But **ip-up** is useful for automating the procedures that send and download mail from a server on the Net. If you have your own dialup account, then you'll want to save connect time by running the **sendmail** *(24.7.1)* and **fetchmail** *(24.11.1)* commands from this script rather than manually.

Tip

You may sometimes get the message that the modem is locked. In that case, the error message will tell you to delete the file /var/lock/LCK..modem. Follow the directive. If the write bit on /dev/modem gets disabled, then enable it with **chmod a+w /dev/modem**.

23.10 PAP and CHAP Authentication

Most ISPs use some form of authentication to verify the identity of the host. PPP supports two forms of authentication:

- **Password Authentication Protocol** (PAP). In this system, the text password and the username are sent across the network for authentication.
- **Challenge Handshake Authentication Protocol** (CHAP). This is a two-way authentication scheme where the password is not sent over the network.

Both PAP and CHAP make use of a **shared secret** that is known to both client and server. This is often the user's password and, for PAP, is stored in the file /etc/ppp/pap-secrets. Here's a typical line from the file:

```
henry       starisp.com        my:pass,word
```

The first field is the user's hostname. If the client's machine is not on the Net (as is the case with dialup connections), the ISP's machine doesn't need to know this name. PPP can be invoked to interpret this field as the username as registered with the ISP rather than a hostname. The second field is the ISP's FQDN; a * here matches all ISPs. The third field contains the shared secret, in this case, the password. The fourth field is generally kept blank.

When a user dials up to the ISP, the password is sent in clear text to the ISP's end. The link is set up only if the password matches the one the ISP maintains in its own /etc/ppp/pap-secrets file.

PAP security is just better than no security at all as a packet sniffer can intercept the text password that is transmitted. Admittedly, it's easier to do this on an Ethernet network than on a telephone line, but then it's vulnerable to attack just the same. Even though PAP is still widely used, CHAP provides a more secure form of authentication.

PPP uses CHAP as the default authentication protocol. CHAP doesn't actually exchange passwords. Rather, the server sends a **challenge string** to the client. The client responds by hashing (encrypting) the challenge string and the shared secret which it maintains in a similar form in /etc/ppp/chap-secrets. The server also carries out a similar exercise at its end since it knows the shared secret as well. It then compares its own computed hash with the one received from the client. The link is activated when the two patterns match.

To use either form of authentication, **pppd** at the server end must be invoked with the auth (authentication) option. However, the client side must invoke it with the user (here user henry) option. Since the authentication is done by computing rather than by logging in, the previous **dip** and **chat** scripts must be modified to delete all code that relates to the *expect-send* strings. For **dip**, you can remove everything after CONNECT but retain the **mode PPP** command. You'll also need to use the /etc/ppp/options file for placing more options. The **chat** script doesn't need to have anything after CONNECT.

Caution

Since the files pap-secrets and chap-secrets contain the password or the challenge strings, they must be unreadable to all except root. Otherwise, the system will be as insecure as one used without any authentication.

23.11   The Network File System

The facilities to log in remotely and transfer files using TCP/IP are often not enough. It's impractical to transfer a large database. It would be much better if the remote file system could be mounted on the local file system so the user wouldn't need to access the remote system with any special commands. Sun Microsystems felt this need and pioneered the concept of the **Network File System** (NFS), which has since been ported to practically all flavors of UNIX.

A network file system mounts a remote file system on a local directory. This provides the illusion that they are locally connected. For instance, if the /datab file system on host *fredo* is mounted locally on the directory /oracle, you'll not know whether /oracle is a local or a remote file system. No special commands are necessary to access these files on the remote (mounted) file system.

The NFS facility is useful for some reasons. Instead of encouraging users to make copies of files (as in **ftp**), NFS allows users working on several computers to share files. This means you can have a number of large disks on a few computers that can be accessed by others. It also makes system maintenance and backup easier because the administrator needs to back up and maintain a single set of files rather than back up identical copies on multiple machines.

Unlike local mounting, NFS is not restricted to mounting only file systems. *It allows you to mount any remote directory even if the directory doesn't constitute a separate file system.* Users may be allowed read or read-write permission on a directory. You can also specify the hosts permitted to use the facility. However, NFS doesn't set permissions at the user level. If you have allowed access to a host, then you are trusting all users on that host. This makes NFS somewhat insecure, especially when providing write access.

Note

When you run out of disk space on an overloaded system, instead of adding a separate hard disk, you can add a separate machine itself and then remotely mount its file systems. The advantage is that your system is up all the time.

23.11.1 Setting Up NFS

NFS is handled mainly by two daemons **mountd** and **nfsd** at the server side (**rpc.mountd** and **rpc.nfsd** in Linux). **mountd** validates the user request, while **nfsd** actually serves the client by mounting and unmounting file systems.

The commands used to handle NFS file systems are the same (**mount** and **umount**), but used here with some modifications. Most systems use BSD-type NFS, which *exports* file systems rather than Sun's Solaris which *shares* them. In this chapter, we'll discuss the BSD system, which is used by a host of vendors like HP-UX, IRIX and SCO, as well as Linux.

When the client issues a mount request, **mountd** checks up the server's /etc/exports file for verifying the access rights of the client. This file contains a line for every exported directory that can be mounted remotely. It can also specify the type of access permitted and the hosts authorized to mount the directory. Here are some typical entries from /etc/exports:

```
/                                    Read-write access to root for all hosts!
/project3/doc
/java/programs    -ro              Read-only access to all hosts
/hrd/html   -access=fredo:tessio   Access only to hosts fredo and tessio
/prog/html   -rw=michael           Read-write access to host michael
```

The format in Linux is different; it follows the directory name with a space-delimited list of one or more hosts. Each hostname is accompanied by the type of permission in parentheses. The first two lines are the same on this system too and are thus not shown:

```
/java/programs  (ro)               Read-only access to all
/hrd/html   fredo(rw) tessio(rw)
/projects       *.planets.com(rw)  All hosts in planets.com domain
```

While the first line specifies read-only permission for all machines, the second one provides read-write access to the hosts *fredo* and *tessio*. The last line allows read-write access to all hosts in the *planets.com* domain.

Once the directory is mounted, access is controlled by **nfsd**. Make sure that both **mountd** and a sufficient number of **nfsd** processes are running and then export the directories in /etc/exports with the **exportfs** command:

```
exportfs -a                        Red Hat uses same command
```

If your system doesn't have the **exportfs** command, then you need to locate the script that contains statements starting the **mountd** and **nfsd** daemons. If this script doesn't have a restart feature, then "stop" the daemons and "start" them again by providing these words as arguments to the script.

Once the server is ready, the client simply has to execute the **mount** command. This time we have to specify the file system type as nfs. Here, we try a soft mount (soft) in the background (bg) in read-only mode:

```
mount -r -F nfs -o soft,bg sunny:/project3/doc /fredo/project3
```

Soft mounting ensures that the client doesn't retry the operation if mounting fails. This mode is recommended for reading documentation. Here, even though the directory was available for mounting in read-write mode, **mount**'s -r option makes sure that /etc/exports is overruled. You can also use the remount option, which along with the other **mount** options, has already been discussed *(21.10.3).*

Like local file systems, NFS file systems can also be specified in /etc/fstab. **mount** then need not be used with such a complex set of options. The above mounting action can be performed automatically at boot time if fstab contains this entry:

```
sunny:/project3/doc  /fredo/project3 nfs ro,soft,bg 0 0
```

NFS is the most common way of sharing files across the network. It can be quite cost-effective in that it is often used to store a single copy of software on a mountable file system. The advantage here is that updates to the software are carried out at only one place. Some organizations use NFS to export the mail spool directory /var/mail for centralizing their mail.

Tip

If you are using NFS to access your own files on a remote file system, make sure your own UID and GUID match the ones on the server. If they don't, then the ls -l listing will show them as numbers rather than names. Moreover, you may not have the required access rights on your own files. In that case, you'd better modify /etc/passwd to have matching UIDs and GUIDs.

SUMMARY

The functioning of a TCP/IP network is controlled mainly by two protocols—*Transmission Control Protocol* (TCP) and *Internet Protocol* (IP). TCP is a reliable protocol. It retransmits lost segments if not received in time at the other end. IP takes care of packet addressing and forwards a packet to the nearest router if necessary.

The number of octets used to represent the network address and the value of the first octet determine the class (A, B and C) of a network. A separate set of network addresses are reserved for use by local internets. These addresses are not used on the Internet.

Every network needs separate IP addresses for *loopback* and *broadcast*. The *subnet mask* interprets an IP address to reflect whether any bits have been borrowed from the host address to form part of the network address.

The network interface card has a unique MAC address to which the IP address has to be converted for a message to reach a host. When configuring the interface, you may need to specify the IRQ and the I/O address, which should not conflict with those used by other devices of the machine.

ifconfig sets the IP address and the subnet mask of the network interface. It is also used to activate and deactivate an interface. **ping** and **netstat** are used to check the connectivity of the network.

The kernel maintains a *routing table*, which is looked up by IP for routing purposes. **route** sets up routes to a network and displays the routing table. The table indicates the gateways that have to be used for routing packets destined for external networks. A *default* route is provided in the routing table in case the lookup fails.

Many TCP/IP services like **telnet**, **ftp** and **pop3** are invoked by **inetd** by reading entries in /etc/inetd.conf. The daemons are often started by a *wrapper* program (like **tcpd**) rather than directly. The port numbers used by these services are specified in /etc/services.

The *Point-to-Point Protocol* (PPP) makes TCP/IP facilities available on a telephone line. **pppd** uses *hardware flow control*, but not *software flow control*. Most ISPs use **pppd** to provide dynamic IP addresses at both ends of the link. On invocation and before termination, **pppd** executes the **/etc/ppp/ip-up** and **/etc/ppp/ip-down** commands, respectively.

To connect to the Internet, the name server addresses have to be specified in /etc/resolv.conf. **dip** and **chat** are two script-based tools that use *expect-send* string pairs to automate the login procedure. **pppd** invokes the **chat** script, while **dip** can start the **pppd** daemon from the script itself. PPP connectivity should be checked with **netstat -rn** and **ping**.

Most ISPs use either PAP or CHAP to authenticate the user. PAP sends a clear text password stored in /etc/ppp/pap-secrets, while CHAP makes a computation using the *challenge string* and *shared secret* which is held in /etc/ppp/chap-secrets. The files are maintained at both ends of the link. CHAP is much more secure than PAP.

The Network File system (NFS) lets you mount a remote file system or a directory on a local directory. Directories along with their access rights are maintained in /etc/exports and exported with **exportfs**. NFS provides no user-level access. /etc/fstab, **mount** and **umount** are used in nearly identical manner as in a standalone host.

SELF-TEST

23.1　Name the class of network to which these IP addresses belong: (i) 202.54.9.1, (ii) 107.35.45.78, (iii) 34.67.102.34.

23.2　Can you have 11.23.34.45 and 172.26.0.6 as IP addresses of hosts on the Internet?

23.3　What are the two hardware parameters of the network interface card that you may need to set manually before configuring TCP/IP on your machine?

23.4　How do you find out the IRQ and I/O address for the network interface card of your system?

23.5　How will you disable the **ftp** service?

23.6　What protocol is mostly used in a TCP/IP dialup connection, and which command activates the service?

23.7　With which Hayes-modem command do you dial?

23.8　What does /etc/exports contain, and how can you make **mountd** read this file after you have made changes to it?

EXERCISES

23.1   How do you find out your machine's MAC address?

23.2   What is a *broadcast*, and what IP address does it use?

23.3   What is the significance of the *loopback address*?

23.4   If you are setting up a Class C intranet, what would the first two octets be if you were following the official guidelines?

23.5   How will you deactivate your network without using any of the *rc* scripts?

23.6   If **ping** shows some "packet loss," what could that indicate?

23.7   Your machine is connected to another one with the IP address 192.168.0.1 which is connected to the Internet. Assuming that the gateway machine allows you to pass packets to the Internet, how will you set up routing on your machine in SVR4 and Linux?

23.8   How do you find out the IP address of your router?

23.9   How will you disable the **telnet** service on your machine?

23.10   You are not able to run the **/usr/sbin/pppd** command from your unprivileged user account. What could be the possible reasons?

23.11   You are able to connect to an ftp site on the Internet using only the IP address, but not the FQDN. What setting have you forgotten to make considering that the name service is running in your network?

23.12   Why is CHAP authentication superior to PAP?

23.13   You need to connect to an ftp site on the Internet from a script but have to make sure the word ppp0 shows in the **netstat -rn** output before executing the **ftp** command. How do you do that?

23.14   Use a single-line **perl** program to change the password of all your .chat and .dip scripts from s1o3n5y8 to j2n98d0k2.

23.15   How will you use **mount** on an SVR4 system to access a remote directory /usr/doc on host *uranus* in read-only mode?

KEY TERMS

broadcast address *(23.1)*

Challenge Handshake Authentication Protocol **(CHAP)** *(23.10)*

challenge string *(23.10)*

connection *(23.1)*

default route *(23.5)*

dynamic addressing *(23.8)*

dynamic routing *(23.5)*

Ethernet address *(23.1)*

hardware flow control *(23.8)*

host address *(23.1)*

Internet Protocol (IP) *(23.1)*

IP address *(23.1)*

localhost *(23.1)*

loopback address *(23.1)*

MAC address *(23.1)*

name server *(23.9)*

network address *(23.1)*

network class *(23.1)*

Network File System (NFS) *(23.11)*

Password Authentication Protocol (PAP) *(23.10)*

Point-to-Point Protocol (PPP) *(23.8)*

resolver *(23.9.1)*

routing table *(23.5)*

shared secret *(23.10)*

software flow control *(23.8)*

static routing *(23.5)*

subnet mask *(23.1)*

Transmission Control Protocol (TCP) *(23.1)*

## CHAPTER 24

Going Further—Building the Internet Server

In the concluding chapter of the book, we'll use UNIX to do what it's best known for today—providing the Internet services. UNIX systems have long played a predominant role in the provision of these services. Until recently, practically all Internet servers were UNIX machines. UNIX dominated this sphere even though the technology involved was nonproprietary and based on open standards.

We take up here three important services that form the backbone of the Internet—DNS (name service), mail and Web services. An entire book is easily devoted to each one of them, so we can't possibly hope to cover most of their features. However, we'll consider their important subsets—just enough to not only understand how they work but also to set up these services "with your own hands." Fortunately, fragmentation in this arena is minimal, so what we discuss here should apply to any UNIX system. Since all Internet services come free with Linux, we'll use Linux as our Internet server.

To build our Internet server in an incremental and coherent manner, we'll work with a real-world application involving fictitious companies with fictitious domain names. Even though two of the services (mail and Web) run straight out of the box, we need to know more about them. There is a great deal of material detailed in this chapter, but the author has tried to simplify matters to the extent possible.

Objectives
- Understand the requirements of an organization for mail and Web services. *(24.1)*
- Learn how DNS uses name servers to handle *zonal* data. *(24.2)*
- Configure a *master name server. (24.3)*
- Configure the *resolver* and handle the **named** daemon. *(24.5 and 24.6)*
- Learn how **sendmail** sends and receives mail. *(24.7)*
- Use /etc/sendmail.cf to handle some common requirements. *(24.8)*
- Use *aliases* to forward mail. *(24.9)*
- Set up a mail server for a host connected to the Internet and for one that uses a dialup line. *(24.10)*
- Use **fetchmail** to download mail from a POP server. *(24.11.1)*
- Understand how HTTP works and configure httpd.conf to handle some of the common Web server functions. *(24.13 and 24.14)*
- Set up *virtual hosts* and understand the techniques used in controlling directory access. *(24.14.6 and 24.15)*

24.1   The Network at Rational Planets

Rational Planets Inc. has an extensive network directly connected to the Internet through a leased line. The company has been assigned the domain name *planets.com* and now intends to set up Internet services on its own network. In this network, the hosts *saturn* and *uranus* will perform the name service. *jupiter* and *saturn* will host the mail service. Among them, *saturn* and *jupiter* are the preferred servers for the respective category. *neptune* will host the Web service.

The rest of the network is placed behind a **firewall**—a computer that protects the internal network from attacks outside. *jupiter* acts as the firewall and provides forwarding facilities which let some machines in the internal network access the Net through this gateway. Some of these workstations use Windows, are switched off at night and have to download their mail from *jupiter*. A few workstations use Linux, are up all the time, and have mail automatically forwarded to them from *jupiter*. One user uses a dialup line to connect to the network from her machine *mercury* at home.

Since Rational Planets has a pretty large setup, it has decided to lease some of its space and services. A smaller organization, Rational Velvet, has just obtained its own domain name *velvet.com*. Since Velvet doesn't have a direct connection to the Internet, their management has decided to take advantage of the facilities available at Planets. Planets will offer Velvet 20 MB of disk space for hosting their Web service, and another 20 MB for receiving all mail on their behalf. *jupiter* accepts mail for Velvet too, and will have a number of FQDNs—*jupiter.planets.com*, *mail.planets.com*, *mail.velvet.com* and *velvet.com*.

Planets offers an unlimited number of mailboxes to Velvet on their server within the constraint of 20 MB. An email message can be addressed to anyone in Velvet using *user@velvet.com*. Likewise, a user on Planets is also addressed as *user@planets.com*. To be able to retrieve mail from Planet's site, Velvet has signed up with a local ISP having the FQDN *scarletisp.com*. This ISP also offers Velvet a free email account *velvet@scarletisp.com*. Velvet uses PPP to intermittently connect to the ISP and download mail from two sources—from Planet's server for its own domain, and from the singular mailbox maintained at the ISP.

After some time, Velvet decides to use the 20MB that Planets has earmarked for them to host its own Web site. The host *neptune* will then have three FQDNs—*neptune.planets.com*, *www.planets.com* and *www.velvet.com*. We'll implement most of our assumptions, but for the time being we have enough material to make a decent beginning. Have a close look at Fig. 24.1 before you proceed.

24.2   The Domain Name Service (DNS)

The Internet doesn't use /etc/hosts for hostname-address resolution. It uses DNS *(11.1.3)*, which utilizes a huge distributed database of these mappings. The system owes it origin to Paul Mockapetris, who wrote its specification and first implementation. However, Kevin Dunlap later wrote the most popular implementation called *BIND* (Berkeley Internet Name Domain) for Berkeley UNIX. BIND 8 is now shipped with practically all UNIX machines.

Apart from maintaining the hostname-address database, BIND also specifies the servers that handle mail for a domain. It may seem incredible, but a message addressed to *henry@neptune.planets.com* doesn't necessarily land up in the host *neptune*. BIND

F I G U R E 24.1 *The Network at Rational Planets*

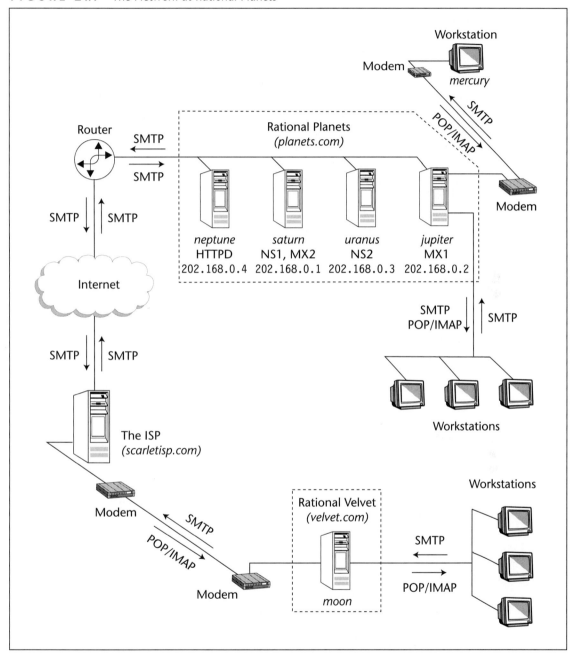

specifies one or more **mail exchangers** (hosts which receive mail) in order of preference so that the hosts are tried out in the right order. Further, if BIND is not able to
resolve an FQDN, it must be able to refer the problem to some other host running the
same service.

24.2.1 How DNS Works

DNS divides the domain namespace into **zones** with corresponding delegation of authority for that zone. The administrator of every zone has the responsibility of maintaining one or more **name servers**—databases containing the name-address information of that zone. The **master** (or primary) **name server** contains the latest information. The **slave** (or secondary) **name server** obtains it from the primary through a **zonal transfer**. It also serves as a backup in the event of failure of the primary. There is a third type of name server—**caching-only**, which merely diverts queries to a special group of 13 master name servers. We'll consider the setup of all three types in the upcoming sections.

The difference between a domain and a zone is quite subtle but must be understood. Let's consider that a domain *birds.edu* is further divided into two sub-domains, *parrots.birds.edu* and *cuckoo.birds.edu*. The administrator at *birds.edu* has decided to delegate the management of *cuckoo.birds.edu* while retaining it for *parrots.birds.edu*. There are two distinct zones here—*cuckoo.birds.edu* and *birds.edu*. Here, the *birds.edu* zone includes the *parrots.birds.edu* sub-domain, but not *cuckoo.birds.edu*. The zones together present a unified picture of the entire domain in the same way multiple file systems combine to form a single file system.

Every zone has its own group of name servers (master and slave), and the answers they provide are **authoritative** (correct) for that zone. A name server is queried by a **resolver**, which acts on behalf of the application to obtain the IP address of a host. It is not a separate program by itself, but a set of library routines that are linked into the applications like **telnet** and **ftp**. Usually, multiple name servers have to be queried to obtain an IP address. This is a job best done by a name server, so the resolver depends on the local name server for doing all the work.

When queried, a name server may be able to perform the resolution, but if it can't, it's not designed to give up. It must be able to provide the IP address (a *referral*) of another name server that would take you one step "closer" to the desired host. If this server can't provide the answer either, it too has to refer the matter to yet another one. The client-server architecture in DNS ensures that the referrals and the linkages between zones are properly exploited till the address is finally resolved.

In the above *birds.edu* domain, if the name server for the *birds.edu* zone is queried for the IP address of a host in the *cuckoo.birds.edu* zone, it obviously wouldn't know the answer. But it must be able to provide the IP address of the name server for the *cuckoo.birds.edu* zone that will know the answer.

The resolution follows a hierarchical pattern. If the local server can't provide the address of *www.cuckoo.birds.edu* (here, *www* is the host), it will check from its records whether it knows the name servers for *cuckoo.birds.edu*, then *birds.edu*, and so forth. At some point this has to stop, and the buck stops at the **root name servers**. These servers know the name servers of all the top-level domains like *com*, *edu*, *ca*, *gb* and so forth. *All* name servers on the Internet have the IP addresses of the root name servers, and will directly contact them when all resolution efforts fail.

Now consider that a host queries the local name server at *cuckoo.birds.edu* to know the address of *www.planets.com*. It obviously won't know and will contact the root name servers directly. One of them will return the IP addresses of the *com* name servers. The local name server now queries the *com* name server, which then refers it to the *planets.com* name server. This server knows the address of *www.planets.com* and returns the answer. The whole thing happens fast in spite of the fact that each of the root name servers handles several thousand queries every second. (There are just 13 of them, and they all run BSD UNIX.)

Note

Some of the root name servers not only provide the IP addresses of the name servers of the top-level domains, but are actually name servers of these domains.

24.3 Setting Up DNS—Configuring the Master Server

BIND, the name service in UNIX, is controlled by the **named** daemon. If **ps -e** (**ps ax** in Linux) shows **named** running, then BIND is running on your system. The latest release is BIND 8, which uses a version number four greater than its predecessor—BIND 4. Even though **named** is run from one of the *rc* scripts, a shell script **ndc** is also available with many implementations. For testing your BIND configuration, you'll find **ndc** quite convenient.

The system uses the configuration file /etc/named.conf (/etc/named.boot in BIND 4), and between two and four additional files containing the hostname-IP address mappings. We'll configure BIND 8 for each of the server types—master, slave and caching-only. Note that a machine can host only a single type of BIND service.

/etc/named.conf—the main file used by **named**—is like the superblock of the file system. It contains summary information like the type of server hosted by the machine, the zones for which it possesses records and the name and location of the database files. Depending on the type of name server, these are the files that could be used by **named**:

- The *hints* file which contains the IP addresses and the FQDNs of the root name servers. **named** always keeps a list of these servers in its cache so it can use them when it is unable to resolve hostnames on its own.
- The *localhost* file which translates the loopback address 127.0.0.1 to the pseudo-hostname *localhost*.
- The *zone* file containing the main database of all hosts in the zone serviced by this server. This file also contains the IP addresses of the name servers and mail servers of the zone. Each zone will have a separate zone file.
- The *reverse lookup* file which maps IP addresses to their corresponding hostnames. Some applications (like **rsh**) need to perform this translation. Each zone will also have its own reverse lookup file.

The master server requires all four files, while the slave server needs to have only the first two. The slave creates the zone and reverse lookup files by loading them from the master server. The caching-only server needs just the hints file, but usually also has the localhost file. We'll now configure each of the name servers for the domain *planets.com* with the network address 202.168.0 (rather, 202.168.0.0).

For networks connected directly to the Internet, you need one of the hosts to run as a master server. We'll first create the four files, house them in a separate directory, and then create the configuration file (named.conf) specifying them and their location. The files can have any name except for the main configuration file /etc/named.conf. *saturn* will act as the master server.

24.3.1   The Hints File

The hints file contains a list of the root name servers in a format understood by **named**. There are 13 of them there on the Internet, and they provide the name server addresses of all the top-level domains. If you want to know the IP address of the name server of *netscape.com*, they can tell you that. We'll call this file named.cache:

```
# cat named.cache
.                      3600000   IN  NS    A.ROOT-SERVERS.NET.
A.ROOT-SERVERS.NET.    3600000       A     198.41.0.4
.                      3600000       NS    B.ROOT-SERVERS.NET.
B.ROOT-SERVERS.NET.    3600000       A     128.9.0.107
.                      3600000       NS    C.ROOT-SERVERS.NET.
C.ROOT-SERVERS.NET.    3600000       A     192.33.4.12
.....
.                      3600000       NS    M.ROOT-SERVERS.NET.
M.ROOT-SERVERS.NET.    3600000       A     202.12.27.33
```

The contents have been edited to show the entries for four of the root name servers. When **named** starts, it reads this file, contacts one of the root name servers listed there and then gets the latest list. It then keeps this list in its cache. You should periodically get the latest file from *ftp://ftp.internic.net/domain/named.root*. You don't have to edit this file; it's always in the format understood by **named**.

For every root server, there are two records—NS and A, and we'll discuss them shortly. The A record holds both the IP address and the FQDN of the server. This is how DNS maintains address mappings, and we'll see the format repeated in the zone file.

Note

On your Linux machine, you'll find the hints file shipped with your distribution as /var/named/named.ca or /var/named/root.hint. You can change the name if you want.

24.3.2   The Localhost File

The localhost file provides the information needed to perform the resolution of the machine's loopback address. **named** should be able to translate the address 127.0.0.1 to the name *localhost*. We'll call this file planets.local:

```
# cat planets.local
@          IN            SOA        localhost.       root.localhost. (
                                    2000061601       ; Serial number
                                    28800            ; Refresh
                                    1400             ; Retry
                                    604800           ; Expire
                                    86400)           ; TTL
           IN            NS         localhost.
1          IN            PTR        localhost.
```

This file format is shared by two other files used by the master server, so you should understand the way it's structured. The file opens with the **Start of Authority** (SOA) record, which has the @ as the first character in the line. This @ refers to the current **origin**—the zone represented by this file. In our case, this origin is the *planets.com* zone. This is followed by the keywords IN (Internet) and SOA. The hostname follows next (localhost.), followed by the email address (root.localhost.) of the user to whom mail should be sent.

There are two more things to note here. The last two names are terminated by a dot. In general, you must make sure the FQDN of a host always ends with a dot when used in these configuration files. If it does not, then **named** understands it to be a host-name, and it tries to affix a domain name to it. Also note that the email address is shown as root.localhost. instead of root@localhost because the @ indicates the origin in **named**.

The SOA record has five fields enclosed within parentheses (comments shown in ;). The serial number must be updated every time a change is made to this file. The slave server periodically checks up the master server's files for this entry to decide whether it should reload the database. You can have a simple serial number or a date-based one with the *YYYYMMDDNN* format where *NN* indicates the serial number.

The refresh cycle implies that the slave server will check the serial number every 28,800 seconds to decide whether it should go in for a zonal transfer. Ideally, this should be a low value, but it need not be so any longer. You can have a notify statement in /etc/named.conf, which informs the slave server that a change has occurred.

The slave server will retry to fetch the data every 1400 seconds if the master server fails to respond. It should also continue to respond to name server queries for another 604,800 seconds (7 days) if the master server is down and the slave server is unable to update its files. The TTL (Time-to-Live) field shows the default value used by all records that don't have this field specified. This here is set to one day.

The SOA record is followed by two more records. The first is the NS (name server) record which shows the localhost itself as the name server for the zone. We'll explain the PTR (pointer) record later, but for the time being accept it as the record that does reverse resolution for the *0.0.127.in-addr.arpa* reverse domain. Here, the host with the address 1 (i.e., 127.0.0.1) is translated to the name *localhost*.

24.3.3   The Zone File

The zone file is the one where all the hostname-address mappings are kept—the one which replaces most of the functionality of /etc/hosts. We must have a separate zone file for the zone *planets.com*. This file is a bit complex (Fig. 24.2), so have a look at it before we embark on its dissection.

The file has been divided here into three sections. It contains all the ingredients you need to know to set up a master name server for a medium-sized network. The SOA record marks the FQDN of the master server as *saturn.planets.com*, and all email related to BIND must be addressed to *root@saturn.planets.com*. The serial number and the time-related parameters have already been discussed.

A zone file is characterized by the presence of **resource records** (RR); you have seen some of them already. Each resource record has four to five fields. The record type is shown in the third field, and IN invariably shows up as the second one. The first and last fields contain the hostname and IP addresses. We find four types of RRs here:

FIGURE 24.2 `planets.master`: *The Zone File*

```
@          IN     SOA      saturn.planets.com.     root.saturn.planets.com. (
                                  3              ; Serial number
                                  28800          ; Refresh
                                  1200           ; Retry
                                  604800         ; Expire
                                  86400)         ; TTL
; Name servers and mail servers
                  IN       NS          saturn.planets.com.
                  IN       NS          uranus.planets.com.
                  IN       MX   10     jupiter.planets.com.
                  IN       MX   20     saturn.planets.com.
; Hosts of this zone
localhost         IN       A           127.0.0.1
saturn            IN       A           202.168.0.1
jupiter           IN       A           202.168.0.2
uranus            IN       A           202.168.0.3
planets.com.      IN       A           202.168.0.3
neptune           IN       A           202.168.0.4
                  IN       MX   10     jupiter.planets.com.
; Aliases
mail              IN       CNAME       jupiter.planets.com.
www               IN       CNAME       neptune.planets.com.
ftp               IN       CNAME       uranus.planets.com.
```

- NS—The name server record. This record is used to indicate the location of the master and slave servers.
- A—The address record. This contains the hostname-address mapping in a slightly enlarged format as compared to /etc/hosts.
- MX—The mail exchanger record. DNS also specifies the servers meant to receive mail for a domain.
- CNAME—The alias that you can use in place of the **canonical** (official) **name** of a host. For instance, even if we access *neptune* as *www.planets.com*, the canonical name for *www.planets.com* continues to be *neptune.planets.com*.

There are two name server (NS) records here. The first one refers to the master server on *saturn.planets.com* and the slave server on *uranus.planets.com*. Since they are complete FQDNs by themselves, they have to be followed by a dot. The first field is missing for both of them. This field is optional, and when you don't provide it, **named** understands it to represent the last zone addressed (in this case, the current zone *planets.com*).

The mail exchanger records (MX) come next. *jupiter* is the most preferred mail server having a priority of 10. The master name server *saturn* is also the backup mail server, but with a lower priority of 20. **named** will direct all incoming mail for the *planets.com* zone first to *jupiter*, failing which mail will be accepted by *saturn*. If the workstations don't have access to the Internet, then the network administrator has to set up a connection between *saturn* and the inner subnet in case *jupiter* goes down.

The next section contains the database with the hostnames on the left and the IP addresses on the right. Most hostnames here don't have a dot, which means that **named** will append the domain name before looking up its IP address. One of them (*neptune*) contains a separate MX record too. BIND allows this, which means that all mail addressed to *user@neptune.planets.com* will also be accepted by *jupiter*. Note that *jupiter* also accepts mail in the form *user@planets.com*.

You'll expect hostnames to have aliases, and BIND offers them through the CNAME record. This record has the alias on the left and the canonical name of the host on the right. It lets you use *www.planets.com* to access the Web site hosted on *neptune*. Here, *www* simply acts as an alias for the host *neptune*. You can create aliases with A records too, but CNAME has the advantage that allows you to change the IP address of *jupiter* without needing to modify the CNAME entry.

There is one unusual entry showing a domain name without a hostname— *planets.com*. Since this is a complete FQDN by itself, it needs to be terminated by a dot. Even though *planets* is not a hostname, you are permitted to access the host *uranus* as *planets.com* in addition to *uranus.planets.com* and *ftp.planets.com*. This is something that we often do on the Internet; we do use *internic.net* in addition to *www.internic.net*.

Caution

Never have a CNAME record point to another CNAME record. It must point to an A record only. Also, MX records must specify the canonical name of a host and not its CNAME (the alias).

24.3.4 The Reverse Zone File

The fourth file that we ought to have is the one required for reverse resolution, i.e., converting an IP address to a domain name. Many UNIX tools need to do that, and there is a special zone file for that purpose. **named** performs all reverse resolution in the *in-addr.arpa* domain. It sounds strange, but then that's how it is. The reverse domain for *planets.com* is to be treated as *0.168.202.in-addr.arpa*—with the IP octets reversed.

It makes some sense to reverse these octets because domain names and IP addresses are structured in opposite ways. The left-most octet in the IP address is most significant, while the same is true for the right-most domain. Reversing the structure of the IP addresses brings it in line with the domain names. The file planets.reverse shows you the reverse entries:

```
# cat planets.reverse
@       IN              SOA     saturn.planets.com.     root.planets.com. (
                                        1               ; Serial number
                                        28800           ; Refresh
                                        7200            ; Retry
                                        604800          ; Expire
                                        86400)          ; TTL

                IN      NS      saturn.planets.com.
                IN      NS      uranus.planets.com.
        1       IN      PTR     saturn.planets.com.
        2       IN      PTR     jupiter.planets.com.
```

```
3               IN         PTR      uranus.planets.com.
4               IN         PTR      neptune.planets.com.
```

This file shows you the entries for the *0.168.202.in-addr.arpa* domain. Apart from NS records, this file features **pointer** records (PTR) to perform reverse resolution. Since we are dealing with a Class C network here, the last octet of the IP address shows up in the first column for these PTR records.

Note

The first column of the PTR records in the reverse resolution file actually contains the host part of the IP address in reversed form. If you have a Class B network 152.167.0.0, your reverse domain would be *167.152.in-addr.arpa*. A host with the IP address 152.167.34.56 would then have 56.34 as the first column in this file.

24.3.5   `named.conf`: The Main Configuration File

Now that we have created all the files we need, we have to create our summary file `/etc/named.conf`. This file specifies the location of the database files and the purpose they serve. The structure of this file has changed considerably between BIND 4 and BIND 8. Fig. 24.3 shows the BIND 8 version.

      The file contains groups of statements enclosed within curly braces and terminated with a semicolon. Note that the closing curly brace itself has to be terminated with a **;** too. The file contains one `zone` statement for every zone the server handles,

FIGURE 24.3   `/etc/named.conf`: *A BIND 8 Version*

```
options {
        directory "/var/named" ;
};
zone "." {
        type hint ;              // used to be specified w/ "cache"
        file "named.cache" ;
};
zone "planets.com" {
        type master ;           // what used to be called "primary"
        file "planets.master" ;
};
zone "0.168.202.in-addr.arpa" {
        type master ;
        file "planets.reverse" ;
};
zone "0.0.127.in-addr.arpa" {
        type master ;
        file "planets.local" ;
};
```

but begins with an `options` statement. This statement merely states that all zone files are located in `/var/named`. You could choose a different directory name if you want, but you'd hardly ever want to do so. Comments are made in C++-style by preceding them with `//`.

Each file we have discussed pertains to a zone as understood by **named**. The `.` (root) and *planets.com* zones are meant for forward resolution, while those using the *in-addr.arpa* domain are meant for reverse resolution. All files are of the master type except the cache file, which loads the IP addresses of root name servers in the machine's cache. The locations of the files are shown relative to the `/var/named` directory as specified by the `options` statement. We won't go into further details or discuss the other options available here since this configuration should suffice for most purposes.

24.4 The Secondary and Caching Servers

The zone file of the master server on *saturn* defines *uranus* as the slave server. The configurations for master and slave are broadly similar; the slave also has the cache and localhost files with identical contents. However, the slave creates the zone and reverse zone files by loading them from the master server. The two entries for forward and reverse resolution in `/etc/named.conf` on *uranus* look like this:

```
zone "planets.com" {
        type slave;                     // This is slave now
        file "planets.slave";           // This file will be created
        master { 202.168.0.1 };         // after loading it from here
};
zone "0.168.202.in-addr.arpa" {
        type slave ;                    // Same comments apply here
        file "planets.slave.reverse";
        master { 202.168.0.1 };
};
```

There are two differences here. The `type` is slave, and the `master` statement is used to load the zone files from the master server. The slave just needs to know the IP address of the master. The files `planets.slave` and `planets.slave.reverse` are created in the secondary by this zonal transfer. You can know whether your slave is working properly by examining the contents of these files.

Even though the above files are defined to be of slave type, the file for the reverse domain *0.0.127.in-addr.arpa* will continue to be of the master type. The `options` statement and the `zone` statement for the hints file remain unchanged.

The caching-only server's configuration is simpler still. It uses just the hints file (and optionally the localhost file). Accordingly, there's a single `zone` statement in `/etc/named.conf` pointing to this file. The `options` statement continues to remain the same.

24.5 Configuring the Resolver

The resolver on UNIX systems uses the configuration file `/etc/resolv.conf`. This file was introduced in the previous chapter *(23.9.1)* when setting up a host for connecting to the Internet. Every host in the *planets.com* network will have these entries in their resolv.conf:

```
search planets.com
nameserver 202.168.0.1
nameserver 202.168.0.3
```

The nameserver entries point to the hosts *saturn* and *uranus*. The resolver will try the first name server listed before it tries the second one. The search statement here makes possible the use of aliases and short names. If you use **ftp** or **telnet** with a name which doesn't have a dot, the domains specified (here, only one) on the search line are appended to the name and the DNS namespace is searched again. This means that you can use **ftp uranus** in addition to **ftp uranus.planets.com**.

Linux systems additionally use another file, /etc/host.conf ("host," not "hosts"). This file contains simply two lines:

```
order hosts bind
multi on
```

The order statement determines the sequencing of resolution. Here, /etc/hosts will be searched before the name server is accessed. We'll ignore the next line.

24.6   ndc **and** nslookup: **Testing the Configuration**

On Linux systems, **named** stores its PID in /var/run/named.pid. This means you can use the hangup signal to kill and restart the daemon—**kill -HUP `cat /var/run/named.pid`**. However, **ndc** offers a better way of handling this daemon. This is a shell script which accepts the arguments start, stop and restart:

```
ndc start
ndc stop
ndc restart                              Same as ndc stop followed by ndc start
```

You can also use the **nslookup** command to test whether **named** knows the name of the name servers and mail exchangers. This command can also be used noninteractively with the FQDN to obtain the IP address of a host. We'll use it interactively here and set the type to ns to look for the name servers:

```
# nslookup
Default Server: saturn.planets.com
Address: 202.168.0.1
> set type=ns                                         Only name server records
> planets.com
Server: saturn.planets.com
Address: 202.168.0.1

planets.com      nameserver = uranus.planets.com
planets.com      nameserver = saturn.planets.com
uranus.planets.com      internet address = 202.168.0.3
saturn.planets.com      internet address = 202.168.0.1
```

When we set `type` to `mx`, we'll know whether **named** knows the mail exchangers:

```
> set type=mx                                        Only mail exchanger records
> planets.com
planets.com       preference = 20, mail exchanger = saturn.planets.com
planets.com       preference = 10, mail exchanger = jupiter.planets.com
    .........                                        Name server lines deleted
saturn.planets.com       internet address = 202.168.0.1
jupiter.planets.com      internet address = 202.168.0.2
```

To test your configuration, you are probably better off using these commands. Here, **nslookup** has identified both name servers and mail exchangers correctly. Now access some of the machines, both with singular host names and complete FQDNs. For instance, you can enter `www.planets.com` on your browser to see if a Web server is running on *neptune*. You can also use **ftp uranus** to see if the resolver expands the hostname to its FQDN.

Tip

To test whether name service is running properly, use **nslookup** with an FQDN like this: **nslookup ftp.planets.com** and see whether **nslookup** outputs the IP address of the host.

24.7 The Mail Service

Email is probably the first service that you'll be asked to set up (apart from BIND which mail must first see running) on your Internet server. Even though Internet mail is somewhat complex, setting up a mail server for a small organization doesn't need to be so. In the present scenario, Rational Planets also handles Velvet's mail, which does add a degree of complexity to the setup. However, if you have been able to come this far, you'll most certainly make it.

The mechanism of mail transmission and delivery has already been discussed in Section 13.6. To recollect the essentials, Internet mail is the handiwork of three agencies:

- The Mail User Agent (MUA), which composes and reads mail.
- The Mail Transport Agent (MTA), which both sends and receives mail.
- The Mail Delivery Agent (MDA), which receives mail from the MTA and delivers it to the users' mailboxes.

Before you proceed with the configuration of this somewhat complex setup, just have a look at Fig. 24.1 to understand the relationships between the mail agents. The MTA's job today is handled universally by SMTP (Simple Mail Transfer Protocol). **sendmail** is the most common implementation of SMTP. In the forthcoming sections, we'll discuss and configure **sendmail**.

When a user connects to a network intermittently—often through a dialup line—it's not possible for mail to reach the user directly. A fourth agency comes into play to fetch the mail from the remote server. The two protocols used to store and fetch mail in this manner are POP (Post Office Protocol) and IMAP (Internet Message Access Protocol). **fetchmail** is the standard POP/IMAP client for Linux systems. We'll learn to configure **fetchmail** to retrieve mail from a POP3 (the latest implementation used universally) server.

24.7.1   sendmail: The Universal MTA

In a network, users on workstations generally submit their mail to a **hub** (a mail server), which has direct access to the outside world. Similarly, the workstations don't receive mail directly either; all incoming mail comes to the hub. This approach shields the individual user from the hassles involved in handling mail. If a mail message can't be sent, it's the hub's job to keep trying for five days before informing the sender.

When the hub routes messages, it rewrites the sender's address so that it appears to have originated from the hub. In other words, it would rewrite the address *henry@neptune.planets.com* to *henry@jupiter.planets.com*, where *jupiter* is the hub at Planets for handling mail. The world then doesn't know the machine that henry actually used to send the mail—a useful security feature. This means that henry can move to a different host and can still use the same email address. If the hub handles mail for the entire domain *planets.com*, then most organizations hide the hub's name too—*henry@planets.com*.

Since incoming mail is also routed through the hub, users have three options:

- View messages on the hub after logging in with **telnet** or **rlogin**. All users at Planets can do that if they have accounts on the hub.
- Request that mail be forwarded to their machines. For this, their own machines must be up all the time.
- Fetch mail from a POP/IMAP server running on the hub. This is the only way Velvet can retrieve mail from Planet's mail server. Users on Planets can use this facility too if they don't want mail forwarded to their machines.

The above was a gentle introduction to **sendmail**, the most common MTA for UNIX systems. There are other MTAs available on UNIX and Linux systems like MMDF and **smail**, but **sendmail** handles the bulk of Internet mail. It was written by Eric Allman at Berkeley and is still maintained by him. **sendmail** is an extremely complex and bizarre program—even by UNIX standards. People shudder at the thought of editing its configuration file (but we won't).

Unlike some other protocols like UUCP, **sendmail** does not use intermediate hosts. It communicates with another MTA at the receiving end, and on confirmation, transports mail *directly* to the receiving MTA. That program may or may not be another **sendmail** program, but it has to understand SMTP. Depending on the forwarding facilities that may be set up, mail may be handled by multiple MTAs before the MDA finally takes over. If a message can't be delivered, **sendmail** will queue the message and try a number of times at regular intervals before notifying the user about its failure.

sendmail uses the concept of *aliasing* to forward mail to one or more users located anywhere. Aliases are maintained in the file /etc/aliases; **sendmail** reads a variant of this file when it receives a message.

24.7.2   Starting and Stopping sendmail

sendmail resides in /usr/sbin (/usr/lib in Solaris). Like **pppd**, it has both server and client components, but it can function in both modes simultaneously in a single invocation. It runs as a server daemon from one of the *rc* scripts to listen to all incoming mail at port 25. If **sendmail** were to receive only incoming mail and not send the outgoing, it has to be invoked in this manner:

```
/usr/sbin/sendmail -bd                                          Daemon mode
```

The -bd option makes **sendmail** run as a daemon process. **sendmail**, like any MTA, doesn't perform mail delivery. Unless it is forwarding mail to another MTA, it hands over mail to the delivery program. UNIX systems maintain a user's mail in a single text file in /var/spool/mail (/var/mail in SVR4). A message for henry is appended to the file /var/spool/mail/henry.

Outgoing mail is spooled to the directory /var/spool/mqueue. If **sendmail** were to send only outgoing mail, then it would have to run as a client in one of these two ways:

```
/usr/sbin/sendmail -q                                     One time invocation
/usr/sbin/sendmail -q 15m                        Examine queue every 15 minutes
```

In the first case, **sendmail** processes the queue as a one-time exercise. You can use the **cron** services to run this command at regular intervals. Alternatively, you can use the second form which looks at the queue every 15 minutes and flushes it. Although running **sendmail** in the daemon mode requires root permission, the -q option can be used by all users.

Even if **sendmail** is run as a daemon with the -bd option, you can invoke it again with the -q option. In many cases, the same machine handles both incoming and outgoing mail. This is the most common way of invoking **sendmail** on a host that's permanently connected to the Internet:

```
/usr/sbin/sendmail -bd -q 15m
```

The behavior of **sendmail** is controlled by /etc/sendmail.cf (/etc/mail/sendmail.cf in Solaris). When you change the contents of this file, make sure that you kill and restart **sendmail**. This can be done by executing the relevant script (say, **/etc/rc.d/init.d/sendmail**) with the restart argument. If the *rc* script on your machine supports only the start and stop arguments, then you can try killing **sendmail** with the SIGHUP signal after locating the PID from the **ps** command.

On Linux systems, **sendmail** stores—in two separate lines in /var/run/sendmail.pid—both the PID and the command line used to execute it. Kill the PID stored in the first line and then execute the contents of the second line:

```
kill `head -1 /var/run/sendmail.pid`                       Stops sendmail
`tail -1 /var/run/sendmail.pid`                            Starts sendmail
```

We haven't used command substitution in the way shown in the second line, but this is a smart way of executing a command line that's embedded in a file. Smarter still would be to create an alias for it.

24.7.3   `mailq`: Viewing the Mail Queue

The mail queue can be viewed with the **mailq** command. This is only a symbolic link to the **sendmail** command, and is really equivalent to running **sendmail -bp**:

```
# mailq
              Mail Queue (1 request)
--Q-ID-- --Size-- ----Q-Time---- ------------Sender/Recipient------------
QAA00943      478 Fri Dec 10 16:22 <sumit@saturn.planets.com>
                                <XLDEL/TMH/VIBHA@tmh.satyam.net.in>
```

This displays the message-id (QAA00943) and the sender's email address in the first line showing the job details. The recipient is shown in the second line. The message-id is embedded in the names of two files which **sendmail** creates for each message. A listing of /var/spool/mqueue shows these two files:

```
# ls /var/spool/mqueue
dfQAA00943
qfQAA00943
```

Every message is held as two files in this directory. The "qf" file contains the mail headers while the "df" file contains the contents. Every user can run this command to view the list of all spooled messages. Unfortunately, there's no command for removing messages from the queue. If a message has to be deleted, the administrator has to use **rm** on the corresponding "df" and "qf" files.

24.8   sendmail.cf: **The Configuration File**

The meat of **sendmail** is found in its configuration file /etc/sendmail.cf. This file, which has terrorized a lot of people, has nearly a thousand lines containing some of the most cryptic code you'd have ever seen. Fortunately, **sendmail** can be set up on most small and medium systems without your ever having to understand most of its contents. The ones you need to know are taken up in the forthcoming paragraphs.

You rarely have to write a sendmail.cf from scratch; all UNIX systems come with a preconfigured file. You need to change just a handful of lines there to get **sendmail** going. However, many users shy away from doing that too. Realizing the need to simplify **sendmail** configuration, the developers of **sendmail** created the **m4** macro-processor. Here, you set some variables in a separate file and let **m4** generate sendmail.cf. We'll not discuss **m4** and prefer to face and edit sendmail.cf directly.

sendmail.cf is divided into a number of sections, each dealing with a different aspect of its configuration. In this section, we'll learn to interpret some of its macros and classes. We'll also encounter some other parameters when we configure our mail server. **sendmail** is different from other configurations scripts; all statements must start from column 1.

24.8.1   Macros

Macros can be considered simply as variables, and they are found at the beginning of the file. All macro definitions start with a D (the letter M used by sendmail.cf stands for mailer), and you can easily locate them by using **grep "^D" /etc/sendmail.cf**. Some of the important macros are shown below:

```
Dj$w.planets.COM
DSscarletisp.com
```

```
DMplanets.com
DnMAILER-DAEMON
DZ8.9.3                                                sendmail's version number
```

The letter D is immediately followed by a single character macro name and then its value—all without intervening spaces. Here, S is set to scarletisp.com, and Z has the value 8.9.3. Like shell variables, all macro variables are evaluated with a $, and you'll find them referenced in the various segments of sendmail.cf.

Many **sendmail** macros begin with a lowercase letter. You can already see one of them—$w. All lowercase macros are not defined in the file, but are defined internally within **sendmail**. The header section has a number of them. Here are some lines that show how **sendmail** uses macros to determine the format of the message headers:

```
H?D?Date: $a
H?F?From: $?x$x <$g>$|$g$.
H?x?Full-Name: $x
H?M?Message-Id: <$t.$i@$j>
```

Each header line is identified by an H, followed by a flag enclosed within ?s and the header template. $a stores the system date in RFC 822 format. $g is the sender's address and $x the full name. The Message-Id is a long character string typically having values like <199908230446.KAA00913@mail.hill.com>. It is derived from the date and time expressed numerically ($t), the queue-id ($i) and the FQDN of the host ($j). You can well appreciate that no two email messages can ever have identical Message-Ids.

Note

The From: line in the message header makes interesting reading. Here, the value is set conditionally. It's either $x <$g> (the RFC 822 format) or $g depending on whether $x is set or not. $?, $| and $. act as the if, else and endif keywords of any if construct. The interpretation is this: "If x exists ($?x), the value is $x <$g> else ($|) it is $g endif ($.)." If the full name doesn't appear in the From: line, then this is the line you need to examine.

24.8.2 Classes

sendmail also uses the letter C to denote a class. Like a macro, this too is followed by a single character and then a list of one or more values. Here are some of the classes that will help you understand the working of **sendmail** better:

```
CO @ % !
Cwlocalhost mail.planets.com planets.com velvet.com
CE root
```

The first class O (the letter "Oh") contains three values separated by spaces. This class prohibits you from using the characters @, % and ! in the username component of an email address.

The class w includes the FQDNs of all hosts for which this host is expected to receive mail. You can specify all these FQDNs in one line, but when there are too many of them, you can use the file class (F) instead. The file class uses the character F with the same single letter (here, w) to indicate that the list is to be taken from a file. Here's how you would probably use w if you had a hundred FQDNs to handle:

```
Fw/etc/sendmail.cw
```

At Rational Planets, all mail is received by *jupiter* and its alias *mail*. While there's a specific MX record *(24.3.3)* pointing to the canonical name *jupiter*, there's none pointing to the alias *mail*. (MX records can't point to aliased hosts.) Once you add `mail.planets.com` to the alias class (either with Cw or Fw), the system will also receive mail addressed to *user@mail.planets.com*. Note that here it also accepts mail addressed to *user@velvet.com*. This requires some additional configuration by way of placing an entry for Velvet in `/etc/mailertable`, but we'll ignore these issues in this text.

24.8.3 Options

sendmail supports over a hundred options that define the location of its files, the disposal of error messages and timeouts. Options are defined with the letter O. The definition has changed from version 8.7. An option is expressed in either of these ways:

```
OA/etc/aliases
O AliasFile=/etc/aliases
```
Pre-ver 8.7
Version 8.7 onwards

The first form uses a single letter and the value without any intervening spaces. Here, the option OA has the value `/etc/aliases`. The second form uses a complete word `AliasFile` as the option name. Moreover, it is preceded by a space and followed by an =. Case here is insignificant; `Aliasfile` and `aliasfile` have the same meaning. Here are some of the important options:

```
O HelpFile=/usr/lib/sendmail.hf
O ForwardPath=$z/.forward.$w:$z/.forward
O QueueDirectory=/var/spool/mqueue
O Timeout.queuewarn=4h
O Timeout.queuereturn=5d
```

The second line specifies the path that **sendmail** has to follow in locating the `.forward` file. It uses two macros $z and $w. You can very nearly guess what these macros represent: $w represents the hostname and $z the home directory.

You must have come across messages from the MAILER-DAEMON expressing its inability to deliver a message. The last two options determine how long **sendmail** tries delivering mail before giving up. If **sendmail** can't deliver mail within four hours, it will issue a warning message to the sender, but will keep trying. If it still can't get through in five days, it gives up and the mail is deleted from the mqueue directory.

24.9 Aliases

sendmail has an extremely flexible and versatile feature in routing mail to any user on any host. This is possible due to the **aliasing** facility, which is represented by the file `/etc/aliases`. Each line of the file is divided into two parts. The left part contains the username that needs to be aliased and the right contains the destination. Some entries in the file throw up a few surprises as well:

```
postmaster: root
mailer-daemon: postmaster
```

```
enquiry: henry
charlie: charlie@neptune.planets.com
friends: romeo,juliet@yahoo.com,jack,jill,andrew
navlist: :include: /home/nav/subscriber.lst
hegel: /dev/null
```

The entries here illustrate the various ways you can use this file. Every username is followed by a : and then by whitespace. The right side contains the expansion of the alias. This expansion may lead to multiple usernames or even filenames. All mail addressed to enquiry is forwarded to henry.

The primary mail server for the *planets.com* domain is *jupiter (24.3.3)*. So mail addressed to charlie would normally be spooled in *jupiter*. Aliasing here redirects it to the host *neptune*. This alias has some significance. Even though all users are received at the hub as *user@planets.com*, aliasing lets you redirect some or all of them to the machines where they actually "belong" to.

When **sendmail** inspects the header of a received message, it first checks the username in the To: field with /etc/aliases. It expands the alias and then continues to check whether the expansion leads to yet another alias. Here, mail addressed to mailer-daemon ultimately lands in root's mailbox because postmaster is further aliased to root.

Let's now turn to the other aliases. Mail addressed to friends is received by five users. One of them is not even in the local domain but on the Internet; **sendmail** allows this. Friends here represents a *mailing list* which allows a group of users to be addressed with a single name. Five users are good enough to accommodate in /etc/aliases, but when there are five hundred of them, then they are better placed in a file. Using the :include: keyword, you can direct **sendmail** to look up the file subscriber.lst for expanding the alias navlist.

The recipient can be a file too. If hegel has left the organization without leaving behind his new address, then all mail addressed to him should be quashed. And there's no better way of doing that than by directing the message to /dev/null.

The administrator can modify this file to add or drop aliases as and when users join or leave. But then she has to compile it with the **newaliases** command. The command is run without any arguments. Like **mailq**, **newaliases** is yet another link to **sendmail** and runs **sendmail -bi**. It creates the file aliases.db in binary format. **sendmail** reads aliases.db rather than aliases when it inspects a mail header.

Caution

Never change the aliases postmaster and mailer-daemon that you'll find in every aliases file.

Note

Beside /etc/aliases, every user can do her own forwarding by placing the name of the destination email address in $HOME/.forward. Temporary forwarding is best done by .forward without reference to the administrator. However, when a user leaves the organization or is transferred, /etc/aliases is a better choice because the user's account may be deleted and her home directory may be removed. The .forward will then go away too.

24.10 Setting Up the Mail Server for *planets.com*

In our *planets.com* network, the MX record in the domain's database *(24.3.3)* assigns *jupiter* and *saturn* the responsibility of handling mail for the entire domain. *jupiter* has a higher priority (10) than *saturn* (20). Since all hosts forward their mail to *jupiter*, they need not run **sendmail** in daemon mode (-bd), but only in the queue mode (with -q). Only *jupiter* and *saturn* need to run **sendmail** in daemon mode.

In this setup, all hosts except *jupiter* and *saturn* can do with a simple sendmail.cf configuration. For instance, the file in *neptune* should contain a line stating the mail is to be forwarded to a "smart" relay host—the host *jupiter*. This is achieved with the S macro on *neptune*'s sendmail.cf:

DSjupiter.planets.com   *Sets the smart relay*

Why do we need a **relay server**? Hosts which are not connected to the Internet or lack the capability to deliver mail need one which has neither limitation. Sending mail can often be a tough proposition. The receiving machine may be down, or there may be no route to the host on account of line breakdowns. A responsible mail server (which a relay server is) has to keep trying for a reasonable period of time to contact the MTA on the other side before it gives up.

It is generally the organization's policy to hide the host name in the email address. In that case, *jupiter* must be told that it has to **masquerade** as *planets.com* rather than *jupiter.planets.com*. You have to set the M macro on *jupiter* in this way:

DMplanets.com   *Masquerades as planets.com*

This means that a user henry on *jupiter* sending out mail will have the sender's name rewritten to *henry@planets.com* instead of *henry@jupiter.planets.com*. This is fine for users on *jupiter*, but Planets may want to have a uniform structure for senders of the entire *planets.com* domain—including those on *neptune*, *uranus*, *saturn* and so forth. In that case, this masquerading has to be done for all hosts which forward their mail to *jupiter*. This time we use the class M:

CM neptune.planets.com saturn.planets.com uranus.planets.com

Note

To be able to masquerade an entire domain with the M class (CM), you must make sure that usernames across the entire organization are unique. This is also a healthy way of organizing user accounts. If usernames are not unique across the domain, then you can't use CM.

Planets' mail service is now ready for its own use. But Planets also has to handle Velvet's mail service, and **sendmail** must know that. This is the job of the w class:

Cwlocalhost planets.com velvet.com

That's all there is to it in the mail configuration. However, we aren't ready yet as we still have to decide about the disposal of received mail.

In our sample configuration, *jupiter* has a permanent connection to the Internet and holds mail for all users in /var/spool/mail. How do users access that mail? If users log in to *jupiter* with **telnet**, they can view their mail using any MUA like **elm** or **pine**. If they are using Netscape (or the MUAs native to their machines), then they have to download their mail on to their machines. There are a number of solutions, and Planets can choose to have different solutions for different workstations:

- If a host is always up and connected to *jupiter*, then you can use /etc/aliases to forward mail for those users who belong to that host. *jupiter* then need not have all these users in its /etc/passwd.
- If all hosts are connected to *jupiter* permanently, then the entire mail can either be forwarded to them, or the users may be allowed the mount the /var/spool/mail filesystem remotely using NFS.
- If a host connects to *jupiter* intermittently—probably through a dialup line—then *jupiter* has to act as a POP or IMAP server as well. The users on this host can then fetch their mail using the POP or IMAP protocols and must have accounts on the host *jupiter*.

We know how to use /etc/aliases, and we also know how to mount an NFS filesystem. Now, refer to Figure 24.1, and you'll note that the host *mercury* connects to *jupiter* through a dialup line. This represents the third option, and hosts using this option require a separate mail configuration.

24.11   POP and IMAP: The Protocols for Offline Use

While the incoming mail server has to be permanently connected to the Internet (otherwise, received mail will bounce), workstations need not always be connected to this server. Users often switch off their machines at night, thus eliminating all chances of mail forwarding through /etc/aliases. Individuals too connect to their ISP's mail server at regular intervals through a dialup line. These situations demand "pulling" mail rather than "pushing" it. POP and IMAP are the protocols that one uses here.

In Planet's network, if users are not allowed to mount /var/spool/mail remotely, then *jupiter* has to hold mail in a POP or IMAP server. We'll consider POP3 (the latest available) as it is the standard on most Internet servers; IMAP is yet to be adopted as a superior standard. When POP3 is enabled, the mail file locations remain the same except that they can be fetched from a remote machine with this protocol.

POP3 is started by **inetd** from /etc/inetd.conf. For it to run, *jupiter* must contain in this file a line similar to these:

```
pop3      stream  tcp     nowait  root    /usr/sbin/tcpd  /usr/sbin/popper -s
pop-3     stream  tcp     nowait  root    /usr/sbin/tcpd  ipop3d
```

In these setups on Red Hat and SuSE Linux, the wrapper program **tcpd** runs the **popper** or **ipop3d** program *(23.7)*. POP3 uses port number 110, and this should be reflected in a corresponding entry in /etc/services:

```
pop3            110/tcp         # POP version 3
pop-3           110/tcp         # POP version 3
```

Make sure that the line is not commented in *jupiter*'s /etc/inetd.conf. We'll now consider the mail configuration for hosts that need to download mail from *jupiter*'s

POP server. This includes both hosts connecting through a dialup line (like *mercury*) as well as those who are connected directly but still prefer to use POP.

24.11.1   `fetchmail`: A POP/IMAP Client

Linux uses a smart program named **`fetchmail`** for fetching mail from a POP or IMAP server. The client program requires the username, the protocol and the FQDN of the mail server as arguments. This is how user romeo on *mercury* connects to *jupiter* to retrieve his mail:

```
$ fetchmail -u romeo -p POP3 jupiter
Enter password for romeo@jupiter: *******
2 messages for romeo at jupiter (12140 octets).
reading message 1 of 2 (2354 octets) .. flushed
reading message 2 of 2 (9786 octets) ......... flushed
```

`fetchmail` prompts for the password which is not echoed to the terminal. It then proceeds to fetch the mail from the POP server. The messages are flushed (deleted) from the server, being **`fetchmail`**'s default behavior. Only newer messages are fetched in this invocation.

   `fetchmail` serves as the connecting link between SMTP running on a host like *mercury* (or *moon*) and SMTP running on the mail server *jupiter* or the ISP's server (like *scarletisp*). However, the overall interface is quite uniform and no stages are bypassed. Let's make no mistake about this; *mercury* too must run **sendmail** in daemon mode and **`fetchmail`** has to hand over the retrieved mail to **sendmail**. **sendmail** will then pass on the mail to a delivery program like **procmail**. This would have been the case had *mercury* been directly connected to *jupiter*. The same considerations apply to the host *moon*, which handles Velvet's mail.

   When you are experimenting with your network, you'll probably want these messages to be kept on the server (`-k`) till you are sure of what you are doing. By default, **`fetchmail`** retrieves only newer messages, but you can override that too and ask it to get all messages (`-a`). You can then later flush them out (`-F`):

```
fetchmail -u romeo -p POP3 -k jupiter.planets.com        Keeps all messages
fetchmail -u romeo -p POP3 -a jupiter.planets.com          Gets all messages
fetchmail -u velvet -p POP3 -F mail.scarletisp.com       Deletes all messages
```

The retrieved mail is now available in the text file `/var/spool/mail/`*username*. romeo can now use any of the character-based clients like **elm** and **pine** to view mail. With Netscape, it's a different story as it expects all mail to be located in `$HOME/nsmail`. However, using symbolic links you can make any mail file located anywhere visible in Netscape. Moreover, Netscape can directly fetch its mail from *jupiter* without taking the *fetchmail-sendmail* route.

   You would probably want to run **`fetchmail`** in daemon mode and transmit the password (in clear text) through a script. **`fetchmail`** uses `.fetchmailrc` where all **`fetchmail`** options can be stored. Here is a sample entry using POP3 that leaves the messages on the server:

```
poll jupiter.planets.com proto POP3
user romeo with password d276y45t
keep                                                    Like the -k option
```

The poll statement takes the mail server as an argument, and proto specifies the type of protocol used. Because the password here is stored as clear text, the file must be made unreadable to group and the world. In any case, **fetchmail** won't run if the permissions of the file are not set to 600.

Note

If *mercury* is also running the POP service, then mail fetched from the POP server on *jupiter* is held in *mercury*'s POP server. Another host can then fetch mail from *mercury* (and store it in another POP server too).

24.12 Setting Up the Mail System at Velvet

We now have to configure the mail server on Velvet's host *moon* to send and receive mail. Note that Velvet can access Planets' host *jupiter* and the ISP's host only through the dialup PPP account. The scenario is different from the previous one in that this time mail has to be downloaded from two sources:

- From the POP server on *jupiter* where Velvet has a *multidrop* mailbox (a mailbox shared by multiple users). Velvet too has to service a number of users using email addresses of the form *user@velvet.com*.
- From the POP server running on the ISP's host *mail.scarletisp.com* where Velvet has a dialup PPP account with the email address *velvet@scarletisp.com*.

For Velvet to send mail, the ISP has to act as the smart relay host. sendmail.cf on *moon* thus has to be configured so that all outgoing mail from *moon* is forwarded to this relay host using PPP. Masquerading also has to be implemented on *moon* so that all addresses appear to be of the form *user@velvet.com*:

```
Dsmail.scarletisp.com                                    The relay host
DMvelvet.com                                          Enables masquerading
```

Unlike the host *jupiter* in the *planets.com* domain, *moon* connects to the Internet (through the ISP) only intermittently—the reason why it needs a relay host. This time, **sendmail** running on *moon* must be told that mailing is "expensive," and that it must not attempt to deliver mail right away on receipt. This requires that you change this option:

```
O HoldExpensive=True
```

You have to make some changes in the mailer definitions too. Mailers are defined by M, and there are four types of SMTP mailers defined in sendmail.cf:

```
Msmtp,          P=[IPC], F=mDFMuXe, S=11/31, R=21, E=\r\n, L=990,
                T=DNS/RFC822/SMTP,
                A=IPC $h
```

```
Mesmtp,          P=[IPC], F=mDFMuXae, S=11/31, R=21, E=\r\n, L=990,
                 T=DNS/RFC822/SMTP,
                 A=IPC $h
Msmtp8,          P=[IPC], F=mDFMuX8e, S=11/31, R=21, E=\r\n, L=990,
                 T=DNS/RFC822/SMTP,
                 A=IPC $h
Mrelay,          P=[IPC], F=mDFMuXa8e, S=11/31, R=61, E=\r\n, L=2040,
                 T=DNS/RFC822/SMTP,
                 A=IPC $h
```

The smtp mailer handles normal SMTP mail. esmtp uses extended SMTP. Unencoded 8-bit mail is now handled by smtp8. The relay mailer routes all mail through the relay host. Each mailer definition also has a number of arguments. P shows [IPC] as the path of the mailer program; this represents the **sendmail** program. S and R show the rules **sendmail** uses to rewrite sender and recipient headers.

The other arguments show that individual lines of a message are terminated by \r\n (E), and that lines can't exceed 990 characters (L). Hostnames are resolved with DNS, the email addresses are of the RFC 822-type, and the **sendmail** command itself (SMTP) is used to execute the mailer.

F represents the flags applicable for the mailer. Many of these flags are common to macros like $a, $b and so on. We have not disturbed any of the default settings except that we have added an e at the end. This makes the mailer expensive, and it won't try to connect to deliver mail instantly, but rather wait for **sendmail -q** to run.

Note

Starting with Version 8.9, **sendmail** doesn't relay by default, and prints the message Relay access denied. If you want the feature enabled so that other networks can still route their mail through your mail server, then enter the names of their domains or their network addresses in /etc/mail/relay-domains, and restart **sendmail**.

Mail delivery is now performed by writing a script which dials out to the ISP, starts the PPP service at both ends and then executes the **sendmail -q** command. You can use **dip**, **chat** (or **wvdial**, a new tool) for dialing, and execute the script from your crontab files. Since **pppd** executes **/etc/ppp/ip-up** on connection, you can place the **sendmail** statement there as well. Note that **sendmail** is always running in daemon mode (**sendmail -bd**).

A word here about the **multidrop mailbox** that Velvet has on *jupiter*. **sendmail** allows email addressed to multiple users in a single domain to be forwarded to a *single* user's account. All we have to do is to ask **fetchmail** to get mail from this account. Since we have two email boxes to deal with, one at *mail.velvet.com* (an alias for *jupiter*), and the other at *mail.scarletisp.com*, .fetchmailrc on *moon* will have two sets of statements:

```
poll mail.scarletisp.com proto POP3
user velvet with password bnet6797
poll jupiter.planets.com proto POP3                          or mail.velvet.com
no dns aka velvet.com                                  This statement is needed
user pop1244238 password hf789bfd is * here
```

The first set downloads Velvet's mail from the ISP's mail server. The second set uses the mailbox username pop1244238 that Planets has assigned to Velvet. Since this mailbox contains mail of multiple users, **fetchmail** has to inspect every mail header and then ensure that mail is distributed to the mailboxes of different users. The * implies this distribution. If you have a username here, then all mail will be dumped to that user's mailbox.

If a POP server is running on *moon*, then individual users from their Windows machines can download their mail using the POP client features built into Netscape Messenger and Outlook Express.

Note

Netscape Messenger is also a POP client and can also fetch mail from a POP server. However, **fetchmail** is superior because it can retrieve mail from multiple servers in a single invocation. Netscape Communicator 6 will also have this feature. But **fetchmail** can also retrieve mail from a multidrop mailbox, which Netscape can't.

24.13   The Web Service

The Web is the most popular service on the Internet. Web servers are commonly known as **httpd servers**—named after the daemon which runs on port 80. There are several types of httpd servers in use on the Web, and many of them are based on the original design from NCSA (the NCSA server). The original server had a number of flaws which required patches to be applied on them. A team of people performed this task in a systematic manner and created "a patchy server." They called it Apache, which today accounts for more than half of all httpd servers on the Web. Apache is the standard server available in all Linux systems. Versions have been developed for all UNIX flavors (*http://www.apache.org*).

The Web server uses the HTTP protocol to handle a request from the client—the browser. Generally, the request is for fetching an HTML document and its associated graphics. Using the help of an external CGI program *(20.20)*, the Web server may serve dynamic HTML output too. A Web server running on a single machine can also serve as multiple Web sites. Security is thus an exceedingly important issue, and Apache has a comprehensive scheme to enforce security at the directory, host and user levels. We'll now acquaint ourselves with most of these features to set up a Web server ourselves.

24.13.1   Apache: The Patchy Server

Apache on Linux systems is located as **httpd** in /usr/sbin. Like **ftp**, **telnet** and **pop-3**, it can be started by **inetd**, but the server is usually run in the stand-alone mode at boot time from one of the *rc* scripts. **httpd** runs as root, but it spawns separate **httpd** processes to serve client requests, as extracts from the **ps axf** command output would reveal:

```
270  ?  S    0:03 /usr/sbin/httpd -f /etc/httpd/httpd.conf -D SSL
280  ?  SW   0:00  \_ (httpd)
281  ?  SW   0:00  \_ (httpd)
282  ?  SW   0:00  \_ (httpd)
283  ?  SW   0:00  \_ (httpd)
284  ?  SW   0:00  \_ (httpd)
```

There are five additional processes here, all having 270 as their PPID—the PID of the initial one run from the *rc* script. Like **named** and **sendmail**, Apache stores the PID of the main **httpd** process in a file—/var/run/httpd.pid. This means you can kill the process with **kill `cat /var/run/httpd/pid`**. You can also use the hangup signal to restart the process after you have made changes to its configuration files (**kill -HUP `cat /var/run/httpd/pid`**).

Apache's behavior is controlled by three configuration files—httpd.conf, srm.conf and access.conf—a legacy that it inherited from the NCSA server. However, the *directives* (syntax) used in these files are common to all three. From version 1.3 onwards, Apache is shipped with a single configuration file httpd.conf. The file is located in /etc/httpd/conf in Red Hat and /etc/httpd in SuSE.

By default, Apache comes fully configured on your Linux system, and may even be running unless you had decided otherwise during the installation of the system. There's not much that you have to change in its configuration files. However, in large setups, one machine may act as the Web server for multiple domains—a feature allowed by Apache. In that case, you need to make separate entries in these files for each *virtual host* and control its directory access rights. You may even need to tune certain parameters for efficient operation.

24.14 httpd.conf: The Configuration File

In these sections, we'll discuss the parameters (Apache calls them *directives*) not by the sequence they occur in the file, but instead by grouping them by their function.

24.14.1 Some Basic Settings

Apache uses the ServerRoot directive to set the directory where the configuration files are located. Make sure the files are placed there:

```
ServerRoot /etc/httpd
```

Apache first looks for httpd.conf, then srm.conf and access.conf. Even if you move all contents into httpd.conf, Apache may still look for the other two files unless you direct it to ignore them:

```
ResourceConfig /dev/null
AccessConfig /dev/null
```

There are also separate directives for the location of **httpd**'s PID file and its access and error log files:

```
PidFile /var/run/httpd/pid
ErrorLog /var/log/httpd/error_log
CustomLog /var/log/httpd/access_log common
```

Apache uses port 80. All port numbers below 1024 are considered to be privileged ports. However, it's the master **httpd** process that runs with root privileges. The child **httpd** processes that actually do the work always run with normal user privileges. As a safety measure, make sure the UID and GUID used by **httpd** are not used by any other user. Red Hat uses nobody for both:

```
User nobody                                    nobody to be in /etc/passwd
Group nobody                                    nobody to be in /etc/group
```

The Webmaster's (the person responsible for maintaining the Web server) address is set by default to *root@localhost*. This is the address the user will often see when she encounters a problem on the server. Since the Webmaster may not use the root account, and the host has its own FQDN, you should set the ServerAdmin and ServerName directives to meaningful values:

```
ServerName www.planets.com
ServerAdmin webmaster@planets.com
```

ServerName is the name returned to the client by the server. For instance, even if the Web server is running on the host *neptune*, you would want users to see the name *www.planets.com* on their URL window. Before you set ServerName to return a name that is different from the canonical name of the host, make sure the alias (here, www) features in the DNS used to access the Web server (as a CNAME record). The zone file does list www as the alias *(24.3.3)*, so we can legitimately set ServerName as above.

24.14.2   Loading Modules

Apache is composed of a number of modules, many of which are built into it during the software building process. These modules provide the basic functionality of the Web server. Many of the directives are module-specific, and you can't expect a particular directive to work unless the respective module is available. Starting with version 1.3, Apache can also dynamically load modules at run time, so you can start with a smaller executable and add only those modules you require.

There are two directives that make these modules available. The LoadModule directive loads the executable module—the object file with the extension .so, and you'll find lines like these:

```
LoadModule mime_module        /usr/lib/apache/mod_mime.so
LoadModule cgi_module         /usr/lib/apache/mod_cgi.so
LoadModule proxy_module       /usr/lib/apache/libproxy.so
LoadModule auth_module        /usr/lib/apache/mod_auth.so
```

For each module, a corresponding AddModule directive should also be placed. This directive loads the source program that was used to create the executable module. Source filenames always end with .c:

```
AddModule mod_mime.c
AddModule mod_cgi.c
AddModule mod_proxy.c
AddModule mod_auth.c
```

There's no need to load all modules; that unnecessarily degrades server performance. Load just the modules that you require. For instance, there's no need to load cgi_module if your site doesn't use CGI.

24.14.3   Resource Locations

Besides these configuration files, Apache needs a separate directory for storing the server's Web pages—the HTML documents. This is known as the **document root** directory. The placeholder for HTML files is set with DocumentRoot:

```
DocumentRoot /home/httpd/html
```

This means that when you access a Web page with the URL *http://www.planets.com/survey.html*, you are actually accessing the file /home/httpd/html/survey.html on the file system. Apache's security feature doesn't allow you to move up this hierarchy and access a file in, say, /usr/sbin. (Anonymous ftp also doesn't allow that.)

CGI programs are responsible for most of the break-ins on the Web, and they need to be kept in a directory separate from DocumentRoot. This is invariably the directory cgi-bin, and is set with ScriptAlias:

```
ScriptAlias /cgi-bin/ /home/httpd/cgi-bin/
```

ScriptAlias sets the alias for a directory containing CGI programs only. It can't be used to define aliases for other directories. Icons can have their own directory too, but this time the aliasing has to be done with Alias:

```
Alias /icons/ /home/httpd/icons/
```

The Alias statement is useful for setting the path of any directory (except the ones containing CGI programs).

One host can serve multiple users, and these users need separate directories for their pages. This is determined by UserDir, and the default is set to public_html:

```
UserDir public_html
```

This directory is to be created in the user's home directory. So if Apache encounters a URL request for *www.planets.com/~juliet*, it has to offer the *default* Web page from the directory /home/juliet/public html (assuming home directories are placed in /home). Apache also permits selective access to "UserDir" directories:

```
UserDir disable                                    Disables all users
UserDir enable henry romeo juliet                   except these three
```

Apache allows users to override the security restrictions that it imposes. It specifies the name of the file that contains user-defined restrictions:

```
AccessFileName .htaccess
```

This means that every user can place a `.htaccess` file in every directory whose access rights she wants to set individually. This file can contain many of the directives used in the configuration file. But they will apply only to that directory and all its subdirectories.

24.14.4 File Types

What is the default Web page? When a URL ends with only a directory name, Apache uses the directive `DirectoryIndex` to look for one or more files in that directory. By default, this is set to `index.html`, but in sites containing several users, it's common to find a comprehensive set of defaults:

```
DirectoryIndex default.htm index.htm index.html index.cgi welcome.html
```

To accommodate Windows 3.1 users, the setting also accepts three character extensions. If none of the files are found in the directory, Apache displays a listing of that directory. There are wonderful options that control the display and let you add your own cosmetic touches, but we'll gloss over them except note that it's best to leave this setting on:

```
FancyIndexing on
```

Apache defines new encoded file types, and it handles them on its own. For instance, files compressed with **compress** and **gzip** can be uncompressed on-the-fly by the browser itself without invoking the **uncompress** and **gunzip** programs:

```
AddEncoding x-compress Z
AddEncoding x-gzip gz
```

Both Mosaic and Netscape can do this decompression automatically. So if you click on a `.gz` file in a directory listing from your browser, you'll be able to see the uncompressed file instantly.

The preceding discussions apply well to a host serving Web pages of a single site. Large installations often serve several sites using the concept of *virtual hosting*. In such cases, each site will have a different location for all these directories—often under their own home directory. We'll have a look at the configuration of a virtual host later.

24.14.5 Tuning the Server

Glittering content will invite lots of hits on the site. It's quite common for many sites to record several hundred thousand hits in a single day. The default Apache configuration won't allow this as it has to spawn separate **httpd** child daemons for servicing each client request. Rather than wait for a client request to spawn such a process, a number of processes are kept ready to reduce the startup time. This is controlled by these settings:

```
MinSpareServers 5
MaxSpareServers 20
StartServers 8
```

At any time, five processes will be idling and waiting to serve a request. For a busy site, you have to adjust the value of the maximum number of server processes that need to be maintained. The system also starts eight processes during startup.

Apart from the above, you also need to set a limit on the maximum number of clients that **httpd** can serve. The default is set to 150:

```
MaxClients 150
```

HTTP runs on the TCP protocol *(23.1)*, which means a connection has to be set up before data can be transferred. When the user clicks on a link, a new connection is set up, thereby increasing the file transfer time. HTTP 1.1 supports the **keepalive** feature which maintains a persistent connection. The behavior of this persistent connection is controlled by these directives:

```
KeepAlive On                                                    This setting must be on
KeepAliveTimeout 15
```

The second setting implies that the current connection will be held for 15 seconds for the next request to arrive. In any case, all requests and acknowledgements must be completed within five minutes:

```
Timeout 300
```

Congestion on the network can be eased by using IP addresses rather than hostnames in the logs:

```
HostnameLookups Off
```

This setting implies that an incoming connection will not invoke a DNS lookup, thereby improving the server's response time.

24.15 Virtual Hosting

All sites on the Web are not hosted on individual machines. Apache supports **virtual hosts** on a single machine, and it's common to find a single host accommodating over a thousand sites. The host may have multiple IP addresses, with each IP address representing one site. Alternatively, it can have a single IP address with multiple domain names. You can set many server parameters for every virtual host with the <VirtualHost> directive (note the angular brackets this time).

Velvet has now decided to use the 20 MB of space that Planets has agreed to provide on their server for hosting Web content. We'll assume that the site *www.velvet.com* has its own individual IP address. This address must feature as an A record in the DNS pointing to *www.planets.com*. A set of directives can be defined separately between the <VirtualHost> and </VirtualHost> tags:

```
<VirtualHost www.velvet.com>
    ServerName www.velvet.com
    ServerAdmin webmaster@velvet.com
    DocumentRoot /home/velvet/www
```

```
    TransferLog /home/velvet/logs/access-log
    ScriptAlias /cgi-bin/ /home/velvet/www/cgi-bin/
</VirtualHost>
```

You can use the IP address in the first directive itself instead of `www.velvet.com`. The `ServerName` changes to `www.velvet.com` from `www.planets.com` when the server receives a request for this site. This site also has its own `DocumentRoot` and `cgi-bin` directories. Presumably, Velvet has a user account velvet in Planets' `/etc/passwd`. By having a home directory-based hosting arrangement, Planets can decentralize administration and let Velvet manage its own site. This generally means that Velvet should have permissions to connect to its virtual domain using **telnet** and **ftp**.

For every virtual host, there has to be a separate section like the one above. Barring a few exceptions like `ServerRoot`, `ServerType` and the parameters used in tuning Apache, practically any `httpd.conf` directive can be used here.

24.16   Directory Access Control

Apache, through `access.conf`, can and is often used to set access restrictions on directories containing documents and CGI programs. In addition, it allows users to override the systemwide restrictions on a per directory basis. Access restrictions are specified between the `<Directory>` and `</Directory>` tags, and a few typical ones for a directory containing HTML files could look like this:

```
<Directory /home/httpd/html>
  Options Indexes FollowSymLinks
  AllowOverride None                                        Can't use .htaccess
  order deny,allow
  deny from all
  allow from hillinfo.com
</Directory>
```

The `Options` statement specifies the options permitted for this directory and all its subdirectories. The server generates a list of files in a directory if it can't find the file `index.html` (Indexes). It also uses a symbolic link in just the same way it handles an ordinary file (`FollowSymLinks`). `AllowOverride` determines whether a user is allowed to override these options. Here, no user can (None), but the `cgi-bin` directory permits every user to override these options:

```
<Directory /home/httpd/cgi-bin>
  AllowOverride All
  Options ExecCGI
</Directory>
```

The setting `AllowOverride All` here implies that every user can nullify these restrictions by placing similar directives in their local file `.htaccess`. When the server retrieves a file from any directory, it first looks for this file. If present, and if the overriding feature is set, then the server applies the statements placed in this file. It often makes sense to let users configure their own directories because the server doesn't have to be restarted when they change the `.htaccess` files.

Notice that the cgi-bin directory uses a special option setting (ExecCGI). Any directory having the ExecCGI setting can be used to hold CGI programs. CGI programs are a big security threat on the Web, and it's necessary that permissions to run CGI programs from a specific directory be set explicitly, rather than by default. However, the statement is redundant here as it is already implied by the ScriptAlias statement that refers to the same directory.

You can set access rights for a directory tree and then override them for a specific subdirectory:

```
Alias /web/docs /home/html/docs

<Directory /web/docs>
     Options Indexes FollowSymLinks
     AllowOverride None
</Directory>

<Directory /web/docs/d1>
     AllowOverride All
</Directory>
```

The server looks for .htaccess in the /web/docs/d1 directory but not in any other subdirectory of /web/docs. This improves server performance.

The order, allow and deny statements are used to define hosts that may be allowed to access documents or run programs in this directory. order determines the sequence in which the access rules are implemented. Here, the deny rule is applied first and then the allow rule. When allowing access to only a handful of hosts, it's usual to deny all users the right first and then allow access to some. Here, only *hillinfo.com* is permitted to access files in the directory. To allow access to all, just use allow from all.

Besides imposing host restrictions, Apache can also require user authentication for accessing a directory. Users then have to provide a username and a password to use certain services; you must have seen all this on the Web already. Apache has user authentication schemes that use the **htpasswd** program. These are some of its advanced features that we can't cover in this text.

Tip

If you don't want any server options for a specific directory to be overridden, just use AllowOverride None on that directory. This can provide a significant boost to server performance as Apache will not then look for .htaccess files in any of the subdirectories of this directory. It increases security as well.

SUMMARY

The Internet uses the Domain Name Service (DNS) to resolve FQDNs to IP addresses and vice versa. The information is held in a set of *name servers*. A domain is divided into *zones*, and the *master* server is authoritative for the zone. The *slave* server loads its information from the master by a *zonal transfer*.

The querying is done by a *resolver*, which is a set of library routines built into the TCP/IP application. It uses the file /etc/resolv.conf. The resolution follows a hierarchical pattern, and when the local name server fails to provide an answer, the root name servers are queried.

BIND is the most common implementation of DNS and uses the **named** daemon. The *hints* file contains the IP addresses and FQDNs of the root name servers and is maintained by every name server in its cache. The *zone* file contains IP address-hostname mappings. The *reverse lookup* and *localhost* files perform reverse resolution—converting the IP address to the FQDN, or 127.0.0.1 to *localhost*. DNS also specifies the servers meant to receive mail for a domain.

The database files use name server (NS) records to specify the IP addresses of the name servers and mail exchanger (MX) records to provide pointers to the mail servers. The address (A) and pointer (PTR) records map addresses to FQDNs, and vice versa. The *canonical name* (CNAME) record is used to provide aliases. The location of all files and the type of name server are specified in /etc/named.conf. **ndc** can start and stop **named**, while **nslookup** can be used to test the setup.

sendmail is the universal transport agent, and **procmail** handles delivery on Linux systems. Mail is fetched from a remote site with the *Post Office Protocol* (POP)—often using a dialup line.

A central *hub* (mail server) generally sends and receives mail on behalf of all hosts. It is often configured to hide the hostname in the email address. The hub may forward mail to individual hosts or offer a file system to be mounted with NFS. It can also act as a POP/IMAP server.

sendmail runs as a daemon (-bd) at port 25 for receiving mail and as an SMTP client (-q) for flushing the mail queue. The queue is maintained in /var/spool/mqueue. **sendmail** takes instructions from /etc/sendmail.cf and performs mail forwarding using /etc/aliases. Aliases are used to redirect mail to one or more users, a mailing list or a file.

sendmail.cf uses macros (D) to define a smart relay host (DS) and perform masquerading (DM). Lowercase macro letters are defined internally. A class is used for defining the domains (Cw) for which **sendmail** receives mail. With options (O), you can set the number of times **sendmail** will try to deliver a message before notifying the failure (O Timeout.queuereturn).

Linux systems use **fetchmail** and .fetchmailrc for retrieving mail from a POP/IMAP server. You can decide whether to keep messages (-k) or retrieve all of them (-a). **fetchmail** is used to get mail for an entire domain held in a single mailbox and then distribute it to the individual mailboxes.

Apache is the most widely used Web server on the Internet. It runs the **httpd** daemon at port 80 and uses the HTTP protocol. **httpd** spawns another **httpd** process in nonprivileged mode to handle a client request. The configuration is set in httpd.conf, but many systems use srm.conf and access.conf as well. Apache is flexible enough to load only the modules required at runtime (LoadModule and AddModule).

Configuration files are held in the server's root directory (ServerRoot). Location of the HTML files is set by DocumentRoot. CGI programs are kept in a separate directory for security reasons (ScriptAlias). Users can keep their own files in separate directories (UserDir).

When a URL doesn't end in a filename, the server looks for the file index.html unless otherwise specified (DirectoryIndex). Apache and modern browsers can decompress `.Z` and `.gz` files on-the-fly (`AddEncoding`). It's because of `KeepAlive` that HTTP 1.1 can support *persistent* connections till the `KeepAliveTimeout` period.

Apache supports *virtual hosting* (`<VirtualHost>`) by which multiple domains can be hosted on a single server, either with a single IP address or different IP addresses. Every virtual domain can have its own settings for document locations and access rights.

Every directory (`<Directory>`) can have its own access restrictions too. `Options` determine whether CGI programs are permitted to run from a directory (`ExecCGI`) or a directory listing is allowed (`Indexes`). A user may or may not be allowed to override these options (`AllowOverride`). One or more sites may be allowed (`allow from`) or denied access (`deny from`) to a directory.

SELF-TEST

24.1   What is the role of the slave name server and how does it obtain its data?

24.2   How does **ftp** get the IP addresses of the name servers?

24.3   How does DNS specify the mail servers that are meant to receive mail for a domain?

24.4   How do you define several names for the same host?

24.5   Who is responsible for delivery? Name some important delivery programs.

24.6   Where is outgoing mail stored, and how do you view the queue?

24.7   How will you notify **sendmail** that it has to receive mail for a hundred domains?

24.8   How will you check whether **sendmail** or POP is running on a system?

24.9   You defined forwarding in /etc/aliases, and it doesn't work. What mistake could you have made?

24.10   How many **httpd** processes will be kept ready on a system?

24.11   How do you set the Web server's root directory for HTML documents?

EXERCISES

24.1   What is the difference between a *domain* and a *zone*? How does DNS handle them?

24.2   What is a *caching-only* name server?

24.3   How do the root name servers help in the resolution process?

24.4   When will you need to convert an IP address to an FQDN?

24.5   How does the slave server know that the master server entries have been modified?

24.6   Mail addressed to *user@hillinfo.com* is handled by a host *mail.hillinfo.com*. But which host will accept mail addressed to *user@www.hillinfo.com*?

24.7   If you are able to access a site with **telnet edison** in addition to **telnet edison.hillinfo.com**, what could the reason be? Assume that there are no entries in /etc/hosts.

24.8   How will you invoke **sendmail** to receive mail and flush the queue every half hour?

24.9   If SMTP delivers mail directly to another SMTP, why does mail sometimes take a few days to reach a person?

24.10   A user wants to hide her hostname when sending out mail and wants her ISP to handle her mail. What should she do?

24.11   You want to be informed within an hour that mail has not been delivered. Which setting do you need to change?

24.12   How does a client using Netscape Messenger need to invoke **sendmail** to send mail to the hub?

24.13   What is the role of /etc/passwd in an incoming mail server?

24.14   How do you configure Apache to let a user melinda access Web pages placed in her own home directory? How is the directory accessed in a URL?

24.15   How will you make Apache serve the file default.html when a URL doesn't contain a filename?

24.16   How do you configure your server to maintain persistent connections?

24.17   What is the significance of the ScriptAlias statement?

24.18   How do you disable access to the cgi-bin directory from the domain *velvet.com*?

24.19   How can you enable CGI execution on a directory?

KEY TERMS

authoritative answer *(24.2.1)*

caching-only name server *(24.2.1)*

canonical name *(24.3.3)*

document root *(24.14.3)*

domain masquerading *(24.10)*

firewall *(24.1)*

httpd servers *(24.13)*

hub *(24.7.1)*

keepalive connection *(24.14.5)*

mail alias *(24.9)*

mail exchanger *(24.2)*

mail relay server *(24.10)*

master name server *(24.2.1)*

multidrop mailbox *(24.12)*

name server *(24.2.1)*

origin *(24.3.2)*

pointer record *(24.3.4)*

resolver *(24.2.1)*

resource record *(24.3.3)*

root name server *(24.2.1)*

slave name server *(24.2.1)*

Start of Authority *(24.3.2)*

virtual host *(24.15)*

zonal transfer *(24.2.1)*

zone *(24.2.1)*

The C Shell—
Programming Constructs

The C shell was developed at the University of California, Berkeley, by William Joy, the architect of **vi**. Both the Korn shell and bash have drawn heavily from the features of this shell. Linux offers a vastly superior C shell, **tcsh**. We have discussed the environment-related features of this shell in Chapter 17; in this appendix we cover its programming constructs.

Computation

The C shell can handle integers for computations. Variable assignment is made with **set** or @:

```
% set x=5
% @ y = 10                                              A space after @
% @ sum=$x + $y
% @ product = $x * $y
% @ quotient = $y/$x                                    Space around / required
@: Badly formed number
% @ quotient = $y / $x
```

Incrementing numbers is done in these ways:

```
@ x = $x + 1
@ x++
@ x ++
```

The @ must be followed by whitespace even if the = need not have any around it. There must also be whitespace on either side of the operand (i.e., the +, -, *, / and % symbols). Variable values are echoed normally with the **echo** statement.

Arrays

The C shell has a number of variables—some unique to itself and some having similar counterparts in the other shells. You have learned how to set and evaluate these variables in Chapter 17, but you would have observed that one variable (path) is set a little differently:

```
set path = (/bin /usr/bin /usr/local/bin /usr/dt/bin .)
```

The above list is actually an *array* supported by this shell. path is normally referred to as a variable, but it can also be considered to be an array of five elements. The first element is accessed by $path[1], the second by $path[2], and so on. The number of elements in the array is indicated by the parameter $#, followed immediately by the variable (or array) name. Let's look at a few examples:

```
% echo $path
/bin /usr/bin /usr/local/bin /usr/dt/bin .
% echo $path[4]
/usr/dt/bin
% echo $#path
5
```

Values can be put into an array with the **set** statement, and **shift** also works with arrays:

```
% set numb = ( 9876 2345 6213 )          Like set 9876 2345 6213 in the other shells
% echo $numb[1]
9876
% echo $#numb                                      Entire list stored in $numb[*]
3
% shift numb                                             Uses array name
% echo $numb[1]
2345
```

Executing a Script

By default, scripts written in the C shell language are executed by the Bourne shell. (Linux uses bash to execute a **tcsh** script.) There are two ways of getting around this; either execute the script with the **csh** command, or place the interpreter specification at the beginning of every C shell script:

```
csh script_name
#!/bin/csh
```

Most C shells support the more convenient second form, but if your version doesn't support it, then the only option left is to use the **csh** command itself.

The if Statement

The **if** statement has a different form here. First, the keyword **then** must be in the *same* line as **if**. Second, the statement terminator is **endif** and not **fi**. Finally, the condition being tested usually has to be enclosed in a matched pair of parentheses:

```
% cat filesize.csh
#!/bin/csh
# Program: filesize.csh - Converts file blocks to size in bytes
```

```
if ( $#argv != 2 ) then              # Condition tested with != instead of -ne
    echo Two parameters required
else
    @ size = $1 * 512
    echo Size of $2 is $size bytes
endif
% filesize.csh 124 tulec04
Size of tulec04 is 63488 bytes
```

Numeric comparison is made with the C-like operators >, == and !=, and so on, rather than the ones Bourne uses (-gt, -lt etc.). $#argv (and not $#) is set to the number of arguments passed to a script. The arguments are individually accessed with $argv[1], $argv[2] and so on. To maintain compatibility with the other shells, the C shell also lets you access them as $1 and $2, and so forth.

You can have single-line conditionals when there is no **else** clause:

```
if ( $#argv == 2 ) @ size = $1 * 512 ; echo Size of $2 is $size bytes
```

When executing a UNIX command as the control command, the command itself should be surrounded by a matched pair of curly braces and not parentheses:

```
if { grep "director" emp.lst } then
```

Finally, remember, that there is no **test** statement or its [ ] equivalent in this shell. However, some of the file attributes can be tested here. You can use **if (-r foo)** to test if the file foo is readable, **if (! -d bar)** to check whether bar is not a directory, and so on. For the complete list of file tests, look up Appendix D.

The switch **Statement**

The **switch** statement (like **case**) matches an expression for more than one alternative, and uses the keywords **endsw**, **case** and **breaksw**. This three-option menu provides a simple example:

```
% cat menu.csh
#!/bin/csh
set choice = $argv[1]            # Option supplied as argument to script
switch ($choice)                 # Like case $choice
case 1:
    ls -l
    breaksw                      # Stops further matching
case 2:
    ps -f
    breaksw
case 3:                          # Can also use default: for the last option
    exit
    breaksw
endsw
```

case has a different use here and is terminated by a colon. **breaksw** breaks control out of the construct after a match is found and the matching actions performed. If this word is not provided, the actions related to *all* options are performed. This makes no sense in most cases, so make sure it's there. Often the last **case** option is used to perform some action—usually aborting the program. In that case, the specific value of the variable choice doesn't matter, and you can use the **default** keyword.

The while and foreach Loops

There are two loops—**while** and **foreach** (instead of **for**). Both loops have three major differences with their counterparts in the other shells:

- The loop condition (or the list) is to be enclosed within parentheses.
- The **do** keyword is not used.
- The loop is terminated with **end** instead of **done**.

Let's consider the **while** loop first. We'll enter a simple sequence at the prompt:

```
% set x = 5
% while ( $x > 3 )                          Can also use while { true }
?   ps -f                                       PS2 for C shell is a ?
?   sleep 5
? end
```

The **foreach** loop also has differences with its Bourne rival, but has been emulated by **perl**. The keyword **foreach** replaces **for**, and the **in** keyword is not required. The example in Section 18.16 can be reframed like this:

```
% foreach file (chap20 chap21 chap22 chap23)
?   cp $file ${file}.bak
?   echo $file copied to $file.bak
? end
```

There are other ways of using a list:

```
foreach item ( `cat clist` )
foreach fname ( *.c )                      All C programs in current directory
foreach fname ( $* )                                    Script arguments
```

The repeat Statement

If a single command has to be repeated a finite number of times, you can use the **repeat** statement:

```
% repeat 3 date
Mon Jan 17 22:40:52 EST 2000
Mon Jan 17 22:40:52 EST 2000
Mon Jan 17 22:40:52 EST 2000
```

The goto Statement

You can use the **goto** statement also. Though this construct is hardly used by programmers today, it's often the best way to wriggle out if used with caution. Let's consider this script:

```
% cat gotoexamp.csh
#!/bin/csh
if ( $#argv == 0 ) then                              # No arguments entered
   goto endblock
else
   grep $1 emp.lst
   exit
endif
endblock:
echo "You have not keyed in an argument"
```

The **exit** statement makes sure that after **grep** has completed execution, control doesn't "fall through" and result in execution of the **echo** command. If you don't place it there, the error message will appear irrespective of whether an argument was supplied or not.

The onintr **Statement**

The **onintr** statement (**trap** in other shells) specifies the commands to be executed when an interrupt signal is sent to the script. It is normally placed at the beginning of a shell script:

```
% cat onintr.csh
#!/bin/csh
onintr cleanup
cut -c1-10 index > $$
cut -c21- index > $$.1
paste $$ $$.1 > pastelist
rm $$ $$.1
exit                                 # Required to stop intrusion into cleanup

cleanup:
rm $$ $$.1
echo "Program interrupted"
```

Like the **goto** statement, the **onintr** statement is followed by a label. Execution branches to that label when the interrupt key is pressed. You may want to ignore the signal and continue processing. In that case, you should make the program immune to such signals by using **onintr** with a -:

```
onintr -
```

The C shell has been completely superseded in power and versatility by the Korn shell and bash which have more powerful programming constructs. If you are looking for an improved C shell, then use **tcsh** offered by Linux.

vi/vim and emacs Command Reference

While each editor has its own unique features, there is considerable overlap of their functions. This appendix makes a comparative presentation of the *editing* features of the **vi/vim** and **emacs** editors. This excludes the nonediting features of **emacs** (like the **dired** function or the mail handling feature). Many of the commands here can be used with a *repeat factor* (**vi**) or the *digit argument* (**emacs**). Commands that act on a region apply to **emacs** and **vim** only, but not **vi**. For details, look up the two chapters (4 and 5) where most of these commands have been explained. For convenience, commands and their customization parameters are grouped together. Commands that operate on sentences and paragraphs have not been considered.

When you encounter a fully-worded **emacs** command in this appendix, you'll have to precede it with *[Alt-x]*, and this has not been indicated explicitly. But the variables that need to be set with **set-variable** have been shown. All variables used with **set-variable** can also be placed in .emacs using the **setq** command.

Here, the *[Alt]* key has been used with **emacs** to signify the *[Meta]* key. Use the key (like *[Esc]*) that actually works on your system.

Navigation

vi Command	Function	emacs Command
h (or *[Backspace]*)	Move cursor left	*[Ctrl-b]*
l (or *[Spacebar]*)	Move cursor right	*[Ctrl-f]*
k (or *[Ctrl-p]*)	Move cursor up	*[Ctrl-p]*
j (or *[Ctrl-n]*)	Move cursor down	*[Ctrl-n]*
[Ctrl-f]	Scroll full page forward	*[Ctrl-v]*
[Ctrl-b]	Scroll full page backward	*[Alt-v]*
[Ctrl-d]	Scroll half page forward	—
[Ctrl-u]	Scroll half page backward	—
1G	Move to beginning of file	*[Alt-<]*
40G	Move to line 40	goto-line 40
G	Move to end of file	*[Alt->]*
—	Toggle line number display mode	line-number-mode
[Ctrl-g]	Display current line number and percentage of file	what-line
:set number (nu)	Show all lines numbered	—

Navigation along a Line

The **B**, **E** and **W** commands in **vi** perform the same functions as their lowercase counterparts except that punctuation is ignored. There's no equivalent punctuation ignoring feature in **emacs**.

vi Command	Function	emacs Command
b	Move back to beginning of word	[Alt-b]
e	Move forward to end of word	[Alt-f]
w	Move forward to beginning of word	—
0 or |	Move to beginning of line	[Ctrl-a]
30|	Move to column 30	[Ctrl-a][Alt-30][Ctrl-f]
^	Move to first character of first word in line	[Alt-m]
$	Move to end of line	[Ctrl-e]

Inserting Text

Unlike **vi**, **emacs** is always in the "input mode." The **emacs** commands shown here merely take you to a specific point in a line from where you can begin your insertion. Insertion of text in **emacs** is shown as *text*. Insertion of a control character is shown here for *[Ctrl-b]*.

vi Command	Function	emacs Command
i	Insert text to left of cursor	*text*
20i-*[Esc]*	Insert 20 hyphens	*[Alt-20]* -
I	Insert text at beginning of line	*[Ctrl-a] text*
a	Append text to right of cursor	*[Ctrl-f] text*
A	Append text at end of line	*[Ctrl-e] text*
o	Open line below	*[Ctrl-e][Enter]*
0	Open line above	*[Ctrl-a][Enter]*
[Ctrl-v][Ctrl-b]	Insert *[Ctrl-b]*	*[Ctrl-q][Ctrl-b]*
[Ctrl-v][Esc]	Insert *[Esc]*	*[Ctrl-q][Esc]*
:set showmode	Display message when **vi** is in input mode	—
:set sm	Show momentarily match to a) and }	blink-matching paren t (with set-variable)
:set ts=*n*	Set tab stops to *n* (default: 8)	edit-tab-stops
:set ai	Next line starts at previous indented level	—

Deleting and Moving Text

All the editing actions in this section can be undone. However, *[Ctrl-d]*, the command that deletes a single character in **emacs** (first entry), doesn't constitute a kill operation. A character deleted with *[Ctrl-d]* can't be restored from the kill ring. However, when the command is preceded by the digit argument, the deletion can be restored.

vi Command	Function	emacs Command
x	Delete character under cursor	*[Ctrl-d]* or *[Delete]*
6x	Delete character under cursor and five characters on right	*[Alt-6][Ctrl-d]*

Deleting and Moving Text (continued)

vi Command	Function	emacs Command
X	Delete previous character	—
dd	Delete current line	*[Ctrl-a][Ctrl-k][Ctrl-k]*
4dd	Delete four lines	*[Alt-4][Ctrl-k]*
64dd	Delete 64 lines	*[Ctrl-u][Ctrl-u][Ctrl-u][Ctrl-k]*
dw	Delete word	*[Alt-d]*
—	Delete previous word	*[Alt][Delete]* or *[Alt][Backspace]*
d0 (d and zero)	Delete to beginning of line	*[Alt-0][Ctrl-k]* (Alt and zero)
d$	Delete to end of line	*[Ctrl-k]*
—	Delete blank lines	*[Ctrl-x][Ctrl-o]*
d	Delete a region (**vim** only)	*[Ctrl-w]*
p	Put deleted text on right (or below in **vi**)	*[Ctrl-y]*
P	Put deleted text above or left	—
"add	Delete current line to buffer a	*[Ctrl-u][Ctrl-x]* xa (on region)
"ap	Restore contents from buffer a	*[Ctrl-u][Ctrl-x]* ga
—	Preserve *n* sections of deleted/copied text in kill ring	kill-ring-max *n* (with set-variable)
ddp	Interchange current line with next	*[Ctrl-n][Ctrl-x][Ctrl-t]*
kddp	Interchange current line with previous	*[Ctrl-x][Ctrl-t]*
J	Join current line with next line	*[Ctrl-e][Ctrl-d]*
kJ	Join current line with previous line	*[Alt-^]*
xp	Transpose two characters	*[Ctrl-t]*
—	Transpose two words	*[Alt-t]*
—	Center line	center-line

Copying Text

vi Command	Function	emacs Command
yy	Copy current line	Requires a region (see below)
6yy	Copy six lines	As above
yw	Copy a word	As above
y	Copy a region (**vim** only)	*[Alt-w]*
p	Put copied text on right (or below in **vi**)	*[Ctrl-y]*
P	Put copied text on left or above	—
"ayy	Copy current line to buffer a	*[Ctrl-x]* xa (on region)
"ap	Restore contents from buffer a	*[Ctrl-x]* ga

Changing, Reading In and Filtering Text

vi Command	Function	emacs Command
r*ch*	Replace single character under cursor with *ch*	*[Ctrl-d]* ch
R	Replace text from cursor to right	Use overwrite-mode, then *text*

Changing, Reading In and Filtering Text (continued)

vi Command	Function	emacs Command
s	Replace single character under cursor with any number of characters	*[Ctrl-d] text*
S	Replace entire line	*[Ctrl-a][Ctrl-k] text*
cw	Change a word	*[Alt-d] text*
c	Change text of region (**vim** only)	—
~	Reverse case of scanned text or region	—
—	Convert word to uppercase	*[Alt-u]*
—	Convert word to lowercase	*[Alt-l]*
—	Capitalize first character of word	*[Alt-c]*
!navigation_cmd cmd	Run command *cmd* on region or section terminated by *navigation_cmd*	*[Ctrl-u][Alt-l] cmd*
—	Run *cmd* on region; output in separate window	*[Alt-l] cmd*
!navigation_cmd sort	Sort region or section terminated by *navigation_cmd*	sort-lines
!tr '[a-z]' '[A-Z]'	Convert region to uppercase (**vim** only)	*[Ctrl-x][Ctrl-u]*
!tr '[A-Z]' '[a-z]'	Convert region to lowercase (**vim** only)	*[Ctrl-x][Ctrl-l]*
:r foo	Read file foo below current line	*[Ctrl-x]* i foo
:r !head -3 foo	Read first three lines of foo below current line	*[Ctrl-u][Alt-!]* head -3 foo

Starting the Editor

vi Command	Function	emacs Command
vi +100 foo	Open file at line 200	emacs +100 foo
vi +/*pat* foo	Open file at first occurrence of pattern *pat*	—
vi + foo	Open file at end	—
—	Load henry's .emacs	emacs -u henry foo
—	Don't load .emacs	emacs -q foo
vi -R foo	Open file in read-only mode	—

Saving and Quitting

vi Command	Function	emacs Command
:w	Save file and remain in editing mode	*[Ctrl-x][Ctrl-s]*
:w bar	Like *Save As .....* in Microsoft Windows	*[Ctrl-x][Ctrl-w]*
:w! bar	As above, but overwrite existing file bar	—
:*n1,n2*w foo	Write lines *n1* to *n2* to file foo	write-region (on region)
:*n1,n2*w >> foo	Append lines *n1* to *n2* to file foo	append-to-file (on region)
:.w foo	Write current line to file foo	—
:$w foo	Write last line to file foo	—
:x	Save file and quit editing mode	*[Ctrl-u][Ctrl-x][Ctrl-c]*
:wq	As above	—

Saving and Quitting (continued)

vi Command	Function	emacs Command
:q	Quit editing mode when no changes are made to file	[Ctrl-x][Ctrl-c]
:q!	Quit editing mode but after abandoning changes	As above, but enter n and yes at prompts
—	Enable/disable autosaving mode	auto-save-default (t or nil) (with set-variable)
—	Set autosave interval to n keystrokes	auto-save-interval n (with set-variable)
—	Set autosave interval to n seconds	auto-save-timeout n (with set-variable)
—	Recover autosaved file	recover-file

Editing Multiple Files

In **vi**, you can't use **:e**, **:n** and **:rew** unless the current file is saved (and autowrite is not set). The **!** placed after the command overrides the safety feature. **emacs** lets you freely move from one file to another without saving.

vi Command	Function	emacs Command
:e foo	Stop editing current file and edit file foo	[Ctrl-x][Ctrl-f]
:e! foo	As above, but after abandoning changes made to current file	Saving not necessary
—	Replace current buffer with another file	[Ctrl-x][Ctrl-v]
:e!	Load last saved edition of current file	revert-buffer
[Ctrl-^]	Return to most recently edited file	[Ctrl-x] b [Enter]
:n	Edit next file (when invoked with multiple filenames)	[Ctrl-x] b and select from list
:set autowrite (aw)	Write current file automatically whenever switching files (with :n in **vi**)	Not necessary
:rew	Rewind file list to start editing first file (when invoked with multiple filenames)	—
—	Kill current buffer	[Ctrl-x] k

Multiple Windows (emacs **and** vim)

vi Command	Function	emacs Command
:sp	Split current window in two	[Ctrl-x] 2
:new	Open a new blank window	[Ctrl-x] b
[Ctrl-w][Ctrl-w]	Toggle between windows	[Ctrl-x] o
:on	Make current window the only window	[Ctrl-x] 1
:q	Quit current window	[Ctrl-x] 0 (zero)
:qa	Quit all windows	—
:xa	Save and quit all windows	[Ctrl-x][Ctrl-c] and then !
—	Scroll text forward in other window	[Ctrl][Alt] v

*Multiple Windows (*emacs *and* vim*) (continued)*

vi Command	Function	emacs Command
[Ctrl-w] +	Increase window size	*[Ctrl-x] ^*
[Ctrl-w] –	Decrease window size (by *n* lines in **emacs**)	*[Ctrl-u] –n [Ctrl-x] ^*
—	Open file in another window	*[Ctrl-x] 4 [Ctrl-f]*

Search and Repeat

Unlike **emacs**, **vi** uses the same search and repeat techniques for strings and regular expressions. **emacs** can also make a search incremental. **vi** uses separate key sequences for searching for a character in a line.

vi Command	Function	emacs Command
/pat	Nonincremental search forward for string *pat*	*[Ctrl-s][Enter] pat*
/pat	As above, but *pat* is a regular expression	*[Ctrl][Alt]* s *[Enter]pat*
?pat	Nonincremental search backward for string *pat*	*[Ctrl-r][Enter] pat*
?pat	As above, but *pat* is a regular expression	*[Ctrl][Alt]* r *[Enter]pat*
—	Incremental search forward for string *pat*	*[Ctrl-s] pat*
—	As above, but *pat* is a regular expression	*[Ctrl][Alt]* s *pat*
—	Incremental search backward for string *pat*	*[Ctrl-r] pat*
—	As above, but *pat* is a regular expression	*[Ctrl][Alt]* r *pat*
n	Repeat string search in same/forward direction	*[Ctrl-s]*
N	Repeat string search in opposite/backward direction	*[Ctrl-r]*
n	Repeat regular expression search in same/forward direction	*[Ctrl][Alt]* s *[Enter][Enter]*
N	Repeat regular expression search in opposite/backward direction	*[Ctrl][Alt]* r *[Enter][Enter]*
—	Search for word following cursor	*[Ctrl-s][Ctrl-w]*
—	Cancel search	*[Esc]*
:set wrapscan (ws)	Continue pattern search by moving to other end of file	—
:set ignorecase (ic)	Ignore case when searching	case-fold-search t (with set-variable)
:set magic	Retain meanings of regular expression characters	—
f*c*	Search forward for character *c*	*[Ctrl-s] c*
F*c*	Search backward for character *c*	*[Ctrl-r] c*
;	Repeat last forward search for character	*[Ctrl-s]*
,	Repeat last reverse search for character	*[Ctrl-r]*

Substitution

vi Command	Function	emacs Command
:1,$s/s1/s2/g	Replace string *s1* with *s2* globally	replace-string
:1,$s/s1/s2/g	As above, but *s1* is a regular expression	replace-regexp
:1,$s/s1/s2/gc	Interactive replacement	*[Alt- %]*

Substitution (continued)

vi Command	Function	emacs Command
:1,$s/s1/s2/gc	As above, but *s1* is a regular expression	query-replace-regexp
—	Preserve original case of letters when replacing	case-replace t (with set-variable)
:s	Repeat last substitution on current line (**vim** only)	—

Marks and Bookmarks

vi Command	Function	emacs Command
ma	Set mark a	*[Ctrl-x]*/a
'a	Move to mark a	*[Ctrl-x]* ja
' '	Toggle between current and previous positions	*[Ctrl-x][Ctrl-x]*
—	Set bookmark	*[Ctrl-x]* rm
—	Jump to bookmark	*[Ctrl-x]* rb

Redoing and Undoing

vi Command	Function	emacs Command
.	Repeat last command (**emacs** command with *[Alt-x]*)	*[Ctrl-x][Esc][Esc]*
u	Undo last editing command	*[Ctrl-x]* u or *[Ctrl--]*
[Ctrl-r]	Redo last undo (**vim** only)	As above but only after all undoing is complete
U	Undo all changes made to current line	—
"4p	Restore 4th recent deletion from buffer (complete lines in **vi**)	*[Ctrl-u]* 4 *[Ctrl-y]*
u. after initial "1p	Undo previous restoration and restore text from next buffer (complete lines in **vi**)	*[Alt-y]* after initial *[Ctrl-y]*

Abbreviating Text

vi Command	Function	emacs Command
—	Enable (toggle in **emacs**) abbreviation mode	abbrev-mode
:ab *stg name*	Abbreviate *name* to *stg*	*stg [Ctrl-x]* aig *name* (ail for local abbreviation)
—	Expand abbreviation from string available in buffer	*[Alt-/]*
:ab	List all abbreviations	list-abbrevs
:unab *stg*	Kill abbreviation *stg*	Delete abbreviation with edit-abbrevs
—	Kill all abbreviations	kill-all-abbrevs
—	Save all current abbreviations	write-abbrev-file
—	Read file containing abbreviations	read-abbrev-file
—	Save all future abbreviations	save-abbrevs t (with set-variable)

Macros and Key Mapping

vi Command	Function	emacs Command
Enter a command sequence, then "ayy	Define a macro (named a in **vi**)	*[Ctrl-x]* (*commands [Ctrl-x]*)
@a	Run last defined macro (named a in **vi**)	*[Ctrl-x]* e
—	Name last defined macro to *macroname*	name-last-kbd-macro
@m	Run macro m (**vi**) or *macroname* (**emacs**)	*macroname* (with *[Alt-x]*)
:map *key commands*	Map *key* to *commands* (**vi**) or *macroname* (**emacs**)	global-set-key, enter *key* and *macroname*
:map! *key commands*	Map *key* to *commands* in input mode	As above
Place the :map command in .exrc	Save macro in file	insert-kbd-macro
—	Load file containing macros	load-file
:map	Display all Command Mode maps	—
:map!	Display all Input Mode maps	—
:unmap *key*	Kill Command Mode map *key*	—
:unmap! *key*	Kill Input Mode map *key*	—

Interface To UNIX

The editor can be suspended with *[Ctrl-z]* only for those shells that enable job control.

vi Command	Function	emacs Command
:!*cmd*	Run UNIX command *cmd*	*[Alt-!]* cmd
:!%	Execute current file as a shell or **perl** script	No shortcut
:sh	Escape to UNIX shell	shell
[Ctrl-z]	Suspend editor	*[Ctrl-z]* or *[Ctrl-x][Ctrl-z]*
:!cc %	Compile currently edited C program	compile
:!javac %	Compile currently edited Java program	No shortcut

Help (emacs only)

vi Command	Function	emacs Command
—	Function performed by keystroke (detailed)	*[Ctrl-h]* k
—	Function performed by keystroke (one-line)	*[Ctrl-h]* c
—	Function performed by command	*[Ctrl-h]* f
—	Key binding available for command	*[Ctrl-h]* w
—	Function of variable and its current setting	*[Ctrl-h]* v
—	Commands that use a concept	*[Ctrl-h]* a
—	Run tutorial	*[Ctrl-h]* t
—	Run info reader	*[Ctrl-h]* i

Miscellaneous

vi Command	Function	emacs Command
—	Cancel a sequence	*[Ctrl-g]*
:set all	Show all set options (**vi**) or variables (**emacs**)	list-options
[Ctrl-l]	Redraw the screen	*[Ctrl-l]*
v	Define start of region (**vim** only)	*[Ctrl-@]* or *[Ctrl][Spacebar]*
—	Complete command from string *stg* used with *[Alt-x]*	*stg [Tab]*
:set ro	Change to read-only mode (**vi**), toggle mode (**emacs**)	*[Ctrl-x][Ctrl-q]*

APPENDIX C

The Regular Expression Superset

Regular expressions are used by the editors **vi/vim** and **emacs**, and the filters **grep**, **egrep**, **sed**, **awk** and **perl**. Unfortunately, they use different subsets of this collection, and most people are not quite sure of the metacharacters that a command recognizes and the ones it doesn't. This appendix was prepared after trying out each and every metacharacter with each of the commands—an exercise that revealed errors (mostly of omission) in the official documentation of these commands. Examples have often been provided to ease understanding.

Basic Regular Expressions

Symbols	vi	emacs	grep	sed	egrep	awk	perl	vim	grep	sed	gawk	Matches
*	•	•	•	•	•	•	•	•	•	•	•	Zero or more occurrences of previous character
g*	•	•	•	•	•	•	•	•	•	•	•	Nothing or g, gg, ggg etc.
gg*	•	•	•	•	•	•	•	•	•	•	•	g, gg, ggg etc.
.	•	•	•	•	•	•	•	•	•	•	•	A single character
.*	•	•	•	•	•	•	•	•	•	•	•	Nothing or any number of characters
[abc]	•	•	•	•	•	•	•	•	•	•	•	a or b or c
[1-3]	•	•	•	•	•	•	•	•	•	•	•	A digit between 1 and 3
[^z]	•	•	•	•	•	•	•	•	•	•	•	Any character except Z
[^a-zA-Z]	•	•	•	•	•	•	•	•	•	•	•	A non-alphabetic character
^DM	•	•	•	•	•	•	•	•	•	•	•	DM at beginning of line
bash$	•	•	•	•	•	•	•	•	•	•	•	bash at end of line

(Linux columns: vim, grep, sed, gawk)

REGULAR EXPRESSIONS

Extended Regular Expressions

Symbols	vi	emacs	grep	sed	egrep	awk	perl	Linux vim	Linux grep	Linux sed	Linux gawk	Matches
+		•			•	•	•				•	One or more occurrences of previous character
g+		•			•	•	•				•	At least one g
g\+								•	•	•		As above
?		•			•	•	•				•	Zero or one occurrence of previous character
g?		•			•	•	•				•	Nothing or one g
g\?									•	•		As above
GIF|JPEG					•	•	•				•	GIF or JPEG
GIF\\\|JPEG		•						•	•	•		As above
wood(cock|house)					•	•	•				•	woodcock or woodhouse
wood\\(cock\\\|house\\)		•						•	•	•		As above
\<pat	•	•						•	•	•	•	Pattern *pat* at beginning of word
pat\>	•	•						•	•	•	•	Pattern *pat* at end of word

Interval and Tagged Regular Expressions

These are advanced regular expressions not used by **egrep** and **awk**. **gawk** and **perl** also accept the Interval Regular Expression but drop the \ in front of the curly brace. **gawk** additionally requires the use of the --posix or -W re-interval option. **perl** drops the \ in front of the (and) as well.

Symbols	vi	emacs	grep	sed	egrep	awk	perl	Linux vim	Linux grep	Linux sed	Linux gawk	Matches
\{*m*\}	•		•	•				•	•	•		*m* occurrences of the previous character
{*m*}							•				•	As above
^.\{9\}nobody	•		•	•				•	•	•		nobody after skipping nine characters from line beginning
^.{9}nobody							•				•	As above
\{*m*,\}	•		•	•				•	•	•		At least *m* occurrences of the previous character
{*m*,}							•				•	As above
\{*m*,*n*\}	•		•	•				•	•	•		Between *m* and *n* occurrences of the previous character
{*m*,*n*}							•				•	As above
\(*exp*\)	•	•	•	•				•	•	•		*exp* and attaches tag \1, \2 etc. to *exp*
(*exp*)							•					As above, but also uses $1, $2 etc.

Escape Sequences

Symbols	vi	emacs	grep	sed	egrep	awk	perl	vim	grep	sed	gawk	Matches
\b		•					•		•	•		On word boundary
wood\b		•					•		•	•		wood but not woodcock
\B		•					•		•	•	•	On non-word boundary
wood\B		•					•		•	•	•	woodcock but not wood
\w		•					•	•	•	•	•	A word character (same as [a-zA-Z0-9_])
\W		•					•	•	•	•	•	A non-word character (same as [^a-zA-Z0-9_])
\d							•	•				A digit (same as [0-9])
\D							•	•				A non-digit (same as [^0-9])
\s							•	•				A whitespace character (same as [□ ⇥]])
\S							•	•				A non-whitespace character (same as [^ □ ⇥])
\t		•					•	•			•	A tab (same as ⇥)
\n							•				•	A newline ([Ctrl-j])
\r							•				•	A carriage return ([Ctrl-m])
\f							•				•	A formfeed ([Ctrl-l])
\nnn							•				•	ASCII octal value nnn
\014							•				•	ASCII octal value 14
\xnn							•				•	ASCII hex value xnn

POSIX Character Classes

Symbols	vi	emacs	grep	sed	egrep	awk	perl	vim	grep	sed	gawk	Matches
[[:alpha:]]								•	•	•	•	An alphabetic character
[[:lower:]]								•	•	•	•	A lowercase alphabetic character
[[:upper:]]								•	•	•	•	An uppercase alphabetic character
[[:digit:]]								•	•	•	•	A numeric character
[[:alnum:]]								•	•	•	•	An alphanumeric character
[[:space:]]								•	•	•	•	A whitespace character including formfeed
[[:cntrl:]]									•	•	•	A control character
[[:blank:]]								•	•	•	•	A space or tab
[[:print:]]								•	•	•	•	A printable character

POSIX Character Classes (continued)

| Symbols | vi | emacs | grep | sed | egrep | awk | perl | Linux | | | | Matches |
								vim	grep	sed	gawk	
`[[:punct:]]`								•	•	•	•	A punctuation character (not a space, letter, digit or control character)
`[[:xdigit:]]`								•	•	•	•	An hexadecimal digit

The Shell Reference

I n this appendix, we present the features of the four shells—Bourne shell (sh), C shell (csh), Korn shell (ksh) and bash (bash). sh is the standard programming language, but csh keeps ticking because of its arguably superior history substitution features. ksh supports in-line editing of commands instead, and it offers several advanced and useful features. bash offers the best of both worlds—the programming language of sh as well as the interactive features of csh. Most of these features were presented in Chapters 8, 10, 17, 18 and 19; they are consolidated, summarized and compared here.

Command Execution Methods

A command can run in many ways—sequentially, conditionally or by using input from another command. Scripts may run in the same or a different sub-shell. You can also bypass an alias or function and execute the external command or built-in. Note that **nohup** and **command** are not built into sh, but they may often exist as external commands (like in Solaris). Here *cmd, cmd1* and *cmd2* signify commands.

Command	Shells	Execute
cmd1 ; *cmd2*	All	*cmd2* after *cmd1*
cmd1 | *cmd2*	All	*cmd2* with input from standard output of *cmd1*
cmd1 && *cmd2*	All	*cmd2* only if *cmd1* returns success
cmd1 || *cmd2*	All	*cmd2* only if *cmd1* returns failure
cmd1 `cmd2`	All	*cmd1* with arguments from standard output of *cmd2*
cmd1 $(*cmd2*)	ksh, bash	As above
(*cmd1*; *cmd2*)	All	*cmd1*, then *cmd2*—both in a sub-shell
{ *cmd1*; *cmd2*; }	sh, ksh, bash	*cmd1*, then *cmd2*—both in the current shell
cmd &	All	*cmd* in background (logout permitted in csh)
nohup *cmd* &	ksh, csh, bash	*cmd* in background (log out permitted)
. *script*	sh, ksh, bash	*script* in current shell (bash also uses source)
source *script*	csh, bash	*script* in current shell
cmd	All	external command or built-in ignoring alias of same name
command *cmd*	ksh, csh, bash	external command or built-in ignoring function (also alias in bash and csh) of same name

Redirection

The shell uses three streams that represent input, output and error. You can prevent files from being overwritten and also merge the output and error streams to handle them collectively.

sh, ksh, bash	csh	Significance
> *file*	> *file*	Send output to *file*.
>> *file*	>> *file*	Append output to *file*.
< *file*	< *file*	Take input from *file*.
<< *mark*	<< *mark*	Take input from following lines up to string *mark* (here document).
set -o noclobber	set noclobber	Don't overwrite files with > and >> (not in sh).
set +o noclobber	unset noclobber	Reverse noclobber setting (not in sh).
>| *file*	>! *file*	Send output to *file* even if noclobber is set (not in sh).
2> *file*	—	Send error messages to *file*.
> *file1* 2> *file2*	—	Send output to *file1* and error to *file2*.
> *file* 2>&1	>& *file*	Send both output and error to *file*.
2> *file* 1>&2	>& *file*	As above.
>| *file* 2>&1	>&! *file*	Send both output and error to *file* even if noclobber is set (not in sh).
>&*n*	—	Send output to *file* descriptor *n*.

Filename Metacharacters

The filename metacharacters are divided into two groups. The entries in the first group are generally common to all shells and are used by commands that use one or more filenames as arguments. They are also used by the **case** conditional to match *strings* and the **for** loop to match filenames in the current directory. Note that a dot at the beginning of a filename has to be matched explicitly.

sh, ksh, bash	csh	Matches
*	*	Any number of characters including none
?	?	A single character
.???*	.???*	Files beginning with a dot followed by at least three characters
[*ijk*]	[*ijk*]	A single character—either an *i, j* or *k* (ranges like a-z, 0-9 permitted)
[!*ijk*]	—	A single character that is not an *i, j* or *k* (ranges permitted)
*.[!oc]	—	All files with extensions except C programs and object files

The features of the second group don't apply to sh, and some don't apply to csh either. If you are using bash, then you need to make the setting **shopt -s extglob** before using the negation operator ! at the beginning of the pattern (in three examples below).

ksh, bash	csh	Significance
{p1,p2,p3}	{p1,p2,p3}	Matches files *p1*, *p2* or *p3*.
calc.{sh,pl,awk}	calc.{sh,pl,awk}	Matches calc.sh, calc.pl or calc.awk.
!(*pat*)	—	Matches all files except *pat*.
!(*p1*|*p2*|*p3*)	—	Matches all files except *p1*, *p2* or *p3*.
!(*.GIF|*.JPEG)	—	Matches all files except those ending with .GIF or .JPEG.
~	~	Matches home directory of current user.
vi ~/.alias	vi ~/.alias	Edit .alias located in home directory.
cd ~*user*	cd ~*user*	Switch to home directory of *user*.
~-	—	Previous directory.
vi ~-/.profile	—	Edit .profile located in previously visited directory.
cd ~-	—	Switch to previous directory.
cd -	—	As above.

Variable and Array Handling

UNIX variables have no type. That's why variables containing numerals can be treated both as strings and numbers. This section features the arithmetic functions, string handling, arrays and special parameters. Some of these features apply to the *ksh93* version of ksh which you may or may not have on your system. Here, *var* signifies a variable.

Initializing Variables

Variables can be divided into two types—local and global (environmental). csh uses different statements for handling these variables and can maintain both a local and global variable having the same name.

sh, ksh, bash	csh	Significance
var=value	set *var=value*	Assign *value* to local variable *var*.
var=value	setenv *var value*	Assign *value* to environmental variable *var*.
export *var*	setenv *var value*	Pass *value* of *var* to all sub-shells.
export	setenv	Display exported/environment variables.
unset *var*	unset *var*	Unset local variable *var*.
unset *var*	unsetenv *var*	Unset environment variable *var*.
read *var*	set *var* = $<	Read keyboard input into *var*.

Integer Arithmetic

Except for sh, all shells use the +, -, *, / and % operators for performing integer arithmetic. They also use the increment and decrement operators (++ and --). sh users have to depend on **expr** for performing both integer arithmetic and some of the string handling functions. POSIX specifies the use of (( )) rather than **let**, but the last example doesn't use the $—a form not recommended by POSIX. This form works only with later versions of bash and *ksh93*.

ksh, bash	csh	Significance
let z=x+y	@ z = $x + $y	Variable z assigned to sum of x and y
let x=x+1	@ x++	Increment x by 1
z=$((x+y))	@ z = $x + $y	z assigned to sum of x and y
z=$((x/y))	@ z = $x / $y	z assigned to quotient of $x/$y
((x++))	@ x++	Increment x by 1 (bash, *ksh93*)

String Manipulation

This is divided into two groups. The first group evaluates a variable *var* differently depending on whether it is set to a non-null value. The second group presents the superior string handling features of ksh and bash. The first six entries in this group replace or delete a pattern *pat* from a string where *pat* can be a wild-card expression.

sh, ksh, bash	csh	Evaluates to
${*var*:+*pat*}	—	*pat* if *var* assigned a non-null value
${*var*:-*pat*}	—	*pat* if *var* is unassigned or null
${*var*:=*pat*}	—	As above, but set *var* to *pat*
${*var*:?*pat*}	—	$*var* if *var* is set, otherwise print *pat* and abort script
—	${?*var*}	0 if *var* is unassigned; otherwise 1

ksh, bash	Evaluates to
${*var*#*pat*}	Segment of *var* remaining after deleting shortest segment matching *pat* at beginning
${*var*##*pat*}	As above but after deleting longest segment
${*var*%*pat*}	Segment of *var* remaining after deleting shortest segment matching *pat* at end
${*var*%%*pat*}	As above but after deleting longest segment
${*var*/*pat*}	*var* after deleting first match of *pat* (bash, *ksh93*)
${*var*/*s1*/*s2*}	*var* after replacing first occurrence of string *s1* with *s2* (bash, *ksh93*)
${#*var*}	Length of *var* (bash, *ksh93*)
${*var*:*x*:*y*}	Substring of length *y* from position *x* in *var* (bash, *ksh93*)

Array Handling

The first index of an array is 0 for ksh and bash, but 1 for csh. You can independently set individual array elements in ksh and bash, but csh allows you to access a range of elements or the last array element without knowing its index.

ksh, bash	csh	Significance
var=(*val1 val2* ...)	set *var*=(*val1 val2* ...)	Set array *var* to values *val1*, *val2*, etc.
unset *var*	unset *var*	Destroy *var*.
var[*n*]=*value*	—	Assign *value* to *n*th element.
${*var*[*n*]}	$*var*[*n*]	*n*th element.
${*var*[*]}	$*var*[*]	All elements.
${*var*[@]}	$*var*	As above.
${#*var*[@]}	$#*var*	Number of elements.
—	$*var*[$#*var*]	Last element.
—	$*var*[*m-n*]	Elements *m* to *n* (*m*- and -*n* permitted).

Special Parameters and Variables

The shell uses a number of special parameters that are set automatically. Command line arguments to shell scripts are accepted into some of these parameters inside the script. Shells other than csh can also set their values using the **set** statement. The other parameters relate to processes. csh accesses the last command line argument with a more intuitive form than the other shells do.

sh, ksh, bash	csh	Significance
$1, $2, etc.	$argv[1], $argv[2], etc.	Command line arguments numbered 1, 2, etc.
$*	$* or $argv[*]	All command line arguments
$#	$#argv	Number of command line arguments
—	$argv[$#argv]	Last command line argument; other shells need to use *var*=`eval echo \\$$#`
$0	$0	Name of executed command
"$@"	—	Treat multiword quoted argument as one argument
$?	$status	Exit status of last command
$$	$$	PID of current shell
$!	—	PID of last background job
—	$<	Input read from keyboard

Command History

History is absent in sh, and the features of ksh are rather limited compared to csh and bash. However, ksh allows in-line editing of the command line using **vi**- and **emacs**-like facilities. The features of bash and csh here are virtually identical, but bash offers the best of both worlds because it too offers in-line editing. Here, *stg*, *stg1* and *stg2* denote strings.

Repeating Events

csh, bash	ksh	Significance
history *n*	history -*n*	Display recent commands or *n* commands.
!!	r	Repeat last command.
!*n*	r *n*	Repeat event number *n*.
!*n*:p	—	Display event *n* without executing it.
!-*n*	r -*n*	Repeat *n*th previous event.
!-2	r -2	Repeat command prior to the previous one.
!*com*	r *com*	Repeat last command beginning with *com*.
!?*stg*?	—	Repeat last command with string *stg* embedded.
!?mtime?:p	—	Display last command with mtime embedded without executing it.

Modifying Previous Command Lines

csh, bash	ksh	Execute
^stg1^stg2	r stg1=stg2	Previous command after replacing *stg1* with *stg2*
!com:s/stg1/stg2	r com stg1=stg2	Last command beginning with *com* after replacing first occurrence of *stg1* with *stg2*
!com:gs/stg1/stg2	—	As above, but after globally replacing *stg1* with *stg2*
!! *arg*	r *arg*	Previous command with argument *arg* appended to command line
!cut | sort	r cut | sort	Last **cut** command but after piping it to **sort**
cmd !$	*cmd* $_	*cmd* with last argument of previous command ($_ used by bash also)

Using Individual Arguments of Previous Commands

This versatile command and argument extraction feature lets you run a new or previous command with any *argument* of any previous command. An argument of a previous command can be run as a command as well. Arguments are extracted using the general :*n* feature where *n* is a single number or a range. :^ (or :1) and :$ refer to the first and last argument, but :0 singles out the command only. This facility is not available in ksh, but only in csh and bash.

csh, bash	Execute
cmd !*	*cmd* with all arguments of previous command
cmd !$	*cmd* with last argument of previous command
cmd $_	As above (bash only)
cmd !:*n*	*cmd* with *n*th argument of previous command
gzip !:4	**gzip** with fourth argument of previous command
cmd !:$	*cmd* with last argument of previous command
cmd !:*m-n*	*cmd* with *m*th up to *n*th argument of previous command
compress !ls:3-$	**compress** with all but first two arguments of last **ls** command
cmd !:*m-*	*cmd* with *m*th argument up to all but last argument of previous command
cmd !*m*:*n*	*cmd* with *n*th argument of event *m*
!*m1*:0 !*m2*:*n*	command of event *m1* with *n*th argument of event *m2*
!!:*n*	*n*th argument of previous command as a command

Truncating Pathnames

If an argument of a previous command is a file pathname, csh and bash let you extract various components of the pathname. Extensions can also be separated from their base filenames and extracted separately. While csh permits the use of these facilities with variables too, bash works only with arguments of previous commands.

csh, bash	Execute
cmd !$:h	*cmd* with head of last argument of previous command
cmd !$:t	*cmd* with tail (filename) of last argument of previous command
cp !$!$:t.txt	**cp** to copy last argument of previous command with a .txt affixed
cmd !$:r	*cmd* with root of last argument of previous command
echo !$:e	**echo** with extension of last argument of previous command (without dot)
echo $*var*:h	**echo** to display head of pathname stored in variable *var* (csh only)

In-Line Command Editing

ksh and bash allow previous commands to be displayed on screen. You can then edit them using the built-in **vi**- and **emacs**-like editing facilities. Only one mode can be activated at a time by using the command **set -o vi** or **set -o emacs**. The essential commands that you can use in these modes are displayed in Table 17.4.

The Environment

The working environment of the shell is determined by entries in its startup files, its variables and the modes in which it is set. ksh and bash easily provide the best working environment of them all. The startup scripts used by these shells (along with the ones used before logging out) are shown in the last three entries in Table 17.1.

Environment/Built-In Variables

These variables are conventionally represented in uppercase. However, csh often features the same variable both in lowercase and uppercase. It uses lowercase variables for its own use, but external programs use the uppercase ones. Four of its variables shown here are actually arrays. Change of setting in one sometimes affects the other, but not always. ksh and bash use many additional variables.

sh, ksh, bash	csh	Significance
CDPATH	cdpath=(*dir1 dir2* ..)	List of directories looked up when using **cd** *dir*
HOME	home	User's home directory
IFS	—	Internal field separator (used by **set**)
LOGNAME	user	User's login name
MAIL	mail=(*n files*)	User's mailbox file (one or more *files* in csh)
MAILCHECK	mail=(*n files*)	How often mailbox file checked (*n* in seconds)
MAILPATH	—	One or more colon delimited mailbox files; can also include message to be printed
PATH	path=(*dir1 dir2* ..)	List of directories searched when a command is executed
PS1	prompt	Primary prompt string
PS2	—	Secondary prompt string (usually ? in csh)
SHELL	shell	User's login shell and the escape shell for programs like **vi** and **mail**
TERM	term	Type of terminal
USER	user	User's login name (bash)

ksh, bash	csh	Significance
BASH_ENV	—	Environment file read by sub-shells (bash)
EDITOR	—	Editor used for in-line command editing in ksh (read after VISUAL; not of much use in bash)
ENV	—	Environment file read by sub-shells (ksh)
HISTFILE	—	History file (csh uses .history)
HISTFILESIZE	savehist	Number of commands saved in history file upon logout (ksh uses HISTSIZE)
HISTSIZE	history	Number of commands saved in memory (in history file in ksh)
LINENO	—	Line number in script or function
OLDPWD	—	Previous directory
PPID	—	PID of the current shell's parent
PWD	cwd	Current directory
REPLY	—	Variable used by read when used without argument
VISUAL	—	Editor used for in-line command editing in ksh (overrides EDITOR; not used in bash)

Shell Modes

A mode in ksh and bash is set by using **set -o** with a keyword as argument (e.g., **set -o vi**). csh simply uses **set** with the keyword (without the =; e.g., **set filec**). These keywords are listed below. Settings are turned off by using **set +o** *keyword* (ksh, bash) or **unset** *keyword* (csh). Many of these settings in ksh and bash can also be turned on by using **set** with a single letter option.

ksh, bash	csh	Significance
emacs	—	Set in-line command editor to emacs.
vi	—	Set in-line command editor to vi.
ignoreeof	ignoreeof	Ignore the eof character for logging out; only **exit** permitted.
noclobber	noclobber	Protect files from being overwritten with > and >>.
—	filec	Turn on filename completion.
noglob	noglob	Don't expand wild cards; treat them literally.
nolog	—	Don't store function definitions in history file (ksh).
notify	notify	Notify job completion immediately and not at next prompt (not in ksh).
verbose	—	Display each script line as it is executed.
xtrace	—	Display command line as executed, preceded by a + (same as **set -x**).

The Comparison Tests

The shells provide wide support for comparing strings, integers and testing of many of the file attributes. They are used with the **test** statement or its [ ] synonym, usually in tandem with the **if**, **while** and **until** statements. This is how you'll be using them:

```
while [ $x -lt 10 ] ; do                                    sh, ksh, bash
if ( -e .profile ) then                                              csh
```

Integer Tests

sh, ksh, bash	csh	Significance
-eq	==	Equal to
-ne	!=	Not equal to
-gt	>	Greater than
-ge	>=	Greater than or equal to
-lt	<	Less than
-le	<=	Less than or equal to

String Tests

The last four examples explicitly show the use of the [[ ]] operators. They permit the use of wild cards for string matching and the conditional operators && and || for evaluating multiple conditions inside them. These forms work with the *ksh93* version of the Korn shell and later versions of bash (offered in SuSE Linux 6.4).

sh, ksh, bash	csh	Evaluates to true if . . .
stg	*stg*	string *stg* is assigned and not null.
-n *stg*	—	*stg* is not a null string.
-z *stg*	—	*stg* is a null string.
stg1 = *stg2*	*stg1* == *stg2*	*stg1* is equal to *stg2*.
stg1 != *stg2*	*stg1* != *stg2*	*stg1* not equal to *stg2*.
[[*stg* == *exp*]]	*stg* =~ *exp*	*stg* = *exp*, where *exp* can be a wild-card pattern (not in sh).
[[*stg* != *exp*]]	*stg* !~ *exp*	*stg* doesn't match the wild-card expression *exp* (not in sh).
[[*stg1* < *stg2*]]	—	*stg1* precedes *stg2* in ASCII collating sequence (not in sh).
[[*stg1* > *stg2*]]	—	*stg1* follows *stg2* in ASCII collating sequence (not in sh).

File Tests

sh, ksh, bash	csh	Evaluates to true if . . .
-e *file*	-e *file*	*file* exists (not in sh).
-f *file*	-f *file*	*file* is a regular file.
-d *file*	-d *file*	*file* is a directory.
-b *file*	—	*file* is block special.
-c *file*	—	*file* is character special.
-r *file*	-r *file*	*file* is readable.
-w *file*	-w *file*	*file* is writable.
-x *file*	-x *file*	*file* is executable.
-O *file*	-o *file*	*file* is owned by user (not in sh).
-s *file*	! -z *file*	*file* has a size greater than zero.
-L *file*	—	*file* is a symbolic link (ksh, bash).
-u *file*	—	*file* has SUID bit set.
-k *file*	—	*file* has sticky bit set.

sh, ksh, bash	csh	Evaluates to true if . . .
file1 -nt *file2*	—	*file1* is newer than *file2* (ksh, bash).
file1 -ot *file2*	—	*file1* is older than *file2* (ksh, bash).
file1 -ef *file2*	—	*file1* is linked to *file2* (ksh, bash).

Internal Commands

This final section presents the internal commands of the shells. Multiple options are shown separated by a |. Some constructs like **select**, **function** and **typeset** are not part of the POSIX specification and have been left out. However, alternatives to these constructs are available. The placeholders *cmd, var, exp* and *stg* have their usual significance.

The commands **fg**, **bg**, **kill**, **stop** and **wait** use *jobids* where a *jobid* is a % sign followed by the job number (%*n*), a command beginning with a string *s* (%*s*), a command containing string *s* (%?*s*), or the current job (%%).

Command	Shells	Significance
. *file*	sh, ksh, bash	Execute file in the current shell.
[ ]	sh, ksh, bash	Synonym for test statement.
[[ ]]	ksh, bash	As above, but permit more elaborate testing.
alias *name*	ksh, csh, bash	Display all alias definitions or of *name* if *name* specified.
alias *name=cmd*	ksh, bash	Define alias *name* as *cmd*.
alias *name cmd*	csh	As above.
bg *jobids*	ksh, csh, bash	Move current job or *jobids* to background.
break *n*	All	Exits current or *n*th (not in csh) for, while or until enclosing loop.

case *string* in
  pat1) *commands1* ;;
  .....
  patn) *commandsn* ;;
esac
	sh, ksh, bash	Execute *commandsn* if *string* matches pattern *patn*. *patn* can also be a wild-card expression. Multiple patterns in a single option are separated by the |. A * as an option matches everything unmatched previously.

cd	All	Change to home directory.
cd *dir*	All	Change to directory *dir*.
cd -	ksh, bash	Change to previous directory.
cd ~/*user*	ksh, csh, bash	Change to home directory of *user*.
command *cmd*	ksh, bash	Execute *cmd* bypassing alias or function.
continue *n*	All	Start execution from top of current or *n*th (except in csh) for, while or until enclosing loop.
echo *ops stg*	All	Display message *stg*. csh doesn't support escape sequences, but bash needs -e option for them.
eval *cmd*	All	Evaluate *cmd* twice. Required when variable contains special characters.
exec *cmd*	All	Replace current shell with *cmd*.
exec *n> file*	sh, ksh, bash	Associate file descriptor *n* with *file*.
export	sh, ksh, bash	Display all exported variables.
export *var*	sh, ksh, bash	Pass value of $*var* to sub-shells.

Command	Shells	Significance
exit *n*	All	Terminate current shell with exit status 0 or *n* if *n* specified.
fg *jobid*	ksh, csh, bash	Move current job or *jobid* to foreground.
for *var* in *list*; do *commands* done	sh, ksh, bash	Assign *var* with each value from *list* and execute *commands* between do and done. See also break and continue.
foreach *var* (*list*) *commands* end	csh	As above, but execute *commands* between foreach and end. See also break and continue.
functions	ksh	Display all function definitions.

function_name() {
commands
}
	sh, ksh, bash	Define function *function_name* as a group of *commands*.
		Accepts positional parameters $1, $2, etc., and
		optionally returns an integer with the return statement.

goto *stg*	csh	Execute command after line beginning with string *stg* followed by :
history -*n* history *n*	ksh, bash csh	Display list of immediate events or last *n* events if *n* specified. As above.
if *condition* ; then *commands* *options* fi	sh, ksh, bash	Conditional. If *condition* is true, then execute *commands*. *options* include testing for alternate conditions with elif and else. See Section 18.8.

if (*condition*) then
  commands
  options
endif
	csh	As above, but *options* use the else if and else
		statements. See Appendix A.

jobs -1	ksh, csh, bash	Display all jobs; with PIDs if -1 specified.
kill -*n* *jobids*|*pids*	ksh, csh, bash	Kill one or more processes with *jobids* or *pids*, optionally with signal *n*. -9 makes sure of kill.
let *var*=*exp*	ksh, bash	Assign computed result of *exp* to *var*. *exp* uses the operators +, -, *, / and %.
logout	csh	Terminate login shell.
nice +*n*|-*n* *cmd*	All	Run *cmd* with lower priority by default, or change priority by *n* units if *n* specified.
nohup *cmd*	ksh, csh	Run *cmd* in background even when logged out.
notify	csh	Report background job completion immediately.
onintr -|*label*	csh	Handle interrupt signal 2. Script branches to *label* or ignores signal (-).
printf *fmt values*	ksh, bash	Display formatted *values* using a C-like *fmt* format string.
pwd	All	Display current directory.
repeat *n cmd*	csh	Execute *cmd* *n* times.
read	ksh, bash	Read keyboard input to script into variable REPLY.
read *var*	sh, ksh, bash	As above, but input assigned to *var*.
set	All	Display all (local in csh) variables.
set -o *mode*	ksh, bash	Set a shell mode. See *Shell Modes*.

Command	Shells	Significance
set *exp*	sh, ksh, bash	Set positional parameters $1, $2 etc. to words in *exp*.
set *var*	csh	Set a shell mode. See *Shell Modes*.
set *var* = $<	csh	Read keyboard input to script into *var*.
set *var* = *value*	csh	Assign value to local variable *var*.
setenv	csh	Display all environment variables.
setenv *var value*	csh	Assign *value* to environment variable *var*.
shift	All	Shift positional parameters to left; $2 becomes $1, etc.
shift *n*	sh, ksh, bash	As above, but shift *n* places to left.
shift *var*	csh	Shift elements of array *var* to left.
source *file*	csh, bash	Execute file in current shell.
stop *jobids*	ksh, csh, bash	Suspend background jobs with *jobids*.
suspend	ksh, csh, bash	Suspend current foreground job (same as *[Ctrl-z]*).

switch (*string*)
  case *pat1*:
    commands1
    breaksw
    ....
  case *patn*:
    commandsn
    breaksw
endsw
	csh	Execute *commandsn* if *string* matches pattern *patn*. switch falls through and executes subsequent commands until it encounters a breaksw. The last option (*patn*) can be replaced by default, which matches everything unmatched previously.

test	sh, ksh, bash	Synonym for []. See The Comparison Tests.
trap *cmds sigs*	sh, ksh, bash	Signal handler. Execute *cmds* when receiving signals *sigs*. ' ' as *cmds* makes script immune. Signal 0 executes *cmds* on exiting the current shell.
type *cmd*	All	Reveal whether *cmd* is an external or internal command, alias or function.
ulimit *ops*	All	Set or display a resource limit.
umask *nnn*	All	Display file creation mask or set mask to octal notation *nnn*.
unalias *name*	ksh, csh, bash	Erase alias definition *name*.
unset *name*	All	Unset variable or array *name*.
unset -f *name*	sh, ksh, bash	Unset function *name*.
until *condition* ; do *commands* done	sh, ksh, bash	Execute *commands* between do and done until *condition* is true. See also break and continue.
wait	All	Pause execution until all background jobs complete.
wait *pids*	sh, ksh, bash	Pause execution until completion of jobs with PIDs *pids*.
while *condition* ; do *commands* done	sh, ksh, bash	Execute *commands* between do and done as long as *condition* is true. See also break and continue.
while (*condition*) *commands* end	csh	Execute *commands* between while and end as long as *condition* is true. See also break and continue.

The HOWTO

How to do or display	Command	Page no
abbreviate a command sequence	alias	501
add a user account *(super user only)*	useradd	677
add a user group *(super user only)*	groupadd	676
address all users *(super user only)*	wall	675
administer printer *(super user only)*	lpadmin	705
	lpc	711
arithmetic (integer) computation noninteractively	expr	558
arithmetic computation interactively	bc	63
	xcalc	358
arithmetic computation using the shell	let	585
assign values to positional parameters	set	580
associate a stream with a file	exec	605
back up files specified in command line	tar	691
back up files with list from standard input	cpio	688
beginning of file	head	271
calendar of month or year	cal	61
cancel print job	cancel	184
	lprm	184, 710
change case of text	tr	278
change current directory	cd *dirname*	170
change current directory to home directory	cd	171
change file's group ownership	chgrp	211
change file's last modification or access time	touch	213
change file's ownership	chown	210
change file's permissions	chmod	201
change login shell without involving administrator	chsh	488
change own password	passwd	53
change password of any user *(super user only)*	passwd *usname*	674

How to do or display	Command	Page no
chat between multiple users in a network	irc	407
chat between two users in a network	talk	323
check current directory	pwd	168
check file system integrity *(super user only)*	fsck	666
clear screen	tput clear	60
command documentation	man	40
command documentation in multiple levels	info	45
command history	history	506
command introduction in single line	whatis	48
command type (external, internal or alias)	type	33
commands containing keyword	apropos	48
compress file (to .gz)	gzip	188
compress file (to .Z)	compress	187
compress multiple files to a single file (to .zip)	zip	188
concatenate files	cat	181
configure network interface *(super user only)*	ifconfig	721
control access to X server	xhost	347
convert between IP address and FQDN	nslookup	751
convert file from DOS to UNIX	dos2unix	284
convert file from UNIX to DOS	unix2dos	284
copy directory tree	cp -r	178
copy file	cp	177
copy file between machines	ftp	329
copy file between machines without authentication	rcp	336
copy file to and from DOS diskette	doscp	687
	mcopy	687
copy floppy diskette or tape media	dd	686
copy multiple text sections in X	xclipboard	357
count number of lines containing a pattern	grep -c	436
count number of lines, words and characters	wc	263
create a file	cat >	181
	vi	67
	emacs	113
create array-like numbered variables	eval	601
create file system *(super user only)*	mkfs	662
create links to a file	ln	214
create or modify disk partitions	fdisk	660
	format	663
create specification file for **cron**	crontab	313
create symbolic links to a file	ln -s	216
cut columns or fields from file	cut	273
debug a shell script	set -x	607

How to do or display	Command	Page no
default file permissions	umask	207
delay command execution in a script	sleep	561
device name of current terminal	tty	56
dial out to ISP for connecting to Internet	minicom	729
	chat	732
	dip	730
difference between two files (as **sed**-like instructions)	diff	269
difference between two files (character-wise list)	cmp	267
directory list	ls -l | grep "^d"	444
disable print queue from accepting jobs	reject	708
	lpc disable	711
disable printer	disable	708
	lpc stop	712
disk space utilization	du	186, 698
echo a message	echo	237
edit a file	vi	67
	emacs	113
enable or disable terminal for **talk**	mesg	324
enable print queue for accepting jobs	accept	708
	lpc enable	711
enable printer	enable	708
	lpc start	712
end of file	tail	272
execute command in background and log out	nohup	304
execute command on remote machine without logging in	rsh	336
execute command with arguments from standard input	xargs	699
execute commands from a shell in X window	xterm	353
execute shell script without spawning sub-shell	. (dot)	523
	source	523
fetch mail from POP or IMAP server	fetchmail	760
file attributes	ls -l	197
file classification according to data type	file	182
file content	cat	181
file content (compressed) (.Z or .gz)	zcat	188
file content in DOS diskette	doscat	687
	mtype	688
file content in *k* columns	pr -*k*	267
file content one page at a time	more	260
	less	262
file content with headings and page numbers	pr	266
file list	ls	193
file list containing a pattern	grep -l	438

How to do or display	Command	Page no
file list in DOS diskette	dosdir	687
	mdir	687
find files by name, last modification or access time	find	218, 698
format DOS floppy diskette	dosformat	688
	mformat	688
format UNIX floppy diskette	fdformat	685
free disk space	df	185
free space in memory and swap	top	303
handle network news	tin	401
	netscape	404
handle signal from a shell script	trap	608
increase priority of a job *(super user only)*	nice	305
input data to a shell script interactively	read	539
join two files laterally	paste	274
kill a job	See "terminate"	
lines common to two files or unique to one	comm	270
lines containing one or more of multiple patterns	egrep	446
	fgrep	446
lines containing pattern	grep	434
lines in ASCII collating sequence	sort	275
lines in double space	pr -d -t	267
lines in numeric sequence	sort -n	277
lines in reverse order	tail -r	272
lines not containing pattern	grep -v	438
lines sorted ignoring case	sort -f	279
lines that are repeated	uniq -d	282
lines that occur only once	uniq -u	282
lock terminal without logging out	lock	57
log a session	script	59
log in to remote machine after authentication	telnet	326
log in to remote machine without using password	rlogin	329
mail message	mail	368
	elm	369
	pine	372
	netscape	379
mail message to all senders when recipient is away	vacation	387
mail queue	mailq	753
mail servers for a domain	nslookup	751
maintain engagement diary	calendar	62
maintain routes in routing table *(super user only)*	route	724
manipulate individual fields in a line	awk	467
	perl	613

How to do or display	Command	Page no
maximum file size	ulimit	675
modify a user account *(super user only)*	usermod	678
modify a user group *(super user only)*	groupmod	677
monitor growth of a file	tail -f	272
mount file system	mount	663
move files to another directory	mv	180
move job to background	bg	310
move job to foreground	fg	309
multiple segments from a file	sed	448
name of local host	hostname	320
name servers for a domain	nslookup	750
network statistics	netstat	725
number lines except empty lines	nl	283
number lines including empty lines	pr -n -t	267
octal value of a character	od	264
operating system name	uname	60
operating system release	uname -r	40
pass variable value to sub-shell	export	491
	setenv	492
position cursor on screen	tput cup	60
print file	lp	183
	lpr	184
print queue	lpstat	707
	lpq	184, 709
process ancestry	ps -f	299
	ps f	302
process attributes	ps	298
process HTML form data	perl	613
reduce priority of a job	nice	305
reload X resources file	xrdb	360
remove a user account *(super user only)*	userdel	678
remove a user group *(super user only)*	groupdel	677
remove duplicate lines	sort -u	277
remove duplicate lines from sorted file	uniq	281
remove empty directory	rmdir	176
remove empty or blank lines	grep -v	438
	sed	448
remove file	rm	179
remove newline character from text	tr -d	280
remove nonempty directory	rm -r	179
rename file or directory	mv	180

How to do or display	Command	Page no
replace current shell with another program	exec	604
replace pattern	See "substitute"	
restore files from backup media	cpio	688
	tar	691
routing table *(super user only)*	route -n	732
schedule job for one-time execution	at	310
schedule job for repeated execution	cron	312
schedule one-time job when system load permits	batch	311
search a file for one or more patterns	See "lines containing"	
set default file permissions *(super user only)*	umask	207
set hostname *(super user only)*	hostname	721
set maximum file size *(super user only)*	ulimit	675
set run level of system *(super user only)*	init	682
set system date *(super user only)*	date	674
set terminal characteristics	stty	57
shift positional parameters to next lower-numbered one	shift	582
shut down system *(super user only)*	shutdown	684
	init	684
sound a beep	echo "\007"	237
spell-check document	spell	284
	ispell	285
split a stream into two	tee	248
squeeze multiple spaces to single space	tr -s	280
start X Window system	startx	345
	xinit	345
string length	expr	558
substitute one character for another	tr	278
substitute one pattern for another	sed	455
substring extracted from a larger string	expr	559
substring position within a larger string	expr	559
super user from a nonprivileged account	su	672
system date	date	61
system load of remote machines	xload	358
system memory usage	top	303
system run level	who -r	682
	runlevel	682
system usage and user information	w	56
terminate an X window	xkill	359
terminate last background job	kill $!	308
terminate login session	exit	9
	logout	9
terminate process	kill	307

How to do or display	Command	Page no
terminate shell script	exit	544
test connectivity of a host	ping	722
time taken to execute a program	time	314
uncompress .gz file	gunzip	188
uncompress .Z file	uncompress	187
uncompress .zip file	unzip	188
unmount file system	umount	664
user information even when not logged in	finger	325
user names only	users	56
users and their activities	who	55
World Wide Web pages with graphics	netscape	412
World Wide Web pages without graphics	lynx	412
write buffer contents to disk *(super user only)*	sync	668
write different segments of file to different files	sed	454

The ASCII Character Set

This appendix lists the values of the first 128 characters of the ASCII character set in decimal, hexadecimal and octal. Octal values are used by the UNIX commands **awk**, **echo**, **perl** and **tr**, while **od** displays characters in octal. Many of these commands also use escape sequences of the form \x as shown for some characters under the *Remarks* column. **awk** and **perl** also use hexadecimal values.

Character	Decimal	Hex	Octal	Remarks
(null)	0	00	000	Null
[Ctrl-a]	1	01	001	
[Ctrl-b]	2	02	002	
[Ctrl-c]	3	03	003	
[Ctrl-d]	4	04	004	
[Ctrl-e]	5	05	005	
[Ctrl-f]	6	06	006	
[Ctrl-g]	7	07	007	Bell (\a)
[Ctrl-h]	8	08	010	Backspace (\b)
[Ctrl-i]	9	09	011	Tab (\t)
[Ctrl-j]	10	0A	012	Newline (\n) (LF)
[Ctrl-k]	11	0B	013	Vertical tab (\v)
[Ctrl-l]	12	0C	014	Formfeed (\f) (FF)
[Ctrl-m]	13	0D	015	Carriage return (\r) (CR)
[Ctrl-n]	14	0E	016	
[Ctrl-o]	15	0F	017	
[Ctrl-p]	16	10	020	
[Ctrl-q]	17	11	021	
[Ctrl-r]	18	12	022	
[Ctrl-s]	19	13	023	
[Ctrl-t]	20	14	024	
[Ctrl-u]	21	15	025	
[Ctrl-v]	22	16	026	
[Ctrl-w]	23	17	027	

ASCII SET

Character	Decimal	Hex	Octal	Remarks
[Ctrl-x]	24	18	030	
[Ctrl-y]	25	19	031	
[Ctrl-z]	26	1A	032	
[Ctrl-[ ]	27	1B	033	Escape
[Ctrl-\]	29	1C	034	
[Ctrl-]]	29	1D	035	
[Ctrl-^]	30	1E	036	
[Ctrl-_]	31	1F	037	
(space)	32	20	040	Space
!	33	21	041	Exclamation mark or bang
"	34	22	042	Double quote
#	35	23	043	Pound sign
$	36	24	044	Dollar sign
%	37	25	045	Percent
&	38	26	046	Ampersand
'	39	27	047	Single quote
(	40	28	050	Left parenthesis
)	41	29	051	Right parenthesis
*	42	2A	052	Asterisk
+	43	2B	053	Plus sign
,	44	2C	054	Comma
-	45	2D	055	Hyphen
.	46	2E	056	Period
/	47	2F	057	Slash
0	48	30	060	
1	49	31	061	
2	50	32	062	
3	51	33	063	
4	52	34	064	
5	53	35	065	
6	54	36	066	
7	55	37	067	
8	56	38	070	
9	57	39	071	
:	58	3A	072	Colon
;	59	3B	073	Semicolon
<	60	3C	074	Lef chevron
=	61	3D	075	Equal sign
>	62	3E	076	Right chevron
?	63	3F	077	Question mark

Character	Decimal	Hex	Octal	Remarks
@	64	40	100	At sign
A	65	41	101	
B	66	42	102	
C	67	43	103	
D	68	44	104	
E	69	45	105	
F	70	46	106	
G	71	47	107	
H	72	48	110	
I	73	49	111	
J	74	4A	112	
K	75	4B	113	
L	76	4C	114	
M	77	4D	115	
N	78	4E	116	
O	79	4F	117	
P	80	50	120	
Q	81	51	121	
R	82	52	122	
S	83	53	123	
T	84	54	124	
U	85	55	125	
V	86	56	126	
W	87	57	127	
X	88	58	130	
Y	89	59	131	
Z	90	5A	132	
[	91	5B	133	Left square bracket
\	92	5C	134	Backslash
]	93	5D	135	Right square bracket
^	94	5E	136	Caret or Hat
_	95	5F	137	Underscore
`	96	60	140	Backquote or Backtick
a	97	61	141	
b	98	62	142	
c	99	63	143	
d	100	64	144	
e	101	65	145	
f	102	66	146	
g	103	67	147	
h	104	68	150	

Character	Decimal	Hex	Octal	Remarks
i	105	69	151	
j	106	6A	152	
k	107	6B	153	
l	108	6C	154	
m	109	6D	155	
n	110	6E	156	
o	111	6F	157	
p	112	70	160	
q	113	71	161	
r	114	72	162	
s	115	73	163	
t	116	74	164	
u	117	75	165	
v	118	76	166	
w	119	77	167	
x	120	78	170	
y	121	79	171	
z	122	7A	172	
{	123	7B	173	Left curly brace
|	124	7C	174	Vertical bar or Pipe
}	125	7D	175	Right curly brace
~	126	7E	176	Tilde
	127	7F	177	Delete or Rubout

Glossary

absolute pathname A pathname which begins with a /, indicating that the file must be referenced in an absolute manner—from root. See also **relative pathname**.

access time One of the time stamps of a file stored in the inode representing the date and time a file was last accessed. A file is considered accessed if it is read, written or executed, and the access time is displayed by the **ls -lu** command.

action A component of a **sed**, **awk** or **perl** instruction which acts on text specified by an address. It normally uses a single character to represent an action for **sed**, but could be a complete program in case of **awk** and **perl**. Also sometimes known as an **internal command**.

address A component of an **sed**, **awk** or **perl** instruction which specifies the lines to be affected by the action. The specification could be made with a single line number or a range of them, or with a regular expression or a pair of them, or any combination of the two.

alias Term used to refer to another name of a command sequence, a hostname or an email address. Aliasing is available in the C shell, Korn shell and bash to abbreviate long command sequences. DNS uses aliasing to provide a host with another name. **sendmail** uses aliasing to forward mail to another address.

anonymous ftp A public ftp site where users use the login name anonymous and the email address as the password to gain access. Most downloadable software are hosted in these sites. Doesn't permit uploading of files.

Apache The most popular Web server used on the Internet and the standard on Linux systems. Supports persistent connections, virtual hosting and directory access control. Represented by the **httpd** daemon. See also **httpd server**.

archie A TCP/IP application that locates any downloadable file on the Internet. **archie** searches most of the anonymous ftp servers on the Net and produces a list of absolute pathnames and FQDNs of the file found. Obsoleted by the Web.

archive Term used to a store a group of files as a single unit—either on magnetic media or as a single disk file. Refers to such units created by **tar** and **cpio**.

argument The words following a command. It can be an option, an expression, an instruction, a program or one or more filenames.

ASCII collating sequence The sequence used by ASCII (American Standard Code for Information Interchange) to number characters. Control characters occupy the top slots, followed by numerals, uppercase letters, and then lowercase. Sequence followed by **sort**, **ls**, the character class used by wild cards and regular expressions, and any UNIX command which sorts its output.

attachment A file sent along with an email message. Attachments can be binary files and can be viewed by a mail client either **inline** or using a **plugin** or a **helper application**.

autosave Feature of the **emacs** editor that saves the buffer periodically in a separate file. The autosaved file has a **#** on either side of its name and can be recovered with the **recover-file** command of the editor.

background An environment where a program runs without being waited for by its parent. A command, when terminated by the & symbol, is understood by the shell to run in the background. Unless run with the **nohup** command, a background job terminates when the user logs out of the system—a restriction that doesn't apply to the C shell and bash.

base64 A form of encoding used by the modern mailers to convert binary attachments to text form. It converts three bytes of data to four six-bit characters and increases the size of the file by a third.

BIND The most widely used DNS implementation (currently BIND 8). Shipped with most UNIX systems for providing name service. See also **domain name system** and **name server**.

birth Term used to refer to the creation of a process. The process is created when the command representing it is invoked and dies when command execution is complete.

block device A hard disk, tape unit or floppy drive where output is written into and read from in units of blocks rather than bytes. Data reading is also attempted first from a buffer cache. Indicated by the character b in the first character of the permissions field of the listing. See also **character device**.

bookmark An invisible mark left in a Web document which allows a user to jump to that location directly without going through intermediate links. **emacs** also uses bookmarks to directly call up a file at a specific line location.

boot block A special area in every file system. For the main file system, this block contains the boot procedure and the partition table, while for others, it is left blank.

broadcast A message relayed by TCP/IP to all machines in a network to get the MAC address of a machine. All the bits of the host portion of the IP address are set to 1 for determining the broadcast address.

browser A program used to view HTML pages of the World Wide Web. Common Web browsers include Netscape and Internet Explorer (for Microsoft Windows and selected UNIX flavors). Linux is shipped with **lynx**, Arena and Netscape. Mosaic was the first Web browser.

BSD UNIX (Berkeley Software Distribution) A flavor of UNIX from the University of California, Berkeley. Berkeley eventually rewrote the entire system from scratch and introduced a number of enhancements like the **vi** editor, C shell, *r*-utilities, PPP and symbolic links. TCP/IP was first available on BSD UNIX.

buffer A temporary storage area in memory or disk used to hold data. Used by **vi** and **emacs** to make a copy of a file before editing. Buffers are used for reading and writing data to disk and storing superblock and inode data.

cache A facility offered by many applications to hold frequently requested information in memory, rather than on disk, thus speeding up data transfer. Term used in TCP/IP networking, especially for name servers. Netscape also uses a cache to store recently retrieved Web pages.

Challenge Handshake Authentication Protocol (CHAP) An authentication scheme using the concept of a *shared secret* and *challenge string*. CHAP makes a calculation from the challenge string and shared secret stored in /etc/chap-secrets and allows access only when the calculations at both ends match. CHAP is quite secure and is getting popular with ISPs. See also **Password Authentication Protocol**.

character The smallest unit of information that can be found in any system. The press of a key generates a single character, while ASCII has a set of 128 of them.

character device A terminal or printer where output is written into and read from in streams of characters. The buffer cache is ignored and the data is read directly. Indicated by the character **c** in the first character of the permissions field of the listing. See also **block device**.

chat See **Internet Relay Chat**.

child process The process created by the parent process. The created process inherits some of the environmental parameters of its parent, but environmental changes made in the child are not available in the parent.

client-server architecture A networked configuration of two or more computers working together. The client computer runs a program which requests a service from a server computer, running a server program. Term used in TCP/IP and the Internet. X Window treats the concept in a reverse manner. See also **X server** and **X client**.

command Normally the first word entered at the prompt. It is usually an executable file, but can also include the built-in statements (also known as **internal commands**) of the shell and some other commands (like **mail**, **vi**, etc.)

command line A complete sequence of a command, its options, filenames and other arguments that are specified at the prompt of the shell. The shell executes a command only when it encounters a complete command line.

command mode One of the three modes available in the **vi** editor to let keystrokes be interpreted as commands to act on text. When a key is pressed in this mode, it doesn't show up on screen but its effect does.

command substitution A secondary command enclosed within a pair of backquotes (` `` `). The shell executes the command so enclosed and places the command text where it occurs with the output the command generates. It can be used to provide arguments to a command.

Common Desktop Environment (CDE) A standardized look and feel of the entire desktop under the X Window system now adopted by most UNIX vendors. It features a Front Panel from which applications can be launched, a File Manager and a Workspace Switch to allow the use of multiple desktops. The window manager **dtwm** used by CDE is based on Motif.

Common Gateway Interface (CGI) The interface offered by a Web server to pass on form data to an external application. The application processes the data and often sends back the results to the client browser. **perl** is the most common language used for CGI.

completion A feature of the **emacs** editor, bash and the Korn shell to enter as much text as to make it unique and let the expansion be performed automatically. For the shells, the completion is effected both for a file and a command that is available in PATH.

concatenation The combination of two or more entities. Term used in connection with the **cat** command and shell variables.

context address A form of addressing used by **sed**, **awk** and **perl** which uses a regular expression enclosed by a pair of /s. The lines containing the expression are affected by the action.

control command A command used in the command line of a shell, **awk** and **perl** conditional or loop to determine the control flow of the construct.

control file A text file where some commands take their instructions from. .exrc, /etc/sendmail.cf, /etc/inittab and /etc/resolv.conf are some of the control files to be found in a UNIX system.

cron The chronograph of the UNIX system. It executes the commands listed in a control file (crontab) at a frequency specified by the various fields in the file. It shouldn't be invoked directly, not even by the super user. See also **crontab**.

crontab A control file named after the user-id containing all instructions that need to be executed periodically, and their frequency of execution. The **cron** command looks at this table every minute to execute any command scheduled for execution.

current directory The directory in which the user is placed after using the **cd** command with an argument. Usually set to the home directory during login time. See also **home directory**.

daemon A process that runs periodically without a user specifically requesting it. It is usually not associated with a specific terminal. **cron**, **init**, **pppd**, **inetd**, **sendmail** and **lpsched** are important daemons that keep the system running.

DARPA The research arm of the US Defense Department responsible for the initial work that ultimately led to the formation of the Internet. Tools developed by DARPA include **telnet** and **ftp**.

datagram Same as **packet**.

death Term used to refer to the termination of a process. The process dies when the command representing it has completed execution.

default route Term used in connection with routing to provide a default exit path for all packets not meant for the local network. PPP uses it as an option (`defaultroute`) to guide all packets meant for the Internet to its interface. Every host also maintains a routing table that provides a similar default route.

device driver A set of routines built into the UNIX kernel to handle all devices. The kernel calls up the right device driver and passes on the proper arguments to it. These parameters are indicated by the major and minor numbers of the device listing. See also **major number** and **minor number**.

device file One of the three types of files of the UNIX system representing a device. Provides a communication channel so that any interaction with the disk file actually results in activation of the physical device.

digit argument A numeric prefix used by an **emacs** command to repeat the command as many times. In **vi**, known as the **repeat factor**.

directory file One of the three types of files of the UNIX system containing no data, but houses the names of other files and subdirectories. For each file, it contains the inode number and the filename. Writing into a directory file is possible only by the kernel.

DNS Same as **Domain Name System**.

document root The absolute pathname in the Web server that holds the HTML documents. Controlled by the directive `DocumentRoot` in the Apache configuration.

domain A common string used by several hosts as part of their fully qualified hostnames. Examples of top-level domains on the Internet are *com*, *edu*, *org* and so on. See also **zone**.

Domain Name System (DNS) A service available in a TCP/IP network which uses the concept of **domains** and **zones** to describe uniquely the name of a host in a network. Also provides facility to convert these hostnames to IP addresses, and vice versa. The database containing the mappings is distributed in a large network with consequent delegation of authority.

empty regular expression A null string signified by two /s, which indicates that the string to be acted upon is the same as the last string searched. Used by **sed** in performing substitution.

encapsulation A process by which information is added to a packet in a TCP/IP network while moving down the protocol stack. Each layer adds its own header and trailer at the sending end, which are stripped off at the receiving end.

encryption A method of encoding a string of characters into a randomly generated character sequence. Used for storing the password of every authorized user of the system.

environment variable A shell variable that determines the nature of the environment of a user. Some of them are automatically set by the shell, though they can also be reassigned by the user. Value of such a variable is available in all sub-shells.

escape sequence A character preceded by a \ which imparts a special meaning to the character. Escape sequences are used by **echo**, **awk** and **perl**. For instance, \t represents a tab, and \n implies a newline.

escaping The use of the \ immediately before a character to indicate that the following character should be treated literally. This property is used by the shell and some filters. In most cases, it removes the special meaning of a character, but sometimes is also used to emphasize it. See also **quoting**.

Ethernet address Same as **MAC address.**

ex mode   Same as **Last Line Mode.**

exec A system call used by a process to overwrite itself with the code of the called process. It is also a shell built-in statement which reassigns the standard input and output of a process. It uses file descriptors rather than physical filenames, and is useful for handling I/O.

exit status A value returned by a command, shell script or a shell function after execution. A value 0 indicates successful (true) execution, while any other value indicates unsuccessful (false) execution. Same as **return value.**

export A built-in shell command which makes the environment of the parent process available in the child process. The statement is used with variables.

extended regular expression An enhanced regular expression used by **egrep**, **awk** and **perl** which enables the specification of multiple patterns and permits the use of groups. Uses the **metacharacters** ?, +, (,) and |.

FAQ A collection of frequently asked questions that are maintained by volunteers on Net News on virtually every topic.

file A container for storing information. An ordinary file contains data. A directory file contains the inode number and the filename of every file in it. Access to a device file implies accessing the physical device. Often used to mean an ordinary file.

file attributes A set of parameters stored in the inode which describes the characteristics of a file. This consists of the type, ownership, permissions, time stamps, size, number of links and an array of 15 disk block addresses.

file ownership One of the attributes of a file. The user creating or copying a file is generally the owner as well. The owner of a file has certain privileges denied others. Ownership can be surrendered to others, but can't be restored once given away.

file permission A three-tiered protection mechanism which determines the read, write and executable permissions of a file. A set of these permissions is also available for each of three categories of users—**user**, **group** and **others**. The permissions can be altered only by the owner of the file with the **chmod** command.

file system A hierarchical structure of files and directories having its separate root directory. Every hard disk has at least one file system in it, which is attached to the main file system with the **mount** command.

file time stamps A set of three dates and times representing the date of last modification, access and change of inode of a file. This information is stored in the inode and revealed with the **ls** command.

File Transfer Protocol (FTP) A TCP/IP application that transfers files between two remote machines. Also features a command by the name **ftp**.

filehandle The logical name of a file used by program statements in **perl**. Can be used to name redirected input and output. The **write**, **print** and **printf** statements use a filehandle to write output to the physical file or a pipeline pointed to by the filehandle.

filter A UNIX command which takes a character stream as standard input, manipulates its contents, and generates a similar stream as standard output. The shell's redirection and piping features can be used with these commands. A filter is unaware of the source and destination of its data.

firewall A machine running special software to protect an internal network from attacks outside. Hosts on the internal network have to connect to the external world through the firewall. Can be configured with additional software to provide selective access and also act as a proxy server.

foreground An environment where a job runs with its parent waiting for its execution to complete. Normally, you can run only one job in the foreground.

fork A system call used by a process to make an exact copy of itself. The copied process inherits the open files of its parent, the current directory and the exported variables, but has a different PID.

fragmentation A process by which packets are broken down into smaller units at a layer in the TCP/IP protocol stack. This usually happens before encapsulation because the network can handle only small packets.

free list A list of inodes maintained in the superblock of the file system which can be released by the kernel immediately for creating or appending to a file.

Free Software Foundation Same as **GNU**.

fully qualified domain name (FQDN) A set of dot-delimited strings representing the domains and sub-domains to which the host belongs. The FQDN of a host (like *www.altavista.com*) is unique in the Internet.

gateway A computer that belongs to multiple networks and has at least two network interface cards. A gateway routes packets from one network to another. Same as **router**.

GET A method of sending form data to a Web server. Data is sent as *name=value* pairs and is available in the QUERY_STRING variable of the Web server. There are restrictions on the size of the query string when this method is used. See also **POST**.

getty A process that runs at every free terminal to monitor the next login. It **execs** the `login` program whenever a user tries to log in.

GNU An organization founded by Richard Stallman (the name of which expands to **GNU**'s **N**ot **U**NIX), but is now known as the Free Software Foundation. Many of the tools available on Linux have been developed by GNU or distributed under its license. The GNU license requires all developers to make the source code public.

graphical user interface (GUI) The component of the X Window system that controls its look and feel. GUI looks are determined by a special client—the **window manager**.

group A category of user understood by the **chmod** command when handling file permissions. More than one user may belong to a group, and one set of file permissions is associated with this category. The numeric representation is stored in `/etc/passwd` and `/etc/group`, while the name is stored in the latter. See also **owner** and **others**.

group-id (GUID) The group name or number of the user, which is allotted by the system administrator when creating a user account. The name and its numeric representation are maintained in `/etc/group`, while the numeric value is also available in `/etc/passwd`.

hard link See **link**.

helper application An external program invoked by a browser to handle a special file format that it sees in the file's extension. Unlike a **plugin**, a helper application views files in a separate window. The file's extension, content type and the external program needed to handle it are specified in `/etc/mime.types` and `/etc/mailcap`.

here document A form of standard input used by many commands, using the << symbol. The input to the command forms part of the command line itself. It is especially useful when used with commands that don't accept an input filename as argument.

hints file The file used by BIND containing the FQDNs and IP addresses of the root name servers. Every machine running BIND must have this data in its cache.

history The facility to store, recall and execute previous commands in the C shell, Korn shell and bash. Also features a command by that name in these shells.

home directory A field specified in `/etc/passwd` to indicate the directory where a user is placed on login. Also used by the **cd** command when used without arguments. Same as **login directory**.

home page Term used to refer to the first page presented to the user on connecting to a Web site.

host A computer or a device in a network having a separate IP address.

hostname The name of a host which is unique in the network. Often used on the Internet with a series of dot-delimited strings to represent a **fully qualified domain name**. Features a command by that name which both displays and sets the hostname.

hosts file Refers to the file /etc/hosts that contains the hostname-IP address mappings.

httpd server A server running the **httpd** daemon for hosting the Web service. The World Wide Web runs on httpd servers. The server sends all documents and graphics requested by a client browser and passes on form data to a CGI application. The main **httpd** daemon spawns a separate child **httpd** daemon to handle each request. Same as **Web server**. See also **Apache**.

hub A central machine that receives mail from a group of hosts and centrally handles their delivery. It often handles all incoming mail and may forward the received mail to the hosts. A hub often rewrites the sender's address either to hide the hostname or to make it appear to have originated from the hub.

hypertext A link placed in one document with the <A HREF> tag which points to a location in another document in the same machine or another. The World Wide Web is a collection of these documents. See also **Web page**.

HyperText Markup Language (HTML) The universal language for coding Web documents. It is characterized by the presence of tags which can transfer control to another document in another machine. HTML documents can be used to view animation or video or play audio.

HyperText Transfer Protocol (HTTP) Sits on top of the TCP/IP protocol stack to retrieve HTML documents from hosts on the Web. It is *stateless* in that a connection has no knowledge of the state of the previous connection. HTTP 1.1 supports **persistent connections**.

icon A small object representing an X client in an inactive state. Double-clicking on an icon activates the window of the client and displays it on the screen.

in-line editing Feature available in the Korn shell and bash to recall and edit previous commands with **vi-** and **emacs**-like commands.

in-place editing Term used in **perl** to edit a file and write the output back to the same file without using redirection.

incremental search A fast and efficient search mechanism available in **emacs**. The search commences as soon as a character is entered and the cursor immediately settles on the first instance of the string that has been entered up to that point.

infinite loop A **while** or **until** loop which never terminates. The **break** (**last** in **perl**) statement is used to switch control out of the loop.

init A process having the PID number 1, which is responsible for the creation of all major processes of the system. **init** runs all the system's daemons and the **getty** process at the terminal ports. It takes instructions from /etc/inittab. It can also be used as a command to set the system to a specific **run level**.

inline The placement of a graphic beside the text in a browser window without using a separate window or application. GIF and JPEG files are displayed in-line by Netscape.

inode A structure maintained in a special area of the disk for storing the attributes of a file. This table contains for every file its permissions, ownership details, time stamps and the number of links. However, it doesn't contain the filename.

inode number A unique number identifying an inode for a file. This number refers to the location of the inode in the inode list. It is displayed with the -i option of **ls**.

input mode One of the three modes of the **vi** editor. In this mode, any key depression is interpreted as input and displayed on the screen. The mode is terminated by pressing the *[Esc]* key. See also **command mode** and **last line mode**.

instruction A combination of an **address** and an **action**. The address specifies the lines to be affected by the action. Used by **sed**, **awk** and **perl**.

interface program A shell script that filters data for printing. The interface program formats the data, supplies the codes needed by the printer and often calls up an external application to print the file.

internal command Name given to a sub-command of many UNIX tools like the **vi**, **emacs**, **more**, **mail** and **sed** commands, and the shell.

Internet The super network of networks connected by the TCP/IP protocol with facilities of email, file transfer, remote login, Net News, IRC and the World Wide Web. All the major networks of the world are connected in this way. See also **World Wide Web**.

internet Two or more networks connected by the TCP/IP protocol. All the Internet facilities of **ftp**, **telnet**, Web browsing and email are also available on an internet. Same as **intranet**.

internet address Same as **IP address**.

Internet Daemon (inetd) A daemon that listens on multiple ports and invokes the other daemons **ftp**, **telnet** and the POP service. **inetd** uses /etc/inetd.conf, which can be used to enable or disable a service.

Internet Protocol (IP) An important member of the TCP/IP protocol suite which handles routing of packets. IP provides a route to the network rather than a route to the host. It has no error-detection or recovery facilities.

Internet Relay Chat (IRC) A service on the Internet that enables multiple users to engage themselves in an on-line text-based conversation. Chat rooms are grouped into channels and messages sent by each member of a channel reaches all channel members in real time. The **irc** command is the most commonly used IRC client.

interrupt The sending of a signal to a process with the intention of terminating it. A specific key is assigned this job, usually *[Ctrl-c]* or *[Delete]*, though it can be reassigned with the **stty** command. Has the signal number 2.

interval regular expression (IRE) A regular expression that uses a single or a comma-delimited pair of numbers, enclosed by a matched pair of escaped curly braces (\{ and \}). The two numbers indicate the minimum and maximum number of times the single character preceding it can occur. Used by **grep**, **sed** and **perl** commands. **perl** drops the \ in its implementation.

intranet Same as **internet**.

IP address A string of four dot-delimited octets used to describe the logical address of a machine in a TCP/IP network. All fully qualified domain names are converted to this address before data can reach the host. It is finally converted to the Ethernet address at the receiving end. Same as **internet address**.

iteration The repeating of a loop's instruction set. The statements inside the loop are repeated as long as the condition specified in the command line of the loop remains true. Term used in connection with the `while`, `until` and `for` loops.

job control A feature provided in most shells (except Bourne) of moving jobs between foreground and background, suspending and killing them. A suspended job can be moved to foreground or background with **fg** or **bg**, respectively.

keepalive Same as **persistent connection**.

kernel The part of the UNIX operating system which is responsible for the creation and management of files and processes. It interacts directly with the machine hardware. It is represented by the file `unix`, `genunix` or `vmlinuz`, which is loaded into memory when the machine is booted.

key binding The association of an **emacs** command with a key sequence. When a valid key sequence is pressed, **emacs** internally executes the command *bound* to the key.

kill The termination of a process by sending a signal to it. UNIX also features a command of the name, which uses a signal number and the process PID to kill it. Usually kills all child processes too once the parent is terminated. Now a built-in feature of most shells.

kill ring A temporary storage area in **emacs** that stores up to the last 30 deletions (normally) and copies. Most deletion operations send deleted data to the kill ring. Entries in the kill ring can be restored.

kill script An *rc* script beginning with K that is used to kill a service. See also **rc script**.

last line mode A mode available in the **vi** editor to let **ex** commands be used to act on text. An indispensable mode for substitution, handling multiple files and customizing the editor. In **vi**, the mode is invoked by pressing a colon. Also known as **ex mode**.

line A sequence of characters terminated by the newline character.

line address A form of addressing used by **sed**, **awk** and **perl** to specify a single line or a group of contiguous lines. It requires a single line number or a pair of them to limit the boundaries of the text.

link A file attribute stored in the inode that allows a file to be referred to by more than one name. One of the attributes of a file that is maintained in the inode. Also features a command by the name `ln`. Same as **hard link**. See also **symbolic link**.

listing The output obtained with the `ls -l` command showing seven attributes of a file.

logical block The unit used for quantifying a set of bytes used in disk I/O operations. The figure is normally 1024 bytes, which implies that a file containing 1 byte occupies one logical block and two physical blocks in the disk. See also **physical block**.

login A process that overlays the **getty** program when the user enters a login name. It execs the shell process on successful login.

login directory Same as **home directory**.

login name Same as **user-id**.

loopback address A fictitious network interface available in every machine. It "loops back" a message addressed to 127.0.0.1 and allows all networking services to run on a stand-alone host.

MAC address A 48-bit address of the network interface card, which is unique throughout the world. All IP addresses have to be converted to these addresses before they can be understood by the receiving machine. Same as **Ethernet address**.

magic Term used in **vi** to refer to the special meaning of a character used in a regular expression. The magic is turned off by using the last line mode command **:set nomagic**.

Mail Delivery Agent (MDA) The agency responsible for delivering mail to the user. Receives a mail message from the Mail Transport Agent and appends it to a text file in /var/mail (/var/spool/mail in Linux). **mail**, **deliver** and **procmail** are common delivery agents. See also **Mail Transport Agent**.

Mail Transport Agent (MTA) The agency responsible for transporting mail across a network. One MTA hands over mail to another MTA before the mail can be delivered. SMTP is the standard protocol used by MTAs and **sendmail** its most common implementation. See also **Mail Delivery Agent**.

Mail User Agent (MUA) The client program used to send and receive mail. The MUA looks at the spool directory in /var/mail (/var/spool/mail in Linux) for locating received mail. It hands over outgoing mail to the Mail Transport Agent. **mail**, **elm**, **pine** and Netscape Messenger are common MUAs.

mailbox A text file named after the username, usually in /var/mail (/var/spool/mail in Linux) that contains all mail received by the user. Binary attachments are held in this file in encoded condition.

mailing list A service on the Internet which centrally maintains the list of subscribers. Mailing lists are organized by topic. A message addressed to the list reaches all its members automatically. **listserv**, **listproc** and **majordomo** are the most popular list programs.

major number One of the parameters of the listing of a device file which indicates the device driver required to access the device. Similar devices have the same major number. See also **minor number**.

meta key A control key of the keyboard used in combination with other keys to invoke an **emacs** command. On PCs, this key is represented either by the *[Esc]* or *[Alt]* key.

metacharacter The name given to a group of characters which means something special to the shell. The shell acts on these characters before executing the command. The meaning of any of these characters is reversed by preceding it with a \. The concept also extends to special characters used by certain commands as part of their syntax. See also **wild card**.

minibuffer The last line in the **emacs** screen which is used to display system messages and the command sequences entered by a user. Search text is entered at the minibuffer. Preceded by the **mode line**.

minor number One of the parameters of the listing of a device file which indicates the special characteristics of the device. Can be interpreted to mean the parameters passed on to the **device driver**. See also **major number**.

mode line The next to bottom-most line in the **emacs** screen which is used to display the filename, line number, the modification status and the mode of the editor. Shows up in reverse video.

modem A device (**mo**dulator-**dem**odulator) that converts analog signals to digital, and vice versa. Used for connecting to the Internet or any TCP/IP network through a telephone line.

modification time One of the time stamps of a file stored in the inode which represents the date and time the contents of a file were last modified. One of the attributes displayed by the listing.

mounting The process of attaching a stand-alone file system to the main file system. Its root directory after mounting becomes the directory of the file system at which mounting took place. Also features a command by the name **mount**, which is used by the system during booting to integrate all stand-alone systems with the main file system.

MULTICS An operating system whose development work was aborted to give way to the UNIX operating system. Many of the features of UNIX owe their origin to MULTICS.

Multipurpose Internet Mail Extensions (MIME) A standard used on the Internet to encode and decode binary files. Also useful in encoding multiple data formats in a *single* mail message. Used to mail multimedia attachments. MIME formats are stored in /etc/mime.types.

name server A dedicated service used on the Internet to convert the FQDN of a host into its IP address, and vice versa. A name server is queried by a resolver. The name server may either have the answer or it has to provide the address of another name server. See also **resolver**.

Netscape A suite of programs from the company of the same name. This suite known as Netscape Communicator includes Netscape Navigator for browsing the Web and Netscape Messenger for handling mail and newsgroups. Invoked by the **netscape** command.

Network File System (NFS) A TCP/IP application that lets users mount a directory of a remote file system on a local directory. Access rights are controlled by /etc/exports in the remote system.

Network News Transfer Protocol (NNTP) The TCP/IP protocol used to handle Net News or newsgroups. One news server fetches news from another news server. Netscape Messenger also acts as an NNTP client, but **tin** and **trn** are the common character-based NNTP clients.

newline The character generated by hitting the *[Enter]* key or *[Ctrl-j]*. Used as the delimiter between two lines and forms one of the characters of **whitespace**.

newsgroup An offline discussion group on the Internet which originates from the UNIX-based USENET. A message doesn't reach out to all members but only to those who download them from a news server. News uses the NNTP protocol. **tin**, **trn** and Netscape Messenger are popular news readers.

node Term used to describe any network device.

nonprivileged user An ordinary user having no super user privileges.

option A string normally starting with a -, which changes the default behavior of a command. It also forms one of its arguments. Multiple options can generally be combined with a single - symbol. Some commands use options beginning with a + symbol, and some don't use either.

ordinary file The most common file of the UNIX system represented by programs, data and text. It contains as much data as one puts into it, but doesn't contain the end-of-file mark or any of the file's attributes. Also known as **regular file** or even **file**.

others A category of user understood by the **chmod** command when handling file permissions. A user who is neither the owner of a file nor belongs to the group of the group owner is in this category. One set of file permissions is associated with this category. See also **owner** and **group**.

overlay The final step required in creating a process. Principle used by **exec** (both the shell statement and the system call) to replace the original program code with the new code.

owner The creator of a file having complete authority over determining its contents and permissions. Understood as **user** by the **chmod** command when handling file permissions. The string and numeric representations are stored in /etc/passwd. See also **group** and **others**.

packet Term applied to describe a fragmented unit of data in a TCP/IP network. Used synonymously with **datagram**.

pager A tool that displays output one screen at a time. **more** and **less** are the standard pagers on UNIX and Linux systems. Both offer search facilities and allow editing of the file using the **vi** editor. The original pager, **pg**, is now obsolete.

parent process The process which creates subsequent processes. Normally, the parent waits for the termination of the created process (unless run in the background). Termination of the parent normally terminates all its children.

partition A separate area of the hard disk that holds a file system. Data from one partition can't spill over to another partition. There can be between four and eight partitions in a disk. Linux supports a single *extended partition* that can hold multiple *logical partitions*.

password A supposedly secret code used by every user at the time of logging in. The code is not flashed on the terminal, but is stored in an encrypted manner in /etc/shadow. Also features a command with a similar name (**passwd**) to change the password.

password aging A system of setting conditions for change of password. Usually, there is a maximum and minimum time for this change. Implemented by using options with the **passwd** command.

Password Authentication Protocol (PAP) A scheme used by PPP for authenticating hosts. ISPs use the concept of a shared secret stored in /etc/ppp/pap-secrets at both ends to allow or disallow access to the Internet. PAP is not very secure as the password is sent across the network in clear text. See also **Challenge Handshake Authentication Protocol**.

PATH A shell variable that contains a colon-delimited list of directories that the shell looks through to locate a command invoked by a user. The PATH generally includes /bin and /usr/bin for nonprivileged users, and /sbin and /usr/sbin for the super user.

pathname A sequence of one or more filenames using a / as a delimiter. All except the last filename have to be directories. See also **relative pathname** and **absolute pathname**.

persistent connection A feature available in HTTP 1.1 that allows multiple resources to be fetched in a single connection. The server holds the connection for a certain time to allow further requests. Persistent connections speed up Web access. Same as **keepalive**.

physical block The unit used by several UNIX commands for quantifying data stored in disk. For most systems this expands to 512 bytes (1024 in Linux). **ls**, **df**, **du** and **find** report in physical blocks.

ping The sending of packets to a remote host to check the connectivity of the network. Also features a command by that name.

pipeline A sequence of two or more commands used with one or more | symbols so that the input of one command comes from the output of another. See also **standard input** and **standard output**.

plugin A small program installed in a browser to handle special file formats which can't be handled by the browser. Unlike a **helper application**, a plugin can't be used to edit a file.

Point-to-Point Protocol (PPP) A TCP/IP protocol that runs on the serial port—often through a modem. Users usually connect to the Internet through a PPP link between their machines and their ISPs. PPP is represented by the **pppd** command which runs both as server and client.

port number A number used to identify a TCP/IP service and defined in /etc/services. A packet has two port numbers, one for each end of the channel. Client port numbers are allotted in a random manner. See also **socket**.

positional parameters The external arguments to a shell script which are read into a series of special variables designated as $1, $2, $3, and so forth. $* represents the entire string and $# signifies the number of parameters set.

POSIX A set of standard interfaces based on the UNIX operating system. POSIX compliance ensures that a set of programs developed on one machine can be moved to another without recoding. POSIX.1 represents the standard for the application programming interface for the C language. POSIX.2 provides the interface for the shell and utilities.

POST A method of sending form data to a Web server. Data is sent as a string of *name=value* pairs and is fed as standard input to a CGI program. There are no restrictions on the size of the string when this method is used. See also **GET**.

Post Office Protocol (POP) The TCP/IP protocol used for fetching mail from an offline or on-line mail server. POP is often used over a dialup line to fetch Internet mail. The POP server is invoked by the Internet Daemon (**inetd**). Netscape has the POP client built-in, but **fetchmail** is the standard POP client for Linux systems.

process An instance of a running program. Usually required to run a command. Most of the shell's internal commands are executed without creating a process.

profile A startup file used and maintained by every user. Has the name .profile, .login or .bash_profile in the home directory. The instructions contained in this file are executed during login time without spawning a sub-shell.

prompt A string consisting of one or more characters showing the position of the cursor. The appearance of a prompt generally indicates that the previous command has completed its run. The prompt can be customized by setting the value of the PS1 or prompt variable.

query string A string that sends form data to a Web server as *name=value* pairs. The string is available in the QUERY_STRING environment variable when the **GET** method is used, but is fed as standard input when **POST** is used.

quoting The principle of enclosing a group of characters in single or double quotes to remove their special meaning. Though the shell ignores all special characters enclosed in single quotes, double quotes permit evaluation of $ as a variable and ` for command substitution.

r-utilities A set of TCP/IP tools developed by Berkeley as alternatives to the DARPA set. The tools include **rlogin**, **rcp** and **rsh**. Access to a remote system through these utilities is controlled by /etc/hosts.equiv and $HOME/.rhosts on the remote machine.

rc script A set of shell scripts available in an rc*n*.d directory (where *n* indicates the run level) in /etc that are used to set a machine to a specific run level. These scripts run the daemons that should run for that level and kill the ones that shouldn't. See also **start script** and **stop script**.

recursion A characteristic feature of some UNIX commands to descend a specified directory to access all subdirectories under this directory, and beyond. `ls`, `rm`, `chmod`, `chown` and `chgrp` use a special option to do that, while `find` and `tar` do it compulsorily.

redirection Term used in the shell to reassign the input and output of a command. The default source and destination of a data stream can be redirected to point to a disk file.

region An editing area in `vim` and `emacs` marked for some action to take place. The region may be copied, deleted, moved or filtered through some external command. `vim` highlights the region but `emacs` doesn't.

regular expression An ambiguous expression formed with some special and ordinary characters, which is expanded by a command (and not by the shell) to match more than one string. Conceptually similar to the shell's **wild cards**, it also features a facility to match the pattern at a certain location in a line. A regular expression is always quoted to prevent its interpretation by the shell. See also **metacharacter**.

regular file Same as **ordinary file**.

relative pathname A pathname which defines the location of a file with respect to the current directory. Uses the symbols . and .. to refer to the current and parent directories, respectively. See also **absolute pathname**.

remote login Connecting to a remote machine using a username and password. All commands entered after logging in are actually executed on the remote machine. See also **telnet**.

repeat factor A feature available in the `vi` editor and the `more` and `less` commands of using a number to prefix any command. It usually repeats the command that number of times. In `emacs`, it is known as the **digit argument**.

resolver A set of library routines used by a TCP/IP application to query a **name server** for resolving a domain name to the IP address. Is represented by the file `/etc/resolv.conf`.

resource record A record in the database files used by **BIND**. The A record converts the FQDN to the IP address. The PTR does the reverse. CNAME is used to provide aliases, while MX specifies the servers that receive mail for the zone.

return value Same as **exit status**.

root The top-most directory in every file system which has no parent. Indicated by the / symbol. Also signifies a user who uses the login name root to log on to the super user account. The / is the home directory of the root user too (except in Linux).

root name server A server running **BIND** that specifies the name servers of the top-level domains like *.com*, *.edu*, *.org* etc. Thirteen of them handle all top-level name server queries on the Internet.

root window The main window in the X Window system which occupies the entire screen. All other windows are displayed on this window and can be considered to be its children. Often, referred to as *desktop*.

router Same as **gateway**.

routing The sending of packets to a gateway or a router when the packet belongs to a different network. The routing table also provides a default route for all packets that can't be matched with explicit routes.

run level Term used to refer to the various states that a UNIX system can be in. The run level is determined by the argument of the **init** command. Different *rc* **scripts** are executed depending on the value of this run level.

scrollbar A widget of the X Window system represented by a bar on the side of a window. The mouse is used on this bar to scroll text forward and back.

sendmail The most common implementation of the SMTP protocol. **sendmail** runs in daemon mode to receive mail and a client to send mail. The configuration is controlled by /etc/sendmail.cf. **sendmail** also uses /etc/aliases to forward mail to any user on any host.

server See **client-server architecture**.

set-user-id (SUID) A special mode assigned to a file. The user executing the file acquires the powers of the owner of the file as long as the program is active. A principle used by UNIX to let users modify important system files by using a specific command, rather than directly. Indicated by the letter s in the permissions field.

shell The command interpreter of the UNIX system, which runs perpetually at every logged-in terminal. The shell processes a user request and interacts with the kernel to execute the command. It also possesses a programming capability. Four types of shells are discussed in this book.

shell function A group of statements executed as a bunch in the current shell. A shell function accepts parameters and can return only a boolean value. It is always executed in the current shell.

shell procedure Same as **shell script**.

shell program Same as **shell script**.

shell script An ordinary file containing a set of commands, which is executed in an interpretive manner in a sub-shell. All the shell's internal commands and external UNIX commands can be specified in a script. Also known as a **shell program** or **shell procedure**.

signal The means of communicating with a process to notify that an event has occurred. Signals are generated by pressing the interrupt key, or by using the **kill** command. The **kill -l** command shows all signals that apply to a system.

signature file A .signature file in a user's home directory. It is used to enter a person's details that must accompany every mail message. Most mail user agents are configured to automatically attach the file with every outgoing message.

Simple Mail Transfer Protocol (SMTP) The TCP/IP protocol used to transport email data across the Internet. SMTP communicates with the SMTP server at the other end and *directly* delivers the message. **sendmail** is the most common implementation of SMTP. See also **Mail Transport Agent**.

sleep Term used to refer to the temporary suspension of a process. Also features a command by that name.

socket A unique combination of two port numbers and two IP addresses, one each for the source and destination. No two connections can have the same socket. See also **port number**.

spam Junk mail that a user receives in abundance—more than what she'd like to have. Many mail user agents like Netscape offer spam filters that search for strings in a message, and on success, deletes them or moves them somewhere else.

spawn The creating of a child process to execute a command whose death is waited for by its parent. However, most of the internal statements of the shell are executed without creating a process. See also **birth**.

standard error The destination used by the diagnostic (error) output stream to write its output. Includes all error messages generated by UNIX commands. The default destination of this stream is the terminal but can be redirected to any file.

standard input The source opened by the shell to accept information as a stream of characters for input to a command. By default, the keyboard is assigned this source, but it can also come from a file, a **pipeline** or a **here document**.

standard output The destination used by commands to send output to as a stream of characters. Used by all UNIX commands which send output to the terminal. The default destination can also be reassigned to divert output to another file or a **pipeline**.

start script An **rc script** beginning with S used to start a service.

sticky bit A special mode assigned to a file or directory. The executable code of an ordinary file gets stuck in the swap area once it has been executed. A directory with the sticky bit set can be shared by a group of users, where one user can't delete or modify another user's files. Indicated by the letter t in the permissions field of the listing.

sub-shell A second shell created by the parent shell. Normally required for executing a shell script or a group of commands with the ( ) operators. Changes made in a sub-shell are not available in the parent.

subnet mask The IP address of a host in a TCP/IP network which has all the bits of the network address set to 1. The mask determines whether a network is subnetted or not.

subroutine A group of statements executed as a bunch in **perl**—like a shell function. Subroutines use arguments which are stored in the array @_. **perl** uses the & symbol to call a subroutine.

super user Same as **system administrator**.

superblock A special area in every file system which reflects its size and status—like the details of free blocks and inodes. Written regularly by the **sync** command with the system's memory table.

suspend The process of temporary stopping of a job. The job may later be killed, moved to the background or started in the foreground. This feature is available in the C shell, Korn shell and bash.

swapping The process of moving currently inactive processes from memory to the swap area of the disk. Also refers to the transfer of these processes from the temporary area to memory when ready for execution. The swap area is organized in a series of contiguous blocks in a separate file system.

symbolic link A file which points to the location of another file or directory. Unlike **hard links**, a symbolic link can link files across file systems. Can be used to link directories also. See also **link**.

sync Term used in connection with the file system and processes. The kernel uses the command by that name to write the superblock and inode data from memory to disk. Two **sync**s are enough to complete the writing operation.

system administrator The person responsible for the management of system resources. The administrator can change any file attribute and kill any user process. Uses a special user account (generally, root) to perform administrative duties. Also known as **super user**.

system call A basic routine defined in the kernel which lets a user remain ignorant of all complex processes in a UNIX system. A handful of such routines perform important tasks like file handling, creating a pipe or generating a process. All commands and programs are written in terms of system calls.

system process A process which runs in the system during booting without being specifically requested for by a user. `init`, `getty`, `cron` and `lpsched` are some of the system processes.

tab A single character which simulates a contiguous set of spaces. Generated by hitting a specific key or *[Ctrl-i]*, and forms one of the characters of **whitespace**. Useful for aligning columns.

tagged regular expression (TRE) Term used to indicate the grouping of a regular expression with an escaped pair of parentheses (\ (and \ )). This group is repeated elsewhere in the line by using the tag *n*, where *n* is a number between 1 and 9. Used by **grep**, **sed** and **perl** commands. **perl** also uses the $ apart from the \ to remember the patterns till the next grouping is done.

TCP/IP Expands to Transmission Control Protocol/Internet Protocol—a collection of protocols used for networking computers using different operating systems and different hardware. Ensures reliable transmission with full error-correction facilities. TCP and IP are two of the most important protocols in this suite.

telnet A TCP/IP application that enables a user to log on to a remote machine after supplying a username and password. After logging in, the user can use the remote machine as if it is a local one. All files are created on the remote machine.

The Open Group Owner of the UNIX standard and the originator of the UNIX98 specification. Includes X/OPEN in its fold. Also maintains the X Window system.

thread Term used to group messages that are exchanged in response to one another. Threads are encountered both in email and newsgroup messages. Many mail user agents and news readers like Netscape can group and view messages by threads.

toggle switch A command that reverses the effect of its immediate previous invocation. **emacs** has a number of commands that act as toggle switches.

top-level domains All domains under the root (.) domain. These include the generic domains *com*, *edu*, *org*, *net* etc., as well as the 2-character country domains like *in*, *au*, *de*, *ca* etc.

Transmission Control Protocol (TCP) One of the most important protocols of the TCP/IP family responsible for transporting data. It breaks data into segments and assembles them at the other end. The transmission is wholly reliable as lost segments are retransmitted.

trusted host A host trusted by a remote host to access its resources. When a host is trusted, all users of the host are also trusted. Trusted hosts are a security threat in a network.

Uniform Resource Locator (URL) A string entered in a separate window on the Web browser to access a Web resource. Comprises the protocol, the FQDN of the site and the pathname of the file. *http://* is the standard protocol prefix used in the URL, but can be *ftp://* or *telnet://* as well.

unmounting The process of disengaging a file system from the main file system. The command **umount** achieves this dismounting, and is used by the system during shutdown of the system. The system administrator unmounts a file system before conducting an integrity check on it.

user equivalence Term used in the context of the **r-utilities** to control a user's access to a like-to-like account on a remote host. If a user has user equivalence, then she is allowed to use **rlogin** to log in to her own account in a remote host without using a password. User equivalence is controlled by /etc/hosts.equiv and $HOME/.rhosts on the remote host.

user-id (UID) The name used by a user to gain access to the system. A list of authorized names is maintained in /etc/passwd along with their numeric representations. Also known as **login name** and **username**.

username Same as **user-id**.

virtual console A system of using multiple screens and logins from a single UNIX machine. A new screen is opened by using *[Alt]* and a function key.

virtual host The facility available on many **httpd servers** including **Apache** to host multiple sites on a single machine. Each virtual host can have its own server name, cgi-bin directory and document root. A virtual host can have the same IP address as the main host or a different one.

wait Term used to refer to the inaction of a parent process while a child is running. Normally the parent waits for the death of the child. Also features a shell built-in command of that name.

Web page An HTML document presented in the form of a page at every Web site and viewed with a browser. It contains text, graphics and animation, and can point to audio and video resources. A page has links with other pages—often on different machines. Pages can be used to create forms for user input.

Web server Same as **httpd server**.

Web site One or more machines belonging to an organization that host httpd services. Maintains all documents and other files related to the organization. Can also maintain links to other Web sites for access to related information.

whitespace A contiguous sequence of spaces, tabs or newlines which is set by the IFS variable. Used as delimiter by many filters and the shell to parse command line arguments. Also used by the **set** statement to assign its arguments to positional parameters.

widget Term used to define a user interface object in the X Window system. It comprises menus, scrollbars and buttons. Athena and Motif are the two common types of widget sets available.

wild card A special character used by the shell to match a group of filenames with a single expression. The * and ? are commonly used wild cards used for framing expressions. See also **metacharacter**.

window manager The special X client program which controls the look and feel of all X clients. It puts a frame around every window and enables window sizing and movement. Until the **dtwm** of CDE took over, **mwm** was the most popular window manager program. Linux used **fvwm** as its standard window manger till KDE and GNOME took over.

word A contiguous string of characters not containing **whitespace**. **wc** features an option to count in units of words, while some GNU filters (Appendix C) use special symbols to match one. A quoted string is understood by the shell as a single word irrespective of the number of actual words it may contain.

World Wide Web A service on the **Internet** featuring a collection of linked documents and images. The Web uses the HTTP protocol and requires a browser to view pages. Hypertext transports users to another document at the click of a mouse. Currently, the most active and exciting area of the Internet.

wraparound A feature provided by the **vi** and **emacs** editors for resuming the search for a pattern from the other end of a file. The entire file is thus searched irrespective of the cursor position at the time of commencement of search. Can be suppressed in **vi** by using the last line mode command **:set nowraparound**.

X client An X program which performs a specific function and uses the X server for display. **xterm** and **xclock** are common X clients found in every X Window system.

X server The program in X Window which controls the display including the monitor, mouse and keyboard. X clients write their output to this program. If the display changes, only the server needs to change and not the clients.

X Window System The graphical component of the UNIX system. X clients write their output to the server, which is responsible for their display on separate windows. Netscape requires this system to handle mail and browse the Web.

zipped file Any file compressed with the **compress**, **gzip** or **zip** command. A UNIX zipped file commonly has the extension `.Z`, `.gz` or `.zip`.

zonal transfer The act of transferring DNS data from the *master name server* to the *slave name server*. The transfer is also effected by BIND's `notify` statement and helps to keep both name servers in "sync." See also **name server**.

zone That part of a domain administered separately and handled by its own **name server**. The name server for a zone is authoritative for that zone. See also **domain**.

Solutions to Self-Test Questions

Chapter 1

1.1   The application programs and the users.
1.2   The ASCII value.
1.3   The *[Ctrl]* and *[Alt]* keys.
1.4   The machine's name.
1.5   You can, but that should be avoided.
1.6   Not necessarily; the password could be incorrect too.
1.7   Use *[Ctrl-c]*, and if it doesn't work, use *[Del]* or *[Delete]*.
1.8   Use **who am i** or **whoami**.
1.9   Use **ls -l.**
1.10 **cat** is used to view the contents of a file. When used with two filenames, it displays the contents of the first file before the second.
1.11 Ken Thompson and Dennis Ritchie.
1.12 Because it was then prevented by the US Government to sell computer software.
1.13 From the University of California, Berkeley.
1.14 Solaris and SunOS.
1.15 SCO UNIX, Intel Solaris and Linux.
1.16 X/Open, now part of The Open Group.
1.17 Richard Stallman and Linux Torvalds.
1.18 Software developers distributing products under that license must make the source code public.
1.19 The kernel.
1.20 Because it is written in C, a high-level language. A program written in a high-level language on one machine can run without any major modifications on another machine.
1.21 System V (AT&T) and BSD (Berkeley). SunOS is based on BSD, but Solaris is based on AT&T's SVR4.
1.22 (i) **unix** or **genunix** (ii) **vmlinuz**.
1.23 Multitasking means that a user can run more than one job at a time.
1.24 Because complex jobs can be handled by connecting a number of these simple ones.

1.25   X Window.
1.26   The shell, **perl**, **tcl** and **python**.
1.27   Red Hat, SuSE and Caldera.

Chapter 2

2.1   The : must be a command that does nothing—a null command.
2.2   Normally not; UNIX is case-sensitive.
2.3   Of course, UNIX doesn't care about extensions.
2.4   **mkdir** and **rmdir**.
2.5   PATH is a system variable which stores a list of directories that the shell searches to locate a command.
2.6   The colon (:).
2.7   No, commands and arguments must be separated by a space. However, you can create **ls-l** as an *alias* to **ls -l**. *(17.4)*
2.8   Three options (-l, -u and -t).
2.9   Linux commands often use two hyphens before an option.
2.10   Sometimes they can be preceded with + or contain an =.
2.11   Sometimes, some commands can't execute without options (like **cut**).
2.12   The command line.
2.13   **awk** and **perl**.
2.14   Use **uname -r**.
2.15   Because the commands there are most often used by users and would be located faster.
2.16   No, commands can be stored in the type-ahead buffer and are automatically executed in sequence.
2.17   The documentation of a command that's viewed on the screen when **man** is used with the command name.
2.18   The **info** command.
2.19   Try using **apropos** with a keyword.

Chapter 3

3.1   When the system administrator invokes the command.
3.2   In the file /etc/shadow.
3.3   Eleven days were skipped in September for adjustment purposes.
3.4   Only if you are the system administrator.
3.5   **calendar** takes input from the file calendar in the user's current directory.
3.6   Both **clear** and **tput clear**.
3.7   The name of the operating system.
3.8   The **w** command.
3.9   Use the **script** command with the filename as argument.
3.10   Use the **tty** command.
3.11   Use the **lock** command (not available in Solaris).
3.12   Make the setting scale=3.
3.13   Use **w henry**.
3.14   Use the **users** command (not available in Solaris).

Chapter 4

4.1   Use **R**, enter the text and press *[Esc]*.
4.2   Move to the first line with **1G**, and then press **0** (the letter 0).
4.3   Take the cursor to **d**, and then use **rt**.
4.4   Use **S**, enter the new text, and then press *[Esc]*.
4.5   Use the Last Line Mode command **:q!**.
4.6   Use **40|**.
4.7   Use **6k**.
4.8   Use *[Ctrl-l]*.
4.9   Use **:.w foo***[Enter]*.
4.10 Use **10yw**.
4.11 They are operators and are used in combination with other commands.
4.12 Use **:1,$s/Internet/Web/g**.
4.13 Use **d1G.**
4.14 Use **:e!**.
4.15 Regions, multiple windows and the history facility in the Last Line Mode.
4.16 Use *[Ctrl-r]*.

Chapter 5

5.1   That the buffer is unmodified.
5.2   Use *[Ctrl-g]* to cancel the command.
5.3   Because it invokes the help facility.
5.4   Use *[Alt-x]*overwrite-mode*[Enter]*.
5.5   Use *[Ctrl-x][Ctrl-w]* and then enter foo2.
5.6   Use *[Ctrl-k]*.
5.7   Use *[Ctrl-a][Ctrl-k]*.
5.8   Use *[Ctrl-u][Ctrl-u][Alt-d]*.
5.9   Use *[Ctrl-a][Alt-40][Ctrl-f]*.
5.10 Use *[Ctrl-v]* (forward) and *[Alt-v]* (backward).
5.11 Use *[Alt->]*.
5.12 First use *[Ctrl-e]* to move to the end of the line and then insert the string.
5.13 Use the *query-replace* facility—*[Alt-%]*, followed by the string.
5.14 Use *[Alt-x]*revert-buffer.
5.15 Use *[Alt-x]*replace-string*[Enter]* and then enter the two strings. Use the command completion feature repl*[Tab]*s*[Tab]* for entering replace-string.
5.16 Use *[Alt-!]* and then the **date** command.

Chapter 6

6.1   The computer's main memory.
6.2   255 characters on modern systems.
6.3   Yes, UNIX is sensitive to case.
6.4   The root directory.
6.5   The system always has these files in every directory and refuses to create them.
6.6   The linefeed or newline character.

6.7   Absolutely legal, but the last `bar` must be an ordinary file and the rest must be directories.

6.8   It simply switches to the home directory.

6.9   Yes, provided you have the directories `cd`, `mkdir` and `rmdir` as a chain created under the current directory.

6.10   Yes, it shows all files in the parent directory.

6.11   Only some of them; the others simply won't work.

6.12   **man mkdir** will suggest using **mkdir -p share/man/cat1**. The -p option creates all subdirectories in one shot.

6.13   No, you have to move up before you delete it. However, Linux allows it; use **rmdir.** from the directory itself.

6.14   Use **cp -r bar1 bar2**.

6.15   Sure, it will; **mv** can also rename directories. But if `bar2` exists, then `bar1` becomes a subdirectory of `bar2`.

6.16   Use **cat -v foo**.

6.17   The files can be divided into *block special* and *character special* types.

6.18   A file compressed with **gzip**.

Chapter 7

7.1   Numerals first, uppercase and then lowercase.

7.2   The -F option marks directories with a / and executables with an *.

7.3   Those names beginning with a dot.

7.4   The output of the **ls -l** command.

7.5   Use **ls -R /**.

7.6   Use **ls ..** to list files in the parent directory.

7.7   By the d in the first character of the permissions field.

7.8   Only the owner of the file or the super user.

7.9   By default, not the hidden files. You have to use the -a option also to list them.

7.10   When the file is more than a year old (six months in Linux).

7.11   She requires group write permission on the directory containing the filename.

7.12   You can do that in two ways:

        (i) `chmod 700 foo`
        (ii) `chmod u+x,go-r foo`

7.13   Your directory has write permission for them.

7.14   Use **ls -i**.

7.15   In `/etc/passwd` and `/etc/group`.

7.16   Use **chown -R henry ***.

7.17   Use **touch -m 09301030 foo**.

7.18   It will create a file `foo` with the current system date and time as its last modification and access times. If the file exists, it will change these time stamps.

7.19   All file attributes like permissions, links, ownership and time stamps but not the filename.

7.20   The file has three names but only a single copy in disk.

7.21   With the **rm** command.

7.22   Use **find / -name "*.html" -o -name "*.java" -print**.

Chapter 8

8.1   Because they mean nothing to the command.

8.2   It expands it to match all files in the current directory.

8.3   Use `chap[a-cx-z]`.

8.4   Not the ones beginning with a dot.

8.5   Use `ls ????*`.

8.6   The **find** command uses a wild-card expression as a parameter to the `-name` keyword.

8.7   The contents are overwritten.

8.8   No problem; the file is created.

8.9   Break up the line at suitable places, but before pressing the *[Enter]* key, enter a \.

8.10 This is another way of executing **bc < bar > foo**. It's a legitimate command.

8.11 Redirect the standard error with 2> to `/dev/null`.

8.12 No, you can't. | and `more` are considered to be arguments of **ls**.

8.13 In the second case, variable evaluation is prevented by single quotes.

8.14 Use two commands in a pipeline—**who | wc -l**.

8.15 No, it doesn't. The shell interprets x as a command and = and 10 as its two arguments.

8.16 The first sets the variable `directory` to the string pwd. The second sets it to the absolute pathname of the current directory.

8.17 bash is the standard shell in Linux.

8.18 You didn't use the `-e` option with **echo**.

Chapter 9

9.1   After pressing v to invoke the **vi** editor.

9.2   Use **/Internet***[Enter]*.

9.3   Use **n** repeatedly.

9.4   A sequence of characters not containing a space, tab or newline.

9.5   Use `lines=`wc -l foo`` or `set lines = `wc -l foo`` (C shell).

9.6   Create a file with these characters and then use **od -bc foo**.

9.7   Use **pr -t -d foo**.

9.8   That the two files are identical.

9.9   Use **comm -12 foo1 foo2**.

9.10 Use **echo "The line length of shortlist is `head -1 shortlist | wc -c`"**.

9.11 **head** picks up 10 lines from each file, but precedes each group with a header that shows the filename.

9.12 Many versions of **tail** use the `-r` option to present lines in reverse order.

9.13 Use **tail -f install_log.1st**.

9.14 No, either the `-c` or `-f` option has to be specified, not both.

9.15 You can, but the command that will be executed is **paste foo1 foo2**.

9.16 Use **sort -u foo**.

9.17 Use **sort -t"|" +4.0 shortlist**.

9.18 A line in a DOS file is terminated by the carriage return-linefeed (CR-LF) characters. A UNIX file uses linefeed as the newline character.

9.19 Use **spell** (System V) and **ispell** (Linux).

Chapter 10

10.1   They are **fork** and **exec**.
10.2   Use **echo $$**.
10.3   When executing a shell script.
10.4   The **getty** process.
10.5   **init**, **lpsched**, **inetd** and **cron** aren't associated with a terminal.
10.6   Use **ps | tail +2**.
10.7   Because it shows the name of the file that the user is working on.
10.8   Only if you are the super user.
10.9   The **-9** or **-SIGKILL** option.
10.10   Only if you are the super user.
10.11   Use **kill -l** (the letter l).
10.12   The user is probably using the Bourne shell which doesn't support job control.
10.13   First press *[Ctrl-z]* to come to the shell prompt. Enter **fg** to return to **vi**.
10.14   You can't know the name of the job.
10.15   Use **at 8 pm tomorrow < dial.sh**.
10.16   Use the interrupt key, but not *[Ctrl-d]*.
10.17   Use the **time** command with both, and note the real time.

Chapter 11

11.1   Both in displaying and setting the hostname.
11.2   A socket consists of a set of four numbers—the IP addresses and port numbers of the client and server.
11.3   The file has to be maintained in each and every host of the network.
11.4   A fully qualified domain name. It consists of a string of domains separated by dots.
11.5   Yes, DNS is insensitive to case.
11.6   **sendmail** for handling mail, **httpd** for Web service and **inetd** for **ftp** and **telnet**.
11.7   Use **talk brenda@uranus**.
11.8   You have to leave behind your leave details in the files **.plan** and **.project**.
11.9   Use **finger @saturn**.
11.10   Use *[Ctrl-]]*.
11.11   Use the **uname -n** or **hostname** command to display the machine's name.
11.12   Enter this string as the URL in the browser window:

        telnet://saturn.planets.com

11.13   Have identical user accounts on both machines.
11.14   No, **ftp** uses **/bin/ls**.
11.15   Use **lcd bar**.
11.16   You can't upload files to an anonymous ftp site.
11.17   It runs the **date** command on a remote host *jupiter* and saves the output remotely in the file **.date**.

Chapter 12

12.1   Because X uses a bit-mapped display where every pixel can be manipulated individually.

12.2   They are **startx** and **xinit**. You can use **xdm** only if you are the root user.

12.3   By pointing the mouse on the root window and clicking one of the mouse buttons.

12.4   The X server.

12.5   Yes, provided the X server is running on HP-UX.

12.6   **xhost** enables or disables the writing of the display by users on other machines. **xhost +** allows access to all clients.

12.7   By the color of its title bar. Only one window will have this color.

12.8   Press *[Alt]* and then move a window by dragging its title bar. The window doesn't get selected but still moves.

12.9   A checkbox permits multiple selection options but not a radio button.

12.10 By clicking on the left button of the title bar of any window.

12.11 It's the Motif window manager that has been standard on UNIX systems before the arrival of CDE.

12.12 Use **xterm -sb -sl 1000**.

12.13 Place the entry **xterm &** in $HOME/.xinitrc.

12.14 The resource settings for clients invoked by that user.

Chapter 13

13.1   They are ordinary files where mail is appended to.

13.2   That the message has been seen.

13.3   From the directory /var/mail (SVR4) or /var/spool/mail (Linux).

13.4   The first sends a mail to the user and the second views your mailbox.

13.5   Use **ps -e | mail charlie**.

13.6   In $HOME/.elm/elmrc.

13.7   After composing your message, use *[Ctrl-j]* and then enter the filename. The cursor must be in the header area.

13.8   Because they can handle multimedia files as attachments.

13.9   Remove the .forward file.

13.10 To the Mail Delivery Agent (MDA).

13.11 Use **netscape -messenger &** from an **xterm** window.

Chapter 14

14.1   They are *com*, *net* and *org*.

14.2   Never; this is the administrative address. Messages have to be addressed to the list's address.

14.3   News messages build up so fast that the administrator has to make space for new messages by deleting the old ones.

14.4   Send a message to *misc.test*.

14.5   A document containing the frequently asked questions of a newsgroup, compiled by volunteers from newsgroup postings.

14.6   Only if both users are in the same IRC network.

14.7   Because it doesn't have to handle graphics, and graphics consume a lot of network bandwidth.

14.8   The HyperText Transfer Protocol (HTTP) at port number 80.

14.9   Keep the *Back* button pressed with the mouse left button. A menu presents all the visited pages in sequence from where you should select the one you require.

14.10   Bookmark the site.

14.11   No, hypertext links can refer to pictures, and even pictures can refer to other pictures.

14.12   Generally, it's the file `index.html`.

14.13   Use the generic name *localhost* in place of the FQDN here—*http://localhost*.

14.14   Because one connection has no knowledge of the previous one.

14.15   It is `Content-Type: text/html`.

14.16   Because the language simply advises the browser by specifying the *meaning* of the content. The browser has to interpret this advice in its own way.

14.17   A graphic acting as a hyperlink where different parts of the graphic point to different resources.

14.18   Place your cursor on the suspected graphic and then right-click on it. If you find an option *Save Image As*, then it's a graphic.

Chapter 15

15.1   **grep** searches for a from the files b and c.

15.2   Set `count=`cat foo[123] | grep -c "HTML"``. (C shell users should prefix the statement with **set**.)

15.3   Use **grep -li "a href" ***.

15.4   Most certainly. Otherwise the shell will try to open a file name TABLE.

15.5   Only in Linux. Use **grep -A 5 "<TABLE>" foo**.

15.6   One or more occurrences of g.

15.7   Use **grep "harriso*n*" foo**.

15.8   The longest pattern starting with a and ending with b, as close to the left of the line as possible.

15.9   Use

    (i) grep "................" foo (16 dots)
    (ii) grep ".\{16\}" foo

15.10   Use **egrep "(lock|har)wood" foo**.

15.11   When the search expression is a simple string and not a regular expression.

15.12   Fill up a file with patterns in exactly the same way they are used in the command line, and then use the commands with the -f option.

15.13   Use **sed 'p' foo**.

15.14   Use **sed -n '$!p' foo**.

15.15   Use this command:

    sed 'a\

A blank line here

    ' foo

15.16   Use **sed 's/Linux/Red Hat &/g' foo**.

15.17   Use **grep UNIX foo | tail -1** to search for the last occurrence of the pattern UNIX in file foo.

Chapter 16

16.1   They are identical; both print the entire line.

16.2   The **sort** command must be placed within double quotes.

16.3   Use **awk '{ x= NR % 2 ; if (x == 1) print }' foo**.

16.4   Use this command:

```
awk -F"|" 'substr($5,0,2) == "09" || substr($5,0,2) == "12"' empn.lst.
```

16.5   Use **awk 'length > 100 && length < 150' foo**.

16.6   Use **ls -l | awk '{tot += $5} END { print tot}'**.

16.7   Use command substitution:

```
x=`awk -F"|" '{ x+= $6 } END { print x/NR }' emp.lst`
```

16.8   Use this pipeline:

```
echo "DOCUMENT LIST" | \
awk '{ for (k = 1 ; k < (55 - length($0)) / 2 ; k++)
        printf "%s"," "
     print $0 }'
```

Chapter 17

17.1   The file vt220 will be found in /usr/lib/terminfo/v.

17.2   As often as specified by mail (C shell) or MAILCHECK (other shells).

17.3   Make the setting set PAGER = less (C shell) or PAGER=less (other shells).

17.4   The variable user (C shell) or LOGNAME (other shells).

17.5   Make the setting **set -o noclobber** (bash or Korn) or **set noclobber** (C shell).

17.6   No, sub-shells read only the environment file.

17.7   When it is made available to all sub-shells with the **export** command or defined with the **setenv** statement (C shell).

17.8   Only .bash_profile.

17.9   Use (i) set history = 200 (ii) HISTSIZE=200 (iii) Korn stores commands only in a file.

17.10 Use (i) !! (ii) r (iii) !!.

17.11 (i) Any of the three: set -o vi, VISUAL=vi or EDITOR=vi (ii) Only set -o vi.

17.12 Use **cd ~henry**.

17.13 :h extracts the directory component of a pathname (the head), and :t extracts the base filename (the tail) in the C shell and bash.

Chapter 18

18.1   The values are x10$ and 1010.

18.2   There's a program with the same name in a directory, which is placed earlier in the PATH list than the current one. The script in the current directory was not executed at all. Use **./foo.sh** to execute the right script.

18.3   Use the statement #!/bin/ksh in the first line of the script.

18.4   The shell will continuously spawn sub-shells till the system is able to handle so many of them.

18.5 $# is 5 and $* expands to the string -l -t bar1 bar2 bar3 provided all the files exist. Combining the options brings down $# to 4 and changes $* to -lt bar1 bar2 bar3.

18.6   The exit status is an integer that represents the success or failure of a command. It has the value 0 when the command executes successfully and is stored in the parameter $?.

18.7   True, because there's nothing to execute; errors are produced only when you do something.

18.8   Only **grep** returns a false exit status on being unable to locate a pattern; the others return true values.

18.9   The external command are **expr**, **sleep** and **basename**. They are most useful when used inside shell scripts.

18.10 Yes, the shell accepts standard input; in fact, that's what it uses most of the time.

18.11 Create a file foo with two lines containing the string and the filename, and then use **emp4.sh < foo**.

18.12 Use **bc < $1 | paste -d= $1 -** in the script.

18.13 This sets up an infinite loop since a value greater than 0 is considered to be true.

18.14 Just provide ten words as a list to **for**; the command *cmd* will be executed 10 times:

```
for x in 0 1 2 3 4 5 6 7 8 9 ; do
     cmd
done
```

18.15 The variable x is not used inside the loop. Usually, the variable is also used inside, but there is no compulsion to use it.

Chapter 19

19.1   It makes sense; it stores the output of the **set** command itself in the positional parameters.

19.2   Use ${12} in the Korn and bash shells. For the Bourne shell, use **shift 3** and then access $9.

19.3   If **grep** fails to find the pattern A HREF, then **set** will operate with no arguments and display all shell variables on the terminal.

19.4   The current directory is one of the environmental parameters inherited by a child process. Since the child cannot alter the environment of its parent, the original directory has to be restored after the death of the script, which is executed in a sub-shell. To make the change permanent, execute the script with the **.** command.

19.5   Export the variable with **export**.

19.6   **echo** shows nothing. **script** runs in a sub-shell, and the value of a variable defined there is not available in the parent (login) shell.

19.7   The command was executed probably in the Bourne or C shells. It evaluates the length of the string stored in $x when used in bash or Korn.

19.8   If a script is invoked without any argument, $1 would be null and flname would be set to emp.lst.

19.9   When the volume of input is quite small or the command doesn't accept a file-name as argument.

19.10   Function **rd()** is shown below:

```
rd() {
        dir=`pwd`
        cd ..
        rm -r $dir
}
```

19.11   Use the **.** or **source** command to execute the script.

19.12   Run the program from the .profile with **exec**.

Chapter 20

20.1   The variable x should be written as $x. It's meant to print 2^32, i.e., 4294967296.

20.2   Use **perl -ne 'print "$.\t" . $_' foo**.

20.3   Use this program:

```
#!/usr/bin/perl -n
split(/:/) ;
print if $_[3] == 100 ;
```

20.4   Use **perl -e 'print "UNIX" x 20 . "\n" ;'**.

20.5   Use **perl -p -i -e "tr/[a-z]/[A-Z]/" foo**.

20.6   This program uses a **for** loop:

```
#!/usr/bin/perl
print ("Enter a number: ") ;
$number = <STDIN> ;
if ( $number > 0 ) {
    for ( $x = 1 ; $x <= $number ; $x++ ) {
            print "$x\n" ;
    }
} else {
    print "Not a positive number\n" ;
}
```

20.7   Here, we use **split** with a null string (//):

```
#!/usr/bin/perl
print ("Enter a string: ") ;
```

```perl
$string = <STDIN> ;
chop ($string) ;
@arr = split (//, $string) ;
$length = @arr ;
for ( $x = 0 ; $x < $length ; $x++ ) {
    print "$arr[$x]\n" ;
}
```

20.8   Use this program:

```perl
#!/usr/bin/perl
$number = 1 ;
while ( $number != 0 ) {
    print ("Enter a number: ") ;
    $number = <STDIN> ;
    chop ($number) ;
    if ( $number != 0 ) {
        $total+= $number ;
    }
}
print "The total is $total\n" ;
```

20.9   Make use of the && and || operators:

```perl
#!/usr/bin/perl
print ( "Enter a year: " ) ;
$year = <STDIN> ;
$remainder4 = $year % 4 ;
$remainder100 = $year % 100 ;
$remainder400 = $year % 400 ;
if ( ($remainder4 == 0 && $remainder100 != 0) || ($remainder400 == 0) ) {
    print "It is a leap year\n" ;
} else {
    print "It is not a leap year\n" ;
}
```

20.10   ! missing in interpreter line (1), " missing (2), ; missing (3), { missing (5), /n
used instead of \n (6). Line numbers are shown in parentheses.

20.11   Use this program:

```perl
#!/usr/bin/perl
print "String : ";
$a = <STDIN>;
print "Number of times : ";
chop ($b = <STDIN>);
$c = $a x $b;
print "The result is : \n$c";
```

Chapter 21

21.1 /dev/fd0 represents the default floppy drive.

21.2 (i) /dev/fd0135ds18 & /dev/dsk/f0q18dt (SVR4) (ii) /dev/fd0H1440 (Linux).

21.3 An extended partition contains a number of independent *logical* partitions. Thus, you can have multiple file systems in a single extended partition.

21.4 The filename is not stored in the inode but only in the directory.

21.5 The link count is decremented by one.

21.6 In the superblock.

21.7 /stand or /kernel (SVR4), /boot (Linux).

21.8 By using the -i option of **ls**.

21.9 Four (IDE) and eight (SCSI).

21.10 The **mkfs** command.

21.11 Unmounting is not possible when the user executing **umount** is placed in a directory inside the file system or any user has a file open in it.

21.12 **fsck** dumps unconnected files to /lost+found.

21.13 Only in single-user mode.

Chapter 22

22.1 In /sbin and /usr/sbin. Older systems will have them in /etc.

22.2 **calendar** in super user mode looks up all users' calendar files, and mails the relevant output to the user.

22.3 In /etc/shadow.

22.4 By using **wall** with the message contents.

22.5 Use **useradd -u 212 -g dialout -d /home/john -s /bin/bash -m john**.

22.6 With the **chsh** command (not available in Solaris).

22.7 The kernel is represented by unix or genunix (SVR4) and vmlinuz (Linux).

22.8 Look for the line containing initdefault in the *action* field of /etc/inittab. The run level specified in that line is the default run level.

22.9 Use *[Ctrl][Alt][Del]*.

22.10 Use **shutdown -y -g0**.

22.11 **init** keeps the system at specific states (run levels) and spawns **getty** processes at the terminal ports.

22.12 Run level 0 shuts down a system, but state 6 also reboots it.

22.13 No, you can't because **lpsched** won't work in single-user mode.

22.14 Use **telinit q** or **init q** to make **init** reread inittab.

Chapter 23

23.1 (i) Class C (ii) Class A (iii) Class A

23.2 You can have the first one, but the second one is reserved for internets.

23.3 The IRQ and the I/O address.

23.4 Use **ifconfig -a**.

23.5 By commenting the line pertaining to **ftp** in /etc/inetd.conf.

23.6 PPP, the Point-to-Point Protocol. The **pppd** command invokes the service.

23.7 Use **ATDT** (tone dialing) or **ATDP** (pulse dialing).

23.8   /etc/exports shows the directories that can be mounted remotely, and specifies the access rights of the client. You can use the **exportfs -a** command to
make the changed information available to the **mount** daemons. If the command
is not available, you have to invoke the relevant "start" script in the rc*n*.d directory with the restart argument.

Chapter 24

24.1   The slave server serves as a backup of the master server and obtains data from
the master through a zonal transfer.

24.2   **ftp** operates through a resolver which reads the name server entries from
/etc/resolv.conf.

24.3   The MX records are used to specify the addresses of the mail servers and their
priority. The server with the lower priority number is tried before the higher
ones.

24.4   The CNAME record is used to define aliases for hostnames.

24.5   The Mail Delivery Agent (MDA) takes mail from SMTP and performs delivery.
mail, **deliver** and **procmail** are common mail delivery programs.

24.6   Mail is spooled in /var/spool/mqueue, and the list is viewed with the **mailq**
command.

24.7   Define all the domains in a file /etc/sendmail.cw and define the file with
Fw/etc/sendmail.cw.

24.8   Use **telnet** *hostname* 25 and **telnet** *hostname* 110, and observe the messages.

24.9   You have not compiled the file with **newaliases**.

24.10   As many as determined by MinSpareServers in httpd.conf.

24.11   With the DocumentRoot directive.

Bibliography

General Reading

The UNIX Programming Environment by Brian Kernighan and Rob Pike (Prentice Hall), 1984, Englewood Cliffs, New Jersey.

The Design of the UNIX Operating System by Maurice Bach (Prentice Hall), 1986, Englewood Cliffs, New Jersey.

The UNIX Operating System by Kaare Christian (John Wiley), 1988, New York.

Open Computing UNIX Unbound by Harley Hahn (Osborne McGraw-Hill), 1994, Berkeley, California.

UNIX System V: A Practical Guide, 3rd Edition, by Mark G. Sobell (Addison-Wesley), 1995, Menlo Park, California.

UNIX System V Release 4: An Introduction, 2nd Edition, by Kenneth Rosen, Richard Rosinski & James Farber (Osborne McGraw Hill), 1996, Berkeley, California.

UNIX Power Tools by Jerry Peek, Tim O'Reilly and Mike Loukides (O'Reilly and Associates), 1994, Sebastopol, California.

Open Computing's Best UNIX Tips Ever by Kenneth Rosen, Richard Rosinski and Douglas Host (Osborne McGraw-Hill), 1994, Berkeley, California.

Running Linux, Third Edition, by Matt Welsh, Matthias Kalle Dalheimer and Lar Kaufman (O'Reilly & Associates), 1999, Sebastopol, California.

Using Linux, Fifth Edition, by Jack Tackett and David Gunter (Que Corporation), 2000, Indianapolis, Indiana.

Red Hat Linux 6 Unleashed by David Pitts, Bill Ball et al. (Sams Publishing), 1999.

Using UNIX, Special Edition, by Peter Kuo (Lead Author) (Que Corporation), 1998, Indianapolis, Indiana.

Topical Reading

A Guide to vi by Dan Sonnenschein (Prentice Hall), 1987, Englewood Cliffs, New Jersey.

GNU Emacs—UNIX Text Editing and Programming by M. Schoonover, J. S. Bowie and W. R. Arnold (Addison-Wesley), 1992, Reading, Massachusetts.

Learning GNU Emacs, 2nd Edition, by Debra Cameron, Bill Rosenblatt and Eric Raymond (O'Reilly & Associates), 1996, Sebastopol, California.

UNIX Application Programming by Ray Swartz (SAMS), 1990, Carmel, Indiana.

Learning the Korn Shell by Bill Rosenblatt (O'Reilly & Associates), 1994, Sebastopol, California.

Learning the bash Shell by Cameron Newham and Bill Rosenblatt (O'Reilly & Associates), 1998, Sebastopol, California.

Programming Perl by Larry Wall and Randal Schwartz (O'Reilly & Associates), 1991, Sebastopol, California.

Learning Perl by Randal Schwartz (O'Reilly & Associates), 1993, Sebastopol, California.

Teach Yourself Perl 5 in 21 Days by David Till (SAMS Publishing), 1996, Indianapolis, Indiana.

Perl 5 Interactive Course by Jon Orwant (Waite Group), 1996.

Teach Yourself CGI Programming with Perl 5 in a Week by Eric Herrman (Sams.net Publishing), 1997.

The X Window System User's Guide—Motif Edition by Valerie Quercia and Tim O'Reilly (O'Reilly & Associates), 1993, Sebastopol, California.

TCP/IP Networking and the Internet

TCP/IP Network Administration by Craig Hunt (O'Reilly & Associates), 1998, Sebastopol, California.

Linux Network Servers by Craig Hunt (Network Press), 1999, Alameda, California.

DNS and BIND, Third Edition, by Paul Albitz and Cricket Liu (O'Reilly & Associates), 1998, Sebastopol, California.

sendmail by Bryan Costales with Eric Allman (O'Reilly & Associates), 1997, Sebastopol, California.

Internet Secrets by John Levine and Corol Baroudi (IDG Books Worldwide), 1996, Foster City, California.

The Whole Internet—User's Guide and Catalog by Ed Krol (O'Reilly & Associates), 1994, Sebastopol, California.

Harley Hahn's The Internet Complete Reference, Second Edition, by Harley Hahn (Osborne McGraw-Hill), 1996, Berkeley, California.

System Administration

UNIX System V Release 4 Administration by David Fiedler and Bruce Hunter (Hayden Books), 1995, Indianapolis, Indiana.

UNIX System Administration Handbook by Evi Nemeth, Garth Snyder, Scott Seebass and Trent Hein (Prentice Hall PTR), 1995, Upper Saddle River, New Jersey.

Essential System Administration by Æleen Frisch (O'Reilly & Associates), 1995, Sebastopol, California.

UNIX System Administrator's Bible by Yves Lepage and Paul Iarrera (IDG Books Worldwide), 1998, Foster City, California.

UNIX System Administrator's Edition by Robin Birk and David B. Horvath et al. (Sams Publishing), 1997.

System Performance Tuning by Mike Loukides (O'Reilly & Associates), 1992, Sebastopol, California.

Journals and Papers

"The UNIX Time-Sharing System" by Dennis Ritchie and Ken Thompson (*Bell System Technical Journal,* Vol. 57, No. 6), 1978, Murray Hill, New Jersey.

"UNIX Implementation" by Ken Thompson (*Bell System Technical Journal,* Vol. 57, No. 6), 1978, Murray Hill, New Jersey.

"A Retrospective" by Dennis Ritchie (*Bell System Technical Journal,* Vol. 57, No. 6), 1978, Murray Hill, New Jersey.

"The UNIX Shell" by Steve Bourne (*Bell System Technical Journal,* Vol. 57, No. 6), 1978, Murray Hill, New Jersey.

Awk—A Pattern Scanning and Processing Language Programmer's Manual by Alfred Aho, Peter Weinberger and Brian Kernighan (Computing Science Technical Report No. 118 of AT&T Bell Labs), Murray Hill, New Jersey.

vi Index

Symbols are listed in the order in which they appear in the ASCII code.
In the alphabetical section of the index, symbols are ignored.

emacs Index

Symbols are listed in the order in which they appear in the ASCII code.
In the alphabetical section of the index, symbols are ignored.

#, 121
* symbol, 140
* * (double asterisks), 119
$ anchoring character, 139
--- on the mode line, 114
^ anchoring character, 139

abbrev-mode variable, 156, 157
abbreviation mode, 153
[Alt] key
   compared to *[Ctrl]*, 128
   substituting for the *[Meta]* key,
    116
[Alt-!], 148
[Alt-%], 141, 142
[Alt-<], 126, 127
[Alt->], 126, 127
[Alt-^], 128
[Alt-0] [Ctrl-k], 129
[Alt-b], 125, 127
[Alt-c], 128, 132, 133
[Alt-d], 128
[Alt-f], 125, 127
[Alt-l], 128, 132, 133, 153
[Alt-u], 128, 132, 133
[Alt-v], 124
[Alt-w], 128, 131
[Alt-x], 121
[Alt-x], 116–117
[Alt-y], 152
anchoring characters, 139
auto-save-timeout variable,
  155–156
autosave feature, 120–121, 820

[Backspace] key, 119
blank lines
   generating with *[Ctrl-n]*, 123
   removing a group of, 129, 130
blink-matching-paren variable,
  156, 157
bookmarks, 150–151, 787
buffers
   associated with files, 118
   deleting the contents of entire, 131
   handling, 145–146, 147
   killing the current, 147
   relationship to windows, 142–143
   replacing with the last autosaved
    file, 121
   setting entire as regions, 128

call-last-kbd-macro command,
  155
capitalizing a single character, 132,
  133
case, changing, 132–133
case conversion regions, 133
case-fold-search variable, 156
character class ([ ]), 139
characters, 132, 133
command completion feature,
  133–135
command output, placing in a file, 147
command reference, 781–789
command sequences, cancelling, 117
commands
   binding to a key sequence, 154
   entering directly, 116–117

prefixing numbers, 122
   recalling previously issued, 117
completion feature, 117, 822
consecutive deletions, storing in the
  kill ring, 130
control keys, 115, 120
crashes, recovering from, 120–121
[Ctrl-_], 128, 135
[Ctrl--], 128, 135
[Ctrl-@], 127, 128
[Ctrl-a], 125, 127
[Ctrl] [Alt] s, 140–141
[Ctrl-b], 123, 124, 125
[Ctrl-d], 119, 128
[Ctrl-e], 125, 127
[Ctrl-f], 123, 124, 125
[Ctrl-g], 117
[Ctrl-h], 119, 148
[Ctrl-h] a, 148
[Ctrl-h] c, 148
[Ctrl-h] f (function), 148, 149
[Ctrl-h] i (info), 148, 150
[Ctrl-h] k (key), 148–149
[Ctrl-h] t (tutorial), 150
[Ctrl-h] v, 148
[Ctrl-h] w **where-is**, 148,
  149–150
[Ctrl-k], 129
[Ctrl-k] [Ctrl-k], 128, 129
[Ctrl] key, 115, 128
[Ctrl-l], 124
[Ctrl-n], 123, 124
[Ctrl-p], 123, 124
[Ctrl-r], 136, 139
[Ctrl-s], 136, 137, 139

Commands and Key Terms

Symbols are listed in the order in which they appear in the ASCII code.
In the alphabetical section of the index, symbols are ignored.

COMMANDS AND
KEY TERMS

C Shell

Symbols are listed in the order in which they appear in the ASCII code.
In the alphabetical section of the index, symbols are ignored.

Korn Shell

Symbols are listed in the order in which they appear in the ASCII code.
In the alphabetical section of the index, symbols are ignored.

bash

Symbols are listed in the order in which they appear in the ASCII code.
In the alphabetical section of the index, symbols are ignored.

Comprehensive Index

Symbols are listed in the order in which they appear in the ASCII code.
In the alphabetical section of the index, symbols are ignored.